America's
Top-Rated Cities:
A Statistical Handbook

Volume 1

2011
Eighteenth Edition

America's
Top-Rated Cities:
A Statistical Handbook

Volume 1: Southern Region

A UNIVERSAL REFERENCE BOOK

Grey House
Publishing

PUBLISHER: Leslie Mackenzie
EDITORIAL DIRECTOR: Laura Mars
EDITOR: David Garoogian

CONTRIBUTING WRITER: Allison Blake
RESEARCH ASSISTANTS: Jacqueline Diaz; Alyssa Garoogian
MARKETING DIRECTOR: Jessica Moody

A Universal Reference Book
Grey House Publishing, Inc.
4919 Route 22
Amenia, NY 12501
518.789.8700
Fax 845.373.6390
www.greyhouse.com
e-mail: books @greyhouse.com

Eighteenth Edition
Printed in Canada

Publisher's Cataloging-in-Publication Data
(Prepared by The Donohue Group, Inc.)

America's top-rated cities. Vol. I, Southern region : a statistical handbook.. -- 1992-

v. : ill. ; cm.
Annual, 1995-
Irregular, 1992-1993
ISSN: 1082-7102

1. Cities and towns--Ratings--Southern States--Statistics--Periodicals. 2. Cities and towns--Southern States--Statistics--Periodicals. 3. Social indicators--Southern States--Periodicals. 4. Quality of life--Southern States--Statistics--Periodicals. 5. Southern States--Social conditions--Statistics--Periodicals. I. Title: America's top rated cities. II. Title: Southern region

HT123.5.S6 A44
307.76/0973/05   421 1948   95644648

4-Volume Set   ISBN: 978-1-59237-747-3
Volume 1   ISBN: 978-1-59237-748-0
Volume 2   ISBN: 978-1-59237-749-7
Volume 3   ISBN: 978-1-59237-750-3
Volume 4   ISBN: 978-1-59237-751-0

Athens, Georgia

Atlanta, Georgia

Austin, Texas

Birmingham, Alabama

Charleston, South Carolina

Chattanooga, Tennessee

Columbia, South Carolina

Dallas, Texas

El Paso, Texas

Fort Lauderdale, Florida

Fort Worth, Texas

Gainesville, Florida

Knoxville, Tennessee

Nashville, Tennessee

Miami, Florida

New Orleans, Louisiana

Savannah, Georgia

Tampa, Florida

Introduction

This eighteenth edition of *America's Top-Rated Cities* is a concise, statistical, 4-volume work identifying America's top-rated cities with populations over 100,000. It profiles 100 cities that have received high marks for business and living from prominent publications, such as *Places Rated Almanac* and *Cities Ranked & Rated,* from surveys appearing in over 200 sources, such as *Fortune, U. S. News & World Report, Men's Health, Forbes, Travel + Leisure* and the *Wall Street Journal,* and from first-hand visits, interviews and reports.

Praise for previous editions:

> *"...this reference tool has clearly proven its worth to a wide audience ranging from businesspeople and corporations planning to launch, relocate, or expand their operations to market researchers, real estate professionals, urban planners, job-seekers, students, and anyone else interested in access to more than 3,600 pages of reliable, attractively presented statistical infomation about larger U.S. cities."*

—ARBA

Each volume covers a different region of the country—Southern, Western, Central and Eastern—and includes a detailed Table of Contents, City Chapters, Appendices, and Maps. Each City Chapter incorporates information from hundreds of resources to create the following major sections:

- **Background**—lively narrative of significant, up-to-date news for both businesses and residents. Each background combines historical facts with up-to-the-minute development, "known-for" annual events, and an annual weather report.
- **Rankings**—fun-to-read, bulleted survey results from over 200 books and magazines, such as general (Most Affordable Cities), specific (Great Golf Cities), and everything in between (Top Cities to Defy Death).
- **Statistical Tables**—115 tables and detailed topics, with several new and expanded topics, offer an unparalleled view of each city's Business and Living Environments. They are carefully organized with data that is easy to read and understand.
- **Appendices**—five in all, follow each volume of City Chapters. These range from listings of Metropolitan Statistical Areas to Comparative Statistics for all 100 cities.

This new edition of *America's Top Rated Cities* includes cites that ranked highest and received the most points, using our unique weighting system. Cities new to this edition are: New Orleans, LA; Plano, TX; Irvine, CA; Bellevue, WA; Naperville, IL; Overland Park, KS; and Cary, NC. Two cities in this editon— Gainesville, FL and Cambridge, MA—have never before been included as a top rated city. Note that three cities do not meet our population criteria of 100,000 (Boulder, Edison and Fargo) but their extraordinarily high rankings prevailed.

BACKGROUND

Each city begins with an informative **Background** that combines history with current events. These narratives reflect changes that have occurred during the past year, and touch on the city's environment, politics, employment, cultural offerings, climate, and often include interesting trivia. For example, both Presidents Franklin and Theodore Roosevelt went to Harvard, Gatorade was invented to hydrate University of Florida's football team (the Gators), and New Orleans is nicknamed "Hollywood South" for the 35 films that were in production at presstime.

RANKINGS

This section has rankings from a possible 289 (up from 231) books, articles, and reports. For easy reference, these Rankings are categorized into 17 topics that have been reorganized somewhat, to allow more specificity: *General; Business/Finance; Children/Family; Culture/Performing Arts; Dating/Romance; Education; Environment; Health/Fitness; Pet; Real Estate; Safety; Seniors/Retirement; Sports/Recreation; Technology; Transportation; Women/Minorities; Miscellaneous.*

The Rankings are presented in an easy-to-read, bulleted format and include results from both annual surveys and one-shot studies. **Best Walking . . . Best for Jobs . . . Best for Hispanics . . . Most Creative . . . Most Fun . . . Safest . . . Best to Save Money . . . Most Polite . . . Best to Retire . . . Best for Dating . . . Most Vegetarian-Friendly . . . Least Stressful . . . Best Sleeping . . . Best to Ride out a Recession . . . Best to Earn a Living . . . Sex Happy . . . Most Political . . . Most Charitable . . . Most Miserable . . . Most Tax Friendly . . . Highest Foreclosure Rates . . . Best for Telecommuters . . . Most Road Rage . . . Greediest . . . Gayest . . . Most Literate . . . Most Tattooed . . . and more.**

This 2011 edition also includes a number of new Rankings, such as **Cities With the Best Broadband, Most Livable Cities for Wheelchair Users,** and **Best Cities for Starter Homes.** While most rankings are from this year or last, you will find a few that are 5 years—or more—old. We decided to keep in those one-time rankings that are either particularly interesting or rank something that is not likely to change much over the long term.

Sources for these Rankings include both well-known magazines and other media, including *Forbes, Fortune, Inc. Magazine, Working Mother, Popular Science, Prevention, Field & Stream, Business Week, Kiplinger's Personal Finance, Men's Journal,* and *Travel + Leisure,* as well as resources not as well known, such as the *Asthma & Allergy Foundation of America, Christopher & Dana Reeve Foundation, The Advocate, Black Enterprise, National Civic League, The National Coalition for the Homeless, Center for Digital Government, U.S. Conference of Mayors, Milken Institue,* and the *Centre for International Competitiveness.*

STATISTICAL TABLES

Each city chapter includes a possible 115 tables and detailed topics—65 in BUSINESS and 50 in LIVING. Nearly 95% of statistical data has been updated. New topics include *Metropolitan Area Exports* and *Best Law Schools.* Expanded topics include the addition of: asian/white and hispanic/white to *Segregation* statistics; Black-owned Asset Management Firms to *Minority Business Opportunity;* metropolitan area data to *Building Permits;* and dentists and DOs to *Distribution of Physicians.*

Business Environment includes hard facts and figures on 12 topics, including City Finances, Demographics, Income, Economy, Employment, and Real Estate. *Living Environment* includes 11 topics, such as Cost of Living, Housing, Health, Education, Safety, Recreation, and Sports Teams.

To compile the Statistical Tables, our editors have again turned to a wide range of sources, some well known, such as the *U.S. Census Bureau, U.S. Environmental Protection Agency, Centers for Disease Control and Prevention,* and the *Federal Bureau of Investigation,* and some more obscure, like *The Tax Foundation, The Council for Community and Economic Research, Claritas,* and *Glenmary Research Center.*

APPENDICES
- **Appendix A**—*Counties*
- **Appendix B**—*Metropolitan Area Definitions*
- **Appendix C**—*Chambers of Commerce and Economic Development Organizations*: Addresses, phone, fax, web sites of these resources help readers find more detailed information on each city.
- **Appendix D**—*State Departments of Labor and Employment*: Additional economic and employment data, with address, phone and web site for easy access.
- **Appendix E**—*Comparative Statistics*: City-by-city comparison comprised of 73 tables. All volumes include all 100 cities.

Material provided by public and private agencies and organizations was supplemented by original research, numerous library sources and Internet sites. *America's Top-Rated Cities, 2011*, is designed for a wide range of readers: private individuals considering relocating a residence or business; professionals considering expanding their businesses or changing careers; corporations considering relocation, opening up additional offices or creating new divisions; government agencies; general and market researchers; real estate consultants; human resource personnel; urban planners; investors; and urban government students.

Western United States

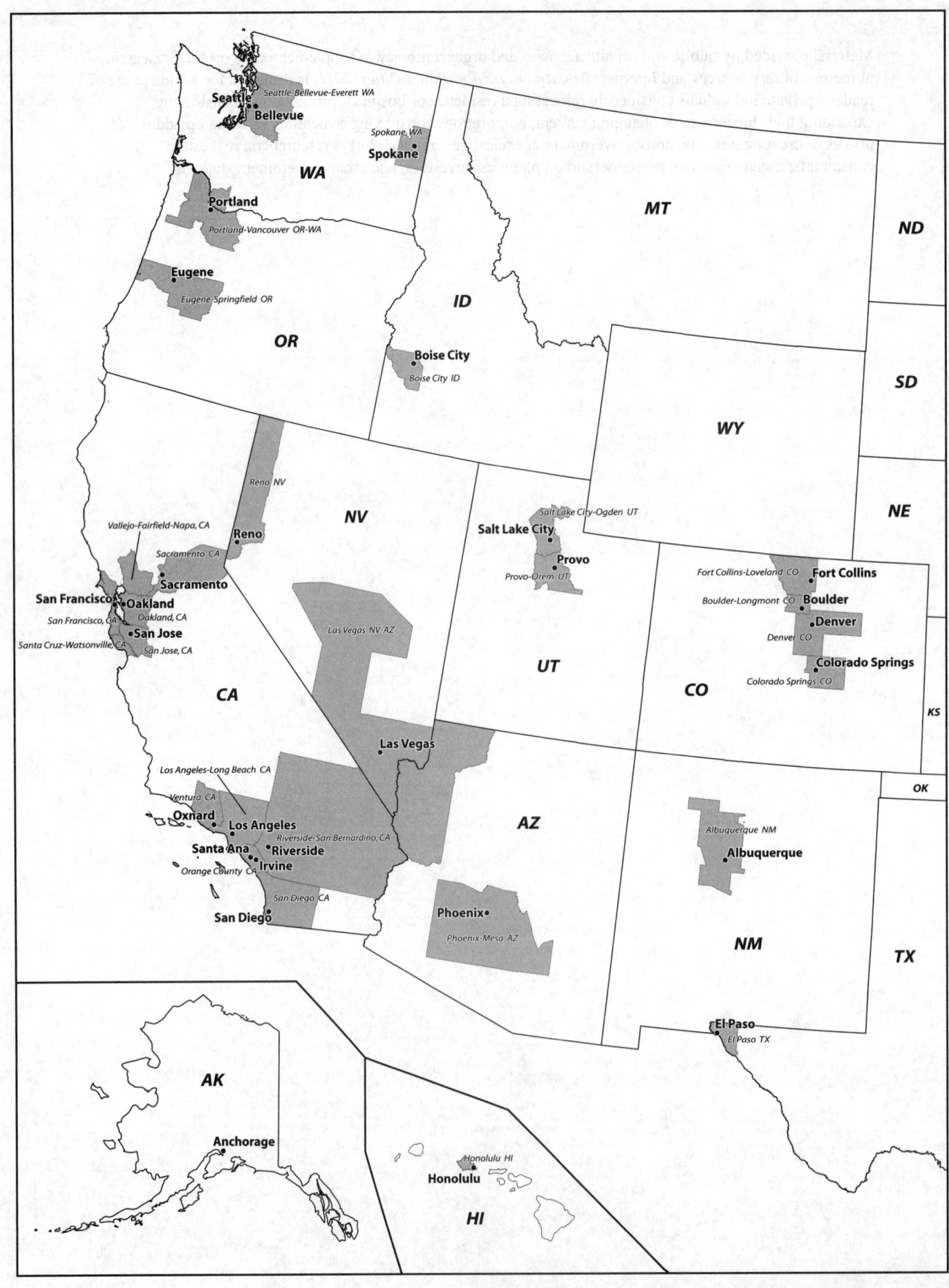

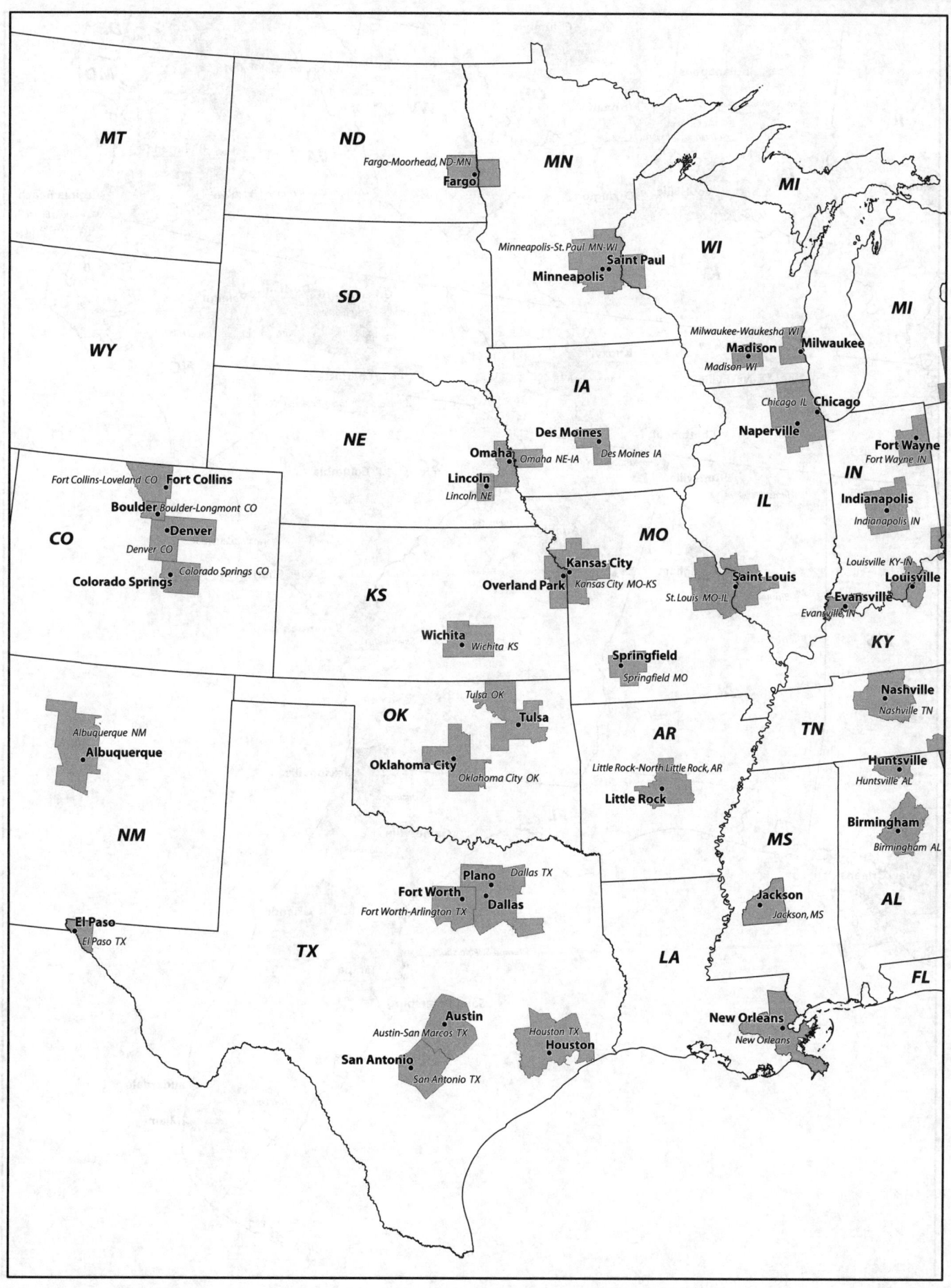

Southeastern United States

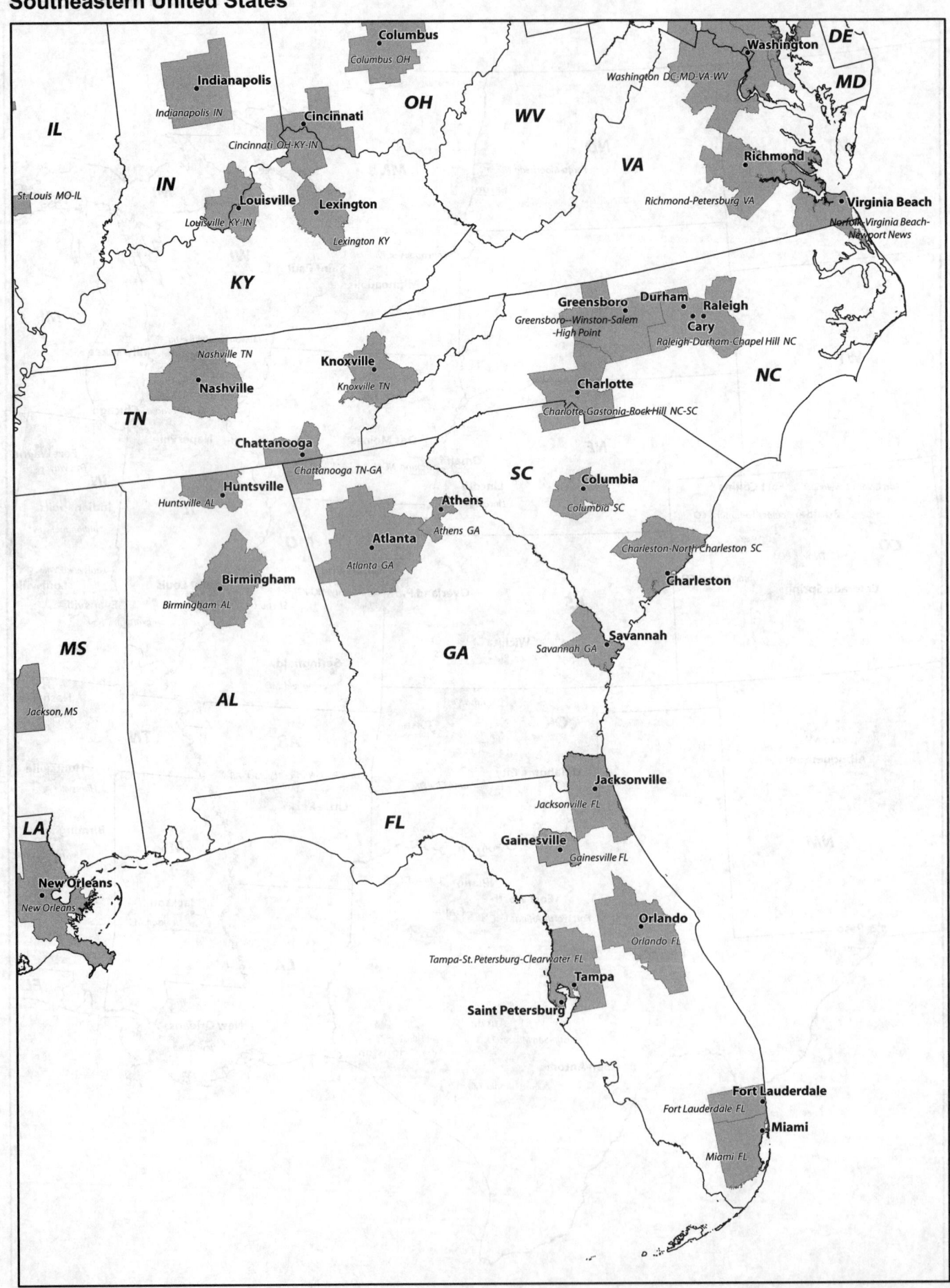

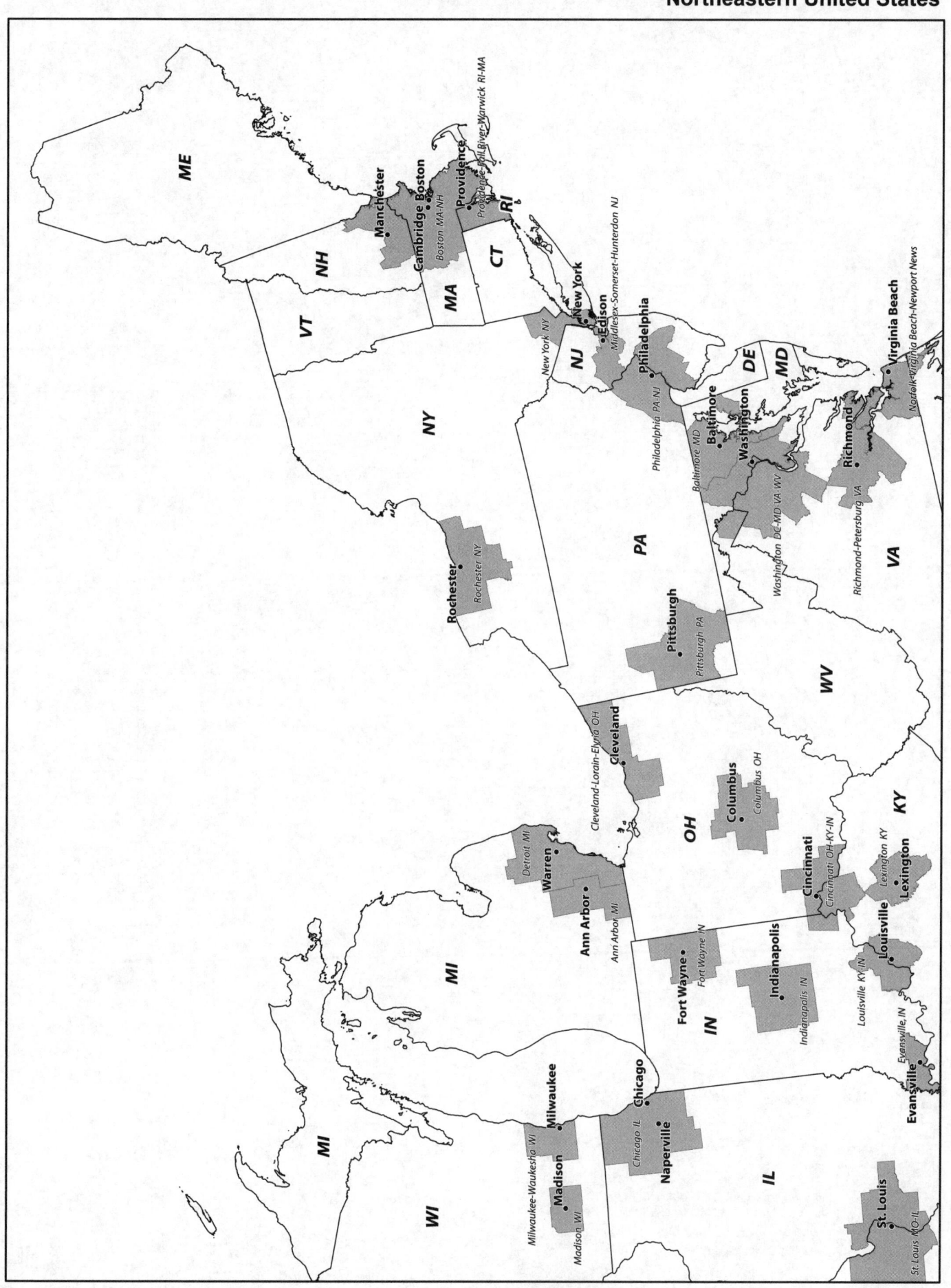

Athens, Georgia

Background

Athens, home to the University of Georgia, retains its old charms while cultivating the new. Antebellum homes that grace the city still stand because Gen. William Tecumseh Sherman's March to the Sea took a route that left this northeast Georgia town intact (while burning Atlanta, about 60 miles to the southwest). The Athens Music History Walking Tour, available through the local convention and visitors' bureau, stops at Weaver D's soul food restaurant with the slogan, "Automatic for the People," that went national as the name of locally-grown REM's 1992 album. The college music scene that spawned the B-52s and the Indigo Girls in the 1970s and 1980s, continues to support a thriving music industry. In 2002, the *New York Times* called Athens "Live Music Central."

Present-day Athens started as a small settlement where an old Cherokee trail crossed the Oconee River. In 1785 the state's General Assembly chartered the university, which established a campus here in 1801. Three years later, the school held its first graduation ceremony. The city was named for the ancient Greece's center of learning.

Undoubtedly the major influence in the city and surrounding Clarke County, the University of Georgia is also the area's largest employer. The comprehensive land grant and sea-grant institution offers all levels of degree programs in numerous disciplines. Other educational institutions in Athens are the Navy Supply School, Athens Technical College, and branches of Piedmont College and Old Dominion University.

Other major employers are focused on health care, government, and manufacturing. They include Athens Regional Medical Center and St. Mary's Health Care System, which have enlarged their facilities and specialized in areas including oncology, pediatrics and heart disease. In March 2010, St. Mary's was the first area hospital to implement the next generation of minimally invasive surgery using a hi-tech assistive robot. Manufacturing is a major employment sector; significant employers include poultry producers Pilgrim's Pride and Gold Kist, which operate local processing plants. Major expansions in the last several years include projects by building insulation makers CertainTeed, Oliver Rubber, and PB Corp./SKAPS Industries, which makes erosion control fencing.

The city's official government merged with its home county in 1991, creating the Unified Government of Athens-Clark County.

With its shops, boutiques and restaurants, Athens offers plenty to do. The Georgia State Museum of Art, Museum of Natural History, and the State Botanical Garden here are affiliated with the university. The restored 1910 Morton Theater once hosted Cab Calloway, Duke Ellington, and Louis Armstrong, and now hosts dramatic and musical performances. Undoubtedly the strong presence of young people in Athens has contributed to the burgeoning artistic scene there. The city center is home to bars, galleries, cafes, and music venues that cater to the city's creative climate. The annual AthFest in June, hosts 120 bands to support local education. The city's charms, attractive to all ages, have not gone unnoticed by the media. Athens has been named one of the best places for small business, the best college town for retirees, and the best place to recapture your youth.

The climate is mild, with average temperatures about 20 degrees warmer than the U.S. average. Snowfall is next to nothing, but precipitation is at its highest from January-March. Spring is lovely, with three to four inches of rain, sunshine up to 70 percent of the time starting in April, and temperatures averaging in the 70s.

Rankings

General Rankings

- Athens was ranked #29 out of 375 metro areas in *Cities Ranked & Rated*. Criteria: cost of living; climate; crime; transportation; economy and jobs; education; arts and culture; health and healthcare; leisure; quality of life. *Cities Ranked & Rated, 2nd Edition, 2007*

- Athens was ranked #209 out of 379 metro areas in *Places Rated Almanac*. Criteria: health care; education; recreation; transportation; ambience; climate; crime; housing costs; jobs. *Places Rated Almanac, 7th Edition, 2007*

- The Athens metro area was selected one of America's "Best Cities" by *Kiplinger's Personal Finance*. Criteria: stable employment; income growth; cost of living; percentage of workforce in the creative class (scientists, engineers, educators, writers, artists, entertainers, etc.). *Kiplinger's Personal Finance, "Best Cities 2009: It's All About Jobs," July 2009*

Business/Finance Rankings

- *American City Business Journals* ranked America's 261 largest cities in terms of their resident's wealth. Athens ranked #190. Criteria: per capita income; median household income; percentage of households with annual incomes of $200,000 or more; median home value. *American City Business Journals, www.bizjournals.com, "Where the Money Is: America's Wealth Centers," August 18, 2008*

- The Athens metro area appeared on the Milken Institute "2010 Best Performing Metros" list. Rank: #32 out of 179 small metro areas. Criteria: job growth; wage and salary growth; high-tech output growth. *Milken Institute, "2010 Best Performing Metros"*

- *Forbes* ranked 184 smaller metro areas in the U.S. in terms of the "Best Small Places for Business and Careers." The Athens metro area was ranked #26. Criteria: 12 metrics including costs (business and living), job growth (past and projected), income growth, educational attainment, projected economic growth, crime, cultural and recreational opportunities, net migration patterns, percentage of subprime mortgages handed out over a three-year period, and the number of highly ranked four-year colleges. *Forbes, "Best Small Places for Business and Careers," April 14, 2010*

Culture/Performing Arts Rankings

- Athens was selected as one of "America's Top 25 Arts Destinations." The city ranked #18 in the mid-sized city (population 100,000 to 499,999) category. Criteria: readers' top choices for arts travel destinations based on the richness and variety of visual arts sites, activities and events. *American Style, "America's Top 25 Arts Destinations," May 2010*

Environmental Rankings

- Athens was selected as one of 22 "Smarter Cities" for energy by the Natural Resources Defense Council." Criteria: investment in green power; energy efficiency measures; conservation. *Natural Resources Defense Council, "2010 Smarter Cities," July 19, 2010*

- Athens was selected as one of "America's 50 Greenest Cities" by *Popular Science*. The city ranked #33. Criteria: electricity; transportation; green living; recycling and green perspective. *Popular Science, February 2008*

- The Athens metro area appeared in *Country Home's* "Best Green Places" report. The area ranked #144 out of 379. Criteria: official energy policies; green power; green buildings; availability of fresh, locally grown food. *Country Home, "Best Green Places," 2008*

- Athens was highlighted as one of the top 25 cleanest metro areas for short-term particle pollution (24-hour PM 2.5) in the U.S. Monitors in these cities reported no days with unhealthful PM 2.5 levels. *American Lung Association, State of the Air 2011*

Real Estate Rankings

- Athens appeared on ApartmentRatings.com "Top College Towns & Cities" for renters list in 2010." The area ranked #2. Overall satisfaction ratings were ranked using thousands of user submitted scores for hundreds of apartment complexes located in cities and towns that are home to the 100 largest four-year institutions in the U.S. *ApartmentRatings.com, "2010 College Town Renter Satisfaction Rankings"*

Safety Rankings

- The National Insurance Crime Bureau ranked 366 metro areas in the U.S. in terms of per capita rates of vehicle theft. The Athens metro area ranked #117 (#1 = highest rate). Criteria: number of vehicle theft offenses per 100,000 inhabitants. *National Insurance Crime Bureau, "Hot Spots," May 17, 2010*

Seniors/Retirement Rankings

- Athens was identified as one of "The Top 100 Places to Retire" by *Topretirements.com* The list reflects the 100 cities (out of 625+ total cities reviewed) that visitors to the website are most interested in for retirement. *Topretirements.com, "2011 Best Places to Retire List: The Sunbelt Rules"*

- Athens was selected as one of the best places to retire by *Money*. The city was ranked #20 out of 25. Criteria: notable lifelong-learning programs; low taxes; affordable housing; high-quality health care; rich intellectual environment. *CNNMoney, "Best Places to Retire 2010"*

- Athens was identified as one of the best places to retire in *Retirement Places Rated*. Criteria: population above 10,000; attractiveness to older adults; affordability; climate and natural endowments; personal safety. The city was ranked #64 out of 200. *Retirement Places Rated, 7th Edition, 2007*

Sports/Recreation Rankings

- Athens appeared on the *Sporting News* list of the "Best Sports Cities" for 2010. The area ranked #70 out of 402 cities in the U.S. *Sporting News* takes a 12-month snapshot, roughly October to October, of each city's sports, putting a heavy premium on regular-season won-lost records (from the most recently completed season). Other criteria include: playoff berths, bowl appearances and tournament bids; championships; applicable power ratings; quality of competition; overall fan fervor as measured in part by attendance as percentage of venue capacity; abundance of teams (rewarding quality over quantity); stadium and arena quality; ticket availability and prices; franchise ownership; and marquee appeal of athletes. *Sporting News, "Best Sports Cities 2010," October, 2010*

- *Golf Digest* ranked 330 metro areas in the U.S. in terms of golf. The Athens metro area was ranked #198. Criteria: access to golf; weather; value of golf; and quality of golf. *Golf Digest, "Metro Golf Rankings," August 2005*

Business Environment

CITY FINANCES

City Government Finances

Component	2008 ($000)	2008 ($ per capita)
Total Revenues	219,337	1,923
Total Expenditures	218,110	1,912
Debt Outstanding	57,713	506
Cash and Securities[1]	186,267	1,633

Note: (1) Cash and security holdings of a government at the close of its fiscal year, including those of its dependent agencies, utilities, and liquor stores.
Source: U.S Census Bureau, State & Local Government Finances 2008

City Government Revenue by Source

Source	2008 ($000)	2008 ($ per capita)
General Revenue		
From Federal Government	9,797	86
From State Government	14,126	124
From Local Governments	44,698	392
Taxes		
Property	43,117	378
Sales and Gross Receipts	19,768	173
Personal Income	0	0
Corporate Income	0	0
Motor Vehicle License	0	0
Other Taxes	4,103	36
Current Charges	45,047	395
Liquor Store	0	0
Utility	18,934	166
Employee Retirement	0	0

Source: U.S Census Bureau, State & Local Government Finances 2008

City Government Expenditures by Function

Function	2008 ($000)	2008 ($ per capita)	2008 (%)
General Direct Expenditures			
Air Transportation	1,158	10	0.5
Corrections	11,701	103	5.4
Education	0	0	0.0
Employment Security Administration	0	0	0.0
Financial Administration	4,454	39	2.0
Fire Protection	12,666	111	5.8
General Public Buildings	5,441	48	2.5
Governmental Administration, Other	12,367	108	5.7
Health	11,766	103	5.4
Highways	13,909	122	6.4
Hospitals	0	0	0.0
Housing and Community Development	6,553	57	3.0
Interest on General Debt	367	3	0.2
Judicial and Legal	8,464	74	3.9
Libraries	1,636	14	0.8
Parking	888	8	0.4
Parks and Recreation	11,757	103	5.4
Police Protection	24,027	211	11.0
Public Welfare	551	5	0.3
Sewerage	19,408	170	8.9
Solid Waste Management	6,600	58	3.0
Veterans' Services	0	0	0.0
Liquor Store	0	0	0.0
Utility	27,172	238	12.5
Employee Retirement	0	0	0.0

Source: U.S Census Bureau, State & Local Government Finances 2008

Municipal Bond Ratings

Area	Moody's	S&P	Fitch
City	n/a	n/a	n/a

Rating Systems (shown in declining order of credit quality): Moody's– Aaa, Aa, A, Baa, Ba, B, Caa, Ca, C (numerical modifiers 1, 2, and 3 are added to letter-rating); S&P– AAA, AA, A, BBB, BB, B, CCC, CC, C; Fitch– AAA, AA, A, BBB, BB, B, CCC, CC, C. Ratings may be modified by the addition of a plus or minus sign to show relative standing within the major rating categories.
Notes: n/a Not available; (1) Not reviewed; (2) Issuer Rating/No General Obligation; (3) Standard and Poor's Issue Credit Rating (ICR) is a current opinion of an obliger with respect to a specific financial obligation, a specific class of financial obligations, or a specific financial program.
Source: U.S. Census Bureau, 2011 Statistical Abstract, Bond Ratings for City Governments by Largest Cities: 2009

DEMOGRAPHICS

Population Growth

Area	1990 Census	2000 Census	2010 Estimate	2015 Projection	Population Growth (%) 2000-2010	Population Growth (%) 2010-2015
City	86,561	100,266	115,741	122,911	15.4	6.2
MSA[1]	136,025	166,079	193,746	206,795	16.7	6.7
U.S.	248,709,873	281,421,906	309,038,974	321,675,005	9.8	4.1

Note: (1) Metropolitan Statistical Area - see Appendix B for areas included
Source: Claritas, Inc.

Number of Households and Average Household Size

Area	2010 Estimate	2010 Average Household Size
City	45,380	2.35
MSA[1]	74,219	2.48
U.S.	116,136,617	2.59

Note: (1) Metropolitan Statistical Area - see Appendix B for areas included
Source: Claritas, Inc.

Race and Ethnicity

Area	White Alone[2] (%)	Black Alone[2] (%)	Asian Alone[2] (%)	Other Race Alone[2] (%)	Hispanic[3] (%)
City	65.0	24.9	3.4	6.7	9.5
MSA[1]	73.3	18.9	2.5	5.2	7.1
U.S.	72.3	12.4	4.4	10.9	15.8

Note: Figures are 2010 estimates; (1) Metropolitan Statistical Area - see Appendix B for areas included (2) Alone is defined as not being in combination with one or more other races; (3) May be of any race.
Source: Claritas, Inc.

Segregation

Type	Segregation Indices[1] 1990	2000	2010	2010 Rank[2]	Percent Change 1990-2000	1990-2010	2000-2010
Black/White	n/a	n/a	n/a	n/a	n/a	n/a	n/a
Asian/White	n/a	n/a	n/a	n/a	n/a	n/a	n/a
Hispanic/White	n/a	n/a	n/a	n/a	n/a	n/a	n/a

Note: Figures are based on an analysis of 1990, 2000, and 2010 Census Decennial Census tract data by William H. Frey, Brookings Institution and the University of Michigan Social Science Data Analysis Network. In this analysis all racial groups (whites, blacks, and asians) are non-Hispanic members of those races. Hispanics are shown as a separate category; All figures cover the Metropolitan Statistical Area (see Appendix B for areas included); (1) Segregation Indices are Dissimilarity Indices that measure the degree to which the minority group is distributed differently than whites across census tracts. They range from 0 (complete integration) to 100 (complete [segregation) where the value indicates the percentage of the minority group that needs to move to be distributed exactly like whites; (2) Ranges from 1 (most segregated) to 102 (least segregated); n/a not available.
Source: www.CensusScope.org

Ancestry

Area	German	Irish	English	American	Italian	Polish	French	Scottish
City	9.8	9.3	11.3	6.2	2.4	1.4	1.8	3.4
MSA[1]	9.6	10.2	11.8	10.3	2.1	1.3	1.6	3.2
U.S.	16.6	12.0	9.1	6.1	5.9	3.3	3.1	1.9

Note: The top eight ancestries in the U.S. are shown. Figures are percentages and include multiple ancestry (e.g. if a person reported being Irish and Italian, they were included in both columns); (1) Metropolitan Statistical Area - see Appendix B for areas included
Source: U.S. Census Bureau, 2007-2009 American Community Survey 3-Year Estimates

Foreign-Born Population

Area	Any Foreign Country	Percent of Population Born in							
		Mexico	Asia	Europe	Carribean	South America	Central America[2]	Africa	Canada
City	10.2	3.3	2.5	1.4	0.4	1.1	0.7	0.5	0.3
MSA[1]	7.4	2.5	1.8	1.0	0.3	0.8	0.4	0.3	0.2
U.S.	12.5	3.8	3.4	1.6	1.1	0.8	0.9	0.5	0.3

Note: (1) Metropolitan Statistical Area - see Appendix B for areas included; (2) Excludes Mexico.
Source: U.S. Census Bureau, 2007-2009 American Community Survey 3-Year Estimates

Marriage Status

Area	Never Married	Now Married[2]	Separated	Widowed	Divorced
City	56.3	30.0	1.7	3.8	8.2
MSA[1]	45.1	40.2	1.8	4.2	8.7
U.S.	31.4	49.7	2.2	6.2	10.6

Note: Figures are percentages and cover the population 15 years of age and older;
(1) Metropolitan Statistical Area - see Appendix B for areas included; (2) Excludes separated
Source: U.S. Census Bureau, 2007-2009 American Community Survey 3-Year Estimates

Age Distribution and Median Age

Area	Percent of Population							Median Age
	Under Age 5	Age 5 to 17	Age 18 to 34	Age 35 to 49	Age 50 to 64	Age 65 to 79	80 Years and Over	
City	6.7	11.7	47.2	14.1	11.8	6.0	2.5	24.5
MSA[1]	6.6	14.9	36.3	17.5	15.0	7.3	2.4	28.5
U.S.	6.9	17.5	23.3	21.4	18.1	9.1	3.7	36.7

Note: (1) Metropolitan Statistical Area - see Appendix B for areas included
Source: U.S. Census Bureau, 2007-2009 American Community Survey 3-Year Estimates

Male/Female Ratio

Area	Males	Females	Males per 100 Females
City	56,697	59,044	96.0
MSA[1]	95,037	98,709	96.3
U.S.	152,401,520	156,637,454	97.3

Note: Figures are 2010 estimates; (1) Metropolitan Statistical Area - see Appendix B for areas included
Source: Claritas, Inc.

Religion

Area	Catholic	Southern Baptist	United Meth- odist	ELCA[1]	LDS[2]	Presby- terian Church USA	Jewish Est.	Muslim Est.
County	4.9	12.8	7.0	0.4	0.5	2.5	0.4	0.3
U.S.	22.0	7.1	3.7	1.8	1.5	1.1	2.2	0.6

Note: Figures are the number of adherents as a percentage of the total population; Adherents are defined as all members, including full members, their children and the estimated number of other participants who are not considered members (e.g. the baptized, those not confirmed, those regularly attending services, etc.); (1) Evangelical Lutheran Church in America; (2) The Church of Jesus Christ of Latter Day Saints Source: Reprinted with permission from Religious Congregations and Membership in the United States 2000 (Nashville, Glenmary Research Center, 2002) Copyright Association of Statisticians of American Religious Bodies. All rights reserved.

ECONOMY

Gross Metropolitan Product

Area	2006	2007	2008	2009	2009 Rank[2]
MSA[1]	5.7	5.9	6.3	6.3	227

Note: Figures are in billions of dollars; (1) Athens-Clarke County, GA Metropolitan Statistical Area - see Appendix B for areas included; (2) Rank ranges from 1 to 363 Source: The U.S. Conference of Mayors, "Pace of Economic Recovery: GMP and Jobs," January 2010

Economic Growth

Area	2006-2008 (%)	2009 (%)	2010 (%)	Rank[2]
MSA[1]	2.0	-0.1	3.3	107
U.S.	1.3	-2.5	2.2	–

Note: Figures are real Gross Metropolitan Product growth rates and represent annual average percent change; (1) Athens-Clarke County, GA Metropolitan Statistical Area - see Appendix B for areas included; (2) Rank ranges from 1 to 363 Source: The U.S. Conference of Mayors, "Pace of Economic Recovery: GMP and Jobs," January 2010

Metropolitan Area Exports

Area	2005	2006	2007	2008	2009	2009 Rank[2]
MSA[1]	228.5	152.0	182.2	171.4	214.6	252

Note: Figures are in millions of dollars; (1) Athens-Clarke County, GA Metropolitan Statistical Area - see Appendix B for areas included; (2) Rank ranges from 1 to 374 Source: U.S. Department of Commerce, International Trade Administration, Office of Trade & Industry Information, Manufacturing & Services

INCOME

Per Capita/Median/Average Income

Area	Per Capita ($)	Median Household ($)	Average Household ($)
City	20,572	34,179	51,390
MSA[1]	22,696	41,542	58,456
U.S.	27,034	52,795	71,071

Note: Figures are 2010 estimates; (1) Metropolitan Statistical Area - see Appendix B for areas included Source: Claritas, Inc.

Household Income Distribution

Area	Under $15,000	$15,000 -24,999	$25,000 -34,999	$35,000 -49,999	$50,000 -74,999	$75,000 -99,000	$100,000 -149,999	$150,000 and up
City	25.5	13.7	11.7	14.0	15.6	7.4	7.3	4.7
MSA[1]	19.8	12.3	11.4	14.7	17.4	9.5	9.1	5.7
U.S.	12.1	10.2	10.6	15.0	19.5	12.5	12.1	8.0

Note: Figures are 2010 estimates; (1) Metropolitan Statistical Area - see Appendix B for areas included Source: Claritas, Inc.

Poverty Rates by Age

Area	All Ages	Under 18 Years Old	18 to 64 Years Old	65 Years and Over
City	34.7	6.5	27.2	1.1
MSA[1]	25.5	5.3	18.8	1.4
U.S.	13.6	4.7	7.7	1.2

Note: Figures are percent of population with income during the previous 12 months below poverty level and only include population for whom poverty status is determined; (1) Metropolitan Statistical Area - see Appendix B for areas included
Source: U.S. Census Bureau, 2007-2009 American Community Survey 3-Year Estimates

Personal Bankruptcy Filing Rate

Area	2006	2007	2008	2009	2010
Clarke County	2.19	2.67	2.91	3.47	3.50
U.S.	2.00	2.73	3.53	4.60	4.96

Note: Numbers are per 1,000 population and include Chapter 7 and Chapter 13 filings
Source: Federal Deposit Insurance Corporation, Regional Economic Conditions, March 17, 2011

EMPLOYMENT

Labor Force and Employment

Area	Civilian Labor Force			Workers Employed		
	Dec. 2009	Dec. 2010	% Chg.	Dec. 2009	Dec. 2010	% Chg.
City	64,003	64,416	0.6	59,181	59,484	0.5
MSA[1]	106,230	106,744	0.5	98,149	98,651	0.5
U.S.	152,693,000	153,156,000	0.3	137,953,000	139,159,000	0.9

Note: Data is not seasonally adjusted and covers workers 16 years of age and older;
(1) Metropolitan Statistical Area - see Appendix B for areas included
Source: Bureau of Labor Statistics, http://stats.bls.gov

Unemployment Rate

Area	2010											
	Jan.	Feb.	Mar.	Apr.	May	Jun.	Jul.	Aug.	Sep.	Oct.	Nov.	Dec.
City	8.3	8.3	7.9	7.5	7.7	8.4	8.3	8.0	7.6	7.6	7.6	7.7
MSA[1]	8.3	8.3	7.8	7.4	7.5	8.0	8.0	7.9	7.5	7.6	7.6	7.6
U.S.	10.6	10.4	10.2	9.5	9.3	9.6	9.7	9.5	9.2	9.0	9.3	9.1

Note: Data is not seasonally adjusted and covers workers 16 years of age and older; All figures are percentages; (1) Metropolitan Statistical Area - see Appendix B for areas included
Source: Bureau of Labor Statistics, http://stats.bls.gov

Projected Unemployment Rate

Area	2007 (%)	2009 (%)	2011 (%)	2013 (%)
MSA[1]	3.9	7.2	7.8	6.7

Note: (1) Metropolitan Statistical Area - see Appendix B for areas included
Source: The U.S. Conference of Mayors, "Pace of Economic Recovery: GMP and Jobs," January 2010

Employment by Occupation

Occupation Classification	City (%)	MSA[1] (%)	U.S. (%)
Sales and Office	22.1	22.9	25.4
Professional and Related	29.5	26.1	21.0
Service	21.3	19.4	17.2
Production, Transportation, and Material Moving	10.6	11.1	12.3
Management, Business, and Financial	11.2	12.6	14.1
Construction, Extraction, and Maintenance	5.1	7.6	9.2
Farming, Forestry, and Fishing	0.3	0.3	0.7

Note: Figures cover employed civilians 16 years of age and older;
(1) Metropolitan Statistical Area - see Appendix B for areas included
Source: U.S. Census Bureau, 2007-2009 American Community Survey 3-Year Estimates

Employment by Industry

Sector	MSA[1]		U.S.
	Number of Employees	Percent of Total	Percent of Total
Government	24,600	30.0	17.2
Education and Health Services	n/a	n/a	15.2
Professional and Business Services	6,900	8.4	13.0
Retail Trade	9,500	11.6	11.4
Leisure and Hospitality	7,800	9.5	9.7
Manufacturing	n/a	n/a	8.8
Financial Activities	n/a	n/a	5.8
Wholesale Trade	n/a	n/a	4.2
Construction	n/a	n/a	4.1
Other Services	n/a	n/a	4.1
Transportation and Utilities	n/a	n/a	3.7
Information	n/a	n/a	2.1
Mining and Logging	n/a	n/a	0.6

Note: Figures cover non-farm employment as of December 2010 and are not seasonally adjusted;
(1) Metropolitan Statistical Area - see Appendix B for areas included; n/a not available
Source: Bureau of Labor Statistics, http://stats.bls.gov

Occupations with Greatest Projected Employment Growth: 2006 - 2016

Occupation[1]	2006 Employment	2016 Projected Employment	Numeric Employment Change	Percent Employment Change
Combined food preparation and serving workers, including fast food	95,500	124,650	29,150	30.5
Retail salespersons	127,750	153,800	26,050	20.4
Customer service representatives	83,640	105,060	21,420	25.6
Registered nurses	61,770	81,670	19,900	32.2
Waiters and waitresses	67,030	85,420	18,390	27.4
Elementary school teachers, except special education	54,220	70,440	16,220	29.9
Office clerks, general	88,680	102,290	13,610	15.3
Janitors and cleaners, except maids and housekeeping cleaners	60,840	73,160	12,320	20.2
Nursing aides, orderlies, and attendants	38,510	48,910	10,400	27.0
Child care workers	35,890	45,770	9,880	27.5

Note: Projections cover Georgia; (1) Sorted by numeric employment change
Source: www.projectionscentral.com, State Occupational Projections, 2006-2016 Long-Term Projections

Fastest Growing Occupations: 2006 - 2016

Occupation[1]	2006 Employment	2016 Projected Employment	Numeric Employment Change	Percent Employment Change
Skin care specialists	1,570	2,560	990	63.1
Network systems and data communications analysts	8,570	13,260	4,690	54.7
Home health aides	7,720	11,780	4,060	52.6
Medical assistants	11,990	17,450	5,460	45.5
Veterinary technologists and technicians	2,160	3,140	980	45.4
Mental health and substance abuse social workers	1,260	1,780	520	41.3
Computer software engineers, applications	11,160	15,730	4,570	40.9
Physician assistants	2,160	3,020	860	39.8
Veterinarians	1,820	2,530	710	39.0
Physical therapist assistants	1,350	1,870	520	38.5

Note: Projections cover Georgia; (1) Sorted by percent employment change and excludes occupations with numeric employment change less than 400
Source: www.projectionscentral.com, State Occupational Projections, 2006-2016 Long-Term Projections

Average Wages

Occupation	$/Hr.	Occupation	$/Hr.
Accountants and Auditors	23.32	Maids and Housekeeping Cleaners	9.06
Automotive Mechanics	19.39	Maintenance and Repair Workers	16.00
Bookkeepers	14.66	Marketing Managers	42.63
Carpenters	18.82	Nuclear Medicine Technologists	n/a
Cashiers	8.48	Nurses, Licensed Practical	18.29
Clerks, General Office	11.71	Nurses, Registered	27.10
Clerks, Receptionists/Information	11.38	Nursing Aides/Orderlies/Attendants	9.71
Clerks, Shipping/Receiving	14.02	Packers and Packagers, Hand	10.11
Computer Programmers	22.69	Physical Therapists	30.60
Computer Support Specialists	19.12	Postal Service Mail Carriers	22.52
Computer Systems Analysts	30.78	Real Estate Brokers	13.14
Cooks, Restaurant	10.10	Retail Salespersons	10.66
Dentists	n/a	Sales Reps., Exc. Tech./Scientific	25.81
Electrical Engineers	36.85	Sales Reps., Tech./Scientific	26.79
Electricians	19.37	Secretaries, Exc. Legal/Med./Exec.	12.80
Financial Managers	46.62	Security Guards	13.07
First-Line Supervisors/Mgrs., Sales	16.47	Surgeons	105.18
Food Preparation Workers	9.64	Teacher Assistants	9.30
General and Operations Managers	41.13	Teachers, Elementary School	26.20
Hairdressers/Cosmetologists	13.85	Teachers, Secondary School	27.20
Internists	66.22	Telemarketers	9.19
Janitors and Cleaners	10.92	Truck Drivers, Heavy/Tractor-Trailer	18.59
Landscaping/Groundskeeping Workers	11.32	Truck Drivers, Light/Delivery Svcs.	15.23
Lawyers	n/a	Waiters and Waitresses	7.84

Note: Wage data covers the Athens-Clarke County, GA - see Appendix B for areas included. Hourly wages for elementary/secondary school teachers and teacher assistants were calculated by the editors from annual wage data assuming a 40 hour work week; n/a not available.
Source: Bureau of Labor Statistics, Metro Area Occupational Employment and Wage Estimates, May 2009

RESIDENTIAL REAL ESTATE

Building Permits

Area	Single-Family			Multi-Family			Total		
	2009	2010	Pct. Chg.	2009	2010	Pct. Chg.	2009	2010	Pct. Chg.
City	90	94	4.4	18	0	-100.0	108	94	-13.0
MSA[1]	277	226	-18.4	20	0	-100.0	297	226	-23.9
U.S.	441,100	447,300	1.4	141,900	157,300	10.9	583,000	604,600	3.7

Note: (1) Metropolitan Statistical Area - see Appendix B for areas included; figures represent new, privately-owned housing units authorized (unadjusted data); All permit data are based on estimates with imputation.
Source: U.S. Census Bureau, Manufacturing, Mining, and Construction Statistics, Building Permits, 2009, 2010

Homeownership Rate

Area	2005 (%)	2006 (%)	2007 (%)	2008 (%)	2009 (%)	2010 (%)
MSA[1]	n/a	n/a	n/a	n/a	n/a	n/a
U.S.	68.9	68.8	68.1	67.8	67.4	66.9

Note: (1) Metropolitan Statistical Area - see Appendix B for areas included
Source: U.S. Census Bureau, Housing Vacancies and Homeownership Annual Statistics: 2010

Housing Vacancy Rates

Area	Gross Vacancy Rate[2] (%)			Year-Round Vacancy Rate[3] (%)			Rental Vacancy Rate[4] (%)			Homeowner Vacancy Rate[5] (%)		
	2008	2009	2010	2008	2009	2010	2008	2009	2010	2008	2009	2010
MSA[1]	n/a	n/a	n/a	n/a	n/a	n/a	n/a	n/a	n/a	n/a	n/a	n/a
U.S.	14.4	14.5	14.3	11.1	11.3	11.3	10.0	10.6	10.2	2.8	2.6	2.6

Note: (1) Metropolitan Statistical Area - see Appendix B for areas included; (2) The percentage of the total housing inventory that is vacant; (3) The percentage of the housing inventory (excluding seasonal units) that is year-round vacant; (4) The percentage of rental inventory that is vacant for rent; (5) The percentage of homeowner inventory that is vacant for sale; n/a not available
Source: U.S. Census Bureau, Housing Vacancies and Homeownership Annual Statistics: 2010

State Corporate Income Tax Rates

State	Tax Rate (%)	Income Brackets ($)	Num. of Brackets	Financial Institution Tax Rate (%)[a]	Federal Income Tax Ded.
Georgia	6.0	Flat rate	1	6.0	No

Note: Tax rates as of January 1, 2011; (a) Rates listed are the tax rates applied to financial institutions or excise taxes based on income. Some states have other taxes based upon the value of deposits or shares.
Source: Federation of Tax Administrators, "State Corporate Income Tax Rates, 2011"

State Individual Income Tax Rates

State	Tax Rate (%)	Income Brackets ($)	Num. of Brackets	Personal Exempt. ($)[1] Single	Personal Exempt. ($)[1] Dependents	Fed. Inc. Tax Ded.
Georgia	1.0 - 6.0	750 (h) - 7,001 (h)	6	2,700	3,000	No

Note: Tax rates as of January 1, 2011; Local- and county-level taxes are not included; n/a not applicable; (1) Married joint filers generally receive double the single exemption; (h) The Georgia income brackets reported are for single individuals. For married couples filing jointly, the same tax rates apply to income brackets ranging from $1,000, to $10,000.
Source: Federation of Tax Administrators, "State Individual Income Tax Rates, 2011"

Various State and Local Tax Rates

State	State and Local Sales and Use (%)	State Sales and Use (%)	Gasoline[1] (¢/gal.)	Cigarette[2] ($/pack)	Spirits[3] ($/gal.)	Wine[4] ($/gal.)	Beer[5] ($/gal.)
Georgia	7.0	4.00	20.8	0.37	3.79	1.51	1.01 (l)

Note: All tax rates as of January 1, 2011 except Spirits (Sept. 1, 2010); (1) The American Petroleum Institute has developed a methodology for determining the average tax rate on a gallon of fuel. Rates may include any of the following: excise taxes, environmental fees, storage tank fees, other fees or taxes, general sales tax, and local taxes. In states where gasoline is subject to the general sales tax, or where the fuel tax is based on the average sale price, the average rate determined by API is sensitive to changes in the price of gasoline. States that fully or partially apply general sales taxes to gasoline: CA, CO, GA, IL, IN, MI, NY; (2) The federal excise tax of $1.0066 per pack and local taxes are not included; (3) Rates are those applicable to off-premise sales of 40% alcohol by volume (a.b.v.) distilled spirits in 750ml containers. Local excise taxes are excluded; (4) Rates are those applicable to off-premise sales of 11% a.b.v. non-carbonated wine in 750ml containers; (5) Rates are those applicable to off-premise sales of 4.7% a.b.v. beer in 12 ounce containers; (l) Includes statewide local rates in Alabama ($0.52) and Georgia ($0.53).
Source: Tax Foundation, 2011 Facts & Figures: How Does Your State Compare?

State-Local Tax Burdens

Area	Rate (%)	Rank[1]	Per Capita Taxes Paid to Home State ($)	Total State and Local Per Capita Taxes Paid ($)	Per Capita Income ($)
Georgia	9.1	32	2,411	3,350	36,738
U.S. Average	9.8	-	3,057	4,160	42,539

Note: Figures cover 2009; (1) Rank ranges from 1 to 50 where 1 is highest tax burden
Source: Tax Foundation, State-Local Tax Burdens, All States, 2009

State Business Tax Climate Index Rankings

State	Overall Rank	Corporate Tax Index Rank	Individual Income Tax Index Rank	Sales Tax Index Rank	Unemployment Insurance Tax Index Rank	Property Tax Index Rank
Georgia	25	8	30	23	22	38

Note: The index is a measure of how each state's tax laws affect economic performance. The lower the rank, the more favorable a state's tax system is for business. All ranks are for fiscal years. States without a given tax are given a ranking of 1.
Source: Tax Foundation, Tax Foundation Background Paper, No. 60, "2011 State Business Tax Climate Index"

**COMMERCIAL
UTILITIES**

Typical Monthly Electric Bills

Area	Commercial Service ($/month)		Industrial Service ($/month)	
	3 kW demand 1,000 kWh	40 kW demand 14,000 kWh	1,000 kW demand 200,000 kWh	50,000 kW demand 15,000,000 kWh
City	n/a	n/a	n/a	n/a
Average[1]	135	1,576	23,741	1,402,202

Note: Based on total rates in effect July 1, 2010; (1) average based on 182 utilities surveyed; n/a not available
Source: Edison Electric Institute, Typical Bills and Average Rates Report, Summer 2010

TRANSPORTATION

Means of Transportation to Work

Area	Car/Truck/Van		Public Transportation			Bicycle	Walked	Other Means	Worked at Home
	Drove Alone	Car-pooled	Bus	Subway	Railroad				
City	72.7	11.6	4.2	0.0	0.0	1.4	5.6	1.1	3.3
MSA[1]	75.6	12.1	2.6	0.0	0.0	0.9	3.7	0.9	4.1
U.S.	75.8	10.4	2.7	1.7	0.5	0.5	2.9	1.2	4.1

Note: Figures are percentages and cover workers 16 years of age and older;
(1) Metropolitan Statistical Area - see Appendix B for areas included
Source: U.S. Census Bureau, 2007-2009 American Community Survey 3-Year Estimates

Travel Time to Work

Area	Less Than 15 Minutes	15 to 29 Minutes	30 to 44 Minutes	45 to 59 Minutes	60 to 89 Minutes	90 Minutes or More
City	47.9	35.4	9.5	2.1	2.5	2.7
MSA[1]	40.3	38.2	12.6	3.4	3.0	2.5
U.S.	28.5	36.2	19.7	7.5	5.6	2.5

Note: Figures are percentages and include workers 16 years old and over;
(1) Metropolitan Statistical Area - see Appendix B for areas included
Source: U.S. Census Bureau, 2007-2009 American Community Survey 3-Year Estimates

Travel Time Index

Area	1982	1999	2008	2009
Urban Area[1]	n/a	n/a	n/a	n/a
Average[2]	1.08	1.20	1.20	1.20

Note: Travel Time Index—the ratio of travel time in the peak period to the travel time at free-flow conditions. A value of 1.30 indicates a 20-minute free-flow trip takes 26 minutes in the peak. Free-flow speeds (60 mph on freeways and 35 mph on principal arterials) are used as the comparison threshold; (1) Covers the Athens-Clarke County urban area; (2) average of 439 urban areas
Source: Texas Transportation Institute, Urban Mobility Report 2010, December 2010

Public Transportation

Agency Name / Mode of Transportation	Vehicles Operated in Maximum Service	Annual Unlinked Passenger Trips ('000)	Annual Passenger Miles ('000)
Athens Transit System			
Demand response	3	8.5	47.8
Bus	22	1,839.0	5,789.9

Note: Figures include both directly operated and purchased transportation
Source: Federal Transit Administration, National Transit Database, 2009

Air Transportation

Airport Name and Code / Type of Service	Passenger Airlines[1]	Passenger Enplanements	Freight Carriers[2]	Freight (lbs.)
Athens Municipal (AHN)				
Domestic service (U.S. carriers - 2010)	4	4,356	0	0
International service (U.S. carriers - 2009)	0	0	0	0

Note: (1) Includes all U.S.-based major, minor and commuter airlines that carried at least one passenger during the year; (2) Includes all U.S.-based airlines and freight carriers that transported at least one pound of freight during the year
Source: Bureau of Transportation Statistics, The Intermodal Transportation Database, Air Carriers: T-100 Domestic Market (U.S. Carriers), 2010; Bureau of Transportation Statistics, The Intermodal Transportation Database, Air Carriers: T-100 International Market (U.S. Carriers), 2009

Other Transportation Statistics

Interstate highways:	CR-82 connecting to I-85 (18 miles)
Amtrak service:	No
Major waterways/ports:	None

Source: Amtrak.com; Google Maps

BUSINESSES

Major Business Headquarters

Company Name	Rankings Fortune[1]	Forbes[2]
No companies listed	-	-

Note: (1) Fortune 500—companies that produce a 10-K are ranked 1 to 500 based on 2010 revenue; (2) all private companies with at least $2 billion in annual revenue are ranked 1 to 223; companies listed are headquartered in the city; dashes indicate no ranking
Source: Fortune, "Fortune 500," May 23, 2011; Forbes, "America's Largest Private Companies," November 3, 2010

Minority- and Women-Owned Businesses

Group	All Firms — Firms	All Firms — Sales ($000)	Firms with Paid Employees — Firms	Firms with Paid Employees — Sales ($000)	Employees	Payroll ($000)
Asian	330	285,670	161	280,037	1,813	40,491
Black	(s)	(s)	(s)	(s)	(s)	(s)
Hispanic	311	22,829	16	11,624	81	2,166
Women	2,687	605,533	366	562,480	4,810	119,645
All Firms	10,181	8,756,927	2,435	8,454,434	48,844	1,391,992

Note: Figures cover firms located in the city; minority- and women-owned business are defined as firms in which the corresponding group own 51% or more of the stock or equity of the company; (s) estimates are suppressed when publication standards are not met
Source: U.S. Census Bureau, 2007 Economic Census, Survey of Business Owners

HOTELS

Hotels/Motels

Area	5 Star Num.	5 Star Pct.3	4 Star Num.	4 Star Pct.3	3 Star Num.	3 Star Pct.3	2 Star Num.	2 Star Pct.3	1 Star Num.	1 Star Pct.3	Not Rated Num.	Not Rated Pct.3
City[1]	0	0.0	0	0.0	7	20.0	20	57.1	1	2.9	7	20.0
Total[2]	119	0.7	927	5.8	4,906	30.5	7,992	49.7	526	3.3	1,625	10.1

Note: (1) Figures cover Athens and vicinity; (2) Figures cover all 100 cities in this book; (3) Percentage of hotels which are a given star rating; Star ratings are determined by expedia.com and offer an indication of the general quality of a particular hotel.
Source: expedia.com, May 5, 2011

EVENT SITES

Major Stadiums, Arenas, and Auditoriums

Name	Max. Capacity
Sanford Stadium	92,746

Source: Original research

Convention Centers

Name	Overall Space (sq. ft.)	Exhibit Space (sq. ft.)	Meeting Space (sq. ft.)	Meeting Rooms

There are no major convention centers.

Source: Original research

Living Environment

COST OF LIVING

Cost of Living Index

Composite Index	Groceries	Housing	Utilities	Trans-portation	Health Care	Misc. Goods/Services
n/a	n/a	n/a	n/a	n/a	n/a	n/a

Note: U.S. = 100; n/a not available
Source: The Council for Community and Economic Research, ACCRA Cost of Living Index, 2010

Grocery Prices

Area[1]	T-Bone Steak ($/pound)	Frying Chicken ($/pound)	Whole Milk ($/half gal.)	Eggs ($/dozen)	Orange Juice ($/64 oz.)	Coffee ($/11.5 oz.)
City[2]	n/a	n/a	n/a	n/a	n/a	n/a
Avg.	9.04	1.16	2.02	1.47	3.08	3.65
Min.	6.97	0.84	1.46	0.96	2.39	2.64
Max.	13.93	2.51	3.58	3.01	4.94	6.32

*Note: (1) Values for the local area are compared with the average, minimum and maximum values for all 338 areas in the Cost of Living Index; n/a not available; (2) Figures cover the Athens GA urban area; **T-Bone Steak** (price per pound); **Frying Chicken** (price per pound, whole fryer); **Whole Milk** (half gallon carton); **Eggs** (price per dozen, Grade A, large); **Orange Juice** (64 oz. Tropicana or Florida Natural); **Coffee** (11.5 oz. can, vacuum-packed, Maxwell House, Hills Bros, or Folgers).*
Source: The Council for Community and Economic Research, ACCRA Cost of Living Index, 2010

Housing and Utility Costs

Area[1]	New Home Price ($)	Apartment Rent ($/month)	All Electric ($/month)	Part Electric ($/month)	Other Energy ($/month)	Telephone ($/month)
City[2]	n/a	n/a	n/a	n/a	n/a	n/a
Avg.	293,442	810	166.39	91.93	83.82	26.93
Min.	182,545	453	119.21	44.47	36.85	17.98
Max.	1,123,114	2,776	307.53	218.20	313.90	39.15

*Note: (1) Values for the local area are compared with the average, minimum and maximum values for all 338 areas in the Cost of Living Index; n/a not available; (2) Figures cover the Athens GA urban area; **New Home Price** (2,400 sf living area, 8,000 sf lot, in urban area with full utilities); **Apartment Rent** (950 sf 2 bedroom/1.5 or 2 bath, unfurnished, excluding all utilities except water); **All Electric** (average monthly cost for an all-electric home); **Part Electric** (average monthly cost for a part-electric home); **Other Energy** (average monthly cost for natural gas, fuel oil, coal, wood, and any other forms of energy except electricity); **Telephone** (price includes basic monthly rate for a private residential line plus additional local usage charges incurred by a family of four).*
Source: The Council for Community and Economic Research, ACCRA Cost of Living Index, 2010

Health Care, Transportation, and Other Costs

Area[1]	Doctor ($/visit)	Dentist ($/visit)	Optometrist ($/visit)	Gasoline ($/gallon)	Beauty Salon ($/visit)	Men's Shirt ($)
City[2]	n/a	n/a	n/a	n/a	n/a	n/a
Avg.	89.44	78.95	87.40	2.73	31.92	24.83
Min.	57.00	54.25	48.32	2.44	19.17	13.67
Max.	149.90	136.73	174.22	3.75	62.81	47.89

*Note: (1) Values for the local area are compared with the average, minimum and maximum values for all 338 areas in the Cost of Living Index; n/a not available; (2) Figures cover the Athens GA urban area; **Doctor** (general practitioners routine exam of an established patient); **Dentist** (adult teeth cleaning and periodic oral examination); **Optometrist** (full vision eye exam for established adult patient); **Gasoline** (one gallon regular unleaded, national brand, including all taxes, cash price at self-service pump if available); **Beauty Salon** (woman's shampoo, trim, and blow-dry); **Men's Shirt** (cotton/polyester dress shirt, pinpoint weave, long sleeves).*
Source: The Council for Community and Economic Research, ACCRA Cost of Living Index, 2010

HOUSING

House Price Index (HPI)

Area	National Ranking[2]	Quarterly Change (%)	One-Year Change (%)	Five-Year Change (%)
MSA[1]	209	-0.77	-2.38	-0.02
U.S.[3]	-	-0.84	-3.95	-11.45

Note: The HPI is a weighted repeat sales index. It measures average price changes in repeat sales or refinancings on the same properties. This information is obtained by reviewing repeat mortgage transactions on single-family properties whose mortgages have been purchased or securitized by Fannie Mae or Freddie Mac in January 1975; (1) Metropolitan/Micropolitan Statistical Area - see Appendix B for areas included; (2) Rankings are based on annual percentage change for all metro areas containing at least 15,000 transactions over the last 10 years and ranges from 1 to 309; (3) figures based on a weighted average of Census Division estimates; all figures are for the period ending December 31, 2010
Source: Federal Housing Finance Agency, House Price Index, February 24, 2011

House Price Valuations

Area	Q4 2005 Price ($000)	Q4 2005 Over-valuation	Q4 2006 Price ($000)	Q4 2006 Over-valuation	Q4 2007 Price ($000)	Q4 2007 Over-valuation	Q4 2008 Price ($000)	Q4 2008 Over-valuation	Q4 2009 Price ($000)	Q4 2009 Over-valuation
MSA[1]	132.7	2.5	138.5	1.3	137.5	-4.4	128.8	-11.8	124.4	-15.9

Note: Figures show the percentage of over- or under-valuation of single family homes relative to statistically normal house values (e.g. a value of 23.6 indicates that house values are 23.6% overvalued). Statistically normal house values are based on house prices, interest rates, household incomes, population densities, and any historical premiums or discounts metropolitan areas have exhibited over time; (1) Figures cover the Athens-Clarke County, GA Metropolitan Statistical Area - see Appendix B for areas included
Source: Global Insight/PNC Financial Services Group, House Prices in America: 4th Quarter 2009 Update

Median Single-Family Home Prices

Area	2008	2009	2010p	Percent Change 2009 to 2010
MSA[1]	n/a	n/a	n/a	n/a
U.S. Average	196.6	172.1	173.2	0.6

Note: Figures are median sales prices of existing single-family homes in thousands of dollars; (p) preliminary; n/a not available; (1) Metropolitan Statistical Area - see Appendix B for areas included
Source: National Association of Realtors, Median Sales Price of Existing Single-Family Homes for Metropolitan Areas, 4th Quarter 2010

Median Apartment Condo-Coop Home Prices

Area	2008	2009	2010p	Percent Change 2009 to 2010
MSA[1]	n/a	n/a	n/a	n/a
U.S. Average	209.8	175.6	171.7	-2.2

Note: Figures are median sales prices of existing apartment condo-coop homes in thousands of dollars; (p) preliminary; n/a not available; (1) Metropolitan Statistical Area - see Appendix B for areas included
Source: National Association of Realtors, Median Sales Price of Existing Apartment Condo-Coop Homes for Metropolitan Areas, 4th Quarter 2010

Year Housing Structure Built

Area	2000 or Later	1990 -1999	1980 -1989	1970 -1979	1960 -1969	1950 -1959	1940 -1949	Before 1940	Median Year
City	20.4	18.7	15.3	17.1	11.8	7.2	3.1	6.5	1983
MSA[1]	17.1	22.0	18.4	17.1	10.1	5.5	2.7	7.2	1984
U.S.	12.5	14.0	14.2	16.5	11.4	11.3	5.8	14.3	1974

Note: Figures are percentages except for Median Year; (1) Metropolitan Statistical Area - see Appendix B for areas included
Source: U.S. Census Bureau, 2007-2009 American Community Survey 3-Year Estimates

HEALTH

Health Risk Data

Category	MSA[1] (%)	U.S. (%)
Adults who have been told they have high blood pressure	n/a	28.7
Adults who have been told they have high blood cholesterol	n/a	37.5
Adults who have been told they have diabetes[3]	n/a	8.3
Adults who have been told they have arthritis	n/a	26.0
Adults who have been told they currently have asthma	n/a	8.8
Adults who are current smokers	n/a	17.9
Adults who are heavy drinkers[4]	n/a	5.1
Adults who are binge drinkers[5]	n/a	15.8
Adults who are overweight (BMI 25.0 - 29.9)	n/a	36.2
Adults who are obese (BMI 30.0 - 99.8)	n/a	26.9
Adults who participated in any physical activities in the past month	n/a	76.2
Adults 50+ who have ever had a sigmoidoscopy or colonoscopy[2]	n/a	62.2
Women 40+ who have had a mammogram within the past two years[2]	n/a	76.0
Adults age 18–64 who have any kind of health care coverage	n/a	83.1

Note: Data as of 2009 unless otherwise noted; n/a not available; (1) Figures cover the Athens-Clarke County, GA Metropolitan Statistical Area - see Appendix B for areas included; (2) Data as of 2008; (3) Figures do not include pregnancy-related, borderline, or pre-diabetes; (4) Heavy drinkers are classified as males having more than two drinks per day or females having more than one drink per day; (5) Binge drinkers are classified as males having five or more drinks on one occasion or females having four or more drinks on one occasion
Source: Centers for Disease Control and Prevention, Behaviorial Risk Factor Surveillance System, SMART: Selected Metropolitan/Micropolitan Area Risk Trends, 2008, 2009

Mortality Rates for the Top 10 Causes of Death in the U.S.

ICD-10[a] Sub-Chapter	ICD-10[a] Code	Age-Adjusted Mortality Rate[1] per 100,000 population	
		County[2]	U.S.
Malignant neoplasms	C00-C97	172.7	180.9
Ischaemic heart diseases	I20-I25	87.3	135.0
Other forms of heart disease	I30-I51	75.4	50.0
Cerebrovascular diseases	I60-I69	48.2	44.1
Chronic lower respiratory diseases	J40-J47	33.0	41.5
Other degenerative diseases of the nervous system	G30-G31	20.4	23.6
Diabetes mellitus	E10-E14	19.1	23.5
Other external causes of accidental injury	W00-X59	16.4	23.5
Organic, including symptomatic, mental disorders	F01-F09	32.3	22.2
Influenza and pneumonia	J09-J18	9.4	18.1

Note: (a) ICD-10 = International Classification of Diseases 10th Revision; (1) Mortality rates are a three year average covering 2005-2007; (2) Figures cover Clarke County
Source: Centers for Disease Control and Prevention, National Center for Health Statistics. Compressed Mortality File 1999-2007. CDC WONDER On-line Database, compiled from Compressed Mortality File 1999-2007 Series 20 No. 2M, 2010.

Mortality Rates for Selected Causes of Death

ICD-10[a] Sub-Chapter	ICD-10[a] Code	Age-Adjusted Mortality Rate[1] per 100,000 population	
		County[2]	U.S.
Assault	X85-Y09	*6.0	6.0
Human immunodeficiency virus (HIV) disease	B20-B24	*5.1	4.0
Hypertensive diseases	I10-I15	23.3	18.0
Intentional self-harm	X60-X84	12.7	11.0
Malnutrition	E40-E46	*0.7	0.8
Obesity and other hyperalimentation	E65-E68	*0.8	1.5
Transport accidents	V01-V99	13.9	15.6
Viral hepatitis	B15-B19	*2.7	2.1

Note: (a) ICD-10 = International Classification of Diseases 10th Revision; (1) Mortality rates are a three year average covering 2005-2007; (2) Figures cover Clarke County; (*) Unreliable data as per CDC
Source: Centers for Disease Control and Prevention, National Center for Health Statistics. Compressed Mortality File 1999-2007. CDC WONDER On-line Database, compiled from Compressed Mortality File 1999-2007 Series 20 No. 2M, 2010.

Distribution of Physicians and Dentists

Area[1]	Dentists[2]	D.O.[3]	M.D.[4]				
			Total	Family/ General Practice	Pediatrics	Medical Specialties	Surgical Specialties
Local (number)	54	12	268	22	11	88	85
Local (rate[5])	4.8	1.0	23.3	1.9	1.0	7.6	7.4
U.S. (rate[5])	4.5	1.9	18.3	2.5	1.4	6.8	4.1

Note: Data as of 2008 unless noted; (1) Local data covers Clarke County; (2) Data as of 2007; (3) Doctor of Osteopathic Medicine; (4) Includes active, non-federal, patient-care, office-based Doctors of Medicine; (5) rate per 10,000 population
Source: Area Resource File (ARF). 2009-2010 Release. U.S. Department of Health and Human Services, Health Resources and Services Administration, Bureau of Health Professions, Rockville, MD, August 2010

Hospitals

Athens has the following hospitals: 2 general medical and surgical; 1 long-term acute care.
AHA Guide to the Healthcare Field 2010

EDUCATION

Public School District Statistics

District Name	Schls	Pupils	Pupil/ Teacher Ratio	Minority Pupils[1] (%)	Free Lunch Eligible[2] (%)	IEP[3] (%)
Clarke County	21	12,262	12.0	80.5	66.8	12.8

Note: Table includes school districts with 2,000 or more students; (1) Percentage of students that are not non-Hispanic white; (2) Percentage of students that are eligible for the free lunch program; (3) Percentage of students that have an Individualized Education Program.
Source: U.S. Department of Education, National Center for Education Statistics, Common Core of Data, Local Education Agency (School District) Universe Survey: School Year 2008-2009; U.S. Department of Education, National Center for Education Statistics, Common Core of Data, Public Elementary/Secondary School Universe Survey: School Year 2008-2009

Top Public High Schools

High School Name	Index[1]	Rank[1]	Subsidized Lunch (%)[2]	E&E (%)[3]
Cedar Shoals	1.140	1561	73.0	16.0
Clarke Central	1.512	1138	68.0	19.9

Note: (1) Public schools are ranked according to a ratio that is the number of Advanced Placement, International Baccalaureate, and/or Cambridge tests taken by all students at a school in 2009 divided by the number of graduating seniors. All of the schools on the list have an index of at least 1.000; they are in the top six percent of public schools measured this way. The rankings range from 1 to 1,734; (2) Percentage of students receiving federally subsidized meals; (3) E & E stands for equity and excellence percentage: the portion of all graduating seniors at a school that had at least one passing grade on one AP or IB test; (4) Schools that offer International Baccalaureate or Cambridge exams; (5) School is unranked, but has been identified by Newsweek as one of the nation's most elite public high schools.
Source: Newsweek Online, "Top High Schools 2010"

Highest Level of Education

Area	Less than H.S.	H.S. Diploma	Some College, No Deg.	Associate Degree	Bachelors Degree	Masters Degree	Profess. School Degree	Doctorate Degree
City	15.5	22.0	16.4	4.9	22.4	10.5	3.4	5.1
MSA[1]	17.1	26.7	16.6	4.7	18.8	9.1	2.8	4.1
U.S.	15.3	29.0	20.7	7.5	17.4	7.0	1.9	1.1

Note: Figures are 2010 estimated percentages and cover persons age 25 and over; (1) Metropolitan Statistical Area - see Appendix B for areas included
Source: Claritas, Inc.

Educational Attainment by Race

Area	High School Graduate (%)					Bachelor's Degree (%)				
	Total	White	Black	Asian	Hisp.[2]	Total	White	Black	Asian	Hisp.[2]
City	84.7	93.3	74.5	96.7	51.8	40.9	55.6	12.3	81.7	18.2
MSA[1]	82.8	87.6	72.0	97.2	50.0	34.1	40.4	11.5	77.8	16.6
U.S.	84.9	90.0	80.7	85.5	60.7	27.8	30.9	17.5	49.7	12.7

Note: Figures shown cover persons 25 years old and over; (1) Metropolitan Statistical Area - see Appendix B for areas included; (2) people of Hispanic origin can be of any race
Source: U.S. Census Bureau, 2007-2009 American Community Survey 3-Year Estimates

School Enrollment by Grade and Control

Area	Preschool (%)		Kindergarten (%)		Grades 1 - 4 (%)		Grades 5 - 8 (%)		Grades 9 - 12 (%)	
	Public	Private	Public	Private	Public	Private	Public	Private	Public	Private
City	62.3	37.7	79.3	20.7	89.8	10.2	87.4	12.6	91.3	8.7
MSA[1]	52.9	47.1	82.5	17.5	89.2	10.8	89.6	10.4	91.1	8.9
U.S.	54.3	45.7	86.4	13.6	88.9	11.1	89.1	10.9	90.2	9.8

Note: Figures shown cover persons 3 years old and over; (1) Metropolitan Statistical Area - see Appendix B for areas included
Source: U.S. Census Bureau, 2007-2009 American Community Survey 3-Year Estimates

Average Salaries of Public School Classroom Teachers

Area	2009-10		2010-11		Percent Change 2009-10 to 2010-11	Percent Change 2000-01 to 2010-11
	Dollars	Rank[1]	Dollars	Rank[1]		
Georgia	53,112	18	53,906	18	1.50	27.7
U.S. Average	55,202	-	56,069	-	1.57	29.3

Note: (1) State rank ranges from 1 to 51 where 1 indicates highest salary.
Source: National Education Association, Rankings & Estimates: Rankings of the States 2010 and Estimates of School Statistics 2011, December 2010

Higher Education

Four-Year Colleges			Two-Year Colleges			Medical Schools[1]	Law Schools[2]	Voc/ Tech[3]
Public	Private Non-profit	Private For-profit	Public	Private Non-profit	Private For-profit			
1	0	0	1	0	0	0	1	1

Note: Figures cover institutions located within the city limits and include main campuses only; (1) includes schools accredited by the Liaison Committee on Medical Education and the American Osteopathic Association; (2) includes American Bar Association-accredited law schools; (3) includes all schools with programs that are less than 2 years.
Source: National Center for Education Statistics, Integrated Postsecondary Education System (IPEDS) Peer Analysis System, 2010-11; U.S. News & World Report, Medical School Directory, 2011; U.S. News & World Report, Law School Directory, 2011

According to *U.S. News & World Report,* the Athens-Clarke County, GA Metropolitan Statistical Area is home to one of the top 197 national universities in the U.S.: **University of Georgia** (#56). The rankings are based on quantitative measurements such as peer assessment, retention, faculty resources, student selectivity, financial resources, graduation rate, and alumni giving rate. *U.S. News & World Report, "America's Best Colleges 2011"*

According to *U.S. News & World Report,* the Athens-Clarke County, GA Metropolitan Statistical Area is home to one of the top 50 law schools in the U.S.: **University of Georgia** (#35). The rankings are based on a weighted average of 10 measures of quality: peer assessment score; assessment score by lawyers/judges; median LSAT scores; median undergrad GPA; acceptance rate; employment rates for graduates; bar passage rate; faculty resources; expenditures per student; student/faculty ratio; and library resources. *U.S. News & World Report, "America's Best Law Schools 2011"*

According to *Forbes,* the Athens-Clarke County, GA Metropolitan Statistical Area is home to one of the top 75 business schools in the U.S.: **Georgia (Terry)** (#50). The rankings are based on the return on investment that graduates of the Class of 2004 received (median salary five years after graduation). *Forbes, "Best Business Schools," August 5, 2009*

**PRESIDENTIAL
ELECTION**

2008 Presidential Election Results

Area	Obama	McCain	Nader	Other
Clarke County	64.8	33.6	0.1	1.5
U.S.	52.9	45.6	0.6	0.9

Note: Results are percentages and may not add to 100% due to rounding
Source: Dave Leip's Atlas of U.S. Presidential Elections, www.uselectionatlas.org

EMPLOYERS

Major Employers

Company Name	Industry	Type of Site
Athens Regional Med Ctr	General medical and surgical hospitals	Headquarters
Athens-Clarke County Unified	Executive offices	Headquarters
Carrier Corporation	Refrigeration and heating equipment	Branch
Certainteed Corporation	Mineral wool	Branch
College of Veterinary Medicine	Colleges and universities	Branch
General Time Corporation	Watches, clocks, watchcases, and parts	Branch
Georgia Board of Regents	Colleges and universities	Headquarters
Georgia Power Company	Electric services	Branch
Island Apparel	Men's and boy's trousers and slacks	Single
Mclane	Groceries, general line	Single
Pilgrims Pride Corporation	Poultry slaughtering and processing	Branch
Power Partners	Transformers, except electric	Single
Richard Russell Ag Res Ctr	Regulation of agricultural marketing	Branch
St Marys Health Care Sys	General medical and surgical hospitals	Headquarters
UGA Foods & Nutrition	Vocational schools, nec	Branch
UGA Housing Dept	Colleges and universities	Branch
University Ga Athc Assn	Membership organizations, nec	Single
University of Georgia	Colleges and universities	Branch
Wal-Mart	Department stores	Branch

Note: Companies shown are located within the Athens metropolitan area; nec = not elsewhere classified.
Source: www.zapdata.com, January 2011

PUBLIC SAFETY

Crime Rate

Area	All Crimes	Violent Crimes				Property Crimes		
		Murder	Forcible Rape	Robbery	Aggrav. Assault	Burglary	Larceny -Theft	Motor Vehicle Theft
City	5,339.6	8.7	36.7	135.3	231.4	1,673.7	3,014.7	239.2
Suburbs[1]	2,987.4	1.3	15.7	24.8	297.8	590.4	1,929.3	128.0
Metro[2]	4,397.3	5.8	28.3	91.1	258.0	1,239.7	2,579.9	194.7
U.S.	3,465.5	5.0	28.7	133.0	262.8	716.3	2,060.9	258.8

Note: Figures are crimes per 100,000 population; (1) All areas within the metro area that are located outside
the city limits; (2) Metropolitan Statistical Area - see Appendix B for areas included
Source: FBI Uniform Crime Reports, 2009

Hate Crimes

Area	Number of Quarters Reported	Bias Motivation				
		Race	Religion	Sexual Orientation	Ethnicity	Disability
City	n/a	n/a	n/a	n/a	n/a	n/a

Note: n/a not available.
Source: Federal Bureau of Investigation, Hate Crime Statistics 2009

Identity Theft Consumer Complaints

Area	Complaints	Complaints per 100,000 Population	Rank[2]
MSA[1]	159	84.8	125
U.S.	250,854	81.3	-

Note: (1) Metropolitan Statistical Area - see Appendix B for areas included; (2) Rank ranges from 1 to 384
where 1 indicates greatest number of complaints per 100,000 population
Source: Federal Trade Commission, Consumer Sentinel Network Data Book for January - December 2010

RECREATION

Culture

Dance[1]	Theatre[1]	Instrumental Music[1]	Vocal Music[1]	Series/ Festivals	Museums	Zoos and Aquariums[2]
2	2	0	0	1	5	0

Note: (1) Number of professional perfoming groups; (2) AZA-accredited
Source: The Grey House Performing Arts Directory, 2011-2012; Official Museum Directory, 2010; American Association of Museums, AAM Member Museums, March 2011; Association of Zoos & Aquariums, AZA Member Zoos & Aquariums, May 2011

Professional Sports Teams

Team Name	League
No teams are located in the metro area	

Source: Original research

CLIMATE

Average and Extreme Temperatures

Temperature	Jan	Feb	Mar	Apr	May	Jun	Jul	Aug	Sep	Oct	Nov	Dec	Yr.
Extreme High (°F)	79	80	85	93	95	101	105	102	98	95	84	77	105
Average High (°F)	52	56	64	73	80	86	88	88	82	73	63	54	72
Average Temp. (°F)	43	46	53	62	70	77	79	79	73	63	53	45	62
Average Low (°F)	33	36	42	51	59	66	70	69	64	52	42	35	52
Extreme Low (°F)	-8	5	10	26	37	46	53	55	36	28	3	0	-8

Note: Figures cover the years 1945-1990
Source: National Climatic Data Center, International Station Meteorological Climate Summary, 9/96

Average Precipitation/Snowfall/Humidity

Precip./Humidity	Jan	Feb	Mar	Apr	May	Jun	Jul	Aug	Sep	Oct	Nov	Dec	Yr.
Avg. Precip. (in.)	4.7	4.6	5.7	4.3	4.0	3.5	5.1	3.6	3.4	2.8	3.8	4.2	49.8
Avg. Snowfall (in.)	1	1	Tr	Tr	0	0	0	0	0	0	Tr	Tr	2
Avg. Rel. Hum. 7am (%)	79	77	78	78	82	83	88	89	88	84	81	79	82
Avg. Rel. Hum. 4pm (%)	56	50	48	45	49	52	57	56	56	51	52	55	52

Note: Figures cover the years 1945-1990; Tr = Trace amounts (<0.05 in. of rain; <0.5 in. of snow)
Source: National Climatic Data Center, International Station Meteorological Climate Summary, 9/96

Weather Conditions

Temperature			Daytime Sky			Precipitation		
10°F & below	32°F & below	90°F & above	Clear	Partly cloudy	Cloudy	0.01 inch or more precip.	0.1 inch or more snow/ice	Thunder-storms
1	49	38	98	147	120	116	3	48

Note: Figures are average number of days per year and cover the years 1945-1990
Source: National Climatic Data Center, International Station Meteorological Climate Summary, 9/96

HAZARDOUS WASTE

Superfund Sites

Athens has no sites on the EPA's Superfund Final National Priorities List.
U.S. Environmental Protection Agency, Final National Priorities List, April 1, 2011

**AIR & WATER
QUALITY**

Air Quality Index

| Area | Percent of Days when Air Quality was...[2] | | | | AQI Statistics | |
	Good	Moderate	Unhealthy for Sensitive Groups	Unhealthy	Maximum	Median
Area[1]	65.2	33.1	1.6	0.0	116	43

*Note: The Air Quality Index (AQI) is an index for reporting daily air quality. EPA calculates the AQI for five major air pollutants regulated by the Clean Air Act: ground-level ozone, particle pollution (also known as particulate matter), carbon monoxide, sulfur dioxide, and nitrogen dioxide. The AQI runs from 0 to 500. The higher the AQI value, the greater the level of air pollution and the greater the health concern. There are six AQI categories: "Good" The AQI is between 0 and 50. Air quality is considered satisfactory; "Moderate" The AQI is between 51 and 100. Air quality is acceptable; "Unhealthy for Sensitive Groups" When AQI values are between 101 and 150, members of sensitive groups may experience health effects; "Unhealthy" When AQI values are between 151 and 200 everyone may begin to experience health effects; "Very Unhealthy" AQI values between 201 and 300 trigger a health alert; "Hazardous" AQI values over 300 trigger health warnings of emergency conditions; (1) Data covers Clarke County; (2) Based on 305 days with AQI data in 2008; The EPA has suspended data updates while it assesses its data systems, including AirData reports and maps.
Source: U.S. Environmental Protection Agency, AirData Report, 2008*

Air Quality Index Pollutants

| Area | Percent of Days when AQI Pollutant was...[2] | | | | | |
	Carbon Monoxide	Nitrogen Dioxide	Ozone	Sulfur Dioxide	Particulate Matter 2.5	Particulate Matter 10
Area[1]	0.0	0.0	55.1	0.0	44.9	0.0

*Note: The Air Quality Index (AQI) is an index for reporting daily air quality. EPA calculates the AQI for five major air pollutants regulated by the Clean Air Act: ground-level ozone, particle pollution (also known as particulate matter), carbon monoxide, sulfur dioxide, and nitrogen dioxide. The AQI runs from 0 to 500. The higher the AQI value, the greater the level of air pollution and the greater the health concern; (1) Data covers Clarke County; (2) Based on 305 days with AQI data in 2008; The EPA has suspended data updates while it assesses its data systems, including AirData reports and maps.
Source: U.S. Environmental Protection Agency, AirData Report, 2008*

Air Quality Index Trends

| Area | Trend Sites (days) | | | | | | | | All Sites (days) |
	2002	2003	2004	2005	2006	2007	2008	2009	2009
MSA[1]	n/a	n/a	n/a	n/a	n/a	n/a	n/a	n/a	n/a

*Note: Figures are the number of days the AQI value exceeded 100 in a given year. An AQI value greater than 100 indicates that air quality would have been in the unhealthful range on that day. Data from exceptional events are included. These counts are presented in two ways. First, the counts are based on sites having an adequate record of monitoring data during the trend period (trend sites). These counts represent the relative change in the number of days with AQI values greater than 100. In the last column, the counts are based on all sites with data in the most recent year (because it is possible for a site to have data in the most recent year but not enough data to be a trend site); (1) Data covers the Athens-Clarke County, GA Metropolitan Statistical Area - see Appendix B for areas included; n/a not available.
Source: U.S. Environmental Protection Agency, Office of Air and Radiation, Air Quality Index Information, "Number of Days with Air Quality Index Values Greater than 100 and Trend Sites, 1990-2009, and at All Sites in 2009"*

Maximum Air Pollutant Concentrations

	Particulate Matter 10 (ug/m^3)	Particulate Matter 2.5 (ug/m^3)	Ozone (ppm)	Carbon Monoxide (ppm)	Sulfur Dioxide (ppm)	Nitrogen Dioxide (ppm)	Lead (ug/m^3)
MSA[1] Level	n/a	20	0.067	n/a	n/a	n/a	n/a
NAAQS[2]	150	35	0.075	9	0.140	0.053	0.15
Met NAAQS[2]	Yes	Yes	Yes	n/a	n/a	n/a	n/a

*Note: Data from exceptional events are not included; (1) Data covers the Athens-Clarke County, GA Metropolitan Statistical Area - see Appendix B for areas included; (2) National Ambient Air Quality Standards; n/a not available
Concentrations: Particulate Matter 10 (coarse particulate) - highest second maximum 24-hour concentration; Particulate Matter 2.5 (fine particulate) - highest 98th percentile 24-hour concentration; Ozone - highest fourth daily maximum 8-hour concentration; Carbon Monoxide - highest second maximum non-overlapping 8-hour concentration; Sulfur Dioxide - highest second maximum 24-hour concentration; Nitrogen Dioxide - highest arithmetic mean concentration; Lead - maximum running 3-month average
Units: ppm = parts per million; ug/m^3 = micrograms per cubic meter
Source: U.S. Environmental Protection Agency, CBSA Factbook 2009, Air Quality Statistics by City, 2009*

Drinking Water

Water System Name	Pop. Served	Primary Water Source Type	Violations[1]	
			Health Based	Monitoring/ Reporting
Athens-Clarke Co. Water System	102,811	Surface	0	0

Note: (1) Based on violation data from January 1, 2010 to December 31, 2010 (includes unresolved violations from earlier years)
Source: U.S. Environmental Protection Agency, Office of Ground Water and Drinking Water, Safe Drinking Water Information System (based on data extracted May 9, 2011)

Atlanta, Georgia

Background

Atlanta was born of a rough-and-tumble past, first as a natural outgrowth of a thriving railroad network in the 1840s, and second as a resilient go-getter that proudly rose again above the rubble of the Civil War.

Blanketed over the rolling hills of the Piedmont Plateau, at the foot of the Blue Ridge Mountains, Georgia's capital stands 1,000 feet above sea level. Atlanta is located in the northwest corner of Georgia where the terrain is rolling to hilly, and slopes downward to the east, west, and south.

Atlanta proper begins at the "terminus," or zero mile mark, of the now defunct Western and Atlantic Railroad Line. However its metropolitan area comprises 28 counties that include Fulton, DeKalb, Clayton and Gwinnet, among others. Population-wise, Atlanta is the largest city in the southeast United States, and has been growing at a steady rate for the last decade. In 2007, the census bureau declared Atlanta the fastest growing metropolitan area in the nation. Understandably, the city contributes to nearly two thirds of the state's economy.

Within the city itself, Atlanta's has a diversified economy that allows for employment in a variety of sectors such as manufacturing, retail, and government. The city hosts many of the nation's Fortune 500 company headquarters, including Home Depot, United Parcel Service, Coca-Cola, Delta Air Lines, and Southern Co., as well as the nation's Centers for Disease Control and Prevention (CDC).

These accomplishments are the result of an involved city government that seeks to work closely with its business community, due in part to a change in the city charter in 1974, when greater administrative powers were vested in the mayoral office, and the city inaugurated its first black mayor.

As middle class residents, both white and black, continue to move to the suburbs separating themselves from Atlanta's old downtown, the city faces the complex issue of where it plans to move as an urban center in light of the conflict between the city and its surroundings.

While schools in the city remain predominantly black and schools in its suburbs predominantly white, Atlanta boasts a racially progressive climate. The Martin Luther King, Jr. Historic Site and Preservation District is located in the Sweet Auburn neighborhood, which includes King's birth home and the Ebenezer Baptist Church, where both he and his father preached. The city's consortium of black colleges that includes Morehouse College and the Interdenominational Theological Center testifies to the city's appreciation for a people who have always been one-third of Atlanta's population.

Indeed, King is one of Atlanta's two Nobel Peace Prize winners. The second, former President Jimmy Carter, famously of Plains, Georgia, also brings his name to Atlanta as namesake to the Carter Center. Devoted to human rights, the center is operated with neighboring Emory University, and sits adjacent to the Jimmy Carter Library and Museum on a hill overlooking the city. Habitat for Humanity, also founded by Carter, moved its international administrative headquarters to Atlanta in 2006.

Hartsfield-Jackson Atlanta International Airport, the world's busiest passenger airport, underwent significant expansion in recent years. MARTA, the city's public transport system, is the nation's 9th largest and transports on average 500,000 passengers daily on a 48-mile, 38-station rapid rail system with connections to hundreds of bus routes.

The Appalachian chain of mountains, the Gulf of Mexico, and the Atlantic Ocean influence Atlanta's climate. Temperatures are moderate to hot throughout the year, but extended periods of heat are unusual and 100-degree heat is rarely experienced. Atlanta winters are mild with a few, short-lived cold spells. Summers can be humid. A rare event occurred in March 2008, when a tornado caused considerable damage to the city.

Rankings

General Rankings

- Atlanta was ranked #54 out of 375 metro areas in *Cities Ranked & Rated*. Criteria: cost of living; climate; crime; transportation; economy and jobs; education; arts and culture; health and healthcare; leisure; quality of life. *Cities Ranked & Rated, 2nd Edition, 2007*

- Atlanta was ranked #21 out of 379 metro areas in *Places Rated Almanac*. Criteria: health care; education; recreation; transportation; ambience; climate; crime; housing costs; jobs. *Places Rated Almanac, 7th Edition, 2007*

- *Men's Health Living* ranked 100 U.S. cities in terms of quality of life. Atlanta was ranked #64 and received a grade of C-. Criteria: number of fitness facilities; air quality; number of physicians; male/female ratio; education levels; household income; cost of living. *Men's Health Living, Spring 2008*

- Atlanta was identified as one of the top places to live in the U.S. by Harris Interactive. The city ranked #7 out of 15. Criteria: 2,620 adults (age 18 and over) were polled and asked "if you could live in or near any city in the country except the one you live in or nearest to now, which city would you choose?" The poll was conducted online within the U.S. between September 14 and 20, 2010. *Harris Interactive, October 20, 2010*

Business/Finance Rankings

- Experian ranked the top 20 major U.S metropolitan areas by average debt per consumer. The Atlanta metro area was ranked #4. Criteria: average debt per consumer. Debt for this study includes credit cards, auto loans and personal loans. It does not include mortgages. *Experian, May 13, 2010*

- Atlanta was identified as one of the top 25 U.S. cities with the most credit card debt by credit reporting bureau Experian. The city was ranked #3. *Experian, March 4, 2011*

- A.G. Edwards ranked America's 500 top-performing communities based on their residents' personal savings and investing behavior. The Atlanta metro area ranked #135 with an index score of 105.06 (national average = 100.00). A dozen statistical factors were measured including: participation in retirement savings plans; personal debt levels; and home ownership. *A.G. Edwards, "2007 Nest Egg Index," September 12, 2007*

- Atlanta was cited as one of America's top metros for new and expanded facility projects in 2010. The area ranked #6 in the large metro area category (population over 1 million). *Site Selection, "2010 Top Metros," March 2011*

- Atlanta was identified as one of the "Top 10 Cities for New Grads." The city ranked #1. Criteria: concentration of young adults (age 20 to 24); inventory of jobs requiring less than one year of experience; average cost of rent for a one bedroom apartment. *CareerBuilder.com, "Top 10 Cities for New Grads," June 5, 2010*

- Atlanta was identified as one of the best cities for new college graduates. The city ranked #4. Criteria: cost of living; average annual salary; unemployment rate; number of employers looking to hire people at entry-level. *Business Week, "The Best Cities for New Grads," July 20, 2010*

- Atlanta was selected as one of the best cities in the world for telecommuting. The city ranked #11. The editors at *Cartridge Save* (printer technology news, guides and reviews) identified the 20 best cities in which to be an at-home, tech-using employee. *Cartridge Save, "20 of the Best Cities in the World for Telecommuting," May 14, 2008*

- *American City Business Journals* ranked America's 261 largest cities in terms of their resident's wealth. Atlanta ranked #52. Criteria: per capita income; median household income; percentage of households with annual incomes of $200,000 or more; median home value. *American City Business Journals, www.bizjournals.com, "Where the Money Is: America's Wealth Centers," August 18, 2008*

- The Atlanta metro area appeared on the Milken Institute "2010 Best Performing Metros" list. Rank: #126 out of 200 large metro areas. Criteria: job growth; wage and salary growth; high-tech output growth. *Milken Institute, "2010 Best Performing Metros"*

- The Atlanta metro area was selected as one of the best cities for entrepreneurs in America by *Inc. Magazine*. Criteria: job-growth data for 335 metro areas was analyzed for: recent growth trend (the current and prior year's employment growth rates, with the current year emphasized); mid-term growth (the average annual 2002-2007 growth rate); long-term trend (the sum of the 2002-2007 and 1996-2001 employment growth rates multiplied by the ratio of the 1996-2001 growth rate over the 2002-2007 growth rate); current year growth. The Atlanta metro area ranked #16 among large metro areas and #85 overall. *Inc. Magazine, "The Best Cities for Doing Business," July 2008*

- Atlanta was identified as one of the top 10 cities with the greatest number of *Inc. 500* companies per million residents. The city ranked #8. *Inc. Magazine, September 2008*

- Atlanta was ranked #95 out of 145 regions worldwide in terms of its "Knowledge Competitiveness Index." The index attempts to measure the knowledge-based development taking place throughout the world and is based on 19 measures of economic performance that indicate a region's ability to translate its knowledge capacity into economic value. *Centre for International Competitiveness, World Knowledge Competitiveness Index 2008*

- *Forbes* ranked the 200 most populous metro areas in the U.S. in terms of the "Best Places for Business and Careers." The Atlanta metro area was ranked #27. Criteria: 12 metrics including costs (business and living), job growth (past and projected), income growth, educational attainment, projected economic growth, crime, cultural and recreational opportunities, net migration patterns, percentage of subprime mortgages handed out over a three-year period, and the number of highly ranked four-year colleges. *Forbes, "Best Places for Business and Careers," April 14, 2010*

Children/Family Rankings

- The Atlanta metro area was selected as one of the "Best Cities for Relocating Families" by Worldwide ERC and Primacy Relocation. The 2008 study looked at nearly 50 factors important to relocating families including: recent job growth; nearby top-ranked colleges; in-state tuition for four-year public colleges; population growth since 2000; pediatricians per 100,000 population; and a Green Living index. *Worldwide ERC and Primacy Relocation, "2008 Best Cities for Relocating Families"*

- *Fit Pregnancy* magazine ranked the 50 best U.S. cities in which to have a baby. Atlanta was ranked #15. Criteria: access to hospitals and doctors; affordability; birthing options; breastfeeding; child care; fertility laws/resources; maternal and infant health risk; parks/stroller friendliness; safety. *Fit Pregnancy, "The Best Cities in America to Have a Baby 2008"*

Culture/Performing Arts Rankings

- Atlanta was selected as one of "America's Top 25 Arts Destinations." The city ranked #9 in the big city (population 500,000 and over) category. Criteria: readers' top choices for arts travel destinations based on the richness and variety of visual arts sites, activities and events. *American Style, "America's Top 25 Arts Destinations," May 2010*

Dating/Romance Rankings

- Atlanta appeared on *Men's Health's* list of the most sex-happy cities in America. The city ranked #21 of 100. Criteria: condom sales; birth rates; sex toy sales; rates of chlamydia, gonorrhea, and syphilis. *Men's Health, "America's Most Sex-Happy Cities," October 2010*

- *Men's Health* ranked 100 U.S. cities in terms of best (and worst) marriages. Atlanta was ranked #66 (#1 = worst marriages). Criteria: rate of failed marriages; stringency of divorce laws; percentage of population who've split; number of licensed marriage and family therapists. *Men's Health, "Splitsville, USA," May 2010*

- Eli Lily and Company, in partnership with Sperling's BestPlaces, ranked the nation's 50 largest metro areas in terms of the "Most Romantic Cities for Baby Boomers." The Atlanta metro area ranked #20. Criteria: marriage and divorce rates among "baby boomers" age 45 to 60; great restaurants; dance studios; chocolate, jewelry and flower sales. *Eli Lily and Company, "Most Romantic Cities for Baby Boomers," April 20, 2007*

- The Atlanta metro area was selected as one of the "Best Cities for Relocating Singles" by Worldwide ERC and Primacy Relocation. The area ranked #6 out of the 100 largest metro areas in the U.S. Areas were selected based on the following criteria: recent job growth; recent singles population growth; overall population growth; affordable rental housing; cost-of-living index; expanded arts and recreation opportunities; ratio of single men and single women; affordability of quality higher education (including state residency requirements); diversity index; climate; population density. *Worldwide ERC and Primacy Relocation, "2008 Best Cities for Relocating Singles"*

- *Forbes* ranked the 40 most populous urbanized areas in the U.S. in terms of the "Best Cities for Singles." The Atlanta metro area ranked #6. Criteria: number of singles; cost of living alone; nightlife; culture; job growth; coolness; and online dating participation. *Forbes.com, "Best Cities for Singles," July 27, 2009*

Education Rankings

- Atlanta was selected as one of "America's Most Literate Cities." The city ranked #4 out of the 75 largest U.S. cities. Criteria: number of booksellers; library resources; Internet resources; educational attainment; periodical publishing resources; newspaper circulation. *Central Connecticut State University, "America's Most Literate Cities 2010"*

- Atlanta was identified as one of the 100 "smartest" metro areas in the U.S. The area ranked #30. Criteria: the editors rated the collective brainpower of the 100 largest metro area in the U.S based on their residents' educational attainment. *American City Business Journals, www.bizjournals.com, April 14, 2008*

- Atlanta was identified as one of "America's Brainiest Bastions" by *Portfolio.com*. The metro area ranked #42 out of 200. Portfolio.com analyzed levels of educational attainment in the nation's 200 largest metropolitan areas. The editors established scores for five levels of educational attainment, based on relative earning power of adult workers age 25 or older. Scores were determined by comparing the median income for all workers with the median income for those workers at a specified educational level. *Portfolio.com, "America's Brainiest Bastions," December 1, 2010*

- *Forbes* ranked the largest metro areas in the U.S. in terms of the "Best Cities for Young Professionals." The Atlanta metro area ranked #9 out of 10. Graduates from six elite schools (Harvard, Stanford, Princeton, Rice, Northwestern and Duke) were tracked ten years after graduation to see where they settled down. Those rankings were combined with several other statistics: job growth; unemployment rate; average salary of college graduates; cost of living; number of large companies that are located in the city. *Forbes.com, "Best Cities for Young Professionals," June 17, 2010*

Environmental Rankings

- The Atlanta metro area was identified as one of "The Ten Biggest American Cities that are Running Out of Water" by *24/7 Wall St.* The metro area ranked #9 out of 10. *24/7 Wall St.* did an analysis of the water supply and consumption in the 30 largest metropolitan areas in the U.S. Criteria include: projected water demand as a share of available precipitation; groundwater use as a share or projected available precipitation; susceptibility to drought; projected increase in freshwater withdrawls; projected increase in summer water deficit. The editors chose ten cities that are likely to face severe shortages in the relatively near-term future. *24/7 Wall St., "The Ten Biggest American Cities that are Running Out of Water," November 1, 2010*

- Atlanta was selected as one of 22 "Smarter Cities" for energy by the Natural Resources Defense Council." Criteria: investment in green power; energy efficiency measures; conservation. *Natural Resources Defense Council, "2010 Smarter Cities," July 19, 2010*

- Atlanta was selected as one of North America's most vegetarian- and vegan-friendly large cities (population 300,000 or more). The city was ranked #4. Criteria: number of vegetarian restaurants and vegetarian-friendly restaurants per capita; input from PETA supporters and staff members on the quality of the options. *People for the Ethical Treatment of Animals, "North America's Best Vegetarian- and Vegan-Friendly Cities," July 23, 2010*

- *American City Business Journal* ranked 43 metropolitan areas in terms of their "greenness." The Atlanta metro area ranked #32. Criteria: Forty-one metros in which *ACBJ* has business weeklies, plus Indianapolis and Cleveland, were ranked based on 20 different indicators such as adoption of green technologies, utilization of environmentally sound practices, and air and water quality. *American City Business Journals, "Green City Index," March 11, 2010*

- 100 of the largest metro areas in the U.S. were analyzed in terms of their current drought severity. The Atlanta metro area ranked #12 (#1 = driest). The rankings were based on statistics such as long-term precipitation trends and patterns and the Palmer drought indices. *Sperling's BestPlaces, www.BestPlaces.net, "America's Drought-Riskiest Cities," November 2007*

- The Atlanta metro area appeared in *Country Home's* "Best Green Places" report. The area ranked #210 out of 379. Criteria: official energy policies; green power; green buildings; availability of fresh, locally grown food. *Country Home, "Best Green Places," 2008*

- Atlanta was highlighted as one of the 25 most ozone-polluted metro areas in the U.S. The area ranked #23. *American Lung Association, State of the Air 2011*

Health/Fitness Rankings

- *Cooking Light* magazine ranked the 20 American cities that best fit their philosophy to eat smart, be fit, and live well. Atlanta ranked #16. Criteria: healthfulness and exercise data; restaurant ratings; farmers' market listings; parks and recreation data. *Cooking Light, "Best Cities Awards," 2007*

- Atlanta was selected as one of the 25 fittest cities in America by *Men's Fitness Online*. It ranked #21 out of America's 50 largest cities. Criteria: fitness centers and sport stores; nutrition; sports participation; TV viewing; overweight/sedentary; junk food; air quality; geography; commute; parks and open space; city recreational facilities; access to healthcare; motivation; mayor and city initiatives; state obesity initiatives. *Men's Fitness Online, 2009 Fittest/Fattest Cities*

- Atlanta was identified as a "2011 Asthma Capital." The area ranked #13 out of the nation's 100 largest metropolitan areas. Twelve factors were used to identify the most challenging places to live for people with asthma: estimated prevalence; self-reported prevalence; crude death rate for asthma; annual pollen score; annual air quality; public smoking laws; number of board-certified asthma specialists; school inhaler access laws; rescue medication use; controller medication use; uninsured rate; poverty rate. *Asthma and Allergy Foundation of America, "2011 Asthma Capitals"*

- Atlanta was identified as a 2009 "Spring Allergy Capital." The area ranked #59 out of 100. Three groups of factors were used to identify the most severe cities for people with allergies during the spring season: annual pollen levels; medicine utilization; access to board-certified allergists. *Asthma and Allergy Foundation of America, "Spring Allergy Capitals 2009"*

- Atlanta was identified as a 2010 "Fall Allergy Capital." The area ranked #53 out of 100. Three groups of factors were used to identify the most severe cities for people with allergies during the fall season: annual pollen levels; medicine utilization; access to board-certified allergists. *Asthma and Allergy Foundation of America, "Fall Allergy Capitals 2010"*

- *Men's Health* ranked 100 U.S. cities in terms of the quality of their tap water. Atlanta was ranked #33 and received a grade of B. Criteria: levels of total coliform bacteria, arsenic, lead, total trihalomethanes (linked to cancer), and halo-acetic acids; number of EPA water-system violations from 1995 to 2005. *Men's Health, March 2007*

- Atlanta was selected as one of America's noisiest cities by *Men's Health*. The city ranked #7 of 10. Criteria: laws limiting excessive noise; traffic congestion levels; airports' overnight flight curfews; percentage of people who report sleeping seven hours or less. *Men's Health, "Ranking America's Cities: America's Noisiest Cities," May 2009*

- Ortho-McNeil Neurologics, in partnership with Sperling's BestPlaces, analyzed 110 metro areas and identified those U.S. cities with the highest prevalence of factors that are most commonly associated with migraine headaches. The Atlanta metro area ranked #33. Criteria: number of migraine-related drug prescriptions per capita; lifestyle factors that can contribute to migraines; environmental factors that can trigger migraines; and consumption of migraine-triggering foods. *Ortho-McNeil Neurologics, "America's Migraine Hot Spots," March 14, 2006*

- An analysis of the "Best & Worst Cities for Sleep" was conducted by Sperling's BestPlaces. The study ranked America's 50 most populated metro areas. The Atlanta metro area ranked #50 (#1 = best city for sleep). Criteria: number of days residents didn't get enough rest or sleep during the past month; average length of daily commute; divorce rate; unemployment rate. *Sperling's BestPlaces, www.BestPlaces.net, "Best & Worst Cities for Sleep," 2006*

- The Atlanta metropolitan area was selected as one of the best metros for hospital care in America by HealthGrades. The rankings are based on a comprehensive study of patient death and complication rates in the nation's nearly 5,000 hospitals. Hospitals performing in the top 5% nationwide across 26 different medical procedures and diagnoses were identified. HealthGrades then ranked cities by the highest percentage of these Distinguished Hospitals for Clinical Excellence™. The Atlanta metro area ranked #27. *HealthGrades.com, "America's Top 50 Cities for Hospital Care," January 26, 2011*

- *Men's Health* ranked 100 U.S. cities in terms of cities "Where the Food is Sickening." Atlanta was ranked #68 and received a grade of C-. The magazine arrived at their ratings by looking at data compiled by the Community Health Status Indicator Project to determine outbreaks of E. coli, salmonella-, and shigella-related infections. They then checked the CDC's Wonder database to see how many people died from tainted food. Finally, the magazine found out which states have adopted the current version of the FDA's uniform Food Code, which contains the most up-to-date rules for keeping restaurant kitchens clean. *Men's Health, October 2005*

- The Atlanta metro area was identified as one of "America's Most Obese Cities" by *Forbes*. The magazine analyzed BMI (body mass index) data from the CDC in the 50 most populated metro areas in the U.S. and ranked the top 20. The area ranked #16. *Forbes, "America's Most Obese Cities," November 26, 2007*

- The American Academy of Dermatology ranked 26 U.S. metropolitan regions in terms of their residents knowledge, attitude and behaviors towards tanning, sun protection and skin cancer detection. The Atlanta metro area ranked #7. The results of the study are based on an online survey of over 7,000 adults nationwide. *American Academy of Dermatology, "Suntelligence: How Sun Smart is Your City," May 3, 2010*

- Scarborough Research, a leading market research firm, identified the top local markets for organic consumers. The Atlanta DMA (Designated Market Area) ranked in the top 15 with 21% of adults reporting that they used any organic food product in their household during the past month. *Scarborough Research, October 10, 2007*

- The Atlanta metro area appeared in the 2010 Gallup-Healthways Well-Being Index. The index, based on interviews with more than 353,000 Americans during 2009, asked individuals to assess their jobs, finances, physical health, emotional state of mind and communities. The metro area ranked #37 out of 162. Criteria: life evaluation; emotional health; work environment; physical health; healthy behaviors; basic access (basic needs optimal for a healthy life, such as access to food and medicine, having health insurance and feeling safe while walking at night). *Gallup-Healthways, "Well-Being Index 2010"*

- The Atlanta metro area was identified as one of "America's Most Stressful Cities" by *Forbes*. The metro area ranked #22. Criteria: median home price drop; unemployment rates; cost of living; air quality; sunny days; population density. *Forbes.com, "America's Most Stressful Cities," August 20, 2009*

- The Atlanta metro area was identified as one of "America's 20 Most Sedentary Cities" by *Forbes*. The metro area ranked #17. Criteria: percentage of overweight or obese people; percentage of people who had not engaged in any physical activity in the past 30 days; average number of hours of TV watched per week. *Forbes.com, "America's Most Sedentary Cities," October 29, 2007*

- *Men's Health* examined the nation's largest 100 cities and identified the 10 cities at lowest risk of erectile dysfunction. Atlanta ranked #4. Criteria: percentage of current male smokers; percentage of adults with a BMI of at least 30; percentage of adults with diabetes; percentage of men working out three or more times per week; percentage of urologists per 100,000 men; number of ED drug prescriptions filled in 2007. *Men's Health, "Ranking America's Cities: Cities that Need Viagara," April 2009*

- 50 of the largest metro areas in the U.S. were analyzed in terms of their health and fitness by the American College of Sports Medicine in their "American Fitness Index." The Atlanta metro area ranked #16 (#1 = healthiest). Criteria: preventative health behaviors; levels of chronic disease; health care access; community resources and policies that support physical activity. *American College of Sports Medicine, "Health and Community Fitness Status of the 50 Largest Metropolitan Areas," May 24, 2010*

- Atlanta was selected as one of the "20 Most Livable U.S. Cities for Wheelchair Users" by the Christopher & Dana Reeve Foundation. The city ranked #20. Criteria: Medicaid eligibility and spending; access to physicians and rehabilitation facilities; access to fitness facilities and recreation; access to paratransit; percentage of people living with disabilities who are employed; clean air; climate. *Christopher & Dana Reeve Foundation, "20 Most Livable U.S. Cities for Wheelchair Users," July 26, 2010*

Real Estate Rankings

- *Fortune* ranked the 100 largest metro areas in the U.S. in terms of projected median home price change in 2010. The Atlanta metro area ranked #41. *Fortune, "The 2010 Housing Outlook," December 9, 2009*

- Atlanta was selected as one of the 10 best U.S. cities for real estate investment. The city ranked #9. *Association of Foreign Investors in Real Estate, "AFIRE News," January/February, 2011*

- Atlanta appeared on ApartmentRatings.com "Top Cities for Renters" list in 2009." The area ranked #52. Overall satisfaction ratings were ranked using thousands of user submitted scores for hundreds of apartment complexes located in the 100 most populated U.S. municipalities. *ApartmentRatings.com, "2009 Renter Satisfaction Rankings"*

- Atlanta appeared on ApartmentRatings.com "Top College Towns & Cities" for renters list in 2010." The area ranked #54. Overall satisfaction ratings were ranked using thousands of user submitted scores for hundreds of apartment complexes located in cities and towns that are home to the 100 largest four-year institutions in the U.S. *ApartmentRatings.com, "2010 College Town Renter Satisfaction Rankings"*

- The nation's largest metro areas were analyzed in terms of the percentage of households entering some stage of foreclosure in 2010. The Atlanta metro area ranked #25 out of 206 (#1 = highest foreclosure rate). *RealtyTrac, 2010 Year-End Metropolitan Foreclosure Market Report, January 27, 2011*

- The Atlanta metro area was identified as one of the "Best Cities to Buy a Home" by *Forbes*. The metro area ranked #10. Criteria: 2-year home price appreciation; vacancy rates; spread between monthly rent and mortgage payment at the median level. *Forbes.com, "Best Cities to Buy a Home," July 22, 2008*

- The Atlanta metro area appeared in a *Wall Street Journal* article ranking cities by "housing stress." The metro area was ranked #18 (#1 = most stress). Criteria: fraction of mortgage-holding homeowners with a monthly housing payment in excess of 30 percent of income; percentage of people without health insurance; unemployment rate. *The Wall Street Journal, "Which Cities Face Biggest Housing Risk," October 5, 2010*

- The Center for Housing Policy ranked 210 U.S metropolitan areas by the fair market rent for a two-bedroom unit. The Atlanta metro area was ranked #78. (#1 = most expensive) with a rent of $912. Criteria: Fair Market Rent (FMR) in effect during the fourth quarter of 2009 based on HUD's fiscal year 2010 FMRs. *The Center for Housing Policy, "Paycheck to Paycheck: Most to Least Expensive Rental Markets in 2009"*

- The Atlanta metro area was identified as one of the worst housing markets of the decade by *Forbes*. The metro area ranked #0. Criteria: decrease in housing values per square foot since January 2000. *Forbes, "America's 5 Best (and Worst) Housing Markets of the Decade," December 7, 2010*

- The Atlanta metro area was identified as one of the top 20 cities in terms of decreasing home equity. The metro area was ranked #15. Criteria: percentage of home equity relative to the home's current value. *Forbes.com, "Where Americans are Losing Home Equity Most," May 1, 2010*

- The Atlanta metro area was identified as one of the markets with the worst expected performance in home prices over the next 12 months. *Local Market Monitor, "First Quarter Home Price Forecast for Largest US Markets," March 2, 2011*

Safety Rankings

- Symantec, the makers of Norton, in partnership with Sperling's BestPlaces, ranked the 50 largest cities in the U.S. in terms of their vulnerability to cybercrime. The city ranked #6. Criteria: number of cyberattacks and potential infections; level of Internet access; expenditures on computer hardware and software; wireless hotspots; broadband connectivity; Internet usage; online purchases. *Symantec, "10 Riskiest Cities for Cybercrime," March 22, 2010*

- Allstate ranked the 200 largest cities in America in terms of driver safety. Atlanta ranked #146. In addition, drivers were 22.4% more likely to have had an accident compared to the national average. Allstate researchers analyzed internal property damage reported claims over a two-year period (from January 2007 to December 2008) to ensure the findings would not be affected by external influences such as weather or road construction. A weighted average of the two-year numbers determined the annual percentages. The report defines an auto crash as any collision resulting in a property damage claim. *Allstate, "The 2010 Allstate America's Best Drivers Report™"*

- Atlanta was identified as one of America's "11 Most Dangerous Cities" by *U.S. News*. The city ranked #2. Criteria: crime risk was calculated using the most recent seven years (2003-2009) of FBI crime reporting data. The data includes both property crimes and violent crimes. *U.S. News & World Report, "The 11 Most Dangerous Cities," February 16, 2011*

- Atlanta was identified as one of the most dangerous large cities in America by CQ Press. All 34 cities with populations of 500,000 or more that reported crime rates in 2009 for murder, rape, robbery, aggravated assault, burglary, and motor vehicle thefts were ranked. The city ranked #5 out of the top 10. *CQ Press, City Crime Rankings 2010-2011*

- The National Insurance Crime Bureau ranked 366 metro areas in the U.S. in terms of per capita rates of vehicle theft. The Atlanta metro area ranked #45 (#1 = highest rate). Criteria: number of vehicle theft offenses per 100,000 inhabitants. *National Insurance Crime Bureau, "Hot Spots," May 17, 2010*

- The Atlanta metro area was identified as one of the "The Most Dangerous Metro Areas for Pedestrians" by Transportation for America and the Surface Transportation Policy Partnership. The metro area ranked #10 out of 52 metro areas with over 1 million residents. Criteria: area's population divided by the number of pedestrian fatalities in that area. *Transportation for America and the Surface Transportation Policy Partnership, "Dangerous by Design: Solving the Epidemic of Preventable Pedestrian Deaths (and Making Great Neighborhoods)," November 11, 2009*

Seniors/Retirement Rankings

- The Atlanta metro area was identified as one of "America's Most Affordable Places to Retire" by *Forbes*. The metro area ranked #9. Criteria: housing affordability; inflation; number of persons over 65 who are employed; net migration for persons over 65; percent of persons over 65 living below poverty level; doctors per capita; number of citizens tapping their Medicare benefits per thousand people. *Forbes.com, "America's Most Affordable Places to Retire," September 5, 2008*

- The Atlanta metro area was selected as one of "America's Best Places to Grow Old" by *Forbes*. The area was ranked #9 out of 10. Criteria: housing affordability; inflationary pressures; number of persons over 65 who are currently employed; net migration for persons over 65; percent of seniors living below poverty level; doctors per capita; number of citizens tapping their Medicare benefits per 1,000 people. *Forbes, "America's Best Places to Grow Old," December 12, 2008*

- Atlanta was selected as one of "5 Great Places to Live." Criteria includes: mass-transit systems so people can drive less; expanded sidewalks to encourage walking; better health care; wide range of mixed-use housing. *AARP The Magazine, September/October 2007*

- The Atlanta metro area was selected as one of "The 10 Most Affordable Cities for Long-Term Care" by *U.S. News & World Report*. Criteria: costs at nursing homes, assisted living facilities, and adult day health care facilities; cost for licensed home health aides. *U.S. News & Word Report, "The 10 Most Affordable Cities for Long-Term Care," May 17, 2010*

Sports/Recreation Rankings

- Atlanta was selected as one of "The Most Miserable Sports Cities" by *Forbes*. The city was ranked #2. Criteria: postseason losses; years since last title; ratio of cumulative seasons to championships won. Contenders were limited to cities with at least 75 cumulative seasons in the four major sports leagues. *Forbes, "The Most Miserable Sports Cities," February 28, 2011*

- Atlanta appeared on the *Sporting News* list of the "Best Sports Cities" for 2010. The area ranked #8 out of 402 cities in the U.S. *Sporting News* takes a 12-month snapshot, roughly October to October, of each city's sports, putting a heavy premium on regular-season won-lost records (from the most recently completed season). Other criteria include: playoff berths, bowl appearances and tournament bids; championships; applicable power ratings; quality of competition; overall fan fervor as measured in part by attendance as percentage of venue capacity; abundance of teams (rewarding quality over quantity); stadium and arena quality; ticket availability and prices; franchise ownership; and marquee appeal of athletes. *Sporting News, "Best Sports Cities 2010," October, 2010*

- Atlanta was chosen as one of America's 25 best cities for running. The city was ranked #20. Criteria: number of running clubs per city; amount of land set aside for park usage; air quality; weather; crime rates; and results from a *Runner's World* poll in which readers ranked their favorite running cities. *Runner's World, "The 25 Best Running Cities in America," July 2005*

- Turner Field (Atlanta Braves) was selected as one of PETA's "2010 Top 10 Vegetarian-Friendly Ballparks." The park ranked #6. *People for the Ethical Treatment of Animals, "2010 Top 10 Vegetarian-Friendly Ballparks"*

- Atlanta was selected as one of the most playful cities in the U.S. by KaBOOM! The organization's Playful City USA initiative is a national recognition program that honors cities and towns across the nation for a vision, plan and commitment to creating an agenda for play. Cities were recognized based on a pledge to five specific commitments to play: creating a local play commission or task force; designing an annual action plan for play; conducting a play space audit; outlining a financial investment in play for the current fiscal year; and proclaiming and celebrating an annual "play day." *KaBOOM! National Campaign for Play, "2010 Playful City USA Communities"*

- *Golf Digest* ranked 330 metro areas in the U.S. in terms of golf. The Atlanta metro area was ranked #281. Criteria: access to golf; weather; value of golf; and quality of golf. *Golf Digest, "Metro Golf Rankings," August 2005*

- *Golf.com* and the research arm of the National Golf Foundation analyzed the 50 largest metropolitan areas in the U.S. in terms of golf. The Atlanta metro area ranked #8. Criteria: weather; affordability; quality of courses; accessibility; number of courses designed by esteemed architects; availability; crowdedness. *Golf.com, November 15, 2007*

Technology Rankings

- The Atlanta metro area was selected as one of "America's Most Wired Cities" by *Forbes*. The metro area was ranked #2 out of 20. Criteria: percentage of Internet users with high-speed access; number of companies providing high-speed Internet; number of public wireless hot spots. *Forbes, "America's Most Wired Cities," March 2, 2010*

- Scarborough Research, a leading market research firm, identified the Atlanta DMA (Designated Market Area) as one of the top markets for text messaging with more than 50% of cell phone subscribers age 18+ utilizing the text messaging feature on their phone. *Scarborough Research, November 24, 2008*

Transportation Rankings

- Atlanta was identified as one of America's worst cities for speed traps by the National Motorists Association. One city from each state was selected based on data from the National Speed Trap Exchange. The NSTE collects driver reported speed trap locations. *National Motorists Association, "The Worst Speed Trap Cities in North America," September 2010*

- Atlanta was selected as one of the "Least Courteous Cities (Worst Road Rage)" in the U.S. by AutoVantage. The city ranked #4. Criteria: 2,518 consumers were interviewed in 25 major metropolitan areas about their views on road rage. *AutoVantage, "2009 AutoVantage Road Rage Survey"*

- The Atlanta metro area appeared on *Forbes* list of the best and worst cities for commuters. The metro area ranked #58 out of 60 (#1 is best). Criteria: travel time; road congestion; travel delays. *Forbes.com, "Best and Worst Cities for Commuters," February 16, 2010*

Women/Minorities Rankings

- Atlanta was ranked #33 out of 100 metro areas in *SELF Magazine's* ranking of America's healthiest places for women." A panel of experts came up with more than 50 criteria including death and disease rates, environmental indicators, community resources, and lifestyle habits. *SELF Magazine, "Secrets of America's Healthiest Women," December 2008*

- Atlanta was selected as one of the "Gayest Cities in America" by *The Advocate*. The city ranked #7 out of 15. Criteria: gay.com profiles; listed officiants for gay weddings within a 50 mile radius; elected openly gay officials; Tegan and Sara performances over the past five years; lesbian bars; gay and gay-friendly religious congregations; entries in YellowPages.com with "gay" in the business name or description. *The Advocate, "Gayest Cities in America," February 2011*

- Atlanta appeared on *Black Enterprise's* list of the "Ten Best Cities for African Americans." The top picks were culled from more than 2,000 interactive surveys completed on www.blackenterprise.com and by editorial staff evaluation. The editors weighed the following criteria as it pertained to African Americans in each city: median household income; percentage of households earning more than $100,000; percentage of businesses owned; percentage of college graduates; unemployment rates; home loan rejections; and homeownership rates. *Black Enterprise, May 2007*

Miscellaneous Rankings

- Energizer Holdings, the makers of Edge® shave gel, in partnership with Sperling's BestPlaces, ranked 50 major metro areas in terms of everyday irritations. The Atlanta metro area ranked #1. Criteria: humidity levels; weather conditions; incidence of traffic delays and congestion; average commute times; frequency of flight delays and cancellations; rates of sleeplessness; underemployment; pollens and allergens; pests; comedy clubs per capita. *Energizer Holdings, "Most Irritation Prone Cities," July 23, 2010*

- Mars Chocolate North America, the makers of COMBOS®, in partnership with Sperling's BestPlaces, ranked 50 major metro areas in terms of their "manliness." The Atlanta metro area ranked #32. Criteria: number of home improvement stores, steak houses, pickup trucks, motorcycles, and manly occupations (fire fighters, police officers, construction workers, EMP personnel) per capita; salty snack sales; sports TV viewing habits. *Mars Chocolate North America, "America's Manliest Cities," June 22, 2010*

- The Atlanta metro area appeared in AutoMD.com's ranking of the "Best and Worst Cities for Auto Repair." The metro area ranked #35 (#1 is best). The 50 most-populated metro areas in the U.S. were ranked on three critical factors: repair affordability; price disparity range; shop integrity factor. *AutoMD.com, "Advocacy for Repair Shop Fairness Report," February 24, 2010*

- Atlanta was selected as one of America's "10 Meanest Cities" by the National Coalition for the Homeless and The National Law Center on Homelessness & Poverty. The city was ranked #4. Criteria: the number of anti-homeless laws; the enforcement of those laws and severity of penalties; the general political climate towards homeless people; local advocate support for the meanest designation; the city's history of criminalization measures; and the existence of pending or recently enacted criminalization legislation in the city. *National Coalition for the Homeless and The National Law Center on Homelessness & Poverty, "Homes Not Handcuffs: The Criminalization of Homelessness in U.S. Cities," July 2009*

- The Atlanta metro area appeared on *Forbes* list of "America's Drunkest Cities." The area ranked #28. Criteria: 35 of the largest continental U.S. metro areas were chosen based on availability of data and geographic diversity. Each metro was ranked in five areas: state laws; drinkers; heavy drinkers; binge drinkers; and alcoholism. *Forbes.com, "America's Drunkest Cities," August 22, 2006*

- Scarborough Research, a leading market research firm, identified the top local markets for frequent fast food restaurant patronage. The Atlanta DMA (Designated Market Area) ranked in the top 10 with consumers reporting an average of 6.2 visits within the past 30 days. *Scarborough Research, May 31, 2006*

- Scarborough Research, a leading market research firm, identified the top local markets for frequent sit-down restaurant patronage. The Atlanta DMA (Designated Market Area) ranked in the top 10 with consumers reporting an average of 4.1 visits within the past 30 days. *Scarborough Research, May 31, 2006*

Business Environment

CITY FINANCES

City Government Finances

Component	2008 ($000)	2008 ($ per capita)
Total Revenues	1,957,826	3,771
Total Expenditures	2,499,255	4,814
Debt Outstanding	6,321,477	12,177
Cash and Securities[1]	5,291,064	10,192

Note: (1) Cash and security holdings of a government at the close of its fiscal year, including those of its dependent agencies, utilities, and liquor stores.
Source: U.S Census Bureau, State & Local Government Finances 2008

City Government Revenue by Source

Source	2008 ($000)	2008 ($ per capita)
General Revenue		
From Federal Government	34,317	66
From State Government	29,999	58
From Local Governments	108,699	209
Taxes		
Property	261,028	503
Sales and Gross Receipts	124,210	239
Personal Income	0	0
Corporate Income	0	0
Motor Vehicle License	0	0
Other Taxes	86,824	167
Current Charges	876,798	1,689
Liquor Store	0	0
Utility	276,171	532
Employee Retirement	-20,480	-39

Source: U.S Census Bureau, State & Local Government Finances 2008

City Government Expenditures by Function

Function	2008 ($000)	2008 ($ per capita)	2008 (%)
General Direct Expenditures			
Air Transportation	646,996	1,246	25.9
Corrections	44,534	86	1.8
Education	0	0	0.0
Employment Security Administration	0	0	0.0
Financial Administration	15,571	30	0.6
Fire Protection	85,672	165	3.4
General Public Buildings	15,937	31	0.6
Governmental Administration, Other	127,382	245	5.1
Health	2,717	5	0.1
Highways	61,723	119	2.5
Hospitals	0	0	0.0
Housing and Community Development	28,737	55	1.1
Interest on General Debt	164,504	317	6.6
Judicial and Legal	24,383	47	1.0
Libraries	0	0	0.0
Parking	0	0	0.0
Parks and Recreation	91,385	176	3.7
Police Protection	200,531	386	8.0
Public Welfare	13,016	25	0.5
Sewerage	249,038	480	10.0
Solid Waste Management	46,158	89	1.8
Veterans' Services	0	0	0.0
Liquor Store	0	0	0.0
Utility	382,316	736	15.3
Employee Retirement	142,999	275	5.7

Source: U.S Census Bureau, State & Local Government Finances 2008

Municipal Bond Ratings

Area	Moody's	S&P	Fitch
City	A1	A	n/a

Rating Systems (shown in declining order of credit quality): Moody's– Aaa, Aa, A, Baa, Ba, B, Caa, Ca, C (numerical modifiers 1, 2, and 3 are added to letter-rating); S&P– AAA, AA, A, BBB, BB, B, CCC, CC, C; Fitch– AAA, AA, A, BBB, BB, B, CCC, CC, C. Ratings may be modified by the addition of a plus or minus sign to show relative standing within the major rating categories.
Notes: n/a Not available; (1) Not reviewed; (2) Issuer Rating/No General Obligation; (3) Standard and Poor's Issue Credit Rating (ICR) is a current opinion of an obliger with respect to a specific financial obligation, a specific class of financial obligations, or a specific financial program.
Source: U.S. Census Bureau, 2011 Statistical Abstract, Bond Ratings for City Governments by Largest Cities: 2009

DEMOGRAPHICS

Population Growth

Area	1990 Census	2000 Census	2010 Estimate	2015 Projection	Population Growth (%) 2000-2010	2010-2015
City	394,092	416,474	541,696	602,248	30.1	11.2
MSA[1]	3,069,411	4,247,981	5,569,195	6,182,135	31.1	11.0
U.S.	248,709,873	281,421,906	309,038,974	321,675,005	9.8	4.1

Note: (1) Metropolitan Statistical Area - see Appendix B for areas included
Source: Claritas, Inc.

Number of Households and Average Household Size

Area	2010 Estimate	2010 Average Household Size
City	217,657	2.34
MSA[1]	2,005,649	2.73
U.S.	116,136,617	2.59

Note: (1) Metropolitan Statistical Area - see Appendix B for areas included
Source: Claritas, Inc.

Race and Ethnicity

Area	White Alone[2] (%)	Black Alone[2] (%)	Asian Alone[2] (%)	Other Race Alone[2] (%)	Hispanic[3] (%)
City	37.0	54.6	2.8	5.6	7.2
MSA[1]	57.9	31.0	4.1	7.0	9.9
U.S.	72.3	12.4	4.4	10.9	15.8

Note: Figures are 2010 estimates; (1) Metropolitan Statistical Area - see Appendix B for areas included (2) Alone is defined as not being in combination with one or more other races; (3) May be of any race.
Source: Claritas, Inc.

Segregation

Type	Segregation Indices[1] 1990	2000	2010	2010 Rank[2]	Percent Change 1990-2000	1990-2010	2000-2010
Black/White	66.3	64.3	59.0	41	-2.0	-7.2	-5.3
Asian/White	42.5	46.9	48.5	10	4.4	6.0	1.5
Hispanic/White	35.3	51.6	49.5	27	16.3	14.1	-2.1

Note: Figures are based on an analysis of 1990, 2000, and 2010 Census Decennial Census tract data by William H. Frey, Brookings Institution and the University of Michigan Social Science Data Analysis Network. In this analysis all racial groups (whites, blacks, and asians) are non-Hispanic members of those races. Hispanics are shown as a separate category; All figures cover the Metropolitan Statistical Area (see Appendix B for areas included); (1) Segregation Indices are Dissimilarity Indices that measure the degree to which the minority group is distributed differently than whites aross census tracts. They range from 0 (complete integration) to 100 (complete [segregation) where the value indicates the percentage of the minority group that needs to move to be distributed exactly like whites; (2) Ranges from 1 (most segregated) to 102 (least segregated); n/a not available.
Source: www.CensusScope.org

Ancestry

Area	German	Irish	English	American	Italian	Polish	French	Scottish
City	7.5	6.2	8.4	6.5	2.4	1.3	2.1	2.1
MSA[1]	8.6	8.8	8.6	9.3	2.9	1.4	1.8	2.0
U.S.	16.6	12.0	9.1	6.1	5.9	3.3	3.1	1.9

Note: The top eight ancestries in the U.S. are shown. Figures are percentages and include multiple ancestry (e.g. if a person reported being Irish and Italian, they were included in both columns); (1) Metropolitan Statistical Area - see Appendix B for areas included
Source: U.S. Census Bureau, 2007-2009 American Community Survey 3-Year Estimates

Foreign-Born Population

Area	Any Foreign Country	Mexico	Asia	Europe	Carribean	South America	Central America[2]	Africa	Canada
City	7.4	1.8	2.1	1.3	0.5	0.5	0.4	0.6	0.2
MSA[1]	12.8	3.4	3.4	1.3	1.2	1.0	1.1	1.2	0.2
U.S.	12.5	3.8	3.4	1.6	1.1	0.8	0.9	0.5	0.3

Note: (1) Metropolitan Statistical Area - see Appendix B for areas included; (2) Excludes Mexico.
Source: U.S. Census Bureau, 2007-2009 American Community Survey 3-Year Estimates

Marriage Status

Area	Never Married	Now Married[2]	Separated	Widowed	Divorced
City	53.7	27.4	2.4	5.1	11.4
MSA[1]	33.5	48.4	2.2	4.7	11.1
U.S.	31.4	49.7	2.2	6.2	10.6

Note: Figures are percentages and cover the population 15 years of age and older; (1) Metropolitan Statistical Area - see Appendix B for areas included; (2) Excludes separated
Source: U.S. Census Bureau, 2007-2009 American Community Survey 3-Year Estimates

Age Distribution and Median Age

Area	Under Age 5	Age 5 to 17	Age 18 to 34	Age 35 to 49	Age 50 to 64	Age 65 to 79	80 Years and Over	Median Age
City	6.6	13.5	31.9	23.9	15.9	5.9	2.3	33.9
MSA[1]	7.9	19.3	24.0	24.1	16.4	6.3	2.1	34.2
U.S.	6.9	17.5	23.3	21.4	18.1	9.1	3.7	36.7

Note: (1) Metropolitan Statistical Area - see Appendix B for areas included
Source: U.S. Census Bureau, 2007-2009 American Community Survey 3-Year Estimates

Male/Female Ratio

Area	Males	Females	Males per 100 Females
City	271,536	270,160	100.5
MSA[1]	2,751,690	2,817,505	97.7
U.S.	152,401,520	156,637,454	97.3

Note: Figures are 2010 estimates; (1) Metropolitan Statistical Area - see Appendix B for areas included
Source: Claritas, Inc.

Religion

Area	Catholic	Southern Baptist	United Meth-odist	ELCA[1]	LDS[2]	Presby-terian Church USA	Jewish Est.	Muslim Est.
County	8.8	10.0	9.2	0.8	0.3	3.7	8.1	2.7
U.S.	22.0	7.1	3.7	1.8	1.5	1.1	2.2	0.6

Note: Figures are the number of adherents as a percentage of the total population; Adherents are defined as all members, including full members, their children and the estimated number of other participants who are not considered members (e.g. the baptized, those not confirmed, those regularly attending services, etc.);
(1) Evangelical Lutheran Church in America; (2) The Church of Jesus Christ of Latter Day Saints
Source: Reprinted with permission from Religious Congregations and Membership in the United States 2000 (Nashville, Glenmary Research Center, 2002) Copyright Association of Statisticians of American Religious Bodies. All rights reserved.

ECONOMY

Gross Metropolitan Product

Area	2006	2007	2008	2009	2009 Rank[2]
MSA[1]	255.4	267.3	269.8	262.7	10

Note: Figures are in billions of dollars; (1) Atlanta-Sandy Springs-Marietta, GA Metropolitan Statistical Area - see Appendix B for areas included; (2) Rank ranges from 1 to 363
Source: The U.S. Conference of Mayors, "Pace of Economic Recovery: GMP and Jobs," January 2010

Economic Growth

Area	2006-2008 (%)	2009 (%)	2010 (%)	Rank[2]
MSA[1]	0.5	-3.6	2.1	233
U.S.	1.3	-2.5	2.2	–

Note: Figures are real Gross Metropolitan Product growth rates and represent annual average percent change; (1) Atlanta-Sandy Springs-Marietta, GA Metropolitan Statistical Area - see Appendix B for areas included; (2) Rank ranges from 1 to 363
Source: The U.S. Conference of Mayors, "Pace of Economic Recovery: GMP and Jobs," January 2010

Metropolitan Area Exports

Area	2005	2006	2007	2008	2009	2009 Rank[2]
MSA[1]	11,063.0	11,393.6	12,551.0	14,432.9	13,405.9	18

Note: Figures are in millions of dollars; (1) Atlanta-Sandy Springs-Marietta, GA Metropolitan Statistical Area - see Appendix B for areas included; (2) Rank ranges from 1 to 374
Source: U.S. Department of Commerce, International Trade Administration, Office of Trade & Industry Information, Manufacturing & Services

INCOME

Per Capita/Median/Average Income

Area	Per Capita ($)	Median Household ($)	Average Household ($)
City	32,441	46,961	79,465
MSA[1]	28,777	60,647	79,200
U.S.	27,034	52,795	71,071

Note: Figures are 2010 estimates; (1) Metropolitan Statistical Area - see Appendix B for areas included
Source: Claritas, Inc.

Household Income Distribution

Area	Percent of Households Earning							
	Under $15,000	$15,000 -24,999	$25,000 -34,999	$35,000 -49,999	$50,000 -74,999	$75,000 -99,000	$100,000 -149,999	$150,000 and up
City	19.0	10.9	9.9	12.8	14.4	9.7	10.4	12.8
MSA[1]	9.0	7.8	9.3	14.9	21.1	14.1	14.2	9.6
U.S.	12.1	10.2	10.6	15.0	19.5	12.5	12.1	8.0

Note: Figures are 2010 estimates; (1) Metropolitan Statistical Area - see Appendix B for areas included
Source: Claritas, Inc.

Poverty Rates by Age

Area	All Ages	Under 18 Years Old	18 to 64 Years Old	65 Years and Over
City	20.8	6.2	13.1	1.5
MSA[1]	12.2	4.6	6.8	0.8
U.S.	13.6	4.7	7.7	1.2

Note: Figures are percent of population with income during the previous 12 months below poverty level and only include population for whom poverty status is determined; (1) Metropolitan Statistical Area - see Appendix B for areas included
Source: U.S. Census Bureau, 2007-2009 American Community Survey 3-Year Estimates

Personal Bankruptcy Filing Rate

Area	2006	2007	2008	2009	2010
Fulton County	3.32	4.29	4.99	6.53	7.25
U.S.	2.00	2.73	3.53	4.60	4.96

Note: Numbers are per 1,000 population and include Chapter 7 and Chapter 13 filings
Source: Federal Deposit Insurance Corporation, Regional Economic Conditions, March 17, 2011

EMPLOYMENT

Labor Force and Employment

Area	Civilian Labor Force			Workers Employed		
	Dec. 2009	Dec. 2010	% Chg.	Dec. 2009	Dec. 2010	% Chg.
City	233,074	232,329	-0.3	207,104	206,028	-0.5
MSA[1]	2,678,487	2,661,869	-0.6	2,404,347	2,391,846	-0.5
U.S.	152,693,000	153,156,000	0.3	137,953,000	139,159,000	0.9

Note: Data is not seasonally adjusted and covers workers 16 years of age and older;
(1) Metropolitan Statistical Area - see Appendix B for areas included
Source: Bureau of Labor Statistics, http://stats.bls.gov

Unemployment Rate

Area	2010											
	Jan.	Feb.	Mar.	Apr.	May	Jun.	Jul.	Aug.	Sep.	Oct.	Nov.	Dec.
City	11.8	11.3	10.8	10.4	10.8	11.5	11.6	11.7	11.3	11.2	11.4	11.3
MSA[1]	10.7	10.5	10.1	9.7	9.8	10.3	10.4	10.4	10.3	10.2	10.3	10.1
U.S.	10.6	10.4	10.2	9.5	9.3	9.6	9.7	9.5	9.2	9.0	9.3	9.1

Note: Data is not seasonally adjusted and covers workers 16 years of age and older; All figures are percentages; (1) Metropolitan Statistical Area - see Appendix B for areas included
Source: Bureau of Labor Statistics, http://stats.bls.gov

Projected Unemployment Rate

Area	2007 (%)	2009 (%)	2011 (%)	2013 (%)
MSA[1]	4.8	10.8	9.2	7.4

Note: (1) Metropolitan Statistical Area - see Appendix B for areas included
Source: The U.S. Conference of Mayors, "Pace of Economic Recovery: GMP and Jobs," January 2010

Employment by Occupation

Occupation Classification	City (%)	MSA[1] (%)	U.S. (%)
Sales and Office	23.8	27.0	25.4
Professional and Related	27.6	21.0	21.0
Service	16.3	14.9	17.2
Production, Transportation, and Material Moving	6.6	10.6	12.3
Management, Business, and Financial	20.5	17.2	14.1
Construction, Extraction, and Maintenance	5.0	9.2	9.2
Farming, Forestry, and Fishing	0.1	0.1	0.7

Note: Figures cover employed civilians 16 years of age and older;
(1) Metropolitan Statistical Area - see Appendix B for areas included
Source: U.S. Census Bureau, 2007-2009 American Community Survey 3-Year Estimates

Employment by Industry

Sector	MSA[1] Number of Employees	MSA[1] Percent of Total	U.S. Percent of Total
Government	320,200	14.2	17.2
Education and Health Services	278,400	12.3	15.2
Professional and Business Services	379,400	16.8	13.0
Retail Trade	253,100	11.2	11.4
Leisure and Hospitality	216,700	9.6	9.7
Manufacturing	143,900	6.4	8.8
Financial Activities	138,500	6.1	5.8
Wholesale Trade	145,100	6.4	4.2
Construction	85,900	3.8	4.1
Other Services	91,900	4.1	4.1
Transportation and Utilities	126,600	5.6	3.7
Information	78,400	3.5	2.1
Mining and Logging	1,300	0.1	0.6

Note: Figures cover non-farm employment as of December 2010 and are not seasonally adjusted;
(1) Metropolitan Statistical Area - see Appendix B for areas included
Source: Bureau of Labor Statistics, http://stats.bls.gov

Occupations with Greatest Projected Employment Growth: 2006 - 2016

Occupation[1]	2006 Employment	2016 Projected Employment	Numeric Employment Change	Percent Employment Change
Combined food preparation and serving workers, including fast food	95,500	124,650	29,150	30.5
Retail salespersons	127,750	153,800	26,050	20.4
Customer service representatives	83,640	105,060	21,420	25.6
Registered nurses	61,770	81,670	19,900	32.2
Waiters and waitresses	67,030	85,420	18,390	27.4
Elementary school teachers, except special education	54,220	70,440	16,220	29.9
Office clerks, general	88,680	102,290	13,610	15.3
Janitors and cleaners, except maids and housekeeping cleaners	60,840	73,160	12,320	20.2
Nursing aides, orderlies, and attendants	38,510	48,910	10,400	27.0
Child care workers	35,890	45,770	9,880	27.5

Note: Projections cover Georgia; (1) Sorted by numeric employment change
Source: www.projectionscentral.com, State Occupational Projections, 2006-2016 Long-Term Projections

Fastest Growing Occupations: 2006 - 2016

Occupation[1]	2006 Employment	2016 Projected Employment	Numeric Employment Change	Percent Employment Change
Skin care specialists	1,570	2,560	990	63.1
Network systems and data communications analysts	8,570	13,260	4,690	54.7
Home health aides	7,720	11,780	4,060	52.6
Medical assistants	11,990	17,450	5,460	45.5
Veterinary technologists and technicians	2,160	3,140	980	45.4
Mental health and substance abuse social workers	1,260	1,780	520	41.3
Computer software engineers, applications	11,160	15,730	4,570	40.9
Physician assistants	2,160	3,020	860	39.8
Veterinarians	1,820	2,530	710	39.0
Physical therapist assistants	1,350	1,870	520	38.5

Note: Projections cover Georgia; (1) Sorted by percent employment change and excludes occupations with numeric employment change less than 400
Source: www.projectionscentral.com, State Occupational Projections, 2006-2016 Long-Term Projections

Average Wages

Occupation	$/Hr.	Occupation	$/Hr.
Accountants and Auditors	34.69	Maids and Housekeeping Cleaners	8.86
Automotive Mechanics	18.42	Maintenance and Repair Workers	18.06
Bookkeepers	17.23	Marketing Managers	54.65
Carpenters	18.27	Nuclear Medicine Technologists	32.23
Cashiers	8.78	Nurses, Licensed Practical	18.51
Clerks, General Office	12.46	Nurses, Registered	30.40
Clerks, Receptionists/Information	12.89	Nursing Aides/Orderlies/Attendants	11.04
Clerks, Shipping/Receiving	14.20	Packers and Packagers, Hand	10.62
Computer Programmers	36.34	Physical Therapists	36.36
Computer Support Specialists	23.74	Postal Service Mail Carriers	23.04
Computer Systems Analysts	40.47	Real Estate Brokers	45.55
Cooks, Restaurant	10.59	Retail Salespersons	11.77
Dentists	n/a	Sales Reps., Exc. Tech./Scientific	30.49
Electrical Engineers	41.82	Sales Reps., Tech./Scientific	40.13
Electricians	20.97	Secretaries, Exc. Legal/Med./Exec.	14.10
Financial Managers	54.94	Security Guards	11.16
First-Line Supervisors/Mgrs., Sales	18.05	Surgeons	104.46
Food Preparation Workers	9.90	Teacher Assistants	9.80
General and Operations Managers	50.36	Teachers, Elementary School	25.70
Hairdressers/Cosmetologists	13.28	Teachers, Secondary School	26.40
Internists	88.19	Telemarketers	15.43
Janitors and Cleaners	10.44	Truck Drivers, Heavy/Tractor-Trailer	20.50
Landscaping/Groundskeeping Workers	11.55	Truck Drivers, Light/Delivery Svcs.	15.18
Lawyers	70.58	Waiters and Waitresses	9.44

Note: Wage data covers the Atlanta-Sandy Springs-Marietta, GA - see Appendix B for areas included. Hourly wages for elementary/secondary school teachers and teacher assistants were calculated by the editors from annual wage data assuming a 40 hour work week; n/a not available.
Source: Bureau of Labor Statistics, Metro Area Occupational Employment and Wage Estimates, May 2009

RESIDENTIAL REAL ESTATE

Building Permits

Area	Single-Family			Multi-Family			Total		
	2009	2010	Pct. Chg.	2009	2010	Pct. Chg.	2009	2010	Pct. Chg.
City	169	83	-50.9	750	196	-73.9	919	279	-69.6
MSA[1]	5,421	6,384	17.8	1,112	1,191	7.1	6,533	7,575	15.9
U.S.	441,100	447,300	1.4	141,900	157,300	10.9	583,000	604,600	3.7

Note: (1) Metropolitan Statistical Area - see Appendix B for areas included; figures represent new, privately-owned housing units authorized (unadjusted data); All permit data are based on estimates with imputation.
Source: U.S. Census Bureau, Manufacturing, Mining, and Construction Statistics, Building Permits, 2009, 2010

Homeownership Rate

Area	2005 (%)	2006 (%)	2007 (%)	2008 (%)	2009 (%)	2010 (%)
MSA[1]	66.4	67.9	66.4	67.5	67.7	67.2
U.S.	68.9	68.8	68.1	67.8	67.4	66.9

Note: (1) Metropolitan Statistical Area - see Appendix B for areas included
Source: U.S. Census Bureau, Housing Vacancies and Homeownership Annual Statistics: 2010

Housing Vacancy Rates

Area	Gross Vacancy Rate[2] (%)			Year-Round Vacancy Rate[3] (%)			Rental Vacancy Rate[4] (%)			Homeowner Vacancy Rate[5] (%)		
	2008	2009	2010	2008	2009	2010	2008	2009	2010	2008	2009	2010
MSA[1]	12.6	13.0	11.7	12.4	12.8	11.4	16.1	16.6	13.8	4.8	4.1	3.0
U.S.	14.4	14.5	14.3	11.1	11.3	11.3	10.0	10.6	10.2	2.8	2.6	2.6

Note: (1) Metropolitan Statistical Area - see Appendix B for areas included; (2) The percentage of the total housing inventory that is vacant; (3) The percentage of the housing inventory (excluding seasonal units) that is year-round vacant; (4) The percentage of rental inventory that is vacant for rent; (5) The percentage of homeowner inventory that is vacant for sale; n/a not available
Source: U.S. Census Bureau, Housing Vacancies and Homeownership Annual Statistics: 2010

State Corporate Income Tax Rates

State	Tax Rate (%)	Income Brackets ($)	Num. of Brackets	Financial Institution Tax Rate (%)[a]	Federal Income Tax Ded.
Georgia	6.0	Flat rate	1	6.0	No

Note: Tax rates as of January 1, 2011; (a) Rates listed are the tax rates applied to financial institutions or excise taxes based on income. Some states have other taxes based upon the value of deposits or shares.
Source: Federation of Tax Administrators, "State Corporate Income Tax Rates, 2011"

State Individual Income Tax Rates

State	Tax Rate (%)	Income Brackets ($)	Num. of Brackets	Personal Exempt. ($)[1] Single	Personal Exempt. ($)[1] Dependents	Fed. Inc. Tax Ded.
Georgia	1.0 - 6.0	750 (h) - 7,001 (h)	6	2,700	3,000	No

Note: Tax rates as of January 1, 2011; Local- and county-level taxes are not included; n/a not applicable; (1) Married joint filers generally receive double the single exemption; (h) The Georgia income brackets reported are for single individuals. For married couples filing jointly, the same tax rates apply to income brackets ranging from $1,000, to $10,000.
Source: Federation of Tax Administrators, "State Individual Income Tax Rates, 2011"

Various State and Local Tax Rates

State	State and Local Sales and Use (%)	State Sales and Use (%)	Gasoline[1] (¢/gal.)	Cigarette[2] ($/pack)	Spirits[3] ($/gal.)	Wine[4] ($/gal.)	Beer[5] ($/gal.)
Georgia	8.0	4.00	20.8	0.37	3.79	1.51	1.01 (l)

Note: All tax rates as of January 1, 2011 except Spirits (Sept. 1, 2010); (1) The American Petroleum Institute has developed a methodology for determining the average tax rate on a gallon of fuel. Rates may include any of the following: excise taxes, environmental fees, storage tank fees, other fees or taxes, general sales tax, and local taxes. In states where gasoline is subject to the general sales tax, or where the fuel tax is based on the average sale price, the average rate determined by API is sensitive to changes in the price of gasoline. States that fully or partially apply general sales taxes to gasoline: CA, CO, GA, IL, IN, MI, NY; (2) The federal excise tax of $1.0066 per pack and local taxes are not included; (3) Rates are those applicable to off-premise sales of 40% alcohol by volume (a.b.v.) distilled spirits in 750ml containers. Local excise taxes are excluded; (4) Rates are those applicable to off-premise sales of 11% a.b.v. non-carbonated wine in 750ml containers; (5) Rates are those applicable to off-premise sales of 4.7% a.b.v. beer in 12 ounce containers; (l) Includes statewide local rates in Alabama ($0.52) and Georgia ($0.53).
Source: Tax Foundation, 2011 Facts & Figures: How Does Your State Compare?

State-Local Tax Burdens

Area	Rate (%)	Rank[1]	Per Capita Taxes Paid to Home State ($)	Total State and Local Per Capita Taxes Paid ($)	Per Capita Income ($)
Georgia	9.1	32	2,411	3,350	36,738
U.S. Average	9.8	-	3,057	4,160	42,539

Note: Figures cover 2009; (1) Rank ranges from 1 to 50 where 1 is highest tax burden
Source: Tax Foundation, State-Local Tax Burdens, All States, 2009

State Business Tax Climate Index Rankings

State	Overall Rank	Corporate Tax Index Rank	Individual Income Tax Index Rank	Sales Tax Index Rank	Unemployment Insurance Tax Index Rank	Property Tax Index Rank
Georgia	25	8	30	23	22	38

Note: The index is a measure of how each state's tax laws affect economic performance. The lower the rank, the more favorable a state's tax system is for business. All ranks are for fiscal years. States without a given tax are given a ranking of 1.
Source: Tax Foundation, Tax Foundation Background Paper, No. 60, "2011 State Business Tax Climate Index"

COMMERCIAL REAL ESTATE

Office Market

Market Area	Inventory (sq. ft.)	Vacant (sq. ft.)	Vac. Rate (%)	Under Constr. (sq. ft.)	Asking Rent ($/sf/yr) Class A	Asking Rent ($/sf/yr) Class B
Atlanta	144,409,878	32,958,711	22.8	-	22.77	17.48

Source: Grubb & Ellis, Office Markets Trends, 1st Quarter 2011

Industrial Market

Market Area	Inventory (sq. ft.)	Vacant (sq. ft.)	Vac. Rate (%)	Under Constr. (sq. ft.)	Asking Rent ($/sf/yr) WH/Dist	Asking Rent ($/sf/yr) R&D/Flex
Atlanta	588,854,035	84,369,402	14.3	-	3.34	6.76

Source: Grubb & Ellis, Industrial Markets Trends, 4th Quarter 2010

COMMERCIAL UTILITIES

Typical Monthly Electric Bills

Area	Commercial Service ($/month) 3 kW demand 1,000 kWh	Commercial Service ($/month) 40 kW demand 14,000 kWh	Industrial Service ($/month) 1,000 kW demand 200,000 kWh	Industrial Service ($/month) 50,000 kW demand 15,000,000 kWh
City	153	1,980	25,423	1,372,795
Average[1]	135	1,576	23,741	1,402,202

Note: Based on total rates in effect July 1, 2010; (1) average based on 182 utilities surveyed
Source: Edison Electric Institute, Typical Bills and Average Rates Report, Summer 2010

TRANSPORTATION

Means of Transportation to Work

Area	Car/Truck/Van Drove Alone	Car/Truck/Van Car-pooled	Public Transportation Bus	Public Transportation Subway	Public Transportation Railroad	Bicycle	Walked	Other Means	Worked at Home
City	67.2	7.6	9.2	2.5	0.3	0.8	4.2	1.5	6.4
MSA[1]	77.1	10.8	2.7	0.7	0.1	0.2	1.4	1.6	5.3
U.S.	75.8	10.4	2.7	1.7	0.5	0.5	2.9	1.2	4.1

Note: Figures are percentages and cover workers 16 years of age and older;
(1) Metropolitan Statistical Area - see Appendix B for areas included
Source: U.S. Census Bureau, 2007-2009 American Community Survey 3-Year Estimates

Travel Time to Work

Area	Less Than 15 Minutes	15 to 29 Minutes	30 to 44 Minutes	45 to 59 Minutes	60 to 89 Minutes	90 Minutes or More
City	23.9	42.4	20.5	6.1	4.3	2.9
MSA[1]	19.2	33.0	24.3	11.3	8.8	3.4
U.S.	28.5	36.2	19.7	7.5	5.6	2.5

Note: Figures are percentages and include workers 16 years old and over;
(1) Metropolitan Statistical Area - see Appendix B for areas included
Source: U.S. Census Bureau, 2007-2009 American Community Survey 3-Year Estimates

Travel Time Index

Area	1982	1999	2008	2009
Urban Area[1]	1.08	1.23	1.23	1.22
Average[2]	1.08	1.20	1.20	1.20

Note: Travel Time Index—the ratio of travel time in the peak period to the travel time at free-flow conditions. A value of 1.30 indicates a 20-minute free-flow trip takes 26 minutes in the peak. Free-flow speeds (60 mph on freeways and 35 mph on principal arterials) are used as the comparison threshold; (1) Covers the Atlanta-Sandy Springs-Marietta urban area; (2) average of 439 urban areas
Source: Texas Transportation Institute, Urban Mobility Report 2010, December 2010

Public Transportation

Agency Name / Mode of Transportation	Vehicles Operated in Maximum Service	Annual Unlinked Passenger Trips ('000)	Annual Passenger Miles ('000)
Metropolitan Atlanta Rapid Transit Authority (MARTA)			
Demand response	126	479.5	6,581.1
Heavy rail	182	83,346.5	527,022.8
Bus	507	72,716.4	285,048.2

Note: Figures include both directly operated and purchased transportation
Source: Federal Transit Administration, National Transit Database, 2009

Air Transportation

Airport Name and Code / Type of Service	Passenger Airlines[1]	Passenger Enplanements	Freight Carriers[2]	Freight (lbs.)
Hartsfield-Jackson Atlanta International Airport (ATL)				
Domestic service (U.S. carriers - 2010)	33	38,513,467	29	298,413,978
International service (U.S. carriers - 2009)	18	3,920,046	11	124,138,195

Note: (1) Includes all U.S.-based major, minor and commuter airlines that carried at least one passenger during the year; (2) Includes all U.S.-based airlines and freight carriers that transported at least one pound of freight during the year
Source: Bureau of Transportation Statistics, The Intermodal Transportation Database, Air Carriers: T-100 Domestic Market (U.S. Carriers), 2010; Bureau of Transportation Statistics, The Intermodal Transportation Database, Air Carriers: T-100 International Market (U.S. Carriers), 2009

Other Transportation Statistics

Interstate highways:	I-20; I-75; I-85
Amtrak service:	Yes
Major waterways/ports:	None

Source: Amtrak.com; Google Maps

BUSINESSES

Major Business Headquarters

Company Name	Rankings	
	Fortune[1]	Forbes[2]
Coca-Cola	70	-
Coca-Cola Enterprises	347	-
Cox Enterprises	-	14
Delta Air Lines	88	-
First Data	236	-
First Data	-	26
Genuine Parts	215	-
Home Depot	30	-
Newell Rubbermaid	397	-
RaceTrac Petroleum	-	63
Southern	147	-
SunTrust Banks	244	-
United Parcel Service	48	-

Note: (1) Fortune 500—companies that produce a 10-K are ranked 1 to 500 based on 2010 revenue; (2) all private companies with at least $2 billion in annual revenue are ranked 1 to 223; companies listed are headquartered in the city; dashes indicate no ranking
Source: Fortune, "Fortune 500," May 23, 2011; Forbes, "America's Largest Private Companies," November 3, 2010

Fast-Growing Businesses

According to *Inc.*, Atlanta is home to five of America's 500 fastest-growing private companies: **Clinical Resources; Principle Solutions Group; The Intersect Group; Vendormate; Vocalocity**. Criteria: must be an independent, privately-held, for-profit, U.S. corporation, proprietorship or partnership; revenues of at least $80,000 in 2006 and $2 million in 2009; four-year operating/sales history; holding companies, regulated banks, and utilities were excluded. *Inc., "America's 500 Fastest-Growing Private Companies," September 2010*

According to *Fortune*, Atlanta is home to one of the 100 fastest-growing companies in the world: **Ebix**. Companies were ranked by their revenue growth rate; their EPS growth rate; and their three-year annualized total return to investors for the period ended June 30, 2010. Criteria for inclusion: a company, foreign or domestic, must trade on a major U.S. stock exchange; file quarterly reports with the SEC; have a minimum market capitalization of $250 million; have a stock price of at least $5 on June 30, 2010; have been trading continuously since June 30, 2007; have revenue and net income for the four quarters ended on or before April 30, 2010, of at least $50 million and $10 million, respectively; and have posted a compound annual growth in revenue and earnings per share of at least 15% annually over the three years ended on or before April 30, 2010. REITs, limited-liability companies, limited parterships, companies about to be acquired, and companies that lost money in the quarter ended April 30, 2010 were excluded. *Fortune, "100 Fastest-Growing Companies," September 6, 2010*

According to *Fortune*, Atlanta is home to two of America's 100 fastest-growing small public companies: **Ebix; Transcend Services**. Companies were ranked by their three-year annualized rates of revenue growth and total return to investors for the period ended December 31, 2008. Criteria for inclusion: revenues of less than $200 million; stock price of at least $1. Banks, real-estate firms and adult entertainment companies were excluded. Also excluded were companies with losses in any of the four quarters ended on or before December 31, 2008. *Fortune Small Business, "America's Fastest-Growing Small Public Companies," July/August 2009*

According to Deloitte, Atlanta is home to four of North America's 500 fastest-growing high-technology companies: **A.D.A.M; Cbeyond; Ebix; SecureWorks**. Companies are ranked by percentage growth in revenue over a five-year period. Criteria for inclusion: company must be headquartered within North America; company must own proprietary intellectual property or proprietary technology that contributes to a significant portion of the company's operating revenue or devotes a significant proportion of revenues to research and development of technology; company must have been in business for a minumum of five years with 2005 operating revenues of at least $50,000 USD/CD and 2009 operating revenues of at least $5 million USD/CD. *Deloitte Touche Tohmatsu, 2010 Deloitte Technology Fast 500*[TM]

Minority Business Opportunity

Atlanta is home to five companies which are on the Black Enterprise Industrial/Service 100 list (100 largest companies based on gross sales): **H.J. Russell & Co.; The Gourmet Cos.; Carter Brothers; B&S Electric Supply; Jackmont Hospitality**. Criteria: operational in previous calendar year; at least 51% black-owned and manufactures/owns the product it sells or provides industrial or consumer services. Brokerages, real estate firms and firms that provide professional services are not eligible. *Black Enterprise, B.E. 100s, 2010*

Atlanta is home to two companies which are on the Black Enterprise Auto Dealer 60 list (60 largest dealers based on gross sales): **Mercedes-Benz of Buckhead; Malcolm Cunningham Automotive Group**. Criteria: company must be operational in previous calendar year and at least 51% black-owned. *Black Enterprise, B.E. 100s, 2010*

Atlanta is home to two companies which are on the Black Enterprise Bank 25 list (25 largest banks based on total assets, capital, deposits and loans, including mortgage-backed securities for the calendar year): **Capitol City Bank & Trust Co.; Citizens Bancshares Corp.** Criteria: commercial banks or savings and loans that are classified by the Federal Reserve as black institutions and have been fully operational for the previous calendar year. *Black Enterprise, B.E. 100s, 2010*

Atlanta is home to two companies which are on the Black Enterprise Asset Manager 15 list (15 largest asset management firms based on assets under management): **EARNEST Partners; Herndon Capital Management**. Criteria: company must be operational in previous calendar year and at least 51% black-owned. *Black Enterprise, B.E. 100s, 2010*

Atlanta is home to four companies which are on the *Hispanic Business 500* list (500 largest U.S. Hispanic-owned companies based on 2009 revenue): **The Zaid Group; PS Energy Group; CAPE; Precision 2000**. Companies included must show at least 51 percent ownership by Hispanic U.S. citizens, and must maintain headquarters in one of the 50 states or Washington, D.C. *Hispanic Business, "Hispanic Business 500," June 2010*

Atlanta is home to one company which is on the *Hispanic Business* Fastest-Growing 100 list (greatest sales growth from 2005 to 2009): **The Zaid Group**. Companies included must show at least 51 percent ownership by Hispanic U.S. citizens, and must maintain headquarters in one of the 50 states or Washington, D.C. In addition, companies must have minimum revenues of $200,000 for calendar year 2005. *Hispanic Business, July/August 2010*

Minority- and Women-Owned Businesses

Group	All Firms		Firms with Paid Employees			
	Firms	Sales ($000)	Firms	Sales ($000)	Employees	Payroll ($000)
Asian	2,257	1,178,708	1,025	1,131,161	5,837	164,452
Black	15,738	1,256,723	981	895,035	7,367	230,657
Hispanic	1,240	415,116	200	356,231	2,051	78,188
Women	17,047	5,316,681	2,348	4,800,357	24,541	851,096
All Firms	50,970	105,935,891	12,828	103,541,312	348,044	19,837,778

Note: Figures cover firms located in the city; minority- and women-owned business are defined as firms in which the corresponding group own 51% or more of the stock or equity of the company
Source: U.S. Census Bureau, 2007 Economic Census, Survey of Business Owners

HOTELS

Hotels/Motels

Area	5 Star		4 Star		3 Star		2 Star		1 Star		Not Rated	
	Num.	Pct.3	Num.	Pct.3	Num.	Pct.3	Num.	Pct.3	Num.	Pct.3	Num.	Pct.3
City[1]	4	0.8	19	3.7	150	29.4	283	55.5	18	3.5	36	7.1
Total[2]	119	0.7	927	5.8	4,906	30.5	7,992	49.7	526	3.3	1,625	10.1

Note: (1) Figures cover Atlanta and vicinity; (2) Figures cover all 100 cities in this book; (3) Percentage of hotels which are a given star rating; Star ratings are determined by expedia.com and offer an indication of the general quality of a particular hotel.
Source: expedia.com, May 5, 2011

The Atlanta metro area is home to five of the top 218 hotels in the U.S. according to *Travel & Leisure*: **Ritz-Carlton Lodge, Reynolds Plantation** (#143); **Four Seasons Hotel, Atlanta** (#152); **Ritz-Carlton, Buckhead** (#167); **Ritz-Carlton, Atlanta** (#169); **InterContinental Buckhead Atlanta** (#193). Criteria: service; location; rooms; food; and value. *Travel & Leisure, "T+L 500, The World's Best Hotels 2011"*

The Atlanta metro area is home to four of the top 100 hotels in the U.S. according to *Condé Nast Traveler*: **Ritz-Carlton** (#27); **InterContinental Buckhead** (#63); **Four Seasons** (#87); **Mansion on Peachtree** (#96). The selections are based on over 25,000 responses to the magazine's annual Readers' Choice Survey. *Condé Nast Traveler, "2010 Readers' Choice Awards"*

EVENT SITES

Major Stadiums, Arenas, and Auditoriums

Name	Max. Capacity
Alexander Memorial Coliseum	9,191
B.T. Harvey Stadium	9,000
Bobby Dodd Stadium at Historic Grant Field	55,000
Boisfeuillet Jones Atlanta Civic Center	4,600
Forbes Arena	6,000
Georgia Dome	71,228
Philips Arena	21,000
Russ Chandler Stadium	4,157
Turner Field	50,096

Source: Original research

Convention Centers

Name	Overall Space (sq. ft.)	Exhibit Space (sq. ft.)	Meeting Space (sq. ft.)	Meeting Rooms
AmericasMart Atlanta	n/a	n/a	441,000	38
Cobb Galleria Centre	320,000	20,000	144,000	20
Georgia International Convention Center	n/a	16,000	150,000	n/a
Georgia World Congress Center	3,900,000	n/a	1,400,000	106

Note: n/a not available
Source: Original research

Living Environment

COST OF LIVING

Cost of Living Index

Composite Index	Groceries	Housing	Utilities	Trans-portation	Health Care	Misc. Goods/ Services
95.6	96.2	90.7	86.3	99.3	103.3	100.3

Note: U.S. = 100; Figures cover the Atlanta GA urban area.
Source: The Council for Community and Economic Research, ACCRA Cost of Living Index, 2010

Grocery Prices

Area[1]	T-Bone Steak ($/pound)	Frying Chicken ($/pound)	Whole Milk ($/half gal.)	Eggs ($/dozen)	Orange Juice ($/64 oz.)	Coffee ($/11.5 oz.)
City[2]	9.76	1.17	1.75	1.16	3.18	3.49
Avg.	9.04	1.16	2.02	1.47	3.08	3.65
Min.	6.97	0.84	1.46	0.96	2.39	2.64
Max.	13.93	2.51	3.58	3.01	4.94	6.32

Note: (1) Values for the local area are compared with the average, minimum and maximum values for all 338 areas in the Cost of Living Index; (2) Figures cover the Atlanta GA urban area; **T-Bone Steak** *(price per pound);* **Frying Chicken** *(price per pound, whole fryer);* **Whole Milk** *(half gallon carton);* **Eggs** *(price per dozen, Grade A, large);* **Orange Juice** *(64 oz. Tropicana or Florida Natural);* **Coffee** *(11.5 oz. can, vacuum-packed, Maxwell House, Hills Bros, or Folgers).*
Source: The Council for Community and Economic Research, ACCRA Cost of Living Index, 2010

Housing and Utility Costs

Area[1]	New Home Price ($)	Apartment Rent ($/month)	All Electric ($/month)	Part Electric ($/month)	Other Energy ($/month)	Telephone ($/month)
City[2]	261,224	790	-	88.54	54.81	25.06
Avg.	293,442	810	166.39	91.93	83.82	26.93
Min.	182,545	453	119.21	44.47	36.85	17.98
Max.	1,123,114	2,776	307.53	218.20	313.90	39.15

Note: (1) Values for the local area are compared with the average, minimum and maximum values for all 338 areas in the Cost of Living Index; (2) Figures cover the Atlanta GA urban area; **New Home Price** *(2,400 sf living area, 8,000 sf lot, in urban area with full utilities);* **Apartment Rent** *(950 sf 2 bedroom/1.5 or 2 bath, unfurnished, excluding all utilities except water);* **All Electric** *(average monthly cost for an all-electric home);* **Part Electric** *(average monthly cost for a part-electric home);* **Other Energy** *(average monthly cost for natural gas, fuel oil, coal, wood, and any other forms of energy except electricity);* **Telephone** *(price includes basic monthly rate for a private residential line plus additional local usage charges incurred by a family of four).*
Source: The Council for Community and Economic Research, ACCRA Cost of Living Index, 2010

Health Care, Transportation, and Other Costs

Area[1]	Doctor ($/visit)	Dentist ($/visit)	Optometrist ($/visit)	Gasoline ($/gallon)	Beauty Salon ($/visit)	Men's Shirt ($)
City[2]	87.08	88.73	70.82	2.63	42.99	22.31
Avg.	89.44	78.95	87.40	2.73	31.92	24.83
Min.	57.00	54.25	48.32	2.44	19.17	13.67
Max.	149.90	136.73	174.22	3.75	62.81	47.89

Note: (1) Values for the local area are compared with the average, minimum and maximum values for all 338 areas in the Cost of Living Index; (2) Figures cover the Atlanta GA urban area; **Doctor** *(general practitioners routine exam of an established patient);* **Dentist** *(adult teeth cleaning and periodic oral examination);* **Optometrist** *(full vision eye exam for established adult patient);* **Gasoline** *(one gallon regular unleaded, national brand, including all taxes, cash price at self-service pump if available);* **Beauty Salon** *(woman's shampoo, trim, and blow-dry);* **Men's Shirt** *(cotton/polyester dress shirt, pinpoint weave, long sleeves).*
Source: The Council for Community and Economic Research, ACCRA Cost of Living Index, 2010

HOUSING

House Price Index (HPI)

Area	National Ranking[2]	Quarterly Change (%)	One-Year Change (%)	Five-Year Change (%)
MSA[1]	257	-1.69	-4.34	-9.92
U.S.[3]	-	-0.84	-3.95	-11.45

Note: The HPI is a weighted repeat sales index. It measures average price changes in repeat sales or refinancings on the same properties. This information is obtained by reviewing repeat mortgage transactions on single-family properties whose mortgages have been purchased or securitized by Fannie Mae or Freddie Mac in January 1975; (1) Metropolitan/Micropolitan Statistical Area - see Appendix B for areas included; (2) Rankings are based on annual percentage change for all metro areas containing at least 15,000 transactions over the last 10 years and ranges from 1 to 309; (3) figures based on a weighted average of Census Division estimates; all figures are for the period ending December 31, 2010
Source: Federal Housing Finance Agency, House Price Index, February 24, 2011

House Price Valuations

Area	Q4 2005 Price ($000)	Q4 2005 Over-valuation	Q4 2006 Price ($000)	Q4 2006 Over-valuation	Q4 2007 Price ($000)	Q4 2007 Over-valuation	Q4 2008 Price ($000)	Q4 2008 Over-valuation	Q4 2009 Price ($000)	Q4 2009 Over-valuation
MSA[1]	172.9	-3.4	177.0	-4.7	171.9	-10.7	153.2	-20.3	149.1	-21.9

Note: Figures show the percentage of over- or under-valuation of single family homes relative to statistically normal house values (e.g. a value of 23.6 indicates that house values are 23.6% overvalued). Statistically normal house values are based on house prices, interest rates, household incomes, population densities, and any historical premiums or discounts metropolitan areas have exhibited over time; (1) Figures cover the Atlanta-Sandy Springs-Marietta, GA Metropolitan Statistical Area - see Appendix B for areas included
Source: Global Insight/PNC Financial Services Group, House Prices in America: 4th Quarter 2009 Update

Median Single-Family Home Prices

Area	2008	2009	2010[p]	Percent Change 2009 to 2010
MSA[1]	149.5	123.5	114.8	-7.0
U.S. Average	196.6	172.1	173.2	0.6

Note: Figures are median sales prices of existing single-family homes in thousands of dollars; (p) preliminary; n/a not available; (1) Metropolitan Statistical Area - see Appendix B for areas included
Source: National Association of Realtors, Median Sales Price of Existing Single-Family Homes for Metropolitan Areas, 4th Quarter 2010

Median Apartment Condo-Coop Home Prices

Area	2008	2009	2010[p]	Percent Change 2009 to 2010
MSA[1]	n/a	n/a	n/a	n/a
U.S. Average	209.8	175.6	171.7	-2.2

Note: Figures are median sales prices of existing apartment condo-coop homes in thousands of dollars; (p) preliminary; n/a not available; (1) Metropolitan Statistical Area - see Appendix B for areas included
Source: National Association of Realtors, Median Sales Price of Existing Apartment Condo-Coop Homes for Metropolitan Areas, 4th Quarter 2010

Year Housing Structure Built

Area	2000 or Later	1990 -1999	1980 -1989	1970 -1979	1960 -1969	1950 -1959	1940 -1949	Before 1940	Median Year
City	18.7	9.4	8.6	10.5	15.4	14.4	7.2	15.8	1968
MSA[1]	23.7	21.8	19.2	13.8	9.2	6.0	2.4	3.9	1988
U.S.	12.5	14.0	14.2	16.5	11.4	11.3	5.8	14.3	1974

Note: Figures are percentages except for Median Year; (1) Metropolitan Statistical Area - see Appendix B for areas included
Source: U.S. Census Bureau, 2007-2009 American Community Survey 3-Year Estimates

HEALTH

Health Risk Data

Category	MSA[1] (%)	U.S. (%)
Adults who have been told they have high blood pressure	27.4	28.7
Adults who have been told they have high blood cholesterol	37.0	37.5
Adults who have been told they have diabetes[3]	7.9	8.3
Adults who have been told they have arthritis	20.3	26.0
Adults who have been told they currently have asthma	6.5	8.8
Adults who are current smokers	14.6	17.9
Adults who are heavy drinkers[4]	3.6	5.1
Adults who are binge drinkers[5]	11.6	15.8
Adults who are overweight (BMI 25.0 - 29.9)	38.9	36.2
Adults who are obese (BMI 30.0 - 99.8)	25.1	26.9
Adults who participated in any physical activities in the past month	77.8	76.2
Adults 50+ who have ever had a sigmoidoscopy or colonoscopy[2]	64.7	62.2
Women 40+ who have had a mammogram within the past two years[2]	79.0	76.0
Adults age 18–64 who have any kind of health care coverage	80.1	83.1

Note: Data as of 2009 unless otherwise noted; (1) Figures cover the Atlanta-Sandy Springs-Marietta, GA Metropolitan Statistical Area - see Appendix B for areas included; (2) Data as of 2008; (3) Figures do not include pregnancy-related, borderline, or pre-diabetes; (4) Heavy drinkers are classified as males having more than two drinks per day or females having more than one drink per day; (5) Binge drinkers are classified as males having five or more drinks on one occasion or females having four or more drinks on one occasion
Source: Centers for Disease Control and Prevention, Behaviorial Risk Factor Surveillance System, SMART: Selected Metropolitan/Micropolitan Area Risk Trends, 2008, 2009

Mortality Rates for the Top 10 Causes of Death in the U.S.

ICD-10[a] Sub-Chapter	ICD-10[a] Code	Age-Adjusted Mortality Rate[1] per 100,000 population	
		County[2]	U.S.
Malignant neoplasms	C00-C97	165.2	180.9
Ischaemic heart diseases	I20-I25	87.7	135.0
Other forms of heart disease	I30-I51	69.7	50.0
Cerebrovascular diseases	I60-I69	46.2	44.1
Chronic lower respiratory diseases	J40-J47	31.3	41.5
Other degenerative diseases of the nervous system	G30-G31	23.3	23.6
Diabetes mellitus	E10-E14	19.7	23.5
Other external causes of accidental injury	W00-X59	23.8	23.5
Organic, including symptomatic, mental disorders	F01-F09	38.2	22.2
Influenza and pneumonia	J09-J18	18.4	18.1

Note: (a) ICD-10 = International Classification of Diseases 10th Revision; (1) Mortality rates are a three year average covering 2005-2007; (2) Figures cover Fulton County
Source: Centers for Disease Control and Prevention, National Center for Health Statistics. Compressed Mortality File 1999-2007. CDC WONDER On-line Database, compiled from Compressed Mortality File 1999-2007 Series 20 No. 2M, 2010.

Mortality Rates for Selected Causes of Death

ICD-10[a] Sub-Chapter	ICD-10[a] Code	Age-Adjusted Mortality Rate[1] per 100,000 population	
		County[2]	U.S.
Assault	X85-Y09	12.2	6.0
Human immunodeficiency virus (HIV) disease	B20-B24	18.1	4.0
Hypertensive diseases	I10-I15	41.6	18.0
Intentional self-harm	X60-X84	7.6	11.0
Malnutrition	E40-E46	1.1	0.8
Obesity and other hyperalimentation	E65-E68	1.4	1.5
Transport accidents	V01-V99	12.6	15.6
Viral hepatitis	B15-B19	1.5	2.1

Note: (a) ICD-10 = International Classification of Diseases 10th Revision; (1) Mortality rates are a three year average covering 2005-2007; (2) Figures cover Fulton County
Source: Centers for Disease Control and Prevention, National Center for Health Statistics. Compressed Mortality File 1999-2007. CDC WONDER On-line Database, compiled from Compressed Mortality File 1999-2007 Series 20 No. 2M, 2010.

Distribution of Physicians and Dentists

Area[1]	Dentists[2]	D.O.[3]	M.D.[4]				
			Total	Family/ General Practice	Pediatrics	Medical Specialties	Surgical Specialties
Local (number)	563	80	3,160	185	226	1,163	862
Local (rate[5])	5.7	0.8	31.2	1.8	2.2	11.5	8.5
U.S. (rate[5])	4.5	1.9	18.3	2.5	1.4	6.8	4.1

Note: Data as of 2008 unless noted; (1) Local data covers Fulton County; (2) Data as of 2007; (3) Doctor of Osteopathic Medicine; (4) Includes active, non-federal, patient-care, office-based Doctors of Medicine; (5) rate per 10,000 population
Source: Area Resource File (ARF). 2009-2010 Release. U.S. Department of Health and Human Services, Health Resources and Services Administration, Bureau of Health Professions, Rockville, MD, August 2010

Hospitals

Atlanta has the following hospitals: 8 general medical and surgical; 1 psychiatric; 1 rehabilitation; 1 alcoholism and other chemical dependency; 2 long-term acute care; 2 other specialty; 1 children's general; 1 children's psychiatric.
AHA Guide to the Healthcare Field 2010

According to *U.S. News,* the Atlanta-Sandy Springs-Marietta, GA Metropolitan Statistical Area is home to two of the best hospitals in the U.S.: **Emory University Hospital**; **Shepherd Center**. The hospitals listed were highly ranked in at least one adult specialty. *U.S. News Online, "America's Best Hospitals 2010-11"*

According to *U.S. News,* the Atlanta-Sandy Springs-Marietta, GA Metropolitan Statistical Area is home to one of the best children's hospitals in the U.S.: **Children's Healthcare of Atlanta**. The hospital listed was highly ranked in at least one pediatric specialty. *U.S. News Online, "America's Best Children's Hospitals 2010-11"*

EDUCATION

Public School District Statistics

District Name	Schls	Pupils	Pupil/ Teacher Ratio	Minority Pupils[1] (%)	Free Lunch Eligible[2] (%)	IEP[3] (%)
Atlanta Public Schools	107	49,032	13.0	89.8	71.7	8.9
Fulton County	98	88,299	13.5	64.9	34.2	10.3

Note: Table includes school districts with 2,000 or more students; (1) Percentage of students that are not non-Hispanic white; (2) Percentage of students that are eligible for the free lunch program; (3) Percentage of students that have an Individualized Education Program.
Source: U.S. Department of Education, National Center for Education Statistics, Common Core of Data, Local Education Agency (School District) Universe Survey: School Year 2008-2009; U.S. Department of Education, National Center for Education Statistics, Common Core of Data, Public Elementary/Secondary School Universe Survey: School Year 2008-2009

Top Public High Schools

High School Name	Index[1]	Rank[1]	Subsidized Lunch (%)[2]	E&E (%)[3]
Druid Hills[4]	2.367	479	49.5	33.3
North Springs	2.199	578	45.0	43.4
Riverwood[4]	3.541	149	24.0	49.8

Note: (1) Public schools are ranked according to a ratio that is the number of Advanced Placement, International Baccalaureate, and/or Cambridge tests taken by all students at a school in 2009 divided by the number of graduating seniors. All of the schools on the list have an index of at least 1.000; they are in the top six percent of public schools measured this way. The rankings range from 1 to 1,734; (2) Percentage of students receiving federally subsidized meals; (3) E & E stands for equity and excellence percentage: the portion of all graduating seniors at a school that had at least one passing grade on one AP or IB test; (4) Schools that offer International Baccalaureate or Cambridge exams; (5) School is unranked, but has been identified by Newsweek as one of the nation's most elite public high schools.
Source: Newsweek Online, "Top High Schools 2010"

Highest Level of Education

Area	Less than H.S.	H.S. Diploma	Some College, No Deg.	Associate Degree	Bachelors Degree	Masters Degree	Profess. School Degree	Doctorate Degree
City	16.7	24.1	14.7	3.9	24.5	10.6	3.7	1.9
MSA[1]	13.0	26.1	20.1	6.6	22.5	8.4	2.1	1.1
U.S.	15.3	29.0	20.7	7.5	17.4	7.0	1.9	1.1

Note: Figures are 2010 estimated percentages and cover persons age 25 and over; (1) Metropolitan Statistical Area - see Appendix B for areas included
Source: Claritas, Inc.

Educational Attainment by Race

Area	High School Graduate (%)					Bachelor's Degree (%)				
	Total	White	Black	Asian	Hisp.[2]	Total	White	Black	Asian	Hisp.[2]
City	86.9	97.7	78.4	88.9	62.7	47.1	76.2	18.9	70.9	27.8
MSA[1]	86.8	90.6	87.2	86.5	56.8	34.2	39.9	25.5	51.9	15.6
U.S.	84.9	90.0	80.7	85.5	60.7	27.8	30.9	17.5	49.7	12.7

Note: Figures shown cover persons 25 years old and over; (1) Metropolitan Statistical Area - see Appendix B for areas included; (2) people of Hispanic origin can be of any race
Source: U.S. Census Bureau, 2007-2009 American Community Survey 3-Year Estimates

School Enrollment by Grade and Control

Area	Preschool (%)		Kindergarten (%)		Grades 1 - 4 (%)		Grades 5 - 8 (%)		Grades 9 - 12 (%)	
	Public	Private	Public	Private	Public	Private	Public	Private	Public	Private
City	44.5	55.5	74.8	25.2	83.2	16.8	81.1	18.9	78.8	21.2
MSA[1]	46.2	53.8	84.7	15.3	89.0	11.0	88.6	11.4	89.4	10.6
U.S.	54.3	45.7	86.4	13.6	88.9	11.1	89.1	10.9	90.2	9.8

Note: Figures shown cover persons 3 years old and over; (1) Metropolitan Statistical Area - see Appendix B for areas included
Source: U.S. Census Bureau, 2007-2009 American Community Survey 3-Year Estimates

Average Salaries of Public School Classroom Teachers

Area	2009-10		2010-11		Percent Change 2009-10 to 2010-11	Percent Change 2000-01 to 2010-11
	Dollars	Rank[1]	Dollars	Rank[1]		
Georgia	53,112	18	53,906	18	1.50	27.7
U.S. Average	55,202	-	56,069	-	1.57	29.3

Note: (1) State rank ranges from 1 to 51 where 1 indicates highest salary.
Source: National Education Association, Rankings & Estimates: Rankings of the States 2010 and Estimates of School Statistics 2011, December 2010

Higher Education

Four-Year Colleges			Two-Year Colleges			Medical Schools[1]	Law Schools[2]	Voc/ Tech[3]
Public	Private Non-profit	Private For-profit	Public	Private Non-profit	Private For-profit			
2	10	10	3	0	6	2	3	6

Note: Figures cover institutions located within the city limits and include main campuses only; (1) includes schools accredited by the Liaison Committee on Medical Education and the American Osteopathic Association; (2) includes American Bar Association-accredited law schools; (3) includes all schools with programs that are less than 2 years.
Source: National Center for Education Statistics, Integrated Postsecondary Education System (IPEDS) Peer Analysis System, 2010-11; U.S. News & World Report, Medical School Directory, 2011; U.S. News & World Report, Law School Directory, 2011

According to *U.S. News & World Report*, the Atlanta-Sandy Springs-Marietta, GA Metropolitan Statistical Area is home to two of the top 197 national universities in the U.S.: **Emory University** (#20); **Georgia Institute of Technology** (#35). The rankings are based on quantitative measurements such as peer assessment, retention, faculty resources, student selectivity, financial resources, graduation rate, and alumni giving rate. *U.S. News & World Report, "America's Best Colleges 2011"*

According to *U.S. News & World Report,* the Atlanta-Sandy Springs-Marietta, GA Metropolitan Statistical Area is home to four of the top 189 liberal arts colleges in the U.S.: **Spelman College** (#59); **Agnes Scott College** (#67); **Morehouse College** (#127); **Oglethorpe University** (#166). The rankings are based on quantitative measurements such as peer assessment, retention, faculty resources, student selectivity, financial resources, graduation rate, and alumni giving rate. *U.S. News & World Report, "America's Best Colleges 2011"*

According to *U.S. News & World Report,* the Atlanta-Sandy Springs-Marietta, GA Metropolitan Statistical Area is home to one of the top 50 law schools in the U.S.: **Emory University** (#30). The rankings are based on a weighted average of 10 measures of quality: peer assessment score; assessment score by lawyers/judges; median LSAT scores; median undergrad GPA; acceptance rate; employment rates for graduates; bar passage rate; faculty resources; expenditures per student; student/faculty ratio; and library resources. *U.S. News & World Report, "America's Best Law Schools 2011"*

According to *Forbes,* the Atlanta-Sandy Springs-Marietta, GA Metropolitan Statistical Area is home to two of the top 75 business schools in the U.S.: **Emory (Goizueta)** (#22); **Georgia Tech** (#44). The rankings are based on the return on investment that graduates of the Class of 2004 received (median salary five years after graduation). *Forbes, "Best Business Schools," August 5, 2009*

PRESIDENTIAL ELECTION

2008 Presidential Election Results

Area	Obama	McCain	Nader	Other
Fulton County	67.1	32.1	0.0	0.8
U.S.	52.9	45.6	0.6	0.9

Note: Results are percentages and may not add to 100% due to rounding
Source: Dave Leip's Atlas of U.S. Presidential Elections, www.uselectionatlas.org

EMPLOYERS

Major Employers

Company Name	Industry	Type of Site
A S A Holdings	Air transportation, scheduled	Single
Accountemps	Employment agencies	Branch
Apartments Com	Miscellaneous personal services	Single
Aquilex Holdings	Holding companies, nec	Headquarters
Avondale Mills	Yarn spinning mills	Single
Clayton County Public Schools	Elementary and secondary schools	Headquarters
Coca-Cola	Flavoring extracts and syrups, nec	Headquarters
Dekalb Regional Healthcare Sys	Management services	Headquarters
Delta Airlines	Air transportation, scheduled	Headquarters
Department of Behavioral Healt	Administration of public health programs	Branch
Emory University Hosp Midtown	General medical and surgical hospitals	Single
Georgia-Pacific	Sanitary paper products	Headquarters
Grady Health System	General medical and surgical hospitals	Headquarters
Gwinnett County Administration	Legislative bodies	Branch
HSS Group	Help supply services	Single
IRS Service Center	Finance, taxation, and monetary policy	Branch
LMAero	Repair services, nec	Single
Materials Research Engineer	Regulation, administration of transportation	Branch
Office of Regional Director	Land, mineral, and wildlife conservation	Branch
Piedmont Hospital	General medical and surgical hospitals	Headquarters
Turner Broadcasting System	Motion picture and tape distribution	Headquarters
USAG Fort Mcpherson	National security	Branch
Villagers Hardware	Lumber and other building materials	Headquarters

Note: Companies shown are located within the Atlanta metropolitan area; nec = not elsewhere classified.
Source: www.zapdata.com, January 2011

Best Companies to Work For

Alston & Bird; Children's Healthcare of Atlanta, headquartered in Atlanta, are among the "100 Best Companies to Work For." To pick the 100 Best Companies to Work For, *Fortune* partnered with the Great Place to Work Institute. Three hundred eleven companies participated in this year's survey. Most of a company's score (two-thirds) is based on the results of the Institute's Trust Index survey, which is sent to a random sample of employees from each company. The survey asks questions related to their attitudes about management's credibility, job satisfaction, and camaraderie. The other third of the scoring is based on the company's responses to the Institute's Culture Audit, which includes detailed questions about pay and benefit programs, and a series of open-ended questions about hiring practices, internal communication, training, recognition programs, and diversity efforts. Any company that is at least seven years old with more than 1,000 U.S. employees is eligible. *Fortune, "100 Best Companies to Work For," February 7, 2011*

Children's Healthcare of Atlanta; Turner Broadcasting System, headquartered in Atlanta, are among the "100 Best Companies for Working Mothers." Criteria: workforce profile; benefits; child care; women's issues and advancement; flexible work; paid time off and leaves; company culture; and work-life programs. This year *Working Mother* gave particular weight to child care, flexibility, and paid time off and leaves. *Working Mother, "100 Best Companies 2010"*

GA Department of Human Resources; Manheim, headquartered in Atlanta, are among the "50 Best Employers for Workers Over 50." Criteria: recruiting practices; opportunities for training, education, and career development; workplace accommodations; alternative work options, such as flexible scheduling, job sharing, and phased retirement; employee health and pension benefits; and retiree benefits. Any employer with at least 50 employees based in the U.S. is eligible. This includes for-profit companies, not-for-profit organizations, and government employers. *AARP, "2009 AARP Best Employers for Workers Over 50"*

Southern Company, headquartered in Atlanta, is among the "100 Best Places to Work in IT." To qualify, companies, both public and private, had to have a minimum of 50 IT employees. Companies were selected based on average salary and bonus increases, the percentage of IT employees receiving promotions, IT staff turnover rates, training and development programs, and the percentage of women and minorities in IT staff and management positions. In addition, information was collected on how the organizations reward outstanding performance, how their retention programs are structured and what benefits they offer. *Computerworld, "100 Best Places to Work in IT 2010"*

PUBLIC SAFETY

Crime Rate

Area	All Crimes	Violent Crimes				Property Crimes		
		Murder	Forcible Rape	Robbery	Aggrav. Assault	Burglary	Larceny -Theft	Motor Vehicle Theft
City	7,362.6	14.5	24.4	492.9	618.4	1,648.0	3,528.8	1,035.6
Suburbs[1]	3,601.8	5.0	20.9	140.7	193.6	912.2	1,998.9	330.4
Metro[2]	3,980.2	5.9	21.3	176.1	236.4	986.3	2,152.8	401.4
U.S.	3,465.5	5.0	28.7	133.0	262.8	716.3	2,060.9	258.8

Note: Figures are crimes per 100,000 population; (1) All areas within the metro area that are located outside the city limits; (2) Metropolitan Statistical Area - see Appendix B for areas included
Source: FBI Uniform Crime Reports, 2009

Hate Crimes

Area	Number of Quarters Reported	Bias Motivation				
		Race	Religion	Sexual Orientation	Ethnicity	Disability
City	4	1	0	0	0	0

Source: Federal Bureau of Investigation, Hate Crime Statistics 2009

Identity Theft Consumer Complaints

Area	Complaints	Complaints per 100,000 Population	Rank[2]
MSA[1]	6,584	124.7	19
U.S.	250,854	81.3	-

Note: (1) Metropolitan Statistical Area - see Appendix B for areas included; (2) Rank ranges from 1 to 384 where 1 indicates greatest number of complaints per 100,000 population
Source: Federal Trade Commission, Consumer Sentinel Network Data Book for January - December 2010

RECREATION

Culture

Dance[1]	Theatre[1]	Instrumental Music[1]	Vocal Music[1]	Series/ Festivals	Museums	Zoos and Aquariums[2]
4	20	6	7	9	22	2

Note: (1) Number of professional perfoming groups; (2) AZA-accredited
Source: The Grey House Performing Arts Directory, 2011-2012; Official Museum Directory, 2010; American Association of Museums, AAM Member Museums, March 2011; Association of Zoos & Aquariums, AZA Member Zoos & Aquariums, May 2011

Professional Sports Teams

Team Name	League
Atlanta Braves	Major League Baseball (MLB)
Atlanta Falcons	National Football League (NFL)
Atlanta Hawks	National Basketball Association (NBA)
Atlanta Thrashers	National Hockey League (NHL)

Note: Includes teams located in the Atlanta metro area.
Source: Original research

CLIMATE

Average and Extreme Temperatures

Temperature	Jan	Feb	Mar	Apr	May	Jun	Jul	Aug	Sep	Oct	Nov	Dec	Yr.
Extreme High (°F)	79	80	85	93	95	101	105	102	98	95	84	77	105
Average High (°F)	52	56	64	73	80	86	88	88	82	73	63	54	72
Average Temp. (°F)	43	46	53	62	70	77	79	79	73	63	53	45	62
Average Low (°F)	33	36	42	51	59	66	70	69	64	52	42	35	52
Extreme Low (°F)	-8	5	10	26	37	46	53	55	36	28	3	0	-8

Note: Figures cover the years 1945-1990
Source: National Climatic Data Center, International Station Meteorological Climate Summary, 9/96

Average Precipitation/Snowfall/Humidity

Precip./Humidity	Jan	Feb	Mar	Apr	May	Jun	Jul	Aug	Sep	Oct	Nov	Dec	Yr.
Avg. Precip. (in.)	4.7	4.6	5.7	4.3	4.0	3.5	5.1	3.6	3.4	2.8	3.8	4.2	49.8
Avg. Snowfall (in.)	1	1	Tr	Tr	0	0	0	0	0	0	Tr	Tr	2
Avg. Rel. Hum. 7am (%)	79	77	78	78	82	83	88	89	88	84	81	79	82
Avg. Rel. Hum. 4pm (%)	56	50	48	45	49	52	57	56	56	51	52	55	52

Note: Figures cover the years 1945-1990; Tr = Trace amounts (<0.05 in. of rain; <0.5 in. of snow)
Source: National Climatic Data Center, International Station Meteorological Climate Summary, 9/96

Weather Conditions

Temperature			Daytime Sky			Precipitation		
10°F & below	32°F & below	90°F & above	Clear	Partly cloudy	Cloudy	0.01 inch or more precip.	0.1 inch or more snow/ice	Thunder-storms
1	49	38	98	147	120	116	3	48

Note: Figures are average number of days per year and cover the years 1945-1990
Source: National Climatic Data Center, International Station Meteorological Climate Summary, 9/96

HAZARDOUS WASTE

Superfund Sites

Atlanta has no sites on the EPA's Superfund Final National Priorities List.
U.S. Environmental Protection Agency, Final National Priorities List, April 1, 2011

**AIR & WATER
QUALITY**

Air Quality Index

| Area | Percent of Days when Air Quality was...[2] | | | | AQI Statistics | |
	Good	Moderate	Unhealthy for Sensitive Groups	Unhealthy	Maximum	Median
Area[1]	51.5	43.9	3.9	0.7	174	49

*Note: The Air Quality Index (AQI) is an index for reporting daily air quality. EPA calculates the AQI for five major air pollutants regulated by the Clean Air Act: ground-level ozone, particle pollution (also known as particulate matter), carbon monoxide, sulfur dioxide, and nitrogen dioxide. The AQI runs from 0 to 500. The higher the AQI value, the greater the level of air pollution and the greater the health concern. There are six AQI categories: "Good" The AQI is between 0 and 50. Air quality is considered satisfactory; "Moderate" The AQI is between 51 and 100. Air quality is acceptable; "Unhealthy for Sensitive Groups" When AQI values are between 101 and 150, members of sensitive groups may experience health effects; "Unhealthy" When AQI values are between 151 and 200 everyone may begin to experience health effects; "Very Unhealthy" AQI values between 201 and 300 trigger a health alert; "Hazardous" AQI values over 300 trigger health warnings of emergency conditions; (1) Data covers Fulton County; (2) Based on 305 days with AQI data in 2008; The EPA has suspended data updates while it assesses its data systems, including AirData reports and maps.
Source: U.S. Environmental Protection Agency, AirData Report, 2008*

Air Quality Index Pollutants

| Area | Percent of Days when AQI Pollutant was...[2] | | | | | |
	Carbon Monoxide	Nitrogen Dioxide	Ozone	Sulfur Dioxide	Particulate Matter 2.5	Particulate Matter 10
Area[1]	0.0	0.0	31.5	0.3	67.2	1.0

*Note: The Air Quality Index (AQI) is an index for reporting daily air quality. EPA calculates the AQI for five major air pollutants regulated by the Clean Air Act: ground-level ozone, particle pollution (also known as particulate matter), carbon monoxide, sulfur dioxide, and nitrogen dioxide. The AQI runs from 0 to 500. The higher the AQI value, the greater the level of air pollution and the greater the health concern; (1) Data covers Fulton County; (2) Based on 305 days with AQI data in 2008; The EPA has suspended data updates while it assesses its data systems, including AirData reports and maps.
Source: U.S. Environmental Protection Agency, AirData Report, 2008*

Air Quality Index Trends

| Area | Trend Sites (days) | | | | | | | | All Sites (days) |
	2002	2003	2004	2005	2006	2007	2008	2009	2009
MSA[1]	44	24	22	32	46	40	25	11	16

*Note: Figures are the number of days the AQI value exceeded 100 in a given year. An AQI value greater than 100 indicates that air quality would have been in the unhealthful range on that day. Data from exceptional events are included. These counts are presented in two ways. First, the counts are based on sites having an adequate record of monitoring data during the trend period (trend sites). These counts represent the relative change in the number of days with AQI values greater than 100. In the last column, the counts are based on all sites with data in the most recent year (because it is possible for a site to have data in the most recent year but not enough data to be a trend site); (1) Data covers the Atlanta-Sandy Springs-Marietta, GA Metropolitan Statistical Area - see Appendix B for areas included
Source: U.S. Environmental Protection Agency, Office of Air and Radiation, Air Quality Index Information, "Number of Days with Air Quality Index Values Greater than 100 and Trend Sites, 1990-2009, and at All Sites in 2009"*

Maximum Air Pollutant Concentrations

	Particulate Matter 10 (ug/m^3)	Particulate Matter 2.5 (ug/m^3)	Ozone (ppm)	Carbon Monoxide (ppm)	Sulfur Dioxide (ppm)	Nitrogen Dioxide (ppm)	Lead (ug/m^3)
MSA[1] Level	42	26	0.077	2	0.01	0.011	0
NAAQS[2]	150	35	0.075	9	0.140	0.053	0.15
Met NAAQS[2]	Yes	Yes	No	Yes	Yes	Yes	Yes

*Note: Data from exceptional events are not included; (1) Data covers the Atlanta-Sandy Springs-Marietta, GA Metropolitan Statistical Area - see Appendix B for areas included; (2) National Ambient Air Quality Standards; n/a not available
Concentrations: Particulate Matter 10 (coarse particulate) - highest second maximum 24-hour concentration; Particulate Matter 2.5 (fine particulate) - highest 98th percentile 24-hour concentration; Ozone - highest fourth daily maximum 8-hour concentration; Carbon Monoxide - highest second maximum non-overlapping 8-hour concentration; Sulfur Dioxide - highest second maximum 24-hour concentration; Nitrogen Dioxide - highest arithmetic mean concentration; Lead - maximum running 3-month average
Units: ppm = parts per million; ug/m^3 = micrograms per cubic meter
Source: U.S. Environmental Protection Agency, CBSA Factbook 2009, Air Quality Statistics by City, 2009*

Drinking Water

Water System Name	Pop. Served	Primary Water Source Type	Violations[1]	
			Health Based	Monitoring/ Reporting
Atlanta	650,000	Surface	0	0

Note: (1) Based on violation data from January 1, 2010 to December 31, 2010 (includes unresolved violations from earlier years)

Source: U.S. Environmental Protection Agency, Office of Ground Water and Drinking Water, Safe Drinking Water Information System (based on data extracted May 9, 2011)

Austin, Texas

Background

Starting out in 1730 as a peaceful Spanish mission on the north bank of the Colorado River in south-central Texas, Austin soon engaged in an imbroglio of territorial wars, beginning when the "Father of Texas," Stephen F. Austin, annexed the territory from Mexico in 1833 as his own. Later, the Republic of Texas named the territory Austin in honor of the colonizer, and conferred upon it state capital status. Challenges to this decision ensued, ranging from an invasion by the Mexican government to reclaim its land, to Sam Houston's call that the capital ought to move from Austin to Houston.

During peaceful times, however, Austin has been called the "City of the Violet Crown." Coined by the short story writer, William Sydney Porter, or O. Henry, the name refers to the purple mist that circles the surrounding hills of the Colorado River Valley.

This city of technological innovation is home to a strong computer and electronics industry. Austin offers more free wireless spots—including its city parks—per capita than any other city in the nation. Austin's technology focus has traditionally drawn numerous high-tech companies, including 360Commerce, Silicon Laboratories, the wireless industry association Wi-Fi Alliance, and Dell Computer, the largest private employer in Central Texas. The 3M Electro Communications Market Center and Visual Systems Divisions are also based in Austin. Samsung Electronics' major computer chip plant was built in Austin in the late 1990s. The plant fabrication line has been extended and a new plant was just completed. It is the size of nine football fields, which makes it the largest in the U.S. It is the company's only semiconductor manufacturing plant located outside of Korea. Along with this technology growth has come the problem of increased traffic, especially on Interstate 35, the main highway linking the U.S. and Mexico. A recently developed 89-mile bypass has helped to relieve some of the traffic difficulties long associated with I-35. In March 2010, the City Council approved an economic development incentive proposal for Facebook, the social media network, to establish an Austin-based sales and operations facility.

In addition to its traditional business community, Austin is home to the main campus of the University of Texas. The university provides Austin with even further diverse lifestyles; today there is a solid mix of white-collar workers, students, professors, blue-collar workers, musicians and artists, and members of the booming tech industry who all call themselves Austinites.

The influx of young people centered on university life has contributed to the city's growth as a thriving live music scene. It is so important to the city that its local government maintains the Austin Music Commission to promote the local music industry.

Not only does the popular PBS music series Austin City Limits hail from the city, but also a notable industry conference takes place here each spring. The South by Southwest Conference (SXSW) showcases more than 2,000 performers at 90+ venues throughout the city. The growing film and interactive industries have been added to the conference in recent years.

The civic-minded city, whose mayor is working toward making Austin the nation's fittest city, is operating from a new city hall, which was completed in late 2004. The building, at about 115,000 square feet, is also home to a public plaza facing Town Lake. One of the town's cultural hubs, the Long Center for the Performing Arts, underwent renovation in 2006, and reopened in 2008.

It is most likely Austinites' pride in their creative and independent culture that has spawned a movement to keep the city from too much corporate development. The slogan "Keep Austin Weird" was adopted by the Austin Independent Business Alliance in 2003 as a way to promote local and alternative business.

The city sits at a desirable location along the Colorado River, and many recreational activities center on the water. For instance, Austin boasts three spring-fed swimming pools enjoyed by its residents, as well as the Lance Armstrong Crosstown Bikeway, named for the seven-time winner of the Tour de France. The city is working on a six-mile bike route through downtown Austin, which will add to the town's more than 100 miles of bike paths. There are dozens of projects currently either under construction or being planned for downtown Austin.

The climate of Austin is subtropical with hot summers. Winters are mild, with below-freezing temperatures occurring on an average of 25 days a year. Cold spells are short, seldom lasting more than two days. Daytime temperatures in summer are hot, while summer nights are usually pleasant.

Rankings

General Rankings

- Austin was ranked #103 out of 375 metro areas in *Cities Ranked & Rated*. Criteria: cost of living; climate; crime; transportation; economy and jobs; education; arts and culture; health and healthcare; leisure; quality of life. *Cities Ranked & Rated, 2nd Edition, 2007*

- Austin was ranked #35 out of 379 metro areas in *Places Rated Almanac*. Criteria: health care; education; recreation; transportation; ambience; climate; crime; housing costs; jobs. *Places Rated Almanac, 7th Edition, 2007*

- The Austin metro area was selected as one of the best cities to relocate to in America by Sperling's BestPlaces. The metro area ranked #5 out of 10. Criteria: unemployment; cost of living; crime rates; population health; cultural events; economic stability. *Sperling's BestPlaces, www.BestPlaces.net, "The Best Cities to Relocate to in America," October 2010*

- The Austin metro area was selected one of America's "Best Cities to Live, Work and Play" by *Kiplinger's Personal Finance*. Criteria: population growth; percentage of workforce in the creative class (scientists, engineers, educators, writers, artists, entertainers, etc.); job quality; income growth; cost of living. *Kiplinger's Personal Finance, "Best Cities to Live, Work and Play," July 2008*

- The Austin metro area was selected one of America's "Best Cities" by *Kiplinger's Personal Finance*. Criteria: stable employment; income growth; cost of living; percentage of workforce in the creative class (scientists, engineers, educators, writers, artists, entertainers, etc.). *Kiplinger's Personal Finance, "Best Cities 2009: It's All About Jobs," July 2009*

- *Men's Health Living* ranked 100 U.S. cities in terms of quality of life. Austin was ranked #32 and received a grade of C+. Criteria: number of fitness facilities; air quality; number of physicians; male/female ratio; education levels; household income; cost of living. *Men's Health Living, Spring 2008*

- Austin was selected as one of the "10 Best Cities for the Next Decade" by Kiplinger's Personal Finance. The city ranked #1. Criteria: innovation factor (smart people, great ideas, and collaboration between governments, universities, and businesses); economic growth and growth potential; creativity in music, arts and culture; neighborhoods and recreational facilities that rank high for "coolness." *Kiplinger's Personal Finance, "10 Best Cities for the Next Decade," July 2010*

- Austin was selected as one of "America's Top 100 Places to Live" by RelocateAmerica.com. Cities and towns nominated to be great places to live along with their key data regarding education, employment, economy, crime, parks, recreation and housing were reviewed, rated and judged by the Relocate-America.com editorial staff. *Relocate-America.com, "RelocateAmerica's Top 100 Places to Live in 2010"*

- Austin was selected as one of "America's Favorite Cities." The city ranked #10 in the "Quality of Life and Visitor Experience" category. Respondents to an online survey were asked to rate 35 top urban destinations in the U.S from a visitor's perspective. Criteria: noteworthy neighborhoods; skyline/views; public parks and outdoor access; cleanliness; public transportation and pedestrian friendliness; safety; weather; peace and quiet; people-watching; environmental friendliness. *Travelandleisure.com, "America's Favorite Cities 2010," November 2010*

- Austin was selected as one of "America's Favorite Cities." The city ranked #4 in the "People" category. Respondents to an online survey were asked to rate 35 top urban destinations in the U.S. from a visitor's perspective. Criteria: attractive; friendly; stylish; intelligent; athletic/active; diverse. *Travelandleisure.com, "America's Favorite Cities 2010," November 2010*

- Austin was selected as one of "America's Favorite Cities." The city ranked #2 in the "Nightlife" category. Respondents to an online survey were asked to rate 35 top urban destinations in the U.S. from a visitor's perspective. Criteria: cocktail hour; live music/concerts and bands; singles/bar scene. *Travelandleisure.com, "America's Favorite Cities 2010," November 2010*

- The U.S. Conference of Mayors and Waste Management sponsor the City Livability Awards Program. The awards recognize and honor mayors for exemplary leadership in developing and implementing programs that improve the quality of life in America's cities. Austin received an Outstanding Achievement Award in the large cities category. *U.S Conference of Mayors, "2010 City Livability Awards"*

Business/Finance Rankings

- Austin was identified as one of the 20 strongest-performing metro areas during the recession and recovery from December 2007 through December 2010. Criteria: percent change in employment; percentage point change in unemployment rate; percent change in gross metropolitan product; percent change in House Price Index. *Brookings Institution, MetroMonitor: Tracking Economic Recession and Recovery in America's 100 Largest Metropolitan Areas, March 2011*

- The Austin metro area was identified as one of 10 "Cities Where the Recession is Easing." The metro area was ranked #1. Criteria: job growth; goods produced; home sale prices; unemployment rates. *Forbes.com, "Cities Where the Recession is Easing," March 3, 2010*

- Austin was identified as one of America's "10 Best Cities to Get a Job" by *U.S. News*. The city ranked #6. Criteria: number of available jobs; unemployment rate. *U.S. News & World Report, "10 Best Cities to Get a Job," February 1, 2011*

- Austin was identified as one of the top 25 U.S. cities with the most credit card debt by credit reporting bureau Experian. The city was ranked #8. *Experian, March 4, 2011*

- A.G. Edwards ranked America's 500 top-performing communities based on their residents' personal savings and investing behavior. The Austin metro area ranked #395 with an index score of 97.15 (national average = 100.00). A dozen statistical factors were measured including: participation in retirement savings plans; personal debt levels; and home ownership. *A.G. Edwards, "2007 Nest Egg Index," September 12, 2007*

- Austin was identified as one of the best cities for new college graduates. The city ranked #5. Criteria: cost of living; average annual salary; unemployment rate; number of employers looking to hire people at entry-level. *Business Week, "The Best Cities for New Grads," July 20, 2010*

- Austin was identified as one of "The Most Inventive Towns in America." The city ranked #3. Criteria: places with the most patents overall, combining those of large companies and individual inventors. *The Wall Street Journal, July 22, 2006*

- Austin was selected as one of the best cities in the world for telecommuting. The city ranked #2. The editors at *Cartridge Save* (printer technology news, guides and reviews) identified the 20 best cities in which to be an at-home, tech-using employee. *Cartridge Save, "20 of the Best Cities in the World for Telecommuting," May 14, 2008*

- *American City Business Journals* ranked America's 261 largest cities in terms of their resident's wealth. Austin ranked #111. Criteria: per capita income; median household income; percentage of households with annual incomes of $200,000 or more; median home value. *American City Business Journals, www.bizjournals.com, "Where the Money Is: America's Wealth Centers," August 18, 2008*

- The Austin metro area appeared on the Milken Institute "2010 Best Performing Metros" list. Rank: #2 out of 200 large metro areas. Criteria: job growth; wage and salary growth; high-tech output growth. *Milken Institute, "2010 Best Performing Metros"*

- The Austin metro area was selected as one of the best cities for entrepreneurs in America by *Inc. Magazine*. Criteria: job-growth data for 335 metro areas was analyzed for: recent growth trend (the current and prior year's employment growth rates, with the current year emphasized); mid-term growth (the average annual 2002-2007 growth rate); long-term trend (the sum of the 2002-2007 and 1996-2001 employment growth rates multiplied by the ratio of the 1996-2001 growth rate over the 2002-2007 growth rate); current year growth. The Austin metro area ranked #2 among large metro areas and #19 overall. *Inc. Magazine, "The Best Cities for Doing Business," July 2008*

- Austin was identified as one of the top 10 cities with the greatest number of *Inc.* 500 companies per million residents. The city ranked #2. *Inc. Magazine, September 2008*

- Austin was ranked #42 out of 145 regions worldwide in terms of its "Knowledge Competitiveness Index." The index attempts to measure the knowledge-based development taking place throughout the world and is based on 19 measures of economic performance that indicate a region's ability to translate its knowledge capacity into economic value. *Centre for International Competitiveness, World Knowledge Competitiveness Index 2008*

- *Forbes* ranked the 200 most populous metro areas in the U.S. in terms of the "Best Places for Business and Careers." The Austin metro area was ranked #10. Criteria: 12 metrics including costs (business and living), job growth (past and projected), income growth, educational attainment, projected economic growth, crime, cultural and recreational opportunities, net migration patterns, percentage of subprime mortgages handed out over a three-year period, and the number of highly ranked four-year colleges. *Forbes, "Best Places for Business and Careers," April 14, 2010*

Children/Family Rankings

- Austin was selected as one of the 10 best cities to raise children in the U.S. by *KidFriendlyCities.org*. Criteria: education; environment; health; employment; crime; diversity; cost of living. *KidFriendlyCities.org, "Top Rated Kid/Family Friendly Cities 2009"*

- The Austin metro area was selected as one of the "Best Cities for Relocating Families" by Worldwide ERC and Primacy Relocation. The 2008 study looked at nearly 50 factors important to relocating families including: recent job growth; nearby top-ranked colleges; in-state tuition for four-year public colleges; population growth since 2000; pediatricians per 100,000 population; and a Green Living index. *Worldwide ERC and Primacy Relocation, "2008 Best Cities for Relocating Families"*

- *Fit Pregnancy* magazine ranked the 50 best U.S. cities in which to have a baby. Austin was ranked #9. Criteria: access to hospitals and doctors; affordability; birthing options; breastfeeding; child care; fertility laws/resources; maternal and infant health risk; parks/stroller friendliness; safety. *Fit Pregnancy, "The Best Cities in America to Have a Baby 2008"*

Culture/Performing Arts Rankings

- Austin was selected as one of 25 best U.S. cities to live, work and make movies. The city was ranked #5. Criteria: cost of living; average salary; unemployment rate; job growth; median home price; crime rate; number of film schools, festivals, movie-related vendors and local movie theaters; current production scene (i.e. production days, size of talent pool); financial incentives for shooting in a particular area. *MovieMaker Magazine, "10 Best Cities to Live, Work & Make Movies in 2010," January 18, 2010*

- Austin was selected as one of "America's Top 25 Arts Destinations." The city ranked #14 in the big city (population 500,000 and over) category. Criteria: readers' top choices for arts travel destinations based on the richness and variety of visual arts sites, activities and events. *American Style, "America's Top 25 Arts Destinations," May 2010*

Dating/Romance Rankings

- Austin appeared on *Men's Health's* list of the most sex-happy cities in America. The city ranked #1 of 100. Criteria: condom sales; birth rates; sex toy sales; rates of chlamydia, gonorrhea, and syphilis. *Men's Health, "America's Most Sex-Happy Cities," October 2010*

- Austin was selected as one of the best cities for single women in America by *SingleMindedWomen.com*. The city ranked #10. Criteria: ratio of women to men; singles population; healthy lifestyle; employment opportunities; cost of living; access to travel; entertainment options; social opportunities. *SingleMindedWomen.com, "Top 10 Cities for Single Women," 2010*

- *Men's Health* ranked 100 U.S. cities in terms of best (and worst) marriages. Austin was ranked #84 (#1 = worst marriages). Criteria: rate of failed marriages; stringency of divorce laws; percentage of population who've split; number of licensed marriage and family therapists. *Men's Health, "Splitsville, USA," May 2010*

- Eli Lily and Company, in partnership with Sperling's BestPlaces, ranked the nation's 50 largest metro areas in terms of the "Most Romantic Cities for Baby Boomers." The Austin metro area ranked #32. Criteria: marriage and divorce rates among "baby boomers" age 45 to 60; great restaurants; dance studios; chocolate, jewelry and flower sales. *Eli Lily and Company, "Most Romantic Cities for Baby Boomers," April 20, 2007*

- The Austin metro area was selected as one of the "Best Cities for Relocating Singles" by Worldwide ERC and Primacy Relocation. The area ranked #33 out of the 100 largest metro areas in the U.S. Areas were selected based on the following criteria: recent job growth; recent singles population growth; overall population growth; affordable rental housing; cost-of-living index; expanded arts and recreation opportunities; ratio of single men and single women; affordability of quality higher education (including state residency requirements); diversity index; climate; population density. *Worldwide ERC and Primacy Relocation, "2008 Best Cities for Relocating Singles"*

- *Forbes* ranked the 40 most populous urbanized areas in the U.S. in terms of the "Best Cities for Singles." The Austin metro area ranked #11. Criteria: number of singles; cost of living alone; nightlife; culture; job growth; coolness; and online dating participation. *Forbes.com, "Best Cities for Singles," July 27, 2009*

Education Rankings

- Austin was selected as one of "America's Most Literate Cities." The city ranked #21 out of the 75 largest U.S. cities. Criteria: number of booksellers; library resources; Internet resources; educational attainment; periodical publishing resources; newspaper circulation. *Central Connecticut State University, "America's Most Literate Cities 2010"*

- Austin was identified as one of the 100 "smartest" metro areas in the U.S. The area ranked #12. Criteria: the editors rated the collective brainpower of the 100 largest metro area in the U.S based on their residents' educational attainment. *American City Business Journals, www.bizjournals.com, April 14, 2008*

- Austin was identified as one of "America's Smartest Cities" by *The Daily Beast*. The metro area ranked #7 out of 55. The editors ranked metropolitan areas with one million or more residents on the following criteria: percentage of residents over age 25 with bachelor's or graduate degrees; non-fiction book sales; ratio of institutions of higher education; libraries per capita. *The Daily Beast, "America's Smartest Cities," October 24, 2010*

- Austin was identified as one of "America's Brainiest Bastions" by *Portfolio.com*. The metro area ranked #22 out of 200. Portfolio.com analyzed levels of educational attainment in the nation's 200 largest metropolitan areas. The editors established scores for five levels of educational attainment, based on relative earning power of adult workers age 25 or older. Scores were determined by comparing the median income for all workers with the median income for those workers at a specified educational level. *Portfolio.com, "America's Brainiest Bastions," December 1, 2010*

- Austin was identified as one of "America's Smartest Cities" by *CNNMoney.com*. The area ranked #6. Criteria: percentage of residents with bachelors or graduate degrees. *CNNMoney.com, "America's Smartest Cities," October 1, 2010*

- Austin was identified one of America's smartest cities" by *Forbes*. The area ranked #24 out of 25. Criteria: percentage of the population age 25 and over with at least a bachelor's degree. *Forbes.com, "The Smartest Cities in America," February 8, 2008*

- *Forbes* ranked the largest metro areas in the U.S. in terms of the "Best Cities for Young Professionals." The Austin metro area ranked #10out of 10. Graduates from six elite schools (Harvard, Stanford, Princeton, Rice, Northwestern and Duke) were tracked ten years after graduation to see where they settled down. Those rankings were combined with several other statistics: job growth; unemployment rate; average salary of college graduates; cost of living; number of large companies that are located in the city. *Forbes.com, "Best Cities for Young Professionals," June 17, 2010*

Environmental Rankings

- Austin was selected as one of 22 "Smarter Cities" for energy by the Natural Resources Defense Council." The city appeared as one of 12 cities in the large city (population 250,000 and over) category. Criteria: investment in green power; energy efficiency measures; conservation. *Natural Resources Defense Council, "2010 Smarter Cities," July 19, 2010*

- *American City Business Journal* ranked 43 metropolitan areas in terms of their "greenness." The Austin metro area ranked #4. Criteria: Forty-one metros in which *ACBJ* has business weeklies, plus Indianapolis and Cleveland, were ranked based on 20 different indicators such as adoption of green technologies, utilization of environmentally sound practices, and air and water quality. *American City Business Journals, "Green City Index," March 11, 2010*

- Austin was selected as one of "America's 50 Greenest Cities" by *Popular Science*. The city ranked #10. Criteria: electricity; transportation; green living; recycling and green perspective. *Popular Science, February 2008*

- 100 of the largest metro areas in the U.S. were analyzed in terms of their current drought severity. The Austin metro area ranked #98 (#1 = driest). The rankings were based on statistics such as long-term precipitation trends and patterns and the Palmer drought indices. *Sperling's BestPlaces, www.BestPlaces.net, "America's Drought-Riskiest Cities," November 2007*

- The Austin metro area appeared in *Country Home's* "Best Green Places" report. The area ranked #33 out of 379. Criteria: official energy policies; green power; green buildings; availability of fresh, locally grown food. *Country Home, "Best Green Places," 2008*

- Austin was highlighted as one of the top 25 cleanest metro areas for short-term particle pollution (24-hour PM 2.5) in the U.S. Monitors in these cities reported no days with unhealthful PM 2.5 levels. *American Lung Association, State of the Air 2011*

Health/Fitness Rankings

- Austin was identified as one of "America's Heart-Healthiest Cities" by *Men's Journal*. The city ranked #2 out of 8. Criteria: easy access to the outdoors; strong park and trail system; clear culture of activity (i.e. outdoor festivals, street fairs, bike racks and local distance races); city should be dense (good walkability), but not big (too stressful). *Men's Journal, "Where You Live is Key," August 2006*

- The American Podiatric Medical Association and *Prevention* magazine ranked 100 American cities based on walkability. Nineteen walking criteria were evaluated including the percentage of adults who walk to work, number of parks per square mile, number of trails for walking and hiking, air pollution, use of mass transit, crime rate, pedestrian fatalities, and percentage of adults who walk for fitness. Austin ranked #23. *Prevention, "The Best Walking Cities of 2009," May 2009; American Podiatric Medical Association, "2009 Best Fitness-Walking Cities," April 7, 2009*

- *Cooking Light* magazine ranked the 20 American cities that best fit their philosophy to eat smart, be fit, and live well. Austin ranked #17. Criteria: healthfulness and exercise data; restaurant ratings; farmers' market listings; parks and recreation data. *Cooking Light, "Best Cities Awards," 2007*

- Austin was selected as one of the 25 fittest cities in America by *Men's Fitness Online*. It ranked #17 out of America's 50 largest cities. Criteria: fitness centers and sport stores; nutrition; sports participation; TV viewing; overweight/sedentary; junk food; air quality; geography; commute; parks and open space; city recreational facilities; access to healthcare; motivation; mayor and city initiatives; state obesity initiatives. *Men's Fitness Online, 2009 Fittest/Fattest Cities*

- Austin was identified as a "2011 Asthma Capital." The area ranked #94 out of the nation's 100 largest metropolitan areas. Twelve factors were used to identify the most challenging places to live for people with asthma: estimated prevalence; self-reported prevalence; crude death rate for asthma; annual pollen score; annual air quality; public smoking laws; number of board-certified asthma specialists; school inhaler access laws; rescue medication use; controller medication use; uninsured rate; poverty rate. *Asthma and Allergy Foundation of America, "2011 Asthma Capitals"*

- Austin was identified as a 2009 "Spring Allergy Capital." The area ranked #71 out of 100. Three groups of factors were used to identify the most severe cities for people with allergies during the spring season: annual pollen levels; medicine utilization; access to board-certified allergists. *Asthma and Allergy Foundation of America, "Spring Allergy Capitals 2009"*

- Austin was identified as a 2010 "Fall Allergy Capital." The area ranked #51 out of 100. Three groups of factors were used to identify the most severe cities for people with allergies during the fall season: annual pollen levels; medicine utilization; access to board-certified allergists. *Asthma and Allergy Foundation of America, "Fall Allergy Capitals 2010"*

- *Men's Health* examined 100 U.S. cities and selected the best and worst cities for men. Austin was ranked among the ten best at #7. Criteria: dozens of statistical parameters of long life in the categories of health, quality of life, and fitness. *Men's Health, "The 10 Best and Worst Cities for Men 2011," January/February 2011*

- *Men's Health* examined 100 U.S. cities and selected the best and worst cities for women. Austin was ranked among the ten best at #5. Criteria: dozens of statistical parameters of long life in the categories of health, quality of life, and fitness. *Men's Health, "The 10 Best and Worst Cities for Women 2011," January/February 2011*

- *Men's Health* ranked 100 U.S. cities in terms of the quality of their tap water. Austin was ranked #50 and received a grade of C. Criteria: levels of total coliform bacteria, arsenic, lead, total trihalomethanes (linked to cancer), and halo-acetic acids; number of EPA water-system violations from 1995 to 2005. *Men's Health, March 2007*

- Ortho-McNeil Neurologics, in partnership with Sperling's BestPlaces, analyzed 110 metro areas and identified those U.S. cities with the highest prevalence of factors that are most commonly associated with migraine headaches. The Austin metro area ranked #65. Criteria: number of migraine-related drug prescriptions per capita; lifestyle factors that can contribute to migraines; environmental factors that can trigger migraines; and consumption of migraine-triggering foods. *Ortho-McNeil Neurologics, "America's Migraine Hot Spots," March 14, 2006*

- An analysis of the "Best & Worst Cities for Sleep" was conducted by Sperling's BestPlaces. The study ranked America's 50 most populated metro areas. The Austin metro area ranked #14 (#1 = best city for sleep). Criteria: number of days residents didn't get enough rest or sleep during the past month; average length of daily commute; divorce rate; unemployment rate. *Sperling's BestPlaces, www.BestPlaces.net, "Best & Worst Cities for Sleep," 2006*

- *Men's Health* ranked 100 U.S. cities in terms of cities "Where the Food is Sickening." Austin was ranked #82 and received a grade of D. The magazine arrived at their ratings by looking at data compiled by the Community Health Status Indicator Project to determine outbreaks of E. coli, salmonella-, and shigella-related infections. They then checked the CDC's Wonder database to see how many people died from tainted food. Finally, the magazine found out which states have adopted the current version of the FDA's uniform Food Code, which contains the most up-to-date rules for keeping restaurant kitchens clean. *Men's Health, October 2005*

- The Austin metro area was identified as one of "America's Most Obese Cities" by *Forbes*. The magazine analyzed BMI (body mass index) data from the CDC in the 50 most populated metro areas in the U.S. and ranked the top 20. The area ranked #18. *Forbes, "America's Most Obese Cities," November 26, 2007*

- Scarborough Research, a leading market research firm, identified the top local markets for organic consumers. The Austin DMA (Designated Market Area) ranked in the top 15 with 23% of adults reporting that they used any organic food product in their household during the past month. *Scarborough Research, October 10, 2007*

- The Austin metro area appeared in the 2010 Gallup-Healthways Well-Being Index. The index, based on interviews with more than 353,000 Americans during 2009, asked individuals to assess their jobs, finances, physical health, emotional state of mind and communities. The metro area ranked #45 out of 162. Criteria: life evaluation; emotional health; work environment; physical health; healthy behaviors; basic access (basic needs optimal for a healthy life, such as access to food and medicine, having health insurance and feeling safe while walking at night). *Gallup-Healthways, "Well-Being Index 2010"*

- The Austin metro area was identified as one of "America's Most Stressful Cities" by *Forbes*. The metro area ranked #40. Criteria: median home price drop; unemployment rates; cost of living; air quality; sunny days; population density. *Forbes.com, "America's Most Stressful Cities," August 20, 2009*

- 50 of the largest metro areas in the U.S. were analyzed in terms of their health and fitness by the American College of Sports Medicine in their "American Fitness Index." The Austin metro area ranked #10 (#1 = healthiest). Criteria: preventative health behaviors; levels of chronic disease; health care access; community resources and policies that support physical activity. *American College of Sports Medicine, "Health and Community Fitness Status of the 50 Largest Metropolitan Areas," May 24, 2010*

Pet Rankings

- Austin was selected as one of "The Best Cities for Dogs." The city was ranked #7. Criteria: number of dogs, dog parks, pet (and pet supply) stores, animal shelters, boarding and daycare facilities, and veterinarians; incidence of heartworm. *Men's Health, "The Best Cities for Dogs," June 2007*

- Austin was identified as one of North America's most accommodating cities for travelers with pets. The city was ranked #3. Criteria: number of AAA Approved and Diamond rated pet-friendly hotels. *AAA, Traveling with your Pet: The AAA PetBook, 2006*

Real Estate Rankings

- *Fortune* ranked the 100 largest metro areas in the U.S. in terms of projected median home price change in 2010. The Austin metro area ranked #26. *Fortune, "The 2010 Housing Outlook," December 9, 2009*

- The Austin metro area was identified as one of the "10 Hottest Condo Markets" in the U.S. The area ranked #2 out of 63 markets with a price appreciation rate of 12.3%. Criteria: year-over-year change of median sales price of existing apartment condo-coop homes between the 4th quarter of 2009 and the 4th quarter of 2010. *National Association of Realtors, Median Sales Price of Existing Apartment Condo-Coop Homes for Metropolitan Areas, 4th Quarter 2010*

- Austin appeared on ApartmentRatings.com "Top Cities for Renters" list in 2009." The area ranked #57. Overall satisfaction ratings were ranked using thousands of user submitted scores for hundreds of apartment complexes located in the 100 most populated U.S. municipalities. *ApartmentRatings.com, "2009 Renter Satisfaction Rankings"*

- Austin appeared on ApartmentRatings.com "Top College Towns & Cities" for renters list in 2010." The area ranked #43. Overall satisfaction ratings were ranked using thousands of user submitted scores for hundreds of apartment complexes located in cities and towns that are home to the 100 largest four-year institutions in the U.S. *ApartmentRatings.com, "2010 College Town Renter Satisfaction Rankings"*

- The Austin metro area was identified as one of "America's Best Housing Markets" by *Forbes*. The metro area ranked #10. Criteria: housing affordability; rising home prices; percentage of foreclosures. *Forbes.com, "America's Best Housing Markets," February 19, 2010*

- The nation's largest metro areas were analyzed in terms of the percentage of households entering some stage of foreclosure in 2010. The Austin metro area ranked #113 out of 206 (#1 = highest foreclosure rate). *RealtyTrac, 2010 Year-End Metropolitan Foreclosure Market Report, January 27, 2011*

- The Austin metro area was identified as one of the "Best Cities to Buy a Home" by *Forbes*. The metro area ranked #2. Criteria: 2-year home price appreciation; vacancy rates; spread between monthly rent and mortgage payment at the median level. *Forbes.com, "Best Cities to Buy a Home," July 22, 2008*

- The Austin metro area appeared in a *Wall Street Journal* article ranking cities by "housing stress." The metro area was ranked #26 (#1 = most stress). Criteria: fraction of mortgage-holding homeowners with a monthly housing payment in excess of 30 percent of income; percentage of people without health insurance; unemployment rate. *The Wall Street Journal, "Which Cities Face Biggest Housing Risk," October 5, 2010*

- The Center for Housing Policy ranked 210 U.S metropolitan areas by the fair market rent for a two-bedroom unit. The Austin metro area was ranked #65. (#1 = most expensive) with a rent of $954. Criteria: Fair Market Rent (FMR) in effect during the fourth quarter of 2009 based on HUD's fiscal year 2010 FMRs. *The Center for Housing Policy, "Paycheck to Paycheck: Most to Least Expensive Rental Markets in 2009"*

Safety Rankings

- Symantec, the makers of Norton, in partnership with Sperling's BestPlaces, ranked the 50 largest cities in the U.S. in terms of their vulnerability to cybercrime. The city ranked #9. Criteria: number of cyberattacks and potential infections; level of Internet access; expenditures on computer hardware and software; wireless hotspots; broadband connectivity; Internet usage; online purchases. *Symantec, "10 Riskiest Cities for Cybercrime," March 22, 2010*

- Farmers Insurance Group of Companies, in partnership with Sperling's BestPlaces, ranked 379 metro areas and identified the "Most Secure U.S. Place to Live." The Austin metro area ranked #4 out of the top 20 in the large metro area category (500,000 or more residents). Criteria: crime statistics; extreme weather; risk of natural disasters; housing depreciation; foreclosures; environmental hazards; terrorist threats; air quality; life expectancy; job loss numbers. *Farmers Insurance Group, "Most Secure U.S. Places to Live 2010"*

- Allstate ranked the 200 largest cities in America in terms of driver safety. Austin ranked #170. In addition, drivers were 34.0% more likely to have had an accident compared to the national average. Allstate researchers analyzed internal property damage reported claims over a two-year period (from January 2007 to December 2008) to ensure the findings would not be affected by external influences such as weather or road construction. A weighted average of the two-year numbers determined the annual percentages. The report defines an auto crash as any collision resulting in a property damage claim. *Allstate, "The 2010 Allstate America's Best Drivers Report™"*

- Austin was identified as one of the safest large cities in America by CQ Press. All 34 cities with populations of 500,000 or more that reported crime rates in 2009 for murder, rape, robbery, aggravated assault, burglary, and motor vehicle thefts were ranked. The city ranked #6 out of the top 10. *CQ Press, City Crime Rankings 2010-2011*

- The National Insurance Crime Bureau ranked 366 metro areas in the U.S. in terms of per capita rates of vehicle theft. The Austin metro area ranked #153 (#1 = highest rate). Criteria: number of vehicle theft offenses per 100,000 inhabitants. *National Insurance Crime Bureau, "Hot Spots," May 17, 2010*

- The Austin metro area was identified as one of the "The Most Dangerous Metro Areas for Pedestrians" by Transportation for America and the Surface Transportation Policy Partnership. The metro area ranked #19 out of 52 metro areas with over 1 million residents. Criteria: area's population divided by the number of pedestrian fatalities in that area. *Transportation for America and the Surface Transportation Policy Partnership, "Dangerous by Design: Solving the Epidemic of Preventable Pedestrian Deaths (and Making Great Neighborhoods)," November 11, 2009*

Seniors/Retirement Rankings

- Austin was identified as one of "The Top 100 Places to Retire" by *Topretirements.com* The list reflects the 100 cities (out of 625+ total cities reviewed) that visitors to the website are most interested in for retirement. *Topretirements.com, "2011 Best Places to Retire List: The Sunbelt Rules"*

- Austin was selected as one of the best places to retire by *Money*. The city was ranked #9 out of 25. Criteria: notable lifelong-learning programs; low taxes; affordable housing; high-quality health care; rich intellectual environment. *CNNMoney, "Best Places to Retire 2010"*

- The Austin metro area was selected as one of the "Best Places for Military Retirees" by *U.S. News*. The area was ranked #3 out of 10. Criteria: climate; health resources; health indicators; crime levels; local school performance; recreational resources; arts and culture; airport and mass transit resources; susceptibility to natural disasters; military facilities and base amenities; VA medical services; tax policies affecting military pensions, unemployment trends; higher education resources; overall affordability; housing costs; home price trends; economic stability. *U.S. News & Word Report, "Best Places for Military Retirees," December 8, 2010*

Sports/Recreation Rankings

- Austin appeared on the *Sporting News* list of the "Best Sports Cities" for 2010. The area ranked #43 out of 402 cities in the U.S. *Sporting News* takes a 12-month snapshot, roughly October to October, of each city's sports, putting a heavy premium on regular-season won-lost records (from the most recently completed season). Other criteria include: playoff berths, bowl appearances and tournament bids; championships; applicable power ratings; quality of competition; overall fan fervor as measured in part by attendance as percentage of venue capacity; abundance of teams (rewarding quality over quantity); stadium and arena quality; ticket availability and prices; franchise ownership; and marquee appeal of athletes. *Sporting News, "Best Sports Cities 2010," October, 2010*

- Austin was selected as one of the five best boat cities to live in (in the U.S.). The city ranked #5. Criteria: climate; scenery; fishing; boat communities with water access. *Best Boat Ne.ws, "The 5 Best Boat Cities to Live In (in the U.S.)," April 16, 2010*

- Austin was chosen as one of America's 25 best cities for running. The city was ranked #11. Criteria: number of running clubs per city; amount of land set aside for park usage; air quality; weather; crime rates; and results from a *Runner's World* poll in which readers ranked their favorite running cities. *Runner's World, "The 25 Best Running Cities in America," July 2005*

- Austin was chosen as a bicycle friendly community by the League of American Bicyclists. A Bicycle Friendly Community welcomes cyclists by providing safe accommodation for cycling and encouraging people to bike for transportation and recreation. There are four award levels: Platinum; Gold; Silver; and Bronze. The community achieved an award level of Silver. *League of American Bicyclists, "Bicycle Friendly Community Master List," September 2010*

- Austin was chosen as one of America's 10 best places to live and boat. Criteria: boating opportunities; boat-friendly regulations; water access; availability of waterfront homes; health of the local economy; and overall lifestyle for boaters. *Boating Magazine, "10 Best Places to Live and Boat," June 2010*

- Austin was chosen as one of America's best cities for bicycling. The city ranked #11 out of 50. Criteria: number of segregated bike lanes, municipal bike racks, and bike boulevards; vibrant and diverse bike culture; smart, savvy bike shops; interviews with national and local advocates, bike shops and other experts. Note: only cities with populations of 100,000 or more were considered. *Bicycling, "America's Best Bike Cities," April 2010*

- *Golf Digest* ranked 330 metro areas in the U.S. in terms of golf. The Austin metro area was ranked #241. Criteria: access to golf; weather; value of golf; and quality of golf. *Golf Digest, "Metro Golf Rankings," August 2005*

- *Golf.com* and the research arm of the National Golf Foundation analyzed the 50 largest metropolitan areas in the U.S. in terms of golf. The Austin metro area ranked #1. Criteria: weather; affordability; quality of courses; accessibility; number of courses designed by esteemed architects; availability; crowdedness. *Golf.com, November 15, 2007*

Technology Rankings

- The Austin metro area was selected as one of "America's Most Wired Cities" by *Forbes*. The metro area was ranked #20 out of 20. Criteria: percentage of Internet users with high-speed access; number of companies providing high-speed Internet; number of public wireless hot spots. *Forbes, "America's Most Wired Cities," March 2, 2010*

- The Austin metro area was selected as one of "America's Most Innovative Cities" by *Forbes*. The metro area was ranked #2 out of 20. Criteria: patents per capita; venture capital investment per capita; ratio of high-tech, science and "creative" jobs. *Forbes, "America's Most Innovative Cities," May 24, 2010*

- The Austin metro area was identified as one of the "Top 14 Nano Metros" in the U.S. by the Project on Emerging Nanotechnologies. The metro area is home to 24 companies, universities, government laboratories and/or organizations working in nanotechnology. *Project on Emerging Nanotechnologies, "Nano Metros 2009"*

Transportation Rankings

- Austin was identified as one of America's "10 Best Cities for Public Transportation" by *U.S. News*. The city ranked #9. The ten cities selected had the best combination of public transportation investment, ridership, and safety. *U.S. News & World Report, "10 Best Cities for Public Transportation," February 8, 2011*

- The Austin metro area appeared on *Forbes* list of the best and worst cities for commuters. The metro area ranked #27 out of 60 (#1 is best). Criteria: travel time; road congestion; travel delays. *Forbes.com, "Best and Worst Cities for Commuters," February 16, 2010*

Women/Minorities Rankings

- Austin was ranked #36 out of 100 metro areas in *SELF Magazine's* ranking of America's healthiest places for women." A panel of experts came up with more than 50 criteria including death and disease rates, environmental indicators, community resources, and lifestyle habits. *SELF Magazine, "Secrets of America's Healthiest Women," December 2008*

- Austin was selected as one of the "Top 10 Cities for Hispanics." Criteria: the prospect of a good job; a safe place to raise a family; a manageable cost of living; the ability to buy and keep a home; a culture of inclusion where Hispanics are highly represented; resources to help start a business; the presence of Hispanic or Spanish-language media; representation of Hispanic needs on local government; a thriving arts and culture community; air quality; energy costs; city's state of health and rates of obesity. *Hispanic Magazine, August 2008*

Miscellaneous Rankings

- Energizer Holdings, the makers of Edge® shave gel, in partnership with Sperling's BestPlaces, ranked 50 major metro areas in terms of everyday irritations. The Austin metro area ranked #32. Criteria: humidity levels; weather conditions; incidence of traffic delays and congestion; average commute times; frequency of flight delays and cancellations; rates of sleeplessness; underemployment; pollens and allergens; pests; comedy clubs per capita. *Energizer Holdings, "Most Irritation Prone Cities," July 23, 2010*

- Austin was selected as one of the most tattooed cities in America by *TotalBeauty.com*. The city was ranked #6. Criteria: number of tattoo and permanent makeup shops per capita; number of tattoo conventions hosted. *TotalBeauty.com, "Top 10 Most Tattooed Cities in America," August 2010*

- The Austin metro area appeared in AutoMD.com's ranking of the "Best and Worst Cities for Auto Repair." The metro area ranked #5 (#1 is best). The 50 most-populated metro areas in the U.S. were ranked on three critical factors: repair affordability; price disparity range; shop integrity factor. *AutoMD.com, "Advocacy for Repair Shop Fairness Report," February 24, 2010*

- Austin appeared on Procter & Gamble's list of the "Top-20 All-Time Sweatiest Cities." The city was ranked #16. The rankings are based on computer simulations of the amount of sweat a person of average height and weight would produce walking around for an hour in the average temperatures during the summer months, based on historical weather data during June, July and August from 2001-2008 for each city. *Procter & Gamble, Old Spice Press Release, "Top-20 All-Time Sweatiest Cities," July 1, 2009*

- The Austin metro area appeared on *Forbes* list of "America's Drunkest Cities." The area ranked #5. Criteria: 35 of the largest continental U.S. metro areas were chosen based on availability of data and geographic diversity. Each metro was ranked in five areas: state laws; drinkers; heavy drinkers; binge drinkers; and alcoholism. *Forbes.com, "America's Drunkest Cities," August 22, 2006*

- Scarborough Research, a leading market research firm, identified the top local markets for gift card purchasers. The Austin DMA (Designated Market Area) ranked in the top 10 with 54% of consumers reporting that they purchased a gift card within the past 12 months. *Scarborough Research, November 15, 2006*

- Scarborough Research, a leading market research firm, identified the top local markets for frequent fast food restaurant patronage. The Austin DMA (Designated Market Area) ranked in the top 10 with consumers reporting an average of 6.3 visits within the past 30 days. *Scarborough Research, May 31, 2006*

- Scarborough Research, a leading market research firm, identified the top local markets for frequent sit-down restaurant patronage. The Austin DMA (Designated Market Area) ranked in the top 10 with consumers reporting an average of 4.0 visits within the past 30 days. *Scarborough Research, May 31, 2006*

Business Environment

CITY FINANCES

City Government Finances

Component	2008 ($000)	2008 ($ per capita)
Total Revenues	2,688,459	3,618
Total Expenditures	2,555,922	3,440
Debt Outstanding	4,534,854	6,103
Cash and Securities[1]	3,818,441	5,139

Note: (1) Cash and security holdings of a government at the close of its fiscal year, including those of its dependent agencies, utilities, and liquor stores.
Source: U.S Census Bureau, State & Local Government Finances 2008

City Government Revenue by Source

Source	2008 ($000)	2008 ($ per capita)
General Revenue		
From Federal Government	60,992	82
From State Government	24,309	33
From Local Governments	43,591	59
Taxes		
Property	251,403	338
Sales and Gross Receipts	235,092	316
Personal Income	0	0
Corporate Income	0	0
Motor Vehicle License	0	0
Other Taxes	25,635	34
Current Charges	450,455	606
Liquor Store	0	0
Utility	1,194,838	1,608
Employee Retirement	232,029	312

Source: U.S Census Bureau, State & Local Government Finances 2008

City Government Expenditures by Function

Function	2008 ($000)	2008 ($ per capita)	2008 (%)
General Direct Expenditures			
Air Transportation	67,292	91	2.6
Corrections	0	0	0.0
Education	0	0	0.0
Employment Security Administration	0	0	0.0
Financial Administration	27,329	37	1.1
Fire Protection	109,719	148	4.3
General Public Buildings	0	0	0.0
Governmental Administration, Other	28,839	39	1.1
Health	135,506	182	5.3
Highways	63,916	86	2.5
Hospitals	729	1	0.0
Housing and Community Development	26,920	36	1.1
Interest on General Debt	73,908	99	2.9
Judicial and Legal	20,732	28	0.8
Libraries	23,223	31	0.9
Parking	175	< 1	< 0.1
Parks and Recreation	103,804	140	4.1
Police Protection	199,360	268	7.8
Public Welfare	0	0	0.0
Sewerage	125,342	169	4.9
Solid Waste Management	54,975	74	2.2
Veterans' Services	0	0	0.0
Liquor Store	0	0	0.0
Utility	1,222,913	1,646	47.8
Employee Retirement	123,464	166	4.8

Source: U.S Census Bureau, State & Local Government Finances 2008

Municipal Bond Ratings

Area	Moody's	S&P	Fitch
City	Aa1	AAA	n/a

Rating Systems (shown in declining order of credit quality): Moody's– Aaa, Aa, A, Baa, Ba, B, Caa, Ca, C (numerical modifiers 1, 2, and 3 are added to letter-rating); S&P– AAA, AA, A, BBB, BB, B, CCC, CC, C; Fitch– AAA, AA, A, BBB, BB, B, CCC, CC, C. Ratings may be modified by the addition of a plus or minus sign to show relative standing within the major rating categories.
Notes: n/a Not available; (1) Not reviewed; (2) Issuer Rating/No General Obligation; (3) Standard and Poor's Issue Credit Rating (ICR) is a current opinion of an obliger with respect to a specific financial obligation, a specific class of financial obligations, or a specific financial program.
Source: U.S. Census Bureau, 2011 Statistical Abstract, Bond Ratings for City Governments by Largest Cities: 2009

DEMOGRAPHICS

Population Growth

Area	1990 Census	2000 Census	2010 Estimate	2015 Projection	Population Growth (%)	
					2000-2010	2010-2015
City	499,053	656,562	764,479	824,376	16.4	7.8
MSA[1]	846,217	1,249,763	1,703,994	1,921,939	36.3	12.8
U.S.	248,709,873	281,421,906	309,038,974	321,675,005	9.8	4.1

Note: (1) Metropolitan Statistical Area - see Appendix B for areas included
Source: Claritas, Inc.

Number of Households and Average Household Size

Area	2010 Estimate	2010 Average Household Size
City	308,268	2.41
MSA[1]	629,606	2.64
U.S.	116,136,617	2.59

Note: (1) Metropolitan Statistical Area - see Appendix B for areas included
Source: Claritas, Inc.

Race and Ethnicity

Area	White Alone[2] (%)	Black Alone[2] (%)	Asian Alone[2] (%)	Other Race Alone[2] (%)	Hispanic[3] (%)
City	62.0	8.0	5.9	24.1	36.2
MSA[1]	69.5	7.3	4.5	18.7	30.5
U.S.	72.3	12.4	4.4	10.9	15.8

Note: Figures are 2010 estimates; (1) Metropolitan Statistical Area - see Appendix B for areas included (2) Alone is defined as not being in combination with one or more other races; (3) May be of any race.
Source: Claritas, Inc.

Segregation

Type	Segregation Indices[1]				Percent Change		
	1990	2000	2010	2010 Rank[2]	1990-2000	1990-2010	2000-2010
Black/White	54.1	52.1	50.1	70	-1.9	-4.0	-2.1
Asian/White	39.4	42.3	41.2	49	2.9	1.8	-1.2
Hispanic/White	41.7	45.6	43.2	51	3.9	1.5	-2.4

Note: Figures are based on an analysis of 1990, 2000, and 2010 Census Decennial Census tract data by William H. Frey, Brookings Institution and the University of Michigan Social Science Data Analysis Network. In this analysis all racial groups (whites, blacks, and asians) are non-Hispanic members of those races. Hispanics are shown as a separate category; All figures cover the Metropolitan Statistical Area (see Appendix B for areas included); (1) Segregation Indices are Dissimilarity Indices that measure the degree to which the minority group is distributed differently than whites aross census tracts. They range from 0 (complete integration) to 100 (complete [segregation) where the value indicates the percentage of the minority group that needs to move to be distributed exactly like whites; (2) Ranges from 1 (most segregated) to 102 (least segregated); n/a not available.
Source: www.CensusScope.org

Ancestry

Area	German	Irish	English	American	Italian	Polish	French	Scottish
City	13.1	8.6	9.2	3.1	2.8	1.7	2.9	2.5
MSA[1]	16.1	9.8	9.9	4.1	2.8	1.7	3.0	2.7
U.S.	16.6	12.0	9.1	6.1	5.9	3.3	3.1	1.9

Note: The top eight ancestries in the U.S. are shown. Figures are percentages and include multiple ancestry (e.g. if a person reported being Irish and Italian, they were included in both columns); (1) Metropolitan Statistical Area - see Appendix B for areas included
Source: U.S. Census Bureau, 2007-2009 American Community Survey 3-Year Estimates

Foreign-Born Population

Area	Percent of Population Born in								
	Any Foreign Country	Mexico	Asia	Europe	Carribean	South America	Central America[2]	Africa	Canada
City	19.8	10.9	4.4	1.1	0.3	0.5	1.7	0.6	0.3
MSA[1]	14.5	7.7	3.3	1.1	0.2	0.4	1.0	0.5	0.2
U.S.	12.5	3.8	3.4	1.6	1.1	0.8	0.9	0.5	0.3

Note: (1) Metropolitan Statistical Area - see Appendix B for areas included; (2) Excludes Mexico.
Source: U.S. Census Bureau, 2007-2009 American Community Survey 3-Year Estimates

Marriage Status

Area	Never Married	Now Married[2]	Separated	Widowed	Divorced
City	42.5	41.8	2.0	3.4	10.3
MSA[1]	35.3	48.3	1.9	3.8	10.7
U.S.	31.4	49.7	2.2	6.2	10.6

Note: Figures are percentages and cover the population 15 years of age and older; (1) Metropolitan Statistical Area - see Appendix B for areas included; (2) Excludes separated
Source: U.S. Census Bureau, 2007-2009 American Community Survey 3-Year Estimates

Age Distribution and Median Age

Area	Percent of Population							Median Age
	Under Age 5	Age 5 to 17	Age 18 to 34	Age 35 to 49	Age 50 to 64	Age 65 to 79	80 Years and Over	
City	7.7	14.2	36.5	21.4	13.5	4.6	2.0	30.9
MSA[1]	7.9	17.3	29.7	22.5	14.9	5.7	2.1	32.2
U.S.	6.9	17.5	23.3	21.4	18.1	9.1	3.7	36.7

Note: (1) Metropolitan Statistical Area - see Appendix B for areas included
Source: U.S. Census Bureau, 2007-2009 American Community Survey 3-Year Estimates

Male/Female Ratio

Area	Males	Females	Males per 100 Females
City	392,918	371,561	105.7
MSA[1]	863,629	840,365	102.8
U.S.	152,401,520	156,637,454	97.3

Note: Figures are 2010 estimates; (1) Metropolitan Statistical Area - see Appendix B for areas included
Source: Claritas, Inc.

Religion

Area	Catholic	Southern Baptist	United Methodist	ELCA[1]	LDS[2]	Presbyterian Church USA	Jewish Est.	Muslim Est.
County	20.4	9.5	2.7	1.5	0.6	1.3	1.7	0.4
U.S.	22.0	7.1	3.7	1.8	1.5	1.1	2.2	0.6

Note: Figures are the number of adherents as a percentage of the total population; Adherents are defined as all members, including full members, their children and the estimated number of other participants who are not considered members (e.g. the baptized, those not confirmed, those regularly attending services, etc.);
(1) Evangelical Lutheran Church in America; (2) The Church of Jesus Christ of Latter Day Saints
Source: Reprinted with permission from Religious Congregations and Membership in the United States 2000 (Nashville, Glenmary Research Center, 2002) Copyright Association of Statisticians of American Religious Bodies. All rights reserved.

ECONOMY

Gross Metropolitan Product

Area	2006	2007	2008	2009	2009 Rank[2]
MSA[1]	71.3	75.8	80.1	81.6	35

Note: Figures are in billions of dollars; (1) Austin-Round Rock, TX Metropolitan Statistical Area - see Appendix B for areas included; (2) Rank ranges from 1 to 363
Source: The U.S. Conference of Mayors, "Pace of Economic Recovery: GMP and Jobs," January 2010

Economic Growth

Area	2006-2008 (%)	2009 (%)	2010 (%)	Rank[2]
MSA[1]	4.8	0.5	4.1	17
U.S.	1.3	-2.5	2.2	–

Note: Figures are real Gross Metropolitan Product growth rates and represent annual average percent change; (1) Austin-Round Rock, TX Metropolitan Statistical Area - see Appendix B for areas included; (2) Rank ranges from 1 to 363
Source: The U.S. Conference of Mayors, "Pace of Economic Recovery: GMP and Jobs," January 2010

Metropolitan Area Exports

Area	2005	2006	2007	2008	2009	2009 Rank[2]
MSA[1]	7,687.0	8,204.6	8,428.6	7,405.5	5,963.7	35

Note: Figures are in millions of dollars; (1) Austin-Round Rock, TX Metropolitan Statistical Area - see Appendix B for areas included; (2) Rank ranges from 1 to 374
Source: U.S. Department of Commerce, International Trade Administration, Office of Trade & Industry Information, Manufacturing & Services

INCOME

Per Capita/Median/Average Income

Area	Per Capita ($)	Median Household ($)	Average Household ($)
City	28,216	49,571	69,121
MSA[1]	28,552	58,887	76,594
U.S.	27,034	52,795	71,071

Note: Figures are 2010 estimates; (1) Metropolitan Statistical Area - see Appendix B for areas included
Source: Claritas, Inc.

Household Income Distribution

Area	Percent of Households Earning							
	Under $15,000	$15,000 -24,999	$25,000 -34,999	$35,000 -49,999	$50,000 -74,999	$75,000 -99,000	$100,000 -149,999	$150,000 and up
City	12.9	10.1	11.5	15.9	19.1	11.5	11.3	7.7
MSA[1]	10.0	8.3	9.7	14.9	20.2	13.9	14.2	8.9
U.S.	12.1	10.2	10.6	15.0	19.5	12.5	12.1	8.0

Note: Figures are 2010 estimates; (1) Metropolitan Statistical Area - see Appendix B for areas included
Source: Claritas, Inc.

Poverty Rates by Age

Area	All Ages	Under 18 Years Old	18 to 64 Years Old	65 Years and Over
City	17.4	5.5	11.3	0.6
MSA[1]	13.2	4.3	8.3	0.5
U.S.	13.6	4.7	7.7	1.2

Note: Figures are percent of population with income during the previous 12 months below poverty level and only include population for whom poverty status is determined; (1) Metropolitan Statistical Area - see Appendix B for areas included
Source: U.S. Census Bureau, 2007-2009 American Community Survey 3-Year Estimates

Personal Bankruptcy Filing Rate

Area	2006	2007	2008	2009	2010
Travis County	1.25	1.31	1.33	1.78	1.83
U.S.	2.00	2.73	3.53	4.60	4.96

Note: Numbers are per 1,000 population and include Chapter 7 and Chapter 13 filings
Source: Federal Deposit Insurance Corporation, Regional Economic Conditions, March 17, 2011

EMPLOYMENT

Labor Force and Employment

Area	Civilian Labor Force			Workers Employed		
	Dec. 2009	Dec. 2010	% Chg.	Dec. 2009	Dec. 2010	% Chg.
City	423,893	429,920	1.4	397,108	402,844	1.4
MSA[1]	890,415	902,646	1.4	828,542	840,510	1.4
U.S.	152,693,000	153,156,000	0.3	137,953,000	139,159,000	0.9

Note: Data is not seasonally adjusted and covers workers 16 years of age and older; (1) Metropolitan Statistical Area - see Appendix B for areas included
Source: Bureau of Labor Statistics, http://stats.bls.gov

Unemployment Rate

Area	2010											
	Jan.	Feb.	Mar.	Apr.	May	Jun.	Jul.	Aug.	Sep.	Oct.	Nov.	Dec.
City	6.9	6.7	6.5	6.3	6.3	6.8	6.8	6.7	6.5	6.4	6.6	6.3
MSA[1]	7.6	7.3	7.2	6.9	6.9	7.3	7.3	7.2	7.0	6.9	7.1	6.9
U.S.	10.6	10.4	10.2	9.5	9.3	9.6	9.7	9.5	9.2	9.0	9.3	9.1

Note: Data is not seasonally adjusted and covers workers 16 years of age and older; All figures are percentages; (1) Metropolitan Statistical Area - see Appendix B for areas included
Source: Bureau of Labor Statistics, http://stats.bls.gov

Projected Unemployment Rate

Area	2007 (%)	2009 (%)	2011 (%)	2013 (%)
MSA[1]	3.8	7.7	7.2	6.1

Note: (1) Metropolitan Statistical Area - see Appendix B for areas included
Source: The U.S. Conference of Mayors, "Pace of Economic Recovery: GMP and Jobs," January 2010

Employment by Occupation

Occupation Classification	City (%)	MSA[1] (%)	U.S. (%)
Sales and Office	22.7	24.8	25.4
Professional and Related	27.3	24.9	21.0
Service	17.0	15.6	17.2
Production, Transportation, and Material Moving	6.5	7.6	12.3
Management, Business, and Financial	15.9	17.0	14.1
Construction, Extraction, and Maintenance	10.6	10.0	9.2
Farming, Forestry, and Fishing	0.1	0.2	0.7

Note: Figures cover employed civilians 16 years of age and older; (1) Metropolitan Statistical Area - see Appendix B for areas included
Source: U.S. Census Bureau, 2007-2009 American Community Survey 3-Year Estimates

Employment by Industry

Sector	MSA[1]		U.S.
	Number of Employees	Percent of Total	Percent of Total
Government	170,800	22.2	17.2
Education and Health Services	89,300	11.6	15.2
Professional and Business Services	108,600	14.1	13.0
Retail Trade	84,100	10.9	11.4
Leisure and Hospitality	82,700	10.7	9.7
Manufacturing	47,700	6.2	8.8
Financial Activities	42,200	5.5	5.8
Wholesale Trade	39,900	5.2	4.2
Construction	n/a	n/a	4.1
Other Services	34,000	4.4	4.1
Transportation and Utilities	13,300	1.7	3.7
Information	19,600	2.5	2.1
Mining and Logging	n/a	n/a	0.6

Note: Figures cover non-farm employment as of December 2010 and are not seasonally adjusted;
(1) Metropolitan Statistical Area - see Appendix B for areas included; n/a not available
Source: Bureau of Labor Statistics, http://stats.bls.gov

Occupations with Greatest Projected Employment Growth: 2006 - 2016

Occupation[1]	2006 Employment	2016 Projected Employment	Numeric Employment Change	Percent Employment Change
Combined food preparation and serving workers, including fast food	270,530	359,050	88,520	32.7
Retail salespersons	332,750	411,350	78,600	23.6
Personal and home care aides	133,050	207,850	74,800	56.2
Customer service representatives	214,440	280,060	65,620	30.6
Elementary school teachers, except special education	145,430	207,710	62,280	42.8
Registered nurses	157,840	217,430	59,590	37.8
Waiters and waitresses	174,140	227,790	53,650	30.8
Child care workers	145,500	189,730	44,230	30.4
Office clerks, general	194,610	236,670	42,060	21.6
Postsecondary teachers	113,400	153,130	39,730	35.0

Note: Projections cover Texas; (1) Sorted by numeric employment change
Source: www.projectionscentral.com, State Occupational Projections, 2006-2016 Long-Term Projections

Fastest Growing Occupations: 2006 - 2016

Occupation[1]	2006 Employment	2016 Projected Employment	Numeric Employment Change	Percent Employment Change
Personal and home care aides	133,050	207,850	74,800	56.2
Network systems and data communications analysts	17,750	27,620	9,870	55.6
Medical assistants	34,790	53,500	18,710	53.8
Special education teachers, preschool, kindergarten, and elementary school	13,750	20,560	6,810	49.5
Physical therapist assistants	3,780	5,570	1,790	47.4
Special education teachers, middle school	6,270	9,170	2,900	46.3
Computer software engineers, applications	30,900	45,200	14,300	46.3
Physician assistants	3,810	5,540	1,730	45.4
Kindergarten teachers, except special education	12,850	18,690	5,840	45.4
Pharmacy technicians	24,420	35,050	10,630	43.5

Note: Projections cover Texas; (1) Sorted by percent employment change and excludes occupations with
numeric employment change less than 1500
Source: www.projectionscentral.com, State Occupational Projections, 2006-2016 Long-Term Projections

Average Wages

Occupation	$/Hr.	Occupation	$/Hr.
Accountants and Auditors	33.18	Maids and Housekeeping Cleaners	8.55
Automotive Mechanics	19.83	Maintenance and Repair Workers	15.69
Bookkeepers	17.32	Marketing Managers	68.24
Carpenters	15.33	Nuclear Medicine Technologists	35.72
Cashiers	9.03	Nurses, Licensed Practical	20.21
Clerks, General Office	14.90	Nurses, Registered	30.08
Clerks, Receptionists/Information	13.37	Nursing Aides/Orderlies/Attendants	10.97
Clerks, Shipping/Receiving	13.36	Packers and Packagers, Hand	9.92
Computer Programmers	40.31	Physical Therapists	31.37
Computer Support Specialists	23.20	Postal Service Mail Carriers	23.42
Computer Systems Analysts	38.45	Real Estate Brokers	n/a
Cooks, Restaurant	9.84	Retail Salespersons	11.55
Dentists	n/a	Sales Reps., Exc. Tech./Scientific	32.49
Electrical Engineers	48.73	Sales Reps., Tech./Scientific	31.01
Electricians	19.58	Secretaries, Exc. Legal/Med./Exec.	14.13
Financial Managers	56.64	Security Guards	12.84
First-Line Supervisors/Mgrs., Sales	19.14	Surgeons	102.13
Food Preparation Workers	8.94	Teacher Assistants	11.70
General and Operations Managers	57.02	Teachers, Elementary School	23.40
Hairdressers/Cosmetologists	13.80	Teachers, Secondary School	24.40
Internists	78.95	Telemarketers	14.04
Janitors and Cleaners	10.32	Truck Drivers, Heavy/Tractor-Trailer	16.91
Landscaping/Groundskeeping Workers	11.31	Truck Drivers, Light/Delivery Svcs.	14.15
Lawyers	57.65	Waiters and Waitresses	8.51

Note: Wage data covers the Austin-Round Rock, TX - see Appendix B for areas included. Hourly wages for elementary/secondary school teachers and teacher assistants were calculated by the editors from annual wage data assuming a 40 hour work week; n/a not available.
Source: Bureau of Labor Statistics, Metro Area Occupational Employment and Wage Estimates, May 2009

RESIDENTIAL REAL ESTATE

Building Permits

Area	Single-Family			Multi-Family			Total		
	2009	2010	Pct. Chg.	2009	2010	Pct. Chg.	2009	2010	Pct. Chg.
City	1,951	1,664	-14.7	1,588	1,110	-30.1	3,539	2,774	-21.6
MSA[1]	6,678	6,200	-7.2	2,080	2,586	24.3	8,758	8,786	0.3
U.S.	441,100	447,300	1.4	141,900	157,300	10.9	583,000	604,600	3.7

Note: (1) Metropolitan Statistical Area - see Appendix B for areas included; figures represent new, privately-owned housing units authorized (unadjusted data); All permit data are based on estimates with imputation.
Source: U.S. Census Bureau, Manufacturing, Mining, and Construction Statistics, Building Permits, 2009, 2010

Homeownership Rate

Area	2005 (%)	2006 (%)	2007 (%)	2008 (%)	2009 (%)	2010 (%)
MSA[1]	63.9	66.7	66.4	65.5	64.0	65.8
U.S.	68.9	68.8	68.1	67.8	67.4	66.9

Note: (1) Metropolitan Statistical Area - see Appendix B for areas included
Source: U.S. Census Bureau, Housing Vacancies and Homeownership Annual Statistics: 2010

Housing Vacancy Rates

Area	Gross Vacancy Rate[2] (%)			Year-Round Vacancy Rate[3] (%)			Rental Vacancy Rate[4] (%)			Homeowner Vacancy Rate[5] (%)		
	2008	2009	2010	2008	2009	2010	2008	2009	2010	2008	2009	2010
MSA[1]	11.4	12.8	15.8	11.0	12.7	15.7	11.8	12.2	11.8	2.3	1.6	1.9
U.S.	14.4	14.5	14.3	11.1	11.3	11.3	10.0	10.6	10.2	2.8	2.6	2.6

Note: (1) Metropolitan Statistical Area - see Appendix B for areas included; (2) The percentage of the total housing inventory that is vacant; (3) The percentage of the housing inventory (excluding seasonal units) that is year-round vacant; (4) The percentage of rental inventory that is vacant for rent; (5) The percentage of homeowner inventory that is vacant for sale; n/a not available
Source: U.S. Census Bureau, Housing Vacancies and Homeownership Annual Statistics: 2010

State Corporate Income Tax Rates

State	Tax Rate (%)	Income Brackets ($)	Num. of Brackets	Financial Institution Tax Rate (%)[a]	Federal Income Tax Ded.
Texas	(y)	–	-	(y)	No

Note: Tax rates as of January 1, 2011; (a) Rates listed are the tax rates applied to financial institutions or excise taxes based on income. Some states have other taxes based upon the value of deposits or shares; (y) Texas imposes a Franchise Tax, otherwise known as margin tax, imposed on entities with more than $1,000,000 total revenues at rate of 1%, or 0.5% for entities primarily engaged in retail or wholesale trade, on lesser of 70% of total revenues or 100%of gross receipts after deductions for either compensation or cost of goods sold.
Source: Federation of Tax Administrators, "State Corporate Income Tax Rates, 2011"

State Individual Income Tax Rates

State	Tax Rate (%)	Income Brackets ($)	Num. of Brackets	Personal Exempt. ($)[1] Single	Personal Exempt. ($)[1] Dependents	Fed. Inc. Tax Ded.
Texas – No State Income Tax						

Note: Tax rates as of January 1, 2011; Local- and county-level taxes are not included; n/a not applicable;
(1) Married joint filers generally receive double the single exemption
Source: Federation of Tax Administrators, "State Individual Income Tax Rates, 2011"

Various State and Local Tax Rates

State	State and Local Sales and Use (%)	State Sales and Use (%)	Gasoline[1] (¢/gal.)	Cigarette[2] ($/pack)	Spirits[3] ($/gal.)	Wine[4] ($/gal.)	Beer[5] ($/gal.)
Texas	8.25	6.25	20.0	1.41	2.40	0.20	0.20

Note: All tax rates as of January 1, 2011 except Spirits (Sept. 1, 2010); (1) The American Petroleum Institute has developed a methodology for determining the average tax rate on a gallon of fuel. Rates may include any of the following: excise taxes, environmental fees, storage tank fees, other fees or taxes, general sales tax, and local taxes. In states where gasoline is subject to the general sales tax, or where the fuel tax is based on the average sale price, the average rate determined by API is sensitive to changes in the price of gasoline. States that fully or partially apply general sales taxes to gasoline: CA, CO, GA, IL, IN, MI, NY; (2) The federal excise tax of $1.0066 per pack and local taxes are not included; (3) Rates are those applicable to off-premise sales of 40% alcohol by volume (a.b.v.) distilled spirits in 750ml containers. Local excise taxes are excluded; (4) Rates are those applicable to off-premise sales of 11% a.b.v. non-carbonated wine in 750ml containers; (5) Rates are those applicable to off-premise sales of 4.7% a.b.v. beer in 12 ounce containers.
Source: Tax Foundation, 2011 Facts & Figures: How Does Your State Compare?

State-Local Tax Burdens

Area	Rate (%)	Rank[1]	Per Capita Taxes Paid to Home State ($)	Total State and Local Per Capita Taxes Paid ($)	Per Capita Income ($)
Texas	7.9	45	2,248	3,197	40,498
U.S. Average	9.8	-	3,057	4,160	42,539

Note: Figures cover 2009; (1) Rank ranges from 1 to 50 where 1 is highest tax burden
Source: Tax Foundation, State-Local Tax Burdens, All States, 2009

State Business Tax Climate Index Rankings

State	Overall Rank	Corporate Tax Index Rank	Individual Income Tax Index Rank	Sales Tax Index Rank	Unemployment Insurance Tax Index Rank	Property Tax Index Rank
Texas	13	46	7	37	15	29

Note: The index is a measure of how each state's tax laws affect economic performance. The lower the rank, the more favorable a state's tax system is for business. All ranks are for fiscal years. States without a given tax are given a ranking of 1.
Source: Tax Foundation, Tax Foundation Background Paper, No. 60, "2011 State Business Tax Climate Index"

COMMERCIAL REAL ESTATE

Office Market

Market Area	Inventory (sq. ft.)	Vacant (sq. ft.)	Vac. Rate (%)	Under Constr. (sq. ft.)	Asking Rent ($/sf/yr) Class A	Asking Rent ($/sf/yr) Class B
Austin	43,495,312	7,902,566	18.2	-	28.09	21.09

Source: Grubb & Ellis, Office Markets Trends, 1st Quarter 2011

Industrial Market

Market Area	Inventory (sq. ft.)	Vacant (sq. ft.)	Vac. Rate (%)	Under Constr. (sq. ft.)	Asking Rent ($/sf/yr) WH/Dist	R&D/Flex
Austin	77,820,171	10,217,017	13.1	637,440	5.67	9.15

Source: Grubb & Ellis, Industrial Markets Trends, 1st Quarter 2011

COMMERCIAL UTILITIES

Typical Monthly Electric Bills

Area	Commercial Service ($/month) 40 kW demand 5,000 kWh	500 kW demand 100,000 kWh	Industrial Service ($/month) 5,000 kW demand 1,500,000 kWh	70,000 kW demand 50,000,000 kWh
City	779	11,778	134,710	3,348,700

Note: Based on rates in effect January 1, 2010
Source: Memphis Light, Gas and Water, 2010 Utility Bill Comparisons for Selected U.S. Cities

TRANSPORTATION

Means of Transportation to Work

Area	Car/Truck/Van Drove Alone	Car-pooled	Public Transportation Bus	Subway	Railroad	Bicycle	Walked	Other Means	Worked at Home
City	71.2	12.0	5.1	0.0	0.0	1.2	2.0	3.1	5.4
MSA[1]	74.5	12.4	2.9	0.0	0.0	0.7	1.6	2.2	5.7
U.S.	75.8	10.4	2.7	1.7	0.5	0.5	2.9	1.2	4.1

Note: Figures are percentages and cover workers 16 years of age and older;
(1) Metropolitan Statistical Area - see Appendix B for areas included
Source: U.S. Census Bureau, 2007-2009 American Community Survey 3-Year Estimates

Travel Time to Work

Area	Less Than 15 Minutes	15 to 29 Minutes	30 to 44 Minutes	45 to 59 Minutes	60 to 89 Minutes	90 Minutes or More
City	26.4	44.6	19.7	4.7	2.9	1.7
MSA[1]	24.7	39.0	22.3	7.6	4.5	1.8
U.S.	28.5	36.2	19.7	7.5	5.6	2.5

Note: Figures are percentages and include workers 16 years old and over;
(1) Metropolitan Statistical Area - see Appendix B for areas included
Source: U.S. Census Bureau, 2007-2009 American Community Survey 3-Year Estimates

Travel Time Index

Area	1982	1999	2008	2009
Urban Area[1]	1.08	1.23	1.27	1.28
Average[2]	1.08	1.20	1.20	1.20

Note: Travel Time Index—the ratio of travel time in the peak period to the travel time at free-flow conditions. A value of 1.30 indicates a 20-minute free-flow trip takes 26 minutes in the peak. Free-flow speeds (60 mph on freeways and 35 mph on principal arterials) are used as the comparison threshold; (1) Covers the Austin-Round Rock urban area; (2) average of 439 urban areas
Source: Texas Transportation Institute, Urban Mobility Report 2010, December 2010

Public Transportation

Agency Name / Mode of Transportation	Vehicles Operated in Maximum Service	Annual Unlinked Passenger Trips ('000)	Annual Passenger Miles ('000)
Capital Metropolitan Transportation Authority (CMTA)			
Demand response	408	257.8	1,725.0
Demand response	94	445.1	3,299.5
Bus	211	25,686.7	125,799.3
Bus	133	12,730.8	45,335.6
Vanpool	140	318.3	7,330.7

Note: Figures include both directly operated and purchased transportation
Source: Federal Transit Administration, National Transit Database, 2009

Air Transportation

Airport Name and Code / Type of Service	Passenger Airlines[1]	Passenger Enplanements	Freight Carriers[2]	Freight (lbs.)
Austin-Bergstrom International (AUS)				
Domestic service (U.S. carriers - 2010)	34	4,194,455	18	78,114,192
International service (U.S. carriers - 2009)	7	487	1	6,106,910

Note: (1) Includes all U.S.-based major, minor and commuter airlines that carried at least one passenger during the year; (2) Includes all U.S.-based airlines and freight carriers that transported at least one pound of freight during the year
Source: Bureau of Transportation Statistics, The Intermodal Transportation Database, Air Carriers: T-100 Domestic Market (U.S. Carriers), 2010; Bureau of Transportation Statistics, The Intermodal Transportation Database, Air Carriers: T-100 International Market (U.S. Carriers), 2009

Other Transportation Statistics

Interstate highways:	I-35
Amtrak service:	Yes
Major waterways/ports:	None

Source: Amtrak.com; Google Maps

BUSINESSES

Major Business Headquarters

Company Name	Rankings	
	Fortune[1]	Forbes[2]
Freescale Semiconductor	-	104
Whole Foods Market	273	-

Note: (1) Fortune 500—companies that produce a 10-K are ranked 1 to 500 based on 2010 revenue; (2) all private companies with at least $2 billion in annual revenue are ranked 1 to 223; companies listed are headquartered in the city; dashes indicate no ranking
Source: Fortune, "Fortune 500," May 23, 2011; Forbes, "America's Largest Private Companies," November 3, 2010

Fast-Growing Businesses

According to *Inc.*, Austin is home to 12 of America's 500 fastest-growing private companies: **All Web Leads; Arrow Glass & Mirror; BancVue; Birds Barbershop; Charity Dynamics; CLEAResult Consulting; Consero; Dexter Field Services; Kinnser Software; Q2ebanking; Smiley Media; uShip**. Criteria: must be an independent, privately-held, for-profit, U.S. corporation, proprietorship or partnership; revenues of at least $80,000 in 2006 and $2 million in 2009; four-year operating/sales history; holding companies, regulated banks, and utilities were excluded. *Inc., "America's 500 Fastest-Growing Private Companies," September 2010*

According to *Fortune*, Austin is home to two of the 100 fastest-growing companies in the world: **EZCORP; Luminex**. Companies were ranked by their revenue growth rate; their EPS growth rate; and their three-year annualized total return to investors for the period ended June 30, 2010. Criteria for inclusion: a company, foreign or domestic, must trade on a major U.S. stock exchange; file quarterly reports with the SEC; have a minimum market capitalization of $250 million; have a stock price of at least $5 on June 30, 2010; have been trading continuously since June 30, 2007; have revenue and net income for the four quarters ended on or before April 30, 2010, of at least $50 million and $10 million, respectively; and have posted a compound annual growth in revenue and earnings per share of at least 15% annually over the three years ended on or before April 30, 2010. REITs, limited-liability companies, limited parterships, companies about to be acquired, and companies that lost money in the quarter ended April 30, 2010 were excluded. *Fortune, "100 Fastest-Growing Companies," September 6, 2010*

According to *Fortune*, Austin is home to one of America's 100 fastest-growing small public companies: **American Physicians**. Companies were ranked by their three-year annualized rates of revenue growth and total return to investors for the period ended December 31, 2008. Criteria for inclusion: revenues of less than $200 million; stock price of at least $1. Banks, real-estate firms and adult entertainment companies were excluded. Also excluded were companies with losses in any of the four quarters ended on or before December 31, 2008. *Fortune Small Business, "America's Fastest-Growing Small Public Companies," July/August 2009*

According to Deloitte, Austin is home to five of North America's 500 fastest-growing high-technology companies: **LibreDigital; Luminex Corporation; Medical Present Value (MPV); Smiley Media; SolarWinds**. Companies are ranked by percentage growth in revenue over a five-year period. Criteria for inclusion: company must be headquartered within North America; company must own proprietary intellectual property or proprietary technology that contributes to a significant portion of the company's operating revenue or devotes a significant proportion of revenues to research and development of technology; company must have been in business for a minumum of five years with 2005 operating revenues of at least $50,000 USD/CD and 2009 operating revenues of at least $5 million USD/CD. *Deloitte Touche Tohmatsu, 2010 Deloitte Technology Fast 500*^{TM}

Minority Business Opportunity

Austin is home to two companies which are on the Black Enterprise Auto Dealer 60 list (60 largest dealers based on gross sales): **JMC Auto Group**; **Davis Motorcars of Austin**. Criteria: company must be operational in previous calendar year and at least 51% black-owned. *Black Enterprise, B.E. 100s, 2010*

Austin is home to one company which is on the *Hispanic Business 500* list (500 largest U.S. Hispanic-owned companies based on 2009 revenue): **Tramex Travel**. Companies included must show at least 51 percent ownership by Hispanic U.S. citizens, and must maintain headquarters in one of the 50 states or Washington, D.C. *Hispanic Business, "Hispanic Business 500," June 2010*

Minority- and Women-Owned Businesses

Group	All Firms		Firms with Paid Employees			
	Firms	Sales ($000)	Firms	Sales ($000)	Employees	Payroll ($000)
Asian	3,978	4,406,130	1,300	4,272,428	10,264	272,468
Black	3,118	505,907	240	450,953	2,879	71,712
Hispanic	10,526	1,467,445	1,233	1,059,525	10,337	295,270
Women	22,702	4,060,836	3,114	3,414,864	26,603	906,128
All Firms	80,582	127,872,644	18,394	124,575,830	425,034	19,188,961

Note: Figures cover firms located in the city; minority- and women-owned business are defined as firms in which the corresponding group own 51% or more of the stock or equity of the company
Source: U.S. Census Bureau, 2007 Economic Census, Survey of Business Owners

HOTELS

Hotels/Motels

Area	5 Star		4 Star		3 Star		2 Star		1 Star		Not Rated	
	Num.	Pct.3	Num.	Pct.3	Num.	Pct.3	Num.	Pct.3	Num.	Pct.3	Num.	Pct.3
City[1]	0	0.0	16	7.3	59	26.9	117	53.4	6	2.7	21	9.6
Total[2]	119	0.7	927	5.8	4,906	30.5	7,992	49.7	526	3.3	1,625	10.1

Note: (1) Figures cover Austin and vicinity; (2) Figures cover all 100 cities in this book; (3) Percentage of hotels which are a given star rating; Star ratings are determined by expedia.com and offer an indication of the general quality of a particular hotel.
Source: expedia.com, May 5, 2011

The Austin metro area is home to one of the top 218 hotels in the U.S. according to *Travel & Leisure*: **Four Seasons Hotel, Austin** (#42). Criteria: service; location; rooms; food; and value. *Travel & Leisure, "T+L 500, The World's Best Hotels 2011"*

The Austin metro area is home to one of the top 100 hotels in the U.S. according to *Condé Nast Traveler*: **Four Seasons** (#75). The selections are based on over 25,000 responses to the magazine's annual Readers' Choice Survey. *Condé Nast Traveler, "2010 Readers' Choice Awards"*

EVENT SITES

Major Stadiums, Arenas, and Auditoriums

Name	Max. Capacity
Darrell K. Royal-Texas Memorial Stadium	100,119
Frank Erwin Center	17,829

Source: Original research

Convention Centers

Name	Overall Space (sq. ft.)	Exhibit Space (sq. ft.)	Meeting Space (sq. ft.)	Meeting Rooms
Austin Convention Center	881,400	37,170	246,097	54

Source: Original research

Living Environment

COST OF LIVING

Cost of Living Index

Composite Index	Groceries	Housing	Utilities	Trans-portation	Health Care	Misc. Goods/ Services
95.5	89.3	85.1	110.7	100.2	100.3	100.4

Note: U.S. = 100; Figures cover the Austin TX urban area.
Source: The Council for Community and Economic Research, ACCRA Cost of Living Index, 2010

Grocery Prices

Area[1]	T-Bone Steak ($/pound)	Frying Chicken ($/pound)	Whole Milk ($/half gal.)	Eggs ($/dozen)	Orange Juice ($/64 oz.)	Coffee ($/11.5 oz.)
City[2]	8.82	1.13	2.29	1.32	2.72	3.08
Avg.	9.04	1.16	2.02	1.47	3.08	3.65
Min.	6.97	0.84	1.46	0.96	2.39	2.64
Max.	13.93	2.51	3.58	3.01	4.94	6.32

Note: (1) Values for the local area are compared with the average, minimum and maximum values for all 338 areas in the Cost of Living Index; (2) Figures cover the Austin TX urban area; **T-Bone Steak** *(price per pound);* **Frying Chicken** *(price per pound, whole fryer);* **Whole Milk** *(half gallon carton);* **Eggs** *(price per dozen, Grade A, large);* **Orange Juice** *(64 oz. Tropicana or Florida Natural);* **Coffee** *(11.5 oz. can, vacuum-packed, Maxwell House, Hills Bros, or Folgers).*
Source: The Council for Community and Economic Research, ACCRA Cost of Living Index, 2010

Housing and Utility Costs

Area[1]	New Home Price ($)	Apartment Rent ($/month)	All Electric ($/month)	Part Electric ($/month)	Other Energy ($/month)	Telephone ($/month)
City[2]	231,855	925	-	97.77	116.32	24.18
Avg.	293,442	810	166.39	91.93	83.82	26.93
Min.	182,545	453	119.21	44.47	36.85	17.98
Max.	1,123,114	2,776	307.53	218.20	313.90	39.15

Note: (1) Values for the local area are compared with the average, minimum and maximum values for all 338 areas in the Cost of Living Index; (2) Figures cover the Austin TX urban area; **New Home Price** *(2,400 sf living area, 8,000 sf lot, in urban area with full utilities);* **Apartment Rent** *(950 sf 2 bedroom/1.5 or 2 bath, unfurnished, excluding all utilities except water);* **All Electric** *(average monthly cost for an all-electric home);* **Part Electric** *(average monthly cost for a part-electric home);* **Other Energy** *(average monthly cost for natural gas, fuel oil, coal, wood, and any other forms of energy except electricity);* **Telephone** *(price includes basic monthly rate for a private residential line plus additional local usage charges incurred by a family of four).*
Source: The Council for Community and Economic Research, ACCRA Cost of Living Index, 2010

Health Care, Transportation, and Other Costs

Area[1]	Doctor ($/visit)	Dentist ($/visit)	Optometrist ($/visit)	Gasoline ($/gallon)	Beauty Salon ($/visit)	Men's Shirt ($)
City[2]	84.28	82.40	94.34	2.61	46.72	21.07
Avg.	89.44	78.95	87.40	2.73	31.92	24.83
Min.	57.00	54.25	48.32	2.44	19.17	13.67
Max.	149.90	136.73	174.22	3.75	62.81	47.89

Note: (1) Values for the local area are compared with the average, minimum and maximum values for all 338 areas in the Cost of Living Index; (2) Figures cover the Austin TX urban area; **Doctor** *(general practitioners routine exam of an established patient);* **Dentist** *(adult teeth cleaning and periodic oral examination);* **Optometrist** *(full vision eye exam for established adult patient);* **Gasoline** *(one gallon regular unleaded, national brand, including all taxes, cash price at self-service pump if available);* **Beauty Salon** *(woman's shampoo, trim, and blow-dry);* **Men's Shirt** *(cotton/polyester dress shirt, pinpoint weave, long sleeves).*
Source: The Council for Community and Economic Research, ACCRA Cost of Living Index, 2010

HOUSING

House Price Index (HPI)

Area	National Ranking[2]	Quarterly Change (%)	One-Year Change (%)	Five-Year Change (%)
MSA[1]	139	-1.05	-0.74	18.78
U.S.[3]	-	-0.84	-3.95	-11.45

Note: The HPI is a weighted repeat sales index. It measures average price changes in repeat sales or refinancings on the same properties. This information is obtained by reviewing repeat mortgage transactions on single-family properties whose mortgages have been purchased or securitized by Fannie Mae or Freddie Mac in January 1975; (1) Metropolitan/Micropolitan Statistical Area - see Appendix B for areas included; (2) Rankings are based on annual percentage change for all metro areas containing at least 15,000 transactions over the last 10 years and ranges from 1 to 309; (3) figures based on a weighted average of Census Division estimates; all figures are for the period ending December 31, 2010
Source: Federal Housing Finance Agency, House Price Index, February 24, 2011

House Price Valuations

Area	Q4 2005 Price ($000)	Q4 2005 Over-valuation	Q4 2006 Price ($000)	Q4 2006 Over-valuation	Q4 2007 Price ($000)	Q4 2007 Over-valuation	Q4 2008 Price ($000)	Q4 2008 Over-valuation	Q4 2009 Price ($000)	Q4 2009 Over-valuation
MSA[1]	148.8	-10.8	163.3	-7.1	174.1	-4.4	177.4	-2.9	177.0	-2.2

Note: Figures show the percentage of over- or under-valuation of single family homes relative to statistically normal house values (e.g. a value of 23.6 indicates that house values are 23.6% overvalued). Statistically normal house values are based on house prices, interest rates, household incomes, population densities, and any historical premiums or discounts metropolitan areas have exhibited over time; (1) Figures cover the Austin-Round Rock, TX Metropolitan Statistical Area - see Appendix B for areas included
Source: Global Insight/PNC Financial Services Group, House Prices in America: 4th Quarter 2009 Update

Median Single-Family Home Prices

Area	2008	2009	2010P	Percent Change 2009 to 2010
MSA[1]	188.6	187.4	193.6	3.3
U.S. Average	196.6	172.1	173.2	0.6

Note: Figures are median sales prices of existing single-family homes in thousands of dollars; (p) preliminary; n/a not available; (1) Metropolitan Statistical Area - see Appendix B for areas included
Source: National Association of Realtors, Median Sales Price of Existing Single-Family Homes for Metropolitan Areas, 4th Quarter 2010

Median Apartment Condo-Coop Home Prices

Area	2008	2009	2010P	Percent Change 2009 to 2010
MSA[1]	170.2	150.9	155.5	3.0
U.S. Average	209.8	175.6	171.7	-2.2

Note: Figures are median sales prices of existing apartment condo-coop homes in thousands of dollars; (p) preliminary; n/a not available; (1) Metropolitan Statistical Area - see Appendix B for areas included
Source: National Association of Realtors, Median Sales Price of Existing Apartment Condo-Coop Homes for Metropolitan Areas, 4th Quarter 2010

Year Housing Structure Built

Area	2000 or Later	1990 -1999	1980 -1989	1970 -1979	1960 -1969	1950 -1959	1940 -1949	Before 1940	Median Year
City	17.8	15.7	22.3	21.7	9.5	6.4	3.4	3.3	1983
MSA[1]	26.6	20.7	20.1	16.3	6.4	4.6	2.4	2.9	1989
U.S.	12.5	14.0	14.2	16.5	11.4	11.3	5.8	14.3	1974

Note: Figures are percentages except for Median Year; (1) Metropolitan Statistical Area - see Appendix B for areas included
Source: U.S. Census Bureau, 2007-2009 American Community Survey 3-Year Estimates

HEALTH

Health Risk Data

Category	MSA[1] (%)	U.S. (%)
Adults who have been told they have high blood pressure	27.8	28.7
Adults who have been told they have high blood cholesterol	37.9	37.5
Adults who have been told they have diabetes[3]	5.8	8.3
Adults who have been told they have arthritis	18.6	26.0
Adults who have been told they currently have asthma	7.3	8.8
Adults who are current smokers	14.2	17.9
Adults who are heavy drinkers[4]	6.8	5.1
Adults who are binge drinkers[5]	20.4	15.8
Adults who are overweight (BMI 25.0 - 29.9)	34.6	36.2
Adults who are obese (BMI 30.0 - 99.8)	26.6	26.9
Adults who participated in any physical activities in the past month	81.8	76.2
Adults 50+ who have ever had a sigmoidoscopy or colonoscopy[2]	67.4	62.2
Women 40+ who have had a mammogram within the past two years[2]	81.4	76.0
Adults age 18–64 who have any kind of health care coverage	81.4	83.1

Note: Data as of 2009 unless otherwise noted; (1) Figures cover the Austin-Round Rock, TX Metropolitan Statistical Area - see Appendix B for areas included; (2) Data as of 2008; (3) Figures do not include pregnancy-related, borderline, or pre-diabetes; (4) Heavy drinkers are classified as males having more than two drinks per day or females having more than one drink per day; (5) Binge drinkers are classified as males having five or more drinks on one occasion or females having four or more drinks on one occasion
Source: Centers for Disease Control and Prevention, Behaviorial Risk Factor Surveillance System, SMART: Selected Metropolitan/Micropolitan Area Risk Trends, 2008, 2009

Mortality Rates for the Top 10 Causes of Death in the U.S.

ICD-10[a] Sub-Chapter	ICD-10[a] Code	Age-Adjusted Mortality Rate[1] per 100,000 population	
		County[2]	U.S.
Malignant neoplasms	C00-C97	159.4	180.9
Ischaemic heart diseases	I20-I25	103.9	135.0
Other forms of heart disease	I30-I51	40.7	50.0
Cerebrovascular diseases	I60-I69	47.9	44.1
Chronic lower respiratory diseases	J40-J47	36.5	41.5
Other degenerative diseases of the nervous system	G30-G31	28.5	23.6
Diabetes mellitus	E10-E14	19.7	23.5
Other external causes of accidental injury	W00-X59	25.3	23.5
Organic, including symptomatic, mental disorders	F01-F09	41.9	22.2
Influenza and pneumonia	J09-J18	13.2	18.1

Note: (a) ICD-10 = International Classification of Diseases 10th Revision; (1) Mortality rates are a three year average covering 2005-2007; (2) Figures cover Travis County
Source: Centers for Disease Control and Prevention, National Center for Health Statistics. Compressed Mortality File 1999-2007. CDC WONDER On-line Database, compiled from Compressed Mortality File 1999-2007 Series 20 No. 2M, 2010.

Mortality Rates for Selected Causes of Death

ICD-10[a] Sub-Chapter	ICD-10[a] Code	Age-Adjusted Mortality Rate[1] per 100,000 population	
		County[2]	U.S.
Assault	X85-Y09	2.7	6.0
Human immunodeficiency virus (HIV) disease	B20-B24	4.1	4.0
Hypertensive diseases	I10-I15	16.9	18.0
Intentional self-harm	X60-X84	11.9	11.0
Malnutrition	E40-E46	*0.7	0.8
Obesity and other hyperalimentation	E65-E68	1.2	1.5
Transport accidents	V01-V99	11.6	15.6
Viral hepatitis	B15-B19	2.5	2.1

Note: (a) ICD-10 = International Classification of Diseases 10th Revision; (1) Mortality rates are a three year average covering 2005-2007; (2) Figures cover Travis County; (*) Unreliable data as per CDC
Source: Centers for Disease Control and Prevention, National Center for Health Statistics. Compressed Mortality File 1999-2007. CDC WONDER On-line Database, compiled from Compressed Mortality File 1999-2007 Series 20 No. 2M, 2010.

Distribution of Physicians and Dentists

Area[1]	Dentists[2]	D.O.[3]	M.D.[4]				
			Total	Family/ General Practice	Pediatrics	Medical Specialties	Surgical Specialties
Local (number)	440	124	2,261	286	174	769	516
Local (rate[5])	4.5	1.2	22.6	2.9	1.7	7.7	5.2
U.S. (rate[5])	4.5	1.9	18.3	2.5	1.4	6.8	4.1

Note: Data as of 2008 unless noted; (1) Local data covers Travis County; (2) Data as of 2007; (3) Doctor of Osteopathic Medicine; (4) Includes active, non-federal, patient-care, office-based Doctors of Medicine; (5) rate per 10,000 population
Source: Area Resource File (ARF). 2009-2010 Release. U.S. Department of Health and Human Services, Health Resources and Services Administration, Bureau of Health Professions, Rockville, MD, August 2010

Hospitals

Austin has the following hospitals: 9 general medical and surgical; 2 psychiatric; 2 rehabilitation; 1 orthopedic; 2 long-term acute care; 1 other specialty; 1 children's general; 1 children's other specialty.
AHA Guide to the Healthcare Field 2010

EDUCATION

Public School District Statistics

District Name	Schls	Pupils	Pupil/ Teacher Ratio	Minority Pupils[1] (%)	Free Lunch Eligible[2] (%)	IEP[3] (%)
Austin ISD	120	83,483	14.2	74.3	54.5	9.4
Eanes ISD	9	7,346	13.3	18.8	1.7	8.0
Lake Travis ISD	9	6,145	14.8	21.9	10.2	7.9

Note: Table includes school districts with 2,000 or more students; (1) Percentage of students that are not non-Hispanic white; (2) Percentage of students that are eligible for the free lunch program; (3) Percentage of students that have an Individualized Education Program.
Source: U.S. Department of Education, National Center for Education Statistics, Common Core of Data, Local Education Agency (School District) Universe Survey: School Year 2008-2009; U.S. Department of Education, National Center for Education Statistics, Common Core of Data, Public Elementary/Secondary School Universe Survey: School Year 2008-2009

Top Public High Schools

High School Name	Index[1]	Rank[1]	Subsidized Lunch (%)[2]	E&E (%)[3]
James Bowie	1.785	869	15.0	37.2
L. C. Anderson[4]	2.721	327	22.0	38.7
Lake Travis	1.740	914	11.6	45.0
Liberal Arts and Science Academy	5.077	54	25.0	93.9
McCallum	1.669	986	38.0	27.7
McNeil	2.179	596	19.0	42.4
NYOS (Not Your Ordinary School) Charter	1.348	1317	40.0	18.5
Stephen F. Austin	1.673	983	36.0	28.5
W. Charles Akins	1.304	1366	65.0	13.3
Westlake	4.887	59	2.0	64.6
Westwood[4]	4.145	91	11.0	63.8

Note: (1) Public schools are ranked according to a ratio that is the number of Advanced Placement, International Baccalaureate, and/or Cambridge tests taken by all students at a school in 2009 divided by the number of graduating seniors. All of the schools on the list have an index of at least 1.000; they are in the top six percent of public schools measured this way. The rankings range from 1 to 1,734; (2) Percentage of students receiving federally subsidized meals; (3) E & E stands for equity and excellence percentage: the portion of all graduating seniors at a school that had at least one passing grade on one AP or IB test; (4) Schools that offer International Baccalaureate or Cambridge exams; (5) School is unranked, but has been identified by Newsweek as one of the nation's most elite public high schools.
Source: Newsweek Online, "Top High Schools 2010"

Highest Level of Education

Area	Less than H.S.	H.S. Diploma	Some College, No Deg.	Associate Degree	Bachelors Degree	Masters Degree	Profess. School Degree	Doctorate Degree
City	15.9	16.8	18.9	5.6	26.1	11.1	3.0	2.5
MSA[1]	13.7	20.2	21.3	6.6	24.7	9.4	2.3	1.8
U.S.	15.3	29.0	20.7	7.5	17.4	7.0	1.9	1.1

Note: Figures are 2010 estimated percentages and cover persons age 25 and over; (1) Metropolitan Statistical Area - see Appendix B for areas included
Source: Claritas, Inc.

Educational Attainment by Race

Area	High School Graduate (%)					Bachelor's Degree (%)				
	Total	White	Black	Asian	Hisp.[2]	Total	White	Black	Asian	Hisp.[2]
City	84.0	96.2	83.1	92.5	59.3	43.3	57.6	20.7	71.1	16.9
MSA[1]	86.3	95.6	85.5	91.4	63.0	38.4	47.7	21.3	66.9	15.7
U.S.	84.9	90.0	80.7	85.5	60.7	27.8	30.9	17.5	49.7	12.7

Note: Figures shown cover persons 25 years old and over; (1) Metropolitan Statistical Area - see Appendix B for areas included; (2) people of Hispanic origin can be of any race
Source: U.S. Census Bureau, 2007-2009 American Community Survey 3-Year Estimates

School Enrollment by Grade and Control

Area	Preschool (%)		Kindergarten (%)		Grades 1 - 4 (%)		Grades 5 - 8 (%)		Grades 9 - 12 (%)	
	Public	Private	Public	Private	Public	Private	Public	Private	Public	Private
City	56.9	43.1	91.7	8.3	91.9	8.1	92.1	7.9	93.2	6.8
MSA[1]	49.9	50.1	90.8	9.2	92.2	7.8	91.9	8.1	93.4	6.6
U.S.	54.3	45.7	86.4	13.6	88.9	11.1	89.1	10.9	90.2	9.8

Note: Figures shown cover persons 3 years old and over; (1) Metropolitan Statistical Area - see Appendix B for areas included
Source: U.S. Census Bureau, 2007-2009 American Community Survey 3-Year Estimates

Average Salaries of Public School Classroom Teachers

Area	2009-10		2010-11		Percent Change 2009-10 to 2010-11	Percent Change 2000-01 to 2010-11
	Dollars	Rank[1]	Dollars	Rank[1]		
Texas	48,261	31	48,261	34	0.00	25.8
U.S. Average	55,202	-	56,069	-	1.57	29.3

Note: (1) State rank ranges from 1 to 51 where 1 indicates highest salary.
Source: National Education Association, Rankings & Estimates: Rankings of the States 2010 and Estimates of School Statistics 2011, December 2010

Higher Education

Four-Year Colleges			Two-Year Colleges			Medical Schools[1]	Law Schools[2]	Voc/ Tech[3]
Public	Private Non-profit	Private For-profit	Public	Private Non-profit	Private For-profit			
1	6	7	1	0	6	0	1	10

Note: Figures cover institutions located within the city limits and include main campuses only; (1) includes schools accredited by the Liaison Committee on Medical Education and the American Osteopathic Association; (2) includes American Bar Association-accredited law schools; (3) includes all schools with programs that are less than 2 years.
Source: National Center for Education Statistics, Integrated Postsecondary Education System (IPEDS) Peer Analysis System, 2010-11; U.S. News & World Report, Medical School Directory, 2011; U.S. News & World Report, Law School Directory, 2011

According to *U.S. News & World Report,* the Austin-Round Rock, TX Metropolitan Statistical Area is home to one of the top 197 national universities in the U.S.: **University of Texas—Austin** (#45). The rankings are based on quantitative measurements such as peer assessment, retention, faculty resources, student selectivity, financial resources, graduation rate, and alumni giving rate. *U.S. News & World Report, "America's Best Colleges 2011"*

According to *U.S. News & World Report,* the Austin-Round Rock, TX Metropolitan Statistical Area is home to one of the top 189 liberal arts colleges in the U.S.: **Southwestern University** (#62). The rankings are based on quantitative measurements such as peer assessment, retention, faculty resources, student selectivity, financial resources, graduation rate, and alumni giving rate. *U.S. News & World Report, "America's Best Colleges 2011"*

According to *U.S. News & World Report,* the Austin-Round Rock, TX Metropolitan Statistical Area is home to one of the top 50 law schools in the U.S.: **University of Texas—Austin** (#14). The rankings are based on a weighted average of 10 measures of quality: peer assessment score; assessment score by lawyers/judges; median LSAT scores; median undergrad GPA; acceptance rate; employment rates for graduates; bar passage rate; faculty resources; expenditures per student; student/faculty ratio; and library resources. *U.S. News & World Report, "America's Best Law Schools 2011"*

According to *Forbes,* the Austin-Round Rock, TX Metropolitan Statistical Area is home to one of the top 75 business schools in the U.S.: **Texas-Austin (McCombs)** (#11). The rankings are based on the return on investment that graduates of the Class of 2004 received (median salary five years after graduation). *Forbes, "Best Business Schools," August 5, 2009*

PRESIDENTIAL ELECTION

2008 Presidential Election Results

Area	Obama	McCain	Nader	Other
Travis County	63.5	34.3	0.2	2.0
U.S.	52.9	45.6	0.6	0.9

Note: Results are percentages and may not add to 100% due to rounding
Source: Dave Leip's Atlas of U.S. Presidential Elections, www.uselectionatlas.org

EMPLOYERS

Major Employers

Company Name	Industry	Type of Site
3M	Paper; coated and laminated, nec	Branch
Attorney General Texas	Legal counsel and prosecution	Branch
Center for Subsurface Modeling	Elementary and secondary schools	Branch
Compliance Center	Finance, taxation, and monetary policy	Branch
Dell	Computer and software stores	Branch
Department Mechanical Engrg	Colleges and universities	Branch
Eltech	Computer peripheral equipment, nec	Single
Envirnmntal Qlty Texas Comm On	Air, water, and solid waste management	Headquarters
Freescale Semiconductor	Commercial physical research	Branch
Freescale Semiconductor	Semiconductors and related devices	Headquarters
Gracywoods Nursing Center	Nursing and personal care, nec	Single
H H S	Building maintenance services, nec	Single
H H S C	Administration of public health programs	Headquarters
Lieutenant Governor Office	Legislative bodies	Headquarters
Nextel	Radiotelephone communication	Single
Public Safety Texas Department	Police protection	Headquarters
State Farm Insurance	Fire, marine, and casualty insurance	Branch
UT Utilities & Energy Man	Electric services	Branch
Workforce Commission Texas	Regulation, miscellaneous commercial sectors	Headquarters

Note: Companies shown are located within the Austin metropolitan area; nec = not elsewhere classified.
Source: www.zapdata.com, January 2011

Best Companies to Work For

National Instruments; Whole Foods Market, headquartered in Austin, are among the "100 Best Companies to Work For." To pick the 100 Best Companies to Work For, *Fortune* partnered with the Great Place to Work Institute. Three hundred eleven companies participated in this year's survey. Most of a company's score (two-thirds) is based on the results of the Institute's Trust Index survey, which is sent to a random sample of employees from each company. The survey asks questions related to their attitudes about management's credibility, job satisfaction, and camaraderie. The other third of the scoring is based on the company's responses to the Institute's Culture Audit, which includes detailed questions about pay and benefit programs, and a series of open-ended questions about hiring practices, internal communication, training, recognition programs, and diversity efforts. Any company that is at least seven years old with more than 1,000 U.S. employees is eligible. *Fortune, "100 Best Companies to Work For," February 7, 2011*

PUBLIC SAFETY

Crime Rate

Area	All Crimes	Violent Crimes				Property Crimes		
		Murder	Forcible Rape	Robbery	Aggrav. Assault	Burglary	Larceny -Theft	Motor Vehicle Theft
City	6,768.8	2.9	34.5	184.0	302.0	1,138.3	4,818.7	288.6
Suburbs[1]	2,420.3	2.0	20.3	27.2	169.3	496.5	1,617.1	87.9
Metro[2]	4,380.9	2.4	26.7	97.9	229.1	785.9	3,060.6	178.4
U.S.	3,465.5	5.0	28.7	133.0	262.8	716.3	2,060.9	258.8

Note: Figures are crimes per 100,000 population; (1) All areas within the metro area that are located outside the city limits; (2) Metropolitan Statistical Area - see Appendix B for areas included
Source: FBI Uniform Crime Reports, 2009

Hate Crimes

Area	Number of Quarters Reported	Bias Motivation				
		Race	Religion	Sexual Orientation	Ethnicity	Disability
City	4	3	1	4	3	0

Source: Federal Bureau of Investigation, Hate Crime Statistics 2009

Identity Theft Consumer Complaints

Area	Complaints	Complaints per 100,000 Population	Rank[2]
MSA[1]	1,284	80.3	150
U.S.	250,854	81.3	-

Note: (1) Metropolitan Statistical Area - see Appendix B for areas included; (2) Rank ranges from 1 to 384 where 1 indicates greatest number of complaints per 100,000 population
Source: Federal Trade Commission, Consumer Sentinel Network Data Book for January - December 2010

RECREATION

Culture

Dance[1]	Theatre[1]	Instrumental Music[1]	Vocal Music[1]	Series/ Festivals	Museums	Zoos and Aquariums[2]
3	7	3	2	5	17	0

Note: (1) Number of professional performing groups; (2) AZA-accredited
Source: The Grey House Performing Arts Directory, 2011-2012; Official Museum Directory, 2010; American Association of Museums, AAM Member Museums, March 2011; Association of Zoos & Aquariums, AZA Member Zoos & Aquariums, May 2011

Professional Sports Teams

Team Name	League
No teams are located in the metro area	

Source: Original research

CLIMATE

Average and Extreme Temperatures

Temperature	Jan	Feb	Mar	Apr	May	Jun	Jul	Aug	Sep	Oct	Nov	Dec	Yr.
Extreme High (°F)	90	97	98	98	100	105	109	106	104	98	91	90	109
Average High (°F)	60	64	72	79	85	91	95	96	90	81	70	63	79
Average Temp. (°F)	50	53	61	69	75	82	85	85	80	70	60	52	69
Average Low (°F)	39	43	50	58	65	72	74	74	69	59	49	41	58
Extreme Low (°F)	-2	7	18	35	43	53	64	61	47	32	20	4	-2

Note: Figures cover the years 1948-1990
Source: National Climatic Data Center, International Station Meteorological Climate Summary, 9/96

Average Precipitation/Snowfall/Humidity

Precip./Humidity	Jan	Feb	Mar	Apr	May	Jun	Jul	Aug	Sep	Oct	Nov	Dec	Yr.
Avg. Precip. (in.)	1.6	2.3	1.8	2.9	4.3	3.5	1.9	1.9	3.3	3.5	2.1	1.9	31.1
Avg. Snowfall (in.)	1	Tr	Tr	0	0	0	0	0	0	0	Tr	Tr	1
Avg. Rel. Hum. 6am (%)	79	80	79	83	88	89	88	87	86	84	81	79	84
Avg. Rel. Hum. 3pm (%)	53	51	47	50	53	49	43	42	47	47	49	51	48

Note: Figures cover the years 1948-1990; Tr = Trace amounts (<0.05 in. of rain; <0.5 in. of snow)
Source: National Climatic Data Center, International Station Meteorological Climate Summary, 9/96

Weather Conditions

Temperature			Daytime Sky			Precipitation		
10°F & below	32°F & below	90°F & above	Clear	Partly cloudy	Cloudy	0.01 inch or more precip.	0.1 inch or more snow/ice	Thunder-storms
<1	20	111	105	148	112	83	1	41

Note: Figures are average number of days per year and cover the years 1948-1990
Source: National Climatic Data Center, International Station Meteorological Climate Summary, 9/96

HAZARDOUS WASTE

Superfund Sites

Austin has no sites on the EPA's Superfund Final National Priorities List.
U.S. Environmental Protection Agency, Final National Priorities List, April 1, 2011

AIR & WATER QUALITY

Air Quality Index

Area	Percent of Days when Air Quality was...[2]				AQI Statistics	
	Good	Moderate	Unhealthy for Sensitive Groups	Unhealthy	Maximum	Median
Area[1]	76.8	22.5	0.7	0.0	106	40

Note: The Air Quality Index (AQI) is an index for reporting daily air quality. EPA calculates the AQI for five major air pollutants regulated by the Clean Air Act: ground-level ozone, particle pollution (also known as particulate matter), carbon monoxide, sulfur dioxide, and nitrogen dioxide. The AQI runs from 0 to 500. The higher the AQI value, the greater the level of air pollution and the greater the health concern. There are six AQI categories: "Good" The AQI is between 0 and 50. Air quality is considered satisfactory; "Moderate" The AQI is between 51 and 100. Air quality is acceptable; "Unhealthy for Sensitive Groups" When AQI values are between 101 and 150, members of sensitive groups may experience health effects; "Unhealthy" When AQI values are between 151 and 200 everyone may begin to experience health effects; "Very Unhealthy" AQI values between 201 and 300 trigger a health alert; "Hazardous" AQI values over 300 trigger health warnings of emergency conditions; (1) Data covers Travis County; (2) Based on 306 days with AQI data in 2008; The EPA has suspended data updates while it assesses its data systems, including AirData reports and maps.
Source: U.S. Environmental Protection Agency, AirData Report, 2008

Air Quality Index Pollutants

Area	Percent of Days when AQI Pollutant was...[2]					
	Carbon Monoxide	Nitrogen Dioxide	Ozone	Sulfur Dioxide	Particulate Matter 2.5	Particulate Matter 10
Area[1]	0.3	0.0	68.3	0.0	31.4	0.0

Note: The Air Quality Index (AQI) is an index for reporting daily air quality. EPA calculates the AQI for five major air pollutants regulated by the Clean Air Act: ground-level ozone, particle pollution (also known as particulate matter), carbon monoxide, sulfur dioxide, and nitrogen dioxide. The AQI runs from 0 to 500. The higher the AQI value, the greater the level of air pollution and the greater the health concern; (1) Data covers Travis County; (2) Based on 306 days with AQI data in 2008; The EPA has suspended data updates while it assesses its data systems, including AirData reports and maps.
Source: U.S. Environmental Protection Agency, AirData Report, 2008

Air Quality Index Trends

| Area | Trend Sites (days) | | | | | | | | All Sites (days) |
	2002	2003	2004	2005	2006	2007	2008	2009	2009
MSA[1]	8	9	8	9	13	4	2	4	5

Note: Figures are the number of days the AQI value exceeded 100 in a given year. An AQI value greater than 100 indicates that air quality would have been in the unhealthful range on that day. Data from exceptional events are included. These counts are presented in two ways. First, the counts are based on sites having an adequate record of monitoring data during the trend period (trend sites). These counts represent the relative change in the number of days with AQI values greater than 100. In the last column, the counts are based on all sites with data in the most recent year (because it is possible for a site to have data in the most recent year but not enough data to be a trend site); (1) Data covers the Austin-Round Rock, TX Metropolitan Statistical Area - see Appendix B for areas included
Source: U.S. Environmental Protection Agency, Office of Air and Radiation, Air Quality Index Information, "Number of Days with Air Quality Index Values Greater than 100 and Trend Sites, 1990-2009, and at All Sites in 2009"

Maximum Air Pollutant Concentrations

	Particulate Matter 10 (ug/m^3)	Particulate Matter 2.5 (ug/m^3)	Ozone (ppm)	Carbon Monoxide (ppm)	Sulfur Dioxide (ppm)	Nitrogen Dioxide (ppm)	Lead (ug/m^3)
MSA[1] Level	41	27	0.076	0	n/a	0.003	n/a
NAAQS[2]	150	35	0.075	9	0.140	0.053	0.15
Met NAAQS[2]	Yes	Yes	No	Yes	n/a	Yes	n/a

Note: Data from exceptional events are not included; (1) Data covers the Austin-Round Rock, TX Metropolitan Statistical Area - see Appendix B for areas included; (2) National Ambient Air Quality Standards; n/a not available
Concentrations: Particulate Matter 10 (coarse particulate) - highest second maximum 24-hour concentration; Particulate Matter 2.5 (fine particulate) - highest 98th percentile 24-hour concentration; Ozone - highest fourth daily maximum 8-hour concentration; Carbon Monoxide - highest second maximum non-overlapping 8-hour concentration; Sulfur Dioxide - highest second maximum 24-hour concentration; Nitrogen Dioxide - highest arithmetic mean concentration; Lead - maximum running 3-month average
Units: ppm = parts per million; ug/m^3 = micrograms per cubic meter
Source: U.S. Environmental Protection Agency, CBSA Factbook 2009, Air Quality Statistics by City, 2009

Drinking Water

| Water System Name | Pop. Served | Primary Water Source Type | Violations[1] | |
			Health Based	Monitoring/ Reporting
Austin Water & Wastewater	780,647	Surface	0	0

Note: (1) Based on violation data from January 1, 2010 to December 31, 2010 (includes unresolved violations from earlier years)
Source: U.S. Environmental Protection Agency, Office of Ground Water and Drinking Water, Safe Drinking Water Information System (based on data extracted May 9, 2011)

Birmingham, Alabama

Background

Lying in the South's Appalachian Ridge and Valley, Birmingham's founding reaches back to 1813, and it was named after the industrial city in England. During the Civil War, a small iron factory was developed. Realizing the potential of an area rich in iron ore and coal, businessmen founded the city in 1871. Birmingham expanded, but tragedy struck when a cholera epidemic and the economic depression of 1873 simultaneously hit the area. The city nearly collapsed.

A change in fortunes occurred in 1880 when railroads crisscrossed the area and the state's first blast furnace began spewing out iron. The decade of the 1880s saw great demands for iron, which helped expand the city's manufacturing base. The population rose so miraculously, from a few thousand in 1880 to over 100,000 in 1910, that Birmingham earned the sobriquet, the Magic City. In the early 1960s the city was the scene of dramatic developments in the civil rights movement.

Race relations have improved markedly since then, as the city's electorate in 1979 chose Richard Arrington, Jr., as its first African-American mayor, and the black middle class has expanded in recent years. The Birmingham Civil Rights Institute, a research library and exhibition center, opened in 1992, further helping to bind the city's racial wounds.

Due to its location in the mineral-rich Jones Valley, Birmingham became the most important steel and iron manufacturing site in the South in the late nineteenth century and through much of the twentieth. Atop Red Mountain to the south, as a dedication to the importance of the industry, stands a cast-iron statue, the largest in the world, of the Roman deity Vulcan, patron of ironsmiths. After a six-year closure, the rehabilitated Vulcan Park & Museum opened in 2004.

Many of the city's employees work in nearly 900 factories, producing such items as chemicals, transportation equipment, and pipe, in addition to the still important manufacture of steel and iron. The city's economy also features a large financial sector, with two major, and many smaller, banks located here, helping to rank the city as a major U.S. banking center.

Honda Corp. chose Lincoln, 45 minutes east of Birmingham, for its factory that produces Odyssey mini-vans, Pilot sport utility vehicles and Ridgeline pickup trucks. The first Odyssey rolled off the assembly line in 2001 to great success. The region's growing automobile manufacturing presence includes Mercedes-Benz U.S. International, Hyundai Motor Manufacturing and Toyota Motor Manufacturing.

Higher education in the city includes the local campus of the University of Alabama at Birmingham, the city's largest employer. In 1945, the university opened its Medical Center, which experienced great expansion in the late 1970s and early 1980s. Also located here is Samford University, Alabama's largest privately supported institution for higher learning and closely aligned with the Southern Baptist Convention.

Furthering the city's cultural life are the Birmingham Botanical Gardens, and the Birmingham Museum of Art with a wide-ranging collection of pieces from 5,000 BC to the present. The city hosts numerous cultural festivals, featuring music, film and literature. City Stages, a world-renowned music festival, is held annually on Father's Day weekend. Autumn brings about the Sidewalk Moving Picture Festival of film and the Taste of 4th Avenue Jazz Festival-held simultaneously in different neighborhoods of the Birmingham. The city has been home to the Southern Heritage Festival for nearly 50 years, a cultural festival celebrating the artistic legacy of Birmingham's African-American community.

The metropolitan area possesses a mild climate, enduring less rain than do some other parts of the state, although it is still relatively abundant. Summers tend to be hot and humid, as is expected in the Deep South. Because of its location on the edge of the Appalachian Range, however, Birmingham's winters are cooler than one would expect in a subtropical region, with temperatures ranging from freezing to moderate.

Rankings

General Rankings

- Birmingham was ranked #223 out of 375 metro areas in *Cities Ranked & Rated*. Criteria: cost of living; climate; crime; transportation; economy and jobs; education; arts and culture; health and healthcare; leisure; quality of life. *Cities Ranked & Rated, 2nd Edition, 2007*

- Birmingham was ranked #53 out of 379 metro areas in *Places Rated Almanac*. Criteria: health care; education; recreation; transportation; ambience; climate; crime; housing costs; jobs. *Places Rated Almanac, 7th Edition, 2007*

- *Men's Health Living* ranked 100 U.S. cities in terms of quality of life. Birmingham was ranked #88 and received a grade of D. Criteria: number of fitness facilities; air quality; number of physicians; male/female ratio; education levels; household income; cost of living. *Men's Health Living, Spring 2008*

Business/Finance Rankings

- A.G. Edwards ranked America's 500 top-performing communities based on their residents' personal savings and investing behavior. The Birmingham metro area ranked #500 with an index score of 94.47 (national average = 100.00). A dozen statistical factors were measured including: participation in retirement savings plans; personal debt levels; and home ownership. *A.G. Edwards, "2007 Nest Egg Index," September 12, 2007*

- Birmingham was identified as one of the "Happiest Cities to Work" by CareerBliss.com, an online community for career advancement. The city ranked #10 out of 10. CareerBliss.com conducted independent company reviews from employees all over the country to collect data on eight specific factors of workplace happiness: growth opportunities, compensation, benefits, work-life balance, career advancement, senior management, job security, and whether the employee would recommend the company to others. The numbers were combined to find an average rating of overall workplace happiness for each city. *CareerBliss.com, "Happiest and Unhappiest Cities to Work," February 1, 2011*

- *American City Business Journals* ranked America's 261 largest cities in terms of their resident's wealth. Birmingham ranked #248. Criteria: per capita income; median household income; percentage of households with annual incomes of $200,000 or more; median home value. *American City Business Journals, www.bizjournals.com, "Where the Money Is: America's Wealth Centers," August 18, 2008*

- The Birmingham metro area appeared on the Milken Institute "2010 Best Performing Metros" list. Rank: #177 out of 200 large metro areas. Criteria: job growth; wage and salary growth; high-tech output growth. *Milken Institute, "2010 Best Performing Metros"*

- *Forbes* ranked the 200 most populous metro areas in the U.S. in terms of the "Best Places for Business and Careers." The Birmingham metro area was ranked #78. Criteria: 12 metrics including costs (business and living), job growth (past and projected), income growth, educational attainment, projected economic growth, crime, cultural and recreational opportunities, net migration patterns, percentage of subprime mortgages handed out over a three-year period, and the number of highly ranked four-year colleges. *Forbes, "Best Places for Business and Careers," April 14, 2010*

Children/Family Rankings

- The Birmingham metro area was selected as one of the "Best Cities for Relocating Families" by Worldwide ERC and Primacy Relocation. The 2008 study looked at nearly 50 factors important to relocating families including: recent job growth; nearby top-ranked colleges; in-state tuition for four-year public colleges; population growth since 2000; pediatricians per 100,000 population; and a Green Living index. *Worldwide ERC and Primacy Relocation, "2008 Best Cities for Relocating Families"*

Dating/Romance Rankings

- Birmingham appeared on *Men's Health's* list of the most sex-happy cities in America. The city ranked #49 of 100. Criteria: condom sales; birth rates; sex toy sales; rates of chlamydia, gonorrhea, and syphilis. *Men's Health, "America's Most Sex-Happy Cities," October 2010*

- *Men's Health* ranked 100 U.S. cities in terms of best (and worst) marriages. Birmingham was ranked #17 (#1 = worst marriages). Criteria: rate of failed marriages; stringency of divorce laws; percentage of population who've split; number of licensed marriage and family therapists. *Men's Health, "Splitsville, USA," May 2010*

- Eli Lily and Company, in partnership with Sperling's BestPlaces, ranked the nation's 50 largest metro areas in terms of the "Most Romantic Cities for Baby Boomers." The Birmingham metro area ranked #36. Criteria: marriage and divorce rates among "baby boomers" age 45 to 60; great restaurants; dance studios; chocolate, jewelry and flower sales. *Eli Lily and Company, "Most Romantic Cities for Baby Boomers," April 20, 2007*

- The Birmingham metro area was selected as one of the "Best Cities for Relocating Singles" by Worldwide ERC and Primacy Relocation. The area ranked #47 out of the 100 largest metro areas in the U.S. Areas were selected based on the following criteria: recent job growth; recent singles population growth; overall population growth; affordable rental housing; cost-of-living index; expanded arts and recreation opportunities; ratio of single men and single women; affordability of quality higher education (including state residency requirements); diversity index; climate; population density. *Worldwide ERC and Primacy Relocation, "2008 Best Cities for Relocating Singles"*

Education Rankings

- Birmingham was identified as one of the 100 "smartest" metro areas in the U.S. The area ranked #68. Criteria: the editors rated the collective brainpower of the 100 largest metro area in the U.S based on their residents' educational attainment. *American City Business Journals, www.bizjournals.com, April 14, 2008*

- Birmingham was identified as one of "America's Brainiest Bastions" by *Portfolio.com*. The metro area ranked #112 out of 200. Portfolio.com analyzed levels of educational attainment in the nation's 200 largest metropolitan areas. The editors established scores for five levels of educational attainment, based on relative earning power of adult workers age 25 or older. Scores were determined by comparing the median income for all workers with the median income for those workers at a specified educational level. *Portfolio.com, "America's Brainiest Bastions," December 1, 2010*

Environmental Rankings

- The Birmingham metro area was identified as one of "America's Dirtiest Cities" by *Forbes*. The metro area ranked #7 out of 10. Criteria: short-term particulate pollution; year-round particulate pollution; ozone pollution. *Forbes, "America's Dirtiest Cities," November 16, 2010*

- Birmingham was selected as one of 22 "Smarter Cities" for energy by the Natural Resources Defense Council." Criteria: investment in green power; energy efficiency measures; conservation. *Natural Resources Defense Council, "2010 Smarter Cities," July 19, 2010*

- *American City Business Journal* ranked 43 metropolitan areas in terms of their "greenness." The Birmingham metro area ranked #38. Criteria: Forty-one metros in which *ACBJ* has business weeklies, plus Indianapolis and Cleveland, were ranked based on 20 different indicators such as adoption of green technologies, utilization of environmentally sound practices, and air and water quality. *American City Business Journals, "Green City Index," March 11, 2010*

- 100 of the largest metro areas in the U.S. were analyzed in terms of their current drought severity. The Birmingham metro area ranked #8 (#1 = driest). The rankings were based on statistics such as long-term precipitation trends and patterns and the Palmer drought indices. *Sperling's BestPlaces, www.BestPlaces.net, "America's Drought-Riskiest Cities," November 2007*

- The Birmingham metro area appeared in *Country Home's* "Best Green Places" report. The area ranked #320 out of 379. Criteria: official energy policies; green power; green buildings; availability of fresh, locally grown food. *Country Home, "Best Green Places," 2008*

- Birmingham was highlighted as one of the 25 metro areas most polluted by short-term particle pollution (24-hour PM 2.5) in the U.S. The area ranked #8. *American Lung Association, State of the Air 2011*

- Birmingham was highlighted as one of the 25 metro areas most polluted by year-round particle pollution (Annual PM 2.5) in the U.S. The area ranked #8. *American Lung Association, State of the Air 2011*

- Birmingham was highlighted as one of the 25 most ozone-polluted metro areas in the U.S. The area ranked #21. *American Lung Association, State of the Air 2011*

Health/Fitness Rankings

- Birmingham was identified as a "2011 Asthma Capital." The area ranked #14 out of the nation's 100 largest metropolitan areas. Twelve factors were used to identify the most challenging places to live for people with asthma: estimated prevalence; self-reported prevalence; crude death rate for asthma; annual pollen score; annual air quality; public smoking laws; number of board-certified asthma specialists; school inhaler access laws; rescue medication use; controller medication use; uninsured rate; poverty rate. *Asthma and Allergy Foundation of America, "2011 Asthma Capitals"*

- Birmingham was identified as a 2009 "Spring Allergy Capital." The area ranked #14 out of 100. Three groups of factors were used to identify the most severe cities for people with allergies during the spring season: annual pollen levels; medicine utilization; access to board-certified allergists. *Asthma and Allergy Foundation of America, "Spring Allergy Capitals 2009"*

- Birmingham was identified as a 2010 "Fall Allergy Capital." The area ranked #18 out of 100. Three groups of factors were used to identify the most severe cities for people with allergies during the fall season: annual pollen levels; medicine utilization; access to board-certified allergists. *Asthma and Allergy Foundation of America, "Fall Allergy Capitals 2010"*

- *Men's Health* examined 100 U.S. cities and selected the best and worst cities for men. Birmingham was ranked among the ten worst at #3. Criteria: dozens of statistical parameters of long life in the categories of health, quality of life, and fitness. *Men's Health, "The 10 Best and Worst Cities for Men 2011," January/February 2011*

- *Men's Health* examined 100 U.S. cities and selected the best and worst cities for women. Birmingham was ranked among the ten worst at #6. Criteria: dozens of statistical parameters of long life in the categories of health, quality of life, and fitness. *Men's Health, "The 10 Best and Worst Cities for Women 2011," January/February 2011*

- *Men's Health* ranked 100 U.S. cities in terms of the quality of their tap water. Birmingham was ranked #12 and received a grade of B. Criteria: levels of total coliform bacteria, arsenic, lead, total trihalomethanes (linked to cancer), and halo-acetic acids; number of EPA water-system violations from 1995 to 2005. *Men's Health, March 2007*

- Ortho-McNeil Neurologics, in partnership with Sperling's BestPlaces, analyzed 110 metro areas and identified those U.S. cities with the highest prevalence of factors that are most commonly associated with migraine headaches. The Birmingham metro area ranked #11. Criteria: number of migraine-related drug prescriptions per capita; lifestyle factors that can contribute to migraines; environmental factors that can trigger migraines; and consumption of migraine-triggering foods. *Ortho-McNeil Neurologics, "America's Migraine Hot Spots," March 14, 2006*

- *Men's Health* ranked 100 U.S. cities in terms of cities "Where the Food is Sickening." Birmingham was ranked #26 and received a grade of C+. The magazine arrived at their ratings by looking at data compiled by the Community Health Status Indicator Project to determine outbreaks of E. coli, salmonella-, and shigella-related infections. They then checked the CDC's Wonder database to see how many people died from tainted food. Finally, the magazine found out which states have adopted the current version of the FDA's uniform Food Code, which contains the most up-to-date rules for keeping restaurant kitchens clean. *Men's Health, October 2005*

- The Birmingham metro area was identified as one of "America's Most Obese Cities" by *Forbes*. The magazine analyzed BMI (body mass index) data from the CDC in the 50 most populated metro areas in the U.S. and ranked the top 20. The area ranked #2. *Forbes, "America's Most Obese Cities," November 26, 2007*

- The Birmingham metro area appeared in the 2010 Gallup-Healthways Well-Being Index. The index, based on interviews with more than 353,000 Americans during 2009, asked individuals to assess their jobs, finances, physical health, emotional state of mind and communities. The metro area ranked #117 out of 162. Criteria: life evaluation; emotional health; work environment; physical health; healthy behaviors; basic access (basic needs optimal for a healthy life, such as access to food and medicine, having health insurance and feeling safe while walking at night). *Gallup-Healthways, "Well-Being Index 2010"*

- The Birmingham metro area was identified as one of "America's 20 Most Sedentary Cities" by *Forbes*. The metro area ranked #5. Criteria: percentage of overweight or obese people; percentage of people who had not engaged in any physical activity in the past 30 days; average number of hours of TV watched per week. *Forbes.com, "America's Most Sedentary Cities," October 29, 2007*

- 50 of the largest metro areas in the U.S. were analyzed in terms of their health and fitness by the American College of Sports Medicine in their "American Fitness Index." The Birmingham metro area ranked #49 (#1 = healthiest). Criteria: preventative health behaviors; levels of chronic disease; health care access; community resources and policies that support physical activity. *American College of Sports Medicine, "Health and Community Fitness Status of the 50 Largest Metropolitan Areas," May 24, 2010*

- Birmingham was selected as one of the "20 Most Livable U.S. Cities for Wheelchair Users" by the Christopher & Dana Reeve Foundation. The city ranked #7. Criteria: Medicaid eligibility and spending; access to physicians and rehabilitation facilities; access to fitness facilities and recreation; access to paratransit; percentage of people living with disabilities who are employed; clean air; climate. *Christopher & Dana Reeve Foundation, "20 Most Livable U.S. Cities for Wheelchair Users," July 26, 2010*

- *The Daily Beast* identified the 30 U.S metro areas with the worst smoking habits. The Birmingham metro area ranked #8. Sixty urban centers with populations of more than one million were ranked based on the following criteria: number of smokers; number of cigarettes smoked per day; fewest attempts to quit. *The Daily Beast, "30 Cities With Smoking Problems," January 3, 2011*

Real Estate Rankings

- *Fortune* ranked the 100 largest metro areas in the U.S. in terms of projected median home price change in 2010. The Birmingham metro area ranked #3. *Fortune, "The 2010 Housing Outlook," December 9, 2009*

- Birmingham appeared on ApartmentRatings.com "Top Cities for Renters" list in 2009." The area ranked #67. Overall satisfaction ratings were ranked using thousands of user submitted scores for hundreds of apartment complexes located in the 100 most populated U.S. municipalities. *ApartmentRatings.com, "2009 Renter Satisfaction Rankings"*

- The nation's largest metro areas were analyzed in terms of the percentage of households entering some stage of foreclosure in 2010. The Birmingham metro area ranked #103 out of 206 (#1 = highest foreclosure rate). *RealtyTrac, 2010 Year-End Metropolitan Foreclosure Market Report, January 27, 2011*

- The Birmingham metro area appeared in a *Wall Street Journal* article ranking cities by "housing stress." The metro area was ranked #31 (#1 = most stress). Criteria: fraction of mortgage-holding homeowners with a monthly housing payment in excess of 30 percent of income; percentage of people without health insurance; unemployment rate. *The Wall Street Journal, "Which Cities Face Biggest Housing Risk," October 5, 2010*

- The Center for Housing Policy ranked 210 U.S metropolitan areas by the fair market rent for a two-bedroom unit. The Birmingham metro area was ranked #144. (#1 = most expensive) with a rent of $735. Criteria: Fair Market Rent (FMR) in effect during the fourth quarter of 2009 based on HUD's fiscal year 2010 FMRs. *The Center for Housing Policy, "Paycheck to Paycheck: Most to Least Expensive Rental Markets in 2009"*

Safety Rankings

- Allstate ranked the 200 largest cities in America in terms of driver safety. Birmingham ranked #17. In addition, drivers were 11.7% less likely to have had an accident compared to the national average. Allstate researchers analyzed internal property damage reported claims over a two-year period (from January 2007 to December 2008) to ensure the findings would not be affected by external influences such as weather or road construction. A weighted average of the two-year numbers determined the annual percentages. The report defines an auto crash as any collision resulting in a property damage claim. *Allstate, "The 2010 Allstate America's Best Drivers Report™"*

- Birmingham was identified as one of America's "11 Most Dangerous Cities" by *U.S. News*. The city ranked #3. Criteria: crime risk was calculated using the most recent seven years (2003-2009) of FBI crime reporting data. The data includes both property crimes and violent crimes. *U.S. News & World Report, "The 11 Most Dangerous Cities," February 16, 2011*

- Birmingham was identified as one of the most dangerous mid-size cities in America by CQ Press. All 234 cities with populations of 100,000 to 499,999 that reported crime rates in 2009 for murder, rape, robbery, aggravated assault, burglary, and motor vehicle thefts were ranked. The city ranked #6 out of the top 10. *CQ Press, City Crime Rankings 2010-2011*

- The National Insurance Crime Bureau ranked 366 metro areas in the U.S. in terms of per capita rates of vehicle theft. The Birmingham metro area ranked #60 (#1 = highest rate). Criteria: number of vehicle theft offenses per 100,000 inhabitants. *National Insurance Crime Bureau, "Hot Spots," May 17, 2010*

- The Birmingham metro area was identified as one of the "The Most Dangerous Metro Areas for Pedestrians" by Transportation for America and the Surface Transportation Policy Partnership. The metro area ranked #9 out of 52 metro areas with over 1 million residents. Criteria: area's population divided by the number of pedestrian fatalities in that area. *Transportation for America and the Surface Transportation Policy Partnership, "Dangerous by Design: Solving the Epidemic of Preventable Pedestrian Deaths (and Making Great Neighborhoods)," November 11, 2009*

Sports/Recreation Rankings

- Birmingham appeared on the *Sporting News* list of the "Best Sports Cities" for 2010. The area ranked #113 out of 402 cities in the U.S. *Sporting News* takes a 12-month snapshot, roughly October to October, of each city's sports, putting a heavy premium on regular-season won-lost records (from the most recently completed season). Other criteria include: playoff berths, bowl appearances and tournament bids; championships; applicable power ratings; quality of competition; overall fan fervor as measured in part by attendance as percentage of venue capacity; abundance of teams (rewarding quality over quantity); stadium and arena quality; ticket availability and prices; franchise ownership; and marquee appeal of athletes. *Sporting News, "Best Sports Cities 2010," October, 2010*

- Scarborough Sports Marketing, a leading market research firm, identified the Birmingham DMA (Designated Market Area) as one of the top markets for sports with more than 60% of adults reporting that they are "very" interested in any of the sports measured by Scarborough. *Scarborough Sports Marketing, October 1, 2008*

- *Golf Digest* ranked 330 metro areas in the U.S. in terms of golf. The Birmingham metro area was ranked #104. Criteria: access to golf; weather; value of golf; and quality of golf. *Golf Digest, "Metro Golf Rankings," August 2005*

Transportation Rankings

- The Birmingham metro area appeared on *Forbes* list of the best and worst cities for commuters. The metro area ranked #52 out of 60 (#1 is best). Criteria: travel time; road congestion; travel delays. *Forbes.com, "Best and Worst Cities for Commuters," February 16, 2010*

Women/Minorities Rankings

● Birmingham was ranked #87 out of 100 metro areas in *SELF Magazine's* ranking of America's healthiest places for women." A panel of experts came up with more than 50 criteria including death and disease rates, environmental indicators, community resources, and lifestyle habits. *SELF Magazine, "Secrets of America's Healthiest Women," December 2008*

Miscellaneous Rankings

● Energizer Holdings, the makers of Edge® shave gel, in partnership with Sperling's BestPlaces, ranked 50 major metro areas in terms of everyday irritations. The Birmingham metro area ranked #8. Criteria: humidity levels; weather conditions; incidence of traffic delays and congestion; average commute times; frequency of flight delays and cancellations; rates of sleeplessness; underemployment; pollens and allergens; pests; comedy clubs per capita. *Energizer Holdings, "Most Irritation Prone Cities," July 23, 2010*

● Mars Chocolate North America, the makers of COMBOS®, in partnership with Sperling's BestPlaces, ranked 50 major metro areas in terms of their "manliness." The Birmingham metro area ranked #18. Criteria: number of home improvement stores, steak houses, pickup trucks, motorcycles, and manly occupations (fire fighters, police officers, construction workers, EMP personnel) per capita; salty snack sales; sports TV viewing habits. *Mars Chocolate North America, "America's Manliest Cities," June 22, 2010*

● Birmingham appeared on Procter & Gamble's list of the "Top-20 All-Time Sweatiest Cities." The city was ranked #17. The rankings are based on computer simulations of the amount of sweat a person of average height and weight would produce walking around for an hour in the average temperatures during the summer months, based on historical weather data during June, July and August from 2001-2008 for each city. *Procter & Gamble, Old Spice Press Release, "Top-20 All-Time Sweatiest Cities," July 1, 2009*

● Scarborough Research, a leading market research firm, identified the top local markets for frequent fast food restaurant patronage. The Birmingham DMA (Designated Market Area) ranked in the top 10 with consumers reporting an average of 6.5 visits within the past 30 days. *Scarborough Research, May 31, 2006*

Business Environment

CITY FINANCES

City Government Finances

Component	2008 ($000)	2008 ($ per capita)
Total Revenues	633,551	2,757
Total Expenditures	622,536	2,709
Debt Outstanding	1,306,047	5,683
Cash and Securities[1]	1,827,540	7,953

Note: (1) Cash and security holdings of a government at the close of its fiscal year, including those of its dependent agencies, utilities, and liquor stores.
Source: U.S Census Bureau, State & Local Government Finances 2008

City Government Revenue by Source

Source	2008 ($000)	2008 ($ per capita)
General Revenue		
From Federal Government	26,630	116
From State Government	7,551	33
From Local Governments	7,515	33
Taxes		
Property	62,698	273
Sales and Gross Receipts	129,732	565
Personal Income	76,918	335
Corporate Income	0	0
Motor Vehicle License	0	0
Other Taxes	167,981	731
Current Charges	31,679	138
Liquor Store	0	0
Utility	115,015	501
Employee Retirement	-16,171	-70

Source: U.S Census Bureau, State & Local Government Finances 2008

City Government Expenditures by Function

Function	2008 ($000)	2008 ($ per capita)	2008 (%)
General Direct Expenditures			
Air Transportation	0	0	0.0
Corrections	7,957	35	1.3
Education	0	0	0.0
Employment Security Administration	0	0	0.0
Financial Administration	8,637	38	1.4
Fire Protection	50,928	222	8.2
General Public Buildings	4,115	18	0.7
Governmental Administration, Other	49,272	214	7.9
Health	1,580	7	0.3
Highways	47,272	206	7.6
Hospitals	0	0	0.0
Housing and Community Development	2,279	10	0.4
Interest on General Debt	37,226	162	6.0
Judicial and Legal	7,229	31	1.2
Libraries	15,864	69	2.5
Parking	11,381	50	1.8
Parks and Recreation	40,541	176	6.5
Police Protection	71,991	313	11.6
Public Welfare	386	2	0.1
Sewerage	3,543	15	0.6
Solid Waste Management	20,854	91	3.3
Veterans' Services	0	0	0.0
Liquor Store	0	0	0.0
Utility	102,788	447	16.5
Employee Retirement	63,391	276	10.2

Source: U.S Census Bureau, State & Local Government Finances 2008

Municipal Bond Ratings

Area	Moody's	S&P	Fitch
City	Aa3	AA	AA-

Rating Systems (shown in declining order of credit quality): Moody's– Aaa, Aa, A, Baa, Ba, B, Caa, Ca, C (numerical modifiers 1, 2, and 3 are added to letter-rating); S&P– AAA, AA, A, BBB, BB, B, CCC, CC, C; Fitch– AAA, AA, A, BBB, BB, B, CCC, CC, C. Ratings may be modified by the addition of a plus or minus sign to show relative standing within the major rating categories.
Notes: n/a Not available; (1) Not reviewed; (2) Issuer Rating/No General Obligation; (3) Standard and Poor's Issue Credit Rating (ICR) is a current opinion of an obliger with respect to a specific financial obligation, a specific class of financial obligations, or a specific financial program.
Source: U.S. Census Bureau, 2011 Statistical Abstract, Bond Ratings for City Governments by Largest Cities: 2009

DEMOGRAPHICS

Population Growth

Area	1990 Census	2000 Census	2010 Estimate	2015 Projection	Population Growth (%) 2000-2010	2010-2015
City	266,532	242,820	227,529	220,329	-6.3	-3.2
MSA[1]	956,894	1,052,238	1,130,075	1,161,967	7.4	2.8
U.S.	248,709,873	281,421,906	309,038,974	321,675,005	9.8	4.1

Note: (1) Metropolitan Statistical Area - see Appendix B for areas included
Source: Claritas, Inc.

Number of Households and Average Household Size

Area	2010 Estimate	2010 Average Household Size
City	94,113	2.32
MSA[1]	449,542	2.46
U.S.	116,136,617	2.59

Note: (1) Metropolitan Statistical Area - see Appendix B for areas included
Source: Claritas, Inc.

Race and Ethnicity

Area	White Alone[2] (%)	Black Alone[2] (%)	Asian Alone[2] (%)	Other Race Alone[2] (%)	Hispanic[3] (%)
City	21.2	75.0	1.0	2.8	3.3
MSA[1]	68.0	28.1	1.1	2.8	3.4
U.S.	72.3	12.4	4.4	10.9	15.8

Note: Figures are 2010 estimates; (1) Metropolitan Statistical Area - see Appendix B for areas included (2) Alone is defined as not being in combination with one or more other races; (3) May be of any race.
Source: Claritas, Inc.

Segregation

Type	Segregation Indices[1] 1990	2000	2010	2010 Rank[2]	Percent Change 1990-2000	1990-2010	2000-2010
Black/White	70.3	69.1	65.8	16	-1.2	-4.5	-3.3
Asian/White	48.7	49.9	47.1	15	1.2	-1.6	-2.7
Hispanic/White	28.8	44.5	44.5	47	15.7	15.7	0.0

Note: Figures are based on an analysis of 1990, 2000, and 2010 Census Decennial Census tract data by William H. Frey, Brookings Institution and the University of Michigan Social Science Data Analysis Network. In this analysis all racial groups (whites, blacks, and asians) are non-Hispanic members of those races. Hispanics are shown as a separate category; All figures cover the Metropolitan Statistical Area (see Appendix B for areas included); (1) Segregation Indices are Dissimilarity Indices that measure the degree to which the minority group is distributed differently than whites aross census tracts. They range from 0 (complete integration) to 100 (complete [segregation) where the value indicates the percentage of the minority group that needs to move to be distributed exactly like whites; (2) Ranges from 1 (most segregated) to 102 (least segregated); n/a not available.
Source: www.CensusScope.org

Ancestry

Area	German	Irish	English	American	Italian	Polish	French	Scottish
City	3.2	4.5	4.5	3.5	1.0	0.5	1.0	1.5
MSA[1]	8.0	10.3	10.3	11.5	2.5	0.8	1.8	2.5
U.S.	16.6	12.0	9.1	6.1	5.9	3.3	3.1	1.9

Note: The top eight ancestries in the U.S. are shown. Figures are percentages and include multiple ancestry (e.g. if a person reported being Irish and Italian, they were included in both columns); (1) Metropolitan Statistical Area - see Appendix B for areas included
Source: U.S. Census Bureau, 2007-2009 American Community Survey 3-Year Estimates

Foreign-Born Population

Area	Any Foreign Country	Mexico	Asia	Europe	Carribean	South America	Central America[2]	Africa	Canada
City	n/a	n/a	n/a	n/a	n/a	n/a	n/a	n/a	n/a
MSA[1]	3.7	1.6	1.0	0.4	0.1	0.2	0.2	0.2	0.1
U.S.	12.5	3.8	3.4	1.6	1.1	0.8	0.9	0.5	0.3

Note: (1) Metropolitan Statistical Area - see Appendix B for areas included; (2) Excludes Mexico.
Source: U.S. Census Bureau, 2007-2009 American Community Survey 3-Year Estimates

Marriage Status

Area	Never Married	Now Married[2]	Separated	Widowed	Divorced
City	42.7	31.4	3.9	8.3	13.7
MSA[1]	28.0	50.3	2.4	7.3	12.0
U.S.	31.4	49.7	2.2	6.2	10.6

Note: Figures are percentages and cover the population 15 years of age and older; (1) Metropolitan Statistical Area - see Appendix B for areas included; (2) Excludes separated
Source: U.S. Census Bureau, 2007-2009 American Community Survey 3-Year Estimates

Age Distribution and Median Age

Area	Under Age 5	Age 5 to 17	Age 18 to 34	Age 35 to 49	Age 50 to 64	Age 65 to 79	80 Years and Over	Median Age
City	6.6	15.3	27.2	19.3	18.7	8.7	4.2	35.7
MSA[1]	6.9	17.3	23.0	21.3	18.6	9.2	3.6	37.1
U.S.	6.9	17.5	23.3	21.4	18.1	9.1	3.7	36.7

Note: (1) Metropolitan Statistical Area - see Appendix B for areas included
Source: U.S. Census Bureau, 2007-2009 American Community Survey 3-Year Estimates

Male/Female Ratio

Area	Males	Females	Males per 100 Females
City	106,257	121,272	87.6
MSA[1]	545,521	584,554	93.3
U.S.	152,401,520	156,637,454	97.3

Note: Figures are 2010 estimates; (1) Metropolitan Statistical Area - see Appendix B for areas included
Source: Claritas, Inc.

Religion

Area	Catholic	Southern Baptist	United Methodist	ELCA[1]	LDS[2]	Presbyterian Church USA	Jewish Est.	Muslim Est.
County	6.7	29.7	8.0	0.2	0.3	1.5	0.8	0.3
U.S.	22.0	7.1	3.7	1.8	1.5	1.1	2.2	0.6

Note: Figures are the number of adherents as a percentage of the total population; Adherents are defined as all members, including full members, their children and the estimated number of other participants who are not considered members (e.g. the baptized, those not confirmed, those regularly attending services, etc.);
(1) Evangelical Lutheran Church in America; (2) The Church of Jesus Christ of Latter Day Saints
Source: Reprinted with permission from Religious Congregations and Membership in the United States 2000 (Nashville, Glenmary Research Center, 2002) Copyright Association of Statisticians of American Religious Bodies. All rights reserved.

ECONOMY

Gross Metropolitan Product

Area	2006	2007	2008	2009	2009 Rank[2]
MSA[1]	51.2	53.1	54.3	54.2	49

Note: Figures are in billions of dollars; (1) Birmingham-Hoover, AL Metropolitan Statistical Area - see Appendix B for areas included; (2) Rank ranges from 1 to 363
Source: The U.S. Conference of Mayors, "Pace of Economic Recovery: GMP and Jobs," January 2010

Economic Growth

Area	2006-2008 (%)	2009 (%)	2010 (%)	Rank[2]
MSA[1]	-0.1	-1.1	2.0	271
U.S.	1.3	-2.5	2.2	–

Note: Figures are real Gross Metropolitan Product growth rates and represent annual average percent change; (1) Birmingham-Hoover, AL Metropolitan Statistical Area - see Appendix B for areas included; (2) Rank ranges from 1 to 363
Source: The U.S. Conference of Mayors, "Pace of Economic Recovery: GMP and Jobs," January 2010

Metropolitan Area Exports

Area	2005	2006	2007	2008	2009	2009 Rank[2]
MSA[1]	796.2	754.2	674.1	1,422.2	1,449.9	97

Note: Figures are in millions of dollars; (1) Birmingham-Hoover, AL Metropolitan Statistical Area - see Appendix B for areas included; (2) Rank ranges from 1 to 374
Source: U.S. Department of Commerce, International Trade Administration, Office of Trade & Industry Information, Manufacturing & Services

INCOME

Per Capita/Median/Average Income

Area	Per Capita ($)	Median Household ($)	Average Household ($)
City	19,179	32,829	44,974
MSA[1]	26,848	48,852	66,891
U.S.	27,034	52,795	71,071

Note: Figures are 2010 estimates; (1) Metropolitan Statistical Area - see Appendix B for areas included
Source: Claritas, Inc.

Household Income Distribution

Area	Percent of Households Earning							
	Under $15,000	$15,000 -24,999	$25,000 -34,999	$35,000 -49,999	$50,000 -74,999	$75,000 -99,000	$100,000 -149,999	$150,000 and up
City	24.8	14.8	13.2	16.6	15.6	7.1	5.2	2.7
MSA[1]	14.5	10.5	10.9	15.3	18.9	11.8	11.0	7.1
U.S.	12.1	10.2	10.6	15.0	19.5	12.5	12.1	8.0

Note: Figures are 2010 estimates; (1) Metropolitan Statistical Area - see Appendix B for areas included
Source: Claritas, Inc.

Poverty Rates by Age

Area	All Ages	Under 18 Years Old	18 to 64 Years Old	65 Years and Over
City	24.7	8.2	14.2	2.3
MSA[1]	13.3	4.5	7.5	1.3
U.S.	13.6	4.7	7.7	1.2

Note: Figures are percent of population with income during the previous 12 months below poverty level and only include population for whom poverty status is determined; (1) Metropolitan Statistical Area - see Appendix B for areas included
Source: U.S. Census Bureau, 2007-2009 American Community Survey 3-Year Estimates

Personal Bankruptcy Filing Rate

Area	2006	2007	2008	2009	2010
Jefferson County	6.78	7.50	7.93	8.87	8.75
U.S.	2.00	2.73	3.53	4.60	4.96

Note: Numbers are per 1,000 population and include Chapter 7 and Chapter 13 filings
Source: Federal Deposit Insurance Corporation, Regional Economic Conditions, March 17, 2011

EMPLOYMENT

Labor Force and Employment

Area	Civilian Labor Force			Workers Employed		
	Dec. 2009	Dec. 2010	% Chg.	Dec. 2009	Dec. 2010	% Chg.
City	96,666	95,172	-1.5	85,595	85,368	-0.3
MSA[1]	522,117	514,559	-1.4	473,277	472,020	-0.3
U.S.	152,693,000	153,156,000	0.3	137,953,000	139,159,000	0.9

Note: Data is not seasonally adjusted and covers workers 16 years of age and older;
(1) Metropolitan Statistical Area - see Appendix B for areas included
Source: Bureau of Labor Statistics, http://stats.bls.gov

Unemployment Rate

Area	2010											
	Jan.	Feb.	Mar.	Apr.	May	Jun.	Jul.	Aug.	Sep.	Oct.	Nov.	Dec.
City	12.1	11.6	11.4	10.9	10.9	11.5	11.6	11.7	11.2	10.9	10.8	10.3
MSA[1]	10.1	9.8	9.5	8.7	8.6	9.3	8.9	9.0	8.7	8.5	8.5	8.3
U.S.	10.6	10.4	10.2	9.5	9.3	9.6	9.7	9.5	9.2	9.0	9.3	9.1

Note: Data is not seasonally adjusted and covers workers 16 years of age and older; All figures are percentages; (1) Metropolitan Statistical Area - see Appendix B for areas included
Source: Bureau of Labor Statistics, http://stats.bls.gov

Projected Unemployment Rate

Area	2007 (%)	2009 (%)	2011 (%)	2013 (%)
MSA[1]	3.4	10.8	9.1	7.1

Note: (1) Metropolitan Statistical Area - see Appendix B for areas included
Source: The U.S. Conference of Mayors, "Pace of Economic Recovery: GMP and Jobs," January 2010

Employment by Occupation

Occupation Classification	City (%)	MSA[1] (%)	U.S. (%)
Sales and Office	27.1	28.5	25.4
Professional and Related	20.0	20.4	21.0
Service	20.6	14.8	17.2
Production, Transportation, and Material Moving	14.2	12.2	12.3
Management, Business, and Financial	9.7	13.6	14.1
Construction, Extraction, and Maintenance	8.2	10.3	9.2
Farming, Forestry, and Fishing	0.1	0.2	0.7

Note: Figures cover employed civilians 16 years of age and older;
(1) Metropolitan Statistical Area - see Appendix B for areas included
Source: U.S. Census Bureau, 2007-2009 American Community Survey 3-Year Estimates

Employment by Industry

Sector	MSA[1]		U.S.
	Number of Employees	Percent of Total	Percent of Total
Government	84,100	17.1	17.2
Education and Health Services	66,400	13.5	15.2
Professional and Business Services	59,100	12.0	13.0
Retail Trade	59,900	12.2	11.4
Leisure and Hospitality	42,200	8.6	9.7
Manufacturing	34,400	7.0	8.8
Financial Activities	36,800	7.5	5.8
Wholesale Trade	28,500	5.8	4.2
Construction	23,900	4.9	4.1
Other Services	23,400	4.8	4.1
Transportation and Utilities	20,700	4.2	3.7
Information	9,200	1.9	2.1
Mining and Logging	2,900	0.6	0.6

Note: Figures cover non-farm employment as of December 2010 and are not seasonally adjusted;
(1) Metropolitan Statistical Area - see Appendix B for areas included
Source: Bureau of Labor Statistics, http://stats.bls.gov

Occupations with Greatest Projected Employment Growth: 2006 - 2016

Occupation[1]	2006 Employment	2016 Projected Employment	Numeric Employment Change	Percent Employment Change
Retail salespersons	62,340	76,190	13,850	22.2
Registered nurses	40,320	51,850	11,530	28.6
Combined food preparation and serving workers, including fast food	46,230	57,130	10,900	23.6
Team assemblers	34,390	43,620	9,230	26.8
Office clerks, general	41,770	48,650	6,880	16.5
Janitors and cleaners, except maids and housekeeping cleaners	33,260	39,960	6,700	20.1
Waiters and waitresses	28,900	35,370	6,470	22.4
Truck drivers, heavy and tractor-trailer	41,030	47,240	6,210	15.1
Bookkeeping, accounting, and auditing clerks	31,730	37,770	6,040	19.0
Customer service representatives	22,790	28,770	5,980	26.2

Note: Projections cover Alabama; (1) Sorted by numeric employment change
Source: www.projectionscentral.com, State Occupational Projections, 2006-2016 Long-Term Projections

Fastest Growing Occupations: 2006 - 2016

Occupation[1]	2006 Employment	2016 Projected Employment	Numeric Employment Change	Percent Employment Change
Network systems and data communications analysts	2,770	4,230	1,460	52.7
Veterinary technologists and technicians	940	1,430	490	52.1
Home health aides	9,590	14,210	4,620	48.2
Medical assistants	5,230	7,750	2,520	48.2
Computer software engineers, applications	3,670	5,420	1,750	47.7
Physical therapist assistants	1,220	1,720	500	41.0
Welding, soldering, and brazing machine setters, operators, and tenders	2,940	4,090	1,150	39.1
Dental hygienists	2,860	3,970	1,110	38.8
Dental assistants	2,850	3,950	1,100	38.6
Fitness trainers and aerobics instructors	2,750	3,790	1,040	37.8

Note: Projections cover Alabama; (1) Sorted by percent employment change and excludes occupations with numeric employment change less than 250
Source: www.projectionscentral.com, State Occupational Projections, 2006-2016 Long-Term Projections

Average Wages

Occupation	$/Hr.	Occupation	$/Hr.
Accountants and Auditors	29.30	Maids and Housekeeping Cleaners	8.68
Automotive Mechanics	17.60	Maintenance and Repair Workers	16.68
Bookkeepers	16.00	Marketing Managers	47.83
Carpenters	16.90	Nuclear Medicine Technologists	28.93
Cashiers	8.45	Nurses, Licensed Practical	17.28
Clerks, General Office	10.70	Nurses, Registered	29.32
Clerks, Receptionists/Information	11.94	Nursing Aides/Orderlies/Attendants	10.69
Clerks, Shipping/Receiving	13.64	Packers and Packagers, Hand	9.24
Computer Programmers	34.26	Physical Therapists	35.41
Computer Support Specialists	22.28	Postal Service Mail Carriers	22.96
Computer Systems Analysts	33.65	Real Estate Brokers	27.08
Cooks, Restaurant	9.60	Retail Salespersons	11.51
Dentists	n/a	Sales Reps., Exc. Tech./Scientific	26.29
Electrical Engineers	39.66	Sales Reps., Tech./Scientific	33.34
Electricians	20.08	Secretaries, Exc. Legal/Med./Exec.	14.90
Financial Managers	52.31	Security Guards	10.29
First-Line Supervisors/Mgrs., Sales	17.64	Surgeons	105.78
Food Preparation Workers	8.66	Teacher Assistants	9.40
General and Operations Managers	50.35	Teachers, Elementary School	23.50
Hairdressers/Cosmetologists	16.66	Teachers, Secondary School	23.90
Internists	102.88	Telemarketers	11.42
Janitors and Cleaners	9.71	Truck Drivers, Heavy/Tractor-Trailer	19.17
Landscaping/Groundskeeping Workers	11.06	Truck Drivers, Light/Delivery Svcs.	13.84
Lawyers	63.17	Waiters and Waitresses	7.88

Note: Wage data covers the Birmingham-Hoover, AL - see Appendix B for areas included. Hourly wages for elementary/secondary school teachers and teacher assistants were calculated by the editors from annual wage data assuming a 40 hour work week; n/a not available.
Source: Bureau of Labor Statistics, Metro Area Occupational Employment and Wage Estimates, May 2009

RESIDENTIAL REAL ESTATE

Building Permits

Area	Single-Family			Multi-Family			Total		
	2009	2010	Pct. Chg.	2009	2010	Pct. Chg.	2009	2010	Pct. Chg.
City	75	110	46.7	62	347	459.7	137	457	233.6
MSA[1]	1,683	1,563	-7.1	124	361	191.1	1,807	1,924	6.5
U.S.	441,100	447,300	1.4	141,900	157,300	10.9	583,000	604,600	3.7

Note: (1) Metropolitan Statistical Area - see Appendix B for areas included; figures represent new, privately-owned housing units authorized (unadjusted data); All permit data are based on estimates with imputation.
Source: U.S. Census Bureau, Manufacturing, Mining, and Construction Statistics, Building Permits, 2009, 2010

Homeownership Rate

Area	2005 (%)	2006 (%)	2007 (%)	2008 (%)	2009 (%)	2010 (%)
MSA[1]	75.1	76.1	75.0	73.3	75.1	76.2
U.S.	68.9	68.8	68.1	67.8	67.4	66.9

Note: (1) Metropolitan Statistical Area - see Appendix B for areas included
Source: U.S. Census Bureau, Housing Vacancies and Homeownership Annual Statistics: 2010

Housing Vacancy Rates

Area	Gross Vacancy Rate[2] (%)			Year-Round Vacancy Rate[3] (%)			Rental Vacancy Rate[4] (%)			Homeowner Vacancy Rate[5] (%)		
	2008	2009	2010	2008	2009	2010	2008	2009	2010	2008	2009	2010
MSA[1]	14.3	12.9	14.8	13.2	11.4	13.5	10.6	13.1	8.8	3.3	2.2	2.3
U.S.	14.4	14.5	14.3	11.1	11.3	11.3	10.0	10.6	10.2	2.8	2.6	2.6

Note: (1) Metropolitan Statistical Area - see Appendix B for areas included; (2) The percentage of the total housing inventory that is vacant; (3) The percentage of the housing inventory (excluding seasonal units) that is year-round vacant; (4) The percentage of rental inventory that is vacant for rent; (5) The percentage of homeowner inventory that is vacant for sale; n/a not available
Source: U.S. Census Bureau, Housing Vacancies and Homeownership Annual Statistics: 2010

State Corporate Income Tax Rates

State	Tax Rate (%)	Income Brackets ($)	Num. of Brackets	Financial Institution Tax Rate (%)[a]	Federal Income Tax Ded.
Alabama	6.5	Flat rate	1	6.5	Yes

Note: Tax rates as of January 1, 2011; (a) Rates listed are the tax rates applied to financial institutions or excise taxes based on income. Some states have other taxes based upon the value of deposits or shares.
Source: Federation of Tax Administrators, "State Corporate Income Tax Rates, 2011"

State Individual Income Tax Rates

State	Tax Rate (%)	Income Brackets ($)	Num. of Brackets	Personal Exempt. ($)[1] Single	Personal Exempt. ($)[1] Dependents	Fed. Inc. Tax Ded.
Alabama	2.0 - 5.0	500 (b) - 3,001 (b)	3	1,500	500 (e)	Yes

Note: Tax rates as of January 1, 2011; Local- and county-level taxes are not included; n/a not applicable; (1) Married joint filers generally receive double the single exemption; (b) For joint returns, taxes are twice the tax on half the couple's income; (e) In Alabama, the per-dependent exemption is $1,000 for taxpayers with state AGI of $20,000 or less, $500 with AGI from $20,001 to $100,000, and $300 with AGI over $100,000.
Source: Federation of Tax Administrators, "State Individual Income Tax Rates, 2011"

Various State and Local Tax Rates

State	State and Local Sales and Use (%)	State Sales and Use (%)	Gasoline[1] (¢/gal.)	Cigarette[2] ($/pack)	Spirits[3] ($/gal.)	Wine[4] ($/gal.)	Beer[5] ($/gal.)
Alabama	10	4.00	20.9	0.43	18.94 (g)	1.70 (k)	1.05 (l)

Note: All tax rates as of January 1, 2011 except Spirits (Sept. 1, 2010); (1) The American Petroleum Institute has developed a methodology for determining the average tax rate on a gallon of fuel. Rates may include any of the following: excise taxes, environmental fees, storage tank fees, other fees or taxes, general sales tax, and local taxes. In states where gasoline is subject to the general sales tax, or where the fuel tax is based on the average sale price, the average rate determined by API is sensitive to changes in the price of gasoline. States that fully or partially apply general sales taxes to gasoline: CA, CO, GA, IL, IN, MI, NY; (2) The federal excise tax of $1.0066 per pack and local taxes are not included; (3) Rates are those applicable to off-premise sales of 40% alcohol by volume (a.b.v.) distilled spirits in 750ml containers. Local excise taxes are excluded; (4) Rates are those applicable to off-premise sales of 11% a.b.v. non-carbonated wine in 750ml containers; (5) Rates are those applicable to off-premise sales of 4.7% a.b.v. beer in 12 ounce containers; (g) States where the government controls sales. In control states, products are subject to ad valorem mark-up and excise taxes. The excise tax rate is calculated using a methodology developed by the Distilled Spirits Council of the United States; (k) Includes $0.26 statewide local rate in Alabama; (l) Includes statewide local rates in Alabama ($0.52) and Georgia ($0.53).
Source: Tax Foundation, 2011 Facts & Figures: How Does Your State Compare?

State-Local Tax Burdens

Area	Rate (%)	Rank[1]	Per Capita Taxes Paid to Home State ($)	Total State and Local Per Capita Taxes Paid ($)	Per Capita Income ($)
Alabama	8.5	40	2,029	2,967	34,911
U.S. Average	9.8	-	3,057	4,160	42,539

Note: Figures cover 2009; (1) Rank ranges from 1 to 50 where 1 is highest tax burden
Source: Tax Foundation, State-Local Tax Burdens, All States, 2009

State Business Tax Climate Index Rankings

State	Overall Rank	Corporate Tax Index Rank	Individual Income Tax Index Rank	Sales Tax Index Rank	Unemployment Insurance Tax Index Rank	Property Tax Index Rank
Alabama	28	24	18	40	10	9

Note: The index is a measure of how each state's tax laws affect economic performance. The lower the rank, the more favorable a state's tax system is for business. All ranks are for fiscal years. States without a given tax are given a ranking of 1.
Source: Tax Foundation, Tax Foundation Background Paper, No. 60, "2011 State Business Tax Climate Index"

COMMERCIAL UTILITIES

Typical Monthly Electric Bills

Area	Commercial Service ($/month)		Industrial Service ($/month)	
	3 kW demand 1,000 kWh	40 kW demand 14,000 kWh	1,000 kW demand 200,000 kWh	50,000 kW demand 15,000,000 kWh
City	153	1,545	17,199	1,107,142
Average[1]	135	1,576	23,741	1,402,202

Note: Based on total rates in effect July 1, 2010; (1) average based on 182 utilities surveyed
Source: Edison Electric Institute, Typical Bills and Average Rates Report, Summer 2010

TRANSPORTATION

Means of Transportation to Work

Area	Car/Truck/Van		Public Transportation			Bicycle	Walked	Other Means	Worked at Home
	Drove Alone	Car-pooled	Bus	Subway	Railroad				
City	79.2	14.4	2.4	0.0	0.0	0.1	2.2	0.4	1.3
MSA[1]	83.3	11.5	0.7	0.0	0.0	0.1	1.1	0.6	2.7
U.S.	75.8	10.4	2.7	1.7	0.5	0.5	2.9	1.2	4.1

Note: Figures are percentages and cover workers 16 years of age and older;
(1) Metropolitan Statistical Area - see Appendix B for areas included
Source: U.S. Census Bureau, 2007-2009 American Community Survey 3-Year Estimates

Travel Time to Work

Area	Less Than 15 Minutes	15 to 29 Minutes	30 to 44 Minutes	45 to 59 Minutes	60 to 89 Minutes	90 Minutes or More
City	25.0	49.2	19.1	3.5	2.1	1.2
MSA[1]	21.7	39.7	23.2	8.8	4.5	2.0
U.S.	28.5	36.2	19.7	7.5	5.6	2.5

Note: Figures are percentages and include workers 16 years old and over;
(1) Metropolitan Statistical Area - see Appendix B for areas included
Source: U.S. Census Bureau, 2007-2009 American Community Survey 3-Year Estimates

Travel Time Index

Area	1982	1999	2008	2009
Urban Area[1]	1.04	1.12	1.14	1.14
Average[2]	1.08	1.20	1.20	1.20

Note: Travel Time Index—the ratio of travel time in the peak period to the travel time at free-flow conditions. A value of 1.30 indicates a 20-minute free-flow trip takes 26 minutes in the peak. Free-flow speeds (60 mph on freeways and 35 mph on principal arterials) are used as the comparison threshold; (1) Covers the Birmingham-Hoover urban area; (2) average of 439 urban areas
Source: Texas Transportation Institute, Urban Mobility Report 2010, December 2010

Public Transportation

Agency Name / Mode of Transportation	Vehicles Operated in Maximum Service	Annual Unlinked Passenger Trips ('000)	Annual Passenger Miles ('000)
Birminghan-Jefferson Co. Transit Authority (MAX)			
Demand response	26	137.0	979.4
Bus	71	2,805.1	14,642.8

Note: Figures include both directly operated and purchased transportation
Source: Federal Transit Administration, National Transit Database, 2009

Air Transportation

Airport Name and Code / Type of Service	Passenger Airlines[1]	Passenger Enplanements	Freight Carriers[2]	Freight (lbs.)
Birmingham International (BHM)				
Domestic service (U.S. carriers - 2010)	30	1,442,361	16	22,423,596
International service (U.S. carriers - 2009)	7	433	0	0

Note: (1) Includes all U.S.-based major, minor and commuter airlines that carried at least one passenger during the year; (2) Includes all U.S.-based airlines and freight carriers that transported at least one pound of freight during the year
Source: Bureau of Transportation Statistics, The Intermodal Transportation Database, Air Carriers: T-100 Domestic Market (U.S. Carriers), 2010; Bureau of Transportation Statistics, The Intermodal Transportation Database, Air Carriers: T-100 International Market (U.S. Carriers), 2009

Other Transportation Statistics

Interstate highways:	I-65; I-59; I-20
Amtrak service:	Yes
Major waterways/ports:	None

Source: Amtrak.com; Google Maps

BUSINESSES

Major Business Headquarters

Company Name	Rankings	
	Fortune[1]	Forbes[2]
Brasfield & Gorrie	-	215
Drummond	-	145
Ebsco Industries	-	190
Regions Financial	293	-

Note: (1) Fortune 500—companies that produce a 10-K are ranked 1 to 500 based on 2010 revenue; (2) all private companies with at least $2 billion in annual revenue are ranked 1 to 223; companies listed are headquartered in the city; dashes indicate no ranking
Source: Fortune, "Fortune 500," May 23, 2011; Forbes, "America's Largest Private Companies," November 3, 2010

Fast-Growing Businesses

According to *Inc.*, Birmingham is home to one of America's 500 fastest-growing private companies: **South Cypress**. Criteria: must be an independent, privately-held, for-profit, U.S. corporation, proprietorship or partnership; revenues of at least $80,000 in 2006 and $2 million in 2009; four-year operating/sales history; holding companies, regulated banks, and utilities were excluded. *Inc., "America's 500 Fastest-Growing Private Companies," September 2010*

According to Deloitte, Birmingham is home to two of North America's 500 fastest-growing high-technology companies: **BioCryst Pharmaceuticals; MEDSEEK**. Companies are ranked by percentage growth in revenue over a five-year period. Criteria for inclusion: company must be headquartered within North America; company must own proprietary intellectual property or proprietary technology that contributes to a significant portion of the company's operating revenue or devotes a significant proportion of revenues to research and development of technology; company must have been in business for a minumum of five years with 2005 operating revenues of at least $50,000 USD/CD and 2009 operating revenues of at least $5 million USD/CD. *Deloitte Touche Tohmatsu, 2010 Deloitte Technology Fast 500[TM]*

Minority- and Women-Owned Businesses

Group	All Firms		Firms with Paid Employees			
	Firms	Sales ($000)	Firms	Sales ($000)	Employees	Payroll ($000)
Asian	543	188,131	194	170,267	1,307	33,082
Black	7,583	302,996	306	168,727	2,156	49,329
Hispanic	255	57,080	40	42,866	340	6,574
Women	6,347	1,372,582	698	1,252,090	7,019	250,586
All Firms	20,088	62,529,577	5,890	61,940,230	183,113	8,400,946

Note: Figures cover firms located in the city; minority- and women-owned business are defined as firms in which the corresponding group own 51% or more of the stock or equity of the company
Source: U.S. Census Bureau, 2007 Economic Census, Survey of Business Owners

HOTELS

Hotels/Motels

Area	5 Star		4 Star		3 Star		2 Star		1 Star		Not Rated	
	Num.	Pct.3	Num.	Pct.3	Num.	Pct.3	Num.	Pct.3	Num.	Pct.3	Num.	Pct.3
City[1]	0	0.0	1	0.9	0	0.0	33	28.2	79	67.5	4	3.4
Total[2]	119	0.7	927	5.8	4,906	30.5	7,992	49.7	526	3.3	1,625	10.1

Note: (1) Figures cover Birmingham and vicinity; (2) Figures cover all 100 cities in this book; (3) Percentage of hotels which are a given star rating; Star ratings are determined by expedia.com and offer an indication of the general quality of a particular hotel.
Source: expedia.com, May 5, 2011

EVENT SITES

Major Stadiums, Arenas, and Auditoriums

Name	Max. Capacity
Boutwell Municipal Auditorium	7,000
Harbert Center	1,000
Legion Field	71,594
Regions Park	16,000

Source: Original research

Convention Centers

Name	Overall Space (sq. ft.)	Exhibit Space (sq. ft.)	Meeting Space (sq. ft.)	Meeting Rooms
Birmingham Jefferson Convention Complex	320,000	100,000	220,000	74

Source: Original research

Living Environment

COST OF LIVING

Cost of Living Index

Composite Index	Groceries	Housing	Utilities	Trans-portation	Health Care	Misc. Goods/Services
90.8	93.5	73.2	105.7	93.5	87.9	100.3

Note: U.S. = 100; Figures cover the Birmingham AL urban area.
Source: The Council for Community and Economic Research, ACCRA Cost of Living Index, 2010

Grocery Prices

Area[1]	T-Bone Steak ($/pound)	Frying Chicken ($/pound)	Whole Milk ($/half gal.)	Eggs ($/dozen)	Orange Juice ($/64 oz.)	Coffee ($/11.5 oz.)
City[2]	8.04	1.10	2.14	1.50	2.82	3.29
Avg.	9.04	1.16	2.02	1.47	3.08	3.65
Min.	6.97	0.84	1.46	0.96	2.39	2.64
Max.	13.93	2.51	3.58	3.01	4.94	6.32

*Note: (1) Values for the local area are compared with the average, minimum and maximum values for all 338 areas in the Cost of Living Index; (2) Figures cover the Birmingham AL urban area; **T-Bone Steak** (price per pound); **Frying Chicken** (price per pound, whole fryer); **Whole Milk** (half gallon carton); **Eggs** (price per dozen, Grade A, large); **Orange Juice** (64 oz. Tropicana or Florida Natural); **Coffee** (11.5 oz. can, vacuum-packed, Maxwell House, Hills Bros, or Folgers).*
Source: The Council for Community and Economic Research, ACCRA Cost of Living Index, 2010

Housing and Utility Costs

Area[1]	New Home Price ($)	Apartment Rent ($/month)	All Electric ($/month)	Part Electric ($/month)	Other Energy ($/month)	Telephone ($/month)
City[2]	205,371	694	-	114.09	85.95	24.33
Avg.	293,442	810	166.39	91.93	83.82	26.93
Min.	182,545	453	119.21	44.47	36.85	17.98
Max.	1,123,114	2,776	307.53	218.20	313.90	39.15

*Note: (1) Values for the local area are compared with the average, minimum and maximum values for all 338 areas in the Cost of Living Index; (2) Figures cover the Birmingham AL urban area; **New Home Price** (2,400 sf living area, 8,000 sf lot, in urban area with full utilities); **Apartment Rent** (950 sf 2 bedroom/1.5 or 2 bath, unfurnished, excluding all utilities except water); **All Electric** (average monthly cost for an all-electric home); **Part Electric** (average monthly cost for a part-electric home); **Other Energy** (average monthly cost for natural gas, fuel oil, coal, wood, and any other forms of energy except electricity); **Telephone** (price includes basic monthly rate for a private residential line plus additional local usage charges incurred by a family of four).*
Source: The Council for Community and Economic Research, ACCRA Cost of Living Index, 2010

Health Care, Transportation, and Other Costs

Area[1]	Doctor ($/visit)	Dentist ($/visit)	Optometrist ($/visit)	Gasoline ($/gallon)	Beauty Salon ($/visit)	Men's Shirt ($)
City[2]	75.67	64.72	91.35	2.63	31.44	30.25
Avg.	89.44	78.95	87.40	2.73	31.92	24.83
Min.	57.00	54.25	48.32	2.44	19.17	13.67
Max.	149.90	136.73	174.22	3.75	62.81	47.89

*Note: (1) Values for the local area are compared with the average, minimum and maximum values for all 338 areas in the Cost of Living Index; (2) Figures cover the Birmingham AL urban area; **Doctor** (general practitioners routine exam of an established patient); **Dentist** (adult teeth cleaning and periodic oral examination); **Optometrist** (full vision eye exam for established adult patient); **Gasoline** (one gallon regular unleaded, national brand, including all taxes, cash price at self-service pump if available); **Beauty Salon** (woman's shampoo, trim, and blow-dry); **Men's Shirt** (cotton/polyester dress shirt, pinpoint weave, long sleeves).*
Source: The Council for Community and Economic Research, ACCRA Cost of Living Index, 2010

HOUSING

House Price Index (HPI)

Area	National Ranking[2]	Quarterly Change (%)	One-Year Change (%)	Five-Year Change (%)
MSA[1]	220	-0.48	-2.71	2.11
U.S.[3]	-	-0.84	-3.95	-11.45

Note: The HPI is a weighted repeat sales index. It measures average price changes in repeat sales or refinancings on the same properties. This information is obtained by reviewing repeat mortgage transactions on single-family properties whose mortgages have been purchased or securitized by Fannie Mae or Freddie Mac in January 1975; (1) Metropolitan/Micropolitan Statistical Area - see Appendix B for areas included; (2) Rankings are based on annual percentage change for all metro areas containing at least 15,000 transactions over the last 10 years and ranges from 1 to 309; (3) figures based on a weighted average of Census Division estimates; all figures are for the period ending December 31, 2010
Source: Federal Housing Finance Agency, House Price Index, February 24, 2011

House Price Valuations

Area	Q4 2005 Price ($000)	Q4 2005 Over-valuation	Q4 2006 Price ($000)	Q4 2006 Over-valuation	Q4 2007 Price ($000)	Q4 2007 Over-valuation	Q4 2008 Price ($000)	Q4 2008 Over-valuation	Q4 2009 Price ($000)	Q4 2009 Over-valuation
MSA[1]	119.0	-5.0	125.3	-4.3	125.8	-8.9	121.7	-13.2	123.3	-14.0

Note: Figures show the percentage of over- or under-valuation of single family homes relative to statistically normal house values (e.g. a value of 23.6 indicates that house values are 23.6% overvalued). Statistically normal house values are based on house prices, interest rates, household incomes, population densities, and any historical premiums or discounts metropolitan areas have exhibited over time; (1) Figures cover the Birmingham-Hoover, AL Metropolitan Statistical Area - see Appendix B for areas included
Source: Global Insight/PNC Financial Services Group, House Prices in America: 4th Quarter 2009 Update

Median Single-Family Home Prices

Area	2008	2009	2010p	Percent Change 2009 to 2010
MSA[1]	153.9	146.1	143.0	-2.1
U.S. Average	196.6	172.1	173.2	0.6

Note: Figures are median sales prices of existing single-family homes in thousands of dollars; (p) preliminary; n/a not available; (1) Metropolitan Statistical Area - see Appendix B for areas included
Source: National Association of Realtors, Median Sales Price of Existing Single-Family Homes for Metropolitan Areas, 4th Quarter 2010

Median Apartment Condo-Coop Home Prices

Area	2008	2009	2010p	Percent Change 2009 to 2010
MSA[1]	n/a	n/a	n/a	n/a
U.S. Average	209.8	175.6	171.7	-2.2

Note: Figures are median sales prices of existing apartment condo-coop homes in thousands of dollars; (p) preliminary; n/a not available; (1) Metropolitan Statistical Area - see Appendix B for areas included
Source: National Association of Realtors, Median Sales Price of Existing Apartment Condo-Coop Homes for Metropolitan Areas, 4th Quarter 2010

Year Housing Structure Built

Area	2000 or Later	1990 -1999	1980 -1989	1970 -1979	1960 -1969	1950 -1959	1940 -1949	Before 1940	Median Year
City	4.6	5.5	10.7	16.0	16.0	19.6	10.2	17.5	1962
MSA[1]	13.0	17.1	14.2	18.0	12.4	11.4	5.6	8.1	1977
U.S.	12.5	14.0	14.2	16.5	11.4	11.3	5.8	14.3	1974

Note: Figures are percentages except for Median Year; (1) Metropolitan Statistical Area - see Appendix B for areas included
Source: U.S. Census Bureau, 2007-2009 American Community Survey 3-Year Estimates

HEALTH

Health Risk Data

Category	MSA[1] (%)	U.S. (%)
Adults who have been told they have high blood pressure	37.8	28.7
Adults who have been told they have high blood cholesterol	39.5	37.5
Adults who have been told they have diabetes[3]	10.2	8.3
Adults who have been told they have arthritis	33.2	26.0
Adults who have been told they currently have asthma	8.1	8.8
Adults who are current smokers	21.8	17.9
Adults who are heavy drinkers[4]	2.8	5.1
Adults who are binge drinkers[5]	11.7	15.8
Adults who are overweight (BMI 25.0 - 29.9)	37.3	36.2
Adults who are obese (BMI 30.0 - 99.8)	31.2	26.9
Adults who participated in any physical activities in the past month	70.4	76.2
Adults 50+ who have ever had a sigmoidoscopy or colonoscopy[2]	65.7	62.2
Women 40+ who have had a mammogram within the past two years[2]	80.4	76.0
Adults age 18–64 who have any kind of health care coverage	84.8	83.1

Note: Data as of 2009 unless otherwise noted; (1) Figures cover the Birmingham-Hoover, AL Metropolitan Statistical Area - see Appendix B for areas included; (2) Data as of 2008; (3) Figures do not include pregnancy-related, borderline, or pre-diabetes; (4) Heavy drinkers are classified as males having more than two drinks per day or females having more than one drink per day; (5) Binge drinkers are classified as males having five or more drinks on one occasion or females having four or more drinks on one occasion
Source: Centers for Disease Control and Prevention, Behaviorial Risk Factor Surveillance System, SMART: Selected Metropolitan/Micropolitan Area Risk Trends, 2008, 2009

Mortality Rates for the Top 10 Causes of Death in the U.S.

ICD-10[a] Sub-Chapter	ICD-10[a] Code	Age-Adjusted Mortality Rate[1] per 100,000 population	
		County[2]	U.S.
Malignant neoplasms	C00-C97	195.4	180.9
Ischaemic heart diseases	I20-I25	104.7	135.0
Other forms of heart disease	I30-I51	96.4	50.0
Cerebrovascular diseases	I60-I69	63.5	44.1
Chronic lower respiratory diseases	J40-J47	42.0	41.5
Other degenerative diseases of the nervous system	G30-G31	28.9	23.6
Diabetes mellitus	E10-E14	30.7	23.5
Other external causes of accidental injury	W00-X59	27.1	23.5
Organic, including symptomatic, mental disorders	F01-F09	32.5	22.2
Influenza and pneumonia	J09-J18	18.3	18.1

Note: (a) ICD-10 = International Classification of Diseases 10th Revision; (1) Mortality rates are a three year average covering 2005-2007; (2) Figures cover Jefferson County
Source: Centers for Disease Control and Prevention, National Center for Health Statistics. Compressed Mortality File 1999-2007. CDC WONDER On-line Database, compiled from Compressed Mortality File 1999-2007 Series 20 No. 2M, 2010.

Mortality Rates for Selected Causes of Death

ICD-10[a] Sub-Chapter	ICD-10[a] Code	Age-Adjusted Mortality Rate[1] per 100,000 population	
		County[2]	U.S.
Assault	X85-Y09	20.7	6.0
Human immunodeficiency virus (HIV) disease	B20-B24	6.2	4.0
Hypertensive diseases	I10-I15	20.0	18.0
Intentional self-harm	X60-X84	11.1	11.0
Malnutrition	E40-E46	1.8	0.8
Obesity and other hyperalimentation	E65-E68	1.6	1.5
Transport accidents	V01-V99	20.0	15.6
Viral hepatitis	B15-B19	2.2	2.1

Note: (a) ICD-10 = International Classification of Diseases 10th Revision; (1) Mortality rates are a three year average covering 2005-2007; (2) Figures cover Jefferson County
Source: Centers for Disease Control and Prevention, National Center for Health Statistics. Compressed Mortality File 1999-2007. CDC WONDER On-line Database, compiled from Compressed Mortality File 1999-2007 Series 20 No. 2M, 2010.

Distribution of Physicians and Dentists

Area[1]	Dentists[2]	D.O.[3]	M.D.[4]				
			Total	Family/ General Practice	Pediatrics	Medical Specialties	Surgical Specialties
Local (number)	375	65	2,100	137	156	835	566
Local (rate[5])	5.7	1.0	31.7	2.1	2.4	12.6	8.5
U.S. (rate[5])	4.5	1.9	18.3	2.5	1.4	6.8	4.1

Note: Data as of 2008 unless noted; (1) Local data covers Jefferson County; (2) Data as of 2007; (3) Doctor of Osteopathic Medicine; (4) Includes active, non-federal, patient-care, office-based Doctors of Medicine; (5) rate per 10,000 population
Source: Area Resource File (ARF). 2009-2010 Release. U.S. Department of Health and Human Services, Health Resources and Services Administration, Bureau of Health Professions, Rockville, MD, August 2010

Hospitals

Birmingham has the following hospitals: 9 general medical and surgical; 1 psychiatric; 1 eye, ear, nose and throat; 1 rehabilitation; 2 long-term acute care; 1 children's general.
AHA Guide to the Healthcare Field 2010

According to *U.S. News,* the Birmingham-Hoover, AL Metropolitan Statistical Area is home to one of the best hospitals in the U.S.: **University of Alabama Hospital at Birmingham**. The hospital listed was highly ranked in at least one adult specialty. *U.S. News Online, "America's Best Hospitals 2010-11"*

According to *U.S. News,* the Birmingham-Hoover, AL Metropolitan Statistical Area is home to one of the best children's hospitals in the U.S.: **Children's Hospital of Alabama at UAB**. The hospital listed was highly ranked in at least one pediatric specialty. *U.S. News Online, "America's Best Children's Hospitals 2010-11"*

EDUCATION

Public School District Statistics

District Name	Schls	Pupils	Pupil/ Teacher Ratio	Minority Pupils[1] (%)	Free Lunch Eligible[2] (%)	IEP[3] (%)
Birmingham City	83	27,440	16.3	99.0	75.3	0.5
Jefferson County	59	36,174	16.1	45.5	31.6	0.5

Note: Table includes school districts with 2,000 or more students; (1) Percentage of students that are not non-Hispanic white; (2) Percentage of students that are eligible for the free lunch program; (3) Percentage of students that have an Individualized Education Program.
Source: U.S. Department of Education, National Center for Education Statistics, Common Core of Data, Local Education Agency (School District) Universe Survey: School Year 2008-2009; U.S. Department of Education, National Center for Education Statistics, Common Core of Data, Public Elementary/Secondary School Universe Survey: School Year 2008-2009

Top Public High Schools

High School Name	Index[1]	Rank[1]	Subsidized Lunch (%)[2]	E&E (%)[3]
Mountain Brook	2.551	387	0.0	53.4
Oak Mountain	1.661	992	6.0	28.0

Note: (1) Public schools are ranked according to a ratio that is the number of Advanced Placement, International Baccalaureate, and/or Cambridge tests taken by all students at a school in 2009 divided by the number of graduating seniors. All of the schools on the list have an index of at least 1.000; they are in the top six percent of public schools measured this way. The rankings range from 1 to 1,734; (2) Percentage of students receiving federally subsidized meals; (3) E & E stands for equity and excellence percentage: the portion of all graduating seniors at a school that had at least one passing grade on one AP or IB test; (4) Schools that offer International Baccalaureate or Cambridge exams; (5) School is unranked, but has been identified by Newsweek as one of the nation's most elite public high schools.
Source: Newsweek Online, "Top High Schools 2010"

Highest Level of Education

Area	Less than H.S.	H.S. Diploma	Some College, No Deg.	Associate Degree	Bachelors Degree	Masters Degree	Profess. School Degree	Doctorate Degree
City	17.0	29.2	24.6	7.1	13.8	5.4	1.9	1.1
MSA[1]	15.1	29.6	22.5	6.8	16.8	6.2	2.2	0.9
U.S.	15.3	29.0	20.7	7.5	17.4	7.0	1.9	1.1

Note: Figures are 2010 estimated percentages and cover persons age 25 and over; (1) Metropolitan Statistical Area - see Appendix B for areas included
Source: Claritas, Inc.

Educational Attainment by Race

Area	High School Graduate (%)					Bachelor's Degree (%)				
	Total	White	Black	Asian	Hisp.[2]	Total	White	Black	Asian	Hisp.[2]
City	82.9	88.8	81.0	n/a	57.8	21.7	38.9	13.6	n/a	18.4
MSA[1]	84.8	86.5	82.4	94.2	58.3	26.3	29.7	16.7	67.2	16.2
U.S.	84.9	90.0	80.7	85.5	60.7	27.8	30.9	17.5	49.7	12.7

Note: Figures shown cover persons 25 years old and over; (1) Metropolitan Statistical Area - see Appendix B for areas included; (2) people of Hispanic origin can be of any race
Source: U.S. Census Bureau, 2007-2009 American Community Survey 3-Year Estimates

School Enrollment by Grade and Control

Area	Preschool (%)		Kindergarten (%)		Grades 1 - 4 (%)		Grades 5 - 8 (%)		Grades 9 - 12 (%)	
	Public	Private	Public	Private	Public	Private	Public	Private	Public	Private
City	53.1	46.9	82.1	17.9	89.9	10.1	84.8	15.2	89.4	10.6
MSA[1]	41.8	58.2	84.2	15.8	90.1	9.9	89.0	11.0	87.6	12.4
U.S.	54.3	45.7	86.4	13.6	88.9	11.1	89.1	10.9	90.2	9.8

Note: Figures shown cover persons 3 years old and over; (1) Metropolitan Statistical Area - see Appendix B for areas included
Source: U.S. Census Bureau, 2007-2009 American Community Survey 3-Year Estimates

Average Salaries of Public School Classroom Teachers

Area	2009-10		2010-11		Percent Change 2009-10 to 2010-11	Percent Change 2000-01 to 2010-11
	Dollars	Rank[1]	Dollars	Rank[1]		
Alabama	47,571	33	48,282	33	1.50	30.1
U.S. Average	55,202	-	56,069	-	1.57	29.3

Note: (1) State rank ranges from 1 to 51 where 1 indicates highest salary.
Source: National Education Association, Rankings & Estimates: Rankings of the States 2010 and Estimates of School Statistics 2011, December 2010

Higher Education

Four-Year Colleges			Two-Year Colleges			Medical Schools[1]	Law Schools[2]	Voc/ Tech[3]
Public	Private Non-profit	Private For-profit	Public	Private Non-profit	Private For-profit			
1	3	4	2	0	1	1	1	1

Note: Figures cover institutions located within the city limits and include main campuses only; (1) includes schools accredited by the Liaison Committee on Medical Education and the American Osteopathic Association; (2) includes American Bar Association-accredited law schools; (3) includes all schools with programs that are less than 2 years.
Source: National Center for Education Statistics, Integrated Postsecondary Education System (IPEDS) Peer Analysis System, 2010-11; U.S. News & World Report, Medical School Directory, 2011; U.S. News & World Report, Law School Directory, 2011

According to *U.S. News & World Report*, the Birmingham-Hoover, AL Metropolitan Statistical Area is home to two of the top 197 national universities in the U.S.: **Samford University** (#104); **University of Alabama—Birmingham** (#151). The rankings are based on quantitative measurements such as peer assessment, retention, faculty resources, student selectivity, financial resources, graduation rate, and alumni giving rate. *U.S. News & World Report, "America's Best Colleges 2011"*

According to *U.S. News & World Report,* the Birmingham-Hoover, AL Metropolitan Statistical Area is home to one of the top 189 liberal arts colleges in the U.S.: **Birmingham-Southern College** (#93). The rankings are based on quantitative measurements such as peer assessment, retention, faculty resources, student selectivity, financial resources, graduation rate, and alumni giving rate. *U.S. News & World Report, "America's Best Colleges 2011"*

PRESIDENTIAL ELECTION

2008 Presidential Election Results

Area	Obama	McCain	Nader	Other
Jefferson County	52.2	47.1	0.2	0.6
U.S.	52.9	45.6	0.6	0.9

Note: Results are percentages and may not add to 100% due to rounding
Source: Dave Leip's Atlas of U.S. Presidential Elections, www.uselectionatlas.org

EMPLOYERS

Major Employers

Company Name	Industry	Type of Site
Alabama Power Company	Electric services	Headquarters
BE&K Construction Company	Industrial buildings and warehouses	Single
Bethea Power Products	Noncurrent-carrying wiring devices	Single
Birmingham V A Medical Center	Administration of veterans' affairs	Branch
Blue Cross	Accident and health insurance	Headquarters
Childrens Hospital	Specialty hospitals, except psychiatric	Headquarters
Childrens Hospital of Alabama	Specialty hospitals, except psychiatric	Branch
Community Hospices America	Skilled nursing care facilities	Single
County of Jefferson	Executive offices	Headquarters
Creative Ideas for Living	Homefurnishings	Single
Ebsco Subscription Service	Business services, nec	Headquarters
G & R Mineral Services	Building maintenance services, nec	Single
General Welding Company	Welding repair	Single
Healthsouth Medical Center	General medical and surgical hospitals	Single
Infinity Group	Insurance agents, brokers, and service	Headquarters
Naphcare	Offices and clinics of medical doctors	Single
Newspaper Holdings	Newspapers	Headquarters
Protective Life Corporation	Life insurance	Headquarters
Shelby Baptist Medical Center	General medical and surgical hospitals	Headquarters
Southern Cleaning Service	Building maintenance services, nec	Single
St Vincents East	Specialty outpatient clinics, nec	Branch
St Vincents East	General medical and surgical hospitals	Headquarters
St Vincents Health System	General medical and surgical hospitals	Headquarters
State Farm Insurance	Fire, marine, and casualty insurance	Branch
Tyson	Poultry slaughtering and processing	Branch
UPS	Courier services, except by air	Branch

Note: Companies shown are located within the Birmingham metropolitan area; nec = not elsewhere classified.
Source: www.zapdata.com, January 2011

PUBLIC SAFETY

Crime Rate

Area	All Crimes	Violent Crimes				Property Crimes		
		Murder	Forcible Rape	Robbery	Aggrav. Assault	Burglary	Larceny -Theft	Motor Vehicle Theft
City	9,223.2	28.6	87.1	505.8	615.3	2,207.4	5,078.0	701.1
Suburbs[1]	4,024.9	4.4	26.0	114.7	212.8	988.3	2,464.0	214.8
Metro[2]	5,070.2	9.3	38.3	193.3	293.7	1,233.4	2,989.6	312.5
U.S.	3,465.5	5.0	28.7	133.0	262.8	716.3	2,060.9	258.8

Note: Figures are crimes per 100,000 population; (1) All areas within the metro area that are located outside the city limits; (2) Metropolitan Statistical Area - see Appendix B for areas included
Source: FBI Uniform Crime Reports, 2009

Hate Crimes

Area	Number of Quarters Reported	Bias Motivation				
		Race	Religion	Sexual Orientation	Ethnicity	Disability
City	n/a	n/a	n/a	n/a	n/a	n/a

Note: n/a not available.
Source: Federal Bureau of Investigation, Hate Crime Statistics 2009

Identity Theft Consumer Complaints

Area	Complaints	Complaints per 100,000 Population	Rank[2]
MSA[1]	928	83.7	130
U.S.	250,854	81.3	-

Note: (1) Metropolitan Statistical Area - see Appendix B for areas included; (2) Rank ranges from 1 to 384 where 1 indicates greatest number of complaints per 100,000 population
Source: Federal Trade Commission, Consumer Sentinel Network Data Book for January - December 2010

RECREATION

Culture

Dance[1]	Theatre[1]	Instrumental Music[1]	Vocal Music[1]	Series/ Festivals	Museums	Zoos and Aquariums[2]
1	3	2	2	2	10	1

Note: (1) Number of professional performing groups; (2) AZA-accredited
Source: The Grey House Performing Arts Directory, 2011-2012; Official Museum Directory, 2010; American Association of Museums, AAM Member Museums, March 2011; Association of Zoos & Aquariums, AZA Member Zoos & Aquariums, May 2011

Professional Sports Teams

Team Name	League

No teams are located in the metro area
Source: Original research

CLIMATE

Average and Extreme Temperatures

Temperature	Jan	Feb	Mar	Apr	May	Jun	Jul	Aug	Sep	Oct	Nov	Dec	Yr.
Extreme High (°F)	81	83	89	92	99	102	106	103	100	94	84	80	106
Average High (°F)	53	58	66	75	82	88	90	90	84	75	64	56	74
Average Temp. (°F)	43	47	54	63	70	77	80	80	74	63	53	46	63
Average Low (°F)	33	36	42	50	58	66	70	69	63	51	41	35	51
Extreme Low (°F)	-6	3	2	26	36	42	51	52	37	27	5	1	-6

Note: Figures cover the years 1948-1995
Source: National Climatic Data Center, International Station Meteorological Climate Summary, 9/96

Average Precipitation/Snowfall/Humidity

Precip./Humidity	Jan	Feb	Mar	Apr	May	Jun	Jul	Aug	Sep	Oct	Nov	Dec	Yr.
Avg. Precip. (in.)	5.0	4.8	5.9	4.6	4.4	3.8	5.1	3.8	4.1	2.9	4.3	4.8	53.5
Avg. Snowfall (in.)	1	Tr	Tr	Tr	0	0	0	0	0	Tr	Tr	Tr	2
Avg. Rel. Hum. 7am (%)	82	81	78	76	76	78	81	82	81	82	82	82	80
Avg. Rel. Hum. 4pm (%)	57	53	48	46	51	54	58	55	54	50	52	58	53

Note: Figures cover the years 1948-1995; Tr = Trace amounts (<0.05 in. of rain; <0.5 in. of snow)
Source: National Climatic Data Center, International Station Meteorological Climate Summary, 9/96

Weather Conditions

Temperature			Daytime Sky			Precipitation		
10°F & below	32°F & below	90°F & above	Clear	Partly cloudy	Cloudy	0.01 inch or more precip.	0.1 inch or more snow/ice	Thunder-storms
1	57	59	91	161	113	119	1	57

Note: Figures are average number of days per year and cover the years 1948-1995
Source: National Climatic Data Center, International Station Meteorological Climate Summary, 9/96

**HAZARDOUS
WASTE**

Superfund Sites

Birmingham has no sites on the EPA's Superfund Final National Priorities List.
U.S. Environmental Protection Agency, Final National Priorities List, April 1, 2011

**AIR & WATER
QUALITY**

Air Quality Index

| Area | Percent of Days when Air Quality was...[2] | | | | AQI Statistics | |
	Good	Moderate	Unhealthy for Sensitive Groups	Unhealthy	Maximum	Median
Area[1]	35.1	60.1	4.8	0.0	150	58

*Note: The Air Quality Index (AQI) is an index for reporting daily air quality. EPA calculates the AQI for five major air pollutants regulated by the Clean Air Act: ground-level ozone, particle pollution (also known as particulate matter), carbon monoxide, sulfur dioxide, and nitrogen dioxide. The AQI runs from 0 to 500. The higher the AQI value, the greater the level of air pollution and the greater the health concern. There are six AQI categories: "Good" The AQI is between 0 and 50. Air quality is considered satisfactory; "Moderate" The AQI is between 51 and 100. Air quality is acceptable; "Unhealthy for Sensitive Groups" When AQI values are between 101 and 150, members of sensitive groups may experience health effects; "Unhealthy" When AQI values are between 151 and 200 everyone may begin to experience health effects; "Very Unhealthy" AQI values between 201 and 300 trigger a health alert; "Hazardous" AQI values over 300 trigger health warnings of emergency conditions; (1) Data covers Jefferson County; (2) Based on 336 days with AQI data in 2008; The EPA has suspended data updates while it assesses its data systems, including AirData reports and maps.
Source: U.S. Environmental Protection Agency, AirData Report, 2008*

Air Quality Index Pollutants

| Area | Percent of Days when AQI Pollutant was...[2] | | | | | |
	Carbon Monoxide	Nitrogen Dioxide	Ozone	Sulfur Dioxide	Particulate Matter 2.5	Particulate Matter 10
Area[1]	9.8	0.0	26.5	0.3	49.1	14.3

*Note: The Air Quality Index (AQI) is an index for reporting daily air quality. EPA calculates the AQI for five major air pollutants regulated by the Clean Air Act: ground-level ozone, particle pollution (also known as particulate matter), carbon monoxide, sulfur dioxide, and nitrogen dioxide. The AQI runs from 0 to 500. The higher the AQI value, the greater the level of air pollution and the greater the health concern; (1) Data covers Jefferson County; (2) Based on 336 days with AQI data in 2008; The EPA has suspended data updates while it assesses its data systems, including AirData reports and maps.
Source: U.S. Environmental Protection Agency, AirData Report, 2008*

Air Quality Index Trends

| Area | Trend Sites (days) | | | | | | | | All Sites (days) |
	2002	2003	2004	2005	2006	2007	2008	2009	2009
MSA[1]	28	31	17	37	36	41	12	5	5

*Note: Figures are the number of days the AQI value exceeded 100 in a given year. An AQI value greater than 100 indicates that air quality would have been in the unhealthful range on that day. Data from exceptional events are included. These counts are presented in two ways. First, the counts are based on sites having an adequate record of monitoring data during the trend period (trend sites). These counts represent the relative change in the number of days with AQI values greater than 100. In the last column, the counts are based on all sites with data in the most recent year (because it is possible for a site to have data in the most recent year but not enough data to be a trend site); (1) Data covers the Birmingham-Hoover, AL Metropolitan Statistical Area - see Appendix B for areas included
Source: U.S. Environmental Protection Agency, Office of Air and Radiation, Air Quality Index Information, "Number of Days with Air Quality Index Values Greater than 100 and Trend Sites, 1990-2009, and at All Sites in 2009"*

Maximum Air Pollutant Concentrations

	Particulate Matter 10 (ug/m^3)	Particulate Matter 2.5 (ug/m^3)	Ozone (ppm)	Carbon Monoxide (ppm)	Sulfur Dioxide (ppm)	Nitrogen Dioxide (ppm)	Lead (ug/m^3)
MSA[1] Level	126	25	0.07	7	0.008	n/a	n/a
NAAQS[2]	150	35	0.075	9	0.140	0.053	0.15
Met NAAQS[2]	Yes	Yes	Yes	Yes	Yes	n/a	n/a

Note: Data from exceptional events are not included; (1) Data covers the Birmingham-Hoover, AL Metropolitan Statistical Area - see Appendix B for areas included; (2) National Ambient Air Quality Standards; n/a not available
Concentrations: Particulate Matter 10 (coarse particulate) - highest second maximum 24-hour concentration; Particulate Matter 2.5 (fine particulate) - highest 98th percentile 24-hour concentration; Ozone - highest fourth daily maximum 8-hour concentration; Carbon Monoxide - highest second maximum non-overlapping 8-hour concentration; Sulfur Dioxide - highest second maximum 24-hour concentration; Nitrogen Dioxide - highest arithmetic mean concentration; Lead - maximum running 3-month average
Units: ppm = parts per million; ug/m^3 = micrograms per cubic meter
Source: U.S. Environmental Protection Agency, CBSA Factbook 2009, Air Quality Statistics by City, 2009

Drinking Water

Water System Name	Pop. Served	Primary Water Source Type	Violations[1] Health Based	Violations[1] Monitoring/ Reporting
Birmingham Water Works Board	601,089	Surface	0	0

Note: (1) Based on violation data from January 1, 2010 to December 31, 2010 (includes unresolved violations from earlier years)
Source: U.S. Environmental Protection Agency, Office of Ground Water and Drinking Water, Safe Drinking Water Information System (based on data extracted May 9, 2011)

Charleston, South Carolina

Background

Charleston, South Carolina is located on the state's Atlantic coastline, 110 miles southeast of Columbia and 100 miles north of Savannah, Georgia. The city, named for King Charles II of England, is the county seat of Charleston County. Charleston is located on a bay at the end of a peninsula between the Ashley and Cooper rivers. The terrain is low-lying and coastal with nearby islands and inlets.

In 1670, English colonists established a nearby settlement, and subsequently moved to Charleston's present site. Charleston became an early trading center for rice, indigo, cotton and other goods. As the plantation economy grew, Charleston became a slave-trading center. In 1861, the Confederacy fired the cannon shot that launched the Civil War from the city's Battery, aimed at the Union's Fort Sumter in Charleston Harbor. Charleston was under siege during the Civil War, and experienced many difficulties during Reconstruction. Manufacturing industries including textiles and ironwork became important in the nineteenth century.

Charleston is part of a larger metropolitan area that includes North Charleston and Mount Pleasant and covers Charleston, Berkley and Dorchester counties. This area is a regional commercial and cultural center and a southern transportation hub whose port is among the nation's busiest shipping facilities. Charleston's other contemporary economic sectors include manufacturing, health care, business and professional services, defense activity, retail and wholesale trade, tourism, education and construction.

Charleston is a popular tourist area, based on its scenery, history and recreation. The city's center is well known for its historic neighborhoods with distinctive early southern architecture and ambiance. As one of the first American cities in the early twentieth century to actively encourage historic restoration and preservation, Charleston has more recently undertaken numerous revitalization initiatives, including the Charleston Place Hotel and retail complex, and Waterfront Park. North Charleston and other communities are also growing with industry and suburban development.

The founding of the Charleston Naval Shipyard stimulated a military-based economy after 1901. Numerous other defense facilities were later established, including the Charleston Air Force Base, located in North Charleston. Several military facilities were closed in the 1990s, including the shipyard, although other defense-related operations have remained.

In 2000, the Confederate submarine the *HL Hunley,* which sank in 1864, was raised, and brought to a conservation laboratory at the old Charleston Naval Base. Author Patricia Cornwell has taken a great interest in the project, and is involved in the current planning of a museum to house the submarine. Also in development is an International Museum of African American History, proposed to sit across from Liberty Square.

Charleston is a center for health care and medical research. SPAWAR (US Navy Space and Naval Warfare Systems Command) is the area's largest single employer followed by the Medical University of South Carolina, founded in 1824, with approximately 8,000 employees. Other area educational institutions include The College of Charleston, The Citadel Military College, Trident Technical College, Charleston Southern University, and a campus of Johnson and Wales University offering culinary and hospitality education.

The Charleston area has numerous parks, including one with a skateboard center, and public waterfront areas. Coastal recreation activities such as boating, swimming, fishing and beaches are popular, as are golf and other land sports.

The Charleston Museum is the nation's oldest, founded in 1773. There are also several former plantations in the area, including Boone Hall Plantation, Drayton Hall, Magnolia Plantation, and Middleton Place. Other attractions include the South Carolina Aquarium with its IMAX Theater, the American Military Museum, the Drayton Hall Plantation Museum, the Gibbes Museum of Art and the Karpeles Manuscript Museum. A North Charleston Convention Center and Performing Arts Center complex opened in 1999. Cultural organizations include the Spoleto Festival USA annual summer arts festival. The third annual Charleston International Film Festival, CIFF, was held in April 2010.)

The Arthur Ravenel Jr. Bridge is the longest cable-stayed bridge in all of the Americas, running across Charleston's Cooper River.

The nearby Atlantic Ocean moderates the climate, especially in winter, and keeps summer a bit cooler than expected. Expect Indian summers in fall, and a possible hurricane, while spring sharply turns from the cold winds of March to lovely May. Severe storms are possible.

Rankings

General Rankings

- Charleston was ranked #174 out of 375 metro areas in *Cities Ranked & Rated*. Criteria: cost of living; climate; crime; transportation; economy and jobs; education; arts and culture; health and healthcare; leisure; quality of life. *Cities Ranked & Rated, 2nd Edition, 2007*

- Charleston was ranked #76 out of 379 metro areas in *Places Rated Almanac*. Criteria: health care; education; recreation; transportation; ambience; climate; crime; housing costs; jobs. *Places Rated Almanac, 7th Edition, 2007*

- Charleston was selected as one of "America's Top 100 Places to Live" by RelocateAmerica.com. Cities and towns nominated to be great places to live along with their key data regarding education, employment, economy, crime, parks, recreation and housing were reviewed, rated and judged by the Relocate-America.com editorial staff. *Relocate-America.com, "RelocateAmerica's Top 100 Places to Live in 2010"*

- Charleston was chosen as one of America's best cities by "Outside Magazine" in the Best for Surfing in the East category. Criteria: educational attainment; cost of living; cultural vibrancy; economic resilience; housing market sanity; sport-specific facts such as the miles of trail within a hour's drive, frequency of group rides, and proximity to worthy ski areas. *Outside Magazine, "Best Towns 2010," August 2010*

- Charleston was selected as one of "America's Favorite Cities." The city ranked #2 in the "Quality of Life and Visitor Experience" category. Respondents to an online survey were asked to rate 35 top urban destinations in the U.S from a visitor's perspective. Criteria: noteworthy neighborhoods; skyline/views; public parks and outdoor access; cleanliness; public transportation and pedestrian friendliness; safety; weather; peace and quiet; people-watching; environmental friendliness. *Travelandleisure.com, "America's Favorite Cities 2010," November 2010*

- Charleston was selected as one of "America's Favorite Cities." The city ranked #2 in the "People" category. Respondents to an online survey were asked to rate 35 top urban destinations in the U.S. from a visitor's perspective. Criteria: attractive; friendly; stylish; intelligent; athletic/active; diverse. *Travelandleisure.com, "America's Favorite Cities 2010," November 2010*

- Charleston was selected as one of "America's Favorite Cities." The city ranked #9 in the "Food/Dining" category. Respondents to an online survey were asked to rate 35 top urban destinations in the U.S. from a visitor's perspective. Criteria: big-name restaurants; ethnic food; farmers' markets; neighborhood joints and cafes. *Travelandleisure.com, "America's Favorite Cities 2010," November 2010*

- Charleston appeared on *National Geographic Adventure's* list of the "50 Best Places to Live + Play." *National Geographic Adventure, September 2008*

- Charleston appeared on *Travel + Leisure's* list of the ten best cities in the continental U.S. and Canada. The city was ranked #3. Criteria: activities/attractions; culture/arts; restaurants/food; people; and value. *Travel + Leisure, "The World's Best Awards 2010"*

- *Condé Nast Traveler* polled thousands of readers for travel satisfaction. American cities were ranked based on the following criteria: friendliness; atmosphere/ambiance; culture/sites; restaurants; lodging; and shopping. Charleston appeared in the top 10, ranking #2. *Condé Nast Traveler, 2010 Readers' Choice Awards*

Business/Finance Rankings

- A.G. Edwards ranked America's 500 top-performing communities based on their residents' personal savings and investing behavior. The Charleston metro area ranked #424 with an index score of 96.25 (national average = 100.00). A dozen statistical factors were measured including: participation in retirement savings plans; personal debt levels; and home ownership. *A.G. Edwards, "2007 Nest Egg Index," September 12, 2007*

- Charleston was cited as one of America's top metros for new and expanded facility projects in 2010. The area ranked #10 in the mid-sized metro area category (population 200,000 to 1 million). *Site Selection, "2010 Top Metros," March 2011*

- Charleston was selected as one of the "100 Best Places to Live and Launch" in the U.S. The city ranked #81. The editors at *Fortune Small Business* ranked 296 Census-designated metro areas by business friendliness (Launching Score, % New Businesses) and lifestyle offerings (Living Score). Then they picked the town within each of the top 100 metro areas that best blends business and pleasure. *Fortune Small Business, "100 Best Places to Live and Launch 2008," April 2008*

- The Charleston metro area appeared on the Milken Institute "2010 Best Performing Metros" list. Rank: #19 out of 200 large metro areas. Criteria: job growth; wage and salary growth; high-tech output growth. *Milken Institute, "2010 Best Performing Metros"*

- The Charleston metro area was selected as one of the best cities for entrepreneurs in America by *Inc. Magazine*. Criteria: job-growth data for 335 metro areas was analyzed for: recent growth trend (the current and prior year's employment growth rates, with the current year emphasized); mid-term growth (the average annual 2002-2007 growth rate); long-term trend (the sum of the 2002-2007 and 1996-2001 employment growth rates multiplied by the ratio of the 1996-2001 growth rate over the 2002-2007 growth rate); current year growth. The Charleston metro area ranked #6 among mid-sized metro areas and #35 overall. *Inc. Magazine, "The Best Cities for Doing Business," July 2008*

- *Forbes* ranked the 200 most populous metro areas in the U.S. in terms of the "Best Places for Business and Careers." The Charleston metro area was ranked #63. Criteria: 12 metrics including costs (business and living), job growth (past and projected), income growth, educational attainment, projected economic growth, crime, cultural and recreational opportunities, net migration patterns, percentage of subprime mortgages handed out over a three-year period, and the number of highly ranked four-year colleges. *Forbes, "Best Places for Business and Careers," April 14, 2010*

Children/Family Rankings

- The Charleston metro area was selected as one of the "Best Cities for Relocating Families" by Worldwide ERC and Primacy Relocation. The 2008 study looked at nearly 50 factors important to relocating families including: recent job growth; nearby top-ranked colleges; in-state tuition for four-year public colleges; population growth since 2000; pediatricians per 100,000 population; and a Green Living index. *Worldwide ERC and Primacy Relocation, "2008 Best Cities for Relocating Families"*

Culture/Performing Arts Rankings

- Charleston was selected as one of "America's Favorite Cities." The city ranked #5 in the "Culture" category. Respondents to an online survey were asked to rate 35 top urban destinations in the U.S. from a visitor's perspective. Criteria: classical music; live music/bands; theater; museums/galleries; historical sites/monuments. *Travelandleisure.com, "America's Favorite Cities 2010," November 2010*

- Charleston was selected as one of "America's Top 25 Arts Destinations." The city ranked #7 in the mid-sized city (population 100,000 to 499,999) category. Criteria: readers' top choices for arts travel destinations based on the richness and variety of visual arts sites, activities and events. *American Style, "America's Top 25 Arts Destinations," May 2010*

Dating/Romance Rankings

- The Charleston metro area was selected as one of the "Best Cities for Relocating Singles" by Worldwide ERC and Primacy Relocation. The area ranked #16 out of the 100 largest metro areas in the U.S. Areas were selected based on the following criteria: recent job growth; recent singles population growth; overall population growth; affordable rental housing; cost-of-living index; expanded arts and recreation opportunities; ratio of single men and single women; affordability of quality higher education (including state residency requirements); diversity index; climate; population density. *Worldwide ERC and Primacy Relocation, "2008 Best Cities for Relocating Singles"*

Education Rankings

- Charleston was identified as one of the 100 "smartest" metro areas in the U.S. The area ranked #51. Criteria: the editors rated the collective brainpower of the 100 largest metro area in the U.S based on their residents' educational attainment. *American City Business Journals, www.bizjournals.com, April 14, 2008*

- Charleston was identified as one of "America's Brainiest Bastions" by *Portfolio.com*. The metro area ranked #67 out of 200. Portfolio.com analyzed levels of educational attainment in the nation's 200 largest metropolitan areas. The editors established scores for five levels of educational attainment, based on relative earning power of adult workers age 25 or older. Scores were determined by comparing the median income for all workers with the median income for those workers at a specified educational level. *Portfolio.com, "America's Brainiest Bastions," December 1, 2010*

Environmental Rankings

- Charleston was selected as one of 22 "Smarter Cities" for energy by the Natural Resources Defense Council." Criteria: investment in green power; energy efficiency measures; conservation. *Natural Resources Defense Council, "2010 Smarter Cities," July 19, 2010*

- 100 of the largest metro areas in the U.S. were analyzed in terms of their current drought severity. The Charleston metro area ranked #36 (#1 = driest). The rankings were based on statistics such as long-term precipitation trends and patterns and the Palmer drought indices. *Sperling's BestPlaces, www.BestPlaces.net, "America's Drought-Riskiest Cities," November 2007*

- The U.S. Conference of Mayors and Wal-Mart Stores sponsor the Mayors' Climate Protection Awards Program. The awards recognize and honor mayors for outstanding and innovative practices that mayors are taking to increase energy efficiency in their cities, and to help curb global warming. Charleston was a Large City Best Practice Model. *U.S. Conference of Mayors, "2009 Mayors' Climate Protection Awards Program"*

- The Charleston metro area appeared in *Country Home's* "Best Green Places" report. The area ranked #146 out of 379. Criteria: official energy policies; green power; green buildings; availability of fresh, locally grown food. *Country Home, "Best Green Places," 2008*

Health/Fitness Rankings

- Charleston was identified as a "2011 Asthma Capital." The area ranked #66 out of the nation's 100 largest metropolitan areas. Twelve factors were used to identify the most challenging places to live for people with asthma: estimated prevalence; self-reported prevalence; crude death rate for asthma; annual pollen score; annual air quality; public smoking laws; number of board-certified asthma specialists; school inhaler access laws; rescue medication use; controller medication use; uninsured rate; poverty rate. *Asthma and Allergy Foundation of America, "2011 Asthma Capitals"*

- Charleston was identified as a 2009 "Spring Allergy Capital." The area ranked #38 out of 100. Three groups of factors were used to identify the most severe cities for people with allergies during the spring season: annual pollen levels; medicine utilization; access to board-certified allergists. *Asthma and Allergy Foundation of America, "Spring Allergy Capitals 2009"*

- Charleston was identified as a 2010 "Fall Allergy Capital." The area ranked #43 out of 100. Three groups of factors were used to identify the most severe cities for people with allergies during the fall season: annual pollen levels; medicine utilization; access to board-certified allergists. *Asthma and Allergy Foundation of America, "Fall Allergy Capitals 2010"*

- Ortho-McNeil Neurologics, in partnership with Sperling's BestPlaces, analyzed 110 metro areas and identified those U.S. cities with the highest prevalence of factors that are most commonly associated with migraine headaches. The Charleston metro area ranked #56. Criteria: number of migraine-related drug prescriptions per capita; lifestyle factors that can contribute to migraines; environmental factors that can trigger migraines; and consumption of migraine-triggering foods. *Ortho-McNeil Neurologics, "America's Migraine Hot Spots," March 14, 2006*

- The Charleston metro area appeared in the 2010 Gallup-Healthways Well-Being Index. The index, based on interviews with more than 353,000 Americans during 2009, asked individuals to assess their jobs, finances, physical health, emotional state of mind and communities. The metro area ranked #46 out of 162. Criteria: life evaluation; emotional health; work environment; physical health; healthy behaviors; basic access (basic needs optimal for a healthy life, such as access to food and medicine, having health insurance and feeling safe while walking at night). *Gallup-Healthways, "Well-Being Index 2010"*

Real Estate Rankings

- The Charleston metro area was identified as one of the "25 Hottest Housing Markets" in the U.S. The area ranked #14 out of 160 markets with a home price appreciation rate of 8.1%. Criteria: year-over-year change of median sales price of existing single-family homes between the 4th quarter of 2009 and the 4th quarter of 2010. *National Association of Realtors, Median Sales Price of Existing Single-Family Homes for Metropolitan Areas, 4th Quarter 2010*

- The nation's largest metro areas were analyzed in terms of the percentage of households entering some stage of foreclosure in 2010. The Charleston metro area ranked #48 out of 206 (#1 = highest foreclosure rate). *RealtyTrac, 2010 Year-End Metropolitan Foreclosure Market Report, January 27, 2011*

- The Charleston metro area was identified as one of "10 Housing Markets for the Next Decade" by *U.S. News and World Report*. The metro area was ranked #7. Criteria: 10-year home price projections from 2009 to 2019. *U.S. News and World Report, "10 Housing Markets for the Next Decade," March 2010*

- The Center for Housing Policy ranked 210 U.S metropolitan areas by the fair market rent for a two-bedroom unit. The Charleston metro area was ranked #88. (#1 = most expensive) with a rent of $863. Criteria: Fair Market Rent (FMR) in effect during the fourth quarter of 2009 based on HUD's fiscal year 2010 FMRs. *The Center for Housing Policy, "Paycheck to Paycheck: Most to Least Expensive Rental Markets in 2009"*

Safety Rankings

- The National Insurance Crime Bureau ranked 366 metro areas in the U.S. in terms of per capita rates of vehicle theft. The Charleston metro area ranked #51 (#1 = highest rate). Criteria: number of vehicle theft offenses per 100,000 inhabitants. *National Insurance Crime Bureau, "Hot Spots," May 17, 2010*

Seniors/Retirement Rankings

- Charleston was selected as one of "10 Historic Places to Retire" by *U.S. News & World Report*. The editors looked for places filled with museums, libraries, and national historic monuments that also offer a good quality of life and plenty of amenities for seniors. *U.S. News & World Report, "10 Historic Places to Retire," September 6, 2010*

- Charleston was identified as one of "The Top 100 Places to Retire" by *Topretirements.com* The list reflects the 100 cities (out of 625+ total cities reviewed) that visitors to the website are most interested in for retirement. *Topretirements.com, "2011 Best Places to Retire List: The Sunbelt Rules"*

- Charleston was identified as one of the best places to retire in *Retirement Places Rated*. Criteria: population above 10,000; attractiveness to older adults; affordability; climate and natural endowments; personal safety. The city was ranked #4 out of 200. *Retirement Places Rated, 7th Edition, 2007*

- Charleston was selected as one of "The Best Retirement Places" by *Forbes*. The magazine considered a wide range of factors such as climate, availability of doctors, driving environment, and crime rates, but focused especially on tax burden and cost of living. *Forbes, "The Best Retirement Places," March 27, 2011*

Sports/Recreation Rankings

- Charleston appeared on the *Sporting News* list of the "Best Sports Cities" for 2010. The area ranked #185 out of 402 cities in the U.S. *Sporting News* takes a 12-month snapshot, roughly October to October, of each city's sports, putting a heavy premium on regular-season won-lost records (from the most recently completed season). Other criteria include: playoff berths, bowl appearances and tournament bids; championships; applicable power ratings; quality of competition; overall fan fervor as measured in part by attendance as percentage of venue capacity; abundance of teams (rewarding quality over quantity); stadium and arena quality; ticket availability and prices; franchise ownership; and marquee appeal of athletes. *Sporting News, "Best Sports Cities 2010," October, 2010*

- Charleston was chosen as a bicycle friendly community by the League of American Bicyclists. A Bicycle Friendly Community welcomes cyclists by providing safe accommodation for cycling and encouraging people to bike for transportation and recreation. There are four award levels: Platinum; Gold; Silver; and Bronze. The community achieved an award level of Bronze. *League of American Bicyclists, "Bicycle Friendly Community Master List," September 2010*

- Charleston was chosen as one of America's best cities for bicycling. The city ranked #29 out of 50. Criteria: number of segregated bike lanes, municipal bike racks, and bike boulevards; vibrant and diverse bike culture; smart, savvy bike shops; interviews with national and local advocates, bike shops and other experts. Note: only cities with populations of 100,000 or more were considered. *Bicycling, "America's Best Bike Cities," April 2010*

- *Golf Digest* ranked 330 metro areas in the U.S. in terms of golf. The Charleston metro area was ranked #109. Criteria: access to golf; weather; value of golf; and quality of golf. *Golf Digest, "Metro Golf Rankings," August 2005*

Women/Minorities Rankings

- Charleston was ranked #62 out of 100 metro areas in *SELF Magazine's* ranking of America's healthiest places for women." A panel of experts came up with more than 50 criteria including death and disease rates, environmental indicators, community resources, and lifestyle habits. *SELF Magazine, "Secrets of America's Healthiest Women," December 2008*

Miscellaneous Rankings

- Charleston was selected as one of America's best-mannered cities. The area ranked #1. The general public determined the winners by casting votes online and by mail. *The Charleston School of Protocol and Etiquette, "2010 Most Mannerly City in America Contest," February 7, 2011*

Business Environment

CITY FINANCES

City Government Finances

Component	2008 ($000)	2008 ($ per capita)
Total Revenues	265,506	2,413
Total Expenditures	347,725	3,161
Debt Outstanding	1,020,223	9,273
Cash and Securities[1]	201,648	1,833

Note: (1) Cash and security holdings of a government at the close of its fiscal year, including those of its dependent agencies, utilities, and liquor stores.
Source: U.S Census Bureau, State & Local Government Finances 2008

City Government Revenue by Source

Source	2008 ($000)	2008 ($ per capita)
General Revenue		
From Federal Government	5,383	49
From State Government	19,784	180
From Local Governments	2,438	22
Taxes		
Property	47,210	429
Sales and Gross Receipts	19,632	178
Personal Income	0	0
Corporate Income	0	0
Motor Vehicle License	0	0
Other Taxes	31,585	287
Current Charges	23,283	212
Liquor Store	0	0
Utility	90,315	821
Employee Retirement	0	0

Source: U.S Census Bureau, State & Local Government Finances 2008

City Government Expenditures by Function

Function	2008 ($000)	2008 ($ per capita)	2008 (%)
General Direct Expenditures			
Air Transportation	0	0	0.0
Corrections	0	0	0.0
Education	0	0	0.0
Employment Security Administration	0	0	0.0
Financial Administration	3,674	33	1.1
Fire Protection	14,262	130	4.1
General Public Buildings	1,994	18	0.6
Governmental Administration, Other	3,720	34	1.1
Health	0	0	0.0
Highways	7,226	66	2.1
Hospitals	0	0	0.0
Housing and Community Development	6,387	58	1.8
Interest on General Debt	29,148	265	8.4
Judicial and Legal	1,208	11	0.3
Libraries	0	0	0.0
Parking	7,198	65	2.1
Parks and Recreation	22,597	205	6.5
Police Protection	31,712	288	9.1
Public Welfare	853	8	0.2
Sewerage	2,646	24	0.8
Solid Waste Management	3,835	35	1.1
Veterans' Services	0	0	0.0
Liquor Store	0	0	0.0
Utility	168,257	1,529	48.4
Employee Retirement	0	0	0.0

Source: U.S Census Bureau, State & Local Government Finances 2008

Municipal Bond Ratings

Area	Moody's	S&P	Fitch
City	Aa1	AAA	n/a

Rating Systems (shown in declining order of credit quality): Moody's– Aaa, Aa, A, Baa, Ba, B, Caa, Ca, C (numerical modifiers 1, 2, and 3 are added to letter-rating); S&P– AAA, AA, A, BBB, BB, B, CCC, CC, C; Fitch– AAA, AA, A, BBB, BB, B, CCC, CC, C. Ratings may be modified by the addition of a plus or minus sign to show relative standing within the major rating categories.
Notes: n/a Not available; (1) Not reviewed; (2) Issuer Rating/No General Obligation; (3) Standard and Poor's Issue Credit Rating (ICR) is a current opinion of an obliger with respect to a specific financial obligation, a specific class of financial obligations, or a specific financial program.
Source: City of Charleston, South Carolina, Comprehensive Annual Financial Report, Fiscal Year Ended December 31, 2009

DEMOGRAPHICS

Population Growth

Area	1990 Census	2000 Census	2010 Estimate	2015 Projection	Population Growth (%) 2000-2010	2010-2015
City	96,102	96,650	111,528	116,709	15.4	4.6
MSA[1]	506,875	549,033	663,996	718,900	20.9	8.3
U.S.	248,709,873	281,421,906	309,038,974	321,675,005	9.8	4.1

Note: (1) Metropolitan Statistical Area - see Appendix B for areas included
Source: Claritas, Inc.

Number of Households and Average Household Size

Area	2010 Estimate	2010 Average Household Size
City	47,704	2.21
MSA[1]	258,984	2.48
U.S.	116,136,617	2.59

Note: (1) Metropolitan Statistical Area - see Appendix B for areas included
Source: Claritas, Inc.

Race and Ethnicity

Area	White Alone[2] (%)	Black Alone[2] (%)	Asian Alone[2] (%)	Other Race Alone[2] (%)	Hispanic[3] (%)
City	66.4	29.8	1.3	2.4	2.5
MSA[1]	66.3	28.2	1.6	3.9	3.9
U.S.	72.3	12.4	4.4	10.9	15.8

Note: Figures are 2010 estimates; (1) Metropolitan Statistical Area - see Appendix B for areas included (2) Alone is defined as not being in combination with one or more other races; (3) May be of any race.
Source: Claritas, Inc.

Segregation

Type	Segregation Indices[1] 1990	2000	2010	2010 Rank[2]	Percent Change 1990-2000	1990-2010	2000-2010
Black/White	47.4	44.2	41.5	88	-3.2	-5.9	-2.7
Asian/White	34.4	34.2	33.4	84	-0.3	-1.1	-0.8
Hispanic/White	26.6	32.2	39.8	66	5.6	13.2	7.6

Note: Figures are based on an analysis of 1990, 2000, and 2010 Census Decennial Census tract data by William H. Frey, Brookings Institution and the University of Michigan Social Science Data Analysis Network. In this analysis all racial groups (whites, blacks, and asians) are non-Hispanic members of those races. Hispanics are shown as a separate category; All figures cover the Metropolitan Statistical Area (see Appendix B for areas included); (1) Segregation Indices are Dissimilarity Indices that measure the degree to which the minority group is distributed differently than whites aross census tracts. They range from 0 (complete integration) to 100 (complete [segregation) where the value indicates the percentage of the minority group that needs to move to be distributed exactly like whites; (2) Ranges from 1 (most segregated) to 102 (least segregated); n/a not available.
Source: www.CensusScope.org

Ancestry

Area	German	Irish	English	American	Italian	Polish	French	Scottish
City	12.7	11.6	12.7	10.9	3.9	1.8	2.6	3.7
MSA[1]	11.8	10.3	10.3	11.4	3.5	1.6	2.7	2.8
U.S.	16.6	12.0	9.1	6.1	5.9	3.3	3.1	1.9

Note: The top eight ancestries in the U.S. are shown. Figures are percentages and include multiple ancestry (e.g. if a person reported being Irish and Italian, they were included in both columns); (1) Metropolitan Statistical Area - see Appendix B for areas included
Source: U.S. Census Bureau, 2007-2009 American Community Survey 3-Year Estimates

Foreign-Born Population

Area	Percent of Population Born in								
	Any Foreign Country	Mexico	Asia	Europe	Carribean	South America	Central America[2]	Africa	Canada
City	n/a	n/a	n/a	n/a	n/a	n/a	n/a	n/a	n/a
MSA[1]	4.8	1.2	1.2	1.1	0.2	0.4	0.3	0.1	0.2
U.S.	12.5	3.8	3.4	1.6	1.1	0.8	0.9	0.5	0.3

Note: (1) Metropolitan Statistical Area - see Appendix B for areas included; (2) Excludes Mexico.
Source: U.S. Census Bureau, 2007-2009 American Community Survey 3-Year Estimates

Marriage Status

Area	Never Married	Now Married[2]	Separated	Widowed	Divorced
City	42.4	39.2	3.2	5.8	9.4
MSA[1]	34.2	46.5	3.1	5.8	10.4
U.S.	31.4	49.7	2.2	6.2	10.6

Note: Figures are percentages and cover the population 15 years of age and older; (1) Metropolitan Statistical Area - see Appendix B for areas included; (2) Excludes separated
Source: U.S. Census Bureau, 2007-2009 American Community Survey 3-Year Estimates

Age Distribution and Median Age

Area	Percent of Population							Median Age
	Under Age 5	Age 5 to 17	Age 18 to 34	Age 35 to 49	Age 50 to 64	Age 65 to 79	80 Years and Over	
City	6.5	13.2	34.4	17.2	16.5	8.5	3.6	32.3
MSA[1]	7.1	16.5	26.6	20.8	17.8	8.4	2.9	34.9
U.S.	6.9	17.5	23.3	21.4	18.1	9.1	3.7	36.7

Note: (1) Metropolitan Statistical Area - see Appendix B for areas included
Source: U.S. Census Bureau, 2007-2009 American Community Survey 3-Year Estimates

Male/Female Ratio

Area	Males	Females	Males per 100 Females
City	53,386	58,142	91.8
MSA[1]	324,572	339,424	95.6
U.S.	152,401,520	156,637,454	97.3

Note: Figures are 2010 estimates; (1) Metropolitan Statistical Area - see Appendix B for areas included
Source: Claritas, Inc.

Religion

Area	Catholic	Southern Baptist	United Meth-odist	ELCA[1]	LDS[2]	Presby-terian Church USA	Jewish Est.	Muslim Est.
County	7.7	11.6	5.7	1.9	0.5	3.9	1.6	0.7
U.S.	22.0	7.1	3.7	1.8	1.5	1.1	2.2	0.6

Note: Figures are the number of adherents as a percentage of the total population; Adherents are defined as all members, including full members, their children and the estimated number of other participants who are not considered members (e.g. the baptized, those not confirmed, those regularly attending services, etc.);
(1) Evangelical Lutheran Church in America; (2) The Church of Jesus Christ of Latter Day Saints
Source: Reprinted with permission from Religious Congregations and Membership in the United States 2000 (Nashville, Glenmary Research Center, 2002) Copyright Association of Statisticians of American Religious Bodies. All rights reserved.

ECONOMY

Gross Metropolitan Product

Area	2006	2007	2008	2009	2009 Rank[2]
MSA[1]	23.9	25.4	26.3	26.3	81

Note: Figures are in billions of dollars; (1) Charleston-North Charleston, SC Metropolitan Statistical Area - see Appendix B for areas included; (2) Rank ranges from 1 to 363
Source: The U.S. Conference of Mayors, "Pace of Economic Recovery: GMP and Jobs," January 2010

Economic Growth

Area	2006-2008 (%)	2009 (%)	2010 (%)	Rank[2]
MSA[1]	2.3	-1.2	2.9	87
U.S.	1.3	-2.5	2.2	–

Note: Figures are real Gross Metropolitan Product growth rates and represent annual average percent change; (1) Charleston-North Charleston, SC Metropolitan Statistical Area - see Appendix B for areas included; (2) Rank ranges from 1 to 363
Source: The U.S. Conference of Mayors, "Pace of Economic Recovery: GMP and Jobs," January 2010

Metropolitan Area Exports

Area	2005	2006	2007	2008	2009	2009 Rank[2]
MSA[1]	1,414.5	1,615.3	1,842.9	2,005.5	1,455.7	96

Note: Figures are in millions of dollars; (1) Charleston-North Charleston, SC Metropolitan Statistical Area - see Appendix B for areas included; (2) Rank ranges from 1 to 374
Source: U.S. Department of Commerce, International Trade Administration, Office of Trade & Industry Information, Manufacturing & Services

INCOME

Per Capita/Median/Average Income

Area	Per Capita ($)	Median Household ($)	Average Household ($)
City	28,499	46,576	65,745
MSA[1]	26,406	51,277	66,897
U.S.	27,034	52,795	71,071

Note: Figures are 2010 estimates; (1) Metropolitan Statistical Area - see Appendix B for areas included
Source: Claritas, Inc.

Household Income Distribution

Area	Percent of Households Earning							
	Under $15,000	$15,000 -24,999	$25,000 -34,999	$35,000 -49,999	$50,000 -74,999	$75,000 -99,000	$100,000 -149,999	$150,000 and up
City	17.6	10.5	10.6	14.6	17.9	10.9	10.3	7.6
MSA[1]	12.9	9.9	10.7	15.5	20.2	13.0	11.2	6.6
U.S.	12.1	10.2	10.6	15.0	19.5	12.5	12.1	8.0

Note: Figures are 2010 estimates; (1) Metropolitan Statistical Area - see Appendix B for areas included
Source: Claritas, Inc.

Poverty Rates by Age

Area	All Ages	Under 18 Years Old	18 to 64 Years Old	65 Years and Over
City	17.1	5.1	10.6	1.4
MSA[1]	14.1	5.1	7.8	1.2
U.S.	13.6	4.7	7.7	1.2

Note: Figures are percent of population with income during the previous 12 months below poverty level and only include population for whom poverty status is determined; (1) Metropolitan Statistical Area - see Appendix B for areas included
Source: U.S. Census Bureau, 2007-2009 American Community Survey 3-Year Estimates

Personal Bankruptcy Filing Rate

Area	2006	2007	2008	2009	2010
Charleston County	0.89	1.22	1.42	1.67	1.84
U.S.	2.00	2.73	3.53	4.60	4.96

Note: Numbers are per 1,000 population and include Chapter 7 and Chapter 13 filings
Source: Federal Deposit Insurance Corporation, Regional Economic Conditions, March 17, 2011

EMPLOYMENT

Labor Force and Employment

Area	Civilian Labor Force			Workers Employed		
	Dec. 2009	Dec. 2010	% Chg.	Dec. 2009	Dec. 2010	% Chg.
City	57,124	58,080	1.7	52,237	53,354	2.1
MSA[1]	315,516	319,849	1.4	284,914	291,009	2.1
U.S.	152,693,000	153,156,000	0.3	137,953,000	139,159,000	0.9

Note: Data is not seasonally adjusted and covers workers 16 years of age and older;
(1) Metropolitan Statistical Area - see Appendix B for areas included
Source: Bureau of Labor Statistics, http://stats.bls.gov

Unemployment Rate

Area	2010											
	Jan.	Feb.	Mar.	Apr.	May	Jun.	Jul.	Aug.	Sep.	Oct.	Nov.	Dec.
City	9.1	9.1	8.4	7.6	8.2	8.6	8.7	9.0	8.1	8.3	8.3	8.1
MSA[1]	10.2	10.1	9.4	8.7	8.9	9.4	9.4	9.8	9.1	9.1	9.3	9.0
U.S.	10.6	10.4	10.2	9.5	9.3	9.6	9.7	9.5	9.2	9.0	9.3	9.1

Note: Data is not seasonally adjusted and covers workers 16 years of age and older; All figures are percentages; (1) Metropolitan Statistical Area - see Appendix B for areas included
Source: Bureau of Labor Statistics, http://stats.bls.gov

Projected Unemployment Rate

Area	2007 (%)	2009 (%)	2011 (%)	2013 (%)
MSA[1]	4.5	10.0	9.0	7.0

Note: (1) Metropolitan Statistical Area - see Appendix B for areas included
Source: The U.S. Conference of Mayors, "Pace of Economic Recovery: GMP and Jobs," January 2010

Employment by Occupation

Occupation Classification	City (%)	MSA[1] (%)	U.S. (%)
Sales and Office	24.7	26.0	25.4
Professional and Related	27.2	20.9	21.0
Service	18.1	17.1	17.2
Production, Transportation, and Material Moving	7.1	11.9	12.3
Management, Business, and Financial	16.3	13.6	14.1
Construction, Extraction, and Maintenance	6.2	10.4	9.2
Farming, Forestry, and Fishing	0.3	0.3	0.7

Note: Figures cover employed civilians 16 years of age and older;
(1) Metropolitan Statistical Area - see Appendix B for areas included
Source: U.S. Census Bureau, 2007-2009 American Community Survey 3-Year Estimates

Employment by Industry

| Sector | MSA[1] | | U.S. |
	Number of Employees	Percent of Total	Percent of Total
Government	58,700	20.6	17.2
Education and Health Services	33,100	11.6	15.2
Professional and Business Services	41,900	14.7	13.0
Retail Trade	35,800	12.5	11.4
Leisure and Hospitality	33,800	11.8	9.7
Manufacturing	21,200	7.4	8.8
Financial Activities	12,200	4.3	5.8
Wholesale Trade	8,100	2.8	4.2
Construction	n/a	n/a	4.1
Other Services	10,500	3.7	4.1
Transportation and Utilities	11,500	4.0	3.7
Information	5,000	1.8	2.1
Mining and Logging	n/a	n/a	0.6

Note: Figures cover non-farm employment as of December 2010 and are not seasonally adjusted;
(1) Metropolitan Statistical Area - see Appendix B for areas included; n/a not available
Source: Bureau of Labor Statistics, http://stats.bls.gov

Occupations with Greatest Projected Employment Growth: 2006 - 2016

Occupation[1]	2006 Employment	2016 Projected Employment	Numeric Employment Change	Percent Employment Change
Retail salespersons	64,600	74,610	10,010	15.5
Customer service representatives	28,150	36,950	8,800	31.3
Combined food preparation and serving workers, including fast food	31,560	37,950	6,390	20.2
Registered nurses	33,310	39,660	6,350	19.1
Postsecondary teachers	17,680	22,760	5,080	28.7
Office clerks, general	39,060	44,110	5,050	12.9
Janitors and cleaners, except maids and housekeeping cleaners	31,110	35,900	4,790	15.4
Truck drivers, heavy and tractor-trailer	25,640	30,390	4,750	18.5
Waiters and waitresses	38,830	42,780	3,950	10.2
Sales representatives, wholesale and manufacturing, except technical and scientific products	17,250	21,120	3,870	22.4

Note: Projections cover South Carolina; (1) Sorted by numeric employment change
Source: www.projectionscentral.com, State Occupational Projections, 2006-2016 Long-Term Projections

Fastest Growing Occupations: 2006 - 2016

Occupation[1]	2006 Employment	2016 Projected Employment	Numeric Employment Change	Percent Employment Change
Ambulance drivers and attendants, except emergency medical technicians	950	1,630	680	71.6
Network systems and data communications analysts	2,320	3,770	1,450	62.5
Chiropractors	660	1,070	410	62.1
Occupational therapist assistants	400	640	240	60.0
Audio and video equipment technicians	350	550	200	57.1
Pharmacy technicians	4,720	7,200	2,480	52.5
Physical therapist assistants	940	1,430	490	52.1
Veterinary technologists and technicians	790	1,190	400	50.6
Multi-media artists and animators	520	780	260	50.0
Self-enrichment education teachers	1,730	2,490	760	43.9

Note: Projections cover South Carolina; (1) Sorted by percent employment change and excludes occupations
with numeric employment change less than 200
Source: www.projectionscentral.com, State Occupational Projections, 2006-2016 Long-Term Projections

Average Wages

Occupation	$/Hr.	Occupation	$/Hr.
Accountants and Auditors	27.47	Maids and Housekeeping Cleaners	9.29
Automotive Mechanics	17.68	Maintenance and Repair Workers	16.27
Bookkeepers	15.90	Marketing Managers	51.12
Carpenters	17.07	Nuclear Medicine Technologists	30.41
Cashiers	8.31	Nurses, Licensed Practical	18.77
Clerks, General Office	12.24	Nurses, Registered	31.18
Clerks, Receptionists/Information	11.86	Nursing Aides/Orderlies/Attendants	11.15
Clerks, Shipping/Receiving	14.27	Packers and Packagers, Hand	9.63
Computer Programmers	30.73	Physical Therapists	32.54
Computer Support Specialists	20.22	Postal Service Mail Carriers	22.71
Computer Systems Analysts	30.71	Real Estate Brokers	26.40
Cooks, Restaurant	11.14	Retail Salespersons	12.13
Dentists	n/a	Sales Reps., Exc. Tech./Scientific	25.55
Electrical Engineers	37.24	Sales Reps., Tech./Scientific	31.99
Electricians	19.36	Secretaries, Exc. Legal/Med./Exec.	15.19
Financial Managers	45.45	Security Guards	12.21
First-Line Supervisors/Mgrs., Sales	19.16	Surgeons	n/a
Food Preparation Workers	8.76	Teacher Assistants	10.00
General and Operations Managers	46.29	Teachers, Elementary School	20.70
Hairdressers/Cosmetologists	17.92	Teachers, Secondary School	23.30
Internists	101.56	Telemarketers	10.94
Janitors and Cleaners	9.51	Truck Drivers, Heavy/Tractor-Trailer	17.24
Landscaping/Groundskeeping Workers	10.91	Truck Drivers, Light/Delivery Svcs.	12.76
Lawyers	56.44	Waiters and Waitresses	9.48

Note: Wage data covers the Charleston-North Charleston-Summerville, SC - see Appendix B for areas included. Hourly wages for elementary/secondary school teachers and teacher assistants were calculated by the editors from annual wage data assuming a 40 hour work week; n/a not available.
Source: Bureau of Labor Statistics, Metro Area Occupational Employment and Wage Estimates, May 2009

RESIDENTIAL REAL ESTATE

Building Permits

Area	Single-Family			Multi-Family			Total		
	2009	2010	Pct. Chg.	2009	2010	Pct. Chg.	2009	2010	Pct. Chg.
City	399	400	0.3	162	164	1.2	561	564	0.5
MSA[1]	2,732	2,787	2.0	217	273	25.8	2,949	3,060	3.8
U.S.	441,100	447,300	1.4	141,900	157,300	10.9	583,000	604,600	3.7

Note: (1) Metropolitan Statistical Area - see Appendix B for areas included; figures represent new, privately-owned housing units authorized (unadjusted data); All permit data are based on estimates with imputation.
Source: U.S. Census Bureau, Manufacturing, Mining, and Construction Statistics, Building Permits, 2009, 2010

Homeownership Rate

Area	2005 (%)	2006 (%)	2007 (%)	2008 (%)	2009 (%)	2010 (%)
MSA[1]	n/a	n/a	n/a	n/a	n/a	n/a
U.S.	68.9	68.8	68.1	67.8	67.4	66.9

Note: (1) Metropolitan Statistical Area - see Appendix B for areas included
Source: U.S. Census Bureau, Housing Vacancies and Homeownership Annual Statistics: 2010

Housing Vacancy Rates

Area	Gross Vacancy Rate[2] (%)			Year-Round Vacancy Rate[3] (%)			Rental Vacancy Rate[4] (%)			Homeowner Vacancy Rate[5] (%)		
	2008	2009	2010	2008	2009	2010	2008	2009	2010	2008	2009	2010
MSA[1]	n/a	n/a	n/a	n/a	n/a	n/a	n/a	n/a	n/a	n/a	n/a	n/a
U.S.	14.4	14.5	14.3	11.1	11.3	11.3	10.0	10.6	10.2	2.8	2.6	2.6

Note: (1) Metropolitan Statistical Area - see Appendix B for areas included; (2) The percentage of the total housing inventory that is vacant; (3) The percentage of the housing inventory (excluding seasonal units) that is year-round vacant; (4) The percentage of rental inventory that is vacant for rent; (5) The percentage of homeowner inventory that is vacant for sale; n/a not available
Source: U.S. Census Bureau, Housing Vacancies and Homeownership Annual Statistics: 2010

State Corporate Income Tax Rates

State	Tax Rate (%)	Income Brackets ($)	Num. of Brackets	Financial Institution Tax Rate (%)[a]	Federal Income Tax Ded.
South Carolina	5.0	Flat rate	1	4.5 (x)	No

Note: Tax rates as of January 1, 2011; (a) Rates listed are the tax rates applied to financial institutions or excise taxes based on income. Some states have other taxes based upon the value of deposits or shares; (x) South Carolina taxes savings and loans at a 6% rate.
Source: Federation of Tax Administrators, "State Corporate Income Tax Rates, 2011"

State Individual Income Tax Rates

State	Tax Rate (%)	Income Brackets ($)	Num. of Brackets	Personal Exempt. ($)[1] Single	Personal Exempt. ($)[1] Dependents	Fed. Inc. Tax Ded.
South Carolina (a)	0.0 - 7.0	2,740 - 13,701	6	3,650 (d)	3,650 (d)	No

Note: Tax rates as of January 1, 2011; Local- and county-level taxes are not included; n/a not applicable; (1) Married joint filers generally receive double the single exemption; (a) 17 states have statutory provision for automatically adjusting to the rate of inflation the dollar values of the income tax brackets, standard deductions, and/or personal exemptions. Massachusetts, Michigan, and Nebraska index the personal exemption only. Oregon does not index the income brackets for $125,000 and over. Because the inflation-adjustments for 2011 are not yet available in most cases, the table reports the 2010 amounts, unless 2011 is specified in a footnote; (d) These states use the personal exemption amounts provided in the federal Internal Revenue Code.
Source: Federation of Tax Administrators, "State Individual Income Tax Rates, 2011"

Various State and Local Tax Rates

State	State and Local Sales and Use (%)	State Sales and Use (%)	Gasoline[1] (¢/gal.)	Cigarette[2] ($/pack)	Spirits[3] ($/gal.)	Wine[4] ($/gal.)	Beer[5] ($/gal.)
South Carolina	8.5	6.00	16.8	0.57	4.97 (i)	1.08	0.77

Note: All tax rates as of January 1, 2011 except Spirits (Sept. 1, 2010); (1) The American Petroleum Institute has developed a methodology for determining the average tax rate on a gallon of fuel. Rates may include any of the following: excise taxes, environmental fees, storage tank fees, other fees or taxes, general sales tax, and local taxes. In states where gasoline is subject to the general sales tax, or where the fuel tax is based on the average sale price, the average rate determined by API is sensitive to changes in the price of gasoline. States that fully or partially apply general sales taxes to gasoline: CA, CO, GA, IL, IN, MI, NY; (2) The federal excise tax of $1.0066 per pack and local taxes are not included; (3) Rates are those applicable to off-premise sales of 40% alcohol by volume (a.b.v.) distilled spirits in 750ml containers. Local excise taxes are excluded; (4) Rates are those applicable to off-premise sales of 11% a.b.v. non-carbonated wine in 750ml containers; (5) Rates are those applicable to off-premise sales of 4.7% a.b.v. beer in 12 ounce containers; (i) Includes a wholesale tax of $5.36 per case.
Source: Tax Foundation, 2011 Facts & Figures: How Does Your State Compare?

State-Local Tax Burdens

Area	Rate (%)	Rank[1]	Per Capita Taxes Paid to Home State ($)	Total State and Local Per Capita Taxes Paid ($)	Per Capita Income ($)
South Carolina	8.1	43	1,845	2,742	33,954
U.S. Average	9.8	-	3,057	4,160	42,539

Note: Figures cover 2009; (1) Rank ranges from 1 to 50 where 1 is highest tax burden
Source: Tax Foundation, State-Local Tax Burdens, All States, 2009

State Business Tax Climate Index Rankings

State	Overall Rank	Corporate Tax Index Rank	Individual Income Tax Index Rank	Sales Tax Index Rank	Unemployment Insurance Tax Index Rank	Property Tax Index Rank
South Carolina	24	9	27	22	43	23

Note: The index is a measure of how each state's tax laws affect economic performance. The lower the rank, the more favorable a state's tax system is for business. All ranks are for fiscal years. States without a given tax are given a ranking of 1.
Source: Tax Foundation, Tax Foundation Background Paper, No. 60, "2011 State Business Tax Climate Index"

**COMMERCIAL
REAL ESTATE**

Office Market

Market Area	Inventory (sq. ft.)	Vacant (sq. ft.)	Vac. Rate (%)	Under Constr. (sq. ft.)	Asking Rent ($/sf/yr)	
					Class A	Class B
Charleston	9,294,239	1,392,476	15.0	120,500	23.21	18.73

Source: Grubb & Ellis, Office Markets Trends, 1st Quarter 2011

Industrial Market

Market Area	Inventory (sq. ft.)	Vacant (sq. ft.)	Vac. Rate (%)	Under Constr. (sq. ft.)	Asking Rent ($/sf/yr)	
					WH/Dist	R&D/Flex
Charleston	42,877,673	5,774,903	13.5	1,018,000	4.11	6.60

Source: Grubb & Ellis, Industrial Markets Trends, 1st Quarter 2011

**COMMERCIAL
UTILITIES**

Typical Monthly Electric Bills

Area	Commercial Service ($/month)		Industrial Service ($/month)	
	3 kW demand 1,000 kWh	40 kW demand 14,000 kWh	1,000 kW demand 200,000 kWh	50,000 kW demand 15,000,000 kWh
City	127	1,628	26,157	1,300,950
Average[1]	135	1,576	23,741	1,402,202

Note: Based on total rates in effect July 1, 2010; (1) average based on 182 utilities surveyed
Source: Edison Electric Institute, Typical Bills and Average Rates Report, Summer 2010

TRANSPORTATION

Means of Transportation to Work

Area	Car/Truck/Van		Public Transportation			Bicycle	Walked	Other Means	Worked at Home
	Drove Alone	Car-pooled	Bus	Subway	Railroad				
City	78.7	7.8	2.8	0.0	0.0	1.3	4.5	1.4	3.4
MSA[1]	81.2	9.6	1.3	0.0	0.0	0.5	2.4	1.2	3.7
U.S.	75.8	10.4	2.7	1.7	0.5	0.5	2.9	1.2	4.1

Note: Figures are percentages and cover workers 16 years of age and older;
(1) Metropolitan Statistical Area - see Appendix B for areas included
Source: U.S. Census Bureau, 2007-2009 American Community Survey 3-Year Estimates

Travel Time to Work

Area	Less Than 15 Minutes	15 to 29 Minutes	30 to 44 Minutes	45 to 59 Minutes	60 to 89 Minutes	90 Minutes or More
City	31.0	46.9	15.6	3.8	1.4	1.3
MSA[1]	25.0	39.5	22.6	7.8	3.5	1.6
U.S.	28.5	36.2	19.7	7.5	5.6	2.5

Note: Figures are percentages and include workers 16 years old and over;
(1) Metropolitan Statistical Area - see Appendix B for areas included
Source: U.S. Census Bureau, 2007-2009 American Community Survey 3-Year Estimates

Travel Time Index

Area	1982	1999	2008	2009
Urban Area[1]	1.09	1.16	1.15	1.15
Average[2]	1.08	1.20	1.20	1.20

Note: Travel Time Index—the ratio of travel time in the peak period to the travel time at
free-flow conditions. A value of 1.30 indicates a 20-minute free-flow trip takes 26 minutes
in the peak. Free-flow speeds (60 mph on freeways and 35 mph on principal arterials)
are used as the comparison threshold; (1) Covers the Charleston-North Charleston urban area;
(2) average of 439 urban areas
Source: Texas Transportation Institute, Urban Mobility Report 2010, December 2010

Public Transportation

Agency Name / Mode of Transportation	Vehicles Operated in Maximum Service	Annual Unlinked Passenger Trips ('000)	Annual Passenger Miles ('000)
Charleston Area Regional Transportation (CARTA)			
Demand response	17	73.5	766.0
Bus	66	3,990.4	15,083.1

Note: Figures include both directly operated and purchased transportation
Source: Federal Transit Administration, National Transit Database, 2009

Air Transportation

Airport Name and Code / Type of Service	Passenger Airlines[1]	Passenger Enplanements	Freight Carriers[2]	Freight (lbs.)
Charleston International Airport (CHS)				
Domestic service (U.S. carriers - 2010)	27	1,010,238	17	4,728,556
International service (U.S. carriers - 2009)	5	1,161	4	6,690,049

Note: (1) Includes all U.S.-based major, minor and commuter airlines that carried at least one passenger during the year; (2) Includes all U.S.-based airlines and freight carriers that transported at least one pound of freight during the year
Source: Bureau of Transportation Statistics, The Intermodal Transportation Database, Air Carriers: T-100 Domestic Market (U.S. Carriers), 2010; Bureau of Transportation Statistics, The Intermodal Transportation Database, Air Carriers: T-100 International Market (U.S. Carriers), 2009

Other Transportation Statistics

Interstate highways:	I-26; I-95
Amtrak service:	Yes (station is located in North Charleston)
Major waterways/ports:	Atlantic Ocean

Source: Amtrak.com; Google Maps

BUSINESSES

Major Business Headquarters

Company Name	Rankings	
	Fortune[1]	Forbes[2]
No companies listed	-	-

Note: (1) Fortune 500—companies that produce a 10-K are ranked 1 to 500 based on 2010 revenue; (2) all private companies with at least $2 billion in annual revenue are ranked 1 to 223; companies listed are headquartered in the city; dashes indicate no ranking
Source: Fortune, "Fortune 500," May 23, 2011; Forbes, "America's Largest Private Companies," November 3, 2010

Minority- and Women-Owned Businesses

Group	All Firms		Firms with Paid Employees			
	Firms	Sales ($000)	Firms	Sales ($000)	Employees	Payroll ($000)
Asian	230	97,937	57	89,149	866	16,742
Black	1,081	64,190	114	37,962	479	11,292
Hispanic	(s)	(s)	(s)	(s)	(s)	(s)
Women	3,766	640,119	657	544,193	4,477	108,612
All Firms	13,392	11,088,365	3,844	10,554,855	62,244	2,129,311

Note: Figures cover firms located in the city; minority- and women-owned business are defined as firms in which the corresponding group own 51% or more of the stock or equity of the company; (s) estimates are suppressed when publication standards are not met
Source: U.S. Census Bureau, 2007 Economic Census, Survey of Business Owners

HOTELS

Hotels/Motels

Area	5 Star		4 Star		3 Star		2 Star		1 Star		Not Rated	
	Num.	Pct.3	Num.	Pct.3	Num.	Pct.3	Num.	Pct.3	Num.	Pct.3	Num.	Pct.3
City[1]	2	1.4	12	8.3	48	33.1	69	47.6	3	2.1	11	7.6
Total[2]	119	0.7	927	5.8	4,906	30.5	7,992	49.7	526	3.3	1,625	10.1

Note: (1) Figures cover Charleston and vicinity; (2) Figures cover all 100 cities in this book; (3) Percentage of hotels which are a given star rating; Star ratings are determined by expedia.com and offer an indication of the general quality of a particular hotel.
Source: expedia.com, May 5, 2011

The Charleston metro area is home to three of the top 218 hotels in the U.S. according to *Travel & Leisure*: **Charleston Place** (#40); **Planters Inn** (#63); **Sanctuary at Kiawah Island Golf Resort** (#86). Criteria: service; location; rooms; food; and value. *Travel & Leisure, "T+L 500, The World's Best Hotels 2011"*

The Charleston metro area is home to four of the top 100 hotels in the U.S. according to *Condé Nast Traveler*: **Charleston Place** (#18); **French Quarter Inn** (#42); **Planters Inn** (#42); **Market Pavilion Hotel** (#95). The selections are based on over 25,000 responses to the magazine's annual Readers' Choice Survey. *Condé Nast Traveler, "2010 Readers' Choice Awards"*

EVENT SITES

Convention Centers

Name	Overall Space (sq. ft.)	Exhibit Space (sq. ft.)	Meeting Space (sq. ft.)	Meeting Rooms
Charleston Area Convention Center Complex	n/a	n/a	76,960	n/a

Note: n/a not available
Source: Original research

Living Environment

COST OF LIVING

Cost of Living Index

Composite Index	Groceries	Housing	Utilities	Trans-portation	Health Care	Misc. Goods/Services
98.3	105.7	92.6	96.6	93.9	104.4	101.5

Note: U.S. = 100; Figures cover the Charleston-North Charleston metro area.
Source: The Council for Community and Economic Research, ACCRA Cost of Living Index, 2010

Grocery Prices

Area[1]	T-Bone Steak ($/pound)	Frying Chicken ($/pound)	Whole Milk ($/half gal.)	Eggs ($/dozen)	Orange Juice ($/64 oz.)	Coffee ($/11.5 oz.)
City[2]	8.36	1.27	2.28	1.51	3.11	3.42
Avg.	9.04	1.16	2.02	1.47	3.08	3.65
Min.	6.97	0.84	1.46	0.96	2.39	2.64
Max.	13.93	2.51	3.58	3.01	4.94	6.32

Note: (1) Values for the local area are compared with the average, minimum and maximum values for all 338 areas in the Cost of Living Index; (2) Figures cover the Charleston-North Charleston metro area; **T-Bone Steak** *(price per pound);* **Frying Chicken** *(price per pound, whole fryer);* **Whole Milk** *(half gallon carton);* **Eggs** *(price per dozen, Grade A, large);* **Orange Juice** *(64 oz. Tropicana or Florida Natural);* **Coffee** *(11.5 oz. can, vacuum-packed, Maxwell House, Hills Bros, or Folgers).*
Source: The Council for Community and Economic Research, ACCRA Cost of Living Index, 2010

Housing and Utility Costs

Area[1]	New Home Price ($)	Apartment Rent ($/month)	All Electric ($/month)	Part Electric ($/month)	Other Energy ($/month)	Telephone ($/month)
City[2]	264,161	899	176.55	-	-	23.82
Avg.	293,442	810	166.39	91.93	83.82	26.93
Min.	182,545	453	119.21	44.47	36.85	17.98
Max.	1,123,114	2,776	307.53	218.20	313.90	39.15

Note: (1) Values for the local area are compared with the average, minimum and maximum values for all 338 areas in the Cost of Living Index; (2) Figures cover the Charleston-North Charleston metro area; **New Home Price** *(2,400 sf living area, 8,000 sf lot, in urban area with full utilities);* **Apartment Rent** *(950 sf 2 bedroom/1.5 or 2 bath, unfurnished, excluding all utilities except water);* **All Electric** *(average monthly cost for an all-electric home);* **Part Electric** *(average monthly cost for a part-electric home);* **Other Energy** *(average monthly cost for natural gas, fuel oil, coal, wood, and any other forms of energy except electricity);* **Telephone** *(price includes basic monthly rate for a private residential line plus additional local usage charges incurred by a family of four).*
Source: The Council for Community and Economic Research, ACCRA Cost of Living Index, 2010

Health Care, Transportation, and Other Costs

Area[1]	Doctor ($/visit)	Dentist ($/visit)	Optometrist ($/visit)	Gasoline ($/gallon)	Beauty Salon ($/visit)	Men's Shirt ($)
City[2]	92.61	83.33	91.20	2.57	44.42	25.75
Avg.	89.44	78.95	87.40	2.73	31.92	24.83
Min.	57.00	54.25	48.32	2.44	19.17	13.67
Max.	149.90	136.73	174.22	3.75	62.81	47.89

Note: (1) Values for the local area are compared with the average, minimum and maximum values for all 338 areas in the Cost of Living Index; (2) Figures cover the Charleston-North Charleston metro area; **Doctor** *(general practitioners routine exam of an established patient);* **Dentist** *(adult teeth cleaning and periodic oral examination);* **Optometrist** *(full vision eye exam for established adult patient);* **Gasoline** *(one gallon regular unleaded, national brand, including all taxes, cash price at self-service pump if available);* **Beauty Salon** *(woman's shampoo, trim, and blow-dry);* **Men's Shirt** *(cotton/polyester dress shirt, pinpoint weave, long sleeves).*
Source: The Council for Community and Economic Research, ACCRA Cost of Living Index, 2010

HOUSING

House Price Index (HPI)

Area	National Ranking[2]	Quarterly Change (%)	One-Year Change (%)	Five-Year Change (%)
MSA[1]	228	-1.13	-2.96	-3.61
U.S.[3]	-	-0.84	-3.95	-11.45

Note: The HPI is a weighted repeat sales index. It measures average price changes in repeat sales or refinancings on the same properties. This information is obtained by reviewing repeat mortgage transactions on single-family properties whose mortgages have been purchased or securitized by Fannie Mae or Freddie Mac in January 1975; (1) Metropolitan/Micropolitan Statistical Area - see Appendix B for areas included; (2) Rankings are based on annual percentage change for all metro areas containing at least 15,000 transactions over the last 10 years and ranges from 1 to 309; (3) figures based on a weighted average of Census Division estimates; all figures are for the period ending December 31, 2010
Source: Federal Housing Finance Agency, House Price Index, February 24, 2011

House Price Valuations

Area	Q4 2005 Price ($000)	Q4 2005 Over-valuation	Q4 2006 Price ($000)	Q4 2006 Over-valuation	Q4 2007 Price ($000)	Q4 2007 Over-valuation	Q4 2008 Price ($000)	Q4 2008 Over-valuation	Q4 2009 Price ($000)	Q4 2009 Over-valuation
MSA[1]	159.8	18.5	170.7	19.6	172.0	14.1	161.1	3.5	154.2	-2.0

Note: Figures show the percentage of over- or under-valuation of single family homes relative to statistically normal house values (e.g. a value of 23.6 indicates that house values are 23.6% overvalued). Statistically normal house values are based on house prices, interest rates, household incomes, population densities, and any historical premiums or discounts metropolitan areas have exhibited over time; (1) Figures cover the Charleston-North Charleston, SC Metropolitan Statistical Area - see Appendix B for areas included
Source: Global Insight/PNC Financial Services Group, House Prices in America: 4th Quarter 2009 Update

Median Single-Family Home Prices

Area	2008	2009	2010p	Percent Change 2009 to 2010
MSA[1]	206.2	192.7	200.5	4.0
U.S. Average	196.6	172.1	173.2	0.6

Note: Figures are median sales prices of existing single-family homes in thousands of dollars; (p) preliminary; n/a not available; (1) Metropolitan Statistical Area - see Appendix B for areas included
Source: National Association of Realtors, Median Sales Price of Existing Single-Family Homes for Metropolitan Areas, 4th Quarter 2010

Median Apartment Condo-Coop Home Prices

Area	2008	2009	2010p	Percent Change 2009 to 2010
MSA[1]	n/a	n/a	n/a	n/a
U.S. Average	209.8	175.6	171.7	-2.2

Note: Figures are median sales prices of existing apartment condo-coop homes in thousands of dollars; (p) preliminary; n/a not available; (1) Metropolitan Statistical Area - see Appendix B for areas included
Source: National Association of Realtors, Median Sales Price of Existing Apartment Condo-Coop Homes for Metropolitan Areas, 4th Quarter 2010

Year Housing Structure Built

Area	2000 or Later	1990-1999	1980-1989	1970-1979	1960-1969	1950-1959	1940-1949	Before 1940	Median Year
City	22.6	13.3	13.4	11.9	9.2	8.3	5.0	16.4	1979
MSA[1]	21.1	17.3	20.0	15.8	9.9	6.8	3.7	5.4	1984
U.S.	12.5	14.0	14.2	16.5	11.4	11.3	5.8	14.3	1974

Note: Figures are percentages except for Median Year; (1) Metropolitan Statistical Area - see Appendix B for areas included
Source: U.S. Census Bureau, 2007-2009 American Community Survey 3-Year Estimates

HEALTH

Health Risk Data

Category	MSA[1] (%)	U.S. (%)
Adults who have been told they have high blood pressure	30.8	28.7
Adults who have been told they have high blood cholesterol	43.9	37.5
Adults who have been told they have diabetes[3]	10.0	8.3
Adults who have been told they have arthritis	27.2	26.0
Adults who have been told they currently have asthma	6.9	8.8
Adults who are current smokers	17.5	17.9
Adults who are heavy drinkers[4]	5.4	5.1
Adults who are binge drinkers[5]	16.5	15.8
Adults who are overweight (BMI 25.0 - 29.9)	35.4	36.2
Adults who are obese (BMI 30.0 - 99.8)	28.6	26.9
Adults who participated in any physical activities in the past month	78.1	76.2
Adults 50+ who have ever had a sigmoidoscopy or colonoscopy[2]	69.0	62.2
Women 40+ who have had a mammogram within the past two years[2]	75.0	76.0
Adults age 18–64 who have any kind of health care coverage	88.0	83.1

Note: Data as of 2009 unless otherwise noted; (1) Figures cover the Charleston-North Charleston, SC Metropolitan Statistical Area - see Appendix B for areas included; (2) Data as of 2008; (3) Figures do not include pregnancy-related, borderline, or pre-diabetes; (4) Heavy drinkers are classified as males having more than two drinks per day or females having more than one drink per day; (5) Binge drinkers are classified as males having five or more drinks on one occasion or females having four or more drinks on one occasion
Source: Centers for Disease Control and Prevention, Behaviorial Risk Factor Surveillance System, SMART: Selected Metropolitan/Micropolitan Area Risk Trends, 2008, 2009

Mortality Rates for the Top 10 Causes of Death in the U.S.

ICD-10[a] Sub-Chapter	ICD-10[a] Code	Age-Adjusted Mortality Rate[1] per 100,000 population County[2]	U.S.
Malignant neoplasms	C00-C97	184.0	180.9
Ischaemic heart diseases	I20-I25	99.1	135.0
Other forms of heart disease	I30-I51	54.4	50.0
Cerebrovascular diseases	I60-I69	55.0	44.1
Chronic lower respiratory diseases	J40-J47	38.6	41.5
Other degenerative diseases of the nervous system	G30-G31	34.9	23.6
Diabetes mellitus	E10-E14	26.7	23.5
Other external causes of accidental injury	W00-X59	27.3	23.5
Organic, including symptomatic, mental disorders	F01-F09	31.1	22.2
Influenza and pneumonia	J09-J18	12.1	18.1

Note: (a) ICD-10 = International Classification of Diseases 10th Revision; (1) Mortality rates are a three year average covering 2005-2007; (2) Figures cover Charleston County
Source: Centers for Disease Control and Prevention, National Center for Health Statistics. Compressed Mortality File 1999-2007. CDC WONDER On-line Database, compiled from Compressed Mortality File 1999-2007 Series 20 No. 2M, 2010.

Mortality Rates for Selected Causes of Death

ICD-10[a] Sub-Chapter	ICD-10[a] Code	Age-Adjusted Mortality Rate[1] per 100,000 population County[2]	U.S.
Assault	X85-Y09	12.3	6.0
Human immunodeficiency virus (HIV) disease	B20-B24	8.0	4.0
Hypertensive diseases	I10-I15	16.3	18.0
Intentional self-harm	X60-X84	11.9	11.0
Malnutrition	E40-E46	*0.8	0.8
Obesity and other hyperalimentation	E65-E68	*1.2	1.5
Transport accidents	V01-V99	21.0	15.6
Viral hepatitis	B15-B19	*1.4	2.1

Note: (a) ICD-10 = International Classification of Diseases 10th Revision; (1) Mortality rates are a three year average covering 2005-2007; (2) Figures cover Charleston County; (*) Unreliable data as per CDC
Source: Centers for Disease Control and Prevention, National Center for Health Statistics. Compressed Mortality File 1999-2007. CDC WONDER On-line Database, compiled from Compressed Mortality File 1999-2007 Series 20 No. 2M, 2010.

Distribution of Physicians and Dentists

Area[1]	Dentists[2]	D.O.[3]	M.D.[4]				
			Total	Family/ General Practice	Pediatrics	Medical Specialties	Surgical Specialties
Local (number)	244	73	1,424	117	93	474	353
Local (rate[5])	7.1	2.1	40.7	3.3	2.7	13.6	10.1
U.S. (rate[5])	4.5	1.9	18.3	2.5	1.4	6.8	4.1

Note: Data as of 2008 unless noted; (1) Local data covers Charleston County; (2) Data as of 2007; (3) Doctor of Osteopathic Medicine; (4) Includes active, non-federal, patient-care, office-based Doctors of Medicine; (5) rate per 10,000 population
Source: Area Resource File (ARF). 2009-2010 Release. U.S. Department of Health and Human Services, Health Resources and Services Administration, Bureau of Health Professions, Rockville, MD, August 2010

Hospitals

Charleston has the following hospitals: 6 general medical and surgical; 1 psychiatric; 1 rehabilitation; 1 long-term acute care.
AHA Guide to the Healthcare Field 2010

According to *U.S. News,* the Charleston-North Charleston, SC Metropolitan Statistical Area is home to one of the best hospitals in the U.S.: **Medical University of South Carolina**. The hospital listed was highly ranked in at least one adult specialty. *U.S. News Online, "America's Best Hospitals 2010-11"*

According to *U.S. News,* the Charleston-North Charleston, SC Metropolitan Statistical Area is home to one of the best children's hospitals in the U.S.: **Medical University of South Carolina Children's Hospital**. The hospital listed was highly ranked in at least one pediatric specialty. *U.S. News Online, "America's Best Children's Hospitals 2010-11"*

EDUCATION

Public School District Statistics

District Name	Schls	Pupils	Pupil/ Teacher Ratio	Minority Pupils[1] (%)	Free Lunch Eligible[2] (%)	IEP[3] (%)
Charleston 01	81	42,303	13.2	57.8	42.7	11.3

Note: Table includes school districts with 2,000 or more students; (1) Percentage of students that are not non-Hispanic white; (2) Percentage of students that are eligible for the free lunch program; (3) Percentage of students that have an Individualized Education Program.
Source: U.S. Department of Education, National Center for Education Statistics, Common Core of Data, Local Education Agency (School District) Universe Survey: School Year 2008-2009; U.S. Department of Education, National Center for Education Statistics, Common Core of Data, Public Elementary/Secondary School Universe Survey: School Year 2008-2009

Highest Level of Education

Area	Less than H.S.	H.S. Diploma	Some College, No Deg.	Associate Degree	Bachelors Degree	Masters Degree	Profess. School Degree	Doctorate Degree
City	11.6	22.5	18.7	7.2	24.1	9.5	4.1	2.4
MSA[1]	12.5	29.3	20.8	8.7	18.1	7.1	2.2	1.3
U.S.	15.3	29.0	20.7	7.5	17.4	7.0	1.9	1.1

Note: Figures are 2010 estimated percentages and cover persons age 25 and over; (1) Metropolitan Statistical Area - see Appendix B for areas included
Source: Claritas, Inc.

Educational Attainment by Race

Area	High School Graduate (%)					Bachelor's Degree (%)				
	Total	White	Black	Asian	Hisp.[2]	Total	White	Black	Asian	Hisp.[2]
City	91.2	96.2	76.1	95.5	80.6	46.7	56.5	18.6	57.1	18.7
MSA[1]	87.5	91.9	78.9	83.0	66.1	29.7	36.2	13.7	40.9	15.5
U.S.	84.9	90.0	80.7	85.5	60.7	27.8	30.9	17.5	49.7	12.7

Note: Figures shown cover persons 25 years old and over; (1) Metropolitan Statistical Area - see Appendix B for areas included; (2) people of Hispanic origin can be of any race
Source: U.S. Census Bureau, 2007-2009 American Community Survey 3-Year Estimates

School Enrollment by Grade and Control

Area	Preschool (%)		Kindergarten (%)		Grades 1 - 4 (%)		Grades 5 - 8 (%)		Grades 9 - 12 (%)	
	Public	Private	Public	Private	Public	Private	Public	Private	Public	Private
City	44.8	55.2	65.2	34.8	82.6	17.4	83.8	16.2	78.3	21.7
MSA[1]	46.9	53.1	80.8	19.2	85.5	14.5	85.7	14.3	86.8	13.2
U.S.	54.3	45.7	86.4	13.6	88.9	11.1	89.1	10.9	90.2	9.8

Note: Figures shown cover persons 3 years old and over; (1) Metropolitan Statistical Area - see Appendix B for areas included
Source: U.S. Census Bureau, 2007-2009 American Community Survey 3-Year Estimates

Average Salaries of Public School Classroom Teachers

Area	2009-10		2010-11		Percent Change 2009-10 to 2010-11	Percent Change 2000-01 to 2010-11
	Dollars	Rank[1]	Dollars	Rank[1]		
South Carolina	47,508	34	49,434	31	4.05	30.3
U.S. Average	55,202	-	56,069	-	1.57	29.3

Note: (1) State rank ranges from 1 to 51 where 1 indicates highest salary.
Source: National Education Association, Rankings & Estimates: Rankings of the States 2010 and Estimates of School Statistics 2011, December 2010

Higher Education

Four-Year Colleges			Two-Year Colleges			Medical Schools[1]	Law Schools[2]	Voc/ Tech[3]
Public	Private Non-profit	Private For-profit	Public	Private Non-profit	Private For-profit			
3	1	2	1	0	0	1	1	3

Note: Figures cover institutions located within the city limits and include main campuses only; (1) includes schools accredited by the Liaison Committee on Medical Education and the American Osteopathic Association; (2) includes American Bar Association-accredited law schools; (3) includes all schools with programs that are less than 2 years.
Source: National Center for Education Statistics, Integrated Postsecondary Education System (IPEDS) Peer Analysis System, 2010-11; U.S. News & World Report, Medical School Directory, 2011; U.S. News & World Report, Law School Directory, 2011

PRESIDENTIAL ELECTION

2008 Presidential Election Results

Area	Obama	McCain	Nader	Other
Charleston County	53.5	45.2	0.3	1.0
U.S.	52.9	45.6	0.6	0.9

Note: Results are percentages and may not add to 100% due to rounding
Source: Dave Leip's Atlas of U.S. Presidential Elections, www.uselectionatlas.org

EMPLOYERS

Major Employers

Company Name	Industry	Type of Site
Alcoa	Primary aluminum	Branch
Alternative Staffing	Help supply services	Headquarters
Behr Heat Transfer Systems	Motor vehicle parts and accessories	Headquarters
Campground At James Island	Trailer parks and campsites	Single
Charleston County Sheriffs Off	Police protection	Branch
Cummins	Internal combustion engines, nec	Branch
Doctors Care	Offices and clinics of medical doctors	Branch
Human Resources Department	Management services	Branch
Kiawah Island Golf Tnnis Rsort	Hotels and motels	Headquarters
Medical Center	Special warehousing and storage, nec	Branch
Medical University SC	General medical and surgical hospitals	Headquarters
Medical University SC	Hospital and medical service plans	Branch
Naval Nclear Pwr Training Unit	National security	Branch
Oral Surgery Clinic	Offices and clinics of medical doctors	Branch
Pediatric Plmnlgy Allrgy	General medical and surgical hospitals	Branch
Ralph H Johnson V A Med Ctr	General medical and surgical hospitals	Branch
Six Continents Hotel	Hotels and motels	Branch
South Carolina Ports Authority	Regulation, administration of transportation	Branch
Trident Health Systems	General medical and surgical hospitals	Headquarters
University of Charleston	Colleges and universities	Headquarters
Verizon Wireless	Radiotelephone communication	Branch
Wild Dunes Resort	Management services	Branch

Note: Companies shown are located within the Charleston metropolitan area; nec = not elsewhere classified.
Source: www.zapdata.com, January 2011

PUBLIC SAFETY

Crime Rate

Area	All Crimes	Violent Crimes				Property Crimes		
		Murder	Forcible Rape	Robbery	Aggrav. Assault	Burglary	Larceny -Theft	Motor Vehicle Theft
City	4,034.1	7.9	27.3	191.8	296.4	497.9	2,772.7	240.1
Suburbs[1]	n/a	4.9	34.2	153.8	442.7	n/a	2,555.0	328.7
Metro[2]	n/a	5.5	33.0	160.4	417.5	n/a	2,592.5	313.5
U.S.	3,465.5	5.0	28.7	133.0	262.8	716.3	2,060.9	258.8

Note: Figures are crimes per 100,000 population; (1) All areas within the metro area that are located outside the city limits; (2) Metropolitan Statistical Area - see Appendix B for areas included
Source: FBI Uniform Crime Reports, 2009

Hate Crimes

Area	Number of Quarters Reported	Bias Motivation				
		Race	Religion	Sexual Orientation	Ethnicity	Disability
City	4	0	0	0	0	0

Source: Federal Bureau of Investigation, Hate Crime Statistics 2009

Identity Theft Consumer Complaints

Area	Complaints	Complaints per 100,000 Population	Rank[2]
MSA[1]	405	64.3	241
U.S.	250,854	81.3	-

Note: (1) Metropolitan Statistical Area - see Appendix B for areas included; (2) Rank ranges from 1 to 384 where 1 indicates greatest number of complaints per 100,000 population
Source: Federal Trade Commission, Consumer Sentinel Network Data Book for January - December 2010

RECREATION

Culture

Dance[1]	Theatre[1]	Instrumental Music[1]	Vocal Music[1]	Series/ Festivals	Museums	Zoos and Aquariums[2]
2	1	2	0	4	12	1

Note: (1) Number of professional perfoming groups; (2) AZA-accredited
Source: The Grey House Performing Arts Directory, 2011-2012; Official Museum Directory, 2010; American Association of Museums, AAM Member Museums, March 2011; Association of Zoos & Aquariums, AZA Member Zoos & Aquariums, May 2011

Professional Sports Teams

Team Name	League

No teams are located in the metro area
Source: Original research

CLIMATE

Average and Extreme Temperatures

Temperature	Jan	Feb	Mar	Apr	May	Jun	Jul	Aug	Sep	Oct	Nov	Dec	Yr.
Extreme High (°F)	83	87	90	94	98	101	104	102	97	94	88	83	104
Average High (°F)	59	62	68	76	83	88	90	89	85	77	69	61	76
Average Temp. (°F)	49	51	57	65	73	78	81	81	76	67	58	51	66
Average Low (°F)	38	40	46	53	62	69	72	72	67	56	46	39	55
Extreme Low (°F)	6	12	15	30	36	50	58	56	42	27	15	8	6

Note: Figures cover the years 1945-1995
Source: National Climatic Data Center, International Station Meteorological Climate Summary, 9/96

Average Precipitation/Snowfall/Humidity

Precip./Humidity	Jan	Feb	Mar	Apr	May	Jun	Jul	Aug	Sep	Oct	Nov	Dec	Yr.
Avg. Precip. (in.)	3.5	3.1	4.4	2.8	4.1	6.0	7.2	6.9	5.6	3.1	2.5	3.1	52.1
Avg. Snowfall (in.)	Tr	Tr	Tr	0	0	0	0	0	0	0	Tr	Tr	1
Avg. Rel. Hum. 7am (%)	83	81	83	84	85	86	88	90	91	89	86	83	86
Avg. Rel. Hum. 4pm (%)	55	52	51	51	56	62	66	66	65	58	56	55	58

Note: Figures cover the years 1945-1995; Tr = Trace amounts (<0.05 in. of rain; <0.5 in. of snow)
Source: National Climatic Data Center, International Station Meteorological Climate Summary, 9/96

Weather Conditions

Temperature			Daytime Sky			Precipitation		
10°F & below	32°F & below	90°F & above	Clear	Partly cloudy	Cloudy	0.01 inch or more precip.	0.1 inch or more snow/ice	Thunder-storms
< 1	33	53	89	162	114	114	1	59

Note: Figures are average number of days per year and cover the years 1945-1995
Source: National Climatic Data Center, International Station Meteorological Climate Summary, 9/96

HAZARDOUS WASTE

Superfund Sites

Charleston has one hazardous waste site on the EPA's Superfund Final National Priorities List: **Koppers Co., Inc. (Charleston Plant)**. *U.S. Environmental Protection Agency, Final National Priorities List, April 1, 2011*

AIR & WATER QUALITY

Air Quality Index

Area	Percent of Days when Air Quality was...[2]				AQI Statistics	
	Good	Moderate	Unhealthy for Sensitive Groups	Unhealthy	Maximum	Median
Area[1]	78.4	21.6	0.0	0.0	100	41

Note: The Air Quality Index (AQI) is an index for reporting daily air quality. EPA calculates the AQI for five major air pollutants regulated by the Clean Air Act: ground-level ozone, particle pollution (also known as particulate matter), carbon monoxide, sulfur dioxide, and nitrogen dioxide. The AQI runs from 0 to 500. The higher the AQI value, the greater the level of air pollution and the greater the health concern. There are six AQI categories: "Good" The AQI is between 0 and 50. Air quality is considered satisfactory; "Moderate" The AQI is between 51 and 100. Air quality is acceptable; "Unhealthy for Sensitive Groups" When AQI values are between 101 and 150, members of sensitive groups may experience health effects; "Unhealthy" When AQI values are between 151 and 200 everyone may begin to experience health effects; "Very Unhealthy" AQI values between 201 and 300 trigger a health alert; "Hazardous" AQI values over 300 trigger health warnings of emergency conditions; (1) Data covers Charleston County; (2) Based on 366 days with AQI data in 2008; The EPA has suspended data updates while it assesses its data systems, including AirData reports and maps.
Source: U.S. Environmental Protection Agency, AirData Report, 2008

Air Quality Index Pollutants

Area	Percent of Days when AQI Pollutant was...[2]					
	Carbon Monoxide	Nitrogen Dioxide	Ozone	Sulfur Dioxide	Particulate Matter 2.5	Particulate Matter 10
Area[1]	0.0	0.0	53.6	0.0	46.4	0.0

Note: The Air Quality Index (AQI) is an index for reporting daily air quality. EPA calculates the AQI for five major air pollutants regulated by the Clean Air Act: ground-level ozone, particle pollution (also known as particulate matter), carbon monoxide, sulfur dioxide, and nitrogen dioxide. The AQI runs from 0 to 500. The higher the AQI value, the greater the level of air pollution and the greater the health concern; (1) Data covers Charleston County; (2) Based on 366 days with AQI data in 2008; The EPA has suspended data updates while it assesses its data systems, including AirData reports and maps.
Source: U.S. Environmental Protection Agency, AirData Report, 2008

Air Quality Index Trends

Area	Trend Sites (days)								All Sites (days)
	2002	2003	2004	2005	2006	2007	2008	2009	2009
MSA[1]	4	3	3	8	9	5	1	0	0

Note: Figures are the number of days the AQI value exceeded 100 in a given year. An AQI value greater than 100 indicates that air quality would have been in the unhealthful range on that day. Data from exceptional events are included. These counts are presented in two ways. First, the counts are based on sites having an adequate record of monitoring data during the trend period (trend sites). These counts represent the relative change in the number of days with AQI values greater than 100. In the last column, the counts are based on all sites with data in the most recent year (because it is possible for a site to have data in the most recent year but not enough data to be a trend site); (1) Data covers the Charleston-North Charleston, SC Metropolitan Statistical Area - see Appendix B for areas included
Source: U.S. Environmental Protection Agency, Office of Air and Radiation, Air Quality Index Information, "Number of Days with Air Quality Index Values Greater than 100 and Trend Sites, 1990-2009, and at All Sites in 2009"

Maximum Air Pollutant Concentrations

	Particulate Matter 10 (ug/m³)	Particulate Matter 2.5 (ug/m³)	Ozone (ppm)	Carbon Monoxide (ppm)	Sulfur Dioxide (ppm)	Nitrogen Dioxide (ppm)	Lead (ug/m³)
MSA[1] Level	43	22	0.063	0	0.006	0.008	0.01
NAAQS[2]	150	35	0.075	9	0.140	0.053	0.15
Met NAAQS[2]	Yes	Yes	Yes	Yes	Yes	Yes	Yes

Note: Data from exceptional events are not included; (1) Data covers the Charleston-North Charleston, SC Metropolitan Statistical Area - see Appendix B for areas included; (2) National Ambient Air Quality Standards; n/a not available
Concentrations: Particulate Matter 10 (coarse particulate) - highest second maximum 24-hour concentration; Particulate Matter 2.5 (fine particulate) - highest 98th percentile 24-hour concentration; Ozone - highest fourth daily maximum 8-hour concentration; Carbon Monoxide - highest second maximum non-overlapping 8-hour concentration; Sulfur Dioxide - highest second maximum 24-hour concentration; Nitrogen Dioxide - highest arithmetic mean concentration; Lead - maximum running 3-month average
Units: ppm = parts per million; ug/m³ = micrograms per cubic meter
Source: U.S. Environmental Protection Agency, CBSA Factbook 2009, Air Quality Statistics by City, 2009

Drinking Water

| Water System Name | Pop. Served | Primary Water Source Type | Violations[1] | |
			Health Based	Monitoring/ Reporting
Charleston Water System	226,551	Surface	0	0

Note: (1) Based on violation data from January 1, 2010 to December 31, 2010 (includes unresolved violations from earlier years)
Source: U.S. Environmental Protection Agency, Office of Ground Water and Drinking Water, Safe Drinking Water Information System (based on data extracted May 9, 2011)

Chattanooga, Tennessee

Background

Chattanooga is located on the Tennessee River near the Georgia border. Its name derives from a Cherokee word meaning "rock rising to a point," which refers to nearby Lookout Mountain. The city rests in a valley ringed by Lookout and Signal mountains, and by Missionary Ridge. Chattanooga is a dynamic tourist, financial, services, and manufacturing center, with unique features of a prosperous and innovative community.

In 1803, John Brown, a half-Cherokee, set up a ferry that became an important crossroads between Southern and Eastern markets, and Chattanooga soon established itself as a modest but important salt-trading center. The city was incorporated in 1839. With the construction in 1849 of a Western and Atlantic Railroad link to other cities, Chattanooga became a major rail hub, distributing many Southern products, such as bacon, flour, iron, whiskey, and, increasingly, cotton, throughout the South Atlantic Eastern seaboard.

During the Civil War, Union troops took the city, and it was from here that General Sherman began his march to the sea. The major battles of Chickamauga and Chattanooga were fought nearby, and the nation's first national military park commemorating these battles is close by. Chattanooga's postwar economy was revived first by coal and iron, and later by the building of the Tennessee Valley Authority dams and associated projects, which resulted in considerable industrial expansion.

The current local economy of Chattanooga is a diversified mix of health care, service, and manufacturing. Chattanooga's three large hospitals (Erlanger Hospital, Packridge Hospital and Memorial Hospital) offer many employment opportunities in the healthcare field. BlueCross BlueShield is also located in the city. Chattanooga is the home of Coca Cola's first bottling plant (still operating today). Volkswagen opened is newest U.S. manufacturing plant in Chattanooga in 2011, which is expected to produce 150,000 Passats annually.

Chattanooga has been dubbed one of America's most "Enlightened Towns" by the *Utne Reader,* and is often held up as a model of sustainable community development. One of the most pedestrian-friendly and walkable cities in the Southeast, Chattanooga has developed a Green Space Master Plan, including tree-lined boulevards, parks and a network of walking and biking paths. The 120-year old Walnut Street Walking Bridge—the longest pedestrian bridge in the nation—is one of several downtown bridges that carry pedestrians over the Tennessee River. The bridges link the more than 20 miles of reclaimed riverfront that make up the new Tennessee Riverpark—a pedestrian wonderland of bicycle and pedestrian paths, nature trails, picnic areas, a sculpture garden, and an aquarium.

One key to the city's renaissance has been the revitalization of its historic theaters and inns, and the construction of Riverwalk, a waterfront park lined by once-abandoned factories. The Riverwalk is part of a nationally celebrated revival of a once industrially-blighted area. Herons and mallards are now seen nesting along 75 miles of greenways in the previously polluted landscape. Further recent improvement to the Tennessee River waterfront includes expansion of the Tennessee Aquarium to include the story of the Tennessee River and the Gulf of Mexico, the renovated Hunter Museum of American Art, and The Passage, a multi-million dollar waterfront revitalization that includes under- and over-ground walks and trails.

The city is also home to The Houston Museum of Decorative Art—the legacy of Anna Safley Houston, which displays rare antique glass and ceramic pieces.

On the sports front, Chattanooga has been home to the U.S. women's Olympic rowing team, a professional soccer team, and sports teams from the University of Tennessee at Chattanooga. In addition to a campus of the University of Tennessee at Chattanooga, established in 1886, Tennessee Temple University and a thriving community college are also here.

No description of Chattanooga would be complete without mention of the Chattanooga Choo Choo Complex, an old station, and now part of a hotel, which features the world's largest HO gauge model railroad layout.

Chattanooga's nearby mountains tend to moderate the winters, by retarding the flow of cold air from the north and west. As a result, winters, though cool, are slightly warmer than nearby locations of similar elevation. Snowfall tends to melt fairly quickly and ice storms are not uncommon. Summers are warm to hot, with afternoon thunderstorms. Annual precipitation is fairly heavy.

Rankings

General Rankings

- Chattanooga was ranked #219 out of 375 metro areas in *Cities Ranked & Rated*. Criteria: cost of living; climate; crime; transportation; economy and jobs; education; arts and culture; health and healthcare; leisure; quality of life. *Cities Ranked & Rated, 2nd Edition, 2007*

- Chattanooga was ranked #122 out of 379 metro areas in *Places Rated Almanac*. Criteria: health care; education; recreation; transportation; ambience; climate; crime; housing costs; jobs. *Places Rated Almanac, 7th Edition, 2007*

- Chattanooga was chosen as one of America's best cities by "Outside Magazine" in the Best Overall in the East (Runner-up) category. Criteria: educational attainment; cost of living; cultural vibrancy; economic resilience; housing market sanity; sport-specific facts such as the miles of trail within a hour's drive, frequency of group rides, and proximity to worthy ski areas. *Outside Magazine, "Best Towns 2010," August 2010*

- Chattanooga appeared on *National Geographic Adventure's* list of the "50 Best Places to Live + Play." *National Geographic Adventure, September 2008*

Business/Finance Rankings

- Chattanooga was selected as one of the best places to start a business by *CNNMoney.com*. Criteria: compelling incentives to would-be entrepreneurs. *CNNMoney.com, "8 Great Cities to Start a Business," 2010*

- *American City Business Journals* ranked America's 261 largest cities in terms of their resident's wealth. Chattanooga ranked #195. Criteria: per capita income; median household income; percentage of households with annual incomes of $200,000 or more; median home value. *American City Business Journals, www.bizjournals.com, "Where the Money Is: America's Wealth Centers," August 18, 2008*

- The Chattanooga metro area appeared on the Milken Institute "2010 Best Performing Metros" list. Rank: #133 out of 200 large metro areas. Criteria: job growth; wage and salary growth; high-tech output growth. *Milken Institute, "2010 Best Performing Metros"*

- *Forbes* ranked the 200 most populous metro areas in the U.S. in terms of the "Best Places for Business and Careers." The Chattanooga metro area was ranked #132. Criteria: 12 metrics including costs (business and living), job growth (past and projected), income growth, educational attainment, projected economic growth, crime, cultural and recreational opportunities, net migration patterns, percentage of subprime mortgages handed out over a three-year period, and the number of highly ranked four-year colleges. *Forbes, "Best Places for Business and Careers," April 14, 2010*

Children/Family Rankings

- The Chattanooga metro area was selected as one of the "Best Cities for Relocating Families" by Worldwide ERC and Primacy Relocation. The 2008 study looked at nearly 50 factors important to relocating families including: recent job growth; nearby top-ranked colleges; in-state tuition for four-year public colleges; population growth since 2000; pediatricians per 100,000 population; and a Green Living index. *Worldwide ERC and Primacy Relocation, "2008 Best Cities for Relocating Families"*

Culture/Performing Arts Rankings

- Chattanooga was selected as one of "America's Top 25 Arts Destinations." The city ranked #4 in the mid-sized city (population 100,000 to 499,999) category. Criteria: readers' top choices for arts travel destinations based on the richness and variety of visual arts sites, activities and events. *American Style, "America's Top 25 Arts Destinations," May 2010*

Education Rankings

- Chattanooga was identified as one of the 100 "smartest" metro areas in the U.S. The area ranked #88. Criteria: the editors rated the collective brainpower of the 100 largest metro area in the U.S based on their residents' educational attainment. *American City Business Journals, www.bizjournals.com, April 14, 2008*

- Chattanooga was identified as one of "America's Brainiest Bastions" by *Portfolio.com*. The metro area ranked #156 out of 200. Portfolio.com analyzed levels of educational attainment in the nation's 200 largest metropolitan areas. The editors established scores for five levels of educational attainment, based on relative earning power of adult workers age 25 or older. Scores were determined by comparing the median income for all workers with the median income for those workers at a specified educational level. *Portfolio.com, "America's Brainiest Bastions," December 1, 2010*

Environmental Rankings

- Chattanooga was selected as one of 22 "Smarter Cities" for energy by the Natural Resources Defense Council." Criteria: investment in green power; energy efficiency measures; conservation. *Natural Resources Defense Council, "2010 Smarter Cities," July 19, 2010*

- 100 of the largest metro areas in the U.S. were analyzed in terms of their current drought severity. The Chattanooga metro area ranked #7 (#1 = driest). The rankings were based on statistics such as long-term precipitation trends and patterns and the Palmer drought indices. *Sperling's BestPlaces, www.BestPlaces.net, "America's Drought-Riskiest Cities," November 2007*

- The U.S. Conference of Mayors and Wal-Mart Stores sponsor the Mayors' Climate Protection Awards Program. The awards recognize and honor mayors for outstanding and innovative practices that mayors are taking to increase energy efficiency in their cities, and to help curb global warming. Chattanooga was a Large City Best Practice Model. *U.S. Conference of Mayors, "2009 Mayors' Climate Protection Awards Program"*

- The Chattanooga metro area appeared in *Country Home's* "Best Green Places" report. The area ranked #260 out of 379. Criteria: official energy policies; green power; green buildings; availability of fresh, locally grown food. *Country Home, "Best Green Places," 2008*

Health/Fitness Rankings

- Chattanooga was given "Well City USA" status by The Wellness Councils of America, whose objective is to engage entire business communities in building healthy workforces. Well City status is met when a minimum of 20 employers who collectively employ at least 20% of the city's workforce become designated Well Workplaces within a three-year period. To date, eleven communities have achieved Well City USA status. *The Wellness Councils of America, Well City USA, 2011*

- Chattanooga was identified as a "2011 Asthma Capital." The area ranked #4 out of the nation's 100 largest metropolitan areas. Twelve factors were used to identify the most challenging places to live for people with asthma: estimated prevalence; self-reported prevalence; crude death rate for asthma; annual pollen score; annual air quality; public smoking laws; number of board-certified asthma specialists; school inhaler access laws; rescue medication use; controller medication use; uninsured rate; poverty rate. *Asthma and Allergy Foundation of America, "2011 Asthma Capitals"*

- Chattanooga was identified as a 2009 "Spring Allergy Capital." The area ranked #17 out of 100. Three groups of factors were used to identify the most severe cities for people with allergies during the spring season: annual pollen levels; medicine utilization; access to board-certified allergists. *Asthma and Allergy Foundation of America, "Spring Allergy Capitals 2009"*

- Chattanooga was identified as a 2010 "Fall Allergy Capital." The area ranked #13 out of 100. Three groups of factors were used to identify the most severe cities for people with allergies during the fall season: annual pollen levels; medicine utilization; access to board-certified allergists. *Asthma and Allergy Foundation of America, "Fall Allergy Capitals 2010"*

- Ortho-McNeil Neurologics, in partnership with Sperling's BestPlaces, analyzed 110 metro areas and identified those U.S. cities with the highest prevalence of factors that are most commonly associated with migraine headaches. The Chattanooga metro area ranked #8. Criteria: number of migraine-related drug prescriptions per capita; lifestyle factors that can contribute to migraines; environmental factors that can trigger migraines; and consumption of migraine-triggering foods. *Ortho-McNeil Neurologics, "America's Migraine Hot Spots," March 14, 2006*

- The Chattanooga metropolitan area was selected as one of the best metros for hospital care in America by HealthGrades. The rankings are based on a comprehensive study of patient death and complication rates in the nation's nearly 5,000 hospitals. Hospitals performing in the top 5% nationwide across 26 different medical procedures and diagnoses were identified. HealthGrades then ranked cities by the highest percentage of these Distinguished Hospitals for Clinical Excellence™. The Chattanooga metro area ranked #9. *HealthGrades.com, "America's Top 50 Cities for Hospital Care," January 26, 2011*

- The Chattanooga metro area appeared in the 2010 Gallup-Healthways Well-Being Index. The index, based on interviews with more than 353,000 Americans during 2009, asked individuals to assess their jobs, finances, physical health, emotional state of mind and communities. The metro area ranked #136 out of 162. Criteria: life evaluation; emotional health; work environment; physical health; healthy behaviors; basic access (basic needs optimal for a healthy life, such as access to food and medicine, having health insurance and feeling safe while walking at night). *Gallup-Healthways, "Well-Being Index 2010"*

Real Estate Rankings

- The Chattanooga metro area was identified as one of the least expensive places to rent in the U.S. The area ranked #136 out of 10 markets with an average effective rent of $580 per month. The rental figures cover apartment properties in complexes with 40 or more units (20 or more units in California and Arizona). The figures are blended average rents, which include all unit sizes. Effective rents include free rent incentives and other landlord concessions. *Wall Street Journal Online, January 17, 2008*

- The nation's largest metro areas were analyzed in terms of the percentage of households entering some stage of foreclosure in 2010. The Chattanooga metro area ranked #109 out of 206 (#1 = highest foreclosure rate). *RealtyTrac, 2010 Year-End Metropolitan Foreclosure Market Report, January 27, 2011*

- The Center for Housing Policy ranked 210 U.S metropolitan areas by the fair market rent for a two-bedroom unit. The Chattanooga metro area was ranked #181. (#1 = most expensive) with a rent of $669. Criteria: Fair Market Rent (FMR) in effect during the fourth quarter of 2009 based on HUD's fiscal year 2010 FMRs. *The Center for Housing Policy, "Paycheck to Paycheck: Most to Least Expensive Rental Markets in 2009"*

Safety Rankings

- Allstate ranked the 200 largest cities in America in terms of driver safety. Chattanooga ranked #2. In addition, drivers were 22.7% less likely to have had an accident compared to the national average. Allstate researchers analyzed internal property damage reported claims over a two-year period (from January 2007 to December 2008) to ensure the findings would not be affected by external influences such as weather or road construction. A weighted average of the two-year numbers determined the annual percentages. The report defines an auto crash as any collision resulting in a property damage claim. *Allstate, "The 2010 Allstate America's Best Drivers Report™"*

- The National Insurance Crime Bureau ranked 366 metro areas in the U.S. in terms of per capita rates of vehicle theft. The Chattanooga metro area ranked #94 (#1 = highest rate). Criteria: number of vehicle theft offenses per 100,000 inhabitants. *National Insurance Crime Bureau, "Hot Spots," May 17, 2010*

Seniors/Retirement Rankings

- Chattanooga was identified as one of "The Top 100 Places to Retire" by *Topretirements.com* The list reflects the 100 cities (out of 625+ total cities reviewed) that visitors to the website are most interested in for retirement. *Topretirements.com, "2011 Best Places to Retire List: The Sunbelt Rules"*

Sports/Recreation Rankings

- Chattanooga appeared on the *Sporting News* list of the "Best Sports Cities" for 2010. The area ranked #200 out of 402 cities in the U.S. *Sporting News* takes a 12-month snapshot, roughly October to October, of each city's sports, putting a heavy premium on regular-season won-lost records (from the most recently completed season). Other criteria include: playoff berths, bowl appearances and tournament bids; championships; applicable power ratings; quality of competition; overall fan fervor as measured in part by attendance as percentage of venue capacity; abundance of teams (rewarding quality over quantity); stadium and arena quality; ticket availability and prices; franchise ownership; and marquee appeal of athletes. *Sporting News, "Best Sports Cities 2010," October, 2010*

- Chattanooga was chosen as a bicycle friendly community by the League of American Bicyclists. A Bicycle Friendly Community welcomes cyclists by providing safe accommodation for cycling and encouraging people to bike for transportation and recreation. There are four award levels: Platinum; Gold; Silver; and Bronze. The community achieved an award level of Bronze. *League of American Bicyclists, "Bicycle Friendly Community Master List," September 2010*

- Chattanooga was chosen as one of America's best cities for bicycling. The city ranked #22 out of 50. Criteria: number of segregated bike lanes, municipal bike racks, and bike boulevards; vibrant and diverse bike culture; smart, savvy bike shops; interviews with national and local advocates, bike shops and other experts. Note: only cities with populations of 100,000 or more were considered. *Bicycling, "America's Best Bike Cities," April 2010*

- *Golf Digest* ranked 330 metro areas in the U.S. in terms of golf. The Chattanooga metro area was ranked #106. Criteria: access to golf; weather; value of golf; and quality of golf. *Golf Digest, "Metro Golf Rankings," August 2005*

Technology Rankings

- Scarborough Research, a leading market research firm, identified the Chattanooga DMA (Designated Market Area) as one of the top markets for text messaging with more than 50% of cell phone subscribers age 18+ utilizing the text messaging feature on their phone. *Scarborough Research, November 24, 2008*

Business Environment

CITY FINANCES

City Government Finances

Component	2008 ($000)	2008 ($ per capita)
Total Revenues	845,142	4,975
Total Expenditures	859,753	5,061
Debt Outstanding	876,066	5,157
Cash and Securities[1]	952,900	5,609

Note: (1) Cash and security holdings of a government at the close of its fiscal year, including those of its dependent agencies, utilities, and liquor stores.
Source: U.S Census Bureau, State & Local Government Finances 2008

City Government Revenue by Source

Source	2008 ($000)	2008 ($ per capita)
General Revenue		
From Federal Government	22,617	133
From State Government	34,635	204
From Local Governments	46,915	276
Taxes		
Property	91,668	540
Sales and Gross Receipts	13,773	81
Personal Income	0	0
Corporate Income	0	0
Motor Vehicle License	346	2
Other Taxes	7,644	45
Current Charges	113,408	668
Liquor Store	0	0
Utility	490,170	2,885
Employee Retirement	-16,227	-96

Source: U.S Census Bureau, State & Local Government Finances 2008

City Government Expenditures by Function

Function	2008 ($000)	2008 ($ per capita)	2008 (%)
General Direct Expenditures			
Air Transportation	8,909	52	1.0
Corrections	0	0	0.0
Education	0	0	0.0
Employment Security Administration	0	0	0.0
Financial Administration	7,812	46	0.9
Fire Protection	28,415	167	3.3
General Public Buildings	1,986	12	0.2
Governmental Administration, Other	51,887	305	6.0
Health	3,421	20	0.4
Highways	17,395	102	2.0
Hospitals	0	0	0.0
Housing and Community Development	7,747	46	0.9
Interest on General Debt	20,514	121	2.4
Judicial and Legal	4,271	25	0.5
Libraries	5,628	33	0.7
Parking	1,241	7	0.1
Parks and Recreation	26,417	156	3.1
Police Protection	45,983	271	5.3
Public Welfare	13,330	78	1.6
Sewerage	37,989	224	4.4
Solid Waste Management	17,849	105	2.1
Veterans' Services	0	0	0.0
Liquor Store	0	0	0.0
Utility	496,319	2,922	57.7
Employee Retirement	30,086	177	3.5

Source: U.S Census Bureau, State & Local Government Finances 2008

Municipal Bond Ratings

Area	Moody's	S&P	Fitch
City	Aa2	AA+	AA+

Rating Systems (shown in declining order of credit quality): Moody's– Aaa, Aa, A, Baa, Ba, B, Caa, Ca, C (numerical modifiers 1, 2, and 3 are added to letter-rating); S&P– AAA, AA, A, BBB, BB, B, CCC, CC, C; Fitch– AAA, AA, A, BBB, BB, B, CCC, CC, C. Ratings may be modified by the addition of a plus or minus sign to show relative standing within the major rating categories.
Notes: n/a Not available; (1) Not reviewed; (2) Issuer Rating/No General Obligation; (3) Standard and Poor's Issue Credit Rating (ICR) is a current opinion of an obliger with respect to a specific financial obligation, a specific class of financial obligations, or a specific financial program.
Source: City of Chattanooga, Tennessee, Comprehensive Annual Financial Report, Fiscal Year Ended June 30, 2010

DEMOGRAPHICS

Population Growth

Area	1990 Census	2000 Census	2010 Estimate	2015 Projection	Population Growth (%) 2000-2010	2010-2015
City	152,695	155,554	172,489	179,545	10.9	4.1
MSA[1]	433,166	476,531	525,589	546,663	10.3	4.0
U.S.	248,709,873	281,421,906	309,038,974	321,675,005	9.8	4.1

Note: (1) Metropolitan Statistical Area - see Appendix B for areas included
Source: Claritas, Inc.

Number of Households and Average Household Size

Area	2010 Estimate	2010 Average Household Size
City	73,828	2.26
MSA[1]	212,905	2.41
U.S.	116,136,617	2.59

Note: (1) Metropolitan Statistical Area - see Appendix B for areas included
Source: Claritas, Inc.

Race and Ethnicity

Area	White Alone[2] (%)	Black Alone[2] (%)	Asian Alone[2] (%)	Other Race Alone[2] (%)	Hispanic[3] (%)
City	59.4	34.6	1.8	4.1	4.0
MSA[1]	82.0	14.0	1.2	2.8	2.6
U.S.	72.3	12.4	4.4	10.9	15.8

Note: Figures are 2010 estimates; (1) Metropolitan Statistical Area - see Appendix B for areas included (2) Alone is defined as not being in combination with one or more other races; (3) May be of any race.
Source: Claritas, Inc.

Segregation

Type	Segregation Indices[1] 1990	2000	2010	2010 Rank[2]	Percent Change 1990-2000	1990-2010	2000-2010
Black/White	72.3	69.3	64.6	25	-3.0	-7.7	-4.8
Asian/White	40.0	41.7	37.7	68	1.7	-2.3	-4.0
Hispanic/White	26.5	33.9	38.8	72	7.3	12.3	5.0

Note: Figures are based on an analysis of 1990, 2000, and 2010 Census Decennial Census tract data by William H. Frey, Brookings Institution and the University of Michigan Social Science Data Analysis Network. In this analysis all racial groups (whites, blacks, and asians) are non-Hispanic members of those races. Hispanics are shown as a separate category; All figures cover the Metropolitan Statistical Area (see Appendix B for areas included); (1) Segregation Indices are Dissimilarity Indices that measure the degree to which the minority group is distributed differently than whites aross census tracts. They range from 0 (complete integration) to 100 (complete [segregation) where the value indicates the percentage of the minority group that needs to move to be distributed exactly like whites; (2) Ranges from 1 (most segregated) to 102 (least segregated); n/a not available.
Source: www.CensusScope.org

Ancestry

Area	German	Irish	English	American	Italian	Polish	French	Scottish
City	8.5	8.2	8.2	11.7	1.7	0.9	1.8	2.1
MSA[1]	10.7	13.2	11.1	17.3	1.6	0.9	2.1	2.5
U.S.	16.6	12.0	9.1	6.1	5.9	3.3	3.1	1.9

Note: The top eight ancestries in the U.S. are shown. Figures are percentages and include multiple ancestry (e.g. if a person reported being Irish and Italian, they were included in both columns); (1) Metropolitan Statistical Area - see Appendix B for areas included
Source: U.S. Census Bureau, 2007-2009 American Community Survey 3-Year Estimates

Foreign-Born Population

Area	Percent of Population Born in								
	Any Foreign Country	Mexico	Asia	Europe	Carribean	South America	Central America[2]	Africa	Canada
City	n/a	n/a	n/a	n/a	n/a	n/a	n/a	n/a	n/a
MSA[1]	3.3	0.6	1.0	0.7	0.1	0.2	0.3	0.2	0.1
U.S.	12.5	3.8	3.4	1.6	1.1	0.8	0.9	0.5	0.3

Note: (1) Metropolitan Statistical Area - see Appendix B for areas included; (2) Excludes Mexico.
Source: U.S. Census Bureau, 2007-2009 American Community Survey 3-Year Estimates

Marriage Status

Area	Never Married	Now Married[2]	Separated	Widowed	Divorced
City	34.4	40.8	3.1	8.0	13.7
MSA[1]	26.1	52.0	2.1	7.3	12.4
U.S.	31.4	49.7	2.2	6.2	10.6

Note: Figures are percentages and cover the population 15 years of age and older;
(1) Metropolitan Statistical Area - see Appendix B for areas included; (2) Excludes separated
Source: U.S. Census Bureau, 2007-2009 American Community Survey 3-Year Estimates

Age Distribution and Median Age

Area	Percent of Population							Median Age
	Under Age 5	Age 5 to 17	Age 18 to 34	Age 35 to 49	Age 50 to 64	Age 65 to 79	80 Years and Over	
City	6.7	14.7	25.4	19.3	18.9	10.6	4.3	37.9
MSA[1]	6.3	16.6	22.0	20.9	19.9	10.7	3.7	38.9
U.S.	6.9	17.5	23.3	21.4	18.1	9.1	3.7	36.7

Note: (1) Metropolitan Statistical Area - see Appendix B for areas included
Source: U.S. Census Bureau, 2007-2009 American Community Survey 3-Year Estimates

Male/Female Ratio

Area	Males	Females	Males per 100 Females
City	82,066	90,423	90.8
MSA[1]	253,697	271,892	93.3
U.S.	152,401,520	156,637,454	97.3

Note: Figures are 2010 estimates; (1) Metropolitan Statistical Area - see Appendix B for areas included
Source: Claritas, Inc.

Religion

Area	Catholic	Southern Baptist	United Methodist	ELCA[1]	LDS[2]	Presbyterian Church USA	Jewish Est.	Muslim Est.
County	3.2	21.6	8.0	0.3	0.2	1.3	0.5	0.7
U.S.	22.0	7.1	3.7	1.8	1.5	1.1	2.2	0.6

Note: Figures are the number of adherents as a percentage of the total population; Adherents are defined as all members, including full members, their children and the estimated number of other participants who are not considered members (e.g. the baptized, those not confirmed, those regularly attending services, etc.); (1) Evangelical Lutheran Church in America; (2) The Church of Jesus Christ of Latter Day Saints Source: Reprinted with permission from Religious Congregations and Membership in the United States 2000 (Nashville, Glenmary Research Center, 2002) Copyright Association of Statisticians of American Religious Bodies. All rights reserved.

ECONOMY

Gross Metropolitan Product

Area	2006	2007	2008	2009	2009 Rank[2]
MSA[1]	19.6	20.4	20.8	20.7	96

Note: Figures are in billions of dollars; (1) Chattanooga, TN-GA Metropolitan Statistical Area - see Appendix B for areas included; (2) Rank ranges from 1 to 363 Source: The U.S. Conference of Mayors, "Pace of Economic Recovery: GMP and Jobs," January 2010

Economic Growth

Area	2006-2008 (%)	2009 (%)	2010 (%)	Rank[2]
MSA[1]	0.5	-1.5	2.2	231
U.S.	1.3	-2.5	2.2	–

Note: Figures are real Gross Metropolitan Product growth rates and represent annual average percent change; (1) Chattanooga, TN-GA Metropolitan Statistical Area - see Appendix B for areas included; (2) Rank ranges from 1 to 363 Source: The U.S. Conference of Mayors, "Pace of Economic Recovery: GMP and Jobs," January 2010

Metropolitan Area Exports

Area	2005	2006	2007	2008	2009	2009 Rank[2]
MSA[1]	540.1	709.6	809.2	1,053.2	660.7	162

Note: Figures are in millions of dollars; (1) Chattanooga, TN-GA Metropolitan Statistical Area - see Appendix B for areas included; (2) Rank ranges from 1 to 374 Source: U.S. Department of Commerce, International Trade Administration, Office of Trade & Industry Information, Manufacturing & Services

INCOME

Per Capita/Median/Average Income

Area	Per Capita ($)	Median Household ($)	Average Household ($)
City	23,775	39,230	54,822
MSA[1]	24,326	45,291	59,503
U.S.	27,034	52,795	71,071

Note: Figures are 2010 estimates; (1) Metropolitan Statistical Area - see Appendix B for areas included Source: Claritas, Inc.

Household Income Distribution

Area	Percent of Households Earning							
	Under $15,000	$15,000 -24,999	$25,000 -34,999	$35,000 -49,999	$50,000 -74,999	$75,000 -99,000	$100,000 -149,999	$150,000 and up
City	18.9	13.6	13.0	16.1	17.4	9.2	7.1	4.7
MSA[1]	14.6	11.8	12.4	16.4	20.4	10.7	8.9	4.8
U.S.	12.1	10.2	10.6	15.0	19.5	12.5	12.1	8.0

Note: Figures are 2010 estimates; (1) Metropolitan Statistical Area - see Appendix B for areas included Source: Claritas, Inc.

Poverty Rates by Age

Area	All Ages	Under 18 Years Old	18 to 64 Years Old	65 Years and Over
City	22.1	7.4	12.5	2.2
MSA[1]	14.9	5.0	8.4	1.5
U.S.	13.6	4.7	7.7	1.2

Note: Figures are percent of population with income during the previous 12 months below poverty level and only include population for whom poverty status is determined; (1) Metropolitan Statistical Area - see Appendix B for areas included
Source: U.S. Census Bureau, 2007-2009 American Community Survey 3-Year Estimates

Personal Bankruptcy Filing Rate

Area	2006	2007	2008	2009	2010
Hamilton County	5.63	6.80	8.05	9.25	8.60
U.S.	2.00	2.73	3.53	4.60	4.96

Note: Numbers are per 1,000 population and include Chapter 7 and Chapter 13 filings
Source: Federal Deposit Insurance Corporation, Regional Economic Conditions, March 17, 2011

EMPLOYMENT

Labor Force and Employment

Area	Civilian Labor Force			Workers Employed		
	Dec. 2009	Dec. 2010	% Chg.	Dec. 2009	Dec. 2010	% Chg.
City	78,201	79,478	1.6	70,720	72,941	3.1
MSA[1]	256,306	260,152	1.5	232,609	238,684	2.6
U.S.	152,693,000	153,156,000	0.3	137,953,000	139,159,000	0.9

Note: Data is not seasonally adjusted and covers workers 16 years of age and older;
(1) Metropolitan Statistical Area - see Appendix B for areas included
Source: Bureau of Labor Statistics, http://stats.bls.gov

Unemployment Rate

Area	2010											
	Jan.	Feb.	Mar.	Apr.	May	Jun.	Jul.	Aug.	Sep.	Oct.	Nov.	Dec.
City	10.4	10.1	10.1	9.4	9.0	9.7	9.1	9.5	8.4	8.5	8.7	8.2
MSA[1]	9.7	9.5	9.2	8.7	8.4	8.7	8.5	8.8	8.2	8.2	8.4	8.3
U.S.	10.6	10.4	10.2	9.5	9.3	9.6	9.7	9.5	9.2	9.0	9.3	9.1

Note: Data is not seasonally adjusted and covers workers 16 years of age and older; All figures are percentages; (1) Metropolitan Statistical Area - see Appendix B for areas included
Source: Bureau of Labor Statistics, http://stats.bls.gov

Projected Unemployment Rate

Area	2007 (%)	2009 (%)	2011 (%)	2013 (%)
MSA[1]	4.7	9.8	9.1	7.5

Note: (1) Metropolitan Statistical Area - see Appendix B for areas included
Source: The U.S. Conference of Mayors, "Pace of Economic Recovery: GMP and Jobs," January 2010

Employment by Occupation

Occupation Classification	City (%)	MSA[1] (%)	U.S. (%)
Sales and Office	24.7	25.7	25.4
Professional and Related	20.6	19.6	21.0
Service	21.1	17.5	17.2
Production, Transportation, and Material Moving	13.9	14.9	12.3
Management, Business, and Financial	13.7	13.7	14.1
Construction, Extraction, and Maintenance	5.9	8.4	9.2
Farming, Forestry, and Fishing	0.2	0.2	0.7

Note: Figures cover employed civilians 16 years of age and older;
(1) Metropolitan Statistical Area - see Appendix B for areas included
Source: U.S. Census Bureau, 2007-2009 American Community Survey 3-Year Estimates

Employment by Industry

| Sector | MSA[1] | | U.S. |
	Number of Employees	Percent of Total	Percent of Total
Government	36,300	15.6	17.2
Education and Health Services	31,500	13.6	15.2
Professional and Business Services	22,000	9.5	13.0
Retail Trade	24,600	10.6	11.4
Leisure and Hospitality	23,100	9.9	9.7
Manufacturing	28,000	12.1	8.8
Financial Activities	17,500	7.5	5.8
Wholesale Trade	8,400	3.6	4.2
Construction	n/a	n/a	4.1
Other Services	10,800	4.7	4.1
Transportation and Utilities	17,400	7.5	3.7
Information	3,700	1.6	2.1
Mining and Logging	n/a	n/a	0.6

Note: Figures cover non-farm employment as of December 2010 and are not seasonally adjusted;
(1) Metropolitan Statistical Area - see Appendix B for areas included; n/a not available
Source: Bureau of Labor Statistics, http://stats.bls.gov

Occupations with Greatest Projected Employment Growth: 2006 - 2016

Occupation[1]	2006 Employment	2016 Projected Employment	Numeric Employment Change	Percent Employment Change
Retail salespersons	85,980	104,710	18,730	21.8
Customer service representatives	48,360	62,400	14,040	29.0
Registered nurses	51,960	65,410	13,450	25.9
Combined food preparation and serving workers, including fast food	56,290	68,360	12,070	21.4
Truck drivers, heavy and tractor-trailer	73,170	83,140	9,970	13.6
Waiters and waitresses	49,750	58,960	9,210	18.5
Office clerks, general	56,220	64,620	8,400	14.9
Elementary school teachers, except special education	30,740	38,000	7,260	23.6
Nursing aides, orderlies, and attendants	31,850	38,580	6,730	21.1
Janitors and cleaners, except maids and housekeeping cleaners	42,750	48,660	5,910	13.8

Note: Projections cover Tennessee; (1) Sorted by numeric employment change
Source: www.projectionscentral.com, State Occupational Projections, 2006-2016 Long-Term Projections

Fastest Growing Occupations: 2006 - 2016

Occupation[1]	2006 Employment	2016 Projected Employment	Numeric Employment Change	Percent Employment Change
Pharmacy technicians	7,970	12,540	4,570	57.3
Environmental engineers	900	1,410	510	56.7
Network systems and data communications analysts	2,810	4,340	1,530	54.4
Home health aides	10,760	15,610	4,850	45.1
Animal trainers	730	1,040	310	42.5
Pharmacists	5,640	7,960	2,320	41.1
Computer software engineers, applications	3,310	4,630	1,320	39.9
Paralegals and legal assistants	3,730	5,180	1,450	38.9
Financial analysts	2,220	3,080	860	38.7
Personal financial advisors	1,440	1,980	540	37.5

Note: Projections cover Tennessee; (1) Sorted by percent employment change and excludes occupations with numeric employment change less than 300
Source: www.projectionscentral.com, State Occupational Projections, 2006-2016 Long-Term Projections

Average Wages

Occupation	$/Hr.	Occupation	$/Hr.
Accountants and Auditors	26.11	Maids and Housekeeping Cleaners	8.56
Automotive Mechanics	15.57	Maintenance and Repair Workers	15.99
Bookkeepers	14.79	Marketing Managers	35.49
Carpenters	15.63	Nuclear Medicine Technologists	30.29
Cashiers	7.98	Nurses, Licensed Practical	17.14
Clerks, General Office	12.50	Nurses, Registered	27.68
Clerks, Receptionists/Information	11.47	Nursing Aides/Orderlies/Attendants	10.68
Clerks, Shipping/Receiving	13.00	Packers and Packagers, Hand	10.52
Computer Programmers	27.35	Physical Therapists	38.23
Computer Support Specialists	19.96	Postal Service Mail Carriers	23.58
Computer Systems Analysts	28.82	Real Estate Brokers	n/a
Cooks, Restaurant	10.03	Retail Salespersons	11.62
Dentists	n/a	Sales Reps., Exc. Tech./Scientific	26.59
Electrical Engineers	37.88	Sales Reps., Tech./Scientific	33.14
Electricians	21.53	Secretaries, Exc. Legal/Med./Exec.	13.72
Financial Managers	36.52	Security Guards	12.40
First-Line Supervisors/Mgrs., Sales	16.54	Surgeons	112.14
Food Preparation Workers	8.41	Teacher Assistants	8.20
General and Operations Managers	44.57	Teachers, Elementary School	23.00
Hairdressers/Cosmetologists	11.59	Teachers, Secondary School	23.00
Internists	93.68	Telemarketers	11.30
Janitors and Cleaners	11.83	Truck Drivers, Heavy/Tractor-Trailer	18.21
Landscaping/Groundskeeping Workers	10.16	Truck Drivers, Light/Delivery Svcs.	15.64
Lawyers	71.32	Waiters and Waitresses	8.35

Note: Wage data covers the Chattanooga, TN-GA - see Appendix B for areas included. Hourly wages for elementary/secondary school teachers and teacher assistants were calculated by the editors from annual wage data assuming a 40 hour work week; n/a not available.
Source: Bureau of Labor Statistics, Metro Area Occupational Employment and Wage Estimates, May 2009

**RESIDENTIAL
REAL ESTATE**

Building Permits

Area	Single-Family			Multi-Family			Total		
	2009	2010	Pct. Chg.	2009	2010	Pct. Chg.	2009	2010	Pct. Chg.
City	207	206	-0.5	62	67	8.1	269	273	1.5
MSA[1]	994	955	-3.9	132	131	-0.8	1,126	1,086	-3.6
U.S.	441,100	447,300	1.4	141,900	157,300	10.9	583,000	604,600	3.7

Note: (1) Metropolitan Statistical Area - see Appendix B for areas included; figures represent new, privately-owned housing units authorized (unadjusted data); All permit data are based on estimates with imputation.
Source: U.S. Census Bureau, Manufacturing, Mining, and Construction Statistics, Building Permits, 2009, 2010

Homeownership Rate

Area	2005 (%)	2006 (%)	2007 (%)	2008 (%)	2009 (%)	2010 (%)
MSA[1]	n/a	n/a	n/a	n/a	n/a	n/a
U.S.	68.9	68.8	68.1	67.8	67.4	66.9

Note: (1) Metropolitan Statistical Area - see Appendix B for areas included
Source: U.S. Census Bureau, Housing Vacancies and Homeownership Annual Statistics: 2010

Housing Vacancy Rates

Area	Gross Vacancy Rate[2] (%)			Year-Round Vacancy Rate[3] (%)			Rental Vacancy Rate[4] (%)			Homeowner Vacancy Rate[5] (%)		
	2008	2009	2010	2008	2009	2010	2008	2009	2010	2008	2009	2010
MSA[1]	n/a	n/a	n/a	n/a	n/a	n/a	n/a	n/a	n/a	n/a	n/a	n/a
U.S.	14.4	14.5	14.3	11.1	11.3	11.3	10.0	10.6	10.2	2.8	2.6	2.6

Note: (1) Metropolitan Statistical Area - see Appendix B for areas included; (2) The percentage of the total housing inventory that is vacant; (3) The percentage of the housing inventory (excluding seasonal units) that is year-round vacant; (4) The percentage of rental inventory that is vacant for rent; (5) The percentage of homeowner inventory that is vacant for sale; n/a not available
Source: U.S. Census Bureau, Housing Vacancies and Homeownership Annual Statistics: 2010

State Corporate Income Tax Rates

State	Tax Rate (%)	Income Brackets ($)	Num. of Brackets	Financial Institution Tax Rate (%)[a]	Federal Income Tax Ded.
Tennessee	6.5	Flat rate	1	6.5	No

Note: Tax rates as of January 1, 2011; (a) Rates listed are the tax rates applied to financial institutions or excise taxes based on income. Some states have other taxes based upon the value of deposits or shares.
Source: Federation of Tax Administrators, "State Corporate Income Tax Rates, 2011"

State Individual Income Tax Rates

State	Tax Rate (%)	Income Brackets ($)	Num. of Brackets	Personal Exempt. ($)[1] Single	Personal Exempt. ($)[1] Dependents	Fed. Inc. Tax Ded.

Tennessee – State Income Tax of 6% on Dividends and Interest Income Only

Note: Tax rates as of January 1, 2011; Local- and county-level taxes are not included; n/a not applicable;
(1) Married joint filers generally receive double the single exemption
Source: Federation of Tax Administrators, "State Individual Income Tax Rates, 2011"

Various State and Local Tax Rates

State	State and Local Sales and Use (%)	State Sales and Use (%)	Gasoline[1] (¢/gal.)	Cigarette[2] ($/pack)	Spirits[3] ($/gal.)	Wine[4] ($/gal.)	Beer[5] ($/gal.)
Tennessee	9.25	7.00	21.4	0.62	4.46	1.27	0.14

Note: All tax rates as of January 1, 2011 except Spirits (Sept. 1, 2010); (1) The American Petroleum Institute has developed a methodology for determining the average tax rate on a gallon of fuel. Rates may include any of the following: excise taxes, environmental fees, storage tank fees, other fees or taxes, general sales tax, and local taxes. In states where gasoline is subject to the general sales tax, or where the fuel tax is based on the average sale price, the average rate determined by API is sensitive to changes in the price of gasoline. States that fully or partially apply general sales taxes to gasoline: CA, CO, GA, IL, IN, MI, NY; (2) The federal excise tax of $1.0066 per pack and local taxes are not included; (3) Rates are those applicable to off-premise sales of 40% alcohol by volume (a.b.v.) distilled spirits in 750ml containers. Local excise taxes are excluded; (4) Rates are those applicable to off-premise sales of 11% a.b.v. non-carbonated wine in 750ml containers; (5) Rates are those applicable to off-premise sales of 4.7% a.b.v. beer in 12 ounce containers.
Source: Tax Foundation, 2011 Facts & Figures: How Does Your State Compare?

State-Local Tax Burdens

Area	Rate (%)	Rank[1]	Per Capita Taxes Paid to Home State ($)	Total State and Local Per Capita Taxes Paid ($)	Per Capita Income ($)
Tennessee	7.6	47	1,851	2,752	36,157
U.S. Average	9.8	-	3,057	4,160	42,539

Note: Figures cover 2009; (1) Rank ranges from 1 to 50 where 1 is highest tax burden
Source: Tax Foundation, State-Local Tax Burdens, All States, 2009

State Business Tax Climate Index Rankings

State	Overall Rank	Corporate Tax Index Rank	Individual Income Tax Index Rank	Sales Tax Index Rank	Unemployment Insurance Tax Index Rank	Property Tax Index Rank
Tennessee	27	11	8	47	35	50

Note: The index is a measure of how each state's tax laws affect economic performance. The lower the rank, the more favorable a state's tax system is for business. All ranks are for fiscal years. States without a given tax are given a ranking of 1.
Source: Tax Foundation, Tax Foundation Background Paper, No. 60, "2011 State Business Tax Climate Index"

COMMERCIAL UTILITIES

Typical Monthly Electric Bills

Area	Commercial Service ($/month) 40 kW demand 5,000 kWh	Commercial Service ($/month) 500 kW demand 100,000 kWh	Industrial Service ($/month) 5,000 kW demand 1,500,000 kWh	Industrial Service ($/month) 70,000 kW demand 50,000,000 kWh
City	443	11,164	131,485	2,623,860

Note: Based on rates in effect January 1, 2010
Source: Memphis Light, Gas and Water, 2010 Utility Bill Comparisons for Selected U.S. Cities

TRANSPORTATION

Means of Transportation to Work

Area	Car/Truck/Van		Public Transportation			Bicycle	Walked	Other Means	Worked at Home
	Drove Alone	Car-pooled	Bus	Subway	Railroad				
City	80.9	10.9	2.0	0.0	0.0	0.4	2.5	1.1	2.1
MSA[1]	82.9	10.7	0.8	0.0	0.0	0.2	1.7	0.8	2.9
U.S.	75.8	10.4	2.7	1.7	0.5	0.5	2.9	1.2	4.1

Note: Figures are percentages and cover workers 16 years of age and older;
(1) Metropolitan Statistical Area - see Appendix B for areas included
Source: U.S. Census Bureau, 2007-2009 American Community Survey 3-Year Estimates

Travel Time to Work

Area	Less Than 15 Minutes	15 to 29 Minutes	30 to 44 Minutes	45 to 59 Minutes	60 to 89 Minutes	90 Minutes or More
City	36.2	47.6	12.0	2.1	1.0	1.0
MSA[1]	27.0	43.9	20.2	5.4	2.3	1.4
U.S.	28.5	36.2	19.7	7.5	5.6	2.5

Note: Figures are percentages and include workers 16 years old and over;
(1) Metropolitan Statistical Area - see Appendix B for areas included
Source: U.S. Census Bureau, 2007-2009 American Community Survey 3-Year Estimates

Travel Time Index

Area	1982	1999	2008	2009
Urban Area[1]	n/a	n/a	n/a	n/a
Average[2]	1.08	1.20	1.20	1.20

Note: Travel Time Index—the ratio of travel time in the peak period to the travel time at free-flow conditions. A value of 1.30 indicates a 20-minute free-flow trip takes 26 minutes in the peak. Free-flow speeds (60 mph on freeways and 35 mph on principal arterials) are used as the comparison threshold; (1) Covers the Chattanooga urban area; (2) average of 439 urban areas
Source: Texas Transportation Institute, Urban Mobility Report 2010, December 2010

Public Transportation

Agency Name / Mode of Transportation	Vehicles Operated in Maximum Service	Annual Unlinked Passenger Trips ('000)	Annual Passenger Miles ('000)
Chattanooga Area Regional Transportation Authority (CARTA)			
Demand response	7	25.5	130.6
Demand response	12	43.6	326.6
Inclined plane	2	374.6	374.6
Bus	49	2,698.4	9,779.8

Note: Figures include both directly operated and purchased transportation
Source: Federal Transit Administration, National Transit Database, 2009

Air Transportation

Airport Name and Code / Type of Service	Passenger Airlines[1]	Passenger Enplanements	Freight Carriers[2]	Freight (lbs.)
Chattanooga Metropolitan (Lovell Field) (CHA)				
Domestic service (U.S. carriers - 2010)	15	292,528	6	2,243,937
International service (U.S. carriers - 2009)	2	441	0	0

Note: (1) Includes all U.S.-based major, minor and commuter airlines that carried at least one passenger during the year; (2) Includes all U.S.-based airlines and freight carriers that transported at least one pound of freight during the year
Source: Bureau of Transportation Statistics, The Intermodal Transportation Database, Air Carriers: T-100 Domestic Market (U.S. Carriers), 2010; Bureau of Transportation Statistics, The Intermodal Transportation Database, Air Carriers: T-100 International Market (U.S. Carriers), 2009

Other Transportation Statistics

Interstate highways:	I-24; I-59; I-75
Amtrak service:	Bus connection
Major waterways/ports:	Tennessee River

Source: Amtrak.com; Google Maps

BUSINESSES

Major Business Headquarters

Company Name	Rankings	
	Fortune[1]	Forbes[2]
Unum Group	239	-

Note: (1) Fortune 500—companies that produce a 10-K are ranked 1 to 500 based on 2010 revenue; (2) all private companies with at least $2 billion in annual revenue are ranked 1 to 223; companies listed are headquartered in the city; dashes indicate no ranking
Source: Fortune, "Fortune 500," May 23, 2011; Forbes, "America's Largest Private Companies," November 3, 2010

Fast-Growing Businesses

According to *Inc.*, Chattanooga is home to one of America's 500 fastest-growing private companies: **Access America Transport**. Criteria: must be an independent, privately-held, for-profit, U.S. corporation, proprietorship or partnership; revenues of at least $80,000 in 2006 and $2 million in 2009; four-year operating/sales history; holding companies, regulated banks, and utilities were excluded. *Inc., "America's 500 Fastest-Growing Private Companies," September 2010*

Minority- and Women-Owned Businesses

Group	All Firms		Firms with Paid Employees			
	Firms	Sales ($000)	Firms	Sales ($000)	Employees	Payroll ($000)
Asian	607	296,599	220	273,479	1,686	45,804
Black	2,602	105,825	109	57,206	612	12,919
Hispanic	202	59,284	39	45,924	803	11,940
Women	4,087	957,996	529	871,128	5,963	152,697
All Firms	17,465	32,558,893	5,409	31,976,419	150,925	5,387,918

Note: Figures cover firms located in the city; minority- and women-owned business are defined as firms in which the corresponding group own 51% or more of the stock or equity of the company
Source: U.S. Census Bureau, 2007 Economic Census, Survey of Business Owners

HOTELS

Hotels/Motels

Area	5 Star		4 Star		3 Star		2 Star		1 Star		Not Rated	
	Num.	Pct.3	Num.	Pct.3	Num.	Pct.3	Num.	Pct.3	Num.	Pct.3	Num.	Pct.3
City[1]	0	0.0	0	0.0	17	16.3	62	59.6	8	7.7	17	16.3
Total[2]	119	0.7	927	5.8	4,906	30.5	7,992	49.7	526	3.3	1,625	10.1

Note: (1) Figures cover Chattanooga and vicinity; (2) Figures cover all 100 cities in this book; (3) Percentage of hotels which are a given star rating; Star ratings are determined by expedia.com and offer an indication of the general quality of a particular hotel.
Source: expedia.com, May 5, 2011

EVENT SITES

Major Stadiums, Arenas, and Auditoriums

Name	Max. Capacity
AT&T Field	6,362
UTC McKenzie Arena	11,218

Source: Original research

Convention Centers

Name	Overall Space (sq. ft.)	Exhibit Space (sq. ft.)	Meeting Space (sq. ft.)	Meeting Rooms
Chattanooga Convention Center	312,000	25,580	100,800	21

Source: Original research

Living Environment

COST OF LIVING

Cost of Living Index

Composite Index	Groceries	Housing	Utilities	Trans-portation	Health Care	Misc. Goods/ Services
91.1	97.4	84.0	82.5	96.4	93.3	95.7

Note: U.S. = 100; Figures cover the Chattanooga TN urban area.
Source: The Council for Community and Economic Research, ACCRA Cost of Living Index, 2010

Grocery Prices

Area[1]	T-Bone Steak ($/pound)	Frying Chicken ($/pound)	Whole Milk ($/half gal.)	Eggs ($/dozen)	Orange Juice ($/64 oz.)	Coffee ($/11.5 oz.)
City[2]	9.11	1.12	2.29	1.34	2.96	3.45
Avg.	9.04	1.16	2.02	1.47	3.08	3.65
Min.	6.97	0.84	1.46	0.96	2.39	2.64
Max.	13.93	2.51	3.58	3.01	4.94	6.32

*Note: (1) Values for the local area are compared with the average, minimum and maximum values for all 338 areas in the Cost of Living Index; (2) Figures cover the Chattanooga TN urban area; **T-Bone Steak** (price per pound); **Frying Chicken** (price per pound, whole fryer); **Whole Milk** (half gallon carton); **Eggs** (price per dozen, Grade A, large); **Orange Juice** (64 oz. Tropicana or Florida Natural); **Coffee** (11.5 oz. can, vacuum-packed, Maxwell House, Hills Bros, or Folgers).*
Source: The Council for Community and Economic Research, ACCRA Cost of Living Index, 2010

Housing and Utility Costs

Area[1]	New Home Price ($)	Apartment Rent ($/month)	All Electric ($/month)	Part Electric ($/month)	Other Energy ($/month)	Telephone ($/month)
City[2]	242,572	716	-	63.46	80.12	22.23
Avg.	293,442	810	166.39	91.93	83.82	26.93
Min.	182,545	453	119.21	44.47	36.85	17.98
Max.	1,123,114	2,776	307.53	218.20	313.90	39.15

*Note: (1) Values for the local area are compared with the average, minimum and maximum values for all 338 areas in the Cost of Living Index; (2) Figures cover the Chattanooga TN urban area; **New Home Price** (2,400 sf living area, 8,000 sf lot, in urban area with full utilities); **Apartment Rent** (950 sf 2 bedroom/1.5 or 2 bath, unfurnished, excluding all utilities except water); **All Electric** (average monthly cost for an all-electric home); **Part Electric** (average monthly cost for a part-electric home); **Other Energy** (average monthly cost for natural gas, fuel oil, coal, wood, and any other forms of energy except electricity); **Telephone** (price includes basic monthly rate for a private residential line plus additional local usage charges incurred by a family of four).*
Source: The Council for Community and Economic Research, ACCRA Cost of Living Index, 2010

Health Care, Transportation, and Other Costs

Area[1]	Doctor ($/visit)	Dentist ($/visit)	Optometrist ($/visit)	Gasoline ($/gallon)	Beauty Salon ($/visit)	Men's Shirt ($)
City[2]	96.93	60.00	89.47	2.55	38.33	25.56
Avg.	89.44	78.95	87.40	2.73	31.92	24.83
Min.	57.00	54.25	48.32	2.44	19.17	13.67
Max.	149.90	136.73	174.22	3.75	62.81	47.89

*Note: (1) Values for the local area are compared with the average, minimum and maximum values for all 338 areas in the Cost of Living Index; (2) Figures cover the Chattanooga TN urban area; **Doctor** (general practitioners routine exam of an established patient); **Dentist** (adult teeth cleaning and periodic oral examination); **Optometrist** (full vision eye exam for established adult patient); **Gasoline** (one gallon regular unleaded, national brand, including all taxes, cash price at self-service pump if available); **Beauty Salon** (woman's shampoo, trim, and blow-dry); **Men's Shirt** (cotton/polyester dress shirt, pinpoint weave, long sleeves).*
Source: The Council for Community and Economic Research, ACCRA Cost of Living Index, 2010

HOUSING

House Price Index (HPI)

Area	National Ranking[2]	Quarterly Change (%)	One-Year Change (%)	Five-Year Change (%)
MSA[1]	65	-0.75	0.37	5.48
U.S.[3]	-	-0.84	-3.95	-11.45

Note: The HPI is a weighted repeat sales index. It measures average price changes in repeat sales or refinancings on the same properties. This information is obtained by reviewing repeat mortgage transactions on single-family properties whose mortgages have been purchased or securitized by Fannie Mae or Freddie Mac in January 1975; (1) Metropolitan/Micropolitan Statistical Area - see Appendix B for areas included; (2) Rankings are based on annual percentage change for all metro areas containing at least 15,000 transactions over the last 10 years and ranges from 1 to 309; (3) figures based on a weighted average of Census Division estimates; all figures are for the period ending December 31, 2010
Source: Federal Housing Finance Agency, House Price Index, February 24, 2011

House Price Valuations

Area	Q4 2005 Price ($000)	Q4 2005 Over-valuation	Q4 2006 Price ($000)	Q4 2006 Over-valuation	Q4 2007 Price ($000)	Q4 2007 Over-valuation	Q4 2008 Price ($000)	Q4 2008 Over-valuation	Q4 2009 Price ($000)	Q4 2009 Over-valuation
MSA[1]	114.7	4.2	119.3	2.0	120.4	-2.0	115.2	-6.3	117.0	-6.8

Note: Figures show the percentage of over- or under-valuation of single family homes relative to statistically normal house values (e.g. a value of 23.6 indicates that house values are 23.6% overvalued). Statistically normal house values are based on house prices, interest rates, household incomes, population densities, and any historical premiums or discounts metropolitan areas have exhibited over time; (1) Figures cover the Chattanooga, TN-GA Metropolitan Statistical Area - see Appendix B for areas included
Source: Global Insight/PNC Financial Services Group, House Prices in America: 4th Quarter 2009 Update

Median Single-Family Home Prices

Area	2008	2009	2010[p]	Percent Change 2009 to 2010
MSA[1]	129.1	122.6	121.4	-1.0
U.S. Average	196.6	172.1	173.2	0.6

Note: Figures are median sales prices of existing single-family homes in thousands of dollars; (p) preliminary; n/a not available; (1) Metropolitan Statistical Area - see Appendix B for areas included
Source: National Association of Realtors, Median Sales Price of Existing Single-Family Homes for Metropolitan Areas, 4th Quarter 2010

Median Apartment Condo-Coop Home Prices

Area	2008	2009	2010[p]	Percent Change 2009 to 2010
MSA[1]	n/a	n/a	n/a	n/a
U.S. Average	209.8	175.6	171.7	-2.2

Note: Figures are median sales prices of existing apartment condo-coop homes in thousands of dollars; (p) preliminary; n/a not available; (1) Metropolitan Statistical Area - see Appendix B for areas included
Source: National Association of Realtors, Median Sales Price of Existing Apartment Condo-Coop Homes for Metropolitan Areas, 4th Quarter 2010

Year Housing Structure Built

Area	2000 or Later	1990 -1999	1980 -1989	1970 -1979	1960 -1969	1950 -1959	1940 -1949	Before 1940	Median Year
City	9.4	9.0	11.4	15.9	15.7	14.6	8.1	16.0	1967
MSA[1]	13.0	15.5	14.4	17.6	12.9	11.4	6.5	8.8	1976
U.S.	12.5	14.0	14.2	16.5	11.4	11.3	5.8	14.3	1974

Note: Figures are percentages except for Median Year; (1) Metropolitan Statistical Area - see Appendix B for areas included
Source: U.S. Census Bureau, 2007-2009 American Community Survey 3-Year Estimates

HEALTH

Health Risk Data

Category	MSA[1] (%)	U.S. (%)
Adults who have been told they have high blood pressure	35.4	28.7
Adults who have been told they have high blood cholesterol	39.4	37.5
Adults who have been told they have diabetes[3]	13.1	8.3
Adults who have been told they have arthritis	29.2	26.0
Adults who have been told they currently have asthma	9.3	8.8
Adults who are current smokers	24.5	17.9
Adults who are heavy drinkers[4]	6.2	5.1
Adults who are binge drinkers[5]	13.7	15.8
Adults who are overweight (BMI 25.0 - 29.9)	28.7	36.2
Adults who are obese (BMI 30.0 - 99.8)	32.7	26.9
Adults who participated in any physical activities in the past month	67.9	76.2
Adults 50+ who have ever had a sigmoidoscopy or colonoscopy[2]	n/a	62.2
Women 40+ who have had a mammogram within the past two years[2]	n/a	76.0
Adults age 18–64 who have any kind of health care coverage	82.6	83.1

Note: Data as of 2009 unless otherwise noted; n/a not available; (1) Figures cover the Chattanooga, TN-GA Metropolitan Statistical Area - see Appendix B for areas included; (2) Data as of 2008; (3) Figures do not include pregnancy-related, borderline, or pre-diabetes; (4) Heavy drinkers are classified as males having more than two drinks per day or females having more than one drink per day; (5) Binge drinkers are classified as males having five or more drinks on one occasion or females having four or more drinks on one occasion
Source: Centers for Disease Control and Prevention, Behaviorial Risk Factor Surveillance System, SMART: Selected Metropolitan/Micropolitan Area Risk Trends, 2008, 2009

Mortality Rates for the Top 10 Causes of Death in the U.S.

ICD-10[a] Sub-Chapter	ICD-10[a] Code	Age-Adjusted Mortality Rate[1] per 100,000 population	
		County[2]	U.S.
Malignant neoplasms	C00-C97	186.6	180.9
Ischaemic heart diseases	I20-I25	136.5	135.0
Other forms of heart disease	I30-I51	43.5	50.0
Cerebrovascular diseases	I60-I69	51.9	44.1
Chronic lower respiratory diseases	J40-J47	51.9	41.5
Other degenerative diseases of the nervous system	G30-G31	52.6	23.6
Diabetes mellitus	E10-E14	23.7	23.5
Other external causes of accidental injury	W00-X59	23.3	23.5
Organic, including symptomatic, mental disorders	F01-F09	19.7	22.2
Influenza and pneumonia	J09-J18	15.5	18.1

Note: (a) ICD-10 = International Classification of Diseases 10th Revision; (1) Mortality rates are a three year average covering 2005-2007; (2) Figures cover Hamilton County
Source: Centers for Disease Control and Prevention, National Center for Health Statistics. Compressed Mortality File 1999-2007. CDC WONDER On-line Database, compiled from Compressed Mortality File 1999-2007 Series 20 No. 2M, 2010.

Mortality Rates for Selected Causes of Death

ICD-10[a] Sub-Chapter	ICD-10[a] Code	Age-Adjusted Mortality Rate[1] per 100,000 population	
		County[2]	U.S.
Assault	X85-Y09	6.3	6.0
Human immunodeficiency virus (HIV) disease	B20-B24	3.5	4.0
Hypertensive diseases	I10-I15	26.8	18.0
Intentional self-harm	X60-X84	11.0	11.0
Malnutrition	E40-E46	*0.9	0.8
Obesity and other hyperalimentation	E65-E68	2.2	1.5
Transport accidents	V01-V99	14.8	15.6
Viral hepatitis	B15-B19	2.4	2.1

Note: (a) ICD-10 = International Classification of Diseases 10th Revision; (1) Mortality rates are a three year average covering 2005-2007; (2) Figures cover Hamilton County; (*) Unreliable data as per CDC
Source: Centers for Disease Control and Prevention, National Center for Health Statistics. Compressed Mortality File 1999-2007. CDC WONDER On-line Database, compiled from Compressed Mortality File 1999-2007 Series 20 No. 2M, 2010.

Distribution of Physicians and Dentists

Area[1]	Dentists[2]	D.O.[3]	M.D.[4]				
			Total	Family/General Practice	Pediatrics	Medical Specialties	Surgical Specialties
Local (number)	158	62	909	89	71	349	234
Local (rate[5])	4.8	1.9	27.2	2.7	2.1	10.4	7.0
U.S. (rate[5])	4.5	1.9	18.3	2.5	1.4	6.8	4.1

Note: Data as of 2008 unless noted; (1) Local data covers Hamilton County; (2) Data as of 2007; (3) Doctor of Osteopathic Medicine; (4) Includes active, non-federal, patient-care, office-based Doctors of Medicine; (5) rate per 10,000 population
Source: Area Resource File (ARF). 2009-2010 Release. U.S. Department of Health and Human Services, Health Resources and Services Administration, Bureau of Health Professions, Rockville, MD, August 2010

Hospitals

Chattanooga has the following hospitals: 3 general medical and surgical; 2 psychiatric; 2 rehabilitation; 1 long-term acute care.
AHA Guide to the Healthcare Field 2010

EDUCATION

Public School District Statistics

District Name	Schls	Pupils	Pupil/Teacher Ratio	Minority Pupils[1] (%)	Free Lunch Eligible[2] (%)	IEP[3] (%)
Hamilton County School Distrct	77	41,547	14.5	40.6	43.5	11.6

Note: Table includes school districts with 2,000 or more students; (1) Percentage of students that are not non-Hispanic white; (2) Percentage of students that are eligible for the free lunch program; (3) Percentage of students that have an Individualized Education Program.
Source: U.S. Department of Education, National Center for Education Statistics, Common Core of Data, Local Education Agency (School District) Universe Survey: School Year 2008-2009; U.S. Department of Education, National Center for Education Statistics, Common Core of Data, Public Elementary/Secondary School Universe Survey: School Year 2008-2009

Highest Level of Education

Area	Less than H.S.	H.S. Diploma	Some College, No Deg.	Associate Degree	Bachelors Degree	Masters Degree	Profess. School Degree	Doctorate Degree
City	15.5	28.6	24.1	6.0	16.9	5.7	2.0	1.2
MSA[1]	17.0	30.5	23.6	6.7	14.8	5.1	1.6	0.8
U.S.	15.3	29.0	20.7	7.5	17.4	7.0	1.9	1.1

Note: Figures are 2010 estimated percentages and cover persons age 25 and over; (1) Metropolitan Statistical Area - see Appendix B for areas included
Source: Claritas, Inc.

Educational Attainment by Race

Area	High School Graduate (%)					Bachelor's Degree (%)				
	Total	White	Black	Asian	Hisp.[2]	Total	White	Black	Asian	Hisp.[2]
City	82.7	87.1	76.7	88.7	45.4	26.2	33.3	11.9	54.4	7.2
MSA[1]	82.7	84.1	77.8	87.7	53.5	22.6	23.8	13.7	54.5	12.4
U.S.	84.9	90.0	80.7	85.5	60.7	27.8	30.9	17.5	49.7	12.7

Note: Figures shown cover persons 25 years old and over; (1) Metropolitan Statistical Area - see Appendix B for areas included; (2) people of Hispanic origin can be of any race
Source: U.S. Census Bureau, 2007-2009 American Community Survey 3-Year Estimates

School Enrollment by Grade and Control

Area	Preschool (%)		Kindergarten (%)		Grades 1 - 4 (%)		Grades 5 - 8 (%)		Grades 9 - 12 (%)	
	Public	Private	Public	Private	Public	Private	Public	Private	Public	Private
City	67.9	32.1	93.1	6.9	87.2	12.8	82.5	17.5	76.6	23.4
MSA[1]	59.7	40.3	89.7	10.3	88.1	11.9	82.9	17.1	78.6	21.4
U.S.	54.3	45.7	86.4	13.6	88.9	11.1	89.1	10.9	90.2	9.8

Note: Figures shown cover persons 3 years old and over; (1) Metropolitan Statistical Area - see Appendix B for areas included
Source: U.S. Census Bureau, 2007-2009 American Community Survey 3-Year Estimates

Average Salaries of Public School Classroom Teachers

Area	2009-10		2010-11		Percent Change 2009-10 to 2010-11	Percent Change 2000-01 to 2010-11
	Dollars	Rank[1]	Dollars	Rank[1]		
Tennessee	46,290	40	47,043	43	1.63	25.7
U.S. Average	55,202	-	56,069	-	1.57	29.3

Note: (1) State rank ranges from 1 to 51 where 1 indicates highest salary.
Source: National Education Association, Rankings & Estimates: Rankings of the States 2010
and Estimates of School Statistics 2011, December 2010

Higher Education

Four-Year Colleges			Two-Year Colleges			Medical Schools[1]	Law Schools[2]	Voc/ Tech[3]
Public	Private Non-profit	Private For-profit	Public	Private Non-profit	Private For-profit			
1	2	3	1	0	2	0	0	1

Note: Figures cover institutions located within the city limits and include main campuses only; (1) includes schools accredited by the Liaison Committee on Medical Education and the American Osteopathic Association; (2) includes American Bar Association-accredited law schools; (3) includes all schools with programs that are less than 2 years.
Source: National Center for Education Statistics, Integrated Postsecondary Education System (IPEDS) Peer Analysis System, 2010-11; U.S. News & World Report, Medical School Directory, 2011; U.S. News & World Report, Law School Directory, 2011

PRESIDENTIAL ELECTION

2008 Presidential Election Results

Area	Obama	McCain	Nader	Other
Hamilton County	43.6	55.4	0.3	0.7
U.S.	52.9	45.6	0.6	0.9

Note: Results are percentages and may not add to 100% due to rounding
Source: Dave Leip's Atlas of U.S. Presidential Elections, www.uselectionatlas.org

EMPLOYERS

Major Employers

Company Name	Industry	Type of Site
Advantage Personnel Cons	Management consulting services	Single
Astec International	Construction machinery	Single
Bluecross Blueshield Tenn	Hospital and medical service plans	Headquarters
Chattanooga Resident Agency	Public order and safety, nec	Branch
County Executive Office	Regulation, administration of utilities	Branch
Erlanger Medical Center	General medical and surgical hospitals	Branch
Further Processing	Poultry slaughtering and processing	Branch
Kenco Logistic Services	General warehousing and storage	Single
Mall Shopping Center	Nonresidential building operators	Headquarters
Mayors Office	Executive offices	Headquarters
Mckee Foods Corporation	Bread, cake, and related products	Headquarters
Nu-Foam Products	Plastics foam products	Single
Orange Grove Center	Job training and related services	Single
Parkridge Medical Center	General medical and surgical hospitals	Headquarters
Provident	Life insurance	Headquarters
Public Works Dept	Urban and community development	Branch
Seaboard Farms of Chattanooga	Poultry slaughtering and processing	Branch
Shaw Industries Group	Yarn spinning mills	Branch
Tennessee Valley Authority	Electric services	Branch
TVA	Electric services	Branch
Vision Care Holdings	Personal credit institutions	Branch

Note: Companies shown are located within the Chattanooga metropolitan area; nec = not elsewhere classified.
Source: www.zapdata.com, January 2011

PUBLIC SAFETY

Crime Rate

Area	All Crimes	Violent Crimes				Property Crimes		
		Murder	Forcible Rape	Robbery	Aggrav. Assault	Burglary	Larceny -Theft	Motor Vehicle Theft
City	8,485.8	9.9	30.7	310.1	688.0	1,731.2	5,186.7	529.2
Suburbs[1]	3,117.7	2.0	21.9	28.5	317.2	674.4	1,897.5	176.2
Metro[2]	4,886.0	4.6	24.8	121.2	439.3	1,022.6	2,981.0	292.5
U.S.	3,465.5	5.0	28.7	133.0	262.8	716.3	2,060.9	258.8

Note: Figures are crimes per 100,000 population; (1) All areas within the metro area that are located outside the city limits; (2) Metropolitan Statistical Area - see Appendix B for areas included
Source: FBI Uniform Crime Reports, 2009

Hate Crimes

Area	Number of Quarters Reported	Bias Motivation				
		Race	Religion	Sexual Orientation	Ethnicity	Disability
City	4	1	0	0	0	1

Source: Federal Bureau of Investigation, Hate Crime Statistics 2009

Identity Theft Consumer Complaints

Area	Complaints	Complaints per 100,000 Population	Rank[2]
MSA[1]	372	72.3	187
U.S.	250,854	81.3	-

Note: (1) Metropolitan Statistical Area - see Appendix B for areas included; (2) Rank ranges from 1 to 384 where 1 indicates greatest number of complaints per 100,000 population
Source: Federal Trade Commission, Consumer Sentinel Network Data Book for January - December 2010

RECREATION

Culture

Dance[1]	Theatre[1]	Instrumental Music[1]	Vocal Music[1]	Series/ Festivals	Museums	Zoos and Aquariums[2]
3	1	1	2	2	9	2

Note: (1) Number of professional performing groups; (2) AZA-accredited
Source: The Grey House Performing Arts Directory, 2011-2012; Official Museum Directory, 2010; American Association of Museums, AAM Member Museums, March 2011; Association of Zoos & Aquariums, AZA Member Zoos & Aquariums, May 2011

Professional Sports Teams

Team Name	League

No teams are located in the metro area
Source: Original research

CLIMATE

Average and Extreme Temperatures

Temperature	Jan	Feb	Mar	Apr	May	Jun	Jul	Aug	Sep	Oct	Nov	Dec	Yr.
Extreme High (°F)	78	79	87	92	97	104	106	104	102	94	84	78	106
Average High (°F)	49	53	62	72	80	87	90	89	83	72	61	51	71
Average Temp. (°F)	39	43	51	60	68	76	79	78	72	61	50	42	60
Average Low (°F)	29	32	39	47	56	64	68	68	61	48	38	32	49
Extreme Low (°F)	-10	1	8	26	34	41	51	53	36	22	4	-2	-10

Note: Figures cover the years 1948-1990
Source: National Climatic Data Center, International Station Meteorological Climate Summary, 9/96

Average Precipitation/Snowfall/Humidity

Precip./Humidity	Jan	Feb	Mar	Apr	May	Jun	Jul	Aug	Sep	Oct	Nov	Dec	Yr.
Avg. Precip. (in.)	5.3	5.0	5.9	4.3	4.1	3.6	4.8	3.5	4.2	3.2	4.5	5.1	53.3
Avg. Snowfall (in.)	2	1	Tr	Tr	0	0	0	0	0	Tr	Tr	1	4
Avg. Rel. Hum. 7am (%)	81	81	81	83	88	89	90	92	92	91	86	83	86
Avg. Rel. Hum. 4pm (%)	58	53	48	44	50	52	55	55	55	50	52	57	52

Note: Figures cover the years 1948-1990; Tr = Trace amounts (<0.05 in. of rain; <0.5 in. of snow)
Source: National Climatic Data Center, International Station Meteorological Climate Summary, 9/96

Weather Conditions

Temperature			Daytime Sky			Precipitation		
10°F & below	32°F & below	90°F & above	Clear	Partly cloudy	Cloudy	0.01 inch or more precip.	0.1 inch or more snow/ice	Thunder-storms
2	73	48	88	141	136	120	3	55

Note: Figures are average number of days per year and cover the years 1948-1990
Source: National Climatic Data Center, International Station Meteorological Climate Summary, 9/96

HAZARDOUS WASTE

Superfund Sites

Chattanooga has one hazardous waste site on the EPA's Superfund Final National Priorities List: **Tennessee Products**. *U.S. Environmental Protection Agency, Final National Priorities List, April 1, 2011*

AIR & WATER QUALITY

Air Quality Index

Area	Percent of Days when Air Quality was...[2]				AQI Statistics	
	Good	Moderate	Unhealthy for Sensitive Groups	Unhealthy	Maximum	Median
Area[1]	63.9	33.8	2.0	0.3	156	45

Note: The Air Quality Index (AQI) is an index for reporting daily air quality. EPA calculates the AQI for five major air pollutants regulated by the Clean Air Act: ground-level ozone, particle pollution (also known as particulate matter), carbon monoxide, sulfur dioxide, and nitrogen dioxide. The AQI runs from 0 to 500. The higher the AQI value, the greater the level of air pollution and the greater the health concern. There are six AQI categories: "Good" The AQI is between 0 and 50. Air quality is considered satisfactory; "Moderate" The AQI is between 51 and 100. Air quality is acceptable; "Unhealthy for Sensitive Groups" When AQI values are between 101 and 150, members of sensitive groups may experience health effects; "Unhealthy" When AQI values are between 151 and 200 everyone may begin to experience health effects; "Very Unhealthy" AQI values between 201 and 300 trigger a health alert; "Hazardous" AQI values over 300 trigger health warnings of emergency conditions; (1) Data covers Hamilton County; (2) Based on 305 days with AQI data in 2008; The EPA has suspended data updates while it assesses its data systems, including AirData reports and maps.
Source: U.S. Environmental Protection Agency, AirData Report, 2008

Air Quality Index Pollutants

Area	Percent of Days when AQI Pollutant was...[2]					
	Carbon Monoxide	Nitrogen Dioxide	Ozone	Sulfur Dioxide	Particulate Matter 2.5	Particulate Matter 10
Area[1]	0.0	0.0	55.4	0.0	44.6	0.0

Note: The Air Quality Index (AQI) is an index for reporting daily air quality. EPA calculates the AQI for five major air pollutants regulated by the Clean Air Act: ground-level ozone, particle pollution (also known as particulate matter), carbon monoxide, sulfur dioxide, and nitrogen dioxide. The AQI runs from 0 to 500. The higher the AQI value, the greater the level of air pollution and the greater the health concern; (1) Data covers Hamilton County; (2) Based on 305 days with AQI data in 2008; The EPA has suspended data updates while it assesses its data systems, including AirData reports and maps.
Source: U.S. Environmental Protection Agency, AirData Report, 2008

Air Quality Index Trends

Area	Trend Sites (days)								All Sites (days)
	2002	2003	2004	2005	2006	2007	2008	2009	2009
MSA[1]	n/a	n/a	n/a	n/a	n/a	n/a	n/a	n/a	n/a

Note: Figures are the number of days the AQI value exceeded 100 in a given year. An AQI value greater than 100 indicates that air quality would have been in the unhealthful range on that day. Data from exceptional events are included. These counts are presented in two ways. First, the counts are based on sites having an adequate record of monitoring data during the trend period (trend sites). These counts represent the relative change in the number of days with AQI values greater than 100. In the last column, the counts are based on all sites with data in the most recent year (because it is possible for a site to have data in the most recent year but not enough data to be a trend site); (1) Data covers the Chattanooga, TN-GA Metropolitan Statistical Area - see Appendix B for areas included; n/a not available.
Source: U.S. Environmental Protection Agency, Office of Air and Radiation, Air Quality Index Information, "Number of Days with Air Quality Index Values Greater than 100 and Trend Sites, 1990-2009, and at All Sites in 2009"

Maximum Air Pollutant Concentrations

	Particulate Matter 10 (ug/m^3)	Particulate Matter 2.5 (ug/m^3)	Ozone (ppm)	Carbon Monoxide (ppm)	Sulfur Dioxide (ppm)	Nitrogen Dioxide (ppm)	Lead (ug/m^3)
MSA[1] Level	23	24	0.07	n/a	n/a	n/a	n/a
NAAQS[2]	150	35	0.075	9	0.140	0.053	0.15
Met NAAQS[2]	Yes	Yes	Yes	n/a	n/a	n/a	n/a

Note: Data from exceptional events are not included; (1) Data covers the Chattanooga, TN-GA Metropolitan Statistical Area - see Appendix B for areas included; (2) National Ambient Air Quality Standards; n/a not available
Concentrations: Particulate Matter 10 (coarse particulate) - highest second maximum 24-hour concentration; Particulate Matter 2.5 (fine particulate) - highest 98th percentile 24-hour concentration; Ozone - highest fourth daily maximum 8-hour concentration; Carbon Monoxide - highest second maximum non-overlapping 8-hour concentration; Sulfur Dioxide - highest second maximum 24-hour concentration; Nitrogen Dioxide - highest arithmetic mean concentration; Lead - maximum running 3-month average
Units: ppm = parts per million; ug/m^3 = micrograms per cubic meter
Source: U.S. Environmental Protection Agency, CBSA Factbook 2009, Air Quality Statistics by City, 2009

Drinking Water

Water System Name	Pop. Served	Primary Water Source Type	Violations[1]	
			Health Based	Monitoring/ Reporting
Tenn-American Water Co.	178,126	Surface	0	0

Note: (1) Based on violation data from January 1, 2010 to December 31, 2010 (includes unresolved violations from earlier years)
Source: U.S. Environmental Protection Agency, Office of Ground Water and Drinking Water, Safe Drinking Water Information System (based on data extracted May 9, 2011)

Columbia, South Carolina

Background

Columbia, on the Congaree River, is South Carolina's capital and largest city, and the seat of Richland County. It is a center for local and state government, and an important financial, insurance, and medical center.

The region has been a trade center from at least 1718, when a trading post opened just south of the present-day city. In 1754, a ferry was established to facilitate contact with the surrounding settlements, and in 1786, when the new state government introduced a bill to create a state capital, Columbia was chosen. Located at almost the dead center of the state, Columbia represented a compromise between South Carolinians on the coast and those in the interior.

The city was planned from the ground up and was originally designed to rest along the river in 400 blocks, which were then divided into half-acre lots. Buyers were required to build houses at least 30 feet long and 18 feet wide within three years, or face penalties. The main thoroughfares were 150 feet wide, and the other streets were also designed generously. Most of this spacious layout still survives, lending an expansive feel to the city as a whole. Columbia, only the second planned city in the United States, achieved a population of nearly 1,000 just after 1800. It was chartered as a town in 1805, and first governed by a mayor, or "intendent," John Taylor, who later served in the state general assembly, in the U.S. Congress, and, finally, as governor of the state.

By 1854, Columbia was a full-fledged chartered city with an elected mayor and six aldermen, a full-time police force, one schoolteacher who was also the city's attorney, and a waterworks, which pumped water via steam engine to a wooden tank and thence by iron and lead pipes to homes and businesses in the area.

Columbia was staunchly Confederate during the Civil War, and in 1865 it was attacked by General Sherman's troops and set ablaze by both Union attackers and Confederate evacuees. After the war and Reconstruction, Columbia saw a revitalization as the state's industrial and farm products hub.

Blue Cross and Blue Shield of S.C. and Palmetto Health, with its two hospitals, Palmetto Richland and Palmetto Baptist, are major employers. Other large employers include SCANA Corp., the area's electricity and natural gas utility; Fort Jackson, the U.S. Army's largest training installation; Humana/TriCare; and the United Parcel Service. Colonial Supplemental Insurance, the second-largest supplemental insurance company in the nation, is based here.

Columbia is the area's cultural center, hosting theaters, galleries, dance companies, and an orchestra. The Columbia Museum of Art is a major regional museum, and the Koger Center for the Arts at the University of South Carolina holds year-round theater, music, and dance productions. The city's Town Theatre is the country's oldest community theatre in continuous use. Annual music festivals include Main Street Jazz, which attracts world-renowned musicians to Columbia, and City Lights, a fall festival that focuses on local musical talent. The Columbia Festival of the Arts is an up-and-coming 11-day festival geared at promoting visual and performance art from the city and its surroundings.

The South Carolina State Museum offers exhibits in natural history, art, science, and technology. Nearing completion is a multi-million dollar observatory/planetarium and large-format OPT theater project including both a 55-foot domed theater in the planetarium and a 3-D theater.

Major historic architecture in Columbia includes the City Hall, designed by President Ulysses S. Grant's federal architect, Alfred Bult Mullet, and the Lutheran Survey Print Building. City officials are planning to redevelop the site of a former 178-acre mental hospital into one of the state capital's largest neighborhoods. For this future development, 1,200 residential units and over 800,000 square feet of retail and office space are planned. The region's economy will also benefit by the currently under-construction University of South Carolina's 200-acre Innovista research campus, which will focus on biomedical, environmental, nanotechnology sectors and future fuels. The city also offers 500 acres of parklands. The Charlie W. Johnson Stadium, home of Benedict College's soccer team, was completed and dedicated in 2006. The Carolina Stadium, USC's new baseball facility and the largest baseball stadium in the state, was completed in February 2009.

The city is home to the University of South Carolina, Lutheran Theological Seminary, Columbia College, Benedict College, Allen University, and Columbia International University.

Located about 150 miles southeast of the Appalachian Mountains, Columbia has a relatively temperate climate. Summers are long and often hot and humid with frequent thunderstorms, thanks to the Bermuda high-pressure force. Winters are mild with little snow, while spring is changeable and can include infrequent tornadoes or hail. Fall is considered the most pleasant season.

Rankings

General Rankings

- Columbia was ranked #110 out of 375 metro areas in *Cities Ranked & Rated*. Criteria: cost of living; climate; crime; transportation; economy and jobs; education; arts and culture; health and healthcare; leisure; quality of life. *Cities Ranked & Rated, 2nd Edition, 2007*

- Columbia was ranked #54 out of 379 metro areas in *Places Rated Almanac*. Criteria: health care; education; recreation; transportation; ambience; climate; crime; housing costs; jobs. *Places Rated Almanac, 7th Edition, 2007*

- *Men's Health Living* ranked 100 U.S. cities in terms of quality of life. Columbia was ranked #39 and received a grade of C+. Criteria: number of fitness facilities; air quality; number of physicians; male/female ratio; education levels; household income; cost of living. *Men's Health Living, Spring 2008*

Business/Finance Rankings

- Columbia was identified as one of the 20 strongest-performing metro areas during the recession and recovery from December 2007 through December 2010. Criteria: percent change in employment; percentage point change in unemployment rate; percent change in gross metropolitan product; percent change in House Price Index. *Brookings Institution, MetroMonitor: Tracking Economic Recession and Recovery in America's 100 Largest Metropolitan Areas, March 2011*

- A.G. Edwards ranked America's 500 top-performing communities based on their residents' personal savings and investing behavior. The Columbia metro area ranked #387 with an index score of 97.25 (national average = 100.00). A dozen statistical factors were measured including: participation in retirement savings plans; personal debt levels; and home ownership. *A.G. Edwards, "2007 Nest Egg Index," September 12, 2007*

- *American City Business Journals* ranked America's 261 largest cities in terms of their resident's wealth. Columbia ranked #164. Criteria: per capita income; median household income; percentage of households with annual incomes of $200,000 or more; median home value. *American City Business Journals, www.bizjournals.com, "Where the Money Is: America's Wealth Centers," August 18, 2008*

- The Columbia metro area appeared on the Milken Institute "2010 Best Performing Metros" list. Rank: #65 out of 200 large metro areas. Criteria: job growth; wage and salary growth; high-tech output growth. *Milken Institute, "2010 Best Performing Metros"*

- The Columbia metro area was selected as one of the best cities for entrepreneurs in America by *Inc. Magazine*. Criteria: job-growth data for 335 metro areas was analyzed for: recent growth trend (the current and prior year's employment growth rates, with the current year emphasized); mid-term growth (the average annual 2002-2007 growth rate); long-term trend (the sum of the 2002-2007 and 1996-2001 employment growth rates multiplied by the ratio of the 1996-2001 growth rate over the 2002-2007 growth rate); current year growth. The Columbia metro area ranked #19 among mid-sized metro areas and #79 overall. *Inc. Magazine, "The Best Cities for Doing Business," July 2008*

- *Forbes* ranked the 200 most populous metro areas in the U.S. in terms of the "Best Places for Business and Careers." The Columbia metro area was ranked #59. Criteria: 12 metrics including costs (business and living), job growth (past and projected), income growth, educational attainment, projected economic growth, crime, cultural and recreational opportunities, net migration patterns, percentage of subprime mortgages handed out over a three-year period, and the number of highly ranked four-year colleges. *Forbes, "Best Places for Business and Careers," April 14, 2010*

Children/Family Rankings

- The Columbia metro area was selected as one of the "Best Cities for Relocating Families" by Worldwide ERC and Primacy Relocation. The 2008 study looked at nearly 50 factors important to relocating families including: recent job growth; nearby top-ranked colleges; in-state tuition for four-year public colleges; population growth since 2000; pediatricians per 100,000 population; and a Green Living index. *Worldwide ERC and Primacy Relocation, "2008 Best Cities for Relocating Families"*

Dating/Romance Rankings

- Columbia was selected as one of the most romantic cities in America by *Amazon.com*. The city ranked #6 of 20. Cities with populations greater than 100,000 were evaluated based on per capita sales of romance novels and relationship books, romantic comedy movies, Barry White albums, and sexual wellness products. *Amazon.com, "Top 20 Most Romantic Cities in America," February 8, 2011*

- Columbia appeared on *Men's Health's* list of the most sex-happy cities in America. The city ranked #32 of 100. Criteria: condom sales; birth rates; sex toy sales; rates of chlamydia, gonorrhea, and syphilis. *Men's Health, "America's Most Sex-Happy Cities," October 2010*

- *Men's Health* ranked 100 U.S. cities in terms of best (and worst) marriages. Columbia was ranked #99 (#1 = worst marriages). Criteria: rate of failed marriages; stringency of divorce laws; percentage of population who've split; number of licensed marriage and family therapists. *Men's Health, "Splitsville, USA," May 2010*

- The Columbia metro area was selected as one of the "Best Cities for Relocating Singles" by Worldwide ERC and Primacy Relocation. The area ranked #50 out of the 100 largest metro areas in the U.S. Areas were selected based on the following criteria: recent job growth; recent singles population growth; overall population growth; affordable rental housing; cost-of-living index; expanded arts and recreation opportunities; ratio of single men and single women; affordability of quality higher education (including state residency requirements); diversity index; climate; population density. *Worldwide ERC and Primacy Relocation, "2008 Best Cities for Relocating Singles"*

Education Rankings

- Columbia was identified as one of the 100 "smartest" metro areas in the U.S. The area ranked #48. Criteria: the editors rated the collective brainpower of the 100 largest metro area in the U.S based on their residents' educational attainment. *American City Business Journals, www.bizjournals.com, April 14, 2008*

- Columbia was identified as one of "America's Brainiest Bastions" by *Portfolio.com*. The metro area ranked #54 out of 200. Portfolio.com analyzed levels of educational attainment in the nation's 200 largest metropolitan areas. The editors established scores for five levels of educational attainment, based on relative earning power of adult workers age 25 or older. Scores were determined by comparing the median income for all workers with the median income for those workers at a specified educational level. *Portfolio.com, "America's Brainiest Bastions," December 1, 2010*

Environmental Rankings

- Columbia was selected as one of 22 "Smarter Cities" for energy by the Natural Resources Defense Council." Criteria: investment in green power; energy efficiency measures; conservation. *Natural Resources Defense Council, "2010 Smarter Cities," July 19, 2010*

- 100 of the largest metro areas in the U.S. were analyzed in terms of their current drought severity. The Columbia metro area ranked #22 (#1 = driest). The rankings were based on statistics such as long-term precipitation trends and patterns and the Palmer drought indices. *Sperling's BestPlaces, www.BestPlaces.net, "America's Drought-Riskiest Cities," November 2007*

- The Columbia metro area appeared in *Country Home's* "Best Green Places" report. The area ranked #152 out of 379. Criteria: official energy policies; green power; green buildings; availability of fresh, locally grown food. *Country Home, "Best Green Places," 2008*

Health/Fitness Rankings

- Columbia was identified as a "2011 Asthma Capital." The area ranked #54 out of the nation's 100 largest metropolitan areas. Twelve factors were used to identify the most challenging places to live for people with asthma: estimated prevalence; self-reported prevalence; crude death rate for asthma; annual pollen score; annual air quality; public smoking laws; number of board-certified asthma specialists; school inhaler access laws; rescue medication use; controller medication use; uninsured rate; poverty rate. *Asthma and Allergy Foundation of America, "2011 Asthma Capitals"*

- Columbia was identified as a 2009 "Spring Allergy Capital." The area ranked #15 out of 100. Three groups of factors were used to identify the most severe cities for people with allergies during the spring season: annual pollen levels; medicine utilization; access to board-certified allergists. *Asthma and Allergy Foundation of America, "Spring Allergy Capitals 2009"*

- Columbia was identified as a 2010 "Fall Allergy Capital." The area ranked #26 out of 100. Three groups of factors were used to identify the most severe cities for people with allergies during the fall season: annual pollen levels; medicine utilization; access to board-certified allergists. *Asthma and Allergy Foundation of America, "Fall Allergy Capitals 2010"*

- *Men's Health* ranked 100 U.S. cities in terms of the quality of their tap water. Columbia was ranked #85 and received a grade of D. Criteria: levels of total coliform bacteria, arsenic, lead, total trihalomethanes (linked to cancer), and halo-acetic acids; number of EPA water-system violations from 1995 to 2005. *Men's Health, March 2007*

- Ortho-McNeil Neurologics, in partnership with Sperling's BestPlaces, analyzed 110 metro areas and identified those U.S. cities with the highest prevalence of factors that are most commonly associated with migraine headaches. The Columbia metro area ranked #27. Criteria: number of migraine-related drug prescriptions per capita; lifestyle factors that can contribute to migraines; environmental factors that can trigger migraines; and consumption of migraine-triggering foods. *Ortho-McNeil Neurologics, "America's Migraine Hot Spots," March 14, 2006*

- The Columbia metro area appeared in the 2010 Gallup-Healthways Well-Being Index. The index, based on interviews with more than 353,000 Americans during 2009, asked individuals to assess their jobs, finances, physical health, emotional state of mind and communities. The metro area ranked #53 out of 162. Criteria: life evaluation; emotional health; work environment; physical health; healthy behaviors; basic access (basic needs optimal for a healthy life, such as access to food and medicine, having health insurance and feeling safe while walking at night). *Gallup-Healthways, "Well-Being Index 2010"*

Real Estate Rankings

- *Fortune* ranked the 100 largest metro areas in the U.S. in terms of projected median home price change in 2010. The Columbia metro area ranked #15. *Fortune, "The 2010 Housing Outlook," December 9, 2009*

- Columbia appeared on ApartmentRatings.com "Top College Towns & Cities" for renters list in 2010." The area ranked #45. Overall satisfaction ratings were ranked using thousands of user submitted scores for hundreds of apartment complexes located in cities and towns that are home to the 100 largest four-year institutions in the U.S. *ApartmentRatings.com, "2010 College Town Renter Satisfaction Rankings"*

- The nation's largest metro areas were analyzed in terms of the percentage of households entering some stage of foreclosure in 2010. The Columbia metro area ranked #108 out of 206 (#1 = highest foreclosure rate). *RealtyTrac, 2010 Year-End Metropolitan Foreclosure Market Report, January 27, 2011*

- The Center for Housing Policy ranked 210 U.S metropolitan areas by the fair market rent for a two-bedroom unit. The Columbia metro area was ranked #130. (#1 = most expensive) with a rent of $767. Criteria: Fair Market Rent (FMR) in effect during the fourth quarter of 2009 based on HUD's fiscal year 2010 FMRs. *The Center for Housing Policy, "Paycheck to Paycheck: Most to Least Expensive Rental Markets in 2009"*

Safety Rankings

- Allstate ranked the 200 largest cities in America in terms of driver safety. Columbia ranked #99. In addition, drivers were 6.2% more likely to have had an accident compared to the national average. Allstate researchers analyzed internal property damage reported claims over a two-year period (from January 2007 to December 2008) to ensure the findings would not be affected by external influences such as weather or road construction. A weighted average of the two-year numbers determined the annual percentages. The report defines an auto crash as any collision resulting in a property damage claim. *Allstate, "The 2010 Allstate America's Best Drivers Report™"*

- The National Insurance Crime Bureau ranked 366 metro areas in the U.S. in terms of per capita rates of vehicle theft. The Columbia metro area ranked #47 (#1 = highest rate). Criteria: number of vehicle theft offenses per 100,000 inhabitants. *National Insurance Crime Bureau, "Hot Spots," May 17, 2010*

Sports/Recreation Rankings

- Columbia appeared on the *Sporting News* list of the "Best Sports Cities" for 2010. The area ranked #84 out of 402 cities in the U.S. *Sporting News* takes a 12-month snapshot, roughly October to October, of each city's sports, putting a heavy premium on regular-season won-lost records (from the most recently completed season). Other criteria include: playoff berths, bowl appearances and tournament bids; championships; applicable power ratings; quality of competition; overall fan fervor as measured in part by attendance as percentage of venue capacity; abundance of teams (rewarding quality over quantity); stadium and arena quality; ticket availability and prices; franchise ownership; and marquee appeal of athletes. *Sporting News, "Best Sports Cities 2010," October, 2010*

- Columbia was chosen as a bicycle friendly community by the League of American Bicyclists. A Bicycle Friendly Community welcomes cyclists by providing safe accommodation for cycling and encouraging people to bike for transportation and recreation. There are four award levels: Platinum; Gold; Silver; and Bronze. The community achieved an award level of Bronze. *League of American Bicyclists, "Bicycle Friendly Community Master List," September 2010*

- *Golf Digest* ranked 330 metro areas in the U.S. in terms of golf. The Columbia metro area was ranked #146. Criteria: access to golf; weather; value of golf; and quality of golf. *Golf Digest, "Metro Golf Rankings," August 2005*

Women/Minorities Rankings

- Columbia was ranked #63 out of 100 metro areas in *SELF Magazine's* ranking of America's healthiest places for women." A panel of experts came up with more than 50 criteria including death and disease rates, environmental indicators, community resources, and lifestyle habits. *SELF Magazine, "Secrets of America's Healthiest Women," December 2008*

Miscellaneous Rankings

- Mars Chocolate North America, the makers of COMBOS®, in partnership with Sperling's BestPlaces, ranked 50 major metro areas in terms of their "manliness." The Columbia metro area ranked #13. Criteria: number of home improvement stores, steak houses, pickup trucks, motorcycles, and manly occupations (fire fighters, police officers, construction workers, EMP personnel) per capita; salty snack sales; sports TV viewing habits. *Mars Chocolate North America, "America's Manliest Cities," June 22, 2010*

Business Environment

CITY FINANCES

City Government Finances

Component	2008 ($000)	2008 ($ per capita)
Total Revenues	244,074	1,955
Total Expenditures	213,485	1,710
Debt Outstanding	275,965	2,211
Cash and Securities[1]	157,303	1,260

Note: (1) Cash and security holdings of a government at the close of its fiscal year, including those of its dependent agencies, utilities, and liquor stores.
Source: U.S Census Bureau, State & Local Government Finances 2008

City Government Revenue by Source

Source	2008 ($000)	2008 ($ per capita)
General Revenue		
From Federal Government	8,143	65
From State Government	14,390	115
From Local Governments	0	0
Taxes		
Property	45,530	365
Sales and Gross Receipts	9,446	76
Personal Income	0	0
Corporate Income	0	0
Motor Vehicle License	0	0
Other Taxes	28,577	229
Current Charges	53,746	431
Liquor Store	0	0
Utility	57,149	458
Employee Retirement	0	0

Source: U.S Census Bureau, State & Local Government Finances 2008

City Government Expenditures by Function

Function	2008 ($000)	2008 ($ per capita)	2008 (%)
General Direct Expenditures			
Air Transportation	0	0	0.0
Corrections	0	0	0.0
Education	0	0	0.0
Employment Security Administration	0	0	0.0
Financial Administration	5,107	41	2.4
Fire Protection	21,588	173	10.1
General Public Buildings	1,350	11	0.6
Governmental Administration, Other	6,108	49	2.9
Health	1,527	12	0.7
Highways	3,355	27	1.6
Hospitals	0	0	0.0
Housing and Community Development	7,102	57	3.3
Interest on General Debt	11,896	95	5.6
Judicial and Legal	4,499	36	2.1
Libraries	0	0	0.0
Parking	4,690	38	2.2
Parks and Recreation	12,621	101	5.9
Police Protection	30,707	246	14.4
Public Welfare	0	0	0.0
Sewerage	13,785	110	6.5
Solid Waste Management	11,663	93	5.5
Veterans' Services	0	0	0.0
Liquor Store	0	0	0.0
Utility	42,985	344	20.1
Employee Retirement	0	0	0.0

Source: U.S Census Bureau, State & Local Government Finances 2008

Municipal Bond Ratings

Area	Moody's	S&P	Fitch
City	Aa2	AA	n/a

Rating Systems (shown in declining order of credit quality): Moody's– Aaa, Aa, A, Baa, Ba, B, Caa, Ca, C (numerical modifiers 1, 2, and 3 are added to letter-rating); S&P– AAA, AA, A, BBB, BB, B, CCC, CC, C; Fitch– AAA, AA, A, BBB, BB, B, CCC, CC, C. Ratings may be modified by the addition of a plus or minus sign to show relative standing within the major rating categories.
Notes: n/a Not available; (1) Not reviewed; (2) Issuer Rating/No General Obligation; (3) Standard and Poor's Issue Credit Rating (ICR) is a current opinion of an obliger with respect to a specific financial obligation, a specific class of financial obligations, or a specific financial program.
Source: City of Columbia, South Carolina, Comprehensive Annual Financial Report, Fiscal Year Ended June 30, 2009

DEMOGRAPHICS

Population Growth

Area	1990 Census	2000 Census	2010 Estimate	2015 Projection	Population Growth (%) 2000-2010	2010-2015
City	115,475	116,278	124,815	130,760	7.3	4.8
MSA[1]	548,325	647,158	744,816	790,857	15.1	6.2
U.S.	248,709,873	281,421,906	309,038,974	321,675,005	9.8	4.1

Note: (1) Metropolitan Statistical Area - see Appendix B for areas included
Source: Claritas, Inc.

Number of Households and Average Household Size

Area	2010 Estimate	2010 Average Household Size
City	46,278	2.12
MSA[1]	290,699	2.44
U.S.	116,136,617	2.59

Note: (1) Metropolitan Statistical Area - see Appendix B for areas included
Source: Claritas, Inc.

Race and Ethnicity

Area	White Alone[2] (%)	Black Alone[2] (%)	Asian Alone[2] (%)	Other Race Alone[2] (%)	Hispanic[3] (%)
City	48.1	45.3	2.3	4.4	4.3
MSA[1]	61.1	33.5	1.6	3.8	4.1
U.S.	72.3	12.4	4.4	10.9	15.8

Note: Figures are 2010 estimates; (1) Metropolitan Statistical Area - see Appendix B for areas included (2) Alone is defined as not being in combination with one or more other races; (3) May be of any race.
Source: Claritas, Inc.

Segregation

Type	Segregation Indices[1] 1990	2000	2010	2010 Rank[2]	Percent Change 1990-2000	1990-2010	2000-2010
Black/White	50.4	48.1	48.8	74	-2.3	-1.6	0.7
Asian/White	43.9	43.8	41.9	46	-0.1	-2.0	-1.9
Hispanic/White	37.7	34.9	34.9	82	-2.8	-2.8	0.0

Note: Figures are based on an analysis of 1990, 2000, and 2010 Census Decennial Census tract data by William H. Frey, Brookings Institution and the University of Michigan Social Science Data Analysis Network. In this analysis all racial groups (whites, blacks, and asians) are non-Hispanic members of those races. Hispanics are shown as a separate category; All figures cover the Metropolitan Statistical Area (see Appendix B for areas included); (1) Segregation Indices are Dissimilarity Indices that measure the degree to which the minority group is distributed differently than whites aross census tracts. They range from 0 (complete integration) to 100 (complete [segregation) where the value indicates the percentage of the minority group that needs to move to be distributed exactly like whites; (2) Ranges from 1 (most segregated) to 102 (least segregated); n/a not available.
Source: www.CensusScope.org

Ancestry

Area	German	Irish	English	American	Italian	Polish	French	Scottish
City	9.8	8.1	9.6	6.3	2.0	1.5	1.8	2.8
MSA[1]	12.2	9.1	9.7	11.6	2.3	1.2	2.0	2.1
U.S.	16.6	12.0	9.1	6.1	5.9	3.3	3.1	1.9

Note: The top eight ancestries in the U.S. are shown. Figures are percentages and include multiple ancestry (e.g. if a person reported being Irish and Italian, they were included in both columns); (1) Metropolitan Statistical Area - see Appendix B for areas included
Source: U.S. Census Bureau, 2007-2009 American Community Survey 3-Year Estimates

Foreign-Born Population

Area	Percent of Population Born in								
	Any Foreign Country	Mexico	Asia	Europe	Carribean	South America	Central America[2]	Africa	Canada
City	n/a	n/a	n/a	n/a	n/a	n/a	n/a	n/a	n/a
MSA[1]	4.7	1.3	1.4	0.8	0.2	0.2	0.4	0.2	0.1
U.S.	12.5	3.8	3.4	1.6	1.1	0.8	0.9	0.5	0.3

Note: (1) Metropolitan Statistical Area - see Appendix B for areas included; (2) Excludes Mexico.
Source: U.S. Census Bureau, 2007-2009 American Community Survey 3-Year Estimates

Marriage Status

Area	Never Married	Now Married[2]	Separated	Widowed	Divorced
City	53.6	29.6	2.9	5.2	8.6
MSA[1]	33.9	47.3	3.1	6.2	9.5
U.S.	31.4	49.7	2.2	6.2	10.6

Note: Figures are percentages and cover the population 15 years of age and older;
(1) Metropolitan Statistical Area - see Appendix B for areas included; (2) Excludes separated
Source: U.S. Census Bureau, 2007-2009 American Community Survey 3-Year Estimates

Age Distribution and Median Age

Area	Percent of Population							Median Age
	Under Age 5	Age 5 to 17	Age 18 to 34	Age 35 to 49	Age 50 to 64	Age 65 to 79	80 Years and Over	
City	5.5	12.7	41.4	17.1	13.8	6.6	2.9	29.0
MSA[1]	6.9	17.6	24.9	21.2	18.1	8.3	3.0	35.5
U.S.	6.9	17.5	23.3	21.4	18.1	9.1	3.7	36.7

Note: (1) Metropolitan Statistical Area - see Appendix B for areas included
Source: U.S. Census Bureau, 2007-2009 American Community Survey 3-Year Estimates

Male/Female Ratio

Area	Males	Females	Males per 100 Females
City	61,996	62,819	98.7
MSA[1]	360,873	383,943	94.0
U.S.	152,401,520	156,637,454	97.3

Note: Figures are 2010 estimates; (1) Metropolitan Statistical Area - see Appendix B for areas included
Source: Claritas, Inc.

Religion

Area	Catholic	Southern Baptist	United Methodist	ELCA[1]	LDS[2]	Presbyterian Church USA	Jewish Est.	Muslim Est.
County	4.0	13.5	7.0	2.7	0.3	3.1	0.9	0.4
U.S.	22.0	7.1	3.7	1.8	1.5	1.1	2.2	0.6

Note: Figures are the number of adherents as a percentage of the total population; Adherents are defined as all members, including full members, their children and the estimated number of other participants who are not considered members (e.g. the baptized, those not confirmed, those regularly attending services, etc.);
(1) Evangelical Lutheran Church in America; (2) The Church of Jesus Christ of Latter Day Saints
Source: Reprinted with permission from Religious Congregations and Membership in the United States 2000 (Nashville, Glenmary Research Center, 2002) Copyright Association of Statisticians of American Religious Bodies. All rights reserved.

ECONOMY

Gross Metropolitan Product

Area	2006	2007	2008	2009	2009 Rank[2]
MSA[1]	28.1	29.0	30.1	30.4	69

Note: Figures are in billions of dollars; (1) Columbia, SC Metropolitan Statistical Area - see Appendix B for areas included; (2) Rank ranges from 1 to 363
Source: The U.S. Conference of Mayors, "Pace of Economic Recovery: GMP and Jobs," January 2010

Economic Growth

Area	2006-2008 (%)	2009 (%)	2010 (%)	Rank[2]
MSA[1]	0.8	-0.1	2.8	205
U.S.	1.3	-2.5	2.2	–

Note: Figures are real Gross Metropolitan Product growth rates and represent annual average percent change; (1) Columbia, SC Metropolitan Statistical Area - see Appendix B for areas included; (2) Rank ranges from 1 to 363
Source: The U.S. Conference of Mayors, "Pace of Economic Recovery: GMP and Jobs," January 2010

Metropolitan Area Exports

Area	2005	2006	2007	2008	2009	2009 Rank[2]
MSA[1]	1,456.0	1,143.5	1,048.0	1,483.5	1,362.5	102

Note: Figures are in millions of dollars; (1) Columbia, SC Metropolitan Statistical Area - see Appendix B for areas included; (2) Rank ranges from 1 to 374
Source: U.S. Department of Commerce, International Trade Administration, Office of Trade & Industry Information, Manufacturing & Services

INCOME

Per Capita/Median/Average Income

Area	Per Capita ($)	Median Household ($)	Average Household ($)
City	23,506	38,709	58,989
MSA[1]	25,589	49,462	64,489
U.S.	27,034	52,795	71,071

Note: Figures are 2010 estimates; (1) Metropolitan Statistical Area - see Appendix B for areas included
Source: Claritas, Inc.

Household Income Distribution

Area	Under $15,000	$15,000 -24,999	$25,000 -34,999	$35,000 -49,999	$50,000 -74,999	$75,000 -99,000	$100,000 -149,999	$150,000 and up
City	20.4	13.6	12.1	15.8	16.2	8.1	7.1	6.7
MSA[1]	12.6	10.5	11.2	16.3	20.5	12.4	11.0	5.5
U.S.	12.1	10.2	10.6	15.0	19.5	12.5	12.1	8.0

Note: Figures are 2010 estimates; (1) Metropolitan Statistical Area - see Appendix B for areas included
Source: Claritas, Inc.

Poverty Rates by Age

Area	All Ages	Under 18 Years Old	18 to 64 Years Old	65 Years and Over
City	21.3	5.5	14.3	1.6
MSA[1]	13.0	4.1	7.7	1.2
U.S.	13.6	4.7	7.7	1.2

Note: Figures are percent of population with income during the previous 12 months below poverty level and only include population for whom poverty status is determined; (1) Metropolitan Statistical Area - see Appendix B for areas included
Source: U.S. Census Bureau, 2007-2009 American Community Survey 3-Year Estimates

Personal Bankruptcy Filing Rate

Area	2006	2007	2008	2009	2010
Richland County	2.11	2.24	2.46	2.42	2.32
U.S.	2.00	2.73	3.53	4.60	4.96

Note: Numbers are per 1,000 population and include Chapter 7 and Chapter 13 filings
Source: Federal Deposit Insurance Corporation, Regional Economic Conditions, March 17, 2011

EMPLOYMENT

Labor Force and Employment

Area	Civilian Labor Force			Workers Employed		
	Dec. 2009	Dec. 2010	% Chg.	Dec. 2009	Dec. 2010	% Chg.
City	54,943	54,922	0.0	49,716	49,714	0.0
MSA[1]	368,248	366,913	-0.4	333,617	333,605	0.0
U.S.	152,693,000	153,156,000	0.3	137,953,000	139,159,000	0.9

Note: Data is not seasonally adjusted and covers workers 16 years of age and older;
(1) Metropolitan Statistical Area - see Appendix B for areas included
Source: Bureau of Labor Statistics, http://stats.bls.gov

Unemployment Rate

Area	2010											
	Jan.	Feb.	Mar.	Apr.	May	Jun.	Jul.	Aug.	Sep.	Oct.	Nov.	Dec.
City	9.6	9.8	9.8	8.9	10.1	10.9	10.8	11.3	9.7	9.9	9.7	9.5
MSA[1]	9.8	9.7	9.3	8.5	8.9	9.4	9.5	9.8	9.1	9.1	9.3	9.1
U.S.	10.6	10.4	10.2	9.5	9.3	9.6	9.7	9.5	9.2	9.0	9.3	9.1

Note: Data is not seasonally adjusted and covers workers 16 years of age and older; All figures are percentages; (1) Metropolitan Statistical Area - see Appendix B for areas included
Source: Bureau of Labor Statistics, http://stats.bls.gov

Projected Unemployment Rate

Area	2007 (%)	2009 (%)	2011 (%)	2013 (%)
MSA[1]	4.9	9.6	8.6	7.0

Note: (1) Metropolitan Statistical Area - see Appendix B for areas included
Source: The U.S. Conference of Mayors, "Pace of Economic Recovery: GMP and Jobs," January 2010

Employment by Occupation

Occupation Classification	City (%)	MSA[1] (%)	U.S. (%)
Sales and Office	25.9	26.3	25.4
Professional and Related	27.1	22.7	21.0
Service	20.5	16.5	17.2
Production, Transportation, and Material Moving	7.2	11.1	12.3
Management, Business, and Financial	14.7	14.3	14.1
Construction, Extraction, and Maintenance	4.5	8.8	9.2
Farming, Forestry, and Fishing	0.1	0.3	0.7

Note: Figures cover employed civilians 16 years of age and older;
(1) Metropolitan Statistical Area - see Appendix B for areas included
Source: U.S. Census Bureau, 2007-2009 American Community Survey 3-Year Estimates

Employment by Industry

| Sector | MSA[1] | | U.S. |
	Number of Employees	Percent of Total	Percent of Total
Government	78,500	22.8	17.2
Education and Health Services	42,800	12.5	15.2
Professional and Business Services	40,000	11.6	13.0
Retail Trade	39,300	11.4	11.4
Leisure and Hospitality	30,800	9.0	9.7
Manufacturing	26,900	7.8	8.8
Financial Activities	27,200	7.9	5.8
Wholesale Trade	13,600	4.0	4.2
Construction	n/a	n/a	4.1
Other Services	13,800	4.0	4.1
Transportation and Utilities	10,600	3.1	3.7
Information	5,500	1.6	2.1
Mining and Logging	n/a	n/a	0.6

Note: Figures cover non-farm employment as of December 2010 and are not seasonally adjusted;
(1) Metropolitan Statistical Area - see Appendix B for areas included; n/a not available
Source: Bureau of Labor Statistics, http://stats.bls.gov

Occupations with Greatest Projected Employment Growth: 2006 - 2016

Occupation[1]	2006 Employment	2016 Projected Employment	Numeric Employment Change	Percent Employment Change
Retail salespersons	64,600	74,610	10,010	15.5
Customer service representatives	28,150	36,950	8,800	31.3
Combined food preparation and serving workers, including fast food	31,560	37,950	6,390	20.2
Registered nurses	33,310	39,660	6,350	19.1
Postsecondary teachers	17,680	22,760	5,080	28.7
Office clerks, general	39,060	44,110	5,050	12.9
Janitors and cleaners, except maids and housekeeping cleaners	31,110	35,900	4,790	15.4
Truck drivers, heavy and tractor-trailer	25,640	30,390	4,750	18.5
Waiters and waitresses	38,830	42,780	3,950	10.2
Sales representatives, wholesale and manufacturing, except technical and scientific products	17,250	21,120	3,870	22.4

Note: Projections cover South Carolina; (1) Sorted by numeric employment change
Source: www.projectionscentral.com, State Occupational Projections, 2006-2016 Long-Term Projections

Fastest Growing Occupations: 2006 - 2016

Occupation[1]	2006 Employment	2016 Projected Employment	Numeric Employment Change	Percent Employment Change
Ambulance drivers and attendants, except emergency medical technicians	950	1,630	680	71.6
Network systems and data communications analysts	2,320	3,770	1,450	62.5
Chiropractors	660	1,070	410	62.1
Occupational therapist assistants	400	640	240	60.0
Audio and video equipment technicians	350	550	200	57.1
Pharmacy technicians	4,720	7,200	2,480	52.5
Physical therapist assistants	940	1,430	490	52.1
Veterinary technologists and technicians	790	1,190	400	50.6
Multi-media artists and animators	520	780	260	50.0
Self-enrichment education teachers	1,730	2,490	760	43.9

Note: Projections cover South Carolina; (1) Sorted by percent employment change and excludes occupations with numeric employment change less than 200
Source: www.projectionscentral.com, State Occupational Projections, 2006-2016 Long-Term Projections

Average Wages

Occupation	$/Hr.	Occupation	$/Hr.
Accountants and Auditors	28.07	Maids and Housekeeping Cleaners	8.89
Automotive Mechanics	16.60	Maintenance and Repair Workers	17.32
Bookkeepers	15.90	Marketing Managers	41.13
Carpenters	16.01	Nuclear Medicine Technologists	29.62
Cashiers	8.08	Nurses, Licensed Practical	19.07
Clerks, General Office	12.81	Nurses, Registered	28.76
Clerks, Receptionists/Information	12.46	Nursing Aides/Orderlies/Attendants	9.96
Clerks, Shipping/Receiving	13.48	Packers and Packagers, Hand	10.00
Computer Programmers	30.60	Physical Therapists	37.11
Computer Support Specialists	20.06	Postal Service Mail Carriers	22.76
Computer Systems Analysts	29.00	Real Estate Brokers	21.11
Cooks, Restaurant	9.61	Retail Salespersons	11.04
Dentists	n/a	Sales Reps., Exc. Tech./Scientific	29.91
Electrical Engineers	42.11	Sales Reps., Tech./Scientific	33.69
Electricians	18.41	Secretaries, Exc. Legal/Med./Exec.	13.98
Financial Managers	45.80	Security Guards	12.42
First-Line Supervisors/Mgrs., Sales	18.68	Surgeons	110.88
Food Preparation Workers	8.08	Teacher Assistants	9.20
General and Operations Managers	49.81	Teachers, Elementary School	22.50
Hairdressers/Cosmetologists	14.80	Teachers, Secondary School	24.30
Internists	106.84	Telemarketers	11.99
Janitors and Cleaners	9.75	Truck Drivers, Heavy/Tractor-Trailer	18.31
Landscaping/Groundskeeping Workers	10.92	Truck Drivers, Light/Delivery Svcs.	13.78
Lawyers	57.22	Waiters and Waitresses	7.67

Note: Wage data covers the Columbia, SC - see Appendix B for areas included. Hourly wages for elementary/secondary school teachers and teacher assistants were calculated by the editors from annual wage data assuming a 40 hour work week; n/a not available.
Source: Bureau of Labor Statistics, Metro Area Occupational Employment and Wage Estimates, May 2009

RESIDENTIAL REAL ESTATE

Building Permits

Area	Single-Family			Multi-Family			Total		
	2009	2010	Pct. Chg.	2009	2010	Pct. Chg.	2009	2010	Pct. Chg.
City	265	203	-23.4	38	96	152.6	303	299	-1.3
MSA[1]	2,583	2,527	-2.2	915	415	-54.6	3,498	2,942	-15.9
U.S.	441,100	447,300	1.4	141,900	157,300	10.9	583,000	604,600	3.7

Note: (1) Metropolitan Statistical Area - see Appendix B for areas included; figures represent new, privately-owned housing units authorized (unadjusted data); All permit data are based on estimates with imputation.
Source: U.S. Census Bureau, Manufacturing, Mining, and Construction Statistics, Building Permits, 2009, 2010

Homeownership Rate

Area	2005 (%)	2006 (%)	2007 (%)	2008 (%)	2009 (%)	2010 (%)
MSA[1]	76.3	72.2	71.1	71.4	71.5	74.1
U.S.	68.9	68.8	68.1	67.8	67.4	66.9

Note: (1) Metropolitan Statistical Area - see Appendix B for areas included
Source: U.S. Census Bureau, Housing Vacancies and Homeownership Annual Statistics: 2010

Housing Vacancy Rates

Area	Gross Vacancy Rate[2] (%)			Year-Round Vacancy Rate[3] (%)			Rental Vacancy Rate[4] (%)			Homeowner Vacancy Rate[5] (%)		
	2008	2009	2010	2008	2009	2010	2008	2009	2010	2008	2009	2010
MSA[1]	13.2	13.3	11.1	12.6	13.0	10.9	6.8	8.4	9.4	3.2	3.1	2.5
U.S.	14.4	14.5	14.3	11.1	11.3	11.3	10.0	10.6	10.2	2.8	2.6	2.6

Note: (1) Metropolitan Statistical Area - see Appendix B for areas included; (2) The percentage of the total housing inventory that is vacant; (3) The percentage of the housing inventory (excluding seasonal units) that is year-round vacant; (4) The percentage of rental inventory that is vacant for rent; (5) The percentage of homeowner inventory that is vacant for sale; n/a not available
Source: U.S. Census Bureau, Housing Vacancies and Homeownership Annual Statistics: 2010

State Corporate Income Tax Rates

State	Tax Rate (%)	Income Brackets ($)	Num. of Brackets	Financial Institution Tax Rate (%)[a]	Federal Income Tax Ded.
South Carolina	5.0	Flat rate	1	4.5 (x)	No

Note: Tax rates as of January 1, 2011; (a) Rates listed are the tax rates applied to financial institutions or excise taxes based on income. Some states have other taxes based upon the value of deposits or shares; (x) South Carolina taxes savings and loans at a 6% rate.
Source: Federation of Tax Administrators, "State Corporate Income Tax Rates, 2011"

State Individual Income Tax Rates

State	Tax Rate (%)	Income Brackets ($)	Num. of Brackets	Personal Exempt. ($)[1] Single	Personal Exempt. ($)[1] Dependents	Fed. Inc. Tax Ded.
South Carolina (a)	0.0 - 7.0	2,740 - 13,701	6	3,650 (d)	3,650 (d)	No

Note: Tax rates as of January 1, 2011; Local- and county-level taxes are not included; n/a not applicable; (1) Married joint filers generally receive double the single exemption; (a) 17 states have statutory provision for automatically adjusting to the rate of inflation the dollar values of the income tax brackets, standard deductions, and/or personal exemptions. Massachusetts, Michigan, and Nebraska index the personal exemption only. Oregon does not index the income brackets for $125,000 and over. Because the inflation-adjustments for 2011 are not yet available in most cases, the table reports the 2010 amounts, unless 2011 is specified in a footnote; (d) These states use the personal exemption amounts provided in the federal Internal Revenue Code.
Source: Federation of Tax Administrators, "State Individual Income Tax Rates, 2011"

Various State and Local Tax Rates

State	State and Local Sales and Use (%)	State Sales and Use (%)	Gasoline[1] (¢/gal.)	Cigarette[2] ($/pack)	Spirits[3] ($/gal.)	Wine[4] ($/gal.)	Beer[5] ($/gal.)
South Carolina	7.0	6.00	16.8	0.57	4.97 (i)	1.08	0.77

Note: All tax rates as of January 1, 2011 except Spirits (Sept. 1, 2010); (1) The American Petroleum Institute has developed a methodology for determining the average tax rate on a gallon of fuel. Rates may include any of the following: excise taxes, environmental fees, storage tank fees, other fees or taxes, general sales tax, and local taxes. In states where gasoline is subject to the general sales tax, or where the fuel tax is based on the average sale price, the average rate determined by API is sensitive to changes in the price of gasoline. States that fully or partially apply general sales taxes to gasoline: CA, CO, GA, IL, IN, MI, NY; (2) The federal excise tax of $1.0066 per pack and local taxes are not included; (3) Rates are those applicable to off-premise sales of 40% alcohol by volume (a.b.v.) distilled spirits in 750ml containers. Local excise taxes are excluded; (4) Rates are those applicable to off-premise sales of 11% a.b.v. non-carbonated wine in 750ml containers; (5) Rates are those applicable to off-premise sales of 4.7% a.b.v. beer in 12 ounce containers; (i) Includes a wholesale tax of $5.36 per case.
Source: Tax Foundation, 2011 Facts & Figures: How Does Your State Compare?

State-Local Tax Burdens

Area	Rate (%)	Rank[1]	Per Capita Taxes Paid to Home State ($)	Total State and Local Per Capita Taxes Paid	Per Capita Income ($)
South Carolina	8.1	43	1,845	2,742	33,954
U.S. Average	9.8	-	3,057	4,160	42,539

Note: Figures cover 2009; (1) Rank ranges from 1 to 50 where 1 is highest tax burden
Source: Tax Foundation, State-Local Tax Burdens, All States, 2009

State Business Tax Climate Index Rankings

State	Overall Rank	Corporate Tax Index Rank	Individual Income Tax Index Rank	Sales Tax Index Rank	Unemployment Insurance Tax Index Rank	Property Tax Index Rank
South Carolina	24	9	27	22	43	23

Note: The index is a measure of how each state's tax laws affect economic performance. The lower the rank, the more favorable a state's tax system is for business. All ranks are for fiscal years. States without a given tax are given a ranking of 1.
Source: Tax Foundation, Tax Foundation Background Paper, No. 60, "2011 State Business Tax Climate Index"

COMMERCIAL REAL ESTATE

Office Market

Market Area	Inventory (sq. ft.)	Vacant (sq. ft.)	Vac. Rate (%)	Under Constr. (sq. ft.)	Asking Rent ($/sf/yr)	
					Class A	Class B
Columbia	11,941,994	2,776,642	23.3	-	18.67	14.99

Source: Grubb & Ellis, Office Markets Trends, 2nd Quarter 2010

COMMERCIAL UTILITIES

Typical Monthly Electric Bills

Area	Commercial Service ($/month)		Industrial Service ($/month)	
	3 kW demand 1,000 kWh	40 kW demand 14,000 kWh	1,000 kW demand 200,000 kWh	50,000 kW demand 15,000,000 kWh
City	n/a	n/a	n/a	n/a
Average[1]	135	1,576	23,741	1,402,202

Note: Based on total rates in effect July 1, 2010; (1) average based on 182 utilities surveyed; n/a not available
Source: Edison Electric Institute, Typical Bills and Average Rates Report, Summer 2010

TRANSPORTATION

Means of Transportation to Work

Area	Car/Truck/Van		Public Transportation			Bicycle	Walked	Other Means	Worked at Home
	Drove Alone	Car-pooled	Bus	Subway	Railroad				
City	65.5	8.8	2.2	0.2	0.0	0.5	4.1	1.7	16.9
MSA[1]	79.5	9.9	0.8	0.1	0.0	0.2	1.6	2.1	5.8
U.S.	75.8	10.4	2.7	1.7	0.5	0.5	2.9	1.2	4.1

Note: Figures are percentages and cover workers 16 years of age and older;
(1) Metropolitan Statistical Area - see Appendix B for areas included
Source: U.S. Census Bureau, 2007-2009 American Community Survey 3-Year Estimates

Travel Time to Work

Area	Less Than 15 Minutes	15 to 29 Minutes	30 to 44 Minutes	45 to 59 Minutes	60 to 89 Minutes	90 Minutes or More
City	41.2	42.9	10.2	2.9	1.4	1.4
MSA[1]	25.9	42.0	21.1	6.5	2.9	1.6
U.S.	28.5	36.2	19.7	7.5	5.6	2.5

Note: Figures are percentages and include workers 16 years old and over;
(1) Metropolitan Statistical Area - see Appendix B for areas included
Source: U.S. Census Bureau, 2007-2009 American Community Survey 3-Year Estimates

Travel Time Index

Area	1982	1999	2008	2009
Urban Area[1]	1.02	1.06	1.08	1.09
Average[2]	1.08	1.20	1.20	1.20

Note: Travel Time Index—the ratio of travel time in the peak period to the travel time at
free-flow conditions. A value of 1.30 indicates a 20-minute free-flow trip takes 26 minutes
in the peak. Free-flow speeds (60 mph on freeways and 35 mph on principal arterials)
are used as the comparison threshold; (1) Covers the Columbia urban area;
(2) average of 439 urban areas
Source: Texas Transportation Institute, Urban Mobility Report 2010, December 2010

Public Transportation

Agency Name / Mode of Transportation	Vehicles Operated in Maximum Service	Annual Unlinked Passenger Trips ('000)	Annual Passenger Miles ('000)
Central Midlands Regional Transit Authority			
Demand response	21	78.2	834.9
Bus	38	2,019.9	10,587.3

Note: Figures include both directly operated and purchased transportation
Source: Federal Transit Administration, National Transit Database, 2009

Air Transportation

Airport Name and Code / Type of Service	Passenger Airlines[1]	Passenger Enplanements	Freight Carriers[2]	Freight (lbs.)
Columbia Metropolitan (CAE)				
Domestic service (U.S. carriers - 2010)	27	480,658	16	71,450,326
International service (U.S. carriers - 2009)	4	671	1	3,168

Note: (1) Includes all U.S.-based major, minor and commuter airlines that carried at least one passenger during the year; (2) Includes all U.S.-based airlines and freight carriers that transported at least one pound of freight during the year
Source: Bureau of Transportation Statistics, The Intermodal Transportation Database, Air Carriers: T-100 Domestic Market (U.S. Carriers), 2010; Bureau of Transportation Statistics, The Intermodal Transportation Database, Air Carriers: T-100 International Market (U.S. Carriers), 2009

Other Transportation Statistics

Interstate highways:	I-20; I-26; I-77
Amtrak service:	Yes
Major waterways/ports:	Congaree River

Source: Amtrak.com; Google Maps

BUSINESSES

Major Business Headquarters

Company Name	Rankings	
	Fortune[1]	Forbes[2]
No companies listed	-	-

Note: (1) Fortune 500—companies that produce a 10-K are ranked 1 to 500 based on 2010 revenue; (2) all private companies with at least $2 billion in annual revenue are ranked 1 to 223; companies listed are headquartered in the city; dashes indicate no ranking
Source: Fortune, "Fortune 500," May 23, 2011; Forbes, "America's Largest Private Companies," November 3, 2010

Minority Business Opportunity

Columbia is home to one company which is on the Black Enterprise Bank 25 list (25 largest banks based on total assets, capital, deposits and loans, including mortgage-backed securities for the calendar year): **South Carolina Community Bank**. Criteria: commercial banks or savings and loans that are classified by the Federal Reserve as black institutions and have been fully operational for the previous calendar year. *Black Enterprise, B.E. 100s, 2010*

Minority- and Women-Owned Businesses

Group	All Firms		Firms with Paid Employees			
	Firms	Sales ($000)	Firms	Sales ($000)	Employees	Payroll ($000)
Asian	299	93,619	118	80,343	599	11,063
Black	2,481	197,421	234	132,808	2,683	39,747
Hispanic	141	205,998	38	202,924	500	15,648
Women	3,094	457,366	672	389,303	4,694	116,649
All Firms	12,783	20,597,163	4,132	20,165,390	96,175	3,692,655

Note: Figures cover firms located in the city; minority- and women-owned business are defined as firms in which the corresponding group own 51% or more of the stock or equity of the company
Source: U.S. Census Bureau, 2007 Economic Census, Survey of Business Owners

HOTELS

Hotels/Motels

Area	5 Star		4 Star		3 Star		2 Star		1 Star		Not Rated	
	Num.	Pct.3	Num.	Pct.3	Num.	Pct.3	Num.	Pct.3	Num.	Pct.3	Num.	Pct.3
City[1]	0	0.0	0	0.0	24	21.8	70	63.6	5	4.5	11	10.0
Total[2]	119	0.7	927	5.8	4,906	30.5	7,992	49.7	526	3.3	1,625	10.1

Note: (1) Figures cover Columbia and vicinity; (2) Figures cover all 100 cities in this book; (3) Percentage of hotels which are a given star rating; Star ratings are determined by expedia.com and offer an indication of the general quality of a particular hotel.
Source: expedia.com, May 5, 2011

EVENT SITES

Major Stadiums, Arenas, and Auditoriums

Name	Max. Capacity
Carolina Coliseum	12,803
Williams-Brice Stadium	80,250

Source: Original research

Convention Centers

Name	Overall Space (sq. ft.)	Exhibit Space (sq. ft.)	Meeting Space (sq. ft.)	Meeting Rooms
Columbia Metropolitan Convention Center	142,500	n/a	24,700	n/a

Note: n/a not available
Source: Original research

Living Environment

COST OF LIVING

Cost of Living Index

Composite Index	Groceries	Housing	Utilities	Trans-portation	Health Care	Misc. Goods/Services
100.4	105.2	82.3	109.0	102.0	106.2	110.6

Note: U.S. = 100; Figures cover the Columbia SC urban area.
Source: The Council for Community and Economic Research, ACCRA Cost of Living Index, 2010

Grocery Prices

Area[1]	T-Bone Steak ($/pound)	Frying Chicken ($/pound)	Whole Milk ($/half gal.)	Eggs ($/dozen)	Orange Juice ($/64 oz.)	Coffee ($/11.5 oz.)
City[2]	9.62	1.28	2.21	1.32	3.22	3.47
Avg.	9.04	1.16	2.02	1.47	3.08	3.65
Min.	6.97	0.84	1.46	0.96	2.39	2.64
Max.	13.93	2.51	3.58	3.01	4.94	6.32

*Note: (1) Values for the local area are compared with the average, minimum and maximum values for all 338 areas in the Cost of Living Index; (2) Figures cover the Columbia SC urban area; **T-Bone Steak** (price per pound); **Frying Chicken** (price per pound, whole fryer); **Whole Milk** (half gallon carton); **Eggs** (price per dozen, Grade A, large); **Orange Juice** (64 oz. Tropicana or Florida Natural); **Coffee** (11.5 oz. can, vacuum-packed, Maxwell House, Hills Bros, or Folgers).*
Source: The Council for Community and Economic Research, ACCRA Cost of Living Index, 2010

Housing and Utility Costs

Area[1]	New Home Price ($)	Apartment Rent ($/month)	All Electric ($/month)	Part Electric ($/month)	Other Energy ($/month)	Telephone ($/month)
City[2]	235,945	752	-	92.81	105.96	27.00
Avg.	293,442	810	166.39	91.93	83.82	26.93
Min.	182,545	453	119.21	44.47	36.85	17.98
Max.	1,123,114	2,776	307.53	218.20	313.90	39.15

*Note: (1) Values for the local area are compared with the average, minimum and maximum values for all 338 areas in the Cost of Living Index; (2) Figures cover the Columbia SC urban area; **New Home Price** (2,400 sf living area, 8,000 sf lot, in urban area with full utilities); **Apartment Rent** (950 sf 2 bedroom/1.5 or 2 bath, unfurnished, excluding all utilities except water); **All Electric** (average monthly cost for an all-electric home); **Part Electric** (average monthly cost for a part-electric home); **Other Energy** (average monthly cost for natural gas, fuel oil, coal, wood, and any other forms of energy except electricity); **Telephone** (price includes basic monthly rate for a private residential line plus additional local usage charges incurred by a family of four).*
Source: The Council for Community and Economic Research, ACCRA Cost of Living Index, 2010

Health Care, Transportation, and Other Costs

Area[1]	Doctor ($/visit)	Dentist ($/visit)	Optometrist ($/visit)	Gasoline ($/gallon)	Beauty Salon ($/visit)	Men's Shirt ($)
City[2]	91.89	86.67	94.83	2.57	30.67	28.29
Avg.	89.44	78.95	87.40	2.73	31.92	24.83
Min.	57.00	54.25	48.32	2.44	19.17	13.67
Max.	149.90	136.73	174.22	3.75	62.81	47.89

*Note: (1) Values for the local area are compared with the average, minimum and maximum values for all 338 areas in the Cost of Living Index; (2) Figures cover the Columbia SC urban area; **Doctor** (general practitioners routine exam of an established patient); **Dentist** (adult teeth cleaning and periodic oral examination); **Optometrist** (full vision eye exam for established adult patient); **Gasoline** (one gallon regular unleaded, national brand, including all taxes, cash price at self-service pump if available); **Beauty Salon** (woman's shampoo, trim, and blow-dry); **Men's Shirt** (cotton/polyester dress shirt, pinpoint weave, long sleeves).*
Source: The Council for Community and Economic Research, ACCRA Cost of Living Index, 2010

HOUSING

House Price Index (HPI)

Area	National Ranking[2]	Quarterly Change (%)	One-Year Change (%)	Five-Year Change (%)
MSA[1]	199	-0.75	-2.09	6.07
U.S.[3]	-	-0.84	-3.95	-11.45

Note: The HPI is a weighted repeat sales index. It measures average price changes in repeat sales or refinancings on the same properties. This information is obtained by reviewing repeat mortgage transactions on single-family properties whose mortgages have been purchased or securitized by Fannie Mae or Freddie Mac in January 1975; (1) Metropolitan/Micropolitan Statistical Area - see Appendix B for areas included; (2) Rankings are based on annual percentage change for all metro areas containing at least 15,000 transactions over the last 10 years and ranges from 1 to 309; (3) figures based on a weighted average of Census Division estimates; all figures are for the period ending December 31, 2010
Source: Federal Housing Finance Agency, House Price Index, February 24, 2011

House Price Valuations

Area	Q4 2005 Price ($000)	Q4 2005 Over-valuation	Q4 2006 Price ($000)	Q4 2006 Over-valuation	Q4 2007 Price ($000)	Q4 2007 Over-valuation	Q4 2008 Price ($000)	Q4 2008 Over-valuation	Q4 2009 Price ($000)	Q4 2009 Over-valuation
MSA[1]	112.3	-2.2	116.9	-3.3	118.7	-5.5	115.9	-9.9	119.0	-9.5

Note: Figures show the percentage of over- or under-valuation of single family homes relative to statistically normal house values (e.g. a value of 23.6 indicates that house values are 23.6% overvalued). Statistically normal house values are based on house prices, interest rates, household incomes, population densities, and any historical premiums or discounts metropolitan areas have exhibited over time; (1) Figures cover the Columbia, SC Metropolitan Statistical Area - see Appendix B for areas included
Source: Global Insight/PNC Financial Services Group, House Prices in America: 4th Quarter 2009 Update

Median Single-Family Home Prices

Area	2008	2009	2010p	Percent Change 2009 to 2010
MSA[1]	145.0	139.2	142.6	2.4
U.S. Average	196.6	172.1	173.2	0.6

Note: Figures are median sales prices of existing single-family homes in thousands of dollars; (p) preliminary; n/a not available; (1) Metropolitan Statistical Area - see Appendix B for areas included
Source: National Association of Realtors, Median Sales Price of Existing Single-Family Homes for Metropolitan Areas, 4th Quarter 2010

Median Apartment Condo-Coop Home Prices

Area	2008	2009	2010p	Percent Change 2009 to 2010
MSA[1]	n/a	n/a	n/a	n/a
U.S. Average	209.8	175.6	171.7	-2.2

Note: Figures are median sales prices of existing apartment condo-coop homes in thousands of dollars; (p) preliminary; n/a not available; (1) Metropolitan Statistical Area - see Appendix B for areas included
Source: National Association of Realtors, Median Sales Price of Existing Apartment Condo-Coop Homes for Metropolitan Areas, 4th Quarter 2010

Year Housing Structure Built

Area	2000 or Later	1990 -1999	1980 -1989	1970 -1979	1960 -1969	1950 -1959	1940 -1949	Before 1940	Median Year
City	12.3	9.2	12.0	11.8	15.0	18.9	9.9	11.0	1967
MSA[1]	17.7	19.1	16.0	18.4	11.3	8.9	4.0	4.6	1982
U.S.	12.5	14.0	14.2	16.5	11.4	11.3	5.8	14.3	1974

Note: Figures are percentages except for Median Year; (1) Metropolitan Statistical Area - see Appendix B for areas included
Source: U.S. Census Bureau, 2007-2009 American Community Survey 3-Year Estimates

HEALTH

Health Risk Data

Category	MSA[1] (%)	U.S. (%)
Adults who have been told they have high blood pressure	29.2	28.7
Adults who have been told they have high blood cholesterol	38.5	37.5
Adults who have been told they have diabetes[3]	11.1	8.3
Adults who have been told they have arthritis	28.8	26.0
Adults who have been told they currently have asthma	4.2	8.8
Adults who are current smokers	17.8	17.9
Adults who are heavy drinkers[4]	4.9	5.1
Adults who are binge drinkers[5]	13.1	15.8
Adults who are overweight (BMI 25.0 - 29.9)	34.5	36.2
Adults who are obese (BMI 30.0 - 99.8)	28.8	26.9
Adults who participated in any physical activities in the past month	73.7	76.2
Adults 50+ who have ever had a sigmoidoscopy or colonoscopy[2]	73.1	62.2
Women 40+ who have had a mammogram within the past two years[2]	80.2	76.0
Adults age 18–64 who have any kind of health care coverage	79.9	83.1

Note: Data as of 2009 unless otherwise noted; (1) Figures cover the Columbia, SC Metropolitan Statistical Area - see Appendix B for areas included; (2) Data as of 2008; (3) Figures do not include pregnancy-related, borderline, or pre-diabetes; (4) Heavy drinkers are classified as males having more than two drinks per day or females having more than one drink per day; (5) Binge drinkers are classified as males having five or more drinks on one occasion or females having four or more drinks on one occasion
Source: Centers for Disease Control and Prevention, Behaviorial Risk Factor Surveillance System, SMART: Selected Metropolitan/Micropolitan Area Risk Trends, 2008, 2009

Mortality Rates for the Top 10 Causes of Death in the U.S.

ICD-10[a] Sub-Chapter	ICD-10[a] Code	Age-Adjusted Mortality Rate[1] per 100,000 population	
		County[2]	U.S.
Malignant neoplasms	C00-C97	196.4	180.9
Ischaemic heart diseases	I20-I25	143.1	135.0
Other forms of heart disease	I30-I51	58.3	50.0
Cerebrovascular diseases	I60-I69	51.0	44.1
Chronic lower respiratory diseases	J40-J47	34.1	41.5
Other degenerative diseases of the nervous system	G30-G31	36.8	23.6
Diabetes mellitus	E10-E14	22.5	23.5
Other external causes of accidental injury	W00-X59	24.0	23.5
Organic, including symptomatic, mental disorders	F01-F09	47.7	22.2
Influenza and pneumonia	J09-J18	12.7	18.1

Note: (a) ICD-10 = International Classification of Diseases 10th Revision; (1) Mortality rates are a three year average covering 2005-2007; (2) Figures cover Richland County
Source: Centers for Disease Control and Prevention, National Center for Health Statistics. Compressed Mortality File 1999-2007. CDC WONDER On-line Database, compiled from Compressed Mortality File 1999-2007 Series 20 No. 2M, 2010.

Mortality Rates for Selected Causes of Death

ICD-10[a] Sub-Chapter	ICD-10[a] Code	Age-Adjusted Mortality Rate[1] per 100,000 population	
		County[2]	U.S.
Assault	X85-Y09	11.1	6.0
Human immunodeficiency virus (HIV) disease	B20-B24	11.3	4.0
Hypertensive diseases	I10-I15	11.4	18.0
Intentional self-harm	X60-X84	8.4	11.0
Malnutrition	E40-E46	*1.3	0.8
Obesity and other hyperalimentation	E65-E68	2.3	1.5
Transport accidents	V01-V99	18.0	15.6
Viral hepatitis	B15-B19	2.3	2.1

Note: (a) ICD-10 = International Classification of Diseases 10th Revision; (1) Mortality rates are a three year average covering 2005-2007; (2) Figures cover Richland County; (*) Unreliable data as per CDC
Source: Centers for Disease Control and Prevention, National Center for Health Statistics. Compressed Mortality File 1999-2007. CDC WONDER On-line Database, compiled from Compressed Mortality File 1999-2007 Series 20 No. 2M, 2010.

Distribution of Physicians and Dentists

Area[1]	Dentists[2]	D.O.[3]	M.D.[4]				
			Total	Family/ General Practice	Pediatrics	Medical Specialties	Surgical Specialties
Local (number)	178	21	958	106	73	361	231
Local (rate[5])	4.9	0.6	26.1	2.9	2.0	9.9	6.3
U.S. (rate[5])	4.5	1.9	18.3	2.5	1.4	6.8	4.1

Note: Data as of 2008 unless noted; (1) Local data covers Richland County; (2) Data as of 2007; (3) Doctor of Osteopathic Medicine; (4) Includes active, non-federal, patient-care, office-based Doctors of Medicine; (5) rate per 10,000 population
Source: Area Resource File (ARF). 2009-2010 Release. U.S. Department of Health and Human Services, Health Resources and Services Administration, Bureau of Health Professions, Rockville, MD, August 2010

Hospitals

Columbia has the following hospitals: 4 general medical and surgical; 2 psychiatric; 1 rehabilitation; 1 long-term acute care.
AHA Guide to the Healthcare Field 2010

EDUCATION

Public School District Statistics

District Name	Schls	Pupils	Pupil/ Teacher Ratio	Minority Pupils[1] (%)	Free Lunch Eligible[2] (%)	IEP[3] (%)
Richland 01	50	24,332	14.4	82.0	56.0	14.4
Richland 02	27	24,516	14.5	68.9	29.9	11.5
SC Public Charter School District	5	2,446	37.9	29.4	34.8	9.4

Note: Table includes school districts with 2,000 or more students; (1) Percentage of students that are not non-Hispanic white; (2) Percentage of students that are eligible for the free lunch program; (3) Percentage of students that have an Individualized Education Program.
Source: U.S. Department of Education, National Center for Education Statistics, Common Core of Data, Local Education Agency (School District) Universe Survey: School Year 2008-2009; U.S. Department of Education, National Center for Education Statistics, Common Core of Data, Public Elementary/Secondary School Universe Survey: School Year 2008-2009

Top Public High Schools

High School Name	Index[1]	Rank[1]	Subsidized Lunch (%)[2]	E&E (%)[3]
A.C. Flora[4]	2.521	397	30.0	20.5
Dreher	1.923	773	32.0	33.0
Irmo[4]	1.680	973	44.0	27.0
Richland Northeast	1.215	1471	41.0	19.3
Spring Valley	1.337	1327	35.0	28.2

Note: (1) Public schools are ranked according to a ratio that is the number of Advanced Placement, International Baccalaureate, and/or Cambridge tests taken by all students at a school in 2009 divided by the number of graduating seniors. All of the schools on the list have an index of at least 1.000; they are in the top six percent of public schools measured this way. The rankings range from 1 to 1,734; (2) Percentage of students receiving federally subsidized meals; (3) E & E stands for equity and excellence percentage: the portion of all graduating seniors at a school that had at least one passing grade on one AP or IB test; (4) Schools that offer International Baccalaureate or Cambridge exams; (5) School is unranked, but has been identified by Newsweek as one of the nation's most elite public high schools.
Source: Newsweek Online, "Top High Schools 2010"

Highest Level of Education

Area	Less than H.S.	H.S. Diploma	Some College, No Deg.	Associate Degree	Bachelors Degree	Masters Degree	Profess. School Degree	Doctorate Degree
City	13.6	21.0	19.9	6.6	22.0	10.8	3.7	2.4
MSA[1]	12.8	27.6	21.1	8.7	18.6	8.0	1.9	1.3
U.S.	15.3	29.0	20.7	7.5	17.4	7.0	1.9	1.1

Note: Figures are 2010 estimated percentages and cover persons age 25 and over; (1) Metropolitan Statistical Area - see Appendix B for areas included
Source: Claritas, Inc.

Educational Attainment by Race

Area	High School Graduate (%)					Bachelor's Degree (%)				
	Total	White	Black	Asian	Hisp.[2]	Total	White	Black	Asian	Hisp.[2]
City	86.1	94.6	75.3	n/a	80.8	40.1	59.4	15.5	n/a	16.5
MSA[1]	87.4	90.9	82.4	86.4	63.6	30.3	34.9	20.6	59.3	16.3
U.S.	84.9	90.0	80.7	85.5	60.7	27.8	30.9	17.5	49.7	12.7

Note: Figures shown cover persons 25 years old and over; (1) Metropolitan Statistical Area - see Appendix B for areas included; (2) people of Hispanic origin can be of any race
Source: U.S. Census Bureau, 2007-2009 American Community Survey 3-Year Estimates

School Enrollment by Grade and Control

Area	Preschool (%)		Kindergarten (%)		Grades 1 - 4 (%)		Grades 5 - 8 (%)		Grades 9 - 12 (%)	
	Public	Private	Public	Private	Public	Private	Public	Private	Public	Private
City	47.1	52.9	78.5	21.5	79.6	20.4	82.6	17.4	93.1	6.9
MSA[1]	55.3	44.7	84.2	15.8	90.3	9.7	91.5	8.5	91.8	8.2
U.S.	54.3	45.7	86.4	13.6	88.9	11.1	89.1	10.9	90.2	9.8

Note: Figures shown cover persons 3 years old and over; (1) Metropolitan Statistical Area - see Appendix B for areas included
Source: U.S. Census Bureau, 2007-2009 American Community Survey 3-Year Estimates

Average Salaries of Public School Classroom Teachers

Area	2009-10		2010-11		Percent Change 2009-10 to 2010-11	Percent Change 2000-01 to 2010-11
	Dollars	Rank[1]	Dollars	Rank[1]		
South Carolina	47,508	34	49,434	31	4.05	30.3
U.S. Average	55,202	-	56,069	-	1.57	29.3

Note: (1) State rank ranges from 1 to 51 where 1 indicates highest salary.
Source: National Education Association, Rankings & Estimates: Rankings of the States 2010 and Estimates of School Statistics 2011, December 2010

Higher Education

Four-Year Colleges			Two-Year Colleges			Medical Schools[1]	Law Schools[2]	Voc/ Tech[3]
Public	Private Non-profit	Private For-profit	Public	Private Non-profit	Private For-profit			
1	6	3	0	0	3	1	1	6

Note: Figures cover institutions located within the city limits and include main campuses only; (1) includes schools accredited by the Liaison Committee on Medical Education and the American Osteopathic Association; (2) includes American Bar Association-accredited law schools; (3) includes all schools with programs that are less than 2 years.
Source: National Center for Education Statistics, Integrated Postsecondary Education System (IPEDS) Peer Analysis System, 2010-11; U.S. News & World Report, Medical School Directory, 2011; U.S. News & World Report, Law School Directory, 2011

According to *U.S. News & World Report,* the Columbia, SC Metropolitan Statistical Area is home to one of the top 197 national universities in the U.S.: **University of South Carolina** (#111). The rankings are based on quantitative measurements such as peer assessment, retention, faculty resources, student selectivity, financial resources, graduation rate, and alumni giving rate. *U.S. News & World Report, "America's Best Colleges 2011"*

According to *Forbes,* the Columbia, SC Metropolitan Statistical Area is home to one of the top 75 business schools in the U.S.: **South Carolina (Moore)** (#67). The rankings are based on the return on investment that graduates of the Class of 2004 received (median salary five years after graduation). *Forbes, "Best Business Schools," August 5, 2009*

PRESIDENTIAL ELECTION

2008 Presidential Election Results

Area	Obama	McCain	Nader	Other
Richland County	64.0	35.1	0.2	0.7
U.S.	52.9	45.6	0.6	0.9

Note: Results are percentages and may not add to 100% due to rounding
Source: Dave Leip's Atlas of U.S. Presidential Elections, www.uselectionatlas.org

EMPLOYERS

Major Employers

Company Name	Industry	Type of Site
Air National Guard	National security	Branch
Amfinity Business Solution	Help supply services	Single
Amick Farms	Livestock services, except veterinary	Single
Blue Cross	Accident and health insurance	Headquarters
Colonial Companies	Accident and health insurance	Headquarters
County of Richland	Executive offices	Headquarters
D O T	Regulation, administration of transportation	Branch
Fort Jackson Army Training Ctr	National security	Branch
Health and Envmtl Ctrl Dept Sc	Administration of public health programs	Headquarters
International Paper	Paper mills	Branch
Johnson Food Services	Eating places	Single
Lexington County Hlth Svc Dst	General medical and surgical hospitals	Headquarters
Michelin Tire	Tires and inner tubes	Branch
Moncrief Army Hospital	General medical and surgical hospitals	Branch
Nelson Mullins Riley & S	Legal services	Headquarters
Palmetto Gba	Hospital and medical service plans	Headquarters
Palmetto-Richland Mem Hosp	General medical and surgical hospitals	Single
SC Department Mental Health	Administration of public health programs	Branch
SC Dept Transportation	Regulation, administration of transportation	Headquarters
University of South Carolina	Colleges and universities	Headquarters
Wm Jennings Bryan Dorn	Administration of veterans' affairs	Branch

Note: Companies shown are located within the Columbia metropolitan area; nec = not elsewhere classified.
Source: www.zapdata.com, January 2011

Best Companies to Work For

Palmetto Health, headquartered in Columbia, is among the "100 Best Places to Work in IT." To qualify, companies, both public and private, had to have a minimum of 50 IT employees. Companies were selected based on average salary and bonus increases, the percentage of IT employees receiving promotions, IT staff turnover rates, training and development programs, and the percentage of women and minorities in IT staff and management positions. In addition, information was collected on how the organizations reward outstanding performance, how their retention programs are structured and what benefits they offer. *Computerworld, "100 Best Places to Work in IT 2010"*

PUBLIC SAFETY

Crime Rate

Area	All Crimes	Violent Crimes				Property Crimes		
		Murder	Forcible Rape	Robbery	Aggrav. Assault	Burglary	Larceny -Theft	Motor Vehicle Theft
City	7,058.7	10.2	53.2	296.4	686.6	1,312.1	4,160.8	539.6
Suburbs[1]	4,273.3	5.5	35.8	108.0	552.0	886.5	2,374.8	310.6
Metro[2]	4,753.6	6.3	38.8	140.5	575.2	959.9	2,682.8	350.0
U.S.	3,465.5	5.0	28.7	133.0	262.8	716.3	2,060.9	258.8

Note: Figures are crimes per 100,000 population; (1) All areas within the metro area that are located outside the city limits; (2) Metropolitan Statistical Area - see Appendix B for areas included
Source: FBI Uniform Crime Reports, 2009

Hate Crimes

Area	Number of Quarters Reported	Bias Motivation				
		Race	Religion	Sexual Orientation	Ethnicity	Disability
City	4	5	1	3	0	0

Source: Federal Bureau of Investigation, Hate Crime Statistics 2009

Identity Theft Consumer Complaints

Area	Complaints	Complaints per 100,000 Population	Rank[2]
MSA[1]	544	76.0	175
U.S.	250,854	81.3	-

Note: (1) Metropolitan Statistical Area - see Appendix B for areas included; (2) Rank ranges from 1 to 384 where 1 indicates greatest number of complaints per 100,000 population
Source: Federal Trade Commission, Consumer Sentinel Network Data Book for January - December 2010

RECREATION

Culture

Dance[1]	Theatre[1]	Instrumental Music[1]	Vocal Music[1]	Series/ Festivals	Museums	Zoos and Aquariums[2]
8	2	0	0	3	11	1

Note: (1) Number of professional perfoming groups; (2) AZA-accredited
Source: The Grey House Performing Arts Directory, 2011-2012; Official Museum Directory, 2010; American Association of Museums, AAM Member Museums, March 2011; Association of Zoos & Aquariums, AZA Member Zoos & Aquariums, May 2011

Professional Sports Teams

Team Name	League

No teams are located in the metro area
Source: Original research

CLIMATE

Average and Extreme Temperatures

Temperature	Jan	Feb	Mar	Apr	May	Jun	Jul	Aug	Sep	Oct	Nov	Dec	Yr.
Extreme High (°F)	84	84	91	94	101	107	107	107	101	101	90	83	107
Average High (°F)	56	60	67	77	84	90	92	91	85	77	67	59	75
Average Temp. (°F)	45	48	55	64	72	78	82	80	75	64	54	47	64
Average Low (°F)	33	35	42	50	59	66	70	69	64	51	41	35	51
Extreme Low (°F)	-1	5	4	26	34	44	54	53	40	23	12	4	-1

Note: Figures cover the years 1948-1990
Source: National Climatic Data Center, International Station Meteorological Climate Summary, 9/96

Average Precipitation/Snowfall/Humidity

Precip./Humidity	Jan	Feb	Mar	Apr	May	Jun	Jul	Aug	Sep	Oct	Nov	Dec	Yr.
Avg. Precip. (in.)	4.0	4.0	4.7	3.4	3.6	4.2	5.5	5.9	4.0	2.9	2.7	3.4	48.3
Avg. Snowfall (in.)	1	1	Tr	0	0	0	0	0	0	0	Tr	Tr	2
Avg. Rel. Hum. 7am (%)	83	83	84	82	84	85	88	91	91	90	88	84	86
Avg. Rel. Hum. 4pm (%)	51	47	44	41	46	50	54	56	54	49	48	51	49

Note: Figures cover the years 1948-1990; Tr = Trace amounts (<0.05 in. of rain; <0.5 in. of snow)
Source: National Climatic Data Center, International Station Meteorological Climate Summary, 9/96

Weather Conditions

Temperature			Daytime Sky			Precipitation		
10°F & below	32°F & below	90°F & above	Clear	Partly cloudy	Cloudy	0.01 inch or more precip.	0.1 inch or more snow/ice	Thunder-storms
< 1	58	77	97	149	119	110	1	53

Note: Figures are average number of days per year and cover the years 1948-1990
Source: National Climatic Data Center, International Station Meteorological Climate Summary, 9/96

HAZARDOUS WASTE

Superfund Sites

Columbia has one hazardous waste site on the EPA's Superfund Final National Priorities List: **SCRDI Bluff Road**. U.S. Environmental Protection Agency, Final National Priorities List, April 1, 2011

**AIR & WATER
QUALITY**

Air Quality Index

Area	Percent of Days when Air Quality was...[2]				AQI Statistics	
	Good	Moderate	Unhealthy for Sensitive Groups	Unhealthy	Maximum	Median
Area[1]	67.5	30.3	2.2	0.0	145	44

*Note: The Air Quality Index (AQI) is an index for reporting daily air quality. EPA calculates the AQI for five major air pollutants regulated by the Clean Air Act: ground-level ozone, particle pollution (also known as particulate matter), carbon monoxide, sulfur dioxide, and nitrogen dioxide. The AQI runs from 0 to 500. The higher the AQI value, the greater the level of air pollution and the greater the health concern. There are six AQI categories: "Good" The AQI is between 0 and 50. Air quality is considered satisfactory; "Moderate" The AQI is between 51 and 100. Air quality is acceptable; "Unhealthy for Sensitive Groups" When AQI values are between 101 and 150, members of sensitive groups may experience health effects; "Unhealthy" When AQI values are between 151 and 200 everyone may begin to experience health effects; "Very Unhealthy" AQI values between 201 and 300 trigger a health alert; "Hazardous" AQI values over 300 trigger health warnings of emergency conditions; (1) Data covers Richland County; (2) Based on 366 days with AQI data in 2008; The EPA has suspended data updates while it assesses its data systems, including AirData reports and maps.
Source: U.S. Environmental Protection Agency, AirData Report, 2008*

Air Quality Index Pollutants

Area	Percent of Days when AQI Pollutant was...[2]					
	Carbon Monoxide	Nitrogen Dioxide	Ozone	Sulfur Dioxide	Particulate Matter 2.5	Particulate Matter 10
Area[1]	0.0	0.0	69.1	0.0	29.8	1.1

*Note: The Air Quality Index (AQI) is an index for reporting daily air quality. EPA calculates the AQI for five major air pollutants regulated by the Clean Air Act: ground-level ozone, particle pollution (also known as particulate matter), carbon monoxide, sulfur dioxide, and nitrogen dioxide. The AQI runs from 0 to 500. The higher the AQI value, the greater the level of air pollution and the greater the health concern; (1) Data covers Richland County; (2) Based on 366 days with AQI data in 2008; The EPA has suspended data updates while it assesses its data systems, including AirData reports and maps.
Source: U.S. Environmental Protection Agency, AirData Report, 2008*

Air Quality Index Trends

Area	Trend Sites (days)								All Sites (days)
	2002	2003	2004	2005	2006	2007	2008	2009	2009
MSA[1]	23	14	17	22	18	14	14	3	3

*Note: Figures are the number of days the AQI value exceeded 100 in a given year. An AQI value greater than 100 indicates that air quality would have been in the unhealthful range on that day. Data from exceptional events are included. These counts are presented in two ways. First, the counts are based on sites having an adequate record of monitoring data during the trend period (trend sites). These counts represent the relative change in the number of days with AQI values greater than 100. In the last column, the counts are based on all sites with data in the most recent year (because it is possible for a site to have data in the most recent year but not enough data to be a trend site); (1) Data covers the Columbia, SC Metropolitan Statistical Area - see Appendix B for areas included
Source: U.S. Environmental Protection Agency, Office of Air and Radiation, Air Quality Index Information, "Number of Days with Air Quality Index Values Greater than 100 and Trend Sites, 1990-2009, and at All Sites in 2009"*

Maximum Air Pollutant Concentrations

	Particulate Matter 10 (ug/m^3)	Particulate Matter 2.5 (ug/m^3)	Ozone (ppm)	Carbon Monoxide (ppm)	Sulfur Dioxide (ppm)	Nitrogen Dioxide (ppm)	Lead (ug/m^3)
MSA[1] Level	62	23	0.066	n/a	0.016	0.005	0
NAAQS[2]	150	35	0.075	9	0.140	0.053	0.15
Met NAAQS[2]	Yes	Yes	Yes	n/a	Yes	Yes	Yes

*Note: Data from exceptional events are not included; (1) Data covers the Columbia, SC Metropolitan Statistical Area - see Appendix B for areas included; (2) National Ambient Air Quality Standards; n/a not available
Concentrations: Particulate Matter 10 (coarse particulate) - highest second maximum 24-hour concentration; Particulate Matter 2.5 (fine particulate) - highest 98th percentile 24-hour concentration; Ozone - highest fourth daily maximum 8-hour concentration; Carbon Monoxide - highest second maximum non-overlapping 8-hour concentration; Sulfur Dioxide - highest second maximum 24-hour concentration; Nitrogen Dioxide - highest arithmetic mean concentration; Lead - maximum running 3-month average
Units: ppm = parts per million; ug/m^3 = micrograms per cubic meter
Source: U.S. Environmental Protection Agency, CBSA Factbook 2009, Air Quality Statistics by City, 2009*

Drinking Water

Water System Name	Pop. Served	Primary Water Source Type	Violations[1]	
			Health Based	Monitoring/ Reporting
City of Columbia	301,500	Surface	0	0

Note: (1) Based on violation data from January 1, 2010 to December 31, 2010 (includes unresolved violations from earlier years)
Source: U.S. Environmental Protection Agency, Office of Ground Water and Drinking Water, Safe Drinking Water Information System (based on data extracted May 9, 2011)

Dallas, Texas

Background

Dallas is one of those cities that offer everything. Founded in 1841 by Tennessee lawyer and trader, John Neely Bryan, Dallas has come to symbolize in modern times all that is big, exciting, and affluent. The city itself is home to 15 billionaires, placing it ninth worldwide among cities with the most billionaires. When combined with the eight billionaires who live in Dallas's neighboring city of Fort Worth, the area has one of the greatest concentrations of billionaires in the world.

Originally one of the largest markets for cotton in the U.S., Dallas moved on to become one of the largest markets for oil in the country. In the 1930s, oil was struck on the eastern fields of Texas. As a result, oil companies were founded and millionaires were made. The face we now associate with Dallas and the state of Texas had emerged.

Today, oil still plays a dominant role in the Dallas economy. Outside of Alaska, Texas holds most of the U.S. oil reserves. For that reason, many oil companies choose to headquarter in the silver skyscrapers of Dallas.

In addition to employment opportunities in the oil industry, the Dallas branch of the Federal Reserve Bank, and a host of other banks and investment firms clustering around the Federal Reserve hub employ thousands. Other opportunities are offered in the aircraft, advertising, motion picture, and publishing industries.

Major employers in the Dallas area include American Airlines (Dallas-Fort Worth Airport); Lockheed Martin (in nearby Fort Worth); University of North Texas in Denton; Parkland Memorial Hospital; and Baylor University Medical center. Vought Aircraft Industries, a major supplier of aircraft components to Boeing, Sikorsky and other aircraft manufacturers, continues to expand its local operations. The city is sometimes referred to as Texas's "Silicon Prairie" because of a high concentration of telecommunications companies including Texas Instruments and regional offices for Alcatel, Ericsson, Fujitsu, MCI, Nokia, Rockwell, Sprint, and Verizon, as well as the national offices of CompUSA and Canadian Nortel. AT&T relocated its headquarters from San Antonio Texas to downtown Dallas in 2008.

The Dallas Convention Center, with more than two million square feet of space, is the largest convention center in Texas with more than 1 million square feet of exhibit area, including nearly 800,000 square feet of same level, contiguous prime exhibit space with more than 3.8 million people attending more than 3,600 conventions and spending more than $4.2 billion annually.

Dallas also offers a busy cultural calendar. A host of independent theater groups is sponsored by Southern Methodist University. The Museum of Art houses an excellent collection of modern art, especially American paintings. The Winspear Opera House, along with 3 other venues that make up the AT&T Performing Arts Center was dedicated on October 12, 2009. The Dallas Opera has showcased Maria Callas, Joan Sutherland, and Monserrat Caballe. The city also contains many historical districts such as the Swiss Avenue District, and elegant buildings such as the City Hall Building designed by I.M. Pei. The most notable event held in Dallas is the State Fair of Texas, which has been held annually at Fair Park since 1886. The fair is a massive event for the state of Texas and brings an estimated $350 million to the city's economy annually.

The area's high concentration of wealth undoubtedly contributes to Dallas's wide array of shopping centers and high-end boutiques. Downtown Dallas is home to many cafes, restaurants and clubs. The city's centrally located "Arts District" is appropriately named for the independent theaters and art galleries located in the neighborhood. While northern districts of the city and the central downtown have seen much urban revival in the last 30 years, neighborhoods south of downtown have not experienced the same growth.

Colleges and universities in the Dallas area include Southern Methodist University, University of Dallas, and University of Texas at Dallas. In 2006, University of North Texas opened a branch in the southern part of the city, in part, to help accelerate development south of downtown Dallas.

The city maintains around 21,000 acres of park land, with over 400 parks.

The climate of Dallas is generally temperate. Occasional periods of extreme cold are short-lived, and extremely high temperatures that sometimes occur in summer usually do not last for extended periods.

Rankings

General Rankings

- Dallas was ranked #132 out of 375 metro areas in *Cities Ranked & Rated*. Criteria: cost of living; climate; crime; transportation; economy and jobs; education; arts and culture; health and healthcare; leisure; quality of life. *Cities Ranked & Rated, 2nd Edition, 2007*

- Dallas was ranked #43 out of 379 metro areas in *Places Rated Almanac*. Criteria: health care; education; recreation; transportation; ambience; climate; crime; housing costs; jobs. *Places Rated Almanac, 7th Edition, 2007*

- *Men's Health Living* ranked 100 U.S. cities in terms of quality of life. Dallas was ranked #97 and received a grade of F. Criteria: number of fitness facilities; air quality; number of physicians; male/female ratio; education levels; household income; cost of living. *Men's Health Living, Spring 2008*

- Dallas was selected as one of "America's Top 100 Places to Live" by RelocateAmerica.com. Cities and towns nominated to be great places to live along with their key data regarding education, employment, economy, crime, parks, recreation and housing were reviewed, rated and judged by the Relocate-America.com editorial staff. *Relocate-America.com, "RelocateAmerica's Top 100 Places to Live in 2010"*

- The U.S. Conference of Mayors and Waste Management sponsor the City Livability Awards Program. The awards recognize and honor mayors for exemplary leadership in developing and implementing programs that improve the quality of life in America's cities. Dallas received an Outstanding Achievement Award in the large cities category. *U.S Conference of Mayors, "2010 City Livability Awards"*

Business/Finance Rankings

- Dallas was identified as one of the 20 strongest-performing metro areas during the recession and recovery from December 2007 through December 2010. Criteria: percent change in employment; percentage point change in unemployment rate; percent change in gross metropolitan product; percent change in House Price Index. *Brookings Institution, MetroMonitor: Tracking Economic Recession and Recovery in America's 100 Largest Metropolitan Areas, March 2011*

- The Dallas metro area was identified as one of 10 "Cities Where the Recession is Easing." The metro area was ranked #3. Criteria: job growth; goods produced; home sale prices; unemployment rates. *Forbes.com, "Cities Where the Recession is Easing," March 3, 2010*

- The Dallas metro area was identified as one of the most affordable major metropolitan areas in America by *Forbes*. The metro area was ranked #14 out of 15. Criteria: median asking price of homes for sale; median salaries of workers with bachelor's degrees or higher compared to a cost-of-living index; unemployment rates. *Forbes.com, "The Most Affordable Cities in America," January 7, 2011*

- Experian ranked the top 20 major U.S metropolitan areas by average debt per consumer. The Dallas metro area was ranked #2. Criteria: average debt per consumer. Debt for this study includes credit cards, auto loans and personal loans. It does not include mortgages. *Experian, May 13, 2010*

- Dallas was identified as one of the top 25 U.S. cities with the most credit card debt by credit reporting bureau Experian. The city was ranked #5. *Experian, March 4, 2011*

- The Dallas metro area was identified as one of the "Best U.S. Cities for Earning a Living" by *Forbes*. The metro area ranked #8. Criteria: median income; cost of living; job growth; number of companies on *Forbes* 400 best big company and 200 best small company lists. *Forbes.com, "Best U.S. Cities for Earning a Living," August 21, 2008*

- A.G. Edwards ranked America's 500 top-performing communities based on their residents' personal savings and investing behavior. The Dallas metro area ranked #353 with an index score of 98.36 (national average = 100.00). A dozen statistical factors were measured including: participation in retirement savings plans; personal debt levels; and home ownership. *A.G. Edwards, "2007 Nest Egg Index," September 12, 2007*

- The Dallas metro area was identified as one of the 10 best cities to find a job in 2009 by *Forbes*. The metro area ranked #10. Criteria: city unemployment rate; number of new jobs created in the previous six months. *Forbes.com, "10 Cities for Job Growth in 2009," January 5, 2009*

- Dallas was cited as one of America's top metros for new and expanded facility projects in 2010. The area ranked #3 in the large metro area category (population over 1 million). *Site Selection, "2010 Top Metros," March 2011*

- Dallas was identified as one of the "Top 10 Cities for New Grads." The city ranked #4. Criteria: concentration of young adults (age 20 to 24); inventory of jobs requiring less than one year of experience; average cost of rent for a one bedroom apartment. *CareerBuilder.com, "Top 10 Cities for New Grads," June 5, 2010*

- Dallas was identified as one of the best cities for new college graduates. The city ranked #3. Criteria: cost of living; average annual salary; unemployment rate; number of employers looking to hire people at entry-level. *Business Week, "The Best Cities for New Grads," July 20, 2010*

- *American City Business Journals* ranked America's 261 largest cities in terms of their resident's wealth. Dallas ranked #147. Criteria: per capita income; median household income; percentage of households with annual incomes of $200,000 or more; median home value. *American City Business Journals, www.bizjournals.com, "Where the Money Is: America's Wealth Centers," August 18, 2008*

- The Dallas metro area appeared on the Milken Institute "2010 Best Performing Metros" list. Rank: #17 out of 200 large metro areas. Criteria: job growth; wage and salary growth; high-tech output growth. *Milken Institute, "2010 Best Performing Metros"*

- The Dallas metro area was selected as one of the best cities for entrepreneurs in America by *Inc. Magazine*. Criteria: job-growth data for 335 metro areas was analyzed for: recent growth trend (the current and prior year's employment growth rates, with the current year emphasized); mid-term growth (the average annual 2002-2007 growth rate); long-term trend (the sum of the 2002-2007 and 1996-2001 employment growth rates multiplied by the ratio of the 1996-2001 growth rate over the 2002-2007 growth rate); current year growth. The Dallas metro area ranked #12 among large metro areas and #57 overall. *Inc. Magazine, "The Best Cities for Doing Business," July 2008*

- Dallas was ranked #52 out of 145 regions worldwide in terms of its "Knowledge Competitiveness Index." The index attempts to measure the knowledge-based development taking place throughout the world and is based on 19 measures of economic performance that indicate a region's ability to translate its knowledge capacity into economic value. *Centre for International Competitiveness, World Knowledge Competitiveness Index 2008*

- *Forbes* ranked the 200 most populous metro areas in the U.S. in terms of the "Best Places for Business and Careers." The Dallas metro area was ranked #26. Criteria: 12 metrics including costs (business and living), job growth (past and projected), income growth, educational attainment, projected economic growth, crime, cultural and recreational opportunities, net migration patterns, percentage of subprime mortgages handed out over a three-year period, and the number of highly ranked four-year colleges. *Forbes, "Best Places for Business and Careers," April 14, 2010*

Children/Family Rankings

- The Dallas metro area was selected as one of the "Best Cities for Relocating Families" by Worldwide ERC and Primacy Relocation. The 2008 study looked at nearly 50 factors important to relocating families including: recent job growth; nearby top-ranked colleges; in-state tuition for four-year public colleges; population growth since 2000; pediatricians per 100,000 population; and a Green Living index. *Worldwide ERC and Primacy Relocation, "2008 Best Cities for Relocating Families"*

- *Fit Pregnancy* magazine ranked the 50 best U.S. cities in which to have a baby. Dallas was ranked #43. Criteria: access to hospitals and doctors; affordability; birthing options; breastfeeding; child care; fertility laws/resources; maternal and infant health risk; parks/stroller friendliness; safety. *Fit Pregnancy, "The Best Cities in America to Have a Baby 2008"*

Culture/Performing Arts Rankings

- Dallas was selected as one of "America's Top 25 Arts Destinations." The city ranked #24 in the big city (population 500,000 and over) category. Criteria: readers' top choices for arts travel destinations based on the richness and variety of visual arts sites, activities and events. *American Style, "America's Top 25 Arts Destinations," May 2010*

Dating/Romance Rankings

- Dallas appeared on *Men's Health's* list of the most sex-happy cities in America. The city ranked #2 of 100. Criteria: condom sales; birth rates; sex toy sales; rates of chlamydia, gonorrhea, and syphilis. *Men's Health, "America's Most Sex-Happy Cities," October 2010*

- Dallas was selected as one of the best cities for single women in America by *SingleMindedWomen.com*. The city ranked #9. Criteria: ratio of women to men; singles population; healthy lifestyle; employment opportunities; cost of living; access to travel; entertainment options; social opportunities. *SingleMindedWomen.com, "Top 10 Cities for Single Women," 2010*

- *Men's Health* ranked 100 U.S. cities in terms of best (and worst) marriages. Dallas was ranked #72 (#1 = worst marriages). Criteria: rate of failed marriages; stringency of divorce laws; percentage of population who've split; number of licensed marriage and family therapists. *Men's Health, "Splitsville, USA," May 2010*

- Eli Lily and Company, in partnership with Sperling's BestPlaces, ranked the nation's 50 largest metro areas in terms of the "Most Romantic Cities for Baby Boomers." The Dallas metro area ranked #9. Criteria: marriage and divorce rates among "baby boomers" age 45 to 60; great restaurants; dance studios; chocolate, jewelry and flower sales. *Eli Lily and Company, "Most Romantic Cities for Baby Boomers," April 20, 2007*

- The Dallas metro area was selected as one of the "Best Cities for Relocating Singles" by Worldwide ERC and Primacy Relocation. The area ranked #37 out of the 100 largest metro areas in the U.S. Areas were selected based on the following criteria: recent job growth; recent singles population growth; overall population growth; affordable rental housing; cost-of-living index; expanded arts and recreation opportunities; ratio of single men and single women; affordability of quality higher education (including state residency requirements); diversity index; climate; population density. *Worldwide ERC and Primacy Relocation, "2008 Best Cities for Relocating Singles"*

- *Forbes* ranked the 40 most populous urbanized areas in the U.S. in terms of the "Best Cities for Singles." The Dallas metro area ranked #17. Criteria: number of singles; cost of living alone; nightlife; culture; job growth; coolness; and online dating participation. *Forbes.com, "Best Cities for Singles," July 27, 2009*

Education Rankings

- Dallas was selected as one of "America's Most Literate Cities." The city ranked #44 out of the 75 largest U.S. cities. Criteria: number of booksellers; library resources; Internet resources; educational attainment; periodical publishing resources; newspaper circulation. *Central Connecticut State University, "America's Most Literate Cities 2010"*

- Dallas was identified as one of the 100 "smartest" metro areas in the U.S. The area ranked #72. Criteria: the editors rated the collective brainpower of the 100 largest metro area in the U.S based on their residents' educational attainment. *American City Business Journals, www.bizjournals.com, April 14, 2008*

- Dallas was identified as one of "America's Brainiest Bastions" by *Portfolio.com*. The metro area ranked #96 out of 200. Portfolio.com analyzed levels of educational attainment in the nation's 200 largest metropolitan areas. The editors established scores for five levels of educational attainment, based on relative earning power of adult workers age 25 or older. Scores were determined by comparing the median income for all workers with the median income for those workers at a specified educational level. *Portfolio.com, "America's Brainiest Bastions," December 1, 2010*

- *Forbes* ranked the largest metro areas in the U.S. in terms of the "Best Cities for Young Professionals." The Dallas metro area ranked #6out of 10. Graduates from six elite schools (Harvard, Stanford, Princeton, Rice, Northwestern and Duke) were tracked ten years after graduation to see where they settled down. Those rankings were combined with several other statistics: job growth; unemployment rate; average salary of college graduates; cost of living; number of large companies that are located in the city. *Forbes.com, "Best Cities for Young Professionals," June 17, 2010*

Environmental Rankings

- Dallas was selected as one of 22 "Smarter Cities" for energy by the Natural Resources Defense Council." The city appeared as one of 12 cities in the large city (population 250,000 and over) category. Criteria: investment in green power; energy efficiency measures; conservation. *Natural Resources Defense Council, "2010 Smarter Cities," July 19, 2010*

- Dallas was selected as one of worst summer weather cities in the U.S. by the *Farmers' Almanac.* The city ranked #3 out of 5. Criteria: average summer and winter temperatures; humidity; precipitation; number of overcast days. The editors only considered cities with populations of 50,000 or more. *Farmers' Almanac, "America's Ten Worst Weather Cities," September 7, 2010*

- *American City Business Journal* ranked 43 metropolitan areas in terms of their "greenness." The Dallas metro area ranked #37. Criteria: Forty-one metros in which *ACBJ* has business weeklies, plus Indianapolis and Cleveland, were ranked based on 20 different indicators such as adoption of green technologies, utilization of environmentally sound practices, and air and water quality. *American City Business Journals, "Green City Index," March 11, 2010*

- 100 of the largest metro areas in the U.S. were analyzed in terms of their current drought severity. The Dallas metro area ranked #97 (#1 = driest). The rankings were based on statistics such as long-term precipitation trends and patterns and the Palmer drought indices. *Sperling's BestPlaces, www.BestPlaces.net, "America's Drought-Riskiest Cities," November 2007*

- The Dallas metro area appeared in *Country Home's* "Best Green Places" report. The area ranked #94 out of 379. Criteria: official energy policies; green power; green buildings; availability of fresh, locally grown food. *Country Home, "Best Green Places," 2008*

- Dallas was highlighted as one of the 25 most ozone-polluted metro areas in the U.S. The area ranked #12. *American Lung Association, State of the Air 2011*

Health/Fitness Rankings

- Dallas was selected as one of the 25 fattest cities in America by *Men's Fitness Online*. It ranked #14 out of America's 50 largest cities. Criteria: fitness centers and sport stores; nutrition; sports participation; TV viewing; overweight/sedentary; junk food; air quality; geography; commute; parks and open space; city recreational facilities; access to healthcare; motivation; mayor and city initiatives; state obesity initiatives. *Men's Fitness Online, 2009 Fittest/Fattest Cities*

- Dallas was identified as a "2011 Asthma Capital." The area ranked #34 out of the nation's 100 largest metropolitan areas. Twelve factors were used to identify the most challenging places to live for people with asthma: estimated prevalence; self-reported prevalence; crude death rate for asthma; annual pollen score; annual air quality; public smoking laws; number of board-certified asthma specialists; school inhaler access laws; rescue medication use; controller medication use; uninsured rate; poverty rate. *Asthma and Allergy Foundation of America, "2011 Asthma Capitals"*

- Dallas was identified as a 2009 "Spring Allergy Capital." The area ranked #50 out of 100. Three groups of factors were used to identify the most severe cities for people with allergies during the spring season: annual pollen levels; medicine utilization; access to board-certified allergists. *Asthma and Allergy Foundation of America, "Spring Allergy Capitals 2009"*

- Dallas was identified as a 2010 "Fall Allergy Capital." The area ranked #33 out of 100. Three groups of factors were used to identify the most severe cities for people with allergies during the fall season: annual pollen levels; medicine utilization; access to board-certified allergists. *Asthma and Allergy Foundation of America, "Fall Allergy Capitals 2010"*

- *Men's Health* ranked 100 U.S. cities in terms of the quality of their tap water. Dallas was ranked #31 and received a grade of B. Criteria: levels of total coliform bacteria, arsenic, lead, total trihalomethanes (linked to cancer), and halo-acetic acids; number of EPA water-system violations from 1995 to 2005. *Men's Health, March 2007*

- Ortho-McNeil Neurologics, in partnership with Sperling's BestPlaces, analyzed 110 metro areas and identified those U.S. cities with the highest prevalence of factors that are most commonly associated with migraine headaches. The Dallas metro area ranked #82. Criteria: number of migraine-related drug prescriptions per capita; lifestyle factors that can contribute to migraines; environmental factors that can trigger migraines; and consumption of migraine-triggering foods. *Ortho-McNeil Neurologics, "America's Migraine Hot Spots," March 14, 2006*

- An analysis of the "Best & Worst Cities for Sleep" was conducted by Sperling's BestPlaces. The study ranked America's 50 most populated metro areas. The Dallas metro area ranked #21 (#1 = best city for sleep). Criteria: number of days residents didn't get enough rest or sleep during the past month; average length of daily commute; divorce rate; unemployment rate. *Sperling's BestPlaces, www.BestPlaces.net, "Best & Worst Cities for Sleep," 2006*

- *Men's Health* ranked 100 U.S. cities in terms of cities "Where the Food is Sickening." Dallas was ranked #16 and received a grade of B-. The magazine arrived at their ratings by looking at data compiled by the Community Health Status Indicator Project to determine outbreaks of E. coli, salmonella-, and shigella-related infections. They then checked the CDC's Wonder database to see how many people died from tainted food. Finally, the magazine found out which states have adopted the current version of the FDA's uniform Food Code, which contains the most up-to-date rules for keeping restaurant kitchens clean. *Men's Health, October 2005*

- The American Academy of Dermatology ranked 26 U.S. metropolitan regions in terms of their residents knowledge, attitude and behaviors towards tanning, sun protection and skin cancer detection. The Dallas metro area ranked #11. The results of the study are based on an online survey of over 7,000 adults nationwide. *American Academy of Dermatology, "Suntelligence: How Sun Smart is Your City," May 3, 2010*

- The Dallas metro area appeared in the 2010 Gallup-Healthways Well-Being Index. The index, based on interviews with more than 353,000 Americans during 2009, asked individuals to assess their jobs, finances, physical health, emotional state of mind and communities. The metro area ranked #41 out of 162. Criteria: life evaluation; emotional health; work environment; physical health; healthy behaviors; basic access (basic needs optimal for a healthy life, such as access to food and medicine, having health insurance and feeling safe while walking at night). *Gallup-Healthways, "Well-Being Index 2010"*

- The Dallas metro area was identified as one of "America's Most Stressful Cities" by *Forbes*. The metro area ranked #36. Criteria: median home price drop; unemployment rates; cost of living; air quality; sunny days; population density. *Forbes.com, "America's Most Stressful Cities," August 20, 2009*

- 50 of the largest metro areas in the U.S. were analyzed in terms of their health and fitness by the American College of Sports Medicine in their "American Fitness Index." The Dallas metro area ranked #40 (#1 = healthiest). Criteria: preventative health behaviors; levels of chronic disease; health care access; community resources and policies that support physical activity. *American College of Sports Medicine, "Health and Community Fitness Status of the 50 Largest Metropolitan Areas," May 24, 2010*

Pet Rankings

- Dallas was identified as one of North America's most accommodating cities for travelers with pets. The city was ranked #6. Criteria: number of AAA Approved and Diamond rated pet-friendly hotels. *AAA, Traveling with your Pet: The AAA PetBook, 2006*

Real Estate Rankings

- *Fortune* ranked the 100 largest metro areas in the U.S. in terms of projected median home price change in 2010. The Dallas metro area ranked #13. *Fortune, "The 2010 Housing Outlook," December 9, 2009*

- Dallas appeared on ApartmentRatings.com "Top Cities for Renters" list in 2009." The area ranked #73. Overall satisfaction ratings were ranked using thousands of user submitted scores for hundreds of apartment complexes located in the 100 most populated U.S. municipalities. *ApartmentRatings.com, "2009 Renter Satisfaction Rankings"*

- The Dallas metro area was identified as one of the "Top 25 Real Estate Investment Markets" by *FinestExperts.com*. The metro area ranked #1. Over 10,000 real estate markets were analyzed to identify the most suitable places for real estate investors to seek stability and growth. Criteria: employment; rental markets; growth levels as offset by foreclosures. *FinestExperts.com, "Top 25 Real Estate Investment Markets," January 7, 2010*

- The Dallas metro area was identified as one of "America's Best Housing Markets" by *Forbes*. The metro area ranked #9. Criteria: housing affordability; rising home prices; percentage of foreclosures. *Forbes.com, "America's Best Housing Markets," February 19, 2010*

- The nation's largest metro areas were analyzed in terms of the percentage of households entering some stage of foreclosure in 2010. The Dallas metro area ranked #98 out of 206 (#1 = highest foreclosure rate). *RealtyTrac, 2010 Year-End Metropolitan Foreclosure Market Report, January 27, 2011*

- The Dallas metro area was identified as one of the "Best Cities to Buy a Home" by *Forbes*. The metro area ranked #6. Criteria: 2-year home price appreciation; vacancy rates; spread between monthly rent and mortgage payment at the median level. *Forbes.com, "Best Cities to Buy a Home," July 22, 2008*

- The Dallas metro area appeared in a *Wall Street Journal* article ranking cities by "housing stress." The metro area was ranked #22 (#1 = most stress). Criteria: fraction of mortgage-holding homeowners with a monthly housing payment in excess of 30 percent of income; percentage of people without health insurance; unemployment rate. *The Wall Street Journal, "Which Cities Face Biggest Housing Risk," October 5, 2010*

- The Center for Housing Policy ranked 210 U.S metropolitan areas by the fair market rent for a two-bedroom unit. The Dallas metro area was ranked #82. (#1 = most expensive) with a rent of $894. Criteria: Fair Market Rent (FMR) in effect during the fourth quarter of 2009 based on HUD's fiscal year 2010 FMRs. *The Center for Housing Policy, "Paycheck to Paycheck: Most to Least Expensive Rental Markets in 2009"*

- The Dallas metro area was identified as one of the markets with the best expected performance in home prices over the next 12 months. *Local Market Monitor, "First Quarter Home Price Forecast for Largest US Markets," March 2, 2011*

Safety Rankings

- Symantec, the makers of Norton, in partnership with Sperling's BestPlaces, ranked the 50 largest cities in the U.S. in terms of their vulnerability to cybercrime. The city ranked #22. Criteria: number of cyberattacks and potential infections; level of Internet access; expenditures on computer hardware and software; wireless hotspots; broadband connectivity; Internet usage; online purchases. *Symantec, "10 Riskiest Cities for Cybercrime," March 22, 2010*

- Allstate ranked the 200 largest cities in America in terms of driver safety. Dallas ranked #173. In addition, drivers were 35.2% more likely to have had an accident compared to the national average. Allstate researchers analyzed internal property damage reported claims over a two-year period (from January 2007 to December 2008) to ensure the findings would not be affected by external influences such as weather or road construction. A weighted average of the two-year numbers determined the annual percentages. The report defines an auto crash as any collision resulting in a property damage claim. *Allstate, "The 2010 Allstate America's Best Drivers Report™"*

- Dallas was identified as one of the least safe places in the U.S. in terms of its vulnerability to natural disasters and weather extremes. The city ranked #2 out of 10. Sperling's BestPlaces analyzed data to show a metro areas' relative tendency to experience natural disasters (hail, tornadoes, high winds, hurricanes, earthquakes, and brush fires) or extreme weather (abundant rain or snowfall or days that are below freezing or above 90 degrees Fahrenheit). *Forbes, "Safest and Least Safe Places in the U.S.," August 30, 2005*

- The National Insurance Crime Bureau ranked 366 metro areas in the U.S. in terms of per capita rates of vehicle theft. The Dallas metro area ranked #39 (#1 = highest rate). Criteria: number of vehicle theft offenses per 100,000 inhabitants. *National Insurance Crime Bureau, "Hot Spots," May 17, 2010*

- The Dallas metro area was identified as one of the "The Most Dangerous Metro Areas for Pedestrians" by Transportation for America and the Surface Transportation Policy Partnership. The metro area ranked #13 out of 52 metro areas with over 1 million residents. Criteria: area's population divided by the number of pedestrian fatalities in that area. *Transportation for America and the Surface Transportation Policy Partnership, "Dangerous by Design: Solving the Epidemic of Preventable Pedestrian Deaths (and Making Great Neighborhoods)," November 11, 2009*

Seniors/Retirement Rankings

- The Dallas metro area was identified as one of "America's Most Affordable Places to Retire" by *Forbes*. The metro area ranked #2. Criteria: housing affordability; inflation; number of persons over 65 who are employed; net migration for persons over 65; percent of persons over 65 living below poverty level; doctors per capita; number of citizens tapping their Medicare benefits per thousand people. *Forbes.com, "America's Most Affordable Places to Retire," September 5, 2008*

- The Dallas metro area was selected as one of "America's Best Places to Grow Old" by *Forbes*. The area was ranked #2 out of 10. Criteria: housing affordability; inflationary pressures; number of persons over 65 who are currently employed; net migration for persons over 65; percent of seniors living below poverty level; doctors per capita; number of citizens tapping their Medicare benefits per 1,000 people. *Forbes, "America's Best Places to Grow Old," December 12, 2008*

- The Dallas metro area was selected as one of "The 10 Most Affordable Cities for Long-Term Care" by *U.S. News & World Report*. Criteria: costs at nursing homes, assisted living facilities, and adult day health care facilities; cost for licensed home health aides. *U.S. News & Word Report, "The 10 Most Affordable Cities for Long-Term Care," May 17, 2010*

Sports/Recreation Rankings

- Dallas appeared on the *Sporting News* list of the "Best Sports Cities" for 2010. The area ranked #5 out of 402 cities in the U.S. *Sporting News* takes a 12-month snapshot, roughly October to October, of each city's sports, putting a heavy premium on regular-season won-lost records (from the most recently completed season). Other criteria include: playoff berths, bowl appearances and tournament bids; championships; applicable power ratings; quality of competition; overall fan fervor as measured in part by attendance as percentage of venue capacity; abundance of teams (rewarding quality over quantity); stadium and arena quality; ticket availability and prices; franchise ownership; and marquee appeal of athletes. *Sporting News, "Best Sports Cities 2010," October, 2010*

- Dallas was chosen as one of America's 25 best cities for running. The city was ranked #15. Criteria: number of running clubs per city; amount of land set aside for park usage; air quality; weather; crime rates; and results from a *Runner's World* poll in which readers ranked their favorite running cities. *Runner's World, "The 25 Best Running Cities in America," July 2005*

- Scarborough Research, a leading market research firm, identified the top local markets for avid NBA fans. The Dallas DMA (Designated Market Area) ranked in the top 10 with 13% of consumers 18 years and over reporting that they are "very interested in the NBA." *Scarborough Research, April 24, 2006*

- *Golf Digest* ranked 330 metro areas in the U.S. in terms of golf. The Dallas metro area was ranked #256. Criteria: access to golf; weather; value of golf; and quality of golf. *Golf Digest, "Metro Golf Rankings," August 2005*

- *Golf.com* and the research arm of the National Golf Foundation analyzed the 50 largest metropolitan areas in the U.S. in terms of golf. The Dallas metro area ranked #4. Criteria: weather; affordability; quality of courses; accessibility; number of courses designed by esteemed architects; availability; crowdedness. *Golf.com, November 15, 2007*

Technology Rankings

- Scarborough Research, a leading market research firm, identified the Dallas DMA (Designated Market Area) as one of the top markets for text messaging with more than 50% of cell phone subscribers age 18+ utilizing the text messaging feature on their phone. *Scarborough Research, November 24, 2008*

Transportation Rankings

- Dallas was selected as one of the "Least Courteous Cities (Worst Road Rage)" in the U.S. by AutoVantage. The city ranked #2. Criteria: 2,518 consumers were interviewed in 25 major metropolitan areas about their views on road rage. *AutoVantage, "2009 AutoVantage Road Rage Survey"*

- The Dallas metro area appeared on *Forbes* list of the best and worst cities for commuters. The metro area ranked #56 out of 60 (#1 is best). Criteria: travel time; road congestion; travel delays. *Forbes.com, "Best and Worst Cities for Commuters," February 16, 2010*

Women/Minorities Rankings

- Dallas was ranked #68 out of 100 metro areas in *SELF Magazine's* ranking of America's healthiest places for women." A panel of experts came up with more than 50 criteria including death and disease rates, environmental indicators, community resources, and lifestyle habits. *SELF Magazine, "Secrets of America's Healthiest Women," December 2008*

- Dallas was selected as one of the 25 healthiest cities for Latinas by *Latina Magazine*. The city ranked #21. Criteria: access to health care; community risk; family and home statistics; air quality; number of parks. *Latina Magazine, May 2007*

- Dallas appeared on *Black Enterprise's* list of the "Ten Best Cities for African Americans." The top picks were culled from more than 2,000 interactive surveys completed on www.blackenterprise.com and by editorial staff evaluation. The editors weighed the following criteria as it pertained to African Americans in each city: median household income; percentage of households earning more than $100,000; percentage of businesses owned; percentage of college graduates; unemployment rates; home loan rejections; and homeownership rates. *Black Enterprise, May 2007*

- Dallas was selected as one of the "Top 10 Cities for Hispanics." Criteria: the prospect of a good job; a safe place to raise a family; a manageable cost of living; the ability to buy and keep a home; a culture of inclusion where Hispanics are highly represented; resources to help start a business; the presence of Hispanic or Spanish-language media; representation of Hispanic needs on local government; a thriving arts and culture community; air quality; energy costs; city's state of health and rates of obesity. *Hispanic Magazine, August 2008*

Miscellaneous Rankings

- Energizer Holdings, the makers of Edge® shave gel, in partnership with Sperling's BestPlaces, ranked 50 major metro areas in terms of everyday irritations. The Dallas metro area ranked #13. Criteria: humidity levels; weather conditions; incidence of traffic delays and congestion; average commute times; frequency of flight delays and cancellations; rates of sleeplessness; underemployment; pollens and allergens; pests; comedy clubs per capita. *Energizer Holdings, "Most Irritation Prone Cities," July 23, 2010*

- Mars Chocolate North America, the makers of COMBOS®, in partnership with Sperling's BestPlaces, ranked 50 major metro areas in terms of their "manliness." The Dallas metro area ranked #39. Criteria: number of home improvement stores, steak houses, pickup trucks, motorcycles, and manly occupations (fire fighters, police officers, construction workers, EMP personnel) per capita; salty snack sales; sports TV viewing habits. *Mars Chocolate North America, "America's Manliest Cities," June 22, 2010*

- The Dallas metro area was selected as one of "America's Greediest Cities" by *Forbes*. The area was ranked #7 out of 10. Criteria: number of Forbes 400 (*Forbes* annual list of the richest Americans) members per capita. *Forbes, "America's Greediest Cities," December 7, 2007*

- Dallas was selected as one of the best cities for shopping in the U.S. by *Forbes*. The city was ranked #3.Criteria: number of major shopping centers; retail locations; Consumer Price Index (CPI); combined state and local sales tax. *Forbes, "America's 25 Best Cities for Shopping," December 13, 2010*

- The Dallas metro area appeared in AutoMD.com's ranking of the "Best and Worst Cities for Auto Repair." The metro area ranked #25 (#1 is best). The 50 most-populated metro areas in the U.S. were ranked on three critical factors: repair affordability; price disparity range; shop integrity factor. *AutoMD.com, "Advocacy for Repair Shop Fairness Report," February 24, 2010*

- Dallas appeared on Procter & Gamble's list of the "Top-20 All-Time Sweatiest Cities." The city was ranked #4. The rankings are based on computer simulations of the amount of sweat a person of average height and weight would produce walking around for an hour in the average temperatures during the summer months, based on historical weather data during June, July and August from 2001-2008 for each city. *Procter & Gamble, Old Spice Press Release, "Top-20 All-Time Sweatiest Cities," July 1, 2009*

- The Dallas metro area appeared on *Forbes* list of "America's Drunkest Cities." The area ranked #27. Criteria: 35 of the largest continental U.S. metro areas were chosen based on availability of data and geographic diversity. Each metro was ranked in five areas: state laws; drinkers; heavy drinkers; binge drinkers; and alcoholism. *Forbes.com, "America's Drunkest Cities," August 22, 2006*

Business Environment

CITY FINANCES

City Government Finances

Component	2008 ($000)	2008 ($ per capita)
Total Revenues	3,164,306	2,551
Total Expenditures	2,974,028	2,397
Debt Outstanding	8,956,826	7,220
Cash and Securities[1]	9,052,523	7,297

Note: (1) Cash and security holdings of a government at the close of its fiscal year, including those of its dependent agencies, utilities, and liquor stores.
Source: U.S Census Bureau, State & Local Government Finances 2008

City Government Revenue by Source

Source	2008 ($000)	2008 ($ per capita)
General Revenue		
From Federal Government	69,315	56
From State Government	61,182	49
From Local Governments	4,685	4
Taxes		
Property	559,874	451
Sales and Gross Receipts	372,041	300
Personal Income	0	0
Corporate Income	0	0
Motor Vehicle License	0	0
Other Taxes	41,274	33
Current Charges	1,096,232	884
Liquor Store	0	0
Utility	222,493	179
Employee Retirement	434,200	350

Source: U.S Census Bureau, State & Local Government Finances 2008

City Government Expenditures by Function

Function	2008 ($000)	2008 ($ per capita)	2008 (%)
General Direct Expenditures			
Air Transportation	504,194	406	17.0
Corrections	2,387	2	0.1
Education	0	0	0.0
Employment Security Administration	0	0	0.0
Financial Administration	32,950	27	1.1
Fire Protection	172,942	139	5.8
General Public Buildings	35,072	28	1.2
Governmental Administration, Other	17,271	14	0.6
Health	40,257	32	1.4
Highways	155,043	125	5.2
Hospitals	0	0	0.0
Housing and Community Development	59,657	48	2.0
Interest on General Debt	377,339	304	12.7
Judicial and Legal	23,399	19	0.8
Libraries	34,761	28	1.2
Parking	2,237	2	0.1
Parks and Recreation	175,625	142	5.9
Police Protection	338,936	273	11.4
Public Welfare	13,913	11	0.5
Sewerage	222,379	179	7.5
Solid Waste Management	58,432	47	2.0
Veterans' Services	0	0	0.0
Liquor Store	0	0	0.0
Utility	326,922	264	11.0
Employee Retirement	282,406	228	9.5

Source: U.S Census Bureau, State & Local Government Finances 2008

Municipal Bond Ratings

Area	Moody's	S&P	Fitch
City	Aa1	AA+	n/a

Rating Systems (shown in declining order of credit quality): Moody's– Aaa, Aa, A, Baa, Ba, B, Caa, Ca, C (numerical modifiers 1, 2, and 3 are added to letter-rating); S&P– AAA, AA, A, BBB, BB, B, CCC, CC, C; Fitch– AAA, AA, A, BBB, BB, B, CCC, CC, C. Ratings may be modified by the addition of a plus or minus sign to show relative standing within the major rating categories.
Notes: n/a Not available; (1) Not reviewed; (2) Issuer Rating/No General Obligation; (3) Standard and Poor's Issue Credit Rating (ICR) is a current opinion of an obliger with respect to a specific financial obligation, a specific class of financial obligations, or a specific financial program.
Source: U.S. Census Bureau, 2011 Statistical Abstract, Bond Ratings for City Governments by Largest Cities: 2009

DEMOGRAPHICS

Population Growth

Area	1990 Census	2000 Census	2010 Estimate	2015 Projection	Population Growth (%) 2000-2010	2010-2015
City	1,006,971	1,188,580	1,297,289	1,357,127	9.1	4.6
MSA[1]	3,989,294	5,161,544	6,493,230	7,129,430	25.8	9.8
U.S.	248,709,873	281,421,906	309,038,974	321,675,005	9.8	4.1

Note: (1) Metropolitan Statistical Area - see Appendix B for areas included
Source: Claritas, Inc.

Number of Households and Average Household Size

Area	2010 Estimate	2010 Average Household Size
City	482,467	2.64
MSA[1]	2,320,136	2.76
U.S.	116,136,617	2.59

Note: (1) Metropolitan Statistical Area - see Appendix B for areas included
Source: Claritas, Inc.

Race and Ethnicity

Area	White Alone[2] (%)	Black Alone[2] (%)	Asian Alone[2] (%)	Other Race Alone[2] (%)	Hispanic[3] (%)
City	48.1	23.0	3.0	25.9	45.8
MSA[1]	64.4	14.0	4.7	16.9	28.1
U.S.	72.3	12.4	4.4	10.9	15.8

Note: Figures are 2010 estimates; (1) Metropolitan Statistical Area - see Appendix B for areas included (2) Alone is defined as not being in combination with one or more other races; (3) May be of any race.
Source: Claritas, Inc.

Segregation

Type	Segregation Indices[1] 1990	2000	2010	2010 Rank[2]	Percent Change 1990-2000	1990-2010	2000-2010
Black/White	62.8	59.8	56.6	48	-3.1	-6.2	-3.2
Asian/White	41.8	45.6	46.6	19	3.8	4.8	1.0
Hispanic/White	48.8	52.3	50.3	24	3.5	1.5	-2.0

Note: Figures are based on an analysis of 1990, 2000, and 2010 Census Decennial Census tract data by William H. Frey, Brookings Institution and the University of Michigan Social Science Data Analysis Network. In this analysis all racial groups (whites, blacks, and asians) are non-Hispanic members of those races. Hispanics are shown as a separate category; All figures cover the Metropolitan Statistical Area (see Appendix B for areas included); (1) Segregation Indices are Dissimilarity Indices that measure the degree to which the minority group is distributed differently than whites aross census tracts. They range from 0 (complete integration) to 100 (complete [segregation) where the value indicates the percentage of the minority group that needs to move to be distributed exactly like whites; (2) Ranges from 1 (most segregated) to 102 (least segregated); n/a not available.
Source: www.CensusScope.org

Ancestry

Area	German	Irish	English	American	Italian	Polish	French	Scottish
City	6.3	4.9	5.4	2.8	1.5	0.9	1.5	1.2
MSA[1]	11.4	8.8	8.6	6.5	2.3	1.2	2.3	1.9
U.S.	16.6	12.0	9.1	6.1	5.9	3.3	3.1	1.9

*Note: The top eight ancestries in the U.S. are shown. Figures are percentages and include multiple ancestry
(e.g. if a person reported being Irish and Italian, they were included in both columns); (1) Metropolitan
Statistical Area - see Appendix B for areas included*
Source: U.S. Census Bureau, 2007-2009 American Community Survey 3-Year Estimates

Foreign-Born Population

Area	Percent of Population Born in								
	Any Foreign Country	Mexico	Asia	Europe	Carribean	South America	Central America[2]	Africa	Canada
City	25.2	18.2	2.3	0.7	0.2	0.4	2.3	1.0	0.1
MSA[1]	17.5	9.8	3.8	0.8	0.2	0.5	1.3	0.8	0.2
U.S.	12.5	3.8	3.4	1.6	1.1	0.8	0.9	0.5	0.3

Note: (1) Metropolitan Statistical Area - see Appendix B for areas included; (2) Excludes Mexico.
Source: U.S. Census Bureau, 2007-2009 American Community Survey 3-Year Estimates

Marriage Status

Area	Never Married	Now Married[2]	Separated	Widowed	Divorced
City	39.1	40.9	3.6	5.2	11.2
MSA[1]	30.9	50.7	2.6	4.7	11.1
U.S.	31.4	49.7	2.2	6.2	10.6

*Note: Figures are percentages and cover the population 15 years of age and older;
(1) Metropolitan Statistical Area - see Appendix B for areas included; (2) Excludes separated*
Source: U.S. Census Bureau, 2007-2009 American Community Survey 3-Year Estimates

Age Distribution and Median Age

Area	Percent of Population							Median Age
	Under Age 5	Age 5 to 17	Age 18 to 34	Age 35 to 49	Age 50 to 64	Age 65 to 79	80 Years and Over	
City	9.5	17.4	29.7	21.0	13.8	5.9	2.7	31.0
MSA[1]	8.4	19.6	25.3	22.8	15.4	6.2	2.2	32.9
U.S.	6.9	17.5	23.3	21.4	18.1	9.1	3.7	36.7

Note: (1) Metropolitan Statistical Area - see Appendix B for areas included
Source: U.S. Census Bureau, 2007-2009 American Community Survey 3-Year Estimates

Male/Female Ratio

Area	Males	Females	Males per 100 Females
City	664,980	632,309	105.2
MSA[1]	3,264,985	3,228,245	101.1
U.S.	152,401,520	156,637,454	97.3

*Note: Figures are 2010 estimates; (1) Metropolitan Statistical Area -
see Appendix B for areas included*
Source: Claritas, Inc.

Religion

Area	Catholic	Southern Baptist	United Meth-odist	ELCA[1]	LDS[2]	Presby-terian Church USA	Jewish Est.	Muslim Est.
County	21.7	12.7	4.8	0.5	0.5	1.3	1.7	1.0
U.S.	22.0	7.1	3.7	1.8	1.5	1.1	2.2	0.6

Note: Figures are the number of adherents as a percentage of the total population; Adherents are defined as all members, including full members, their children and the estimated number of other participants who are not considered members (e.g. the baptized, those not confirmed, those regularly attending services, etc.); (1) Evangelical Lutheran Church in America; (2) The Church of Jesus Christ of Latter Day Saints Source: Reprinted with permission from Religious Congregations and Membership in the United States 2000 (Nashville, Glenmary Research Center, 2002) Copyright Association of Statisticians of American Religious Bodies. All rights reserved.

ECONOMY

Gross Metropolitan Product

Area	2006	2007	2008	2009	2009 Rank[2]
MSA[1]	340.6	362.1	379.9	384.8	6

Note: Figures are in billions of dollars; (1) Dallas-Fort Worth-Arlington, TX Metropolitan Statistical Area - see Appendix B for areas included; (2) Rank ranges from 1 to 363 Source: The U.S. Conference of Mayors, "Pace of Economic Recovery: GMP and Jobs," January 2010

Economic Growth

Area	2006-2008 (%)	2009 (%)	2010 (%)	Rank[2]
MSA[1]	2.7	-0.1	3.7	67
U.S.	1.3	-2.5	2.2	–

Note: Figures are real Gross Metropolitan Product growth rates and represent annual average percent change; (1) Dallas-Fort Worth-Arlington, TX Metropolitan Statistical Area - see Appendix B for areas included; (2) Rank ranges from 1 to 363 Source: The U.S. Conference of Mayors, "Pace of Economic Recovery: GMP and Jobs," January 2010

Metropolitan Area Exports

Area	2005	2006	2007	2008	2009	2009 Rank[2]
MSA[1]	20,541.2	22,461.6	22,079.1	22,503.7	19,881.8	10

Note: Figures are in millions of dollars; (1) Dallas-Fort Worth-Arlington, TX Metropolitan Statistical Area - see Appendix B for areas included; (2) Rank ranges from 1 to 374 Source: U.S. Department of Commerce, International Trade Administration, Office of Trade & Industry Information, Manufacturing & Services

INCOME

Per Capita/Median/Average Income

Area	Per Capita ($)	Median Household ($)	Average Household ($)
City	24,273	43,066	64,560
MSA[1]	27,980	58,202	77,740
U.S.	27,034	52,795	71,071

Note: Figures are 2010 estimates; (1) Metropolitan Statistical Area - see Appendix B for areas included Source: Claritas, Inc.

Household Income Distribution

Area	Percent of Households Earning							
	Under $15,000	$15,000 -24,999	$25,000 -34,999	$35,000 -49,999	$50,000 -74,999	$75,000 -99,000	$100,000 -149,999	$150,000 and up
City	14.6	12.4	13.5	17.5	16.9	9.1	8.6	7.4
MSA[1]	9.4	8.6	10.2	15.3	19.6	13.3	14.1	9.4
U.S.	12.1	10.2	10.6	15.0	19.5	12.5	12.1	8.0

Note: Figures are 2010 estimates; (1) Metropolitan Statistical Area - see Appendix B for areas included Source: Claritas, Inc.

Poverty Rates by Age

Area	All Ages	Under 18 Years Old	18 to 64 Years Old	65 Years and Over
City	22.2	9.2	11.9	1.1
MSA[1]	13.4	5.4	7.2	0.7
U.S.	13.6	4.7	7.7	1.2

Note: Figures are percent of population with income during the previous 12 months below poverty level and only include population for whom poverty status is determined; (1) Metropolitan Statistical Area - see Appendix B for areas included
Source: U.S. Census Bureau, 2007-2009 American Community Survey 3-Year Estimates

Personal Bankruptcy Filing Rate

Area	2006	2007	2008	2009	2010
Dallas County	2.13	2.30	2.29	2.77	2.73
U.S.	2.00	2.73	3.53	4.60	4.96

Note: Numbers are per 1,000 population and include Chapter 7 and Chapter 13 filings
Source: Federal Deposit Insurance Corporation, Regional Economic Conditions, March 17, 2011

EMPLOYMENT

Labor Force and Employment

Area	Civilian Labor Force			Workers Employed		
	Dec. 2009	Dec. 2010	% Chg.	Dec. 2009	Dec. 2010	% Chg.
City	588,889	602,997	2.4	539,610	551,590	2.2
MD[1]	2,109,867	2,158,513	2.3	1,942,343	1,985,464	2.2
U.S.	152,693,000	153,156,000	0.3	137,953,000	139,159,000	0.9

Note: Data is not seasonally adjusted and covers workers 16 years of age and older;
(1) Metropolitan Division - see Appendix B for areas included
Source: Bureau of Labor Statistics, http://stats.bls.gov

Unemployment Rate

Area	2010											
	Jan.	Feb.	Mar.	Apr.	May	Jun.	Jul.	Aug.	Sep.	Oct.	Nov.	Dec.
City	9.2	9.0	8.9	8.6	8.6	9.0	9.0	8.8	8.6	8.5	8.8	8.5
MD[1]	8.7	8.5	8.4	8.1	8.0	8.5	8.5	8.4	8.1	8.0	8.3	8.0
U.S.	10.6	10.4	10.2	9.5	9.3	9.6	9.7	9.5	9.2	9.0	9.3	9.1

Note: Data is not seasonally adjusted and covers workers 16 years of age and older; All figures are percentages; (1) Metropolitan Division - see Appendix B for areas included
Source: Bureau of Labor Statistics, http://stats.bls.gov

Projected Unemployment Rate

Area	2007 (%)	2009 (%)	2011 (%)	2013 (%)
MSA[1]	4.4	8.9	8.3	7.0

Note: (1) Metropolitan Statistical Area - see Appendix B for areas included
Source: The U.S. Conference of Mayors, "Pace of Economic Recovery: GMP and Jobs," January 2010

Employment by Occupation

Occupation Classification	City (%)	MSA[1] (%)	U.S. (%)
Sales and Office	24.4	27.0	25.4
Professional and Related	16.9	19.5	21.0
Service	18.1	15.1	17.2
Production, Transportation, and Material Moving	12.4	11.8	12.3
Management, Business, and Financial	13.7	15.7	14.1
Construction, Extraction, and Maintenance	14.3	10.7	9.2
Farming, Forestry, and Fishing	0.2	0.2	0.7

Note: Figures cover employed civilians 16 years of age and older;
(1) Metropolitan Statistical Area - see Appendix B for areas included
Source: U.S. Census Bureau, 2007-2009 American Community Survey 3-Year Estimates

Employment by Industry

| Sector | MSA[1] | | U.S. |
	Number of Employees	Percent of Total	Percent of Total
Government	276,100	13.4	17.2
Education and Health Services	255,300	12.4	15.2
Professional and Business Services	344,000	16.7	13.0
Retail Trade	210,300	10.2	11.4
Leisure and Hospitality	191,400	9.3	9.7
Manufacturing	162,400	7.9	8.8
Financial Activities	180,400	8.8	5.8
Wholesale Trade	119,900	5.8	4.2
Construction	n/a	n/a	4.1
Other Services	69,100	3.4	4.1
Transportation and Utilities	74,500	3.6	3.7
Information	64,200	3.1	2.1
Mining and Logging	n/a	n/a	0.6

Note: Figures cover non-farm employment as of December 2010 and are not seasonally adjusted;
(1) Metropolitan Statistical Area - see Appendix B for areas included; n/a not available
Source: Bureau of Labor Statistics, http://stats.bls.gov

Occupations with Greatest Projected Employment Growth: 2006 - 2016

Occupation[1]	2006 Employment	2016 Projected Employment	Numeric Employment Change	Percent Employment Change
Combined food preparation and serving workers, including fast food	270,530	359,050	88,520	32.7
Retail salespersons	332,750	411,350	78,600	23.6
Personal and home care aides	133,050	207,850	74,800	56.2
Customer service representatives	214,440	280,060	65,620	30.6
Elementary school teachers, except special education	145,430	207,710	62,280	42.8
Registered nurses	157,840	217,430	59,590	37.8
Waiters and waitresses	174,140	227,790	53,650	30.8
Child care workers	145,500	189,730	44,230	30.4
Office clerks, general	194,610	236,670	42,060	21.6
Postsecondary teachers	113,400	153,130	39,730	35.0

Note: Projections cover Texas; (1) Sorted by numeric employment change
Source: www.projectionscentral.com, State Occupational Projections, 2006-2016 Long-Term Projections

Fastest Growing Occupations: 2006 - 2016

Occupation[1]	2006 Employment	2016 Projected Employment	Numeric Employment Change	Percent Employment Change
Personal and home care aides	133,050	207,850	74,800	56.2
Network systems and data communications analysts	17,750	27,620	9,870	55.6
Medical assistants	34,790	53,500	18,710	53.8
Special education teachers, preschool, kindergarten, and elementary school	13,750	20,560	6,810	49.5
Physical therapist assistants	3,780	5,570	1,790	47.4
Special education teachers, middle school	6,270	9,170	2,900	46.3
Computer software engineers, applications	30,900	45,200	14,300	46.3
Physician assistants	3,810	5,540	1,730	45.4
Kindergarten teachers, except special education	12,850	18,690	5,840	45.4
Pharmacy technicians	24,420	35,050	10,630	43.5

Note: Projections cover Texas; (1) Sorted by percent employment change and excludes occupations with numeric employment change less than 1500
Source: www.projectionscentral.com, State Occupational Projections, 2006-2016 Long-Term Projections

Average Wages

Occupation	$/Hr.	Occupation	$/Hr.
Accountants and Auditors	32.90	Maids and Housekeeping Cleaners	8.89
Automotive Mechanics	18.35	Maintenance and Repair Workers	16.07
Bookkeepers	17.45	Marketing Managers	62.86
Carpenters	15.47	Nuclear Medicine Technologists	31.78
Cashiers	8.69	Nurses, Licensed Practical	22.59
Clerks, General Office	14.40	Nurses, Registered	32.47
Clerks, Receptionists/Information	12.90	Nursing Aides/Orderlies/Attendants	10.99
Clerks, Shipping/Receiving	13.87	Packers and Packagers, Hand	9.89
Computer Programmers	40.97	Physical Therapists	39.65
Computer Support Specialists	24.37	Postal Service Mail Carriers	23.77
Computer Systems Analysts	40.47	Real Estate Brokers	47.56
Cooks, Restaurant	9.77	Retail Salespersons	12.29
Dentists	n/a	Sales Reps., Exc. Tech./Scientific	29.08
Electrical Engineers	46.55	Sales Reps., Tech./Scientific	49.88
Electricians	20.47	Secretaries, Exc. Legal/Med./Exec.	14.58
Financial Managers	59.84	Security Guards	12.72
First-Line Supervisors/Mgrs., Sales	19.44	Surgeons	108.56
Food Preparation Workers	8.61	Teacher Assistants	11.00
General and Operations Managers	59.88	Teachers, Elementary School	25.80
Hairdressers/Cosmetologists	13.15	Teachers, Secondary School	27.00
Internists	100.60	Telemarketers	13.85
Janitors and Cleaners	9.85	Truck Drivers, Heavy/Tractor-Trailer	18.91
Landscaping/Groundskeeping Workers	11.05	Truck Drivers, Light/Delivery Svcs.	15.12
Lawyers	71.15	Waiters and Waitresses	8.67

Note: Wage data covers the Dallas-Plano-Irving, TX Metropolitan Division - see Appendix B for areas included. Hourly wages for elementary/secondary school teachers and teacher assistants were calculated by the editors from annual wage data assuming a 40 hour work week; n/a not available.
Source: Bureau of Labor Statistics, Metro Area Occupational Employment and Wage Estimates, May 2009

RESIDENTIAL REAL ESTATE

Building Permits

Area	Single-Family			Multi-Family			Total		
	2009	2010	Pct. Chg.	2009	2010	Pct. Chg.	2009	2010	Pct. Chg.
City	734	865	17.8	1,037	1,744	68.2	1,771	2,609	47.3
MSA[1]	14,141	14,420	2.0	6,229	5,138	-17.5	20,370	19,558	-4.0
U.S.	441,100	447,300	1.4	141,900	157,300	10.9	583,000	604,600	3.7

Note: (1) Metropolitan Statistical Area - see Appendix B for areas included; figures represent new, privately-owned housing units authorized (unadjusted data); All permit data are based on estimates with imputation.
Source: U.S. Census Bureau, Manufacturing, Mining, and Construction Statistics, Building Permits, 2009, 2010

Homeownership Rate

Area	2005 (%)	2006 (%)	2007 (%)	2008 (%)	2009 (%)	2010 (%)
MSA[1]	62.3	60.7	60.9	60.9	61.6	63.8
U.S.	68.9	68.8	68.1	67.8	67.4	66.9

Note: (1) Metropolitan Statistical Area - see Appendix B for areas included
Source: U.S. Census Bureau, Housing Vacancies and Homeownership Annual Statistics: 2010

Housing Vacancy Rates

Area	Gross Vacancy Rate[2] (%)			Year-Round Vacancy Rate[3] (%)			Rental Vacancy Rate[4] (%)			Homeowner Vacancy Rate[5] (%)		
	2008	2009	2010	2008	2009	2010	2008	2009	2010	2008	2009	2010
MSA[1]	9.5	9.4	10.5	9.4	9.3	10.4	10.5	11.7	13.5	2.8	2.1	2.3
U.S.	14.4	14.5	14.3	11.1	11.3	11.3	10.0	10.6	10.2	2.8	2.6	2.6

Note: (1) Metropolitan Statistical Area - see Appendix B for areas included; (2) The percentage of the total housing inventory that is vacant; (3) The percentage of the housing inventory (excluding seasonal units) that is year-round vacant; (4) The percentage of rental inventory that is vacant for rent; (5) The percentage of homeowner inventory that is vacant for sale; n/a not available
Source: U.S. Census Bureau, Housing Vacancies and Homeownership Annual Statistics: 2010

State Corporate Income Tax Rates

State	Tax Rate (%)	Income Brackets ($)	Num. of Brackets	Financial Institution Tax Rate (%)[a]	Federal Income Tax Ded.
Texas	(y)	–	-	(y)	No

Note: Tax rates as of January 1, 2011; (a) Rates listed are the tax rates applied to financial institutions or excise taxes based on income. Some states have other taxes based upon the value of deposits or shares; (y) Texas imposes a Franchise Tax, otherwise known as margin tax, imposed on entities with more than $1,000,000 total revenues at rate of 1%, or 0.5% for entities primarily engaged in retail or wholesale trade, on lesser of 70% of total revenues or 100% of gross receipts after deductions for either compensation or cost of goods sold.
Source: Federation of Tax Administrators, "State Corporate Income Tax Rates, 2011"

State Individual Income Tax Rates

State	Tax Rate (%)	Income Brackets ($)	Num. of Brackets	Personal Exempt. ($)[1] Single	Personal Exempt. ($)[1] Dependents	Fed. Inc. Tax Ded.
Texas – No State Income Tax						

Note: Tax rates as of January 1, 2011; Local- and county-level taxes are not included; n/a not applicable;
(1) Married joint filers generally receive double the single exemption
Source: Federation of Tax Administrators, "State Individual Income Tax Rates, 2011"

Various State and Local Tax Rates

State	State and Local Sales and Use (%)	State Sales and Use (%)	Gasoline[1] (¢/gal.)	Cigarette[2] ($/pack)	Spirits[3] ($/gal.)	Wine[4] ($/gal.)	Beer[5] ($/gal.)
Texas	8.25	6.25	20.0	1.41	2.40	0.20	0.20

Note: All tax rates as of January 1, 2011 except Spirits (Sept. 1, 2010); (1) The American Petroleum Institute has developed a methodology for determining the average tax rate on a gallon of fuel. Rates may include any of the following: excise taxes, environmental fees, storage tank fees, other fees or taxes, general sales tax, and local taxes. In states where gasoline is subject to the general sales tax, or where the fuel tax is based on the average sale price, the average rate determined by API is sensitive to changes in the price of gasoline. States that fully or partially apply general sales taxes to gasoline: CA, CO, GA, IL, IN, MI, NY; (2) The federal excise tax of $1.0066 per pack and local taxes are not included; (3) Rates are those applicable to off-premise sales of 40% alcohol by volume (a.b.v.) distilled spirits in 750ml containers. Local excise taxes are excluded; (4) Rates are those applicable to off-premise sales of 11% a.b.v. non-carbonated wine in 750ml containers; (5) Rates are those applicable to off-premise sales of 4.7% a.b.v. beer in 12 ounce containers.
Source: Tax Foundation, 2011 Facts & Figures: How Does Your State Compare?

State-Local Tax Burdens

Area	Rate (%)	Rank[1]	Per Capita Taxes Paid to Home State ($)	Total State and Local Per Capita Taxes Paid ($)	Per Capita Income ($)
Texas	7.9	45	2,248	3,197	40,498
U.S. Average	9.8	-	3,057	4,160	42,539

Note: Figures cover 2009; (1) Rank ranges from 1 to 50 where 1 is highest tax burden
Source: Tax Foundation, State-Local Tax Burdens, All States, 2009

State Business Tax Climate Index Rankings

State	Overall Rank	Corporate Tax Index Rank	Individual Income Tax Index Rank	Sales Tax Index Rank	Unemployment Insurance Tax Index Rank	Property Tax Index Rank
Texas	13	46	7	37	15	29

Note: The index is a measure of how each state's tax laws affect economic performance. The lower the rank, the more favorable a state's tax system is for business. All ranks are for fiscal years. States without a given tax are given a ranking of 1.
Source: Tax Foundation, Tax Foundation Background Paper, No. 60, "2011 State Business Tax Climate Index"

COMMERCIAL REAL ESTATE

Office Market

Market Area	Inventory (sq. ft.)	Vacant (sq. ft.)	Vac. Rate (%)	Under Constr. (sq. ft.)	Asking Rent ($/sf/yr) Class A	Asking Rent ($/sf/yr) Class B
Dallas/Fort Worth	190,744,710	43,317,095	22.7	281,600	23.16	17.90

Source: Grubb & Ellis, Office Markets Trends, 1st Quarter 2011

Industrial Market

Market Area	Inventory (sq. ft.)	Vacant (sq. ft.)	Vac. Rate (%)	Under Constr. (sq. ft.)	Asking Rent ($/sf/yr) WH/Dist	R&D/Flex
Dallas/Fort Worth	662,799,900	76,917,306	11.6	1,403,552	3.53	6.46

Source: Grubb & Ellis, Industrial Markets Trends, 1st Quarter 2011

COMMERCIAL UTILITIES

Typical Monthly Electric Bills

Area	Commercial Service ($/month) 3 kW demand 1,000 kWh	40 kW demand 14,000 kWh	Industrial Service ($/month) 1,000 kW demand 200,000 kWh	50,000 kW demand 15,000,000 kWh
City	n/a	n/a	n/a	n/a
Average[1]	135	1,576	23,741	1,402,202

Note: Based on total rates in effect July 1, 2010; (1) average based on 182 utilities surveyed; n/a not available
Source: Edison Electric Institute, Typical Bills and Average Rates Report, Summer 2010

TRANSPORTATION

Means of Transportation to Work

Area	Car/Truck/Van Drove Alone	Car-pooled	Public Transportation Bus	Subway	Railroad	Bicycle	Walked	Other Means	Worked at Home
City	76.4	12.7	3.6	0.3	0.4	0.1	1.8	1.2	3.6
MSA[1]	80.4	11.0	1.2	0.2	0.2	0.2	1.3	1.4	4.1
U.S.	75.8	10.4	2.7	1.7	0.5	0.5	2.9	1.2	4.1

Note: Figures are percentages and cover workers 16 years of age and older;
(1) Metropolitan Statistical Area - see Appendix B for areas included
Source: U.S. Census Bureau, 2007-2009 American Community Survey 3-Year Estimates

Travel Time to Work

Area	Less Than 15 Minutes	15 to 29 Minutes	30 to 44 Minutes	45 to 59 Minutes	60 to 89 Minutes	90 Minutes or More
City	22.2	40.5	23.7	7.0	4.9	1.8
MSA[1]	22.5	36.3	24.0	9.6	5.9	1.7
U.S.	28.5	36.2	19.7	7.5	5.6	2.5

Note: Figures are percentages and include workers 16 years old and over;
(1) Metropolitan Statistical Area - see Appendix B for areas included
Source: U.S. Census Bureau, 2007-2009 American Community Survey 3-Year Estimates

Travel Time Index

Area	1982	1999	2008	2009
Urban Area[1]	1.05	1.19	1.23	1.22
Average[2]	1.08	1.20	1.20	1.20

Note: Travel Time Index—the ratio of travel time in the peak period to the travel time at free-flow conditions. A value of 1.30 indicates a 20-minute free-flow trip takes 26 minutes in the peak. Free-flow speeds (60 mph on freeways and 35 mph on principal arterials) are used as the comparison threshold; (1) Covers the Dallas-Fort Worth-Arlington urban area; (2) average of 439 urban areas
Source: Texas Transportation Institute, Urban Mobility Report 2010, December 2010

Public Transportation

Agency Name / Mode of Transportation	Vehicles Operated in Maximum Service	Annual Unlinked Passenger Trips ('000)	Annual Passenger Miles ('000)
Dallas Area Rapid Transit Authority (DART)			
Commuter rail	21	1,607.2	18,965.4
Demand response	207	1,038.7	14,338.1
Light rail	85	18,965.2	133,364.3
Bus	564	42,517.3	173,242.2
Vanpool	162	880.7	35,337.8

Note: Figures include both directly operated and purchased transportation
Source: Federal Transit Administration, National Transit Database, 2009

Air Transportation

Airport Name and Code / Type of Service	Passenger Airlines[1]	Passenger Enplanements	Freight Carriers[2]	Freight (lbs.)
Dallas-Fort Worth International (DFW)				
Domestic service (U.S. carriers - 2010)	29	24,515,012	29	331,267,166
International service (U.S. carriers - 2009)	14	1,982,583	9	56,792,392
Dallas Love Field (DAL)				
Domestic service (U.S. carriers - 2010)	16	3,780,857	6	9,736,359
International service (U.S. carriers - 2009)	5	519	3	23,275

Note: (1) Includes all U.S.-based major, minor and commuter airlines that carried at least one passenger during the year; (2) Includes all U.S.-based airlines and freight carriers that transported at least one pound of freight during the year
Source: Bureau of Transportation Statistics, The Intermodal Transportation Database, Air Carriers: T-100 Domestic Market (U.S. Carriers), 2010; Bureau of Transportation Statistics, The Intermodal Transportation Database, Air Carriers: T-100 International Market (U.S. Carriers), 2009

Other Transportation Statistics

Interstate highways:	I-20; I-30; I-35E; I-45
Amtrak service:	Yes
Major waterways/ports:	None

Source: Amtrak.com; Google Maps

BUSINESSES

Major Business Headquarters

Company Name	Rankings	
	Fortune[1]	Forbes[2]
AT&T	12	-
Atmos Energy	473	-
Celanese	388	-
Dean Foods	203	-
Energy Future Holdings	292	25
Energy Transfer Equity	351	-
Glazer's Wholesale Drug	-	131
Holly	289	-
Neiman Marcus Group	-	93
Sammons Enterprises	-	138
Southwest Airlines	205	-
Tenet Healthcare	266	-
Texas Instruments	175	-

Note: (1) Fortune 500—companies that produce a 10-K are ranked 1 to 500 based on 2010 revenue; (2) all private companies with at least $2 billion in annual revenue are ranked 1 to 223; companies listed are headquartered in the city; dashes indicate no ranking
Source: Fortune, "Fortune 500," May 23, 2011; Forbes, "America's Largest Private Companies," November 3, 2010

Fast-Growing Businesses

According to *Inc.*, Dallas is home to 11 of America's 500 fastest-growing private companies: **Alsbridge; Ambit Energy; Behavioral Health Group; Ensurity Group; Improving Enterprises; Magic Logix; Pursuit of Excellence; ShopForBags.com; Texas Energy Holdings; The Pursuant Group; Viverae**. Criteria: must be an independent, privately-held, for-profit, U.S. corporation, proprietorship or partnership; revenues of at least $80,000 in 2006 and $2 million in 2009; four-year operating/sales history; holding companies, regulated banks, and utilities were excluded. *Inc., "America's 500 Fastest-Growing Private Companies," September 2010*

According to *Fortune*, Dallas is home to two of America's 100 fastest-growing small public companies: **Holly Energy Partners; United States Lime & Mineral**. Companies were ranked by their three-year annualized rates of revenue growth and total return to investors for the period ended December 31, 2008. Criteria for inclusion: revenues of less than $200 million; stock price of at least $1. Banks, real-estate firms and adult entertainment companies were excluded. Also excluded were companies with losses in any of the four quarters ended on or before December 31, 2008. *Fortune Small Business, "America's Fastest-Growing Small Public Companies," July/August 2009*

According to Deloitte, Dallas is home to three of North America's 500 fastest-growing high-technology companies: **One Technologies; SPEED FC; XENOSOFT TECHNOLOGIES**. Companies are ranked by percentage growth in revenue over a five-year period. Criteria for inclusion: company must be headquartered within North America; company must own proprietary intellectual property or proprietary technology that contributes to a significant portion of the company's operating revenue or devotes a significant proportion of revenues to research and development of technology; company must have been in business for a minumum of five years with 2005 operating revenues of at least $50,000 USD/CD and 2009 operating revenues of at least $5 million USD/CD. *Deloitte Touche Tohmatsu, 2010 Deloitte Technology Fast 500*[TM]

Minority Business Opportunity

Dallas is home to three companies which are on the Black Enterprise Industrial/Service 100 list (100 largest companies based on gross sales): **PrimeSource FSE; Facility Interiors; Parrish McDonald's Restaurants**. Criteria: operational in previous calendar year; at least 51% black-owned and manufactures/owns the product it sells or provides industrial or consumer services. Brokerages, real estate firms and firms that provide professional services are not eligible. *Black Enterprise, B.E. 100s, 2010*

Dallas is home to two companies which are on the Black Enterprise Private Equity 15 list (15 largest private equity firms based on capital under management): **Pharos Capital Group; 21st Century Group**. Criteria: company must be operational in previous calendar year and at least 51% black-owned. *Black Enterprise, B.E. 100s, 2010*

Dallas is home to 10 companies which are on the *Hispanic Business 500* list (500 largest U.S. Hispanic-owned companies based on 2009 revenue): **Pinnacle Technical Resources; Azteca-Omega Group; Gilbert May; Aguirre Roden; Alman Construction Services; ROC Construction; Estrada Hinojosa & Company; Pursuit of Excellence HR; Carrco Painting Contractor; Rocky Duron & Associates**. Companies included must show at least 51 percent ownership by Hispanic U.S. citizens, and must maintain headquarters in one of the 50 states or Washington, D.C. *Hispanic Business, "Hispanic Business 500," June 2010*

Dallas is home to three companies which are on the *Hispanic Business* Fastest-Growing 100 list (greatest sales growth from 2005 to 2009): **Pinnacle Technical Resources; Alman Construction; Gilbert May**. Companies included must show at least 51 percent ownership by Hispanic U.S. citizens, and must maintain headquarters in one of the 50 states or Washington, D.C. In addition, companies must have minimum revenues of $200,000 for calendar year 2005. *Hispanic Business, July/August 2010*

Minority- and Women-Owned Businesses

Group	All Firms		Firms with Paid Employees			
	Firms	Sales ($000)	Firms	Sales ($000)	Employees	Payroll ($000)
Asian	5,977	3,165,560	2,181	3,012,132	15,033	478,254
Black	16,319	1,212,849	770	906,803	7,562	204,412
Hispanic	18,162	3,358,739	1,989	2,603,364	27,163	712,610
Women	33,388	9,072,616	4,058	8,140,079	47,654	1,546,480
All Firms	121,288	185,276,035	26,431	179,315,300	723,979	36,952,454

Note: Figures cover firms located in the city; minority- and women-owned business are defined as firms in which the corresponding group own 51% or more of the stock or equity of the company
Source: U.S. Census Bureau, 2007 Economic Census, Survey of Business Owners

HOTELS

Hotels/Motels

Area	5 Star		4 Star		3 Star		2 Star		1 Star		Not Rated	
	Num.	Pct.3	Num.	Pct.3	Num.	Pct.3	Num.	Pct.3	Num.	Pct.3	Num.	Pct.3
City[1]	3	0.6	30	5.9	155	30.6	279	55.1	10	2.0	29	5.7
Total[2]	119	0.7	927	5.8	4,906	30.5	7,992	49.7	526	3.3	1,625	10.1

Note: (1) Figures cover Dallas and vicinity; (2) Figures cover all 100 cities in this book; (3) Percentage of hotels which are a given star rating; Star ratings are determined by expedia.com and offer an indication of the general quality of a particular hotel.
Source: expedia.com, May 5, 2011

The Dallas metro area is home to six of the top 218 hotels in the U.S. according to *Travel & Leisure*: **Rosewood Mansion on Turtle Creek** (#16); **The Adolphus** (#28); **Rosewood Crescent Hotel** (#76); **Hotel ZaZa, Dallas** (#92); **Omni Mandalay Hotel at Las Colinas** (#177); **Four Seasons Resort and Club Dallas at Las Colinas** (#206). Criteria: service; location; rooms; food; and value. *Travel & Leisure, "T+L 500, The World's Best Hotels 2011"*

The Dallas metro area is home to three of the top 100 hotels in the U.S. according to *Condé Nast Traveler*: **Rosewood Crescent Hotel** (#7); **Rosewood Mansion on Turtle Creek** (#9); **Ritz-Carlton Dallas** (#87). The selections are based on over 25,000 responses to the magazine's annual Readers' Choice Survey. *Condé Nast Traveler, "2010 Readers' Choice Awards"*

EVENT SITES

Major Stadiums, Arenas, and Auditoriums

Name	Max. Capacity
American Airlines Center	20,000
Cotton Bowl	92,100
Superpages.com Center	20,111

Source: Original research

Convention Centers

Name	Overall Space (sq. ft.)	Exhibit Space (sq. ft.)	Meeting Space (sq. ft.)	Meeting Rooms
Dallas Convention Center	2,000,000	n/a	929,726	96

Note: n/a not available
Source: Original research

Living Environment

COST OF LIVING

Cost of Living Index

Composite Index	Groceries	Housing	Utilities	Trans-portation	Health Care	Misc. Goods/ Services
91.9	96.2	70.7	105.5	100.9	103.8	100.4

Note: U.S. = 100; Figures cover the Dallas TX urban area.
Source: The Council for Community and Economic Research, ACCRA Cost of Living Index, 2010

Grocery Prices

Area[1]	T-Bone Steak ($/pound)	Frying Chicken ($/pound)	Whole Milk ($/half gal.)	Eggs ($/dozen)	Orange Juice ($/64 oz.)	Coffee ($/11.5 oz.)
City[2]	8.66	0.98	2.03	1.40	2.89	3.81
Avg.	9.04	1.16	2.02	1.47	3.08	3.65
Min.	6.97	0.84	1.46	0.96	2.39	2.64
Max.	13.93	2.51	3.58	3.01	4.94	6.32

Note: (1) Values for the local area are compared with the average, minimum and maximum values for all 338 areas in the Cost of Living Index; (2) Figures cover the Dallas TX urban area; **T-Bone Steak** (price per pound); **Frying Chicken** (price per pound, whole fryer); **Whole Milk** (half gallon carton); **Eggs** (price per dozen, Grade A, large); **Orange Juice** (64 oz. Tropicana or Florida Natural); **Coffee** (11.5 oz. can, vacuum-packed, Maxwell House, Hills Bros, or Folgers).
Source: The Council for Community and Economic Research, ACCRA Cost of Living Index, 2010

Housing and Utility Costs

Area[1]	New Home Price ($)	Apartment Rent ($/month)	All Electric ($/month)	Part Electric ($/month)	Other Energy ($/month)	Telephone ($/month)
City[2]	197,358	702	-	139.74	44.85	28.15
Avg.	293,442	810	166.39	91.93	83.82	26.93
Min.	182,545	453	119.21	44.47	36.85	17.98
Max.	1,123,114	2,776	307.53	218.20	313.90	39.15

Note: (1) Values for the local area are compared with the average, minimum and maximum values for all 338 areas in the Cost of Living Index; (2) Figures cover the Dallas TX urban area; **New Home Price** (2,400 sf living area, 8,000 sf lot, in urban area with full utilities); **Apartment Rent** (950 sf 2 bedroom/1.5 or 2 bath, unfurnished, excluding all utilities except water); **All Electric** (average monthly cost for an all-electric home); **Part Electric** (average monthly cost for a part-electric home); **Other Energy** (average monthly cost for natural gas, fuel oil, coal, wood, and any other forms of energy except electricity); **Telephone** (price includes basic monthly rate for a private residential line plus additional local usage charges incurred by a family of four).
Source: The Council for Community and Economic Research, ACCRA Cost of Living Index, 2010

Health Care, Transportation, and Other Costs

Area[1]	Doctor ($/visit)	Dentist ($/visit)	Optometrist ($/visit)	Gasoline ($/gallon)	Beauty Salon ($/visit)	Men's Shirt ($)
City[2]	92.71	84.90	90.40	2.58	29.10	24.60
Avg.	89.44	78.95	87.40	2.73	31.92	24.83
Min.	57.00	54.25	48.32	2.44	19.17	13.67
Max.	149.90	136.73	174.22	3.75	62.81	47.89

Note: (1) Values for the local area are compared with the average, minimum and maximum values for all 338 areas in the Cost of Living Index; (2) Figures cover the Dallas TX urban area; **Doctor** (general practitioners routine exam of an established patient); **Dentist** (adult teeth cleaning and periodic oral examination); **Optometrist** (full vision eye exam for established adult patient); **Gasoline** (one gallon regular unleaded, national brand, including all taxes, cash price at self-service pump if available); **Beauty Salon** (woman's shampoo, trim, and blow-dry); **Men's Shirt** (cotton/polyester dress shirt, pinpoint weave, long sleeves).
Source: The Council for Community and Economic Research, ACCRA Cost of Living Index, 2010

HOUSING

House Price Index (HPI)

Area	National Ranking[2]	Quarterly Change (%)	One-Year Change (%)	Five-Year Change (%)
MD[1]	103	-0.43	-0.26	6.73
U.S.[3]	-	-0.84	-3.95	-11.45

Note: The HPI is a weighted repeat sales index. It measures average price changes in repeat sales or refinancings on the same properties. This information is obtained by reviewing repeat mortgage transactions on single-family properties whose mortgages have been purchased or securitized by Fannie Mae or Freddie Mac in January 1975; (1) Metropolitan Division - see Appendix B for areas included; (2) Rankings are based on annual percentage change for all metro areas containing at least 15,000 transactions over the last 10 years and ranges from 1 to 309; (3) figures based on a weighted average of Census Division estimates; all figures are for the period ending December 31, 2010
Source: Federal Housing Finance Agency, House Price Index, February 24, 2011

House Price Valuations

Area	Q4 2005 Price ($000)	Q4 2005 Over-valuation	Q4 2006 Price ($000)	Q4 2006 Over-valuation	Q4 2007 Price ($000)	Q4 2007 Over-valuation	Q4 2008 Price ($000)	Q4 2008 Over-valuation	Q4 2009 Price ($000)	Q4 2009 Over-valuation
MD[1]	127.1	-20.5	131.9	-22.2	134.1	-24.6	136.4	-24.0	137.1	-23.1

Note: Figures show the percentage of over- or under-valuation of single family homes relative to statistically normal house values (e.g. a value of 23.6 indicates that house values are 23.6% overvalued). Statistically normal house values are based on house prices, interest rates, household incomes, population densities, and any historical premiums or discounts metropolitan areas have exhibited over time; (1) Figures cover the Dallas-Plano-Irving, TX Metropolitan Division - see Appendix B for areas included
Source: Global Insight/PNC Financial Services Group, House Prices in America: 4th Quarter 2009 Update

Median Single-Family Home Prices

Area	2008	2009	2010p	Percent Change 2009 to 2010
MSA[1]	145.8	140.5	148.4	5.6
U.S. Average	196.6	172.1	173.2	0.6

Note: Figures are median sales prices of existing single-family homes in thousands of dollars; (p) preliminary; n/a not available; (1) Metropolitan Statistical Area - see Appendix B for areas included
Source: National Association of Realtors, Median Sales Price of Existing Single-Family Homes for Metropolitan Areas, 4th Quarter 2010

Median Apartment Condo-Coop Home Prices

Area	2008	2009	2010p	Percent Change 2009 to 2010
MSA[1]	137.4	130.5	132.6	1.6
U.S. Average	209.8	175.6	171.7	-2.2

Note: Figures are median sales prices of existing apartment condo-coop homes in thousands of dollars; (p) preliminary; n/a not available; (1) Metropolitan Statistical Area - see Appendix B for areas included
Source: National Association of Realtors, Median Sales Price of Existing Apartment Condo-Coop Homes for Metropolitan Areas, 4th Quarter 2010

Year Housing Structure Built

Area	2000 or Later	1990 -1999	1980 -1989	1970 -1979	1960 -1969	1950 -1959	1940 -1949	Before 1940	Median Year
City	10.7	9.3	18.0	19.0	15.6	15.3	6.1	5.9	1974
MSA[1]	20.5	17.0	20.3	16.1	10.4	8.8	3.3	3.5	1984
U.S.	12.5	14.0	14.2	16.5	11.4	11.3	5.8	14.3	1974

Note: Figures are percentages except for Median Year; (1) Metropolitan Statistical Area - see Appendix B for areas included
Source: U.S. Census Bureau, 2007-2009 American Community Survey 3-Year Estimates

HEALTH

Health Risk Data

Category	MSA[1] (%)	U.S. (%)
Adults who have been told they have high blood pressure	25.4	28.7
Adults who have been told they have high blood cholesterol	41.8	37.5
Adults who have been told they have diabetes[3]	8.3	8.3
Adults who have been told they have arthritis	18.5	26.0
Adults who have been told they currently have asthma	7.2	8.8
Adults who are current smokers	16.3	17.9
Adults who are heavy drinkers[4]	4.3	5.1
Adults who are binge drinkers[5]	7.9	15.8
Adults who are overweight (BMI 25.0 - 29.9)	37.0	36.2
Adults who are obese (BMI 30.0 - 99.8)	26.1	26.9
Adults who participated in any physical activities in the past month	77.4	76.2
Adults 50+ who have ever had a sigmoidoscopy or colonoscopy[2]	59.2	62.2
Women 40+ who have had a mammogram within the past two years[2]	76.5	76.0
Adults age 18–64 who have any kind of health care coverage	76.1	83.1

Note: Data as of 2009 unless otherwise noted; (1) Figures cover the Dallas-Plano-Irving, TX Metropolitan Division - see Appendix B for areas included; (2) Data as of 2008; (3) Figures do not include pregnancy-related, borderline, or pre-diabetes; (4) Heavy drinkers are classified as males having more than two drinks per day or females having more than one drink per day; (5) Binge drinkers are classified as males having five or more drinks on one occasion or females having four or more drinks on one occasion
Source: Centers for Disease Control and Prevention, Behaviorial Risk Factor Surveillance System, SMART: Selected Metropolitan/Micropolitan Area Risk Trends, 2008, 2009

Mortality Rates for the Top 10 Causes of Death in the U.S.

ICD-10[a] Sub-Chapter	ICD-10[a] Code	Age-Adjusted Mortality Rate[1] per 100,000 population	
		County[2]	U.S.
Malignant neoplasms	C00-C97	174.3	180.9
Ischaemic heart diseases	I20-I25	127.6	135.0
Other forms of heart disease	I30-I51	47.6	50.0
Cerebrovascular diseases	I60-I69	50.4	44.1
Chronic lower respiratory diseases	J40-J47	37.1	41.5
Other degenerative diseases of the nervous system	G30-G31	32.3	23.6
Diabetes mellitus	E10-E14	22.8	23.5
Other external causes of accidental injury	W00-X59	21.6	23.5
Organic, including symptomatic, mental disorders	F01-F09	28.6	22.2
Influenza and pneumonia	J09-J18	17.5	18.1

Note: (a) ICD-10 = International Classification of Diseases 10th Revision; (1) Mortality rates are a three year average covering 2005-2007; (2) Figures cover Dallas County
Source: Centers for Disease Control and Prevention, National Center for Health Statistics. Compressed Mortality File 1999-2007. CDC WONDER On-line Database, compiled from Compressed Mortality File 1999-2007 Series 20 No. 2M, 2010.

Mortality Rates for Selected Causes of Death

ICD-10[a] Sub-Chapter	ICD-10[a] Code	Age-Adjusted Mortality Rate[1] per 100,000 population	
		County[2]	U.S.
Assault	X85-Y09	9.9	6.0
Human immunodeficiency virus (HIV) disease	B20-B24	7.8	4.0
Hypertensive diseases	I10-I15	25.3	18.0
Intentional self-harm	X60-X84	9.5	11.0
Malnutrition	E40-E46	1.1	0.8
Obesity and other hyperalimentation	E65-E68	1.6	1.5
Transport accidents	V01-V99	12.1	15.6
Viral hepatitis	B15-B19	2.4	2.1

Note: (a) ICD-10 = International Classification of Diseases 10th Revision; (1) Mortality rates are a three year average covering 2005-2007; (2) Figures cover Dallas County
Source: Centers for Disease Control and Prevention, National Center for Health Statistics. Compressed Mortality File 1999-2007. CDC WONDER On-line Database, compiled from Compressed Mortality File 1999-2007 Series 20 No. 2M, 2010.

Distribution of Physicians and Dentists

Area[1]	Dentists[2]	D.O.[3]	M.D.[4]				
			Total	Family/ General Practice	Pediatrics	Medical Specialties	Surgical Specialties
Local (number)	1,068	425	4,513	371	298	1,651	1,114
Local (rate[5])	4.5	1.8	18.7	1.5	1.2	6.8	4.6
U.S. (rate[5])	4.5	1.9	18.3	2.5	1.4	6.8	4.1

Note: Data as of 2008 unless noted; (1) Local data covers Dallas County; (2) Data as of 2007; (3) Doctor of Osteopathic Medicine; (4) Includes active, non-federal, patient-care, office-based Doctors of Medicine; (5) rate per 10,000 population
Source: Area Resource File (ARF). 2009-2010 Release. U.S. Department of Health and Human Services, Health Resources and Services Administration, Bureau of Health Professions, Rockville, MD, August 2010

Hospitals

Dallas has the following hospitals: 14 general medical and surgical; 2 psychiatric; 3 rehabilitation; 1 heart; 6 long-term acute care; 1 children's general; 1 children's other specialty; 1 children's orthopedic.
AHA Guide to the Healthcare Field 2010

According to *U.S. News,* the Dallas-Plano-Irving, TX Metropolitan Division is home to four of the best hospitals in the U.S.: **Baylor Institute for Rehabilitation**; **Baylor University Medical Center**; **Parkland Memorial Hospital**; **University of Texas Southwestern Medical Center**. The hospitals listed were highly ranked in at least one adult specialty. *U.S. News Online, "America's Best Hospitals 2010-11"*

According to *U.S. News,* the Dallas-Plano-Irving, TX Metropolitan Division is home to two of the best children's hospitals in the U.S.: **Children's Medical Center Dallas**; **Children's Medical Center-Texas Scottish Rite Hospital for Children**. The hospitals listed were highly ranked in at least one pediatric specialty. *U.S. News Online, "America's Best Children's Hospitals 2010-11"*

EDUCATION

Public School District Statistics

District Name	Schls	Pupils	Pupil/ Teacher Ratio	Minority Pupils[1] (%)	Free Lunch Eligible[2] (%)	IEP[3] (%)
Dallas ISD	232	157,352	14.4	95.4	78.4	7.4
Highland Park ISD	7	6,331	15.4	7.0	n/a	8.3

Note: Table includes school districts with 2,000 or more students; (1) Percentage of students that are not non-Hispanic white; (2) Percentage of students that are eligible for the free lunch program; (3) Percentage of students that have an Individualized Education Program.
Source: U.S. Department of Education, National Center for Education Statistics, Common Core of Data, Local Education Agency (School District) Universe Survey: School Year 2008-2009; U.S. Department of Education, National Center for Education Statistics, Common Core of Data, Public Elementary/Secondary School Universe Survey: School Year 2008-2009

Top Public High Schools

High School Name	Index[1]	Rank[1]	Subsidized Lunch (%)[2]	E&E (%)[3]
Booker T. Washington School for the Performing and Visual Arts	3.784	114	29.0	67.0
Highland Park	5.613	38	0.0	76.0
Hillcrest	2.704	333	64.0	20.3
Judge Barefoot Sanders Magnet Center for Public Service	3.521	154	58.0	17.6
Lake Highlands	2.065	672	38.0	26.6
School of Business and Management	3.134	222	68.0	31.3
Science/Engineering Magnet	12.080	4	61.0	100.0
Talented and Gifted	14.938	1	28.0	100.0
White	2.789	303	66.0	28.7
Woodrow Wilson	2.435	436	52.0	27.4

Note: (1) Public schools are ranked according to a ratio that is the number of Advanced Placement, International Baccalaureate, and/or Cambridge tests taken by all students at a school in 2009 divided by the number of graduating seniors. All of the schools on the list have an index of at least 1.000; they are in the top six percent of public schools measured this way. The rankings range from 1 to 1,734; (2) Percentage of students receiving federally subsidized meals; (3) E & E stands for equity and excellence percentage: the portion of all graduating seniors at a school that had at least one passing grade on one AP or IB test; (4) Schools that offer International Baccalaureate or Cambridge exams; (5) School is unranked, but has been identified by Newsweek as one of the nation's most elite public high schools.
Source: Newsweek Online, "Top High Schools 2010"

Highest Level of Education

Area	Less than H.S.	H.S. Diploma	Some College, No Deg.	Associate Degree	Bachelors Degree	Masters Degree	Profess. School Degree	Doctorate Degree
City	30.6	20.8	17.3	4.5	17.2	6.3	2.3	0.9
MSA[1]	18.5	23.3	22.2	6.3	20.3	7.0	1.5	0.9
U.S.	15.3	29.0	20.7	7.5	17.4	7.0	1.9	1.1

Note: Figures are 2010 estimated percentages and cover persons age 25 and over; (1) Metropolitan Statistical Area - see Appendix B for areas included
Source: Claritas, Inc.

Educational Attainment by Race

Area	High School Graduate (%)					Bachelor's Degree (%)				
	Total	White	Black	Asian	Hisp.[2]	Total	White	Black	Asian	Hisp.[2]
City	71.8	94.4	80.2	87.4	41.0	28.1	53.7	13.5	60.9	7.4
MSA[1]	81.9	92.7	86.3	88.2	49.9	30.2	38.0	21.2	56.4	9.9
U.S.	84.9	90.0	80.7	85.5	60.7	27.8	30.9	17.5	49.7	12.7

Note: Figures shown cover persons 25 years old and over; (1) Metropolitan Statistical Area - see Appendix B for areas included; (2) people of Hispanic origin can be of any race
Source: U.S. Census Bureau, 2007-2009 American Community Survey 3-Year Estimates

School Enrollment by Grade and Control

Area	Preschool (%)		Kindergarten (%)		Grades 1 - 4 (%)		Grades 5 - 8 (%)		Grades 9 - 12 (%)	
	Public	Private	Public	Private	Public	Private	Public	Private	Public	Private
City	63.8	36.2	88.5	11.5	89.4	10.6	89.9	10.1	89.8	10.2
MSA[1]	50.2	49.8	88.8	11.2	91.4	8.6	92.1	7.9	92.4	7.6
U.S.	54.3	45.7	86.4	13.6	88.9	11.1	89.1	10.9	90.2	9.8

Note: Figures shown cover persons 3 years old and over; (1) Metropolitan Statistical Area - see Appendix B for areas included
Source: U.S. Census Bureau, 2007-2009 American Community Survey 3-Year Estimates

Average Salaries of Public School Classroom Teachers

Area	2009-10		2010-11		Percent Change 2009-10 to 2010-11	Percent Change 2000-01 to 2010-11
	Dollars	Rank[1]	Dollars	Rank[1]		
Texas	48,261	31	48,261	34	0.00	25.8
U.S. Average	55,202	-	56,069	-	1.57	29.3

Note: (1) State rank ranges from 1 to 51 where 1 indicates highest salary.
Source: National Education Association, Rankings & Estimates: Rankings of the States 2010
and Estimates of School Statistics 2011, December 2010

Higher Education

Four-Year Colleges			Two-Year Colleges			Medical Schools[1]	Law Schools[2]	Voc/ Tech[3]
Public	Private Non-profit	Private For-profit	Public	Private Non-profit	Private For-profit			
1	6	3	3	1	12	1	1	13

Note: Figures cover institutions located within the city limits and include main campuses only; (1) includes
schools accredited by the Liaison Committee on Medical Education and the American Osteopathic Association;
(2) includes American Bar Association-accredited law schools; (3) includes all schools with programs that are
less than 2 years.
Source: National Center for Education Statistics, Integrated Postsecondary Education System (IPEDS) Peer
Analysis System, 2010-11; U.S. News & World Report, Medical School Directory, 2011; U.S. News & World
Report, Law School Directory, 2011

According to *U.S. News & World Report,* the Dallas-Plano-Irving, TX Metropolitan Division
is home to two of the top 197 national universities in the U.S.: **Southern Methodist
University** (#56); **University of Texas—Dallas** (#143). The rankings are based on
quantitative measurements such as peer assessment, retention, faculty resources, student
selectivity, financial resources, graduation rate, and alumni giving rate. *U.S. News & World
Report, "America's Best Colleges 2011"*

According to *U.S. News & World Report,* the Dallas-Plano-Irving, TX Metropolitan Division
is home to one of the top 50 law schools in the U.S.: **Southern Methodist University
(Dedman)** (#50). The rankings are based on a weighted average of 10 measures of quality:
peer assessment score; assessment score by lawyers/judges; median LSAT scores; median
undergrad GPA; acceptance rate; employment rates for graduates; bar passage rate; faculty
resources; expenditures per student; student/faculty ratio; and library resources. *U.S. News &
World Report, "America's Best Law Schools 2011"*

According to *Forbes,* the Dallas-Plano-Irving, TX Metropolitan Division is home to one of
the top 75 business schools in the U.S.: **SMU (Cox)** (#33). The rankings are based on the
return on investment that graduates of the Class of 2004 received (median salary five years
after graduation). *Forbes, "Best Business Schools," August 5, 2009*

**PRESIDENTIAL
ELECTION**

2008 Presidential Election Results

Area	Obama	McCain	Nader	Other
Dallas County	57.2	41.9	0.1	0.9
U.S.	52.9	45.6	0.6	0.9

Note: Results are percentages and may not add to 100% due to rounding
Source: Dave Leip's Atlas of U.S. Presidential Elections, www.uselectionatlas.org

EMPLOYERS

Major Employers

Company Name	Industry	Type of Site
Associates Corp North America	Personal credit institutions	Headquarters
Associates First Capital Corp	Mortgage bankers and correspondents	Headquarters
Baylor University Medical Ctr	General medical and surgical hospitals	Headquarters
Dallas Cnty Commissioners Crt	Executive offices	Branch
Dallas County Sheriffs Dept	Police protection	Branch
Emergency Department	General medical and surgical hospitals	Branch
HP Enterprise Services	Data processing and preparation	Headquarters
JC Penney	Department stores	Headquarters
Lockheed Martin Missiles	Aircraft	Branch
North Texas Hcs	Administration of veterans' affairs	Branch
Odyssey Healthcare	Skilled nursing care facilities	Headquarters
Palm Harbor Homes I	Prefabricated wood buildings	Single
Parkland Health & Hospital Sys	General medical and surgical hospitals	Headquarters
Presbyterian Hospital Dallas	General medical and surgical hospitals	Branch
Romanos Macaroni Grill	Eating places	Single
SFG Management Ltd Lblty Co	Fluid milk	Single
South Central Region	Detective and armored car services	Branch
Southwest Airlines	Air transportation, scheduled	Headquarters
Teaching Assistance Office	Colleges and universities	Branch
Texas Instruments	Semiconductors and related devices	Headquarters
The University of Texas At El	Accident and health insurance	Headquarters
Verizon	Telephone communication, except radio	Branch
Verizon	Business consulting, nec	Branch
Verizon Business	Telephone communication, except radio	Branch

Note: Companies shown are located within the Dallas metropolitan area; nec = not elsewhere classified.
Source: www.zapdata.com, January 2011

Best Companies to Work For

Balfour Beatty Construction; TDIndustries, headquartered in Dallas, are among the "100 Best Companies to Work For." To pick the 100 Best Companies to Work For, *Fortune* partnered with the Great Place to Work Institute. Three hundred eleven companies participated in this year's survey. Most of a company's score (two-thirds) is based on the results of the Institute's Trust Index survey, which is sent to a random sample of employees from each company. The survey asks questions related to their attitudes about management's credibility, job satisfaction, and camaraderie. The other third of the scoring is based on the company's responses to the Institute's Culture Audit, which includes detailed questions about pay and benefit programs, and a series of open-ended questions about hiring practices, internal communication, training, recognition programs, and diversity efforts. Any company that is at least seven years old with more than 1,000 U.S. employees is eligible. *Fortune, "100 Best Companies to Work For," February 7, 2011*

Texas Instruments, headquartered in Dallas, is among the "100 Best Companies for Working Mothers." Criteria: workforce profile; benefits; child care; women's issues and advancement; flexible work; paid time off and leaves; company culture; and work-life programs. This year *Working Mother* gave particular weight to child care, flexibility, and paid time off and leaves. *Working Mother, "100 Best Companies 2010"*

Comerica Bank; Southwest Airlines, headquartered in Dallas, are among the "100 Best Places to Work in IT." To qualify, companies, both public and private, had to have a minimum of 50 IT employees. Companies were selected based on average salary and bonus increases, the percentage of IT employees receiving promotions, IT staff turnover rates, training and development programs, and the percentage of women and minorities in IT staff and management positions. In addition, information was collected on how the organizations reward outstanding performance, how their retention programs are structured and what benefits they offer. *Computerworld, "100 Best Places to Work in IT 2010"*

AT&T; Texas Instruments, located in Dallas, are among the "Top Companies for Executive Women." To be named to the list, companies with a minimum of two women on the board complete a comprehensive application that focuses on the number of women in senior ranks (compared to men and to the company population). In addition to assessing corporate programs and policies dedicated to advancing women, NAFE measured results, examining the number of women in each company overall, in senior management, and on its board of directors. They drew particular attention to the number of women with profit-and-loss responsibility. *National Association for Female Executives, "2011 NAFE Top Companies for Executive Women"*

PUBLIC SAFETY

Crime Rate

Area	All Crimes	Violent Crimes				Property Crimes		
		Murder	Forcible Rape	Robbery	Aggrav. Assault	Burglary	Larceny -Theft	Motor Vehicle Theft
City	6,323.1	12.9	37.6	426.3	315.4	1,505.7	3,214.9	810.3
Suburbs[1]	3,327.4	2.3	22.8	73.2	136.4	736.1	2,105.4	251.2
Metro[2]	4,220.1	5.4	27.2	178.4	189.7	965.5	2,436.0	417.8
U.S.	3,465.5	5.0	28.7	133.0	262.8	716.3	2,060.9	258.8

Note: Figures are crimes per 100,000 population; (1) All areas within the metro area that are located outside the city limits; (2) Metropolitan Division - see Appendix B for areas included
Source: FBI Uniform Crime Reports, 2009

Hate Crimes

Area	Number of Quarters Reported	Bias Motivation				
		Race	Religion	Sexual Orientation	Ethnicity	Disability
City	4	3	2	3	3	0

Source: Federal Bureau of Investigation, Hate Crime Statistics 2009

Identity Theft Consumer Complaints

Area	Complaints	Complaints per 100,000 Population	Rank[2]
MSA[1]	6,920	112.6	36
U.S.	250,854	81.3	-

Note: (1) Metropolitan Statistical Area - see Appendix B for areas included; (2) Rank ranges from 1 to 384 where 1 indicates greatest number of complaints per 100,000 population
Source: Federal Trade Commission, Consumer Sentinel Network Data Book for January - December 2010

RECREATION

Culture

Dance[1]	Theatre[1]	Instrumental Music[1]	Vocal Music[1]	Series/ Festivals	Museums	Zoos and Aquariums[2]
2	16	7	3	6	18	2

Note: (1) Number of professional performing groups; (2) AZA-accredited
Source: The Grey House Performing Arts Directory, 2011-2012; Official Museum Directory, 2010; American Association of Museums, AAM Member Museums, March 2011; Association of Zoos & Aquariums, AZA Member Zoos & Aquariums, May 2011

Professional Sports Teams

Team Name	League
Dallas Cowboys	National Football League (NFL)
Dallas Mavericks	National Basketball Association (NBA)
Dallas Stars	National Hockey League (NHL)
FC Dallas	Major League Soccer (MLS)
Texas Rangers	Major League Baseball (MLB)

Note: Includes teams located in the Dallas-Fort Worth metro area.
Source: Original research

CLIMATE

Average and Extreme Temperatures

Temperature	Jan	Feb	Mar	Apr	May	Jun	Jul	Aug	Sep	Oct	Nov	Dec	Yr.
Extreme High (°F)	85	90	100	100	101	112	111	109	107	101	91	87	112
Average High (°F)	55	60	68	76	84	92	96	96	89	79	67	58	77
Average Temp. (°F)	45	50	57	66	74	82	86	86	79	68	56	48	67
Average Low (°F)	35	39	47	56	64	72	76	75	68	57	46	38	56
Extreme Low (°F)	-2	9	12	30	39	53	58	58	42	24	16	0	-2

Note: Figures cover the years 1945-1993
Source: National Climatic Data Center, International Station Meteorological Climate Summary, 9/96

Average Precipitation/Snowfall/Humidity

Precip./Humidity	Jan	Feb	Mar	Apr	May	Jun	Jul	Aug	Sep	Oct	Nov	Dec	Yr.
Avg. Precip. (in.)	1.9	2.3	2.6	3.8	4.9	3.4	2.1	2.3	2.9	3.3	2.3	2.1	33.9
Avg. Snowfall (in.)	1	1	Tr	Tr	0	0	0	0	0	Tr	Tr	Tr	3
Avg. Rel. Hum. 6am (%)	78	77	75	77	82	81	77	76	80	79	78	77	78
Avg. Rel. Hum. 3pm (%)	53	51	47	49	51	48	43	41	46	46	48	51	48

Note: Figures cover the years 1945-1993; Tr = Trace amounts (<0.05 in. of rain; <0.5 in. of snow)
Source: National Climatic Data Center, International Station Meteorological Climate Summary, 9/96

Weather Conditions

Temperature			Daytime Sky			Precipitation		
10°F & below	32°F & below	90°F & above	Clear	Partly cloudy	Cloudy	0.01 inch or more precip.	0.1 inch or more snow/ice	Thunder-storms
1	34	102	108	160	97	78	2	49

Note: Figures are average number of days per year and cover the years 1945-1993
Source: National Climatic Data Center, International Station Meteorological Climate Summary, 9/96

HAZARDOUS WASTE

Superfund Sites

Dallas has one hazardous waste site on the EPA's Superfund Final National Priorities List: **RSR Corp.** *U.S. Environmental Protection Agency, Final National Priorities List, April 1, 2011*

AIR & WATER QUALITY

Air Quality Index

Area	Percent of Days when Air Quality was...[2]				AQI Statistics	
	Good	Moderate	Unhealthy for Sensitive Groups	Unhealthy	Maximum	Median
Area[1]	71.6	26.1	2.3	0.0	145	43

Note: The Air Quality Index (AQI) is an index for reporting daily air quality. EPA calculates the AQI for five major air pollutants regulated by the Clean Air Act: ground-level ozone, particle pollution (also known as particulate matter), carbon monoxide, sulfur dioxide, and nitrogen dioxide. The AQI runs from 0 to 500. The higher the AQI value, the greater the level of air pollution and the greater the health concern. There are six AQI categories: "Good" The AQI is between 0 and 50. Air quality is considered satisfactory; "Moderate" The AQI is between 51 and 100. Air quality is acceptable; "Unhealthy for Sensitive Groups" When AQI values are between 101 and 150, members of sensitive groups may experience health effects; "Unhealthy" When AQI values are between 151 and 200 everyone may begin to experience health effects; "Very Unhealthy" AQI values between 201 and 300 trigger a health alert; "Hazardous" AQI values over 300 trigger health warnings of emergency conditions; (1) Data covers Dallas County; (2) Based on 306 days with AQI data in 2008; The EPA has suspended data updates while it assesses its data systems, including AirData reports and maps.
Source: U.S. Environmental Protection Agency, AirData Report, 2008

Air Quality Index Pollutants

Area	Percent of Days when AQI Pollutant was...[2]					
	Carbon Monoxide	Nitrogen Dioxide	Ozone	Sulfur Dioxide	Particulate Matter 2.5	Particulate Matter 10
Area[1]	0.3	0.0	69.0	0.0	30.7	0.0

Note: The Air Quality Index (AQI) is an index for reporting daily air quality. EPA calculates the AQI for five major air pollutants regulated by the Clean Air Act: ground-level ozone, particle pollution (also known as particulate matter), carbon monoxide, sulfur dioxide, and nitrogen dioxide. The AQI runs from 0 to 500. The higher the AQI value, the greater the level of air pollution and the greater the health concern; (1) Data covers Dallas County; (2) Based on 306 days with AQI data in 2008; The EPA has suspended data updates while it assesses its data systems, including AirData reports and maps.
Source: U.S. Environmental Protection Agency, AirData Report, 2008

Air Quality Index Trends

Area	Trend Sites (days)								All Sites (days)
	2002	2003	2004	2005	2006	2007	2008	2009	2009
MSA[1]	40	40	32	56	39	16	20	19	33

Note: Figures are the number of days the AQI value exceeded 100 in a given year. An AQI value greater than 100 indicates that air quality would have been in the unhealthful range on that day. Data from exceptional events are included. These counts are presented in two ways. First, the counts are based on sites having an adequate record of monitoring data during the trend period (trend sites). These counts represent the relative change in the number of days with AQI values greater than 100. In the last column, the counts are based on all sites with data in the most recent year (because it is possible for a site to have data in the most recent year but not enough data to be a trend site); (1) Data covers the Dallas-Fort Worth-Arlington, TX Metropolitan Statistical Area - see Appendix B for areas included
Source: U.S. Environmental Protection Agency, Office of Air and Radiation, Air Quality Index Information, "Number of Days with Air Quality Index Values Greater than 100 and Trend Sites, 1990-2009, and at All Sites in 2009"

Maximum Air Pollutant Concentrations

	Particulate Matter 10 (ug/m^3)	Particulate Matter 2.5 (ug/m^3)	Ozone (ppm)	Carbon Monoxide (ppm)	Sulfur Dioxide (ppm)	Nitrogen Dioxide (ppm)	Lead (ug/m^3)
MSA[1] Level	43	38	0.091	2	0.004	0.012	0.65
NAAQS[2]	150	35	0.075	9	0.140	0.053	0.15
Met NAAQS[2]	Yes	No	No	Yes	Yes	Yes	No

Note: Data from exceptional events are not included; (1) Data covers the Dallas-Fort Worth-Arlington, TX Metropolitan Statistical Area - see Appendix B for areas included; (2) National Ambient Air Quality Standards; n/a not available; (a) Localized impact from an industrial source in Dallas. Concentration from highest nonpoint source site is 0.14 ug/m^3 in Collin County
Concentrations: Particulate Matter 10 (coarse particulate) - highest second maximum 24-hour concentration; Particulate Matter 2.5 (fine particulate) - highest 98th percentile 24-hour concentration; Ozone - highest fourth daily maximum 8-hour concentration; Carbon Monoxide - highest second maximum non-overlapping 8-hour concentration; Sulfur Dioxide - highest second maximum 24-hour concentration; Nitrogen Dioxide - highest arithmetic mean concentration; Lead - maximum running 3-month average
Units: ppm = parts per million; ug/m^3 = micrograms per cubic meter
Source: U.S. Environmental Protection Agency, CBSA Factbook 2009, Air Quality Statistics by City, 2009

Drinking Water

Water System Name	Pop. Served	Primary Water Source Type	Violations[1]	
			Health Based	Monitoring/ Reporting
Dallas Water Utility	1,280,500	Surface	0	1

Note: (1) Based on violation data from January 1, 2010 to December 31, 2010 (includes unresolved violations from earlier years)
Source: U.S. Environmental Protection Agency, Office of Ground Water and Drinking Water, Safe Drinking Water Information System (based on data extracted May 9, 2011)

El Paso, Texas

Background

El Paso is so named because it sits in a spectacular pass through the Franklin Mountains, at an average elevation of 3,700 feet and in direct view of peaks that rise to 7,200 feet. El Paso is the fourth-largest city in Texas. It lies just south of New Mexico on the Rio Grande and just north of Juarez, Mexico.

The early Spanish explorer Alvar Nunez Cabeza de Vaca (circa 1530) probably passed through this area, but the city was named in 1598 by Juan de Onante, who dubbed it El Paso del Rio del Norte, or The Pass at the River of the North. It was also Onante who declared the area Spanish, on the authority of King Philip II, but a mission was not established until 1649. For some time, El Paso del Norte was the seat of government for northern Mexico, but settlement in and around the present-day city was sparse for many years.

This had changed considerably by 1807, when Zebulon A. Pike, a United States Army officer, was interned in El Paso after being convicted of trespassing on Spanish territory. He found the area pleasant and well tended, with many irrigated fields and vineyards and a thriving trade in brandy and wine. In spite of Pike's stay there, though, El Paso remained for many years a largely Mexican region, escaping most of the military action connected to the Texas Revolution.

In the wake of the Mexican War (1846-1848) and in response to the California gold rush in 1849, El Paso emerged as a significant way station on the road West. A federal garrison, Fort Bliss, was established there in 1849, and was briefly occupied by Confederate sympathizers in 1862. Federal forces quickly reoccupied the fort, however, and the area was firmly controlled by Union armies. El Paso was incorporated in 1873, and after 1881, growth accelerated considerably with the building of rail links through the city, giving rise to ironworks, mills, and breweries.

During the Mexican Revolution (1911), El Paso was an important and disputed city, with Pancho Villa himself a frequent visitor, and many of his followers residents of the town. Mexico's national history, in fact, continued to affect El Paso until 1967 when, by way of settling a historic border dispute, 437 acres of the city was ceded to Mexico. Much of the disputed area on both sides of the border was made into parkland. The U.S. National Parks Service maintains the Chamizal Park on the U.S. side and it plays host to a variety of community events during the year including the Chamizal Film Festival and the summer concert series, Music Under the Stars.

One of the major points of entry to the U.S. from Mexico, El Paso is a vitally important international city and a burgeoning center of rail, road, and air transportation. During the 1990s, the city's economy shifted more toward a service-oriented economy and away from a manufacturing base.

Transportation services and motor freight transportation and warehousing has been increasing, and tourism is becoming a growing segment of the economy. Government and military are also sources of employment, with Ft. Bliss being the largest Air Defense Artillery Training Center in the world. The city hosts the University of Texas at El Paso, and a community college. Cultural amenities include the Tigua Indian Cultural Center, a Wilderness Park Museum, the El Paso Zoo, museums, a symphony orchestra, a ballet company, and many theaters. The city's "Wild West" qualities have long made it a popular destination for musicians-many of whom have recorded albums at El Paso's Sonic Ranch recording studio.

A downtown renovation project began in 2006, with the goal of increasing El Paso's aesthetic appeal. The first stages of this project included building an open-air mall and "lifestyle center" in the city's central area. A Doubletree by Hilton Hotel was completed in 2009, along with renovations of several historic downtown buildings.

In August 2007, El Paso became the site of the world's largest inland desalination plant, designed to produce 27.5 million gallons of fresh water daily making it a critical component of the region's water portfolio.

The weather in El Paso is of the mountain-desert type, with very little precipitation. Summers are hot, humidity is low and winters are mild. However, temperatures in the flat Rio Grande Valley nearby are notably cooler at night year-round. There is plenty of sunshine and clear skies 202 days of the year.

Rankings

General Rankings

- El Paso was ranked #165 out of 375 metro areas in *Cities Ranked & Rated*. Criteria: cost of living; climate; crime; transportation; economy and jobs; education; arts and culture; health and healthcare; leisure; quality of life. *Cities Ranked & Rated, 2nd Edition, 2007*

- El Paso was ranked #127 out of 379 metro areas in *Places Rated Almanac*. Criteria: health care; education; recreation; transportation; ambience; climate; crime; housing costs; jobs. *Places Rated Almanac, 7th Edition, 2007*

- *Men's Health Living* ranked 100 U.S. cities in terms of quality of life. El Paso was ranked #63 and received a grade of C-. Criteria: number of fitness facilities; air quality; number of physicians; male/female ratio; education levels; household income; cost of living. *Men's Health Living, Spring 2008*

- El Paso was selected as an "All-America City" by the National Civic League. The All-America City Award recognizes civic excellence and annually honors 10 communities that best exemplify the spirit of grassroots citizen involvement and cross-sector collaborative problem solving. *National Civic League, 2010 All-America City Awards*

Business/Finance Rankings

- El Paso was identified as one of the 20 strongest-performing metro areas during the recession and recovery from December 2007 through December 2010. Criteria: percent change in employment; percentage point change in unemployment rate; percent change in gross metropolitan product; percent change in House Price Index. *Brookings Institution, MetroMonitor: Tracking Economic Recession and Recovery in America's 100 Largest Metropolitan Areas, March 2011*

- The El Paso metro area was identified as one of the most debt-ridden places in America by credit reporting agency Equifax. The metro area was ranked #5. Criteria: proportion of average yearly income owed to credit card companies. *Equifax, "The Most Debt-Ridden Cities," January 29, 2011*

- El Paso was identified as one of the "Happiest Cities to Work" by CareerBliss.com, an online community for career advancement. The city ranked #7 out of 10. CareerBliss.com conducted independent company reviews from employees all over the country to collect data on eight specific factors of workplace happiness: growth opportunities, compensation, benefits, work-life balance, career advancement, senior management, job security, and whether the employee would recommend the company to others. The numbers were combined to find an average rating of overall workplace happiness for each city. *CareerBliss.com, "Happiest and Unhappiest Cities to Work," February 1, 2011*

- *American City Business Journals* ranked America's 261 largest cities in terms of their resident's wealth. El Paso ranked #244. Criteria: per capita income; median household income; percentage of households with annual incomes of $200,000 or more; median home value. *American City Business Journals, www.bizjournals.com, "Where the Money Is: America's Wealth Centers," August 18, 2008*

- The El Paso metro area appeared on the Milken Institute "2010 Best Performing Metros" list. Rank: #9 out of 200 large metro areas. Criteria: job growth; wage and salary growth; high-tech output growth. *Milken Institute, "2010 Best Performing Metros"*

- The El Paso metro area was selected as one of the best cities for entrepreneurs in America by *Inc. Magazine*. Criteria: job-growth data for 335 metro areas was analyzed for: recent growth trend (the current and prior year's employment growth rates, with the current year emphasized); mid-term growth (the average annual 2002-2007 growth rate); long-term trend (the sum of the 2002-2007 and 1996-2001 employment growth rates multiplied by the ratio of the 1996-2001 growth rate over the 2002-2007 growth rate); current year growth. The El Paso metro area ranked #26 among mid-sized metro areas and #96 overall. *Inc. Magazine, "The Best Cities for Doing Business," July 2008*

- *Forbes* ranked the 200 most populous metro areas in the U.S. in terms of the "Best Places for Business and Careers." The El Paso metro area was ranked #113. Criteria: 12 metrics including costs (business and living), job growth (past and projected), income growth, educational attainment, projected economic growth, crime, cultural and recreational opportunities, net migration patterns, percentage of subprime mortgages handed out over a three-year period, and the number of highly ranked four-year colleges. *Forbes, "Best Places for Business and Careers," April 14, 2010*

Children/Family Rankings

- The El Paso metro area was selected as one of the "Best Cities for Relocating Families" by Worldwide ERC and Primacy Relocation. The 2008 study looked at nearly 50 factors important to relocating families including: recent job growth; nearby top-ranked colleges; in-state tuition for four-year public colleges; population growth since 2000; pediatricians per 100,000 population; and a Green Living index. *Worldwide ERC and Primacy Relocation, "2008 Best Cities for Relocating Families"*

- *Fit Pregnancy* magazine ranked the 50 best U.S. cities in which to have a baby. El Paso was ranked #34. Criteria: access to hospitals and doctors; affordability; birthing options; breastfeeding; child care; fertility laws/resources; maternal and infant health risk; parks/stroller friendliness; safety. *Fit Pregnancy, "The Best Cities in America to Have a Baby 2008"*

Dating/Romance Rankings

- El Paso appeared on *Men's Health's* list of the most sex-happy cities in America. The city ranked #27 of 100. Criteria: condom sales; birth rates; sex toy sales; rates of chlamydia, gonorrhea, and syphilis. *Men's Health, "America's Most Sex-Happy Cities," October 2010*

- *Men's Health* ranked 100 U.S. cities in terms of best (and worst) marriages. El Paso was ranked #98 (#1 = worst marriages). Criteria: rate of failed marriages; stringency of divorce laws; percentage of population who've split; number of licensed marriage and family therapists. *Men's Health, "Splitsville, USA," May 2010*

- The El Paso metro area was selected as one of the "Best Cities for Relocating Singles" by Worldwide ERC and Primacy Relocation. The area ranked #79 out of the 100 largest metro areas in the U.S. Areas were selected based on the following criteria: recent job growth; recent singles population growth; overall population growth; affordable rental housing; cost-of-living index; expanded arts and recreation opportunities; ratio of single men and single women; affordability of quality higher education (including state residency requirements); diversity index; climate; population density. *Worldwide ERC and Primacy Relocation, "2008 Best Cities for Relocating Singles"*

Education Rankings

- El Paso was selected as one of "America's Most Literate Cities." The city ranked #69 out of the 75 largest U.S. cities. Criteria: number of booksellers; library resources; Internet resources; educational attainment; periodical publishing resources; newspaper circulation. *Central Connecticut State University, "America's Most Literate Cities 2010"*

- El Paso was identified as one of the 100 "smartest" metro areas in the U.S. The area ranked #96. Criteria: the editors rated the collective brainpower of the 100 largest metro area in the U.S based on their residents' educational attainment. *American City Business Journals, www.bizjournals.com, April 14, 2008*

- El Paso was identified as one of "America's Brainiest Bastions" by *Portfolio.com.* The metro area ranked #186 out of 200. Portfolio.com analyzed levels of educational attainment in the nation's 200 largest metropolitan areas. The editors established scores for five levels of educational attainment, based on relative earning power of adult workers age 25 or older. Scores were determined by comparing the median income for all workers with the median income for those workers at a specified educational level. *Portfolio.com, "America's Brainiest Bastions," December 1, 2010*

Environmental Rankings

- El Paso was selected as one of 22 "Smarter Cities" for energy by the Natural Resources Defense Council." The city appeared as one of 12 cities in the large city (population 250,000 and over) category. Criteria: investment in green power; energy efficiency measures; conservation. *Natural Resources Defense Council, "2010 Smarter Cities," July 19, 2010*

- 100 of the largest metro areas in the U.S. were analyzed in terms of their current drought severity. The El Paso metro area ranked #95 (#1 = driest). The rankings were based on statistics such as long-term precipitation trends and patterns and the Palmer drought indices. *Sperling's BestPlaces, www.BestPlaces.net, "America's Drought-Riskiest Cities," November 2007*

- The El Paso metro area appeared in *Country Home's* "Best Green Places" report. The area ranked #156 out of 379. Criteria: official energy policies; green power; green buildings; availability of fresh, locally grown food. *Country Home, "Best Green Places," 2008*

Health/Fitness Rankings

- El Paso was selected as one of the 25 fattest cities in America by *Men's Fitness Online*. It ranked #7 out of America's 50 largest cities. Criteria: fitness centers and sport stores; nutrition; sports participation; TV viewing; overweight/sedentary; junk food; air quality; geography; commute; parks and open space; city recreational facilities; access to healthcare; motivation; mayor and city initiatives; state obesity initiatives. *Men's Fitness Online, 2009 Fittest/Fattest Cities*

- El Paso was identified as a "2011 Asthma Capital." The area ranked #50 out of the nation's 100 largest metropolitan areas. Twelve factors were used to identify the most challenging places to live for people with asthma: estimated prevalence; self-reported prevalence; crude death rate for asthma; annual pollen score; annual air quality; public smoking laws; number of board-certified asthma specialists; school inhaler access laws; rescue medication use; controller medication use; uninsured rate; poverty rate. *Asthma and Allergy Foundation of America, "2011 Asthma Capitals"*

- El Paso was identified as a 2009 "Spring Allergy Capital." The area ranked #68 out of 100. Three groups of factors were used to identify the most severe cities for people with allergies during the spring season: annual pollen levels; medicine utilization; access to board-certified allergists. *Asthma and Allergy Foundation of America, "Spring Allergy Capitals 2009"*

- El Paso was identified as a 2010 "Fall Allergy Capital." The area ranked #35 out of 100. Three groups of factors were used to identify the most severe cities for people with allergies during the fall season: annual pollen levels; medicine utilization; access to board-certified allergists. *Asthma and Allergy Foundation of America, "Fall Allergy Capitals 2010"*

- *Men's Health* ranked 100 U.S. cities in terms of the quality of their tap water. El Paso was ranked #73 and received a grade of C. Criteria: levels of total coliform bacteria, arsenic, lead, total trihalomethanes (linked to cancer), and halo-acetic acids; number of EPA water-system violations from 1995 to 2005. *Men's Health, March 2007*

- Ortho-McNeil Neurologics, in partnership with Sperling's BestPlaces, analyzed 110 metro areas and identified those U.S. cities with the highest prevalence of factors that are most commonly associated with migraine headaches. The El Paso metro area ranked #107. Criteria: number of migraine-related drug prescriptions per capita; lifestyle factors that can contribute to migraines; environmental factors that can trigger migraines; and consumption of migraine-triggering foods. *Ortho-McNeil Neurologics, "America's Migraine Hot Spots," March 14, 2006*

- *Men's Health* ranked 100 U.S. cities in terms of cities "Where the Food is Sickening." El Paso was ranked #72 and received a grade of D+. The magazine arrived at their ratings by looking at data compiled by the Community Health Status Indicator Project to determine outbreaks of E. coli, salmonella-, and shigella-related infections. They then checked the CDC's Wonder database to see how many people died from tainted food. Finally, the magazine found out which states have adopted the current version of the FDA's uniform Food Code, which contains the most up-to-date rules for keeping restaurant kitchens clean. *Men's Health, October 2005*

- *Men's Health* examined the nation's largest 100 cities and identified the cities with the best and worst teeth. El Paso was ranked among the ten worst at #6. Criteria: annual dentist visits; canceled appointments; regular flossers; fluoride usage; dental extractions. *Men's Health, April 2008*

- Scarborough Research, a leading market research firm, identified the top local markets for diabetes medication purchasers. The El Paso DMA (Designated Market Area) ranked in the top 13 with 10% of consumers reporting that they purchased medication for diabetes within the past 12 months. *Scarborough Research, March 19, 2007*

- The El Paso metro area appeared in the 2010 Gallup-Healthways Well-Being Index. The index, based on interviews with more than 353,000 Americans during 2009, asked individuals to assess their jobs, finances, physical health, emotional state of mind and communities. The metro area ranked #70 out of 162. Criteria: life evaluation; emotional health; work environment; physical health; healthy behaviors; basic access (basic needs optimal for a healthy life, such as access to food and medicine, having health insurance and feeling safe while walking at night). *Gallup-Healthways, "Well-Being Index 2010"*

Real Estate Rankings

- *Fortune* ranked the 100 largest metro areas in the U.S. in terms of projected median home price change in 2010. The El Paso metro area ranked #33. *Fortune, "The 2010 Housing Outlook," December 9, 2009*

- El Paso appeared on ApartmentRatings.com "Top Cities for Renters" list in 2009." The area ranked #75. Overall satisfaction ratings were ranked using thousands of user submitted scores for hundreds of apartment complexes located in the 100 most populated U.S. municipalities. *ApartmentRatings.com, "2009 Renter Satisfaction Rankings"*

- The nation's largest metro areas were analyzed in terms of the percentage of households entering some stage of foreclosure in 2010. The El Paso metro area ranked #193 out of 206 (#1 = highest foreclosure rate). *RealtyTrac, 2010 Year-End Metropolitan Foreclosure Market Report, January 27, 2011*

- The Center for Housing Policy ranked 210 U.S metropolitan areas by the fair market rent for a two-bedroom unit. The El Paso metro area was ranked #208. (#1 = most expensive) with a rent of $598. Criteria: Fair Market Rent (FMR) in effect during the fourth quarter of 2009 based on HUD's fiscal year 2010 FMRs. *The Center for Housing Policy, "Paycheck to Paycheck: Most to Least Expensive Rental Markets in 2009"*

- The El Paso metro area was identified as one of the markets with the best expected performance in home prices over the next 12 months. *Local Market Monitor, "First Quarter Home Price Forecast for Largest US Markets," March 2, 2011*

Safety Rankings

- Symantec, the makers of Norton, in partnership with Sperling's BestPlaces, ranked the 50 largest cities in the U.S. in terms of their vulnerability to cybercrime. The city ranked #49. Criteria: number of cyberattacks and potential infections; level of Internet access; expenditures on computer hardware and software; wireless hotspots; broadband connectivity; Internet usage; online purchases. *Symantec, "10 Riskiest Cities for Cybercrime," March 22, 2010*

- Farmers Insurance Group of Companies, in partnership with Sperling's BestPlaces, ranked 379 metro areas and identified the "Most Secure U.S. Place to Live." The El Paso metro area ranked #8 out of the top 20 in the large metro area category (500,000 or more residents). Criteria: crime statistics; extreme weather; risk of natural disasters; housing depreciation; foreclosures; environmental hazards; terrorist threats; air quality; life expectancy; job loss numbers. *Farmers Insurance Group, "Most Secure U.S. Places to Live 2010"*

- Allstate ranked the 200 largest cities in America in terms of driver safety. El Paso ranked #77. In addition, drivers were 2.2% more likely to have had an accident compared to the national average. Allstate researchers analyzed internal property damage reported claims over a two-year period (from January 2007 to December 2008) to ensure the findings would not be affected by external influences such as weather or road construction. A weighted average of the two-year numbers determined the annual percentages. The report defines an auto crash as any collision resulting in a property damage claim. *Allstate, "The 2010 Allstate America's Best Drivers Report™"*

- El Paso was identified as one of the safest large cities in America by CQ Press. All 34 cities with populations of 500,000 or more that reported crime rates in 2009 for murder, rape, robbery, aggravated assault, burglary, and motor vehicle thefts were ranked. The city ranked #1 out of the top 10. *CQ Press, City Crime Rankings 2010-2011*

- The National Insurance Crime Bureau ranked 366 metro areas in the U.S. in terms of per capita rates of vehicle theft. The El Paso metro area ranked #27 (#1 = highest rate). Criteria: number of vehicle theft offenses per 100,000 inhabitants. *National Insurance Crime Bureau, "Hot Spots," May 17, 2010*

Sports/Recreation Rankings

- El Paso appeared on the *Sporting News* list of the "Best Sports Cities" for 2010. The area ranked #101 out of 402 cities in the U.S. *Sporting News* takes a 12-month snapshot, roughly October to October, of each city's sports, putting a heavy premium on regular-season won-lost records (from the most recently completed season). Other criteria include: playoff berths, bowl appearances and tournament bids; championships; applicable power ratings; quality of competition; overall fan fervor as measured in part by attendance as percentage of venue capacity; abundance of teams (rewarding quality over quantity); stadium and arena quality; ticket availability and prices; franchise ownership; and marquee appeal of athletes. *Sporting News, "Best Sports Cities 2010," October, 2010*

- Scarborough Research, a leading market research firm, identified the top local markets for avid NBA fans. The El Paso DMA (Designated Market Area) ranked in the top 10 with 13% of consumers 18 years and over reporting that they are "very interested in the NBA." *Scarborough Research, April 24, 2006*

- *Golf Digest* ranked 330 metro areas in the U.S. in terms of golf. The El Paso metro area was ranked #203. Criteria: access to golf; weather; value of golf; and quality of golf. *Golf Digest, "Metro Golf Rankings," August 2005*

Technology Rankings

- Scarborough Research, a leading market research firm, identified the El Paso DMA (Designated Market Area) as one of the top markets for text messaging with more than 50% of cell phone subscribers age 18+ utilizing the text messaging feature on their phone. *Scarborough Research, November 24, 2008*

Women/Minorities Rankings

- El Paso was ranked #75 out of 100 metro areas in *SELF Magazine's* ranking of America's healthiest places for women." A panel of experts came up with more than 50 criteria including death and disease rates, environmental indicators, community resources, and lifestyle habits. *SELF Magazine, "Secrets of America's Healthiest Women," December 2008*

Miscellaneous Rankings

- The El Paso metro area appeared in AutoMD.com's ranking of the "Best and Worst Cities for Auto Repair." The metro area ranked #13 (#1 is best). The 50 most-populated metro areas in the U.S. were ranked on three critical factors: repair affordability; price disparity range; shop integrity factor. *AutoMD.com, "Advocacy for Repair Shop Fairness Report," February 24, 2010*

- *Men's Health* examined the nation's largest 100 cities and identified "America's Most Political Cities." El Paso was ranked among the ten least political at #3. Criteria: percentage of active registered voters; percentage of ballots counted of active registration; percentage of income donated to 2008 presidential election; campaign spending; percentage of registrants who voted in the 2008 primaries; percentage of voters in the 2004/2006 Senate election; percentage of voters in the 2004-2007 gubernatorial election. *Men's Health, "Ranking America's Cities: America's Most Political Cities," October 2008*

- El Paso appeared on Procter & Gamble's list of the "Top-20 All-Time Sweatiest Cities." The city was ranked #13. The rankings are based on computer simulations of the amount of sweat a person of average height and weight would produce walking around for an hour in the average temperatures during the summer months, based on historical weather data during June, July and August from 2001-2008 for each city. *Procter & Gamble, Old Spice Press Release, "Top-20 All-Time Sweatiest Cities," July 1, 2009*

Business Environment

CITY FINANCES

City Government Finances

Component	2008 ($000)	2008 ($ per capita)
Total Revenues	885,260	1,459
Total Expenditures	872,674	1,438
Debt Outstanding	1,281,223	2,111
Cash and Securities[1]	1,643,603	2,708

Note: (1) Cash and security holdings of a government at the close of its fiscal year, including those of its dependent agencies, utilities, and liquor stores.
Source: U.S Census Bureau, State & Local Government Finances 2008

City Government Revenue by Source

Source	2008 ($000)	2008 ($ per capita)
General Revenue		
From Federal Government	47,291	78
From State Government	21,102	35
From Local Governments	2,634	4
Taxes		
Property	160,980	265
Sales and Gross Receipts	151,301	249
Personal Income	0	0
Corporate Income	0	0
Motor Vehicle License	0	0
Other Taxes	12,544	21
Current Charges	154,356	254
Liquor Store	0	0
Utility	75,936	125
Employee Retirement	194,534	321

Source: U.S Census Bureau, State & Local Government Finances 2008

City Government Expenditures by Function

Function	2008 ($000)	2008 ($ per capita)	2008 (%)
General Direct Expenditures			
Air Transportation	52,863	87	6.1
Corrections	0	0	0.0
Education	0	0	0.0
Employment Security Administration	0	0	0.0
Financial Administration	8,009	13	0.9
Fire Protection	62,843	104	7.2
General Public Buildings	15,784	26	1.8
Governmental Administration, Other	12,247	20	1.4
Health	23,232	38	2.7
Highways	50,613	83	5.8
Hospitals	0	0	0.0
Housing and Community Development	18,345	30	2.1
Interest on General Debt	32,569	54	3.7
Judicial and Legal	8,723	14	1.0
Libraries	9,011	15	1.0
Parking	0	0	0.0
Parks and Recreation	49,245	81	5.6
Police Protection	96,386	159	11.0
Public Welfare	0	0	0.0
Sewerage	46,520	77	5.3
Solid Waste Management	28,987	48	3.3
Veterans' Services	0	0	0.0
Liquor Store	0	0	0.0
Utility	253,476	418	29.0
Employee Retirement	72,204	119	8.3

Source: U.S Census Bureau, State & Local Government Finances 2008

Municipal Bond Ratings

Area	Moody's	S&P	Fitch
City	Aa3	AA	AA-

Rating Systems (shown in declining order of credit quality): Moody's– Aaa, Aa, A, Baa, Ba, B, Caa, Ca, C (numerical modifiers 1, 2, and 3 are added to letter-rating); S&P– AAA, AA, A, BBB, BB, B, CCC, CC, C; Fitch– AAA, AA, A, BBB, BB, B, CCC, CC, C. Ratings may be modified by the addition of a plus or minus sign to show relative standing within the major rating categories.
Notes: n/a Not available; (1) Not reviewed; (2) Issuer Rating/No General Obligation; (3) Standard and Poor's Issue Credit Rating (ICR) is a current opinion of an obliger with respect to a specific financial obligation, a specific class of financial obligations, or a specific financial program.
Source: U.S. Census Bureau, 2011 Statistical Abstract, Bond Ratings for City Governments by Largest Cities: 2009

DEMOGRAPHICS

Population Growth

Area	1990 Census	2000 Census	2010 Estimate	2015 Projection	Population Growth (%) 2000-2010	Population Growth (%) 2010-2015
City	515,541	563,662	614,938	640,686	9.1	4.2
MSA[1]	591,610	679,622	764,048	803,756	12.4	5.2
U.S.	248,709,873	281,421,906	309,038,974	321,675,005	9.8	4.1

Note: (1) Metropolitan Statistical Area - see Appendix B for areas included
Source: Claritas, Inc.

Number of Households and Average Household Size

Area	2010 Estimate	2010 Average Household Size
City	202,980	3.00
MSA[1]	240,413	3.12
U.S.	116,136,617	2.59

Note: (1) Metropolitan Statistical Area - see Appendix B for areas included
Source: Claritas, Inc.

Race and Ethnicity

Area	White Alone[2] (%)	Black Alone[2] (%)	Asian Alone[2] (%)	Other Race Alone[2] (%)	Hispanic[3] (%)
City	72.2	2.8	1.2	23.7	80.4
MSA[1]	72.9	2.7	1.1	23.3	82.2
U.S.	72.3	12.4	4.4	10.9	15.8

Note: Figures are 2010 estimates; (1) Metropolitan Statistical Area - see Appendix B for areas included (2) Alone is defined as not being in combination with one or more other races; (3) May be of any race.
Source: Claritas, Inc.

Segregation

Type	Segregation Indices[1] 1990	2000	2010	2010 Rank[2]	Percent Change 1990-2000	1990-2010	2000-2010
Black/White	37.5	36.2	30.7	100	-1.3	-6.8	-5.5
Asian/White	23.8	21.9	22.2	100	-1.9	-1.7	0.2
Hispanic/White	49.7	45.2	43.3	50	-4.5	-6.5	-1.9

Note: Figures are based on an analysis of 1990, 2000, and 2010 Census Decennial Census tract data by William H. Frey, Brookings Institution and the University of Michigan Social Science Data Analysis Network. In this analysis all racial groups (whites, blacks, and asians) are non-Hispanic members of those races. Hispanics are shown as a separate category; All figures cover the Metropolitan Statistical Area (see Appendix B for areas included); (1) Segregation Indices are Dissimilarity Indices that measure the degree to which the minority group is distributed differently than whites aross census tracts. They range from 0 (complete integration) to 100 (complete [segregation) where the value indicates the percentage of the minority group that needs to move to be distributed exactly like whites; (2) Ranges from 1 (most segregated) to 102 (least segregated); n/a not available.
Source: www.CensusScope.org

Ancestry

Area	German	Irish	English	American	Italian	Polish	French	Scottish
City	4.1	2.8	2.4	3.4	1.0	0.5	0.7	0.5
MSA[1]	3.8	2.6	2.2	3.3	0.9	0.5	0.7	0.5
U.S.	16.6	12.0	9.1	6.1	5.9	3.3	3.1	1.9

Note: The top eight ancestries in the U.S. are shown. Figures are percentages and include multiple ancestry (e.g. if a person reported being Irish and Italian, they were included in both columns); (1) Metropolitan Statistical Area - see Appendix B for areas included
Source: U.S. Census Bureau, 2007-2009 American Community Survey 3-Year Estimates

Foreign-Born Population

Area	Percent of Population Born in								
	Any Foreign Country	Mexico	Asia	Europe	Carribean	South America	Central America[2]	Africa	Canada
City	25.4	22.7	1.1	0.7	0.2	0.2	0.3	0.1	0.0
MSA[1]	26.3	24.0	1.0	0.6	0.2	0.2	0.3	0.1	0.0
U.S.	12.5	3.8	3.4	1.6	1.1	0.8	0.9	0.5	0.3

Note: (1) Metropolitan Statistical Area - see Appendix B for areas included; (2) Excludes Mexico.
Source: U.S. Census Bureau, 2007-2009 American Community Survey 3-Year Estimates

Marriage Status

Area	Never Married	Now Married[2]	Separated	Widowed	Divorced
City	30.9	49.1	3.5	6.0	10.5
MSA[1]	30.9	49.8	3.6	5.8	9.9
U.S.	31.4	49.7	2.2	6.2	10.6

Note: Figures are percentages and cover the population 15 years of age and older;
(1) Metropolitan Statistical Area - see Appendix B for areas included; (2) Excludes separated
Source: U.S. Census Bureau, 2007-2009 American Community Survey 3-Year Estimates

Age Distribution and Median Age

Area	Percent of Population							Median Age
	Under Age 5	Age 5 to 17	Age 18 to 34	Age 35 to 49	Age 50 to 64	Age 65 to 79	80 Years and Over	
City	9.6	21.1	23.3	19.6	15.0	8.3	3.1	31.8
MSA[1]	9.9	21.6	23.8	19.5	14.6	7.7	2.9	30.8
U.S.	6.9	17.5	23.3	21.4	18.1	9.1	3.7	36.7

Note: (1) Metropolitan Statistical Area - see Appendix B for areas included
Source: U.S. Census Bureau, 2007-2009 American Community Survey 3-Year Estimates

Male/Female Ratio

Area	Males	Females	Males per 100 Females
City	291,638	323,300	90.2
MSA[1]	367,257	396,791	92.6
U.S.	152,401,520	156,637,454	97.3

Note: Figures are 2010 estimates; (1) Metropolitan Statistical Area - see Appendix B for areas included
Source: Claritas, Inc.

Religion

Area	Catholic	Southern Baptist	United Meth-odist	ELCA[1]	LDS[2]	Presby-terian Church USA	Jewish Est.	Muslim Est.
County	51.5	3.6	1.3	0.2	0.8	0.4	0.7	0.1
U.S.	22.0	7.1	3.7	1.8	1.5	1.1	2.2	0.6

Note: Figures are the number of adherents as a percentage of the total population; Adherents are defined as all members, including full members, their children and the estimated number of other participants who are not considered members (e.g. the baptized, those not confirmed, those regularly attending services, etc.); (1) Evangelical Lutheran Church in America; (2) The Church of Jesus Christ of Latter Day Saints
Source: Reprinted with permission from Religious Congregations and Membership in the United States 2000 (Nashville, Glenmary Research Center, 2002) Copyright Association of Statisticians of American Religious Bodies. All rights reserved.

ECONOMY

Gross Metropolitan Product

Area	2006	2007	2008	2009	2009 Rank[2]
MSA[1]	23.2	24.6	26.4	26.9	79

Note: Figures are in billions of dollars; (1) El Paso, TX Metropolitan Statistical Area - see Appendix B for areas included; (2) Rank ranges from 1 to 363
Source: The U.S. Conference of Mayors, "Pace of Economic Recovery: GMP and Jobs," January 2010

Economic Growth

Area	2006-2008 (%)	2009 (%)	2010 (%)	Rank[2]
MSA[1]	3.6	0.6	4.7	37
U.S.	1.3	-2.5	2.2	–

Note: Figures are real Gross Metropolitan Product growth rates and represent annual average percent change; (1) El Paso, TX Metropolitan Statistical Area - see Appendix B for areas included; (2) Rank ranges from 1 to 363
Source: The U.S. Conference of Mayors, "Pace of Economic Recovery: GMP and Jobs," January 2010

Metropolitan Area Exports

Area	2005	2006	2007	2008	2009	2009 Rank[2]
MSA[1]	9,654.6	10,105.8	9,608.0	9,390.5	7,748.0	31

Note: Figures are in millions of dollars; (1) El Paso, TX Metropolitan Statistical Area - see Appendix B for areas included; (2) Rank ranges from 1 to 374
Source: U.S. Department of Commerce, International Trade Administration, Office of Trade & Industry Information, Manufacturing & Services

INCOME

Per Capita/Median/Average Income

Area	Per Capita ($)	Median Household ($)	Average Household ($)
City	17,492	38,566	52,557
MSA[1]	16,178	36,981	50,645
U.S.	27,034	52,795	71,071

Note: Figures are 2010 estimates; (1) Metropolitan Statistical Area - see Appendix B for areas included
Source: Claritas, Inc.

Household Income Distribution

Area	Percent of Households Earning							
	Under $15,000	$15,000 -24,999	$25,000 -34,999	$35,000 -49,999	$50,000 -74,999	$75,000 -99,000	$100,000 -149,999	$150,000 and up
City	18.7	14.1	13.3	16.2	17.7	8.9	7.5	3.6
MSA[1]	18.8	15.2	13.9	16.4	17.1	8.4	6.9	3.3
U.S.	12.1	10.2	10.6	15.0	19.5	12.5	12.1	8.0

Note: Figures are 2010 estimates; (1) Metropolitan Statistical Area - see Appendix B for areas included
Source: Claritas, Inc.

Poverty Rates by Age

Area	All Ages	Under 18 Years Old	18 to 64 Years Old	65 Years and Over
City	24.8	10.8	11.6	2.4
MSA[1]	25.9	11.4	12.2	2.3
U.S.	13.6	4.7	7.7	1.2

Note: Figures are percent of population with income during the previous 12 months below poverty level and only include population for whom poverty status is determined; (1) Metropolitan Statistical Area - see Appendix B for areas included
Source: U.S. Census Bureau, 2007-2009 American Community Survey 3-Year Estimates

Personal Bankruptcy Filing Rate

Area	2006	2007	2008	2009	2010
El Paso County	2.11	2.28	3.00	3.89	3.59
U.S.	2.00	2.73	3.53	4.60	4.96

Note: Numbers are per 1,000 population and include Chapter 7 and Chapter 13 filings
Source: Federal Deposit Insurance Corporation, Regional Economic Conditions, March 17, 2011

EMPLOYMENT

Labor Force and Employment

Area	Civilian Labor Force			Workers Employed		
	Dec. 2009	Dec. 2010	% Chg.	Dec. 2009	Dec. 2010	% Chg.
City	265,934	274,211	3.1	244,163	249,990	2.4
MSA[1]	312,104	322,362	3.3	284,426	291,214	2.4
U.S.	152,693,000	153,156,000	0.3	137,953,000	139,159,000	0.9

Note: Data is not seasonally adjusted and covers workers 16 years of age and older;
(1) Metropolitan Statistical Area - see Appendix B for areas included
Source: Bureau of Labor Statistics, http://stats.bls.gov

Unemployment Rate

Area	2010											
	Jan.	Feb.	Mar.	Apr.	May	Jun.	Jul.	Aug.	Sep.	Oct.	Nov.	Dec.
City	8.8	8.6	8.5	8.2	8.1	8.8	9.0	8.9	8.7	8.7	9.0	8.8
MSA[1]	9.6	9.4	9.3	8.9	9.0	9.6	9.9	9.8	9.6	9.5	9.9	9.7
U.S.	10.6	10.4	10.2	9.5	9.3	9.6	9.7	9.5	9.2	9.0	9.3	9.1

Note: Data is not seasonally adjusted and covers workers 16 years of age and older; All figures are percentages; (1) Metropolitan Statistical Area - see Appendix B for areas included
Source: Bureau of Labor Statistics, http://stats.bls.gov

Projected Unemployment Rate

Area	2007 (%)	2009 (%)	2011 (%)	2013 (%)
MSA[1]	5.7	10.3	10.3	9.1

Note: (1) Metropolitan Statistical Area - see Appendix B for areas included
Source: The U.S. Conference of Mayors, "Pace of Economic Recovery: GMP and Jobs," January 2010

Employment by Occupation

Occupation Classification	City (%)	MSA[1] (%)	U.S. (%)
Sales and Office	28.3	27.6	25.4
Professional and Related	19.2	18.0	21.0
Service	19.8	19.7	17.2
Production, Transportation, and Material Moving	11.9	13.3	12.3
Management, Business, and Financial	11.7	10.9	14.1
Construction, Extraction, and Maintenance	8.9	10.1	9.2
Farming, Forestry, and Fishing	0.1	0.4	0.7

Note: Figures cover employed civilians 16 years of age and older;
(1) Metropolitan Statistical Area - see Appendix B for areas included
Source: U.S. Census Bureau, 2007-2009 American Community Survey 3-Year Estimates

Employment by Industry

Sector	MSA[1] Number of Employees	MSA[1] Percent of Total	U.S. Percent of Total
Government	72,000	25.5	17.2
Education and Health Services	36,100	12.8	15.2
Professional and Business Services	31,300	11.1	13.0
Retail Trade	35,200	12.5	11.4
Leisure and Hospitality	27,600	9.8	9.7
Manufacturing	16,800	5.9	8.8
Financial Activities	11,500	4.1	5.8
Wholesale Trade	9,900	3.5	4.2
Construction	n/a	n/a	4.1
Other Services	9,400	3.3	4.1
Transportation and Utilities	12,500	4.4	3.7
Information	5,000	1.8	2.1
Mining and Logging	n/a	n/a	0.6

Note: Figures cover non-farm employment as of December 2010 and are not seasonally adjusted;
(1) Metropolitan Statistical Area - see Appendix B for areas included; n/a not available
Source: Bureau of Labor Statistics, http://stats.bls.gov

Occupations with Greatest Projected Employment Growth: 2006 - 2016

Occupation[1]	2006 Employment	2016 Projected Employment	Numeric Employment Change	Percent Employment Change
Combined food preparation and serving workers, including fast food	270,530	359,050	88,520	32.7
Retail salespersons	332,750	411,350	78,600	23.6
Personal and home care aides	133,050	207,850	74,800	56.2
Customer service representatives	214,440	280,060	65,620	30.6
Elementary school teachers, except special education	145,430	207,710	62,280	42.8
Registered nurses	157,840	217,430	59,590	37.8
Waiters and waitresses	174,140	227,790	53,650	30.8
Child care workers	145,500	189,730	44,230	30.4
Office clerks, general	194,610	236,670	42,060	21.6
Postsecondary teachers	113,400	153,130	39,730	35.0

Note: Projections cover Texas; (1) Sorted by numeric employment change
Source: www.projectionscentral.com, State Occupational Projections, 2006-2016 Long-Term Projections

Fastest Growing Occupations: 2006 - 2016

Occupation[1]	2006 Employment	2016 Projected Employment	Numeric Employment Change	Percent Employment Change
Personal and home care aides	133,050	207,850	74,800	56.2
Network systems and data communications analysts	17,750	27,620	9,870	55.6
Medical assistants	34,790	53,500	18,710	53.8
Special education teachers, preschool, kindergarten, and elementary school	13,750	20,560	6,810	49.5
Physical therapist assistants	3,780	5,570	1,790	47.4
Special education teachers, middle school	6,270	9,170	2,900	46.3
Computer software engineers, applications	30,900	45,200	14,300	46.3
Physician assistants	3,810	5,540	1,730	45.4
Kindergarten teachers, except special education	12,850	18,690	5,840	45.4
Pharmacy technicians	24,420	35,050	10,630	43.5

Note: Projections cover Texas; (1) Sorted by percent employment change and excludes occupations with numeric employment change less than 1500
Source: www.projectionscentral.com, State Occupational Projections, 2006-2016 Long-Term Projections

Average Wages

Occupation	$/Hr.	Occupation	$/Hr.
Accountants and Auditors	26.06	Maids and Housekeeping Cleaners	7.90
Automotive Mechanics	14.53	Maintenance and Repair Workers	12.63
Bookkeepers	13.72	Marketing Managers	46.65
Carpenters	12.34	Nuclear Medicine Technologists	28.66
Cashiers	8.01	Nurses, Licensed Practical	20.24
Clerks, General Office	11.05	Nurses, Registered	29.25
Clerks, Receptionists/Information	9.73	Nursing Aides/Orderlies/Attendants	9.42
Clerks, Shipping/Receiving	10.33	Packers and Packagers, Hand	7.99
Computer Programmers	26.78	Physical Therapists	45.85
Computer Support Specialists	18.53	Postal Service Mail Carriers	24.22
Computer Systems Analysts	28.71	Real Estate Brokers	n/a
Cooks, Restaurant	9.13	Retail Salespersons	10.16
Dentists	n/a	Sales Reps., Exc. Tech./Scientific	20.50
Electrical Engineers	37.87	Sales Reps., Tech./Scientific	32.72
Electricians	18.30	Secretaries, Exc. Legal/Med./Exec.	11.84
Financial Managers	38.11	Security Guards	11.74
First-Line Supervisors/Mgrs., Sales	18.31	Surgeons	105.11
Food Preparation Workers	7.68	Teacher Assistants	11.60
General and Operations Managers	41.98	Teachers, Elementary School	24.80
Hairdressers/Cosmetologists	9.77	Teachers, Secondary School	25.40
Internists	105.34	Telemarketers	9.30
Janitors and Cleaners	9.45	Truck Drivers, Heavy/Tractor-Trailer	18.92
Landscaping/Groundskeeping Workers	9.68	Truck Drivers, Light/Delivery Svcs.	11.49
Lawyers	63.58	Waiters and Waitresses	7.85

Note: Wage data covers the El Paso, TX - see Appendix B for areas included. Hourly wages for elementary/secondary school teachers and teacher assistants were calculated by the editors from annual wage data assuming a 40 hour work week; n/a not available.
Source: Bureau of Labor Statistics, Metro Area Occupational Employment and Wage Estimates, May 2009

RESIDENTIAL REAL ESTATE

Building Permits

Area	Single-Family			Multi-Family			Total		
	2009	2010	Pct. Chg.	2009	2010	Pct. Chg.	2009	2010	Pct. Chg.
City	2,330	2,478	6.4	551	1,584	187.5	2,881	4,062	41.0
MSA[1]	2,640	2,961	12.2	551	1,588	188.2	3,191	4,549	42.6
U.S.	441,100	447,300	1.4	141,900	157,300	10.9	583,000	604,600	3.7

Note: (1) Metropolitan Statistical Area - see Appendix B for areas included; figures represent new, privately-owned housing units authorized (unadjusted data); All permit data are based on estimates with imputation.
Source: U.S. Census Bureau, Manufacturing, Mining, and Construction Statistics, Building Permits, 2009, 2010

Homeownership Rate

Area	2005 (%)	2006 (%)	2007 (%)	2008 (%)	2009 (%)	2010 (%)
MSA[1]	72.6	65.0	68.2	64.8	63.8	70.1
U.S.	68.9	68.8	68.1	67.8	67.4	66.9

Note: (1) Metropolitan Statistical Area - see Appendix B for areas included
Source: U.S. Census Bureau, Housing Vacancies and Homeownership Annual Statistics: 2010

Housing Vacancy Rates

Area	Gross Vacancy Rate[2] (%)			Year-Round Vacancy Rate[3] (%)			Rental Vacancy Rate[4] (%)			Homeowner Vacancy Rate[5] (%)		
	2008	2009	2010	2008	2009	2010	2008	2009	2010	2008	2009	2010
MSA[1]	9.0	8.6	7.0	9.0	8.4	6.9	9.5	9.6	5.8	3.0	2.5	1.4
U.S.	14.4	14.5	14.3	11.1	11.3	11.3	10.0	10.6	10.2	2.8	2.6	2.6

Note: (1) Metropolitan Statistical Area - see Appendix B for areas included; (2) The percentage of the total housing inventory that is vacant; (3) The percentage of the housing inventory (excluding seasonal units) that is year-round vacant; (4) The percentage of rental inventory that is vacant for rent; (5) The percentage of homeowner inventory that is vacant for sale; n/a not available
Source: U.S. Census Bureau, Housing Vacancies and Homeownership Annual Statistics: 2010

State Corporate Income Tax Rates

State	Tax Rate (%)	Income Brackets ($)	Num. of Brackets	Financial Institution Tax Rate (%)[a]	Federal Income Tax Ded.
Texas	(y)	–	-	(y)	No

Note: Tax rates as of January 1, 2011; (a) Rates listed are the tax rates applied to financial institutions or excise taxes based on income. Some states have other taxes based upon the value of deposits or shares; (y) Texas imposes a Franchise Tax, otherwise known as margin tax, imposed on entities with more than $1,000,000 total revenues at rate of 1%, or 0.5% for entities primarily engaged in retail or wholesale trade, on lesser of 70% of total revenues or 100% of gross receipts after deductions for either compensation or cost of goods sold.
Source: Federation of Tax Administrators, "State Corporate Income Tax Rates, 2011"

State Individual Income Tax Rates

State	Tax Rate (%)	Income Brackets ($)	Num. of Brackets	Personal Exempt. ($)[1] Single	Personal Exempt. ($)[1] Dependents	Fed. Inc. Tax Ded.
Texas – No State Income Tax						

Note: Tax rates as of January 1, 2011; Local- and county-level taxes are not included; n/a not applicable; (1) Married joint filers generally receive double the single exemption
Source: Federation of Tax Administrators, "State Individual Income Tax Rates, 2011"

Various State and Local Tax Rates

State	State and Local Sales and Use (%)	State Sales and Use (%)	Gasoline[1] (¢/gal.)	Cigarette[2] ($/pack)	Spirits[3] ($/gal.)	Wine[4] ($/gal.)	Beer[5] ($/gal.)
Texas	8.25	6.25	20.0	1.41	2.40	0.20	0.20

Note: All tax rates as of January 1, 2011 except Spirits (Sept. 1, 2010); (1) The American Petroleum Institute has developed a methodology for determining the average tax rate on a gallon of fuel. Rates may include any of the following: excise taxes, environmental fees, storage tank fees, other fees or taxes, general sales tax, and local taxes. In states where gasoline is subject to the general sales tax, or where the fuel tax is based on the average sale price, the average rate determined by API is sensitive to changes in the price of gasoline. States that fully or partially apply general sales taxes to gasoline: CA, CO, GA, IL, IN, MI, NY; (2) The federal excise tax of $1.0066 per pack and local taxes are not included; (3) Rates are those applicable to off-premise sales of 40% alcohol by volume (a.b.v.) distilled spirits in 750ml containers. Local excise taxes are excluded; (4) Rates are those applicable to off-premise sales of 11% a.b.v. non-carbonated wine in 750ml containers; (5) Rates are those applicable to off-premise sales of 4.7% a.b.v. beer in 12 ounce containers.
Source: Tax Foundation, 2011 Facts & Figures: How Does Your State Compare?

State-Local Tax Burdens

Area	Rate (%)	Rank[1]	Per Capita Taxes Paid to Home State ($)	Total State and Local Per Capita Taxes Paid ($)	Per Capita Income ($)
Texas	7.9	45	2,248	3,197	40,498
U.S. Average	9.8	-	3,057	4,160	42,539

Note: Figures cover 2009; (1) Rank ranges from 1 to 50 where 1 is highest tax burden
Source: Tax Foundation, State-Local Tax Burdens, All States, 2009

State Business Tax Climate Index Rankings

State	Overall Rank	Corporate Tax Index Rank	Individual Income Tax Index Rank	Sales Tax Index Rank	Unemployment Insurance Tax Index Rank	Property Tax Index Rank
Texas	13	46	7	37	15	29

Note: The index is a measure of how each state's tax laws affect economic performance. The lower the rank, the more favorable a state's tax system is for business. All ranks are for fiscal years. States without a given tax are given a ranking of 1.
Source: Tax Foundation, Tax Foundation Background Paper, No. 60, "2011 State Business Tax Climate Index"

COMMERCIAL REAL ESTATE

Industrial Market

Market Area	Inventory (sq. ft.)	Vacant (sq. ft.)	Vac. Rate (%)	Under Constr. (sq. ft.)	Asking Rent ($/sf/yr) WH/Dist	Asking Rent ($/sf/yr) R&D/Flex
El Paso	57,182,259	7,212,297	12.6	-	3.21	-

Source: Grubb & Ellis, Industrial Markets Trends, 4th Quarter 2010

**COMMERCIAL
UTILITIES**

Typical Monthly Electric Bills

Area	Commercial Service ($/month)		Industrial Service ($/month)	
	3 kW demand 1,000 kWh	40 kW demand 14,000 kWh	1,000 kW demand 200,000 kWh	50,000 kW demand 15,000,000 kWh
City	157	1,699	32,881	1,949,160
Average[1]	135	1,576	23,741	1,402,202

Note: Based on total rates in effect July 1, 2010; (1) average based on 182 utilities surveyed
Source: Edison Electric Institute, Typical Bills and Average Rates Report, Summer 2010

TRANSPORTATION

Means of Transportation to Work

Area	Car/Truck/Van		Public Transportation			Bicycle	Walked	Other Means	Worked at Home
	Drove Alone	Car-pooled	Bus	Subway	Railroad				
City	80.0	10.4	2.2	0.0	0.0	0.2	2.2	2.5	2.5
MSA[1]	79.5	10.8	1.9	0.0	0.0	0.2	2.1	2.7	2.8
U.S.	75.8	10.4	2.7	1.7	0.5	0.5	2.9	1.2	4.1

Note: Figures are percentages and cover workers 16 years of age and older;
(1) Metropolitan Statistical Area - see Appendix B for areas included
Source: U.S. Census Bureau, 2007-2009 American Community Survey 3-Year Estimates

Travel Time to Work

Area	Less Than 15 Minutes	15 to 29 Minutes	30 to 44 Minutes	45 to 59 Minutes	60 to 89 Minutes	90 Minutes or More
City	24.9	47.0	21.3	3.7	1.9	1.2
MSA[1]	24.3	45.5	22.6	4.4	2.2	1.2
U.S.	28.5	36.2	19.7	7.5	5.6	2.5

Note: Figures are percentages and include workers 16 years old and over;
(1) Metropolitan Statistical Area - see Appendix B for areas included
Source: U.S. Census Bureau, 2007-2009 American Community Survey 3-Year Estimates

Travel Time Index

Area	1982	1999	2008	2009
Urban Area[1]	1.03	1.14	1.15	1.15
Average[2]	1.08	1.20	1.20	1.20

Note: Travel Time Index—the ratio of travel time in the peak period to the travel time at
free-flow conditions. A value of 1.30 indicates a 20-minute free-flow trip takes 26 minutes
in the peak. Free-flow speeds (60 mph on freeways and 35 mph on principal arterials)
are used as the comparison threshold; (1) Covers the El Paso urban area;
(2) average of 439 urban areas
Source: Texas Transportation Institute, Urban Mobility Report 2010, December 2010

Public Transportation

Agency Name / Mode of Transportation	Vehicles Operated in Maximum Service	Annual Unlinked Passenger Trips ('000)	Annual Passenger Miles ('000)
Mass Transit Department-City of El Paso (Sun Metro)			
Demand response	20	19.0	205.6
Demand response	47	225.2	2,095.0
Bus	118	12,179.8	62,193.1

Note: Figures include both directly operated and purchased transportation
Source: Federal Transit Administration, National Transit Database, 2009

Air Transportation

Airport Name and Code / Type of Service	Passenger Airlines[1]	Passenger Enplanements	Freight Carriers[2]	Freight (lbs.)
El Paso International (ELP)				
Domestic service (U.S. carriers - 2010)	21	1,504,267	18	89,020,649
International service (U.S. carriers - 2009)	6	246	5	1,391,131

Note: (1) Includes all U.S.-based major, minor and commuter airlines that carried at least one passenger during the year; (2) Includes all U.S.-based airlines and freight carriers that transported at least one pound of freight during the year
Source: Bureau of Transportation Statistics, The Intermodal Transportation Database, Air Carriers: T-100 Domestic Market (U.S. Carriers), 2010; Bureau of Transportation Statistics, The Intermodal Transportation Database, Air Carriers: T-100 International Market (U.S. Carriers), 2009

Other Transportation Statistics

Interstate highways: I-10
Amtrak service: Yes
Major waterways/ports: Rio Grande
Source: Amtrak.com; Google Maps

BUSINESSES

Major Business Headquarters

Company Name	Rankings Fortune[1]	Forbes[2]
Western Refining	298	-

Note: (1) Fortune 500—companies that produce a 10-K are ranked 1 to 500 based on 2010 revenue; (2) all private companies with at least $2 billion in annual revenue are ranked 1 to 223; companies listed are headquartered in the city; dashes indicate no ranking
Source: Fortune, "Fortune 500," May 23, 2011; Forbes, "America's Largest Private Companies," November 3, 2010

Minority Business Opportunity

El Paso is home to seven companies which are on the *Hispanic Business 500* list (500 largest U.S. Hispanic-owned companies based on 2009 revenue): **Fred Loya Insurance**; **Pro Auto Dealers**; **Bravo Southwest**; **RMPersonnel**; **Miratek Corporation**; **dmDickason Personnel Services.**; **Human Capital International**. Companies included must show at least 51 percent ownership by Hispanic U.S. citizens, and must maintain headquarters in one of the 50 states or Washington, D.C. *Hispanic Business, "Hispanic Business 500," June 2010*

El Paso is home to three companies which are on the *Hispanic Business* Fastest-Growing 100 list (greatest sales growth from 2005 to 2009): **Pro Auto Dealers**; **Fred Loya Insurance**; **Miratek Corporation**. Companies included must show at least 51 percent ownership by Hispanic U.S. citizens, and must maintain headquarters in one of the 50 states or Washington, D.C. In addition, companies must have minimum revenues of $200,000 for calendar year 2005. *Hispanic Business, July/August 2010*

Minority- and Women-Owned Businesses

Group	All Firms Firms	Sales ($000)	Firms with Paid Employees Firms	Sales ($000)	Employees	Payroll ($000)
Asian	1,116	191,108	433	174,717	2,836	43,467
Black	1,197	57,643	(s)	(s)	(s)	(s)
Hispanic	31,640	5,521,058	3,924	4,565,644	29,777	798,704
Women	14,792	1,952,682	1,609	1,638,631	17,694	375,970
All Firms	52,919	45,727,653	9,368	44,068,193	182,451	5,020,183

Note: Figures cover firms located in the city; minority- and women-owned business are defined as firms in which the corresponding group own 51% or more of the stock or equity of the company; (s) estimates are suppressed when publication standards are not met
Source: U.S. Census Bureau, 2007 Economic Census, Survey of Business Owners

HOTELS

Hotels/Motels

Area	5 Star		4 Star		3 Star		2 Star		1 Star		Not Rated	
	Num.	Pct.3	Num.	Pct.3	Num.	Pct.3	Num.	Pct.3	Num.	Pct.3	Num.	Pct.3
City[1]	0	0.0	0	0.0	17	26.6	39	60.9	1	1.6	7	10.9
Total[2]	119	0.7	927	5.8	4,906	30.5	7,992	49.7	526	3.3	1,625	10.1

Note: (1) Figures cover El Paso and vicinity; (2) Figures cover all 100 cities in this book; (3) Percentage of hotels which are a given star rating; Star ratings are determined by expedia.com and offer an indication of the general quality of a particular hotel.
Source: expedia.com, May 5, 2011

EVENT SITES

Major Stadiums, Arenas, and Auditoriums

Name	Max. Capacity
Cohen Stadium	10,000
El Paso County Coliseum	7,000
Magoffin Auditorium	1,200
Sun Bowl Stadium	52,000

Source: Original research

Convention Centers

Name	Overall Space (sq. ft.)	Exhibit Space (sq. ft.)	Meeting Space (sq. ft.)	Meeting Rooms
Judson F. Williams Convention Center	n/a	14,900	80,000	17

Note: n/a not available
Source: Original research

Living Environment

COST OF LIVING

Cost of Living Index

Composite Index	Groceries	Housing	Utilities	Trans-portation	Health Care	Misc. Goods/ Services
90.4	99.9	86.0	88.1	97.0	95.4	88.5

Note: U.S. = 100; Figures cover the El Paso TX urban area.
Source: The Council for Community and Economic Research, ACCRA Cost of Living Index, 2010

Grocery Prices

Area[1]	T-Bone Steak ($/pound)	Frying Chicken ($/pound)	Whole Milk ($/half gal.)	Eggs ($/dozen)	Orange Juice ($/64 oz.)	Coffee ($/11.5 oz.)
City[2]	8.78	0.90	1.88	1.59	2.88	3.91
Avg.	9.04	1.16	2.02	1.47	3.08	3.65
Min.	6.97	0.84	1.46	0.96	2.39	2.64
Max.	13.93	2.51	3.58	3.01	4.94	6.32

*Note: (1) Values for the local area are compared with the average, minimum and maximum values for all 338 areas in the Cost of Living Index; (2) Figures cover the El Paso TX urban area; **T-Bone Steak** (price per pound); **Frying Chicken** (price per pound, whole fryer); **Whole Milk** (half gallon carton); **Eggs** (price per dozen, Grade A, large); **Orange Juice** (64 oz. Tropicana or Florida Natural); **Coffee** (11.5 oz. can, vacuum-packed, Maxwell House, Hills Bros, or Folgers).*
Source: The Council for Community and Economic Research, ACCRA Cost of Living Index, 2010

Housing and Utility Costs

Area[1]	New Home Price ($)	Apartment Rent ($/month)	All Electric ($/month)	Part Electric ($/month)	Other Energy ($/month)	Telephone ($/month)
City[2]	235,174	825	-	102.64	38.19	26.95
Avg.	293,442	810	166.39	91.93	83.82	26.93
Min.	182,545	453	119.21	44.47	36.85	17.98
Max.	1,123,114	2,776	307.53	218.20	313.90	39.15

*Note: (1) Values for the local area are compared with the average, minimum and maximum values for all 338 areas in the Cost of Living Index; (2) Figures cover the El Paso TX urban area; **New Home Price** (2,400 sf living area, 8,000 sf lot, in urban area with full utilities); **Apartment Rent** (950 sf 2 bedroom/1.5 or 2 bath, unfurnished, excluding all utilities except water); **All Electric** (average monthly cost for an all-electric home); **Part Electric** (average monthly cost for a part-electric home); **Other Energy** (average monthly cost for natural gas, fuel oil, coal, wood, and any other forms of energy except electricity); **Telephone** (price includes basic monthly rate for a private residential line plus additional local usage charges incurred by a family of four).*
Source: The Council for Community and Economic Research, ACCRA Cost of Living Index, 2010

Health Care, Transportation, and Other Costs

Area[1]	Doctor ($/visit)	Dentist ($/visit)	Optometrist ($/visit)	Gasoline ($/gallon)	Beauty Salon ($/visit)	Men's Shirt ($)
City[2]	85.28	74.89	74.25	2.69	31.89	23.91
Avg.	89.44	78.95	87.40	2.73	31.92	24.83
Min.	57.00	54.25	48.32	2.44	19.17	13.67
Max.	149.90	136.73	174.22	3.75	62.81	47.89

*Note: (1) Values for the local area are compared with the average, minimum and maximum values for all 338 areas in the Cost of Living Index; (2) Figures cover the El Paso TX urban area; **Doctor** (general practitioners routine exam of an established patient); **Dentist** (adult teeth cleaning and periodic oral examination); **Optometrist** (full vision eye exam for established adult patient); **Gasoline** (one gallon regular unleaded, national brand, including all taxes, cash price at self-service pump if available); **Beauty Salon** (woman's shampoo, trim, and blow-dry); **Men's Shirt** (cotton/polyester dress shirt, pinpoint weave, long sleeves).*
Source: The Council for Community and Economic Research, ACCRA Cost of Living Index, 2010

HOUSING

House Price Index (HPI)

Area	National Ranking[2]	Quarterly Change (%)	One-Year Change (%)	Five-Year Change (%)
MSA[1]	99	0.47	-0.21	17.20
U.S.[3]	-	-0.84	-3.95	-11.45

Note: The HPI is a weighted repeat sales index. It measures average price changes in repeat sales or refinancings on the same properties. This information is obtained by reviewing repeat mortgage transactions on single-family properties whose mortgages have been purchased or securitized by Fannie Mae or Freddie Mac in January 1975; (1) Metropolitan/Micropolitan Statistical Area - see Appendix B for areas included; (2) Rankings are based on annual percentage change for all metro areas containing at least 15,000 transactions over the last 10 years and ranges from 1 to 309; (3) figures based on a weighted average of Census Division estimates; all figures are for the period ending December 31, 2010
Source: Federal Housing Finance Agency, House Price Index, February 24, 2011

House Price Valuations

Area	Q4 2005 Price ($000)	Q4 2005 Over-valuation	Q4 2006 Price ($000)	Q4 2006 Over-valuation	Q4 2007 Price ($000)	Q4 2007 Over-valuation	Q4 2008 Price ($000)	Q4 2008 Over-valuation	Q4 2009 Price ($000)	Q4 2009 Over-valuation
MSA[1]	89.6	-17.8	104.6	-9.0	109.4	-8.5	106.0	-11.3	104.6	-13.2

Note: Figures show the percentage of over- or under-valuation of single family homes relative to statistically normal house values (e.g. a value of 23.6 indicates that house values are 23.6% overvalued). Statistically normal house values are based on house prices, interest rates, household incomes, population densities, and any historical premiums or discounts metropolitan areas have exhibited over time; (1) Figures cover the El Paso, TX Metropolitan Statistical Area - see Appendix B for areas included
Source: Global Insight/PNC Financial Services Group, House Prices in America: 4th Quarter 2009 Update

Median Single-Family Home Prices

Area	2008	2009	2010p	Percent Change 2009 to 2010
MSA[1]	137.5	132.6	134.3	1.3
U.S. Average	196.6	172.1	173.2	0.6

Note: Figures are median sales prices of existing single-family homes in thousands of dollars; (p) preliminary; n/a not available; (1) Metropolitan Statistical Area - see Appendix B for areas included
Source: National Association of Realtors, Median Sales Price of Existing Single-Family Homes for Metropolitan Areas, 4th Quarter 2010

Median Apartment Condo-Coop Home Prices

Area	2008	2009	2010p	Percent Change 2009 to 2010
MSA[1]	n/a	n/a	n/a	n/a
U.S. Average	209.8	175.6	171.7	-2.2

Note: Figures are median sales prices of existing apartment condo-coop homes in thousands of dollars; (p) preliminary; n/a not available; (1) Metropolitan Statistical Area - see Appendix B for areas included
Source: National Association of Realtors, Median Sales Price of Existing Apartment Condo-Coop Homes for Metropolitan Areas, 4th Quarter 2010

Year Housing Structure Built

Area	2000 or Later	1990 -1999	1980 -1989	1970 -1979	1960 -1969	1950 -1959	1940 -1949	Before 1940	Median Year
City	13.7	13.4	15.5	20.5	13.3	13.2	4.2	6.1	1976
MSA[1]	15.5	14.7	16.4	19.7	12.3	11.8	4.1	5.5	1978
U.S.	12.5	14.0	14.2	16.5	11.4	11.3	5.8	14.3	1974

Note: Figures are percentages except for Median Year; (1) Metropolitan Statistical Area - see Appendix B for areas included
Source: U.S. Census Bureau, 2007-2009 American Community Survey 3-Year Estimates

HEALTH

Health Risk Data

Category	MSA[1] (%)	U.S. (%)
Adults who have been told they have high blood pressure	29.1	28.7
Adults who have been told they have high blood cholesterol	40.4	37.5
Adults who have been told they have diabetes[3]	12.4	8.3
Adults who have been told they have arthritis	20.5	26.0
Adults who have been told they currently have asthma	6.6	8.8
Adults who are current smokers	15.2	17.9
Adults who are heavy drinkers[4]	4.0	5.1
Adults who are binge drinkers[5]	13.5	15.8
Adults who are overweight (BMI 25.0 - 29.9)	35.9	36.2
Adults who are obese (BMI 30.0 - 99.8)	28.4	26.9
Adults who participated in any physical activities in the past month	76.4	76.2
Adults 50+ who have ever had a sigmoidoscopy or colonoscopy[2]	50.7	62.2
Women 40+ who have had a mammogram within the past two years[2]	71.2	76.0
Adults age 18–64 who have any kind of health care coverage	58.4	83.1

Note: Data as of 2009 unless otherwise noted; (1) Figures cover the El Paso, TX Metropolitan Statistical Area - see Appendix B for areas included; (2) Data as of 2008; (3) Figures do not include pregnancy-related, borderline, or pre-diabetes; (4) Heavy drinkers are classified as males having more than two drinks per day or females having more than one drink per day; (5) Binge drinkers are classified as males having five or more drinks on one occasion or females having four or more drinks on one occasion
Source: Centers for Disease Control and Prevention, Behaviorial Risk Factor Surveillance System, SMART: Selected Metropolitan/Micropolitan Area Risk Trends, 2008, 2009

Mortality Rates for the Top 10 Causes of Death in the U.S.

ICD-10[a] Sub-Chapter	ICD-10[a] Code	Age-Adjusted Mortality Rate[1] per 100,000 population	
		County[2]	U.S.
Malignant neoplasms	C00-C97	153.5	180.9
Ischaemic heart diseases	I20-I25	102.6	135.0
Other forms of heart disease	I30-I51	39.9	50.0
Cerebrovascular diseases	I60-I69	40.6	44.1
Chronic lower respiratory diseases	J40-J47	33.8	41.5
Other degenerative diseases of the nervous system	G30-G31	23.2	23.6
Diabetes mellitus	E10-E14	35.8	23.5
Other external causes of accidental injury	W00-X59	18.9	23.5
Organic, including symptomatic, mental disorders	F01-F09	15.6	22.2
Influenza and pneumonia	J09-J18	10.9	18.1

Note: (a) ICD-10 = International Classification of Diseases 10th Revision; (1) Mortality rates are a three year average covering 2005-2007; (2) Figures cover El Paso County
Source: Centers for Disease Control and Prevention, National Center for Health Statistics. Compressed Mortality File 1999-2007. CDC WONDER On-line Database, compiled from Compressed Mortality File 1999-2007 Series 20 No. 2M, 2010.

Mortality Rates for Selected Causes of Death

ICD-10[a] Sub-Chapter	ICD-10[a] Code	Age-Adjusted Mortality Rate[1] per 100,000 population	
		County[2]	U.S.
Assault	X85-Y09	3.3	6.0
Human immunodeficiency virus (HIV) disease	B20-B24	4.1	4.0
Hypertensive diseases	I10-I15	29.1	18.0
Intentional self-harm	X60-X84	8.4	11.0
Malnutrition	E40-E46	1.9	0.8
Obesity and other hyperalimentation	E65-E68	2.0	1.5
Transport accidents	V01-V99	13.8	15.6
Viral hepatitis	B15-B19	3.8	2.1

Note: (a) ICD-10 = International Classification of Diseases 10th Revision; (1) Mortality rates are a three year average covering 2005-2007; (2) Figures cover El Paso County
Source: Centers for Disease Control and Prevention, National Center for Health Statistics. Compressed Mortality File 1999-2007. CDC WONDER On-line Database, compiled from Compressed Mortality File 1999-2007 Series 20 No. 2M, 2010.

Distribution of Physicians and Dentists

Area[1]	Dentists[2]	D.O.[3]	M.D.[4]				
			Total	Family/ General Practice	Pediatrics	Medical Specialties	Surgical Specialties
Local (number)	121	99	851	95	78	324	231
Local (rate[5])	1.7	1.3	11.5	1.3	1.1	4.4	3.1
U.S. (rate[5])	4.5	1.9	18.3	2.5	1.4	6.8	4.1

Note: Data as of 2008 unless noted; (1) Local data covers El Paso County; (2) Data as of 2007; (3) Doctor of Osteopathic Medicine; (4) Includes active, non-federal, patient-care, office-based Doctors of Medicine; (5) rate per 10,000 population
Source: Area Resource File (ARF). 2009-2010 Release. U.S. Department of Health and Human Services, Health Resources and Services Administration, Bureau of Health Professions, Rockville, MD, August 2010

Hospitals

El Paso has the following hospitals: 8 general medical and surgical; 1 psychiatric; 2 rehabilitation; 1 orthopedic; 2 long-term acute care.
AHA Guide to the Healthcare Field 2010

EDUCATION

Public School District Statistics

District Name	Schls	Pupils	Pupil/ Teacher Ratio	Minority Pupils[1] (%)	Free Lunch Eligible[2] (%)	IEP[3] (%)
Canutillo ISD	9	5,745	14.8	95.1	69.1	8.4
Clint ISD	13	10,899	17.1	96.9	57.5	7.9
El Paso ISD	93	62,322	14.2	87.8	58.2	8.5
Socorro ISD	42	39,771	16.4	96.0	59.5	8.4
Ysleta ISD	63	44,592	14.7	94.6	50.2	10.5

Note: Table includes school districts with 2,000 or more students; (1) Percentage of students that are not non-Hispanic white; (2) Percentage of students that are eligible for the free lunch program; (3) Percentage of students that have an Individualized Education Program.
Source: U.S. Department of Education, National Center for Education Statistics, Common Core of Data, Local Education Agency (School District) Universe Survey: School Year 2008-2009; U.S. Department of Education, National Center for Education Statistics, Common Core of Data, Public Elementary/Secondary School Universe Survey: School Year 2008-2009

Highest Level of Education

Area	Less than H.S.	H.S. Diploma	Some College, No Deg.	Associate Degree	Bachelors Degree	Masters Degree	Profess. School Degree	Doctorate Degree
City	25.8	23.8	22.2	6.6	14.2	5.4	1.4	0.6
MSA[1]	29.0	24.2	21.2	6.3	12.7	4.8	1.2	0.5
U.S.	15.3	29.0	20.7	7.5	17.4	7.0	1.9	1.1

Note: Figures are 2010 estimated percentages and cover persons age 25 and over; (1) Metropolitan Statistical Area - see Appendix B for areas included
Source: Claritas, Inc.

Educational Attainment by Race

Area	High School Graduate (%)					Bachelor's Degree (%)				
	Total	White	Black	Asian	Hisp.[2]	Total	White	Black	Asian	Hisp.[2]
City	74.0	94.3	93.4	84.4	68.2	21.8	38.3	26.0	50.6	17.2
MSA[1]	71.3	94.0	92.6	83.6	65.4	19.7	37.1	25.6	49.0	15.3
U.S.	84.9	90.0	80.7	85.5	60.7	27.8	30.9	17.5	49.7	12.7

Note: Figures shown cover persons 25 years old and over; (1) Metropolitan Statistical Area - see Appendix B for areas included; (2) people of Hispanic origin can be of any race
Source: U.S. Census Bureau, 2007-2009 American Community Survey 3-Year Estimates

School Enrollment by Grade and Control

Area	Preschool (%) Public	Preschool (%) Private	Kindergarten (%) Public	Kindergarten (%) Private	Grades 1 - 4 (%) Public	Grades 1 - 4 (%) Private	Grades 5 - 8 (%) Public	Grades 5 - 8 (%) Private	Grades 9 - 12 (%) Public	Grades 9 - 12 (%) Private
City	81.1	18.9	91.2	8.8	95.6	4.4	94.5	5.5	96.0	4.0
MSA[1]	83.8	16.2	92.5	7.5	96.1	3.9	95.2	4.8	96.4	3.6
U.S.	54.3	45.7	86.4	13.6	88.9	11.1	89.1	10.9	90.2	9.8

Note: Figures shown cover persons 3 years old and over; (1) Metropolitan Statistical Area - see Appendix B for areas included
Source: U.S. Census Bureau, 2007-2009 American Community Survey 3-Year Estimates

Average Salaries of Public School Classroom Teachers

Area	2009-10 Dollars	2009-10 Rank[1]	2010-11 Dollars	2010-11 Rank[1]	Percent Change 2009-10 to 2010-11	Percent Change 2000-01 to 2010-11
Texas	48,261	31	48,261	34	0.00	25.8
U.S. Average	55,202	-	56,069	-	1.57	29.3

Note: (1) State rank ranges from 1 to 51 where 1 indicates highest salary.
Source: National Education Association, Rankings & Estimates: Rankings of the States 2010
and Estimates of School Statistics 2011, December 2010

Higher Education

Four-Year Colleges Public	Four-Year Colleges Private Non-profit	Four-Year Colleges Private For-profit	Two-Year Colleges Public	Two-Year Colleges Private Non-profit	Two-Year Colleges Private For-profit	Medical Schools[1]	Law Schools[2]	Voc/ Tech[3]
1	0	0	1	0	8	0	0	4

Note: Figures cover institutions located within the city limits and include main campuses only; (1) includes schools accredited by the Liaison Committee on Medical Education and the American Osteopathic Association; (2) includes American Bar Association-accredited law schools; (3) includes all schools with programs that are less than 2 years.
Source: National Center for Education Statistics, Integrated Postsecondary Education System (IPEDS) Peer Analysis System, 2010-11; U.S. News & World Report, Medical School Directory, 2011; U.S. News & World Report, Law School Directory, 2011

PRESIDENTIAL ELECTION

2008 Presidential Election Results

Area	Obama	McCain	Nader	Other
El Paso County	65.7	33.3	0.1	0.9
U.S.	52.9	45.6	0.6	0.9

Note: Results are percentages and may not add to 100% due to rounding
Source: Dave Leip's Atlas of U.S. Presidential Elections, www.uselectionatlas.org

EMPLOYERS

Major Employers

Company Name	Industry	Type of Site
ADP	Data processing and preparation	Branch
AHAC	Employment agencies	Single
City of El Paso	Executive offices	Headquarters
Delphi	Motor vehicle parts and accessories	Branch
Delphi	Engine electrical equipment	Headquarters
El Paso Border Patrol	Finance, taxation, and monetary policy	Branch
Elcom	Electronic components, nec	Single
GE	Motors and generators	Branch
Genpact	Data processing and preparation	Headquarters
Lear Furukawa Corporation	Public building and related furniture	Single
Phillips Consumer Electronics	Radio and t.v. communications equipment	Single
Providence Memorial Hospital	Offices and clinics of medical doctors	Branch
R E Thomason General Hospital	General medical and surgical hospitals	Headquarters
Speaking Rock Csino Entrmt Ctr	Amusement and recreation, nec	Branch
The University of Texas	Colleges and universities	Headquarters
Time Warner	Cable and other pay television services	Headquarters
United Retail Incorporated	Catalog and mail-order houses	Branch
University of Texas System	Colleges and universities	Branch
US Post Office	U.S. postal service	Branch
Verizon Business	Telephone communication, except radio	Branch

Note: Companies shown are located within the El Paso metropolitan area; nec = not elsewhere classified.
Source: www.zapdata.com, January 2011

PUBLIC SAFETY

Crime Rate

Area	All Crimes	Violent Crimes				Property Crimes		
		Murder	Forcible Rape	Robbery	Aggrav. Assault	Burglary	Larceny -Theft	Motor Vehicle Theft
City	3,451.5	1.9	29.4	73.0	352.9	321.7	2,367.0	305.4
Suburbs[1]	2,938.7	3.1	37.4	45.0	275.3	611.5	1,776.6	189.9
Metro[2]	3,361.8	2.1	30.8	68.1	339.4	372.4	2,263.7	285.2
U.S.	3,465.5	5.0	28.7	133.0	262.8	716.3	2,060.9	258.8

Note: Figures are crimes per 100,000 population; (1) All areas within the metro area that are located outside the city limits; (2) Metropolitan Statistical Area - see Appendix B for areas included
Source: FBI Uniform Crime Reports, 2009

Hate Crimes

Area	Number of Quarters Reported	Bias Motivation				
		Race	Religion	Sexual Orientation	Ethnicity	Disability
City	4	0	1	2	0	0

Source: Federal Bureau of Investigation, Hate Crime Statistics 2009

Identity Theft Consumer Complaints

Area	Complaints	Complaints per 100,000 Population	Rank[2]
MSA[1]	951	129.4	15
U.S.	250,854	81.3	-

Note: (1) Metropolitan Statistical Area - see Appendix B for areas included; (2) Rank ranges from 1 to 384 where 1 indicates greatest number of complaints per 100,000 population
Source: Federal Trade Commission, Consumer Sentinel Network Data Book for January - December 2010

RECREATION

Culture

Dance[1]	Theatre[1]	Instrumental Music[1]	Vocal Music[1]	Series/ Festivals	Museums	Zoos and Aquariums[2]
0	2	2	0	5	9	1

Note: (1) Number of professional perfoming groups; (2) AZA-accredited
Source: The Grey House Performing Arts Directory, 2011-2012; Official Museum Directory, 2010; American Association of Museums, AAM Member Museums, March 2011; Association of Zoos & Aquariums, AZA Member Zoos & Aquariums, May 2011

Professional Sports Teams

Team Name	League
No teams are located in the metro area	

Source: Original research

CLIMATE

Average and Extreme Temperatures

Temperature	Jan	Feb	Mar	Apr	May	Jun	Jul	Aug	Sep	Oct	Nov	Dec	Yr.
Extreme High (°F)	80	83	89	98	104	114	112	108	104	96	87	80	114
Average High (°F)	57	63	70	79	87	96	95	93	88	79	66	58	78
Average Temp. (°F)	44	49	56	64	73	81	83	81	75	65	52	45	64
Average Low (°F)	31	35	41	49	58	66	70	68	62	50	38	32	50
Extreme Low (°F)	-8	8	14	23	31	46	57	56	42	25	1	5	-8

Note: Figures cover the years 1948-1995
Source: National Climatic Data Center, International Station Meteorological Climate Summary, 9/96

Average Precipitation/Snowfall/Humidity

Precip./Humidity	Jan	Feb	Mar	Apr	May	Jun	Jul	Aug	Sep	Oct	Nov	Dec	Yr.
Avg. Precip. (in.)	0.4	0.4	0.3	0.2	0.3	0.7	1.6	1.5	1.4	0.7	0.3	0.6	8.6
Avg. Snowfall (in.)	1	1	Tr	Tr	0	0	0	0	0	Tr	1	2	6
Avg. Rel. Hum. 6am (%)	68	60	50	43	44	46	63	69	72	66	63	68	59
Avg. Rel. Hum. 3pm (%)	34	27	21	17	17	17	28	30	32	29	30	36	26

Note: Figures cover the years 1948-1995; Tr = Trace amounts (<0.05 in. of rain; <0.5 in. of snow)
Source: National Climatic Data Center, International Station Meteorological Climate Summary, 9/96

Weather Conditions

Temperature			Daytime Sky			Precipitation		
10°F & below	32°F & below	90°F & above	Clear	Partly cloudy	Cloudy	0.01 inch or more precip.	0.1 inch or more snow/ice	Thunder-storms
1	59	106	147	164	54	49	3	35

Note: Figures are average number of days per year and cover the years 1948-1995
Source: National Climatic Data Center, International Station Meteorological Climate Summary, 9/96

HAZARDOUS WASTE

Superfund Sites

El Paso has no sites on the EPA's Superfund Final National Priorities List.
U.S. Environmental Protection Agency, Final National Priorities List, April 1, 2011

AIR & WATER QUALITY

Air Quality Index

Area	Percent of Days when Air Quality was...[2]				AQI Statistics	
	Good	Moderate	Unhealthy for Sensitive Groups	Unhealthy	Maximum	Median
Area[1]	47.7	47.1	5.2	0.0	147	52

Note: The Air Quality Index (AQI) is an index for reporting daily air quality. EPA calculates the AQI for five major air pollutants regulated by the Clean Air Act: ground-level ozone, particle pollution (also known as particulate matter), carbon monoxide, sulfur dioxide, and nitrogen dioxide. The AQI runs from 0 to 500. The higher the AQI value, the greater the level of air pollution and the greater the health concern. There are six AQI categories: "Good" The AQI is between 0 and 50. Air quality is considered satisfactory; "Moderate" The AQI is between 51 and 100. Air quality is acceptable; "Unhealthy for Sensitive Groups" When AQI values are between 101 and 150, members of sensitive groups may experience health effects; "Unhealthy" When AQI values are between 151 and 200 everyone may begin to experience health effects; "Very Unhealthy" AQI values between 201 and 300 trigger a health alert; "Hazardous" AQI values over 300 trigger health warnings of emergency conditions; (1) Data covers El Paso County; (2) Based on 306 days with AQI data in 2008; The EPA has suspended data updates while it assesses its data systems, including AirData reports and maps.
Source: U.S. Environmental Protection Agency, AirData Report, 2008

Air Quality Index Pollutants

Area	Percent of Days when AQI Pollutant was...[2]					
	Carbon Monoxide	Nitrogen Dioxide	Ozone	Sulfur Dioxide	Particulate Matter 2.5	Particulate Matter 10
Area[1]	0.3	0.0	44.1	0.0	38.2	17.3

Note: The Air Quality Index (AQI) is an index for reporting daily air quality. EPA calculates the AQI for five major air pollutants regulated by the Clean Air Act: ground-level ozone, particle pollution (also known as particulate matter), carbon monoxide, sulfur dioxide, and nitrogen dioxide. The AQI runs from 0 to 500. The higher the AQI value, the greater the level of air pollution and the greater the health concern; (1) Data covers El Paso County; (2) Based on 306 days with AQI data in 2008; The EPA has suspended data updates while it assesses its data systems, including AirData reports and maps.
Source: U.S. Environmental Protection Agency, AirData Report, 2008

Air Quality Index Trends

Area	Trend Sites (days)								All Sites (days)
	2002	2003	2004	2005	2006	2007	2008	2009	2009
MSA[1]	15	13	5	10	10	8	8	2	3

Note: Figures are the number of days the AQI value exceeded 100 in a given year. An AQI value greater than 100 indicates that air quality would have been in the unhealthful range on that day. Data from exceptional events are included. These counts are presented in two ways. First, the counts are based on sites having an adequate record of monitoring data during the trend period (trend sites). These counts represent the relative change in the number of days with AQI values greater than 100. In the last column, the counts are based on all sites with data in the most recent year (because it is possible for a site to have data in the most recent year but not enough data to be a trend site); (1) Data covers the El Paso, TX Metropolitan Statistical Area - see Appendix B for areas included
Source: U.S. Environmental Protection Agency, Office of Air and Radiation, Air Quality Index Information, "Number of Days with Air Quality Index Values Greater than 100 and Trend Sites, 1990-2009, and at All Sites in 2009"

Maximum Air Pollutant Concentrations

	Particulate Matter 10 (ug/m^3)	Particulate Matter 2.5 (ug/m^3)	Ozone (ppm)	Carbon Monoxide (ppm)	Sulfur Dioxide (ppm)	Nitrogen Dioxide (ppm)	Lead (ug/m^3)
MSA[1] Level	90	41	0.072	4	0.004	0.016	0.04
NAAQS[2]	150	35	0.075	9	0.140	0.053	0.15
Met NAAQS[2]	Yes	No	Yes	Yes	Yes	Yes	Yes

Note: Data from exceptional events are not included; (1) Data covers the El Paso, TX Metropolitan Statistical Area - see Appendix B for areas included; (2) National Ambient Air Quality Standards; n/a not available Concentrations: Particulate Matter 10 (coarse particulate) - highest second maximum 24-hour concentration; Particulate Matter 2.5 (fine particulate) - highest 98th percentile 24-hour concentration; Ozone - highest fourth daily maximum 8-hour concentration; Carbon Monoxide - highest second maximum non-overlapping 8-hour concentration; Sulfur Dioxide - highest second maximum 24-hour concentration; Nitrogen Dioxide - highest arithmetic mean concentration; Lead - maximum running 3-month average
Units: ppm = parts per million; ug/m^3 = micrograms per cubic meter
Source: U.S. Environmental Protection Agency, CBSA Factbook 2009, Air Quality Statistics by City, 2009

Drinking Water

Water System Name	Pop. Served	Primary Water Source Type	Violations[1]	
			Health Based	Monitoring/ Reporting
El Paso Water Utilities	630,000	Surface	1	0

Note: (1) Based on violation data from January 1, 2010 to December 31, 2010 (includes unresolved violations from earlier years)
Source: U.S. Environmental Protection Agency, Office of Ground Water and Drinking Water, Safe Drinking Water Information System (based on data extracted May 9, 2011)

Fort Lauderdale, Florida

Background

Located on the Atlantic Ocean in southeast Florida, Fort Lauderdale is a city of tiny residential islands, canals, and yacht basins, and is called the "Venice of America."

Originally built as a fortification in 1837 for the Seminole War, Fort Lauderdale eased into more peaceful times as a top tourist spot. Photos of students on spring break, cars cruising "The Strip," and tan young men and women on the beach stimulated the imagination of people around the world.

Tourism remains robust in Fort Lauderdale. Resort hotels include the Seminole Hard Rock Hotel & Casino Hollywood, now infamous as the site of Anna Nicole Smith's high-profile death, the Hilton Fort Lauderdale Beach Resort, and the Fort Lauderdale Grande Hotel & Yacht Club, which opened in 2007. Several other luxury resorts are under construction, including The Marriott Ocean Village and Resort, a conference, retail and hotel complex on six acres of Hollywood Beach oceanfront and Intracoastal Waterway.

Fort Lauderdale is renowned for its resort culture and vibrant nightlife. The city has held on to its reputation as a college spring break hotspot, despite legislation passed over two decades ago outlawing the unruly disturbances that once occurred every spring. While it still attracts spring breakers looking for sunny days and wild nights, Fort Lauderdale is far less impacted by the influx of college students today than it was during the birth of MTV.

Nearby Port Everglades was the winter homeport for the Queen Elizabeth II—Cunard Line's $800 million flagship. The ship is now a first class hotel and entertainment center in Dubai. Port Everglades currently hosts a total of 48 cruise ships from 17 different cruise lines.

Fashionable Las Olas Boulevard, the main artery of downtown, is full of shops and restaurants and a quaint street on which to stroll. The Museum of Art is a handsome modern edifice that showcases nineteenth- and twentieth-century paintings and Japanese objects d'art, and is noted as having the largest U.S. collection of artwork from Copenhagen, Brussels, and Amsterdam. The Museum of Discovery and Science includes the Blockbuster IMAX® Theater, compliments of the multi-corporation mogul Wayne Huizenga, and is fascinating to children of all ages. And the Broward Center for Performing Arts hosts Broadway plays and other major cultural events.

The Fort Lauderdale-Hollywood International Airport, with free Wi-Fi connectivity, is one of the fastest growing in the country, and is also the largest employer in Broward County, with nearly 10,500 employees.

As home to one of the biggest yacht basins in the country, Fort Lauderdale's boating industry stays busy. And, because of its largely residential character, the home improvement industry—concrete, air conditioning, and roofing—plays a large claim to the economy as well.

Fort Lauderdale's climate is primarily subtropical marine, which produces a long, warm summer with abundant rainfall, followed by a mild, dry winter. Hurricanes occasionally affect the area, with most occurring in September and October. Funnel clouds and waterspouts are sometimes sighted during the summer months, but neither causes significant damage. Strong and sometimes spectacular lightning storms occur most often during June, July, and August.

Rankings

General Rankings

- Fort Lauderdale was ranked #158 out of 375 metro areas in *Cities Ranked & Rated*. Criteria: cost of living; climate; crime; transportation; economy and jobs; education; arts and culture; health and healthcare; leisure; quality of life. *Cities Ranked & Rated, 2nd Edition, 2007*

- Fort Lauderdale was ranked #170 out of 379 metro areas in *Places Rated Almanac*. Criteria: health care; education; recreation; transportation; ambience; climate; crime; housing costs; jobs. *Places Rated Almanac, 7th Edition, 2007*

Business/Finance Rankings

- Miami was identified as one of the 20 weakest-performing metro areas during the recession and recovery from December 2007 through December 2010. Criteria: percent change in employment; percentage point change in unemployment rate; percent change in gross metropolitan product; percent change in House Price Index. *Brookings Institution, MetroMonitor: Tracking Economic Recession and Recovery in America's 100 Largest Metropolitan Areas, March 2011*

- Experian ranked the top 20 major U.S metropolitan areas by average debt per consumer. The Miami metro area was ranked #19. Criteria: average debt per consumer. Debt for this study includes credit cards, auto loans and personal loans. It does not include mortgages. *Experian, May 13, 2010*

- A.G. Edwards ranked America's 500 top-performing communities based on their residents' personal savings and investing behavior. The Fort Lauderdale metro area ranked #488 with an index score of 94.81 (national average = 100.00). A dozen statistical factors were measured including: participation in retirement savings plans; personal debt levels; and home ownership. *A.G. Edwards, "2007 Nest Egg Index," September 12, 2007*

- Fort Lauderdale was selected as one of the "100 Best Places to Live and Launch" in the U.S. The city ranked #70. The editors at *Fortune Small Business* ranked 296 Census-designated metro areas by business friendliness (Launching Score, % New Businesses) and lifestyle offerings (Living Score). Then they picked the town within each of the top 100 metro areas that best blends business and pleasure. *Fortune Small Business, "100 Best Places to Live and Launch 2008," April 2008*

- *American City Business Journals* ranked America's 261 largest cities in terms of their resident's wealth. Fort Lauderdale ranked #38. Criteria: per capita income; median household income; percentage of households with annual incomes of $200,000 or more; median home value. *American City Business Journals, www.bizjournals.com, "Where the Money Is: America's Wealth Centers," August 18, 2008*

- The Fort Lauderdale metro area appeared on the Milken Institute "2010 Best Performing Metros" list. Rank: #156 out of 200 large metro areas. Criteria: job growth; wage and salary growth; high-tech output growth. *Milken Institute, "2010 Best Performing Metros"*

- The Fort Lauderdale metro area was selected as one of the best cities for entrepreneurs in America by *Inc. Magazine*. Criteria: job-growth data for 335 metro areas was analyzed for: recent growth trend (the current and prior year's employment growth rates, with the current year emphasized); mid-term growth (the average annual 2002-2007 growth rate); long-term trend (the sum of the 2002-2007 and 1996-2001 employment growth rates multiplied by the ratio of the 1996-2001 growth rate over the 2002-2007 growth rate); current year growth. The Fort Lauderdale metro area ranked #27 among large metro areas and #144 overall. *Inc. Magazine, "The Best Cities for Doing Business," July 2008*

- Fort Lauderdale was ranked #115 out of 145 regions worldwide in terms of its "Knowledge Competitiveness Index." The index attempts to measure the knowledge-based development taking place throughout the world and is based on 19 measures of economic performance that indicate a region's ability to translate its knowledge capacity into economic value. *Centre for International Competitiveness, World Knowledge Competitiveness Index 2008*

- *Forbes* ranked the 200 most populous metro areas in the U.S. in terms of the "Best Places for Business and Careers." The Fort Lauderdale metro area was ranked #175. Criteria: 12 metrics including costs (business and living), job growth (past and projected), income growth, educational attainment, projected economic growth, crime, cultural and recreational opportunities, net migration patterns, percentage of subprime mortgages handed out over a three-year period, and the number of highly ranked four-year colleges. *Forbes, "Best Places for Business and Careers," April 14, 2010*

Children/Family Rankings

- The Fort Lauderdale metro area was selected as one of the "Best Cities for Relocating Families" by Worldwide ERC and Primacy Relocation. The 2008 study looked at nearly 50 factors important to relocating families including: recent job growth; nearby top-ranked colleges; in-state tuition for four-year public colleges; population growth since 2000; pediatricians per 100,000 population; and a Green Living index. *Worldwide ERC and Primacy Relocation, "2008 Best Cities for Relocating Families"*

Dating/Romance Rankings

- Eli Lily and Company, in partnership with Sperling's BestPlaces, ranked the nation's 50 largest metro areas in terms of the "Most Romantic Cities for Baby Boomers." The Miami metro area ranked #49. Criteria: marriage and divorce rates among "baby boomers" age 45 to 60; great restaurants; dance studios; chocolate, jewelry and flower sales. *Eli Lily and Company, "Most Romantic Cities for Baby Boomers," April 20, 2007*

- The Fort Lauderdale metro area was selected as one of the "Best Cities for Relocating Singles" by Worldwide ERC and Primacy Relocation. The area ranked #24 out of the 100 largest metro areas in the U.S. Areas were selected based on the following criteria: recent job growth; recent singles population growth; overall population growth; affordable rental housing; cost-of-living index; expanded arts and recreation opportunities; ratio of single men and single women; affordability of quality higher education (including state residency requirements); diversity index; climate; population density. *Worldwide ERC and Primacy Relocation, "2008 Best Cities for Relocating Singles"*

- *Forbes* ranked the 40 most populous urbanized areas in the U.S. in terms of the "Best Cities for Singles." The Miami metro area ranked #29. Criteria: number of singles; cost of living alone; nightlife; culture; job growth; coolness; and online dating participation. *Forbes.com, "Best Cities for Singles," July 27, 2009*

Education Rankings

- Fort Lauderdale was identified as one of the 100 "smartest" metro areas in the U.S. The area ranked #61. Criteria: the editors rated the collective brainpower of the 100 largest metro area in the U.S based on their residents' educational attainment. *American City Business Journals, www.bizjournals.com, April 14, 2008*

- Fort Lauderdale was identified as one of "America's Brainiest Bastions" by *Portfolio.com*. The metro area ranked #118 out of 200. Portfolio.com analyzed levels of educational attainment in the nation's 200 largest metropolitan areas. The editors established scores for five levels of educational attainment, based on relative earning power of adult workers age 25 or older. Scores were determined by comparing the median income for all workers with the median income for those workers at a specified educational level. *Portfolio.com, "America's Brainiest Bastions," December 1, 2010*

Environmental Rankings

- Fort Lauderdale was selected as one of 22 "Smarter Cities" for energy by the Natural Resources Defense Council." Criteria: investment in green power; energy efficiency measures; conservation. *Natural Resources Defense Council, "2010 Smarter Cities," July 19, 2010*

- *American City Business Journal* ranked 43 metropolitan areas in terms of their "greenness." The Fort Lauderdale metro area ranked #30. Criteria: Forty-one metros in which *ACBJ* has business weeklies, plus Indianapolis and Cleveland, were ranked based on 20 different indicators such as adoption of green technologies, utilization of environmentally sound practices, and air and water quality. *American City Business Journals, "Green City Index," March 11, 2010*

- The Miami metro area was selected as one of "America's Cleanest Cities" by *Forbes*. The metro area ranked #1 out of 10. Criteria: air quality; water quality; per capita spending on Superfund site cleanup and solid-waste management. *Forbes.com, "America's Cleanest Cities," March 11, 2008*

- 100 of the largest metro areas in the U.S. were analyzed in terms of their current drought severity. The Fort Lauderdale metro area ranked #58 (#1 = driest). The rankings were based on statistics such as long-term precipitation trends and patterns and the Palmer drought indices. *Sperling's BestPlaces, www.BestPlaces.net, "America's Drought-Riskiest Cities," November 2007*

- The Fort Lauderdale metro area appeared in *Country Home's* "Best Green Places" report. The area ranked #219 out of 379. Criteria: official energy policies; green power; green buildings; availability of fresh, locally grown food. *Country Home, "Best Green Places," 2008*

Health/Fitness Rankings

- Miami was identified as a "2011 Asthma Capital." The area ranked #61 out of the nation's 100 largest metropolitan areas. Twelve factors were used to identify the most challenging places to live for people with asthma: estimated prevalence; self-reported prevalence; crude death rate for asthma; annual pollen score; annual air quality; public smoking laws; number of board-certified asthma specialists; school inhaler access laws; rescue medication use; controller medication use; uninsured rate; poverty rate. *Asthma and Allergy Foundation of America, "2011 Asthma Capitals"*

- Miami was identified as a 2009 "Spring Allergy Capital." The area ranked #97 out of 100. Three groups of factors were used to identify the most severe cities for people with allergies during the spring season: annual pollen levels; medicine utilization; access to board-certified allergists. *Asthma and Allergy Foundation of America, "Spring Allergy Capitals 2009"*

- Miami was identified as a 2010 "Fall Allergy Capital." The area ranked #88 out of 100. Three groups of factors were used to identify the most severe cities for people with allergies during the fall season: annual pollen levels; medicine utilization; access to board-certified allergists. *Asthma and Allergy Foundation of America, "Fall Allergy Capitals 2010"*

- Ortho-McNeil Neurologics, in partnership with Sperling's BestPlaces, analyzed 110 metro areas and identified those U.S. cities with the highest prevalence of factors that are most commonly associated with migraine headaches. The Fort Lauderdale metro area ranked #104. Criteria: number of migraine-related drug prescriptions per capita; lifestyle factors that can contribute to migraines; environmental factors that can trigger migraines; and consumption of migraine-triggering foods. *Ortho-McNeil Neurologics, "America's Migraine Hot Spots," March 14, 2006*

- An analysis of the "Best & Worst Cities for Sleep" was conducted by Sperling's BestPlaces. The study ranked America's 50 most populated metro areas. The Fort Lauderdale metro area ranked #38 (#1 = best city for sleep). Criteria: number of days residents didn't get enough rest or sleep during the past month; average length of daily commute; divorce rate; unemployment rate. *Sperling's BestPlaces, www.BestPlaces.net, "Best & Worst Cities for Sleep," 2006*

- The Fort Lauderdale metropolitan area was selected as one of the best metros for hospital care in America by HealthGrades. The rankings are based on a comprehensive study of patient death and complication rates in the nation's nearly 5,000 hospitals. Hospitals performing in the top 5% nationwide across 26 different medical procedures and diagnoses were identified. HealthGrades then ranked cities by the highest percentage of these Distinguished Hospitals for Clinical Excellence™. The Fort Lauderdale metro area ranked #19. *HealthGrades.com, "America's Top 50 Cities for Hospital Care," January 26, 2011*

- The American Academy of Dermatology ranked 26 U.S. metropolitan regions in terms of their residents knowledge, attitude and behaviors towards tanning, sun protection and skin cancer detection. The Miami metro area ranked #13. The results of the study are based on an online survey of over 7,000 adults nationwide. *American Academy of Dermatology, "Suntelligence: How Sun Smart is Your City," May 3, 2010*

- The Fort Lauderdale metro area appeared in the 2010 Gallup-Healthways Well-Being Index. The index, based on interviews with more than 353,000 Americans during 2009, asked individuals to assess their jobs, finances, physical health, emotional state of mind and communities. The metro area ranked #121 out of 162. Criteria: life evaluation; emotional health; work environment; physical health; healthy behaviors; basic access (basic needs optimal for a healthy life, such as access to food and medicine, having health insurance and feeling safe while walking at night). *Gallup-Healthways, "Well-Being Index 2010"*

- The Fort Lauderdale metro area was identified as one of "America's Most Stressful Cities" by *Forbes*. The metro area ranked #20. Criteria: median home price drop; unemployment rates; cost of living; air quality; sunny days; population density. *Forbes.com, "America's Most Stressful Cities," August 20, 2009*

- The Miami metro area was identified as one of "America's 20 Most Sedentary Cities" by *Forbes*. The metro area ranked #10. Criteria: percentage of overweight or obese people; percentage of people who had not engaged in any physical activity in the past 30 days; average number of hours of TV watched per week. *Forbes.com, "America's Most Sedentary Cities," October 29, 2007*

- 50 of the largest metro areas in the U.S. were analyzed in terms of their health and fitness by the American College of Sports Medicine in their "American Fitness Index." The Miami metro area ranked #39 (#1 = healthiest). Criteria: preventative health behaviors; levels of chronic disease; health care access; community resources and policies that support physical activity. *American College of Sports Medicine, "Health and Community Fitness Status of the 50 Largest Metropolitan Areas," May 24, 2010*

Real Estate Rankings

- *Fortune* ranked the 100 largest metro areas in the U.S. in terms of projected median home price change in 2010. The Fort Lauderdale metro area ranked #98. *Fortune, "The 2010 Housing Outlook," December 9, 2009*

- Fort Lauderdale appeared on ApartmentRatings.com "Top College Towns & Cities" for renters list in 2010." The area ranked #83. Overall satisfaction ratings were ranked using thousands of user submitted scores for hundreds of apartment complexes located in cities and towns that are home to the 100 largest four-year institutions in the U.S. *ApartmentRatings.com, "2010 College Town Renter Satisfaction Rankings"*

- The Fort Lauderdale metro area was identified as one of "America's 25 Weakest Housing Markets" by *Forbes*. The metro area ranked #4. Criteria: metro areas with populations over 500,000 were ranked based on projected home values through 2011. *Forbes.com, "America's 25 Weakest Housing Markets," January 7, 2009*

- The nation's largest metro areas were analyzed in terms of the percentage of households entering some stage of foreclosure in 2010. The Miami metro area ranked #5 out of 206 (#1 = highest foreclosure rate). *RealtyTrac, 2010 Year-End Metropolitan Foreclosure Market Report, January 27, 2011*

- The Fort Lauderdale metro area appeared in a *Wall Street Journal* article ranking cities by "housing stress." The metro area was ranked #1 (#1 = most stress). Criteria: fraction of mortgage-holding homeowners with a monthly housing payment in excess of 30 percent of income; percentage of people without health insurance; unemployment rate. *The Wall Street Journal, "Which Cities Face Biggest Housing Risk," October 5, 2010*

- The Center for Housing Policy ranked 210 U.S metropolitan areas by the fair market rent for a two-bedroom unit. The Fort Lauderdale metro area was ranked #14. (#1 = most expensive) with a rent of $1,358. Criteria: Fair Market Rent (FMR) in effect during the fourth quarter of 2009 based on HUD's fiscal year 2010 FMRs. *The Center for Housing Policy, "Paycheck to Paycheck: Most to Least Expensive Rental Markets in 2009"*

- The Fort Lauderdale metro area was identified as one of the top 20 cities in terms of decreasing home equity. The metro area was ranked #17. Criteria: percentage of home equity relative to the home's current value. *Forbes.com, "Where Americans are Losing Home Equity Most," May 1, 2010*

- The Fort Lauderdale metro area was identified as one of the markets with the best expected performance in home prices over the next 12 months. *Local Market Monitor, "First Quarter Home Price Forecast for Largest US Markets," March 2, 2011*

Safety Rankings

- Allstate ranked the 200 largest cities in America in terms of driver safety. Fort Lauderdale ranked #123. In addition, drivers were 14.1% more likely to have had an accident compared to the national average. Allstate researchers analyzed internal property damage reported claims over a two-year period (from January 2007 to December 2008) to ensure the findings would not be affected by external influences such as weather or road construction. A weighted average of the two-year numbers determined the annual percentages. The report defines an auto crash as any collision resulting in a property damage claim. *Allstate, "The 2010 Allstate America's Best Drivers Report™"*

- Sperling's BestPlaces analyzed the tracks of tropical storms for the past 100 years and ranked which areas are most likely to be hit by a major hurricane. The Fort Lauderdale metro area ranked #1 out of 10. *Sperling's BestPlaces, www.bestplaces.net, February 2, 2006*

- The National Insurance Crime Bureau ranked 366 metro areas in the U.S. in terms of per capita rates of vehicle theft. The Fort Lauderdale metro area ranked #42 (#1 = highest rate). Criteria: number of vehicle theft offenses per 100,000 inhabitants. *National Insurance Crime Bureau, "Hot Spots," May 17, 2010*

- The Fort Lauderdale metro area was identified as one of the "The Most Dangerous Metro Areas for Pedestrians" by Transportation for America and the Surface Transportation Policy Partnership. The metro area ranked #3 out of 52 metro areas with over 1 million residents. Criteria: area's population divided by the number of pedestrian fatalities in that area. *Transportation for America and the Surface Transportation Policy Partnership, "Dangerous by Design: Solving the Epidemic of Preventable Pedestrian Deaths (and Making Great Neighborhoods)," November 11, 2009*

Seniors/Retirement Rankings

- The Fort Lauderdale metro area was selected as one of the "10 Best Places for Single Seniors to Retire" by *U.S. News & World Report.* Criteria: metro areas with the most single seniors age 55 and over. *U.S. News & World Report, "10 Best Places for Single Seniors to Retire," November 1, 2010*

- Fort Lauderdale was identified as one of "The Top 100 Places to Retire" by *Topretirements.com* The list reflects the 100 cities (out of 625+ total cities reviewed) that visitors to the website are most interested in for retirement. *Topretirements.com, "2011 Best Places to Retire List: The Sunbelt Rules"*

- Fort Lauderdale was selected as one of America's "Top 10 Places for Swinging Single Seniors to Retire" by *U.S. News & World Report.* Criteria: 10 retirement destinations were selected that have plenty of opportunities to meet other singles and fun things to do on a date. *U.S. News & World Report, "Top 10 Places for Swinging Single Seniors to Retire," February 20, 2009*

- The Fort Lauderdale metro area was selected as one of "The 10 Most Affordable Cities for Long-Term Care" by *U.S. News & World Report.* Criteria: costs at nursing homes, assisted living facilities, and adult day health care facilities; cost for licensed home health aides. *U.S. News & Word Report, "The 10 Most Affordable Cities for Long-Term Care," May 17, 2010*

Sports/Recreation Rankings

- Fort Lauderdale was chosen as one of America's 10 best places to live and boat. Criteria: boating opportunities; boat-friendly regulations; water access; availability of waterfront homes; health of the local economy; and overall lifestyle for boaters. *Boating Magazine, "10 Best Places to Live and Boat," June 2010*

- Scarborough Research, a leading market research firm, identified the top local markets for avid NBA fans. The Fort Lauderdale DMA (Designated Market Area) ranked in the top 10 with 13% of consumers 18 years and over reporting that they are "very interested in the NBA." *Scarborough Research, April 24, 2006*

- *Golf Digest* ranked 330 metro areas in the U.S. in terms of golf. The Fort Lauderdale metro area was ranked #266. Criteria: access to golf; weather; value of golf; and quality of golf. *Golf Digest, "Metro Golf Rankings," August 2005*

Technology Rankings

- The Fort Lauderdale metro area was selected as one of "America's Most Wired Cities" by *Forbes*. The metro area was ranked #17 out of 20. Criteria: percentage of Internet users with high-speed access; number of companies providing high-speed Internet; number of public wireless hot spots. *Forbes, "America's Most Wired Cities," March 2, 2010*

Transportation Rankings

- The Fort Lauderdale metro area appeared on *Forbes* list of the best and worst cities for commuters. The metro area ranked #55 out of 60 (#1 is best). Criteria: travel time; road congestion; travel delays. *Forbes.com, "Best and Worst Cities for Commuters," February 16, 2010*

Women/Minorities Rankings

- Fort Lauderdale was ranked #40 out of 100 metro areas in *SELF Magazine's* ranking of America's healthiest places for women." A panel of experts came up with more than 50 criteria including death and disease rates, environmental indicators, community resources, and lifestyle habits. *SELF Magazine, "Secrets of America's Healthiest Women," December 2008*

Miscellaneous Rankings

- Energizer Holdings, the makers of Edge® shave gel, in partnership with Sperling's BestPlaces, ranked 50 major metro areas in terms of everyday irritations. The Miami metro area ranked #14. Criteria: humidity levels; weather conditions; incidence of traffic delays and congestion; average commute times; frequency of flight delays and cancellations; rates of sleeplessness; underemployment; pollens and allergens; pests; comedy clubs per capita. *Energizer Holdings, "Most Irritation Prone Cities," July 23, 2010*

- Mars Chocolate North America, the makers of COMBOS®, in partnership with Sperling's BestPlaces, ranked 50 major metro areas in terms of their "manliness." The Miami metro area ranked #49. Criteria: number of home improvement stores, steak houses, pickup trucks, motorcycles, and manly occupations (fire fighters, police officers, construction workers, EMP personnel) per capita; salty snack sales; sports TV viewing habits. *Mars Chocolate North America, "America's Manliest Cities," June 22, 2010*

- The Miami metro area was selected as one of "America's Greediest Cities" by *Forbes*. The area was ranked #10 out of 10. Criteria: number of Forbes 400 (*Forbes* annual list of the richest Americans) members per capita. *Forbes, "America's Greediest Cities," December 7, 2007*

- The Fort Lauderdale metro area was selected as one of "America's 20 Most Miserable Cities" by *Forbes*. The metro area ranked #13. Criteria: jobless rates; inflation; taxes; commuting times; crime rates; performance by the city's sports teams; weather; pollution; corruption by public officials. *Forbes.com, "America's 20 Most Miserable Cities, 2011" February 2, 2011*

- The Miami metro area appeared on *Forbes* list of "America's Drunkest Cities." The area ranked #33. Criteria: 35 of the largest continental U.S. metro areas were chosen based on availability of data and geographic diversity. Each metro was ranked in five areas: state laws; drinkers; heavy drinkers; binge drinkers; and alcoholism. *Forbes.com, "America's Drunkest Cities," August 22, 2006*

Business Environment

CITY FINANCES

City Government Finances

Component	2008 ($000)	2008 ($ per capita)
Total Revenues	597,622	3,255
Total Expenditures	489,711	2,667
Debt Outstanding	329,492	1,795
Cash and Securities[1]	1,270,553	6,920

Note: (1) Cash and security holdings of a government at the close of its fiscal year, including those of its dependent agencies, utilities, and liquor stores.
Source: U.S Census Bureau, State & Local Government Finances 2008

City Government Revenue by Source

Source	2008 ($000)	2008 ($ per capita)
General Revenue		
From Federal Government	22,631	123
From State Government	20,900	114
From Local Governments	27,853	152
Taxes		
Property	138,130	752
Sales and Gross Receipts	57,464	313
Personal Income	0	0
Corporate Income	0	0
Motor Vehicle License	0	0
Other Taxes	13,351	73
Current Charges	58,390	318
Liquor Store	0	0
Utility	77,983	425
Employee Retirement	109,637	597

Source: U.S Census Bureau, State & Local Government Finances 2008

City Government Expenditures by Function

Function	2008 ($000)	2008 ($ per capita)	2008 (%)
General Direct Expenditures			
Air Transportation	6,214	34	1.3
Corrections	0	0	0.0
Education	0	0	0.0
Employment Security Administration	0	0	0.0
Financial Administration	13,280	72	2.7
Fire Protection	70,787	386	14.5
General Public Buildings	0	0	0.0
Governmental Administration, Other	8,242	45	1.7
Health	29	< 1	< 0.1
Highways	14,556	79	3.0
Hospitals	0	0	0.0
Housing and Community Development	19,764	108	4.0
Interest on General Debt	4,803	26	1.0
Judicial and Legal	3,150	17	0.6
Libraries	0	0	0.0
Parking	8,848	48	1.8
Parks and Recreation	39,227	214	8.0
Police Protection	86,310	470	17.6
Public Welfare	0	0	0.0
Sewerage	0	0	0.0
Solid Waste Management	19,614	107	4.0
Veterans' Services	0	0	0.0
Liquor Store	0	0	0.0
Utility	68,738	374	14.0
Employee Retirement	67,127	366	13.7

Source: U.S Census Bureau, State & Local Government Finances 2008

Municipal Bond Ratings

Area	Moody's	S&P	Fitch
City	n/a	n/a	n/a

Rating Systems (shown in declining order of credit quality): Moody's– Aaa, Aa, A, Baa, Ba, B, Caa, Ca, C (numerical modifiers 1, 2, and 3 are added to letter-rating); S&P– AAA, AA, A, BBB, BB, B, CCC, CC, C; Fitch– AAA, AA, A, BBB, BB, B, CCC, CC, C. Ratings may be modified by the addition of a plus or minus sign to show relative standing within the major rating categories.
Notes: n/a Not available; (1) Not reviewed; (2) Issuer Rating/No General Obligation; (3) Standard and Poor's Issue Credit Rating (ICR) is a current opinion of an obliger with respect to a specific financial obligation, a specific class of financial obligations, or a specific financial program.
Source: U.S. Census Bureau, 2011 Statistical Abstract, Bond Ratings for City Governments by Largest Cities: 2009

DEMOGRAPHICS

Population Growth

Area	1990 Census	2000 Census	2010 Estimate	2015 Projection	Population Growth (%) 2000-2010	Population Growth (%) 2010-2015
City	149,908	152,397	158,684	161,790	4.1	2.0
MSA[1]	4,056,100	5,007,564	5,519,882	5,786,816	10.2	4.8
U.S.	248,709,873	281,421,906	309,038,974	321,675,005	9.8	4.1

Note: (1) Metropolitan Statistical Area - see Appendix B for areas included
Source: Claritas, Inc.

Number of Households and Average Household Size

Area	2010 Estimate	2010 Average Household Size
City	70,385	2.18
MSA[1]	2,058,462	2.64
U.S.	116,136,617	2.59

Note: (1) Metropolitan Statistical Area - see Appendix B for areas included
Source: Claritas, Inc.

Race and Ethnicity

Area	White Alone[2] (%)	Black Alone[2] (%)	Asian Alone[2] (%)	Other Race Alone[2] (%)	Hispanic[3] (%)
City	60.5	30.6	1.2	7.7	12.4
MSA[1]	69.7	19.4	2.1	8.9	40.3
U.S.	72.3	12.4	4.4	10.9	15.8

Note: Figures are 2010 estimates; (1) Metropolitan Statistical Area - see Appendix B for areas included (2) Alone is defined as not being in combination with one or more other races; (3) May be of any race.
Source: Claritas, Inc.

Segregation

Type	Segregation Indices[1] 1990	2000	2010	2010 Rank[2]	Percent Change 1990-2000	1990-2010	2000-2010
Black/White	71.4	69.2	64.8	23	-2.3	-6.6	-4.3
Asian/White	26.8	33.3	34.2	80	6.4	7.3	0.9
Hispanic/White	32.5	59.0	57.4	8	26.5	24.8	-1.6

Note: Figures are based on an analysis of 1990, 2000, and 2010 Census Decennial Census tract data by William H. Frey, Brookings Institution and the University of Michigan Social Science Data Analysis Network. In this analysis all racial groups (whites, blacks, and asians) are non-Hispanic members of those races. Hispanics are shown as a separate category; All figures cover the Metropolitan Statistical Area (see Appendix B for areas included); (1) Segregation Indices are Dissimilarity Indices that measure the degree to which the minority group is distributed differently than whites across census tracts. They range from 0 (complete integration) to 100 (complete [segregation) where the value indicates the percentage of the minority group that needs to move to be distributed exactly like whites; (2) Ranges from 1 (most segregated) to 102 (least segregated); n/a not available.
Source: www.CensusScope.org

Ancestry

Area	German	Irish	English	American	Italian	Polish	French	Scottish
City	9.4	10.4	7.5	7.8	7.8	2.8	2.0	1.8
MSA[1]	6.2	6.0	4.2	4.2	5.9	2.5	1.7	0.9
U.S.	16.6	12.0	9.1	6.1	5.9	3.3	3.1	1.9

Note: The top eight ancestries in the U.S. are shown. Figures are percentages and include multiple ancestry (e.g. if a person reported being Irish and Italian, they were included in both columns); (1) Metropolitan Statistical Area - see Appendix B for areas included
Source: U.S. Census Bureau, 2007-2009 American Community Survey 3-Year Estimates

Foreign-Born Population

Area	Percent of Population Born in								
	Any Foreign Country	Mexico	Asia	Europe	Carribean	South America	Central America[2]	Africa	Canada
City	21.5	0.9	1.7	3.4	8.5	3.2	2.4	0.5	0.9
MSA[1]	36.7	1.2	1.9	2.3	18.6	7.3	4.4	0.4	0.6
U.S.	12.5	3.8	3.4	1.6	1.1	0.8	0.9	0.5	0.3

Note: (1) Metropolitan Statistical Area - see Appendix B for areas included; (2) Excludes Mexico.
Source: U.S. Census Bureau, 2007-2009 American Community Survey 3-Year Estimates

Marriage Status

Area	Never Married	Now Married[2]	Separated	Widowed	Divorced
City	39.0	36.6	2.9	6.2	15.3
MSA[1]	31.9	45.5	2.9	7.5	12.3
U.S.	31.4	49.7	2.2	6.2	10.6

Note: Figures are percentages and cover the population 15 years of age and older;
(1) Metropolitan Statistical Area - see Appendix B for areas included; (2) Excludes separated
Source: U.S. Census Bureau, 2007-2009 American Community Survey 3-Year Estimates

Age Distribution and Median Age

Area	Percent of Population							Median Age
	Under Age 5	Age 5 to 17	Age 18 to 34	Age 35 to 49	Age 50 to 64	Age 65 to 79	80 Years and Over	
City	6.3	13.9	21.6	24.0	20.4	9.4	4.5	40.7
MSA[1]	6.6	16.2	21.6	22.2	17.6	10.4	5.4	39.0
U.S.	6.9	17.5	23.3	21.4	18.1	9.1	3.7	36.7

Note: (1) Metropolitan Statistical Area - see Appendix B for areas included
Source: U.S. Census Bureau, 2007-2009 American Community Survey 3-Year Estimates

Male/Female Ratio

Area	Males	Females	Males per 100 Females
City	83,393	75,291	110.8
MSA[1]	2,682,549	2,837,333	94.5
U.S.	152,401,520	156,637,454	97.3

Note: Figures are 2010 estimates; (1) Metropolitan Statistical Area -
see Appendix B for areas included
Source: Claritas, Inc.

Religion

Area	Catholic	Southern Baptist	United Methodist	ELCA[1]	LDS[2]	Presbyterian Church USA	Jewish Est.	Muslim Est.
County	21.1	3.6	1.2	0.3	0.3	0.4	13.1	0.4
U.S.	22.0	7.1	3.7	1.8	1.5	1.1	2.2	0.6

Note: Figures are the number of adherents as a percentage of the total population; Adherents are defined as all members, including full members, their children and the estimated number of other participants who are not considered members (e.g. the baptized, those not confirmed, those regularly attending services, etc.);
(1) Evangelical Lutheran Church in America; (2) The Church of Jesus Christ of Latter Day Saints
Source: Reprinted with permission from Religious Congregations and Membership in the United States 2000 (Nashville, Glenmary Research Center, 2002) Copyright Association of Statisticians of American Religious Bodies. All rights reserved.

ECONOMY

Gross Metropolitan Product

Area	2006	2007	2008	2009	2009 Rank[2]
MSA[1]	251.5	260.0	261.3	257.2	11

Note: Figures are in billions of dollars; (1) Miami-Fort Lauderdale-Miami Beach, FL Metropolitan Statistical Area - see Appendix B for areas included; (2) Rank ranges from 1 to 363
Source: The U.S. Conference of Mayors, "Pace of Economic Recovery: GMP and Jobs," January 2010

Economic Growth

Area	2006-2008 (%)	2009 (%)	2010 (%)	Rank[2]
MSA[1]	-0.4	-2.5	2.4	294
U.S.	1.3	-2.5	2.2	–

Note: Figures are real Gross Metropolitan Product growth rates and represent annual average percent change; (1) Miami-Fort Lauderdale-Miami Beach, FL Metropolitan Statistical Area - see Appendix B for areas included; (2) Rank ranges from 1 to 363
Source: The U.S. Conference of Mayors, "Pace of Economic Recovery: GMP and Jobs," January 2010

Metropolitan Area Exports

Area	2005	2006	2007	2008	2009	2009 Rank[2]
MSA[1]	20,382.9	23,491.3	26,197.4	33,411.5	31,175.0	5

Note: Figures are in millions of dollars; (1) Miami-Fort Lauderdale-Miami Beach, FL Metropolitan Statistical Area - see Appendix B for areas included; (2) Rank ranges from 1 to 374
Source: U.S. Department of Commerce, International Trade Administration, Office of Trade & Industry Information, Manufacturing & Services

INCOME

Per Capita/Median/Average Income

Area	Per Capita ($)	Median Household ($)	Average Household ($)
City	33,686	49,118	74,854
MSA[1]	27,136	50,324	72,073
U.S.	27,034	52,795	71,071

Note: Figures are 2010 estimates; (1) Metropolitan Statistical Area - see Appendix B for areas included
Source: Claritas, Inc.

Household Income Distribution

Area	Percent of Households Earning							
	Under $15,000	$15,000 -24,999	$25,000 -34,999	$35,000 -49,999	$50,000 -74,999	$75,000 -99,000	$100,000 -149,999	$150,000 and up
City	14.1	11.2	11.2	14.4	18.4	10.7	9.6	10.4
MSA[1]	13.4	10.7	10.9	14.8	18.6	11.4	11.4	8.8
U.S.	12.1	10.2	10.6	15.0	19.5	12.5	12.1	8.0

Note: Figures are 2010 estimates; (1) Metropolitan Statistical Area - see Appendix B for areas included
Source: Claritas, Inc.

Poverty Rates by Age

Area	All Ages	Under 18 Years Old	18 to 64 Years Old	65 Years and Over
City	18.2	6.1	10.4	1.7
MSA[1]	14.2	4.4	7.5	2.3
U.S.	13.6	4.7	7.7	1.2

Note: Figures are percent of population with income during the previous 12 months below poverty level and only include population for whom poverty status is determined; (1) Metropolitan Statistical Area - see Appendix B for areas included
Source: U.S. Census Bureau, 2007-2009 American Community Survey 3-Year Estimates

Personal Bankruptcy Filing Rate

Area	2006	2007	2008	2009	2010
Broward County	1.32	2.21	3.69	5.37	6.71
U.S.	2.00	2.73	3.53	4.60	4.96

Note: Numbers are per 1,000 population and include Chapter 7 and Chapter 13 filings
Source: Federal Deposit Insurance Corporation, Regional Economic Conditions, March 17, 2011

EMPLOYMENT

Labor Force and Employment

Area	Civilian Labor Force			Workers Employed		
	Dec. 2009	Dec. 2010	% Chg.	Dec. 2009	Dec. 2010	% Chg.
City	102,833	103,747	0.9	93,969	94,060	0.1
MD[1]	976,384	985,607	0.9	884,149	885,009	0.1
U.S.	152,693,000	153,156,000	0.3	137,953,000	139,159,000	0.9

Note: Data is not seasonally adjusted and covers workers 16 years of age and older;
(1) Metropolitan Division - see Appendix B for areas included
Source: Bureau of Labor Statistics, http://stats.bls.gov

Unemployment Rate

Area	2010											
	Jan.	Feb.	Mar.	Apr.	May	Jun.	Jul.	Aug.	Sep.	Oct.	Nov.	Dec.
City	9.2	8.9	8.8	8.6	8.5	8.8	9.4	9.5	9.4	9.4	9.9	9.3
MD[1]	10.1	9.9	9.8	9.5	9.5	9.9	10.4	10.5	10.3	10.1	10.7	10.2
U.S.	10.6	10.4	10.2	9.5	9.3	9.6	9.7	9.5	9.2	9.0	9.3	9.1

Note: Data is not seasonally adjusted and covers workers 16 years of age and older; All figures are percentages; (1) Metropolitan Division - see Appendix B for areas included
Source: Bureau of Labor Statistics, http://stats.bls.gov

Projected Unemployment Rate

Area	2007 (%)	2009 (%)	2011 (%)	2013 (%)
MSA[1]	4.5	11.4	10.0	8.0

Note: (1) Metropolitan Statistical Area - see Appendix B for areas included
Source: The U.S. Conference of Mayors, "Pace of Economic Recovery: GMP and Jobs," January 2010

Employment by Occupation

Occupation Classification	City (%)	MSA[1] (%)	U.S. (%)
Sales and Office	28.1	28.7	25.4
Professional and Related	17.9	18.0	21.0
Service	19.4	19.7	17.2
Production, Transportation, and Material Moving	8.2	8.9	12.3
Management, Business, and Financial	17.1	14.6	14.1
Construction, Extraction, and Maintenance	9.2	9.7	9.2
Farming, Forestry, and Fishing	0.1	0.4	0.7

Note: Figures cover employed civilians 16 years of age and older;
(1) Metropolitan Statistical Area - see Appendix B for areas included
Source: U.S. Census Bureau, 2007-2009 American Community Survey 3-Year Estimates

Employment by Industry

| Sector | MSA[1] | | U.S. |
	Number of Employees	Percent of Total	Percent of Total
Government	101,200	14.3	17.2
Education and Health Services	96,100	13.5	15.2
Professional and Business Services	118,200	16.7	13.0
Retail Trade	96,900	13.7	11.4
Leisure and Hospitality	77,200	10.9	9.7
Manufacturing	23,400	3.3	8.8
Financial Activities	53,200	7.5	5.8
Wholesale Trade	43,400	6.1	4.2
Construction	30,300	4.3	4.1
Other Services	30,700	4.3	4.1
Transportation and Utilities	22,400	3.2	3.7
Information	16,400	2.3	2.1
Mining and Logging	n/a	n/a	0.6

Note: Figures cover non-farm employment as of December 2010 and are not seasonally adjusted;
(1) Metropolitan Statistical Area - see Appendix B for areas included; n/a not available
Source: Bureau of Labor Statistics, http://stats.bls.gov

Occupations with Greatest Projected Employment Growth: 2006 - 2016

Occupation[1]	2006 Employment	2016 Projected Employment	Numeric Employment Change	Percent Employment Change
Retail salespersons	283,850	339,780	55,930	19.7
Customer service representatives	162,780	214,600	51,820	31.8
Registered nurses	148,390	190,020	41,630	28.1
Combined food preparation and serving workers, including fast food	163,780	202,670	38,890	23.7
Waiters and waitresses	197,920	232,430	34,510	17.4
Office clerks, general	188,190	221,750	33,560	17.8
Bookkeeping, accounting, and auditing clerks	128,340	153,830	25,490	19.9
Janitors and cleaners, except maids and housekeeping cleaners	124,030	147,970	23,940	19.3
Sales representatives, services, all other	73,650	97,390	23,740	32.2
Executive secretaries and administrative assistants	106,820	129,140	22,320	20.9

Note: Projections cover Florida; (1) Sorted by numeric employment change
Source: www.projectionscentral.com, State Occupational Projections, 2006-2016 Long-Term Projections

Fastest Growing Occupations: 2006 - 2016

Occupation[1]	2006 Employment	2016 Projected Employment	Numeric Employment Change	Percent Employment Change
Network systems and data communications analysts	20,830	33,090	12,260	58.9
Court reporters	2,170	3,430	1,260	58.1
Computer software engineers, applications	17,350	27,250	9,900	57.1
Veterinary technologists and technicians	5,720	8,880	3,160	55.2
Veterinarians	3,280	4,890	1,610	49.1
Home health aides	29,600	42,780	13,180	44.5
Personal and home care aides	10,640	15,220	4,580	43.0
Paralegals and legal assistants	19,240	27,360	8,120	42.2
Pharmacy technicians	21,110	29,950	8,840	41.9
Medical assistants	31,040	43,930	12,890	41.5

Note: Projections cover Florida; (1) Sorted by percent employment change and excludes occupations with numeric employment change less than 900
Source: www.projectionscentral.com, State Occupational Projections, 2006-2016 Long-Term Projections

Average Wages

Occupation	$/Hr.	Occupation	$/Hr.
Accountants and Auditors	30.97	Maids and Housekeeping Cleaners	9.54
Automotive Mechanics	17.83	Maintenance and Repair Workers	16.13
Bookkeepers	17.04	Marketing Managers	56.51
Carpenters	17.86	Nuclear Medicine Technologists	37.48
Cashiers	9.13	Nurses, Licensed Practical	19.56
Clerks, General Office	12.33	Nurses, Registered	31.98
Clerks, Receptionists/Information	13.15	Nursing Aides/Orderlies/Attendants	11.18
Clerks, Shipping/Receiving	13.09	Packers and Packagers, Hand	9.73
Computer Programmers	30.17	Physical Therapists	39.43
Computer Support Specialists	17.34	Postal Service Mail Carriers	24.64
Computer Systems Analysts	33.24	Real Estate Brokers	31.35
Cooks, Restaurant	12.19	Retail Salespersons	13.64
Dentists	n/a	Sales Reps., Exc. Tech./Scientific	26.45
Electrical Engineers	34.90	Sales Reps., Tech./Scientific	34.49
Electricians	19.36	Secretaries, Exc. Legal/Med./Exec.	14.38
Financial Managers	55.87	Security Guards	10.71
First-Line Supervisors/Mgrs., Sales	21.57	Surgeons	115.99
Food Preparation Workers	9.86	Teacher Assistants	9.60
General and Operations Managers	50.46	Teachers, Elementary School	n/a
Hairdressers/Cosmetologists	13.85	Teachers, Secondary School	n/a
Internists	93.92	Telemarketers	10.83
Janitors and Cleaners	10.26	Truck Drivers, Heavy/Tractor-Trailer	18.32
Landscaping/Groundskeeping Workers	11.52	Truck Drivers, Light/Delivery Svcs.	14.33
Lawyers	57.21	Waiters and Waitresses	10.07

Note: Wage data covers the Fort Lauderdale-Pompano Beach-Deerfield Beach, FL Metropolitan Division - see Appendix B for areas included. Hourly wages for elementary/secondary school teachers and teacher assistants were calculated by the editors from annual wage data assuming a 40 hour work week; n/a not available.
Source: Bureau of Labor Statistics, Metro Area Occupational Employment and Wage Estimates, May 2009

RESIDENTIAL REAL ESTATE

Building Permits

Area	Single-Family			Multi-Family			Total		
	2009	2010	Pct. Chg.	2009	2010	Pct. Chg.	2009	2010	Pct. Chg.
City	38	42	10.5	0	0	-	38	42	10.5
MSA[1]	2,289	3,171	38.5	1,586	2,706	70.6	3,875	5,877	51.7
U.S.	441,100	447,300	1.4	141,900	157,300	10.9	583,000	604,600	3.7

Note: (1) Metropolitan Statistical Area - see Appendix B for areas included; figures represent new, privately-owned housing units authorized (unadjusted data); All permit data are based on estimates with imputation.
Source: U.S. Census Bureau, Manufacturing, Mining, and Construction Statistics, Building Permits, 2009, 2010

Homeownership Rate

Area	2005 (%)	2006 (%)	2007 (%)	2008 (%)	2009 (%)	2010 (%)
MSA[1]	69.2	67.4	66.6	66.0	67.1	63.8
U.S.	68.9	68.8	68.1	67.8	67.4	66.9

Note: (1) Metropolitan Statistical Area - see Appendix B for areas included
Source: U.S. Census Bureau, Housing Vacancies and Homeownership Annual Statistics: 2010

Housing Vacancy Rates

Area	Gross Vacancy Rate[2] (%)			Year-Round Vacancy Rate[3] (%)			Rental Vacancy Rate[4] (%)			Homeowner Vacancy Rate[5] (%)		
	2008	2009	2010	2008	2009	2010	2008	2009	2010	2008	2009	2010
MSA[1]	22.1	23.1	21.8	13.1	13.7	13.0	12.1	13.2	10.1	3.8	3.2	3.5
U.S.	14.4	14.5	14.3	11.1	11.3	11.3	10.0	10.6	10.2	2.8	2.6	2.6

Note: (1) Metropolitan Statistical Area - see Appendix B for areas included; (2) The percentage of the total housing inventory that is vacant; (3) The percentage of the housing inventory (excluding seasonal units) that is year-round vacant; (4) The percentage of rental inventory that is vacant for rent; (5) The percentage of homeowner inventory that is vacant for sale; n/a not available
Source: U.S. Census Bureau, Housing Vacancies and Homeownership Annual Statistics: 2010

State Corporate Income Tax Rates

State	Tax Rate (%)	Income Brackets ($)	Num. of Brackets	Financial Institution Tax Rate (%)[a]	Federal Income Tax Ded.
Florida	5.5 (f)	Flat rate	1	5.5 (f)	No

Note: Tax rates as of January 1, 2011; (a) Rates listed are the tax rates applied to financial institutions or excise taxes based on income. Some states have other taxes based upon the value of deposits or shares; (f) An exemption of $5,000 is allowed. Florida's Alternative Minimum Tax rate is 3.3%.
Source: Federation of Tax Administrators, "State Corporate Income Tax Rates, 2011"

State Individual Income Tax Rates

State	Tax Rate (%)	Income Brackets ($)	Num. of Brackets	Personal Exempt. ($)[1] Single	Personal Exempt. ($)[1] Dependents	Fed. Inc. Tax Ded.
Florida – No State Income Tax						

Note: Tax rates as of January 1, 2011; Local- and county-level taxes are not included; n/a not applicable; (1) Married joint filers generally receive double the single exemption
Source: Federation of Tax Administrators, "State Individual Income Tax Rates, 2011"

Various State and Local Tax Rates

State	State and Local Sales and Use (%)	State Sales and Use (%)	Gasoline[1] (¢/gal.)	Cigarette[2] ($/pack)	Spirits[3] ($/gal.)	Wine[4] ($/gal.)	Beer[5] ($/gal.)
Florida	6.0	6.00	34.4	1.34	6.50	2.25	0.48

Note: All tax rates as of January 1, 2011 except Spirits (Sept. 1, 2010); (1) The American Petroleum Institute has developed a methodology for determining the average tax rate on a gallon of fuel. Rates may include any of the following: excise taxes, environmental fees, storage tank fees, other fees or taxes, general sales tax, and local taxes. In states where gasoline is subject to the general sales tax, or where the fuel tax is based on the average sale price, the average rate determined by API is sensitive to changes in the price of gasoline. States that fully or partially apply general sales taxes to gasoline: CA, CO, GA, IL, IN, MI, NY; (2) The federal excise tax of $1.0066 per pack and local taxes are not included; (3) Rates are those applicable to off-premise sales of 40% alcohol by volume (a.b.v.) distilled spirits in 750ml containers. Local excise taxes are excluded; (4) Rates are those applicable to off-premise sales of 11% a.b.v. non-carbonated wine in 750ml containers; (5) Rates are those applicable to off-premise sales of 4.7% a.b.v. beer in 12 ounce containers.
Source: Tax Foundation, 2011 Facts & Figures: How Does Your State Compare?

State-Local Tax Burdens

Area	Rate (%)	Rank[1]	Per Capita Taxes Paid to Home State ($)	Total State and Local Per Capita Taxes Paid ($)	Per Capita Income ($)
Florida	9.2	31	2,713	3,897	42,146
U.S. Average	9.8	-	3,057	4,160	42,539

Note: Figures cover 2009; (1) Rank ranges from 1 to 50 where 1 is highest tax burden
Source: Tax Foundation, State-Local Tax Burdens, All States, 2009

State Business Tax Climate Index Rankings

State	Overall Rank	Corporate Tax Index Rank	Individual Income Tax Index Rank	Sales Tax Index Rank	Unemployment Insurance Tax Index Rank	Property Tax Index Rank
Florida	5	15	1	30	3	28

Note: The index is a measure of how each state's tax laws affect economic performance. The lower the rank, the more favorable a state's tax system is for business. All ranks are for fiscal years. States without a given tax are given a ranking of 1.
Source: Tax Foundation, Tax Foundation Background Paper, No. 60, "2011 State Business Tax Climate Index"

COMMERCIAL REAL ESTATE

Office Market

Market Area	Inventory (sq. ft.)	Vacant (sq. ft.)	Vac. Rate (%)	Under Constr. (sq. ft.)	Asking Rent ($/sf/yr) Class A	Asking Rent ($/sf/yr) Class B
Broward County	33,642,475	5,712,468	17.0	-	30.47	23.27

Source: Grubb & Ellis, Office Markets Trends, 1st Quarter 2011

Industrial Market

Market Area	Inventory (sq. ft.)	Vacant (sq. ft.)	Vac. Rate (%)	Under Constr. (sq. ft.)	Asking Rent ($/sf/yr) WH/Dist	R&D/Flex
Broward County	102,525,592	10,446,197	10.2	-	6.44	8.96

Source: Grubb & Ellis, Industrial Markets Trends, 4th Quarter 2010

COMMERCIAL UTILITIES

Typical Monthly Electric Bills

Area	Commercial Service ($/month) 3 kW demand 1,000 kWh	40 kW demand 14,000 kWh	Industrial Service ($/month) 1,000 kW demand 200,000 kWh	50,000 kW demand 15,000,000 kWh
City	106	1,214	21,777	945,149
Average[1]	135	1,576	23,741	1,402,202

Note: Based on total rates in effect July 1, 2010; (1) average based on 182 utilities surveyed
Source: Edison Electric Institute, Typical Bills and Average Rates Report, Summer 2010

TRANSPORTATION

Means of Transportation to Work

Area	Car/Truck/Van Drove Alone	Car-pooled	Public Transportation Bus	Subway	Railroad	Bicycle	Walked	Other Means	Worked at Home
City	74.0	9.8	4.2	0.0	0.2	1.7	2.4	2.2	5.4
MSA[1]	78.1	10.1	3.3	0.2	0.2	0.5	1.8	1.5	4.3
U.S.	75.8	10.4	2.7	1.7	0.5	0.5	2.9	1.2	4.1

Note: Figures are percentages and cover workers 16 years of age and older;
(1) Metropolitan Statistical Area - see Appendix B for areas included
Source: U.S. Census Bureau, 2007-2009 American Community Survey 3-Year Estimates

Travel Time to Work

Area	Less Than 15 Minutes	15 to 29 Minutes	30 to 44 Minutes	45 to 59 Minutes	60 to 89 Minutes	90 Minutes or More
City	27.7	39.8	20.3	4.9	5.4	1.9
MSA[1]	19.9	36.0	27.0	8.9	6.3	2.0
U.S.	28.5	36.2	19.7	7.5	5.6	2.5

Note: Figures are percentages and include workers 16 years old and over;
(1) Metropolitan Statistical Area - see Appendix B for areas included
Source: U.S. Census Bureau, 2007-2009 American Community Survey 3-Year Estimates

Travel Time Index

Area	1982	1999	2008	2009
Urban Area[1]	1.09	1.24	1.26	1.23
Average[2]	1.08	1.20	1.20	1.20

Note: Travel Time Index—the ratio of travel time in the peak period to the travel time at
free-flow conditions. A value of 1.30 indicates a 20-minute free-flow trip takes 26 minutes
in the peak. Free-flow speeds (60 mph on freeways and 35 mph on principal arterials)
are used as the comparison threshold; (1) Covers the Miami-Fort Lauderdale-Miami Beach urban area;
(2) average of 439 urban areas
Source: Texas Transportation Institute, Urban Mobility Report 2010, December 2010

Public Transportation

Agency Name / Mode of Transportation	Vehicles Operated in Maximum Service	Annual Unlinked Passenger Trips ('000)	Annual Passenger Miles ('000)
Broward County Mass Transit Division (BCT)			
Demand response	231	916.0	9,800.8
Bus	240	36,804.7	166,671.8
South Florida Regional Transportation Authority (TRI-Rail)			
Commuter rail	34	4,223.4	122,469.6
Bus	18	488.1	1,675.0

Note: Figures include both directly operated and purchased transportation
Source: Federal Transit Administration, National Transit Database, 2009

Air Transportation

Airport Name and Code / Type of Service	Passenger Airlines[1]	Passenger Enplanements	Freight Carriers[2]	Freight (lbs.)
Ft. Lauderdale-Hollywood International (FLL)				
Domestic service (U.S. carriers - 2010)	27	9,208,192	15	94,680,743
International service (U.S. carriers - 2009)	12	787,032	2	147,862

Note: (1) Includes all U.S.-based major, minor and commuter airlines that carried at least one passenger during the year; (2) Includes all U.S.-based airlines and freight carriers that transported at least one pound of freight during the year
Source: Bureau of Transportation Statistics, The Intermodal Transportation Database, Air Carriers: T-100 Domestic Market (U.S. Carriers), 2010; Bureau of Transportation Statistics, The Intermodal Transportation Database, Air Carriers: T-100 International Market (U.S. Carriers), 2009

Other Transportation Statistics

Interstate highways:	I-95
Amtrak service:	Yes
Major waterways/ports:	Intracoastal Waterway; Port Everglades

Source: Amtrak.com; Google Maps

BUSINESSES

Major Business Headquarters

Company Name	Rankings	
	Fortune[1]	Forbes[2]
AutoNation	197	-

Note: (1) Fortune 500—companies that produce a 10-K are ranked 1 to 500 based on 2010 revenue; (2) all private companies with at least $2 billion in annual revenue are ranked 1 to 223; companies listed are headquartered in the city; dashes indicate no ranking
Source: Fortune, "Fortune 500," May 23, 2011; Forbes, "America's Largest Private Companies," November 3, 2010

Fast-Growing Businesses

According to *Inc.*, Fort Lauderdale is home to two of America's 500 fastest-growing private companies: **Balance Staffing; Wyngate International**. Criteria: must be an independent, privately-held, for-profit, U.S. corporation, proprietorship or partnership; revenues of at least $80,000 in 2006 and $2 million in 2009; four-year operating/sales history; holding companies, regulated banks, and utilities were excluded. *Inc., "America's 500 Fastest-Growing Private Companies," September 2010*

According to *Fortune*, Fort Lauderdale is home to one of America's 100 fastest-growing small public companies: **Universal Insurance Holdings**. Companies were ranked by their three-year annualized rates of revenue growth and total return to investors for the period ended December 31, 2008. Criteria for inclusion: revenues of less than $200 million; stock price of at least $1. Banks, real-estate firms and adult entertainment companies were excluded. Also excluded were companies with losses in any of the four quarters ended on or before December 31, 2008. *Fortune Small Business, "America's Fastest-Growing Small Public Companies," July/August 2009*

According to Deloitte, Fort Lauderdale is home to one of North America's 500 fast-growing high-technology companies: **OmniComm Systems**. Companies are ranked by percentage growth in revenue over a five-year period. Criteria for inclusion: company must be headquartered within North America; company must own proprietary intellectual property or proprietary technology that contributes to a significant portion of the company's operating revenue or devotes a significant proportion of revenues to research and development of technology; company must have been in business for a minumum of five years with 2005 operating revenues of at least $50,000 USD/CD and 2009 operating revenues of at least $5 million USD/CD. *Deloitte Touche Tohmatsu, 2010 Deloitte Technology Fast 500*[TM]

Minority Business Opportunity

Fort Lauderdale is home to one company which is on the *Hispanic Business 500* list (500 largest U.S. Hispanic-owned companies based on 2009 revenue): **Superior Design International**. Companies included must show at least 51 percent ownership by Hispanic U.S. citizens, and must maintain headquarters in one of the 50 states or Washington, D.C. *Hispanic Business, "Hispanic Business 500," June 2010*

Minority- and Women-Owned Businesses

Group	All Firms		Firms with Paid Employees			
	Firms	Sales ($000)	Firms	Sales ($000)	Employees	Payroll ($000)
Asian	640	343,263	223	314,149	1,270	28,809
Black	3,872	132,943	195	76,548	829	20,404
Hispanic	3,230	940,320	637	862,094	3,882	182,480
Women	7,610	1,120,712	1,519	941,501	8,836	267,356
All Firms	30,171	37,879,711	9,286	36,753,910	150,268	7,636,233

Note: Figures cover firms located in the city; minority- and women-owned business are defined as firms in which the corresponding group own 51% or more of the stock or equity of the company
Source: U.S. Census Bureau, 2007 Economic Census, Survey of Business Owners

HOTELS

Hotels/Motels

Area	5 Star		4 Star		3 Star		2 Star		1 Star		Not Rated	
	Num.	Pct.3	Num.	Pct.3	Num.	Pct.3	Num.	Pct.3	Num.	Pct.3	Num.	Pct.3
City[1]	1	0.4	20	8.8	57	25.1	117	51.5	3	1.3	29	12.8
Total[2]	119	0.7	927	5.8	4,906	30.5	7,992	49.7	526	3.3	1,625	10.1

Note: (1) Figures cover Fort Lauderdale and vicinity; (2) Figures cover all 100 cities in this book; (3) Percentage of hotels which are a given star rating; Star ratings are determined by expedia.com and offer an indication of the general quality of a particular hotel.
Source: expedia.com, May 5, 2011

The Fort Lauderdale metro area is home to one of the top 218 hotels in the U.S. according to *Travel & Leisure*: **Atlantic Resort & Spa** (#100). Criteria: service; location; rooms; food; and value. *Travel & Leisure, "T+L 500, The World's Best Hotels 2011"*

The Fort Lauderdale metro area is home to one of the top 100 hotels in the U.S. according to *Condé Nast Traveler*: **W Fort Lauderdale** (#69). The selections are based on over 25,000 responses to the magazine's annual Readers' Choice Survey. *Condé Nast Traveler, "2010 Readers' Choice Awards"*

EVENT SITES

Major Stadiums, Arenas, and Auditoriums

Name	Max. Capacity
Broward Center for the Performing Arts	3,000
Fort Lauderdale Stadium	8,340
Lockhart Stadium	18,500
War Memorial Auditorium	2,110

Source: Original research

Convention Centers

Name	Overall Space (sq. ft.)	Exhibit Space (sq. ft.)	Meeting Space (sq. ft.)	Meeting Rooms
Broward County Convention Center	600,000	n/a	n/a	n/a

Note: n/a not available
Source: Original research

Living Environment

COST OF LIVING

Cost of Living Index

Composite Index	Groceries	Housing	Utilities	Trans-portation	Health Care	Misc. Goods/ Services
115.7	112.5	144.0	92.5	106.3	102.4	103.7

Note: U.S. = 100; Figures cover the Fort Lauderdale FL urban area.
Source: The Council for Community and Economic Research, ACCRA Cost of Living Index, 2010

Grocery Prices

Area[1]	T-Bone Steak ($/pound)	Frying Chicken ($/pound)	Whole Milk ($/half gal.)	Eggs ($/dozen)	Orange Juice ($/64 oz.)	Coffee ($/11.5 oz.)
City[2]	10.42	1.43	2.50	1.67	3.13	3.28
Avg.	9.04	1.16	2.02	1.47	3.08	3.65
Min.	6.97	0.84	1.46	0.96	2.39	2.64
Max.	13.93	2.51	3.58	3.01	4.94	6.32

*Note: (1) Values for the local area are compared with the average, minimum and maximum values for all 338 areas in the Cost of Living Index; (2) Figures cover the Fort Lauderdale FL urban area; **T-Bone Steak** (price per pound); **Frying Chicken** (price per pound, whole fryer); **Whole Milk** (half gallon carton); **Eggs** (price per dozen, Grade A, large); **Orange Juice** (64 oz. Tropicana or Florida Natural); **Coffee** (11.5 oz. can, vacuum-packed, Maxwell House, Hills Bros, or Folgers).*
Source: The Council for Community and Economic Research, ACCRA Cost of Living Index, 2010

Housing and Utility Costs

Area[1]	New Home Price ($)	Apartment Rent ($/month)	All Electric ($/month)	Part Electric ($/month)	Other Energy ($/month)	Telephone ($/month)
City[2]	396,553	1,299	170.81	-	-	22.37
Avg.	293,442	810	166.39	91.93	83.82	26.93
Min.	182,545	453	119.21	44.47	36.85	17.98
Max.	1,123,114	2,776	307.53	218.20	313.90	39.15

*Note: (1) Values for the local area are compared with the average, minimum and maximum values for all 338 areas in the Cost of Living Index; (2) Figures cover the Fort Lauderdale FL urban area; **New Home Price** (2,400 sf living area, 8,000 sf lot, in urban area with full utilities); **Apartment Rent** (950 sf 2 bedroom/1.5 or 2 bath, unfurnished, excluding all utilities except water); **All Electric** (average monthly cost for an all-electric home); **Part Electric** (average monthly cost for a part-electric home); **Other Energy** (average monthly cost for natural gas, fuel oil, coal, wood, and any other forms of energy except electricity); **Telephone** (price includes basic monthly rate for a private residential line plus additional local usage charges incurred by a family of four).*
Source: The Council for Community and Economic Research, ACCRA Cost of Living Index, 2010

Health Care, Transportation, and Other Costs

Area[1]	Doctor ($/visit)	Dentist ($/visit)	Optometrist ($/visit)	Gasoline ($/gallon)	Beauty Salon ($/visit)	Men's Shirt ($)
City[2]	81.32	86.62	98.08	2.80	40.80	18.84
Avg.	89.44	78.95	87.40	2.73	31.92	24.83
Min.	57.00	54.25	48.32	2.44	19.17	13.67
Max.	149.90	136.73	174.22	3.75	62.81	47.89

*Note: (1) Values for the local area are compared with the average, minimum and maximum values for all 338 areas in the Cost of Living Index; (2) Figures cover the Fort Lauderdale FL urban area; **Doctor** (general practitioners routine exam of an established patient); **Dentist** (adult teeth cleaning and periodic oral examination); **Optometrist** (full vision eye exam for established adult patient); **Gasoline** (one gallon regular unleaded, national brand, including all taxes, cash price at self-service pump if available); **Beauty Salon** (woman's shampoo, trim, and blow-dry); **Men's Shirt** (cotton/polyester dress shirt, pinpoint weave, long sleeves).*
Source: The Council for Community and Economic Research, ACCRA Cost of Living Index, 2010

HOUSING

House Price Index (HPI)

Area	National Ranking[2]	Quarterly Change (%)	One-Year Change (%)	Five-Year Change (%)
MD[1]	142	-1.77	-0.80	-37.99
U.S.[3]	-	-0.84	-3.95	-11.45

Note: The HPI is a weighted repeat sales index. It measures average price changes in repeat sales or refinancings on the same properties. This information is obtained by reviewing repeat mortgage transactions on single-family properties whose mortgages have been purchased or securitized by Fannie Mae or Freddie Mac in January 1975; (1) Metropolitan Division - see Appendix B for areas included; (2) Rankings are based on annual percentage change for all metro areas containing at least 15,000 transactions over the last 10 years and ranges from 1 to 309; (3) figures based on a weighted average of Census Division estimates; all figures are for the period ending December 31, 2010
Source: Federal Housing Finance Agency, House Price Index, February 24, 2011

House Price Valuations

Area	Q4 2005 Price ($000)	Q4 2005 Over-valuation	Q4 2006 Price ($000)	Q4 2006 Over-valuation	Q4 2007 Price ($000)	Q4 2007 Over-valuation	Q4 2008 Price ($000)	Q4 2008 Over-valuation	Q4 2009 Price ($000)	Q4 2009 Over-valuation
MD[1]	259.4	41.9	268.7	39.5	237.6	22.1	161.2	-16.5	146.6	-24.0

Note: Figures show the percentage of over- or under-valuation of single family homes relative to statistically normal house values (e.g. a value of 23.6 indicates that house values are 23.6% overvalued). Statistically normal house values are based on house prices, interest rates, household incomes, population densities, and any historical premiums or discounts metropolitan areas have exhibited over time; (1) Figures cover the Fort Lauderdale-Pompano Beach-Deerfield Beach, FL Metropolitan Division - see Appendix B for areas included
Source: Global Insight/PNC Financial Services Group, House Prices in America: 4th Quarter 2009 Update

Median Single-Family Home Prices

Area	2008	2009	2010[p]	Percent Change 2009 to 2010
MSA[1]	285.1	211.2	200.8	-4.9
U.S. Average	196.6	172.1	173.2	0.6

Note: Figures are median sales prices of existing single-family homes in thousands of dollars; (p) preliminary; n/a not available; (1) Metropolitan Statistical Area - see Appendix B for areas included
Source: National Association of Realtors, Median Sales Price of Existing Single-Family Homes for Metropolitan Areas, 4th Quarter 2010

Median Apartment Condo-Coop Home Prices

Area	2008	2009	2010[p]	Percent Change 2009 to 2010
MSA[1]	161.6	107.4	92.2	-14.2
U.S. Average	209.8	175.6	171.7	-2.2

Note: Figures are median sales prices of existing apartment condo-coop homes in thousands of dollars; (p) preliminary; n/a not available; (1) Metropolitan Statistical Area - see Appendix B for areas included
Source: National Association of Realtors, Median Sales Price of Existing Apartment Condo-Coop Homes for Metropolitan Areas, 4th Quarter 2010

Year Housing Structure Built

Area	2000 or Later	1990 -1999	1980 -1989	1970 -1979	1960 -1969	1950 -1959	1940 -1949	Before 1940	Median Year
City	11.1	4.9	6.7	22.2	26.2	23.3	4.1	1.5	1968
MSA[1]	12.4	14.6	19.7	23.5	13.0	10.9	3.6	2.2	1979
U.S.	12.5	14.0	14.2	16.5	11.4	11.3	5.8	14.3	1974

Note: Figures are percentages except for Median Year; (1) Metropolitan Statistical Area - see Appendix B for areas included
Source: U.S. Census Bureau, 2007-2009 American Community Survey 3-Year Estimates

HEALTH

Health Risk Data

Category	MSA[1] (%)	U.S. (%)
Adults who have been told they have high blood pressure	31.8	28.7
Adults who have been told they have high blood cholesterol	38.2	37.5
Adults who have been told they have diabetes[3]	10.3	8.3
Adults who have been told they have arthritis	22.1	26.0
Adults who have been told they currently have asthma	4.6	8.8
Adults who are current smokers	11.3	17.9
Adults who are heavy drinkers[4]	3.1	5.1
Adults who are binge drinkers[5]	12.0	15.8
Adults who are overweight (BMI 25.0 - 29.9)	38.1	36.2
Adults who are obese (BMI 30.0 - 99.8)	23.7	26.9
Adults who participated in any physical activities in the past month	75.5	76.2
Adults 50+ who have ever had a sigmoidoscopy or colonoscopy[2]	58.8	62.2
Women 40+ who have had a mammogram within the past two years[2]	83.0	76.0
Adults age 18–64 who have any kind of health care coverage	80.7	83.1

Note: Data as of 2009 unless otherwise noted; (1) Figures cover the Miami-Fort Lauderdale-Miami Beach, FL Metropolitan Statistical Area - see Appendix B for areas included; (2) Data as of 2008; (3) Figures do not include pregnancy-related, borderline, or pre-diabetes; (4) Heavy drinkers are classified as males having more than two drinks per day or females having more than one drink per day; (5) Binge drinkers are classified as males having five or more drinks on one occasion or females having four or more drinks on one occasion
Source: Centers for Disease Control and Prevention, Behaviorial Risk Factor Surveillance System, SMART: Selected Metropolitan/Micropolitan Area Risk Trends, 2008, 2009

Mortality Rates for the Top 10 Causes of Death in the U.S.

ICD-10[a] Sub-Chapter	ICD-10[a] Code	Age-Adjusted Mortality Rate[1] per 100,000 population	
		County[2]	U.S.
Malignant neoplasms	C00-C97	165.5	180.9
Ischaemic heart diseases	I20-I25	134.2	135.0
Other forms of heart disease	I30-I51	33.8	50.0
Cerebrovascular diseases	I60-I69	38.1	44.1
Chronic lower respiratory diseases	J40-J47	31.3	41.5
Other degenerative diseases of the nervous system	G30-G31	24.7	23.6
Diabetes mellitus	E10-E14	18.3	23.5
Other external causes of accidental injury	W00-X59	23.8	23.5
Organic, including symptomatic, mental disorders	F01-F09	11.8	22.2
Influenza and pneumonia	J09-J18	7.2	18.1

Note: (a) ICD-10 = International Classification of Diseases 10th Revision; (1) Mortality rates are a three year average covering 2005-2007; (2) Figures cover Broward County
Source: Centers for Disease Control and Prevention, National Center for Health Statistics. Compressed Mortality File 1999-2007. CDC WONDER On-line Database, compiled from Compressed Mortality File 1999-2007 Series 20 No. 2M, 2010.

Mortality Rates for Selected Causes of Death

ICD-10[a] Sub-Chapter	ICD-10[a] Code	Age-Adjusted Mortality Rate[1] per 100,000 population	
		County[2]	U.S.
Assault	X85-Y09	5.5	6.0
Human immunodeficiency virus (HIV) disease	B20-B24	15.3	4.0
Hypertensive diseases	I10-I15	13.8	18.0
Intentional self-harm	X60-X84	10.6	11.0
Malnutrition	E40-E46	*0.2	0.8
Obesity and other hyperalimentation	E65-E68	1.7	1.5
Transport accidents	V01-V99	17.0	15.6
Viral hepatitis	B15-B19	2.1	2.1

Note: (a) ICD-10 = International Classification of Diseases 10th Revision; (1) Mortality rates are a three year average covering 2005-2007; (2) Figures cover Broward County; (*) Unreliable data as per CDC
Source: Centers for Disease Control and Prevention, National Center for Health Statistics. Compressed Mortality File 1999-2007. CDC WONDER On-line Database, compiled from Compressed Mortality File 1999-2007 Series 20 No. 2M, 2010.

Distribution of Physicians and Dentists

Area[1]	Dentists[2]	D.O.[3]	M.D.[4]				
			Total	Family/ General Practice	Pediatrics	Medical Specialties	Surgical Specialties
Local (number)	878	592	3,416	279	284	1,463	787
Local (rate[5])	5.0	3.4	19.5	1.6	1.6	8.3	4.5
U.S. (rate[5])	4.5	1.9	18.3	2.5	1.4	6.8	4.1

Note: Data as of 2008 unless noted; (1) Local data covers Broward County; (2) Data as of 2007; (3) Doctor of Osteopathic Medicine; (4) Includes active, non-federal, patient-care, office-based Doctors of Medicine; (5) rate per 10,000 population
Source: Area Resource File (ARF). 2009-2010 Release. U.S. Department of Health and Human Services, Health Resources and Services Administration, Bureau of Health Professions, Rockville, MD, August 2010

Hospitals

Fort Lauderdale has the following hospitals: 4 general medical and surgical; 2 psychiatric; 1 rehabilitation; 1 long-term acute care.
AHA Guide to the Healthcare Field 2010

According to *U.S. News,* the Fort Lauderdale-Pompano Beach-Deerfield Beach, FL Metropolitan Division is home to one of the best hospitals in the U.S.: **Cleveland Clinic Florida**. The hospital listed was highly ranked in at least one adult specialty. *U.S. News Online, "America's Best Hospitals 2010-11"*

EDUCATION

Public School District Statistics

District Name	Schls	Pupils	Pupil/ Teacher Ratio	Minority Pupils[1] (%)	Free Lunch Eligible[2] (%)	IEP[3] (%)
Broward	303	256,351	13.7	70.6	38.6	12.1

Note: Table includes school districts with 2,000 or more students; (1) Percentage of students that are not non-Hispanic white; (2) Percentage of students that are eligible for the free lunch program; (3) Percentage of students that have an Individualized Education Program.
Source: U.S. Department of Education, National Center for Education Statistics, Common Core of Data, Local Education Agency (School District) Universe Survey: School Year 2008-2009; U.S. Department of Education, National Center for Education Statistics, Common Core of Data, Public Elementary/Secondary School Universe Survey: School Year 2008-2009

Top Public High Schools

High School Name	Index[1]	Rank[1]	Subsidized Lunch (%)[2]	E&E (%)[3]
Fort Lauderdale[4]	3.681	130	61.0	29.9
Stranahan	3.076	235	76.0	17.1

Note: (1) Public schools are ranked according to a ratio that is the number of Advanced Placement, International Baccalaureate, and/or Cambridge tests taken by all students at a school in 2009 divided by the number of graduating seniors. All of the schools on the list have an index of at least 1.000; they are in the top six percent of public schools measured this way. The rankings range from 1 to 1,734; (2) Percentage of students receiving federally subsidized meals; (3) E & E stands for equity and excellence percentage: the portion of all graduating seniors at a school that had at least one passing grade on one AP or IB test; (4) Schools that offer International Baccalaureate or Cambridge exams; (5) School is unranked, but has been identified by Newsweek as one of the nation's most elite public high schools.
Source: Newsweek Online, "Top High Schools 2010"

Highest Level of Education

Area	Less than H.S.	H.S. Diploma	Some College, No Deg.	Associate Degree	Bachelors Degree	Masters Degree	Profess. School Degree	Doctorate Degree
City	17.0	25.9	18.8	6.9	19.9	7.2	3.2	1.0
MSA[1]	17.5	27.6	17.7	8.1	18.7	6.5	2.8	1.1
U.S.	15.3	29.0	20.7	7.5	17.4	7.0	1.9	1.1

Note: Figures are 2010 estimated percentages and cover persons age 25 and over; (1) Metropolitan Statistical Area - see Appendix B for areas included
Source: Claritas, Inc.

Educational Attainment by Race

Area	High School Graduate (%)					Bachelor's Degree (%)				
	Total	White	Black	Asian	Hisp.[2]	Total	White	Black	Asian	Hisp.[2]
City	84.7	94.3	65.8	90.1	73.4	31.2	41.6	8.3	51.2	21.2
MSA[1]	82.5	92.2	75.7	87.1	74.5	28.6	36.9	17.2	48.0	23.6
U.S.	84.9	90.0	80.7	85.5	60.7	27.8	30.9	17.5	49.7	12.7

Note: Figures shown cover persons 25 years old and over; (1) Metropolitan Statistical Area - see Appendix B for areas included; (2) people of Hispanic origin can be of any race
Source: U.S. Census Bureau, 2007-2009 American Community Survey 3-Year Estimates

School Enrollment by Grade and Control

Area	Preschool (%)		Kindergarten (%)		Grades 1 - 4 (%)		Grades 5 - 8 (%)		Grades 9 - 12 (%)	
	Public	Private	Public	Private	Public	Private	Public	Private	Public	Private
City	46.8	53.2	81.2	18.8	84.4	15.6	81.4	18.6	79.6	20.4
MSA[1]	43.2	56.8	82.2	17.8	86.8	13.2	86.1	13.9	87.1	12.9
U.S.	54.3	45.7	86.4	13.6	88.9	11.1	89.1	10.9	90.2	9.8

Note: Figures shown cover persons 3 years old and over; (1) Metropolitan Statistical Area - see Appendix B for areas included
Source: U.S. Census Bureau, 2007-2009 American Community Survey 3-Year Estimates

Average Salaries of Public School Classroom Teachers

Area	2009-10		2010-11		Percent Change 2009-10 to 2010-11	Percent Change 2000-01 to 2010-11
	Dollars	Rank[1]	Dollars	Rank[1]		
Florida	46,708	37	46,702	47	-0.01	22.2
U.S. Average	55,202	-	56,069	-	1.57	29.3

Note: (1) State rank ranges from 1 to 51 where 1 indicates highest salary.
Source: National Education Association, Rankings & Estimates: Rankings of the States 2010 and Estimates of School Statistics 2011, December 2010

Higher Education

Four-Year Colleges			Two-Year Colleges			Medical Schools[1]	Law Schools[2]	Voc/ Tech[3]
Public	Private Non-profit	Private For-profit	Public	Private Non-profit	Private For-profit			
1	3	3	0	0	3	1	1	1

Note: Figures cover institutions located within the city limits and include main campuses only; (1) includes schools accredited by the Liaison Committee on Medical Education and the American Osteopathic Association; (2) includes American Bar Association-accredited law schools; (3) includes all schools with programs that are less than 2 years.
Source: National Center for Education Statistics, Integrated Postsecondary Education System (IPEDS) Peer Analysis System, 2010-11; U.S. News & World Report, Medical School Directory, 2011; U.S. News & World Report, Law School Directory, 2011

PRESIDENTIAL ELECTION

2008 Presidential Election Results

Area	Obama	McCain	Nader	Other
Broward County	67.0	32.3	0.2	0.4
U.S.	52.9	45.6	0.6	0.9

Note: Results are percentages and may not add to 100% due to rounding
Source: Dave Leip's Atlas of U.S. Presidential Elections, www.uselectionatlas.org

EMPLOYERS

Major Employers

Company Name	Industry	Type of Site
Amisub	General medical and surgical hospitals	Headquarters
Amtrust Financial Corporation	Federal savings institutions	Branch
Andrx Pharmaceuticals	Analytical instruments	Single
Answer Group	Custom computer programming services	Headquarters
Broadspire	Health and allied services, nec	Headquarters
Broward General Medical Center	Offices and clinics of medical doctors	Branch
Checks In Motion	Accounting, auditing, and bookkeeping	Single
City of Fort Lauderdale	Executive offices	Headquarters
Columbia Hca	General medical and surgical hospitals	Single
DFA Holdings	Liquor stores	Branch
Diplomat Country Club & Spa	Membership sports and recreation clubs	Single
Diplomat Resort & Country Club	Hotels and motels	Single
Florida Medical Center	General medical and surgical hospitals	Headquarters
Holy Cross Hospital	General medical and surgical hospitals	Headquarters
JM Family Enterprises	Automobiles and other motor vehicles	Headquarters
Lynn Rgnal Cncer Ctr Boca Rton	General medical and surgical hospitals	Headquarters
Mail Terminal Services	Business services, nec	Single
Mednax	Offices and clinics of medical doctors	Headquarters
Memorial Hospital West	General medical and surgical hospitals	Branch
Motorola	Radio and t.v. communications equipment	Branch
North Brwrd Hsp Aux Gift Shop	General medical and surgical hospitals	Branch
Nova Southeastern Univ	Colleges and universities	Headquarters
Pompano Park Racing	Racing, including track operation	Single
University Hospital & Med Ctr	General medical and surgical hospitals	Single

Note: Companies shown are located within the Fort Lauderdale metropolitan area; nec = not elsewhere classified.
Source: www.zapdata.com, January 2011

PUBLIC SAFETY

Crime Rate

Area	All Crimes	Violent Crimes				Property Crimes		
		Murder	Forcible Rape	Robbery	Aggrav. Assault	Burglary	Larceny -Theft	Motor Vehicle Theft
City	6,480.2	7.1	30.6	374.4	397.4	1,589.0	3,706.1	375.5
Suburbs[1]	4,294.5	4.0	24.4	171.7	315.7	832.7	2,662.4	283.6
Metro[2]	4,523.1	4.3	25.1	192.9	324.3	911.8	2,771.5	293.2
U.S.	3,465.5	5.0	28.7	133.0	262.8	716.3	2,060.9	258.8

Note: Figures are crimes per 100,000 population; (1) All areas within the metro area that are located outside the city limits; (2) Metropolitan Division - see Appendix B for areas included
Source: FBI Uniform Crime Reports, 2009

Hate Crimes

Area	Number of Quarters Reported	Bias Motivation				
		Race	Religion	Sexual Orientation	Ethnicity	Disability
City	4	0	0	0	0	0

Source: Federal Bureau of Investigation, Hate Crime Statistics 2009

Identity Theft Consumer Complaints

Area	Complaints	Complaints per 100,000 Population	Rank[2]
MSA[1]	9,972	184.2	1
U.S.	250,854	81.3	-

Note: (1) Metropolitan Statistical Area - see Appendix B for areas included; (2) Rank ranges from 1 to 384 where 1 indicates greatest number of complaints per 100,000 population
Source: Federal Trade Commission, Consumer Sentinel Network Data Book for January - December 2010

RECREATION

Culture

Dance[1]	Theatre[1]	Instrumental Music[1]	Vocal Music[1]	Series/ Festivals	Museums	Zoos and Aquariums[2]
0	2	1	1	3	8	0

Note: (1) Number of professional perfoming groups; (2) AZA-accredited
Source: The Grey House Performing Arts Directory, 2011-2012; Official Museum Directory, 2010; American Association of Museums, AAM Member Museums, March 2011; Association of Zoos & Aquariums, AZA Member Zoos & Aquariums, May 2011

Professional Sports Teams

Team Name	League
Florida Marlins	Major League Baseball (MLB)
Florida Panthers	National Hockey League (NHL)
Miami Dolphins	National Football League (NFL)
Miami Heat	National Basketball Association (NBA)

Note: Includes teams located in the Miami-Fort Lauderdale metro area.
Source: Original research

CLIMATE

Average and Extreme Temperatures

Temperature	Jan	Feb	Mar	Apr	May	Jun	Jul	Aug	Sep	Oct	Nov	Dec	Yr.
Extreme High (°F)	88	89	92	96	95	98	98	98	97	95	89	87	98
Average High (°F)	75	77	79	82	85	88	89	90	88	85	80	77	83
Average Temp. (°F)	68	69	72	75	79	82	83	83	82	78	73	69	76
Average Low (°F)	59	60	64	68	72	75	76	76	76	72	66	61	69
Extreme Low (°F)	30	35	32	42	55	60	69	68	68	53	39	30	30

Note: Figures cover the years 1948-1990
Source: National Climatic Data Center, International Station Meteorological Climate Summary, 9/96

Average Precipitation/Snowfall/Humidity

Precip./Humidity	Jan	Feb	Mar	Apr	May	Jun	Jul	Aug	Sep	Oct	Nov	Dec	Yr.
Avg. Precip. (in.)	1.9	2.0	2.3	3.0	6.2	8.7	6.1	7.5	8.2	6.6	2.7	1.8	57.1
Avg. Snowfall (in.)	0	0	0	0	0	0	0	0	0	0	0	0	0
Avg. Rel. Hum. 7am (%)	84	84	82	80	81	84	84	86	88	87	85	84	84
Avg. Rel. Hum. 4pm (%)	59	57	57	57	62	68	66	67	69	65	63	60	63

Note: Figures cover the years 1948-1990; Tr = Trace amounts (<0.05 in. of rain; <0.5 in. of snow)
Source: National Climatic Data Center, International Station Meteorological Climate Summary, 9/96

Weather Conditions

Temperature			Daytime Sky			Precipitation		
32°F & below	45°F & below	90°F & above	Clear	Partly cloudy	Cloudy	0.01 inch or more precip.	0.1 inch or more snow/ice	Thunder-storms
< 1	7	55	48	263	54	128	0	74

Note: Figures are average number of days per year and cover the years 1948-1990
Source: National Climatic Data Center, International Station Meteorological Climate Summary, 9/96

HAZARDOUS WASTE

Superfund Sites

Fort Lauderdale has three hazardous waste sites on the EPA's Superfund Final National Priorities List: **Florida Petroleum Reprocessors; Hollingsworth Solderless Terminal; Wingate Road Municipal Incinerator Dump**. *U.S. Environmental Protection Agency, Final National Priorities List, April 1, 2011*

**AIR & WATER
QUALITY**

Air Quality Index

Area	Percent of Days when Air Quality was...[2]				AQI Statistics	
	Good	Moderate	Unhealthy for Sensitive Groups	Unhealthy	Maximum	Median
Area[1]	90.9	8.7	0.4	0.0	145	32

*Note: The Air Quality Index (AQI) is an index for reporting daily air quality. EPA calculates the AQI for five major air pollutants regulated by the Clean Air Act: ground-level ozone, particle pollution (also known as particulate matter), carbon monoxide, sulfur dioxide, and nitrogen dioxide. The AQI runs from 0 to 500. The higher the AQI value, the greater the level of air pollution and the greater the health concern. There are six AQI categories: "Good" The AQI is between 0 and 50. Air quality is considered satisfactory; "Moderate" The AQI is between 51 and 100. Air quality is acceptable; "Unhealthy for Sensitive Groups" When AQI values are between 101 and 150, members of sensitive groups may experience health effects; "Unhealthy" When AQI values are between 151 and 200 everyone may begin to experience health effects; "Very Unhealthy" AQI values between 201 and 300 trigger a health alert; "Hazardous" AQI values over 300 trigger health warnings of emergency conditions; (1) Data covers Broward County; (2) Based on 275 days with AQI data in 2008; The EPA has suspended data updates while it assesses its data systems, including AirData reports and maps.
Source: U.S. Environmental Protection Agency, AirData Report, 2008*

Air Quality Index Pollutants

Area	Percent of Days when AQI Pollutant was...[2]					
	Carbon Monoxide	Nitrogen Dioxide	Ozone	Sulfur Dioxide	Particulate Matter 2.5	Particulate Matter 10
Area[1]	0.4	0.0	65.5	0.0	28.7	5.5

*Note: The Air Quality Index (AQI) is an index for reporting daily air quality. EPA calculates the AQI for five major air pollutants regulated by the Clean Air Act: ground-level ozone, particle pollution (also known as particulate matter), carbon monoxide, sulfur dioxide, and nitrogen dioxide. The AQI runs from 0 to 500. The higher the AQI value, the greater the level of air pollution and the greater the health concern; (1) Data covers Broward County; (2) Based on 275 days with AQI data in 2008; The EPA has suspended data updates while it assesses its data systems, including AirData reports and maps.
Source: U.S. Environmental Protection Agency, AirData Report, 2008*

Air Quality Index Trends

Area	Trend Sites (days)								All Sites (days)
	2002	2003	2004	2005	2006	2007	2008	2009	2009
MSA[1]	5	4	11	4	11	10	5	2	2

*Note: Figures are the number of days the AQI value exceeded 100 in a given year. An AQI value greater than 100 indicates that air quality would have been in the unhealthful range on that day. Data from exceptional events are included. These counts are presented in two ways. First, the counts are based on sites having an adequate record of monitoring data during the trend period (trend sites). These counts represent the relative change in the number of days with AQI values greater than 100. In the last column, the counts are based on all sites with data in the most recent year (because it is possible for a site to have data in the most recent year but not enough data to be a trend site); (1) Data covers the Miami-Fort Lauderdale-Miami Beach, FL Metropolitan Statistical Area - see Appendix B for areas included
Source: U.S. Environmental Protection Agency, Office of Air and Radiation, Air Quality Index Information, "Number of Days with Air Quality Index Values Greater than 100 and Trend Sites, 1990-2009, and at All Sites in 2009"*

Maximum Air Pollutant Concentrations

	Particulate Matter 10 (ug/m^3)	Particulate Matter 2.5 (ug/m^3)	Ozone (ppm)	Carbon Monoxide (ppm)	Sulfur Dioxide (ppm)	Nitrogen Dioxide (ppm)	Lead (ug/m^3)
MSA[1] Level	65	16	0.064	2	0.014	0.009	n/a
NAAQS[2]	150	35	0.075	9	0.140	0.053	0.15
Met NAAQS[2]	Yes	Yes	Yes	Yes	Yes	Yes	n/a

*Note: Data from exceptional events are not included; (1) Data covers the Miami-Fort Lauderdale-Miami Beach, FL Metropolitan Statistical Area - see Appendix B for areas included; (2) National Ambient Air Quality Standards; n/a not available
Concentrations: Particulate Matter 10 (coarse particulate) - highest second maximum 24-hour concentration; Particulate Matter 2.5 (fine particulate) - highest 98th percentile 24-hour concentration; Ozone - highest fourth daily maximum 8-hour concentration; Carbon Monoxide - highest second maximum non-overlapping 8-hour concentration; Sulfur Dioxide - highest second maximum 24-hour concentration; Nitrogen Dioxide - highest arithmetic mean concentration; Lead - maximum running 3-month average
Units: ppm = parts per million; ug/m^3 = micrograms per cubic meter
Source: U.S. Environmental Protection Agency, CBSA Factbook 2009, Air Quality Statistics by City, 2009*

Drinking Water

Water System Name	Pop. Served	Primary Water Source Type	Violations[1]	
			Health Based	Monitoring/ Reporting
City of Fort Lauderdale	172,680	Ground	0	0

Note: (1) Based on violation data from January 1, 2010 to December 31, 2010 (includes unresolved violations from earlier years)
Source: U.S. Environmental Protection Agency, Office of Ground Water and Drinking Water, Safe Drinking Water Information System (based on data extracted May 9, 2011)

Fort Worth, Texas

Background

Fort Worth lies in north central Texas near the headwaters of the Trinity River. Despite its modern skyscrapers, multiple freeways, shopping malls, and extensive industry, the city is known for its easygoing, Western atmosphere.

The area has seen many travelers. Nomadic Native Americans of the plains rode through on horses bred from those brought by Spanish explorers. The 1840s saw American-Anglos settle in the region. On June 6, 1849, Major Ripley A. Arnold and his U.S. Cavalry troop established an outpost on the Trinity River to protect settlers moving westward. The fort was named for General William J. Worth, Commander of the U.S. Army's Texas department. When the fort was abandoned in 1853, settlers moved in and converted the vacant barracks into trading establishments and homes, stealing the county seat from Birdville (an act made legal in the 1860 election).

In the 1860s, Fort Worth, which was close to the Chisholm Trail, became an oasis for cowboys traveling to and from Kansas. Although the town's growth virtually stopped during the Civil War, Fort Worth was incorporated as a city in 1873. In a race against time, the final 26 miles of the Texas & Pacific Line were completed and Fort Worth survived to be a part of the West Texas oil boom in 1917.

Real prosperity followed at the end of World War II, when the city became a center for a number of military installations. Aviation has been the city's principal source of economic growth. The city's leading industries include the manufacture of aircraft, automobiles, machinery, and containers, as well as food processing and brewing. Emerging economic sectors in the new century include semiconductor manufacturing, communications equipment manufacturing, corporate offices, and distribution.

Major corporations here include Pier 1 Imports, American Airlines, RadioShack, Bell Helicopter Textron, and Lockheed Martin.

Since it first began testing DNA samples in 2003, the DNA Identity Laboratory at the University of North Texas Health Science Center has made nearly 100 matches, helping to solve missing-persons cases and closing criminal cases. The university is also home to the national Osteopathic Research Center, the only academic DNA Lab qualified to work with the FBI, the Texas Center for Health Disparities and the Health Institutes of Texas. Other colleges in Fort Worth include Texas Christian University, Southwestern Baptist Seminary, and Texas Wesleyan University.

After a long period of planning, Fort Worth's most comprehensive mixed-use project at Walsh Ranch, is nearing completion. With designs for residential, commercial, office and retail development, the project is named after the original owners of the property, F. Howard and Mary D. Walsh, who were well-known ranchers, philanthropists and civic leaders.

The Omni Fort Worth Hotel opened in January of 2009, and is the first new hotel in the city in over 20 years. It was host to the 2011 AFC champion Pittsburgh Steelers during Super Bowl XLV.

Winter temperatures and rainfall are both modified by the northeast-northwest mountain barrier, which prevents shallow cold air masses from crossing over from the west. Summer temperatures vary with cloud and shower activity, but are generally mild. Summer precipitation is largely from local thunderstorms and varies from year to year. Damaging rains are infrequent. Hurricanes have produced heavy rainfall, but are usually not accompanied by destructive winds.

Rankings

General Rankings

- Fort Worth was ranked #133 out of 375 metro areas in *Cities Ranked & Rated*. Criteria: cost of living; climate; crime; transportation; economy and jobs; education; arts and culture; health and healthcare; leisure; quality of life. *Cities Ranked & Rated, 2nd Edition, 2007*

- Fort Worth was ranked #92 out of 379 metro areas in *Places Rated Almanac*. Criteria: health care; education; recreation; transportation; ambience; climate; crime; housing costs; jobs. *Places Rated Almanac, 7th Edition, 2007*

- The Fort Worth metro area was selected as one of the best cities to relocate to in America by Sperling's BestPlaces. The metro area ranked #4 out of 10. Criteria: unemployment; cost of living; crime rates; population health; cultural events; economic stability. *Sperling's BestPlaces, www.BestPlaces.net, "The Best Cities to Relocate to in America," October 2010*

- *Men's Health Living* ranked 100 U.S. cities in terms of quality of life. Fort Worth was ranked #85 and received a grade of D. Criteria: number of fitness facilities; air quality; number of physicians; male/female ratio; education levels; household income; cost of living. *Men's Health Living, Spring 2008*

- Fort Worth was selected as one of "America's Top 100 Places to Live" by RelocateAmerica.com. Cities and towns nominated to be great places to live along with their key data regarding education, employment, economy, crime, parks, recreation and housing were reviewed, rated and judged by the Relocate-America.com editorial staff. *Relocate-America.com, "RelocateAmerica's Top 100 Places to Live in 2010"*

Business/Finance Rankings

- Dallas was identified as one of the 20 strongest-performing metro areas during the recession and recovery from December 2007 through December 2010. Criteria: percent change in employment; percentage point change in unemployment rate; percent change in gross metropolitan product; percent change in House Price Index. *Brookings Institution, MetroMonitor: Tracking Economic Recession and Recovery in America's 100 Largest Metropolitan Areas, March 2011*

- The Fort Worth metro area was identified as one of 10 "Cities Where the Recession is Easing." The metro area was ranked #3. Criteria: job growth; goods produced; home sale prices; unemployment rates. *Forbes.com, "Cities Where the Recession is Easing," March 3, 2010*

- The Fort Worth metro area was identified as one of the most affordable major metropolitan areas in America by *Forbes*. The metro area was ranked #14 out of 15. Criteria: median asking price of homes for sale; median salaries of workers with bachelor's degrees or higher compared to a cost-of-living index; unemployment rates. *Forbes.com, "The Most Affordable Cities in America," January 7, 2011*

- Experian ranked the top 20 major U.S metropolitan areas by average debt per consumer. The Dallas metro area was ranked #2. Criteria: average debt per consumer. Debt for this study includes credit cards, auto loans and personal loans. It does not include mortgages. *Experian, May 13, 2010*

- The Dallas metro area was identified as one of the "Best U.S. Cities for Earning a Living" by *Forbes*. The metro area ranked #8. Criteria: median income; cost of living; job growth; number of companies on *Forbes* 400 best big company and 200 best small company lists. *Forbes.com, "Best U.S. Cities for Earning a Living," August 21, 2008*

- A.G. Edwards ranked America's 500 top-performing communities based on their residents' personal savings and investing behavior. The Fort Worth metro area ranked #353 with an index score of 98.36 (national average = 100.00). A dozen statistical factors were measured including: participation in retirement savings plans; personal debt levels; and home ownership. *A.G. Edwards, "2007 Nest Egg Index," September 12, 2007*

- The Dallas metro area was identified as one of the 10 best cities to find a job in 2009 by *Forbes*. The metro area ranked #10. Criteria: city unemployment rate; number of new jobs created in the previous six months. *Forbes.com, "10 Cities for Job Growth in 2009," January 5, 2009*

- Fort Worth was cited as one of America's top metros for new and expanded facility projects in 2010. The area ranked #3 in the large metro area category (population over 1 million). *Site Selection, "2010 Top Metros," March 2011*

- Fort Worth was identified as one of the best cities for new college graduates. The city ranked #10. Criteria: cost of living; average annual salary; unemployment rate; number of employers looking to hire people at entry-level. *Business Week, "The Best Cities for New Grads," July 20, 2010*

- Fort Worth was selected as one of the "100 Best Places to Live and Launch" in the U.S. The city ranked #9. The editors at *Fortune Small Business* ranked 296 Census-designated metro areas by business friendliness (Launching Score, % New Businesses) and lifestyle offerings (Living Score). Then they picked the town within each of the top 100 metro areas that best blends business and pleasure. *Fortune Small Business, "100 Best Places to Live and Launch 2008," April 2008*

- *American City Business Journals* ranked America's 261 largest cities in terms of their resident's wealth. Fort Worth ranked #178. Criteria: per capita income; median household income; percentage of households with annual incomes of $200,000 or more; median home value. *American City Business Journals, www.bizjournals.com, "Where the Money Is: America's Wealth Centers," August 18, 2008*

- The Fort Worth metro area appeared on the Milken Institute "2010 Best Performing Metros" list. Rank: #23 out of 200 large metro areas. Criteria: job growth; wage and salary growth; high-tech output growth. *Milken Institute, "2010 Best Performing Metros"*

- The Fort Worth metro area was selected as one of the best cities for entrepreneurs in America by *Inc. Magazine*. Criteria: job-growth data for 335 metro areas was analyzed for: recent growth trend (the current and prior year's employment growth rates, with the current year emphasized); mid-term growth (the average annual 2002-2007 growth rate); long-term trend (the sum of the 2002-2007 and 1996-2001 employment growth rates multiplied by the ratio of the 1996-2001 growth rate over the 2002-2007 growth rate); current year growth. The Fort Worth metro area ranked #9 among large metro areas and #50 overall. *Inc. Magazine, "The Best Cities for Doing Business," July 2008*

- Fort Worth was ranked #52 out of 145 regions worldwide in terms of its "Knowledge Competitiveness Index." The index attempts to measure the knowledge-based development taking place throughout the world and is based on 19 measures of economic performance that indicate a region's ability to translate its knowledge capacity into economic value. *Centre for International Competitiveness, World Knowledge Competitiveness Index 2008*

- *Forbes* ranked the 200 most populous metro areas in the U.S. in terms of the "Best Places for Business and Careers." The Fort Worth metro area was ranked #34. Criteria: 12 metrics including costs (business and living), job growth (past and projected), income growth, educational attainment, projected economic growth, crime, cultural and recreational opportunities, net migration patterns, percentage of subprime mortgages handed out over a three-year period, and the number of highly ranked four-year colleges. *Forbes, "Best Places for Business and Careers," April 14, 2010*

Children/Family Rankings

- The Fort Worth metro area was selected as one of the "Best Cities for Relocating Families" by Worldwide ERC and Primacy Relocation. The 2008 study looked at nearly 50 factors important to relocating families including: recent job growth; nearby top-ranked colleges; in-state tuition for four-year public colleges; population growth since 2000; pediatricians per 100,000 population; and a Green Living index. *Worldwide ERC and Primacy Relocation, "2008 Best Cities for Relocating Families"*

- *Fit Pregnancy* magazine ranked the 50 best U.S. cities in which to have a baby. Fort Worth was ranked #45. Criteria: access to hospitals and doctors; affordability; birthing options; breastfeeding; child care; fertility laws/resources; maternal and infant health risk; parks/stroller friendliness; safety. *Fit Pregnancy, "The Best Cities in America to Have a Baby 2008"*

- Fort Worth was chosen as one of America's "100 Best Communities for Young People." The winners were selected based upon detailed information provided about each community's efforts to fulfill five essential promises critical to the well-being of young people: caring adults who are actively involved in their lives; safe places in which to learn and grow; a healthy start toward adulthood; an effective education that builds marketable skills; and opportunities to help others. *America's Promise Alliance, "100 Best Communities for Young People, 2010"*

Dating/Romance Rankings

- Fort Worth appeared on *Men's Health's* list of the most sex-happy cities in America. The city ranked #12 of 100. Criteria: condom sales; birth rates; sex toy sales; rates of chlamydia, gonorrhea, and syphilis. *Men's Health, "America's Most Sex-Happy Cities," October 2010*

- *Men's Health* ranked 100 U.S. cities in terms of best (and worst) marriages. Fort Worth was ranked #45 (#1 = worst marriages). Criteria: rate of failed marriages; stringency of divorce laws; percentage of population who've split; number of licensed marriage and family therapists. *Men's Health, "Splitsville, USA," May 2010*

- Eli Lily and Company, in partnership with Sperling's BestPlaces, ranked the nation's 50 largest metro areas in terms of the "Most Romantic Cities for Baby Boomers." The Dallas metro area ranked #9. Criteria: marriage and divorce rates among "baby boomers" age 45 to 60; great restaurants; dance studios; chocolate, jewelry and flower sales. *Eli Lily and Company, "Most Romantic Cities for Baby Boomers," April 20, 2007*

- The Fort Worth metro area was selected as one of the "Best Cities for Relocating Singles" by Worldwide ERC and Primacy Relocation. The area ranked #46 out of the 100 largest metro areas in the U.S. Areas were selected based on the following criteria: recent job growth; recent singles population growth; overall population growth; affordable rental housing; cost-of-living index; expanded arts and recreation opportunities; ratio of single men and single women; affordability of quality higher education (including state residency requirements); diversity index; climate; population density. *Worldwide ERC and Primacy Relocation, "2008 Best Cities for Relocating Singles"*

- *Forbes* ranked the 40 most populous urbanized areas in the U.S. in terms of the "Best Cities for Singles." The Dallas metro area ranked #17. Criteria: number of singles; cost of living alone; nightlife; culture; job growth; coolness; and online dating participation. *Forbes.com, "Best Cities for Singles," July 27, 2009*

Education Rankings

- Fort Worth was selected as one of "America's Most Literate Cities." The city ranked #50 out of the 75 largest U.S. cities. Criteria: number of booksellers; library resources; Internet resources; educational attainment; periodical publishing resources; newspaper circulation. *Central Connecticut State University, "America's Most Literate Cities 2010"*

- Fort Worth was identified as one of the 100 "smartest" metro areas in the U.S. The area ranked #72. Criteria: the editors rated the collective brainpower of the 100 largest metro area in the U.S based on their residents' educational attainment. *American City Business Journals, www.bizjournals.com, April 14, 2008*

- Fort Worth was identified as one of "America's Brainiest Bastions" by *Portfolio.com*. The metro area ranked #96 out of 200. Portfolio.com analyzed levels of educational attainment in the nation's 200 largest metropolitan areas. The editors established scores for five levels of educational attainment, based on relative earning power of adult workers age 25 or older. Scores were determined by comparing the median income for all workers with the median income for those workers at a specified educational level. *Portfolio.com, "America's Brainiest Bastions," December 1, 2010*

- *Forbes* ranked the largest metro areas in the U.S. in terms of the "Best Cities for Young Professionals." The Dallas metro area ranked #6out of 10. Graduates from six elite schools (Harvard, Stanford, Princeton, Rice, Northwestern and Duke) were tracked ten years after graduation to see where they settled down. Those rankings were combined with several other statistics: job growth; unemployment rate; average salary of college graduates; cost of living; number of large companies that are located in the city. *Forbes.com, "Best Cities for Young Professionals," June 17, 2010*

Environmental Rankings

- The Fort Worth metro area was identified as one of "The Ten Biggest American Cities that are Running Out of Water" by *24/7 Wall St.* The metro area ranked #6 out of 10. *24/7 Wall St.* did an analysis of the water supply and consumption in the 30 largest metropolitan areas in the U.S. Criteria include: projected water demand as a share of available precipitation; groundwater use as a share or projected available precipitation; susceptibility to drought; projected increase in freshwater withdrawls; projected increase in summer water deficit. The editors chose ten cities that are likely to face severe shortages in the relatively near-term future. *24/7 Wall St., "The Ten Biggest American Cities that are Running Out of Water," November 1, 2010*

- Fort Worth was selected as one of 22 "Smarter Cities" for energy by the Natural Resources Defense Council." Criteria: investment in green power; energy efficiency measures; conservation. *Natural Resources Defense Council, "2010 Smarter Cities," July 19, 2010*

- *American City Business Journal* ranked 43 metropolitan areas in terms of their "greenness." The Fort Worth metro area ranked #37. Criteria: Forty-one metros in which *ACBJ* has business weeklies, plus Indianapolis and Cleveland, were ranked based on 20 different indicators such as adoption of green technologies, utilization of environmentally sound practices, and air and water quality. *American City Business Journals, "Green City Index," March 11, 2010*

- Fort Worth was selected as one of "America's 50 Greenest Cities" by *Popular Science.* The city ranked #15. Criteria: electricity; transportation; green living; recycling and green perspective. *Popular Science, February 2008*

- 100 of the largest metro areas in the U.S. were analyzed in terms of their current drought severity. The Fort Worth metro area ranked #97 (#1 = driest). The rankings were based on statistics such as long-term precipitation trends and patterns and the Palmer drought indices. *Sperling's BestPlaces, www.BestPlaces.net, "America's Drought-Riskiest Cities," November 2007*

- The Fort Worth metro area appeared in *Country Home's* "Best Green Places" report. The area ranked #171 out of 379. Criteria: official energy policies; green power; green buildings; availability of fresh, locally grown food. *Country Home, "Best Green Places," 2008*

- Fort Worth was highlighted as one of the 25 most ozone-polluted metro areas in the U.S. The area ranked #12. *American Lung Association, State of the Air 2011*

Health/Fitness Rankings

- Fort Worth was selected as one of the 25 fattest cities in America by *Men's Fitness Online.* It ranked #14 out of America's 50 largest cities. Criteria: fitness centers and sport stores; nutrition; sports participation; TV viewing; overweight/sedentary; junk food; air quality; geography; commute; parks and open space; city recreational facilities; access to healthcare; motivation; mayor and city initiatives; state obesity initiatives. *Men's Fitness Online, 2009 Fittest/Fattest Cities*

- Dallas was identified as a "2011 Asthma Capital." The area ranked #34 out of the nation's 100 largest metropolitan areas. Twelve factors were used to identify the most challenging places to live for people with asthma: estimated prevalence; self-reported prevalence; crude death rate for asthma; annual pollen score; annual air quality; public smoking laws; number of board-certified asthma specialists; school inhaler access laws; rescue medication use; controller medication use; uninsured rate; poverty rate. *Asthma and Allergy Foundation of America, "2011 Asthma Capitals"*

- Dallas was identified as a 2009 "Spring Allergy Capital." The area ranked #50 out of 100. Three groups of factors were used to identify the most severe cities for people with allergies during the spring season: annual pollen levels; medicine utilization; access to board-certified allergists. *Asthma and Allergy Foundation of America, "Spring Allergy Capitals 2009"*

- Dallas was identified as a 2010 "Fall Allergy Capital." The area ranked #33 out of 100. Three groups of factors were used to identify the most severe cities for people with allergies during the fall season: annual pollen levels; medicine utilization; access to board-certified allergists. *Asthma and Allergy Foundation of America, "Fall Allergy Capitals 2010"*

- *Men's Health* ranked 100 U.S. cities in terms of the quality of their tap water. Fort Worth was ranked #64 and received a grade of C. Criteria: levels of total coliform bacteria, arsenic, lead, total trihalomethanes (linked to cancer), and halo-acetic acids; number of EPA water-system violations from 1995 to 2005. *Men's Health, March 2007*

- Ortho-McNeil Neurologics, in partnership with Sperling's BestPlaces, analyzed 110 metro areas and identified those U.S. cities with the highest prevalence of factors that are most commonly associated with migraine headaches. The Fort Worth metro area ranked #82. Criteria: number of migraine-related drug prescriptions per capita; lifestyle factors that can contribute to migraines; environmental factors that can trigger migraines; and consumption of migraine-triggering foods. *Ortho-McNeil Neurologics, "America's Migraine Hot Spots," March 14, 2006*

- An analysis of the "Best & Worst Cities for Sleep" was conducted by Sperling's BestPlaces. The study ranked America's 50 most populated metro areas. The Fort Worth metro area ranked #40 (#1 = best city for sleep). Criteria: number of days residents didn't get enough rest or sleep during the past month; average length of daily commute; divorce rate; unemployment rate. *Sperling's BestPlaces, www.BestPlaces.net, "Best & Worst Cities for Sleep," 2006*

- *Men's Health* ranked 100 U.S. cities in terms of cities "Where the Food is Sickening." Fort Worth was ranked #10 and received a grade of B+. The magazine arrived at their ratings by looking at data compiled by the Community Health Status Indicator Project to determine outbreaks of E. coli, salmonella-, and shigella-related infections. They then checked the CDC's Wonder database to see how many people died from tainted food. Finally, the magazine found out which states have adopted the current version of the FDA's uniform Food Code, which contains the most up-to-date rules for keeping restaurant kitchens clean. *Men's Health, October 2005*

- The American Academy of Dermatology ranked 26 U.S. metropolitan regions in terms of their residents knowledge, attitude and behaviors towards tanning, sun protection and skin cancer detection. The Dallas metro area ranked #11. The results of the study are based on an online survey of over 7,000 adults nationwide. *American Academy of Dermatology, "Suntelligence: How Sun Smart is Your City," May 3, 2010*

- The Fort Worth metro area appeared in the 2010 Gallup-Healthways Well-Being Index. The index, based on interviews with more than 353,000 Americans during 2009, asked individuals to assess their jobs, finances, physical health, emotional state of mind and communities. The metro area ranked #41 out of 162. Criteria: life evaluation; emotional health; work environment; physical health; healthy behaviors; basic access (basic needs optimal for a healthy life, such as access to food and medicine, having health insurance and feeling safe while walking at night). *Gallup-Healthways, "Well-Being Index 2010"*

- The Fort Worth metro area was identified as one of "America's Most Stressful Cities" by *Forbes*. The metro area ranked #36. Criteria: median home price drop; unemployment rates; cost of living; air quality; sunny days; population density. *Forbes.com, "America's Most Stressful Cities," August 20, 2009*

- *Men's Health* examined the nation's largest 100 cities and identified the 10 cities at highest risk of erectile dysfunction. Fort Worth ranked #5. Criteria: percentage of current male smokers; percentage of adults with a BMI of at least 30; percentage of adults with diabetes; percentage of men working out three or more times per week; percentage of urologists per 100,000 men; number of ED drug prescriptions filled in 2007. *Men's Health, "Ranking America's Cities: Cities that Need Viagara," April 2009*

- 50 of the largest metro areas in the U.S. were analyzed in terms of their health and fitness by the American College of Sports Medicine in their "American Fitness Index." The Dallas metro area ranked #40 (#1 = healthiest). Criteria: preventative health behaviors; levels of chronic disease; health care access; community resources and policies that support physical activity. *American College of Sports Medicine, "Health and Community Fitness Status of the 50 Largest Metropolitan Areas," May 24, 2010*

- Fort Worth was selected as one of the "20 Most Livable U.S. Cities for Wheelchair Users" by the Christopher & Dana Reeve Foundation. The city ranked #14. Criteria: Medicaid eligibility and spending; access to physicians and rehabilitation facilities; access to fitness facilities and recreation; access to paratransit; percentage of people living with disabilities who are employed; clean air; climate. *Christopher & Dana Reeve Foundation, "20 Most Livable U.S. Cities for Wheelchair Users," July 26, 2010*

Real Estate Rankings

- *Fortune* ranked the 100 largest metro areas in the U.S. in terms of projected median home price change in 2010. The Fort Worth metro area ranked #14. *Fortune, "The 2010 Housing Outlook," December 9, 2009*

- Fort Worth appeared on ApartmentRatings.com "Top Cities for Renters" list in 2009." The area ranked #28. Overall satisfaction ratings were ranked using thousands of user submitted scores for hundreds of apartment complexes located in the 100 most populated U.S. municipalities. *ApartmentRatings.com, "2009 Renter Satisfaction Rankings"*

- The Fort Worth metro area was identified as one of the "Top 25 Real Estate Investment Markets" by *FinestExperts.com*. The metro area ranked #1. Over 10,000 real estate markets were analyzed to identify the most suitable places for real estate investors to seek stability and growth. Criteria: employment; rental markets; growth levels as offset by foreclosures. *FinestExperts.com, "Top 25 Real Estate Investment Markets," January 7, 2010*

- The Fort Worth metro area was identified as one of "America's Best Housing Markets" by *Forbes*. The metro area ranked #9. Criteria: housing affordability; rising home prices; percentage of foreclosures. *Forbes.com, "America's Best Housing Markets," February 19, 2010*

- The nation's largest metro areas were analyzed in terms of the percentage of households entering some stage of foreclosure in 2010. The Dallas metro area ranked #98 out of 206 (#1 = highest foreclosure rate). *RealtyTrac, 2010 Year-End Metropolitan Foreclosure Market Report, January 27, 2011*

- The Dallas metro area was identified as one of the "Best Cities to Buy a Home" by *Forbes*. The metro area ranked #6. Criteria: 2-year home price appreciation; vacancy rates; spread between monthly rent and mortgage payment at the median level. *Forbes.com, "Best Cities to Buy a Home," July 22, 2008*

- The Fort Worth metro area was identified as one of the 10 best cities for "Real Estate Steals" in the U.S. by *U.S. News and World Report*. The metro area was ranked #9. Criteria: average and quarterly price-to-income ratios. *U.S. News and World Report, "10 Cities for Real Estate Steals," February 18, 2010*

- The Fort Worth metro area appeared in a *Wall Street Journal* article ranking cities by "housing stress." The metro area was ranked #22 (#1 = most stress). Criteria: fraction of mortgage-holding homeowners with a monthly housing payment in excess of 30 percent of income; percentage of people without health insurance; unemployment rate. *The Wall Street Journal, "Which Cities Face Biggest Housing Risk," October 5, 2010*

- The Center for Housing Policy ranked 210 U.S metropolitan areas by the fair market rent for a two-bedroom unit. The Fort Worth metro area was ranked #90. (#1 = most expensive) with a rent of $861. Criteria: Fair Market Rent (FMR) in effect during the fourth quarter of 2009 based on HUD's fiscal year 2010 FMRs. *The Center for Housing Policy, "Paycheck to Paycheck: Most to Least Expensive Rental Markets in 2009"*

- The Dallas metro area was identified as one of the markets with the best expected performance in home prices over the next 12 months. *Local Market Monitor, "First Quarter Home Price Forecast for Largest US Markets," March 2, 2011*

Safety Rankings

- Symantec, the makers of Norton, in partnership with Sperling's BestPlaces, ranked the 50 largest cities in the U.S. in terms of their vulnerability to cybercrime. The city ranked #46. Criteria: number of cyberattacks and potential infections; level of Internet access; expenditures on computer hardware and software; wireless hotspots; broadband connectivity; Internet usage; online purchases. *Symantec, "10 Riskiest Cities for Cybercrime," March 22, 2010*

- Allstate ranked the 200 largest cities in America in terms of driver safety. Fort Worth ranked #140. In addition, drivers were 19.2% more likely to have had an accident compared to the national average. Allstate researchers analyzed internal property damage reported claims over a two-year period (from January 2007 to December 2008) to ensure the findings would not be affected by external influences such as weather or road construction. A weighted average of the two-year numbers determined the annual percentages. The report defines an auto crash as any collision resulting in a property damage claim. *Allstate, "The 2010 Allstate America's Best Drivers Report™"*

- Dallas was identified as one of the least safe places in the U.S. in terms of its vulnerability to natural disasters and weather extremes. The city ranked #2 out of 10. Sperling's BestPlaces analyzed data to show a metro areas' relative tendency to experience natural disasters (hail, tornadoes, high winds, hurricanes, earthquakes, and brush fires) or extreme weather (abundant rain or snowfall or days that are below freezing or above 90 degrees Fahrenheit). *Forbes, "Safest and Least Safe Places in the U.S.," August 30, 2005*

- Fort Worth was identified as one of the safest large cities in America by CQ Press. All 34 cities with populations of 500,000 or more that reported crime rates in 2009 for murder, rape, robbery, aggravated assault, burglary, and motor vehicle thefts were ranked. The city ranked #10 out of the top 10. *CQ Press, City Crime Rankings 2010-2011*

- The National Insurance Crime Bureau ranked 366 metro areas in the U.S. in terms of per capita rates of vehicle theft. The Fort Worth metro area ranked #39 (#1 = highest rate). Criteria: number of vehicle theft offenses per 100,000 inhabitants. *National Insurance Crime Bureau, "Hot Spots," May 17, 2010*

- The Fort Worth metro area was identified as one of the "The Most Dangerous Metro Areas for Pedestrians" by Transportation for America and the Surface Transportation Policy Partnership. The metro area ranked #13 out of 52 metro areas with over 1 million residents. Criteria: area's population divided by the number of pedestrian fatalities in that area. *Transportation for America and the Surface Transportation Policy Partnership, "Dangerous by Design: Solving the Epidemic of Preventable Pedestrian Deaths (and Making Great Neighborhoods)," November 11, 2009*

Seniors/Retirement Rankings

- The Dallas metro area was identified as one of "America's Most Affordable Places to Retire" by *Forbes*. The metro area ranked #2. Criteria: housing affordability; inflation; number of persons over 65 who are employed; net migration for persons over 65; percent of persons over 65 living below poverty level; doctors per capita; number of citizens tapping their Medicare benefits per thousand people. *Forbes.com, "America's Most Affordable Places to Retire," September 5, 2008*

- The Dallas metro area was selected as one of "America's Best Places to Grow Old" by *Forbes*. The area was ranked #2 out of 10. Criteria: housing affordability; inflationary pressures; number of persons over 65 who are currently employed; net migration for persons over 65; percent of seniors living below poverty level; doctors per capita; number of citizens tapping their Medicare benefits per 1,000 people. *Forbes, "America's Best Places to Grow Old," December 12, 2008*

- The Fort Worth metro area was selected as one of "The 10 Most Affordable Cities for Long-Term Care" by *U.S. News & World Report*. Criteria: costs at nursing homes, assisted living facilities, and adult day health care facilities; cost for licensed home health aides. *U.S. News & Word Report, "The 10 Most Affordable Cities for Long-Term Care," May 17, 2010*

Sports/Recreation Rankings

- Fort Worth appeared on the *Sporting News* list of the "Best Sports Cities" for 2010. The area ranked #5 out of 402 cities in the U.S. *Sporting News* takes a 12-month snapshot, roughly October to October, of each city's sports, putting a heavy premium on regular-season won-lost records (from the most recently completed season). Other criteria include: playoff berths, bowl appearances and tournament bids; championships; applicable power ratings; quality of competition; overall fan fervor as measured in part by attendance as percentage of venue capacity; abundance of teams (rewarding quality over quantity); stadium and arena quality; ticket availability and prices; franchise ownership; and marquee appeal of athletes. *Sporting News, "Best Sports Cities 2010," October, 2010*

- Scarborough Research, a leading market research firm, identified the top local markets for avid NBA fans. The Fort Worth DMA (Designated Market Area) ranked in the top 10 with 13% of consumers 18 years and over reporting that they are "very interested in the NBA." *Scarborough Research, April 24, 2006*

- *Golf Digest* ranked 330 metro areas in the U.S. in terms of golf. The Fort Worth metro area was ranked #243. Criteria: access to golf; weather; value of golf; and quality of golf. *Golf Digest, "Metro Golf Rankings," August 2005*

- *Golf.com* and the research arm of the National Golf Foundation analyzed the 50 largest metropolitan areas in the U.S. in terms of golf. The Dallas metro area ranked #4. Criteria: weather; affordability; quality of courses; accessibility; number of courses designed by esteemed architects; availability; crowdedness. *Golf.com, November 15, 2007*

Technology Rankings

- Fort Worth was selected as a 2010 Digital Cities Survey winner. The city ranked #10 in the large city (250,000 or more population) category. The survey examined and assessed how city governments are utilizing information technology to operate and deliver quality service to their customers and citizens. Survey questions focused on implementation and adoption of online service delivery; planning and governance; and the infrastructure and architecture that make the transformation to digital government possible. *Center for Digital Government, "2010 Digital Cities Survey"*

- Scarborough Research, a leading market research firm, identified the Fort Worth DMA (Designated Market Area) as one of the top markets for text messaging with more than 50% of cell phone subscribers age 18+ utilizing the text messaging feature on their phone. *Scarborough Research, November 24, 2008*

Transportation Rankings

- Fort Worth was selected as one of the "Least Courteous Cities (Worst Road Rage)" in the U.S. by AutoVantage. The city ranked #2. Criteria: 2,518 consumers were interviewed in 25 major metropolitan areas about their views on road rage. *AutoVantage, "2009 AutoVantage Road Rage Survey"*

- The Fort Worth metro area appeared on *Forbes* list of the best and worst cities for commuters. The metro area ranked #56 out of 60 (#1 is best). Criteria: travel time; road congestion; travel delays. *Forbes.com, "Best and Worst Cities for Commuters," February 16, 2010*

Women/Minorities Rankings

- Fort Worth was ranked #88 out of 100 metro areas in *SELF Magazine's* ranking of America's healthiest places for women." A panel of experts came up with more than 50 criteria including death and disease rates, environmental indicators, community resources, and lifestyle habits. *SELF Magazine, "Secrets of America's Healthiest Women," December 2008*

- Dallas appeared on *Black Enterprise's* list of the "Ten Best Cities for African Americans." The top picks were culled from more than 2,000 interactive surveys completed on www.blackenterprise.com and by editorial staff evaluation. The editors weighed the following criteria as it pertained to African Americans in each city: median household income; percentage of households earning more than $100,000; percentage of businesses owned; percentage of college graduates; unemployment rates; home loan rejections; and homeownership rates. *Black Enterprise, May 2007*

Miscellaneous Rankings

- Proctor & Gamble, the makers of Pepto-Bismol, in partnership with Sperling's BestPlaces, ranked the nation's 100 most populated metro areas in terms of the "Best Places for Thanksgiving Celebrations." The Fort Worth metro area ranked #4. Criteria: turkey consumption per capita; increase in inbound air traffic during Thanksgiving; Pepto-Bismol sales; results from a consumer poll of 4,800 Americans recording the number of people attending Thanksgiving, the number of dishes served, and ways people intended to celebrate. *Proctor & Gamble, "Top 10 Best Places for Thanksgiving Celebrations," November 18, 2010*

- Energizer Holdings, the makers of Edge® shave gel, in partnership with Sperling's BestPlaces, ranked 50 major metro areas in terms of everyday irritations. The Dallas metro area ranked #13. Criteria: humidity levels; weather conditions; incidence of traffic delays and congestion; average commute times; frequency of flight delays and cancellations; rates of sleeplessness; underemployment; pollens and allergens; pests; comedy clubs per capita. *Energizer Holdings, "Most Irritation Prone Cities," July 23, 2010*

- Mars Chocolate North America, the makers of COMBOS®, in partnership with Sperling's BestPlaces, ranked 50 major metro areas in terms of their "manliness." The Dallas metro area ranked #39. Criteria: number of home improvement stores, steak houses, pickup trucks, motorcycles, and manly occupations (fire fighters, police officers, construction workers, EMP personnel) per capita; salty snack sales; sports TV viewing habits. *Mars Chocolate North America, "America's Manliest Cities," June 22, 2010*

- The Dallas metro area was selected as one of "America's Greediest Cities" by *Forbes*. The area was ranked #7 out of 10. Criteria: number of Forbes 400 (*Forbes* annual list of the richest Americans) members per capita. *Forbes, "America's Greediest Cities," December 7, 2007*

- The Dallas metro area appeared in AutoMD.com's ranking of the "Best and Worst Cities for Auto Repair." The metro area ranked #34 (#1 is best). The 50 most-populated metro areas in the U.S. were ranked on three critical factors: repair affordability; price disparity range; shop integrity factor. *AutoMD.com, "Advocacy for Repair Shop Fairness Report," February 24, 2010*

- The Fort Worth metro area appeared on *Forbes* list of "America's Drunkest Cities." The area ranked #27. Criteria: 35 of the largest continental U.S. metro areas were chosen based on availability of data and geographic diversity. Each metro was ranked in five areas: state laws; drinkers; heavy drinkers; binge drinkers; and alcoholism. *Forbes.com, "America's Drunkest Cities," August 22, 2006*

Business Environment

CITY FINANCES

City Government Finances

Component	2008 ($000)	2008 ($ per capita)
Total Revenues	1,343,091	1,970
Total Expenditures	1,073,127	1,574
Debt Outstanding	1,389,941	2,039
Cash and Securities[1]	2,817,451	4,132

Note: (1) Cash and security holdings of a government at the close of its fiscal year, including those of its dependent agencies, utilities, and liquor stores.
Source: U.S Census Bureau, State & Local Government Finances 2008

City Government Revenue by Source

Source	2008 ($000)	2008 ($ per capita)
General Revenue		
From Federal Government	442	1
From State Government	58,739	86
From Local Governments	267	0
Taxes		
Property	289,411	424
Sales and Gross Receipts	181,058	266
Personal Income	0	0
Corporate Income	0	0
Motor Vehicle License	0	0
Other Taxes	63,525	93
Current Charges	139,571	205
Liquor Store	0	0
Utility	190,183	279
Employee Retirement	301,555	442

Source: U.S Census Bureau, State & Local Government Finances 2008

City Government Expenditures by Function

Function	2008 ($000)	2008 ($ per capita)	2008 (%)
General Direct Expenditures			
Air Transportation	3,647	5	0.3
Corrections	0	0	0.0
Education	0	0	0.0
Employment Security Administration	0	0	0.0
Financial Administration	7,456	11	0.7
Fire Protection	93,751	138	8.7
General Public Buildings	0	0	0.0
Governmental Administration, Other	12,661	19	1.2
Health	12,872	19	1.2
Highways	87,806	129	8.2
Hospitals	0	0	0.0
Housing and Community Development	15,437	23	1.4
Interest on General Debt	25,619	38	2.4
Judicial and Legal	15,806	23	1.5
Libraries	17,048	25	1.6
Parking	339	< 1	< 0.1
Parks and Recreation	49,493	73	4.6
Police Protection	182,542	268	17.0
Public Welfare	0	0	0.0
Sewerage	116,099	170	10.8
Solid Waste Management	42,673	63	4.0
Veterans' Services	0	0	0.0
Liquor Store	0	0	0.0
Utility	197,239	289	18.4
Employee Retirement	95,699	140	8.9

Source: U.S Census Bureau, State & Local Government Finances 2008

Municipal Bond Ratings

Area	Moody's	S&P	Fitch
City	Aa2	AA+	AA

Rating Systems (shown in declining order of credit quality): Moody's– Aaa, Aa, A, Baa, Ba, B, Caa, Ca, C (numerical modifiers 1, 2, and 3 are added to letter-rating); S&P– AAA, AA, A, BBB, BB, B, CCC, CC, C; Fitch– AAA, AA, A, BBB, BB, B, CCC, CC, C. Ratings may be modified by the addition of a plus or minus sign to show relative standing within the major rating categories.
Notes: n/a Not available; (1) Not reviewed; (2) Issuer Rating/No General Obligation; (3) Standard and Poor's Issue Credit Rating (ICR) is a current opinion of an obliger with respect to a specific financial obligation, a specific class of financial obligations, or a specific financial program.
Source: U.S. Census Bureau, 2011 Statistical Abstract, Bond Ratings for City Governments by Largest Cities: 2009

DEMOGRAPHICS

Population Growth

Area	1990 Census	2000 Census	2010 Estimate	2015 Projection	Population Growth (%)	
					2000-2010	2010-2015
City	448,311	534,694	696,039	764,598	30.2	9.8
MSA[1]	3,989,294	5,161,544	6,493,230	7,129,430	25.8	9.8
U.S.	248,709,873	281,421,906	309,038,974	321,675,005	9.8	4.1

Note: (1) Metropolitan Statistical Area - see Appendix B for areas included
Source: Claritas, Inc.

Number of Households and Average Household Size

Area	2010 Estimate	2010 Average Household Size
City	248,820	2.73
MSA[1]	2,320,136	2.76
U.S.	116,136,617	2.59

Note: (1) Metropolitan Statistical Area - see Appendix B for areas included
Source: Claritas, Inc.

Race and Ethnicity

Area	White Alone[2] (%)	Black Alone[2] (%)	Asian Alone[2] (%)	Other Race Alone[2] (%)	Hispanic[3] (%)
City	57.8	18.5	3.2	20.5	35.9
MSA[1]	64.4	14.0	4.7	16.9	28.1
U.S.	72.3	12.4	4.4	10.9	15.8

Note: Figures are 2010 estimates; (1) Metropolitan Statistical Area - see Appendix B for areas included (2) Alone is defined as not being in combination with one or more other races; (3) May be of any race.
Source: Claritas, Inc.

Segregation

Type	Segregation Indices[1]				Percent Change		
	1990	2000	2010	2010 Rank[2]	1990-2000	1990-2010	2000-2010
Black/White	62.8	59.8	56.6	48	-3.1	-6.2	-3.2
Asian/White	41.8	45.6	46.6	19	3.8	4.8	1.0
Hispanic/White	48.8	52.3	50.3	24	3.5	1.5	-2.0

Note: Figures are based on an analysis of 1990, 2000, and 2010 Census Decennial Census tract data by William H. Frey, Brookings Institution and the University of Michigan Social Science Data Analysis Network. In this analysis all racial groups (whites, blacks, and asians) are non-Hispanic members of those races. Hispanics are shown as a separate category; All figures cover the Metropolitan Statistical Area (see Appendix B for areas included); (1) Segregation Indices are Dissimilarity Indices that measure the degree to which the minority group is distributed differently than whites aross census tracts. They range from 0 (complete integration) to 100 (complete [segregation) where the value indicates the percentage of the minority group that needs to move to be distributed exactly like whites; (2) Ranges from 1 (most segregated) to 102 (least segregated); n/a not available.
Source: www.CensusScope.org

Ancestry

Area	German	Irish	English	American	Italian	Polish	French	Scottish
City	9.3	7.2	7.1	7.1	1.9	0.9	1.8	1.8
MSA[1]	11.4	8.8	8.6	6.5	2.3	1.2	2.3	1.9
U.S.	16.6	12.0	9.1	6.1	5.9	3.3	3.1	1.9

Note: The top eight ancestries in the U.S. are shown. Figures are percentages and include multiple ancestry (e.g. if a person reported being Irish and Italian, they were included in both columns); (1) Metropolitan Statistical Area - see Appendix B for areas included
Source: U.S. Census Bureau, 2007-2009 American Community Survey 3-Year Estimates

Foreign-Born Population

Area	Percent of Population Born in								
	Any Foreign Country	Mexico	Asia	Europe	Carribean	South America	Central America[2]	Africa	Canada
City	18.3	12.6	2.6	0.8	0.2	0.4	0.9	0.6	0.1
MSA[1]	17.5	9.8	3.8	0.8	0.2	0.5	1.3	0.8	0.2
U.S.	12.5	3.8	3.4	1.6	1.1	0.8	0.9	0.5	0.3

Note: (1) Metropolitan Statistical Area - see Appendix B for areas included; (2) Excludes Mexico.
Source: U.S. Census Bureau, 2007-2009 American Community Survey 3-Year Estimates

Marriage Status

Area	Never Married	Now Married[2]	Separated	Widowed	Divorced
City	31.6	48.4	3.0	5.0	12.0
MSA[1]	30.9	50.7	2.6	4.7	11.1
U.S.	31.4	49.7	2.2	6.2	10.6

Note: Figures are percentages and cover the population 15 years of age and older; (1) Metropolitan Statistical Area - see Appendix B for areas included; (2) Excludes separated
Source: U.S. Census Bureau, 2007-2009 American Community Survey 3-Year Estimates

Age Distribution and Median Age

Area	Percent of Population							Median Age
	Under Age 5	Age 5 to 17	Age 18 to 34	Age 35 to 49	Age 50 to 64	Age 65 to 79	80 Years and Over	
City	9.8	19.8	27.0	21.3	13.9	5.9	2.3	31.0
MSA[1]	8.4	19.6	25.3	22.8	15.4	6.2	2.2	32.9
U.S.	6.9	17.5	23.3	21.4	18.1	9.1	3.7	36.7

Note: (1) Metropolitan Statistical Area - see Appendix B for areas included
Source: U.S. Census Bureau, 2007-2009 American Community Survey 3-Year Estimates

Male/Female Ratio

Area	Males	Females	Males per 100 Females
City	347,246	348,793	99.6
MSA[1]	3,264,985	3,228,245	101.1
U.S.	152,401,520	156,637,454	97.3

Note: Figures are 2010 estimates; (1) Metropolitan Statistical Area - see Appendix B for areas included
Source: Claritas, Inc.

Religion

Area	Catholic	Southern Baptist	United Meth-odist	ELCA[1]	LDS[2]	Presby-terian Church USA	Jewish Est.	Muslim Est.
County	11.5	18.7	6.8	0.6	0.8	0.8	0.4	1.0
U.S.	22.0	7.1	3.7	1.8	1.5	1.1	2.2	0.6

Note: Figures are the number of adherents as a percentage of the total population; Adherents are defined as all members, including full members, their children and the estimated number of other participants who are not considered members (e.g. the baptized, those not confirmed, those regularly attending services, etc.);
(1) Evangelical Lutheran Church in America; (2) The Church of Jesus Christ of Latter Day Saints
Source: Reprinted with permission from Religious Congregations and Membership in the United States 2000 (Nashville, Glenmary Research Center, 2002) Copyright Association of Statisticians of American Religious Bodies. All rights reserved.

ECONOMY

Gross Metropolitan Product

Area	2006	2007	2008	2009	2009 Rank[2]
MSA[1]	340.6	362.1	379.9	384.8	6

Note: Figures are in billions of dollars; (1) Dallas-Fort Worth-Arlington, TX Metropolitan Statistical Area - see Appendix B for areas included; (2) Rank ranges from 1 to 363
Source: The U.S. Conference of Mayors, "Pace of Economic Recovery: GMP and Jobs," January 2010

Economic Growth

Area	2006-2008 (%)	2009 (%)	2010 (%)	Rank[2]
MSA[1]	2.7	-0.1	3.7	67
U.S.	1.3	-2.5	2.2	–

Note: Figures are real Gross Metropolitan Product growth rates and represent annual average percent change; (1) Dallas-Fort Worth-Arlington, TX Metropolitan Statistical Area - see Appendix B for areas included; (2) Rank ranges from 1 to 363
Source: The U.S. Conference of Mayors, "Pace of Economic Recovery: GMP and Jobs," January 2010

Metropolitan Area Exports

Area	2005	2006	2007	2008	2009	2009 Rank[2]
MSA[1]	20,541.2	22,461.6	22,079.1	22,503.7	19,881.8	10

Note: Figures are in millions of dollars; (1) Dallas-Fort Worth-Arlington, TX Metropolitan Statistical Area - see Appendix B for areas included; (2) Rank ranges from 1 to 374
Source: U.S. Department of Commerce, International Trade Administration, Office of Trade & Industry Information, Manufacturing & Services

INCOME

Per Capita/Median/Average Income

Area	Per Capita ($)	Median Household ($)	Average Household ($)
City	22,786	46,649	62,573
MSA[1]	27,980	58,202	77,740
U.S.	27,034	52,795	71,071

Note: Figures are 2010 estimates; (1) Metropolitan Statistical Area - see Appendix B for areas included
Source: Claritas, Inc.

Household Income Distribution

Area	Percent of Households Earning							
	Under $15,000	$15,000 -24,999	$25,000 -34,999	$35,000 -49,999	$50,000 -74,999	$75,000 -99,000	$100,000 -149,999	$150,000 and up
City	13.4	11.3	12.1	17.0	19.0	11.2	10.5	5.6
MSA[1]	9.4	8.6	10.2	15.3	19.6	13.3	14.1	9.4
U.S.	12.1	10.2	10.6	15.0	19.5	12.5	12.1	8.0

Note: Figures are 2010 estimates; (1) Metropolitan Statistical Area - see Appendix B for areas included
Source: Claritas, Inc.

Poverty Rates by Age

Area	All Ages	Under 18 Years Old	18 to 64 Years Old	65 Years and Over
City	17.3	7.5	8.9	0.9
MSA[1]	13.4	5.4	7.2	0.7
U.S.	13.6	4.7	7.7	1.2

Note: Figures are percent of population with income during the previous 12 months below poverty level and only include population for whom poverty status is determined; (1) Metropolitan Statistical Area - see Appendix B for areas included
Source: U.S. Census Bureau, 2007-2009 American Community Survey 3-Year Estimates

Personal Bankruptcy Filing Rate

Area	2006	2007	2008	2009	2010
Tarrant County	2.44	2.91	3.01	3.73	3.75
U.S.	2.00	2.73	3.53	4.60	4.96

Note: Numbers are per 1,000 population and include Chapter 7 and Chapter 13 filings
Source: Federal Deposit Insurance Corporation, Regional Economic Conditions, March 17, 2011

EMPLOYMENT

Labor Force and Employment

Area	Civilian Labor Force			Workers Employed		
	Dec. 2009	Dec. 2010	% Chg.	Dec. 2009	Dec. 2010	% Chg.
City	332,708	338,904	1.9	306,145	311,270	1.7
MD[1]	1,054,949	1,072,202	1.6	971,158	987,399	1.7
U.S.	152,693,000	153,156,000	0.3	137,953,000	139,159,000	0.9

Note: Data is not seasonally adjusted and covers workers 16 years of age and older;
(1) Metropolitan Division - see Appendix B for areas included
Source: Bureau of Labor Statistics, http://stats.bls.gov

Unemployment Rate

Area	2010											
	Jan.	Feb.	Mar.	Apr.	May	Jun.	Jul.	Aug.	Sep.	Oct.	Nov.	Dec.
City	8.7	8.5	8.4	8.3	8.2	8.7	8.9	8.7	8.3	8.2	8.4	8.2
MD[1]	8.6	8.5	8.4	8.0	8.0	8.5	8.5	8.3	8.1	8.0	8.2	7.9
U.S.	10.6	10.4	10.2	9.5	9.3	9.6	9.7	9.5	9.2	9.0	9.3	9.1

Note: Data is not seasonally adjusted and covers workers 16 years of age and older; All figures are percentages; (1) Metropolitan Division - see Appendix B for areas included
Source: Bureau of Labor Statistics, http://stats.bls.gov

Projected Unemployment Rate

Area	2007 (%)	2009 (%)	2011 (%)	2013 (%)
MSA[1]	4.4	8.9	8.3	7.0

Note: (1) Metropolitan Statistical Area - see Appendix B for areas included
Source: The U.S. Conference of Mayors, "Pace of Economic Recovery: GMP and Jobs," January 2010

Employment by Occupation

Occupation Classification	City (%)	MSA[1] (%)	U.S. (%)
Sales and Office	26.3	27.0	25.4
Professional and Related	18.4	19.5	21.0
Service	16.4	15.1	17.2
Production, Transportation, and Material Moving	14.9	11.8	12.3
Management, Business, and Financial	13.0	15.7	14.1
Construction, Extraction, and Maintenance	10.8	10.7	9.2
Farming, Forestry, and Fishing	0.1	0.2	0.7

Note: Figures cover employed civilians 16 years of age and older;
(1) Metropolitan Statistical Area - see Appendix B for areas included
Source: U.S. Census Bureau, 2007-2009 American Community Survey 3-Year Estimates

Employment by Industry

Sector	MSA[1]		U.S.
	Number of Employees	Percent of Total	Percent of Total
Government	126,400	14.8	17.2
Education and Health Services	108,500	12.7	15.2
Professional and Business Services	91,900	10.7	13.0
Retail Trade	101,800	11.9	11.4
Leisure and Hospitality	89,600	10.5	9.7
Manufacturing	85,900	10.0	8.8
Financial Activities	51,300	6.0	5.8
Wholesale Trade	38,700	4.5	4.2
Construction	n/a	n/a	4.1
Other Services	31,300	3.7	4.1
Transportation and Utilities	63,200	7.4	3.7
Information	13,700	1.6	2.1
Mining and Logging	n/a	n/a	0.6

Note: Figures cover non-farm employment as of December 2010 and are not seasonally adjusted;
(1) Metropolitan Statistical Area - see Appendix B for areas included; n/a not available
Source: Bureau of Labor Statistics, http://stats.bls.gov

Occupations with Greatest Projected Employment Growth: 2006 - 2016

Occupation[1]	2006 Employment	2016 Projected Employment	Numeric Employment Change	Percent Employment Change
Combined food preparation and serving workers, including fast food	270,530	359,050	88,520	32.7
Retail salespersons	332,750	411,350	78,600	23.6
Personal and home care aides	133,050	207,850	74,800	56.2
Customer service representatives	214,440	280,060	65,620	30.6
Elementary school teachers, except special education	145,430	207,710	62,280	42.8
Registered nurses	157,840	217,430	59,590	37.8
Waiters and waitresses	174,140	227,790	53,650	30.8
Child care workers	145,500	189,730	44,230	30.4
Office clerks, general	194,610	236,670	42,060	21.6
Postsecondary teachers	113,400	153,130	39,730	35.0

Note: Projections cover Texas; (1) Sorted by numeric employment change
Source: www.projectionscentral.com, State Occupational Projections, 2006-2016 Long-Term Projections

Fastest Growing Occupations: 2006 - 2016

Occupation[1]	2006 Employment	2016 Projected Employment	Numeric Employment Change	Percent Employment Change
Personal and home care aides	133,050	207,850	74,800	56.2
Network systems and data communications analysts	17,750	27,620	9,870	55.6
Medical assistants	34,790	53,500	18,710	53.8
Special education teachers, preschool, kindergarten, and elementary school	13,750	20,560	6,810	49.5
Physical therapist assistants	3,780	5,570	1,790	47.4
Special education teachers, middle school	6,270	9,170	2,900	46.3
Computer software engineers, applications	30,900	45,200	14,300	46.3
Physician assistants	3,810	5,540	1,730	45.4
Kindergarten teachers, except special education	12,850	18,690	5,840	45.4
Pharmacy technicians	24,420	35,050	10,630	43.5

Note: Projections cover Texas; (1) Sorted by percent employment change and excludes occupations with numeric employment change less than 1500
Source: www.projectionscentral.com, State Occupational Projections, 2006-2016 Long-Term Projections

Average Wages

Occupation	$/Hr.	Occupation	$/Hr.
Accountants and Auditors	33.24	Maids and Housekeeping Cleaners	8.58
Automotive Mechanics	17.40	Maintenance and Repair Workers	15.89
Bookkeepers	16.37	Marketing Managers	51.80
Carpenters	15.32	Nuclear Medicine Technologists	32.89
Cashiers	8.82	Nurses, Licensed Practical	20.16
Clerks, General Office	12.69	Nurses, Registered	30.48
Clerks, Receptionists/Information	12.20	Nursing Aides/Orderlies/Attendants	11.06
Clerks, Shipping/Receiving	14.52	Packers and Packagers, Hand	10.47
Computer Programmers	36.58	Physical Therapists	39.23
Computer Support Specialists	21.45	Postal Service Mail Carriers	23.73
Computer Systems Analysts	39.28	Real Estate Brokers	21.41
Cooks, Restaurant	9.57	Retail Salespersons	11.12
Dentists	n/a	Sales Reps., Exc. Tech./Scientific	29.06
Electrical Engineers	33.73	Sales Reps., Tech./Scientific	42.57
Electricians	20.06	Secretaries, Exc. Legal/Med./Exec.	14.55
Financial Managers	53.16	Security Guards	14.11
First-Line Supervisors/Mgrs., Sales	19.55	Surgeons	89.78
Food Preparation Workers	8.61	Teacher Assistants	9.10
General and Operations Managers	51.90	Teachers, Elementary School	24.30
Hairdressers/Cosmetologists	12.95	Teachers, Secondary School	25.30
Internists	74.08	Telemarketers	10.19
Janitors and Cleaners	10.79	Truck Drivers, Heavy/Tractor-Trailer	19.53
Landscaping/Groundskeeping Workers	10.84	Truck Drivers, Light/Delivery Svcs.	14.57
Lawyers	55.25	Waiters and Waitresses	9.89

Note: Wage data covers the Fort Worth-Arlington, TX Metropolitan Division - see Appendix B for areas included. Hourly wages for elementary/secondary school teachers and teacher assistants were calculated by the editors from annual wage data assuming a 40 hour work week; n/a not available.
Source: Bureau of Labor Statistics, Metro Area Occupational Employment and Wage Estimates, May 2009

RESIDENTIAL REAL ESTATE

Building Permits

Area	Single-Family			Multi-Family			Total		
	2009	2010	Pct. Chg.	2009	2010	Pct. Chg.	2009	2010	Pct. Chg.
City	3,070	2,759	-10.1	973	818	-15.9	4,043	3,577	-11.5
MSA[1]	14,141	14,420	2.0	6,229	5,138	-17.5	20,370	19,558	-4.0
U.S.	441,100	447,300	1.4	141,900	157,300	10.9	583,000	604,600	3.7

Note: (1) Metropolitan Statistical Area - see Appendix B for areas included; figures represent new, privately-owned housing units authorized (unadjusted data); All permit data are based on estimates with imputation.
Source: U.S. Census Bureau, Manufacturing, Mining, and Construction Statistics, Building Permits, 2009, 2010

Homeownership Rate

Area	2005 (%)	2006 (%)	2007 (%)	2008 (%)	2009 (%)	2010 (%)
MSA[1]	62.3	60.7	60.9	60.9	61.6	63.8
U.S.	68.9	68.8	68.1	67.8	67.4	66.9

Note: (1) Metropolitan Statistical Area - see Appendix B for areas included
Source: U.S. Census Bureau, Housing Vacancies and Homeownership Annual Statistics: 2010

Housing Vacancy Rates

Area	Gross Vacancy Rate[2] (%)			Year-Round Vacancy Rate[3] (%)			Rental Vacancy Rate[4] (%)			Homeowner Vacancy Rate[5] (%)		
	2008	2009	2010	2008	2009	2010	2008	2009	2010	2008	2009	2010
MSA[1]	9.5	9.4	10.5	9.4	9.3	10.4	10.5	11.7	13.5	2.8	2.1	2.3
U.S.	14.4	14.5	14.3	11.1	11.3	11.3	10.0	10.6	10.2	2.8	2.6	2.6

Note: (1) Metropolitan Statistical Area - see Appendix B for areas included; (2) The percentage of the total housing inventory that is vacant; (3) The percentage of the housing inventory (excluding seasonal units) that is year-round vacant; (4) The percentage of rental inventory that is vacant for rent; (5) The percentage of homeowner inventory that is vacant for sale; n/a not available
Source: U.S. Census Bureau, Housing Vacancies and Homeownership Annual Statistics: 2010

State Corporate Income Tax Rates

State	Tax Rate (%)	Income Brackets ($)	Num. of Brackets	Financial Institution Tax Rate (%)[a]	Federal Income Tax Ded.
Texas	(y)	–	-	(y)	No

Note: Tax rates as of January 1, 2011; (a) Rates listed are the tax rates applied to financial institutions or excise taxes based on income. Some states have other taxes based upon the value of deposits or shares; (y) Texas imposes a Franchise Tax, otherwise known as margin tax, imposed on entities with more than $1,000,000 total revenues at rate of 1%, or 0.5% for entities primarily engaged in retail or wholesale trade, on lesser of 70% of total revenues or 100% of gross receipts after deductions for either compensation or cost of goods sold.
Source: Federation of Tax Administrators, "State Corporate Income Tax Rates, 2011"

State Individual Income Tax Rates

State	Tax Rate (%)	Income Brackets ($)	Num. of Brackets	Personal Exempt. ($)[1] Single	Personal Exempt. ($)[1] Dependents	Fed. Inc. Tax Ded.

Texas – No State Income Tax

Note: Tax rates as of January 1, 2011; Local- and county-level taxes are not included; n/a not applicable; (1) Married joint filers generally receive double the single exemption
Source: Federation of Tax Administrators, "State Individual Income Tax Rates, 2011"

Various State and Local Tax Rates

State	State and Local Sales and Use (%)	State Sales and Use (%)	Gasoline[1] (¢/gal.)	Cigarette[2] ($/pack)	Spirits[3] ($/gal.)	Wine[4] ($/gal.)	Beer[5] ($/gal.)
Texas	8.25	6.25	20.0	1.41	2.40	0.20	0.20

Note: All tax rates as of January 1, 2011 except Spirits (Sept. 1, 2010); (1) The American Petroleum Institute has developed a methodology for determining the average tax rate on a gallon of fuel. Rates may include any of the following: excise taxes, environmental fees, storage tank fees, other fees or taxes, general sales tax, and local taxes. In states where gasoline is subject to the general sales tax, or where the fuel tax is based on the average sale price, the average rate determined by API is sensitive to changes in the price of gasoline. States that fully or partially apply general sales taxes to gasoline: CA, CO, GA, IL, IN, MI, NY; (2) The federal excise tax of $1.0066 per pack and local taxes are not included; (3) Rates are those applicable to off-premise sales of 40% alcohol by volume (a.b.v.) distilled spirits in 750ml containers. Local excise taxes are excluded; (4) Rates are those applicable to off-premise sales of 11% a.b.v. non-carbonated wine in 750ml containers; (5) Rates are those applicable to off-premise sales of 4.7% a.b.v. beer in 12 ounce containers.
Source: Tax Foundation, 2011 Facts & Figures: How Does Your State Compare?

State-Local Tax Burdens

Area	Rate (%)	Rank[1]	Per Capita Taxes Paid to Home State ($)	Total State and Local Per Capita Taxes Paid ($)	Per Capita Income ($)
Texas	7.9	45	2,248	3,197	40,498
U.S. Average	9.8	-	3,057	4,160	42,539

Note: Figures cover 2009; (1) Rank ranges from 1 to 50 where 1 is highest tax burden
Source: Tax Foundation, State-Local Tax Burdens, All States, 2009

State Business Tax Climate Index Rankings

State	Overall Rank	Corporate Tax Index Rank	Individual Income Tax Index Rank	Sales Tax Index Rank	Unemployment Insurance Tax Index Rank	Property Tax Index Rank
Texas	13	46	7	37	15	29

Note: The index is a measure of how each state's tax laws affect economic performance. The lower the rank, the more favorable a state's tax system is for business. All ranks are for fiscal years. States without a given tax are given a ranking of 1.
Source: Tax Foundation, Tax Foundation Background Paper, No. 60, "2011 State Business Tax Climate Index"

COMMERCIAL REAL ESTATE

Office Market

Market Area	Inventory (sq. ft.)	Vacant (sq. ft.)	Vac. Rate (%)	Under Constr. (sq. ft.)	Asking Rent ($/sf/yr) Class A	Asking Rent ($/sf/yr) Class B
Dallas/Fort Worth	190,744,710	43,317,095	22.7	281,600	23.16	17.90

Source: Grubb & Ellis, Office Markets Trends, 1st Quarter 2011

Industrial Market

Market Area	Inventory (sq. ft.)	Vacant (sq. ft.)	Vac. Rate (%)	Under Constr. (sq. ft.)	Asking Rent ($/sf/yr) WH/Dist	Asking Rent ($/sf/yr) R&D/Flex
Dallas/Fort Worth	662,799,900	76,917,306	11.6	1,403,552	3.53	6.46

Source: Grubb & Ellis, Industrial Markets Trends, 1st Quarter 2011

COMMERCIAL UTILITIES

Typical Monthly Electric Bills

Area	Commercial Service ($/month) 3 kW demand 1,000 kWh	Commercial Service ($/month) 40 kW demand 14,000 kWh	Industrial Service ($/month) 1,000 kW demand 200,000 kWh	Industrial Service ($/month) 50,000 kW demand 15,000,000 kWh
City	n/a	n/a	n/a	n/a
Average[1]	135	1,576	23,741	1,402,202

Note: Based on total rates in effect July 1, 2010; (1) average based on 182 utilities surveyed; n/a not available
Source: Edison Electric Institute, Typical Bills and Average Rates Report, Summer 2010

TRANSPORTATION

Means of Transportation to Work

Area	Car/Truck/Van Drove Alone	Car/Truck/Van Carpooled	Public Transportation Bus	Public Transportation Subway	Public Transportation Railroad	Bicycle	Walked	Other Means	Worked at Home
City	80.4	12.1	1.0	0.0	0.2	0.2	1.2	1.9	3.1
MSA[1]	80.4	11.0	1.2	0.2	0.2	0.2	1.3	1.4	4.1
U.S.	75.8	10.4	2.7	1.7	0.5	0.5	2.9	1.2	4.1

Note: Figures are percentages and cover workers 16 years of age and older;
(1) Metropolitan Statistical Area - see Appendix B for areas included
Source: U.S. Census Bureau, 2007-2009 American Community Survey 3-Year Estimates

Travel Time to Work

Area	Less Than 15 Minutes	15 to 29 Minutes	30 to 44 Minutes	45 to 59 Minutes	60 to 89 Minutes	90 Minutes or More
City	23.3	40.2	21.7	7.7	5.2	1.8
MSA[1]	22.5	36.3	24.0	9.6	5.9	1.7
U.S.	28.5	36.2	19.7	7.5	5.6	2.5

Note: Figures are percentages and include workers 16 years old and over;
(1) Metropolitan Statistical Area - see Appendix B for areas included
Source: U.S. Census Bureau, 2007-2009 American Community Survey 3-Year Estimates

Travel Time Index

Area	1982	1999	2008	2009
Urban Area[1]	1.05	1.19	1.23	1.22
Average[2]	1.08	1.20	1.20	1.20

Note: Travel Time Index—the ratio of travel time in the peak period to the travel time at
free-flow conditions. A value of 1.30 indicates a 20-minute free-flow trip takes 26 minutes
in the peak. Free-flow speeds (60 mph on freeways and 35 mph on principal arterials)
are used as the comparison threshold; (1) Covers the Dallas-Fort Worth-Arlington urban area;
(2) average of 439 urban areas
Source: Texas Transportation Institute, Urban Mobility Report 2010, December 2010

Public Transportation

Agency Name / Mode of Transportation	Vehicles Operated in Maximum Service	Annual Unlinked Passenger Trips ('000)	Annual Passenger Miles ('000)
Fort Worth Transportation Authority (The T)			
Commuter rail	15	1,131.6	18,962.4
Demand response	35	153.6	1,671.3
Demand response	53	242.0	2,197.9
Bus	126	6,292.4	35,218.2
Bus	3	72.3	265.9

Note: Figures include both directly operated and purchased transportation
Source: Federal Transit Administration, National Transit Database, 2009

Air Transportation

Airport Name and Code / Type of Service	Passenger Airlines[1]	Passenger Enplanements	Freight Carriers[2]	Freight (lbs.)
Dallas-Fort Worth International (DFW)				
Domestic service (U.S. carriers - 2010)	29	24,515,012	29	331,267,166
International service (U.S. carriers - 2009)	14	1,982,583	9	56,792,392
Dallas Love Field (DAL)				
Domestic service (U.S. carriers - 2010)	16	3,780,857	6	9,736,359
International service (U.S. carriers - 2009)	5	519	3	23,275

Note: (1) Includes all U.S.-based major, minor and commuter airlines that carried at least one passenger during the year; (2) Includes all U.S.-based airlines and freight carriers that transported at least one pound of freight during the year
Source: Bureau of Transportation Statistics, The Intermodal Transportation Database, Air Carriers: T-100 Domestic Market (U.S. Carriers), 2010; Bureau of Transportation Statistics, The Intermodal Transportation Database, Air Carriers: T-100 International Market (U.S. Carriers), 2009

Other Transportation Statistics

Interstate highways:	I-20; I-35W; I-30
Amtrak service:	Yes
Major waterways/ports:	None

Source: Amtrak.com; Google Maps

BUSINESSES

Major Business Headquarters

Company Name	Rankings	
	Fortune[1]	Forbes[2]
AMR	118	-
Ben E Keith	-	147
D.R. Horton	499	-
RadioShack	492	-

Note: (1) Fortune 500—companies that produce a 10-K are ranked 1 to 500 based on 2010 revenue; (2) all private companies with at least $2 billion in annual revenue are ranked 1 to 223; companies listed are headquartered in the city; dashes indicate no ranking
Source: Fortune, "Fortune 500," May 23, 2011; Forbes, "America's Largest Private Companies," November 3, 2010

Fast-Growing Businesses

According to *Inc.*, Fort Worth is home to two of America's 500 fastest-growing private companies: **ChiroNET; The Penna Group**. Criteria: must be an independent, privately-held, for-profit, U.S. corporation, proprietorship or partnership; revenues of at least $80,000 in 2006 and $2 million in 2009; four-year operating/sales history; holding companies, regulated banks, and utilities were excluded. *Inc., "America's 500 Fastest-Growing Private Companies," September 2010*

According to Deloitte, Fort Worth is home to one of North America's 500 fastest-growing high-technology companies: **ECi Software Solutions**. Companies are ranked by percentage growth in revenue over a five-year period. Criteria for inclusion: company must be headquartered within North America; company must own proprietary intellectual property or proprietary technology that contributes to a significant portion of the company's operating revenue or devotes a significant proportion of revenues to research and development of technology; company must have been in business for a minumum of five years with 2005 operating revenues of at least $50,000 USD/CD and 2009 operating revenues of at least $5 million USD/CD. *Deloitte Touche Tohmatsu, 2010 Deloitte Technology Fast 500*[TM]

Minority Business Opportunity

Fort Worth is home to one company which is on the Black Enterprise Asset Manager 15 list (15 largest asset management firms based on assets under management): **American Beacon Advisors**. Criteria: company must be operational in previous calendar year and at least 51% black-owned. *Black Enterprise, B.E. 100s, 2010*

Fort Worth is home to one company which is on the *Hispanic Business 500* list (500 largest U.S. Hispanic-owned companies based on 2009 revenue): **Thos. S. Byrne Ltd.** Companies included must show at least 51 percent ownership by Hispanic U.S. citizens, and must maintain headquarters in one of the 50 states or Washington, D.C. *Hispanic Business, "Hispanic Business 500," June 2010*

Fort Worth is home to one company which is on the *Hispanic Business* Fastest-Growing 100 list (greatest sales growth from 2005 to 2009): **Thos. S. Byrne Ltd.** Companies included must show at least 51 percent ownership by Hispanic U.S. citizens, and must maintain headquarters in one of the 50 states or Washington, D.C. In addition, companies must have minimum revenues of $200,000 for calendar year 2005. *Hispanic Business, July/August 2010*

Minority- and Women-Owned Businesses

Group	All Firms		Firms with Paid Employees			
	Firms	Sales ($000)	Firms	Sales ($000)	Employees	Payroll ($000)
Asian	2,530	1,131,325	588	1,054,655	2,854	114,999
Black	7,643	209,790	172	92,162	1,219	31,476
Hispanic	8,168	828,355	625	556,625	7,700	171,154
Women	16,515	3,158,441	1,533	2,784,740	13,109	395,861
All Firms	54,916	85,076,401	10,421	83,106,496	311,906	13,847,048

Note: Figures cover firms located in the city; minority- and women-owned business are defined as firms in which the corresponding group own 51% or more of the stock or equity of the company
Source: U.S. Census Bureau, 2007 Economic Census, Survey of Business Owners

HOTELS

Hotels/Motels

Area	5 Star		4 Star		3 Star		2 Star		1 Star		Not Rated	
	Num.	Pct.3	Num.	Pct.3	Num.	Pct.3	Num.	Pct.3	Num.	Pct.3	Num.	Pct.3
City[1]	0	0.0	3	2.3	29	22.7	73	57.0	4	3.1	19	14.8
Total[2]	119	0.7	927	5.8	4,906	30.5	7,992	49.7	526	3.3	1,625	10.1

Note: (1) Figures cover Fort Worth and vicinity; (2) Figures cover all 100 cities in this book; (3) Percentage of hotels which are a given star rating; Star ratings are determined by expedia.com and offer an indication of the general quality of a particular hotel.
Source: expedia.com, May 5, 2011

The Fort Worth metro area is home to one of the top 100 hotels in the U.S. according to *Condé Nast Traveler*: **Omni Fort Worth Hotel** (#87). The selections are based on over 25,000 responses to the magazine's annual Readers' Choice Survey. *Condé Nast Traveler, "2010 Readers' Choice Awards"*

EVENT SITES

Major Stadiums, Arenas, and Auditoriums

Name	Max. Capacity
Amon G. Carter Stadium	44,008
LaGrave Field	4,100

Source: Original research

Convention Centers

Name	Overall Space (sq. ft.)	Exhibit Space (sq. ft.)	Meeting Space (sq. ft.)	Meeting Rooms
Fort Worth Convention Center	n/a	58,849	253,226	41

Note: n/a not available
Source: Original research

Living Environment

COST OF LIVING

Cost of Living Index

Composite Index	Groceries	Housing	Utilities	Trans-portation	Health Care	Misc. Goods/ Services
91.1	89.8	78.0	106.2	97.6	93.8	96.1

Note: U.S. = 100; Figures cover the Fort Worth TX urban area.
Source: The Council for Community and Economic Research, ACCRA Cost of Living Index, 2010

Grocery Prices

Area[1]	T-Bone Steak ($/pound)	Frying Chicken ($/pound)	Whole Milk ($/half gal.)	Eggs ($/dozen)	Orange Juice ($/64 oz.)	Coffee ($/11.5 oz.)
City[2]	8.27	1.03	1.88	1.33	2.83	3.24
Avg.	9.04	1.16	2.02	1.47	3.08	3.65
Min.	6.97	0.84	1.46	0.96	2.39	2.64
Max.	13.93	2.51	3.58	3.01	4.94	6.32

Note: (1) Values for the local area are compared with the average, minimum and maximum values for all 338 areas in the Cost of Living Index; (2) Figures cover the Fort Worth TX urban area; **T-Bone Steak** *(price per pound);* **Frying Chicken** *(price per pound, whole fryer);* **Whole Milk** *(half gallon carton);* **Eggs** *(price per dozen, Grade A, large);* **Orange Juice** *(64 oz. Tropicana or Florida Natural);* **Coffee** *(11.5 oz. can, vacuum-packed, Maxwell House, Hills Bros, or Folgers).*
Source: The Council for Community and Economic Research, ACCRA Cost of Living Index, 2010

Housing and Utility Costs

Area[1]	New Home Price ($)	Apartment Rent ($/month)	All Electric ($/month)	Part Electric ($/month)	Other Energy ($/month)	Telephone ($/month)
City[2]	203,993	902	-	133.63	45.92	29.95
Avg.	293,442	810	166.39	91.93	83.82	26.93
Min.	182,545	453	119.21	44.47	36.85	17.98
Max.	1,123,114	2,776	307.53	218.20	313.90	39.15

Note: (1) Values for the local area are compared with the average, minimum and maximum values for all 338 areas in the Cost of Living Index; (2) Figures cover the Fort Worth TX urban area; **New Home Price** *(2,400 sf living area, 8,000 sf lot, in urban area with full utilities);* **Apartment Rent** *(950 sf 2 bedroom/1.5 or 2 bath, unfurnished, excluding all utilities except water);* **All Electric** *(average monthly cost for an all-electric home);* **Part Electric** *(average monthly cost for a part-electric home);* **Other Energy** *(average monthly cost for natural gas, fuel oil, coal, wood, and any other forms of energy except electricity);* **Telephone** *(price includes basic monthly rate for a private residential line plus additional local usage charges incurred by a family of four).*
Source: The Council for Community and Economic Research, ACCRA Cost of Living Index, 2010

Health Care, Transportation, and Other Costs

Area[1]	Doctor ($/visit)	Dentist ($/visit)	Optometrist ($/visit)	Gasoline ($/gallon)	Beauty Salon ($/visit)	Men's Shirt ($)
City[2]	84.00	76.34	55.72	2.57	34.89	26.37
Avg.	89.44	78.95	87.40	2.73	31.92	24.83
Min.	57.00	54.25	48.32	2.44	19.17	13.67
Max.	149.90	136.73	174.22	3.75	62.81	47.89

Note: (1) Values for the local area are compared with the average, minimum and maximum values for all 338 areas in the Cost of Living Index; (2) Figures cover the Fort Worth TX urban area; **Doctor** *(general practitioners routine exam of an established patient);* **Dentist** *(adult teeth cleaning and periodic oral examination);* **Optometrist** *(full vision eye exam for established adult patient);* **Gasoline** *(one gallon regular unleaded, national brand, including all taxes, cash price at self-service pump if available);* **Beauty Salon** *(woman's shampoo, trim, and blow-dry);* **Men's Shirt** *(cotton/polyester dress shirt, pinpoint weave, long sleeves).*
Source: The Council for Community and Economic Research, ACCRA Cost of Living Index, 2010

HOUSING

House Price Index (HPI)

Area	National Ranking[2]	Quarterly Change (%)	One-Year Change (%)	Five-Year Change (%)
MD[1]	151	-1.07	-1.04	6.70
U.S.[3]	-	-0.84	-3.95	-11.45

Note: The HPI is a weighted repeat sales index. It measures average price changes in repeat sales or refinancings on the same properties. This information is obtained by reviewing repeat mortgage transactions on single-family properties whose mortgages have been purchased or securitized by Fannie Mae or Freddie Mac in January 1975; (1) Metropolitan Division - see Appendix B for areas included; (2) Rankings are based on annual percentage change for all metro areas containing at least 15,000 transactions over the last 10 years and ranges from 1 to 309; (3) figures based on a weighted average of Census Division estimates; all figures are for the period ending December 31, 2010
Source: Federal Housing Finance Agency, House Price Index, February 24, 2011

House Price Valuations

Area	Q4 2005 Price ($000)	Q4 2005 Over-valuation	Q4 2006 Price ($000)	Q4 2006 Over-valuation	Q4 2007 Price ($000)	Q4 2007 Over-valuation	Q4 2008 Price ($000)	Q4 2008 Over-valuation	Q4 2009 Price ($000)	Q4 2009 Over-valuation
MD[1]	105.1	-19.5	110.2	-20.5	112.5	-22.3	112.0	-23.2	112.5	-23.2

Note: Figures show the percentage of over- or under-valuation of single family homes relative to statistically normal house values (e.g. a value of 23.6 indicates that house values are 23.6% overvalued). Statistically normal house values are based on house prices, interest rates, household incomes, population densities, and any historical premiums or discounts metropolitan areas have exhibited over time; (1) Figures cover the Fort Worth-Arlington, TX Metropolitan Division - see Appendix B for areas included
Source: Global Insight/PNC Financial Services Group, House Prices in America: 4th Quarter 2009 Update

Median Single-Family Home Prices

Area	2008	2009	2010p	Percent Change 2009 to 2010
MSA[1]	145.8	140.5	148.4	5.6
U.S. Average	196.6	172.1	173.2	0.6

Note: Figures are median sales prices of existing single-family homes in thousands of dollars; (p) preliminary; n/a not available; (1) Metropolitan Statistical Area - see Appendix B for areas included
Source: National Association of Realtors, Median Sales Price of Existing Single-Family Homes for Metropolitan Areas, 4th Quarter 2010

Median Apartment Condo-Coop Home Prices

Area	2008	2009	2010p	Percent Change 2009 to 2010
MSA[1]	137.4	130.5	132.6	1.6
U.S. Average	209.8	175.6	171.7	-2.2

Note: Figures are median sales prices of existing apartment condo-coop homes in thousands of dollars; (p) preliminary; n/a not available; (1) Metropolitan Statistical Area - see Appendix B for areas included
Source: National Association of Realtors, Median Sales Price of Existing Apartment Condo-Coop Homes for Metropolitan Areas, 4th Quarter 2010

Year Housing Structure Built

Area	2000 or Later	1990-1999	1980-1989	1970-1979	1960-1969	1950-1959	1940-1949	Before 1940	Median Year
City	25.3	10.7	14.9	11.1	9.7	12.8	6.9	8.7	1981
MSA[1]	20.5	17.0	20.3	16.1	10.4	8.8	3.3	3.5	1984
U.S.	12.5	14.0	14.2	16.5	11.4	11.3	5.8	14.3	1974

Note: Figures are percentages except for Median Year; (1) Metropolitan Statistical Area - see Appendix B for areas included
Source: U.S. Census Bureau, 2007-2009 American Community Survey 3-Year Estimates

HEALTH

Health Risk Data

Category	MSA[1] (%)	U.S. (%)
Adults who have been told they have high blood pressure	26.6	28.7
Adults who have been told they have high blood cholesterol	41.0	37.5
Adults who have been told they have diabetes[3]	7.4	8.3
Adults who have been told they have arthritis	27.2	26.0
Adults who have been told they currently have asthma	5.1	8.8
Adults who are current smokers	18.0	17.9
Adults who are heavy drinkers[4]	6.4	5.1
Adults who are binge drinkers[5]	14.8	15.8
Adults who are overweight (BMI 25.0 - 29.9)	41.4	36.2
Adults who are obese (BMI 30.0 - 99.8)	24.7	26.9
Adults who participated in any physical activities in the past month	76.2	76.2
Adults 50+ who have ever had a sigmoidoscopy or colonoscopy[2]	63.8	62.2
Women 40+ who have had a mammogram within the past two years[2]	71.0	76.0
Adults age 18–64 who have any kind of health care coverage	74.9	83.1

Note: Data as of 2009 unless otherwise noted; (1) Figures cover the Fort Worth-Arlington, TX Metropolitan Division - see Appendix B for areas included; (2) Data as of 2008; (3) Figures do not include pregnancy-related, borderline, or pre-diabetes; (4) Heavy drinkers are classified as males having more than two drinks per day or females having more than one drink per day; (5) Binge drinkers are classified as males having five or more drinks on one occasion or females having four or more drinks on one occasion
Source: Centers for Disease Control and Prevention, Behaviorial Risk Factor Surveillance System, SMART: Selected Metropolitan/Micropolitan Area Risk Trends, 2008, 2009

Mortality Rates for the Top 10 Causes of Death in the U.S.

ICD-10[a] Sub-Chapter	ICD-10[a] Code	Age-Adjusted Mortality Rate[1] per 100,000 population	
		County[2]	U.S.
Malignant neoplasms	C00-C97	177.3	180.9
Ischaemic heart diseases	I20-I25	137.4	135.0
Other forms of heart disease	I30-I51	52.0	50.0
Cerebrovascular diseases	I60-I69	58.6	44.1
Chronic lower respiratory diseases	J40-J47	46.8	41.5
Other degenerative diseases of the nervous system	G30-G31	28.1	23.6
Diabetes mellitus	E10-E14	23.8	23.5
Other external causes of accidental injury	W00-X59	18.5	23.5
Organic, including symptomatic, mental disorders	F01-F09	35.5	22.2
Influenza and pneumonia	J09-J18	14.2	18.1

Note: (a) ICD-10 = International Classification of Diseases 10th Revision; (1) Mortality rates are a three year average covering 2005-2007; (2) Figures cover Tarrant County
Source: Centers for Disease Control and Prevention, National Center for Health Statistics. Compressed Mortality File 1999-2007. CDC WONDER On-line Database, compiled from Compressed Mortality File 1999-2007 Series 20 No. 2M, 2010.

Mortality Rates for Selected Causes of Death

ICD-10[a] Sub-Chapter	ICD-10[a] Code	Age-Adjusted Mortality Rate[1] per 100,000 population	
		County[2]	U.S.
Assault	X85-Y09	5.1	6.0
Human immunodeficiency virus (HIV) disease	B20-B24	4.5	4.0
Hypertensive diseases	I10-I15	27.0	18.0
Intentional self-harm	X60-X84	10.8	11.0
Malnutrition	E40-E46	1.7	0.8
Obesity and other hyperalimentation	E65-E68	1.3	1.5
Transport accidents	V01-V99	13.1	15.6
Viral hepatitis	B15-B19	2.6	2.1

Note: (a) ICD-10 = International Classification of Diseases 10th Revision; (1) Mortality rates are a three year average covering 2005-2007; (2) Figures cover Tarrant County
Source: Centers for Disease Control and Prevention, National Center for Health Statistics. Compressed Mortality File 1999-2007. CDC WONDER On-line Database, compiled from Compressed Mortality File 1999-2007 Series 20 No. 2M, 2010.

Distribution of Physicians and Dentists

Area[1]	Dentists[2]	D.O.[3]	M.D.[4]				
			Total	Family/ General Practice	Pediatrics	Medical Specialties	Surgical Specialties
Local (number)	637	632	2,390	306	166	825	628
Local (rate[5])	3.7	3.6	13.7	1.7	0.9	4.7	3.6
U.S. (rate[5])	4.5	1.9	18.3	2.5	1.4	6.8	4.1

Note: Data as of 2008 unless noted; (1) Local data covers Tarrant County; (2) Data as of 2007; (3) Doctor of Osteopathic Medicine; (4) Includes active, non-federal, patient-care, office-based Doctors of Medicine; (5) rate per 10,000 population
Source: Area Resource File (ARF). 2009-2010 Release. U.S. Department of Health and Human Services, Health Resources and Services Administration, Bureau of Health Professions, Rockville, MD, August 2010

Hospitals

Fort Worth has the following hospitals: 7 general medical and surgical; 2 rehabilitation; 1 surgical; 4 long-term acute care; 1 children's general.
AHA Guide to the Healthcare Field 2010

According to *U.S. News*, the Fort Worth-Arlington, TX Metropolitan Division is home to one of the best children's hospitals in the U.S.: **Cook Children's Medical Center**. The hospital listed was highly ranked in at least one pediatric specialty. *U.S. News Online, "America's Best Children's Hospitals 2010-11"*

EDUCATION

Public School District Statistics

District Name	Schls	Pupils	Pupil/ Teacher Ratio	Minority Pupils[1] (%)	Free Lunch Eligible[2] (%)	IEP[3] (%)
Castleberry ISD	8	3,517	16.2	71.7	64.3	7.4
Eagle Mt-Saginaw ISD	23	15,292	16.0	46.6	23.1	8.7
Fort Worth ISD	147	79,285	15.3	86.6	63.3	7.7

Note: Table includes school districts with 2,000 or more students; (1) Percentage of students that are not non-Hispanic white; (2) Percentage of students that are eligible for the free lunch program; (3) Percentage of students that have an Individualized Education Program.
Source: U.S. Department of Education, National Center for Education Statistics, Common Core of Data, Local Education Agency (School District) Universe Survey: School Year 2008-2009; U.S. Department of Education, National Center for Education Statistics, Common Core of Data, Public Elementary/Secondary School Universe Survey: School Year 2008-2009

Top Public High Schools

High School Name	Index[1]	Rank[1]	Subsidized Lunch (%)[2]	E&E (%)[3]
Diamond Hill-Jarvis	2.866	281	87.0	22.4
Fort Worth Academy of Fine Arts	1.541	1111	14.0	67.6
Paschal	3.425	173	41.0	40.3

Note: (1) Public schools are ranked according to a ratio that is the number of Advanced Placement, International Baccalaureate, and/or Cambridge tests taken by all students at a school in 2009 divided by the number of graduating seniors. All of the schools on the list have an index of at least 1.000; they are in the top six percent of public schools measured this way. The rankings range from 1 to 1,734; (2) Percentage of students receiving federally subsidized meals; (3) E & E stands for equity and excellence percentage: the portion of all graduating seniors at a school that had at least one passing grade on one AP or IB test; (4) Schools that offer International Baccalaureate or Cambridge exams; (5) School is unranked, but has been identified by Newsweek as one of the nation's most elite public high schools.
Source: Newsweek Online, "Top High Schools 2010"

Highest Level of Education

Area	Less than H.S.	H.S. Diploma	Some College, No Deg.	Associate Degree	Bachelors Degree	Masters Degree	Profess. School Degree	Doctorate Degree
City	24.7	25.2	21.1	5.5	15.7	5.6	1.4	0.8
MSA[1]	18.5	23.3	22.2	6.3	20.3	7.0	1.5	0.9
U.S.	15.3	29.0	20.7	7.5	17.4	7.0	1.9	1.1

Note: Figures are 2010 estimated percentages and cover persons age 25 and over; (1) Metropolitan Statistical Area - see Appendix B for areas included
Source: Claritas, Inc.

Educational Attainment by Race

Area	High School Graduate (%)					Bachelor's Degree (%)				
	Total	White	Black	Asian	Hisp.[2]	Total	White	Black	Asian	Hisp.[2]
City	77.4	91.9	82.4	83.8	47.4	25.0	37.2	15.5	38.7	7.6
MSA[1]	81.9	92.7	86.3	88.2	49.9	30.2	38.0	21.2	56.4	9.9
U.S.	84.9	90.0	80.7	85.5	60.7	27.8	30.9	17.5	49.7	12.7

Note: Figures shown cover persons 25 years old and over; (1) Metropolitan Statistical Area - see Appendix B for areas included; (2) people of Hispanic origin can be of any race
Source: U.S. Census Bureau, 2007-2009 American Community Survey 3-Year Estimates

School Enrollment by Grade and Control

Area	Preschool (%)		Kindergarten (%)		Grades 1 - 4 (%)		Grades 5 - 8 (%)		Grades 9 - 12 (%)	
	Public	Private	Public	Private	Public	Private	Public	Private	Public	Private
City	58.1	41.9	90.1	9.9	91.5	8.5	92.2	7.8	90.3	9.7
MSA[1]	50.2	49.8	88.8	11.2	91.4	8.6	92.1	7.9	92.4	7.6
U.S.	54.3	45.7	86.4	13.6	88.9	11.1	89.1	10.9	90.2	9.8

Note: Figures shown cover persons 3 years old and over; (1) Metropolitan Statistical Area - see Appendix B for areas included
Source: U.S. Census Bureau, 2007-2009 American Community Survey 3-Year Estimates

Average Salaries of Public School Classroom Teachers

Area	2009-10		2010-11		Percent Change 2009-10 to 2010-11	Percent Change 2000-01 to 2010-11
	Dollars	Rank[1]	Dollars	Rank[1]		
Texas	48,261	31	48,261	34	0.00	25.8
U.S. Average	55,202	-	56,069	-	1.57	29.3

Note: (1) State rank ranges from 1 to 51 where 1 indicates highest salary.
Source: National Education Association, Rankings & Estimates: Rankings of the States 2010 and Estimates of School Statistics 2011, December 2010

Higher Education

Four-Year Colleges			Two-Year Colleges			Medical Schools[1]	Law Schools[2]	Voc/ Tech[3]
Public	Private Non-profit	Private For-profit	Public	Private Non-profit	Private For-profit			
0	3	1	1	0	4	1	1	2

Note: Figures cover institutions located within the city limits and include main campuses only; (1) includes schools accredited by the Liaison Committee on Medical Education and the American Osteopathic Association; (2) includes American Bar Association-accredited law schools; (3) includes all schools with programs that are less than 2 years.
Source: National Center for Education Statistics, Integrated Postsecondary Education System (IPEDS) Peer Analysis System, 2010-11; U.S. News & World Report, Medical School Directory, 2011; U.S. News & World Report, Law School Directory, 2011

According to *U.S. News & World Report,* the Fort Worth-Arlington, TX Metropolitan Division is home to one of the top 197 national universities in the U.S.: **Texas Christian University** (#99). The rankings are based on quantitative measurements such as peer assessment, retention, faculty resources, student selectivity, financial resources, graduation rate, and alumni giving rate. *U.S. News & World Report, "America's Best Colleges 2011"*

According to *Forbes,* the Fort Worth-Arlington, TX Metropolitan Division is home to one of the top 75 business schools in the U.S.: **TCU (Neeley)** (#60). The rankings are based on the return on investment that graduates of the Class of 2004 received (median salary five years after graduation). *Forbes, "Best Business Schools," August 5, 2009*

PRESIDENTIAL ELECTION

2008 Presidential Election Results

Area	Obama	McCain	Nader	Other
Tarrant County	43.7	55.4	0.1	0.8
U.S.	52.9	45.6	0.6	0.9

Note: Results are percentages and may not add to 100% due to rounding
Source: Dave Leip's Atlas of U.S. Presidential Elections, www.uselectionatlas.org

EMPLOYERS

Major Employers

Company Name	Industry	Type of Site
Alcon Holdings	Pharmaceutical preparations	Headquarters
AMR Corporation	Air transportation, scheduled	Headquarters
Arlington Memorial Hospital	General medical and surgical hospitals	Single
BNSF Railway Company	Railroads, line-haul operating	Headquarters
Combat Support Associates	Engineering services	Single
Department of Geology	Colleges and universities	Branch
Gamestop	Catalog and mail-order houses	Headquarters
Gaylord Texan Resort	Hotels and motels	Single
General Motors	Motor vehicles and car bodies	Branch
Harris Medical Laboratory	General medical and surgical hospitals	Headquarters
Jacobs Engineering Group	Engineering services	Branch
John Peter Smith Hospital	Accounting, auditing, and bookkeeping	Branch
John Peter Smith Hospital	General medical and surgical hospitals	Headquarters
Marine Corps United States	National security	Branch
Psychological/Deaf Svcs Dept	Elementary and secondary schools	Branch
Radioshack	Radio, television, and electronic stores	Headquarters
Sabre Travel Info Network	Travel agencies	Headquarters
Texas Pacific Group	Investors, nec	Headquarters
University of North Texas	Offices and clinics of osteopathic physicians	Headquarters
Unt Health Science Center	Offices and clinics of osteopathic physicians	Single
US Dept of the Air Force	National security	Branch

Note: Companies shown are located within the Fort Worth metropolitan area; nec = not elsewhere classified.
Source: www.zapdata.com, January 2011

PUBLIC SAFETY

Crime Rate

Area	All Crimes	Violent Crimes				Property Crimes		
		Murder	Forcible Rape	Robbery	Aggrav. Assault	Burglary	Larceny -Theft	Motor Vehicle Theft
City	5,545.1	6.1	51.1	200.3	327.5	1,408.2	3,257.1	294.7
Suburbs[1]	4,011.3	2.2	28.4	84.9	236.1	837.7	2,584.0	238.1
Metro[2]	4,534.7	3.5	36.1	124.3	267.3	1,032.4	2,813.7	257.4
U.S.	3,465.5	5.0	28.7	133.0	262.8	716.3	2,060.9	258.8

Note: Figures are crimes per 100,000 population; (1) All areas within the metro area that are located outside the city limits; (2) Metropolitan Division - see Appendix B for areas included
Source: FBI Uniform Crime Reports, 2009

Hate Crimes

Area	Number of Quarters Reported	Bias Motivation				
		Race	Religion	Sexual Orientation	Ethnicity	Disability
City	4	3	2	0	1	0

Source: Federal Bureau of Investigation, Hate Crime Statistics 2009

Identity Theft Consumer Complaints

Area	Complaints	Complaints per 100,000 Population	Rank[2]
MSA[1]	6,920	112.6	36
U.S.	250,854	81.3	-

Note: (1) Metropolitan Statistical Area - see Appendix B for areas included; (2) Rank ranges from 1 to 384 where 1 indicates greatest number of complaints per 100,000 population
Source: Federal Trade Commission, Consumer Sentinel Network Data Book for January - December 2010

RECREATION

Culture

Dance[1]	Theatre[1]	Instrumental Music[1]	Vocal Music[1]	Series/ Festivals	Museums	Zoos and Aquariums[2]
3	8	3	3	3	12	1

Note: (1) Number of professional perfoming groups; (2) AZA-accredited
Source: The Grey House Performing Arts Directory, 2011-2012; Official Museum Directory, 2010; American Association of Museums, AAM Member Museums, March 2011; Association of Zoos & Aquariums, AZA Member Zoos & Aquariums, May 2011

Professional Sports Teams

Team Name	League
Dallas Cowboys	National Football League (NFL)
Dallas Mavericks	National Basketball Association (NBA)
Dallas Stars	National Hockey League (NHL)
FC Dallas	Major League Soccer (MLS)
Texas Rangers	Major League Baseball (MLB)

Note: Includes teams located in the Dallas-Fort Worth metro area.
Source: Original research

CLIMATE

Average and Extreme Temperatures

Temperature	Jan	Feb	Mar	Apr	May	Jun	Jul	Aug	Sep	Oct	Nov	Dec	Yr.
Extreme High (°F)	88	88	96	98	103	113	110	108	107	106	89	90	113
Average High (°F)	54	59	67	76	83	92	96	96	88	79	67	58	76
Average Temp. (°F)	44	49	57	66	73	81	85	85	78	68	56	47	66
Average Low (°F)	33	38	45	54	63	71	75	74	67	56	45	37	55
Extreme Low (°F)	4	6	11	29	41	51	59	56	43	29	19	-1	-1

Note: Figures cover the years 1953-1990
Source: National Climatic Data Center, International Station Meteorological Climate Summary, 9/96

Average Precipitation/Snowfall/Humidity

Precip./Humidity	Jan	Feb	Mar	Apr	May	Jun	Jul	Aug	Sep	Oct	Nov	Dec	Yr.
Avg. Precip. (in.)	1.8	2.2	2.6	3.7	4.9	2.8	2.1	1.9	3.0	3.3	2.1	1.7	32.3
Avg. Snowfall (in.)	1	1	Tr	0	0	0	0	0	0	0	Tr	Tr	3
Avg. Rel. Hum. 6am (%)	79	79	79	81	86	85	80	79	83	82	80	79	81
Avg. Rel. Hum. 3pm (%)	52	51	48	50	53	47	42	41	46	47	49	51	48

Note: Figures cover the years 1953-1990; Tr = Trace amounts (<0.05 in. of rain; <0.5 in. of snow)
Source: National Climatic Data Center, International Station Meteorological Climate Summary, 9/96

Weather Conditions

Temperature			Daytime Sky			Precipitation		
10°F & below	32°F & below	90°F & above	Clear	Partly cloudy	Cloudy	0.01 inch or more precip.	0.1 inch or more snow/ice	Thunder-storms
1	40	100	123	136	106	79	3	47

Note: Figures are average number of days per year and cover the years 1953-1990
Source: National Climatic Data Center, International Station Meteorological Climate Summary, 9/96

HAZARDOUS WASTE

Superfund Sites

Fort Worth has one hazardous waste site on the EPA's Superfund Final National Priorities List: **Air Force Plant #4 (General Dynamics)**. *U.S. Environmental Protection Agency, Final National Priorities List, April 1, 2011*

**AIR & WATER
QUALITY**

Air Quality Index

Area	Percent of Days when Air Quality was...[2]				AQI Statistics	
	Good	Moderate	Unhealthy for Sensitive Groups	Unhealthy	Maximum	Median
Area[1]	65.4	27.5	6.9	0.3	156	46

*Note: The Air Quality Index (AQI) is an index for reporting daily air quality. EPA calculates the AQI for five major air pollutants regulated by the Clean Air Act: ground-level ozone, particle pollution (also known as particulate matter), carbon monoxide, sulfur dioxide, and nitrogen dioxide. The AQI runs from 0 to 500. The higher the AQI value, the greater the level of air pollution and the greater the health concern. There are six AQI categories: "Good" The AQI is between 0 and 50. Air quality is considered satisfactory; "Moderate" The AQI is between 51 and 100. Air quality is acceptable; "Unhealthy for Sensitive Groups" When AQI values are between 101 and 150, members of sensitive groups may experience health effects; "Unhealthy" When AQI values are between 151 and 200 everyone may begin to experience health effects; "Very Unhealthy" AQI values between 201 and 300 trigger a health alert; "Hazardous" AQI values over 300 trigger health warnings of emergency conditions; (1) Data covers Tarrant County; (2) Based on 306 days with AQI data in 2008; The EPA has suspended data updates while it assesses its data systems, including AirData reports and maps.
Source: U.S. Environmental Protection Agency, AirData Report, 2008*

Air Quality Index Pollutants

Area	Percent of Days when AQI Pollutant was...[2]					
	Carbon Monoxide	Nitrogen Dioxide	Ozone	Sulfur Dioxide	Particulate Matter 2.5	Particulate Matter 10
Area[1]	0.3	0.0	73.2	0.0	26.5	0.0

*Note: The Air Quality Index (AQI) is an index for reporting daily air quality. EPA calculates the AQI for five major air pollutants regulated by the Clean Air Act: ground-level ozone, particle pollution (also known as particulate matter), carbon monoxide, sulfur dioxide, and nitrogen dioxide. The AQI runs from 0 to 500. The higher the AQI value, the greater the level of air pollution and the greater the health concern; (1) Data covers Tarrant County; (2) Based on 306 days with AQI data in 2008; The EPA has suspended data updates while it assesses its data systems, including AirData reports and maps.
Source: U.S. Environmental Protection Agency, AirData Report, 2008*

Air Quality Index Trends

Area	Trend Sites (days)								All Sites (days)
	2002	2003	2004	2005	2006	2007	2008	2009	2009
MSA[1]	40	40	32	56	39	16	20	19	33

*Note: Figures are the number of days the AQI value exceeded 100 in a given year. An AQI value greater than 100 indicates that air quality would have been in the unhealthful range on that day. Data from exceptional events are included. These counts are presented in two ways. First, the counts are based on sites having an adequate record of monitoring data during the trend period (trend sites). These counts represent the relative change in the number of days with AQI values greater than 100. In the last column, the counts are based on all sites with data in the most recent year (because it is possible for a site to have data in the most recent year but not enough data to be a trend site); (1) Data covers the Dallas-Fort Worth-Arlington, TX Metropolitan Statistical Area - see Appendix B for areas included
Source: U.S. Environmental Protection Agency, Office of Air and Radiation, Air Quality Index Information, "Number of Days with Air Quality Index Values Greater than 100 and Trend Sites, 1990-2009, and at All Sites in 2009"*

Maximum Air Pollutant Concentrations

	Particulate Matter 10 (ug/m³)	Particulate Matter 2.5 (ug/m³)	Ozone (ppm)	Carbon Monoxide (ppm)	Sulfur Dioxide (ppm)	Nitrogen Dioxide (ppm)	Lead (ug/m³)
MSA[1] Level	43	38	0.091	2	0.004	0.012	0.65
NAAQS[2]	150	35	0.075	9	0.140	0.053	0.15
Met NAAQS[2]	Yes	No	No	Yes	Yes	Yes	No

*Note: Data from exceptional events are not included; (1) Data covers the Dallas-Fort Worth-Arlington, TX Metropolitan Statistical Area - see Appendix B for areas included; (2) National Ambient Air Quality Standards; n/a not available; (a) Localized impact from an industrial source in Dallas. Concentration from highest nonpoint source site is 0.14 ug/m³ in Collin County
Concentrations: Particulate Matter 10 (coarse particulate) - highest second maximum 24-hour concentration; Particulate Matter 2.5 (fine particulate) - highest 98th percentile 24-hour concentration; Ozone - highest fourth daily maximum 8-hour concentration; Carbon Monoxide - highest second maximum non-overlapping 8-hour concentration; Sulfur Dioxide - highest second maximum 24-hour concentration; Nitrogen Dioxide - highest arithmetic mean concentration; Lead - maximum running 3-month average
Units: ppm = parts per million; ug/m³ = micrograms per cubic meter
Source: U.S. Environmental Protection Agency, CBSA Factbook 2009, Air Quality Statistics by City, 2009*

Drinking Water

Water System Name	Pop. Served	Primary Water Source Type	Violations[1]	
			Health Based	Monitoring/ Reporting
City of Fort Worth	727,575	Surface	0	0

Note: (1) Based on violation data from January 1, 2010 to December 31, 2010 (includes unresolved violations from earlier years)
Source: U.S. Environmental Protection Agency, Office of Ground Water and Drinking Water, Safe Drinking Water Information System (based on data extracted May 9, 2011)

Gainesville, Florida

Background

Gainesville is the cultural and educational hub of North Florida, located partway between the Atlantic Ocean and Gulf of Mexico. Alachua County's largest city has grown with a population drawn to its subtropical locale and its heartbeat and largest employer, the colossal University of Florida (UF). Innovation is the name of the game when it comes to the region's push for businesses emerging from the university's numerous research centers. In addition, Gainesville is only a short drive to rural Florida habitat. Ten miles south are the bison, alligators, and 270 bird species found at Paynes Prairie Preserve. Plus, North Florida has the world's largest concentration of freshwater springs.

Originally a Timucuan Indian village, present-day Gainesville was part of a Spanish land grant by 1817. The United States annexed Florida in 1825, and just over a quarter-century later came plans for the Florida Railroad. In 1853, the local citizenry opted to create a new county seat along the railroad line, and Gainesville was founded and named for Seminole Indian War General Edmund P. Gaine. After the Civil War, a Union veteran established a successful cotton shipping station here, and in 1906 UF was founded. Through the years, fire and development has destroyed many of Gainesville's early buildings, a few remain including the Hippodrome State Theatre which was once the local Federal Building.

Emerging from the University of Florida (the nation's fifth or sixth largest public university, depending on the source) are projects from dozens of research centers and institutes. An early success was Gatorade, invented in 1965 to hydrate the powerhouse Gator football team (national champions, 2006 and 2008). Alternative energy research draws accolades, and the city proper became the nation's first to implement a solar feed-in tariff, which means consumers who invest in the appropriate technology can sell their electricity back to the utility. Several research buildings are under construction or just completed, with $750 million in recent expenditures. And UF's Center for Movement Disorders and Neurorestoration opened in 2011, thereby integrating ten departments focused on clinical services, research and education to study and cure movement disorders.

Substantial efforts are underway to capture and nurture start-up companies. The Florida Innovation Hub at UF, now under construction, is funded by $8.2 million from the federal Economic Development administration and $5 million from UF. It's slated for a fall 2011 opening and will include the UF Tech Connect, designed to help businesses get started, and its Office of Technology Licensing, to help the push to grow new business.

The Hub is part of the Innovation Square package, a ten-year, 40-acre project situated to bridge the campus and Gainesville's downtown area, and expected to reach more than a million square feet when complete. Two new buildings are in their early stages: the 120,000-square-foot Infusion Technology Center, slated for a 2012 opening, which will share an atrium with the Hub and house existing science and technology companies; and a 120-bed residence hall for students interested in entrepreneurship, designed to accommodate visiting executives and entrepreneurs.

A long list of rankings laud Gainesville's quality of life for young people and retirees. As with many college towns, there's long been a happening music scene. Tom Petty and the Heartbreakers emerged from Gainesville. Cultural resources include the Florida Museum of Natural History, founded in 1891, fueled by donations from interested professors. In addition to its central museum and collections, it operates the Randell Research Center (a significant Calusa Indian archaeological site—and an ancient ecological site—in Lee County northwest of Fort Myers) and the $12 million William W. and Nadine M. McGuire Center for Lepidoptera and Biodiversity that boasts one of the world's largest butterfly and moth collections.

In addition, UF's Harn Museum of Art, opened in 1990, exhibits traveling shows and collections of photography and Ancient American, Asian, African, modern and contemporary art. Also in the city are the Hippodrome State Theatre, showcasing cinema and traveling theater, and the Curtis M. Phillips Center for Performing Arts.

Famously humid, Gainesville's subtropical climate means freezes are not unheard of in winter, with December through February average highs in the 50s. June through August is notably wet, averaging more than six inches of rain the first two months of summer and eight inches in August. Equally notable, Gainesville's inland location tends to mitigate the threat of hurricanes that face Florida's coasts. Temperatures often climb into the 90s from April to October.

Rankings

Business/Finance Rankings

- Gainesville was selected as one of the "100 Best Places to Live and Launch" in the U.S. The city ranked #47. The editors at *Fortune Small Business* ranked 296 Census-designated metro areas by business friendliness (Launching Score, % New Businesses) and lifestyle offerings (Living Score). Then they picked the town within each of the top 100 metro areas that best blends business and pleasure. *Fortune Small Business, "100 Best Places to Live and Launch 2008," April 2008*

- *American City Business Journals* ranked America's 261 largest cities in terms of their resident's wealth. Gainesville ranked #189. Criteria: per capita income; median household income; percentage of households with annual incomes of $200,000 or more; median home value. *American City Business Journals, www.bizjournals.com, "Where the Money Is: America's Wealth Centers," August 18, 2008*

- The Gainesville metro area appeared on the Milken Institute "2010 Best Performing Metros" list. Rank: #86 out of 200 large metro areas. Criteria: job growth; wage and salary growth; high-tech output growth. *Milken Institute, "2010 Best Performing Metros"*

- *Forbes* ranked the 200 most populous metro areas in the U.S. in terms of the "Best Places for Business and Careers." The Gainesville metro area was ranked #43. Criteria: 12 metrics including costs (business and living), job growth (past and projected), income growth, educational attainment, projected economic growth, crime, cultural and recreational opportunities, net migration patterns, percentage of subprime mortgages handed out over a three-year period, and the number of highly ranked four-year colleges. *Forbes, "Best Places for Business and Careers," April 14, 2010*

Dating/Romance Rankings

- Gainesville was selected as one of the most romantic cities in America by *Amazon.com*. The city ranked #9 of 20. Cities with populations greater than 100,000 were evaluated based on per capita sales of romance novels and relationship books, romantic comedy movies, Barry White albums, and sexual wellness products. *Amazon.com, "Top 20 Most Romantic Cities in America," February 8, 2011*

Education Rankings

- Gainesville was identified as one of "America's Brainiest Bastions" by *Portfolio.com*. The metro area ranked #14 out of 200. Portfolio.com analyzed levels of educational attainment in the nation's 200 largest metropolitan areas. The editors established scores for five levels of educational attainment, based on relative earning power of adult workers age 25 or older. Scores were determined by comparing the median income for all workers with the median income for those workers at a specified educational level. *Portfolio.com, "America's Brainiest Bastions," December 1, 2010*

Environmental Rankings

- Gainesville was selected as one of 22 "Smarter Cities" for energy by the Natural Resources Defense Council." Criteria: investment in green power; energy efficiency measures; conservation. *Natural Resources Defense Council, "2010 Smarter Cities," July 19, 2010*

- The Gainesville metro area appeared in *Country Home's* "Best Green Places" report. The area ranked #58 out of 379. Criteria: official energy policies; green power; green buildings; availability of fresh, locally grown food. *Country Home, "Best Green Places," 2008*

Health/Fitness Rankings

- Gainesville was given "Well City USA" status by The Wellness Councils of America, whose objective is to engage entire business communities in building healthy workforces. Well City status is met when a minimum of 20 employers who collectively employ at least 20% of the city's workforce become designated Well Workplaces within a three-year period. To date, eleven communities have achieved Well City USA status. *The Wellness Councils of America, Well City USA, 2011*

Real Estate Rankings

- Gainesville appeared on ApartmentRatings.com "Top College Towns & Cities" for renters list in 2010." The area ranked #26. Overall satisfaction ratings were ranked using thousands of user submitted scores for hundreds of apartment complexes located in cities and towns that are home to the 100 largest four-year institutions in the U.S. *ApartmentRatings.com, "2010 College Town Renter Satisfaction Rankings"*

- The nation's largest metro areas were analyzed in terms of the percentage of households entering some stage of foreclosure in 2010. The Gainesville metro area ranked #72 out of 206 (#1 = highest foreclosure rate). *RealtyTrac, 2010 Year-End Metropolitan Foreclosure Market Report, January 27, 2011*

- The Center for Housing Policy ranked 210 U.S metropolitan areas by the fair market rent for a two-bedroom unit. The Gainesville metro area was ranked #103. (#1 = most expensive) with a rent of $833. Criteria: Fair Market Rent (FMR) in effect during the fourth quarter of 2009 based on HUD's fiscal year 2010 FMRs. *The Center for Housing Policy, "Paycheck to Paycheck: Most to Least Expensive Rental Markets in 2009"*

Safety Rankings

- The National Insurance Crime Bureau ranked 366 metro areas in the U.S. in terms of per capita rates of vehicle theft. The Gainesville metro area ranked #105 (#1 = highest rate). Criteria: number of vehicle theft offenses per 100,000 inhabitants. *National Insurance Crime Bureau, "Hot Spots," May 17, 2010*

Seniors/Retirement Rankings

- Gainesville was identified as one of "The Top 100 Places to Retire" by *Topretirements.com* The list reflects the 100 cities (out of 625+ total cities reviewed) that visitors to the website are most interested in for retirement. *Topretirements.com, "2011 Best Places to Retire List: The Sunbelt Rules"*

Sports/Recreation Rankings

- Gainesville appeared on the *Sporting News* list of the "Best Sports Cities" for 2010. The area ranked #50 out of 402 cities in the U.S. *Sporting News* takes a 12-month snapshot, roughly October to October, of each city's sports, putting a heavy premium on regular-season won-lost records (from the most recently completed season). Other criteria include: playoff berths, bowl appearances and tournament bids; championships; applicable power ratings; quality of competition; overall fan fervor as measured in part by attendance as percentage of venue capacity; abundance of teams (rewarding quality over quantity); stadium and arena quality; ticket availability and prices; franchise ownership; and marquee appeal of athletes. *Sporting News, "Best Sports Cities 2010," October, 2010*

- Gainesville was chosen as a bicycle friendly community by the League of American Bicyclists. A Bicycle Friendly Community welcomes cyclists by providing safe accommodation for cycling and encouraging people to bike for transportation and recreation. There are four award levels: Platinum; Gold; Silver; and Bronze. The community achieved an award level of Silver. *League of American Bicyclists, "Bicycle Friendly Community Master List," September 2010*

- Gainesville was chosen as one of America's best cities for bicycling. The city ranked #16 out of 50. Criteria: number of segregated bike lanes, municipal bike racks, and bike boulevards; vibrant and diverse bike culture; smart, savvy bike shops; interviews with national and local advocates, bike shops and other experts. Note: only cities with populations of 100,000 or more were considered. *Bicycling, "America's Best Bike Cities," April 2010*

Miscellaneous Rankings

- Gainesville was selected as one of America's "10 Meanest Cities" by the National Coalition for the Homeless and The National Law Center on Homelessness & Poverty. The city was ranked #5. Criteria: the number of anti-homeless laws; the enforcement of those laws and severity of penalties; the general political climate towards homeless people; local advocate support for the meanest designation; the city's history of criminalization measures; and the existence of pending or recently enacted criminalization legislation in the city. *National Coalition for the Homeless and The National Law Center on Homelessness & Poverty, "Homes Not Handcuffs: The Criminalization of Homelessness in U.S. Cities," July 2009*

Business Environment

CITY FINANCES

City Government Finances

Component	2008 ($000)	2008 ($ per capita)
Total Revenues	566,691	4,955
Total Expenditures	549,715	4,806
Debt Outstanding	765,787	6,695
Cash and Securities[1]	785,560	6,868

Note: (1) Cash and security holdings of a government at the close of its fiscal year, including those of its dependent agencies, utilities, and liquor stores.
Source: U.S Census Bureau, State & Local Government Finances 2008

City Government Revenue by Source

Source	2008 ($000)	2008 ($ per capita)
General Revenue		
From Federal Government	7,170	63
From State Government	15,174	133
From Local Governments	897	8
Taxes		
Property	25,967	227
Sales and Gross Receipts	23,281	204
Personal Income	0	0
Corporate Income	0	0
Motor Vehicle License	0	0
Other Taxes	6,516	57
Current Charges	63,339	554
Liquor Store	0	0
Utility	277,770	2,429
Employee Retirement	78,094	683

Source: U.S Census Bureau, State & Local Government Finances 2008

City Government Expenditures by Function

Function	2008 ($000)	2008 ($ per capita)	2008 (%)
General Direct Expenditures			
Air Transportation	0	0	0.0
Corrections	0	0	0.0
Education	0	0	0.0
Employment Security Administration	0	0	0.0
Financial Administration	7,137	62	1.3
Fire Protection	13,438	117	2.4
General Public Buildings	3,777	33	0.7
Governmental Administration, Other	5,332	47	1.0
Health	0	0	0.0
Highways	13,588	119	2.5
Hospitals	0	0	0.0
Housing and Community Development	7,007	61	1.3
Interest on General Debt	13,477	118	2.5
Judicial and Legal	1,412	12	0.3
Libraries	0	0	0.0
Parking	337	3	0.1
Parks and Recreation	11,222	98	2.0
Police Protection	36,638	320	6.7
Public Welfare	892	8	0.2
Sewerage	35,093	307	6.4
Solid Waste Management	10,566	92	1.9
Veterans' Services	0	0	0.0
Liquor Store	0	0	0.0
Utility	310,780	2,717	56.5
Employee Retirement	33,670	294	6.1

Source: U.S Census Bureau, State & Local Government Finances 2008

Municipal Bond Ratings

Area	Moody's	S&P	Fitch
City	n/a	n/a	AA-

Rating Systems (shown in declining order of credit quality): Moody's– Aaa, Aa, A, Baa, Ba, B, Caa, Ca, C (numerical modifiers 1, 2, and 3 are added to letter-rating); S&P– AAA, AA, A, BBB, BB, B, CCC, CC, C; Fitch– AAA, AA, A, BBB, BB, B, CCC, CC, C. Ratings may be modified by the addition of a plus or minus sign to show relative standing within the major rating categories.
Notes: n/a Not available; (1) Not reviewed; (2) Issuer Rating/No General Obligation; (3) Standard and Poor's Issue Credit Rating (ICR) is a current opinion of an obliger with respect to a specific financial obligation, a specific class of financial obligations, or a specific financial program.
Source: City of Gainesville, Florida, Comprehensive Annual Financial Report, Fiscal Year Ended September 30, 2010

DEMOGRAPHICS

Population Growth

Area	1990 Census	2000 Census	2010 Estimate	2015 Projection	Population Growth (%) 2000-2010	Population Growth (%) 2010-2015
City	90,519	95,447	100,710	104,346	5.5	3.6
MSA[1]	191,263	232,392	268,606	287,115	15.6	6.9
U.S.	248,709,873	281,421,906	309,038,974	321,675,005	9.8	4.1

Note: (1) Metropolitan Statistical Area - see Appendix B for areas included
Source: Claritas, Inc.

Number of Households and Average Household Size

Area	2010 Estimate	2010 Average Household Size
City	39,809	2.23
MSA[1]	107,906	2.35
U.S.	116,136,617	2.59

Note: (1) Metropolitan Statistical Area - see Appendix B for areas included
Source: Claritas, Inc.

Race and Ethnicity

Area	White Alone[2] (%)	Black Alone[2] (%)	Asian Alone[2] (%)	Other Race Alone[2] (%)	Hispanic[3] (%)
City	65.6	23.9	5.4	5.1	8.3
MSA[1]	72.5	18.5	4.3	4.7	7.3
U.S.	72.3	12.4	4.4	10.9	15.8

Note: Figures are 2010 estimates; (1) Metropolitan Statistical Area - see Appendix B for areas included (2) Alone is defined as not being in combination with one or more other races; (3) May be of any race.
Source: Claritas, Inc.

Segregation

Type	Segregation Indices[1] 1990	2000	2010	2010 Rank[2]	Percent Change 1990-2000	1990-2010	2000-2010
Black/White	n/a	n/a	n/a	n/a	n/a	n/a	n/a
Asian/White	n/a	n/a	n/a	n/a	n/a	n/a	n/a
Hispanic/White	n/a	n/a	n/a	n/a	n/a	n/a	n/a

Note: Figures are based on an analysis of 1990, 2000, and 2010 Census Decennial Census tract data by William H. Frey, Brookings Institution and the University of Michigan Social Science Data Analysis Network. In this analysis all racial groups (whites, blacks, and asians) are non-Hispanic members of those races. Hispanics are shown as a separate category; All figures cover the Metropolitan Statistical Area (see Appendix B for areas included); (1) Segregation Indices are Dissimilarity Indices that measure the degree to which the minority group is distributed differently than whites aross census tracts. They range from 0 (complete integration) to 100 (complete [segregation) where the value indicates the percentage of the minority group that needs to move to be distributed exactly like whites; (2) Ranges from 1 (most segregated) to 102 (least segregated); n/a not available.
Source: www.CensusScope.org

Ancestry

Area	German	Irish	English	American	Italian	Polish	French	Scottish
City	14.0	11.6	10.8	1.7	5.8	3.6	2.5	2.3
MSA[1]	13.8	12.2	11.0	5.0	5.4	2.7	2.7	2.5
U.S.	16.6	12.0	9.1	6.1	5.9	3.3	3.1	1.9

Note: The top eight ancestries in the U.S. are shown. Figures are percentages and include multiple ancestry (e.g. if a person reported being Irish and Italian, they were included in both columns); (1) Metropolitan Statistical Area - see Appendix B for areas included
Source: U.S. Census Bureau, 2007-2009 American Community Survey 3-Year Estimates

Foreign-Born Population

Area	Any Foreign Country	Mexico	Asia	Europe	Carribean	South America	Central America[2]	Africa	Canada
City	10.5	0.3	3.6	1.8	1.4	1.7	0.6	0.4	0.5
MSA[1]	9.2	0.3	3.2	1.7	1.6	1.1	0.5	0.5	0.5
U.S.	12.5	3.8	3.4	1.6	1.1	0.8	0.9	0.5	0.3

Note: (1) Metropolitan Statistical Area - see Appendix B for areas included; (2) Excludes Mexico.
Source: U.S. Census Bureau, 2007-2009 American Community Survey 3-Year Estimates

Marriage Status

Area	Never Married	Now Married[2]	Separated	Widowed	Divorced
City	65.1	22.3	1.3	3.9	7.4
MSA[1]	47.3	37.5	1.3	4.9	9.0
U.S.	31.4	49.7	2.2	6.2	10.6

Note: Figures are percentages and cover the population 15 years of age and older; (1) Metropolitan Statistical Area - see Appendix B for areas included; (2) Excludes separated
Source: U.S. Census Bureau, 2007-2009 American Community Survey 3-Year Estimates

Age Distribution and Median Age

Area	Under Age 5	Age 5 to 17	Age 18 to 34	Age 35 to 49	Age 50 to 64	Age 65 to 79	80 Years and Over	Median Age
City	4.7	9.4	55.1	12.5	10.9	4.6	2.7	23.1
MSA[1]	5.6	13.1	38.0	16.7	15.8	7.5	3.3	28.1
U.S.	6.9	17.5	23.3	21.4	18.1	9.1	3.7	36.7

Note: (1) Metropolitan Statistical Area - see Appendix B for areas included
Source: U.S. Census Bureau, 2007-2009 American Community Survey 3-Year Estimates

Male/Female Ratio

Area	Males	Females	Males per 100 Females
City	49,965	50,745	98.5
MSA[1]	132,771	135,835	97.7
U.S.	152,401,520	156,637,454	97.3

Note: Figures are 2010 estimates; (1) Metropolitan Statistical Area - see Appendix B for areas included
Source: Claritas, Inc.

Religion

Area	Catholic	Southern Baptist	United Meth-odist	ELCA[1]	LDS[2]	Presby-terian Church USA	Jewish Est.	Muslim Est.
County	7.3	11.2	5.4	0.4	0.7	1.1	1.0	0.2
U.S.	22.0	7.1	3.7	1.8	1.5	1.1	2.2	0.6

Note: Figures are the number of adherents as a percentage of the total population; Adherents are defined as all members, including full members, their children and the estimated number of other participants who are not considered members (e.g. the baptized, those not confirmed, those regularly attending services, etc.);
(1) Evangelical Lutheran Church in America; (2) The Church of Jesus Christ of Latter Day Saints
Source: Reprinted with permission from Religious Congregations and Membership in the United States 2000 (Nashville, Glenmary Research Center, 2002) Copyright Association of Statisticians of American Religious Bodies. All rights reserved.

ECONOMY

Gross Metropolitan Product

Area	2006	2007	2008	2009	2009 Rank[2]
MSA[1]	8.9	9.4	9.6	9.5	177

Note: Figures are in billions of dollars; (1) Gainesville, FL Metropolitan Statistical Area - see Appendix B for areas included; (2) Rank ranges from 1 to 363
Source: The U.S. Conference of Mayors, "Pace of Economic Recovery: GMP and Jobs," January 2010

Economic Growth

Area	2006-2008 (%)	2009 (%)	2010 (%)	Rank[2]
MSA[1]	1.1	-2.1	2.0	183
U.S.	1.3	-2.5	2.2	–

Note: Figures are real Gross Metropolitan Product growth rates and represent annual average percent change; (1) Gainesville, FL Metropolitan Statistical Area - see Appendix B for areas included; (2) Rank ranges from 1 to 363
Source: The U.S. Conference of Mayors, "Pace of Economic Recovery: GMP and Jobs," January 2010

Metropolitan Area Exports

Area	2005	2006	2007	2008	2009	2009 Rank[2]
MSA[1]	186.8	191.5	227.5	285.5	233.2	241

Note: Figures are in millions of dollars; (1) Gainesville, FL Metropolitan Statistical Area - see Appendix B for areas included; (2) Rank ranges from 1 to 374
Source: U.S. Department of Commerce, International Trade Administration, Office of Trade & Industry Information, Manufacturing & Services

INCOME

Per Capita/Median/Average Income

Area	Per Capita ($)	Median Household ($)	Average Household ($)
City	21,283	35,378	52,342
MSA[1]	23,875	40,780	58,453
U.S.	27,034	52,795	71,071

Note: Figures are 2010 estimates; (1) Metropolitan Statistical Area - see Appendix B for areas included
Source: Claritas, Inc.

Household Income Distribution

Area	Percent of Households Earning							
	Under $15,000	$15,000 -24,999	$25,000 -34,999	$35,000 -49,999	$50,000 -74,999	$75,000 -99,000	$100,000 -149,999	$150,000 and up
City	23.8	13.7	12.2	14.1	15.4	8.2	7.8	4.8
MSA[1]	20.4	12.2	11.9	14.1	16.8	9.7	8.9	5.9
U.S.	12.1	10.2	10.6	15.0	19.5	12.5	12.1	8.0

Note: Figures are 2010 estimates; (1) Metropolitan Statistical Area - see Appendix B for areas included
Source: Claritas, Inc.

Poverty Rates by Age

Area	All Ages	Under 18 Years Old	18 to 64 Years Old	65 Years and Over
City	36.8	3.9	32.1	0.8
MSA[1]	23.7	3.6	19.1	1.0
U.S.	13.6	4.7	7.7	1.2

Note: Figures are percent of population with income during the previous 12 months below poverty level and only include population for whom poverty status is determined; (1) Metropolitan Statistical Area - see Appendix B for areas included
Source: U.S. Census Bureau, 2007-2009 American Community Survey 3-Year Estimates

Personal Bankruptcy Filing Rate

Area	2006	2007	2008	2009	2010
Alachua County	0.85	1.07	1.48	1.93	1.98
U.S.	2.00	2.73	3.53	4.60	4.96

Note: Numbers are per 1,000 population and include Chapter 7 and Chapter 13 filings
Source: Federal Deposit Insurance Corporation, Regional Economic Conditions, March 17, 2011

EMPLOYMENT

Labor Force and Employment

Area	Civilian Labor Force			Workers Employed		
	Dec. 2009	Dec. 2010	% Chg.	Dec. 2009	Dec. 2010	% Chg.
City	59,685	60,405	1.2	55,174	55,274	0.2
MSA[1]	137,500	138,752	0.9	126,680	126,908	0.2
U.S.	152,693,000	153,156,000	0.3	137,953,000	139,159,000	0.9

Note: Data is not seasonally adjusted and covers workers 16 years of age and older;
(1) Metropolitan Statistical Area - see Appendix B for areas included
Source: Bureau of Labor Statistics, http://stats.bls.gov

Unemployment Rate

Area	2010											
	Jan.	Feb.	Mar.	Apr.	May	Jun.	Jul.	Aug.	Sep.	Oct.	Nov.	Dec.
City	8.1	8.3	7.7	7.0	7.3	8.6	9.5	8.7	8.1	7.7	8.9	8.5
MSA[1]	8.4	8.3	8.0	7.3	7.5	8.4	9.1	8.8	8.3	8.0	8.8	8.5
U.S.	10.6	10.4	10.2	9.5	9.3	9.6	9.7	9.5	9.2	9.0	9.3	9.1

Note: Data is not seasonally adjusted and covers workers 16 years of age and older; All figures are percentages; (1) Metropolitan Statistical Area - see Appendix B for areas included
Source: Bureau of Labor Statistics, http://stats.bls.gov

Projected Unemployment Rate

Area	2007 (%)	2009 (%)	2011 (%)	2013 (%)
MSA[1]	3.3	7.7	6.8	5.3

Note: (1) Metropolitan Statistical Area - see Appendix B for areas included
Source: The U.S. Conference of Mayors, "Pace of Economic Recovery: GMP and Jobs," January 2010

Employment by Occupation

Occupation Classification	City (%)	MSA[1] (%)	U.S. (%)
Sales and Office	22.7	24.1	25.4
Professional and Related	30.3	29.2	21.0
Service	24.5	20.0	17.2
Production, Transportation, and Material Moving	6.7	7.1	12.3
Management, Business, and Financial	10.9	12.8	14.1
Construction, Extraction, and Maintenance	4.3	6.1	9.2
Farming, Forestry, and Fishing	0.5	0.7	0.7

Note: Figures cover employed civilians 16 years of age and older;
(1) Metropolitan Statistical Area - see Appendix B for areas included
Source: U.S. Census Bureau, 2007-2009 American Community Survey 3-Year Estimates

Employment by Industry

Sector	MSA[1]		U.S.
	Number of Employees	Percent of Total	Percent of Total
Government	42,500	33.3	17.2
Education and Health Services	22,500	17.6	15.2
Professional and Business Services	10,600	8.3	13.0
Retail Trade	13,500	10.6	11.4
Leisure and Hospitality	13,200	10.4	9.7
Manufacturing	4,400	3.5	8.8
Financial Activities	6,100	4.8	5.8
Wholesale Trade	2,400	1.9	4.2
Construction	n/a	n/a	4.1
Other Services	4,400	3.5	4.1
Transportation and Utilities	2,300	1.8	3.7
Information	1,500	1.2	2.1
Mining and Logging	n/a	n/a	0.6

Note: Figures cover non-farm employment as of December 2010 and are not seasonally adjusted;
(1) Metropolitan Statistical Area - see Appendix B for areas included; n/a not available
Source: Bureau of Labor Statistics, http://stats.bls.gov

Occupations with Greatest Projected Employment Growth: 2006 - 2016

Occupation[1]	2006 Employment	2016 Projected Employment	Numeric Employment Change	Percent Employment Change
Retail salespersons	283,850	339,780	55,930	19.7
Customer service representatives	162,780	214,600	51,820	31.8
Registered nurses	148,390	190,020	41,630	28.1
Combined food preparation and serving workers, including fast food	163,780	202,670	38,890	23.7
Waiters and waitresses	197,920	232,430	34,510	17.4
Office clerks, general	188,190	221,750	33,560	17.8
Bookkeeping, accounting, and auditing clerks	128,340	153,830	25,490	19.9
Janitors and cleaners, except maids and housekeeping cleaners	124,030	147,970	23,940	19.3
Sales representatives, services, all other	73,650	97,390	23,740	32.2
Executive secretaries and administrative assistants	106,820	129,140	22,320	20.9

Note: Projections cover Florida; (1) Sorted by numeric employment change
Source: www.projectionscentral.com, State Occupational Projections, 2006-2016 Long-Term Projections

Fastest Growing Occupations: 2006 - 2016

Occupation[1]	2006 Employment	2016 Projected Employment	Numeric Employment Change	Percent Employment Change
Network systems and data communications analysts	20,830	33,090	12,260	58.9
Court reporters	2,170	3,430	1,260	58.1
Computer software engineers, applications	17,350	27,250	9,900	57.1
Veterinary technologists and technicians	5,720	8,880	3,160	55.2
Veterinarians	3,280	4,890	1,610	49.1
Home health aides	29,600	42,780	13,180	44.5
Personal and home care aides	10,640	15,220	4,580	43.0
Paralegals and legal assistants	19,240	27,360	8,120	42.2
Pharmacy technicians	21,110	29,950	8,840	41.9
Medical assistants	31,040	43,930	12,890	41.5

Note: Projections cover Florida; (1) Sorted by percent employment change and excludes occupations with numeric employment change less than 900
Source: www.projectionscentral.com, State Occupational Projections, 2006-2016 Long-Term Projections

Average Wages

Occupation	$/Hr.	Occupation	$/Hr.
Accountants and Auditors	26.67	Maids and Housekeeping Cleaners	9.57
Automotive Mechanics	18.76	Maintenance and Repair Workers	14.94
Bookkeepers	15.14	Marketing Managers	51.96
Carpenters	16.34	Nuclear Medicine Technologists	30.56
Cashiers	8.81	Nurses, Licensed Practical	19.17
Clerks, General Office	11.88	Nurses, Registered	29.95
Clerks, Receptionists/Information	12.07	Nursing Aides/Orderlies/Attendants	11.06
Clerks, Shipping/Receiving	11.66	Packers and Packagers, Hand	10.50
Computer Programmers	25.72	Physical Therapists	37.58
Computer Support Specialists	17.01	Postal Service Mail Carriers	22.54
Computer Systems Analysts	28.91	Real Estate Brokers	n/a
Cooks, Restaurant	10.54	Retail Salespersons	12.63
Dentists	n/a	Sales Reps., Exc. Tech./Scientific	27.69
Electrical Engineers	38.34	Sales Reps., Tech./Scientific	35.00
Electricians	19.55	Secretaries, Exc. Legal/Med./Exec.	13.52
Financial Managers	51.42	Security Guards	12.80
First-Line Supervisors/Mgrs., Sales	19.79	Surgeons	n/a
Food Preparation Workers	9.09	Teacher Assistants	10.30
General and Operations Managers	39.63	Teachers, Elementary School	n/a
Hairdressers/Cosmetologists	11.02	Teachers, Secondary School	n/a
Internists	n/a	Telemarketers	8.53
Janitors and Cleaners	10.03	Truck Drivers, Heavy/Tractor-Trailer	14.54
Landscaping/Groundskeeping Workers	10.82	Truck Drivers, Light/Delivery Svcs.	13.62
Lawyers	35.20	Waiters and Waitresses	9.63

Note: Wage data covers the Gainesville, FL - see Appendix B for areas included. Hourly wages for elementary/secondary school teachers and teacher assistants were calculated by the editors from annual wage data assuming a 40 hour work week; n/a not available.
Source: Bureau of Labor Statistics, Metro Area Occupational Employment and Wage Estimates, May 2009

RESIDENTIAL REAL ESTATE

Building Permits

Area	Single-Family			Multi-Family			Total		
	2009	2010	Pct. Chg.	2009	2010	Pct. Chg.	2009	2010	Pct. Chg.
City	45	45	0.0	145	123	-15.2	190	168	-11.6
MSA[1]	384	367	-4.4	145	123	-15.2	529	490	-7.4
U.S.	441,100	447,300	1.4	141,900	157,300	10.9	583,000	604,600	3.7

Note: (1) Metropolitan Statistical Area - see Appendix B for areas included; figures represent new, privately-owned housing units authorized (unadjusted data); All permit data are based on estimates with imputation.
Source: U.S. Census Bureau, Manufacturing, Mining, and Construction Statistics, Building Permits, 2009, 2010

Homeownership Rate

Area	2005 (%)	2006 (%)	2007 (%)	2008 (%)	2009 (%)	2010 (%)
MSA[1]	n/a	n/a	n/a	n/a	n/a	n/a
U.S.	68.9	68.8	68.1	67.8	67.4	66.9

Note: (1) Metropolitan Statistical Area - see Appendix B for areas included
Source: U.S. Census Bureau, Housing Vacancies and Homeownership Annual Statistics: 2010

Housing Vacancy Rates

Area	Gross Vacancy Rate[2] (%)			Year-Round Vacancy Rate[3] (%)			Rental Vacancy Rate[4] (%)			Homeowner Vacancy Rate[5] (%)		
	2008	2009	2010	2008	2009	2010	2008	2009	2010	2008	2009	2010
MSA[1]	n/a	n/a	n/a	n/a	n/a	n/a	n/a	n/a	n/a	n/a	n/a	n/a
U.S.	14.4	14.5	14.3	11.1	11.3	11.3	10.0	10.6	10.2	2.8	2.6	2.6

Note: (1) Metropolitan Statistical Area - see Appendix B for areas included; (2) The percentage of the total housing inventory that is vacant; (3) The percentage of the housing inventory (excluding seasonal units) that is year-round vacant; (4) The percentage of rental inventory that is vacant for rent; (5) The percentage of homeowner inventory that is vacant for sale; n/a not available
Source: U.S. Census Bureau, Housing Vacancies and Homeownership Annual Statistics: 2010

State Corporate Income Tax Rates

State	Tax Rate (%)	Income Brackets ($)	Num. of Brackets	Financial Institution Tax Rate (%)[a]	Federal Income Tax Ded.
Florida	5.5 (f)	Flat rate	1	5.5 (f)	No

Note: Tax rates as of January 1, 2011; (a) Rates listed are the tax rates applied to financial institutions or excise taxes based on income. Some states have other taxes based upon the value of deposits or shares; (f) An exemption of $5,000 is allowed. Florida's Alternative Minimum Tax rate is 3.3%.
Source: Federation of Tax Administrators, "State Corporate Income Tax Rates, 2011"

State Individual Income Tax Rates

State	Tax Rate (%)	Income Brackets ($)	Num. of Brackets	Personal Exempt. ($)[1] Single	Personal Exempt. ($)[1] Dependents	Fed. Inc. Tax Ded.
Florida – No State Income Tax						

Note: Tax rates as of January 1, 2011; Local- and county-level taxes are not included; n/a not applicable; (1) Married joint filers generally receive double the single exemption
Source: Federation of Tax Administrators, "State Individual Income Tax Rates, 2011"

Various State and Local Tax Rates

State	State and Local Sales and Use (%)	State Sales and Use (%)	Gasoline[1] (¢/gal.)	Cigarette[2] ($/pack)	Spirits[3] ($/gal.)	Wine[4] ($/gal.)	Beer[5] ($/gal.)
Florida	6.25	6.00	34.4	1.34	6.50	2.25	0.48

Note: All tax rates as of January 1, 2011 except Spirits (Sept. 1, 2010); (1) The American Petroleum Institute has developed a methodology for determining the average tax rate on a gallon of fuel. Rates may include any of the following: excise taxes, environmental fees, storage tank fees, other fees or taxes, general sales tax, and local taxes. In states where gasoline is subject to the general sales tax, or where the fuel tax is based on the average sale price, the average rate determined by API is sensitive to changes in the price of gasoline. States that fully or partially apply general sales taxes to gasoline: CA, CO, GA, IL, IN, MI, NY; (2) The federal excise tax of $1.0066 per pack and local taxes are not included; (3) Rates are those applicable to off-premise sales of 40% alcohol by volume (a.b.v.) distilled spirits in 750ml containers. Local excise taxes are excluded; (4) Rates are those applicable to off-premise sales of 11% a.b.v. non-carbonated wine in 750ml containers; (5) Rates are those applicable to off-premise sales of 4.7% a.b.v. beer in 12 ounce containers.
Source: Tax Foundation, 2011 Facts & Figures: How Does Your State Compare?

State-Local Tax Burdens

Area	Rate (%)	Rank[1]	Per Capita Taxes Paid to Home State ($)	Total State and Local Per Capita Taxes Paid ($)	Per Capita Income ($)
Florida	9.2	31	2,713	3,897	42,146
U.S. Average	9.8	-	3,057	4,160	42,539

Note: Figures cover 2009; (1) Rank ranges from 1 to 50 where 1 is highest tax burden
Source: Tax Foundation, State-Local Tax Burdens, All States, 2009

State Business Tax Climate Index Rankings

State	Overall Rank	Corporate Tax Index Rank	Individual Income Tax Index Rank	Sales Tax Index Rank	Unemployment Insurance Tax Index Rank	Property Tax Index Rank
Florida	5	15	1	30	3	28

Note: The index is a measure of how each state's tax laws affect economic performance. The lower the rank, the more favorable a state's tax system is for business. All ranks are for fiscal years. States without a given tax are given a ranking of 1.
Source: Tax Foundation, Tax Foundation Background Paper, No. 60, "2011 State Business Tax Climate Index"

COMMERCIAL UTILITIES

Typical Monthly Electric Bills

Area	Commercial Service ($/month) 3 kW demand 1,000 kWh	40 kW demand 14,000 kWh	Industrial Service ($/month) 1,000 kW demand 200,000 kWh	50,000 kW demand 15,000,000 kWh
City	n/a	n/a	n/a	n/a
Average[1]	135	1,576	23,741	1,402,202

Note: Based on total rates in effect July 1, 2010; (1) average based on 182 utilities surveyed; n/a not available
Source: Edison Electric Institute, Typical Bills and Average Rates Report, Summer 2010

TRANSPORTATION

Means of Transportation to Work

Area	Car/Truck/Van		Public Transportation			Bicycle	Walked	Other Means	Worked at Home
	Drove Alone	Car-pooled	Bus	Subway	Railroad				
City	69.8	9.2	5.3	0.0	0.0	5.7	5.5	1.6	2.7
MSA[1]	75.4	11.3	2.8	0.0	0.0	2.9	2.8	1.3	3.4
U.S.	75.8	10.4	2.7	1.7	0.5	0.5	2.9	1.2	4.1

Note: Figures are percentages and cover workers 16 years of age and older;
(1) Metropolitan Statistical Area - see Appendix B for areas included
Source: U.S. Census Bureau, 2007-2009 American Community Survey 3-Year Estimates

Travel Time to Work

Area	Less Than 15 Minutes	15 to 29 Minutes	30 to 44 Minutes	45 to 59 Minutes	60 to 89 Minutes	90 Minutes or More
City	45.4	41.7	8.9	1.8	1.5	0.7
MSA[1]	32.0	43.4	17.0	3.7	2.7	1.2
U.S.	28.5	36.2	19.7	7.5	5.6	2.5

Note: Figures are percentages and include workers 16 years old and over;
(1) Metropolitan Statistical Area - see Appendix B for areas included
Source: U.S. Census Bureau, 2007-2009 American Community Survey 3-Year Estimates

Travel Time Index

Area	1982	1999	2008	2009
Urban Area[1]	n/a	n/a	n/a	n/a
Average[2]	1.08	1.20	1.20	1.20

Note: Travel Time Index—the ratio of travel time in the peak period to the travel time at
free-flow conditions. A value of 1.30 indicates a 20-minute free-flow trip takes 26 minutes
in the peak. Free-flow speeds (60 mph on freeways and 35 mph on principal arterials)
are used as the comparison threshold; (1) Covers the Gainesville urban area;
(2) average of 439 urban areas
Source: Texas Transportation Institute, Urban Mobility Report 2010, December 2010

Public Transportation

Agency Name / Mode of Transportation	Vehicles Operated in Maximum Service	Annual Unlinked Passenger Trips ('000)	Annual Passenger Miles ('000)
Gainesville Regional Transit System (RTS)			
Demand response	22	39.7	325.8
Bus	88	8,940.0	25,031.9

Note: Figures include both directly operated and purchased transportation
Source: Federal Transit Administration, National Transit Database, 2009

Air Transportation

Airport Name and Code / Type of Service	Passenger Airlines[1]	Passenger Enplanements	Freight Carriers[2]	Freight (lbs.)
Gainesville Regional Airport (GNV)				
Domestic service (U.S. carriers - 2010)	13	159,476	4	13,831
International service (U.S. carriers - 2009)	0	0	0	0

Note: (1) Includes all U.S.-based major, minor and commuter airlines that carried at least one passenger during
the year; (2) Includes all U.S.-based airlines and freight carriers that transported at least one pound of freight
during the year
Source: Bureau of Transportation Statistics, The Intermodal Transportation Database, Air Carriers: T-100
Domestic Market (U.S. Carriers), 2010; Bureau of Transportation Statistics, The Intermodal Transportation
Database, Air Carriers: T-100 International Market (U.S. Carriers), 2009

Other Transportation Statistics

Interstate highways:	I-75
Amtrak service:	Yes (train station is located in Waldo
Major waterways/ports:	None

Source: Amtrak.com; Google Maps

BUSINESSES

Major Business Headquarters

Company Name	Rankings	
	Fortune[1]	Forbes[2]
No companies listed	-	-

Note: (1) Fortune 500—companies that produce a 10-K are ranked 1 to 500 based on 2010 revenue; (2) all private companies with at least $2 billion in annual revenue are ranked 1 to 223; companies listed are headquartered in the city; dashes indicate no ranking
Source: Fortune, "Fortune 500," May 23, 2011; Forbes, "America's Largest Private Companies," November 3, 2010

Fast-Growing Businesses

According to *Fortune*, Gainesville is home to one of America's 100 fastest-growing small public companies: **Exactech**. Companies were ranked by their three-year annualized rates of revenue growth and total return to investors for the period ended December 31, 2008. Criteria for inclusion: revenues of less than $200 million; stock price of at least $1. Banks, real-estate firms and adult entertainment companies were excluded. Also excluded were companies with losses in any of the four quarters ended on or before December 31, 2008. *Fortune Small Business, "America's Fastest-Growing Small Public Companies," July/August 2009*

Minority- and Women-Owned Businesses

Group	All Firms		Firms with Paid Employees			
	Firms	Sales ($000)	Firms	Sales ($000)	Employees	Payroll ($000)
Asian	407	97,010	152	93,107	583	12,034
Black	919	146,222	122	135,251	587	17,559
Hispanic	753	207,434	193	168,321	856	28,036
Women	3,387	629,433	498	532,285	4,359	114,296
All Firms	10,980	10,487,232	3,223	10,132,351	60,502	2,196,066

Note: Figures cover firms located in the city; minority- and women-owned business are defined as firms in which the corresponding group own 51% or more of the stock or equity of the company
Source: U.S. Census Bureau, 2007 Economic Census, Survey of Business Owners

HOTELS

Hotels/Motels

Area	5 Star		4 Star		3 Star		2 Star		1 Star		Not Rated	
	Num.	Pct.3	Num.	Pct.3	Num.	Pct.3	Num.	Pct.3	Num.	Pct.3	Num.	Pct.3
City[1]	0	0.0	0	0.0	11	23.9	24	52.2	3	6.5	8	17.4
Total[2]	119	0.7	927	5.8	4,906	30.5	7,992	49.7	526	3.3	1,625	10.1

Note: (1) Figures cover Gainesville and vicinity; (2) Figures cover all 100 cities in this book; (3) Percentage of hotels which are a given star rating; Star ratings are determined by expedia.com and offer an indication of the general quality of a particular hotel.
Source: expedia.com, May 5, 2011

EVENT SITES

Major Stadiums, Arenas, and Auditoriums

Name	Max. Capacity
Ben Hill Griffin Stadium at Florida Field (The Swamp)	88,548
Stephen C. O'Connell Center (O'Dome)	12,000

Source: Original research

Living Environment

COST OF LIVING

Cost of Living Index

Composite Index	Groceries	Housing	Utilities	Trans-portation	Health Care	Misc. Goods/ Services
99.8	106.3	101.8	99.2	103.3	92.7	95.5

Note: U.S. = 100; Figures cover the Gainesville FL urban area.
Source: The Council for Community and Economic Research, ACCRA Cost of Living Index, 2010

Grocery Prices

Area[1]	T-Bone Steak ($/pound)	Frying Chicken ($/pound)	Whole Milk ($/half gal.)	Eggs ($/dozen)	Orange Juice ($/64 oz.)	Coffee ($/11.5 oz.)
City[2]	9.99	1.24	2.43	1.41	3.06	3.57
Avg.	9.04	1.16	2.02	1.47	3.08	3.65
Min.	6.97	0.84	1.46	0.96	2.39	2.64
Max.	13.93	2.51	3.58	3.01	4.94	6.32

Note: (1) Values for the local area are compared with the average, minimum and maximum values for all 338 areas in the Cost of Living Index; (2) Figures cover the Gainesville FL urban area; **T-Bone Steak** *(price per pound);* **Frying Chicken** *(price per pound, whole fryer);* **Whole Milk** *(half gallon carton);* **Eggs** *(price per dozen, Grade A, large);* **Orange Juice** *(64 oz. Tropicana or Florida Natural);* **Coffee** *(11.5 oz. can, vacuum-packed, Maxwell House, Hills Bros, or Folgers).*
Source: The Council for Community and Economic Research, ACCRA Cost of Living Index, 2010

Housing and Utility Costs

Area[1]	New Home Price ($)	Apartment Rent ($/month)	All Electric ($/month)	Part Electric ($/month)	Other Energy ($/month)	Telephone ($/month)
City[2]	282,583	883	-	133.02	50.67	24.00
Avg.	293,442	810	166.39	91.93	83.82	26.93
Min.	182,545	453	119.21	44.47	36.85	17.98
Max.	1,123,114	2,776	307.53	218.20	313.90	39.15

Note: (1) Values for the local area are compared with the average, minimum and maximum values for all 338 areas in the Cost of Living Index; (2) Figures cover the Gainesville FL urban area; **New Home Price** *(2,400 sf living area, 8,000 sf lot, in urban area with full utilities);* **Apartment Rent** *(950 sf 2 bedroom/1.5 or 2 bath, unfurnished, excluding all utilities except water);* **All Electric** *(average monthly cost for an all-electric home);* **Part Electric** *(average monthly cost for a part-electric home);* **Other Energy** *(average monthly cost for natural gas, fuel oil, coal, wood, and any other forms of energy except electricity);* **Telephone** *(price includes basic monthly rate for a private residential line plus additional local usage charges incurred by a family of four).*
Source: The Council for Community and Economic Research, ACCRA Cost of Living Index, 2010

Health Care, Transportation, and Other Costs

Area[1]	Doctor ($/visit)	Dentist ($/visit)	Optometrist ($/visit)	Gasoline ($/gallon)	Beauty Salon ($/visit)	Men's Shirt ($)
City[2]	71.87	75.15	77.39	2.78	37.86	17.76
Avg.	89.44	78.95	87.40	2.73	31.92	24.83
Min.	57.00	54.25	48.32	2.44	19.17	13.67
Max.	149.90	136.73	174.22	3.75	62.81	47.89

Note: (1) Values for the local area are compared with the average, minimum and maximum values for all 338 areas in the Cost of Living Index; (2) Figures cover the Gainesville FL urban area; **Doctor** *(general practitioners routine exam of an established patient);* **Dentist** *(adult teeth cleaning and periodic oral examination);* **Optometrist** *(full vision eye exam for established adult patient);* **Gasoline** *(one gallon regular unleaded, national brand, including all taxes, cash price at self-service pump if available);* **Beauty Salon** *(woman's shampoo, trim, and blow-dry);* **Men's Shirt** *(cotton/polyester dress shirt, pinpoint weave, long sleeves).*
Source: The Council for Community and Economic Research, ACCRA Cost of Living Index, 2010

HOUSING

House Price Index (HPI)

Area	National Ranking[2]	Quarterly Change (%)	One-Year Change (%)	Five-Year Change (%)
MSA[1]	247	1.36	-4.00	-9.19
U.S.[3]	-	-0.84	-3.95	-11.45

Note: The HPI is a weighted repeat sales index. It measures average price changes in repeat sales or refinancings on the same properties. This information is obtained by reviewing repeat mortgage transactions on single-family properties whose mortgages have been purchased or securitized by Fannie Mae or Freddie Mac in January 1975; (1) Metropolitan/Micropolitan Statistical Area - see Appendix B for areas included; (2) Rankings are based on annual percentage change for all metro areas containing at least 15,000 transactions over the last 10 years and ranges from 1 to 309; (3) figures based on a weighted average of Census Division estimates; all figures are for the period ending December 31, 2010
Source: Federal Housing Finance Agency, House Price Index, February 24, 2011

House Price Valuations

Area	Q4 2005 Price ($000)	Q4 2005 Over-valuation	Q4 2006 Price ($000)	Q4 2006 Over-valuation	Q4 2007 Price ($000)	Q4 2007 Over-valuation	Q4 2008 Price ($000)	Q4 2008 Over-valuation	Q4 2009 Price ($000)	Q4 2009 Over-valuation
MSA[1]	159.4	20.2	169.8	17.1	165.7	9.4	140.9	-8.4	135.4	-12.7

Note: Figures show the percentage of over- or under-valuation of single family homes relative to statistically normal house values (e.g. a value of 23.6 indicates that house values are 23.6% overvalued). Statistically normal house values are based on house prices, interest rates, household incomes, population densities, and any historical premiums or discounts metropolitan areas have exhibited over time; (1) Figures cover the Gainesville, FL Metropolitan Statistical Area - see Appendix B for areas included
Source: Global Insight/PNC Financial Services Group, House Prices in America: 4th Quarter 2009 Update

Median Single-Family Home Prices

Area	2008	2009	2010p	Percent Change 2009 to 2010
MSA[1]	188.6	167.6	160.9	-4.0
U.S. Average	196.6	172.1	173.2	0.6

Note: Figures are median sales prices of existing single-family homes in thousands of dollars; (p) preliminary; n/a not available; (1) Metropolitan Statistical Area - see Appendix B for areas included
Source: National Association of Realtors, Median Sales Price of Existing Single-Family Homes for Metropolitan Areas, 4th Quarter 2010

Median Apartment Condo-Coop Home Prices

Area	2008	2009	2010p	Percent Change 2009 to 2010
MSA[1]	n/a	n/a	n/a	n/a
U.S. Average	209.8	175.6	171.7	-2.2

Note: Figures are median sales prices of existing apartment condo-coop homes in thousands of dollars; (p) preliminary; n/a not available; (1) Metropolitan Statistical Area - see Appendix B for areas included
Source: National Association of Realtors, Median Sales Price of Existing Apartment Condo-Coop Homes for Metropolitan Areas, 4th Quarter 2010

Year Housing Structure Built

Area	2000 or Later	1990-1999	1980-1989	1970-1979	1960-1969	1950-1959	1940-1949	Before 1940	Median Year
City	12.2	15.6	19.2	23.0	14.2	10.3	3.0	2.4	1979
MSA[1]	18.8	19.8	21.8	19.4	9.1	6.4	2.1	2.5	1985
U.S.	12.5	14.0	14.2	16.5	11.4	11.3	5.8	14.3	1974

Note: Figures are percentages except for Median Year; (1) Metropolitan Statistical Area - see Appendix B for areas included
Source: U.S. Census Bureau, 2007-2009 American Community Survey 3-Year Estimates

HEALTH

Health Risk Data

Category	MSA[1] (%)	U.S. (%)
Adults who have been told they have high blood pressure	n/a	28.7
Adults who have been told they have high blood cholesterol	n/a	37.5
Adults who have been told they have diabetes[3]	n/a	8.3
Adults who have been told they have arthritis	n/a	26.0
Adults who have been told they currently have asthma	n/a	8.8
Adults who are current smokers	n/a	17.9
Adults who are heavy drinkers[4]	n/a	5.1
Adults who are binge drinkers[5]	n/a	15.8
Adults who are overweight (BMI 25.0 - 29.9)	n/a	36.2
Adults who are obese (BMI 30.0 - 99.8)	n/a	26.9
Adults who participated in any physical activities in the past month	n/a	76.2
Adults 50+ who have ever had a sigmoidoscopy or colonoscopy[2]	n/a	62.2
Women 40+ who have had a mammogram within the past two years[2]	n/a	76.0
Adults age 18–64 who have any kind of health care coverage	n/a	83.1

Note: Data as of 2009 unless otherwise noted; n/a not available; (1) Figures cover the Gainesville, FL Metropolitan Statistical Area - see Appendix B for areas included; (2) Data as of 2008; (3) Figures do not include pregnancy-related, borderline, or pre-diabetes; (4) Heavy drinkers are classified as males having more than two drinks per day or females having more than one drink per day; (5) Binge drinkers are classified as males having five or more drinks on one occasion or females having four or more drinks on one occasion
Source: Centers for Disease Control and Prevention, Behaviorial Risk Factor Surveillance System, SMART: Selected Metropolitan/Micropolitan Area Risk Trends, 2008, 2009

Mortality Rates for the Top 10 Causes of Death in the U.S.

ICD-10[a] Sub-Chapter	ICD-10[a] Code	Age-Adjusted Mortality Rate[1] per 100,000 population	
		County[2]	U.S.
Malignant neoplasms	C00-C97	195.2	180.9
Ischaemic heart diseases	I20-I25	97.9	135.0
Other forms of heart disease	I30-I51	39.6	50.0
Cerebrovascular diseases	I60-I69	48.7	44.1
Chronic lower respiratory diseases	J40-J47	42.9	41.5
Other degenerative diseases of the nervous system	G30-G31	31.5	23.6
Diabetes mellitus	E10-E14	27.4	23.5
Other external causes of accidental injury	W00-X59	28.7	23.5
Organic, including symptomatic, mental disorders	F01-F09	36.2	22.2
Influenza and pneumonia	J09-J18	10.9	18.1

Note: (a) ICD-10 = International Classification of Diseases 10th Revision; (1) Mortality rates are a three year average covering 2005-2007; (2) Figures cover Alachua County
Source: Centers for Disease Control and Prevention, National Center for Health Statistics. Compressed Mortality File 1999-2007. CDC WONDER On-line Database, compiled from Compressed Mortality File 1999-2007 Series 20 No. 2M, 2010.

Mortality Rates for Selected Causes of Death

ICD-10[a] Sub-Chapter	ICD-10[a] Code	Age-Adjusted Mortality Rate[1] per 100,000 population	
		County[2]	U.S.
Assault	X85-Y09	4.7	6.0
Human immunodeficiency virus (HIV) disease	B20-B24	5.3	4.0
Hypertensive diseases	I10-I15	17.2	18.0
Intentional self-harm	X60-X84	12.6	11.0
Malnutrition	E40-E46	*0.8	0.8
Obesity and other hyperalimentation	E65-E68	*2.0	1.5
Transport accidents	V01-V99	18.9	15.6
Viral hepatitis	B15-B19	*2.1	2.1

Note: (a) ICD-10 = International Classification of Diseases 10th Revision; (1) Mortality rates are a three year average covering 2005-2007; (2) Figures cover Alachua County; (*) Unreliable data as per CDC
Source: Centers for Disease Control and Prevention, National Center for Health Statistics. Compressed Mortality File 1999-2007. CDC WONDER On-line Database, compiled from Compressed Mortality File 1999-2007 Series 20 No. 2M, 2010.

Distribution of Physicians and Dentists

Area[1]	Dentists[2]	D.O.[3]	M.D.[4]				
			Total	Family/ General Practice	Pediatrics	Medical Specialties	Surgical Specialties
Local (number)	200	56	961	112	72	357	184
Local (rate[5])	8.3	2.3	39.7	4.6	3.0	14.7	7.6
U.S. (rate[5])	4.5	1.9	18.3	2.5	1.4	6.8	4.1

Note: Data as of 2008 unless noted; (1) Local data covers Alachua County; (2) Data as of 2007; (3) Doctor of Osteopathic Medicine; (4) Includes active, non-federal, patient-care, office-based Doctors of Medicine; (5) rate per 10,000 population
Source: Area Resource File (ARF). 2009-2010 Release. U.S. Department of Health and Human Services, Health Resources and Services Administration, Bureau of Health Professions, Rockville, MD, August 2010

Hospitals

Gainesville has the following hospitals: 2 general medical and surgical; 1 rehabilitation; 1 long-term acute care; 1 other specialty.
AHA Guide to the Healthcare Field 2010

According to *U.S. News,* the Gainesville, FL Metropolitan Statistical Area is home to one of the best hospitals in the U.S.: **Shands at the University of Florida**. The hospital listed was highly ranked in at least one adult specialty. *U.S. News Online, "America's Best Hospitals 2010-11"*

According to *U.S. News,* the Gainesville, FL Metropolitan Statistical Area is home to one of the best children's hospitals in the U.S.: **Shands Children's Hospital at the University of Florida**. The hospital listed was highly ranked in at least one pediatric specialty. *U.S. News Online, "America's Best Children's Hospitals 2010-11"*

EDUCATION

Public School District Statistics

District Name	Schls	Pupils	Pupil/ Teacher Ratio	Minority Pupils[1] (%)	Free Lunch Eligible[2] (%)	IEP[3] (%)
Alachua	64	27,546	13.1	51.3	38.9	17.9

Note: Table includes school districts with 2,000 or more students; (1) Percentage of students that are not non-Hispanic white; (2) Percentage of students that are eligible for the free lunch program; (3) Percentage of students that have an Individualized Education Program.
Source: U.S. Department of Education, National Center for Education Statistics, Common Core of Data, Local Education Agency (School District) Universe Survey: School Year 2008-2009; U.S. Department of Education, National Center for Education Statistics, Common Core of Data, Public Elementary/Secondary School Universe Survey: School Year 2008-2009

Top Public High Schools

High School Name	Index[1]	Rank[1]	Subsidized Lunch (%)[2]	E&E (%)[3]
Buchholz	3.623	137	23.0	52.6
Eastside	7.326	18	42.0	n/a
Gainesville[4]	2.877	279	39.0	29.9

Note: (1) Public schools are ranked according to a ratio that is the number of Advanced Placement, International Baccalaureate, and/or Cambridge tests taken by all students at a school in 2009 divided by the number of graduating seniors. All of the schools on the list have an index of at least 1.000; they are in the top six percent of public schools measured this way. The rankings range from 1 to 1,734; (2) Percentage of students receiving federally subsidized meals; (3) E & E stands for equity and excellence percentage: the portion of all graduating seniors at a school that had at least one passing grade on one AP or IB test; (4) Schools that offer International Baccalaureate or Cambridge exams; (5) School is unranked, but has been identified by Newsweek as one of the nation's most elite public high schools; n/a not available
Source: Newsweek Online, "Top High Schools 2010"

Highest Level of Education

Area	Less than H.S.	H.S. Diploma	Some College, No Deg.	Associate Degree	Bachelors Degree	Masters Degree	Profess. School Degree	Doctorate Degree
City	10.7	17.2	14.7	9.8	23.0	14.7	4.1	6.0
MSA[1]	10.9	21.6	16.2	9.9	21.4	11.7	3.7	4.6
U.S.	15.3	29.0	20.7	7.5	17.4	7.0	1.9	1.1

Note: Figures are 2010 estimated percentages and cover persons age 25 and over; (1) Metropolitan Statistical Area - see Appendix B for areas included
Source: Claritas, Inc.

Educational Attainment by Race

Area	High School Graduate (%)					Bachelor's Degree (%)				
	Total	White	Black	Asian	Hisp.[2]	Total	White	Black	Asian	Hisp.[2]
City	87.5	91.6	77.1	90.3	83.0	42.7	52.2	13.5	65.1	43.0
MSA[1]	88.7	91.3	77.6	94.9	83.3	38.5	42.8	14.6	70.4	37.4
U.S.	84.9	90.0	80.7	85.5	60.7	27.8	30.9	17.5	49.7	12.7

Note: Figures shown cover persons 25 years old and over; (1) Metropolitan Statistical Area - see Appendix B for areas included; (2) people of Hispanic origin can be of any race
Source: U.S. Census Bureau, 2007-2009 American Community Survey 3-Year Estimates

School Enrollment by Grade and Control

Area	Preschool (%)		Kindergarten (%)		Grades 1 - 4 (%)		Grades 5 - 8 (%)		Grades 9 - 12 (%)	
	Public	Private	Public	Private	Public	Private	Public	Private	Public	Private
City	42.4	57.6	85.3	14.7	86.4	13.6	93.1	6.9	93.6	6.4
MSA[1]	45.1	54.9	88.9	11.1	85.6	14.4	85.8	14.2	88.4	11.6
U.S.	54.3	45.7	86.4	13.6	88.9	11.1	89.1	10.9	90.2	9.8

Note: Figures shown cover persons 3 years old and over; (1) Metropolitan Statistical Area - see Appendix B for areas included
Source: U.S. Census Bureau, 2007-2009 American Community Survey 3-Year Estimates

Average Salaries of Public School Classroom Teachers

Area	2009-10		2010-11		Percent Change 2009-10 to 2010-11	Percent Change 2000-01 to 2010-11
	Dollars	Rank[1]	Dollars	Rank[1]		
Florida	46,708	37	46,702	47	-0.01	22.2
U.S. Average	55,202	-	56,069	-	1.57	29.3

Note: (1) State rank ranges from 1 to 51 where 1 indicates highest salary.
Source: National Education Association, Rankings & Estimates: Rankings of the States 2010 and Estimates of School Statistics 2011, December 2010

Higher Education

Four-Year Colleges			Two-Year Colleges			Medical Schools[1]	Law Schools[2]	Voc/ Tech[3]
Public	Private Non-profit	Private For-profit	Public	Private Non-profit	Private For-profit			
2	2	1	0	1	0	1	1	2

Note: Figures cover institutions located within the city limits and include main campuses only; (1) includes schools accredited by the Liaison Committee on Medical Education and the American Osteopathic Association; (2) includes American Bar Association-accredited law schools; (3) includes all schools with programs that are less than 2 years.
Source: National Center for Education Statistics, Integrated Postsecondary Education System (IPEDS) Peer Analysis System, 2010-11; U.S. News & World Report, Medical School Directory, 2011; U.S. News & World Report, Law School Directory, 2011

According to *U.S. News & World Report*, the Gainesville, FL Metropolitan Statistical Area is home to one of the top 197 national universities in the U.S.: **University of Florida** (#53). The rankings are based on quantitative measurements such as peer assessment, retention, faculty resources, student selectivity, financial resources, graduation rate, and alumni giving rate.
U.S. News & World Report, "America's Best Colleges 2011"

According to *U.S. News & World Report*, the Gainesville, FL Metropolitan Statistical Area is home to one of the top 50 law schools in the U.S.: **University of Florida (Levin)** (#47). The rankings are based on a weighted average of 10 measures of quality: peer assessment score; assessment score by lawyers/judges; median LSAT scores; median undergrad GPA; acceptance rate; employment rates for graduates; bar passage rate; faculty resources; expenditures per student; student/faculty ratio; and library resources. *U.S. News & World Report, "America's Best Law Schools 2011"*

According to *Forbes*, the Gainesville, FL Metropolitan Statistical Area is home to one of the top 75 business schools in the U.S.: **Florida (Hough)** (#54). The rankings are based on the return on investment that graduates of the Class of 2004 received (median salary five years after graduation). *Forbes, "Best Business Schools," August 5, 2009*

PRESIDENTIAL ELECTION

2008 Presidential Election Results

Area	Obama	McCain	Nader	Other
Alachua County	60.0	38.5	0.5	1.0
U.S.	52.9	45.6	0.6	0.9

Note: Results are percentages and may not add to 100% due to rounding
Source: Dave Leip's Atlas of U.S. Presidential Elections, www.uselectionatlas.org

EMPLOYERS

Major Employers

Company Name	Industry	Type of Site
Alachua County Sheriffs Office	Police protection	Branch
Chemistry Department	Colleges and universities	Branch
County of Alachua	Executive offices	Branch
Department of Chemistry	Colleges and universities	Branch
Institute of Fam Agriculture	Farm management services	Branch
Malcolm Randall VA Medical Ctr	Civic and social associations	Branch
MPS	Storage batteries	Headquarters
Nationwide	Insurance agents, brokers, and service	Branch
North Florida Regional Hosp	General medical and surgical hospitals	Headquarters
Raiford Prison	Correctional institutions	Branch
Santa Fe College	Junior colleges	Headquarters
Shands at AGH	General medical and surgical hospitals	Branch
Shands at Live Oaks	General medical and surgical hospitals	Headquarters
Tacachale	Administration of social and manpower programs	Branch
UF Physical Plant	Building maintenance services, nec	Branch
University Florida Bookstores	Colleges and universities	Headquarters
University of Florida	Colleges and universities	Branch

Note: Companies shown are located within the Gainesville metropolitan area; nec = not elsewhere classified.
Source: www.zapdata.com, January 2011

PUBLIC SAFETY

Crime Rate

Area	All Crimes	Violent Crimes				Property Crimes		
		Murder	Forcible Rape	Robbery	Aggrav. Assault	Burglary	Larceny -Theft	Motor Vehicle Theft
City	6,541.4	2.6	82.4	207.3	710.5	1,290.1	3,866.7	381.7
Suburbs[1]	3,901.3	2.8	37.5	95.8	486.2	1,036.3	2,054.5	188.2
Metro[2]	5,075.2	2.7	57.5	145.4	585.9	1,149.1	2,860.3	274.3
U.S.	3,465.5	5.0	28.7	133.0	262.8	716.3	2,060.9	258.8

Note: Figures are crimes per 100,000 population; (1) All areas within the metro area that are located outside the city limits; (2) Metropolitan Statistical Area - see Appendix B for areas included
Source: FBI Uniform Crime Reports, 2009

Hate Crimes

Area	Number of Quarters Reported	Bias Motivation				
		Race	Religion	Sexual Orientation	Ethnicity	Disability
City	4	5	1	4	2	0

Source: Federal Bureau of Investigation, Hate Crime Statistics 2009

Identity Theft Consumer Complaints

Area	Complaints	Complaints per 100,000 Population	Rank[2]
MSA[1]	220	85.6	117
U.S.	250,854	81.3	-

Note: (1) Metropolitan Statistical Area - see Appendix B for areas included; (2) Rank ranges from 1 to 384 where 1 indicates greatest number of complaints per 100,000 population
Source: Federal Trade Commission, Consumer Sentinel Network Data Book for January - December 2010

RECREATION

Culture

Dance[1]	Theatre[1]	Instrumental Music[1]	Vocal Music[1]	Series/ Festivals	Museums	Zoos and Aquariums[2]
1	1	1	0	1	4	1

Note: (1) Number of professional perfoming groups; (2) AZA-accredited
Source: The Grey House Performing Arts Directory, 2011-2012; Official Museum Directory, 2010; American Association of Museums, AAM Member Museums, March 2011; Association of Zoos & Aquariums, AZA Member Zoos & Aquariums, May 2011

Professional Sports Teams

Team Name	League
No teams are located in the metro area	

Source: Original research

CLIMATE

Average and Extreme Temperatures

Temperature	Jan	Feb	Mar	Apr	May	Jun	Jul	Aug	Sep	Oct	Nov	Dec	Yr.
Extreme High (°F)	83	85	90	95	98	102	99	99	95	92	88	85	102
Average High (°F)	66	68	74	81	86	89	90	90	87	81	74	68	79
Average Temp. (°F)	55	57	63	69	75	79	81	81	78	71	63	56	69
Average Low (°F)	43	45	50	56	63	69	71	71	69	60	51	44	58
Extreme Low (°F)	10	19	28	35	42	50	62	62	48	33	28	13	10

Note: Figures cover the years 1962-1995
Source: National Climatic Data Center, International Station Meteorological Climate Summary, 9/96

Average Precipitation/Snowfall/Humidity

Precip./Humidity	Jan	Feb	Mar	Apr	May	Jun	Jul	Aug	Sep	Oct	Nov	Dec	Yr.
Avg. Precip. (in.)	3.7	4.0	3.9	2.3	3.3	6.9	6.5	7.7	5.1	2.8	2.2	2.6	50.9
Avg. Snowfall (in.)	0	Tr	0	0	0	0	0	0	0	0	0	Tr	Tr
Avg. Rel. Hum. 7am (%)	90	90	92	92	91	93	94	96	96	94	94	92	93
Avg. Rel. Hum. 4pm (%)	60	55	52	50	51	61	67	67	67	63	63	61	60

Note: Figures cover the years 1962-1995; Tr = Trace amounts (<0.05 in. of rain; <0.5 in. of snow)
Source: National Climatic Data Center, International Station Meteorological Climate Summary, 9/96

Weather Conditions

Temperature			Daytime Sky			Precipitation		
32°F & below	45°F & below	90°F & above	Clear	Partly cloudy	Cloudy	0.01 inch or more precip.	0.1 inch or more snow/ice	Thunder-storms
16	73	77	88	196	81	119	0	78

Note: Figures are average number of days per year and cover the years 1962-1995
Source: National Climatic Data Center, International Station Meteorological Climate Summary, 9/96

HAZARDOUS WASTE

Superfund Sites

Gainesville has one hazardous waste site on the EPA's Superfund Final National Priorities List: **Cabot/Koppers**. *U.S. Environmental Protection Agency, Final National Priorities List, April 1, 2011*

AIR & WATER QUALITY

Air Quality Index

Area	Percent of Days when Air Quality was...[2]				AQI Statistics	
	Good	Moderate	Unhealthy for Sensitive Groups	Unhealthy	Maximum	Median
Area[1]	94.2	5.5	0.4	0.0	101	33

Note: The Air Quality Index (AQI) is an index for reporting daily air quality. EPA calculates the AQI for five major air pollutants regulated by the Clean Air Act: ground-level ozone, particle pollution (also known as particulate matter), carbon monoxide, sulfur dioxide, and nitrogen dioxide. The AQI runs from 0 to 500. The higher the AQI value, the greater the level of air pollution and the greater the health concern. There are six AQI categories: "Good" The AQI is between 0 and 50. Air quality is considered satisfactory; "Moderate" The AQI is between 51 and 100. Air quality is acceptable; "Unhealthy for Sensitive Groups" When AQI values are between 101 and 150, members of sensitive groups may experience health effects; "Unhealthy" When AQI values are between 151 and 200 everyone may begin to experience health effects; "Very Unhealthy" AQI values between 201 and 300 trigger a health alert; "Hazardous" AQI values over 300 trigger health warnings of emergency conditions; (1) Data covers Alachua County; (2) Based on 274 days with AQI data in 2008; The EPA has suspended data updates while it assesses its data systems, including AirData reports and maps.
Source: U.S. Environmental Protection Agency, AirData Report, 2008

Air Quality Index Pollutants

Area	Percent of Days when AQI Pollutant was...[2]					
	Carbon Monoxide	Nitrogen Dioxide	Ozone	Sulfur Dioxide	Particulate Matter 2.5	Particulate Matter 10
Area[1]	0.0	0.0	82.1	0.0	8.8	9.1

Note: The Air Quality Index (AQI) is an index for reporting daily air quality. EPA calculates the AQI for five major air pollutants regulated by the Clean Air Act: ground-level ozone, particle pollution (also known as particulate matter), carbon monoxide, sulfur dioxide, and nitrogen dioxide. The AQI runs from 0 to 500. The higher the AQI value, the greater the level of air pollution and the greater the health concern; (1) Data covers Alachua County; (2) Based on 274 days with AQI data in 2008; The EPA has suspended data updates while it assesses its data systems, including AirData reports and maps.
Source: U.S. Environmental Protection Agency, AirData Report, 2008

Air Quality Index Trends

Area	Trend Sites (days)								All Sites (days)
	2002	2003	2004	2005	2006	2007	2008	2009	2009
MSA[1]	n/a	n/a	n/a	n/a	n/a	n/a	n/a	n/a	n/a

Note: Figures are the number of days the AQI value exceeded 100 in a given year. An AQI value greater than 100 indicates that air quality would have been in the unhealthful range on that day. Data from exceptional events are included. These counts are presented in two ways. First, the counts are based on sites having an adequate record of monitoring data during the trend period (trend sites). These counts represent the relative change in the number of days with AQI values greater than 100. In the last column, the counts are based on all sites with data in the most recent year (because it is possible for a site to have data in the most recent year but not enough data to be a trend site); (1) Data covers the Gainesville, FL Metropolitan Statistical Area - see Appendix B for areas included; n/a not available.
Source: U.S. Environmental Protection Agency, Office of Air and Radiation, Air Quality Index Information, "Number of Days with Air Quality Index Values Greater than 100 and Trend Sites, 1990-2009, and at All Sites in 2009"

Maximum Air Pollutant Concentrations

	Particulate Matter 10 (ug/m^3)	Particulate Matter 2.5 (ug/m^3)	Ozone (ppm)	Carbon Monoxide (ppm)	Sulfur Dioxide (ppm)	Nitrogen Dioxide (ppm)	Lead (ug/m^3)
MSA[1] Level	35	19	0.056	n/a	n/a	n/a	n/a
NAAQS[2]	150	35	0.075	9	0.140	0.053	0.15
Met NAAQS[2]	Yes	Yes	Yes	n/a	n/a	n/a	n/a

Note: Data from exceptional events are not included; (1) Data covers the Gainesville, FL Metropolitan Statistical Area - see Appendix B for areas included; (2) National Ambient Air Quality Standards; n/a not available
Concentrations: Particulate Matter 10 (coarse particulate) - highest second maximum 24-hour concentration; Particulate Matter 2.5 (fine particulate) - highest 98th percentile 24-hour concentration; Ozone - highest fourth daily maximum 8-hour concentration; Carbon Monoxide - highest second maximum non-overlapping 8-hour concentration; Sulfur Dioxide - highest second maximum 24-hour concentration; Nitrogen Dioxide - highest arithmetic mean concentration; Lead - maximum running 3-month average
Units: ppm = parts per million; ug/m^3 = micrograms per cubic meter
Source: U.S. Environmental Protection Agency, CBSA Factbook 2009, Air Quality Statistics by City, 2009

Drinking Water

Water System Name	Pop. Served	Primary Water Source Type	Violations[1]	
			Health Based	Monitoring/ Reporting
GRU - Murphree WTP	178,344	Ground	0	0

Note: (1) Based on violation data from January 1, 2010 to December 31, 2010 (includes unresolved violations from earlier years)
Source: U.S. Environmental Protection Agency, Office of Ground Water and Drinking Water, Safe Drinking Water Information System (based on data extracted May 9, 2011)

Houston, Texas

Background

Back in 1836, brothers John K. and Augustus C. Allen bought a 6,642-acre tract of marshy, mosquito-infested land 56 miles north of the Gulf of Mexico and named it Houston, after the hero of San Jacinto. From that moment on, Houston has experienced continued growth.

By the end of its first year in the Republic of Texas, Houston claimed 1,500 residents, one theater, and interestingly, no churches. The first churches came three years later. By the end of its second year, Houston saw its first steamship, establishing its position as one of the top-ranking ports in the country.

Certainly, Houston owes much to the Houston ship channel, the "golden strip" on which oil refineries, chemical plants, cement factories, and grain elevators conduct their bustling economic activity. The diversity of these industries is a testament to Houston's economy in general.

Tonnage through the Port of Houston has grown to the point of its claim of being number one in the nation for foreign tonnage. The port is important to the cruise industry as well, and the Norwegian Cruise Line has sailed from Houston since 2003.

As Texas' biggest city, Houston has also enjoyed manufacturing expansion in its diversified economy. A revitalized downtown is home to Continental Airlines' worldwide headquarters, bringing in over 3,000 jobs from the suburbs. Landing at Houston's three airports are F-16s, jumbo jets, luxurious corporate jets, home-built aircraft, crop dusters and everything in between.

Not limited to being a manufacturing center, Houston boasts of being one of the major scientific research areas in the world. The presence of the Johnson Space Center has spawned a number of related industries in medical and technological research. The Texas Medical Center oversees a network of 45 medical institutions, including St. Luke's Episcopal Hospital, the Texas Children's Hospital, and the Methodist Hospital.

As a city whose reputation rests upon advanced research, Houston is also devoted to education and the arts. Rice University, for example, whose admission standards rank as one of the highest in the nation, is located in Houston, as are Dominican College and the University of St. Thomas.

Today, this relatively young city is home to a diverse range of ethnicities, including Mexican-American, Nigerian, American-Indian and Pakistani.

Houston also is patron to the Museum of Fine Arts, the Contemporary Arts Museum, and the Houston Ballet and Grand Opera. A host of smaller cultural institutions, such as the Gilbert and Sullivan Society, the Virtuoso Quartet, and the Houston Harpsichord Society enliven the scene. Two privately funded museums, the Holocaust Museum Houston and the Houston Museum of Natural Science, are historical and educational attractions, and a new baseball stadium, Minute Maid Park, was completed in 2000 in the city's downtown.

Houstonians are eagerly embracing continued revitalization. This urban comeback has resulted in a virtual explosion of dining and entertainment options in the heart of the city. The opening of the Bayou Place, Huston's largest entertainment complex, has especially generated excitement, providing a variety of restaurants and entertainment options in one facility. A new highly active urban park opened in 2007 on 12 acres in front of the George R. Brown Convention Center. Reliant Stadium, located in downtown Houston, is home to the NFL's Houston Texans. The stadium hosted Superbowl XXXVIII in 2004 and WrestleMania XXV in the spring of 2009.

Located in the flat coastal plains, Houston's climate is predominantly marine. The terrain includes many small streams and bayous, which, together with the nearness to Galveston Bay, favor the development of fog. Temperatures are moderated by the influence of winds from the Gulf of Mexico, which is 50 miles away. Mild winters are the norm, as is abundant rainfall. Polar air penetrates the area frequently enough to provide variability in the weather.

Rankings

General Rankings

- Houston was ranked #256 out of 375 metro areas in *Cities Ranked & Rated*. Criteria: cost of living; climate; crime; transportation; economy and jobs; education; arts and culture; health and healthcare; leisure; quality of life. *Cities Ranked & Rated, 2nd Edition, 2007*

- Houston was ranked #48 out of 379 metro areas in *Places Rated Almanac*. Criteria: health care; education; recreation; transportation; ambience; climate; crime; housing costs; jobs. *Places Rated Almanac, 7th Edition, 2007*

- The Houston metro area was selected one of America's "Best Cities to Live, Work and Play" by *Kiplinger's Personal Finance*. Criteria: population growth; percentage of workforce in the creative class (scientists, engineers, educators, writers, artists, entertainers, etc.); job quality; income growth; cost of living. *Kiplinger's Personal Finance, "Best Cities to Live, Work and Play," July 2008*

- *Men's Health Living* ranked 100 U.S. cities in terms of quality of life. Houston was ranked #93 and received a grade of F. Criteria: number of fitness facilities; air quality; number of physicians; male/female ratio; education levels; household income; cost of living. *Men's Health Living, Spring 2008*

Business/Finance Rankings

- The Houston metro area was identified as one of 10 "Cities Where the Recession is Easing." The metro area was ranked #4. Criteria: job growth; goods produced; home sale prices; unemployment rates. *Forbes.com, "Cities Where the Recession is Easing," March 3, 2010*

- The Houston metro area was identified as one of the most affordable major metropolitan areas in America by *Forbes*. The metro area was ranked #10 out of 15. Criteria: median asking price of homes for sale; median salaries of workers with bachelor's degrees or higher compared to a cost-of-living index; unemployment rates. *Forbes.com, "The Most Affordable Cities in America," January 7, 2011*

- Experian ranked the top 20 major U.S metropolitan areas by average debt per consumer. The Houston metro area was ranked #6. Criteria: average debt per consumer. Debt for this study includes credit cards, auto loans and personal loans. It does not include mortgages. *Experian, May 13, 2010*

- The Houston metro area was identified as one of the "Best U.S. Cities for Earning a Living" by *Forbes*. The metro area ranked #1. Criteria: median income; cost of living; job growth; number of companies on *Forbes* 400 best big company and 200 best small company lists. *Forbes.com, "Best U.S. Cities for Earning a Living," August 21, 2008*

- A.G. Edwards ranked America's 500 top-performing communities based on their residents' personal savings and investing behavior. The Houston metro area ranked #440 with an index score of 95.95 (national average = 100.00). A dozen statistical factors were measured including: participation in retirement savings plans; personal debt levels; and home ownership. *A.G. Edwards, "2007 Nest Egg Index," September 12, 2007*

- The Houston metro area was identified as one of the 10 best cities to find a job in 2009 by *Forbes*. The metro area ranked #9. Criteria: city unemployment rate; number of new jobs created in the previous six months. *Forbes.com, "10 Cities for Job Growth in 2009," January 5, 2009*

- Houston was cited as one of America's top metros for new and expanded facility projects in 2010. The area ranked #2 in the large metro area category (population over 1 million). *Site Selection, "2010 Top Metros," March 2011*

- Houston was identified as one of the best cities for new college graduates. The city ranked #1. Criteria: cost of living; average annual salary; unemployment rate; number of employers looking to hire people at entry-level. *Business Week, "The Best Cities for New Grads," July 20, 2010*

- Houston was identified as one of "The Most Inventive Towns in America." The city ranked #11. Criteria: places with the most patents overall, combining those of large companies and individual inventors. *The Wall Street Journal, July 22, 2006*

- *American City Business Journals* ranked America's 261 largest cities in terms of their resident's wealth. Houston ranked #170. Criteria: per capita income; median household income; percentage of households with annual incomes of $200,000 or more; median home value. *American City Business Journals, www.bizjournals.com, "Where the Money Is: America's Wealth Centers," August 18, 2008*

- The Houston metro area appeared on the Milken Institute "2010 Best Performing Metros" list. Rank: #10 out of 200 large metro areas. Criteria: job growth; wage and salary growth; high-tech output growth. *Milken Institute, "2010 Best Performing Metros"*

- The Houston metro area was selected as one of the best cities for entrepreneurs in America by *Inc. Magazine*. Criteria: job-growth data for 335 metro areas was analyzed for: recent growth trend (the current and prior year's employment growth rates, with the current year emphasized); mid-term growth (the average annual 2002-2007 growth rate); long-term trend (the sum of the 2002-2007 and 1996-2001 employment growth rates multiplied by the ratio of the 1996-2001 growth rate over the 2002-2007 growth rate); current year growth. The Houston metro area ranked #4 among large metro areas and #28 overall. *Inc. Magazine, "The Best Cities for Doing Business," July 2008*

- Houston was ranked #70 out of 145 regions worldwide in terms of its "Knowledge Competitiveness Index." The index attempts to measure the knowledge-based development taking place throughout the world and is based on 19 measures of economic performance that indicate a region's ability to translate its knowledge capacity into economic value. *Centre for International Competitiveness, World Knowledge Competitiveness Index 2008*

- *Forbes* ranked the 200 most populous metro areas in the U.S. in terms of the "Best Places for Business and Careers." The Houston metro area was ranked #33. Criteria: 12 metrics including costs (business and living), job growth (past and projected), income growth, educational attainment, projected economic growth, crime, cultural and recreational opportunities, net migration patterns, percentage of subprime mortgages handed out over a three-year period, and the number of highly ranked four-year colleges. *Forbes, "Best Places for Business and Careers," April 14, 2010*

Children/Family Rankings

- The Houston metro area was selected as one of the "Best Cities for Relocating Families" by Worldwide ERC and Primacy Relocation. The 2008 study looked at nearly 50 factors important to relocating families including: recent job growth; nearby top-ranked colleges; in-state tuition for four-year public colleges; population growth since 2000; pediatricians per 100,000 population; and a Green Living index. *Worldwide ERC and Primacy Relocation, "2008 Best Cities for Relocating Families"*

- *Fit Pregnancy* magazine ranked the 50 best U.S. cities in which to have a baby. Houston was ranked #35. Criteria: access to hospitals and doctors; affordability; birthing options; breastfeeding; child care; fertility laws/resources; maternal and infant health risk; parks/stroller friendliness; safety. *Fit Pregnancy, "The Best Cities in America to Have a Baby 2008"*

- Houston was chosen as one of America's "100 Best Communities for Young People." The winners were selected based upon detailed information provided about each community's efforts to fulfill five essential promises critical to the well-being of young people: caring adults who are actively involved in their lives; safe places in which to learn and grow; a healthy start toward adulthood; an effective education that builds marketable skills; and opportunities to help others. *America's Promise Alliance, "100 Best Communities for Young People, 2010"*

Dating/Romance Rankings

- Houston appeared on *Men's Health's* list of the most sex-happy cities in America. The city ranked #10 of 100. Criteria: condom sales; birth rates; sex toy sales; rates of chlamydia, gonorrhea, and syphilis. *Men's Health, "America's Most Sex-Happy Cities," October 2010*

- *Men's Health* ranked 100 U.S. cities in terms of best (and worst) marriages. Houston was ranked #78 (#1 = worst marriages). Criteria: rate of failed marriages; stringency of divorce laws; percentage of population who've split; number of licensed marriage and family therapists. *Men's Health, "Splitsville, USA," May 2010*

- Eli Lily and Company, in partnership with Sperling's BestPlaces, ranked the nation's 50 largest metro areas in terms of the "Most Romantic Cities for Baby Boomers." The Houston metro area ranked #10. Criteria: marriage and divorce rates among "baby boomers" age 45 to 60; great restaurants; dance studios; chocolate, jewelry and flower sales. *Eli Lily and Company, "Most Romantic Cities for Baby Boomers," April 20, 2007*

- The Houston metro area was selected as one of the "Best Cities for Relocating Singles" by Worldwide ERC and Primacy Relocation. The area ranked #23 out of the 100 largest metro areas in the U.S. Areas were selected based on the following criteria: recent job growth; recent singles population growth; overall population growth; affordable rental housing; cost-of-living index; expanded arts and recreation opportunities; ratio of single men and single women; affordability of quality higher education (including state residency requirements); diversity index; climate; population density. *Worldwide ERC and Primacy Relocation, "2008 Best Cities for Relocating Singles"*

- *Forbes* ranked the 40 most populous urbanized areas in the U.S. in terms of the "Best Cities for Singles." The Houston metro area ranked #25. Criteria: number of singles; cost of living alone; nightlife; culture; job growth; coolness; and online dating participation. *Forbes.com, "Best Cities for Singles," July 27, 2009*

Education Rankings

- Houston was selected as one of "America's Most Literate Cities." The city ranked #60 out of the 75 largest U.S. cities. Criteria: number of booksellers; library resources; Internet resources; educational attainment; periodical publishing resources; newspaper circulation. *Central Connecticut State University, "America's Most Literate Cities 2010"*

- Houston was identified as one of the 100 "smartest" metro areas in the U.S. The area ranked #83. Criteria: the editors rated the collective brainpower of the 100 largest metro area in the U.S based on their residents' educational attainment. *American City Business Journals, www.bizjournals.com, April 14, 2008*

- Houston was identified as one of "America's Brainiest Bastions" by *Portfolio.com*. The metro area ranked #121 out of 200. Portfolio.com analyzed levels of educational attainment in the nation's 200 largest metropolitan areas. The editors established scores for five levels of educational attainment, based on relative earning power of adult workers age 25 or older. Scores were determined by comparing the median income for all workers with the median income for those workers at a specified educational level. *Portfolio.com, "America's Brainiest Bastions," December 1, 2010*

- *Forbes* ranked the largest metro areas in the U.S. in terms of the "Best Cities for Young Professionals." The Houston metro area ranked #1out of 10. Graduates from six elite schools (Harvard, Stanford, Princeton, Rice, Northwestern and Duke) were tracked ten years after graduation to see where they settled down. Those rankings were combined with several other statistics: job growth; unemployment rate; average salary of college graduates; cost of living; number of large companies that are located in the city. *Forbes.com, "Best Cities for Young Professionals," June 17, 2010*

Environmental Rankings

- The Houston metro area was identified as one of "The Ten Biggest American Cities that are Running Out of Water" by *24/7 Wall St.* The metro area ranked #2 out of 10. *24/7 Wall St.* did an analysis of the water supply and consumption in the 30 largest metropolitan areas in the U.S. Criteria include: projected water demand as a share of available precipitation; groundwater use as a share or projected available precipitation; susceptibility to drought; projected increase in freshwater withdrawls; projected increase in summer water deficit. The editors chose ten cities that are likely to face severe shortages in the relatively near-term future. *24/7 Wall St., "The Ten Biggest American Cities that are Running Out of Water," November 1, 2010*

- Houston was selected as one of 22 "Smarter Cities" for energy by the Natural Resources Defense Council." Criteria: investment in green power; energy efficiency measures; conservation. *Natural Resources Defense Council, "2010 Smarter Cities," July 19, 2010*

- The Houston metro area was selected as one of "America's Most Toxic Cities" by *Forbes*. The metro area ranked #7 out of 10. The 80 largest metropolitan areas were ranked on the following criteria: air quality; water quality; Superfund sites; toxic releases. *Forbes, "America's Most Toxic Cities, 2011," February 28, 2011*

- *American City Business Journal* ranked 43 metropolitan areas in terms of their "greenness." The Houston metro area ranked #26. Criteria: Forty-one metros in which *ACBJ* has business weeklies, plus Indianapolis and Cleveland, were ranked based on 20 different indicators such as adoption of green technologies, utilization of environmentally sound practices, and air and water quality. *American City Business Journals, "Green City Index," March 11, 2010*

- 100 of the largest metro areas in the U.S. were analyzed in terms of their current drought severity. The Houston metro area ranked #96 (#1 = driest). The rankings were based on statistics such as long-term precipitation trends and patterns and the Palmer drought indices. *Sperling's BestPlaces, www.BestPlaces.net, "America's Drought-Riskiest Cities," November 2007*

- The U.S. Conference of Mayors and Wal-Mart Stores sponsor the Mayors' Climate Protection Awards Program. The awards recognize and honor mayors for outstanding and innovative practices that mayors are taking to increase energy efficiency in their cities, and to help curb global warming. Houston was a Large City Best Practice Model. *U.S. Conference of Mayors, "2009 Mayors' Climate Protection Awards Program"*

- *Business Week* identified the 15 metro areas that saw the steepest declines in ground-level ozone pollution between 1990 and 2005. The Houston metro area ranked #4. *Business Week, "America's Most Cleaned-Up Metro Areas," March 23, 2007*

- The Houston metro area appeared in *Country Home's* "Best Green Places" report. The area ranked #122 out of 379. Criteria: official energy policies; green power; green buildings; availability of fresh, locally grown food. *Country Home, "Best Green Places," 2008*

- Houston was highlighted as one of the 25 metro areas most polluted by year-round particle pollution (Annual PM 2.5) in the U.S. The area ranked #17. *American Lung Association, State of the Air 2011*

- Houston was highlighted as one of the 25 most ozone-polluted metro areas in the U.S. The area ranked #8. *American Lung Association, State of the Air 2011*

Health/Fitness Rankings

- Houston was named the winner of the 2007 Accessible America contest by the National Organization on Disability. The city was honored for its successful design of accessible programs, services and facilities for its citizens and visitors with disabilities. *National Organization on Disability, 2007 Accessible America Contest*

- Houston was selected as one of the 25 fattest cities in America by *Men's Fitness Online*. It ranked #6 out of America's 50 largest cities. Criteria: fitness centers and sport stores; nutrition; sports participation; TV viewing; overweight/sedentary; junk food; air quality; geography; commute; parks and open space; city recreational facilities; access to healthcare; motivation; mayor and city initiatives; state obesity initiatives. *Men's Fitness Online, 2009 Fittest/Fattest Cities*

- Houston was identified as a "2011 Asthma Capital." The area ranked #64 out of the nation's 100 largest metropolitan areas. Twelve factors were used to identify the most challenging places to live for people with asthma: estimated prevalence; self-reported prevalence; crude death rate for asthma; annual pollen score; annual air quality; public smoking laws; number of board-certified asthma specialists; school inhaler access laws; rescue medication use; controller medication use; uninsured rate; poverty rate. *Asthma and Allergy Foundation of America, "2011 Asthma Capitals"*

- Houston was identified as a 2009 "Spring Allergy Capital." The area ranked #73 out of 100. Three groups of factors were used to identify the most severe cities for people with allergies during the spring season: annual pollen levels; medicine utilization; access to board-certified allergists. *Asthma and Allergy Foundation of America, "Spring Allergy Capitals 2009"*

- Houston was identified as a 2010 "Fall Allergy Capital." The area ranked #32 out of 100. Three groups of factors were used to identify the most severe cities for people with allergies during the fall season: annual pollen levels; medicine utilization; access to board-certified allergists. *Asthma and Allergy Foundation of America, "Fall Allergy Capitals 2010"*

- *Men's Health* ranked 100 U.S. cities in terms of the quality of their tap water. Houston was ranked #75 and received a grade of C. Criteria: levels of total coliform bacteria, arsenic, lead, total trihalomethanes (linked to cancer), and halo-acetic acids; number of EPA water-system violations from 1995 to 2005. *Men's Health, March 2007*

- Houston was selected as one of America's noisiest cities by *Men's Health*. The city ranked #9 of 10. Criteria: laws limiting excessive noise; traffic congestion levels; airports' overnight flight curfews; percentage of people who report sleeping seven hours or less. *Men's Health, "Ranking America's Cities: America's Noisiest Cities," May 2009*

- Ortho-McNeil Neurologics, in partnership with Sperling's BestPlaces, analyzed 110 metro areas and identified those U.S. cities with the highest prevalence of factors that are most commonly associated with migraine headaches. The Houston metro area ranked #95. Criteria: number of migraine-related drug prescriptions per capita; lifestyle factors that can contribute to migraines; environmental factors that can trigger migraines; and consumption of migraine-triggering foods. *Ortho-McNeil Neurologics, "America's Migraine Hot Spots," March 14, 2006*

- An analysis of the "Best & Worst Cities for Sleep" was conducted by Sperling's BestPlaces. The study ranked America's 50 most populated metro areas. The Houston metro area ranked #48 (#1 = best city for sleep). Criteria: number of days residents didn't get enough rest or sleep during the past month; average length of daily commute; divorce rate; unemployment rate. *Sperling's BestPlaces, www.BestPlaces.net, "Best & Worst Cities for Sleep," 2006*

- The Houston metropolitan area was selected as one of the best metros for hospital care in America by HealthGrades. The rankings are based on a comprehensive study of patient death and complication rates in the nation's nearly 5,000 hospitals. Hospitals performing in the top 5% nationwide across 26 different medical procedures and diagnoses were identified. HealthGrades then ranked cities by the highest percentage of these Distinguished Hospitals for Clinical Excellence™. The Houston metro area ranked #22. *HealthGrades.com, "America's Top 50 Cities for Hospital Care," January 26, 2011*

- *Men's Health* ranked 100 U.S. cities in terms of cities "Where the Food is Sickening." Houston was ranked #49 and received a grade of C. The magazine arrived at their ratings by looking at data compiled by the Community Health Status Indicator Project to determine outbreaks of E. coli, salmonella-, and shigella-related infections. They then checked the CDC's Wonder database to see how many people died from tainted food. Finally, the magazine found out which states have adopted the current version of the FDA's uniform Food Code, which contains the most up-to-date rules for keeping restaurant kitchens clean. *Men's Health, October 2005*

- The American Academy of Dermatology ranked 26 U.S. metropolitan regions in terms of their residents knowledge, attitude and behaviors towards tanning, sun protection and skin cancer detection. The Houston metro area ranked #12. The results of the study are based on an online survey of over 7,000 adults nationwide. *American Academy of Dermatology, "Suntelligence: How Sun Smart is Your City," May 3, 2010*

- The Houston metro area appeared in the 2010 Gallup-Healthways Well-Being Index. The index, based on interviews with more than 353,000 Americans during 2009, asked individuals to assess their jobs, finances, physical health, emotional state of mind and communities. The metro area ranked #68 out of 162. Criteria: life evaluation; emotional health; work environment; physical health; healthy behaviors; basic access (basic needs optimal for a healthy life, such as access to food and medicine, having health insurance and feeling safe while walking at night). *Gallup-Healthways, "Well-Being Index 2010"*

- The Houston metro area was identified as one of "America's Most Stressful Cities" by *Forbes*. The metro area ranked #32. Criteria: median home price drop; unemployment rates; cost of living; air quality; sunny days; population density. *Forbes.com, "America's Most Stressful Cities," August 20, 2009*

- The Houston metro area was identified as one of "America's 20 Most Sedentary Cities" by *Forbes*. The metro area ranked #11. Criteria: percentage of overweight or obese people; percentage of people who had not engaged in any physical activity in the past 30 days; average number of hours of TV watched per week. *Forbes.com, "America's Most Sedentary Cities," October 29, 2007*

- 50 of the largest metro areas in the U.S. were analyzed in terms of their health and fitness by the American College of Sports Medicine in their "American Fitness Index." The Houston metro area ranked #42 (#1 = healthiest). Criteria: preventative health behaviors; levels of chronic disease; health care access; community resources and policies that support physical activity. *American College of Sports Medicine, "Health and Community Fitness Status of the 50 Largest Metropolitan Areas," May 24, 2010*

Pet Rankings

- Houston was identified as one of North America's most accommodating cities for travelers with pets. The city was ranked #1. Criteria: number of AAA Approved and Diamond rated pet-friendly hotels. *AAA, Traveling with your Pet: The AAA PetBook, 2006*

Real Estate Rankings

- *Fortune* ranked the 100 largest metro areas in the U.S. in terms of projected median home price change in 2010. The Houston metro area ranked #6. *Fortune, "The 2010 Housing Outlook," December 9, 2009*

- Houston was selected as one of the 10 best U.S. cities for real estate investment. The city ranked #7. *Association of Foreign Investors in Real Estate, "AFIRE News," January/February, 2011*

- Houston appeared on ApartmentRatings.com "Top Cities for Renters" list in 2009." The area ranked #71. Overall satisfaction ratings were ranked using thousands of user submitted scores for hundreds of apartment complexes located in the 100 most populated U.S. municipalities. *ApartmentRatings.com, "2009 Renter Satisfaction Rankings"*

- Houston appeared on ApartmentRatings.com "Top College Towns & Cities" for renters list in 2010." The area ranked #64. Overall satisfaction ratings were ranked using thousands of user submitted scores for hundreds of apartment complexes located in cities and towns that are home to the 100 largest four-year institutions in the U.S. *ApartmentRatings.com, "2010 College Town Renter Satisfaction Rankings"*

- The Houston metro area was identified as one of the "Top 25 Real Estate Investment Markets" by *FinestExperts.com*. The metro area ranked #4. Over 10,000 real estate markets were analyzed to identify the most suitable places for real estate investors to seek stability and growth. Criteria: employment; rental markets; growth levels as offset by foreclosures. *FinestExperts.com, "Top 25 Real Estate Investment Markets," January 7, 2010*

- The Houston metro area was identified as one of "America's Best Housing Markets" by *Forbes*. The metro area ranked #3. Criteria: housing affordability; rising home prices; percentage of foreclosures. *Forbes.com, "America's Best Housing Markets," February 19, 2010*

- The nation's largest metro areas were analyzed in terms of the percentage of households entering some stage of foreclosure in 2010. The Houston metro area ranked #104 out of 206 (#1 = highest foreclosure rate). *RealtyTrac, 2010 Year-End Metropolitan Foreclosure Market Report, January 27, 2011*

- The Houston metro area was identified as one of the "Best Cities to Buy a Home" by *Forbes*. The metro area ranked #1. Criteria: 2-year home price appreciation; vacancy rates; spread between monthly rent and mortgage payment at the median level. *Forbes.com, "Best Cities to Buy a Home," July 22, 2008*

- The Houston metro area appeared in a *Wall Street Journal* article ranking cities by "housing stress." The metro area was ranked #19 (#1 = most stress). Criteria: fraction of mortgage-holding homeowners with a monthly housing payment in excess of 30 percent of income; percentage of people without health insurance; unemployment rate. *The Wall Street Journal, "Which Cities Face Biggest Housing Risk," October 5, 2010*

- The Center for Housing Policy ranked 210 U.S metropolitan areas by the fair market rent for a two-bedroom unit. The Houston metro area was ranked #84. (#1 = most expensive) with a rent of $892. Criteria: Fair Market Rent (FMR) in effect during the fourth quarter of 2009 based on HUD's fiscal year 2010 FMRs. *The Center for Housing Policy, "Paycheck to Paycheck: Most to Least Expensive Rental Markets in 2009"*

Safety Rankings

- Symantec, the makers of Norton, in partnership with Sperling's BestPlaces, ranked the 50 largest cities in the U.S. in terms of their vulnerability to cybercrime. The city ranked #32. Criteria: number of cyberattacks and potential infections; level of Internet access; expenditures on computer hardware and software; wireless hotspots; broadband connectivity; Internet usage; online purchases. *Symantec, "10 Riskiest Cities for Cybercrime," March 22, 2010*

- Allstate ranked the 200 largest cities in America in terms of driver safety. Houston ranked #161. In addition, drivers were 29.5% more likely to have had an accident compared to the national average. Allstate researchers analyzed internal property damage reported claims over a two-year period (from January 2007 to December 2008) to ensure the findings would not be affected by external influences such as weather or road construction. A weighted average of the two-year numbers determined the annual percentages. The report defines an auto crash as any collision resulting in a property damage claim. *Allstate, "The 2010 Allstate America's Best Drivers Report™"*

- Houston was identified as one of the most dangerous large cities in America by CQ Press. All 34 cities with populations of 500,000 or more that reported crime rates in 2009 for murder, rape, robbery, aggravated assault, burglary, and motor vehicle thefts were ranked. The city ranked #9 out of the top 10. *CQ Press, City Crime Rankings 2010-2011*

- The National Insurance Crime Bureau ranked 366 metro areas in the U.S. in terms of per capita rates of vehicle theft. The Houston metro area ranked #25 (#1 = highest rate). Criteria: number of vehicle theft offenses per 100,000 inhabitants. *National Insurance Crime Bureau, "Hot Spots," May 17, 2010*

- The Houston metro area was identified as one of the "The Most Dangerous Metro Areas for Pedestrians" by Transportation for America and the Surface Transportation Policy Partnership. The metro area ranked #8 out of 52 metro areas with over 1 million residents. Criteria: area's population divided by the number of pedestrian fatalities in that area. *Transportation for America and the Surface Transportation Policy Partnership, "Dangerous by Design: Solving the Epidemic of Preventable Pedestrian Deaths (and Making Great Neighborhoods)," November 11, 2009*

Seniors/Retirement Rankings

- The Houston metro area was identified as one of "America's Most Affordable Places to Retire" by *Forbes*. The metro area ranked #4. Criteria: housing affordability; inflation; number of persons over 65 who are employed; net migration for persons over 65; percent of persons over 65 living below poverty level; doctors per capita; number of citizens tapping their Medicare benefits per thousand people. *Forbes.com, "America's Most Affordable Places to Retire," September 5, 2008*

- The Houston metro area was selected as one of "America's Best Places to Grow Old" by *Forbes*. The area was ranked #4 out of 10. Criteria: housing affordability; inflationary pressures; number of persons over 65 who are currently employed; net migration for persons over 65; percent of seniors living below poverty level; doctors per capita; number of citizens tapping their Medicare benefits per 1,000 people. *Forbes, "America's Best Places to Grow Old," December 12, 2008*

- The Houston metro area was selected as one of "The 10 Most Affordable Cities for Long-Term Care" by *U.S. News & World Report*. Criteria: costs at nursing homes, assisted living facilities, and adult day health care facilities; cost for licensed home health aides. *U.S. News & Word Report, "The 10 Most Affordable Cities for Long-Term Care," May 17, 2010*

Sports/Recreation Rankings

- Houston was selected as one of "The Most Miserable Sports Cities" by *Forbes*. The city was ranked #6. Criteria: postseason losses; years since last title; ratio of cumulative seasons to championships won. Contenders were limited to cities with at least 75 cumulative seasons in the four major sports leagues. *Forbes, "The Most Miserable Sports Cities," February 28, 2011*

- Houston appeared on the *Sporting News* list of the "Best Sports Cities" for 2010. The area ranked #14 out of 402 cities in the U.S. *Sporting News* takes a 12-month snapshot, roughly October to October, of each city's sports, putting a heavy premium on regular-season won-lost records (from the most recently completed season). Other criteria include: playoff berths, bowl appearances and tournament bids; championships; applicable power ratings; quality of competition; overall fan fervor as measured in part by attendance as percentage of venue capacity; abundance of teams (rewarding quality over quantity); stadium and arena quality; ticket availability and prices; franchise ownership; and marquee appeal of athletes. *Sporting News, "Best Sports Cities 2010," October, 2010*

- Houston was chosen as one of America's 25 best cities for running. The city was ranked #21. Criteria: number of running clubs per city; amount of land set aside for park usage; air quality; weather; crime rates; and results from a *Runner's World* poll in which readers ranked their favorite running cities. *Runner's World, "The 25 Best Running Cities in America," July 2005*

- Minute Maid Park (Houston Astros) was selected as one of PETA's "2010 Top 10 Vegetarian-Friendly Ballparks." The park ranked #3. *People for the Ethical Treatment of Animals, "2010 Top 10 Vegetarian-Friendly Ballparks"*

- Scarborough Research, a leading market research firm, identified the top local markets for avid NBA fans. The Houston DMA (Designated Market Area) ranked in the top 10 with 14% of consumers 18 years and over reporting that they are "very interested in the NBA." *Scarborough Research, April 24, 2006*

- *Golf Digest* ranked 330 metro areas in the U.S. in terms of golf. The Houston metro area was ranked #263. Criteria: access to golf; weather; value of golf; and quality of golf. *Golf Digest, "Metro Golf Rankings," August 2005*

Technology Rankings

- The Houston metro area was identified as one of 10 "Top Up-and-Coming Tech Cities" by *Forbes*. The metro area ranked #4. Criteria: regional innovation trends; important patents. *Forbes.com, "Top Up-and-Coming Tech Cities," March 11, 2008*

- The Houston metro area was identified as one of the "Top 14 Nano Metros" in the U.S. by the Project on Emerging Nanotechnologies. The metro area is home to 24 companies, universities, government laboratories and/or organizations working in nanotechnology. *Project on Emerging Nanotechnologies, "Nano Metros 2009"*

Transportation Rankings

- Houston was identified as one of America's worst cities for speed traps by the National Motorists Association. One city from each state was selected based on data from the National Speed Trap Exchange. The NSTE collects driver reported speed trap locations. *National Motorists Association, "The Worst Speed Trap Cities in North America," September 2010*

- The Houston metro area appeared on *Forbes* list of the best and worst cities for commuters. The metro area ranked #53 out of 60 (#1 is best). Criteria: travel time; road congestion; travel delays. *Forbes.com, "Best and Worst Cities for Commuters," February 16, 2010*

Women/Minorities Rankings

- Houston was ranked #86 out of 100 metro areas in *SELF Magazine's* ranking of America's healthiest places for women." A panel of experts came up with more than 50 criteria including death and disease rates, environmental indicators, community resources, and lifestyle habits. *SELF Magazine, "Secrets of America's Healthiest Women," December 2008*

- Houston appeared on *Black Enterprise's* list of the "Ten Best Cities for African Americans." The top picks were culled from more than 2,000 interactive surveys completed on www.blackenterprise.com and by editorial staff evaluation. The editors weighed the following criteria as it pertained to African Americans in each city: median household income; percentage of households earning more than $100,000; percentage of businesses owned; percentage of college graduates; unemployment rates; home loan rejections; and homeownership rates. *Black Enterprise, May 2007*

- Houston was selected as one of the "Top 10 Cities for Hispanics." Criteria: the prospect of a good job; a safe place to raise a family; a manageable cost of living; the ability to buy and keep a home; a culture of inclusion where Hispanics are highly represented; resources to help start a business; the presence of Hispanic or Spanish-language media; representation of Hispanic needs on local government; a thriving arts and culture community; air quality; energy costs; city's state of health and rates of obesity. *Hispanic Magazine, August 2008*

Miscellaneous Rankings

- Energizer Holdings, the makers of Edge® shave gel, in partnership with Sperling's BestPlaces, ranked 50 major metro areas in terms of everyday irritations. The Houston metro area ranked #2. Criteria: humidity levels; weather conditions; incidence of traffic delays and congestion; average commute times; frequency of flight delays and cancellations; rates of sleeplessness; underemployment; pollens and allergens; pests; comedy clubs per capita. *Energizer Holdings, "Most Irritation Prone Cities," July 23, 2010*

- Mars Chocolate North America, the makers of COMBOS®, in partnership with Sperling's BestPlaces, ranked 50 major metro areas in terms of their "manliness." The Houston metro area ranked #24. Criteria: number of home improvement stores, steak houses, pickup trucks, motorcycles, and manly occupations (fire fighters, police officers, construction workers, EMP personnel) per capita; salty snack sales; sports TV viewing habits. *Mars Chocolate North America, "America's Manliest Cities," June 22, 2010*

- Houston was selected as one of the "Worst Hair Cities" by naturallycurly.com. The city was ranked #8. Criteria: humidity levels; pollution; rainfall; average wind speeds; water hardness; beauty salons per capita. *naturallycurly.com, "Best/Worst Hair Cities," April 29, 2009*

- Houston was selected as one of the best cities for shopping in the U.S. by *Forbes.* The city was ranked #1.Criteria: number of major shopping centers; retail locations; Consumer Price Index (CPI); combined state and local sales tax. *Forbes, "America's 25 Best Cities for Shopping," December 13, 2010*

- The Houston metro area appeared in AutoMD.com's ranking of the "Best and Worst Cities for Auto Repair." The metro area ranked #27 (#1 is best). The 50 most-populated metro areas in the U.S. were ranked on three critical factors: repair affordability; price disparity range; shop integrity factor. *AutoMD.com, "Advocacy for Repair Shop Fairness Report," February 24, 2010*

- *Men's Health* examined the nation's largest 100 cities and identified "America's Most Political Cities." Houston was ranked among the ten least political at #9. Criteria: percentage of active registered voters; percentage of ballots counted of active registration; percentage of income donated to 2008 presidential election; campaign spending; percentage of registrants who voted in the 2008 primaries; percentage of voters in the 2004/2006 Senate election; percentage of voters in the 2004-2007 gubernatorial election. *Men's Health, "Ranking America's Cities: America's Most Political Cities," October 2008*

- Houston appeared on Procter & Gamble's list of the "Top-20 All-Time Sweatiest Cities." The city was ranked #5. The rankings are based on computer simulations of the amount of sweat a person of average height and weight would produce walking around for an hour in the average temperatures during the summer months, based on historical weather data during June, July and August from 2001-2008 for each city. *Procter & Gamble, Old Spice Press Release, "Top-20 All-Time Sweatiest Cities," July 1, 2009*

- The Houston metro area appeared on *Forbes* list of "America's Drunkest Cities." The area ranked #18. Criteria: 35 of the largest continental U.S. metro areas were chosen based on availability of data and geographic diversity. Each metro was ranked in five areas: state laws; drinkers; heavy drinkers; binge drinkers; and alcoholism. *Forbes.com, "America's Drunkest Cities," August 22, 2006*

- Scarborough Research, a leading market research firm, identified the top local markets for frequent sit-down restaurant patronage. The Houston DMA (Designated Market Area) ranked in the top 10 with consumers reporting an average of 4.0 visits within the past 30 days. *Scarborough Research, May 31, 2006*

Business Environment

CITY FINANCES

City Government Finances

Component	2008 ($000)	2008 ($ per capita)
Total Revenues	3,910,490	1,771
Total Expenditures	4,384,986	1,986
Debt Outstanding	12,813,681	5,803
Cash and Securities[1]	11,826,932	5,356

Note: (1) Cash and security holdings of a government at the close of its fiscal year, including those of its dependent agencies, utilities, and liquor stores.
Source: U.S Census Bureau, State & Local Government Finances 2008

City Government Revenue by Source

Source	2008 ($000)	2008 ($ per capita)
General Revenue		
From Federal Government	228,448	103
From State Government	72,670	33
From Local Governments	30,512	14
Taxes		
Property	934,980	423
Sales and Gross Receipts	751,471	340
Personal Income	0	0
Corporate Income	0	0
Motor Vehicle License	0	0
Other Taxes	66,420	30
Current Charges	873,397	396
Liquor Store	0	0
Utility	325,344	147
Employee Retirement	196,055	89

Source: U.S Census Bureau, State & Local Government Finances 2008

City Government Expenditures by Function

Function	2008 ($000)	2008 ($ per capita)	2008 (%)
General Direct Expenditures			
Air Transportation	460,088	208	10.5
Corrections	22,284	10	0.5
Education	0	0	0.0
Employment Security Administration	0	0	0.0
Financial Administration	43,951	20	1.0
Fire Protection	338,387	153	7.7
General Public Buildings	47,746	22	1.1
Governmental Administration, Other	42,733	19	1.0
Health	109,111	49	2.5
Highways	157,937	72	3.6
Hospitals	0	0	0.0
Housing and Community Development	88,550	40	2.0
Interest on General Debt	558,784	253	12.7
Judicial and Legal	45,912	21	1.0
Libraries	58,372	26	1.3
Parking	4,110	2	0.1
Parks and Recreation	158,518	72	3.6
Police Protection	601,785	273	13.7
Public Welfare	0	0	0.0
Sewerage	394,650	179	9.0
Solid Waste Management	73,891	33	1.7
Veterans' Services	0	0	0.0
Liquor Store	0	0	0.0
Utility	340,957	154	7.8
Employee Retirement	417,300	189	9.5

Source: U.S Census Bureau, State & Local Government Finances 2008

Municipal Bond Ratings

Area	Moody's	S&P	Fitch
City	Aa3	AA	AA-

Rating Systems (shown in declining order of credit quality): Moody's– Aaa, Aa, A, Baa, Ba, B, Caa, Ca, C (numerical modifiers 1, 2, and 3 are added to letter-rating); S&P– AAA, AA, A, BBB, BB, B, CCC, CC, C; Fitch– AAA, AA, A, BBB, BB, B, CCC, CC, C. Ratings may be modified by the addition of a plus or minus sign to show relative standing within the major rating categories.

Notes: n/a Not available; (1) Not reviewed; (2) Issuer Rating/No General Obligation; (3) Standard and Poor's Issue Credit Rating (ICR) is a current opinion of an obliger with respect to a specific financial obligation, a specific class of financial obligations, or a specific financial program.
Source: U.S. Census Bureau, 2011 Statistical Abstract, Bond Ratings for City Governments by Largest Cities: 2009

DEMOGRAPHICS

Population Growth

Area	1990 Census	2000 Census	2010 Estimate	2015 Projection	Population Growth (%) 2000-2010	2010-2015
City	1,697,610	1,953,631	2,269,768	2,451,441	16.2	8.0
MSA[1]	3,767,335	4,715,407	5,909,705	6,480,092	25.3	9.7
U.S.	248,709,873	281,421,906	309,038,974	321,675,005	9.8	4.1

Note: (1) Metropolitan Statistical Area - see Appendix B for areas included
Source: Claritas, Inc.

Number of Households and Average Household Size

Area	2010 Estimate	2010 Average Household Size
City	818,151	2.73
MSA[1]	2,041,580	2.85
U.S.	116,136,617	2.59

Note: (1) Metropolitan Statistical Area - see Appendix B for areas included
Source: Claritas, Inc.

Race and Ethnicity

Area	White Alone[2] (%)	Black Alone[2] (%)	Asian Alone[2] (%)	Other Race Alone[2] (%)	Hispanic[3] (%)
City	47.2	23.6	5.4	23.7	44.6
MSA[1]	59.0	16.6	5.6	18.8	34.5
U.S.	72.3	12.4	4.4	10.9	15.8

Note: Figures are 2010 estimates; (1) Metropolitan Statistical Area - see Appendix B for areas included (2) Alone is defined as not being in combination with one or more other races; (3) May be of any race.
Source: Claritas, Inc.

Segregation

Type	Segregation Indices[1] 1990	2000	2010	2010 Rank[2]	Percent Change 1990-2000	1990-2010	2000-2010
Black/White	65.5	65.7	61.4	36	0.1	-4.1	-4.2
Asian/White	48.0	51.4	50.4	7	3.4	2.4	-1.0
Hispanic/White	47.8	53.4	52.5	18	5.6	4.7	-0.9

Note: Figures are based on an analysis of 1990, 2000, and 2010 Census Decennial Census tract data by William H. Frey, Brookings Institution and the University of Michigan Social Science Data Analysis Network. In this analysis all racial groups (whites, blacks, and asians) are non-Hispanic members of those races. Hispanics are shown as a separate category; All figures cover the Metropolitan Statistical Area (see Appendix B for areas included); (1) Segregation Indices are Dissimilarity Indices that measure the degree to which the minority group is distributed differently than whites aross census tracts. They range from 0 (complete integration) to 100 (complete [segregation) where the value indicates the percentage of the minority group that needs to move to be distributed exactly like whites; (2) Ranges from 1 (most segregated) to 102 (least segregated); n/a not available.
Source: www.CensusScope.org

Ancestry

Area	German	Irish	English	American	Italian	Polish	French	Scottish
City	6.2	4.4	4.8	2.6	1.6	0.9	1.8	1.1
MSA[1]	10.0	6.9	6.6	4.5	2.3	1.3	2.8	1.4
U.S.	16.6	12.0	9.1	6.1	5.9	3.3	3.1	1.9

Note: The top eight ancestries in the U.S. are shown. Figures are percentages and include multiple ancestry (e.g. if a person reported being Irish and Italian, they were included in both columns); (1) Metropolitan Statistical Area - see Appendix B for areas included
Source: U.S. Census Bureau, 2007-2009 American Community Survey 3-Year Estimates

Foreign-Born Population

Area	Percent of Population Born in								
	Any Foreign Country	Mexico	Asia	Europe	Carribean	South America	Central America[2]	Africa	Canada
City	28.1	13.9	4.9	1.2	0.5	1.0	5.2	1.1	0.2
MSA[1]	21.5	10.2	4.6	1.0	0.5	1.0	3.1	0.8	0.2
U.S.	12.5	3.8	3.4	1.6	1.1	0.8	0.9	0.5	0.3

Note: (1) Metropolitan Statistical Area - see Appendix B for areas included; (2) Excludes Mexico.
Source: U.S. Census Bureau, 2007-2009 American Community Survey 3-Year Estimates

Marriage Status

Area	Never Married	Now Married[2]	Separated	Widowed	Divorced
City	36.9	44.5	3.5	5.0	10.0
MSA[1]	31.1	51.3	2.8	4.7	10.0
U.S.	31.4	49.7	2.2	6.2	10.6

Note: Figures are percentages and cover the population 15 years of age and older:
(1) Metropolitan Statistical Area - see Appendix B for areas included; (2) Excludes separated
Source: U.S. Census Bureau, 2007-2009 American Community Survey 3-Year Estimates

Age Distribution and Median Age

Area	Percent of Population							Median Age
	Under Age 5	Age 5 to 17	Age 18 to 34	Age 35 to 49	Age 50 to 64	Age 65 to 79	80 Years and Over	
City	8.8	18.0	27.9	21.2	15.2	6.5	2.4	32.0
MSA[1]	8.5	20.1	24.6	22.1	16.4	6.3	2.0	32.8
U.S.	6.9	17.5	23.3	21.4	18.1	9.1	3.7	36.7

Note: (1) Metropolitan Statistical Area - see Appendix B for areas included
Source: U.S. Census Bureau, 2007-2009 American Community Survey 3-Year Estimates

Male/Female Ratio

Area	Males	Females	Males per 100 Females
City	1,143,799	1,125,969	101.6
MSA[1]	2,958,164	2,951,541	100.2
U.S.	152,401,520	156,637,454	97.3

Note: Figures are 2010 estimates; (1) Metropolitan Statistical Area - see Appendix B for areas included
Source: Claritas, Inc.

Religion

Area	Catholic	Southern Baptist	United Meth-odist	ELCA[1]	LDS[2]	Presby-terian Church USA	Jewish Est.	Muslim Est.
County	18.2	14.3	5.0	0.5	0.7	1.1	1.1	1.4
U.S.	22.0	7.1	3.7	1.8	1.5	1.1	2.2	0.6

Note: Figures are the number of adherents as a percentage of the total population; Adherents are defined as all members, including full members, their children and the estimated number of other participants who are not considered members (e.g. the baptized, those not confirmed, those regularly attending services, etc.); (1) Evangelical Lutheran Church in America; (2) The Church of Jesus Christ of Latter Day Saints
Source: Reprinted with permission from Religious Congregations and Membership in the United States 2000 (Nashville, Glenmary Research Center, 2002) Copyright Association of Statisticians of American Religious Bodies. All rights reserved.

ECONOMY

Gross Metropolitan Product

Area	2006	2007	2008	2009	2009 Rank[2]
MSA[1]	346.3	375.5	403.2	407.8	4

Note: Figures are in billions of dollars; (1) Houston-Sugar Land-Baytown, TX Metropolitan Statistical Area - see Appendix B for areas included; (2) Rank ranges from 1 to 363
Source: The U.S. Conference of Mayors, "Pace of Economic Recovery: GMP and Jobs," January 2010

Economic Growth

Area	2006-2008 (%)	2009 (%)	2010 (%)	Rank[2]
MSA[1]	2.8	-0.2	3.1	66
U.S.	1.3	-2.5	2.2	–

Note: Figures are real Gross Metropolitan Product growth rates and represent annual average percent change: (1) Houston-Sugar Land-Baytown, TX Metropolitan Statistical Area - see Appendix B for areas included; (2) Rank ranges from 1 to 363
Source: The U.S. Conference of Mayors, "Pace of Economic Recovery: GMP and Jobs," January 2010

Metropolitan Area Exports

Area	2005	2006	2007	2008	2009	2009 Rank[2]
MSA[1]	41,747.9	53,281.0	62,814.7	80,015.1	65,820.9	2

Note: Figures are in millions of dollars; (1) Houston-Sugar Land-Baytown, TX Metropolitan Statistical Area - see Appendix B for areas included; (2) Rank ranges from 1 to 374
Source: U.S. Department of Commerce, International Trade Administration, Office of Trade & Industry Information, Manufacturing & Services

INCOME

Per Capita/Median/Average Income

Area	Per Capita ($)	Median Household ($)	Average Household ($)
City	23,910	44,923	65,640
MSA[1]	26,961	57,150	77,540
U.S.	27,034	52,795	71,071

Note: Figures are 2010 estimates; (1) Metropolitan Statistical Area - see Appendix B for areas included
Source: Claritas, Inc.

Household Income Distribution

Area	Percent of Households Earning							
	Under $15,000	$15,000 -24,999	$25,000 -34,999	$35,000 -49,999	$50,000 -74,999	$75,000 -99,000	$100,000 -149,999	$150,000 and up
City	15.0	11.7	12.5	16.3	17.6	9.7	9.7	7.5
MSA[1]	11.0	9.1	10.1	14.5	18.6	12.6	14.0	10.0
U.S.	12.1	10.2	10.6	15.0	19.5	12.5	12.1	8.0

Note: Figures are 2010 estimates; (1) Metropolitan Statistical Area - see Appendix B for areas included
Source: Claritas, Inc.

Poverty Rates by Age

Area	All Ages	Under 18 Years Old	18 to 64 Years Old	65 Years and Over
City	20.2	8.3	10.6	1.2
MSA[1]	14.7	6.1	7.7	0.9
U.S.	13.6	4.7	7.7	1.2

Note: Figures are percent of population with income during the previous 12 months below poverty level and only include population for whom poverty status is determined; (1) Metropolitan Statistical Area - see Appendix B for areas included
Source: U.S. Census Bureau, 2007-2009 American Community Survey 3-Year Estimates

Personal Bankruptcy Filing Rate

Area	2006	2007	2008	2009	2010
Harris County	1.48	1.72	1.50	1.76	2.07
U.S.	2.00	2.73	3.53	4.60	4.96

Note: Numbers are per 1,000 population and include Chapter 7 and Chapter 13 filings
Source: Federal Deposit Insurance Corporation, Regional Economic Conditions, March 17, 2011

EMPLOYMENT

Labor Force and Employment

Area	Civilian Labor Force			Workers Employed		
	Dec. 2009	Dec. 2010	% Chg.	Dec. 2009	Dec. 2010	% Chg.
City	1,054,206	1,080,233	2.5	972,933	994,389	2.2
MSA[1]	2,849,041	2,917,366	2.4	2,618,530	2,676,277	2.2
U.S.	152,693,000	153,156,000	0.3	137,953,000	139,159,000	0.9

Note: Data is not seasonally adjusted and covers workers 16 years of age and older;
(1) Metropolitan Statistical Area - see Appendix B for areas included
Source: Bureau of Labor Statistics, http://stats.bls.gov

Unemployment Rate

Area	2010											
	Jan.	Feb.	Mar.	Apr.	May	Jun.	Jul.	Aug.	Sep.	Oct.	Nov.	Dec.
City	8.4	8.2	8.2	7.9	7.9	8.4	8.5	8.3	8.1	8.0	8.2	7.9
MSA[1]	8.8	8.6	8.6	8.2	8.2	8.7	8.7	8.6	8.3	8.2	8.5	8.3
U.S.	10.6	10.4	10.2	9.5	9.3	9.6	9.7	9.5	9.2	9.0	9.3	9.1

Note: Data is not seasonally adjusted and covers workers 16 years of age and older; All figures are percentages; (1) Metropolitan Statistical Area - see Appendix B for areas included
Source: Bureau of Labor Statistics, http://stats.bls.gov

Projected Unemployment Rate

Area	2007 (%)	2009 (%)	2011 (%)	2013 (%)
MSA[1]	4.3	8.9	7.9	6.6

Note: (1) Metropolitan Statistical Area - see Appendix B for areas included
Source: The U.S. Conference of Mayors, "Pace of Economic Recovery: GMP and Jobs," January 2010

Employment by Occupation

Occupation Classification	City (%)	MSA[1] (%)	U.S. (%)
Sales and Office	23.5	24.5	25.4
Professional and Related	19.8	20.4	21.0
Service	18.5	16.0	17.2
Production, Transportation, and Material Moving	12.9	12.5	12.3
Management, Business, and Financial	12.3	14.5	14.1
Construction, Extraction, and Maintenance	12.9	11.8	9.2
Farming, Forestry, and Fishing	0.2	0.2	0.7

Note: Figures cover employed civilians 16 years of age and older;
(1) Metropolitan Statistical Area - see Appendix B for areas included
Source: U.S. Census Bureau, 2007-2009 American Community Survey 3-Year Estimates

Employment by Industry

| Sector | MSA[1] | | U.S. |
	Number of Employees	Percent of Total	Percent of Total
Government	385,000	15.0	17.2
Education and Health Services	313,100	12.2	15.2
Professional and Business Services	366,200	14.3	13.0
Retail Trade	273,400	10.6	11.4
Leisure and Hospitality	234,500	9.1	9.7
Manufacturing	218,700	8.5	8.8
Financial Activities	135,400	5.3	5.8
Wholesale Trade	132,400	5.2	4.2
Construction	173,600	6.8	4.1
Other Services	92,400	3.6	4.1
Transportation and Utilities	127,700	5.0	3.7
Information	31,300	1.2	2.1
Mining and Logging	83,500	3.3	0.6

Note: Figures cover non-farm employment as of December 2010 and are not seasonally adjusted;
(1) Metropolitan Statistical Area - see Appendix B for areas included
Source: Bureau of Labor Statistics, http://stats.bls.gov

Occupations with Greatest Projected Employment Growth: 2006 - 2016

Occupation[1]	2006 Employment	2016 Projected Employment	Numeric Employment Change	Percent Employment Change
Combined food preparation and serving workers, including fast food	270,530	359,050	88,520	32.7
Retail salespersons	332,750	411,350	78,600	23.6
Personal and home care aides	133,050	207,850	74,800	56.2
Customer service representatives	214,440	280,060	65,620	30.6
Elementary school teachers, except special education	145,430	207,710	62,280	42.8
Registered nurses	157,840	217,430	59,590	37.8
Waiters and waitresses	174,140	227,790	53,650	30.8
Child care workers	145,500	189,730	44,230	30.4
Office clerks, general	194,610	236,670	42,060	21.6
Postsecondary teachers	113,400	153,130	39,730	35.0

Note: Projections cover Texas; (1) Sorted by numeric employment change
Source: www.projectionscentral.com, State Occupational Projections, 2006-2016 Long-Term Projections

Fastest Growing Occupations: 2006 - 2016

Occupation[1]	2006 Employment	2016 Projected Employment	Numeric Employment Change	Percent Employment Change
Personal and home care aides	133,050	207,850	74,800	56.2
Network systems and data communications analysts	17,750	27,620	9,870	55.6
Medical assistants	34,790	53,500	18,710	53.8
Special education teachers, preschool, kindergarten, and elementary school	13,750	20,560	6,810	49.5
Physical therapist assistants	3,780	5,570	1,790	47.4
Special education teachers, middle school	6,270	9,170	2,900	46.3
Computer software engineers, applications	30,900	45,200	14,300	46.3
Physician assistants	3,810	5,540	1,730	45.4
Kindergarten teachers, except special education	12,850	18,690	5,840	45.4
Pharmacy technicians	24,420	35,050	10,630	43.5

Note: Projections cover Texas; (1) Sorted by percent employment change and excludes occupations with numeric employment change less than 1500
Source: www.projectionscentral.com, State Occupational Projections, 2006-2016 Long-Term Projections

Average Wages

Occupation	$/Hr.	Occupation	$/Hr.
Accountants and Auditors	33.75	Maids and Housekeeping Cleaners	8.51
Automotive Mechanics	19.89	Maintenance and Repair Workers	15.70
Bookkeepers	17.13	Marketing Managers	62.51
Carpenters	16.57	Nuclear Medicine Technologists	31.14
Cashiers	8.56	Nurses, Licensed Practical	20.81
Clerks, General Office	13.55	Nurses, Registered	33.26
Clerks, Receptionists/Information	12.55	Nursing Aides/Orderlies/Attendants	10.86
Clerks, Shipping/Receiving	13.76	Packers and Packagers, Hand	9.54
Computer Programmers	34.99	Physical Therapists	38.52
Computer Support Specialists	23.98	Postal Service Mail Carriers	23.98
Computer Systems Analysts	39.00	Real Estate Brokers	41.68
Cooks, Restaurant	8.85	Retail Salespersons	11.22
Dentists	n/a	Sales Reps., Exc. Tech./Scientific	31.19
Electrical Engineers	43.50	Sales Reps., Tech./Scientific	41.06
Electricians	21.13	Secretaries, Exc. Legal/Med./Exec.	14.22
Financial Managers	58.21	Security Guards	11.25
First-Line Supervisors/Mgrs., Sales	20.21	Surgeons	54.05
Food Preparation Workers	9.51	Teacher Assistants	9.80
General and Operations Managers	57.93	Teachers, Elementary School	24.70
Hairdressers/Cosmetologists	12.57	Teachers, Secondary School	26.30
Internists	88.74	Telemarketers	14.46
Janitors and Cleaners	9.60	Truck Drivers, Heavy/Tractor-Trailer	17.68
Landscaping/Groundskeeping Workers	10.28	Truck Drivers, Light/Delivery Svcs.	15.59
Lawyers	68.96	Waiters and Waitresses	8.80

Note: Wage data covers the Houston-Sugar Land-Baytown, TX - see Appendix B for areas included. Hourly wages for elementary/secondary school teachers and teacher assistants were calculated by the editors from annual wage data assuming a 40 hour work week; n/a not available.
Source: Bureau of Labor Statistics, Metro Area Occupational Employment and Wage Estimates, May 2009

RESIDENTIAL REAL ESTATE

Building Permits

Area	Single-Family			Multi-Family			Total		
	2009	2010	Pct. Chg.	2009	2010	Pct. Chg.	2009	2010	Pct. Chg.
City	2,579	2,452	-4.9	1,710	2,139	25.1	4,289	4,591	7.0
MSA[1]	22,369	22,330	-0.2	4,957	5,122	3.3	27,326	27,452	0.5
U.S.	441,100	447,300	1.4	141,900	157,300	10.9	583,000	604,600	3.7

Note: (1) Metropolitan Statistical Area - see Appendix B for areas included; figures represent new, privately-owned housing units authorized (unadjusted data); All permit data are based on estimates with imputation.
Source: U.S. Census Bureau, Manufacturing, Mining, and Construction Statistics, Building Permits, 2009, 2010

Homeownership Rate

Area	2005 (%)	2006 (%)	2007 (%)	2008 (%)	2009 (%)	2010 (%)
MSA[1]	61.7	63.5	64.5	64.8	63.6	61.4
U.S.	68.9	68.8	68.1	67.8	67.4	66.9

Note: (1) Metropolitan Statistical Area - see Appendix B for areas included
Source: U.S. Census Bureau, Housing Vacancies and Homeownership Annual Statistics: 2010

Housing Vacancy Rates

Area	Gross Vacancy Rate[2] (%)			Year-Round Vacancy Rate[3] (%)			Rental Vacancy Rate[4] (%)			Homeowner Vacancy Rate[5] (%)		
	2008	2009	2010	2008	2009	2010	2008	2009	2010	2008	2009	2010
MSA[1]	12.7	12.5	12.2	12.5	12.3	11.9	15.6	15.6	16.2	2.7	1.9	2.8
U.S.	14.4	14.5	14.3	11.1	11.3	11.3	10.0	10.6	10.2	2.8	2.6	2.6

Note: (1) Metropolitan Statistical Area - see Appendix B for areas included; (2) The percentage of the total housing inventory that is vacant; (3) The percentage of the housing inventory (excluding seasonal units) that is year-round vacant; (4) The percentage of rental inventory that is vacant for rent; (5) The percentage of homeowner inventory that is vacant for sale; n/a not available
Source: U.S. Census Bureau, Housing Vacancies and Homeownership Annual Statistics: 2010

State Corporate Income Tax Rates

State	Tax Rate (%)	Income Brackets ($)	Num. of Brackets	Financial Institution Tax Rate (%)[a]	Federal Income Tax Ded.
Texas	(y)	–	-	(y)	No

Note: Tax rates as of January 1, 2011; (a) Rates listed are the tax rates applied to financial institutions or excise taxes based on income. Some states have other taxes based upon the value of deposits or shares; (y) Texas imposes a Franchise Tax, otherwise known as margin tax, imposed on entities with more than $1,000,000 total revenues at rate of 1%, or 0.5% for entities primarily engaged in retail or wholesale trade, on lesser of 70% of total revenues or 100%of gross receipts after deductions for either compensation or cost of goods sold.
Source: Federation of Tax Administrators, "State Corporate Income Tax Rates, 2011"

State Individual Income Tax Rates

State	Tax Rate (%)	Income Brackets ($)	Num. of Brackets	Personal Exempt. ($)[1] Single	Dependents	Fed. Inc. Tax Ded.
Texas – No State Income Tax						

Note: Tax rates as of January 1, 2011; Local- and county-level taxes are not included; n/a not applicable; (1) Married joint filers generally receive double the single exemption
Source: Federation of Tax Administrators, "State Individual Income Tax Rates, 2011"

Various State and Local Tax Rates

State	State and Local Sales and Use (%)	State Sales and Use (%)	Gasoline[1] (¢/gal.)	Cigarette[2] ($/pack)	Spirits[3] ($/gal.)	Wine[4] ($/gal.)	Beer[5] ($/gal.)
Texas	8.25	6.25	20.0	1.41	2.40	0.20	0.20

Note: All tax rates as of January 1, 2011 except Spirits (Sept. 1, 2010); (1) The American Petroleum Institute has developed a methodology for determining the average tax rate on a gallon of fuel. Rates may include any of the following: excise taxes, environmental fees, storage tank fees, other fees or taxes, general sales tax, and local taxes. In states where gasoline is subject to the general sales tax, or where the fuel tax is based on the average sale price, the average rate determined by API is sensitive to changes in the price of gasoline. States that fully or partially apply general sales taxes to gasoline: CA, CO, GA, IL, IN, MI, NY; (2) The federal excise tax of $1.0066 per pack and local taxes are not included; (3) Rates are those applicable to off-premise sales of 40% alcohol by volume (a.b.v.) distilled spirits in 750ml containers. Local excise taxes are excluded; (4) Rates are those applicable to off-premise sales of 11% a.b.v. non-carbonated wine in 750ml containers; (5) Rates are those applicable to off-premise sales of 4.7% a.b.v. beer in 12 ounce containers.
Source: Tax Foundation, 2011 Facts & Figures: How Does Your State Compare?

State-Local Tax Burdens

Area	Rate (%)	Rank[1]	Per Capita Taxes Paid to Home State ($)	Total State and Local Per Capita Taxes Paid ($)	Per Capita Income ($)
Texas	7.9	45	2,248	3,197	40,498
U.S. Average	9.8	-	3,057	4,160	42,539

Note: Figures cover 2009; (1) Rank ranges from 1 to 50 where 1 is highest tax burden
Source: Tax Foundation, State-Local Tax Burdens, All States, 2009

State Business Tax Climate Index Rankings

State	Overall Rank	Corporate Tax Index Rank	Individual Income Tax Index Rank	Sales Tax Index Rank	Unemployment Insurance Tax Index Rank	Property Tax Index Rank
Texas	13	46	7	37	15	29

Note: The index is a measure of how each state's tax laws affect economic performance. The lower the rank, the more favorable a state's tax system is for business. All ranks are for fiscal years. States without a given tax are given a ranking of 1.
Source: Tax Foundation, Tax Foundation Background Paper, No. 60, "2011 State Business Tax Climate Index"

COMMERCIAL REAL ESTATE

Office Market

Market Area	Inventory (sq. ft.)	Vacant (sq. ft.)	Vac. Rate (%)	Under Constr. (sq. ft.)	Asking Rent ($/sf/yr) Class A	Class B
Houston	170,132,084	27,462,817	16.1	1,252,468	29.33	19.16

Source: Grubb & Ellis, Office Markets Trends, 1st Quarter 2011

Industrial Market

Market Area	Inventory (sq. ft.)	Vacant (sq. ft.)	Vac. Rate (%)	Under Constr. (sq. ft.)	Asking Rent ($/sf/yr) WH/Dist	R&D/Flex
Houston	430,476,061	27,762,068	6.4	608,972	4.50	7.28

Source: Grubb & Ellis, Industrial Markets Trends, 1st Quarter 2011

COMMERCIAL UTILITIES

Typical Monthly Electric Bills

Area	Commercial Service ($/month) 3 kW demand 1,000 kWh	40 kW demand 14,000 kWh	Industrial Service ($/month) 1,000 kW demand 200,000 kWh	50,000 kW demand 15,000,000 kWh
City	n/a	n/a	n/a	n/a
Average[1]	135	1,576	23,741	1,402,202

Note: Based on total rates in effect July 1, 2010; (1) average based on 182 utilities surveyed; n/a not available
Source: Edison Electric Institute, Typical Bills and Average Rates Report, Summer 2010

TRANSPORTATION

Means of Transportation to Work

Area	Car/Truck/Van Drove Alone	Car-pooled	Public Transportation Bus	Subway	Railroad	Bicycle	Walked	Other Means	Worked at Home
City	74.6	13.5	4.3	0.1	0.1	0.4	2.2	1.6	3.2
MSA[1]	78.3	12.3	2.5	0.0	0.0	0.3	1.5	1.6	3.4
U.S.	75.8	10.4	2.7	1.7	0.5	0.5	2.9	1.2	4.1

Note: Figures are percentages and cover workers 16 years of age and older;
(1) Metropolitan Statistical Area - see Appendix B for areas included
Source: U.S. Census Bureau, 2007-2009 American Community Survey 3-Year Estimates

Travel Time to Work

Area	Less Than 15 Minutes	15 to 29 Minutes	30 to 44 Minutes	45 to 59 Minutes	60 to 89 Minutes	90 Minutes or More
City	20.9	39.4	24.9	7.6	5.1	2.0
MSA[1]	20.6	34.7	24.9	10.1	7.4	2.3
U.S.	28.5	36.2	19.7	7.5	5.6	2.5

Note: Figures are percentages and include workers 16 years old and over;
(1) Metropolitan Statistical Area - see Appendix B for areas included
Source: U.S. Census Bureau, 2007-2009 American Community Survey 3-Year Estimates

Travel Time Index

Area	1982	1999	2008	2009
Urban Area[1]	1.18	1.25	1.28	1.25
Average[2]	1.08	1.20	1.20	1.20

Note: Travel Time Index—the ratio of travel time in the peak period to the travel time at
free-flow conditions. A value of 1.30 indicates a 20-minute free-flow trip takes 26 minutes
in the peak. Free-flow speeds (60 mph on freeways and 35 mph on principal arterials)
are used as the comparison threshold; (1) Covers the Houston-Sugar Land-Baytown urban area;
(2) average of 439 urban areas
Source: Texas Transportation Institute, Urban Mobility Report 2010, December 2010

Public Transportation

Agency Name / Mode of Transportation	Vehicles Operated in Maximum Service	Annual Unlinked Passenger Trips ('000)	Annual Passenger Miles ('000)
Metropolitan Transit Authority of Harris County (METRO)			
Demand response	415	1,482.7	16,708.1
Light rail	17	11,613.7	27,501.4
Bus	180	13,847.5	96,624.7
Bus	846	58,947.7	377,494.3
Vanpool	766	2,619.1	71,672.4

Note: Figures include both directly operated and purchased transportation
Source: Federal Transit Administration, National Transit Database, 2009

Air Transportation

Airport Name and Code / Type of Service	Passenger Airlines[1]	Passenger Enplanements	Freight Carriers[2]	Freight (lbs.)
George Bush Intercontinental (IAH)				
Domestic service (U.S. carriers - 2010)	30	15,342,604	31	194,652,392
International service (U.S. carriers - 2009)	16	3,153,429	17	57,496,801
William P. Hobby (HOU)				
Domestic service (U.S. carriers - 2010)	26	4,356,858	9	12,843,632
International service (U.S. carriers - 2009)	4	51	0	0

Note: (1) Includes all U.S.-based major, minor and commuter airlines that carried at least one passenger during the year; (2) Includes all U.S.-based airlines and freight carriers that transported at least one pound of freight during the year
Source: Bureau of Transportation Statistics, The Intermodal Transportation Database, Air Carriers: T-100 Domestic Market (U.S. Carriers), 2010; Bureau of Transportation Statistics, The Intermodal Transportation Database, Air Carriers: T-100 International Market (U.S. Carriers), 2009

Other Transportation Statistics

Interstate highways:	I-10; I-45
Amtrak service:	Yes
Major waterways/ports:	Gulf of Mexico; Port of Houston

Source: Amtrak.com; Google Maps

BUSINESSES

Major Business Headquarters

Company Name	Rankings	
	Fortune[1]	Forbes[2]
Apache	206	-
Baker Hughes	170	-
Calpine	349	-
Cameron International	375	-
CenterPoint Energy	279	-
ConocoPhillips	4	-
EOG Resources	377	-
El Paso	481	-
Enbridge Energy Partners	309	-
Enterprise Products Partners	80	-
Frontier Oil	389	-
Grocers Supply	-	128
Group 1 Automotive	413	-
Gulf States Toyota	-	76
Halliburton	144	-
KBR	242	-
Kinder Morgan	294	-
Marathon Oil	29	-
McJunkin Red Man	-	95
National Oilwell Varco	202	-
Plains All American Pipeline	99	-
Republic National Distributing Company	-	71
Spectra Energy	441	-

Sysco	67	-
Targa Resources	416	-
Waste Management	196	-

Note: (1) Fortune 500—companies that produce a 10-K are ranked 1 to 500 based on 2010 revenue; (2) all private companies with at least $2 billion in annual revenue are ranked 1 to 223; companies listed are headquartered in the city; dashes indicate no ranking
Source: Fortune, "Fortune 500," May 23, 2011; Forbes, "America's Largest Private Companies," November 3, 2010

Fast-Growing Businesses

According to *Inc.*, Houston is home to five of America's 500 fastest-growing private companies: **eCardio Diagnostics; Employer Flexible; GlobaLogix; Psychological Software Solutions; SightLine Health**. Criteria: must be an independent, privately-held, for-profit, U.S. corporation, proprietorship or partnership; revenues of at least $80,000 in 2006 and $2 million in 2009; four-year operating/sales history; holding companies, regulated banks, and utilities were excluded. *Inc., "America's 500 Fastest-Growing Private Companies," September 2010*

According to *Fortune*, Houston is home to one of the 100 fastest-growing companies in the world: **Atwood Oceanics**. Companies were ranked by their revenue growth rate; their EPS growth rate; and their three-year annualized total return to investors for the period ended June 30, 2010. Criteria for inclusion: a company, foreign or domestic, must trade on a major U.S. stock exchange; file quarterly reports with the SEC; have a minimum market capitalization of $250 million; have a stock price of at least $5 on June 30, 2010; have been trading continuously since June 30, 2007; have revenue and net income for the four quarters ended on or before April 30, 2010, of at least $50 million and $10 million, respectively; and have posted a compound annual growth in revenue and earnings per share of at least 15% annually over the three years ended on or before April 30, 2010. REITs, limited-liability companies, limited parterships, companies about to be acquired, and companies that lost money in the quarter ended April 30, 2010 were excluded. *Fortune, "100 Fastest-Growing Companies," September 6, 2010*

According to *Fortune*, Houston is home to two of America's 100 fastest-growing small public companies: **KMG Chemicals; OYO Geospace**. Companies were ranked by their three-year annualized rates of revenue growth and total return to investors for the period ended December 31, 2008. Criteria for inclusion: revenues of less than $200 million; stock price of at least $1. Banks, real-estate firms and adult entertainment companies were excluded. Also excluded were companies with losses in any of the four quarters ended on or before December 31, 2008. *Fortune Small Business, "America's Fastest-Growing Small Public Companies," July/August 2009*

According to Deloitte, Houston is home to seven of North America's 500 fastest-growing high-technology companies: **Additech; Alert Logic; BBS Technologies; Merrick Systems; PreCash; Psychological Software Solutions; RigNet**. Companies are ranked by percentage growth in revenue over a five-year period. Criteria for inclusion: company must be headquartered within North America; company must own proprietary intellectual property or proprietary technology that contributes to a significant portion of the company's operating revenue or devotes a significant proportion of revenues to research and development of technology; company must have been in business for a minumum of five years with 2005 operating revenues of at least $50,000 USD/CD and 2009 operating revenues of at least $5 million USD/CD. *Deloitte Touche Tohmatsu, 2010 Deloitte Technology Fast 500*[TM]

Minority Business Opportunity

Houston is home to one company which is on the Black Enterprise Industrial/Service 100 list (100 largest companies based on gross sales): **CAMAC International Corp.** Criteria: operational in previous calendar year; at least 51% black-owned and manufactures/owns the product it sells or provides industrial or consumer services. Brokerages, real estate firms and firms that provide professional services are not eligible. *Black Enterprise, B.E. 100s, 2010*

Houston is home to two companies which are on the Black Enterprise Auto Dealer 60 list (60 largest dealers based on gross sales): **Barnett Auto Group; Gulfgate Dodge Chrysler Jeep**. Criteria: company must be operational in previous calendar year and at least 51% black-owned. *Black Enterprise, B.E. 100s, 2010*

Houston is home to one company which is on the Black Enterprise Private Equity 15 list (15 largest private equity firms based on capital under management): **Capital Point Partners**. Criteria: company must be operational in previous calendar year and at least 51% black-owned. *Black Enterprise, B.E. 100s, 2010*

Houston is home to one company which is on the Black Enterprise Asset Manager 15 list (15 largest asset management firms based on assets under management): **Smith Graham & Co. Investment Advisors**. Criteria: company must be operational in previous calendar year and at least 51% black-owned. *Black Enterprise, B.E. 100s, 2010*

Houston is home to 20 companies which are on the *Hispanic Business 500* list (500 largest U.S. Hispanic-owned companies based on 2009 revenue): **G&A Partners; MEI Technologies; The Plaza Group; Reytec Construction Resources; Lopez Negrete Communications; Sweetlake Chemicals Ltd.; Taylor & Hill; Marimon Business Systems; MCA Communications; Today's Business Solutions; Traf-Tex; Tejas Office Products; Milam & Co. Painting; Tube America; TruckNation; Luis Auto Colors; Nino Corp. Lodging; Aviles Engineering Corp.; IDC; Aztec Communications Ltd.** Companies included must show at least 51 percent ownership by Hispanic U.S. citizens, and must maintain headquarters in one of the 50 states or Washington, D.C. *Hispanic Business, "Hispanic Business 500," June 2010*

Houston is home to five companies which are on the *Hispanic Business* Fastest-Growing 100 list (greatest sales growth from 2005 to 2009): **IDC; Sweetlake Chemicals Ltd.; G&A Partners; Today's Business Solutions; MEI Technologies.** Companies included must show at least 51 percent ownership by Hispanic U.S. citizens, and must maintain headquarters in one of the 50 states or Washington, D.C. In addition, companies must have minimum revenues of $200,000 for calendar year 2005. *Hispanic Business, July/August 2010*

Minority- and Women-Owned Businesses

Group	All Firms		Firms with Paid Employees			
	Firms	Sales ($000)	Firms	Sales ($000)	Employees	Payroll ($000)
Asian	22,816	10,795,130	6,868	10,054,883	47,334	1,317,577
Black	33,061	2,077,993	1,757	1,492,851	27,498	530,585
Hispanic	51,205	10,505,159	4,071	8,548,735	42,665	1,526,879
Women	63,434	18,013,795	7,358	16,448,338	88,485	3,287,647
All Firms	219,324	514,239,419	48,215	505,797,017	1,443,398	76,246,756

Note: Figures cover firms located in the city; minority- and women-owned business are defined as firms in which the corresponding group own 51% or more of the stock or equity of the company
Source: U.S. Census Bureau, 2007 Economic Census, Survey of Business Owners

HOTELS

Hotels/Motels

Area	5 Star		4 Star		3 Star		2 Star		1 Star		Not Rated	
	Num.	Pct.[3]	Num.	Pct.[3]	Num.	Pct.[3]	Num.	Pct.[3]	Num.	Pct.[3]	Num.	Pct.[3]
City[1]	3	0.6	21	4.0	126	24.3	290	55.9	11	2.1	68	13.1
Total[2]	119	0.7	927	5.8	4,906	30.5	7,992	49.7	526	3.3	1,625	10.1

Note: (1) Figures cover Houston and vicinity; (2) Figures cover all 100 cities in this book; (3) Percentage of hotels which are a given star rating; Star ratings are determined by expedia.com and offer an indication of the general quality of a particular hotel.
Source: expedia.com, May 5, 2011

The Houston metro area is home to two of the top 218 hotels in the U.S. according to *Travel & Leisure*: **Houstonian Hotel, Club & Spa** (#27); **St. Regis, Houston** (#203). Criteria: service; location; rooms; food; and value. *Travel & Leisure, "T+L 500, The World's Best Hotels 2011"*

The Houston metro area is home to two of the top 100 hotels in the U.S. according to *Condé Nast Traveler*: **Hotel Sorella** (#11); **Hotel Icon** (#69). The selections are based on over 25,000 responses to the magazine's annual Readers' Choice Survey. *Condé Nast Traveler, "2010 Readers' Choice Awards"*

EVENT SITES

Major Stadiums, Arenas, and Auditoriums

Name	Max. Capacity
Berry Center	11,000
Hobby Center for the Performing Arts	3,150
Houston Livestock Show & Rodeo Inc.	74,000
John O'Quinn Field at Corbin J. Robertson Stadium	32,000
Majestic Theatre	2,311
Minute Maid Park	40,950
Reliant Arena	5,800
Reliant Astrodome	67,925
Reliant Stadium	72,000
Rice Stadium	70,000
Toyota Center	19,300

Source: Original research

Convention Centers

Name	Overall Space (sq. ft.)	Exhibit Space (sq. ft.)	Meeting Space (sq. ft.)	Meeting Rooms
George R. Brown Convention Center	1,200,000	185,000	862,000	100

Source: Original research

Living Environment

COST OF LIVING

Cost of Living Index

Composite Index	Groceries	Housing	Utilities	Trans- portation	Health Care	Misc. Goods/ Services
92.2	85.1	82.0	97.7	99.2	94.6	99.9

Note: U.S. = 100; Figures cover the Houston TX urban area.
Source: The Council for Community and Economic Research, ACCRA Cost of Living Index, 2010

Grocery Prices

Area[1]	T-Bone Steak ($/pound)	Frying Chicken ($/pound)	Whole Milk ($/half gal.)	Eggs ($/dozen)	Orange Juice ($/64 oz.)	Coffee ($/11.5 oz.)
City[2]	6.97	0.94	1.98	1.31	2.64	2.93
Avg.	9.04	1.16	2.02	1.47	3.08	3.65
Min.	6.97	0.84	1.46	0.96	2.39	2.64
Max.	13.93	2.51	3.58	3.01	4.94	6.32

Note: (1) Values for the local area are compared with the average, minimum and maximum values for all 338 areas in the Cost of Living Index; (2) Figures cover the Houston TX urban area; **T-Bone Steak** *(price per pound);* **Frying Chicken** *(price per pound, whole fryer);* **Whole Milk** *(half gallon carton);* **Eggs** *(price per dozen, Grade A, large);* **Orange Juice** *(64 oz. Tropicana or Florida Natural);* **Coffee** *(11.5 oz. can, vacuum-packed, Maxwell House, Hills Bros, or Folgers).*
Source: The Council for Community and Economic Research, ACCRA Cost of Living Index, 2010

Housing and Utility Costs

Area[1]	New Home Price ($)	Apartment Rent ($/month)	All Electric ($/month)	Part Electric ($/month)	Other Energy ($/month)	Telephone ($/month)
City[2]	224,048	858	-	107.28	49.34	29.82
Avg.	293,442	810	166.39	91.93	83.82	26.93
Min.	182,545	453	119.21	44.47	36.85	17.98
Max.	1,123,114	2,776	307.53	218.20	313.90	39.15

Note: (1) Values for the local area are compared with the average, minimum and maximum values for all 338 areas in the Cost of Living Index; (2) Figures cover the Houston TX urban area; **New Home Price** *(2,400 sf living area, 8,000 sf lot, in urban area with full utilities);* **Apartment Rent** *(950 sf 2 bedroom/1.5 or 2 bath, unfurnished, excluding all utilities except water);* **All Electric** *(average monthly cost for an all-electric home);* **Part Electric** *(average monthly cost for a part-electric home);* **Other Energy** *(average monthly cost for natural gas, fuel oil, coal, wood, and any other forms of energy except electricity);* **Telephone** *(price includes basic monthly rate for a private residential line plus additional local usage charges incurred by a family of four).*
Source: The Council for Community and Economic Research, ACCRA Cost of Living Index, 2010

Health Care, Transportation, and Other Costs

Area[1]	Doctor ($/visit)	Dentist ($/visit)	Optometrist ($/visit)	Gasoline ($/gallon)	Beauty Salon ($/visit)	Men's Shirt ($)
City[2]	76.66	78.10	86.17	2.57	40.20	22.48
Avg.	89.44	78.95	87.40	2.73	31.92	24.83
Min.	57.00	54.25	48.32	2.44	19.17	13.67
Max.	149.90	136.73	174.22	3.75	62.81	47.89

Note: (1) Values for the local area are compared with the average, minimum and maximum values for all 338 areas in the Cost of Living Index; (2) Figures cover the Houston TX urban area; **Doctor** *(general practitioners routine exam of an established patient);* **Dentist** *(adult teeth cleaning and periodic oral examination);* **Optometrist** *(full vision eye exam for established adult patient);* **Gasoline** *(one gallon regular unleaded, national brand, including all taxes, cash price at self-service pump if available);* **Beauty Salon** *(woman's shampoo, trim, and blow-dry);* **Men's Shirt** *(cotton/polyester dress shirt, pinpoint weave, long sleeves).*
Source: The Council for Community and Economic Research, ACCRA Cost of Living Index, 2010

HOUSING

House Price Index (HPI)

Area	National Ranking[2]	Quarterly Change (%)	One-Year Change (%)	Five-Year Change (%)
MSA[1]	122	-0.02	-0.53	14.40
U.S.[3]	-	-0.84	-3.95	-11.45

Note: The HPI is a weighted repeat sales index. It measures average price changes in repeat sales or refinancings on the same properties. This information is obtained by reviewing repeat mortgage transactions on single-family properties whose mortgages have been purchased or securitized by Fannie Mae or Freddie Mac in January 1975; (1) Metropolitan/Micropolitan Statistical Area - see Appendix B for areas included; (2) Rankings are based on annual percentage change for all metro areas containing at least 15,000 transactions over the last 10 years and ranges from 1 to 309; (3) figures based on a weighted average of Census Division estimates; all figures are for the period ending December 31, 2010
Source: Federal Housing Finance Agency, House Price Index, February 24, 2011

House Price Valuations

Area	Q4 2005 Price ($000)	Q4 2005 Over-valuation	Q4 2006 Price ($000)	Q4 2006 Over-valuation	Q4 2007 Price ($000)	Q4 2007 Over-valuation	Q4 2008 Price ($000)	Q4 2008 Over-valuation	Q4 2009 Price ($000)	Q4 2009 Over-valuation
MSA[1]	110.1	-20.4	116.8	-23.4	122.0	-25.0	122.7	-26.3	127.4	-22.7

Note: Figures show the percentage of over- or under-valuation of single family homes relative to statistically normal house values (e.g. a value of 23.6 indicates that house values are 23.6% overvalued). Statistically normal house values are based on house prices, interest rates, household incomes, population densities, and any historical premiums or discounts metropolitan areas have exhibited over time; (1) Figures cover the Houston-Sugar Land-Baytown, TX Metropolitan Statistical Area - see Appendix B for areas included
Source: Global Insight/PNC Financial Services Group, House Prices in America: 4th Quarter 2009 Update

Median Single-Family Home Prices

Area	2008	2009	2010[p]	Percent Change 2009 to 2010
MSA[1]	151.6	153.1	155.0	1.2
U.S. Average	196.6	172.1	173.2	0.6

Note: Figures are median sales prices of existing single-family homes in thousands of dollars; (p) preliminary; n/a not available; (1) Metropolitan Statistical Area - see Appendix B for areas included
Source: National Association of Realtors, Median Sales Price of Existing Single-Family Homes for Metropolitan Areas, 4th Quarter 2010

Median Apartment Condo-Coop Home Prices

Area	2008	2009	2010[p]	Percent Change 2009 to 2010
MSA[1]	132.4	131.0	125.7	-4.0
U.S. Average	209.8	175.6	171.7	-2.2

Note: Figures are median sales prices of existing apartment condo-coop homes in thousands of dollars; (p) preliminary; n/a not available; (1) Metropolitan Statistical Area - see Appendix B for areas included
Source: National Association of Realtors, Median Sales Price of Existing Apartment Condo-Coop Homes for Metropolitan Areas, 4th Quarter 2010

Year Housing Structure Built

Area	2000 or Later	1990 -1999	1980 -1989	1970 -1979	1960 -1969	1950 -1959	1940 -1949	Before 1940	Median Year
City	13.5	9.0	14.4	26.8	15.2	11.8	4.9	4.5	1975
MSA[1]	21.0	14.5	17.5	22.3	10.4	7.9	3.3	3.0	1982
U.S.	12.5	14.0	14.2	16.5	11.4	11.3	5.8	14.3	1974

Note: Figures are percentages except for Median Year; (1) Metropolitan Statistical Area - see Appendix B for areas included
Source: U.S. Census Bureau, 2007-2009 American Community Survey 3-Year Estimates

HEALTH

Health Risk Data

Category	MSA[1] (%)	U.S. (%)
Adults who have been told they have high blood pressure	26.5	28.7
Adults who have been told they have high blood cholesterol	40.6	37.5
Adults who have been told they have diabetes[3]	7.8	8.3
Adults who have been told they have arthritis	18.9	26.0
Adults who have been told they currently have asthma	6.2	8.8
Adults who are current smokers	17.1	17.9
Adults who are heavy drinkers[4]	6.1	5.1
Adults who are binge drinkers[5]	15.9	15.8
Adults who are overweight (BMI 25.0 - 29.9)	37.1	36.2
Adults who are obese (BMI 30.0 - 99.8)	27.3	26.9
Adults who participated in any physical activities in the past month	74.2	76.2
Adults 50+ who have ever had a sigmoidoscopy or colonoscopy[2]	57.8	62.2
Women 40+ who have had a mammogram within the past two years[2]	74.5	76.0
Adults age 18–64 who have any kind of health care coverage	74.7	83.1

Note: Data as of 2009 unless otherwise noted; (1) Figures cover the Houston-Sugar Land-Baytown, TX Metropolitan Statistical Area - see Appendix B for areas included; (2) Data as of 2008; (3) Figures do not include pregnancy-related, borderline, or pre-diabetes; (4) Heavy drinkers are classified as males having more than two drinks per day or females having more than one drink per day; (5) Binge drinkers are classified as males having five or more drinks on one occasion or females having four or more drinks on one occasion
Source: Centers for Disease Control and Prevention, Behaviorial Risk Factor Surveillance System, SMART: Selected Metropolitan/Micropolitan Area Risk Trends, 2008, 2009

Mortality Rates for the Top 10 Causes of Death in the U.S.

ICD-10[a] Sub-Chapter	ICD-10[a] Code	Age-Adjusted Mortality Rate[1] per 100,000 population	
		County[2]	U.S.
Malignant neoplasms	C00-C97	172.2	180.9
Ischaemic heart diseases	I20-I25	125.6	135.0
Other forms of heart disease	I30-I51	54.2	50.0
Cerebrovascular diseases	I60-I69	53.4	44.1
Chronic lower respiratory diseases	J40-J47	32.2	41.5
Other degenerative diseases of the nervous system	G30-G31	24.1	23.6
Diabetes mellitus	E10-E14	23.1	23.5
Other external causes of accidental injury	W00-X59	27.0	23.5
Organic, including symptomatic, mental disorders	F01-F09	27.6	22.2
Influenza and pneumonia	J09-J18	16.8	18.1

Note: (a) ICD-10 = International Classification of Diseases 10th Revision; (1) Mortality rates are a three year average covering 2005-2007; (2) Figures cover Harris County
Source: Centers for Disease Control and Prevention, National Center for Health Statistics. Compressed Mortality File 1999-2007. CDC WONDER On-line Database, compiled from Compressed Mortality File 1999-2007 Series 20 No. 2M, 2010.

Mortality Rates for Selected Causes of Death

ICD-10[a] Sub-Chapter	ICD-10[a] Code	Age-Adjusted Mortality Rate[1] per 100,000 population	
		County[2]	U.S.
Assault	X85-Y09	10.3	6.0
Human immunodeficiency virus (HIV) disease	B20-B24	7.5	4.0
Hypertensive diseases	I10-I15	18.7	18.0
Intentional self-harm	X60-X84	9.6	11.0
Malnutrition	E40-E46	1.5	0.8
Obesity and other hyperalimentation	E65-E68	1.6	1.5
Transport accidents	V01-V99	14.3	15.6
Viral hepatitis	B15-B19	2.8	2.1

Note: (a) ICD-10 = International Classification of Diseases 10th Revision; (1) Mortality rates are a three year average covering 2005-2007; (2) Figures cover Harris County
Source: Centers for Disease Control and Prevention, National Center for Health Statistics. Compressed Mortality File 1999-2007. CDC WONDER On-line Database, compiled from Compressed Mortality File 1999-2007 Series 20 No. 2M, 2010.

Distribution of Physicians and Dentists

Area[1]	Dentists[2]	D.O.[3]	M.D.[4]				
			Total	Family/ General Practice	Pediatrics	Medical Specialties	Surgical Specialties
Local (number)	1,620	317	7,232	772	573	2,708	1,700
Local (rate[5])	4.1	0.8	18.2	1.9	1.4	6.8	4.3
U.S. (rate[5])	4.5	1.9	18.3	2.5	1.4	6.8	4.1

Note: Data as of 2008 unless noted; (1) Local data covers Harris County; (2) Data as of 2007; (3) Doctor of Osteopathic Medicine; (4) Includes active, non-federal, patient-care, office-based Doctors of Medicine; (5) rate per 10,000 population
Source: Area Resource File (ARF). 2009-2010 Release. U.S. Department of Health and Human Services, Health Resources and Services Administration, Bureau of Health Professions, Rockville, MD, August 2010

Hospitals

Houston has the following hospitals: 29 general medical and surgical; 7 psychiatric; 1 obstetrics and gynecology; 1 rehabilitation; 1 orthopedic; 1 cancer; 6 long-term acute care; 1 children's other specialty; 1 children's orthopedic.
AHA Guide to the Healthcare Field 2010

According to *U.S. News,* the Houston-Sugar Land-Baytown, TX Metropolitan Statistical Area is home to eight of the best hospitals in the U.S.: **Memorial Hermann-Texas Medical Center; Menninger Clinic; Methodist Hospital; St. Luke's Episcopal Hospital; TIRR Memorial Hermann; Texas Heart Institute at St. Luke's Episcopal Hospital; Texas Orthopedic Hospital; University of Texas M.D. Anderson Cancer Center**. The hospitals listed were highly ranked in at least one adult specialty. *U.S. News Online, "America's Best Hospitals 2010-11"*

According to *U.S. News,* the Houston-Sugar Land-Baytown, TX Metropolitan Statistical Area is home to three of the best children's hospitals in the U.S.: **Children's Cancer Hospital-University of Texas M.D. Anderson Cancer Center; Children's Memorial Hermann Hospital; Texas Children's Hospital**. The hospitals listed were highly ranked in at least one pediatric specialty. *U.S. News Online, "America's Best Children's Hospitals 2010-11"*

EDUCATION

Public School District Statistics

District Name	Schls	Pupils	Pupil/ Teacher Ratio	Minority Pupils[1] (%)	Free Lunch Eligible[2] (%)	IEP[3] (%)
Aldine ISD	72	61,526	14.8	96.7	72.5	7.4
Alief ISD	45	45,230	14.7	96.4	65.5	8.5
Cypress-Fairbanks ISD	78	100,685	15.7	62.9	33.6	7.4
Galena Park ISD	24	21,350	14.0	93.6	65.8	8.8
Houston ISD	296	200,225	16.7	92.2	52.9	8.4
Kipp Inc Charter	10	2,929	15.3	99.0	77.7	4.0
North Forest ISD	13	7,902	16.9	99.5	99.5	8.7
Sheldon ISD	9	6,206	16.1	86.4	64.1	5.8
Southwest School	5	2,309	23.3	57.1	24.7	9.5
Spring Branch ISD	49	32,409	14.1	68.8	46.9	9.2
Spring ISD	36	33,980	15.2	82.8	51.0	9.6
Yes Preparatory Public Schools	5	2,638	16.2	98.7	61.0	4.7

Note: Table includes school districts with 2,000 or more students; (1) Percentage of students that are not non-Hispanic white; (2) Percentage of students that are eligible for the free lunch program; (3) Percentage of students that have an Individualized Education Program.
Source: U.S. Department of Education, National Center for Education Statistics, Common Core of Data, Local Education Agency (School District) Universe Survey: School Year 2008-2009; U.S. Department of Education, National Center for Education Statistics, Common Core of Data, Public Elementary/Secondary School Universe Survey: School Year 2008-2009

Top Public High Schools

High School Name	Index[1]	Rank[1]	Subsidized Lunch (%)[2]	E&E (%)[3]
Carnegie Vanguard	5.873	30	29.0	77.8
Cesar Chavez	1.898	787	85.0	13.6
Challenge Early College	1.292	1382	58.0	50.7
Charles H Milby	1.188	1510	84.0	15.5
Clear Lake	1.933	768	11.0	26.5
Cypress Creek	1.204	1487	25.0	28.3
Debakey High School for Health Professions	4.569	71	49.0	97.4
Elsik	1.138	1562	70.0	11.6
HS for Law Enforcement and Criminal Justice	1.336	1329	76.0	16.1
Harmony Science Academy	1.229	1453	79.0	10.8
High School for Performing & Visual Arts	2.514	399	18.0	44.6
KIPP Houston	3.384	179	90.0	95.9
Klein Forest	1.101	1606	17.0	11.8
Langham Creek	1.317	1354	35.0	24.5
Memorial	3.119	225	11.0	53.7
Mirabeau B. Lamar[4]	2.175	597	n/a	n/a
Robert E Lee	3.531	152	91.0	22.0
Sam Houston Math, Science & Technology Center	1.412	1260		88.0
Scarborough	1.545	1103	82.0	48.4
Sharpstown	2.191	587	83.0	10.6
Stratford	2.588	376	23.0	44.4
Waltrip	1.215	1470	73.0	69.2
Westbury	2.049	684	74.0	9.6
Westside	2.746	317	44.0	34.5
YES Prep Southeast	3.769	117	76.0	56.1

Note: (1) Public schools are ranked according to a ratio that is the number of Advanced Placement, International Baccalaureate, and/or Cambridge tests taken by all students at a school in 2009 divided by the number of graduating seniors. All of the schools on the list have an index of at least 1.000; they are in the top six percent of public schools measured this way. The rankings range from 1 to 1,734; (2) Percentage of students receiving federally subsidized meals; (3) E & E stands for equity and excellence percentage: the portion of all graduating seniors at a school that had at least one passing grade on one AP or IB test; (4) Schools that offer International Baccalaureate or Cambridge exams; (5) School is unranked, but has been identified by Newsweek as one of the nation's most elite public high schools; n/a not available
Source: Newsweek Online, "Top High Schools 2010"

Highest Level of Education

Area	Less than H.S.	H.S. Diploma	Some College, No Deg.	Associate Degree	Bachelors Degree	Masters Degree	Profess. School Degree	Doctorate Degree
City	27.2	22.6	18.3	4.6	17.3	6.4	2.2	1.4
MSA[1]	20.2	24.6	21.3	6.0	18.7	6.3	1.8	1.2
U.S.	15.3	29.0	20.7	7.5	17.4	7.0	1.9	1.1

Note: Figures are 2010 estimated percentages and cover persons age 25 and over; (1) Metropolitan Statistical Area - see Appendix B for areas included
Source: Claritas, Inc.

Educational Attainment by Race

Area	High School Graduate (%)					Bachelor's Degree (%)				
	Total	White	Black	Asian	Hisp.[2]	Total	White	Black	Asian	Hisp.[2]
City	74.2	94.8	81.7	84.3	47.9	28.6	52.0	16.9	53.2	9.2
MSA[1]	79.9	92.8	85.1	86.2	53.8	28.3	38.5	20.6	52.4	10.2
U.S.	84.9	90.0	80.7	85.5	60.7	27.8	30.9	17.5	49.7	12.7

Note: Figures shown cover persons 25 years old and over; (1) Metropolitan Statistical Area - see Appendix B for areas included; (2) people of Hispanic origin can be of any race
Source: U.S. Census Bureau, 2007-2009 American Community Survey 3-Year Estimates

School Enrollment by Grade and Control

Area	Preschool (%)		Kindergarten (%)		Grades 1 - 4 (%)		Grades 5 - 8 (%)		Grades 9 - 12 (%)	
	Public	Private	Public	Private	Public	Private	Public	Private	Public	Private
City	68.3	31.7	91.9	8.1	92.6	7.4	92.6	7.4	92.6	7.4
MSA[1]	56.6	43.4	90.0	10.0	92.9	7.1	93.0	7.0	93.4	6.6
U.S.	54.3	45.7	86.4	13.6	88.9	11.1	89.1	10.9	90.2	9.8

Note: Figures shown cover persons 3 years old and over; (1) Metropolitan Statistical Area - see Appendix B for areas included
Source: U.S. Census Bureau, 2007-2009 American Community Survey 3-Year Estimates

Average Salaries of Public School Classroom Teachers

Area	2009-10		2010-11		Percent Change 2009-10 to 2010-11	Percent Change 2000-01 to 2010-11
	Dollars	Rank[1]	Dollars	Rank[1]		
Texas	48,261	31	48,261	34	0.00	25.8
U.S. Average	55,202	-	56,069	-	1.57	29.3

Note: (1) State rank ranges from 1 to 51 where 1 indicates highest salary.
Source: National Education Association, Rankings & Estimates: Rankings of the States 2010 and Estimates of School Statistics 2011, December 2010

Higher Education

Four-Year Colleges			Two-Year Colleges			Medical Schools[1]	Law Schools[2]	Voc/ Tech[3]
Public	Private Non-profit	Private For-profit	Public	Private Non-profit	Private For-profit			
6	7	9	1	1	11	2	3	35

Note: Figures cover institutions located within the city limits and include main campuses only; (1) includes schools accredited by the Liaison Committee on Medical Education and the American Osteopathic Association; (2) includes American Bar Association-accredited law schools; (3) includes all schools with programs that are less than 2 years.
Source: National Center for Education Statistics, Integrated Postsecondary Education System (IPEDS) Peer Analysis System, 2010-11; U.S. News & World Report, Medical School Directory, 2011; U.S. News & World Report, Law School Directory, 2011

According to *U.S. News & World Report,* the Houston-Sugar Land-Baytown, TX Metropolitan Statistical Area is home to one of the top 197 national universities in the U.S.: **Rice University** (#17). The rankings are based on quantitative measurements such as peer assessment, retention, faculty resources, student selectivity, financial resources, graduation rate, and alumni giving rate. *U.S. News & World Report, "America's Best Colleges 2011"*

According to *Forbes,* the Houston-Sugar Land-Baytown, TX Metropolitan Statistical Area is home to one of the top 75 business schools in the U.S.: **Rice (Jones)** (#47). The rankings are based on the return on investment that graduates of the Class of 2004 received (median salary five years after graduation). *Forbes, "Best Business Schools," August 5, 2009*

PRESIDENTIAL ELECTION

2008 Presidential Election Results

Area	Obama	McCain	Nader	Other
Harris County	50.4	48.8	0.1	0.7
U.S.	52.9	45.6	0.6	0.9

Note: Results are percentages and may not add to 100% due to rounding
Source: Dave Leip's Atlas of U.S. Presidential Elections, www.uselectionatlas.org

EMPLOYERS

Major Employers

Company Name	Industry	Type of Site
Bechtel Oil Gas and Chem	Heavy construction, nec	Headquarters
Christus Saint Catherine Hosp	Management consulting services	Single
Conocophillips	Petroleum refining	Headquarters
Continental Airlines	Air transportation, scheduled	Headquarters
El Paso E&P Company	Petroleum refining	Headquarters
F Charles Brunicardi Md	Professional organizations	Single
Grey Wolf	Drilling oil and gas wells	Headquarters
Houston V A Medical Center	Administration of veterans' affairs	Branch
Kellogs Brown & Root	Heavy construction, nec	Headquarters
Lyondell Chem Worldwide	Industrial organic chemicals, nec	Single
Mens Warehouse	Nonresidential building operators	Single
Methodist Hospital System The	General medical and surgical hospitals	Headquarters
NASA	Space research and technology	Headquarters
Office of Public Relations	Administration of veterans' affairs	Branch
Philip Industrial Services Usa	Business consulting, nec	Single
Quaker State Corporation	Lubricating oils and greases	Single
Rescue Rooter	Plumbing, heating, air-conditioning	Single
St Lukes Episcopal Health Sy	General medical and surgical hospitals	Headquarters
St Lukes Health Systems	General medical and surgical hospitals	Single
Texas Childrens Health Plan	Offices and clinics of medical doctors	Headquarters
Tracer Industries	Plumbing, heating, air-conditioning	Headquarters
University of Houston System	Colleges and universities	Branch
Wood Group Well Support	Environmental controls	Branch

Note: Companies shown are located within the Houston metropolitan area; nec = not elsewhere classified.
Source: www.zapdata.com, January 2011

Best Companies to Work For

Camden Property Trust; EOG Resources; Men's Wearhouse; The Methodist Hospital System, headquartered in Houston, are among the "100 Best Companies to Work For." To pick the 100 Best Companies to Work For, *Fortune* partnered with the Great Place to Work Institute. Three hundred eleven companies participated in this year's survey. Most of a company's score (two-thirds) is based on the results of the Institute's Trust Index survey, which is sent to a random sample of employees from each company. The survey asks questions related to their attitudes about management's credibility, job satisfaction, and camaraderie. The other third of the scoring is based on the company's responses to the Institute's Culture Audit, which includes detailed questions about pay and benefit programs, and a series of open-ended questions about hiring practices, internal communication, training, recognition programs, and diversity efforts. Any company that is at least seven years old with more than 1,000 U.S. employees is eligible. *Fortune, "100 Best Companies to Work For," February 7, 2011*

MEI Technologies; University of St. Thomas, headquartered in Houston, are among the "50 Best Employers for Workers Over 50." Criteria: recruiting practices; opportunities for training, education, and career development; workplace accommodations; alternative work options, such as flexible scheduling, job sharing, and phased retirement; employee health and pension benefits; and retiree benefits. Any employer with at least 50 employees based in the U.S. is eligible. This includes for-profit companies, not-for-profit organizations, and government employers. *AARP, "2009 AARP Best Employers for Workers Over 50"*

Baker Hughes; Transocean, headquartered in Houston, are among the "100 Best Places to Work in IT." To qualify, companies, both public and private, had to have a minimum of 50 IT employees. Companies were selected based on average salary and bonus increases, the percentage of IT employees receiving promotions, IT staff turnover rates, training and development programs, and the percentage of women and minorities in IT staff and management positions. In addition, information was collected on how the organizations reward outstanding performance, how their retention programs are structured and what benefits they offer. *Computerworld, "100 Best Places to Work in IT 2010"*

PUBLIC SAFETY

Crime Rate

Area	All Crimes	Violent Crimes				Property Crimes		
		Murder	Forcible Rape	Robbery	Aggrav. Assault	Burglary	Larceny -Theft	Motor Vehicle Theft
City	6,444.2	12.6	36.2	499.9	576.8	1,287.7	3,389.0	641.9
Suburbs[1]	3,802.3	4.9	24.9	134.2	277.1	876.1	2,197.5	287.6
Metro[2]	4,827.6	7.9	29.3	276.2	393.4	1,035.8	2,659.9	425.1
U.S.	3,465.5	5.0	28.7	133.0	262.8	716.3	2,060.9	258.8

Note: Figures are crimes per 100,000 population; (1) All areas within the metro area that are located outside the city limits; (2) Metropolitan Statistical Area - see Appendix B for areas included
Source: FBI Uniform Crime Reports, 2009

Hate Crimes

Area	Number of Quarters Reported	Bias Motivation				
		Race	Religion	Sexual Orientation	Ethnicity	Disability
City	4	4	1	5	4	0

Source: Federal Bureau of Investigation, Hate Crime Statistics 2009

Identity Theft Consumer Complaints

Area	Complaints	Complaints per 100,000 Population	Rank[2]
MSA[1]	6,056	107.6	43
U.S.	250,854	81.3	-

Note: (1) Metropolitan Statistical Area - see Appendix B for areas included; (2) Rank ranges from 1 to 384 where 1 indicates greatest number of complaints per 100,000 population
Source: Federal Trade Commission, Consumer Sentinel Network Data Book for January - December 2010

RECREATION

Culture

Dance[1]	Theatre[1]	Instrumental Music[1]	Vocal Music[1]	Series/ Festivals	Museums	Zoos and Aquariums[2]
7	12	6	4	12	22	2

Note: (1) Number of professional performing groups; (2) AZA-accredited
Source: The Grey House Performing Arts Directory, 2011-2012; Official Museum Directory, 2010; American Association of Museums, AAM Member Museums, March 2011; Association of Zoos & Aquariums, AZA Member Zoos & Aquariums, May 2011

Professional Sports Teams

Team Name	League
Houston Astros	Major League Baseball (MLB)
Houston Dynamo	Major League Soccer (MLS)
Houston Rockets	National Basketball Association (NBA)
Houston Texans	National Football League (NFL)

Note: Includes teams located in the Houston metro area.
Source: Original research

CLIMATE

Average and Extreme Temperatures

Temperature	Jan	Feb	Mar	Apr	May	Jun	Jul	Aug	Sep	Oct	Nov	Dec	Yr.
Extreme High (°F)	84	91	91	95	97	103	104	107	102	94	89	83	107
Average High (°F)	61	65	73	79	85	91	93	93	89	81	72	65	79
Average Temp. (°F)	51	54	62	69	75	81	83	83	79	70	61	54	69
Average Low (°F)	41	43	51	58	65	71	73	73	68	58	50	43	58
Extreme Low (°F)	12	20	22	31	44	52	62	62	48	32	19	7	7

Note: Figures cover the years 1969-1990
Source: National Climatic Data Center, International Station Meteorological Climate Summary, 9/96

Average Precipitation/Snowfall/Humidity

Precip./Humidity	Jan	Feb	Mar	Apr	May	Jun	Jul	Aug	Sep	Oct	Nov	Dec	Yr.
Avg. Precip. (in.)	3.3	2.7	3.3	3.3	5.6	4.9	3.7	3.7	4.8	4.7	3.7	3.3	46.9
Avg. Snowfall (in.)	Tr	Tr	0	0	0	0	0	0	0	0	Tr	Tr	Tr
Avg. Rel. Hum. 6am (%)	85	86	87	89	91	92	93	93	93	91	89	86	90
Avg. Rel. Hum. 3pm (%)	58	55	54	54	57	56	55	55	57	53	55	57	55

Note: Figures cover the years 1969-1990; Tr = Trace amounts (<0.05 in. of rain; <0.5 in. of snow)
Source: National Climatic Data Center, International Station Meteorological Climate Summary, 9/96

Weather Conditions

Temperature			Daytime Sky			Precipitation		
32°F & below	45°F & below	90°F & above	Clear	Partly cloudy	Cloudy	0.01 inch or more precip.	0.1 inch or more snow/ice	Thunder-storms
21	87	96	83	168	114	101	1	62

Note: Figures are average number of days per year and cover the years 1969-1990
Source: National Climatic Data Center, International Station Meteorological Climate Summary, 9/96

HAZARDOUS WASTE

Superfund Sites

Houston has seven hazardous waste sites on the EPA's Superfund Final National Priorities List: **Crystal Chemical Co.**; **Geneva Industries/Fuhrmann Energy**; **Jones Road Ground Water Plume**; **Many Diversified Interests, Inc.**; **North Cavalcade Street**; **Sol Lynn/Industrial Transformers**; **South Cavalcade Street**. *U.S. Environmental Protection Agency, Final National Priorities List, April 1, 2011*

AIR & WATER QUALITY

Air Quality Index

Area	Percent of Days when Air Quality was...[2]				AQI Statistics	
	Good	Moderate	Unhealthy for Sensitive Groups	Unhealthy	Maximum	Median
Area[1]	41.8	51.3	6.2	0.7	177	54

Note: The Air Quality Index (AQI) is an index for reporting daily air quality. EPA calculates the AQI for five major air pollutants regulated by the Clean Air Act: ground-level ozone, particle pollution (also known as particulate matter), carbon monoxide, sulfur dioxide, and nitrogen dioxide. The AQI runs from 0 to 500. The higher the AQI value, the greater the level of air pollution and the greater the health concern. There are six AQI categories: "Good" The AQI is between 0 and 50. Air quality is considered satisfactory; "Moderate" The AQI is between 51 and 100. Air quality is acceptable; "Unhealthy for Sensitive Groups" When AQI values are between 101 and 150, members of sensitive groups may experience health effects; "Unhealthy" When AQI values are between 151 and 200 everyone may begin to experience health effects; "Very Unhealthy" AQI values between 201 and 300 trigger a health alert; "Hazardous" AQI values over 300 trigger health warnings of emergency conditions; (1) Data covers Harris County; (2) Based on 306 days with AQI data in 2008; The EPA has suspended data updates while it assesses its data systems, including AirData reports and maps.
Source: U.S. Environmental Protection Agency, AirData Report, 2008

Air Quality Index Pollutants

Area	Percent of Days when AQI Pollutant was...[2]					
	Carbon Monoxide	Nitrogen Dioxide	Ozone	Sulfur Dioxide	Particulate Matter 2.5	Particulate Matter 10
Area[1]	0.7	0.0	45.4	0.0	44.8	9.2

Note: The Air Quality Index (AQI) is an index for reporting daily air quality. EPA calculates the AQI for five major air pollutants regulated by the Clean Air Act: ground-level ozone, particle pollution (also known as particulate matter), carbon monoxide, sulfur dioxide, and nitrogen dioxide. The AQI runs from 0 to 500. The higher the AQI value, the greater the level of air pollution and the greater the health concern; (1) Data covers Harris County; (2) Based on 306 days with AQI data in 2008; The EPA has suspended data updates while it assesses its data systems, including AirData reports and maps.
Source: U.S. Environmental Protection Agency, AirData Report, 2008

Air Quality Index Trends

Area	Trend Sites (days)								All Sites (days)
	2002	2003	2004	2005	2006	2007	2008	2009	2009
MSA[1]	44	55	42	58	35	28	18	18	31

Note: Figures are the number of days the AQI value exceeded 100 in a given year. An AQI value greater than 100 indicates that air quality would have been in the unhealthful range on that day. Data from exceptional events are included. These counts are presented in two ways. First, the counts are based on sites having an adequate record of monitoring data during the trend period (trend sites). These counts represent the relative change in the number of days with AQI values greater than 100. In the last column, the counts are based on all sites with data in the most recent year (because it is possible for a site to have data in the most recent year but not enough data to be a trend site); (1) Data covers the Houston-Sugar Land-Baytown, TX Metropolitan Statistical Area - see Appendix B for areas included
Source: U.S. Environmental Protection Agency, Office of Air and Radiation, Air Quality Index Information, "Number of Days with Air Quality Index Values Greater than 100 and Trend Sites, 1990-2009, and at All Sites in 2009"

Maximum Air Pollutant Concentrations

	Particulate Matter 10 (ug/m³)	Particulate Matter 2.5 (ug/m³)	Ozone (ppm)	Carbon Monoxide (ppm)	Sulfur Dioxide (ppm)	Nitrogen Dioxide (ppm)	Lead (ug/m³)
MSA[1] Level	102	26	0.091	2	0.03	0.014	0.01
NAAQS[2]	150	35	0.075	9	0.140	0.053	0.15
Met NAAQS[2]	Yes	Yes	No	Yes	Yes	Yes	Yes

Note: Data from exceptional events are not included; (1) Data covers the Houston-Sugar Land-Baytown, TX Metropolitan Statistical Area - see Appendix B for areas included; (2) National Ambient Air Quality Standards; n/a not available
Concentrations: Particulate Matter 10 (coarse particulate) - highest second maximum 24-hour concentration; Particulate Matter 2.5 (fine particulate) - highest 98th percentile 24-hour concentration; Ozone - highest fourth daily maximum 8-hour concentration; Carbon Monoxide - highest second maximum non-overlapping 8-hour concentration; Sulfur Dioxide - highest second maximum 24-hour concentration; Nitrogen Dioxide - highest arithmetic mean concentration; Lead - maximum running 3-month average
Units: ppm = parts per million; ug/m³ = micrograms per cubic meter
Source: U.S. Environmental Protection Agency, CBSA Factbook 2009, Air Quality Statistics by City, 2009

Drinking Water

Water System Name	Pop. Served	Primary Water Source Type	Violations[1] Health Based	Violations[1] Monitoring/ Reporting
City of Houston	2,700,000	Surface	0	0

Note: (1) Based on violation data from January 1, 2010 to December 31, 2010 (includes unresolved violations from earlier years)
Source: U.S. Environmental Protection Agency, Office of Ground Water and Drinking Water, Safe Drinking Water Information System (based on data extracted May 9, 2011)

Huntsville, Alabama

Background

The seat of Madison County, Huntsville is richly evocative of the antebellum Deep South. It is also a uniquely cosmopolitan town that remains one of the South's fastest growing, with the highest per capita income in the Southeast.

Huntsville became the seat of Madison County, named for President James Madison, when that jurisdiction was created in 1808. Originally home to Cherokee and Chickasaw Indians, the Huntsville area was rich in forests and game animals. The town itself is named for John Hunt, a Virginia Revolutionary War veteran who built a cabin in 1805 on what is now the corner of Bank Street and Oak Avenue.

The fertility of the valley began to attract both smaller farmers and wealthy plantation investors. Leroy Pope, having donated land to the embryonic municipality, wished to rename it Twickenham, after a London suburb that was home to his relative, the poet Alexander Pope. However, resentment against all things British, which surged following the War of 1812, was sufficient to reestablish Huntsville under its original moniker.

Huntsville was the largest town in the Alabama Territory by 1819, the same year Alabama received statehood. The town was the site of the state's first constitutional convention and briefly served as the state capital. It quickly became a major hub for the sale and processing of corn, tobacco, and cotton, with the last crop becoming the economic mainstay. The establishment of textile mills allowed the town to benefit from both primary production and finished products. In 1852, the last leg of the Memphis and Charleston Railway was completed, establishing Huntsville as a major center in a larger regional marketplace. By the middle of the nineteenth century, the region's planters, merchants, and shippers had transformed Huntsville into one of the main commercial cities in the South.

Because many wealthy residents had remained loyal to the Union at the outset of the Civil War, the town was largely undamaged by occupying forces and, as a result, Huntsville boasts one of the largest collections of undamaged antebellum houses in the South. Walking tours of the Twickenham historic district offer the charms of the 1819 Weeden House Museum and the 1860 Huntsville Depot Museum. Restored nineteenth-century cabins and farm buildings are displayed at the mountaintop Burritt Museum and Park.

Huntsville's U.S. Space and Rocket Center, the state's largest tourist attraction, showcases space technology. It is also the home of Space Camp, providing residential and day camp eductional opportunities for children and adults designed to promote science, engineering, aviation and exploration. The Huntsville Botanical Garden, features year-long floral and aquatic gardens, and the Huntsville Museum of Art features both contemporary and classical exhibits.

The city's modern Von Braun Center hosts national and international trade shows and conventions and local sports teams; it also has a concert hall and playhouse. The city also has an outstanding symphony orchestra.

Institutions of higher learning include the University of Alabama in Huntsville (established 1950), and Oakwood College (1896), while Alabama A&M University (1875) is in nearby Normal, Alabama.

Redstone Arsenal, home to the U.S. Army Aviation and Missile Command, is the main engine that propelled Huntsville into the high-tech hub it is today, and is the United States' most crucial strategic and research site for the development and implementation of rocketry, aviation, and related programs. In 1950, German rocket scientists, most notably the famous Wernher von Braun, came to the Redstone Arsenal to develop rockets for the U.S. Army. Within the decade, the Redstone complex had developed the rocket that launched America's first satellite into space, and later, the rockets that put astronauts into space and eventually landed them on the moon.

Despite the economic downturn of the early 1990s, Huntsville has seen progress on the manufacturing front. More than forty Fortune 500 companies have operations in Huntsville. Since 2003, Toyota in Huntsville has produced that company's only V8 engines outside of Japan, and Target has a major distribution center in town.

Huntsville enjoys a mild, temperate climate. Only four to five weeks during the middle of winter see temperatures below freezing. While substantial winter weather and blizzards were frequent in the 1990s, Huntsville has now gone over 13 years without significant snowfall. Rainfall is fairly abundant.

Rankings

General Rankings

- Huntsville was ranked #211 out of 375 metro areas in *Cities Ranked & Rated*. Criteria: cost of living; climate; crime; transportation; economy and jobs; education; arts and culture; health and healthcare; leisure; quality of life. *Cities Ranked & Rated, 2nd Edition, 2007*

- Huntsville was ranked #97 out of 379 metro areas in *Places Rated Almanac*. Criteria: health care; education; recreation; transportation; ambience; climate; crime; housing costs; jobs. *Places Rated Almanac, 7th Edition, 2007*

- The Huntsville metro area was selected one of America's "Best Cities" by *Kiplinger's Personal Finance*. Criteria: stable employment; income growth; cost of living; percentage of workforce in the creative class (scientists, engineers, educators, writers, artists, entertainers, etc.). *Kiplinger's Personal Finance, "Best Cities 2009: It's All About Jobs," July 2009*

- Huntsville was selected as one of "America's Top 100 Places to Live" by RelocateAmerica.com. Cities and towns nominated to be great places to live along with their key data regarding education, employment, economy, crime, parks, recreation and housing were reviewed, rated and judged by the Relocate-America.com editorial staff. *Relocate-America.com, "RelocateAmerica's Top 100 Places to Live in 2010"*

- Huntsville was selected as one of the "Best Places to Live" by *Men's Journal*. Criteria: "18 towns were selected that are perfecting the art of living well—places where conservation is more important than development, bike makers and breweries and farmers thrive, and Whole Foods is considered a big-box store." *Men's Journal, "Best Place to Live 2011: Think Small, Live Big," April 2011*

Business/Finance Rankings

- The Huntsville metro area was identified as one of the 10 best cities for job growth in 2010 by *USAToday* based on data from *Moody's Economy.com*. The metro area was ranked #2. Criteria: one-year forecast change in jobs from the 4th quarter 2009 to the 4th quarter 2010. *USAToday, "Jobs May Rebound in 2010," April 7, 2010*

- A.G. Edwards ranked America's 500 top-performing communities based on their residents' personal savings and investing behavior. The Huntsville metro area ranked #354 with an index score of 98.33 (national average = 100.00). A dozen statistical factors were measured including: participation in retirement savings plans; personal debt levels; and home ownership. *A.G. Edwards, "2007 Nest Egg Index," September 12, 2007*

- Huntsville was selected as one of the "100 Best Places to Live and Launch" in the U.S. The city ranked #86. The editors at *Fortune Small Business* ranked 296 Census-designated metro areas by business friendliness (Launching Score, % New Businesses) and lifestyle offerings (Living Score). Then they picked the town within each of the top 100 metro areas that best blends business and pleasure. *Fortune Small Business, "100 Best Places to Live and Launch 2008," April 2008*

- *American City Business Journals* ranked America's 261 largest cities in terms of their resident's wealth. Huntsville ranked #129. Criteria: per capita income; median household income; percentage of households with annual incomes of $200,000 or more; median home value. *American City Business Journals, www.bizjournals.com, "Where the Money Is: America's Wealth Centers," August 18, 2008*

- The Huntsville metro area appeared on the Milken Institute "2010 Best Performing Metros" list. Rank: #3 out of 200 large metro areas. Criteria: job growth; wage and salary growth; high-tech output growth. *Milken Institute, "2010 Best Performing Metros"*

- The Huntsville metro area was selected as one of the best cities for entrepreneurs in America by *Inc. Magazine*. Criteria: job-growth data for 335 metro areas was analyzed for: recent growth trend (the current and prior year's employment growth rates, with the current year emphasized); mid-term growth (the average annual 2002-2007 growth rate); long-term trend (the sum of the 2002-2007 and 1996-2001 employment growth rates multiplied by the ratio of the 1996-2001 growth rate over the 2002-2007 growth rate); current year growth. The Huntsville metro area ranked #5 among mid-sized metro areas and #32 overall. *Inc. Magazine, "The Best Cities for Doing Business," July 2008*

- *Forbes* ranked the 200 most populous metro areas in the U.S. in terms of the "Best Places for Business and Careers." The Huntsville metro area was ranked #8. Criteria: 12 metrics including costs (business and living), job growth (past and projected), income growth, educational attainment, projected economic growth, crime, cultural and recreational opportunities, net migration patterns, percentage of subprime mortgages handed out over a three-year period, and the number of highly ranked four-year colleges. *Forbes, "Best Places for Business and Careers," April 14, 2010*

Children/Family Rankings

- The Huntsville metro area was selected as one of the "Best Cities for Relocating Families" by Worldwide ERC and Primacy Relocation. The 2008 study looked at nearly 50 factors important to relocating families including: recent job growth; nearby top-ranked colleges; in-state tuition for four-year public colleges; population growth since 2000; pediatricians per 100,000 population; and a Green Living index. *Worldwide ERC and Primacy Relocation, "2008 Best Cities for Relocating Families"*

- Huntsville was chosen as one of America's "100 Best Communities for Young People." The winners were selected based upon detailed information provided about each community's efforts to fulfill five essential promises critical to the well-being of young people: caring adults who are actively involved in their lives; safe places in which to learn and grow; a healthy start toward adulthood; an effective education that builds marketable skills; and opportunities to help others. *America's Promise Alliance, "100 Best Communities for Young People, 2010"*

Education Rankings

- Huntsville was identified as one of "America's Brainiest Bastions" by *Portfolio.com*. The metro area ranked #38 out of 200. Portfolio.com analyzed levels of educational attainment in the nation's 200 largest metropolitan areas. The editors established scores for five levels of educational attainment, based on relative earning power of adult workers age 25 or older. Scores were determined by comparing the median income for all workers with the median income for those workers at a specified educational level. *Portfolio.com, "America's Brainiest Bastions," December 1, 2010*

Environmental Rankings

- Huntsville was selected as one of 22 "Smarter Cities" for energy by the Natural Resources Defense Council." Criteria: investment in green power; energy efficiency measures; conservation. *Natural Resources Defense Council, "2010 Smarter Cities," July 19, 2010*

- Huntsville was selected as one of "America's 50 Greenest Cities" by *Popular Science*. The city ranked #18. Criteria: electricity; transportation; green living; recycling and green perspective. *Popular Science, February 2008*

- The Huntsville metro area appeared in *Country Home's* "Best Green Places" report. The area ranked #361 out of 379. Criteria: official energy policies; green power; green buildings; availability of fresh, locally grown food. *Country Home, "Best Green Places," 2008*

Health/Fitness Rankings

- The Huntsville metro area appeared in the 2010 Gallup-Healthways Well-Being Index. The index, based on interviews with more than 353,000 Americans during 2009, asked individuals to assess their jobs, finances, physical health, emotional state of mind and communities. The metro area ranked #40 out of 162. Criteria: life evaluation; emotional health; work environment; physical health; healthy behaviors; basic access (basic needs optimal for a healthy life, such as access to food and medicine, having health insurance and feeling safe while walking at night). *Gallup-Healthways, "Well-Being Index 2010"*

Real Estate Rankings

- The nation's largest metro areas were analyzed in terms of the percentage of households entering some stage of foreclosure in 2010. The Huntsville metro area ranked #158 out of 206 (#1 = highest foreclosure rate). *RealtyTrac, 2010 Year-End Metropolitan Foreclosure Market Report, January 27, 2011*

Safety Rankings

- Allstate ranked the 200 largest cities in America in terms of driver safety. Huntsville ranked #8. In addition, drivers were 18.1% less likely to have had an accident compared to the national average. Allstate researchers analyzed internal property damage reported claims over a two-year period (from January 2007 to December 2008) to ensure the findings would not be affected by external influences such as weather or road construction. A weighted average of the two-year numbers determined the annual percentages. The report defines an auto crash as any collision resulting in a property damage claim. *Allstate, "The 2010 Allstate America's Best Drivers Report™"*

- The National Insurance Crime Bureau ranked 366 metro areas in the U.S. in terms of per capita rates of vehicle theft. The Huntsville metro area ranked #133 (#1 = highest rate). Criteria: number of vehicle theft offenses per 100,000 inhabitants. *National Insurance Crime Bureau, "Hot Spots," May 17, 2010*

Seniors/Retirement Rankings

- Huntsville was selected as one of the best places to retire by *Money*. The city was ranked #8 out of 25. Criteria: notable lifelong-learning programs; low taxes; affordable housing; high-quality health care; rich intellectual environment. *CNNMoney, "Best Places to Retire 2010"*

Sports/Recreation Rankings

- Huntsville appeared on the *Sporting News* list of the "Best Sports Cities" for 2010. The area ranked #260 out of 402 cities in the U.S. *Sporting News* takes a 12-month snapshot, roughly October to October, of each city's sports, putting a heavy premium on regular-season won-lost records (from the most recently completed season). Other criteria include: playoff berths, bowl appearances and tournament bids; championships; applicable power ratings; quality of competition; overall fan fervor as measured in part by attendance as percentage of venue capacity; abundance of teams (rewarding quality over quantity); stadium and arena quality; ticket availability and prices; franchise ownership; and marquee appeal of athletes. *Sporting News, "Best Sports Cities 2010," October, 2010*

- *Golf Digest* ranked 330 metro areas in the U.S. in terms of golf. The Huntsville metro area was ranked #177. Criteria: access to golf; weather; value of golf; and quality of golf. *Golf Digest, "Metro Golf Rankings," August 2005*

Business Environment

CITY FINANCES

City Government Finances

Component	2008 ($000)	2008 ($ per capita)
Total Revenues	790,977	4,617
Total Expenditures	745,601	4,352
Debt Outstanding	745,667	4,352
Cash and Securities[1]	420,553	2,455

Note: (1) Cash and security holdings of a government at the close of its fiscal year, including those of its dependent agencies, utilities, and liquor stores.
Source: U.S Census Bureau, State & Local Government Finances 2008

City Government Revenue by Source

Source	2008 ($000)	2008 ($ per capita)
General Revenue		
From Federal Government	3,071	18
From State Government	23,278	136
From Local Governments	3,074	18
Taxes		
Property	43,153	252
Sales and Gross Receipts	152,758	892
Personal Income	0	0
Corporate Income	0	0
Motor Vehicle License	0	0
Other Taxes	26,072	152
Current Charges	54,325	317
Liquor Store	0	0
Utility	446,750	2,608
Employee Retirement	0	0

Source: U.S Census Bureau, State & Local Government Finances 2008

City Government Expenditures by Function

Function	2008 ($000)	2008 ($ per capita)	2008 (%)
General Direct Expenditures			
Air Transportation	0	0	0.0
Corrections	127	1	0.0
Education	0	0	0.0
Employment Security Administration	0	0	0.0
Financial Administration	7,142	42	1.0
Fire Protection	27,922	163	3.7
General Public Buildings	16,926	99	2.3
Governmental Administration, Other	2,380	14	0.3
Health	3,830	22	0.5
Highways	17,176	100	2.3
Hospitals	0	0	0.0
Housing and Community Development	11,542	67	1.5
Interest on General Debt	22,141	129	3.0
Judicial and Legal	4,102	24	0.6
Libraries	5,575	33	0.7
Parking	1,779	10	0.2
Parks and Recreation	19,997	117	2.7
Police Protection	35,622	208	4.8
Public Welfare	0	0	0.0
Sewerage	12,738	74	1.7
Solid Waste Management	10,539	62	1.4
Veterans' Services	0	0	0.0
Liquor Store	0	0	0.0
Utility	465,373	2,716	62.4
Employee Retirement	0	0	0.0

Source: U.S Census Bureau, State & Local Government Finances 2008

Municipal Bond Ratings

Area	Moody's	S&P	Fitch
City	Aaa	AAA	n/a

Rating Systems (shown in declining order of credit quality): Moody's– Aaa, Aa, A, Baa, Ba, B, Caa, Ca, C (numerical modifiers 1, 2, and 3 are added to letter-rating); S&P– AAA, AA, A, BBB, BB, B, CCC, CC, C; Fitch– AAA, AA, A, BBB, BB, B, CCC, CC, C. Ratings may be modified by the addition of a plus or minus sign to show relative standing within the major rating categories.

Notes: n/a Not available; (1) Not reviewed; (2) Issuer Rating/No General Obligation; (3) Standard and Poor's Issue Credit Rating (ICR) is a current opinion of an obliger with respect to a specific financial obligation, a specific class of financial obligations, or a specific financial program.

Source: City of Huntsville, Alabama, Comprehensive Annual Financial Report, Fiscal Year Ended September 30, 2010

DEMOGRAPHICS

Population Growth

Area	1990 Census	2000 Census	2010 Estimate	2015 Projection	Population Growth (%) 2000-2010	Population Growth (%) 2010-2015
City	161,842	158,216	176,195	185,173	11.4	5.1
MSA[1]	293,047	342,376	407,220	437,840	18.9	7.5
U.S.	248,709,873	281,421,906	309,038,974	321,675,005	9.8	4.1

Note: (1) Metropolitan Statistical Area - see Appendix B for areas included
Source: Claritas, Inc.

Number of Households and Average Household Size

Area	2010 Estimate	2010 Average Household Size
City	76,367	2.23
MSA[1]	162,099	2.45
U.S.	116,136,617	2.59

Note: (1) Metropolitan Statistical Area - see Appendix B for areas included
Source: Claritas, Inc.

Race and Ethnicity

Area	White Alone[2] (%)	Black Alone[2] (%)	Asian Alone[2] (%)	Other Race Alone[2] (%)	Hispanic[3] (%)
City	61.5	32.3	2.5	3.7	3.3
MSA[1]	72.2	22.1	1.9	3.8	3.3
U.S.	72.3	12.4	4.4	10.9	15.8

Note: Figures are 2010 estimates; (1) Metropolitan Statistical Area - see Appendix B for areas included (2) Alone is defined as not being in combination with one or more other races; (3) May be of any race.
Source: Claritas, Inc.

Segregation

Type	Segregation Indices[1] 1990	2000	2010	2010 Rank[2]	Percent Change 1990-2000	1990-2010	2000-2010
Black/White	n/a	n/a	n/a	n/a	n/a	n/a	n/a
Asian/White	n/a	n/a	n/a	n/a	n/a	n/a	n/a
Hispanic/White	n/a	n/a	n/a	n/a	n/a	n/a	n/a

Note: Figures are based on an analysis of 1990, 2000, and 2010 Census Decennial Census tract data by William H. Frey, Brookings Institution and the University of Michigan Social Science Data Analysis Network. In this analysis all racial groups (whites, blacks, and asians) are non-Hispanic members of those races. Hispanics are shown as a separate category; All figures cover the Metropolitan Statistical Area (see Appendix B for areas included); (1) Segregation Indices are Dissimilarity Indices that measure the degree to which the minority group is distributed differently than whites aross census tracts. They range from 0 (complete integration) to 100 (complete [segregation) where the value indicates the percentage of the minority group that needs to move to be distributed exactly like whites; (2) Ranges from 1 (most segregated) to 102 (least segregated); n/a not available.
Source: www.CensusScope.org

Ancestry

Area	German	Irish	English	American	Italian	Polish	French	Scottish
City	9.7	10.6	11.5	10.5	2.3	1.0	2.1	2.4
MSA[1]	10.6	11.9	11.1	13.0	2.4	1.2	2.1	2.4
U.S.	16.6	12.0	9.1	6.1	5.9	3.3	3.1	1.9

Note: The top eight ancestries in the U.S. are shown. Figures are percentages and include multiple ancestry (e.g. if a person reported being Irish and Italian, they were included in both columns); (1) Metropolitan Statistical Area - see Appendix B for areas included
Source: U.S. Census Bureau, 2007-2009 American Community Survey 3-Year Estimates

Foreign-Born Population

Area	Percent of Population Born in								
	Any Foreign Country	Mexico	Asia	Europe	Carribean	South America	Central America[2]	Africa	Canada
City	n/a	n/a	n/a	n/a	n/a	n/a	n/a	n/a	n/a
MSA[1]	4.4	1.1	1.6	0.8	0.3	0.1	0.1	0.3	0.2
U.S.	12.5	3.8	3.4	1.6	1.1	0.8	0.9	0.5	0.3

Note: (1) Metropolitan Statistical Area - see Appendix B for areas included; (2) Excludes Mexico.
Source: U.S. Census Bureau, 2007-2009 American Community Survey 3-Year Estimates

Marriage Status

Area	Never Married	Now Married[2]	Separated	Widowed	Divorced
City	32.1	44.5	3.3	6.7	13.4
MSA[1]	27.4	52.0	2.7	5.7	12.2
U.S.	31.4	49.7	2.2	6.2	10.6

Note: Figures are percentages and cover the population 15 years of age and older; (1) Metropolitan Statistical Area - see Appendix B for areas included; (2) Excludes separated
Source: U.S. Census Bureau, 2007-2009 American Community Survey 3-Year Estimates

Age Distribution and Median Age

Area	Percent of Population							Median Age
	Under Age 5	Age 5 to 17	Age 18 to 34	Age 35 to 49	Age 50 to 64	Age 65 to 79	80 Years and Over	
City	6.1	16.0	25.3	20.1	17.8	11.0	3.6	37.0
MSA[1]	6.4	17.7	22.8	22.8	18.0	9.5	2.8	37.3
U.S.	6.9	17.5	23.3	21.4	18.1	9.1	3.7	36.7

Note: (1) Metropolitan Statistical Area - see Appendix B for areas included
Source: U.S. Census Bureau, 2007-2009 American Community Survey 3-Year Estimates

Male/Female Ratio

Area	Males	Females	Males per 100 Females
City	85,298	90,897	93.8
MSA[1]	200,275	206,945	96.8
U.S.	152,401,520	156,637,454	97.3

Note: Figures are 2010 estimates; (1) Metropolitan Statistical Area - see Appendix B for areas included
Source: Claritas, Inc.

Religion

Area	Catholic	Southern Baptist	United Meth-odist	ELCA[1]	LDS[2]	Presby-terian Church USA	Jewish Est.	Muslim Est.
County	5.8	22.4	7.7	0.7	0.8	1.6	0.3	0.4
U.S.	22.0	7.1	3.7	1.8	1.5	1.1	2.2	0.6

Note: Figures are the number of adherents as a percentage of the total population; Adherents are defined as all members, including full members, their children and the estimated number of other participants who are not considered members (e.g. the baptized, those not confirmed, those regularly attending services, etc.); (1) Evangelical Lutheran Church in America; (2) The Church of Jesus Christ of Latter Day Saints
Source: Reprinted with permission from Religious Congregations and Membership in the United States 2000 (Nashville, Glenmary Research Center, 2002) Copyright Association of Statisticians of American Religious Bodies. All rights reserved.

ECONOMY

Gross Metropolitan Product

Area	2006	2007	2008	2009	2009 Rank[2]
MSA[1]	17.2	18.1	19.3	19.6	99

Note: Figures are in billions of dollars; (1) Huntsville, AL Metropolitan Statistical Area - see Appendix B for areas included; (2) Rank ranges from 1 to 363
Source: The U.S. Conference of Mayors, "Pace of Economic Recovery: GMP and Jobs," January 2010

Economic Growth

Area	2006-2008 (%)	2009 (%)	2010 (%)	Rank[2]
MSA[1]	4.8	0.7	2.8	16
U.S.	1.3	-2.5	2.2	–

Note: Figures are real Gross Metropolitan Product growth rates and represent annual average percent change; (1) Huntsville, AL Metropolitan Statistical Area - see Appendix B for areas included; (2) Rank ranges from 1 to 363
Source: The U.S. Conference of Mayors, "Pace of Economic Recovery: GMP and Jobs," January 2010

Metropolitan Area Exports

Area	2005	2006	2007	2008	2009	2009 Rank[2]
MSA[1]	1,104.8	1,251.9	1,052.8	1,079.3	1,136.5	115

Note: Figures are in millions of dollars; (1) Huntsville, AL Metropolitan Statistical Area - see Appendix B for areas included; (2) Rank ranges from 1 to 374
Source: U.S. Department of Commerce, International Trade Administration, Office of Trade & Industry Information, Manufacturing & Services

INCOME

Per Capita/Median/Average Income

Area	Per Capita ($)	Median Household ($)	Average Household ($)
City	29,064	47,856	66,403
MSA[1]	27,794	53,544	69,313
U.S.	27,034	52,795	71,071

Note: Figures are 2010 estimates; (1) Metropolitan Statistical Area - see Appendix B for areas included
Source: Claritas, Inc.

Household Income Distribution

Area	Under $15,000	$15,000 -24,999	$25,000 -34,999	$35,000 -49,999	$50,000 -74,999	$75,000 -99,000	$100,000 -149,999	$150,000 and up
City	14.5	11.6	11.5	14.6	18.3	11.1	11.5	7.1
MSA[1]	12.0	10.2	10.5	14.6	19.1	13.0	13.5	7.1
U.S.	12.1	10.2	10.6	15.0	19.5	12.5	12.1	8.0

Note: Figures are 2010 estimates; (1) Metropolitan Statistical Area - see Appendix B for areas included
Source: Claritas, Inc.

Poverty Rates by Age

Area	All Ages	Under 18 Years Old	18 to 64 Years Old	65 Years and Over
City	15.2	5.1	9.3	0.9
MSA[1]	11.8	4.1	6.9	0.9
U.S.	13.6	4.7	7.7	1.2

Note: Figures are percent of population with income during the previous 12 months below poverty level and only include population for whom poverty status is determined; (1) Metropolitan Statistical Area - see Appendix B for areas included
Source: U.S. Census Bureau, 2007-2009 American Community Survey 3-Year Estimates

Personal Bankruptcy Filing Rate

Area	2006	2007	2008	2009	2010
Madison County	3.21	3.67	4.49	4.99	5.22
U.S.	2.00	2.73	3.53	4.60	4.96

Note: Numbers are per 1,000 population and include Chapter 7 and Chapter 13 filings
Source: Federal Deposit Insurance Corporation, Regional Economic Conditions, March 17, 2011

EMPLOYMENT

Labor Force and Employment

Area	Civilian Labor Force			Workers Employed		
	Dec. 2009	Dec. 2010	% Chg.	Dec. 2009	Dec. 2010	% Chg.
City	91,279	90,774	-0.6	84,445	84,297	-0.2
MSA[1]	208,152	206,531	-0.8	192,028	191,689	-0.2
U.S.	152,693,000	153,156,000	0.3	137,953,000	139,159,000	0.9

Note: Data is not seasonally adjusted and covers workers 16 years of age and older;
(1) Metropolitan Statistical Area - see Appendix B for areas included
Source: Bureau of Labor Statistics, http://stats.bls.gov

Unemployment Rate

Area	2010											
	Jan.	Feb.	Mar.	Apr.	May	Jun.	Jul.	Aug.	Sep.	Oct.	Nov.	Dec.
City	8.2	7.9	7.7	7.0	7.0	7.7	7.6	7.5	7.3	7.1	7.1	7.1
MSA[1]	8.5	8.3	7.9	7.2	7.1	7.5	7.5	7.4	7.3	7.1	7.2	7.2
U.S.	10.6	10.4	10.2	9.5	9.3	9.6	9.7	9.5	9.2	9.0	9.3	9.1

Note: Data is not seasonally adjusted and covers workers 16 years of age and older; All figures are percentages; (1) Metropolitan Statistical Area - see Appendix B for areas included
Source: Bureau of Labor Statistics, http://stats.bls.gov

Projected Unemployment Rate

Area	2007 (%)	2009 (%)	2011 (%)	2013 (%)
MSA[1]	2.9	8.8	7.8	6.0

Note: (1) Metropolitan Statistical Area - see Appendix B for areas included
Source: The U.S. Conference of Mayors, "Pace of Economic Recovery: GMP and Jobs," January 2010

Employment by Occupation

Occupation Classification	City (%)	MSA[1] (%)	U.S. (%)
Sales and Office	24.2	23.7	25.4
Professional and Related	28.0	27.3	21.0
Service	16.5	14.2	17.2
Production, Transportation, and Material Moving	11.0	12.1	12.3
Management, Business, and Financial	14.2	14.6	14.1
Construction, Extraction, and Maintenance	6.0	7.9	9.2
Farming, Forestry, and Fishing	0.1	0.3	0.7

Note: Figures cover employed civilians 16 years of age and older;
(1) Metropolitan Statistical Area - see Appendix B for areas included
Source: U.S. Census Bureau, 2007-2009 American Community Survey 3-Year Estimates

Employment by Industry

Sector	MSA[1]		U.S.
	Number of Employees	Percent of Total	Percent of Total
Government	49,400	23.7	17.2
Education and Health Services	17,100	8.2	15.2
Professional and Business Services	47,800	22.9	13.0
Retail Trade	22,800	10.9	11.4
Leisure and Hospitality	17,300	8.3	9.7
Manufacturing	23,000	11.0	8.8
Financial Activities	6,100	2.9	5.8
Wholesale Trade	5,200	2.5	4.2
Construction	n/a	n/a	4.1
Other Services	7,300	3.5	4.1
Transportation and Utilities	2,600	1.2	3.7
Information	2,600	1.2	2.1
Mining and Logging	n/a	n/a	0.6

Note: Figures cover non-farm employment as of December 2010 and are not seasonally adjusted;
(1) Metropolitan Statistical Area - see Appendix B for areas included; n/a not available
Source: Bureau of Labor Statistics, http://stats.bls.gov

Occupations with Greatest Projected Employment Growth: 2006 - 2016

Occupation[1]	2006 Employment	2016 Projected Employment	Numeric Employment Change	Percent Employment Change
Retail salespersons	62,340	76,190	13,850	22.2
Registered nurses	40,320	51,850	11,530	28.6
Combined food preparation and serving workers, including fast food	46,230	57,130	10,900	23.6
Team assemblers	34,390	43,620	9,230	26.8
Office clerks, general	41,770	48,650	6,880	16.5
Janitors and cleaners, except maids and housekeeping cleaners	33,260	39,960	6,700	20.1
Waiters and waitresses	28,900	35,370	6,470	22.4
Truck drivers, heavy and tractor-trailer	41,030	47,240	6,210	15.1
Bookkeeping, accounting, and auditing clerks	31,730	37,770	6,040	19.0
Customer service representatives	22,790	28,770	5,980	26.2

Note: Projections cover Alabama; (1) Sorted by numeric employment change
Source: www.projectionscentral.com, State Occupational Projections, 2006-2016 Long-Term Projections

Fastest Growing Occupations: 2006 - 2016

Occupation[1]	2006 Employment	2016 Projected Employment	Numeric Employment Change	Percent Employment Change
Network systems and data communications analysts	2,770	4,230	1,460	52.7
Veterinary technologists and technicians	940	1,430	490	52.1
Home health aides	9,590	14,210	4,620	48.2
Medical assistants	5,230	7,750	2,520	48.2
Computer software engineers, applications	3,670	5,420	1,750	47.7
Physical therapist assistants	1,220	1,720	500	41.0
Welding, soldering, and brazing machine setters, operators, and tenders	2,940	4,090	1,150	39.1
Dental hygienists	2,860	3,970	1,110	38.8
Dental assistants	2,850	3,950	1,100	38.6
Fitness trainers and aerobics instructors	2,750	3,790	1,040	37.8

Note: Projections cover Alabama; (1) Sorted by percent employment change and excludes occupations with numeric employment change less than 250
Source: www.projectionscentral.com, State Occupational Projections, 2006-2016 Long-Term Projections

Average Wages

Occupation	$/Hr.	Occupation	$/Hr.
Accountants and Auditors	31.87	Maids and Housekeeping Cleaners	9.09
Automotive Mechanics	17.06	Maintenance and Repair Workers	16.86
Bookkeepers	14.25	Marketing Managers	50.18
Carpenters	14.36	Nuclear Medicine Technologists	29.80
Cashiers	8.14	Nurses, Licensed Practical	16.58
Clerks, General Office	10.79	Nurses, Registered	28.25
Clerks, Receptionists/Information	10.99	Nursing Aides/Orderlies/Attendants	9.69
Clerks, Shipping/Receiving	13.25	Packers and Packagers, Hand	10.43
Computer Programmers	35.81	Physical Therapists	40.91
Computer Support Specialists	20.78	Postal Service Mail Carriers	23.46
Computer Systems Analysts	36.17	Real Estate Brokers	26.82
Cooks, Restaurant	10.63	Retail Salespersons	10.66
Dentists	n/a	Sales Reps., Exc. Tech./Scientific	22.84
Electrical Engineers	42.30	Sales Reps., Tech./Scientific	36.31
Electricians	18.36	Secretaries, Exc. Legal/Med./Exec.	15.05
Financial Managers	53.12	Security Guards	12.85
First-Line Supervisors/Mgrs., Sales	17.80	Surgeons	n/a
Food Preparation Workers	8.24	Teacher Assistants	8.80
General and Operations Managers	50.47	Teachers, Elementary School	24.10
Hairdressers/Cosmetologists	11.90	Teachers, Secondary School	21.10
Internists	n/a	Telemarketers	10.72
Janitors and Cleaners	9.95	Truck Drivers, Heavy/Tractor-Trailer	16.10
Landscaping/Groundskeeping Workers	11.54	Truck Drivers, Light/Delivery Svcs.	13.91
Lawyers	60.29	Waiters and Waitresses	8.97

Note: Wage data covers the Huntsville, AL - see Appendix B for areas included. Hourly wages for elementary/secondary school teachers and teacher assistants were calculated by the editors from annual wage data assuming a 40 hour work week; n/a not available.
Source: Bureau of Labor Statistics, Metro Area Occupational Employment and Wage Estimates, May 2009

RESIDENTIAL REAL ESTATE

Building Permits

Area	Single-Family			Multi-Family			Total		
	2009	2010	Pct. Chg.	2009	2010	Pct. Chg.	2009	2010	Pct. Chg.
City	1,096	1,073	-2.1	324	0	-100.0	1,420	1,073	-24.4
MSA[1]	2,293	2,275	-0.8	695	0	-100.0	2,988	2,275	-23.9
U.S.	441,100	447,300	1.4	141,900	157,300	10.9	583,000	604,600	3.7

Note: (1) Metropolitan Statistical Area - see Appendix B for areas included; figures represent new, privately-owned housing units authorized (unadjusted data); All permit data are based on estimates with imputation.
Source: U.S. Census Bureau, Manufacturing, Mining, and Construction Statistics, Building Permits, 2009, 2010

Homeownership Rate

Area	2005 (%)	2006 (%)	2007 (%)	2008 (%)	2009 (%)	2010 (%)
MSA[1]	n/a	n/a	n/a	n/a	n/a	n/a
U.S.	68.9	68.8	68.1	67.8	67.4	66.9

Note: (1) Metropolitan Statistical Area - see Appendix B for areas included
Source: U.S. Census Bureau, Housing Vacancies and Homeownership Annual Statistics: 2010

Housing Vacancy Rates

Area	Gross Vacancy Rate[2] (%)			Year-Round Vacancy Rate[3] (%)			Rental Vacancy Rate[4] (%)			Homeowner Vacancy Rate[5] (%)		
	2008	2009	2010	2008	2009	2010	2008	2009	2010	2008	2009	2010
MSA[1]	n/a	n/a	n/a	n/a	n/a	n/a	n/a	n/a	n/a	n/a	n/a	n/a
U.S.	14.4	14.5	14.3	11.1	11.3	11.3	10.0	10.6	10.2	2.8	2.6	2.6

Note: (1) Metropolitan Statistical Area - see Appendix B for areas included; (2) The percentage of the total housing inventory that is vacant; (3) The percentage of the housing inventory (excluding seasonal units) that is year-round vacant; (4) The percentage of rental inventory that is vacant for rent; (5) The percentage of homeowner inventory that is vacant for sale; n/a not available
Source: U.S. Census Bureau, Housing Vacancies and Homeownership Annual Statistics: 2010

State Corporate Income Tax Rates

State	Tax Rate (%)	Income Brackets ($)	Num. of Brackets	Financial Institution Tax Rate (%)[a]	Federal Income Tax Ded.
Alabama	6.5	Flat rate	1	6.5	Yes

Note: Tax rates as of January 1, 2011; (a) Rates listed are the tax rates applied to financial institutions or excise taxes based on income. Some states have other taxes based upon the value of deposits or shares.
Source: Federation of Tax Administrators, "State Corporate Income Tax Rates, 2011"

State Individual Income Tax Rates

State	Tax Rate (%)	Income Brackets ($)	Num. of Brackets	Personal Exempt. ($)[1] Single	Personal Exempt. ($)[1] Dependents	Fed. Inc. Tax Ded.
Alabama	2.0 - 5.0	500 (b) - 3,001 (b)	3	1,500	500 (e)	Yes

Note: Tax rates as of January 1, 2011; Local- and county-level taxes are not included; n/a not applicable; (1) Married joint filers generally receive double the single exemption; (b) For joint returns, taxes are twice the tax on half the couple's income; (e) In Alabama, the per-dependent exemption is $1,000 for taxpayers with state AGI of $20,000 or less, $500 with AGI from $20,001 to $100,000, and $300 with AGI over $100,000.
Source: Federation of Tax Administrators, "State Individual Income Tax Rates, 2011"

Various State and Local Tax Rates

State	State and Local Sales and Use (%)	State Sales and Use (%)	Gasoline[1] (¢/gal.)	Cigarette[2] ($/pack)	Spirits[3] ($/gal.)	Wine[4] ($/gal.)	Beer[5] ($/gal.)
Alabama	8.0	4.00	20.9	0.43	18.94 (g)	1.70 (k)	1.05 (l)

Note: All tax rates as of January 1, 2011 except Spirits (Sept. 1, 2010); (1) The American Petroleum Institute has developed a methodology for determining the average tax rate on a gallon of fuel. Rates may include any of the following: excise taxes, environmental fees, storage tank fees, other fees or taxes, general sales tax, and local taxes. In states where gasoline is subject to the general sales tax, or where the fuel tax is based on the average sale price, the average rate determined by API is sensitive to changes in the price of gasoline. States that fully or partially apply general sales taxes to gasoline: CA, CO, GA, IL, IN, MI, NY; (2) The federal excise tax of $1.0066 per pack and local taxes are not included; (3) Rates are those applicable to off-premise sales of 40% alcohol by volume (a.b.v.) distilled spirits in 750ml containers. Local excise taxes are excluded; (4) Rates are those applicable to off-premise sales of 11% a.b.v. non-carbonated wine in 750ml containers; (5) Rates are those applicable to off-premise sales of 4.7% a.b.v. beer in 12 ounce containers; (g) States where the government controls sales. In control states, products are subject to ad valorem mark-up and excise taxes. The excise tax rate is calculated using a methodology developed by the Distilled Spirits Council of the United States; (k) Includes $0.26 statewide local rate in Alabama; (l) Includes statewide local rates in Alabama ($0.52) and Georgia ($0.53).
Source: Tax Foundation, 2011 Facts & Figures: How Does Your State Compare?

State-Local Tax Burdens

Area	Rate (%)	Rank[1]	Per Capita Taxes Paid to Home State ($)	Total State and Local Per Capita Taxes Paid ($)	Per Capita Income ($)
Alabama	8.5	40	2,029	2,967	34,911
U.S. Average	9.8	-	3,057	4,160	42,539

Note: Figures cover 2009; (1) Rank ranges from 1 to 50 where 1 is highest tax burden
Source: Tax Foundation, State-Local Tax Burdens, All States, 2009

State Business Tax Climate Index Rankings

State	Overall Rank	Corporate Tax Index Rank	Individual Income Tax Index Rank	Sales Tax Index Rank	Unemployment Insurance Tax Index Rank	Property Tax Index Rank
Alabama	28	24	18	40	10	9

Note: The index is a measure of how each state's tax laws affect economic performance. The lower the rank, the more favorable a state's tax system is for business. All ranks are for fiscal years. States without a given tax are given a ranking of 1.
Source: Tax Foundation, Tax Foundation Background Paper, No. 60, "2011 State Business Tax Climate Index"

**COMMERCIAL
UTILITIES**

Typical Monthly Electric Bills

Area	Commercial Service ($/month)		Industrial Service ($/month)	
	40 kW demand 5,000 kWh	500 kW demand 100,000 kWh	5,000 kW demand 1,500,000 kWh	70,000 kW demand 50,000,000 kWh
City	407	10,539	109,605	1,964,100

Note: Based on rates in effect January 1, 2010
Source: Memphis Light, Gas and Water, 2010 Utility Bill Comparisons for Selected U.S. Cities

TRANSPORTATION

Means of Transportation to Work

Area	Car/Truck/Van		Public Transportation			Bicycle	Walked	Other Means	Worked at Home
	Drove Alone	Car-pooled	Bus	Subway	Railroad				
City	84.4	9.7	0.6	0.0	0.0	0.1	1.1	1.2	3.0
MSA[1]	85.5	9.7	0.3	0.0	0.0	0.1	1.1	1.0	2.2
U.S.	75.8	10.4	2.7	1.7	0.5	0.5	2.9	1.2	4.1

Note: Figures are percentages and cover workers 16 years of age and older;
(1) Metropolitan Statistical Area - see Appendix B for areas included
Source: U.S. Census Bureau, 2007-2009 American Community Survey 3-Year Estimates

Travel Time to Work

Area	Less Than 15 Minutes	15 to 29 Minutes	30 to 44 Minutes	45 to 59 Minutes	60 to 89 Minutes	90 Minutes or More
City	37.2	47.6	11.4	1.3	1.2	1.3
MSA[1]	28.5	44.3	19.2	5.1	1.6	1.2
U.S.	28.5	36.2	19.7	7.5	5.6	2.5

Note: Figures are percentages and include workers 16 years old and over;
(1) Metropolitan Statistical Area - see Appendix B for areas included
Source: U.S. Census Bureau, 2007-2009 American Community Survey 3-Year Estimates

Travel Time Index

Area	1982	1999	2008	2009
Urban Area[1]	n/a	n/a	n/a	n/a
Average[2]	1.08	1.20	1.20	1.20

*Note: Travel Time Index—the ratio of travel time in the peak period to the travel time at
free-flow conditions. A value of 1.30 indicates a 20-minute free-flow trip takes 26 minutes
in the peak. Free-flow speeds (60 mph on freeways and 35 mph on principal arterials)
are used as the comparison threshold; (1) Covers the Huntsville urban area;
(2) average of 439 urban areas*
Source: Texas Transportation Institute, Urban Mobility Report 2010, December 2010

Public Transportation

Agency Name / Mode of Transportation	Vehicles Operated in Maximum Service	Annual Unlinked Passenger Trips ('000)	Annual Passenger Miles ('000)
City of Huntsville - Public Transportation Division			
Demand response	15	79.9	633.5
Bus	13	325.2	1,640.6

Note: Figures include both directly operated and purchased transportation
Source: Federal Transit Administration, National Transit Database, 2009

Air Transportation

Airport Name and Code / Type of Service	Passenger Airlines[1]	Passenger Enplanements	Freight Carriers[2]	Freight (lbs.)
Huntsville International (HSV)				
Domestic service (U.S. carriers - 2010)	21	605,566	12	6,280,412
International service (U.S. carriers - 2009)	2	85	5	59,247,011

Note: (1) Includes all U.S.-based major, minor and commuter airlines that carried at least one passenger during the year; (2) Includes all U.S.-based airlines and freight carriers that transported at least one pound of freight during the year
Source: Bureau of Transportation Statistics, The Intermodal Transportation Database, Air Carriers: T-100 Domestic Market (U.S. Carriers), 2010; Bureau of Transportation Statistics, The Intermodal Transportation Database, Air Carriers: T-100 International Market (U.S. Carriers), 2009

Other Transportation Statistics

Interstate highways:	I-65
Amtrak service:	No
Major waterways/ports:	Near the Tennessee River (12 miles)

Source: Amtrak.com; Google Maps

BUSINESSES

Major Business Headquarters

Company Name	Rankings	
	Fortune[1]	Forbes[2]
No companies listed	-	-

Note: (1) Fortune 500—companies that produce a 10-K are ranked 1 to 500 based on 2010 revenue; (2) all private companies with at least $2 billion in annual revenue are ranked 1 to 223; companies listed are headquartered in the city; dashes indicate no ranking
Source: Fortune, "Fortune 500," May 23, 2011; Forbes, "America's Largest Private Companies," November 3, 2010

Minority Business Opportunity

Huntsville is home to one company which is on the Black Enterprise Industrial/Service 100 list (100 largest companies based on gross sales): **Tec-Masters**. Criteria: operational in previous calendar year; at least 51% black-owned and manufactures/owns the product it sells or provides industrial or consumer services. Brokerages, real estate firms and firms that provide professional services are not eligible. *Black Enterprise, B.E. 100s, 2010*

Huntsville is home to one company which is on the Black Enterprise Auto Dealer 60 list (60 largest dealers based on gross sales): **Lexus of Huntsville**. Criteria: company must be operational in previous calendar year and at least 51% black-owned. *Black Enterprise, B.E. 100s, 2010*

Huntsville is home to three companies which are on the *Hispanic Business 500* list (500 largest U.S. Hispanic-owned companies based on 2009 revenue): **COLSA Corp.**; **Intuitive Research & Technology Corp.**; **SEI Group**. Companies included must show at least 51 percent ownership by Hispanic U.S. citizens, and must maintain headquarters in one of the 50 states or Washington, D.C. *Hispanic Business, "Hispanic Business 500," June 2010*

Huntsville is home to one company which is on the *Hispanic Business* Fastest-Growing 100 list (greatest sales growth from 2005 to 2009): **Intuitive Research & Technology Corp.** Companies included must show at least 51 percent ownership by Hispanic U.S. citizens, and must maintain headquarters in one of the 50 states or Washington, D.C. In addition, companies must have minimum revenues of $200,000 for calendar year 2005. *Hispanic Business, July/August 2010*

Minority- and Women-Owned Businesses

Group	All Firms		Firms with Paid Employees			
	Firms	Sales ($000)	Firms	Sales ($000)	Employees	Payroll ($000)
Asian	576	413,879	256	390,751	3,129	137,158
Black	2,007	268,991	157	243,092	1,821	77,246
Hispanic	207	260,684	45	254,977	1,705	111,457
Women	4,347	1,211,336	649	1,117,014	7,744	276,445
All Firms	14,557	28,246,971	4,606	27,654,907	122,271	5,235,603

Note: Figures cover firms located in the city; minority- and women-owned business are defined as firms in which the corresponding group own 51% or more of the stock or equity of the company
Source: U.S. Census Bureau, 2007 Economic Census, Survey of Business Owners

HOTELS

Hotels/Motels

Area	5 Star		4 Star		3 Star		2 Star		1 Star		Not Rated	
	Num.	Pct.3	Num.	Pct.3	Num.	Pct.3	Num.	Pct.3	Num.	Pct.3	Num.	Pct.3
City[1]	0	0.0	1	1.4	16	21.6	39	52.7	1	1.4	17	23.0
Total[2]	119	0.7	927	5.8	4,906	30.5	7,992	49.7	526	3.3	1,625	10.1

Note: (1) Figures cover Huntsville and vicinity; (2) Figures cover all 100 cities in this book; (3) Percentage of hotels which are a given star rating; Star ratings are determined by expedia.com and offer an indication of the general quality of a particular hotel.
Source: expedia.com, May 5, 2011

EVENT SITES

Major Stadiums, Arenas, and Auditoriums

Name	Max. Capacity
Joe W Davis Stadium	10,200
Von Braun Center Arena	10,000

Source: Original research

Convention Centers

Name	Overall Space (sq. ft.)	Exhibit Space (sq. ft.)	Meeting Space (sq. ft.)	Meeting Rooms

There are no major convention centers.
Source: Original research

Living Environment

COST OF LIVING

Cost of Living Index

Composite Index	Groceries	Housing	Utilities	Trans-portation	Health Care	Misc. Goods/ Services
91.2	94.9	78.7	86.1	99.7	92.0	99.8

Note: U.S. = 100; Figures cover the Huntsville AL urban area.
Source: The Council for Community and Economic Research, ACCRA Cost of Living Index, 2010

Grocery Prices

Area[1]	T-Bone Steak ($/pound)	Frying Chicken ($/pound)	Whole Milk ($/half gal.)	Eggs ($/dozen)	Orange Juice ($/64 oz.)	Coffee ($/11.5 oz.)
City[2]	9.05	1.12	2.03	1.41	2.66	3.14
Avg.	9.04	1.16	2.02	1.47	3.08	3.65
Min.	6.97	0.84	1.46	0.96	2.39	2.64
Max.	13.93	2.51	3.58	3.01	4.94	6.32

Note: (1) Values for the local area are compared with the average, minimum and maximum values for all 338 areas in the Cost of Living Index; (2) Figures cover the Huntsville AL urban area; **T-Bone Steak** (price per pound); **Frying Chicken** (price per pound, whole fryer); **Whole Milk** (half gallon carton); **Eggs** (price per dozen, Grade A, large); **Orange Juice** (64 oz. Tropicana or Florida Natural); **Coffee** (11.5 oz. can, vacuum-packed, Maxwell House, Hills Bros, or Folgers).
Source: The Council for Community and Economic Research, ACCRA Cost of Living Index, 2010

Housing and Utility Costs

Area[1]	New Home Price ($)	Apartment Rent ($/month)	All Electric ($/month)	Part Electric ($/month)	Other Energy ($/month)	Telephone ($/month)
City[2]	226,779	736	127.90	-	-	28.90
Avg.	293,442	810	166.39	91.93	83.82	26.93
Min.	182,545	453	119.21	44.47	36.85	17.98
Max.	1,123,114	2,776	307.53	218.20	313.90	39.15

Note: (1) Values for the local area are compared with the average, minimum and maximum values for all 338 areas in the Cost of Living Index; (2) Figures cover the Huntsville AL urban area; **New Home Price** (2,400 sf living area, 8,000 sf lot, in urban area with full utilities); **Apartment Rent** (950 sf 2 bedroom/1.5 or 2 bath, unfurnished, excluding all utilities except water); **All Electric** (average monthly cost for an all-electric home); **Part Electric** (average monthly cost for a part-electric home); **Other Energy** (average monthly cost for natural gas, fuel oil, coal, wood, and any other forms of energy except electricity); **Telephone** (price includes basic monthly rate for a private residential line plus additional local usage charges incurred by a family of four).
Source: The Council for Community and Economic Research, ACCRA Cost of Living Index, 2010

Health Care, Transportation, and Other Costs

Area[1]	Doctor ($/visit)	Dentist ($/visit)	Optometrist ($/visit)	Gasoline ($/gallon)	Beauty Salon ($/visit)	Men's Shirt ($)
City[2]	61.56	73.56	94.33	2.73	33.61	20.24
Avg.	89.44	78.95	87.40	2.73	31.92	24.83
Min.	57.00	54.25	48.32	2.44	19.17	13.67
Max.	149.90	136.73	174.22	3.75	62.81	47.89

Note: (1) Values for the local area are compared with the average, minimum and maximum values for all 338 areas in the Cost of Living Index; (2) Figures cover the Huntsville AL urban area; **Doctor** (general practitioners routine exam of an established patient); **Dentist** (adult teeth cleaning and periodic oral examination); **Optometrist** (full vision eye exam for established adult patient); **Gasoline** (one gallon regular unleaded, national brand, including all taxes, cash price at self-service pump if available); **Beauty Salon** (woman's shampoo, trim, and blow-dry); **Men's Shirt** (cotton/polyester dress shirt, pinpoint weave, long sleeves).
Source: The Council for Community and Economic Research, ACCRA Cost of Living Index, 2010

HOUSING

House Price Index (HPI)

Area	National Ranking[2]	Quarterly Change (%)	One-Year Change (%)	Five-Year Change (%)
MSA[1]	131	-0.42	-0.65	15.55
U.S.[3]	-	-0.84	-3.95	-11.45

Note: The HPI is a weighted repeat sales index. It measures average price changes in repeat sales or refinancings on the same properties. This information is obtained by reviewing repeat mortgage transactions on single-family properties whose mortgages have been purchased or securitized by Fannie Mae or Freddie Mac in January 1975; (1) Metropolitan/Micropolitan Statistical Area - see Appendix B for areas included; (2) Rankings are based on annual percentage change for all metro areas containing at least 15,000 transactions over the last 10 years and ranges from 1 to 309; (3) figures based on a weighted average of Census Division estimates; all figures are for the period ending December 31, 2010
Source: Federal Housing Finance Agency, House Price Index, February 24, 2011

House Price Valuations

Area	Q4 2005 Price ($000)	Q4 2005 Over-valuation	Q4 2006 Price ($000)	Q4 2006 Over-valuation	Q4 2007 Price ($000)	Q4 2007 Over-valuation	Q4 2008 Price ($000)	Q4 2008 Over-valuation	Q4 2009 Price ($000)	Q4 2009 Over-valuation
MSA[1]	117.4	-9.5	128.0	-7.2	133.0	-9.7	130.7	-13.4	135.4	-12.4

Note: Figures show the percentage of over- or under-valuation of single family homes relative to statistically normal house values (e.g. a value of 23.6 indicates that house values are 23.6% overvalued). Statistically normal house values are based on house prices, interest rates, household incomes, population densities, and any historical premiums or discounts metropolitan areas have exhibited over time; (1) Figures cover the Huntsville, AL Metropolitan Statistical Area - see Appendix B for areas included
Source: Global Insight/PNC Financial Services Group, House Prices in America: 4th Quarter 2009 Update

Median Single-Family Home Prices

Area	2008	2009	2010p	Percent Change 2009 to 2010
MSA[1]	n/a	n/a	n/a	n/a
U.S. Average	196.6	172.1	173.2	0.6

Note: Figures are median sales prices of existing single-family homes in thousands of dollars; (p) preliminary; n/a not available; (1) Metropolitan Statistical Area - see Appendix B for areas included
Source: National Association of Realtors, Median Sales Price of Existing Single-Family Homes for Metropolitan Areas, 4th Quarter 2010

Median Apartment Condo-Coop Home Prices

Area	2008	2009	2010p	Percent Change 2009 to 2010
MSA[1]	n/a	n/a	n/a	n/a
U.S. Average	209.8	175.6	171.7	-2.2

Note: Figures are median sales prices of existing apartment condo-coop homes in thousands of dollars; (p) preliminary; n/a not available; (1) Metropolitan Statistical Area - see Appendix B for areas included
Source: National Association of Realtors, Median Sales Price of Existing Apartment Condo-Coop Homes for Metropolitan Areas, 4th Quarter 2010

Year Housing Structure Built

Area	2000 or Later	1990 -1999	1980 -1989	1970 -1979	1960 -1969	1950 -1959	1940 -1949	Before 1940	Median Year
City	11.8	11.3	15.8	18.1	24.7	11.6	3.3	3.3	1974
MSA[1]	18.7	18.8	17.7	14.8	16.0	7.9	2.7	3.5	1983
U.S.	12.5	14.0	14.2	16.5	11.4	11.3	5.8	14.3	1974

Note: Figures are percentages except for Median Year; (1) Metropolitan Statistical Area - see Appendix B for areas included
Source: U.S. Census Bureau, 2007-2009 American Community Survey 3-Year Estimates

HEALTH

Health Risk Data

Category	MSA[1] (%)	U.S. (%)
Adults who have been told they have high blood pressure	n/a	28.7
Adults who have been told they have high blood cholesterol	n/a	37.5
Adults who have been told they have diabetes[3]	n/a	8.3
Adults who have been told they have arthritis	n/a	26.0
Adults who have been told they currently have asthma	n/a	8.8
Adults who are current smokers	n/a	17.9
Adults who are heavy drinkers[4]	n/a	5.1
Adults who are binge drinkers[5]	n/a	15.8
Adults who are overweight (BMI 25.0 - 29.9)	n/a	36.2
Adults who are obese (BMI 30.0 - 99.8)	n/a	26.9
Adults who participated in any physical activities in the past month	n/a	76.2
Adults 50+ who have ever had a sigmoidoscopy or colonoscopy[2]	n/a	62.2
Women 40+ who have had a mammogram within the past two years[2]	n/a	76.0
Adults age 18–64 who have any kind of health care coverage	n/a	83.1

Note: Data as of 2009 unless otherwise noted; n/a not available; (1) Figures cover the Huntsville, AL Metropolitan Statistical Area - see Appendix B for areas included; (2) Data as of 2008; (3) Figures do not include pregnancy-related, borderline, or pre-diabetes; (4) Heavy drinkers are classified as males having more than two drinks per day or females having more than one drink per day; (5) Binge drinkers are classified as males having five or more drinks on one occasion or females having four or more drinks on one occasion
Source: Centers for Disease Control and Prevention, Behaviorial Risk Factor Surveillance System, SMART: Selected Metropolitan/Micropolitan Area Risk Trends, 2008, 2009

Mortality Rates for the Top 10 Causes of Death in the U.S.

ICD-10[a] Sub-Chapter	ICD-10[a] Code	Age-Adjusted Mortality Rate[1] per 100,000 population	
		County[2]	U.S.
Malignant neoplasms	C00-C97	183.1	180.9
Ischaemic heart diseases	I20-I25	61.8	135.0
Other forms of heart disease	I30-I51	129.2	50.0
Cerebrovascular diseases	I60-I69	47.9	44.1
Chronic lower respiratory diseases	J40-J47	38.8	41.5
Other degenerative diseases of the nervous system	G30-G31	31.9	23.6
Diabetes mellitus	E10-E14	29.1	23.5
Other external causes of accidental injury	W00-X59	20.0	23.5
Organic, including symptomatic, mental disorders	F01-F09	28.4	22.2
Influenza and pneumonia	J09-J18	17.5	18.1

Note: (a) ICD-10 = International Classification of Diseases 10th Revision; (1) Mortality rates are a three year average covering 2005-2007; (2) Figures cover Madison County
Source: Centers for Disease Control and Prevention, National Center for Health Statistics. Compressed Mortality File 1999-2007. CDC WONDER On-line Database, compiled from Compressed Mortality File 1999-2007 Series 20 No. 2M, 2010.

Mortality Rates for Selected Causes of Death

ICD-10[a] Sub-Chapter	ICD-10[a] Code	Age-Adjusted Mortality Rate[1] per 100,000 population	
		County[2]	U.S.
Assault	X85-Y09	6.2	6.0
Human immunodeficiency virus (HIV) disease	B20-B24	*1.9	4.0
Hypertensive diseases	I10-I15	16.5	18.0
Intentional self-harm	X60-X84	11.2	11.0
Malnutrition	E40-E46	*1.8	0.8
Obesity and other hyperalimentation	E65-E68	*1.1	1.5
Transport accidents	V01-V99	23.0	15.6
Viral hepatitis	B15-B19	2.3	2.1

Note: (a) ICD-10 = International Classification of Diseases 10th Revision; (1) Mortality rates are a three year average covering 2005-2007; (2) Figures cover Madison County; (*) Unreliable data as per CDC
Source: Centers for Disease Control and Prevention, National Center for Health Statistics. Compressed Mortality File 1999-2007. CDC WONDER On-line Database, compiled from Compressed Mortality File 1999-2007 Series 20 No. 2M, 2010.

Distribution of Physicians and Dentists

Area[1]	Dentists[2]	D.O.[3]	M.D.[4]				
			Total	Family/ General Practice	Pediatrics	Medical Specialties	Surgical Specialties
Local (number)	138	29	670	118	44	222	162
Local (rate[5])	4.4	0.9	20.9	3.7	1.4	6.9	5.0
U.S. (rate[5])	4.5	1.9	18.3	2.5	1.4	6.8	4.1

Note: Data as of 2008 unless noted; (1) Local data covers Madison County; (2) Data as of 2007; (3) Doctor of Osteopathic Medicine; (4) Includes active, non-federal, patient-care, office-based Doctors of Medicine; (5) rate per 10,000 population
Source: Area Resource File (ARF). 2009-2010 Release. U.S. Department of Health and Human Services, Health Resources and Services Administration, Bureau of Health Professions, Rockville, MD, August 2010

Hospitals

Huntsville has the following hospitals: 2 general medical and surgical; 1 rehabilitation.
AHA Guide to the Healthcare Field 2010

EDUCATION

Public School District Statistics

District Name	Schls	Pupils	Pupil/ Teacher Ratio	Minority Pupils[1] (%)	Free Lunch Eligible[2] (%)	IEP[3] (%)
Huntsville City	52	23,205	13.0	51.9	36.9	0.7
Madison County	28	19,785	16.4	28.1	21.4	1.0

Note: Table includes school districts with 2,000 or more students; (1) Percentage of students that are not non-Hispanic white; (2) Percentage of students that are eligible for the free lunch program; (3) Percentage of students that have an Individualized Education Program.
Source: U.S. Department of Education, National Center for Education Statistics, Common Core of Data, Local Education Agency (School District) Universe Survey: School Year 2008-2009; U.S. Department of Education, National Center for Education Statistics, Common Core of Data, Public Elementary/Secondary School Universe Survey: School Year 2008-2009

Top Public High Schools

High School Name	Index[1]	Rank[1]	Subsidized Lunch (%)[2]	E&E (%)[3]
Grissom	1.412	1259	7.0	29.3

Note: (1) Public schools are ranked according to a ratio that is the number of Advanced Placement, International Baccalaureate, and/or Cambridge tests taken by all students at a school in 2009 divided by the number of graduating seniors. All of the schools on the list have an index of at least 1.000; they are in the top six percent of public schools measured this way. The rankings range from 1 to 1,734; (2) Percentage of students receiving federally subsidized meals; (3) E & E stands for equity and excellence percentage: the portion of all graduating seniors at a school that had at least one passing grade on one AP or IB test; (4) Schools that offer International Baccalaureate or Cambridge exams; (5) School is unranked, but has been identified by Newsweek as one of the nation's most elite public high schools.
Source: Newsweek Online, "Top High Schools 2010"

Highest Level of Education

Area	Less than H.S.	H.S. Diploma	Some College, No Deg.	Associate Degree	Bachelors Degree	Masters Degree	Profess. School Degree	Doctorate Degree
City	12.0	21.8	21.5	6.3	25.0	9.8	2.1	1.6
MSA[1]	13.6	24.8	21.2	6.5	22.5	8.8	1.4	1.2
U.S.	15.3	29.0	20.7	7.5	17.4	7.0	1.9	1.1

Note: Figures are 2010 estimated percentages and cover persons age 25 and over; (1) Metropolitan Statistical Area - see Appendix B for areas included
Source: Claritas, Inc.

Educational Attainment by Race

Area	High School Graduate (%)					Bachelor's Degree (%)				
	Total	White	Black	Asian	Hisp.[2]	Total	White	Black	Asian	Hisp.[2]
City	87.6	92.4	78.4	92.2	57.5	38.2	45.3	20.9	64.6	17.8
MSA[1]	86.8	88.9	80.7	92.6	63.2	34.0	36.3	25.4	54.0	19.4
U.S.	84.9	90.0	80.7	85.5	60.7	27.8	30.9	17.5	49.7	12.7

Note: Figures shown cover persons 25 years old and over; (1) Metropolitan Statistical Area - see Appendix B for areas included; (2) people of Hispanic origin can be of any race
Source: U.S. Census Bureau, 2007-2009 American Community Survey 3-Year Estimates

School Enrollment by Grade and Control

Area	Preschool (%)		Kindergarten (%)		Grades 1 - 4 (%)		Grades 5 - 8 (%)		Grades 9 - 12 (%)	
	Public	Private	Public	Private	Public	Private	Public	Private	Public	Private
City	44.2	55.8	85.0	15.0	88.9	11.1	84.3	15.7	91.7	8.3
MSA[1]	41.4	58.6	87.4	12.6	89.7	10.3	83.9	16.1	90.0	10.0
U.S.	54.3	45.7	86.4	13.6	88.9	11.1	89.1	10.9	90.2	9.8

Note: Figures shown cover persons 3 years old and over; (1) Metropolitan Statistical Area - see Appendix B for areas included
Source: U.S. Census Bureau, 2007-2009 American Community Survey 3-Year Estimates

Average Salaries of Public School Classroom Teachers

Area	2009-10		2010-11		Percent Change 2009-10 to 2010-11	Percent Change 2000-01 to 2010-11
	Dollars	Rank[1]	Dollars	Rank[1]		
Alabama	47,571	33	48,282	33	1.50	30.1
U.S. Average	55,202	-	56,069	-	1.57	29.3

Note: (1) State rank ranges from 1 to 51 where 1 indicates highest salary.
Source: National Education Association, Rankings & Estimates: Rankings of the States 2010 and Estimates of School Statistics 2011, December 2010

Higher Education

Four-Year Colleges			Two-Year Colleges			Medical Schools[1]	Law Schools[2]	Voc/ Tech[3]
Public	Private Non-profit	Private For-profit	Public	Private Non-profit	Private For-profit			
1	2	1	1	0	0	0	0	0

Note: Figures cover institutions located within the city limits and include main campuses only; (1) includes schools accredited by the Liaison Committee on Medical Education and the American Osteopathic Association; (2) includes American Bar Association-accredited law schools; (3) includes all schools with programs that are less than 2 years.
Source: National Center for Education Statistics, Integrated Postsecondary Education System (IPEDS) Peer Analysis System, 2010-11; U.S. News & World Report, Medical School Directory, 2011; U.S. News & World Report, Law School Directory, 2011

According to *U.S. News & World Report,* the Huntsville, AL Metropolitan Statistical Area is home to one of the top 197 national universities in the U.S.: **University of Alabama—Huntsville** (#179). The rankings are based on quantitative measurements such as peer assessment, retention, faculty resources, student selectivity, financial resources, graduation rate, and alumni giving rate. *U.S. News & World Report, "America's Best Colleges 2011"*

PRESIDENTIAL ELECTION

2008 Presidential Election Results

Area	Obama	McCain	Nader	Other
Madison County	41.9	56.9	0.3	0.9
U.S.	52.9	45.6	0.6	0.9

Note: Results are percentages and may not add to 100% due to rounding
Source: Dave Leip's Atlas of U.S. Presidential Elections, www.uselectionatlas.org

EMPLOYERS

Major Employers

Company Name	Industry	Type of Site
Adtran	Telephone and telegraph apparatus	Headquarters
Amsmi-Rd-Ba	National security	Branch
Avocent Corporation	Computer terminals	Headquarters
Boeing	Aircraft	Branch
Browns Ferry Nuclear Plant	Electric services	Branch
City of Huntsville	Executive offices	Branch
Clerk Treasurer	Legislative bodies	Branch
Colsa Corporation	Commercial physical research	Headquarters
Commander	National security	Branch
Commissioner Dept	Executive offices	Headquarters
Contracting Dept	National security	Branch
Dynetics	Commercial physical research	Headquarters
Huntsville Hosp Women Children	General medical and surgical hospitals	Headquarters
Intergraph Sec Govt and Infra	Prepackaged software	Headquarters
NASA	Space research and technology	Headquarters
SAIC	Data processing and preparation	Branch
SCI Enclosures	Sheet metalwork	Single
Teledyne Brown Engineering	Commercial physical research	Headquarters
United States Dept of Army	National security	Branch
VDO Automotive	Engine electrical equipment	Branch

Note: Companies shown are located within the Huntsville metropolitan area; nec = not elsewhere classified.
Source: www.zapdata.com, January 2011

Best Companies to Work For

Intuitive Research and Technology Corporation, headquartered in Huntsville, is among the "50 Best Employers for Workers Over 50." Criteria: recruiting practices; opportunities for training, education, and career development; workplace accommodations; alternative work options, such as flexible scheduling, job sharing, and phased retirement; employee health and pension benefits; and retiree benefits. Any employer with at least 50 employees based in the U.S. is eligible. This includes for-profit companies, not-for-profit organizations, and government employers. *AARP, "2009 AARP Best Employers for Workers Over 50"*

PUBLIC SAFETY

Crime Rate

Area	All Crimes	Violent Crimes				Property Crimes		
		Murder	Forcible Rape	Robbery	Aggrav. Assault	Burglary	Larceny -Theft	Motor Vehicle Theft
City	6,133.2	7.3	49.8	242.4	352.2	1,411.0	3,569.4	501.1
Suburbs[1]	2,334.9	3.6	17.3	52.4	136.9	587.0	1,405.0	132.9
Metro[2]	4,015.5	5.2	31.7	136.5	232.1	951.5	2,362.6	295.8
U.S.	3,465.5	5.0	28.7	133.0	262.8	716.3	2,060.9	258.8

Note: Figures are crimes per 100,000 population; (1) All areas within the metro area that are located outside the city limits; (2) Metropolitan Statistical Area - see Appendix B for areas included
Source: FBI Uniform Crime Reports, 2009

Hate Crimes

Area	Number of Quarters Reported	Bias Motivation				
		Race	Religion	Sexual Orientation	Ethnicity	Disability
City	4	0	0	0	0	0

Source: Federal Bureau of Investigation, Hate Crime Statistics 2009

Identity Theft Consumer Complaints

Area	Complaints	Complaints per 100,000 Population	Rank[2]
MSA[1]	275	71.1	192
U.S.	250,854	81.3	-

Note: (1) Metropolitan Statistical Area - see Appendix B for areas included; (2) Rank ranges from 1 to 384
where 1 indicates greatest number of complaints per 100,000 population
Source: Federal Trade Commission, Consumer Sentinel Network Data Book for January - December 2010

RECREATION

Culture

Dance[1]	Theatre[1]	Instrumental Music[1]	Vocal Music[1]	Series/ Festivals	Museums	Zoos and Aquariums[2]
1	1	3	1	2	8	0

Note: (1) Number of professional perfoming groups; (2) AZA-accredited
Source: The Grey House Performing Arts Directory, 2011-2012; Official Museum Directory, 2010; American
Association of Museums, AAM Member Museums, March 2011; Association of Zoos & Aquariums, AZA
Member Zoos & Aquariums, May 2011

Professional Sports Teams

Team Name	League

No teams are located in the metro area
Source: Original research

CLIMATE

Average and Extreme Temperatures

Temperature	Jan	Feb	Mar	Apr	May	Jun	Jul	Aug	Sep	Oct	Nov	Dec	Yr.
Extreme High (°F)	76	82	88	92	96	101	104	103	101	91	84	77	104
Average High (°F)	49	54	63	73	80	87	90	89	83	73	62	52	71
Average Temp. (°F)	39	44	52	61	69	76	80	79	73	62	51	43	61
Average Low (°F)	30	33	41	49	58	65	69	68	62	50	40	33	50
Extreme Low (°F)	-11	5	6	26	36	45	53	52	37	28	15	-3	-11

Note: Figures cover the years 1958-1995
Source: National Climatic Data Center, International Station Meteorological Climate Summary, 9/96

Average Precipitation/Snowfall/Humidity

Precip./Humidity	Jan	Feb	Mar	Apr	May	Jun	Jul	Aug	Sep	Oct	Nov	Dec	Yr.
Avg. Precip. (in.)	5.0	5.0	6.6	4.8	5.1	4.3	4.6	3.5	4.1	3.3	4.7	5.7	56.8
Avg. Snowfall (in.)	2	1	1	Tr	0	0	0	0	0	Tr	Tr	1	4
Avg. Rel. Hum. 7am (%)	82	81	79	78	79	81	84	86	85	86	84	81	82
Avg. Rel. Hum. 4pm (%)	60	56	51	46	51	53	56	55	54	51	55	60	54

Note: Figures cover the years 1958-1995; Tr = Trace amounts (<0.05 in. of rain; <0.5 in. of snow)
Source: National Climatic Data Center, International Station Meteorological Climate Summary, 9/96

Weather Conditions

Temperature			Daytime Sky			Precipitation		
10°F & below	32°F & below	90°F & above	Clear	Partly cloudy	Cloudy	0.01 inch or more precip.	0.1 inch or more snow/ice	Thunder-storms
2	66	49	70	118	177	116	2	54

Note: Figures are average number of days per year and cover the years 1958-1995
Source: National Climatic Data Center, International Station Meteorological Climate Summary, 9/96

HAZARDOUS WASTE

Superfund Sites

Huntsville has one hazardous waste site on the EPA's Superfund Final National Priorities
List: **Redstone Arsenal (USARMY/NASA)**. *U.S. Environmental Protection Agency, Final*
National Priorities List, April 1, 2011

AIR & WATER QUALITY

Air Quality Index

| Area | Percent of Days when Air Quality was...[2] | | | | AQI Statistics | |
	Good	Moderate	Unhealthy for Sensitive Groups	Unhealthy	Maximum	Median
Area[1]	75.7	23.8	0.5	0.0	122	41

Note: The Air Quality Index (AQI) is an index for reporting daily air quality. EPA calculates the AQI for five major air pollutants regulated by the Clean Air Act: ground-level ozone, particle pollution (also known as particulate matter), carbon monoxide, sulfur dioxide, and nitrogen dioxide. The AQI runs from 0 to 500. The higher the AQI value, the greater the level of air pollution and the greater the health concern. There are six AQI categories: "Good" The AQI is between 0 and 50. Air quality is considered satisfactory; "Moderate" The AQI is between 51 and 100. Air quality is acceptable; "Unhealthy for Sensitive Groups" When AQI values are between 101 and 150, members of sensitive groups may experience health effects; "Unhealthy" When AQI values are between 151 and 200 everyone may begin to experience health effects; "Very Unhealthy" AQI values between 201 and 300 trigger a health alert; "Hazardous" AQI values over 300 trigger health warnings of emergency conditions; (1) Data covers Madison County; (2) Based on 366 days with AQI data in 2008; The EPA has suspended data updates while it assesses its data systems, including AirData reports and maps.
Source: U.S. Environmental Protection Agency, AirData Report, 2008

Air Quality Index Pollutants

| Area | Percent of Days when AQI Pollutant was...[2] | | | | | |
	Carbon Monoxide	Nitrogen Dioxide	Ozone	Sulfur Dioxide	Particulate Matter 2.5	Particulate Matter 10
Area[1]	0.0	0.0	68.6	0.0	31.4	0.0

Note: The Air Quality Index (AQI) is an index for reporting daily air quality. EPA calculates the AQI for five major air pollutants regulated by the Clean Air Act: ground-level ozone, particle pollution (also known as particulate matter), carbon monoxide, sulfur dioxide, and nitrogen dioxide. The AQI runs from 0 to 500. The higher the AQI value, the greater the level of air pollution and the greater the health concern; (1) Data covers Madison County; (2) Based on 366 days with AQI data in 2008; The EPA has suspended data updates while it assesses its data systems, including AirData reports and maps.
Source: U.S. Environmental Protection Agency, AirData Report, 2008

Air Quality Index Trends

| Area | Trend Sites (days) | | | | | | | | All Sites (days) |
	2002	2003	2004	2005	2006	2007	2008	2009	2009
MSA[1]	n/a	n/a	n/a	n/a	n/a	n/a	n/a	n/a	n/a

Note: Figures are the number of days the AQI value exceeded 100 in a given year. An AQI value greater than 100 indicates that air quality would have been in the unhealthful range on that day. Data from exceptional events are included. These counts are presented in two ways. First, the counts are based on sites having an adequate record of monitoring data during the trend period (trend sites). These counts represent the relative change in the number of days with AQI values greater than 100. In the last column, the counts are based on all sites with data in the most recent year (because it is possible for a site to have data in the most recent year but not enough data to be a trend site); (1) Data covers the Huntsville, AL Metropolitan Statistical Area - see Appendix B for areas included; n/a not available.
Source: U.S. Environmental Protection Agency, Office of Air and Radiation, Air Quality Index Information, "Number of Days with Air Quality Index Values Greater than 100 and Trend Sites, 1990-2009, and at All Sites in 2009"

Maximum Air Pollutant Concentrations

	Particulate Matter 10 (ug/m^3)	Particulate Matter 2.5 (ug/m^3)	Ozone (ppm)	Carbon Monoxide (ppm)	Sulfur Dioxide (ppm)	Nitrogen Dioxide (ppm)	Lead (ug/m^3)
MSA[1] Level	31	21	0.066	n/a	n/a	n/a	n/a
NAAQS[2]	150	35	0.075	9	0.140	0.053	0.15
Met NAAQS[2]	Yes	Yes	Yes	n/a	n/a	n/a	n/a

Note: Data from exceptional events are not included; (1) Data covers the Huntsville, AL Metropolitan Statistical Area - see Appendix B for areas included; (2) National Ambient Air Quality Standards; n/a not available
Concentrations: Particulate Matter 10 (coarse particulate) - highest second maximum 24-hour concentration; Particulate Matter 2.5 (fine particulate) - highest 98th percentile 24-hour concentration; Ozone - highest fourth daily maximum 8-hour concentration; Carbon Monoxide - highest second maximum non-overlapping 8-hour concentration; Sulfur Dioxide - highest second maximum 24-hour concentration; Nitrogen Dioxide - highest arithmetic mean concentration; Lead - maximum running 3-month average
Units: ppm = parts per million; ug/m^3 = micrograms per cubic meter
Source: U.S. Environmental Protection Agency, CBSA Factbook 2009, Air Quality Statistics by City, 2009

Drinking Water

Water System Name	Pop. Served	Primary Water Source Type	Violations[1]	
			Health Based	Monitoring/ Reporting
Huntsville Utilities	219,168	Surface	0	0

Note: (1) Based on violation data from January 1, 2010 to December 31, 2010 (includes unresolved violations from earlier years)

Source: U.S. Environmental Protection Agency, Office of Ground Water and Drinking Water, Safe Drinking Water Information System (based on data extracted May 9, 2011)

Jackson, Mississippi

Background

Jackson, located along the Pearl River in central-western Mississippi, is both the state capital and state's most populous city.

What is now Jackson was originally settled by a French Canadian trader named Louis LeFleur. The settlement was known as both Parkerville and LeFleur's Bluff before it became the state capital and renamed Jackson, after Andrew Jackson, the 7th President of the United States. The state legislature met for the first time in Jackson in 1822. The first railroads in the city were built in 1840, which connected Jackson to nearby cities including Vicksburg, Raymond and Brandon.

At the time of the Civil War, Jackson was a relatively small city but it still served as an important manufacturing center for the Confederate forces. In addition, several important battles took place in the city including the Battle of Jackson in 1863, which was won by the Union army.

The beginning of the twentieth century brought new industries and economic growth to Jackson. In the 1930s, the discovery of natural gas fields near Jackson was an important part of the city's economic prosperity. During World War II, Hawkins Field in Jackson became an important airbase and, in 1941, the Dutch Air Force relocated its Royal Netherlands Military Flying School there because Holland was occupied by Nazi forces.

The 1960s brought dramatic change to Jackson, primarily due to the Civil Rights Movement. The most noteworthy and tragic civil rights event that took place in Jackson was the 1963 assassination of Medgar Evers, a prominent civil rights activist and leader of the Mississippi chapter of the NAACP. Byron De La Beckwith, a white supremacist, was convicted for the murder in 1994.

Other notable events during this decade included the first successful lung transplant, performed in Jackson by Dr. James Hardy at the University of Mississippi Medical Center in 1963, and the Candlestick Park Tornado, which touched down in the Candlestick Shopping Center in 1966 killing nineteen people.

In 1997, Jackson voters elected Harvey Johnson, Jr., the city's first African-American mayor. One of his major proposals was a new convention center to attract businesses to the city. Jackson's original proposal failed, but the convention center was ultimately completed as part of a tax referendum designed to revitalize downtown Jackson. The $65 million facility opened in January of 2009 with over 330,000 square feet of usable space.

Other groups involved with the revitalization program include the Downtown Jackson Partners, comprised of corporate leaders, elected officials and citizens. Currently, over $1 billion in economic development projects are underway, including hotels, residential buildings, museums, a new Federal courthouse and a new Jackson Police Department Headquarters.

Transportation needs in Jackson are served by the Jackson-Evers International Airport, which was renamed in 2004 to honor the assassinated civil rights leader Medgar Evers. Underway is a $19 million Airport Parkway, to connect downtown Jackson to the airport, with train service by Canadian National Railway, Kansas City Southern Railway, and Amtrak.

Performing arts groups in Jackson include the Jackson Symphony Orchestra, Ballet Mississippi, the Mississippi Opera, the Mississippi Chorus and the New Stage Theatre. Other attractions include the Mississippi Museum of Art, the Russell C. Davis Planetarium, the Jackson State University Botanical Gardens and the Jackson Zoo. In addition, the city hosts the USA International Ballet Competition. The competition was founded in 1978 by Tahlia Mara and takes place every four years as part of the International Ballet Competition, which originated in Bulgaria in 1964. The last competition occurred in June of 2010.

Major institutions of higher learning in Jackson include Tougaloo College, Jackson State University, Mississippi College School of Law and the University of Mississippi Medical Center, among others. While the city does not have any major professional sports teams, Millsap College is currently the summer home of the NFL's New Orleans Saints.

The climate in Jackson is generally very hot and humid during the summer and more mild during the winter. Rain is common during all seasons of the year and is usually accompanied by thunderstorms, which can be severe at times. Jackson does receive some snow, although it is generally light. More severe weather sometimes comes in the form of hail, strong winds and even tornadoes, such as the famed Candlestick Park Tornado of 1966.

Rankings

General Rankings

- Jackson was ranked #98 out of 375 metro areas in *Cities Ranked & Rated*. Criteria: cost of living; climate; crime; transportation; economy and jobs; education; arts and culture; health and healthcare; leisure; quality of life. *Cities Ranked & Rated, 2nd Edition, 2007*

- Jackson was ranked #151 out of 379 metro areas in *Places Rated Almanac*. Criteria: health care; education; recreation; transportation; ambience; climate; crime; housing costs; jobs. *Places Rated Almanac, 7th Edition, 2007*

- *Men's Health Living* ranked 100 U.S. cities in terms of quality of life. Jackson was ranked #47 and received a grade of C. Criteria: number of fitness facilities; air quality; number of physicians; male/female ratio; education levels; household income; cost of living. *Men's Health Living, Spring 2008*

Business/Finance Rankings

- Jackson was identified as one of the 20 strongest-performing metro areas during the recession and recovery from December 2007 through December 2010. Criteria: percent change in employment; percentage point change in unemployment rate; percent change in gross metropolitan product; percent change in House Price Index. *Brookings Institution, MetroMonitor: Tracking Economic Recession and Recovery in America's 100 Largest Metropolitan Areas, March 2011*

- *American City Business Journals* ranked America's 261 largest cities in terms of their resident's wealth. Jackson ranked #249. Criteria: per capita income; median household income; percentage of households with annual incomes of $200,000 or more; median home value. *American City Business Journals, www.bizjournals.com, "Where the Money Is: America's Wealth Centers," August 18, 2008*

- The Jackson metro area appeared on the Milken Institute "2010 Best Performing Metros" list. Rank: #66 out of 200 large metro areas. Criteria: job growth; wage and salary growth; high-tech output growth. *Milken Institute, "2010 Best Performing Metros"*

- *Forbes* ranked the 200 most populous metro areas in the U.S. in terms of the "Best Places for Business and Careers." The Jackson metro area was ranked #134. Criteria: 12 metrics including costs (business and living), job growth (past and projected), income growth, educational attainment, projected economic growth, crime, cultural and recreational opportunities, net migration patterns, percentage of subprime mortgages handed out over a three-year period, and the number of highly ranked four-year colleges. *Forbes, "Best Places for Business and Careers," April 14, 2010*

Children/Family Rankings

- The Jackson metro area was selected as one of the "Best Cities for Relocating Families" by Worldwide ERC and Primacy Relocation. The 2008 study looked at nearly 50 factors important to relocating families including: recent job growth; nearby top-ranked colleges; in-state tuition for four-year public colleges; population growth since 2000; pediatricians per 100,000 population; and a Green Living index. *Worldwide ERC and Primacy Relocation, "2008 Best Cities for Relocating Families"*

Dating/Romance Rankings

- Jackson appeared on *Men's Health's* list of the most sex-happy cities in America. The city ranked #25 of 100. Criteria: condom sales; birth rates; sex toy sales; rates of chlamydia, gonorrhea, and syphilis. *Men's Health, "America's Most Sex-Happy Cities," October 2010*

- *Men's Health* ranked 100 U.S. cities in terms of best (and worst) marriages. Jackson was ranked #77 (#1 = worst marriages). Criteria: rate of failed marriages; stringency of divorce laws; percentage of population who've split; number of licensed marriage and family therapists. *Men's Health, "Splitsville, USA," May 2010*

Education Rankings

- Jackson was identified as one of the 100 "smartest" metro areas in the U.S. The area ranked #52. Criteria: the editors rated the collective brainpower of the 100 largest metro area in the U.S based on their residents' educational attainment. *American City Business Journals, www.bizjournals.com, April 14, 2008*

- Jackson was identified as one of "America's Brainiest Bastions" by *Portfolio.com.* The metro area ranked #89 out of 200. Portfolio.com analyzed levels of educational attainment in the nation's 200 largest metropolitan areas. The editors established scores for five levels of educational attainment, based on relative earning power of adult workers age 25 or older. Scores were determined by comparing the median income for all workers with the median income for those workers at a specified educational level. *Portfolio.com, "America's Brainiest Bastions," December 1, 2010*

Environmental Rankings

- Jackson was selected as one of 22 "Smarter Cities" for energy by the Natural Resources Defense Council." Criteria: investment in green power; energy efficiency measures; conservation. *Natural Resources Defense Council, "2010 Smarter Cities," July 19, 2010*

- 100 of the largest metro areas in the U.S. were analyzed in terms of their current drought severity. The Jackson metro area ranked #43 (#1 = driest). The rankings were based on statistics such as long-term precipitation trends and patterns and the Palmer drought indices. *Sperling's BestPlaces, www.BestPlaces.net, "America's Drought-Riskiest Cities," November 2007*

- The Jackson metro area appeared in *Country Home's* "Best Green Places" report. The area ranked #345 out of 379. Criteria: official energy policies; green power; green buildings; availability of fresh, locally grown food. *Country Home, "Best Green Places," 2008*

- Jackson was highlighted as one of the top 25 cleanest metro areas for short-term particle pollution (24-hour PM 2.5) in the U.S. Monitors in these cities reported no days with unhealthful PM 2.5 levels. *American Lung Association, State of the Air 2011*

Health/Fitness Rankings

- Jackson was identified as a "2011 Asthma Capital." The area ranked #87 out of the nation's 100 largest metropolitan areas. Twelve factors were used to identify the most challenging places to live for people with asthma: estimated prevalence; self-reported prevalence; crude death rate for asthma; annual pollen score; annual air quality; public smoking laws; number of board-certified asthma specialists; school inhaler access laws; rescue medication use; controller medication use; uninsured rate; poverty rate. *Asthma and Allergy Foundation of America, "2011 Asthma Capitals"*

- Jackson was identified as a 2009 "Spring Allergy Capital." The area ranked #13 out of 100. Three groups of factors were used to identify the most severe cities for people with allergies during the spring season: annual pollen levels; medicine utilization; access to board-certified allergists. *Asthma and Allergy Foundation of America, "Spring Allergy Capitals 2009"*

- Jackson was identified as a 2010 "Fall Allergy Capital." The area ranked #5 out of 100. Three groups of factors were used to identify the most severe cities for people with allergies during the fall season: annual pollen levels; medicine utilization; access to board-certified allergists. *Asthma and Allergy Foundation of America, "Fall Allergy Capitals 2010"*

- *Men's Health* ranked 100 U.S. cities in terms of the quality of their tap water. Jackson was ranked #60 and received a grade of C. Criteria: levels of total coliform bacteria, arsenic, lead, total trihalomethanes (linked to cancer), and halo-acetic acids; number of EPA water-system violations from 1995 to 2005. *Men's Health, March 2007*

- Jackson was selected as one of the most accident-prone cities in America by *Men's Health*. The city ranked #7 of 10. Criteria: workplace accident rates; traffic fatalities; emergency room visits; accidental poisonings; incidents of drowning; fires; injury-producing falls. *Men's Health, "Ranking America's Cities: Accident City, USA," October 2009*

- Ortho-McNeil Neurologics, in partnership with Sperling's BestPlaces, analyzed 110 metro areas and identified those U.S. cities with the highest prevalence of factors that are most commonly associated with migraine headaches. The Jackson metro area ranked #19. Criteria: number of migraine-related drug prescriptions per capita; lifestyle factors that can contribute to migraines; environmental factors that can trigger migraines; and consumption of migraine-triggering foods. *Ortho-McNeil Neurologics, "America's Migraine Hot Spots," March 14, 2006*

- *Men's Health* examined the nation's largest 100 cities and identified the cities with the best and worst teeth. Jackson was ranked among the ten worst at #5. Criteria: annual dentist visits; canceled appointments; regular flossers; fluoride usage; dental extractions. *Men's Health, April 2008*

Real Estate Rankings

- The nation's largest metro areas were analyzed in terms of the percentage of households entering some stage of foreclosure in 2010. The Jackson metro area ranked #168 out of 206 (#1 = highest foreclosure rate). *RealtyTrac, 2010 Year-End Metropolitan Foreclosure Market Report, January 27, 2011*

- The Center for Housing Policy ranked 210 U.S metropolitan areas by the fair market rent for a two-bedroom unit. The Jackson metro area was ranked #125. (#1 = most expensive) with a rent of $788. Criteria: Fair Market Rent (FMR) in effect during the fourth quarter of 2009 based on HUD's fiscal year 2010 FMRs. *The Center for Housing Policy, "Paycheck to Paycheck: Most to Least Expensive Rental Markets in 2009"*

Safety Rankings

- Allstate ranked the 200 largest cities in America in terms of driver safety. Jackson ranked #182. In addition, drivers were 44.7% more likely to have had an accident compared to the national average. Allstate researchers analyzed internal property damage reported claims over a two-year period (from January 2007 to December 2008) to ensure the findings would not be affected by external influences such as weather or road construction. A weighted average of the two-year numbers determined the annual percentages. The report defines an auto crash as any collision resulting in a property damage claim. *Allstate, "The 2010 Allstate America's Best Drivers Report™"*

- Jackson was identified as one of the least safe places in the U.S. in terms of its vulnerability to natural disasters and weather extremes. The city ranked #3 out of 10. Sperling's BestPlaces analyzed data to show a metro areas' relative tendency to experience natural disasters (hail, tornadoes, high winds, hurricanes, earthquakes, and brush fires) or extreme weather (abundant rain or snowfall or days that are below freezing or above 90 degrees Fahrenheit). *Forbes, "Safest and Least Safe Places in the U.S.," August 30, 2005*

- Jackson was identified as one of the most dangerous mid-size cities in America by CQ Press. All 234 cities with populations of 100,000 to 499,999 that reported crime rates in 2009 for murder, rape, robbery, aggravated assault, burglary, and motor vehicle thefts were ranked. The city ranked #8 out of the top 10. *CQ Press, City Crime Rankings 2010-2011*

- The National Insurance Crime Bureau ranked 366 metro areas in the U.S. in terms of per capita rates of vehicle theft. The Jackson metro area ranked #19 (#1 = highest rate). Criteria: number of vehicle theft offenses per 100,000 inhabitants. *National Insurance Crime Bureau, "Hot Spots," May 17, 2010*

Seniors/Retirement Rankings

- The Jackson metro area was selected as one of the "10 Best Places for Single Seniors to Retire" by *U.S. News & World Report*. Criteria: metro areas with the most single seniors age 55 and over. *U.S. News & World Report, "10 Best Places for Single Seniors to Retire," November 1, 2010*

Sports/Recreation Rankings

- Jackson appeared on the *Sporting News* list of the "Best Sports Cities" for 2010. The area ranked #207 out of 402 cities in the U.S. *Sporting News* takes a 12-month snapshot, roughly October to October, of each city's sports, putting a heavy premium on regular-season won-lost records (from the most recently completed season). Other criteria include: playoff berths, bowl appearances and tournament bids; championships; applicable power ratings; quality of competition; overall fan fervor as measured in part by attendance as percentage of venue capacity; abundance of teams (rewarding quality over quantity); stadium and arena quality; ticket availability and prices; franchise ownership; and marquee appeal of athletes. *Sporting News, "Best Sports Cities 2010," October, 2010*

- *Golf Digest* ranked 330 metro areas in the U.S. in terms of golf. The Jackson metro area was ranked #145. Criteria: access to golf; weather; value of golf; and quality of golf. *Golf Digest, "Metro Golf Rankings," August 2005*

Transportation Rankings

- Jackson was identified as one of America's worst cities for speed traps by the National Motorists Association. One city from each state was selected based on data from the National Speed Trap Exchange. The NSTE collects driver reported speed trap locations. *National Motorists Association, "The Worst Speed Trap Cities in North America," September 2010*

Business Environment

CITY FINANCES

City Government Finances

Component	2008 ($000)	2008 ($ per capita)
Total Revenues	236,121	1,344
Total Expenditures	234,824	1,336
Debt Outstanding	401,952	2,288
Cash and Securities[1]	214,380	1,220

Note: (1) Cash and security holdings of a government at the close of its fiscal year, including those of its dependent agencies, utilities, and liquor stores.
Source: U.S Census Bureau, State & Local Government Finances 2008

City Government Revenue by Source

Source	2008 ($000)	2008 ($ per capita)
General Revenue		
From Federal Government	16,307	93
From State Government	45,387	258
From Local Governments	994	6
Taxes		
Property	63,606	362
Sales and Gross Receipts	9,060	52
Personal Income	0	0
Corporate Income	0	0
Motor Vehicle License	0	0
Other Taxes	2,280	13
Current Charges	62,797	357
Liquor Store	0	0
Utility	18,982	108
Employee Retirement	0	0

Source: U.S Census Bureau, State & Local Government Finances 2008

City Government Expenditures by Function

Function	2008 ($000)	2008 ($ per capita)	2008 (%)
General Direct Expenditures			
Air Transportation	17,584	100	7.5
Corrections	2,626	15	1.1
Education	0	0	0.0
Employment Security Administration	0	0	0.0
Financial Administration	4,940	28	2.1
Fire Protection	21,707	124	9.2
General Public Buildings	2,761	16	1.2
Governmental Administration, Other	9,402	54	4.0
Health	914	5	0.4
Highways	16,803	96	7.2
Hospitals	0	0	0.0
Housing and Community Development	9,852	56	4.2
Interest on General Debt	8,634	49	3.7
Judicial and Legal	4,280	24	1.8
Libraries	0	0	0.0
Parking	0	0	0.0
Parks and Recreation	27,176	155	11.6
Police Protection	25,977	148	11.1
Public Welfare	914	5	0.4
Sewerage	22,416	128	9.5
Solid Waste Management	12,202	69	5.2
Veterans' Services	0	0	0.0
Liquor Store	0	0	0.0
Utility	31,607	180	13.5
Employee Retirement	0	0	0.0

Source: U.S Census Bureau, State & Local Government Finances 2008

Municipal Bond Ratings

Area	Moody's	S&P	Fitch
City	Aa2	AA-	n/a

Rating Systems (shown in declining order of credit quality): Moody's– Aaa, Aa, A, Baa, Ba, B, Caa, Ca, C (numerical modifiers 1, 2, and 3 are added to letter-rating); S&P– AAA, AA, A, BBB, BB, B, CCC, CC, C; Fitch– AAA, AA, A, BBB, BB, B, CCC, CC, C. Ratings may be modified by the addition of a plus or minus sign to show relative standing within the major rating categories.
Notes: n/a Not available; (1) Not reviewed; (2) Issuer Rating/No General Obligation; (3) Standard and Poor's Issue Credit Rating (ICR) is a current opinion of an obliger with respect to a specific financial obligation, a specific class of financial obligations, or a specific financial program.
Source: City of Jackson, Mississippi, Comprehensive Annual Financial Report, Fiscal Year Ended September 30, 2010

DEMOGRAPHICS

Population Growth

Area	1990 Census	2000 Census	2010 Estimate	2015 Projection	Population Growth (%) 2000-2010	Population Growth (%) 2010-2015
City	196,469	184,256	172,029	164,415	-6.6	-4.4
MSA[1]	446,941	497,197	542,333	555,584	9.1	2.4
U.S.	248,709,873	281,421,906	309,038,974	321,675,005	9.8	4.1

Note: (1) Metropolitan Statistical Area - see Appendix B for areas included
Source: Claritas, Inc.

Number of Households and Average Household Size

Area	2010 Estimate	2010 Average Household Size
City	63,694	2.59
MSA[1]	200,786	2.60
U.S.	116,136,617	2.59

Note: (1) Metropolitan Statistical Area - see Appendix B for areas included
Source: Claritas, Inc.

Race and Ethnicity

Area	White Alone[2] (%)	Black Alone[2] (%)	Asian Alone[2] (%)	Other Race Alone[2] (%)	Hispanic[3] (%)
City	19.9	77.7	0.7	1.7	1.4
MSA[1]	50.5	46.9	0.9	1.7	1.7
U.S.	72.3	12.4	4.4	10.9	15.8

Note: Figures are 2010 estimates; (1) Metropolitan Statistical Area - see Appendix B for areas included (2) Alone is defined as not being in combination with one or more other races; (3) May be of any race.
Source: Claritas, Inc.

Segregation

Type	Segregation Indices[1] 1990	2000	2010	2010 Rank[2]	Percent Change 1990-2000	1990-2010	2000-2010
Black/White	62.4	57.5	56.0	51	-5.0	-6.5	-1.5
Asian/White	35.3	38.0	38.9	63	2.7	3.6	1.0
Hispanic/White	26.2	31.6	42.9	52	5.4	16.7	11.4

Note: Figures are based on an analysis of 1990, 2000, and 2010 Census Decennial Census tract data by William H. Frey, Brookings Institution and the University of Michigan Social Science Data Analysis Network. In this analysis all racial groups (whites, blacks, and asians) are non-Hispanic members of those races. Hispanics are shown as a separate category; All figures cover the Metropolitan Statistical Area (see Appendix B for areas included); (1) Segregation Indices are Dissimilarity Indices that measure the degree to which the minority group is distributed differently than whites aross census tracts. They range from 0 (complete integration) to 100 (complete [segregation) where the value indicates the percentage of the minority group that needs to move to be distributed exactly like whites; (2) Ranges from 1 (most segregated) to 102 (least segregated); n/a not available.
Source: www.CensusScope.org

Ancestry

Area	German	Irish	English	American	Italian	Polish	French	Scottish
City	2.3	3.3	3.6	2.4	0.6	0.2	0.9	0.7
MSA[1]	5.8	8.7	7.5	7.5	1.4	0.4	2.0	1.8
U.S.	16.6	12.0	9.1	6.1	5.9	3.3	3.1	1.9

Note: The top eight ancestries in the U.S. are shown. Figures are percentages and include multiple ancestry (e.g. if a person reported being Irish and Italian, they were included in both columns); (1) Metropolitan Statistical Area - see Appendix B for areas included
Source: U.S. Census Bureau, 2007-2009 American Community Survey 3-Year Estimates

Foreign-Born Population

Area	Percent of Population Born in								
	Any Foreign Country	Mexico	Asia	Europe	Carribean	South America	Central America[2]	Africa	Canada
City	n/a	n/a	n/a	n/a	n/a	n/a	n/a	n/a	n/a
MSA[1]	n/a	n/a	n/a	n/a	n/a	n/a	n/a	n/a	n/a
U.S.	12.5	3.8	3.4	1.6	1.1	0.8	0.9	0.5	0.3

Note: (1) Metropolitan Statistical Area - see Appendix B for areas included; (2) Excludes Mexico.
Source: U.S. Census Bureau, 2007-2009 American Community Survey 3-Year Estimates

Marriage Status

Area	Never Married	Now Married[2]	Separated	Widowed	Divorced
City	46.5	31.1	4.1	6.4	12.0
MSA[1]	34.7	44.4	2.9	6.6	11.4
U.S.	31.4	49.7	2.2	6.2	10.6

Note: Figures are percentages and cover the population 15 years of age and older;
(1) Metropolitan Statistical Area - see Appendix B for areas included; (2) Excludes separated
Source: U.S. Census Bureau, 2007-2009 American Community Survey 3-Year Estimates

Age Distribution and Median Age

Area	Percent of Population							Median Age
	Under Age 5	Age 5 to 17	Age 18 to 34	Age 35 to 49	Age 50 to 64	Age 65 to 79	80 Years and Over	
City	8.4	20.0	27.1	18.8	15.7	6.8	3.2	30.9
MSA[1]	7.5	19.1	24.8	20.4	17.1	8.0	3.1	33.9
U.S.	6.9	17.5	23.3	21.4	18.1	9.1	3.7	36.7

Note: (1) Metropolitan Statistical Area - see Appendix B for areas included
Source: U.S. Census Bureau, 2007-2009 American Community Survey 3-Year Estimates

Male/Female Ratio

Area	Males	Females	Males per 100 Females
City	80,500	91,529	88.0
MSA[1]	259,905	282,428	92.0
U.S.	152,401,520	156,637,454	97.3

Note: Figures are 2010 estimates; (1) Metropolitan Statistical Area - see Appendix B for areas included
Source: Claritas, Inc.

Religion

Area	Catholic	Southern Baptist	United Meth-odist	ELCA[1]	LDS[2]	Presby-terian Church USA	Jewish Est.	Muslim Est.
County	3.0	30.1	10.6	0.2	0.3	0.8	0.2	0.5
U.S.	22.0	7.1	3.7	1.8	1.5	1.1	2.2	0.6

Note: Figures are the number of adherents as a percentage of the total population; Adherents are defined as all members, including full members, their children and the estimated number of other participants who are not considered members (e.g. the baptized, those not confirmed, those regularly attending services, etc.);
(1) Evangelical Lutheran Church in America; (2) The Church of Jesus Christ of Latter Day Saints
Source: Reprinted with permission from Religious Congregations and Membership in the United States 2000 (Nashville, Glenmary Research Center, 2002) Copyright Association of Statisticians of American Religious Bodies. All rights reserved.

ECONOMY

Gross Metropolitan Product

Area	2006	2007	2008	2009	2009 Rank[2]
MSA[1]	21.4	22.3	23.1	23.4	87

Note: Figures are in billions of dollars; (1) Jackson, MS Metropolitan Statistical Area - see Appendix B for areas included; (2) Rank ranges from 1 to 363
Source: The U.S. Conference of Mayors, "Pace of Economic Recovery: GMP and Jobs," January 2010

Economic Growth

Area	2006-2008 (%)	2009 (%)	2010 (%)	Rank[2]
MSA[1]	0.7	0.1	2.6	215
U.S.	1.3	-2.5	2.2	–

Note: Figures are real Gross Metropolitan Product growth rates and represent annual average percent change; (1) Jackson, MS Metropolitan Statistical Area - see Appendix B for areas included; (2) Rank ranges from 1 to 363
Source: The U.S. Conference of Mayors, "Pace of Economic Recovery: GMP and Jobs," January 2010

Metropolitan Area Exports

Area	2005	2006	2007	2008	2009	2009 Rank[2]
MSA[1]	904.4	939.9	601.1	676.9	432.3	196

Note: Figures are in millions of dollars; (1) Jackson, MS Metropolitan Statistical Area - see Appendix B for areas included; (2) Rank ranges from 1 to 374
Source: U.S. Department of Commerce, International Trade Administration, Office of Trade & Industry Information, Manufacturing & Services

INCOME

Per Capita/Median/Average Income

Area	Per Capita ($)	Median Household ($)	Average Household ($)
City	18,952	33,672	50,312
MSA[1]	23,298	45,912	62,215
U.S.	27,034	52,795	71,071

Note: Figures are 2010 estimates; (1) Metropolitan Statistical Area - see Appendix B for areas included
Source: Claritas, Inc.

Household Income Distribution

Area	Percent of Households Earning							
	Under $15,000	$15,000 -24,999	$25,000 -34,999	$35,000 -49,999	$50,000 -74,999	$75,000 -99,000	$100,000 -149,999	$150,000 and up
City	23.2	15.0	13.6	16.1	15.3	7.1	5.4	4.3
MSA[1]	15.9	11.3	11.4	15.8	18.7	11.4	9.8	5.8
U.S.	12.1	10.2	10.6	15.0	19.5	12.5	12.1	8.0

Note: Figures are 2010 estimates; (1) Metropolitan Statistical Area - see Appendix B for areas included
Source: Claritas, Inc.

Poverty Rates by Age

Area	All Ages	Under 18 Years Old	18 to 64 Years Old	65 Years and Over
City	27.2	11.4	14.2	1.5
MSA[1]	17.8	6.8	9.6	1.4
U.S.	13.6	4.7	7.7	1.2

Note: Figures are percent of population with income during the previous 12 months below poverty level and only include population for whom poverty status is determined; (1) Metropolitan Statistical Area - see Appendix B for areas included
Source: U.S. Census Bureau, 2007-2009 American Community Survey 3-Year Estimates

Personal Bankruptcy Filing Rate

Area	2006	2007	2008	2009	2010
Hinds County	5.24	6.88	5.82	6.49	6.37
U.S.	2.00	2.73	3.53	4.60	4.96

Note: Numbers are per 1,000 population and include Chapter 7 and Chapter 13 filings
Source: Federal Deposit Insurance Corporation, Regional Economic Conditions, March 17, 2011

EMPLOYMENT

Labor Force and Employment

Area	Civilian Labor Force			Workers Employed		
	Dec. 2009	Dec. 2010	% Chg.	Dec. 2009	Dec. 2010	% Chg.
City	79,941	82,262	2.9	71,929	74,537	3.6
MSA[1]	262,148	269,419	2.8	239,852	248,550	3.6
U.S.	152,693,000	153,156,000	0.3	137,953,000	139,159,000	0.9

Note: Data is not seasonally adjusted and covers workers 16 years of age and older;
(1) Metropolitan Statistical Area - see Appendix B for areas included
Source: Bureau of Labor Statistics, http://stats.bls.gov

Unemployment Rate

Area	2010											
	Jan.	Feb.	Mar.	Apr.	May	Jun.	Jul.	Aug.	Sep.	Oct.	Nov.	Dec.
City	11.3	10.6	10.2	9.6	10.2	10.6	10.9	9.3	9.9	9.8	9.6	9.4
MSA[1]	9.7	9.0	8.6	8.0	8.5	8.8	9.0	7.6	8.1	8.1	7.9	7.7
U.S.	10.6	10.4	10.2	9.5	9.3	9.6	9.7	9.5	9.2	9.0	9.3	9.1

Note: Data is not seasonally adjusted and covers workers 16 years of age and older; All figures are percentages; (1) Metropolitan Statistical Area - see Appendix B for areas included
Source: Bureau of Labor Statistics, http://stats.bls.gov

Projected Unemployment Rate

Area	2007 (%)	2009 (%)	2011 (%)	2013 (%)
MSA[1]	5.0	8.4	8.0	6.7

Note: (1) Metropolitan Statistical Area - see Appendix B for areas included
Source: The U.S. Conference of Mayors, "Pace of Economic Recovery: GMP and Jobs," January 2010

Employment by Occupation

Occupation Classification	City (%)	MSA[1] (%)	U.S. (%)
Sales and Office	27.2	26.9	25.4
Professional and Related	20.3	21.6	21.0
Service	22.2	16.8	17.2
Production, Transportation, and Material Moving	11.9	11.1	12.3
Management, Business, and Financial	9.9	13.8	14.1
Construction, Extraction, and Maintenance	8.4	9.4	9.2
Farming, Forestry, and Fishing	0.1	0.4	0.7

Note: Figures cover employed civilians 16 years of age and older;
(1) Metropolitan Statistical Area - see Appendix B for areas included
Source: U.S. Census Bureau, 2007-2009 American Community Survey 3-Year Estimates

Employment by Industry

Sector	MSA[1]		U.S.
	Number of Employees	Percent of Total	Percent of Total
Government	57,400	22.7	17.2
Education and Health Services	39,300	15.6	15.2
Professional and Business Services	27,600	10.9	13.0
Retail Trade	28,900	11.4	11.4
Leisure and Hospitality	21,200	8.4	9.7
Manufacturing	16,000	6.3	8.8
Financial Activities	15,200	6.0	5.8
Wholesale Trade	10,900	4.3	4.2
Construction	11,000	4.4	4.1
Other Services	9,400	3.7	4.1
Transportation and Utilities	10,300	4.1	3.7
Information	4,600	1.8	2.1
Mining and Logging	900	0.4	0.6

Note: Figures cover non-farm employment as of December 2010 and are not seasonally adjusted;
(1) Metropolitan Statistical Area - see Appendix B for areas included
Source: Bureau of Labor Statistics, http://stats.bls.gov

Occupations with Greatest Projected Employment Growth: 2006 - 2016

Occupation[1]	2006 Employment	2016 Projected Employment	Numeric Employment Change	Percent Employment Change
Retail salespersons	38,720	48,060	9,340	24.1
Registered nurses	27,440	34,330	6,890	25.1
Cashiers, except gaming	47,100	52,550	5,450	11.6
First-line supervisors/managers of retail sales workers	26,950	31,590	4,640	17.2
Janitors and cleaners, except maids and housekeeping cleaners	21,830	26,130	4,300	19.7
Customer service representatives	12,500	16,670	4,170	33.4
Truck drivers, heavy and tractor-trailer	24,290	28,430	4,140	17.0
Bookkeeping, accounting, and auditing clerks	21,000	25,120	4,120	19.6
Nursing aides, orderlies, and attendants	16,640	20,480	3,840	23.1
Food preparation workers	14,910	18,290	3,380	22.7

Note: Projections cover Mississippi; (1) Sorted by numeric employment change
Source: www.projectionscentral.com, State Occupational Projections, 2006-2016 Long-Term Projections

Fastest Growing Occupations: 2006 - 2016

Occupation[1]	2006 Employment	2016 Projected Employment	Numeric Employment Change	Percent Employment Change
Home health aides	3,570	5,410	1,840	51.5
Computer software engineers, applications	1,100	1,640	540	49.1
Network systems and data communications analysts	710	1,020	310	43.7
Pharmacy technicians	2,390	3,370	980	41.0
Veterinarians	610	850	240	39.3
Industrial engineers	1,040	1,440	400	38.5
Medical assistants	2,170	2,990	820	37.8
Correctional officers and jailers	6,220	8,350	2,130	34.2
Customer service representatives	12,500	16,670	4,170	33.4
Network and computer systems administrators	1,260	1,680	420	33.3

Note: Projections cover Mississippi; (1) Sorted by percent employment change and excludes occupations with numeric employment change less than 200
Source: www.projectionscentral.com, State Occupational Projections, 2006-2016 Long-Term Projections

Average Wages

Occupation	$/Hr.	Occupation	$/Hr.
Accountants and Auditors	25.46	Maids and Housekeeping Cleaners	7.89
Automotive Mechanics	15.01	Maintenance and Repair Workers	14.51
Bookkeepers	16.67	Marketing Managers	39.66
Carpenters	14.00	Nuclear Medicine Technologists	29.01
Cashiers	8.39	Nurses, Licensed Practical	17.20
Clerks, General Office	11.34	Nurses, Registered	28.54
Clerks, Receptionists/Information	10.84	Nursing Aides/Orderlies/Attendants	9.62
Clerks, Shipping/Receiving	15.92	Packers and Packagers, Hand	9.05
Computer Programmers	23.99	Physical Therapists	35.77
Computer Support Specialists	19.99	Postal Service Mail Carriers	23.03
Computer Systems Analysts	28.09	Real Estate Brokers	n/a
Cooks, Restaurant	9.27	Retail Salespersons	11.59
Dentists	n/a	Sales Reps., Exc. Tech./Scientific	24.78
Electrical Engineers	36.37	Sales Reps., Tech./Scientific	35.52
Electricians	21.46	Secretaries, Exc. Legal/Med./Exec.	13.05
Financial Managers	39.13	Security Guards	9.37
First-Line Supervisors/Mgrs., Sales	16.82	Surgeons	n/a
Food Preparation Workers	8.02	Teacher Assistants	8.40
General and Operations Managers	44.32	Teachers, Elementary School	20.30
Hairdressers/Cosmetologists	12.60	Teachers, Secondary School	20.40
Internists	n/a	Telemarketers	12.22
Janitors and Cleaners	9.99	Truck Drivers, Heavy/Tractor-Trailer	20.01
Landscaping/Groundskeeping Workers	10.08	Truck Drivers, Light/Delivery Svcs.	13.87
Lawyers	51.56	Waiters and Waitresses	7.70

Note: Wage data covers the Jackson, MS - see Appendix B for areas included. Hourly wages for elementary/secondary school teachers and teacher assistants were calculated by the editors from annual wage data assuming a 40 hour work week; n/a not available.
Source: Bureau of Labor Statistics, Metro Area Occupational Employment and Wage Estimates, May 2009

RESIDENTIAL REAL ESTATE

Building Permits

Area	Single-Family			Multi-Family			Total		
	2009	2010	Pct. Chg.	2009	2010	Pct. Chg.	2009	2010	Pct. Chg.
City	45	42	-6.7	4	88	2,100.0	49	130	165.3
MSA[1]	1,182	1,303	10.2	6	88	1,366.7	1,188	1,391	17.1
U.S.	441,100	447,300	1.4	141,900	157,300	10.9	583,000	604,600	3.7

Note: (1) Metropolitan Statistical Area - see Appendix B for areas included; figures represent new, privately-owned housing units authorized (unadjusted data); All permit data are based on estimates with imputation.
Source: U.S. Census Bureau, Manufacturing, Mining, and Construction Statistics, Building Permits, 2009, 2010

Homeownership Rate

Area	2005 (%)	2006 (%)	2007 (%)	2008 (%)	2009 (%)	2010 (%)
MSA[1]	n/a	n/a	n/a	n/a	n/a	n/a
U.S.	68.9	68.8	68.1	67.8	67.4	66.9

Note: (1) Metropolitan Statistical Area - see Appendix B for areas included
Source: U.S. Census Bureau, Housing Vacancies and Homeownership Annual Statistics: 2010

Housing Vacancy Rates

Area	Gross Vacancy Rate[2] (%)			Year-Round Vacancy Rate[3] (%)			Rental Vacancy Rate[4] (%)			Homeowner Vacancy Rate[5] (%)		
	2008	2009	2010	2008	2009	2010	2008	2009	2010	2008	2009	2010
MSA[1]	n/a	n/a	n/a	n/a	n/a	n/a	n/a	n/a	n/a	n/a	n/a	n/a
U.S.	14.4	14.5	14.3	11.1	11.3	11.3	10.0	10.6	10.2	2.8	2.6	2.6

Note: (1) Metropolitan Statistical Area - see Appendix B for areas included; (2) The percentage of the total housing inventory that is vacant; (3) The percentage of the housing inventory (excluding seasonal units) that is year-round vacant; (4) The percentage of rental inventory that is vacant for rent; (5) The percentage of homeowner inventory that is vacant for sale; n/a not available
Source: U.S. Census Bureau, Housing Vacancies and Homeownership Annual Statistics: 2010

State Corporate Income Tax Rates

State	Tax Rate (%)	Income Brackets ($)	Num. of Brackets	Financial Institution Tax Rate (%)[a]	Federal Income Tax Ded.
Mississippi	3.0 - 5.0	5,000 - 10,001	3	3.0 - 5.0	No

Note: Tax rates as of January 1, 2011; (a) Rates listed are the tax rates applied to financial institutions or excise taxes based on income. Some states have other taxes based upon the value of deposits or shares.
Source: Federation of Tax Administrators, "State Corporate Income Tax Rates, 2011"

State Individual Income Tax Rates

State	Tax Rate (%)	Income Brackets ($)	Num. of Brackets	Personal Exempt. ($)[1] Single	Personal Exempt. ($)[1] Dependents	Fed. Inc. Tax Ded.
Mississippi	3.0 - 5.0	5,000 - 10,001	3	6,000	1,500	No

Note: Tax rates as of January 1, 2011; Local- and county-level taxes are not included; n/a not applicable;
(1) Married joint filers generally receive double the single exemption
Source: Federation of Tax Administrators, "State Individual Income Tax Rates, 2011"

Various State and Local Tax Rates

State	State and Local Sales and Use (%)	State Sales and Use (%)	Gasoline[1] (¢/gal.)	Cigarette[2] ($/pack)	Spirits[3] ($/gal.)	Wine[4] ($/gal.)	Beer[5] ($/gal.)
Mississippi	7.0	7.00	18.8	0.68	7.78 (g)	(j)	0.43

Note: All tax rates as of January 1, 2011 except Spirits (Sept. 1, 2010); (1) The American Petroleum Institute has developed a methodology for determining the average tax rate on a gallon of fuel. Rates may include any of the following: excise taxes, environmental fees, storage tank fees, other fees or taxes, general sales tax, and local taxes. In states where gasoline is subject to the general sales tax, or where the fuel tax is based on the average sale price, the average rate determined by API is sensitive to changes in the price of gasoline. States that fully or partially apply general sales taxes to gasoline: CA, CO, GA, IL, IN, MI, NY; (2) The federal excise tax of $1.0066 per pack and local taxes are not included; (3) Rates are those applicable to off-premise sales of 40% alcohol by volume (a.b.v.) distilled spirits in 750ml containers. Local excise taxes are excluded; (4) Rates are those applicable to off-premise sales of 11% a.b.v. non-carbonated wine in 750ml containers; (5) Rates are those applicable to off-premise sales of 4.7% a.b.v. beer in 12 ounce containers; (g) States where the government controls sales. In control states, products are subject to ad valorem mark-up and excise taxes. The excise tax rate is calculated using a methodology developed by the Distilled Spirits Council of the United States; (j) Control states, where the government controls all sales. Products can be subject to ad valorem mark-up and excise taxes.
Source: Tax Foundation, 2011 Facts & Figures: How Does Your State Compare?

State-Local Tax Burdens

Area	Rate (%)	Rank[1]	Per Capita Taxes Paid to Home State ($)	Total State and Local Per Capita Taxes Paid ($)	Per Capita Income ($)
Mississippi	8.7	36	1,863	2,678	30,689
U.S. Average	9.8	-	3,057	4,160	42,539

Note: Figures cover 2009; (1) Rank ranges from 1 to 50 where 1 is highest tax burden
Source: Tax Foundation, State-Local Tax Burdens, All States, 2009

State Business Tax Climate Index Rankings

State	Overall Rank	Corporate Tax Index Rank	Individual Income Tax Index Rank	Sales Tax Index Rank	Unemployment Insurance Tax Index Rank	Property Tax Index Rank
Mississippi	21	13	19	33	4	31

Note: The index is a measure of how each state's tax laws affect economic performance. The lower the rank, the more favorable a state's tax system is for business. All ranks are for fiscal years. States without a given tax are given a ranking of 1.
Source: Tax Foundation, Tax Foundation Background Paper, No. 60, "2011 State Business Tax Climate Index"

**COMMERCIAL
UTILITIES**

Typical Monthly Electric Bills

Area	Commercial Service ($/month)		Industrial Service ($/month)	
	3 kW demand 1,000 kWh	40 kW demand 14,000 kWh	1,000 kW demand 200,000 kWh	50,000 kW demand 15,000,000 kWh
City	130	1,356	16,701	1,081,050
Average[1]	135	1,576	23,741	1,402,202

Note: Based on total rates in effect July 1, 2010; (1) average based on 182 utilities surveyed
Source: Edison Electric Institute, Typical Bills and Average Rates Report, Summer 2010

TRANSPORTATION

Means of Transportation to Work

Area	Car/Truck/Van		Public Transportation			Bicycle	Walked	Other Means	Worked at Home
	Drove Alone	Car-pooled	Bus	Subway	Railroad				
City	81.9	11.4	0.8	0.0	0.0	0.2	1.5	1.3	2.9
MSA[1]	84.1	9.9	0.5	0.0	0.0	0.1	1.1	1.1	3.1
U.S.	75.8	10.4	2.7	1.7	0.5	0.5	2.9	1.2	4.1

Note: Figures are percentages and cover workers 16 years of age and older;
(1) Metropolitan Statistical Area - see Appendix B for areas included
Source: U.S. Census Bureau, 2007-2009 American Community Survey 3-Year Estimates

Travel Time to Work

Area	Less Than 15 Minutes	15 to 29 Minutes	30 to 44 Minutes	45 to 59 Minutes	60 to 89 Minutes	90 Minutes or More
City	24.6	53.1	17.8	2.3	1.2	1.0
MSA[1]	23.6	45.5	22.0	4.8	2.6	1.5
U.S.	28.5	36.2	19.7	7.5	5.6	2.5

Note: Figures are percentages and include workers 16 years old and over;
(1) Metropolitan Statistical Area - see Appendix B for areas included
Source: U.S. Census Bureau, 2007-2009 American Community Survey 3-Year Estimates

Travel Time Index

Area	1982	1999	2008	2009
Urban Area[1]	1.02	1.06	1.08	1.07
Average[2]	1.08	1.20	1.20	1.20

Note: Travel Time Index—the ratio of travel time in the peak period to the travel time at
free-flow conditions. A value of 1.30 indicates a 20-minute free-flow trip takes 26 minutes
in the peak. Free-flow speeds (60 mph on freeways and 35 mph on principal arterials)
are used as the comparison threshold; (1) Covers the Jackson urban area;
(2) average of 439 urban areas
Source: Texas Transportation Institute, Urban Mobility Report 2010, December 2010

Public Transportation

Agency Name / Mode of Transportation	Vehicles Operated in Maximum Service	Annual Unlinked Passenger Trips ('000)	Annual Passenger Miles ('000)
City of Jackson Transit System (JATRAN)			
Demand response	11	24.8	277.4
Bus	25	516.7	3,404.8

Note: Figures include both directly operated and purchased transportation
Source: Federal Transit Administration, National Transit Database, 2009

Air Transportation

Airport Name and Code / Type of Service	Passenger Airlines[1]	Passenger Enplanements	Freight Carriers[2]	Freight (lbs.)
Jackson International (JAN)				
Domestic service (U.S. carriers - 2010)	18	617,983	7	7,819,449
International service (U.S. carriers - 2009)	2	7	1	1,826

Note: (1) Includes all U.S.-based major, minor and commuter airlines that carried at least one passenger during the year; (2) Includes all U.S.-based airlines and freight carriers that transported at least one pound of freight during the year
Source: Bureau of Transportation Statistics, The Intermodal Transportation Database, Air Carriers: T-100 Domestic Market (U.S. Carriers), 2010; Bureau of Transportation Statistics, The Intermodal Transportation Database, Air Carriers: T-100 International Market (U.S. Carriers), 2009

Other Transportation Statistics

Interstate highways:	I-20; I-55
Amtrak service:	Yes
Major waterways/ports:	None

Source: Amtrak.com; Google Maps

BUSINESSES

Major Business Headquarters

Company Name	Rankings	
	Fortune[1]	Forbes[2]
Ergon	-	86

Note: (1) Fortune 500—companies that produce a 10-K are ranked 1 to 500 based on 2010 revenue; (2) all private companies with at least $2 billion in annual revenue are ranked 1 to 223; companies listed are headquartered in the city; dashes indicate no ranking
Source: Fortune, "Fortune 500," May 23, 2011; Forbes, "America's Largest Private Companies," November 3, 2010

Fast-Growing Businesses

According to *Fortune*, Jackson is home to one of the 100 fastest-growing companies in the world: **Cal-Maine Foods**. Companies were ranked by their revenue growth rate; their EPS growth rate; and their three-year annualized total return to investors for the period ended June 30, 2010. Criteria for inclusion: a company, foreign or domestic, must trade on a major U.S. stock exchange; file quarterly reports with the SEC; have a minimum market capitalization of $250 million; have a stock price of at least $5 on June 30, 2010; have been trading continuously since June 30, 2007; have revenue and net income for the four quarters ended on or before April 30, 2010, of at least $50 million and $10 million, respectively; and have posted a compound annual growth in revenue and earnings per share of at least 15% annually over the three years ended on or before April 30, 2010. REITs, limited-liability companies, limited parterships, companies about to be acquired, and companies that lost money in the quarter ended April 30, 2010 were excluded. *Fortune, "100 Fastest-Growing Companies," September 6, 2010*

Minority- and Women-Owned Businesses

Group	All Firms		Firms with Paid Employees			
	Firms	Sales ($000)	Firms	Sales ($000)	Employees	Payroll ($000)
Asian	306	116,202	185	109,819	954	17,060
Black	6,445	247,392	280	137,873	2,017	44,933
Hispanic	49	16,856	20	15,783	204	3,961
Women	5,313	568,793	549	480,939	4,651	115,101
All Firms	15,385	17,655,303	3,929	17,133,910	85,783	3,047,875

Note: Figures cover firms located in the city; minority- and women-owned business are defined as firms in which the corresponding group own 51% or more of the stock or equity of the company
Source: U.S. Census Bureau, 2007 Economic Census, Survey of Business Owners

HOTELS

Hotels/Motels

Area	5 Star		4 Star		3 Star		2 Star		1 Star		Not Rated	
	Num.	Pct.3	Num.	Pct.3	Num.	Pct.3	Num.	Pct.3	Num.	Pct.3	Num.	Pct.3
City[1]	0	0.0	0	0.0	12	12.0	60	60.0	2	2.0	26	26.0
Total[2]	119	0.7	927	5.8	4,906	30.5	7,992	49.7	526	3.3	1,625	10.1

Note: (1) Figures cover Jackson and vicinity; (2) Figures cover all 100 cities in this book; (3) Percentage of hotels which are a given star rating; Star ratings are determined by expedia.com and offer an indication of the general quality of a particular hotel.
Source: expedia.com, May 5, 2011

EVENT SITES

Major Stadiums, Arenas, and Auditoriums

Name	Max. Capacity
Mississippi Coast Coliseum	15,000
Mississippi Veterans Memorial Stadium	60,492
Smith-Wills Stadium	5,200

Source: Original research

Convention Centers

Name	Overall Space (sq. ft.)	Exhibit Space (sq. ft.)	Meeting Space (sq. ft.)	Meeting Rooms
Jackson Cenvention Complex	330,000	n/a	60,000	n/a
Mississippi Telcom Center	120,000	n/a	n/a	n/a

Note: n/a not available
Source: Original research

Living Environment

COST OF LIVING

Cost of Living Index

Composite Index	Groceries	Housing	Utilities	Trans-portation	Health Care	Misc. Goods/ Services
96.9	93.0	94.0	118.1	92.0	95.7	96.1

Note: U.S. = 100; Figures cover the Jackson MS urban area.
Source: The Council for Community and Economic Research, ACCRA Cost of Living Index, 2010

Grocery Prices

Area[1]	T-Bone Steak ($/pound)	Frying Chicken ($/pound)	Whole Milk ($/half gal.)	Eggs ($/dozen)	Orange Juice ($/64 oz.)	Coffee ($/11.5 oz.)
City[2]	9.13	1.01	2.09	1.33	2.85	3.02
Avg.	9.04	1.16	2.02	1.47	3.08	3.65
Min.	6.97	0.84	1.46	0.96	2.39	2.64
Max.	13.93	2.51	3.58	3.01	4.94	6.32

Note: (1) Values for the local area are compared with the average, minimum and maximum values for all 338 areas in the Cost of Living Index; (2) Figures cover the Jackson MS urban area; **T-Bone Steak** *(price per pound);* **Frying Chicken** *(price per pound, whole fryer);* **Whole Milk** *(half gallon carton);* **Eggs** *(price per dozen, Grade A, large);* **Orange Juice** *(64 oz. Tropicana or Florida Natural);* **Coffee** *(11.5 oz. can, vacuum-packed, Maxwell House, Hills Bros, or Folgers).*
Source: The Council for Community and Economic Research, ACCRA Cost of Living Index, 2010

Housing and Utility Costs

Area[1]	New Home Price ($)	Apartment Rent ($/month)	All Electric ($/month)	Part Electric ($/month)	Other Energy ($/month)	Telephone ($/month)
City[2]	273,992	730	-	94.24	118.02	30.00
Avg.	293,442	810	166.39	91.93	83.82	26.93
Min.	182,545	453	119.21	44.47	36.85	17.98
Max.	1,123,114	2,776	307.53	218.20	313.90	39.15

Note: (1) Values for the local area are compared with the average, minimum and maximum values for all 338 areas in the Cost of Living Index; (2) Figures cover the Jackson MS urban area; **New Home Price** *(2,400 sf living area, 8,000 sf lot, in urban area with full utilities);* **Apartment Rent** *(950 sf 2 bedroom/1.5 or 2 bath, unfurnished, excluding all utilities except water);* **All Electric** *(average monthly cost for an all-electric home);* **Part Electric** *(average monthly cost for a part-electric home);* **Other Energy** *(average monthly cost for natural gas, fuel oil, coal, wood, and any other forms of energy except electricity);* **Telephone** *(price includes basic monthly rate for a private residential line plus additional local usage charges incurred by a family of four).*
Source: The Council for Community and Economic Research, ACCRA Cost of Living Index, 2010

Health Care, Transportation, and Other Costs

Area[1]	Doctor ($/visit)	Dentist ($/visit)	Optometrist ($/visit)	Gasoline ($/gallon)	Beauty Salon ($/visit)	Men's Shirt ($)
City[2]	84.10	76.53	79.21	2.51	31.89	24.62
Avg.	89.44	78.95	87.40	2.73	31.92	24.83
Min.	57.00	54.25	48.32	2.44	19.17	13.67
Max.	149.90	136.73	174.22	3.75	62.81	47.89

Note: (1) Values for the local area are compared with the average, minimum and maximum values for all 338 areas in the Cost of Living Index; (2) Figures cover the Jackson MS urban area; **Doctor** *(general practitioners routine exam of an established patient);* **Dentist** *(adult teeth cleaning and periodic oral examination);* **Optometrist** *(full vision eye exam for established adult patient);* **Gasoline** *(one gallon regular unleaded, national brand, including all taxes, cash price at self-service pump if available);* **Beauty Salon** *(woman's shampoo, trim, and blow-dry);* **Men's Shirt** *(cotton/polyester dress shirt, pinpoint weave, long sleeves).*
Source: The Council for Community and Economic Research, ACCRA Cost of Living Index, 2010

HOUSING

House Price Index (HPI)

Area	National Ranking[2]	Quarterly Change (%)	One-Year Change (%)	Five-Year Change (%)
MSA[1]	123	-1.05	-0.53	6.25
U.S.[3]	-	-0.84	-3.95	-11.45

Note: The HPI is a weighted repeat sales index. It measures average price changes in repeat sales or refinancings on the same properties. This information is obtained by reviewing repeat mortgage transactions on single-family properties whose mortgages have been purchased or securitized by Fannie Mae or Freddie Mac in January 1975; (1) Metropolitan/Micropolitan Statistical Area - see Appendix B for areas included; (2) Rankings are based on annual percentage change for all metro areas containing at least 15,000 transactions over the last 10 years and ranges from 1 to 309; (3) figures based on a weighted average of Census Division estimates; all figures are for the period ending December 31, 2010
Source: Federal Housing Finance Agency, House Price Index, February 24, 2011

House Price Valuations

Area	Q4 2005 Price ($000)	Q4 2005 Over-valuation	Q4 2006 Price ($000)	Q4 2006 Over-valuation	Q4 2007 Price ($000)	Q4 2007 Over-valuation	Q4 2008 Price ($000)	Q4 2008 Over-valuation	Q4 2009 Price ($000)	Q4 2009 Over-valuation
MSA[1]	99.9	-14.4	106.0	-12.9	105.7	-16.4	103.1	-19.4	101.6	-22.5

Note: Figures show the percentage of over- or under-valuation of single family homes relative to statistically normal house values (e.g. a value of 23.6 indicates that house values are 23.6% overvalued). Statistically normal house values are based on house prices, interest rates, household incomes, population densities, and any historical premiums or discounts metropolitan areas have exhibited over time; (1) Figures cover the Jackson, MS Metropolitan Statistical Area - see Appendix B for areas included
Source: Global Insight/PNC Financial Services Group, House Prices in America: 4th Quarter 2009 Update

Median Single-Family Home Prices

Area	2008	2009	2010[p]	Percent Change 2009 to 2010
MSA[1]	128.7	134.9	133.2	-1.3
U.S. Average	196.6	172.1	173.2	0.6

Note: Figures are median sales prices of existing single-family homes in thousands of dollars; (p) preliminary; n/a not available; (1) Metropolitan Statistical Area - see Appendix B for areas included
Source: National Association of Realtors, Median Sales Price of Existing Single-Family Homes for Metropolitan Areas, 4th Quarter 2010

Median Apartment Condo-Coop Home Prices

Area	2008	2009	2010[p]	Percent Change 2009 to 2010
MSA[1]	n/a	n/a	n/a	n/a
U.S. Average	209.8	175.6	171.7	-2.2

Note: Figures are median sales prices of existing apartment condo-coop homes in thousands of dollars; (p) preliminary; n/a not available; (1) Metropolitan Statistical Area - see Appendix B for areas included
Source: National Association of Realtors, Median Sales Price of Existing Apartment Condo-Coop Homes for Metropolitan Areas, 4th Quarter 2010

Year Housing Structure Built

Area	2000 or Later	1990 -1999	1980 -1989	1970 -1979	1960 -1969	1950 -1959	1940 -1949	Before 1940	Median Year
City	5.0	7.7	13.8	25.9	21.6	16.3	6.1	3.7	1971
MSA[1]	15.7	19.1	16.2	20.5	12.9	8.8	3.6	3.3	1981
U.S.	12.5	14.0	14.2	16.5	11.4	11.3	5.8	14.3	1974

Note: Figures are percentages except for Median Year; (1) Metropolitan Statistical Area - see Appendix B for areas included
Source: U.S. Census Bureau, 2007-2009 American Community Survey 3-Year Estimates

HEALTH

Health Risk Data

Category	MSA[1] (%)	U.S. (%)
Adults who have been told they have high blood pressure	36.4	28.7
Adults who have been told they have high blood cholesterol	35.2	37.5
Adults who have been told they have diabetes[3]	10.5	8.3
Adults who have been told they have arthritis	27.9	26.0
Adults who have been told they currently have asthma	9.4	8.8
Adults who are current smokers	20.9	17.9
Adults who are heavy drinkers[4]	3.2	5.1
Adults who are binge drinkers[5]	12.0	15.8
Adults who are overweight (BMI 25.0 - 29.9)	33.6	36.2
Adults who are obese (BMI 30.0 - 99.8)	35.3	26.9
Adults who participated in any physical activities in the past month	67.2	76.2
Adults 50+ who have ever had a sigmoidoscopy or colonoscopy[2]	65.1	62.2
Women 40+ who have had a mammogram within the past two years[2]	77.3	76.0
Adults age 18–64 who have any kind of health care coverage	78.3	83.1

Note: Data as of 2009 unless otherwise noted; (1) Figures cover the Jackson, MS Metropolitan Statistical Area - see Appendix B for areas included; (2) Data as of 2008; (3) Figures do not include pregnancy-related, borderline, or pre-diabetes; (4) Heavy drinkers are classified as males having more than two drinks per day or females having more than one drink per day; (5) Binge drinkers are classified as males having five or more drinks on one occasion or females having four or more drinks on one occasion
Source: Centers for Disease Control and Prevention, Behaviorial Risk Factor Surveillance System, SMART: Selected Metropolitan/Micropolitan Area Risk Trends, 2008, 2009

Mortality Rates for the Top 10 Causes of Death in the U.S.

ICD-10[a] Sub-Chapter	ICD-10[a] Code	Age-Adjusted Mortality Rate[1] per 100,000 population	
		County[2]	U.S.
Malignant neoplasms	C00-C97	162.4	180.9
Ischaemic heart diseases	I20-I25	103.3	135.0
Other forms of heart disease	I30-I51	105.1	50.0
Cerebrovascular diseases	I60-I69	42.9	44.1
Chronic lower respiratory diseases	J40-J47	34.9	41.5
Other degenerative diseases of the nervous system	G30-G31	15.9	23.6
Diabetes mellitus	E10-E14	16.2	23.5
Other external causes of accidental injury	W00-X59	15.7	23.5
Organic, including symptomatic, mental disorders	F01-F09	27.8	22.2
Influenza and pneumonia	J09-J18	18.3	18.1

Note: (a) ICD-10 = International Classification of Diseases 10th Revision; (1) Mortality rates are a three year average covering 2005-2007; (2) Figures cover Hinds County
Source: Centers for Disease Control and Prevention, National Center for Health Statistics. Compressed Mortality File 1999-2007. CDC WONDER On-line Database, compiled from Compressed Mortality File 1999-2007 Series 20 No. 2M, 2010.

Mortality Rates for Selected Causes of Death

ICD-10[a] Sub-Chapter	ICD-10[a] Code	Age-Adjusted Mortality Rate[1] per 100,000 population	
		County[2]	U.S.
Assault	X85-Y09	19.3	6.0
Human immunodeficiency virus (HIV) disease	B20-B24	18.0	4.0
Hypertensive diseases	I10-I15	61.6	18.0
Intentional self-harm	X60-X84	10.0	11.0
Malnutrition	E40-E46	*1.5	0.8
Obesity and other hyperalimentation	E65-E68	*1.6	1.5
Transport accidents	V01-V99	24.7	15.6
Viral hepatitis	B15-B19	*0.7	2.1

Note: (a) ICD-10 = International Classification of Diseases 10th Revision; (1) Mortality rates are a three year average covering 2005-2007; (2) Figures cover Hinds County; (*) Unreliable data as per CDC
Source: Centers for Disease Control and Prevention, National Center for Health Statistics. Compressed Mortality File 1999-2007. CDC WONDER On-line Database, compiled from Compressed Mortality File 1999-2007 Series 20 No. 2M, 2010.

Distribution of Physicians and Dentists

Area[1]	Dentists[2]	D.O.[3]	M.D.[4]				
			Total	Family/ General Practice	Pediatrics	Medical Specialties	Surgical Specialties
Local (number)	123	18	683	62	45	250	183
Local (rate[5])	4.9	0.7	27.6	2.5	1.8	10.1	7.4
U.S. (rate[5])	4.5	1.9	18.3	2.5	1.4	6.8	4.1

Note: Data as of 2008 unless noted; (1) Local data covers Hinds County; (2) Data as of 2007; (3) Doctor of Osteopathic Medicine; (4) Includes active, non-federal, patient-care, office-based Doctors of Medicine; (5) rate per 10,000 population
Source: Area Resource File (ARF). 2009-2010 Release. U.S. Department of Health and Human Services, Health Resources and Services Administration, Bureau of Health Professions, Rockville, MD, August 2010

Hospitals

Jackson has the following hospitals: 5 general medical and surgical; 1 psychiatric; 1 obstetrics and gynecology; 1 rehabilitation; 3 long-term acute care.
AHA Guide to the Healthcare Field 2010

EDUCATION

Public School District Statistics

District Name	Schls	Pupils	Pupil/ Teacher Ratio	Minority Pupils[1] (%)	Free Lunch Eligible[2] (%)	IEP[3] (%)
Jackson Public School Dist	61	30,587	16.0	98.4	79.0	n/a

Note: Table includes school districts with 2,000 or more students; (1) Percentage of students that are not non-Hispanic white; (2) Percentage of students that are eligible for the free lunch program; (3) Percentage of students that have an Individualized Education Program.
Source: U.S. Department of Education, National Center for Education Statistics, Common Core of Data, Local Education Agency (School District) Universe Survey: School Year 2008-2009; U.S. Department of Education, National Center for Education Statistics, Common Core of Data, Public Elementary/Secondary School Universe Survey: School Year 2008-2009

Top Public High Schools

High School Name	Index[1]	Rank[1]	Subsidized Lunch (%)[2]	E&E (%)[3]
Murrah	1.385	1282	67.0	16.0

Note: (1) Public schools are ranked according to a ratio that is the number of Advanced Placement, International Baccalaureate, and/or Cambridge tests taken by all students at a school in 2009 divided by the number of graduating seniors. All of the schools on the list have an index of at least 1.000; they are in the top six percent of public schools measured this way. The rankings range from 1 to 1,734; (2) Percentage of students receiving federally subsidized meals; (3) E & E stands for equity and excellence percentage: the portion of all graduating seniors at a school that had at least one passing grade on one AP or IB test; (4) Schools that offer International Baccalaureate or Cambridge exams; (5) School is unranked, but has been identified by Newsweek as one of the nation's most elite public high schools.
Source: Newsweek Online, "Top High Schools 2010"

Highest Level of Education

Area	Less than H.S.	H.S. Diploma	Some College, No Deg.	Associate Degree	Bachelors Degree	Masters Degree	Profess. School Degree	Doctorate Degree
City	17.4	23.8	23.8	7.1	17.6	6.6	2.6	1.2
MSA[1]	14.9	24.9	22.7	8.4	19.4	6.3	2.3	1.2
U.S.	15.3	29.0	20.7	7.5	17.4	7.0	1.9	1.1

Note: Figures are 2010 estimated percentages and cover persons age 25 and over; (1) Metropolitan Statistical Area - see Appendix B for areas included
Source: Claritas, Inc.

Educational Attainment by Race

Area	High School Graduate (%)					Bachelor's Degree (%)				
	Total	White	Black	Asian	Hisp.[2]	Total	White	Black	Asian	Hisp.[2]
City	82.1	93.1	78.8	n/a	49.0	27.3	51.8	18.9	n/a	15.1
MSA[1]	84.5	90.4	77.9	84.8	47.6	29.0	36.8	18.4	63.7	11.5
U.S.	84.9	90.0	80.7	85.5	60.7	27.8	30.9	17.5	49.7	12.7

Note: Figures shown cover persons 25 years old and over; (1) Metropolitan Statistical Area - see Appendix B for areas included; (2) people of Hispanic origin can be of any race
Source: U.S. Census Bureau, 2007-2009 American Community Survey 3-Year Estimates

School Enrollment by Grade and Control

Area	Preschool (%)		Kindergarten (%)		Grades 1 - 4 (%)		Grades 5 - 8 (%)		Grades 9 - 12 (%)	
	Public	Private	Public	Private	Public	Private	Public	Private	Public	Private
City	76.1	23.9	82.2	17.8	88.7	11.3	83.5	16.5	86.0	14.0
MSA[1]	56.0	44.0	79.4	20.6	86.4	13.6	83.5	16.5	86.6	13.4
U.S.	54.3	45.7	86.4	13.6	88.9	11.1	89.1	10.9	90.2	9.8

Note: Figures shown cover persons 3 years old and over; (1) Metropolitan Statistical Area - see Appendix B for areas included
Source: U.S. Census Bureau, 2007-2009 American Community Survey 3-Year Estimates

Average Salaries of Public School Classroom Teachers

Area	2009-10		2010-11		Percent Change 2009-10 to 2010-11	Percent Change 2000-01 to 2010-11
	Dollars	Rank[1]	Dollars	Rank[1]		
Mississippi	45,644	48	46,818	46	2.57	46.5
U.S. Average	55,202	-	56,069	-	1.57	29.3

Note: (1) State rank ranges from 1 to 51 where 1 indicates highest salary.
Source: National Education Association, Rankings & Estimates: Rankings of the States 2010 and Estimates of School Statistics 2011, December 2010

Higher Education

Four-Year Colleges			Two-Year Colleges			Medical Schools[1]	Law Schools[2]	Voc/ Tech[3]
Public	Private Non-profit	Private For-profit	Public	Private Non-profit	Private For-profit			
2	3	1	0	0	3	1	1	3

Note: Figures cover institutions located within the city limits and include main campuses only; (1) includes schools accredited by the Liaison Committee on Medical Education and the American Osteopathic Association; (2) includes American Bar Association-accredited law schools; (3) includes all schools with programs that are less than 2 years.
Source: National Center for Education Statistics, Integrated Postsecondary Education System (IPEDS) Peer Analysis System, 2010-11; U.S. News & World Report, Medical School Directory, 2011; U.S. News & World Report, Law School Directory, 2011

According to *U.S. News & World Report,* the Jackson, MS Metropolitan Statistical Area is home to two of the top 189 liberal arts colleges in the U.S.: **Millsaps College** (#93); **Tougaloo College** (#166). The rankings are based on quantitative measurements such as peer assessment, retention, faculty resources, student selectivity, financial resources, graduation rate, and alumni giving rate. *U.S. News & World Report, "America's Best Colleges 2011"*

PRESIDENTIAL ELECTION

2008 Presidential Election Results

Area	Obama	McCain	Nader	Other
Hinds County	69.2	30.3	0.1	0.4
U.S.	52.9	45.6	0.6	0.9

Note: Results are percentages and may not add to 100% due to rounding
Source: Dave Leip's Atlas of U.S. Presidential Elections, www.uselectionatlas.org

EMPLOYERS

Major Employers

Company Name	Industry	Type of Site
Bellsouth	Business services, nec	Branch
Blue Cross	Hospital and medical service plans	Headquarters
Central District-Commissioner	Regulation, administration of transportation	Branch
Chief Engineer	Regulation, administration of transportation	Branch
County of Jackson	Executive offices	Branch
Entergy	Electric services	Headquarters
Finance and Accounts	Administration of public health programs	Headquarters
HMA	General medical and surgical hospitals	Headquarters
Hudspeth Retardation Center	Administration of public health programs	Branch
JSU	Colleges and universities	Headquarters
Miss Dept Transportation	Regulation, administration of transportation	Branch
Mississippi Baptist Health Sys	Management services	Headquarters
Oxford Healthcare	Home health care services	Single
Peco Foods of Mississippi	Poultry and poultry products	Branch
River Oaks Health System	General medical and surgical hospitals	Headquarters
Skytel	Radiotelephone communication	Headquarters
Southern Capital Life Insur Co	Investment advice	Single
Southern Healthcare Agency	Help supply services	Single
St Dominic-Jackson Mem Hosp	General medical and surgical hospitals	Single
Transportation Commission	Regulation, administration of transportation	Headquarters
University Mississippi Med Ctr	General medical and surgical hospitals	Single
Vertex Aerospace	Airports, flying fields, and services	Single
Youngwllams Child Support Svcs	Legal services	Single

Note: Companies shown are located within the Jackson metropolitan area; nec = not elsewhere classified.
Source: www.zapdata.com, January 2011

PUBLIC SAFETY

Crime Rate

Area	All Crimes	Violent Crimes				Property Crimes		
		Murder	Forcible Rape	Robbery	Aggrav. Assault	Burglary	Larceny -Theft	Motor Vehicle Theft
City	8,505.3	21.4	71.8	554.4	229.2	2,644.1	4,047.5	936.9
Suburbs[1]	2,287.9	1.9	25.4	36.3	100.1	594.1	1,397.4	132.6
Metro[2]	4,269.2	8.1	40.2	201.4	141.3	1,247.4	2,241.9	388.9
U.S.	3,465.5	5.0	28.7	133.0	262.8	716.3	2,060.9	258.8

Note: Figures are crimes per 100,000 population; (1) All areas within the metro area that are located outside the city limits; (2) Metropolitan Statistical Area - see Appendix B for areas included
Source: FBI Uniform Crime Reports, 2009

Hate Crimes

Area	Number of Quarters Reported	Bias Motivation				
		Race	Religion	Sexual Orientation	Ethnicity	Disability
City	n/a	n/a	n/a	n/a	n/a	n/a

Note: n/a not available.
Source: Federal Bureau of Investigation, Hate Crime Statistics 2009

Identity Theft Consumer Complaints

Area	Complaints	Complaints per 100,000 Population	Rank[2]
MSA[1]	533	99.8	60
U.S.	250,854	81.3	-

Note: (1) Metropolitan Statistical Area - see Appendix B for areas included; (2) Rank ranges from 1 to 384 where 1 indicates greatest number of complaints per 100,000 population
Source: Federal Trade Commission, Consumer Sentinel Network Data Book for January - December 2010

RECREATION

Culture

Dance[1]	Theatre[1]	Instrumental Music[1]	Vocal Music[1]	Series/ Festivals	Museums	Zoos and Aquariums[2]
1	2	2	1	3	11	1

Note: (1) Number of professional perfoming groups; (2) AZA-accredited
Source: The Grey House Performing Arts Directory, 2011-2012; Official Museum Directory, 2010; American Association of Museums, AAM Member Museums, March 2011; Association of Zoos & Aquariums, AZA Member Zoos & Aquariums, May 2011

Professional Sports Teams

Team Name	League

No teams are located in the metro area
Source: Original research

CLIMATE

Average and Extreme Temperatures

Temperature	Jan	Feb	Mar	Apr	May	Jun	Jul	Aug	Sep	Oct	Nov	Dec	Yr.
Extreme High (°F)	82	85	89	94	99	105	106	102	104	95	88	84	106
Average High (°F)	56	60	69	77	84	90	92	92	87	78	68	59	76
Average Temp. (°F)	45	48	57	65	72	79	82	81	76	65	56	49	65
Average Low (°F)	34	36	44	52	60	68	71	70	65	52	44	37	53
Extreme Low (°F)	2	11	15	27	38	47	51	55	35	29	17	4	2

Note: Figures cover the years 1963-1990
Source: National Climatic Data Center, International Station Meteorological Climate Summary, 9/96

Average Precipitation/Snowfall/Humidity

Precip./Humidity	Jan	Feb	Mar	Apr	May	Jun	Jul	Aug	Sep	Oct	Nov	Dec	Yr.
Avg. Precip. (in.)	5.1	4.7	5.8	5.7	5.4	3.0	4.5	3.8	3.6	3.3	4.7	5.8	55.4
Avg. Snowfall (in.)	1	Tr	Tr	Tr	0	0	0	0	0	0	Tr	Tr	1
Avg. Rel. Hum. 6am (%)	87	87	88	90	92	92	93	94	94	93	90	87	91
Avg. Rel. Hum. 3pm (%)	59	54	51	50	53	52	56	56	55	49	52	58	54

Note: Figures cover the years 1963-1990; Tr = Trace amounts (<0.05 in. of rain; <0.5 in. of snow)
Source: National Climatic Data Center, International Station Meteorological Climate Summary, 9/96

Weather Conditions

Temperature			Daytime Sky			Precipitation		
10°F & below	32°F & below	90°F & above	Clear	Partly cloudy	Cloudy	0.01 inch or more precip.	0.1 inch or more snow/ice	Thunder-storms
1	50	84	103	144	118	106	2	68

Note: Figures are average number of days per year and cover the years 1963-1990
Source: National Climatic Data Center, International Station Meteorological Climate Summary, 9/96

HAZARDOUS WASTE

Superfund Sites

Jackson has no sites on the EPA's Superfund Final National Priorities List.
U.S. Environmental Protection Agency, Final National Priorities List, April 1, 2011

AIR & WATER QUALITY

Air Quality Index

| Area | Percent of Days when Air Quality was...[2] | | | | AQI Statistics | |
	Good	Moderate	Unhealthy for Sensitive Groups	Unhealthy	Maximum	Median
Area[1]	74.8	25.2	0.0	0.0	90	39

Note: The Air Quality Index (AQI) is an index for reporting daily air quality. EPA calculates the AQI for five major air pollutants regulated by the Clean Air Act: ground-level ozone, particle pollution (also known as particulate matter), carbon monoxide, sulfur dioxide, and nitrogen dioxide. The AQI runs from 0 to 500. The higher the AQI value, the greater the level of air pollution and the greater the health concern. There are six AQI categories: "Good" The AQI is between 0 and 50. Air quality is considered satisfactory; "Moderate" The AQI is between 51 and 100. Air quality is acceptable; "Unhealthy for Sensitive Groups" When AQI values are between 101 and 150, members of sensitive groups may experience health effects; "Unhealthy" When AQI values are between 151 and 200 everyone may begin to experience health effects; "Very Unhealthy" AQI values between 201 and 300 trigger a health alert; "Hazardous" AQI values over 300 trigger health warnings of emergency conditions; (1) Data covers Hinds County; (2) Based on 330 days with AQI data in 2008; The EPA has suspended data updates while it assesses its data systems, including AirData reports and maps.
Source: U.S. Environmental Protection Agency, AirData Report, 2008

Air Quality Index Pollutants

| Area | Percent of Days when AQI Pollutant was...[2] | | | | | |
	Carbon Monoxide	Nitrogen Dioxide	Ozone	Sulfur Dioxide	Particulate Matter 2.5	Particulate Matter 10
Area[1]	0.0	0.0	24.5	0.0	75.5	0.0

Note: The Air Quality Index (AQI) is an index for reporting daily air quality. EPA calculates the AQI for five major air pollutants regulated by the Clean Air Act: ground-level ozone, particle pollution (also known as particulate matter), carbon monoxide, sulfur dioxide, and nitrogen dioxide. The AQI runs from 0 to 500. The higher the AQI value, the greater the level of air pollution and the greater the health concern; (1) Data covers Hinds County; (2) Based on 330 days with AQI data in 2008; The EPA has suspended data updates while it assesses its data systems, including AirData reports and maps.
Source: U.S. Environmental Protection Agency, AirData Report, 2008

Air Quality Index Trends

| Area | Trend Sites (days) | | | | | | | | All Sites (days) |
	2002	2003	2004	2005	2006	2007	2008	2009	2009
MSA[1]	n/a	n/a	n/a	n/a	n/a	n/a	n/a	n/a	n/a

Note: Figures are the number of days the AQI value exceeded 100 in a given year. An AQI value greater than 100 indicates that air quality would have been in the unhealthful range on that day. Data from exceptional events are included. These counts are presented in two ways. First, the counts are based on sites having an adequate record of monitoring data during the trend period (trend sites). These counts represent the relative change in the number of days with AQI values greater than 100. In the last column, the counts are based on all sites with data in the most recent year (because it is possible for a site to have data in the most recent year but not enough data to be a trend site); (1) Data covers the Jackson, MS Metropolitan Statistical Area - see Appendix B for areas included; n/a not available.
Source: U.S. Environmental Protection Agency, Office of Air and Radiation, Air Quality Index Information, "Number of Days with Air Quality Index Values Greater than 100 and Trend Sites, 1990-2009, and at All Sites in 2009"

Maximum Air Pollutant Concentrations

	Particulate Matter 10 (ug/m^3)	Particulate Matter 2.5 (ug/m^3)	Ozone (ppm)	Carbon Monoxide (ppm)	Sulfur Dioxide (ppm)	Nitrogen Dioxide (ppm)	Lead (ug/m^3)
MSA[1] Level	n/a	23	0.061	n/a	n/a	n/a	n/a
NAAQS[2]	150	35	0.075	9	0.140	0.053	0.15
Met NAAQS[2]	Yes	Yes	Yes	n/a	n/a	n/a	n/a

Note: Data from exceptional events are not included; (1) Data covers the Jackson, MS Metropolitan Statistical Area - see Appendix B for areas included; (2) National Ambient Air Quality Standards; n/a not available
Concentrations: Particulate Matter 10 (coarse particulate) - highest second maximum 24-hour concentration; Particulate Matter 2.5 (fine particulate) - highest 98th percentile 24-hour concentration; Ozone - highest fourth daily maximum 8-hour concentration; Carbon Monoxide - highest second maximum non-overlapping 8-hour concentration; Sulfur Dioxide - highest second maximum 24-hour concentration; Nitrogen Dioxide - highest arithmetic mean concentration; Lead - maximum running 3-month average
Units: ppm = parts per million; ug/m^3 = micrograms per cubic meter
Source: U.S. Environmental Protection Agency, CBSA Factbook 2009, Air Quality Statistics by City, 2009

Drinking Water

Water System Name	Pop. Served	Primary Water Source Type	Violations[1] Health Based	Violations[1] Monitoring/ Reporting
City of Jackson	175,930	Surface	0	0

Note: (1) Based on violation data from January 1, 2010 to December 31, 2010 (includes unresolved violations from earlier years)
Source: U.S. Environmental Protection Agency, Office of Ground Water and Drinking Water, Safe Drinking Water Information System (based on data extracted May 9, 2011)

Jacksonville, Florida

Background

Modern day Jacksonville is largely a product of the reconstruction that occurred during the 1940s after a fire had razed 147 city blocks a few decades earlier. Lying under the modern structures, however, is a history that dates back earlier than the settlement of Plymouth by the Pilgrims.

Located in the northeast part of Florida on the St. John's River, Jacksonville, the largest city in land area in the contiguous United States, was settled by English, Spanish, and French explorers from the sixteenth through the eighteenth centuries. Sites commemorating their presence include: Fort Caroline National Monument, marking the French settlement led by René de Goulaine Laudonniére in 1564; Spanish Pond one-quarter of a mile east of Fort Caroline, where Spanish forces led by Pedro Menendez captured the Fort; and Fort George Island, from which General James Oglethorpe led English attacks against the Spanish during the eighteenth century.

Jacksonville was attractive to these early settlers because of its easy access to the Atlantic Ocean, which meant a favorable port.

Today, Jacksonville remains an advantageous port and is home to Naval Air Station Jacksonville, a major employer in the area. In January of 2009 the Navy announced plans to station a nuclear powered-carrier at the Jacksonville Naval Base, Mayport. Construction has started to accommodate the large ship, which will arrive in 2014.

Jacksonville is the financial hub of Florida. In recent years, companies expanding or relocating in the city have included Flightstar Aircraft Services, Cingular Wireless, CitiCards, and Fidelity National Financial. Other significant employers include the Winn-Dixie corporate headquarters, Blue Cross/Blue Shield of Florida, and Bank of America, which also has a regional banking system headquarters in Jacksonville. The East Coast's largest rail network, CSX Transportation, also maintains its headquarters here.

On the cultural front, Jacksonville boasts a range of options, including the Children's Museum, the Jacksonville Symphony Orchestra, the Gator Bowl, and beach facilities. In 2005, the city welcomed Super Bowl XXXIX to what was then called Alltel Stadium (now Jacksonville Municipal Stadium), home of the NFL's Jacksonville Jaguars. It also hosts the largest urban park system in the United States, providing services at more than 337 locations on more than 80,000 acres located throughout the city. The Jacksonville Jazz Festival, held every April, is the second-largest jazz festival in the nation. The city is home to several theaters, including Little Theatre, which, operating since 1919, is one of the oldest operating community theaters in the nation.

Jacksonville has more than 80,000 acres of parkland throughout the city, and is renowned for its outdoor recreational facilities. The city's most recent park, The Jacksonville Arboretum and Gardens, was opened in the fall of 2008.

Summers are long, warm, and relatively humid. Winters are generally mild, although periodic invasions of cold northern air bring the temperature down. Temperatures along the beaches rarely rise above 90 degrees. Summer coastal thunderstorms usually occur before noon, and move inland in the afternoons. The greatest rainfall, as localized thundershowers, occurs during the summer months. Although the area is in the hurricane belt, this section of the coast has been very fortunate in escaping hurricane-force winds.

Rankings

General Rankings

- Jacksonville was ranked #252 out of 375 metro areas in *Cities Ranked & Rated*. Criteria: cost of living; climate; crime; transportation; economy and jobs; education; arts and culture; health and healthcare; leisure; quality of life. *Cities Ranked & Rated, 2nd Edition, 2007*

- Jacksonville was ranked #83 out of 379 metro areas in *Places Rated Almanac*. Criteria: health care; education; recreation; transportation; ambience; climate; crime; housing costs; jobs. *Places Rated Almanac, 7th Edition, 2007*

- *Men's Health Living* ranked 100 U.S. cities in terms of quality of life. Jacksonville was ranked #61 and received a grade of C-. Criteria: number of fitness facilities; air quality; number of physicians; male/female ratio; education levels; household income; cost of living. *Men's Health Living, Spring 2008*

Business/Finance Rankings

- Jacksonville was identified as one of the top 25 U.S. cities with the most credit card debt by credit reporting bureau Experian. The city was ranked #2. *Experian, March 4, 2011*

- A.G. Edwards ranked America's 500 top-performing communities based on their residents' personal savings and investing behavior. The Jacksonville metro area ranked #342 with an index score of 98.68 (national average = 100.00). A dozen statistical factors were measured including: participation in retirement savings plans; personal debt levels; and home ownership. *A.G. Edwards, "2007 Nest Egg Index," September 12, 2007*

- Jacksonville was identified as one of the "Happiest Cities to Work" by CareerBliss.com, an online community for career advancement. The city ranked #3 out of 10. CareerBliss.com conducted independent company reviews from employees all over the country to collect data on eight specific factors of workplace happiness: growth opportunities, compensation, benefits, work-life balance, career advancement, senior management, job security, and whether the employee would recommend the company to others. The numbers were combined to find an average rating of overall workplace happiness for each city. *CareerBliss.com, "Happiest and Unhappiest Cities to Work," February 1, 2011*

- *American City Business Journals* ranked America's 261 largest cities in terms of their resident's wealth. Jacksonville ranked #160. Criteria: per capita income; median household income; percentage of households with annual incomes of $200,000 or more; median home value. *American City Business Journals, www.bizjournals.com, "Where the Money Is: America's Wealth Centers," August 18, 2008*

- The Jacksonville metro area appeared on the Milken Institute "2010 Best Performing Metros" list. Rank: #120 out of 200 large metro areas. Criteria: job growth; wage and salary growth; high-tech output growth. *Milken Institute, "2010 Best Performing Metros"*

- The Jacksonville metro area was selected as one of the best cities for entrepreneurs in America by *Inc. Magazine*. Criteria: job-growth data for 335 metro areas was analyzed for: recent growth trend (the current and prior year's employment growth rates, with the current year emphasized); mid-term growth (the average annual 2002-2007 growth rate); long-term trend (the sum of the 2002-2007 and 1996-2001 employment growth rates multiplied by the ratio of the 1996-2001 growth rate over the 2002-2007 growth rate); current year growth. The Jacksonville metro area ranked #19 among large metro areas and #102 overall. *Inc. Magazine, "The Best Cities for Doing Business," July 2008*

- Jacksonville was ranked #106 out of 145 regions worldwide in terms of its "Knowledge Competitiveness Index." The index attempts to measure the knowledge-based development taking place throughout the world and is based on 19 measures of economic performance that indicate a region's ability to translate its knowledge capacity into economic value. *Centre for International Competitiveness, World Knowledge Competitiveness Index 2008*

- *Forbes* ranked the 200 most populous metro areas in the U.S. in terms of the "Best Places for Business and Careers." The Jacksonville metro area was ranked #114. Criteria: 12 metrics including costs (business and living), job growth (past and projected), income growth, educational attainment, projected economic growth, crime, cultural and recreational opportunities, net migration patterns, percentage of subprime mortgages handed out over a three-year period, and the number of highly ranked four-year colleges. *Forbes, "Best Places for Business and Careers," April 14, 2010*

- Jacksonville appeared on *Kiplinger's Personal Finance* list of the "Top Ten Tax-Friendly Cities." The city was ranked #6. Criteria: income tax; sales tax; real estate and car/personal property tax. *Kiplinger's Personal Finance, March 1, 2009*

Children/Family Rankings

- Jacksonville was selected as one of the least safe cities for children in America by *Men's Health*. The city ranked #1 of 10. Criteria: accidental death rates for kids ages 5 to 14; number of car seat inspection locations per child; sex offenders per capita; percentage of abused children protected from further abuse; strength of child-restraint and bike-helmet laws. *Men's Health, "The Safest (and Least Safe) Cities for Children," September 2010*

- The Jacksonville metro area was selected as one of the "Best Cities for Relocating Families" by Worldwide ERC and Primacy Relocation. The 2008 study looked at nearly 50 factors important to relocating families including: recent job growth; nearby top-ranked colleges; in-state tuition for four-year public colleges; population growth since 2000; pediatricians per 100,000 population; and a Green Living index. *Worldwide ERC and Primacy Relocation, "2008 Best Cities for Relocating Families"*

- *Fit Pregnancy* magazine ranked the 50 best U.S. cities in which to have a baby. Jacksonville was ranked #11. Criteria: access to hospitals and doctors; affordability; birthing options; breastfeeding; child care; fertility laws/resources; maternal and infant health risk; parks/stroller friendliness; safety. *Fit Pregnancy, "The Best Cities in America to Have a Baby 2008"*

Culture/Performing Arts Rankings

- Jacksonville was selected as one of "America's Top 25 Arts Destinations." The city ranked #25 in the big city (population 500,000 and over) category. Criteria: readers' top choices for arts travel destinations based on the richness and variety of visual arts sites, activities and events. *American Style, "America's Top 25 Arts Destinations," May 2010*

Dating/Romance Rankings

- Jacksonville appeared on *Men's Health's* list of the most sex-happy cities in America. The city ranked #51 of 100. Criteria: condom sales; birth rates; sex toy sales; rates of chlamydia, gonorrhea, and syphilis. *Men's Health, "America's Most Sex-Happy Cities," October 2010*

- *Men's Health* ranked 100 U.S. cities in terms of best (and worst) marriages. Jacksonville was ranked #22 (#1 = worst marriages). Criteria: rate of failed marriages; stringency of divorce laws; percentage of population who've split; number of licensed marriage and family therapists. *Men's Health, "Splitsville, USA," May 2010*

- Eli Lily and Company, in partnership with Sperling's BestPlaces, ranked the nation's 50 largest metro areas in terms of the "Most Romantic Cities for Baby Boomers." The Jacksonville metro area ranked #33. Criteria: marriage and divorce rates among "baby boomers" age 45 to 60; great restaurants; dance studios; chocolate, jewelry and flower sales. *Eli Lily and Company, "Most Romantic Cities for Baby Boomers," April 20, 2007*

- The Jacksonville metro area was selected as one of the "Best Cities for Relocating Singles" by Worldwide ERC and Primacy Relocation. The area ranked #22 out of the 100 largest metro areas in the U.S. Areas were selected based on the following criteria: recent job growth; recent singles population growth; overall population growth; affordable rental housing; cost-of-living index; expanded arts and recreation opportunities; ratio of single men and single women; affordability of quality higher education (including state residency requirements); diversity index; climate; population density. *Worldwide ERC and Primacy Relocation, "2008 Best Cities for Relocating Singles"*

- *Forbes* ranked the 40 most populous urbanized areas in the U.S. in terms of the "Best Cities for Singles." The Jacksonville metro area ranked #40. Criteria: number of singles; cost of living alone; nightlife; culture; job growth; coolness; and online dating participation. *Forbes.com, "Best Cities for Singles," July 27, 2009*

Education Rankings

- Jacksonville was selected as one of "America's Most Literate Cities." The city ranked #49 out of the 75 largest U.S. cities. Criteria: number of booksellers; library resources; Internet resources; educational attainment; periodical publishing resources; newspaper circulation. *Central Connecticut State University, "America's Most Literate Cities 2010"*

- Jacksonville was identified as one of the 100 "smartest" metro areas in the U.S. The area ranked #69. Criteria: the editors rated the collective brainpower of the 100 largest metro area in the U.S based on their residents' educational attainment. *American City Business Journals, www.bizjournals.com, April 14, 2008*

- Jacksonville was identified as one of "America's Brainiest Bastions" by *Portfolio.com*. The metro area ranked #91 out of 200. Portfolio.com analyzed levels of educational attainment in the nation's 200 largest metropolitan areas. The editors established scores for five levels of educational attainment, based on relative earning power of adult workers age 25 or older. Scores were determined by comparing the median income for all workers with the median income for those workers at a specified educational level. *Portfolio.com, "America's Brainiest Bastions," December 1, 2010*

Environmental Rankings

- Jacksonville was selected as one of 22 "Smarter Cities" for energy by the Natural Resources Defense Council." Criteria: investment in green power; energy efficiency measures; conservation. *Natural Resources Defense Council, "2010 Smarter Cities," July 19, 2010*

- *American City Business Journal* ranked 43 metropolitan areas in terms of their "greenness." The Jacksonville metro area ranked #27. Criteria: Forty-one metros in which *ACBJ* has business weeklies, plus Indianapolis and Cleveland, were ranked based on 20 different indicators such as adoption of green technologies, utilization of environmentally sound practices, and air and water quality. *American City Business Journals, "Green City Index," March 11, 2010*

- The Jacksonville metro area was selected as one of "America's Cleanest Cities" by *Forbes*. The metro area ranked #3 out of 10. Criteria: air quality; water quality; per capita spending on Superfund site cleanup and solid-waste management. *Forbes.com, "America's Cleanest Cities," March 11, 2008*

- 100 of the largest metro areas in the U.S. were analyzed in terms of their current drought severity. The Jacksonville metro area ranked #11 (#1 = driest). The rankings were based on statistics such as long-term precipitation trends and patterns and the Palmer drought indices. *Sperling's BestPlaces, www.BestPlaces.net, "America's Drought-Riskiest Cities," November 2007*

- The Jacksonville metro area appeared in *Country Home's* "Best Green Places" report. The area ranked #283 out of 379. Criteria: official energy policies; green power; green buildings; availability of fresh, locally grown food. *Country Home, "Best Green Places," 2008*

Health/Fitness Rankings

- Jacksonville was given "Well City USA" status by The Wellness Councils of America, whose objective is to engage entire business communities in building healthy workforces. Well City status is met when a minimum of 20 employers who collectively employ at least 20% of the city's workforce become designated Well Workplaces within a three-year period. To date, eleven communities have achieved Well City USA status. *The Wellness Councils of America, Well City USA, 2011*

- Jacksonville was selected as one of the 25 fattest cities in America by *Men's Fitness Online*. It ranked #8 out of America's 50 largest cities. Criteria: fitness centers and sport stores; nutrition; sports participation; TV viewing; overweight/sedentary; junk food; air quality; geography; commute; parks and open space; city recreational facilities; access to healthcare; motivation; mayor and city initiatives; state obesity initiatives. *Men's Fitness Online, 2009 Fittest/Fattest Cities*

- Jacksonville was identified as a "2011 Asthma Capital." The area ranked #29 out of the nation's 100 largest metropolitan areas. Twelve factors were used to identify the most challenging places to live for people with asthma: estimated prevalence; self-reported prevalence; crude death rate for asthma; annual pollen score; annual air quality; public smoking laws; number of board-certified asthma specialists; school inhaler access laws; rescue medication use; controller medication use; uninsured rate; poverty rate. *Asthma and Allergy Foundation of America, "2011 Asthma Capitals"*

- Jacksonville was identified as a 2009 "Spring Allergy Capital." The area ranked #63 out of 100. Three groups of factors were used to identify the most severe cities for people with allergies during the spring season: annual pollen levels; medicine utilization; access to board-certified allergists. *Asthma and Allergy Foundation of America, "Spring Allergy Capitals 2009"*

- Jacksonville was identified as a 2010 "Fall Allergy Capital." The area ranked #57 out of 100. Three groups of factors were used to identify the most severe cities for people with allergies during the fall season: annual pollen levels; medicine utilization; access to board-certified allergists. *Asthma and Allergy Foundation of America, "Fall Allergy Capitals 2010"*

- *Men's Health* ranked 100 U.S. cities in terms of the quality of their tap water. Jacksonville was ranked #74 and received a grade of C. Criteria: levels of total coliform bacteria, arsenic, lead, total trihalomethanes (linked to cancer), and halo-acetic acids; number of EPA water-system violations from 1995 to 2005. *Men's Health, March 2007*

- Jacksonville was selected as one of America's noisiest cities by *Men's Health*. The city ranked #10 of 10. Criteria: laws limiting excessive noise; traffic congestion levels; airports' overnight flight curfews; percentage of people who report sleeping seven hours or less. *Men's Health, "Ranking America's Cities: America's Noisiest Cities," May 2009*

- Jacksonville was selected as one of the most accident-prone cities in America by *Men's Health*. The city ranked #2 of 10. Criteria: workplace accident rates; traffic fatalities; emergency room visits; accidental poisonings; incidents of drowning; fires; injury-producing falls. *Men's Health, "Ranking America's Cities: Accident City, USA," October 2009*

- Ortho-McNeil Neurologics, in partnership with Sperling's BestPlaces, analyzed 110 metro areas and identified those U.S. cities with the highest prevalence of factors that are most commonly associated with migraine headaches. The Jacksonville metro area ranked #53. Criteria: number of migraine-related drug prescriptions per capita; lifestyle factors that can contribute to migraines; environmental factors that can trigger migraines; and consumption of migraine-triggering foods. *Ortho-McNeil Neurologics, "America's Migraine Hot Spots," March 14, 2006*

- The Jacksonville metropolitan area was selected as one of the best metros for hospital care in America by HealthGrades. The rankings are based on a comprehensive study of patient death and complication rates in the nation's nearly 5,000 hospitals. Hospitals performing in the top 5% nationwide across 26 different medical procedures and diagnoses were identified. HealthGrades then ranked cities by the highest percentage of these Distinguished Hospitals for Clinical Excellence™. The Jacksonville metro area ranked #29. *HealthGrades.com, "America's Top 50 Cities for Hospital Care," January 26, 2011*

- *Men's Health* ranked 100 U.S. cities in terms of cities "Where the Food is Sickening." Jacksonville was ranked #92 and received a grade of D. The magazine arrived at their ratings by looking at data compiled by the Community Health Status Indicator Project to determine outbreaks of E. coli, salmonella-, and shigella-related infections. They then checked the CDC's Wonder database to see how many people died from tainted food. Finally, the magazine found out which states have adopted the current version of the FDA's uniform Food Code, which contains the most up-to-date rules for keeping restaurant kitchens clean. *Men's Health, October 2005*

- The Jacksonville metro area was identified as one of "America's Most Obese Cities" by *Forbes*. The magazine analyzed BMI (body mass index) data from the CDC in the 50 most populated metro areas in the U.S. and ranked the top 20. The area ranked #6. *Forbes, "America's Most Obese Cities," November 26, 2007*

- The Jacksonville metro area appeared in the 2010 Gallup-Healthways Well-Being Index. The index, based on interviews with more than 353,000 Americans during 2009, asked individuals to assess their jobs, finances, physical health, emotional state of mind and communities. The metro area ranked #134 out of 162. Criteria: life evaluation; emotional health; work environment; physical health; healthy behaviors; basic access (basic needs optimal for a healthy life, such as access to food and medicine, having health insurance and feeling safe while walking at night). *Gallup-Healthways, "Well-Being Index 2010"*

- The Jacksonville metro area was identified as one of "America's Most Stressful Cities" by *Forbes*. The metro area ranked #32. Criteria: median home price drop; unemployment rates; cost of living; air quality; sunny days; population density. *Forbes.com, "America's Most Stressful Cities," August 20, 2009*

- The Jacksonville metro area was identified as one of "America's 20 Most Sedentary Cities" by *Forbes*. The metro area ranked #8. Criteria: percentage of overweight or obese people; percentage of people who had not engaged in any physical activity in the past 30 days; average number of hours of TV watched per week. *Forbes.com, "America's Most Sedentary Cities," October 29, 2007*

- 50 of the largest metro areas in the U.S. were analyzed in terms of their health and fitness by the American College of Sports Medicine in their "American Fitness Index." The Jacksonville metro area ranked #24 (#1 = healthiest). Criteria: preventative health behaviors; levels of chronic disease; health care access; community resources and policies that support physical activity. *American College of Sports Medicine, "Health and Community Fitness Status of the 50 Largest Metropolitan Areas," May 24, 2010*

- *The Daily Beast* identified the 30 U.S metro areas with the worst smoking habits. The Jacksonville metro area ranked #20. Sixty urban centers with populations of more than one million were ranked based on the following criteria: number of smokers; number of cigarettes smoked per day; fewest attempts to quit. *The Daily Beast, "30 Cities With Smoking Problems," January 3, 2011*

Real Estate Rankings

- *Fortune* ranked the 100 largest metro areas in the U.S. in terms of projected median home price change in 2010. The Jacksonville metro area ranked #93. *Fortune, "The 2010 Housing Outlook," December 9, 2009*

- Jacksonville was identified as one of the top 20 metro areas with the lowest rate of house price appreciation in 2010. The area ranked #292 with a one-year price appreciation of -7.2% through the 4th quarter 2010. *Federal Housing Finance Agency, House Price Index, 4th Quarter 2010*

- Jacksonville appeared on ApartmentRatings.com "Top Cities for Renters" list in 2009." The area ranked #30. Overall satisfaction ratings were ranked using thousands of user submitted scores for hundreds of apartment complexes located in the 100 most populated U.S. municipalities. *ApartmentRatings.com, "2009 Renter Satisfaction Rankings"*

- The Jacksonville metro area was identified as one of "America's 25 Weakest Housing Markets" by *Forbes*. The metro area ranked #6. Criteria: metro areas with populations over 500,000 were ranked based on projected home values through 2011. *Forbes.com, "America's 25 Weakest Housing Markets," January 7, 2009*

- The nation's largest metro areas were analyzed in terms of the percentage of households entering some stage of foreclosure in 2010. The Jacksonville metro area ranked #27 out of 206 (#1 = highest foreclosure rate). *RealtyTrac, 2010 Year-End Metropolitan Foreclosure Market Report, January 27, 2011*

- The Jacksonville metro area was identified as one of the "Best Cities to Buy a Home" by *Forbes*. The metro area ranked #9. Criteria: 2-year home price appreciation; vacancy rates; spread between monthly rent and mortgage payment at the median level. *Forbes.com, "Best Cities to Buy a Home," July 22, 2008*

- The Jacksonville metro area appeared in a *Wall Street Journal* article ranking cities by "housing stress." The metro area was ranked #15 (#1 = most stress). Criteria: fraction of mortgage-holding homeowners with a monthly housing payment in excess of 30 percent of income; percentage of people without health insurance; unemployment rate. *The Wall Street Journal, "Which Cities Face Biggest Housing Risk," October 5, 2010*

- The Center for Housing Policy ranked 210 U.S metropolitan areas by the fair market rent for a two-bedroom unit. The Jacksonville metro area was ranked #79. (#1 = most expensive) with a rent of $903. Criteria: Fair Market Rent (FMR) in effect during the fourth quarter of 2009 based on HUD's fiscal year 2010 FMRs. *The Center for Housing Policy, "Paycheck to Paycheck: Most to Least Expensive Rental Markets in 2009"*

- The Jacksonville metro area was identified as one of the markets with the worst expected performance in home prices over the next 12 months. *Local Market Monitor, "First Quarter Home Price Forecast for Largest US Markets," March 2, 2011*

Safety Rankings

- Symantec, the makers of Norton, in partnership with Sperling's BestPlaces, ranked the 50 largest cities in the U.S. in terms of their vulnerability to cybercrime. The city ranked #39. Criteria: number of cyberattacks and potential infections; level of Internet access; expenditures on computer hardware and software; wireless hotspots; broadband connectivity; Internet usage; online purchases. *Symantec, "10 Riskiest Cities for Cybercrime," March 22, 2010*

- Allstate ranked the 200 largest cities in America in terms of driver safety. Jacksonville ranked #69. In addition, drivers were 0.8% more likely to have had an accident compared to the national average. Allstate researchers analyzed internal property damage reported claims over a two-year period (from January 2007 to December 2008) to ensure the findings would not be affected by external influences such as weather or road construction. A weighted average of the two-year numbers determined the annual percentages. The report defines an auto crash as any collision resulting in a property damage claim. *Allstate, "The 2010 Allstate America's Best Drivers Report™"*

- The National Insurance Crime Bureau ranked 366 metro areas in the U.S. in terms of per capita rates of vehicle theft. The Jacksonville metro area ranked #96 (#1 = highest rate). Criteria: number of vehicle theft offenses per 100,000 inhabitants. *National Insurance Crime Bureau, "Hot Spots," May 17, 2010*

- The Jacksonville metro area was identified as one of the "The Most Dangerous Metro Areas for Pedestrians" by Transportation for America and the Surface Transportation Policy Partnership. The metro area ranked #4 out of 52 metro areas with over 1 million residents. Criteria: area's population divided by the number of pedestrian fatalities in that area. *Transportation for America and the Surface Transportation Policy Partnership, "Dangerous by Design: Solving the Epidemic of Preventable Pedestrian Deaths (and Making Great Neighborhoods)," November 11, 2009*

Seniors/Retirement Rankings

- Jacksonville was identified as one of "The Top 100 Places to Retire" by *Topretirements.com* The list reflects the 100 cities (out of 625+ total cities reviewed) that visitors to the website are most interested in for retirement. *Topretirements.com, "2011 Best Places to Retire List: The Sunbelt Rules"*

- Jacksonville was selected as one of "The Best Retirement Places" by *Forbes*. The magazine considered a wide range of factors such as climate, availability of doctors, driving environment, and crime rates, but focused especially on tax burden and cost of living. *Forbes, "The Best Retirement Places," March 27, 2011*

Sports/Recreation Rankings

- Jacksonville appeared on the *Sporting News* list of the "Best Sports Cities" for 2010. The area ranked #49 out of 402 cities in the U.S. *Sporting News* takes a 12-month snapshot, roughly October to October, of each city's sports, putting a heavy premium on regular-season won-lost records (from the most recently completed season). Other criteria include: playoff berths, bowl appearances and tournament bids; championships; applicable power ratings; quality of competition; overall fan fervor as measured in part by attendance as percentage of venue capacity; abundance of teams (rewarding quality over quantity); stadium and arena quality; ticket availability and prices; franchise ownership; and marquee appeal of athletes. *Sporting News, "Best Sports Cities 2010," October, 2010*

- Scarborough Sports Marketing, a leading market research firm, identified the Jacksonville DMA (Designated Market Area) as one of the top markets for sports with more than 60% of adults reporting that they are "very" interested in any of the sports measured by Scarborough. *Scarborough Sports Marketing, October 1, 2008*

- *Golf Digest* ranked 330 metro areas in the U.S. in terms of golf. The Jacksonville metro area was ranked #81. Criteria: access to golf; weather; value of golf; and quality of golf. *Golf Digest, "Metro Golf Rankings," August 2005*

Transportation Rankings

- Jacksonville was identified as one of America's worst cities for speed traps by the National Motorists Association. One city from each state was selected based on data from the National Speed Trap Exchange. The NSTE collects driver reported speed trap locations. *National Motorists Association, "The Worst Speed Trap Cities in North America," September 2010*

- The Jacksonville metro area appeared on *Forbes* list of the best and worst cities for commuters. The metro area ranked #40 out of 60 (#1 is best). Criteria: travel time; road congestion; travel delays. *Forbes.com, "Best and Worst Cities for Commuters," February 16, 2010*

Women/Minorities Rankings

- Jacksonville was ranked #73 out of 100 metro areas in *SELF Magazine's* ranking of America's healthiest places for women." A panel of experts came up with more than 50 criteria including death and disease rates, environmental indicators, community resources, and lifestyle habits. *SELF Magazine, "Secrets of America's Healthiest Women," December 2008*

- Jacksonville appeared on *Black Enterprise's* list of the "Ten Best Cities for African Americans." The top picks were culled from more than 2,000 interactive surveys completed on www.blackenterprise.com and by editorial staff evaluation. The editors weighed the following criteria as it pertained to African Americans in each city: median household income; percentage of households earning more than $100,000; percentage of businesses owned; percentage of college graduates; unemployment rates; home loan rejections; and homeownership rates. *Black Enterprise, May 2007*

Miscellaneous Rankings

- Energizer Holdings, the makers of Edge® shave gel, in partnership with Sperling's BestPlaces, ranked 50 major metro areas in terms of everyday irritations. The Jacksonville metro area ranked #20. Criteria: humidity levels; weather conditions; incidence of traffic delays and congestion; average commute times; frequency of flight delays and cancellations; rates of sleeplessness; underemployment; pollens and allergens; pests; comedy clubs per capita. *Energizer Holdings, "Most Irritation Prone Cities," July 23, 2010*

- Mars Chocolate North America, the makers of COMBOS®, in partnership with Sperling's BestPlaces, ranked 50 major metro areas in terms of their "manliness." The Jacksonville metro area ranked #36. Criteria: number of home improvement stores, steak houses, pickup trucks, motorcycles, and manly occupations (fire fighters, police officers, construction workers, EMP personnel) per capita; salty snack sales; sports TV viewing habits. *Mars Chocolate North America, "America's Manliest Cities," June 22, 2010*

- Jacksonville was selected as one of the best cities for shopping in the U.S. by *Forbes*. The city was ranked #9.Criteria: number of major shopping centers; retail locations; Consumer Price Index (CPI); combined state and local sales tax. *Forbes, "America's 25 Best Cities for Shopping," December 13, 2010*

- The Jacksonville metro area appeared in AutoMD.com's ranking of the "Best and Worst Cities for Auto Repair." The metro area ranked #2 (#1 is best). The 50 most-populated metro areas in the U.S. were ranked on three critical factors: repair affordability; price disparity range; shop integrity factor. *AutoMD.com, "Advocacy for Repair Shop Fairness Report," February 24, 2010*

- The Jacksonville metro area was selected as one of "America's 20 Most Miserable Cities" by *Forbes*. The metro area ranked #19. Criteria: jobless rates; inflation; taxes; commuting times; crime rates; performance by the city's sports teams; weather; pollution; corruption by public officials. *Forbes.com, "America's 20 Most Miserable Cities, 2011" February 2, 2011*

- Scarborough Research, a leading market research firm, identified the top local markets for gift card purchasers. The Jacksonville DMA (Designated Market Area) ranked in the top 10 with 54% of consumers reporting that they purchased a gift card within the past 12 months. *Scarborough Research, November 15, 2006*

Business Environment

CITY FINANCES

City Government Finances

Component	2008 ($000)	2008 ($ per capita)
Total Revenues	3,772,863	4,683
Total Expenditures	3,797,802	4,714
Debt Outstanding	11,550,574	14,338
Cash and Securities[1]	7,550,414	9,372

*Note: (1) Cash and security holdings of a government at the close of its fiscal
year, including those of its dependent agencies, utilities, and liquor stores.*
Source: U.S Census Bureau, State & Local Government Finances 2008

City Government Revenue by Source

Source	2008 ($000)	2008 ($ per capita)
General Revenue		
From Federal Government	72,410	90
From State Government	176,840	220
From Local Governments	353	0
Taxes		
Property	470,227	584
Sales and Gross Receipts	307,652	382
Personal Income	0	0
Corporate Income	0	0
Motor Vehicle License	0	0
Other Taxes	19,531	24
Current Charges	469,347	583
Liquor Store	0	0
Utility	1,411,243	1,752
Employee Retirement	431,461	536

Source: U.S Census Bureau, State & Local Government Finances 2008

City Government Expenditures by Function

Function	2008 ($000)	2008 ($ per capita)	2008 (%)
General Direct Expenditures			
Air Transportation	55,250	69	1.5
Corrections	64,677	80	1.7
Education	0	0	0.0
Employment Security Administration	0	0	0.0
Financial Administration	65,636	81	1.7
Fire Protection	109,570	136	2.9
General Public Buildings	13,223	16	0.3
Governmental Administration, Other	22,920	28	0.6
Health	20,828	26	0.5
Highways	77,844	97	2.0
Hospitals	0	0	0.0
Housing and Community Development	31,864	40	0.8
Interest on General Debt	368,871	458	9.7
Judicial and Legal	42,336	53	1.1
Libraries	29,867	37	0.8
Parking	2,469	3	0.1
Parks and Recreation	56,496	70	1.5
Police Protection	184,025	228	4.8
Public Welfare	84,568	105	2.2
Sewerage	157,417	195	4.1
Solid Waste Management	59,956	74	1.6
Veterans' Services	0	0	0.0
Liquor Store	0	0	0.0
Utility	1,864,012	2,314	49.1
Employee Retirement	206,777	257	5.4

Source: U.S Census Bureau, State & Local Government Finances 2008

Municipal Bond Ratings

Area	Moody's	S&P	Fitch
City	Aa2	AA-	AA

Rating Systems (shown in declining order of credit quality): Moody's– Aaa, Aa, A, Baa, Ba, B, Caa, Ca, C (numerical modifiers 1, 2, and 3 are added to letter-rating); S&P– AAA, AA, A, BBB, BB, B, CCC, CC, C; Fitch– AAA, AA, A, BBB, BB, B, CCC, CC, C. Ratings may be modified by the addition of a plus or minus sign to show relative standing within the major rating categories.
Notes: n/a Not available; (1) Not reviewed; (2) Issuer Rating/No General Obligation; (3) Standard and Poor's Issue Credit Rating (ICR) is a current opinion of an obliger with respect to a specific financial obligation, a specific class of financial obligations, or a specific financial program.
Source: U.S. Census Bureau, 2011 Statistical Abstract, Bond Ratings for City Governments by Largest Cities: 2009

DEMOGRAPHICS

Population Growth

Area	1990 Census	2000 Census	2010 Estimate	2015 Projection	Population Growth (%) 2000-2010	2010-2015
City	635,221	735,617	846,695	902,808	15.1	6.6
MSA[1]	925,213	1,122,750	1,372,183	1,498,271	22.2	9.2
U.S.	248,709,873	281,421,906	309,038,974	321,675,005	9.8	4.1

Note: (1) Metropolitan Statistical Area - see Appendix B for areas included
Source: Claritas, Inc.

Number of Households and Average Household Size

Area	2010 Estimate	2010 Average Household Size
City	333,499	2.50
MSA[1]	536,105	2.52
U.S.	116,136,617	2.59

Note: (1) Metropolitan Statistical Area - see Appendix B for areas included
Source: Claritas, Inc.

Race and Ethnicity

Area	White Alone[2] (%)	Black Alone[2] (%)	Asian Alone[2] (%)	Other Race Alone[2] (%)	Hispanic[3] (%)
City	60.4	30.8	3.5	5.3	6.6
MSA[1]	70.1	22.2	2.9	4.7	6.2
U.S.	72.3	12.4	4.4	10.9	15.8

Note: Figures are 2010 estimates; (1) Metropolitan Statistical Area - see Appendix B for areas included (2) Alone is defined as not being in combination with one or more other races; (3) May be of any race.
Source: Claritas, Inc.

Segregation

Type	Segregation Indices[1] 1990	2000	2010	2010 Rank[2]	Percent Change 1990-2000	1990-2010	2000-2010
Black/White	57.5	53.9	53.1	59	-3.6	-4.4	-0.8
Asian/White	34.2	37.0	37.5	71	2.8	3.2	0.4
Hispanic/White	22.1	26.6	27.6	98	4.6	5.5	1.0

Note: Figures are based on an analysis of 1990, 2000, and 2010 Census Decennial Census tract data by William H. Frey, Brookings Institution and the University of Michigan Social Science Data Analysis Network. In this analysis all racial groups (whites, blacks, and asians) are non-Hispanic members of those races. Hispanics are shown as a separate category; All figures cover the Metropolitan Statistical Area (see Appendix B for areas included); (1) Segregation Indices are Dissimilarity Indices that measure the degree to which the minority group is distributed differently than whites aross census tracts. They range from 0 (complete integration) to 100 (complete [segregation) where the value indicates the percentage of the minority group that needs to move to be distributed exactly like whites; (2) Ranges from 1 (most segregated) to 102 (least segregated); n/a not available.
Source: www.CensusScope.org

Ancestry

Area	German	Irish	English	American	Italian	Polish	French	Scottish
City	10.4	10.6	8.6	6.6	3.7	1.9	2.4	2.1
MSA[1]	12.1	12.4	10.3	8.6	4.6	2.2	2.7	2.4
U.S.	16.6	12.0	9.1	6.1	5.9	3.3	3.1	1.9

Note: The top eight ancestries in the U.S. are shown. Figures are percentages and include multiple ancestry (e.g. if a person reported being Irish and Italian, they were included in both columns); (1) Metropolitan Statistical Area - see Appendix B for areas included
Source: U.S. Census Bureau, 2007-2009 American Community Survey 3-Year Estimates

Foreign-Born Population

Area	Percent of Population Born in								
	Any Foreign Country	Mexico	Asia	Europe	Carribean	South America	Central America[2]	Africa	Canada
City	8.8	0.7	2.9	1.8	1.4	0.8	0.4	0.5	0.1
MSA[1]	7.5	0.6	2.4	1.7	1.1	0.7	0.4	0.3	0.2
U.S.	12.5	3.8	3.4	1.6	1.1	0.8	0.9	0.5	0.3

Note: (1) Metropolitan Statistical Area - see Appendix B for areas included; (2) Excludes Mexico.
Source: U.S. Census Bureau, 2007-2009 American Community Survey 3-Year Estimates

Marriage Status

Area	Never Married	Now Married[2]	Separated	Widowed	Divorced
City	32.2	46.2	2.6	6.0	13.0
MSA[1]	29.3	49.8	2.4	5.9	12.6
U.S.	31.4	49.7	2.2	6.2	10.6

Note: Figures are percentages and cover the population 15 years of age and older;
(1) Metropolitan Statistical Area - see Appendix B for areas included; (2) Excludes separated
Source: U.S. Census Bureau, 2007-2009 American Community Survey 3-Year Estimates

Age Distribution and Median Age

Area	Percent of Population							Median Age
	Under Age 5	Age 5 to 17	Age 18 to 34	Age 35 to 49	Age 50 to 64	Age 65 to 79	80 Years and Over	
City	7.7	17.3	25.6	21.6	17.2	7.6	2.9	34.5
MSA[1]	7.0	17.5	23.3	22.1	18.4	8.4	3.2	36.5
U.S.	6.9	17.5	23.3	21.4	18.1	9.1	3.7	36.7

Note: (1) Metropolitan Statistical Area - see Appendix B for areas included
Source: U.S. Census Bureau, 2007-2009 American Community Survey 3-Year Estimates

Male/Female Ratio

Area	Males	Females	Males per 100 Females
City	410,299	436,396	94.0
MSA[1]	670,200	701,983	95.5
U.S.	152,401,520	156,637,454	97.3

Note: Figures are 2010 estimates; (1) Metropolitan Statistical Area - see Appendix B for areas included
Source: Claritas, Inc.

Religion

Area	Catholic	Southern Baptist	United Methodist	ELCA[1]	LDS[2]	Presbyterian Church USA	Jewish Est.	Muslim Est.
County	8.3	18.4	3.7	0.5	0.7	1.7	0.8	0.3
U.S.	22.0	7.1	3.7	1.8	1.5	1.1	2.2	0.6

Note: Figures are the number of adherents as a percentage of the total population; Adherents are defined as all members, including full members, their children and the estimated number of other participants who are not considered members (e.g. the baptized, those not confirmed, those regularly attending services, etc.); (1) Evangelical Lutheran Church in America; (2) The Church of Jesus Christ of Latter Day Saints
Source: Reprinted with permission from Religious Congregations and Membership in the United States 2000 (Nashville, Glenmary Research Center, 2002) Copyright Association of Statisticians of American Religious Bodies. All rights reserved.

ECONOMY

Gross Metropolitan Product

Area	2006	2007	2008	2009	2009 Rank[2]
MSA[1]	58.2	59.6	59.7	58.6	46

Note: Figures are in billions of dollars; (1) Jacksonville, FL Metropolitan Statistical Area - see Appendix B for areas included; (2) Rank ranges from 1 to 363
Source: The U.S. Conference of Mayors, "Pace of Economic Recovery: GMP and Jobs," January 2010

Economic Growth

Area	2006-2008 (%)	2009 (%)	2010 (%)	Rank[2]
MSA[1]	-1.3	-2.9	2.0	322
U.S.	1.3	-2.5	2.2	–

Note: Figures are real Gross Metropolitan Product growth rates and represent annual average percent change; (1) Jacksonville, FL Metropolitan Statistical Area - see Appendix B for areas included; (2) Rank ranges from 1 to 363
Source: The U.S. Conference of Mayors, "Pace of Economic Recovery: GMP and Jobs," January 2010

Metropolitan Area Exports

Area	2005	2006	2007	2008	2009	2009 Rank[2]
MSA[1]	1,200.6	1,445.9	1,709.3	1,973.5	1,634.4	90

Note: Figures are in millions of dollars; (1) Jacksonville, FL Metropolitan Statistical Area - see Appendix B for areas included; (2) Rank ranges from 1 to 374
Source: U.S. Department of Commerce, International Trade Administration, Office of Trade & Industry Information, Manufacturing & Services

INCOME

Per Capita/Median/Average Income

Area	Per Capita ($)	Median Household ($)	Average Household ($)
City	25,890	50,252	65,168
MSA[1]	27,961	54,624	71,023
U.S.	27,034	52,795	71,071

Note: Figures are 2010 estimates; (1) Metropolitan Statistical Area - see Appendix B for areas included
Source: Claritas, Inc.

Household Income Distribution

Area	Under $15,000	$15,000 -24,999	$25,000 -34,999	$35,000 -49,999	$50,000 -74,999	$75,000 -99,000	$100,000 -149,999	$150,000 and up
City	12.0	9.9	11.5	16.5	21.3	12.4	10.7	5.7
MSA[1]	10.4	9.3	10.7	15.7	21.3	13.2	12.1	7.3
U.S.	12.1	10.2	10.6	15.0	19.5	12.5	12.1	8.0

Note: Figures are 2010 estimates; (1) Metropolitan Statistical Area - see Appendix B for areas included
Source: Claritas, Inc.

Poverty Rates by Age

Area	All Ages	Under 18 Years Old	18 to 64 Years Old	65 Years and Over
City	13.8	5.0	7.8	1.1
MSA[1]	12.0	4.2	6.8	1.0
U.S.	13.6	4.7	7.7	1.2

Note: Figures are percent of population with income during the previous 12 months below poverty level and only include population for whom poverty status is determined; (1) Metropolitan Statistical Area - see Appendix B for areas included
Source: U.S. Census Bureau, 2007-2009 American Community Survey 3-Year Estimates

Personal Bankruptcy Filing Rate

Area	2006	2007	2008	2009	2010
Duval County	2.39	3.47	4.45	5.82	5.91
U.S.	2.00	2.73	3.53	4.60	4.96

Note: Numbers are per 1,000 population and include Chapter 7 and Chapter 13 filings
Source: Federal Deposit Insurance Corporation, Regional Economic Conditions, March 17, 2011

EMPLOYMENT

Labor Force and Employment

Area	Civilian Labor Force			Workers Employed		
	Dec. 2009	Dec. 2010	% Chg.	Dec. 2009	Dec. 2010	% Chg.
City	411,812	417,935	1.5	366,869	371,136	1.2
MSA[1]	676,626	688,236	1.7	604,876	611,911	1.2
U.S.	152,693,000	153,156,000	0.3	137,953,000	139,159,000	0.9

Note: Data is not seasonally adjusted and covers workers 16 years of age and older;
(1) Metropolitan Statistical Area - see Appendix B for areas included
Source: Bureau of Labor Statistics, http://stats.bls.gov

Unemployment Rate

Area	2010											
	Jan.	Feb.	Mar.	Apr.	May	Jun.	Jul.	Aug.	Sep.	Oct.	Nov.	Dec.
City	11.7	11.5	11.5	11.1	11.0	11.4	12.2	12.2	11.5	11.2	11.6	11.2
MSA[1]	11.4	11.3	11.2	10.7	10.6	11.0	11.6	11.7	11.2	11.0	11.5	11.1
U.S.	10.6	10.4	10.2	9.5	9.3	9.6	9.7	9.5	9.2	9.0	9.3	9.1

Note: Data is not seasonally adjusted and covers workers 16 years of age and older; All figures are percentages; (1) Metropolitan Statistical Area - see Appendix B for areas included
Source: Bureau of Labor Statistics, http://stats.bls.gov

Projected Unemployment Rate

Area	2007 (%)	2009 (%)	2011 (%)	2013 (%)
MSA[1]	4.3	11.6	10.1	7.9

Note: (1) Metropolitan Statistical Area - see Appendix B for areas included
Source: The U.S. Conference of Mayors, "Pace of Economic Recovery: GMP and Jobs," January 2010

Employment by Occupation

Occupation Classification	City (%)	MSA[1] (%)	U.S. (%)
Sales and Office	29.7	29.1	25.4
Professional and Related	17.7	18.2	21.0
Service	17.3	17.2	17.2
Production, Transportation, and Material Moving	10.6	9.6	12.3
Management, Business, and Financial	14.9	15.8	14.1
Construction, Extraction, and Maintenance	9.6	9.9	9.2
Farming, Forestry, and Fishing	0.1	0.3	0.7

Note: Figures cover employed civilians 16 years of age and older;
(1) Metropolitan Statistical Area - see Appendix B for areas included
Source: U.S. Census Bureau, 2007-2009 American Community Survey 3-Year Estimates

Employment by Industry

Sector	MSA[1]		U.S.
	Number of Employees	Percent of Total	Percent of Total
Government	77,400	13.2	17.2
Education and Health Services	86,900	14.8	15.2
Professional and Business Services	87,700	14.9	13.0
Retail Trade	70,800	12.1	11.4
Leisure and Hospitality	64,600	11.0	9.7
Manufacturing	27,100	4.6	8.8
Financial Activities	55,600	9.5	5.8
Wholesale Trade	25,500	4.3	4.2
Construction	27,300	4.6	4.1
Other Services	23,400	4.0	4.1
Transportation and Utilities	30,400	5.2	3.7
Information	10,000	1.7	2.1
Mining and Logging	400	0.1	0.6

Note: Figures cover non-farm employment as of December 2010 and are not seasonally adjusted;
(1) Metropolitan Statistical Area - see Appendix B for areas included
Source: Bureau of Labor Statistics, http://stats.bls.gov

Occupations with Greatest Projected Employment Growth: 2006 - 2016

Occupation[1]	2006 Employment	2016 Projected Employment	Numeric Employment Change	Percent Employment Change
Retail salespersons	283,850	339,780	55,930	19.7
Customer service representatives	162,780	214,600	51,820	31.8
Registered nurses	148,390	190,020	41,630	28.1
Combined food preparation and serving workers, including fast food	163,780	202,670	38,890	23.7
Waiters and waitresses	197,920	232,430	34,510	17.4
Office clerks, general	188,190	221,750	33,560	17.8
Bookkeeping, accounting, and auditing clerks	128,340	153,830	25,490	19.9
Janitors and cleaners, except maids and housekeeping cleaners	124,030	147,970	23,940	19.3
Sales representatives, services, all other	73,650	97,390	23,740	32.2
Executive secretaries and administrative assistants	106,820	129,140	22,320	20.9

Note: Projections cover Florida; (1) Sorted by numeric employment change
Source: www.projectionscentral.com, State Occupational Projections, 2006-2016 Long-Term Projections

Fastest Growing Occupations: 2006 - 2016

Occupation[1]	2006 Employment	2016 Projected Employment	Numeric Employment Change	Percent Employment Change
Network systems and data communications analysts	20,830	33,090	12,260	58.9
Court reporters	2,170	3,430	1,260	58.1
Computer software engineers, applications	17,350	27,250	9,900	57.1
Veterinary technologists and technicians	5,720	8,880	3,160	55.2
Veterinarians	3,280	4,890	1,610	49.1
Home health aides	29,600	42,780	13,180	44.5
Personal and home care aides	10,640	15,220	4,580	43.0
Paralegals and legal assistants	19,240	27,360	8,120	42.2
Pharmacy technicians	21,110	29,950	8,840	41.9
Medical assistants	31,040	43,930	12,890	41.5

Note: Projections cover Florida; (1) Sorted by percent employment change and excludes occupations with numeric employment change less than 900
Source: www.projectionscentral.com, State Occupational Projections, 2006-2016 Long-Term Projections

Average Wages

Occupation	$/Hr.	Occupation	$/Hr.
Accountants and Auditors	28.12	Maids and Housekeeping Cleaners	9.21
Automotive Mechanics	17.86	Maintenance and Repair Workers	16.29
Bookkeepers	15.57	Marketing Managers	57.19
Carpenters	17.53	Nuclear Medicine Technologists	31.80
Cashiers	8.65	Nurses, Licensed Practical	19.30
Clerks, General Office	12.07	Nurses, Registered	29.53
Clerks, Receptionists/Information	12.16	Nursing Aides/Orderlies/Attendants	11.71
Clerks, Shipping/Receiving	14.16	Packers and Packagers, Hand	10.60
Computer Programmers	36.10	Physical Therapists	39.56
Computer Support Specialists	19.86	Postal Service Mail Carriers	23.53
Computer Systems Analysts	32.67	Real Estate Brokers	42.61
Cooks, Restaurant	10.88	Retail Salespersons	12.14
Dentists	n/a	Sales Reps., Exc. Tech./Scientific	26.71
Electrical Engineers	35.97	Sales Reps., Tech./Scientific	41.13
Electricians	20.88	Secretaries, Exc. Legal/Med./Exec.	13.97
Financial Managers	52.14	Security Guards	10.42
First-Line Supervisors/Mgrs., Sales	20.05	Surgeons	n/a
Food Preparation Workers	9.09	Teacher Assistants	11.10
General and Operations Managers	45.64	Teachers, Elementary School	22.00
Hairdressers/Cosmetologists	14.87	Teachers, Secondary School	22.70
Internists	n/a	Telemarketers	11.12
Janitors and Cleaners	10.93	Truck Drivers, Heavy/Tractor-Trailer	17.97
Landscaping/Groundskeeping Workers	11.31	Truck Drivers, Light/Delivery Svcs.	13.80
Lawyers	46.55	Waiters and Waitresses	9.71

Note: Wage data covers the Jacksonville, FL - see Appendix B for areas included. Hourly wages for elementary/secondary school teachers and teacher assistants were calculated by the editors from annual wage data assuming a 40 hour work week; n/a not available.
Source: Bureau of Labor Statistics, Metro Area Occupational Employment and Wage Estimates, May 2009

RESIDENTIAL REAL ESTATE

Building Permits

Area	Single-Family			Multi-Family			Total		
	2009	2010	Pct. Chg.	2009	2010	Pct. Chg.	2009	2010	Pct. Chg.
City	1,467	1,397	-4.8	1,171	68	-94.2	2,638	1,465	-44.5
MSA[1]	3,323	3,387	1.9	1,343	219	-83.7	4,666	3,606	-22.7
U.S.	441,100	447,300	1.4	141,900	157,300	10.9	583,000	604,600	3.7

Note: (1) Metropolitan Statistical Area - see Appendix B for areas included; figures represent new, privately-owned housing units authorized (unadjusted data); All permit data are based on estimates with imputation.
Source: U.S. Census Bureau, Manufacturing, Mining, and Construction Statistics, Building Permits, 2009, 2010

Homeownership Rate

Area	2005 (%)	2006 (%)	2007 (%)	2008 (%)	2009 (%)	2010 (%)
MSA[1]	67.9	70.0	70.9	72.1	72.6	70.0
U.S.	68.9	68.8	68.1	67.8	67.4	66.9

Note: (1) Metropolitan Statistical Area - see Appendix B for areas included
Source: U.S. Census Bureau, Housing Vacancies and Homeownership Annual Statistics: 2010

Housing Vacancy Rates

Area	Gross Vacancy Rate[2] (%)			Year-Round Vacancy Rate[3] (%)			Rental Vacancy Rate[4] (%)			Homeowner Vacancy Rate[5] (%)		
	2008	2009	2010	2008	2009	2010	2008	2009	2010	2008	2009	2010
MSA[1]	14.7	14.3	14.9	14.1	13.6	14.6	15.3	15.9	13.9	5.4	3.7	4.6
U.S.	14.4	14.5	14.3	11.1	11.3	11.3	10.0	10.6	10.2	2.8	2.6	2.6

Note: (1) Metropolitan Statistical Area - see Appendix B for areas included; (2) The percentage of the total housing inventory that is vacant; (3) The percentage of the housing inventory (excluding seasonal units) that is year-round vacant; (4) The percentage of rental inventory that is vacant for rent; (5) The percentage of homeowner inventory that is vacant for sale; n/a not available
Source: U.S. Census Bureau, Housing Vacancies and Homeownership Annual Statistics: 2010

State Corporate Income Tax Rates

State	Tax Rate (%)	Income Brackets ($)	Num. of Brackets	Financial Institution Tax Rate (%)[a]	Federal Income Tax Ded.
Florida	5.5 (f)	Flat rate	1	5.5 (f)	No

Note: Tax rates as of January 1, 2011; (a) Rates listed are the tax rates applied to financial institutions or excise taxes based on income. Some states have other taxes based upon the value of deposits or shares; (f) An exemption of $5,000 is allowed. Florida's Alternative Minimum Tax rate is 3.3%.
Source: Federation of Tax Administrators, "State Corporate Income Tax Rates, 2011"

State Individual Income Tax Rates

State	Tax Rate (%)	Income Brackets ($)	Num. of Brackets	Personal Exempt. ($)[1] Single	Personal Exempt. ($)[1] Dependents	Fed. Inc. Tax Ded.
Florida – No State Income Tax						

Note: Tax rates as of January 1, 2011; Local- and county-level taxes are not included; n/a not applicable;
(1) Married joint filers generally receive double the single exemption
Source: Federation of Tax Administrators, "State Individual Income Tax Rates, 2011"

Various State and Local Tax Rates

State	State and Local Sales and Use (%)	State Sales and Use (%)	Gasoline[1] (¢/gal.)	Cigarette[2] ($/pack)	Spirits[3] ($/gal.)	Wine[4] ($/gal.)	Beer[5] ($/gal.)
Florida	7.0	6.00	34.4	1.34	6.50	2.25	0.48

Note: All tax rates as of January 1, 2011 except Spirits (Sept. 1, 2010); (1) The American Petroleum Institute has developed a methodology for determining the average tax rate on a gallon of fuel. Rates may include any of the following: excise taxes, environmental fees, storage tank fees, other fees or taxes, general sales tax, and local taxes. In states where gasoline is subject to the general sales tax, or where the fuel tax is based on the average sale price, the average rate determined by API is sensitive to changes in the price of gasoline. States that fully or partially apply general sales taxes to gasoline: CA, CO, GA, IL, IN, MI, NY; (2) The federal excise tax of $1.0066 per pack and local taxes are not included; (3) Rates are those applicable to off-premise sales of 40% alcohol by volume (a.b.v.) distilled spirits in 750ml containers. Local excise taxes are excluded; (4) Rates are those applicable to off-premise sales of 11% a.b.v. non-carbonated wine in 750ml containers; (5) Rates are those applicable to off-premise sales of 4.7% a.b.v. beer in 12 ounce containers.
Source: Tax Foundation, 2011 Facts & Figures: How Does Your State Compare?

State-Local Tax Burdens

Area	Rate (%)	Rank[1]	Per Capita Taxes Paid to Home State ($)	Total State and Local Per Capita Taxes Paid ($)	Per Capita Income ($)
Florida	9.2	31	2,713	3,897	42,146
U.S. Average	9.8	-	3,057	4,160	42,539

Note: Figures cover 2009; (1) Rank ranges from 1 to 50 where 1 is highest tax burden
Source: Tax Foundation, State-Local Tax Burdens, All States, 2009

State Business Tax Climate Index Rankings

State	Overall Rank	Corporate Tax Index Rank	Individual Income Tax Index Rank	Sales Tax Index Rank	Unemployment Insurance Tax Index Rank	Property Tax Index Rank
Florida	5	15	1	30	3	28

Note: The index is a measure of how each state's tax laws affect economic performance. The lower the rank, the more favorable a state's tax system is for business. All ranks are for fiscal years. States without a given tax are given a ranking of 1.
Source: Tax Foundation, Tax Foundation Background Paper, No. 60, "2011 State Business Tax Climate Index"

COMMERCIAL UTILITIES

Typical Monthly Electric Bills

Area	Commercial Service ($/month) 40 kW demand 5,000 kWh	Commercial Service ($/month) 500 kW demand 100,000 kWh	Industrial Service ($/month) 5,000 kW demand 1,500,000 kWh	Industrial Service ($/month) 70,000 kW demand 50,000,000 kWh
City	538	12,105	161,837	3,656,323

Note: Based on rates in effect January 1, 2010
Source: Memphis Light, Gas and Water, 2010 Utility Bill Comparisons for Selected U.S. Cities

TRANSPORTATION

Means of Transportation to Work

Area	Car/Truck/Van		Public Transportation			Bicycle	Walked	Other Means	Worked at Home
	Drove Alone	Car-pooled	Bus	Subway	Railroad				
City	81.1	11.1	1.6	0.0	0.0	0.4	1.5	1.2	3.0
MSA[1]	81.1	10.5	1.1	0.0	0.0	0.6	1.5	1.5	3.7
U.S.	75.8	10.4	2.7	1.7	0.5	0.5	2.9	1.2	4.1

Note: Figures are percentages and cover workers 16 years of age and older;
(1) Metropolitan Statistical Area - see Appendix B for areas included
Source: U.S. Census Bureau, 2007-2009 American Community Survey 3-Year Estimates

Travel Time to Work

Area	Less Than 15 Minutes	15 to 29 Minutes	30 to 44 Minutes	45 to 59 Minutes	60 to 89 Minutes	90 Minutes or More
City	21.4	45.8	23.2	5.5	2.8	1.3
MSA[1]	22.1	40.0	23.9	8.4	4.0	1.6
U.S.	28.5	36.2	19.7	7.5	5.6	2.5

Note: Figures are percentages and include workers 16 years old and over;
(1) Metropolitan Statistical Area - see Appendix B for areas included
Source: U.S. Census Bureau, 2007-2009 American Community Survey 3-Year Estimates

Travel Time Index

Area	1982	1999	2008	2009
Urban Area[1]	1.06	1.13	1.13	1.12
Average[2]	1.08	1.20	1.20	1.20

Note: Travel Time Index—the ratio of travel time in the peak period to the travel time at free-flow conditions. A value of 1.30 indicates a 20-minute free-flow trip takes 26 minutes in the peak. Free-flow speeds (60 mph on freeways and 35 mph on principal arterials) are used as the comparison threshold; (1) Covers the Jacksonville urban area;
(2) average of 439 urban areas
Source: Texas Transportation Institute, Urban Mobility Report 2010, December 2010

Public Transportation

Agency Name / Mode of Transportation	Vehicles Operated in Maximum Service	Annual Unlinked Passenger Trips ('000)	Annual Passenger Miles ('000)
Jacksonville Transportation Authority (JTA)			
Automated guideway	7	449.7	176.7
Demand response	86	357.9	3,546.6
Bus	162	10,253.9	54,696.6

Note: Figures include both directly operated and purchased transportation
Source: Federal Transit Administration, National Transit Database, 2009

Air Transportation

Airport Name and Code / Type of Service	Passenger Airlines[1]	Passenger Enplanements	Freight Carriers[2]	Freight (lbs.)
Jacksonville International (JAX)				
Domestic service (U.S. carriers - 2010)	31	2,755,042	12	76,416,175
International service (U.S. carriers - 2009)	7	691	1	45

Note: (1) Includes all U.S.-based major, minor and commuter airlines that carried at least one passenger during the year; (2) Includes all U.S.-based airlines and freight carriers that transported at least one pound of freight during the year
Source: Bureau of Transportation Statistics, The Intermodal Transportation Database, Air Carriers: T-100 Domestic Market (U.S. Carriers), 2010; Bureau of Transportation Statistics, The Intermodal Transportation Database, Air Carriers: T-100 International Market (U.S. Carriers), 2009

Other Transportation Statistics

Interstate highways:	I-10; I-95
Amtrak service:	Yes
Major waterways/ports:	St. Johns River

Source: Amtrak.com; Google Maps

BUSINESSES

Major Business Headquarters

Company Name	Rankings	
	Fortune[1]	Forbes[2]
CSX	230	-
Fidelity National Financial	398	-
Fidelity National Information Services	426	-
Winn-Dixie Stores	324	-

Note: (1) Fortune 500—companies that produce a 10-K are ranked 1 to 500 based on 2010 revenue; (2) all private companies with at least $2 billion in annual revenue are ranked 1 to 223; companies listed are headquartered in the city; dashes indicate no ranking
Source: Fortune, "Fortune 500," May 23, 2011; Forbes, "America's Largest Private Companies," November 3, 2010

Fast-Growing Businesses

According to *Inc.*, Jacksonville is home to three of America's 500 fastest-growing private companies: **A. Harold and Associates; Ocenture; SNS Logistics**. Criteria: must be an independent, privately-held, for-profit, U.S. corporation, proprietorship or partnership; revenues of at least $80,000 in 2006 and $2 million in 2009; four-year operating/sales history; holding companies, regulated banks, and utilities were excluded. *Inc., "America's 500 Fastest-Growing Private Companies," September 2010*

According to Deloitte, Jacksonville is home to one of North America's 500 fastest-growing high-technology companies: **Web.com**. Companies are ranked by percentage growth in revenue over a five-year period. Criteria for inclusion: company must be headquartered within North America; company must own proprietary intellectual property or proprietary technology that contributes to a significant portion of the company's operating revenue or devotes a significant proportion of revenues to research and development of technology; company must have been in business for a minumum of five years with 2005 operating revenues of at least $50,000 USD/CD and 2009 operating revenues of at least $5 million USD/CD. *Deloitte Touche Tohmatsu, 2010 Deloitte Technology Fast 500*™

Minority Business Opportunity

Jacksonville is home to one company which is on the Black Enterprise Industrial/Service 100 list (100 largest companies based on gross sales): **Raven Transport Co.** Criteria: operational in previous calendar year; at least 51% black-owned and manufactures/owns the product it sells or provides industrial or consumer services. Brokerages, real estate firms and firms that provide professional services are not eligible. *Black Enterprise, B.E. 100s, 2010*

Jacksonville is home to one company which is on the *Hispanic Business 500* list (500 largest U.S. Hispanic-owned companies based on 2009 revenue): **Information & Computing Services**. Companies included must show at least 51 percent ownership by Hispanic U.S. citizens, and must maintain headquarters in one of the 50 states or Washington, D.C. *Hispanic Business, "Hispanic Business 500," June 2010*

Minority- and Women-Owned Businesses

Group	All Firms		Firms with Paid Employees			
	Firms	Sales ($000)	Firms	Sales ($000)	Employees	Payroll ($000)
Asian	3,271	683,614	869	590,793	5,405	124,593
Black	9,718	373,933	650	208,344	3,220	66,134
Hispanic	4,175	800,765	611	627,534	4,024	117,669
Women	19,155	3,802,252	3,059	3,403,581	22,636	698,117
All Firms	64,114	109,406,895	17,487	107,422,420	431,873	17,495,974

Note: Figures cover firms located in the city; minority- and women-owned business are defined as firms in which the corresponding group own 51% or more of the stock or equity of the company
Source: U.S. Census Bureau, 2007 Economic Census, Survey of Business Owners

HOTELS

Hotels/Motels

Area	5 Star		4 Star		3 Star		2 Star		1 Star		Not Rated	
	Num.	Pct.3	Num.	Pct.3	Num.	Pct.3	Num.	Pct.3	Num.	Pct.3	Num.	Pct.3
City[1]	1	0.6	9	5.2	49	28.3	99	57.2	4	2.3	11	6.4
Total[2]	119	0.7	927	5.8	4,906	30.5	7,992	49.7	526	3.3	1,625	10.1

Note: (1) Figures cover Jacksonville and vicinity; (2) Figures cover all 100 cities in this book; (3) Percentage of hotels which are a given star rating; Star ratings are determined by expedia.com and offer an indication of the general quality of a particular hotel.
Source: expedia.com, May 5, 2011

The Jacksonville metro area is home to three of the top 218 hotels in the U.S. according to *Travel & Leisure*: **Ponte Vedra Inn & Club** (#65); **Ritz-Carlton, Amelia Island** (#73); **Lodge & Club at Ponte Vendra Beach** (#215). Criteria: service; location; rooms; food; and value. *Travel & Leisure, "T+L 500, The World's Best Hotels 2011"*

EVENT SITES

Major Stadiums, Arenas, and Auditoriums

Name	Max. Capacity
Baseball Grounds of Jacksonville	11,000
Florida Theatre	2,403
Jacksonville Municipal Stadium	77,000
Jacksonville Veterans Memorial Arena	15,000
Morocco Shrine Auditorium	3,000
Times-Union Center for the Performing Arts	2,979

Source: Original research

Convention Centers

Name	Overall Space (sq. ft.)	Exhibit Space (sq. ft.)	Meeting Space (sq. ft.)	Meeting Rooms
Prime F. Osborn III Convention Center	296,000	48,000	100,000	22

Source: Original research

Living Environment

COST OF LIVING

Cost of Living Index

Composite Index	Groceries	Housing	Utilities	Trans-portation	Health Care	Misc. Goods/ Services
92.9	102.8	80.0	91.9	103.6	94.5	97.3

Note: U.S. = 100; Figures cover the Jacksonville FL urban area.
Source: The Council for Community and Economic Research, ACCRA Cost of Living Index, 2010

Grocery Prices

Area[1]	T-Bone Steak ($/pound)	Frying Chicken ($/pound)	Whole Milk ($/half gal.)	Eggs ($/dozen)	Orange Juice ($/64 oz.)	Coffee ($/11.5 oz.)
City[2]	9.38	1.27	2.39	1.47	3.03	3.46
Avg.	9.04	1.16	2.02	1.47	3.08	3.65
Min.	6.97	0.84	1.46	0.96	2.39	2.64
Max.	13.93	2.51	3.58	3.01	4.94	6.32

Note: (1) Values for the local area are compared with the average, minimum and maximum values for all 338 areas in the Cost of Living Index; (2) Figures cover the Jacksonville FL urban area; **T-Bone Steak** *(price per pound);* **Frying Chicken** *(price per pound, whole fryer);* **Whole Milk** *(half gallon carton);* **Eggs** *(price per dozen, Grade A, large);* **Orange Juice** *(64 oz. Tropicana or Florida Natural);* **Coffee** *(11.5 oz. can, vacuum-packed, Maxwell House, Hills Bros, or Folgers).*
Source: The Council for Community and Economic Research, ACCRA Cost of Living Index, 2010

Housing and Utility Costs

Area[1]	New Home Price ($)	Apartment Rent ($/month)	All Electric ($/month)	Part Electric ($/month)	Other Energy ($/month)	Telephone ($/month)
City[2]	205,252	933	163.38	-	-	23.88
Avg.	293,442	810	166.39	91.93	83.82	26.93
Min.	182,545	453	119.21	44.47	36.85	17.98
Max.	1,123,114	2,776	307.53	218.20	313.90	39.15

Note: (1) Values for the local area are compared with the average, minimum and maximum values for all 338 areas in the Cost of Living Index; (2) Figures cover the Jacksonville FL urban area; **New Home Price** *(2,400 sf living area, 8,000 sf lot, in urban area with full utilities);* **Apartment Rent** *(950 sf 2 bedroom/1.5 or 2 bath, unfurnished, excluding all utilities except water);* **All Electric** *(average monthly cost for an all-electric home);* **Part Electric** *(average monthly cost for a part-electric home);* **Other Energy** *(average monthly cost for natural gas, fuel oil, coal, wood, and any other forms of energy except electricity);* **Telephone** *(price includes basic monthly rate for a private residential line plus additional local usage charges incurred by a family of four).*
Source: The Council for Community and Economic Research, ACCRA Cost of Living Index, 2010

Health Care, Transportation, and Other Costs

Area[1]	Doctor ($/visit)	Dentist ($/visit)	Optometrist ($/visit)	Gasoline ($/gallon)	Beauty Salon ($/visit)	Men's Shirt ($)
City[2]	71.32	82.84	54.53	2.67	41.87	21.38
Avg.	89.44	78.95	87.40	2.73	31.92	24.83
Min.	57.00	54.25	48.32	2.44	19.17	13.67
Max.	149.90	136.73	174.22	3.75	62.81	47.89

Note: (1) Values for the local area are compared with the average, minimum and maximum values for all 338 areas in the Cost of Living Index; (2) Figures cover the Jacksonville FL urban area; **Doctor** *(general practitioners routine exam of an established patient);* **Dentist** *(adult teeth cleaning and periodic oral examination);* **Optometrist** *(full vision eye exam for established adult patient);* **Gasoline** *(one gallon regular unleaded, national brand, including all taxes, cash price at self-service pump if available);* **Beauty Salon** *(woman's shampoo, trim, and blow-dry);* **Men's Shirt** *(cotton/polyester dress shirt, pinpoint weave, long sleeves).*
Source: The Council for Community and Economic Research, ACCRA Cost of Living Index, 2010

HOUSING

House Price Index (HPI)

Area	National Ranking[2]	Quarterly Change (%)	One-Year Change (%)	Five-Year Change (%)
MSA[1]	292	-2.38	-7.28	-19.37
U.S.[3]	-	-0.84	-3.95	-11.45

Note: The HPI is a weighted repeat sales index. It measures average price changes in repeat sales or refinancings on the same properties. This information is obtained by reviewing repeat mortgage transactions on single-family properties whose mortgages have been purchased or securitized by Fannie Mae or Freddie Mac in January 1975; (1) Metropolitan/Micropolitan Statistical Area - see Appendix B for areas included; (2) Rankings are based on annual percentage change for all metro areas containing at least 15,000 transactions over the last 10 years and ranges from 1 to 309; (3) figures based on a weighted average of Census Division estimates; all figures are for the period ending December 31, 2010
Source: Federal Housing Finance Agency, House Price Index, February 24, 2011

House Price Valuations

Area	Q4 2005 Price ($000)	Q4 2005 Over-valuation	Q4 2006 Price ($000)	Q4 2006 Over-valuation	Q4 2007 Price ($000)	Q4 2007 Over-valuation	Q4 2008 Price ($000)	Q4 2008 Over-valuation	Q4 2009 Price ($000)	Q4 2009 Over-valuation
MSA[1]	176.2	20.5	189.7	18.6	180.0	9.3	151.6	-8.4	137.1	-17.4

Note: Figures show the percentage of over- or under-valuation of single family homes relative to statistically normal house values (e.g. a value of 23.6 indicates that house values are 23.6% overvalued). Statistically normal house values are based on house prices, interest rates, household incomes, population densities, and any historical premiums or discounts metropolitan areas have exhibited over time; (1) Figures cover the Jacksonville, FL Metropolitan Statistical Area - see Appendix B for areas included
Source: Global Insight/PNC Financial Services Group, House Prices in America: 4th Quarter 2009 Update

Median Single-Family Home Prices

Area	2008	2009	2010p	Percent Change 2009 to 2010
MSA[1]	174.6	145.9	138.8	-4.9
U.S. Average	196.6	172.1	173.2	0.6

Note: Figures are median sales prices of existing single-family homes in thousands of dollars; (p) preliminary; n/a not available; (1) Metropolitan Statistical Area - see Appendix B for areas included
Source: National Association of Realtors, Median Sales Price of Existing Single-Family Homes for Metropolitan Areas, 4th Quarter 2010

Median Apartment Condo-Coop Home Prices

Area	2008	2009	2010p	Percent Change 2009 to 2010
MSA[1]	137.2	104.8	73.4	-30.0
U.S. Average	209.8	175.6	171.7	-2.2

Note: Figures are median sales prices of existing apartment condo-coop homes in thousands of dollars; (p) preliminary; n/a not available; (1) Metropolitan Statistical Area - see Appendix B for areas included
Source: National Association of Realtors, Median Sales Price of Existing Apartment Condo-Coop Homes for Metropolitan Areas, 4th Quarter 2010

Year Housing Structure Built

Area	2000 or Later	1990 -1999	1980 -1989	1970 -1979	1960 -1969	1950 -1959	1940 -1949	Before 1940	Median Year
City	19.0	15.6	17.9	13.4	11.4	11.7	5.8	5.3	1981
MSA[1]	21.9	18.1	19.2	14.1	9.3	9.0	4.3	4.2	1985
U.S.	12.5	14.0	14.2	16.5	11.4	11.3	5.8	14.3	1974

Note: Figures are percentages except for Median Year; (1) Metropolitan Statistical Area - see Appendix B for areas included
Source: U.S. Census Bureau, 2007-2009 American Community Survey 3-Year Estimates

HEALTH

Health Risk Data

Category	MSA[1] (%)	U.S. (%)
Adults who have been told they have high blood pressure	26.8	28.7
Adults who have been told they have high blood cholesterol	32.2	37.5
Adults who have been told they have diabetes[3]	10.0	8.3
Adults who have been told they have arthritis	25.5	26.0
Adults who have been told they currently have asthma	9.3	8.8
Adults who are current smokers	21.3	17.9
Adults who are heavy drinkers[4]	6.0	5.1
Adults who are binge drinkers[5]	16.4	15.8
Adults who are overweight (BMI 25.0 - 29.9)	36.3	36.2
Adults who are obese (BMI 30.0 - 99.8)	24.8	26.9
Adults who participated in any physical activities in the past month	75.7	76.2
Adults 50+ who have ever had a sigmoidoscopy or colonoscopy[2]	67.9	62.2
Women 40+ who have had a mammogram within the past two years[2]	79.1	76.0
Adults age 18–64 who have any kind of health care coverage	82.2	83.1

Note: Data as of 2009 unless otherwise noted; (1) Figures cover the Jacksonville, FL Metropolitan Statistical Area - see Appendix B for areas included; (2) Data as of 2008; (3) Figures do not include pregnancy-related, borderline, or pre-diabetes; (4) Heavy drinkers are classified as males having more than two drinks per day or females having more than one drink per day; (5) Binge drinkers are classified as males having five or more drinks on one occasion or females having four or more drinks on one occasion
Source: Centers for Disease Control and Prevention, Behaviorial Risk Factor Surveillance System, SMART: Selected Metropolitan/Micropolitan Area Risk Trends, 2008, 2009

Mortality Rates for the Top 10 Causes of Death in the U.S.

ICD-10[a] Sub-Chapter	ICD-10[a] Code	Age-Adjusted Mortality Rate[1] per 100,000 population County[2]	U.S.
Malignant neoplasms	C00-C97	209.3	180.9
Ischaemic heart diseases	I20-I25	145.0	135.0
Other forms of heart disease	I30-I51	50.0	50.0
Cerebrovascular diseases	I60-I69	50.5	44.1
Chronic lower respiratory diseases	J40-J47	50.5	41.5
Other degenerative diseases of the nervous system	G30-G31	22.5	23.6
Diabetes mellitus	E10-E14	35.8	23.5
Other external causes of accidental injury	W00-X59	30.2	23.5
Organic, including symptomatic, mental disorders	F01-F09	31.5	22.2
Influenza and pneumonia	J09-J18	19.7	18.1

Note: (a) ICD-10 = International Classification of Diseases 10th Revision; (1) Mortality rates are a three year average covering 2005-2007; (2) Figures cover Duval County
Source: Centers for Disease Control and Prevention, National Center for Health Statistics. Compressed Mortality File 1999-2007. CDC WONDER On-line Database, compiled from Compressed Mortality File 1999-2007 Series 20 No. 2M, 2010.

Mortality Rates for Selected Causes of Death

ICD-10[a] Sub-Chapter	ICD-10[a] Code	Age-Adjusted Mortality Rate[1] per 100,000 population County[2]	U.S.
Assault	X85-Y09	14.6	6.0
Human immunodeficiency virus (HIV) disease	B20-B24	12.9	4.0
Hypertensive diseases	I10-I15	31.6	18.0
Intentional self-harm	X60-X84	13.6	11.0
Malnutrition	E40-E46	2.0	0.8
Obesity and other hyperalimentation	E65-E68	2.3	1.5
Transport accidents	V01-V99	18.9	15.6
Viral hepatitis	B15-B19	3.7	2.1

Note: (a) ICD-10 = International Classification of Diseases 10th Revision; (1) Mortality rates are a three year average covering 2005-2007; (2) Figures cover Duval County
Source: Centers for Disease Control and Prevention, National Center for Health Statistics. Compressed Mortality File 1999-2007. CDC WONDER On-line Database, compiled from Compressed Mortality File 1999-2007 Series 20 No. 2M, 2010.

Distribution of Physicians and Dentists

Area[1]	Dentists[2]	D.O.[3]	M.D.[4]				
			Total	Family/ General Practice	Pediatrics	Medical Specialties	Surgical Specialties
Local (number)	318	168	1,883	271	132	684	426
Local (rate[5])	3.7	2.0	22.1	3.2	1.5	8.0	5.0
U.S. (rate[5])	4.5	1.9	18.3	2.5	1.4	6.8	4.1

Note: Data as of 2008 unless noted; (1) Local data covers Duval County; (2) Data as of 2007; (3) Doctor of Osteopathic Medicine; (4) Includes active, non-federal, patient-care, office-based Doctors of Medicine; (5) rate per 10,000 population
Source: Area Resource File (ARF). 2009-2010 Release. U.S. Department of Health and Human Services, Health Resources and Services Administration, Bureau of Health Professions, Rockville, MD, August 2010

Hospitals

Jacksonville has the following hospitals: 7 general medical and surgical; 1 psychiatric; 1 rehabilitation; 1 long-term acute care.
AHA Guide to the Healthcare Field 2010

According to *U.S. News,* the Jacksonville, FL Metropolitan Statistical Area is home to one of the best hospitals in the U.S.: **Mayo Clinic**. The hospital listed was highly ranked in at least one adult specialty. *U.S. News Online, "America's Best Hospitals 2010-11"*

According to *U.S. News,* the Jacksonville, FL Metropolitan Statistical Area is home to one of the best children's hospitals in the U.S.: **Wolfson Children's Hospital**. The hospital listed was highly ranked in at least one pediatric specialty. *U.S. News Online, "America's Best Children's Hospitals 2010-11"*

EDUCATION

Public School District Statistics

District Name	Schls	Pupils	Pupil/ Teacher Ratio	Minority Pupils[1] (%)	Free Lunch Eligible[2] (%)	IEP[3] (%)
Duval	175	122,606	15.4	59.8	37.7	14.3

Note: Table includes school districts with 2,000 or more students; (1) Percentage of students that are not non-Hispanic white; (2) Percentage of students that are eligible for the free lunch program; (3) Percentage of students that have an Individualized Education Program.
Source: U.S. Department of Education, National Center for Education Statistics, Common Core of Data, Local Education Agency (School District) Universe Survey: School Year 2008-2009; U.S. Department of Education, National Center for Education Statistics, Common Core of Data, Public Elementary/Secondary School Universe Survey: School Year 2008-2009

Top Public High Schools

High School Name	Index[1]	Rank[1]	Subsidized Lunch (%)[2]	E&E (%)[3]
Anderson School of Arts	5.716	33	9.4	51.1
Bartram Trail	1.748	907	1.0	41.0
Englewood	1.505	1146	46.0	9.5
Mandarin[4]	4.083	97	12.0	22.2
Paxon School for Advanced Studies[4]	9.513	8	14.0	76.1
Sandalwood	3.189	210	26.0	18.5
Stanton College Prep[4]	12.562	3	10.0	100.0

Note: (1) Public schools are ranked according to a ratio that is the number of Advanced Placement, International Baccalaureate, and/or Cambridge tests taken by all students at a school in 2009 divided by the number of graduating seniors. All of the schools on the list have an index of at least 1.000; they are in the top six percent of public schools measured this way. The rankings range from 1 to 1,734; (2) Percentage of students receiving federally subsidized meals; (3) E & E stands for equity and excellence percentage: the portion of all graduating seniors at a school that had at least one passing grade on one AP or IB test; (4) Schools that offer International Baccalaureate or Cambridge exams; (5) School is unranked, but has been identified by Newsweek as one of the nation's most elite public high schools.
Source: Newsweek Online, "Top High Schools 2010"

Highest Level of Education

Area	Less than H.S.	H.S. Diploma	Some College, No Deg.	Associate Degree	Bachelors Degree	Masters Degree	Profess. School Degree	Doctorate Degree
City	13.2	31.3	23.8	8.4	15.5	5.3	1.6	0.9
MSA[1]	12.3	30.6	23.7	8.5	16.5	5.8	1.7	0.9
U.S.	15.3	29.0	20.7	7.5	17.4	7.0	1.9	1.1

Note: Figures are 2010 estimated percentages and cover persons age 25 and over; (1) Metropolitan Statistical Area - see Appendix B for areas included
Source: Claritas, Inc.

Educational Attainment by Race

Area	High School Graduate (%)					Bachelor's Degree (%)				
	Total	White	Black	Asian	Hisp.[2]	Total	White	Black	Asian	Hisp.[2]
City	86.9	90.1	81.9	85.3	78.1	24.1	26.9	15.2	44.9	21.1
MSA[1]	87.9	90.3	82.0	86.6	78.9	25.9	28.3	15.2	45.3	21.6
U.S.	84.9	90.0	80.7	85.5	60.7	27.8	30.9	17.5	49.7	12.7

Note: Figures shown cover persons 25 years old and over; (1) Metropolitan Statistical Area - see Appendix B for areas included; (2) people of Hispanic origin can be of any race
Source: U.S. Census Bureau, 2007-2009 American Community Survey 3-Year Estimates

School Enrollment by Grade and Control

Area	Preschool (%)		Kindergarten (%)		Grades 1 - 4 (%)		Grades 5 - 8 (%)		Grades 9 - 12 (%)	
	Public	Private	Public	Private	Public	Private	Public	Private	Public	Private
City	50.0	50.0	80.4	19.6	84.5	15.5	80.7	19.3	82.6	17.4
MSA[1]	47.0	53.0	83.8	16.2	86.4	13.6	83.9	16.1	86.4	13.6
U.S.	54.3	45.7	86.4	13.6	88.9	11.1	89.1	10.9	90.2	9.8

Note: Figures shown cover persons 3 years old and over; (1) Metropolitan Statistical Area - see Appendix B for areas included
Source: U.S. Census Bureau, 2007-2009 American Community Survey 3-Year Estimates

Average Salaries of Public School Classroom Teachers

Area	2009-10		2010-11		Percent Change 2009-10 to 2010-11	Percent Change 2000-01 to 2010-11
	Dollars	Rank[1]	Dollars	Rank[1]		
Florida	46,708	37	46,702	47	-0.01	22.2
U.S. Average	55,202	-	56,069	-	1.57	29.3

Note: (1) State rank ranges from 1 to 51 where 1 indicates highest salary.
Source: National Education Association, Rankings & Estimates: Rankings of the States 2010 and Estimates of School Statistics 2011, December 2010

Higher Education

Four-Year Colleges			Two-Year Colleges			Medical Schools[1]	Law Schools[2]	Voc/ Tech[3]
Public	Private Non-profit	Private For-profit	Public	Private Non-profit	Private For-profit			
2	4	5	0	0	8	0	1	9

Note: Figures cover institutions located within the city limits and include main campuses only; (1) includes schools accredited by the Liaison Committee on Medical Education and the American Osteopathic Association; (2) includes American Bar Association-accredited law schools; (3) includes all schools with programs that are less than 2 years.
Source: National Center for Education Statistics, Integrated Postsecondary Education System (IPEDS) Peer Analysis System, 2010-11; U.S. News & World Report, Medical School Directory, 2011; U.S. News & World Report, Law School Directory, 2011

PRESIDENTIAL ELECTION

2008 Presidential Election Results

Area	Obama	McCain	Nader	Other
Duval County	48.6	50.5	0.2	0.6
U.S.	52.9	45.6	0.6	0.9

Note: Results are percentages and may not add to 100% due to rounding
Source: Dave Leip's Atlas of U.S. Presidential Elections, www.uselectionatlas.org

EMPLOYERS

Major Employers

Company Name	Industry	Type of Site
Amelia Island Plantation	Hotels and motels	Single
Baptist Health System	Management services	Headquarters
Blue Cross	Hospital and medical service plans	Branch
Blue Cross and Blue Shield	Hospital and medical service plans	Branch
Chase Manhattan	Mortgage bankers and correspondents	Branch
Coastline Plastics	Plastics materials and resins	Single
FCSO	Management consulting services	Headquarters
FIS	Business services, nec	Headquarters
Fleet Readiness Ctr Southeast	National security	Branch
Jacksonville Electric Auth	Electric services	Branch
Kelley-Clarke	Groceries, general line	Single
Marketplace	Grocery stores	Headquarters
Mayo Clinic Jacksonville	Offices and clinics of medical doctors	Headquarters
Memorial Hosp Jacksonville	General medical and surgical hospitals	Single
National Gibsome	Adhesives and sealants	Single
Navair Depot Jacksonville	National security	Branch
Northrop Grumman Systems Corp	Aircraft	Branch
Saint Johns County School Dst	Elementary and secondary schools	Headquarters
UNF/SBDC	Colleges and universities	Single
University Health Groups	Management services	Headquarters
Vistakon	Ophthalmic goods	Headquarters

Note: Companies shown are located within the Jacksonville metropolitan area; nec = not elsewhere classified.
Source: www.zapdata.com, January 2011

PUBLIC SAFETY

Crime Rate

Area	All Crimes	Violent Crimes				Property Crimes		
		Murder	Forcible Rape	Robbery	Aggrav. Assault	Burglary	Larceny -Theft	Motor Vehicle Theft
City	5,993.7	12.2	26.9	291.2	505.6	1,395.7	3,426.1	335.9
Suburbs[1]	3,447.3	4.1	21.9	71.9	377.1	668.3	2,162.5	141.6
Metro[2]	5,004.1	9.1	25.0	206.0	455.7	1,113.0	2,935.1	260.4
U.S.	3,465.5	5.0	28.7	133.0	262.8	716.3	2,060.9	258.8

Note: Figures are crimes per 100,000 population; (1) All areas within the metro area that are located outside the city limits; (2) Metropolitan Statistical Area - see Appendix B for areas included
Source: FBI Uniform Crime Reports, 2009

Hate Crimes

Area	Number of Quarters Reported	Bias Motivation				
		Race	Religion	Sexual Orientation	Ethnicity	Disability
City	4	2	0	0	0	0

Source: Federal Bureau of Investigation, Hate Crime Statistics 2009

Identity Theft Consumer Complaints

Area	Complaints	Complaints per 100,000 Population	Rank[2]
MSA[1]	1,242	95.5	79
U.S.	250,854	81.3	-

Note: (1) Metropolitan Statistical Area - see Appendix B for areas included; (2) Rank ranges from 1 to 384 where 1 indicates greatest number of complaints per 100,000 population
Source: Federal Trade Commission, Consumer Sentinel Network Data Book for January - December 2010

RECREATION

Culture

Dance[1]	Theatre[1]	Instrumental Music[1]	Vocal Music[1]	Series/ Festivals	Museums	Zoos and Aquariums[2]
2	2	1	0	5	11	1

Note: (1) Number of professional performing groups; (2) AZA-accredited
Source: The Grey House Performing Arts Directory, 2011-2012; Official Museum Directory, 2010; American Association of Museums, AAM Member Museums, March 2011; Association of Zoos & Aquariums, AZA Member Zoos & Aquariums, May 2011

Professional Sports Teams

Team Name	League
Jacksonville Jaguars	National Football League (NFL)

Note: Includes teams located in the Jacksonville metro area.
Source: Original research

CLIMATE

Average and Extreme Temperatures

Temperature	Jan	Feb	Mar	Apr	May	Jun	Jul	Aug	Sep	Oct	Nov	Dec	Yr.
Extreme High (°F)	84	88	91	95	100	103	103	102	98	96	88	84	103
Average High (°F)	65	68	74	80	86	90	92	91	87	80	73	67	79
Average Temp. (°F)	54	57	62	69	75	80	83	82	79	71	62	56	69
Average Low (°F)	43	45	51	57	64	70	73	73	70	61	51	44	58
Extreme Low (°F)	7	22	23	34	45	47	61	63	48	36	21	11	7

Note: Figures cover the years 1948-1990
Source: National Climatic Data Center, International Station Meteorological Climate Summary, 9/96

Average Precipitation/Snowfall/Humidity

Precip./Humidity	Jan	Feb	Mar	Apr	May	Jun	Jul	Aug	Sep	Oct	Nov	Dec	Yr.
Avg. Precip. (in.)	3.0	3.7	3.8	3.0	3.6	5.3	6.2	7.4	7.8	3.7	2.0	2.6	52.0
Avg. Snowfall (in.)	Tr	Tr	Tr	0	0	0	0	0	0	0	0	Tr	0
Avg. Rel. Hum. 7am (%)	86	86	87	86	86	88	89	91	92	91	89	88	88
Avg. Rel. Hum. 4pm (%)	56	53	50	49	54	61	64	65	66	62	58	58	58

Note: Figures cover the years 1948-1990; Tr = Trace amounts (<0.05 in. of rain; <0.5 in. of snow)
Source: National Climatic Data Center, International Station Meteorological Climate Summary, 9/96

Weather Conditions

Temperature			Daytime Sky			Precipitation		
10°F & below	32°F & below	90°F & above	Clear	Partly cloudy	Cloudy	0.01 inch or more precip.	0.1 inch or more snow/ice	Thunder-storms
<1	16	83	86	181	98	114	1	65

Note: Figures are average number of days per year and cover the years 1948-1990
Source: National Climatic Data Center, International Station Meteorological Climate Summary, 9/96

HAZARDOUS WASTE

Superfund Sites

Jacksonville has five hazardous waste sites on the EPA's Superfund Final National Priorities List: **Cecil Field Naval Air Station; Hipps Road Landfill (Duval County); Jacksonville Naval Air Station; Kerr-McGee Chemical Corp - Jacksonville; Pickettville Road Landfill**. *U.S. Environmental Protection Agency, Final National Priorities List, April 1, 2011*

**AIR & WATER
QUALITY**

Air Quality Index

Area	Percent of Days when Air Quality was...[2]				AQI Statistics	
	Good	Moderate	Unhealthy for Sensitive Groups	Unhealthy	Maximum	Median
Area[1]	85.1	14.9	0.0	0.0	100	39

*Note: The Air Quality Index (AQI) is an index for reporting daily air quality. EPA calculates the AQI for five major air pollutants regulated by the Clean Air Act: ground-level ozone, particle pollution (also known as particulate matter), carbon monoxide, sulfur dioxide, and nitrogen dioxide. The AQI runs from 0 to 500. The higher the AQI value, the greater the level of air pollution and the greater the health concern. There are six AQI categories: "Good" The AQI is between 0 and 50. Air quality is considered satisfactory; "Moderate" The AQI is between 51 and 100. Air quality is acceptable; "Unhealthy for Sensitive Groups" When AQI values are between 101 and 150, members of sensitive groups may experience health effects; "Unhealthy" When AQI values are between 151 and 200 everyone may begin to experience health effects; "Very Unhealthy" AQI values between 201 and 300 trigger a health alert; "Hazardous" AQI values over 300 trigger health warnings of emergency conditions; (1) Data covers Duval County; (2) Based on 275 days with AQI data in 2008; The EPA has suspended data updates while it assesses its data systems, including AirData reports and maps.
Source: U.S. Environmental Protection Agency, AirData Report, 2008*

Air Quality Index Pollutants

Area	Percent of Days when AQI Pollutant was...[2]					
	Carbon Monoxide	Nitrogen Dioxide	Ozone	Sulfur Dioxide	Particulate Matter 2.5	Particulate Matter 10
Area[1]	1.1	0.0	66.9	0.0	26.5	5.5

*Note: The Air Quality Index (AQI) is an index for reporting daily air quality. EPA calculates the AQI for five major air pollutants regulated by the Clean Air Act: ground-level ozone, particle pollution (also known as particulate matter), carbon monoxide, sulfur dioxide, and nitrogen dioxide. The AQI runs from 0 to 500. The higher the AQI value, the greater the level of air pollution and the greater the health concern; (1) Data covers Duval County; (2) Based on 275 days with AQI data in 2008; The EPA has suspended data updates while it assesses its data systems, including AirData reports and maps.
Source: U.S. Environmental Protection Agency, AirData Report, 2008*

Air Quality Index Trends

Area	Trend Sites (days)								All Sites (days)
	2002	2003	2004	2005	2006	2007	2008	2009	2009
MSA[1]	57	8	15	20	34	15	10	3	4

*Note: Figures are the number of days the AQI value exceeded 100 in a given year. An AQI value greater than 100 indicates that air quality would have been in the unhealthful range on that day. Data from exceptional events are included. These counts are presented in two ways. First, the counts are based on sites having an adequate record of monitoring data during the trend period (trend sites). These counts represent the relative change in the number of days with AQI values greater than 100. In the last column, the counts are based on all sites with data in the most recent year (because it is possible for a site to have data in the most recent year but not enough data to be a trend site); (1) Data covers the Jacksonville, FL Metropolitan Statistical Area - see Appendix B for areas included
Source: U.S. Environmental Protection Agency, Office of Air and Radiation, Air Quality Index Information, "Number of Days with Air Quality Index Values Greater than 100 and Trend Sites, 1990-2009, and at All Sites in 2009"*

Maximum Air Pollutant Concentrations

	Particulate Matter 10 (ug/m^3)	Particulate Matter 2.5 (ug/m^3)	Ozone (ppm)	Carbon Monoxide (ppm)	Sulfur Dioxide (ppm)	Nitrogen Dioxide (ppm)	Lead (ug/m^3)
MSA[1] Level	61	19	0.065	2	0.022	0.008	n/a
NAAQS[2]	150	35	0.075	9	0.140	0.053	0.15
Met NAAQS[2]	Yes	Yes	Yes	Yes	Yes	Yes	n/a

*Note: Data from exceptional events are not included; (1) Data covers the Jacksonville, FL Metropolitan Statistical Area - see Appendix B for areas included; (2) National Ambient Air Quality Standards; n/a not available
Concentrations: Particulate Matter 10 (coarse particulate) - highest second maximum 24-hour concentration; Particulate Matter 2.5 (fine particulate) - highest 98th percentile 24-hour concentration; Ozone - highest fourth daily maximum 8-hour concentration; Carbon Monoxide - highest second maximum non-overlapping 8-hour concentration; Sulfur Dioxide - highest second maximum 24-hour concentration; Nitrogen Dioxide - highest arithmetic mean concentration; Lead - maximum running 3-month average
Units: ppm = parts per million; ug/m^3 = micrograms per cubic meter
Source: U.S. Environmental Protection Agency, CBSA Factbook 2009, Air Quality Statistics by City, 2009*

Drinking Water

Water System Name	Pop. Served	Primary Water Source Type	Violations[1] Health Based	Monitoring/ Reporting
JEA-Major Grid	800,000	Ground	0	0

Note: (1) Based on violation data from January 1, 2010 to December 31, 2010 (includes unresolved violations from earlier years)

Source: U.S. Environmental Protection Agency, Office of Ground Water and Drinking Water, Safe Drinking Water Information System (based on data extracted May 9, 2011)

Knoxville, Tennessee

Background

Home of the Tennessee Valley Authority, "Bleak House" (Confederate Memorial Hall), and the 1982 World's Fair, Knoxville's central business district reflects every period of its history. Knoxville was settled at the end of the eighteenth century when a flood of pioneers migrated to Tennessee. It soon established itself as the gateway to the West. In 1791, William Blount, its first territorial governor, chose James White's Fort as the capital of the territory, subsequently renaming it for Secretary of War, James Knox.

The city played an important part in the Civil War and was occupied by both the Confederate and Union armies. Knoxville rapidly recovered during Reconstruction and became the business center of the east Tennessee Valley.

Metropolitan Knoxville is home to many widely diversified industries and recently ranked fifth in *Forbes* magazine's Best Places for Business and Careers. Aluminum and clothing constitute the primary manufactured products. Automobile parts and pre-fabricated homes, fiberglass boats, and health-care products are some of its other products.

The U.S. Department of Energy facility at Oak Ridge, which is close by, was built during World War II to develop the atomic bomb. The facility is the area's largest employer, with more than 12,000 people working there. The second- and third-largest employers are educational in nature, including the University of Tennessee, Knoxville, and Knox County Public School System. Combined, they employ more than 17,000 area residents. Other companies based in Knoxville include AC Entertainment, Pilot Corp., and the Tennessee Valley Authority.

Through the years, Knoxville has played host to numerous sports championships: 1988 National Chess Championship for elementary school children; 1993 A.A.U. Junior Olympic Games; 1996 National Gymnastics Championship; and 1997 Super National Scholastic Chess Championships—the largest ever held in the United States and possibly the world. The Kansas City Chiefs won the Superbowl in 1970 and have continued to draw impressive crowds, selling out every home game for the past 17 seasons. Pulitzer Prize-winner James Agee is Knoxville's native son. The author fondly depicts his background in a number of his works.

The city is located where the Holston and French Broad rivers meet to create the Tennessee River, about 110 miles northeast of Chattanooga. It lies in a broad valley between the Cumberland Mountains to the northwest and the Great Smoky Mountains to the southeast. The Cumberland Mountains weaken the force of cold winter air, which frequently moves south of Knoxville, and modifies the hot summer winds common to the plains to the west. The topography also creates winds that are generally light and discourages tornadoes.

Rankings

General Rankings

- Knoxville was ranked #99 out of 375 metro areas in *Cities Ranked & Rated*. Criteria: cost of living; climate; crime; transportation; economy and jobs; education; arts and culture; health and healthcare; leisure; quality of life. *Cities Ranked & Rated, 2nd Edition, 2007*

- Knoxville was ranked #31 out of 379 metro areas in *Places Rated Almanac*. Criteria: health care; education; recreation; transportation; ambience; climate; crime; housing costs; jobs. *Places Rated Almanac, 7th Edition, 2007*

- Knoxville was selected as one of "America's Top 100 Places to Live" by RelocateAmerica.com. Cities and towns nominated to be great places to live along with their key data regarding education, employment, economy, crime, parks, recreation and housing were reviewed, rated and judged by the Relocate-America.com editorial staff. *Relocate-America.com, "RelocateAmerica's Top 100 Places to Live in 2010"*

Business/Finance Rankings

- A.G. Edwards ranked America's 500 top-performing communities based on their residents' personal savings and investing behavior. The Knoxville metro area ranked #404 with an index score of 96.95 (national average = 100.00). A dozen statistical factors were measured including: participation in retirement savings plans; personal debt levels; and home ownership. *A.G. Edwards, "2007 Nest Egg Index," September 12, 2007*

- *American City Business Journals* ranked America's 261 largest cities in terms of their resident's wealth. Knoxville ranked #227. Criteria: per capita income; median household income; percentage of households with annual incomes of $200,000 or more; median home value. *American City Business Journals, www.bizjournals.com, "Where the Money Is: America's Wealth Centers," August 18, 2008*

- The Knoxville metro area appeared on the Milken Institute "2010 Best Performing Metros" list. Rank: #92 out of 200 large metro areas. Criteria: job growth; wage and salary growth; high-tech output growth. *Milken Institute, "2010 Best Performing Metros"*

- *Forbes* ranked the 200 most populous metro areas in the U.S. in terms of the "Best Places for Business and Careers." The Knoxville metro area was ranked #56. Criteria: 12 metrics including costs (business and living), job growth (past and projected), income growth, educational attainment, projected economic growth, crime, cultural and recreational opportunities, net migration patterns, percentage of subprime mortgages handed out over a three-year period, and the number of highly ranked four-year colleges. *Forbes, "Best Places for Business and Careers," April 14, 2010*

Children/Family Rankings

- The Knoxville metro area was selected as one of the "Best Cities for Relocating Families" by Worldwide ERC and Primacy Relocation. The 2008 study looked at nearly 50 factors important to relocating families including: recent job growth; nearby top-ranked colleges; in-state tuition for four-year public colleges; population growth since 2000; pediatricians per 100,000 population; and a Green Living index. *Worldwide ERC and Primacy Relocation, "2008 Best Cities for Relocating Families"*

Dating/Romance Rankings

- Knoxville was selected as one of the most romantic cities in America by *Amazon.com*. The city ranked #2 of 20. Cities with populations greater than 100,000 were evaluated based on per capita sales of romance novels and relationship books, romantic comedy movies, Barry White albums, and sexual wellness products. *Amazon.com, "Top 20 Most Romantic Cities in America," February 8, 2011*

- The Knoxville metro area was selected as one of the "Best Cities for Relocating Singles" by Worldwide ERC and Primacy Relocation. The area ranked #44 out of the 100 largest metro areas in the U.S. Areas were selected based on the following criteria: recent job growth; recent singles population growth; overall population growth; affordable rental housing; cost-of-living index; expanded arts and recreation opportunities; ratio of single men and single women; affordability of quality higher education (including state residency requirements); diversity index; climate; population density. *Worldwide ERC and Primacy Relocation, "2008 Best Cities for Relocating Singles"*

Education Rankings

- Knoxville was identified as one of the 100 "smartest" metro areas in the U.S. The area ranked #62. Criteria: the editors rated the collective brainpower of the 100 largest metro area in the U.S based on their residents' educational attainment. *American City Business Journals, www.bizjournals.com, April 14, 2008*

- Knoxville was identified as one of "America's Brainiest Bastions" by *Portfolio.com.* The metro area ranked #85 out of 200. Portfolio.com analyzed levels of educational attainment in the nation's 200 largest metropolitan areas. The editors established scores for five levels of educational attainment, based on relative earning power of adult workers age 25 or older. Scores were determined by comparing the median income for all workers with the median income for those workers at a specified educational level. *Portfolio.com, "America's Brainiest Bastions," December 1, 2010*

Environmental Rankings

- Knoxville was selected as one of 22 "Smarter Cities" for energy by the Natural Resources Defense Council." Criteria: investment in green power; energy efficiency measures; conservation. *Natural Resources Defense Council, "2010 Smarter Cities," July 19, 2010*

- 100 of the largest metro areas in the U.S. were analyzed in terms of their current drought severity. The Knoxville metro area ranked #10 (#1 = driest). The rankings were based on statistics such as long-term precipitation trends and patterns and the Palmer drought indices. *Sperling's BestPlaces, www.BestPlaces.net, "America's Drought-Riskiest Cities," November 2007*

- The Knoxville metro area appeared in *Country Home's* "Best Green Places" report. The area ranked #209 out of 379. Criteria: official energy policies; green power; green buildings; availability of fresh, locally grown food. *Country Home, "Best Green Places," 2008*

- Knoxville was highlighted as one of the 25 metro areas most polluted by year-round particle pollution (Annual PM 2.5) in the U.S. The area ranked #24. *American Lung Association, State of the Air 2011*

- Knoxville was highlighted as one of the 25 most ozone-polluted metro areas in the U.S. The area ranked #18. *American Lung Association, State of the Air 2011*

Health/Fitness Rankings

- Knoxville was identified as a "2011 Asthma Capital." The area ranked #2 out of the nation's 100 largest metropolitan areas. Twelve factors were used to identify the most challenging places to live for people with asthma: estimated prevalence; self-reported prevalence; crude death rate for asthma; annual pollen score; annual air quality; public smoking laws; number of board-certified asthma specialists; school inhaler access laws; rescue medication use; controller medication use; uninsured rate; poverty rate. *Asthma and Allergy Foundation of America, "2011 Asthma Capitals"*

- Knoxville was identified as a 2009 "Spring Allergy Capital." The area ranked #2 out of 100. Three groups of factors were used to identify the most severe cities for people with allergies during the spring season: annual pollen levels; medicine utilization; access to board-certified allergists. *Asthma and Allergy Foundation of America, "Spring Allergy Capitals 2009"*

- Knoxville was identified as a 2010 "Fall Allergy Capital." The area ranked #4 out of 100. Three groups of factors were used to identify the most severe cities for people with allergies during the fall season: annual pollen levels; medicine utilization; access to board-certified allergists. *Asthma and Allergy Foundation of America, "Fall Allergy Capitals 2010"*

- Ortho-McNeil Neurologics, in partnership with Sperling's BestPlaces, analyzed 110 metro areas and identified those U.S. cities with the highest prevalence of factors that are most commonly associated with migraine headaches. The Knoxville metro area ranked #4. Criteria: number of migraine-related drug prescriptions per capita; lifestyle factors that can contribute to migraines; environmental factors that can trigger migraines; and consumption of migraine-triggering foods. *Ortho-McNeil Neurologics, "America's Migraine Hot Spots," March 14, 2006*

- Scarborough Research, a leading market research firm, identified the top local markets for diabetes medication purchasers. The Knoxville DMA (Designated Market Area) ranked in the top 13 with 14% of consumers reporting that they purchased medication for diabetes within the past 12 months. *Scarborough Research, March 19, 2007*

- The Knoxville metro area appeared in the 2010 Gallup-Healthways Well-Being Index. The index, based on interviews with more than 353,000 Americans during 2009, asked individuals to assess their jobs, finances, physical health, emotional state of mind and communities. The metro area ranked #101 out of 162. Criteria: life evaluation; emotional health; work environment; physical health; healthy behaviors; basic access (basic needs optimal for a healthy life, such as access to food and medicine, having health insurance and feeling safe while walking at night). *Gallup-Healthways, "Well-Being Index 2010"*

- *The Daily Beast* identified the 30 U.S metro areas with the worst smoking habits. The Knoxville metro area ranked #12. Sixty urban centers with populations of more than one million were ranked based on the following criteria: number of smokers; number of cigarettes smoked per day; fewest attempts to quit. *The Daily Beast, "30 Cities With Smoking Problems," January 3, 2011*

Real Estate Rankings

- *Fortune* ranked the 100 largest metro areas in the U.S. in terms of projected median home price change in 2010. The Knoxville metro area ranked #45. *Fortune, "The 2010 Housing Outlook," December 9, 2009*

- Knoxville appeared on ApartmentRatings.com "Top College Towns & Cities" for renters list in 2010." The area ranked #8. Overall satisfaction ratings were ranked using thousands of user submitted scores for hundreds of apartment complexes located in cities and towns that are home to the 100 largest four-year institutions in the U.S. *ApartmentRatings.com, "2010 College Town Renter Satisfaction Rankings"*

- The Knoxville metro area was identified as one of the least expensive places to rent in the U.S. The area ranked #8 out of 10 markets with an average effective rent of $560 per month. The rental figures cover apartment properties in complexes with 40 or more units (20 or more units in California and Arizona). The figures are blended average rents, which include all unit sizes. Effective rents include free rent incentives and other landlord concessions. *Wall Street Journal Online, January 17, 2008*

- The nation's largest metro areas were analyzed in terms of the percentage of households entering some stage of foreclosure in 2010. The Knoxville metro area ranked #138 out of 206 (#1 = highest foreclosure rate). *RealtyTrac, 2010 Year-End Metropolitan Foreclosure Market Report, January 27, 2011*

- The Center for Housing Policy ranked 210 U.S metropolitan areas by the fair market rent for a two-bedroom unit. The Knoxville metro area was ranked #147. (#1 = most expensive) with a rent of $732. Criteria: Fair Market Rent (FMR) in effect during the fourth quarter of 2009 based on HUD's fiscal year 2010 FMRs. *The Center for Housing Policy, "Paycheck to Paycheck: Most to Least Expensive Rental Markets in 2009"*

Safety Rankings

- Allstate ranked the 200 largest cities in America in terms of driver safety. Knoxville ranked #5. In addition, drivers were 19.5% less likely to have had an accident compared to the national average. Allstate researchers analyzed internal property damage reported claims over a two-year period (from January 2007 to December 2008) to ensure the findings would not be affected by external influences such as weather or road construction. A weighted average of the two-year numbers determined the annual percentages. The report defines an auto crash as any collision resulting in a property damage claim. *Allstate, "The 2010 Allstate America's Best Drivers Report™"*

- The National Insurance Crime Bureau ranked 366 metro areas in the U.S. in terms of per capita rates of vehicle theft. The Knoxville metro area ranked #112 (#1 = highest rate). Criteria: number of vehicle theft offenses per 100,000 inhabitants. *National Insurance Crime Bureau, "Hot Spots," May 17, 2010*

Seniors/Retirement Rankings

- Knoxville was identified as one of "The Top 100 Places to Retire" by *Topretirements.com* The list reflects the 100 cities (out of 625+ total cities reviewed) that visitors to the website are most interested in for retirement. *Topretirements.com, "2011 Best Places to Retire List: The Sunbelt Rules"*

Sports/Recreation Rankings

- Knoxville appeared on the *Sporting News* list of the "Best Sports Cities" for 2010. The area ranked #58 out of 402 cities in the U.S. *Sporting News* takes a 12-month snapshot, roughly October to October, of each city's sports, putting a heavy premium on regular-season won-lost records (from the most recently completed season). Other criteria include: playoff berths, bowl appearances and tournament bids; championships; applicable power ratings; quality of competition; overall fan fervor as measured in part by attendance as percentage of venue capacity; abundance of teams (rewarding quality over quantity); stadium and arena quality; ticket availability and prices; franchise ownership; and marquee appeal of athletes. *Sporting News, "Best Sports Cities 2010," October, 2010*

- Knoxville was chosen as a bicycle friendly community by the League of American Bicyclists. A Bicycle Friendly Community welcomes cyclists by providing safe accommodation for cycling and encouraging people to bike for transportation and recreation. There are four award levels: Platinum; Gold; Silver; and Bronze. The community achieved an award level of Bronze. *League of American Bicyclists, "Bicycle Friendly Community Master List," September 2010*

- Knoxville was chosen as one of America's 10 best places to live and boat. Criteria: boating opportunities; boat-friendly regulations; water access; availability of waterfront homes; health of the local economy; and overall lifestyle for boaters. *Boating Magazine, "10 Best Places to Live and Boat," June 2010*

- *Golf Digest* ranked 330 metro areas in the U.S. in terms of golf. The Knoxville metro area was ranked #201. Criteria: access to golf; weather; value of golf; and quality of golf. *Golf Digest, "Metro Golf Rankings," August 2005*

Women/Minorities Rankings

- Knoxville was ranked #32 out of 100 metro areas in *SELF Magazine's* ranking of America's healthiest places for women." A panel of experts came up with more than 50 criteria including death and disease rates, environmental indicators, community resources, and lifestyle habits. *SELF Magazine, "Secrets of America's Healthiest Women," December 2008*

Business Environment

CITY FINANCES

City Government Finances

Component	2008 ($000)	2008 ($ per capita)
Total Revenues	956,609	5,212
Total Expenditures	1,018,287	5,548
Debt Outstanding	740,836	4,036
Cash and Securities[1]	843,978	4,598

*Note: (1) Cash and security holdings of a government at the close of its fiscal
year, including those of its dependent agencies, utilities, and liquor stores.
Source: U.S Census Bureau, State & Local Government Finances 2008*

City Government Revenue by Source

Source	2008 ($000)	2008 ($ per capita)
General Revenue		
From Federal Government	34,505	188
From State Government	39,280	214
From Local Governments	11,628	63
Taxes		
Property	96,054	523
Sales and Gross Receipts	57,501	313
Personal Income	0	0
Corporate Income	0	0
Motor Vehicle License	0	0
Other Taxes	2,307	13
Current Charges	83,122	453
Liquor Store	0	0
Utility	631,649	3,441
Employee Retirement	-28,709	-156

Source: U.S Census Bureau, State & Local Government Finances 2008

City Government Expenditures by Function

Function	2008 ($000)	2008 ($ per capita)	2008 (%)
General Direct Expenditures			
Air Transportation	0	0	0.0
Corrections	0	0	0.0
Education	0	0	0.0
Employment Security Administration	0	0	0.0
Financial Administration	9,899	54	1.0
Fire Protection	29,911	163	2.9
General Public Buildings	0	0	0.0
Governmental Administration, Other	3,865	21	0.4
Health	13	<1	<0.1
Highways	9,101	50	0.9
Hospitals	0	0	0.0
Housing and Community Development	6,511	35	0.6
Interest on General Debt	20,783	113	2.0
Judicial and Legal	2,400	13	0.2
Libraries	0	0	0.0
Parking	641	3	0.1
Parks and Recreation	6,433	35	0.6
Police Protection	45,910	250	4.5
Public Welfare	0	0	0.0
Sewerage	87,965	479	8.6
Solid Waste Management	9,407	51	0.9
Veterans' Services	0	0	0.0
Liquor Store	0	0	0.0
Utility	682,701	3,720	67.0
Employee Retirement	35,200	192	3.5

Source: U.S Census Bureau, State & Local Government Finances 2008

Municipal Bond Ratings

Area	Moody's	S&P	Fitch
City	Aa1	AA+	AAA

Rating Systems (shown in declining order of credit quality): Moody's– Aaa, Aa, A, Baa, Ba, B, Caa, Ca, C (numerical modifiers 1, 2, and 3 are added to letter-rating); S&P– AAA, AA, A, BBB, BB, B, CCC, CC, C; Fitch– AAA, AA, A, BBB, BB, B, CCC, CC, C. Ratings may be modified by the addition of a plus or minus sign to show relative standing within the major rating categories.
Notes: n/a Not available; (1) Not reviewed; (2) Issuer Rating/No General Obligation; (3) Standard and Poor's Issue Credit Rating (ICR) is a current opinion of an obliger with respect to a specific financial obligation, a specific class of financial obligations, or a specific financial program.
Source: City of Knoxville, Tennessee, Comprehensive Annual Financial Report, Fiscal Year Ended June 30, 2010

DEMOGRAPHICS

Population Growth

Area	1990 Census	2000 Census	2010 Estimate	2015 Projection	Population Growth (%) 2000-2010	Population Growth (%) 2010-2015
City	173,288	173,890	185,041	190,587	6.4	3.0
MSA[1]	534,919	616,079	705,932	747,061	14.6	5.8
U.S.	248,709,873	281,421,906	309,038,974	321,675,005	9.8	4.1

Note: (1) Metropolitan Statistical Area - see Appendix B for areas included
Source: Claritas, Inc.

Number of Households and Average Household Size

Area	2010 Estimate	2010 Average Household Size
City	83,624	2.09
MSA[1]	295,527	2.33
U.S.	116,136,617	2.59

Note: (1) Metropolitan Statistical Area - see Appendix B for areas included
Source: Claritas, Inc.

Race and Ethnicity

Area	White Alone[2] (%)	Black Alone[2] (%)	Asian Alone[2] (%)	Other Race Alone[2] (%)	Hispanic[3] (%)
City	76.6	17.2	1.9	4.2	3.3
MSA[1]	89.1	6.6	1.4	2.9	2.5
U.S.	72.3	12.4	4.4	10.9	15.8

Note: Figures are 2010 estimates; (1) Metropolitan Statistical Area - see Appendix B for areas included (2) Alone is defined as not being in combination with one or more other races; (3) May be of any race.
Source: Claritas, Inc.

Segregation

Type	Segregation Indices[1] 1990	2000	2010	2010 Rank[2]	Percent Change 1990-2000	1990-2010	2000-2010
Black/White	60.8	57.2	54.1	54	-3.6	-6.7	-3.1
Asian/White	50.0	43.5	43.3	36	-6.5	-6.7	-0.3
Hispanic/White	26.7	25.4	33.6	86	-1.3	6.9	8.2

Note: Figures are based on an analysis of 1990, 2000, and 2010 Census Decennial Census tract data by William H. Frey, Brookings Institution and the University of Michigan Social Science Data Analysis Network. In this analysis all racial groups (whites, blacks, and asians) are non-Hispanic members of those races. Hispanics are shown as a separate category; All figures cover the Metropolitan Statistical Area (see Appendix B for areas included); (1) Segregation Indices are Dissimilarity Indices that measure the degree to which the minority group is distributed differently than whites aross census tracts. They range from 0 (complete integration) to 100 (complete [segregation) where the value indicates the percentage of the minority group that needs to move to be distributed exactly like whites; (2) Ranges from 1 (most segregated) to 102 (least segregated); n/a not available.
Source: www.CensusScope.org

Ancestry

Area	German	Irish	English	American	Italian	Polish	French	Scottish
City	16.4	12.4	16.2	9.7	2.1	1.4	2.1	2.5
MSA[1]	16.1	13.4	14.8	14.9	2.4	1.5	2.1	2.9
U.S.	16.6	12.0	9.1	6.1	5.9	3.3	3.1	1.9

Note: The top eight ancestries in the U.S. are shown. Figures are percentages and include multiple ancestry (e.g. if a person reported being Irish and Italian, they were included in both columns); (1) Metropolitan Statistical Area - see Appendix B for areas included
Source: U.S. Census Bureau, 2007-2009 American Community Survey 3-Year Estimates

Foreign-Born Population

Area	Any Foreign Country	Mexico	Asia	Europe	Carribean	South America	Central America[2]	Africa	Canada
					Percent of Population Born in				
City	n/a	n/a	n/a	n/a	n/a	n/a	n/a	n/a	n/a
MSA[1]	3.2	0.6	1.2	0.6	0.0	0.1	0.2	0.2	0.2
U.S.	12.5	3.8	3.4	1.6	1.1	0.8	0.9	0.5	0.3

Note: (1) Metropolitan Statistical Area - see Appendix B for areas included; (2) Excludes Mexico.
Source: U.S. Census Bureau, 2007-2009 American Community Survey 3-Year Estimates

Marriage Status

Area	Never Married	Now Married[2]	Separated	Widowed	Divorced
City	40.9	36.7	1.8	7.3	13.3
MSA[1]	27.3	52.4	1.6	6.7	12.0
U.S.	31.4	49.7	2.2	6.2	10.6

Note: Figures are percentages and cover the population 15 years of age and older; (1) Metropolitan Statistical Area - see Appendix B for areas included; (2) Excludes separated
Source: U.S. Census Bureau, 2007-2009 American Community Survey 3-Year Estimates

Age Distribution and Median Age

Area	Under Age 5	Age 5 to 17	Age 18 to 34	Age 35 to 49	Age 50 to 64	Age 65 to 79	80 Years and Over	Median Age
				Percent of Population				
City	6.4	12.8	32.8	18.9	15.5	9.2	4.3	32.8
MSA[1]	6.1	15.9	23.0	21.3	19.5	10.5	3.7	38.7
U.S.	6.9	17.5	23.3	21.4	18.1	9.1	3.7	36.7

Note: (1) Metropolitan Statistical Area - see Appendix B for areas included
Source: U.S. Census Bureau, 2007-2009 American Community Survey 3-Year Estimates

Male/Female Ratio

Area	Males	Females	Males per 100 Females
City	88,777	96,264	92.2
MSA[1]	342,840	363,092	94.4
U.S.	152,401,520	156,637,454	97.3

Note: Figures are 2010 estimates; (1) Metropolitan Statistical Area - see Appendix B for areas included
Source: Claritas, Inc.

Religion

Area	Catholic	Southern Baptist	United Meth-odist	ELCA[1]	LDS[2]	Presby-terian Church USA	Jewish Est.	Muslim Est.
County	4.0	31.5	8.4	0.7	0.4	2.6	0.5	0.9
U.S.	22.0	7.1	3.7	1.8	1.5	1.1	2.2	0.6

Note: Figures are the number of adherents as a percentage of the total population; Adherents are defined as all members, including full members, their children and the estimated number of other participants who are not considered members (e.g. the baptized, those not confirmed, those regularly attending services, etc.);
(1) Evangelical Lutheran Church in America; (2) The Church of Jesus Christ of Latter Day Saints
Source: Reprinted with permission from Religious Congregations and Membership in the United States 2000 (Nashville, Glenmary Research Center, 2002) Copyright Association of Statisticians of American Religious Bodies. All rights reserved.

ECONOMY

Gross Metropolitan Product

Area	2006	2007	2008	2009	2009 Rank[2]
MSA[1]	27.4	28.4	29.6	29.5	70

Note: Figures are in billions of dollars; (1) Knoxville, TN Metropolitan Statistical Area - see Appendix B for areas included; (2) Rank ranges from 1 to 363
Source: The U.S. Conference of Mayors, "Pace of Economic Recovery: GMP and Jobs," January 2010

Economic Growth

Area	2006-2008 (%)	2009 (%)	2010 (%)	Rank[2]
MSA[1]	2.0	-1.4	2.4	111
U.S.	1.3	-2.5	2.2	–

Note: Figures are real Gross Metropolitan Product growth rates and represent annual average percent change; (1) Knoxville, TN Metropolitan Statistical Area - see Appendix B for areas included; (2) Rank ranges from 1 to 363
Source: The U.S. Conference of Mayors, "Pace of Economic Recovery: GMP and Jobs," January 2010

Metropolitan Area Exports

Area	2005	2006	2007	2008	2009	2009 Rank[2]
MSA[1]	1,372.5	2,011.1	2,094.0	2,312.7	1,887.5	79

Note: Figures are in millions of dollars; (1) Knoxville, TN Metropolitan Statistical Area - see Appendix B for areas included; (2) Rank ranges from 1 to 374
Source: U.S. Department of Commerce, International Trade Administration, Office of Trade & Industry Information, Manufacturing & Services

INCOME

Per Capita/Median/Average Income

Area	Per Capita ($)	Median Household ($)	Average Household ($)
City	21,750	32,768	47,008
MSA[1]	26,117	45,934	61,768
U.S.	27,034	52,795	71,071

Note: Figures are 2010 estimates; (1) Metropolitan Statistical Area - see Appendix B for areas included
Source: Claritas, Inc.

Household Income Distribution

Area	Percent of Households Earning							
	Under $15,000	$15,000 -24,999	$25,000 -34,999	$35,000 -49,999	$50,000 -74,999	$75,000 -99,000	$100,000 -149,999	$150,000 and up
City	23.9	15.5	13.6	15.6	15.1	7.3	5.7	3.4
MSA[1]	14.9	11.6	12.0	15.7	19.2	11.0	9.9	5.6
U.S.	12.1	10.2	10.6	15.0	19.5	12.5	12.1	8.0

Note: Figures are 2010 estimates; (1) Metropolitan Statistical Area - see Appendix B for areas included
Source: Claritas, Inc.

Poverty Rates by Age

Area	All Ages	Under 18 Years Old	18 to 64 Years Old	65 Years and Over
City	24.9	6.7	16.8	1.4
MSA[1]	14.4	4.2	9.0	1.1
U.S.	13.6	4.7	7.7	1.2

Note: Figures are percent of population with income during the previous 12 months below poverty level and only include population for whom poverty status is determined; (1) Metropolitan Statistical Area - see Appendix B for areas included
Source: U.S. Census Bureau, 2007-2009 American Community Survey 3-Year Estimates

Personal Bankruptcy Filing Rate

Area	2006	2007	2008	2009	2010
Knox County	2.86	3.97	5.23	5.83	5.42
U.S.	2.00	2.73	3.53	4.60	4.96

Note: Numbers are per 1,000 population and include Chapter 7 and Chapter 13 filings
Source: Federal Deposit Insurance Corporation, Regional Economic Conditions, March 17, 2011

EMPLOYMENT

Labor Force and Employment

Area	Civilian Labor Force			Workers Employed		
	Dec. 2009	Dec. 2010	% Chg.	Dec. 2009	Dec. 2010	% Chg.
City	92,633	94,018	1.5	84,013	86,557	3.0
MSA[1]	360,112	366,095	1.7	329,208	339,180	3.0
U.S.	152,693,000	153,156,000	0.3	137,953,000	139,159,000	0.9

Note: Data is not seasonally adjusted and covers workers 16 years of age and older; (1) Metropolitan Statistical Area - see Appendix B for areas included
Source: Bureau of Labor Statistics, http://stats.bls.gov

Unemployment Rate

Area	2010											
	Jan.	Feb.	Mar.	Apr.	May	Jun.	Jul.	Aug.	Sep.	Oct.	Nov.	Dec.
City	9.8	9.6	9.6	9.2	8.7	9.0	8.7	8.9	8.2	8.0	8.2	7.9
MSA[1]	9.1	8.9	8.8	8.2	7.7	7.9	7.7	7.8	7.3	7.2	7.4	7.4
U.S.	10.6	10.4	10.2	9.5	9.3	9.6	9.7	9.5	9.2	9.0	9.3	9.1

Note: Data is not seasonally adjusted and covers workers 16 years of age and older; All figures are percentages; (1) Metropolitan Statistical Area - see Appendix B for areas included
Source: Bureau of Labor Statistics, http://stats.bls.gov

Projected Unemployment Rate

Area	2007 (%)	2009 (%)	2011 (%)	2013 (%)
MSA[1]	4.2	9.4	8.6	7.0

Note: (1) Metropolitan Statistical Area - see Appendix B for areas included
Source: The U.S. Conference of Mayors, "Pace of Economic Recovery: GMP and Jobs," January 2010

Employment by Occupation

Occupation Classification	City (%)	MSA[1] (%)	U.S. (%)
Sales and Office	28.1	27.9	25.4
Professional and Related	22.7	21.7	21.0
Service	21.5	16.6	17.2
Production, Transportation, and Material Moving	9.6	11.5	12.3
Management, Business, and Financial	10.3	13.5	14.1
Construction, Extraction, and Maintenance	7.7	8.7	9.2
Farming, Forestry, and Fishing	0.1	0.2	0.7

Note: Figures cover employed civilians 16 years of age and older; (1) Metropolitan Statistical Area - see Appendix B for areas included
Source: U.S. Census Bureau, 2007-2009 American Community Survey 3-Year Estimates

Employment by Industry

| Sector | MSA[1] | | U.S. |
	Number of Employees	Percent of Total	Percent of Total
Government	51,300	15.7	17.2
Education and Health Services	45,400	13.9	15.2
Professional and Business Services	45,100	13.8	13.0
Retail Trade	41,600	12.7	11.4
Leisure and Hospitality	34,200	10.5	9.7
Manufacturing	29,300	9.0	8.8
Financial Activities	16,700	5.1	5.8
Wholesale Trade	15,800	4.8	4.2
Construction	n/a	n/a	4.1
Other Services	14,200	4.3	4.1
Transportation and Utilities	11,300	3.5	3.7
Information	5,500	1.7	2.1
Mining and Logging	n/a	n/a	0.6

Note: Figures cover non-farm employment as of December 2010 and are not seasonally adjusted;
(1) Metropolitan Statistical Area - see Appendix B for areas included; n/a not available
Source: Bureau of Labor Statistics, http://stats.bls.gov

Occupations with Greatest Projected Employment Growth: 2006 - 2016

Occupation[1]	2006 Employment	2016 Projected Employment	Numeric Employment Change	Percent Employment Change
Retail salespersons	85,980	104,710	18,730	21.8
Customer service representatives	48,360	62,400	14,040	29.0
Registered nurses	51,960	65,410	13,450	25.9
Combined food preparation and serving workers, including fast food	56,290	68,360	12,070	21.4
Truck drivers, heavy and tractor-trailer	73,170	83,140	9,970	13.6
Waiters and waitresses	49,750	58,960	9,210	18.5
Office clerks, general	56,220	64,620	8,400	14.9
Elementary school teachers, except special education	30,740	38,000	7,260	23.6
Nursing aides, orderlies, and attendants	31,850	38,580	6,730	21.1
Janitors and cleaners, except maids and housekeeping cleaners	42,750	48,660	5,910	13.8

Note: Projections cover Tennessee; (1) Sorted by numeric employment change
Source: www.projectionscentral.com, State Occupational Projections, 2006-2016 Long-Term Projections

Fastest Growing Occupations: 2006 - 2016

Occupation[1]	2006 Employment	2016 Projected Employment	Numeric Employment Change	Percent Employment Change
Pharmacy technicians	7,970	12,540	4,570	57.3
Environmental engineers	900	1,410	510	56.7
Network systems and data communications analysts	2,810	4,340	1,530	54.4
Home health aides	10,760	15,610	4,850	45.1
Animal trainers	730	1,040	310	42.5
Pharmacists	5,640	7,960	2,320	41.1
Computer software engineers, applications	3,310	4,630	1,320	39.9
Paralegals and legal assistants	3,730	5,180	1,450	38.9
Financial analysts	2,220	3,080	860	38.7
Personal financial advisors	1,440	1,980	540	37.5

Note: Projections cover Tennessee; (1) Sorted by percent employment change and excludes occupations with numeric employment change less than 300
Source: www.projectionscentral.com, State Occupational Projections, 2006-2016 Long-Term Projections

Average Wages

Occupation	$/Hr.	Occupation	$/Hr.
Accountants and Auditors	27.11	Maids and Housekeeping Cleaners	8.69
Automotive Mechanics	14.50	Maintenance and Repair Workers	15.66
Bookkeepers	14.79	Marketing Managers	38.33
Carpenters	16.24	Nuclear Medicine Technologists	28.59
Cashiers	8.43	Nurses, Licensed Practical	15.98
Clerks, General Office	13.38	Nurses, Registered	27.15
Clerks, Receptionists/Information	11.81	Nursing Aides/Orderlies/Attendants	10.70
Clerks, Shipping/Receiving	12.68	Packers and Packagers, Hand	8.88
Computer Programmers	30.19	Physical Therapists	33.76
Computer Support Specialists	19.46	Postal Service Mail Carriers	22.90
Computer Systems Analysts	33.40	Real Estate Brokers	24.66
Cooks, Restaurant	10.39	Retail Salespersons	11.56
Dentists	n/a	Sales Reps., Exc. Tech./Scientific	27.78
Electrical Engineers	43.28	Sales Reps., Tech./Scientific	32.41
Electricians	18.98	Secretaries, Exc. Legal/Med./Exec.	13.28
Financial Managers	40.21	Security Guards	10.39
First-Line Supervisors/Mgrs., Sales	17.81	Surgeons	n/a
Food Preparation Workers	9.97	Teacher Assistants	8.40
General and Operations Managers	42.56	Teachers, Elementary School	21.70
Hairdressers/Cosmetologists	15.07	Teachers, Secondary School	22.70
Internists	92.73	Telemarketers	10.10
Janitors and Cleaners	10.11	Truck Drivers, Heavy/Tractor-Trailer	18.33
Landscaping/Groundskeeping Workers	12.39	Truck Drivers, Light/Delivery Svcs.	14.28
Lawyers	55.71	Waiters and Waitresses	7.98

Note: Wage data covers the Knoxville, TN - see Appendix B for areas included. Hourly wages for elementary/secondary school teachers and teacher assistants were calculated by the editors from annual wage data assuming a 40 hour work week; n/a not available.
Source: Bureau of Labor Statistics, Metro Area Occupational Employment and Wage Estimates, May 2009

RESIDENTIAL REAL ESTATE

Building Permits

Area	Single-Family			Multi-Family			Total		
	2009	2010	Pct. Chg.	2009	2010	Pct. Chg.	2009	2010	Pct. Chg.
City	194	192	-1.0	214	650	203.7	408	842	106.4
MSA[1]	1,367	1,452	6.2	560	821	46.6	1,927	2,273	18.0
U.S.	441,100	447,300	1.4	141,900	157,300	10.9	583,000	604,600	3.7

Note: (1) Metropolitan Statistical Area - see Appendix B for areas included; figures represent new, privately-owned housing units authorized (unadjusted data); All permit data are based on estimates with imputation.
Source: U.S. Census Bureau, Manufacturing, Mining, and Construction Statistics, Building Permits, 2009, 2010

Homeownership Rate

Area	2005 (%)	2006 (%)	2007 (%)	2008 (%)	2009 (%)	2010 (%)
MSA[1]	n/a	n/a	n/a	n/a	n/a	n/a
U.S.	68.9	68.8	68.1	67.8	67.4	66.9

Note: (1) Metropolitan Statistical Area - see Appendix B for areas included
Source: U.S. Census Bureau, Housing Vacancies and Homeownership Annual Statistics: 2010

Housing Vacancy Rates

Area	Gross Vacancy Rate[2] (%)			Year-Round Vacancy Rate[3] (%)			Rental Vacancy Rate[4] (%)			Homeowner Vacancy Rate[5] (%)		
	2008	2009	2010	2008	2009	2010	2008	2009	2010	2008	2009	2010
MSA[1]	n/a	n/a	n/a	n/a	n/a	n/a	n/a	n/a	n/a	n/a	n/a	n/a
U.S.	14.4	14.5	14.3	11.1	11.3	11.3	10.0	10.6	10.2	2.8	2.6	2.6

Note: (1) Metropolitan Statistical Area - see Appendix B for areas included; (2) The percentage of the total housing inventory that is vacant; (3) The percentage of the housing inventory (excluding seasonal units) that is year-round vacant; (4) The percentage of rental inventory that is vacant for rent; (5) The percentage of homeowner inventory that is vacant for sale; n/a not available
Source: U.S. Census Bureau, Housing Vacancies and Homeownership Annual Statistics: 2010

State Corporate Income Tax Rates

State	Tax Rate (%)	Income Brackets ($)	Num. of Brackets	Financial Institution Tax Rate (%)[a]	Federal Income Tax Ded.
Tennessee	6.5	Flat rate	1	6.5	No

Note: Tax rates as of January 1, 2011; (a) Rates listed are the tax rates applied to financial institutions or excise taxes based on income. Some states have other taxes based upon the value of deposits or shares.
Source: Federation of Tax Administrators, "State Corporate Income Tax Rates, 2011"

State Individual Income Tax Rates

State	Tax Rate (%)	Income Brackets ($)	Num. of Brackets	Personal Exempt. ($)[1] Single	Personal Exempt. ($)[1] Dependents	Fed. Inc. Tax Ded.
Tennessee – State Income Tax of 6% on Dividends and Interest Income Only						

Note: Tax rates as of January 1, 2011; Local- and county-level taxes are not included; n/a not applicable;
(1) Married joint filers generally receive double the single exemption
Source: Federation of Tax Administrators, "State Individual Income Tax Rates, 2011"

Various State and Local Tax Rates

State	State and Local Sales and Use (%)	State Sales and Use (%)	Gasoline[1] (¢/gal.)	Cigarette[2] ($/pack)	Spirits[3] ($/gal.)	Wine[4] ($/gal.)	Beer[5] ($/gal.)
Tennessee	9.25	7.00	21.4	0.62	4.46	1.27	0.14

Note: All tax rates as of January 1, 2011 except Spirits (Sept. 1, 2010); (1) The American Petroleum Institute has developed a methodology for determining the average tax rate on a gallon of fuel. Rates may include any of the following: excise taxes, environmental fees, storage tank fees, other fees or taxes, general sales tax, and local taxes. In states where gasoline is subject to the general sales tax, or where the fuel tax is based on the average sale price, the average rate determined by API is sensitive to changes in the price of gasoline. States that fully or partially apply general sales taxes to gasoline: CA, CO, GA, IL, IN, MI, NY; (2) The federal excise tax of $1.0066 per pack and local taxes are not included; (3) Rates are those applicable to off-premise sales of 40% alcohol by volume (a.b.v.) distilled spirits in 750ml containers. Local excise taxes are excluded; (4) Rates are those applicable to off-premise sales of 11% a.b.v. non-carbonated wine in 750ml containers; (5) Rates are those applicable to off-premise sales of 4.7% a.b.v. beer in 12 ounce containers.
Source: Tax Foundation, 2011 Facts & Figures: How Does Your State Compare?

State-Local Tax Burdens

Area	Rate (%)	Rank[1]	Per Capita Taxes Paid to Home State ($)	Total State and Local Per Capita Taxes Paid ($)	Per Capita Income ($)
Tennessee	7.6	47	1,851	2,752	36,157
U.S. Average	9.8	-	3,057	4,160	42,539

Note: Figures cover 2009; (1) Rank ranges from 1 to 50 where 1 is highest tax burden
Source: Tax Foundation, State-Local Tax Burdens, All States, 2009

State Business Tax Climate Index Rankings

State	Overall Rank	Corporate Tax Index Rank	Individual Income Tax Index Rank	Sales Tax Index Rank	Unemployment Insurance Tax Index Rank	Property Tax Index Rank
Tennessee	27	11	8	47	35	50

Note: The index is a measure of how each state's tax laws affect economic performance. The lower the rank, the more favorable a state's tax system is for business. All ranks are for fiscal years. States without a given tax are given a ranking of 1.
Source: Tax Foundation, Tax Foundation Background Paper, No. 60, "2011 State Business Tax Climate Index"

COMMERCIAL UTILITIES

Typical Monthly Electric Bills

Area	Commercial Service ($/month) 40 kW demand 5,000 kWh	Commercial Service ($/month) 500 kW demand 100,000 kWh	Industrial Service ($/month) 5,000 kW demand 1,500,000 kWh	Industrial Service ($/month) 70,000 kW demand 50,000,000 kWh
City	438	10,927	131,985	2,031,100

Note: Based on rates in effect January 1, 2010
Source: Memphis Light, Gas and Water, 2010 Utility Bill Comparisons for Selected U.S. Cities

TRANSPORTATION

Means of Transportation to Work

Area	Car/Truck/Van		Public Transportation			Bicycle	Walked	Other Means	Worked at Home
	Drove Alone	Car-pooled	Bus	Subway	Railroad				
City	83.1	8.5	1.3	0.0	0.0	0.7	2.6	1.0	2.8
MSA[1]	84.7	8.9	0.4	0.0	0.0	0.2	1.4	1.1	3.2
U.S.	75.8	10.4	2.7	1.7	0.5	0.5	2.9	1.2	4.1

Note: Figures are percentages and cover workers 16 years of age and older;
(1) Metropolitan Statistical Area - see Appendix B for areas included
Source: U.S. Census Bureau, 2007-2009 American Community Survey 3-Year Estimates

Travel Time to Work

Area	Less Than 15 Minutes	15 to 29 Minutes	30 to 44 Minutes	45 to 59 Minutes	60 to 89 Minutes	90 Minutes or More
City	33.7	49.3	13.0	1.8	1.5	0.7
MSA[1]	27.6	45.6	19.3	4.5	2.0	1.1
U.S.	28.5	36.2	19.7	7.5	5.6	2.5

Note: Figures are percentages and include workers 16 years old and over;
(1) Metropolitan Statistical Area - see Appendix B for areas included
Source: U.S. Census Bureau, 2007-2009 American Community Survey 3-Year Estimates

Travel Time Index

Area	1982	1999	2008	2009
Urban Area[1]	1.04	1.10	1.07	1.06
Average[2]	1.08	1.20	1.20	1.20

Note: Travel Time Index—the ratio of travel time in the peak period to the travel time at free-flow conditions. A value of 1.30 indicates a 20-minute free-flow trip takes 26 minutes in the peak. Free-flow speeds (60 mph on freeways and 35 mph on principal arterials) are used as the comparison threshold; (1) Covers the Knoxville urban area; (2) average of 439 urban areas
Source: Texas Transportation Institute, Urban Mobility Report 2010, December 2010

Public Transportation

Agency Name / Mode of Transportation	Vehicles Operated in Maximum Service	Annual Unlinked Passenger Trips ('000)	Annual Passenger Miles ('000)
Knoxville Area Transit (KAT)			
Demand response	18	49.9	381.6
Bus	76	3,455.0	13,750.9

Note: Figures include both directly operated and purchased transportation
Source: Federal Transit Administration, National Transit Database, 2009

Air Transportation

Airport Name and Code / Type of Service	Passenger Airlines[1]	Passenger Enplanements	Freight Carriers[2]	Freight (lbs.)
McGhee-Tyson Airport (TYS)				
Domestic service (U.S. carriers - 2010)	29	804,249	15	51,173,409
International service (U.S. carriers - 2009)	4	258	1	8,824

Note: (1) Includes all U.S.-based major, minor and commuter airlines that carried at least one passenger during the year; (2) Includes all U.S.-based airlines and freight carriers that transported at least one pound of freight during the year
Source: Bureau of Transportation Statistics, The Intermodal Transportation Database, Air Carriers: T-100 Domestic Market (U.S. Carriers), 2010; Bureau of Transportation Statistics, The Intermodal Transportation Database, Air Carriers: T-100 International Market (U.S. Carriers), 2009

Other Transportation Statistics

Interstate highways:	I-40; I-75
Amtrak service:	No
Major waterways/ports:	Tennessee River; Port of Knoxville

Source: Amtrak.com; Google Maps

BUSINESSES

Major Business Headquarters

Company Name	Rankings	
	Fortune[1]	Forbes[2]
HT Hackney	-	82
Pilot Flying J	-	12

Note: (1) Fortune 500—companies that produce a 10-K are ranked 1 to 500 based on 2010 revenue; (2) all private companies with at least $2 billion in annual revenue are ranked 1 to 223; companies listed are headquartered in the city; dashes indicate no ranking
Source: Fortune, "Fortune 500," May 23, 2011; Forbes, "America's Largest Private Companies," November 3, 2010

Fast-Growing Businesses

According to *Inc.*, Knoxville is home to one of America's 500 fastest-growing private companies: **Physicians' Pharmaceutical**. Criteria: must be an independent, privately-held, for-profit, U.S. corporation, proprietorship or partnership; revenues of at least $80,000 in 2006 and $2 million in 2009; four-year operating/sales history; holding companies, regulated banks, and utilities were excluded. *Inc., "America's 500 Fastest-Growing Private Companies," September 2010*

Minority Business Opportunity

Knoxville is home to one company which is on the *Hispanic Business 500* list (500 largest U.S. Hispanic-owned companies based on 2009 revenue): **ES&H**. Companies included must show at least 51 percent ownership by Hispanic U.S. citizens, and must maintain headquarters in one of the 50 states or Washington, D.C. *Hispanic Business, "Hispanic Business 500," June 2010*

Minority- and Women-Owned Businesses

Group	All Firms		Firms with Paid Employees			
	Firms	Sales ($000)	Firms	Sales ($000)	Employees	Payroll ($000)
Asian	465	103,093	150	89,757	802	20,182
Black	1,573	93,411	78	58,232	1,087	25,160
Hispanic	403	55,970	50	46,234	379	8,749
Women	4,768	1,015,454	765	925,155	8,009	249,725
All Firms	19,873	36,620,468	6,111	35,938,737	156,592	5,372,760

Note: Figures cover firms located in the city; minority- and women-owned business are defined as firms in which the corresponding group own 51% or more of the stock or equity of the company
Source: U.S. Census Bureau, 2007 Economic Census, Survey of Business Owners

HOTELS

Hotels/Motels

Area	5 Star		4 Star		3 Star		2 Star		1 Star		Not Rated	
	Num.	Pct.3	Num.	Pct.3	Num.	Pct.3	Num.	Pct.3	Num.	Pct.3	Num.	Pct.3
City[1]	0	0.0	1	0.9	16	13.7	79	67.5	6	5.1	15	12.8
Total[2]	119	0.7	927	5.8	4,906	30.5	7,992	49.7	526	3.3	1,625	10.1

Note: (1) Figures cover Knoxville and vicinity; (2) Figures cover all 100 cities in this book; (3) Percentage of hotels which are a given star rating; Star ratings are determined by expedia.com and offer an indication of the general quality of a particular hotel.
Source: expedia.com, May 5, 2011

The Knoxville metro area is home to one of the top 218 hotels in the U.S. according to *Travel & Leisure*: **Blackberry Farm** (#29). Criteria: service; location; rooms; food; and value. *Travel & Leisure, "T+L 500, The World's Best Hotels 2011"*

The Knoxville metro area is home to one of the top 100 hotels in the U.S. according to *Condé Nast Traveler*: **Blackberry Farm** (#19). The selections are based on over 25,000 responses to the magazine's annual Readers' Choice Survey. *Condé Nast Traveler, "2010 Readers' Choice Awards"*

EVENT SITES

Major Stadiums, Arenas, and Auditoriums

Name	Max. Capacity
Knoxville Civic Auditorium and Coliseum	10,000
Neyland Stadium	100,011
Thompson-Boling Arena	25,000

Source: Original research

Convention Centers

Name	Overall Space (sq. ft.)	Exhibit Space (sq. ft.)	Meeting Space (sq. ft.)	Meeting Rooms
Knoxville Convention Center	500,545	27,300	119,922	14
Merchants Town Square	n/a	n/a	120,000	n/a

Note: n/a not available
Source: Original research

Living Environment

COST OF LIVING

Cost of Living Index

Composite Index	Groceries	Housing	Utilities	Trans-portation	Health Care	Misc. Goods/Services
89.4	91.4	82.0	95.1	84.2	88.4	95.1

Note: U.S. = 100; Figures cover the Knoxville TN urban area.
Source: The Council for Community and Economic Research, ACCRA Cost of Living Index, 2010

Grocery Prices

Area[1]	T-Bone Steak ($/pound)	Frying Chicken ($/pound)	Whole Milk ($/half gal.)	Eggs ($/dozen)	Orange Juice ($/64 oz.)	Coffee ($/11.5 oz.)
City[2]	8.86	0.99	2.08	1.25	2.76	3.00
Avg.	9.04	1.16	2.02	1.47	3.08	3.65
Min.	6.97	0.84	1.46	0.96	2.39	2.64
Max.	13.93	2.51	3.58	3.01	4.94	6.32

Note: (1) Values for the local area are compared with the average, minimum and maximum values for all 338 areas in the Cost of Living Index; (2) Figures cover the Knoxville TN urban area; **T-Bone Steak** *(price per pound);* **Frying Chicken** *(price per pound, whole fryer);* **Whole Milk** *(half gallon carton);* **Eggs** *(price per dozen, Grade A, large);* **Orange Juice** *(64 oz. Tropicana or Florida Natural);* **Coffee** *(11.5 oz. can, vacuum-packed, Maxwell House, Hills Bros, or Folgers).*
Source: The Council for Community and Economic Research, ACCRA Cost of Living Index, 2010

Housing and Utility Costs

Area[1]	New Home Price ($)	Apartment Rent ($/month)	All Electric ($/month)	Part Electric ($/month)	Other Energy ($/month)	Telephone ($/month)
City[2]	243,677	640	-	69.25	94.34	26.11
Avg.	293,442	810	166.39	91.93	83.82	26.93
Min.	182,545	453	119.21	44.47	36.85	17.98
Max.	1,123,114	2,776	307.53	218.20	313.90	39.15

Note: (1) Values for the local area are compared with the average, minimum and maximum values for all 338 areas in the Cost of Living Index; (2) Figures cover the Knoxville TN urban area; **New Home Price** *(2,400 sf living area, 8,000 sf lot, in urban area with full utilities);* **Apartment Rent** *(950 sf 2 bedroom/1.5 or 2 bath, unfurnished, excluding all utilities except water);* **All Electric** *(average monthly cost for an all-electric home);* **Part Electric** *(average monthly cost for a part-electric home);* **Other Energy** *(average monthly cost for natural gas, fuel oil, coal, wood, and any other forms of energy except electricity);* **Telephone** *(price includes basic monthly rate for a private residential line plus additional local usage charges incurred by a family of four).*
Source: The Council for Community and Economic Research, ACCRA Cost of Living Index, 2010

Health Care, Transportation, and Other Costs

Area[1]	Doctor ($/visit)	Dentist ($/visit)	Optometrist ($/visit)	Gasoline ($/gallon)	Beauty Salon ($/visit)	Men's Shirt ($)
City[2]	77.17	66.13	80.80	2.55	33.60	21.38
Avg.	89.44	78.95	87.40	2.73	31.92	24.83
Min.	57.00	54.25	48.32	2.44	19.17	13.67
Max.	149.90	136.73	174.22	3.75	62.81	47.89

Note: (1) Values for the local area are compared with the average, minimum and maximum values for all 338 areas in the Cost of Living Index; (2) Figures cover the Knoxville TN urban area; **Doctor** *(general practitioners routine exam of an established patient);* **Dentist** *(adult teeth cleaning and periodic oral examination);* **Optometrist** *(full vision eye exam for established adult patient);* **Gasoline** *(one gallon regular unleaded, national brand, including all taxes, cash price at self-service pump if available);* **Beauty Salon** *(woman's shampoo, trim, and blow-dry);* **Men's Shirt** *(cotton/polyester dress shirt, pinpoint weave, long sleeves).*
Source: The Council for Community and Economic Research, ACCRA Cost of Living Index, 2010

HOUSING

House Price Index (HPI)

Area	National Ranking[2]	Quarterly Change (%)	One-Year Change (%)	Five-Year Change (%)
MSA[1]	130	-0.19	-0.65	8.81
U.S.[3]	-	-0.84	-3.95	-11.45

Note: The HPI is a weighted repeat sales index. It measures average price changes in repeat sales or refinancings on the same properties. This information is obtained by reviewing repeat mortgage transactions on single-family properties whose mortgages have been purchased or securitized by Fannie Mae or Freddie Mac in January 1975; (1) Metropolitan/Micropolitan Statistical Area - see Appendix B for areas included; (2) Rankings are based on annual percentage change for all metro areas containing at least 15,000 transactions over the last 10 years and ranges from 1 to 309; (3) figures based on a weighted average of Census Division estimates; all figures are for the period ending December 31, 2010
Source: Federal Housing Finance Agency, House Price Index, February 24, 2011

House Price Valuations

Area	Q4 2005 Price ($000)	Q4 2005 Over-valuation	Q4 2006 Price ($000)	Q4 2006 Over-valuation	Q4 2007 Price ($000)	Q4 2007 Over-valuation	Q4 2008 Price ($000)	Q4 2008 Over-valuation	Q4 2009 Price ($000)	Q4 2009 Over-valuation
MSA[1]	124.5	3.9	133.3	4.7	138.7	3.7	132.2	-0.7	132.9	-2.4

Note: Figures show the percentage of over- or under-valuation of single family homes relative to statistically normal house values (e.g. a value of 23.6 indicates that house values are 23.6% overvalued). Statistically normal house values are based on house prices, interest rates, household incomes, population densities, and any historical premiums or discounts metropolitan areas have exhibited over time; (1) Figures cover the Knoxville, TN Metropolitan Statistical Area - see Appendix B for areas included
Source: Global Insight/PNC Financial Services Group, House Prices in America: 4th Quarter 2009 Update

Median Single-Family Home Prices

Area	2008	2009	2010p	Percent Change 2009 to 2010
MSA[1]	149.1	141.4	140.9	-0.4
U.S. Average	196.6	172.1	173.2	0.6

Note: Figures are median sales prices of existing single-family homes in thousands of dollars; (p) preliminary; n/a not available; (1) Metropolitan Statistical Area - see Appendix B for areas included
Source: National Association of Realtors, Median Sales Price of Existing Single-Family Homes for Metropolitan Areas, 4th Quarter 2010

Median Apartment Condo-Coop Home Prices

Area	2008	2009	2010p	Percent Change 2009 to 2010
MSA[1]	147.8	138.9	136.5	-1.7
U.S. Average	209.8	175.6	171.7	-2.2

Note: Figures are median sales prices of existing apartment condo-coop homes in thousands of dollars; (p) preliminary; n/a not available; (1) Metropolitan Statistical Area - see Appendix B for areas included
Source: National Association of Realtors, Median Sales Price of Existing Apartment Condo-Coop Homes for Metropolitan Areas, 4th Quarter 2010

Year Housing Structure Built

Area	2000 or Later	1990 -1999	1980 -1989	1970 -1979	1960 -1969	1950 -1959	1940 -1949	Before 1940	Median Year
City	10.3	11.6	14.0	20.1	14.2	14.0	7.1	8.7	1973
MSA[1]	14.5	19.7	15.7	17.5	11.2	9.3	6.1	6.0	1980
U.S.	12.5	14.0	14.2	16.5	11.4	11.3	5.8	14.3	1974

Note: Figures are percentages except for Median Year; (1) Metropolitan Statistical Area - see Appendix B for areas included
Source: U.S. Census Bureau, 2007-2009 American Community Survey 3-Year Estimates

HEALTH

Health Risk Data

Category	MSA[1] (%)	U.S. (%)
Adults who have been told they have high blood pressure	n/a	28.7
Adults who have been told they have high blood cholesterol	n/a	37.5
Adults who have been told they have diabetes[3]	n/a	8.3
Adults who have been told they have arthritis	n/a	26.0
Adults who have been told they currently have asthma	n/a	8.8
Adults who are current smokers	n/a	17.9
Adults who are heavy drinkers[4]	n/a	5.1
Adults who are binge drinkers[5]	n/a	15.8
Adults who are overweight (BMI 25.0 - 29.9)	n/a	36.2
Adults who are obese (BMI 30.0 - 99.8)	n/a	26.9
Adults who participated in any physical activities in the past month	n/a	76.2
Adults 50+ who have ever had a sigmoidoscopy or colonoscopy[2]	n/a	62.2
Women 40+ who have had a mammogram within the past two years[2]	n/a	76.0
Adults age 18–64 who have any kind of health care coverage	n/a	83.1

Note: Data as of 2009 unless otherwise noted; n/a not available; (1) Figures cover the Knoxville, TN Metropolitan Statistical Area - see Appendix B for areas included; (2) Data as of 2008; (3) Figures do not include pregnancy-related, borderline, or pre-diabetes; (4) Heavy drinkers are classified as males having more than two drinks per day or females having more than one drink per day; (5) Binge drinkers are classified as males having five or more drinks on one occasion or females having four or more drinks on one occasion
Source: Centers for Disease Control and Prevention, Behaviorial Risk Factor Surveillance System, SMART: Selected Metropolitan/Micropolitan Area Risk Trends, 2008, 2009

Mortality Rates for the Top 10 Causes of Death in the U.S.

ICD-10[a] Sub-Chapter	ICD-10[a] Code	Age-Adjusted Mortality Rate[1] per 100,000 population	
		County[2]	U.S.
Malignant neoplasms	C00-C97	188.7	180.9
Ischaemic heart diseases	I20-I25	134.5	135.0
Other forms of heart disease	I30-I51	35.2	50.0
Cerebrovascular diseases	I60-I69	48.7	44.1
Chronic lower respiratory diseases	J40-J47	49.2	41.5
Other degenerative diseases of the nervous system	G30-G31	35.9	23.6
Diabetes mellitus	E10-E14	20.1	23.5
Other external causes of accidental injury	W00-X59	32.0	23.5
Organic, including symptomatic, mental disorders	F01-F09	25.0	22.2
Influenza and pneumonia	J09-J18	22.7	18.1

Note: (a) ICD-10 = International Classification of Diseases 10th Revision; (1) Mortality rates are a three year average covering 2005-2007; (2) Figures cover Knox County
Source: Centers for Disease Control and Prevention, National Center for Health Statistics. Compressed Mortality File 1999-2007. CDC WONDER On-line Database, compiled from Compressed Mortality File 1999-2007 Series 20 No. 2M, 2010.

Mortality Rates for Selected Causes of Death

ICD-10[a] Sub-Chapter	ICD-10[a] Code	Age-Adjusted Mortality Rate[1] per 100,000 population	
		County[2]	U.S.
Assault	X85-Y09	7.0	6.0
Human immunodeficiency virus (HIV) disease	B20-B24	3.1	4.0
Hypertensive diseases	I10-I15	16.8	18.0
Intentional self-harm	X60-X84	13.6	11.0
Malnutrition	E40-E46	*1.1	0.8
Obesity and other hyperalimentation	E65-E68	1.6	1.5
Transport accidents	V01-V99	17.4	15.6
Viral hepatitis	B15-B19	3.9	2.1

Note: (a) ICD-10 = International Classification of Diseases 10th Revision; (1) Mortality rates are a three year average covering 2005-2007; (2) Figures cover Knox County; (*) Unreliable data as per CDC
Source: Centers for Disease Control and Prevention, National Center for Health Statistics. Compressed Mortality File 1999-2007. CDC WONDER On-line Database, compiled from Compressed Mortality File 1999-2007 Series 20 No. 2M, 2010.

Distribution of Physicians and Dentists

Area[1]	Dentists[2]	D.O.[3]	M.D.[4]				
			Total	Family/General Practice	Pediatrics	Medical Specialties	Surgical Specialties
Local (number)	184	73	1,412	169	87	549	336
Local (rate[5])	4.3	1.7	32.8	3.9	2.0	12.7	7.8
U.S. (rate[5])	4.5	1.9	18.3	2.5	1.4	6.8	4.1

Note: Data as of 2008 unless noted; (1) Local data covers Knox County; (2) Data as of 2007; (3) Doctor of Osteopathic Medicine; (4) Includes active, non-federal, patient-care, office-based Doctors of Medicine; (5) rate per 10,000 population
Source: Area Resource File (ARF). 2009-2010 Release. U.S. Department of Health and Human Services, Health Resources and Services Administration, Bureau of Health Professions, Rockville, MD, August 2010

Hospitals

Knoxville has the following hospitals: 5 general medical and surgical; 1 psychiatric; 1 obstetrics and gynecology; 2 long-term acute care; 1 other specialty; 1 children's other specialty.
AHA Guide to the Healthcare Field 2010

EDUCATION

Public School District Statistics

District Name	Schls	Pupils	Pupil/Teacher Ratio	Minority Pupils[1] (%)	Free Lunch Eligible[2] (%)	IEP[3] (%)
Knox County School District	87	55,535	14.5	20.6	32.7	10.7

Note: Table includes school districts with 2,000 or more students; (1) Percentage of students that are not non-Hispanic white; (2) Percentage of students that are eligible for the free lunch program; (3) Percentage of students that have an Individualized Education Program.
Source: U.S. Department of Education, National Center for Education Statistics, Common Core of Data, Local Education Agency (School District) Universe Survey: School Year 2008-2009; U.S. Department of Education, National Center for Education Statistics, Common Core of Data, Public Elementary/Secondary School Universe Survey: School Year 2008-2009

Top Public High Schools

High School Name	Index[1]	Rank[1]	Subsidized Lunch (%)[2]	E&E (%)[3]
Farragut	1.365	1299	13.0	30.8
West	1.489	1163	43.0	29.0

Note: (1) Public schools are ranked according to a ratio that is the number of Advanced Placement, International Baccalaureate, and/or Cambridge tests taken by all students at a school in 2009 divided by the number of graduating seniors. All of the schools on the list have an index of at least 1.000; they are in the top six percent of public schools measured this way. The rankings range from 1 to 1,734; (2) Percentage of students receiving federally subsidized meals; (3) E & E stands for equity and excellence percentage: the portion of all graduating seniors at a school that had at least one passing grade on one AP or IB test; (4) Schools that offer International Baccalaureate or Cambridge exams; (5) School is unranked, but has been identified by Newsweek as one of the nation's most elite public high schools.
Source: Newsweek Online, "Top High Schools 2010"

Highest Level of Education

Area	Less than H.S.	H.S. Diploma	Some College, No Deg.	Associate Degree	Bachelors Degree	Masters Degree	Profess. School Degree	Doctorate Degree
City	14.8	28.3	20.3	6.5	18.8	7.4	2.2	1.8
MSA[1]	13.5	30.4	20.6	6.9	18.4	6.9	1.8	1.5
U.S.	15.3	29.0	20.7	7.5	17.4	7.0	1.9	1.1

Note: Figures are 2010 estimated percentages and cover persons age 25 and over; (1) Metropolitan Statistical Area - see Appendix B for areas included
Source: Claritas, Inc.

Educational Attainment by Race

Area	High School Graduate (%)					Bachelor's Degree (%)				
	Total	White	Black	Asian	Hisp.[2]	Total	White	Black	Asian	Hisp.[2]
City	85.4	87.2	79.4	86.4	59.0	29.0	32.1	11.5	63.1	14.7
MSA[1]	86.5	87.1	84.5	89.1	64.8	28.2	28.5	18.6	65.4	20.8
U.S.	84.9	90.0	80.7	85.5	60.7	27.8	30.9	17.5	49.7	12.7

Note: Figures shown cover persons 25 years old and over; (1) Metropolitan Statistical Area - see Appendix B for areas included; (2) people of Hispanic origin can be of any race
Source: U.S. Census Bureau, 2007-2009 American Community Survey 3-Year Estimates

School Enrollment by Grade and Control

Area	Preschool (%)		Kindergarten (%)		Grades 1 - 4 (%)		Grades 5 - 8 (%)		Grades 9 - 12 (%)	
	Public	Private	Public	Private	Public	Private	Public	Private	Public	Private
City	45.3	54.7	83.3	16.7	83.8	16.2	86.1	13.9	87.9	12.1
MSA[1]	44.6	55.4	83.3	16.7	88.0	12.0	86.5	13.5	88.3	11.7
U.S.	54.3	45.7	86.4	13.6	88.9	11.1	89.1	10.9	90.2	9.8

Note: Figures shown cover persons 3 years old and over; (1) Metropolitan Statistical Area - see Appendix B for areas included
Source: U.S. Census Bureau, 2007-2009 American Community Survey 3-Year Estimates

Average Salaries of Public School Classroom Teachers

Area	2009-10		2010-11		Percent Change 2009-10 to 2010-11	Percent Change 2000-01 to 2010-11
	Dollars	Rank[1]	Dollars	Rank[1]		
Tennessee	46,290	40	47,043	43	1.63	25.7
U.S. Average	55,202	-	56,069	-	1.57	29.3

Note: (1) State rank ranges from 1 to 51 where 1 indicates highest salary.
Source: National Education Association, Rankings & Estimates: Rankings of the States 2010 and Estimates of School Statistics 2011, December 2010

Higher Education

Four-Year Colleges			Two-Year Colleges			Medical Schools[1]	Law Schools[2]	Voc/ Tech[3]
Public	Private Non-profit	Private For-profit	Public	Private Non-profit	Private For-profit			
1	1	3	2	0	0	0	1	3

Note: Figures cover institutions located within the city limits and include main campuses only; (1) includes schools accredited by the Liaison Committee on Medical Education and the American Osteopathic Association; (2) includes American Bar Association-accredited law schools; (3) includes all schools with programs that are less than 2 years.
Source: National Center for Education Statistics, Integrated Postsecondary Education System (IPEDS) Peer Analysis System, 2010-11; U.S. News & World Report, Medical School Directory, 2011; U.S. News & World Report, Law School Directory, 2011

According to *U.S. News & World Report*, the Knoxville, TN Metropolitan Statistical Area is home to one of the top 197 national universities in the U.S.: **University of Tennessee** (#104). The rankings are based on quantitative measurements such as peer assessment, retention, faculty resources, student selectivity, financial resources, graduation rate, and alumni giving rate. *U.S. News & World Report, "America's Best Colleges 2011"*

According to *U.S. News & World Report*, the Knoxville, TN Metropolitan Statistical Area is home to one of the top 189 liberal arts colleges in the U.S.: **Maryville College** (#174). The rankings are based on quantitative measurements such as peer assessment, retention, faculty resources, student selectivity, financial resources, graduation rate, and alumni giving rate. *U.S. News & World Report, "America's Best Colleges 2011"*

According to *Forbes*, the Knoxville, TN Metropolitan Statistical Area is home to one of the top 75 business schools in the U.S.: **Tennessee** (#42). The rankings are based on the return on investment that graduates of the Class of 2004 received (median salary five years after graduation). *Forbes, "Best Business Schools," August 5, 2009*

PRESIDENTIAL ELECTION

2008 Presidential Election Results

Area	Obama	McCain	Nader	Other
Knox County	37.7	60.7	0.5	1.0
U.S.	52.9	45.6	0.6	0.9

Note: Results are percentages and may not add to 100% due to rounding
Source: Dave Leip's Atlas of U.S. Presidential Elections, www.uselectionatlas.org

EMPLOYERS

Major Employers

Company Name	Industry	Type of Site
Anderson Services	Local trucking, without storage	Single
Apple Jacks 2010	Amusement and recreation, nec	Branch
Baptist Health System	General medical and surgical hospitals	Headquarters
Baptist Hospital East Tenn	General medical and surgical hospitals	Headquarters
Baptist Hospital West	General medical and surgical hospitals	Single
Bechtel Jacobs Company	Facilities support services	Headquarters
Blount County School District	Elementary and secondary schools	Branch
Blount Memorial Hospital	General medical and surgical hospitals	Headquarters
BWXT Y-12	Administration of general economic programs	Branch
County of Blount	Courts	Branch
East Tenn Chld Hosp Assn	Specialty hospitals, except psychiatric	Headquarters
Fort Sanders Regional Med Ctr	General medical and surgical hospitals	Headquarters
Knox County Sheriff	Police protection	Branch
Lockheed Martin Energy Res	Noncommercial research organizations	Single
Oak Ridge National Laboratory	Commercial physical research	Headquarters
Oak Rigde National Laboratory	Commercial physical research	Branch
Oakwood Homes	Mobile homes	Headquarters
Parkwest Medical Center	General medical and surgical hospitals	Headquarters
Prologic Dist Svcs E	Local trucking, without storage	Single
Sheet Metal Workers Local Un 5	Labor organizations	Branch
Southeast Service Corporation	Disinfecting and pest control services	Single
Southern Building Services	Building maintenance services, nec	Branch
Tennessee Valley Authority	Electric services	Headquarters
University Health System	Offices and clinics of medical doctors	Branch
UT Agriculture Extensions Svc	Colleges and universities	Branch
UT Memorial Hospital	General medical and surgical hospitals	Headquarters

Note: Companies shown are located within the Knoxville metropolitan area; nec = not elsewhere classified.
Source: www.zapdata.com, January 2011

PUBLIC SAFETY

Crime Rate

Area	All Crimes	Violent Crimes				Property Crimes		
		Murder	Forcible Rape	Robbery	Aggrav. Assault	Burglary	Larceny -Theft	Motor Vehicle Theft
City	7,418.3	11.8	79.1	355.1	611.8	1,393.1	4,602.1	365.3
Suburbs[1]	2,802.7	1.7	17.6	52.1	220.1	801.1	1,563.4	146.7
Metro[2]	4,024.6	4.4	33.9	132.3	323.8	957.8	2,367.8	204.5
U.S.	3,465.5	5.0	28.7	133.0	262.8	716.3	2,060.9	258.8

Note: Figures are crimes per 100,000 population; (1) All areas within the metro area that are located outside the city limits; (2) Metropolitan Statistical Area - see Appendix B for areas included
Source: FBI Uniform Crime Reports, 2009

Hate Crimes

Area	Number of Quarters Reported	Bias Motivation				
		Race	Religion	Sexual Orientation	Ethnicity	Disability
City	4	3	1	0	0	0

Source: Federal Bureau of Investigation, Hate Crime Statistics 2009

Identity Theft Consumer Complaints

Area	Complaints	Complaints per 100,000 Population	Rank[2]
MSA[1]	406	59.6	270
U.S.	250,854	81.3	-

Note: (1) Metropolitan Statistical Area - see Appendix B for areas included; (2) Rank ranges from 1 to 384 where 1 indicates greatest number of complaints per 100,000 population
Source: Federal Trade Commission, Consumer Sentinel Network Data Book for January - December 2010

RECREATION

Culture

Dance[1]	Theatre[1]	Instrumental Music[1]	Vocal Music[1]	Series/ Festivals	Museums	Zoos and Aquariums[2]
2	6	1	1	2	9	1

Note: (1) Number of professional perfoming groups; (2) AZA-accredited
Source: The Grey House Performing Arts Directory, 2011-2012; Official Museum Directory, 2010; American Association of Museums, AAM Member Museums, March 2011; Association of Zoos & Aquariums, AZA Member Zoos & Aquariums, May 2011

Professional Sports Teams

Team Name	League

No teams are located in the metro area
Source: Original research

CLIMATE

Average and Extreme Temperatures

Temperature	Jan	Feb	Mar	Apr	May	Jun	Jul	Aug	Sep	Oct	Nov	Dec	Yr.
Extreme High (°F)	77	83	86	91	94	102	103	102	103	91	84	80	103
Average High (°F)	47	52	61	71	78	85	88	87	82	71	59	50	69
Average Temp. (°F)	38	42	50	59	67	75	78	77	71	60	49	41	59
Average Low (°F)	29	32	39	47	56	64	68	67	61	48	38	32	48
Extreme Low (°F)	-24	-2	1	22	32	43	49	53	36	25	5	-6	-24

Note: Figures cover the years 1948-1990
Source: National Climatic Data Center, International Station Meteorological Climate Summary, 9/96

Average Precipitation/Snowfall/Humidity

Precip./Humidity	Jan	Feb	Mar	Apr	May	Jun	Jul	Aug	Sep	Oct	Nov	Dec	Yr.
Avg. Precip. (in.)	4.5	4.3	5.0	3.6	3.9	3.8	4.5	3.1	2.9	2.8	3.8	4.5	46.7
Avg. Snowfall (in.)	5	4	2	1	0	0	0	0	0	Tr	1	2	13
Avg. Rel. Hum. 7am (%)	81	80	79	80	85	86	89	91	91	89	84	82	85
Avg. Rel. Hum. 4pm (%)	60	54	50	46	52	54	56	55	54	51	54	59	54

Note: Figures cover the years 1948-1990; Tr = Trace amounts (<0.05 in. of rain; <0.5 in. of snow)
Source: National Climatic Data Center, International Station Meteorological Climate Summary, 9/96

Weather Conditions

Temperature			Daytime Sky			Precipitation		
10°F & below	32°F & below	90°F & above	Clear	Partly cloudy	Cloudy	0.01 inch or more precip.	0.1 inch or more snow/ice	Thunder-storms
3	73	33	85	142	138	125	8	47

Note: Figures are average number of days per year and cover the years 1948-1990
Source: National Climatic Data Center, International Station Meteorological Climate Summary, 9/96

HAZARDOUS WASTE

Superfund Sites

Knoxville has one hazardous waste site on the EPA's Superfund Final National Priorities List: **Smokey Mountain Smelters**. *U.S. Environmental Protection Agency, Final National Priorities List, April 1, 2011*

**AIR & WATER
QUALITY**

Air Quality Index

Area	Percent of Days when Air Quality was...[2]				AQI Statistics	
	Good	Moderate	Unhealthy for Sensitive Groups	Unhealthy	Maximum	Median
Area[1]	58.0	38.7	3.3	0.0	150	46

Note: The Air Quality Index (AQI) is an index for reporting daily air quality. EPA calculates the AQI for five major air pollutants regulated by the Clean Air Act: ground-level ozone, particle pollution (also known as particulate matter), carbon monoxide, sulfur dioxide, and nitrogen dioxide. The AQI runs from 0 to 500. The higher the AQI value, the greater the level of air pollution and the greater the health concern. There are six AQI categories: "Good" The AQI is between 0 and 50. Air quality is considered satisfactory; "Moderate" The AQI is between 51 and 100. Air quality is acceptable; "Unhealthy for Sensitive Groups" When AQI values are between 101 and 150, members of sensitive groups may experience health effects; "Unhealthy" When AQI values are between 151 and 200 everyone may begin to experience health effects; "Very Unhealthy" AQI values between 201 and 300 trigger a health alert; "Hazardous" AQI values over 300 trigger health warnings of emergency conditions; (1) Data covers Knox County; (2) Based on 305 days with AQI data in 2008; The EPA has suspended data updates while it assesses its data systems, including AirData reports and maps.
Source: U.S. Environmental Protection Agency, AirData Report, 2008

Air Quality Index Pollutants

Area	Percent of Days when AQI Pollutant was...[2]					
	Carbon Monoxide	Nitrogen Dioxide	Ozone	Sulfur Dioxide	Particulate Matter 2.5	Particulate Matter 10
Area[1]	0.0	0.0	53.8	0.0	46.2	0.0

Note: The Air Quality Index (AQI) is an index for reporting daily air quality. EPA calculates the AQI for five major air pollutants regulated by the Clean Air Act: ground-level ozone, particle pollution (also known as particulate matter), carbon monoxide, sulfur dioxide, and nitrogen dioxide. The AQI runs from 0 to 500. The higher the AQI value, the greater the level of air pollution and the greater the health concern; (1) Data covers Knox County; (2) Based on 305 days with AQI data in 2008; The EPA has suspended data updates while it assesses its data systems, including AirData reports and maps.
Source: U.S. Environmental Protection Agency, AirData Report, 2008

Air Quality Index Trends

Area	Trend Sites (days)								All Sites (days)
	2002	2003	2004	2005	2006	2007	2008	2009	2009
MSA[1]	118	96	98	101	84	107	80	20	21

Note: Figures are the number of days the AQI value exceeded 100 in a given year. An AQI value greater than 100 indicates that air quality would have been in the unhealthful range on that day. Data from exceptional events are included. These counts are presented in two ways. First, the counts are based on sites having an adequate record of monitoring data during the trend period (trend sites). These counts represent the relative change in the number of days with AQI values greater than 100. In the last column, the counts are based on all sites with data in the most recent year (because it is possible for a site to have data in the most recent year but not enough data to be a trend site); (1) Data covers the Knoxville, TN Metropolitan Statistical Area - see Appendix B for areas included
Source: U.S. Environmental Protection Agency, Office of Air and Radiation, Air Quality Index Information, "Number of Days with Air Quality Index Values Greater than 100 and Trend Sites, 1990-2009, and at All Sites in 2009"

Maximum Air Pollutant Concentrations

	Particulate Matter 10 (ug/m³)	Particulate Matter 2.5 (ug/m³)	Ozone (ppm)	Carbon Monoxide (ppm)	Sulfur Dioxide (ppm)	Nitrogen Dioxide (ppm)	Lead (ug/m³)
MSA[1] Level	60	23	0.069	0	0.003	0.001	0.03
NAAQS[2]	150	35	0.075	9	0.140	0.053	0.15
Met NAAQS[2]	Yes	Yes	Yes	Yes	Yes	Yes	Yes

Note: Data from exceptional events are not included; (1) Data covers the Knoxville, TN Metropolitan Statistical Area - see Appendix B for areas included; (2) National Ambient Air Quality Standards; n/a not available
Concentrations: Particulate Matter 10 (coarse particulate) - highest second maximum 24-hour concentration; Particulate Matter 2.5 (fine particulate) - highest 98th percentile 24-hour concentration; Ozone - highest fourth daily maximum 8-hour concentration; Carbon Monoxide - highest second maximum non-overlapping 8-hour concentration; Sulfur Dioxide - highest second maximum 24-hour concentration; Nitrogen Dioxide - highest arithmetic mean concentration; Lead - maximum running 3-month average
Units: ppm = parts per million; ug/m³ = micrograms per cubic meter
Source: U.S. Environmental Protection Agency, CBSA Factbook 2009, Air Quality Statistics by City, 2009

Drinking Water

Water System Name	Pop. Served	Primary Water Source Type	Violations[1]	
			Health Based	Monitoring/ Reporting
Knoxville Utilities Board	236,338	Surface	0	0

Note: (1) Based on violation data from January 1, 2010 to December 31, 2010 (includes unresolved violations from earlier years)
Source: U.S. Environmental Protection Agency, Office of Ground Water and Drinking Water, Safe Drinking Water Information System (based on data extracted May 9, 2011)

Drinking Water

Miami, Florida

Background

While the majority of Miami's residents used to be Caucasian of European descent, the rapidly growing city now consists of a majority of Latinos. The number of Cubans, Puerto Ricans, and Haitians give the city a flavorful mix with a Latin American and Caribbean accent. The City of Miami has three official languages: English, Spanish, and Haitian Creole.

Thanks to early pioneer Julia Tuttle, railroad magnate Henry Flagler extended the East Coast Railroad beyond Palm Beach. Within 15 years of that decision, Miami became known as the "Gold Coast." The land boom of the 1920s brought wealthy socialites, as well as African-Americans in search of work. Pink- and aquamarine-hued art deco hotels were squeezed onto a tiny tract of land called Miami Beach, and the population of the Miami metro area swelled.

Given Miami's origins in a tourist-oriented economy, many of the activities in which residents engage are "leisurely," including swimming, scuba diving, golf, tennis, and boating. For those who enjoy professional sports, the city is host to the following teams: the Miami Dolphins, football; the Florida Marlins, baseball; the Miami Heat, basketball; and the Florida Panthers, hockey. Cultural activities range from the Miami City Ballet and the Coconut Grove Playhouse to numerous art galleries and museums, including the Bass Museum of Art. Visits to the Villa Vizcaya, a gorgeous palazzo built by industrialist James Deering in the Italian Renaissance style, and to the Miami MetroZoo are popular pastimes.

Miami's prime location on Biscayne Bay in the southeastern United States makes it a perfect nexus for travel and trade. The Port of Miami is a bustling center for many cruise and cargo ships. The Port is also a base for the National Oceanic and Atmospheric Administration. The Miami International Airport is a busy destination point to and from many Latin-American and Caribbean countries.

Miami is still at the trading crossroads of the Western Hemisphere as the chief shipment point for exports and imports with Latin America and the Caribbean. One out of every three North American cruise passengers sails from Miami. Miami was also the host city of the 2003 Free Trade Area of the Americas negotiations, and is one of the leading candidates to become the trading bloc's headquarters.

The sultry, subtropical climate against a backdrop of Spanish, art deco, and modern architecture makes Miami a uniquely cosmopolitan city. The Art Deco Historic District, known as South Beach and located on the tip of Miami Beach, has recently developed an international reputation in the fashion, film, and music industries. Greater Miami is now a national center for film, television, and print production.

In recent years Miami has witnessed its largest real estate boom since the 1920s, especially in the newly created midtown, north of downtown and south of the Design District. Nearly 25,000 new residential units have been added to the downtown skyline since 2005.

Long, warm summers are typical, as are mild, dry winters. The marine influence is evidenced by the narrow daily range of temperature and the rapid warming of cold air masses. During the summer months, rainfall occurs in early morning near the ocean and in early afternoon further inland. Hurricanes occasionally affect the Miami area, usually in September and October, while destructive tornadoes are quite rare. Funnel clouds are occasionally sighted and a few touch the ground briefly, but significant destruction is unusual. Waterspouts are visible from the beaches during the summer months but seldom cause any damage. During June, July, and August, there are numerous beautiful, but dangerous, lightning events.

Rankings

General Rankings

- Miami was ranked #250 out of 375 metro areas in *Cities Ranked & Rated*. Criteria: cost of living; climate; crime; transportation; economy and jobs; education; arts and culture; health and healthcare; leisure; quality of life. *Cities Ranked & Rated, 2nd Edition, 2007*

- Miami was ranked #135 out of 379 metro areas in *Places Rated Almanac*. Criteria: health care; education; recreation; transportation; ambience; climate; crime; housing costs; jobs. *Places Rated Almanac, 7th Edition, 2007*

- *Men's Health Living* ranked 100 U.S. cities in terms of quality of life. Miami was ranked #89 and received a grade of D. Criteria: number of fitness facilities; air quality; number of physicians; male/female ratio; education levels; household income; cost of living. *Men's Health Living, Spring 2008*

- Miami was identified as one of the top places to live in the U.S. by Harris Interactive. The city ranked #13 out of 15. Criteria: 2,620 adults (age 18 and over) were polled and asked "if you could live in or near any city in the country except the one you live in or nearest to now, which city would you choose?" The poll was conducted online within the U.S. between September 14 and 20, 2010. *Harris Interactive, October 20, 2010*

Business/Finance Rankings

- Miami was identified as one of the 20 weakest-performing metro areas during the recession and recovery from December 2007 through December 2010. Criteria: percent change in employment; percentage point change in unemployment rate; percent change in gross metropolitan product; percent change in House Price Index. *Brookings Institution, MetroMonitor: Tracking Economic Recession and Recovery in America's 100 Largest Metropolitan Areas, March 2011*

- Experian ranked the top 20 major U.S metropolitan areas by average debt per consumer. The Miami metro area was ranked #19. Criteria: average debt per consumer. Debt for this study includes credit cards, auto loans and personal loans. It does not include mortgages. *Experian, May 13, 2010*

- Miami was selected as one of the best places to start a business by *CNNMoney.com*. Criteria: compelling incentives to would-be entrepreneurs. *CNNMoney.com, "8 Great Cities to Start a Business," 2010*

- Miami was identified as one of the top 25 U.S. cities with the most credit card debt by credit reporting bureau Experian. The city was ranked #23. *Experian, March 4, 2011*

- A.G. Edwards ranked America's 500 top-performing communities based on their residents' personal savings and investing behavior. The Miami metro area ranked #488 with an index score of 94.81 (national average = 100.00). A dozen statistical factors were measured including: participation in retirement savings plans; personal debt levels; and home ownership. *A.G. Edwards, "2007 Nest Egg Index," September 12, 2007*

- Miami was identified as one of the "Happiest Cities to Work" by CareerBliss.com, an online community for career advancement. The city ranked #4 out of 10. CareerBliss.com conducted independent company reviews from employees all over the country to collect data on eight specific factors of workplace happiness: growth opportunities, compensation, benefits, work-life balance, career advancement, senior management, job security, and whether the employee would recommend the company to others. The numbers were combined to find an average rating of overall workplace happiness for each city. *CareerBliss.com, "Happiest and Unhappiest Cities to Work," February 1, 2011*

- *American City Business Journals* ranked America's 261 largest cities in terms of their resident's wealth. Miami ranked #97. Criteria: per capita income; median household income; percentage of households with annual incomes of $200,000 or more; median home value. *American City Business Journals, www.bizjournals.com, "Where the Money Is: America's Wealth Centers," August 18, 2008*

- The Miami metro area appeared on the Milken Institute "2010 Best Performing Metros" list. Rank: #151 out of 200 large metro areas. Criteria: job growth; wage and salary growth; high-tech output growth. *Milken Institute, "2010 Best Performing Metros"*

- The Miami metro area was selected as one of the best cities for entrepreneurs in America by *Inc. Magazine*. Criteria: job-growth data for 335 metro areas was analyzed for: recent growth trend (the current and prior year's employment growth rates, with the current year emphasized); mid-term growth (the average annual 2002-2007 growth rate); long-term trend (the sum of the 2002-2007 and 1996-2001 employment growth rates multiplied by the ratio of the 1996-2001 growth rate over the 2002-2007 growth rate); current year growth. The Miami metro area ranked #28 among large metro areas and #145 overall. *Inc. Magazine, "The Best Cities for Doing Business," July 2008*

- Miami was ranked #115 out of 145 regions worldwide in terms of its "Knowledge Competitiveness Index." The index attempts to measure the knowledge-based development taking place throughout the world and is based on 19 measures of economic performance that indicate a region's ability to translate its knowledge capacity into economic value. *Centre for International Competitiveness, World Knowledge Competitiveness Index 2008*

- *Forbes* ranked the 200 most populous metro areas in the U.S. in terms of the "Best Places for Business and Careers." The Miami metro area was ranked #152. Criteria: 12 metrics including costs (business and living), job growth (past and projected), income growth, educational attainment, projected economic growth, crime, cultural and recreational opportunities, net migration patterns, percentage of subprime mortgages handed out over a three-year period, and the number of highly ranked four-year colleges. *Forbes, "Best Places for Business and Careers," April 14, 2010*

Children/Family Rankings

- The Miami metro area was selected as one of the "Best Cities for Relocating Families" by Worldwide ERC and Primacy Relocation. The 2008 study looked at nearly 50 factors important to relocating families including: recent job growth; nearby top-ranked colleges; in-state tuition for four-year public colleges; population growth since 2000; pediatricians per 100,000 population; and a Green Living index. *Worldwide ERC and Primacy Relocation, "2008 Best Cities for Relocating Families"*

- *Fit Pregnancy* magazine ranked the 50 best U.S. cities in which to have a baby. Miami was ranked #23. Criteria: access to hospitals and doctors; affordability; birthing options; breastfeeding; child care; fertility laws/resources; maternal and infant health risk; parks/stroller friendliness; safety. *Fit Pregnancy, "The Best Cities in America to Have a Baby 2008"*

Culture/Performing Arts Rankings

- Miami was selected as one of "America's Top 25 Arts Destinations." The city ranked #12 in the mid-sized city (population 100,000 to 499,999) category. Criteria: readers' top choices for arts travel destinations based on the richness and variety of visual arts sites, activities and events. *American Style, "America's Top 25 Arts Destinations," May 2010*

Dating/Romance Rankings

- Miami was selected as one of the most romantic cities in America by *Amazon.com*. The city ranked #4 of 20. Cities with populations greater than 100,000 were evaluated based on per capita sales of romance novels and relationship books, romantic comedy movies, Barry White albums, and sexual wellness products. *Amazon.com, "Top 20 Most Romantic Cities in America," February 8, 2011*

- Miami appeared on *Men's Health's* list of the most sex-happy cities in America. The city ranked #88 of 100. Criteria: condom sales; birth rates; sex toy sales; rates of chlamydia, gonorrhea, and syphilis. *Men's Health, "America's Most Sex-Happy Cities," October 2010*

- *Men's Health* ranked 100 U.S. cities in terms of best (and worst) marriages. Miami was ranked #20 (#1 = worst marriages). Criteria: rate of failed marriages; stringency of divorce laws; percentage of population who've split; number of licensed marriage and family therapists. *Men's Health, "Splitsville, USA," May 2010*

- Eli Lily and Company, in partnership with Sperling's BestPlaces, ranked the nation's 50 largest metro areas in terms of the "Most Romantic Cities for Baby Boomers." The Miami metro area ranked #49. Criteria: marriage and divorce rates among "baby boomers" age 45 to 60; great restaurants; dance studios; chocolate, jewelry and flower sales. *Eli Lily and Company, "Most Romantic Cities for Baby Boomers," April 20, 2007*

- The Miami metro area was selected as one of the "Best Cities for Relocating Singles" by Worldwide ERC and Primacy Relocation. The area ranked #26 out of the 100 largest metro areas in the U.S. Areas were selected based on the following criteria: recent job growth; recent singles population growth; overall population growth; affordable rental housing; cost-of-living index; expanded arts and recreation opportunities; ratio of single men and single women; affordability of quality higher education (including state residency requirements); diversity index; climate; population density. *Worldwide ERC and Primacy Relocation, "2008 Best Cities for Relocating Singles"*

- *Forbes* ranked the 40 most populous urbanized areas in the U.S. in terms of the "Best Cities for Singles." The Miami metro area ranked #29. Criteria: number of singles; cost of living alone; nightlife; culture; job growth; coolness; and online dating participation. *Forbes.com, "Best Cities for Singles," July 27, 2009*

Education Rankings

- Miami was selected as one of "America's Most Literate Cities." The city ranked #29 out of the 75 largest U.S. cities. Criteria: number of booksellers; library resources; Internet resources; educational attainment; periodical publishing resources; newspaper circulation. *Central Connecticut State University, "America's Most Literate Cities 2010"*

- Miami was identified as one of the 100 "smartest" metro areas in the U.S. The area ranked #61. Criteria: the editors rated the collective brainpower of the 100 largest metro area in the U.S based on their residents' educational attainment. *American City Business Journals, www.bizjournals.com, April 14, 2008*

- Miami was identified as one of "America's Brainiest Bastions" by *Portfolio.com.* The metro area ranked #118 out of 200. Portfolio.com analyzed levels of educational attainment in the nation's 200 largest metropolitan areas. The editors established scores for five levels of educational attainment, based on relative earning power of adult workers age 25 or older. Scores were determined by comparing the median income for all workers with the median income for those workers at a specified educational level. *Portfolio.com, "America's Brainiest Bastions," December 1, 2010*

Environmental Rankings

- Miami was selected as one of 22 "Smarter Cities" for energy by the Natural Resources Defense Council." Criteria: investment in green power; energy efficiency measures; conservation. *Natural Resources Defense Council, "2010 Smarter Cities," July 19, 2010*

- Miami was selected as one of worst summer weather cities in the U.S. by the *Farmers' Almanac.* The city ranked #1 out of 5. Criteria: average summer and winter temperatures; humidity; precipitation; number of overcast days. The editors only considered cities with populations of 50,000 or more. *Farmers' Almanac, "America's Ten Worst Weather Cities," September 7, 2010*

- *American City Business Journal* ranked 43 metropolitan areas in terms of their "greenness." The Miami metro area ranked #30. Criteria: Forty-one metros in which *ACBJ* has business weeklies, plus Indianapolis and Cleveland, were ranked based on 20 different indicators such as adoption of green technologies, utilization of environmentally sound practices, and air and water quality. *American City Business Journals, "Green City Index," March 11, 2010*

- The Miami metro area was selected as one of "America's Cleanest Cities" by *Forbes.* The metro area ranked #1 out of 10. Criteria: air quality; water quality; per capita spending on Superfund site cleanup and solid-waste management. *Forbes.com, "America's Cleanest Cities," March 11, 2008*

- 100 of the largest metro areas in the U.S. were analyzed in terms of their current drought severity. The Miami metro area ranked #58 (#1 = driest). The rankings were based on statistics such as long-term precipitation trends and patterns and the Palmer drought indices. *Sperling's BestPlaces, www.BestPlaces.net, "America's Drought-Riskiest Cities," November 2007*

- The Miami metro area appeared in *Country Home's* "Best Green Places" report. The area ranked #121 out of 379. Criteria: official energy policies; green power; green buildings; availability of fresh, locally grown food. *Country Home, "Best Green Places," 2008*

- WeatherBill identified the 10 rainiest cities in the U.S. Miami ranked #7. The study ranked 195 cities in the contiguous 48 states by the amount of rainfall they received annually over a 30-year period. *WeatherBill, May 23, 2007*

Health/Fitness Rankings

- Miami was selected as one of the 25 fattest cities in America by *Men's Fitness Online*. It ranked #1 out of America's 50 largest cities. Criteria: fitness centers and sport stores; nutrition; sports participation; TV viewing; overweight/sedentary; junk food; air quality; geography; commute; parks and open space; city recreational facilities; access to healthcare; motivation; mayor and city initiatives; state obesity initiatives. *Men's Fitness Online, 2009 Fittest/Fattest Cities*

- Miami was identified as a "2011 Asthma Capital." The area ranked #61 out of the nation's 100 largest metropolitan areas. Twelve factors were used to identify the most challenging places to live for people with asthma: estimated prevalence; self-reported prevalence; crude death rate for asthma; annual pollen score; annual air quality; public smoking laws; number of board-certified asthma specialists; school inhaler access laws; rescue medication use; controller medication use; uninsured rate; poverty rate. *Asthma and Allergy Foundation of America, "2011 Asthma Capitals"*

- Miami was identified as a 2009 "Spring Allergy Capital." The area ranked #97 out of 100. Three groups of factors were used to identify the most severe cities for people with allergies during the spring season: annual pollen levels; medicine utilization; access to board-certified allergists. *Asthma and Allergy Foundation of America, "Spring Allergy Capitals 2009"*

- Miami was identified as a 2010 "Fall Allergy Capital." The area ranked #88 out of 100. Three groups of factors were used to identify the most severe cities for people with allergies during the fall season: annual pollen levels; medicine utilization; access to board-certified allergists. *Asthma and Allergy Foundation of America, "Fall Allergy Capitals 2010"*

- *Men's Health* ranked 100 U.S. cities in terms of the quality of their tap water. Miami was ranked #48 and received a grade of C. Criteria: levels of total coliform bacteria, arsenic, lead, total trihalomethanes (linked to cancer), and halo-acetic acids; number of EPA water-system violations from 1995 to 2005. *Men's Health, March 2007*

- Miami was selected as one of America's noisiest cities by *Men's Health*. The city ranked #5 of 10. Criteria: laws limiting excessive noise; traffic congestion levels; airports' overnight flight curfews; percentage of people who report sleeping seven hours or less. *Men's Health, "Ranking America's Cities: America's Noisiest Cities," May 2009*

- Ortho-McNeil Neurologics, in partnership with Sperling's BestPlaces, analyzed 110 metro areas and identified those U.S. cities with the highest prevalence of factors that are most commonly associated with migraine headaches. The Miami metro area ranked #104. Criteria: number of migraine-related drug prescriptions per capita; lifestyle factors that can contribute to migraines; environmental factors that can trigger migraines; and consumption of migraine-triggering foods. *Ortho-McNeil Neurologics, "America's Migraine Hot Spots," March 14, 2006*

- An analysis of the "Best & Worst Cities for Sleep" was conducted by Sperling's BestPlaces. The study ranked America's 50 most populated metro areas. The Miami metro area ranked #8 (#1 = best city for sleep). Criteria: number of days residents didn't get enough rest or sleep during the past month; average length of daily commute; divorce rate; unemployment rate. *Sperling's BestPlaces, www.BestPlaces.net, "Best & Worst Cities for Sleep," 2006*

- The Miami metropolitan area was selected as one of the best metros for hospital care in America by HealthGrades. The rankings are based on a comprehensive study of patient death and complication rates in the nation's nearly 5,000 hospitals. Hospitals performing in the top 5% nationwide across 26 different medical procedures and diagnoses were identified. HealthGrades then ranked cities by the highest percentage of these Distinguished Hospitals for Clinical Excellence™. The Miami metro area ranked #19. *HealthGrades.com, "America's Top 50 Cities for Hospital Care," January 26, 2011*

- *Men's Health* ranked 100 U.S. cities in terms of cities "Where the Food is Sickening." Miami was ranked #45 and received a grade of C. The magazine arrived at their ratings by looking at data compiled by the Community Health Status Indicator Project to determine outbreaks of E. coli, salmonella-, and shigella-related infections. They then checked the CDC's Wonder database to see how many people died from tainted food. Finally, the magazine found out which states have adopted the current version of the FDA's uniform Food Code, which contains the most up-to-date rules for keeping restaurant kitchens clean. *Men's Health, October 2005*

- The American Academy of Dermatology ranked 26 U.S. metropolitan regions in terms of their residents knowledge, attitude and behaviors towards tanning, sun protection and skin cancer detection. The Miami metro area ranked #13. The results of the study are based on an online survey of over 7,000 adults nationwide. *American Academy of Dermatology, "Suntelligence: How Sun Smart is Your City," May 3, 2010*

- The Miami metro area appeared in the 2010 Gallup-Healthways Well-Being Index. The index, based on interviews with more than 353,000 Americans during 2009, asked individuals to assess their jobs, finances, physical health, emotional state of mind and communities. The metro area ranked #121 out of 162. Criteria: life evaluation; emotional health; work environment; physical health; healthy behaviors; basic access (basic needs optimal for a healthy life, such as access to food and medicine, having health insurance and feeling safe while walking at night). *Gallup-Healthways, "Well-Being Index 2010"*

- The Miami metro area was identified as one of "America's Most Stressful Cities" by *Forbes*. The metro area ranked #20. Criteria: median home price drop; unemployment rates; cost of living; air quality; sunny days; population density. *Forbes.com, "America's Most Stressful Cities," August 20, 2009*

- The Miami metro area was identified as one of "America's 20 Most Sedentary Cities" by *Forbes*. The metro area ranked #10. Criteria: percentage of overweight or obese people; percentage of people who had not engaged in any physical activity in the past 30 days; average number of hours of TV watched per week. *Forbes.com, "America's Most Sedentary Cities," October 29, 2007*

- 50 of the largest metro areas in the U.S. were analyzed in terms of their health and fitness by the American College of Sports Medicine in their "American Fitness Index." The Miami metro area ranked #39 (#1 = healthiest). Criteria: preventative health behaviors; levels of chronic disease; health care access; community resources and policies that support physical activity. *American College of Sports Medicine, "Health and Community Fitness Status of the 50 Largest Metropolitan Areas," May 24, 2010*

- Miami was selected as one of the "20 Most Livable U.S. Cities for Wheelchair Users" by the Christopher & Dana Reeve Foundation. The city ranked #11. Criteria: Medicaid eligibility and spending; access to physicians and rehabilitation facilities; access to fitness facilities and recreation; access to paratransit; percentage of people living with disabilities who are employed; clean air; climate. *Christopher & Dana Reeve Foundation, "20 Most Livable U.S. Cities for Wheelchair Users," July 26, 2010*

Real Estate Rankings

- *Fortune* ranked the 100 largest metro areas in the U.S. in terms of projected median home price change in 2010. The Miami metro area ranked #100. *Fortune, "The 2010 Housing Outlook," December 9, 2009*

- Miami was selected as one of the 10 best U.S. cities for real estate investment. The city ranked #8. *Association of Foreign Investors in Real Estate, "AFIRE News," January/February, 2011*

- Miami appeared on ApartmentRatings.com "Top Cities for Renters" list in 2009." The area ranked #76. Overall satisfaction ratings were ranked using thousands of user submitted scores for hundreds of apartment complexes located in the 100 most populated U.S. municipalities. *ApartmentRatings.com, "2009 Renter Satisfaction Rankings"*

- Miami appeared on ApartmentRatings.com "Top College Towns & Cities" for renters list in 2010." The area ranked #68. Overall satisfaction ratings were ranked using thousands of user submitted scores for hundreds of apartment complexes located in cities and towns that are home to the 100 largest four-year institutions in the U.S. *ApartmentRatings.com, "2010 College Town Renter Satisfaction Rankings"*

- The Miami metro area was identified as one of "America's 25 Weakest Housing Markets" by *Forbes*. The metro area ranked #2. Criteria: metro areas with populations over 500,000 were ranked based on projected home values through 2011. *Forbes.com, "America's 25 Weakest Housing Markets," January 7, 2009*

- The nation's largest metro areas were analyzed in terms of the percentage of households entering some stage of foreclosure in 2010. The Miami metro area ranked #5 out of 206 (#1 = highest foreclosure rate). *RealtyTrac, 2010 Year-End Metropolitan Foreclosure Market Report, January 27, 2011*

- The Miami metro area appeared in a *Wall Street Journal* article ranking cities by "housing stress." The metro area was ranked #1 (#1 = most stress). Criteria: fraction of mortgage-holding homeowners with a monthly housing payment in excess of 30 percent of income; percentage of people without health insurance; unemployment rate. *The Wall Street Journal, "Which Cities Face Biggest Housing Risk," October 5, 2010*

- The Center for Housing Policy ranked 210 U.S metropolitan areas by the fair market rent for a two-bedroom unit. The Miami metro area was ranked #26. (#1 = most expensive) with a rent of $1,206. Criteria: Fair Market Rent (FMR) in effect during the fourth quarter of 2009 based on HUD's fiscal year 2010 FMRs. *The Center for Housing Policy, "Paycheck to Paycheck: Most to Least Expensive Rental Markets in 2009"*

- The Miami metro area was identified as one of the top 20 cities in terms of decreasing home equity. The metro area was ranked #19. Criteria: percentage of home equity relative to the home's current value. *Forbes.com, "Where Americans are Losing Home Equity Most," May 1, 2010*

Safety Rankings

- Symantec, the makers of Norton, in partnership with Sperling's BestPlaces, ranked the 50 largest cities in the U.S. in terms of their vulnerability to cybercrime. The city ranked #27. Criteria: number of cyberattacks and potential infections; level of Internet access; expenditures on computer hardware and software; wireless hotspots; broadband connectivity; Internet usage; online purchases. *Symantec, "10 Riskiest Cities for Cybercrime," March 22, 2010*

- Allstate ranked the 200 largest cities in America in terms of driver safety. Miami ranked #171. In addition, drivers were 34.2% more likely to have had an accident compared to the national average. Allstate researchers analyzed internal property damage reported claims over a two-year period (from January 2007 to December 2008) to ensure the findings would not be affected by external influences such as weather or road construction. A weighted average of the two-year numbers determined the annual percentages. The report defines an auto crash as any collision resulting in a property damage claim. *Allstate, "The 2010 Allstate America's Best Drivers Report™"*

- Miami was identified as one of America's "11 Most Dangerous Cities" by *U.S. News*. The city ranked #7. Criteria: crime risk was calculated using the most recent seven years (2003-2009) of FBI crime reporting data. The data includes both property crimes and violent crimes. *U.S. News & World Report, "The 11 Most Dangerous Cities," February 16, 2011*

- Sperling's BestPlaces analyzed the tracks of tropical storms for the past 100 years and ranked which areas are most likely to be hit by a major hurricane. The Miami metro area ranked #1 out of 10. *Sperling's BestPlaces, www.bestplaces.net, February 2, 2006*

- The National Insurance Crime Bureau ranked 366 metro areas in the U.S. in terms of per capita rates of vehicle theft. The Miami metro area ranked #42 (#1 = highest rate). Criteria: number of vehicle theft offenses per 100,000 inhabitants. *National Insurance Crime Bureau, "Hot Spots," May 17, 2010*

- The Miami metro area was identified as one of the "The Most Dangerous Metro Areas for Pedestrians" by Transportation for America and the Surface Transportation Policy Partnership. The metro area ranked #3 out of 52 metro areas with over 1 million residents. Criteria: area's population divided by the number of pedestrian fatalities in that area. *Transportation for America and the Surface Transportation Policy Partnership, "Dangerous by Design: Solving the Epidemic of Preventable Pedestrian Deaths (and Making Great Neighborhoods)," November 11, 2009*

Seniors/Retirement Rankings

- The Miami metro area was selected as one of the "10 Best Places for Single Seniors to Retire" by *U.S. News & World Report*. Criteria: metro areas with the most single seniors age 55 and over. *U.S. News & World Report, "10 Best Places for Single Seniors to Retire," November 1, 2010*

- The Miami metro area was selected as one of "The 10 Most Affordable Cities for Long-Term Care" by *U.S. News & World Report*. Criteria: costs at nursing homes, assisted living facilities, and adult day health care facilities; cost for licensed home health aides. *U.S. News & Word Report, "The 10 Most Affordable Cities for Long-Term Care," May 17, 2010*

Sports/Recreation Rankings

- Miami appeared on the *Sporting News* list of the "Best Sports Cities" for 2010. The area ranked #11 out of 402 cities in the U.S. *Sporting News* takes a 12-month snapshot, roughly October to October, of each city's sports, putting a heavy premium on regular-season won-lost records (from the most recently completed season). Other criteria include: playoff berths, bowl appearances and tournament bids; championships; applicable power ratings; quality of competition; overall fan fervor as measured in part by attendance as percentage of venue capacity; abundance of teams (rewarding quality over quantity); stadium and arena quality; ticket availability and prices; franchise ownership; and marquee appeal of athletes. *Sporting News, "Best Sports Cities 2010," October, 2010*

- Miami was chosen as one of America's best cities for bicycling. The city ranked #44 out of 50. Criteria: number of segregated bike lanes, municipal bike racks, and bike boulevards; vibrant and diverse bike culture; smart, savvy bike shops; interviews with national and local advocates, bike shops and other experts. Note: only cities with populations of 100,000 or more were considered. *Bicycling, "America's Best Bike Cities," April 2010*

- Scarborough Research, a leading market research firm, identified the top local markets for avid NBA fans. The Miami DMA (Designated Market Area) ranked in the top 10 with 13% of consumers 18 years and over reporting that they are "very interested in the NBA." *Scarborough Research, April 24, 2006*

- *Golf Digest* ranked 330 metro areas in the U.S. in terms of golf. The Miami metro area was ranked #307. Criteria: access to golf; weather; value of golf; and quality of golf. *Golf Digest, "Metro Golf Rankings," August 2005*

Technology Rankings

- The Miami metro area was selected as one of "America's Most Wired Cities" by *Forbes*. The metro area was ranked #17 out of 20. Criteria: percentage of Internet users with high-speed access; number of companies providing high-speed Internet; number of public wireless hot spots. *Forbes, "America's Most Wired Cities," March 2, 2010*

Transportation Rankings

- The Miami metro area appeared on *Forbes* list of the best and worst cities for commuters. The metro area ranked #55 out of 60 (#1 is best). Criteria: travel time; road congestion; travel delays. *Forbes.com, "Best and Worst Cities for Commuters," February 16, 2010*

Women/Minorities Rankings

- Miami was ranked #39 out of 100 metro areas in *SELF Magazine's* ranking of America's healthiest places for women." A panel of experts came up with more than 50 criteria including death and disease rates, environmental indicators, community resources, and lifestyle habits. *SELF Magazine, "Secrets of America's Healthiest Women," December 2008*

- Miami was selected as one of the "Gayest Cities in America" by *The Advocate*. The city ranked #15 out of 15. Criteria: gay.com profiles; listed officiants for gay weddings within a 50 mile radius; elected openly gay officials; Tegan and Sara performances over the past five years; lesbian bars; gay and gay-friendly religious congregations; entries in YellowPages.com with "gay" in the business name or description. *The Advocate, "Gayest Cities in America," February 2011*

- Miami was selected as one of the "Top 10 Cities for Hispanics." Criteria: the prospect of a good job; a safe place to raise a family; a manageable cost of living; the ability to buy and keep a home; a culture of inclusion where Hispanics are highly represented; resources to help start a business; the presence of Hispanic or Spanish-language media; representation of Hispanic needs on local government; a thriving arts and culture community; air quality; energy costs; city's state of health and rates of obesity. *Hispanic Magazine, August 2008*

Miscellaneous Rankings

- Energizer Holdings, the makers of Edge® shave gel, in partnership with Sperling's BestPlaces, ranked 50 major metro areas in terms of everyday irritations. The Miami metro area ranked #14. Criteria: humidity levels; weather conditions; incidence of traffic delays and congestion; average commute times; frequency of flight delays and cancellations; rates of sleeplessness; underemployment; pollens and allergens; pests; comedy clubs per capita. *Energizer Holdings, "Most Irritation Prone Cities," July 23, 2010*

- Mars Chocolate North America, the makers of COMBOS®, in partnership with Sperling's BestPlaces, ranked 50 major metro areas in terms of their "manliness." The Miami metro area ranked #49. Criteria: number of home improvement stores, steak houses, pickup trucks, motorcycles, and manly occupations (fire fighters, police officers, construction workers, EMP personnel) per capita; salty snack sales; sports TV viewing habits. *Mars Chocolate North America, "America's Manliest Cities," June 22, 2010*

- Miami was selected as one of the "Best Hair Cities" by naturallycurly.com. The city was ranked #7. Criteria: humidity levels; pollution; rainfall; average wind speeds; water hardness; beauty salons per capita. *naturallycurly.com, "Best/Worst Hair Cities," April 29, 2009*

- The Miami metro area was selected as one of "America's Greediest Cities" by *Forbes*. The area was ranked #10 out of 10. Criteria: number of Forbes 400 (*Forbes* annual list of the richest Americans) members per capita. *Forbes, "America's Greediest Cities," December 7, 2007*

- The Miami metro area appeared in AutoMD.com's ranking of the "Best and Worst Cities for Auto Repair." The metro area ranked #14 (#1 is best). The 50 most-populated metro areas in the U.S. were ranked on three critical factors: repair affordability; price disparity range; shop integrity factor. *AutoMD.com, "Advocacy for Repair Shop Fairness Report," February 24, 2010*

- Miami was identified as one of "America's Vainest Cities" by Forbes.com. The city ranked #3. Criteria: highest number of cosmetic surgeons per 100,000 people in America's 50 largest cities. *Forbes.com, "America's Vainest Cities," November 29, 2007*

- The Miami metro area was selected as one of "America's 20 Most Miserable Cities" by *Forbes*. The metro area ranked #2. Criteria: jobless rates; inflation; taxes; commuting times; crime rates; performance by the city's sports teams; weather; pollution; corruption by public officials. *Forbes.com, "America's 20 Most Miserable Cities, 2011" February 2, 2011*

- Miami appeared on Procter & Gamble's list of the "Top-20 All-Time Sweatiest Cities." The city was ranked #7. The rankings are based on computer simulations of the amount of sweat a person of average height and weight would produce walking around for an hour in the average temperatures during the summer months, based on historical weather data during June, July and August from 2001-2008 for each city. *Procter & Gamble, Old Spice Press Release, "Top-20 All-Time Sweatiest Cities," July 1, 2009*

- The Miami metro area appeared on *Forbes* list of "America's Drunkest Cities." The area ranked #33. Criteria: 35 of the largest continental U.S. metro areas were chosen based on availability of data and geographic diversity. Each metro was ranked in five areas: state laws; drinkers; heavy drinkers; binge drinkers; and alcoholism. *Forbes.com, "America's Drunkest Cities," August 22, 2006*

Business Environment

CITY FINANCES

City Government Finances

Component	2008 ($000)	2008 ($ per capita)
Total Revenues	858,879	2,096
Total Expenditures	862,165	2,104
Debt Outstanding	531,658	1,298
Cash and Securities[1]	2,676,559	6,533

Note: (1) Cash and security holdings of a government at the close of its fiscal year, including those of its dependent agencies, utilities, and liquor stores.
Source: U.S Census Bureau, State & Local Government Finances 2008

City Government Revenue by Source

Source	2008 ($000)	2008 ($ per capita)
General Revenue		
From Federal Government	34,982	85
From State Government	70,855	173
From Local Governments	48,370	118
Taxes		
Property	298,259	728
Sales and Gross Receipts	104,364	255
Personal Income	0	0
Corporate Income	0	0
Motor Vehicle License	0	0
Other Taxes	36,865	90
Current Charges	109,438	267
Liquor Store	0	0
Utility	0	0
Employee Retirement	129,155	315

Source: U.S Census Bureau, State & Local Government Finances 2008

City Government Expenditures by Function

Function	2008 ($000)	2008 ($ per capita)	2008 (%)
General Direct Expenditures			
Air Transportation	0	0	0.0
Corrections	0	0	0.0
Education	0	0	0.0
Employment Security Administration	0	0	0.0
Financial Administration	14,300	35	1.7
Fire Protection	107,347	262	12.5
General Public Buildings	0	0	0.0
Governmental Administration, Other	12,720	31	1.5
Health	0	0	0.0
Highways	35,331	86	4.1
Hospitals	0	0	0.0
Housing and Community Development	48,017	117	5.6
Interest on General Debt	24,346	59	2.8
Judicial and Legal	5,981	15	0.7
Libraries	0	0	0.0
Parking	21,728	53	2.5
Parks and Recreation	116,010	283	13.5
Police Protection	150,731	368	17.5
Public Welfare	0	0	0.0
Sewerage	558	1	0.1
Solid Waste Management	27,519	67	3.2
Veterans' Services	0	0	0.0
Liquor Store	0	0	0.0
Utility	5,124	13	0.6
Employee Retirement	136,945	334	15.9

Source: U.S Census Bureau, State & Local Government Finances 2008

Municipal Bond Ratings

Area	Moody's	S&P	Fitch
City	A2	A+	A

Rating Systems (shown in declining order of credit quality): Moody's– Aaa, Aa, A, Baa, Ba, B, Caa, Ca, C (numerical modifiers 1, 2, and 3 are added to letter-rating); S&P– AAA, AA, A, BBB, BB, B, CCC, CC, C; Fitch– AAA, AA, A, BBB, BB, B, CCC, CC, C. Ratings may be modified by the addition of a plus or minus sign to show relative standing within the major rating categories.
Notes: n/a Not available; (1) Not reviewed; (2) Issuer Rating/No General Obligation; (3) Standard and Poor's Issue Credit Rating (ICR) is a current opinion of an obliger with respect to a specific financial obligation, a specific class of financial obligations, or a specific financial program.
Source: U.S. Census Bureau, 2011 Statistical Abstract, Bond Ratings for City Governments by Largest Cities: 2009

DEMOGRAPHICS

Population Growth

Area	1990 Census	2000 Census	2010 Estimate	2015 Projection	Population Growth (%) 2000-2010	2010-2015
City	358,843	362,470	411,168	434,131	13.4	5.6
MSA[1]	4,056,100	5,007,564	5,519,882	5,786,816	10.2	4.8
U.S.	248,709,873	281,421,906	309,038,974	321,675,005	9.8	4.1

Note: (1) Metropolitan Statistical Area - see Appendix B for areas included
Source: Claritas, Inc.

Number of Households and Average Household Size

Area	2010 Estimate	2010 Average Household Size
City	155,735	2.55
MSA[1]	2,058,462	2.64
U.S.	116,136,617	2.59

Note: (1) Metropolitan Statistical Area - see Appendix B for areas included
Source: Claritas, Inc.

Race and Ethnicity

Area	White Alone[2] (%)	Black Alone[2] (%)	Asian Alone[2] (%)	Other Race Alone[2] (%)	Hispanic[3] (%)
City	70.0	18.2	0.7	11.1	68.9
MSA[1]	69.7	19.4	2.1	8.9	40.3
U.S.	72.3	12.4	4.4	10.9	15.8

Note: Figures are 2010 estimates; (1) Metropolitan Statistical Area - see Appendix B for areas included (2) Alone is defined as not being in combination with one or more other races; (3) May be of any race.
Source: Claritas, Inc.

Segregation

Type	Segregation Indices[1] 1990	2000	2010	2010 Rank[2]	Percent Change 1990-2000	1990-2010	2000-2010
Black/White	71.4	69.2	64.8	23	-2.3	-6.6	-4.3
Asian/White	26.8	33.3	34.2	80	6.4	7.3	0.9
Hispanic/White	32.5	59.0	57.4	8	26.5	24.8	-1.6

Note: Figures are based on an analysis of 1990, 2000, and 2010 Census Decennial Census tract data by William H. Frey, Brookings Institution and the University of Michigan Social Science Data Analysis Network. In this analysis all racial groups (whites, blacks, and asians) are non-Hispanic members of those races. Hispanics are shown as a separate category; All figures cover the Metropolitan Statistical Area (see Appendix B for areas included); (1) Segregation Indices are Dissimilarity Indices that measure the degree to which the minority group is distributed differently than whites aross census tracts. They range from 0 (complete integration) to 100 (complete [segregation) where the value indicates the percentage of the minority group that needs to move to be distributed exactly like whites; (2) Ranges from 1 (most segregated) to 102 (least segregated); n/a not available.
Source: www.CensusScope.org

Ancestry

Area	German	Irish	English	American	Italian	Polish	French	Scottish
City	1.9	1.7	1.1	2.0	1.8	0.6	1.0	0.3
MSA[1]	6.2	6.0	4.2	4.2	5.9	2.5	1.7	0.9
U.S.	16.6	12.0	9.1	6.1	5.9	3.3	3.1	1.9

Note: The top eight ancestries in the U.S. are shown. Figures are percentages and include multiple ancestry (e.g. if a person reported being Irish and Italian, they were included in both columns); (1) Metropolitan Statistical Area - see Appendix B for areas included
Source: U.S. Census Bureau, 2007-2009 American Community Survey 3-Year Estimates

Foreign-Born Population

Area	Percent of Population Born in								
	Any Foreign Country	Mexico	Asia	Europe	Carribean	South America	Central America[2]	Africa	Canada
City	56.7	1.0	0.9	1.6	31.8	7.0	13.9	0.4	0.2
MSA[1]	36.7	1.2	1.9	2.3	18.6	7.3	4.4	0.4	0.6
U.S.	12.5	3.8	3.4	1.6	1.1	0.8	0.9	0.5	0.3

Note: (1) Metropolitan Statistical Area - see Appendix B for areas included; (2) Excludes Mexico.
Source: U.S. Census Bureau, 2007-2009 American Community Survey 3-Year Estimates

Marriage Status

Area	Never Married	Now Married[2]	Separated	Widowed	Divorced
City	37.4	37.6	4.3	7.6	13.0
MSA[1]	31.9	45.5	2.9	7.5	12.3
U.S.	31.4	49.7	2.2	6.2	10.6

Note: Figures are percentages and cover the population 15 years of age and older;
(1) Metropolitan Statistical Area - see Appendix B for areas included; (2) Excludes separated
Source: U.S. Census Bureau, 2007-2009 American Community Survey 3-Year Estimates

Age Distribution and Median Age

Area	Percent of Population							Median Age
	Under Age 5	Age 5 to 17	Age 18 to 34	Age 35 to 49	Age 50 to 64	Age 65 to 79	80 Years and Over	
City	6.9	13.2	24.7	21.5	17.1	11.2	5.4	38.7
MSA[1]	6.6	16.2	21.6	22.2	17.6	10.4	5.4	39.0
U.S.	6.9	17.5	23.3	21.4	18.1	9.1	3.7	36.7

Note: (1) Metropolitan Statistical Area - see Appendix B for areas included
Source: U.S. Census Bureau, 2007-2009 American Community Survey 3-Year Estimates

Male/Female Ratio

Area	Males	Females	Males per 100 Females
City	205,016	206,152	99.4
MSA[1]	2,682,549	2,837,333	94.5
U.S.	152,401,520	156,637,454	97.3

Note: Figures are 2010 estimates; (1) Metropolitan Statistical Area - see Appendix B for areas included
Source: Claritas, Inc.

Religion

Area	Catholic	Southern Baptist	United Methodist	ELCA[1]	LDS[2]	Presbyterian Church USA	Jewish Est.	Muslim Est.
County	24.1	3.6	0.8	0.3	0.3	0.2	5.5	0.3
U.S.	22.0	7.1	3.7	1.8	1.5	1.1	2.2	0.6

Note: Figures are the number of adherents as a percentage of the total population; Adherents are defined as all members, including full members, their children and the estimated number of other participants who are not considered members (e.g. the baptized, those not confirmed, those regularly attending services, etc.);
(1) Evangelical Lutheran Church in America; (2) The Church of Jesus Christ of Latter Day Saints
Source: Reprinted with permission from Religious Congregations and Membership in the United States 2000 (Nashville, Glenmary Research Center, 2002) Copyright Association of Statisticians of American Religious Bodies. All rights reserved.

ECONOMY

Gross Metropolitan Product

Area	2006	2007	2008	2009	2009 Rank[2]
MSA[1]	251.5	260.0	261.3	257.2	11

Note: Figures are in billions of dollars; (1) Miami-Fort Lauderdale-Miami Beach, FL Metropolitan Statistical Area - see Appendix B for areas included; (2) Rank ranges from 1 to 363
Source: The U.S. Conference of Mayors, "Pace of Economic Recovery: GMP and Jobs," January 2010

Economic Growth

Area	2006-2008 (%)	2009 (%)	2010 (%)	Rank[2]
MSA[1]	-0.4	-2.5	2.4	294
U.S.	1.3	-2.5	2.2	–

Note: Figures are real Gross Metropolitan Product growth rates and represent annual average percent change; (1) Miami-Fort Lauderdale-Miami Beach, FL Metropolitan Statistical Area - see Appendix B for areas included; (2) Rank ranges from 1 to 363
Source: The U.S. Conference of Mayors, "Pace of Economic Recovery: GMP and Jobs," January 2010

Metropolitan Area Exports

Area	2005	2006	2007	2008	2009	2009 Rank[2]
MSA[1]	20,382.9	23,491.3	26,197.4	33,411.5	31,175.0	5

Note: Figures are in millions of dollars; (1) Miami-Fort Lauderdale-Miami Beach, FL Metropolitan Statistical Area - see Appendix B for areas included; (2) Rank ranges from 1 to 374
Source: U.S. Department of Commerce, International Trade Administration, Office of Trade & Industry Information, Manufacturing & Services

INCOME

Per Capita/Median/Average Income

Area	Per Capita ($)	Median Household ($)	Average Household ($)
City	19,806	30,447	50,898
MSA[1]	27,136	50,324	72,073
U.S.	27,034	52,795	71,071

Note: Figures are 2010 estimates; (1) Metropolitan Statistical Area - see Appendix B for areas included
Source: Claritas, Inc.

Household Income Distribution

Area	Percent of Households Earning							
	Under $15,000	$15,000 -24,999	$25,000 -34,999	$35,000 -49,999	$50,000 -74,999	$75,000 -99,000	$100,000 -149,999	$150,000 and up
City	28.3	15.1	12.1	13.4	13.0	6.5	6.2	5.4
MSA[1]	13.4	10.7	10.9	14.8	18.6	11.4	11.4	8.8
U.S.	12.1	10.2	10.6	15.0	19.5	12.5	12.1	8.0

Note: Figures are 2010 estimates; (1) Metropolitan Statistical Area - see Appendix B for areas included
Source: Claritas, Inc.

Poverty Rates by Age

Area	All Ages	Under 18 Years Old	18 to 64 Years Old	65 Years and Over
City	25.8	6.9	13.7	5.1
MSA[1]	14.2	4.4	7.5	2.3
U.S.	13.6	4.7	7.7	1.2

Note: Figures are percent of population with income during the previous 12 months below poverty level and only include population for whom poverty status is determined; (1) Metropolitan Statistical Area - see Appendix B for areas included
Source: U.S. Census Bureau, 2007-2009 American Community Survey 3-Year Estimates

Personal Bankruptcy Filing Rate

Area	2006	2007	2008	2009	2010
Miami-Dade County	n/a	n/a	n/a	n/a	n/a
U.S.	2.00	2.73	3.53	4.60	4.96

Note: Numbers are per 1,000 population and include Chapter 7 and Chapter 13 filings; n/a not available
Source: Federal Deposit Insurance Corporation, Regional Economic Conditions, March 17, 2011

EMPLOYMENT

Labor Force and Employment

Area	Civilian Labor Force			Workers Employed		
	Dec. 2009	Dec. 2010	% Chg.	Dec. 2009	Dec. 2010	% Chg.
City	189,231	200,338	5.9	166,259	172,181	3.6
MD[1]	1,236,009	1,303,792	5.5	1,093,648	1,132,600	3.6
U.S.	152,693,000	153,156,000	0.3	137,953,000	139,159,000	0.9

Note: Data is not seasonally adjusted and covers workers 16 years of age and older;
(1) Metropolitan Division - see Appendix B for areas included
Source: Bureau of Labor Statistics, http://stats.bls.gov

Unemployment Rate

Area	2010											
	Jan.	Feb.	Mar.	Apr.	May	Jun.	Jul.	Aug.	Sep.	Oct.	Nov.	Dec.
City	11.7	11.8	12.4	12.3	12.7	13.3	13.7	14.5	13.5	14.1	13.6	14.1
MD[1]	11.1	11.2	11.9	11.8	12.1	12.7	12.9	13.6	12.6	13.1	12.6	13.1
U.S.	10.6	10.4	10.2	9.5	9.3	9.6	9.7	9.5	9.2	9.0	9.3	9.1

Note: Data is not seasonally adjusted and covers workers 16 years of age and older; All figures are percentages; (1) Metropolitan Division - see Appendix B for areas included
Source: Bureau of Labor Statistics, http://stats.bls.gov

Projected Unemployment Rate

Area	2007 (%)	2009 (%)	2011 (%)	2013 (%)
MSA[1]	4.5	11.4	10.0	8.0

Note: (1) Metropolitan Statistical Area - see Appendix B for areas included
Source: The U.S. Conference of Mayors, "Pace of Economic Recovery: GMP and Jobs," January 2010

Employment by Occupation

Occupation Classification	City (%)	MSA[1] (%)	U.S. (%)
Sales and Office	23.9	28.7	25.4
Professional and Related	15.1	18.0	21.0
Service	24.1	19.7	17.2
Production, Transportation, and Material Moving	10.6	8.9	12.3
Management, Business, and Financial	11.9	14.6	14.1
Construction, Extraction, and Maintenance	14.2	9.7	9.2
Farming, Forestry, and Fishing	0.2	0.4	0.7

Note: Figures cover employed civilians 16 years of age and older;
(1) Metropolitan Statistical Area - see Appendix B for areas included
Source: U.S. Census Bureau, 2007-2009 American Community Survey 3-Year Estimates

Employment by Industry

Sector	MSA[1]		U.S.
	Number of Employees	Percent of Total	Percent of Total
Government	151,800	15.2	17.2
Education and Health Services	161,700	16.2	15.2
Professional and Business Services	132,000	13.2	13.0
Retail Trade	127,100	12.8	11.4
Leisure and Hospitality	108,300	10.9	9.7
Manufacturing	34,700	3.5	8.8
Financial Activities	63,400	6.4	5.8
Wholesale Trade	68,900	6.9	4.2
Construction	31,300	3.1	4.1
Other Services	40,200	4.0	4.1
Transportation and Utilities	59,300	6.0	3.7
Information	17,500	1.8	2.1
Mining and Logging	300	<0.1	0.6

Note: Figures cover non-farm employment as of December 2010 and are not seasonally adjusted;
(1) Metropolitan Statistical Area - see Appendix B for areas included
Source: Bureau of Labor Statistics, http://stats.bls.gov

Occupations with Greatest Projected Employment Growth: 2006 - 2016

Occupation[1]	2006 Employment	2016 Projected Employment	Numeric Employment Change	Percent Employment Change
Retail salespersons	283,850	339,780	55,930	19.7
Customer service representatives	162,780	214,600	51,820	31.8
Registered nurses	148,390	190,020	41,630	28.1
Combined food preparation and serving workers, including fast food	163,780	202,670	38,890	23.7
Waiters and waitresses	197,920	232,430	34,510	17.4
Office clerks, general	188,190	221,750	33,560	17.8
Bookkeeping, accounting, and auditing clerks	128,340	153,830	25,490	19.9
Janitors and cleaners, except maids and housekeeping cleaners	124,030	147,970	23,940	19.3
Sales representatives, services, all other	73,650	97,390	23,740	32.2
Executive secretaries and administrative assistants	106,820	129,140	22,320	20.9

Note: Projections cover Florida; (1) Sorted by numeric employment change
Source: www.projectionscentral.com, State Occupational Projections, 2006-2016 Long-Term Projections

Fastest Growing Occupations: 2006 - 2016

Occupation[1]	2006 Employment	2016 Projected Employment	Numeric Employment Change	Percent Employment Change
Network systems and data communications analysts	20,830	33,090	12,260	58.9
Court reporters	2,170	3,430	1,260	58.1
Computer software engineers, applications	17,350	27,250	9,900	57.1
Veterinary technologists and technicians	5,720	8,880	3,160	55.2
Veterinarians	3,280	4,890	1,610	49.1
Home health aides	29,600	42,780	13,180	44.5
Personal and home care aides	10,640	15,220	4,580	43.0
Paralegals and legal assistants	19,240	27,360	8,120	42.2
Pharmacy technicians	21,110	29,950	8,840	41.9
Medical assistants	31,040	43,930	12,890	41.5

Note: Projections cover Florida; (1) Sorted by percent employment change and excludes occupations with numeric employment change less than 900
Source: www.projectionscentral.com, State Occupational Projections, 2006-2016 Long-Term Projections

Average Wages

Occupation	$/Hr.	Occupation	$/Hr.
Accountants and Auditors	33.45	Maids and Housekeeping Cleaners	9.44
Automotive Mechanics	18.46	Maintenance and Repair Workers	15.30
Bookkeepers	16.08	Marketing Managers	54.19
Carpenters	16.30	Nuclear Medicine Technologists	30.26
Cashiers	8.88	Nurses, Licensed Practical	19.83
Clerks, General Office	12.03	Nurses, Registered	32.90
Clerks, Receptionists/Information	11.45	Nursing Aides/Orderlies/Attendants	10.74
Clerks, Shipping/Receiving	12.85	Packers and Packagers, Hand	9.47
Computer Programmers	34.09	Physical Therapists	35.87
Computer Support Specialists	20.14	Postal Service Mail Carriers	24.70
Computer Systems Analysts	33.73	Real Estate Brokers	36.01
Cooks, Restaurant	11.96	Retail Salespersons	13.23
Dentists	n/a	Sales Reps., Exc. Tech./Scientific	27.65
Electrical Engineers	40.21	Sales Reps., Tech./Scientific	31.24
Electricians	20.52	Secretaries, Exc. Legal/Med./Exec.	14.59
Financial Managers	59.51	Security Guards	11.08
First-Line Supervisors/Mgrs., Sales	20.44	Surgeons	97.02
Food Preparation Workers	9.71	Teacher Assistants	10.70
General and Operations Managers	50.23	Teachers, Elementary School	n/a
Hairdressers/Cosmetologists	12.86	Teachers, Secondary School	n/a
Internists	97.31	Telemarketers	12.55
Janitors and Cleaners	9.84	Truck Drivers, Heavy/Tractor-Trailer	18.01
Landscaping/Groundskeeping Workers	10.50	Truck Drivers, Light/Delivery Svcs.	13.06
Lawyers	59.91	Waiters and Waitresses	9.77

Note: Wage data covers the Miami-Miami Beach-Kendall, FL Metropolitan Division - see Appendix B for areas included. Hourly wages for elementary/secondary school teachers and teacher assistants were calculated by the editors from annual wage data assuming a 40 hour work week; n/a not available.
Source: Bureau of Labor Statistics, Metro Area Occupational Employment and Wage Estimates, May 2009

RESIDENTIAL REAL ESTATE

Building Permits

Area	Single-Family			Multi-Family			Total		
	2009	2010	Pct. Chg.	2009	2010	Pct. Chg.	2009	2010	Pct. Chg.
City	28	27	-3.6	280	685	144.6	308	712	131.2
MSA[1]	2,289	3,171	38.5	1,586	2,706	70.6	3,875	5,877	51.7
U.S.	441,100	447,300	1.4	141,900	157,300	10.9	583,000	604,600	3.7

Note: (1) Metropolitan Statistical Area - see Appendix B for areas included; figures represent new, privately-owned housing units authorized (unadjusted data); All permit data are based on estimates with imputation.
Source: U.S. Census Bureau, Manufacturing, Mining, and Construction Statistics, Building Permits, 2009, 2010

Homeownership Rate

Area	2005 (%)	2006 (%)	2007 (%)	2008 (%)	2009 (%)	2010 (%)
MSA[1]	69.2	67.4	66.6	66.0	67.1	63.8
U.S.	68.9	68.8	68.1	67.8	67.4	66.9

Note: (1) Metropolitan Statistical Area - see Appendix B for areas included
Source: U.S. Census Bureau, Housing Vacancies and Homeownership Annual Statistics: 2010

Housing Vacancy Rates

Area	Gross Vacancy Rate[2] (%)			Year-Round Vacancy Rate[3] (%)			Rental Vacancy Rate[4] (%)			Homeowner Vacancy Rate[5] (%)		
	2008	2009	2010	2008	2009	2010	2008	2009	2010	2008	2009	2010
MSA[1]	22.1	23.1	21.8	13.1	13.7	13.0	12.1	13.2	10.1	3.8	3.2	3.5
U.S.	14.4	14.5	14.3	11.1	11.3	11.3	10.0	10.6	10.2	2.8	2.6	2.6

Note: (1) Metropolitan Statistical Area - see Appendix B for areas included; (2) The percentage of the total housing inventory that is vacant; (3) The percentage of the housing inventory (excluding seasonal units) that is year-round vacant; (4) The percentage of rental inventory that is vacant for rent; (5) The percentage of homeowner inventory that is vacant for sale; n/a not available
Source: U.S. Census Bureau, Housing Vacancies and Homeownership Annual Statistics: 2010

State Corporate Income Tax Rates

State	Tax Rate (%)	Income Brackets ($)	Num. of Brackets	Financial Institution Tax Rate (%)[a]	Federal Income Tax Ded.
Florida	5.5 (f)	Flat rate	1	5.5 (f)	No

Note: Tax rates as of January 1, 2011; (a) Rates listed are the tax rates applied to financial institutions or excise taxes based on income. Some states have other taxes based upon the value of deposits or shares; (f) An exemption of $5,000 is allowed. Florida's Alternative Minimum Tax rate is 3.3%.
Source: Federation of Tax Administrators, "State Corporate Income Tax Rates, 2011"

State Individual Income Tax Rates

State	Tax Rate (%)	Income Brackets ($)	Num. of Brackets	Personal Exempt. ($)[1]		Fed. Inc. Tax Ded.
				Single	Dependents	
Florida – No State Income Tax						

Note: Tax rates as of January 1, 2011; Local- and county-level taxes are not included; n/a not applicable; (1) Married joint filers generally receive double the single exemption
Source: Federation of Tax Administrators, "State Individual Income Tax Rates, 2011"

Various State and Local Tax Rates

State	State and Local Sales and Use (%)	State Sales and Use (%)	Gasoline[1] (¢/gal.)	Cigarette[2] ($/pack)	Spirits[3] ($/gal.)	Wine[4] ($/gal.)	Beer[5] ($/gal.)
Florida	7.0	6.00	34.4	1.34	6.50	2.25	0.48

Note: All tax rates as of January 1, 2011 except Spirits (Sept. 1, 2010); (1) The American Petroleum Institute has developed a methodology for determining the average tax rate on a gallon of fuel. Rates may include any of the following: excise taxes, environmental fees, storage tank fees, other fees or taxes, general sales tax, and local taxes. In states where gasoline is subject to the general sales tax, or where the fuel tax is based on the average sale price, the average rate determined by API is sensitive to changes in the price of gasoline. States that fully or partially apply general sales taxes to gasoline: CA, CO, GA, IL, IN, MI, NY; (2) The federal excise tax of $1.0066 per pack and local taxes are not included; (3) Rates are those applicable to off-premise sales of 40% alcohol by volume (a.b.v.) distilled spirits in 750ml containers. Local excise taxes are excluded; (4) Rates are those applicable to off-premise sales of 11% a.b.v. non-carbonated wine in 750ml containers; (5) Rates are those applicable to off-premise sales of 4.7% a.b.v. beer in 12 ounce containers.
Source: Tax Foundation, 2011 Facts & Figures: How Does Your State Compare?

State-Local Tax Burdens

Area	Rate (%)	Rank[1]	Per Capita Taxes Paid to Home State ($)	Total State and Local Per Capita Taxes Paid ($)	Per Capita Income ($)
Florida	9.2	31	2,713	3,897	42,146
U.S. Average	9.8	-	3,057	4,160	42,539

Note: Figures cover 2009; (1) Rank ranges from 1 to 50 where 1 is highest tax burden
Source: Tax Foundation, State-Local Tax Burdens, All States, 2009

State Business Tax Climate Index Rankings

State	Overall Rank	Corporate Tax Index Rank	Individual Income Tax Index Rank	Sales Tax Index Rank	Unemployment Insurance Tax Index Rank	Property Tax Index Rank
Florida	5	15	1	30	3	28

Note: The index is a measure of how each state's tax laws affect economic performance. The lower the rank, the more favorable a state's tax system is for business. All ranks are for fiscal years. States without a given tax are given a ranking of 1.
Source: Tax Foundation, Tax Foundation Background Paper, No. 60, "2011 State Business Tax Climate Index"

COMMERCIAL REAL ESTATE

Office Market

Market Area	Inventory (sq. ft.)	Vacant (sq. ft.)	Vac. Rate (%)	Under Constr. (sq. ft.)	Asking Rent ($/sf/yr)	
					Class A	Class B
Miami-Dade County	48,010,426	9,381,709	19.5	768,924	36.56	26.14

Source: Grubb & Ellis, Office Markets Trends, 1st Quarter 2011

Industrial Market

Market Area	Inventory (sq. ft.)	Vacant (sq. ft.)	Vac. Rate (%)	Under Constr. (sq. ft.)	Asking Rent ($/sf/yr) WH/Dist	R&D/Flex
Miami-Dade County	199,491,492	17,861,885	9.0	-	4.64	8.95

Source: Grubb & Ellis, Industrial Markets Trends, 4th Quarter 2010

COMMERCIAL UTILITIES

Typical Monthly Electric Bills

Area	Commercial Service ($/month) 3 kW demand 1,000 kWh	40 kW demand 14,000 kWh	Industrial Service ($/month) 1,000 kW demand 200,000 kWh	50,000 kW demand 15,000,000 kWh
City	106	1,214	21,777	945,149
Average[1]	135	1,576	23,741	1,402,202

Note: Based on total rates in effect July 1, 2010; (1) average based on 182 utilities surveyed
Source: Edison Electric Institute, Typical Bills and Average Rates Report, Summer 2010

TRANSPORTATION

Means of Transportation to Work

Area	Car/Truck/Van Drove Alone	Car-pooled	Public Transportation Bus	Subway	Railroad	Bicycle	Walked	Other Means	Worked at Home
City	68.9	10.1	10.7	0.5	0.4	0.4	3.8	1.6	3.5
MSA[1]	78.1	10.1	3.3	0.2	0.2	0.5	1.8	1.5	4.3
U.S.	75.8	10.4	2.7	1.7	0.5	0.5	2.9	1.2	4.1

Note: Figures are percentages and cover workers 16 years of age and older;
(1) Metropolitan Statistical Area - see Appendix B for areas included
Source: U.S. Census Bureau, 2007-2009 American Community Survey 3-Year Estimates

Travel Time to Work

Area	Less Than 15 Minutes	15 to 29 Minutes	30 to 44 Minutes	45 to 59 Minutes	60 to 89 Minutes	90 Minutes or More
City	19.2	39.9	24.8	8.4	5.9	1.9
MSA[1]	19.9	36.0	27.0	8.9	6.3	2.0
U.S.	28.5	36.2	19.7	7.5	5.6	2.5

Note: Figures are percentages and include workers 16 years old and over;
(1) Metropolitan Statistical Area - see Appendix B for areas included
Source: U.S. Census Bureau, 2007-2009 American Community Survey 3-Year Estimates

Travel Time Index

Area	1982	1999	2008	2009
Urban Area[1]	1.09	1.24	1.26	1.23
Average[2]	1.08	1.20	1.20	1.20

Note: Travel Time Index—the ratio of travel time in the peak period to the travel time at
free-flow conditions. A value of 1.30 indicates a 20-minute free-flow trip takes 26 minutes
in the peak. Free-flow speeds (60 mph on freeways and 35 mph on principal arterials)
are used as the comparison threshold; (1) Covers the Miami-Fort Lauderdale-Miami Beach urban area;
(2) average of 439 urban areas
Source: Texas Transportation Institute, Urban Mobility Report 2010, December 2010

Public Transportation

Agency Name / Mode of Transportation	Vehicles Operated in Maximum Service	Annual Unlinked Passenger Trips ('000)	Annual Passenger Miles ('000)
Miami-Dade Transit (MDT)			
Automated guideway	21	8,100.1	8,408.2
Demand response	316	1,552.0	16,778.4
Heavy rail	84	18,244.5	132,769.7
Bus	716	75,608.0	391,313.2
South Florida Regional Transportation Authority (TRI-Rail)			
Commuter rail	34	4,223.4	122,469.6
Bus	18	488.1	1,675.0

Note: Figures include both directly operated and purchased transportation
Source: Federal Transit Administration, National Transit Database, 2009

Air Transportation

Airport Name and Code / Type of Service	Passenger Airlines[1]	Passenger Enplanements	Freight Carriers[2]	Freight (lbs.)
Miami International (MIA)				
Domestic service (U.S. carriers - 2010)	29	8,645,358	28	179,645,932
International service (U.S. carriers - 2009)	18	5,129,764	22	768,260,007

Note: (1) Includes all U.S.-based major, minor and commuter airlines that carried at least one passenger during the year; (2) Includes all U.S.-based airlines and freight carriers that transported at least one pound of freight during the year
Source: Bureau of Transportation Statistics, The Intermodal Transportation Database, Air Carriers: T-100 Domestic Market (U.S. Carriers), 2010; Bureau of Transportation Statistics, The Intermodal Transportation Database, Air Carriers: T-100 International Market (U.S. Carriers), 2009

Other Transportation Statistics

Interstate highways: I-95
Amtrak service: Yes
Major waterways/ports: Port of Miami; Atlantic Intracoastal Waterway
Source: Amtrak.com; Google Maps

BUSINESSES

Major Business Headquarters

Company Name	Rankings	
	Fortune[1]	Forbes[2]
Brightstar	-	154
Burger King	-	170
Ryder System	437	-
Southern Wine & Spirits	-	30
World Fuel Services	133	-

Note: (1) Fortune 500—companies that produce a 10-K are ranked 1 to 500 based on 2010 revenue; (2) all private companies with at least $2 billion in annual revenue are ranked 1 to 223; companies listed are headquartered in the city; dashes indicate no ranking
Source: Fortune, "Fortune 500," May 23, 2011; Forbes, "America's Largest Private Companies," November 3, 2010

Fast-Growing Businesses

According to *Inc.*, Miami is home to three of America's 500 fastest-growing private companies: **merchant one; The Retail Outsource; US Media Consulting**. Criteria: must be an independent, privately-held, for-profit, U.S. corporation, proprietorship or partnership; revenues of at least $80,000 in 2006 and $2 million in 2009; four-year operating/sales history; holding companies, regulated banks, and utilities were excluded. *Inc., "America's 500 Fastest-Growing Private Companies," September 2010*

According to Deloitte, Miami is home to two of North America's 500 fastest-growing high-technology companies: **Avisena; Terremark Worldwide**. Companies are ranked by percentage growth in revenue over a five-year period. Criteria for inclusion: company must be headquartered within North America; company must own proprietary intellectual property or proprietary technology that contributes to a significant portion of the company's operating revenue or devotes a significant proportion of revenues to research and development of technology; company must have been in business for a minumum of five years with 2005 operating revenues of at least $50,000 USD/CD and 2009 operating revenues of at least $5 million USD/CD. *Deloitte Touche Tohmatsu, 2010 Deloitte Technology Fast 500*[TM]

Minority Business Opportunity

Miami is home to 67 companies which are on the *Hispanic Business 500* list (500 largest U.S. Hispanic-owned companies based on 2009 revenue): **Brightstar Corp.; Quirch Foods Co.; Precision Trading Corp.; El Dorado Furniture Corp.; MCM; Refricenter of Miami; Rowland Coffee Roasters; First Equity Mortgage Bankers; Headquarter Toyota; Miami Automotive Retail; Tire Group International; Kira; Vila & Son Landscape Corp.; Metro Ford; John Keeler & Co.; R.C. Aluminum Industries; South Dade Automotive; Psychcare; Century Metal & Supplies; Metric Engineering; Link Construction Group; Softech International; AZF Automotive Group; Everglades Steel Corp. & Medley Steel Corp.; Inktel Direct Corp.; Solo Printing; Adonel Concrete Pumping & Finishing of S. FL; Fru-Veg Marketing; Intermarket Corp.; Jorda Enterprises; Express Travel of Miami; Bermello Ajamil & Partners; Original Impressions; Roach Busters Bug Killers of America; Mercedes Electric Supply; Granada Insurance Co.; Protec; Viña & Son Food Distributor; Budget Construction Co.; Rey's Pizza Corp.; Interamerican Bank; LACE Foodservice; Cherokee Enterprises; Plastec USA; Vista Color Corp.; Nital Trading Co.; Gancedo Lumber Co.; South Miami Pharmacy; X-EETO; Florida Lumber Co.; American Fasteners Corp.; Envirowaste Services Group; A&P Consulting Transportation Engineers; ProTranslating.; Island Dairy Distributors; Structural Prestressed Industries; Wendium of Florida; Tire Masters International; Honshy Electric Co.; The Perishable Specialist; F.R. Aleman & Associates; Future Force Personnel; Meridian Partners; Gem Paver Systems; WONEF-Longwood; Beam Radio; T&S Roofing Systems**. Companies included must show at least 51 percent ownership by Hispanic U.S. citizens, and must maintain headquarters in one of the 50 states or Washington, D.C. *Hispanic Business, "Hispanic Business 500," June 2010*

Miami is home to 11 companies which are on the *Hispanic Business* Fastest-Growing 100 list (greatest sales growth from 2005 to 2009): **Link Construction Group; AZF Automotive Group; X-EETO; Cherokee Enterprises; Softech International; ProTranslating; Tire Group International; Solo Printing; Nital Trading Co.; The Perishable Specialist; Century Metal & Supplies**. Companies included must show at least 51 percent ownership by Hispanic U.S. citizens, and must maintain headquarters in one of the 50 states or Washington, D.C. In addition, companies must have minimum revenues of $200,000 for calendar year 2005. *Hispanic Business, July/August 2010*

Minority- and Women-Owned Businesses

Group	All Firms		Firms with Paid Employees			
	Firms	Sales ($000)	Firms	Sales ($000)	Employees	Payroll ($000)
Asian	1,738	629,557	579	586,220	2,895	58,879
Black	9,448	492,059	588	337,832	4,470	75,101
Hispanic	53,237	12,035,979	6,320	10,467,657	35,450	1,128,981
Women	24,414	2,443,049	2,705	1,920,188	14,331	420,472
All Firms	85,146	65,730,894	15,130	62,998,520	321,387	15,802,112

Note: Figures cover firms located in the city; minority- and women-owned business are defined as firms in which the corresponding group own 51% or more of the stock or equity of the company
Source: U.S. Census Bureau, 2007 Economic Census, Survey of Business Owners

HOTELS

Hotels/Motels

Area	5 Star		4 Star		3 Star		2 Star		1 Star		Not Rated	
	Num.	Pct.3	Num.	Pct.3	Num.	Pct.3	Num.	Pct.3	Num.	Pct.3	Num.	Pct.3
City[1]	8	2.3	60	17.0	145	41.2	111	31.5	5	1.4	23	6.5
Total[2]	119	0.7	927	5.8	4,906	30.5	7,992	49.7	526	3.3	1,625	10.1

Note: (1) Figures cover Miami and vicinity; (2) Figures cover all 100 cities in this book; (3) Percentage of hotels which are a given star rating; Star ratings are determined by expedia.com and offer an indication of the general quality of a particular hotel.
Source: expedia.com, May 5, 2011

The Miami metro area is home to five of the top 218 hotels in the U.S. according to *Travel & Leisure*: **Ritz-Carlton, Key Biscayne** (#129); **Four Seasons Hotel, Miami** (#135); **Biltmore Hotel** (#168); **Ritz-Carlton, South Beach** (#185); **W South Beach** (#203). Criteria: service; location; rooms; food; and value. *Travel & Leisure, "T+L 500, The World's Best Hotels 2011"*

The Miami metro area is home to three of the top 100 hotels in the U.S. according to *Condé Nast Traveler*: **The Setai** (#10); **Mandarin Oriental** (#47); **Four Seasons** (#58). The selections are based on over 25,000 responses to the magazine's annual Readers' Choice Survey. *Condé Nast Traveler, "2010 Readers' Choice Awards"*

EVENT SITES

Major Stadiums, Arenas, and Auditoriums

Name	Max. Capacity
American Airlines Arena	19,600
Arnold Hall and Coliseum, Fair Expo Center	7,460
Bayfront Park Amphitheater	6,500
Edwards Hall, Fair Expo Center	5,083
FIU Stadium	18,000
James L. Knight Center	4,646
Sun Life Stadium	36,500
U.S. Century Bank Arena	5,000

Source: Original research

Convention Centers

Name	Overall Space (sq. ft.)	Exhibit Space (sq. ft.)	Meeting Space (sq. ft.)	Meeting Rooms
Coconut Grove Convention Center	n/a	n/a	150,000	n/a
Miami Beach Convention Center	1,000,000	100,000	500,000	70

Note: n/a not available
Source: Original research

Living Environment

COST OF LIVING

Cost of Living Index

Composite Index	Groceries	Housing	Utilities	Trans-portation	Health Care	Misc. Goods/ Services
106.0	110.9	107.7	91.9	108.8	105.7	106.2

Note: U.S. = 100; Figures cover the Miami-Dade County FL urban area.
Source: The Council for Community and Economic Research, ACCRA Cost of Living Index, 2010

Grocery Prices

Area[1]	T-Bone Steak ($/pound)	Frying Chicken ($/pound)	Whole Milk ($/half gal.)	Eggs ($/dozen)	Orange Juice ($/64 oz.)	Coffee ($/11.5 oz.)
City[2]	9.76	1.26	2.44	1.63	3.15	3.44
Avg.	9.04	1.16	2.02	1.47	3.08	3.65
Min.	6.97	0.84	1.46	0.96	2.39	2.64
Max.	13.93	2.51	3.58	3.01	4.94	6.32

Note: (1) Values for the local area are compared with the average, minimum and maximum values for all 338 areas in the Cost of Living Index; (2) Figures cover the Miami-Dade County FL urban area; **T-Bone Steak** *(price per pound);* **Frying Chicken** *(price per pound, whole fryer);* **Whole Milk** *(half gallon carton);* **Eggs** *(price per dozen, Grade A, large);* **Orange Juice** *(64 oz. Tropicana or Florida Natural);* **Coffee** *(11.5 oz. can, vacuum-packed, Maxwell House, Hills Bros, or Folgers).*
Source: The Council for Community and Economic Research, ACCRA Cost of Living Index, 2010

Housing and Utility Costs

Area[1]	New Home Price ($)	Apartment Rent ($/month)	All Electric ($/month)	Part Electric ($/month)	Other Energy ($/month)	Telephone ($/month)
City[2]	266,107	1,433	169.06	-	-	22.44
Avg.	293,442	810	166.39	91.93	83.82	26.93
Min.	182,545	453	119.21	44.47	36.85	17.98
Max.	1,123,114	2,776	307.53	218.20	313.90	39.15

Note: (1) Values for the local area are compared with the average, minimum and maximum values for all 338 areas in the Cost of Living Index; (2) Figures cover the Miami-Dade County FL urban area; **New Home Price** *(2,400 sf living area, 8,000 sf lot, in urban area with full utilities);* **Apartment Rent** *(950 sf 2 bedroom/1.5 or 2 bath, unfurnished, excluding all utilities except water);* **All Electric** *(average monthly cost for an all-electric home);* **Part Electric** *(average monthly cost for a part-electric home);* **Other Energy** *(average monthly cost for natural gas, fuel oil, coal, wood, and any other forms of energy except electricity);* **Telephone** *(price includes basic monthly rate for a private residential line plus additional local usage charges incurred by a family of four).*
Source: The Council for Community and Economic Research, ACCRA Cost of Living Index, 2010

Health Care, Transportation, and Other Costs

Area[1]	Doctor ($/visit)	Dentist ($/visit)	Optometrist ($/visit)	Gasoline ($/gallon)	Beauty Salon ($/visit)	Men's Shirt ($)
City[2]	90.57	89.88	79.93	2.80	45.87	24.40
Avg.	89.44	78.95	87.40	2.73	31.92	24.83
Min.	57.00	54.25	48.32	2.44	19.17	13.67
Max.	149.90	136.73	174.22	3.75	62.81	47.89

Note: (1) Values for the local area are compared with the average, minimum and maximum values for all 338 areas in the Cost of Living Index; (2) Figures cover the Miami-Dade County FL urban area; **Doctor** *(general practitioners routine exam of an established patient);* **Dentist** *(adult teeth cleaning and periodic oral examination);* **Optometrist** *(full vision eye exam for established adult patient);* **Gasoline** *(one gallon regular unleaded, national brand, including all taxes, cash price at self-service pump if available);* **Beauty Salon** *(woman's shampoo, trim, and blow-dry);* **Men's Shirt** *(cotton/polyester dress shirt, pinpoint weave, long sleeves).*
Source: The Council for Community and Economic Research, ACCRA Cost of Living Index, 2010

HOUSING

House Price Index (HPI)

Area	National Ranking[2]	Quarterly Change (%)	One-Year Change (%)	Five-Year Change (%)
MD[1]	249	-1.52	-4.05	-30.80
U.S.[3]	-	-0.84	-3.95	-11.45

Note: The HPI is a weighted repeat sales index. It measures average price changes in repeat sales or refinancings on the same properties. This information is obtained by reviewing repeat mortgage transactions on single-family properties whose mortgages have been purchased or securitized by Fannie Mae or Freddie Mac in January 1975; (1) Metropolitan Division - see Appendix B for areas included; (2) Rankings are based on annual percentage change for all metro areas containing at least 15,000 transactions over the last 10 years and ranges from 1 to 309; (3) figures based on a weighted average of Census Division estimates; all figures are for the period ending December 31, 2010
Source: Federal Housing Finance Agency, House Price Index, February 24, 2011

House Price Valuations

Area	Q4 2005		Q4 2006		Q4 2007		Q4 2008		Q4 2009	
	Price ($000)	Over-valuation	Price ($000)	Over-valuation	Price ($000)	Over-valuation	Price ($000)	Over-valuation	Price ($000)	Over-valuation
MD[1]	281.3	49.4	307.2	48.8	307.4	45.0	206.9	-2.6	180.5	-15.6

Note: Figures show the percentage of over- or under-valuation of single family homes relative to statistically normal house values (e.g. a value of 23.6 indicates that house values are 23.6% overvalued). Statistically normal house values are based on house prices, interest rates, household incomes, population densities, and any historical premiums or discounts metropolitan areas have exhibited over time; (1) Figures cover the Miami-Miami Beach-Kendall, FL Metropolitan Division - see Appendix B for areas included
Source: Global Insight/PNC Financial Services Group, House Prices in America: 4th Quarter 2009 Update

Median Single-Family Home Prices

Area	2008	2009	2010p	Percent Change 2009 to 2010
MSA[1]	285.1	211.2	200.8	-4.9
U.S. Average	196.6	172.1	173.2	0.6

Note: Figures are median sales prices of existing single-family homes in thousands of dollars; (p) preliminary; n/a not available; (1) Metropolitan Statistical Area - see Appendix B for areas included
Source: National Association of Realtors, Median Sales Price of Existing Single-Family Homes for Metropolitan Areas, 4th Quarter 2010

Median Apartment Condo-Coop Home Prices

Area	2008	2009	2010p	Percent Change 2009 to 2010
MSA[1]	161.6	107.4	92.2	-14.2
U.S. Average	209.8	175.6	171.7	-2.2

Note: Figures are median sales prices of existing apartment condo-coop homes in thousands of dollars; (p) preliminary; n/a not available; (1) Metropolitan Statistical Area - see Appendix B for areas included
Source: National Association of Realtors, Median Sales Price of Existing Apartment Condo-Coop Homes for Metropolitan Areas, 4th Quarter 2010

Year Housing Structure Built

Area	2000 or Later	1990 -1999	1980 -1989	1970 -1979	1960 -1969	1950 -1959	1940 -1949	Before 1940	Median Year
City	13.3	6.7	7.9	15.3	11.6	17.5	17.6	10.2	1964
MSA[1]	12.4	14.6	19.7	23.5	13.0	10.9	3.6	2.2	1979
U.S.	12.5	14.0	14.2	16.5	11.4	11.3	5.8	14.3	1974

Note: Figures are percentages except for Median Year; (1) Metropolitan Statistical Area - see Appendix B for areas included
Source: U.S. Census Bureau, 2007-2009 American Community Survey 3-Year Estimates

HEALTH

Health Risk Data

Category	MSA[1] (%)	U.S. (%)
Adults who have been told they have high blood pressure	31.8	28.7
Adults who have been told they have high blood cholesterol	38.2	37.5
Adults who have been told they have diabetes[3]	10.3	8.3
Adults who have been told they have arthritis	22.1	26.0
Adults who have been told they currently have asthma	4.6	8.8
Adults who are current smokers	11.3	17.9
Adults who are heavy drinkers[4]	3.1	5.1
Adults who are binge drinkers[5]	12.0	15.8
Adults who are overweight (BMI 25.0 - 29.9)	38.1	36.2
Adults who are obese (BMI 30.0 - 99.8)	23.7	26.9
Adults who participated in any physical activities in the past month	75.5	76.2
Adults 50+ who have ever had a sigmoidoscopy or colonoscopy[2]	58.8	62.2
Women 40+ who have had a mammogram within the past two years[2]	83.0	76.0
Adults age 18–64 who have any kind of health care coverage	80.7	83.1

Note: Data as of 2009 unless otherwise noted; (1) Figures cover the Miami-Fort Lauderdale-Miami Beach, FL Metropolitan Statistical Area - see Appendix B for areas included; (2) Data as of 2008; (3) Figures do not include pregnancy-related, borderline, or pre-diabetes; (4) Heavy drinkers are classified as males having more than two drinks per day or females having more than one drink per day; (5) Binge drinkers are classified as males having five or more drinks on one occasion or females having four or more drinks on one occasion
Source: Centers for Disease Control and Prevention, Behavioral Risk Factor Surveillance System, SMART: Selected Metropolitan/Micropolitan Area Risk Trends, 2008, 2009

Mortality Rates for the Top 10 Causes of Death in the U.S.

ICD-10[a] Sub-Chapter	ICD-10[a] Code	Age-Adjusted Mortality Rate[1] per 100,000 population	
		County[2]	U.S.
Malignant neoplasms	C00-C97	145.6	180.9
Ischaemic heart diseases	I20-I25	143.7	135.0
Other forms of heart disease	I30-I51	35.5	50.0
Cerebrovascular diseases	I60-I69	32.5	44.1
Chronic lower respiratory diseases	J40-J47	25.2	41.5
Other degenerative diseases of the nervous system	G30-G31	25.2	23.6
Diabetes mellitus	E10-E14	23.3	23.5
Other external causes of accidental injury	W00-X59	16.3	23.5
Organic, including symptomatic, mental disorders	F01-F09	15.3	22.2
Influenza and pneumonia	J09-J18	10.1	18.1

Note: (a) ICD-10 = International Classification of Diseases 10th Revision; (1) Mortality rates are a three year average covering 2005-2007; (2) Figures cover Miami-Dade County
Source: Centers for Disease Control and Prevention, National Center for Health Statistics. Compressed Mortality File 1999-2007. CDC WONDER On-line Database, compiled from Compressed Mortality File 1999-2007 Series 20 No. 2M, 2010.

Mortality Rates for Selected Causes of Death

ICD-10[a] Sub-Chapter	ICD-10[a] Code	Age-Adjusted Mortality Rate[1] per 100,000 population	
		County[2]	U.S.
Assault	X85-Y09	9.2	6.0
Human immunodeficiency virus (HIV) disease	B20-B24	17.1	4.0
Hypertensive diseases	I10-I15	19.0	18.0
Intentional self-harm	X60-X84	8.7	11.0
Malnutrition	E40-E46	0.3	0.8
Obesity and other hyperalimentation	E65-E68	1.3	1.5
Transport accidents	V01-V99	15.8	15.6
Viral hepatitis	B15-B19	2.3	2.1

Note: (a) ICD-10 = International Classification of Diseases 10th Revision; (1) Mortality rates are a three year average covering 2005-2007; (2) Figures cover Miami-Dade County
Source: Centers for Disease Control and Prevention, National Center for Health Statistics. Compressed Mortality File 1999-2007. CDC WONDER On-line Database, compiled from Compressed Mortality File 1999-2007 Series 20 No. 2M, 2010.

Distribution of Physicians and Dentists

Area[1]	Dentists[2]	D.O.[3]	M.D.[4]				
			Total	Family/ General Practice	Pediatrics	Medical Specialties	Surgical Specialties
Local (number)	1,079	336	5,460	680	476	2,224	1,171
Local (rate[5])	4.4	1.4	22.0	2.7	1.9	9.0	4.7
U.S. (rate[5])	4.5	1.9	18.3	2.5	1.4	6.8	4.1

Note: Data as of 2008 unless noted; (1) Local data covers Miami-Dade County; (2) Data as of 2007; (3) Doctor of Osteopathic Medicine; (4) Includes active, non-federal, patient-care, office-based Doctors of Medicine; (5) rate per 10,000 population
Source: Area Resource File (ARF). 2009-2010 Release. U.S. Department of Health and Human Services, Health Resources and Services Administration, Bureau of Health Professions, Rockville, MD, August 2010

Hospitals

Miami has the following hospitals: 12 general medical and surgical; 1 eye, ear, nose and throat; 2 rehabilitation; 2 long-term acute care; 1 children's general.
AHA Guide to the Healthcare Field 2010

According to *U.S. News,* the Miami-Miami Beach-Kendall, FL Metropolitan Division is home to three of the best hospitals in the U.S.: **Bascom Palmer Eye Institute at the University of Miami**; **Mount Sinai Medical Center**; **University of Miami-Jackson Memorial Hospital**. The hospitals listed were highly ranked in at least one adult specialty. *U.S. News Online, "America's Best Hospitals 2010-11"*

According to *U.S. News,* the Miami-Miami Beach-Kendall, FL Metropolitan Division is home to two of the best children's hospitals in the U.S.: **Holtz Children's Hospital at UM-Jackson Memorial Hospital**; **Miami Children's Hospital**. The hospitals listed were highly ranked in at least one pediatric specialty. *U.S. News Online, "America's Best Children's Hospitals 2010-11"*

EDUCATION

Public School District Statistics

District Name	Schls	Pupils	Pupil/ Teacher Ratio	Minority Pupils[1] (%)	Free Lunch Eligible[2] (%)	IEP[3] (%)
Miami-Dade	496	345,525	15.4	90.9	52.8	11.3

Note: Table includes school districts with 2,000 or more students; (1) Percentage of students that are not non-Hispanic white; (2) Percentage of students that are eligible for the free lunch program; (3) Percentage of students that have an Individualized Education Program.
Source: U.S. Department of Education, National Center for Education Statistics, Common Core of Data, Local Education Agency (School District) Universe Survey: School Year 2008-2009; U.S. Department of Education, National Center for Education Statistics, Common Core of Data, Public Elementary/Secondary School Universe Survey: School Year 2008-2009

Top Public High Schools

High School Name	Index[1]	Rank[1]	Subsidized Lunch (%)[2]	E&E (%)[3]
American[4]	1.789	862	69.0	15.3
Coral Reef[4]	5.660	36	45.0	78.0
Design & Architecture Sr High	3.464	164	40.0	100.0
Doral Academy Charter	1.078	1633	52.0	31.4
G. Holmes Braddock[4]	1.550	1099	64.0	17.9
Krop[4]	1.754	903	44.0	33.1
MAST Academy	3.784	115	30.0	67.6
Miami	1.560	1092	85.2	25.0
Miami Central	1.382	1284	78.9	3.0
Miami Coral Park	1.386	1281	62.0	n/a
Miami Edison	1.497	1154	82.0	n/a
Miami Jackson	1.299	1373	83.1	5.0
Miami Killian	2.071	663	45.5	30.0
Miami Palmetto	3.376	180	20.1	55.0
Miami Sunset	1.240	1439	57.5	15.0
New World School of the Arts	2.064	673	30.0	25.0
Robert Morgan	2.132	630	42.6	n/a
School for Advanced Studies	5.309	47	44.0	85.4
Southwest Miami	2.055	681	65.5	n/a

Note: (1) Public schools are ranked according to a ratio that is the number of Advanced Placement, International Baccalaureate, and/or Cambridge tests taken by all students at a school in 2009 divided by the number of graduating seniors. All of the schools on the list have an index of at least 1.000; they are in the top six percent of public schools measured this way. The rankings range from 1 to 1,734; (2) Percentage of students receiving federally subsidized meals; (3) E & E stands for equity and excellence percentage: the portion of all graduating seniors at a school that had at least one passing grade on one AP or IB test; (4) Schools that offer International Baccalaureate or Cambridge exams; (5) School is unranked, but has been identified by Newsweek as one of the nation's most elite public high schools; n/a not available
Source: Newsweek Online, "Top High Schools 2010"

Highest Level of Education

Area	Less than H.S.	H.S. Diploma	Some College, No Deg.	Associate Degree	Bachelors Degree	Masters Degree	Profess. School Degree	Doctorate Degree
City	36.3	25.0	11.2	5.6	13.1	4.7	2.8	1.3
MSA[1]	17.5	27.6	17.7	8.1	18.7	6.5	2.8	1.1
U.S.	15.3	29.0	20.7	7.5	17.4	7.0	1.9	1.1

Note: Figures are 2010 estimated percentages and cover persons age 25 and over; (1) Metropolitan Statistical Area - see Appendix B for areas included
Source: Claritas, Inc.

Educational Attainment by Race

Area	High School Graduate (%)					Bachelor's Degree (%)				
	Total	White	Black	Asian	Hisp.[2]	Total	White	Black	Asian	Hisp.[2]
City	67.9	93.7	62.6	87.1	63.9	23.3	58.9	9.8	62.6	19.3
MSA[1]	82.5	92.2	75.7	87.1	74.5	28.6	36.9	17.2	48.0	23.6
U.S.	84.9	90.0	80.7	85.5	60.7	27.8	30.9	17.5	49.7	12.7

Note: Figures shown cover persons 25 years old and over; (1) Metropolitan Statistical Area - see Appendix B for areas included; (2) people of Hispanic origin can be of any race
Source: U.S. Census Bureau, 2007-2009 American Community Survey 3-Year Estimates

School Enrollment by Grade and Control

Area	Preschool (%)		Kindergarten (%)		Grades 1 - 4 (%)		Grades 5 - 8 (%)		Grades 9 - 12 (%)	
	Public	Private	Public	Private	Public	Private	Public	Private	Public	Private
City	61.4	38.6	86.0	14.0	89.2	10.8	91.2	8.8	89.7	10.3
MSA[1]	43.2	56.8	82.2	17.8	86.8	13.2	86.1	13.9	87.1	12.9
U.S.	54.3	45.7	86.4	13.6	88.9	11.1	89.1	10.9	90.2	9.8

Note: Figures shown cover persons 3 years old and over; (1) Metropolitan Statistical Area - see Appendix B for areas included
Source: U.S. Census Bureau, 2007-2009 American Community Survey 3-Year Estimates

Average Salaries of Public School Classroom Teachers

Area	2009-10		2010-11		Percent Change 2009-10 to 2010-11	Percent Change 2000-01 to 2010-11
	Dollars	Rank[1]	Dollars	Rank[1]		
Florida	46,708	37	46,702	47	-0.01	22.2
U.S. Average	55,202	-	56,069	-	1.57	29.3

Note: (1) State rank ranges from 1 to 51 where 1 indicates highest salary.
*Source: National Education Association, Rankings & Estimates: Rankings of the States 2010
and Estimates of School Statistics 2011, December 2010*

Higher Education

Four-Year Colleges			Two-Year Colleges			Medical Schools[1]	Law Schools[2]	Voc/ Tech[3]
Public	Private Non-profit	Private For-profit	Public	Private Non-profit	Private For-profit			
2	5	5	3	0	11	1	1	21

*Note: Figures cover institutions located within the city limits and include main campuses only; (1) includes
schools accredited by the Liaison Committee on Medical Education and the American Osteopathic Association;
(2) includes American Bar Association-accredited law schools; (3) includes all schools with programs that are
less than 2 years.*
*Source: National Center for Education Statistics, Integrated Postsecondary Education System (IPEDS) Peer
Analysis System, 2010-11; U.S. News & World Report, Medical School Directory, 2011; U.S. News & World
Report, Law School Directory, 2011*

According to *U.S. News & World Report,* the Miami-Miami Beach-Kendall, FL Metropolitan
Division is home to one of the top 197 national universities in the U.S.: **University of Miami**
(#47). The rankings are based on quantitative measurements such as peer assessment,
retention, faculty resources, student selectivity, financial resources, graduation rate, and
alumni giving rate. *U.S. News & World Report, "America's Best Colleges 2011"*

According to *Forbes,* the Miami-Miami Beach-Kendall, FL Metropolitan Division is home to
one of the top 75 business schools in the U.S.: **Miami** (#43). The rankings are based on the
return on investment that graduates of the Class of 2004 received (median salary five years
after graduation). *Forbes, "Best Business Schools," August 5, 2009*

PRESIDENTIAL ELECTION

2008 Presidential Election Results

Area	Obama	McCain	Nader	Other
Miami-Dade County	57.8	41.7	0.2	0.3
U.S.	52.9	45.6	0.6	0.9

Note: Results are percentages and may not add to 100% due to rounding
Source: Dave Leip's Atlas of U.S. Presidential Elections, www.uselectionatlas.org

EMPLOYERS

Major Employers

Company Name	Industry	Type of Site
Aluma Craft Products	Metal doors, sash, and trim	Single
American Woolen Company	Broadwoven fabric mills, wool	Single
Baker Norton US	Pharmaceutical preparations	Single
Baptist Health South Florida	General medical and surgical hospitals	Headquarters
Baptist Hospital Miami	General medical and surgical hospitals	Headquarters
Board of Gov State Univ Sys Of	Colleges and universities	Headquarters
Bursars Office	Colleges and universities	Branch
Cordis Corporation	Surgical and medical instruments	Headquarters
Costa Farms	Ornamental nursery products	Headquarters
Goodwill Industries S Fla	Job training and related services	Headquarters
Interfoods of America	Eating places	Headquarters
Kendall Campus	Junior colleges	Branch
Medical Center Campus	Vocational schools, nec	Branch
Mercy Hospital	General medical and surgical hospitals	Headquarters
Miami Childrens Hospital	Specialty hospitals, except psychiatric	Headquarters
Miami Vamc	General medical and surgical hospitals	Branch
Mount Sinai & Miami Heart	General medical and surgical hospitals	Headquarters
Mount Sinai Med Ctr Fla	General medical and surgical hospitals	Branch
Royal Caribbean Cruises Ltd	Data processing and preparation	Branch
Royal Caribbean International	Deep sea passenger transportation, except ferry	Headquarters
Royal Caribbean International	Deep sea passenger transportation, except ferry	Branch
Sunrise Group The	Residential care	Single
University of Miami Hospital	General medical and surgical hospitals	Branch
Wolfson Campus	Junior colleges	Branch

Note: Companies shown are located within the Miami metropolitan area; nec = not elsewhere classified.
Source: www.zapdata.com, January 2011

Best Companies to Work For

Burger King, headquartered in Miami, is among the "Best Companies for Multicultural Women." *Working Mother* selected 20 companies based on a detailed application completed by each company. Private and public firms based in the United States were eligible to apply. Government agencies, companies in the human resources field and non-autonomous divisions of companies were not eligible. Companies supplied data about the hiring, pay and promotion of multicultural employees. Applications focused on representation of multicultural women, recruitment, retention and advancement programs, and company culture. *Working Mother, "20 Best Companies for Multicultural Women 2010"*

PUBLIC SAFETY

Crime Rate

Area	All Crimes	Violent Crimes				Property Crimes		
		Murder	Forcible Rape	Robbery	Aggrav. Assault	Burglary	Larceny -Theft	Motor Vehicle Theft
City	6,145.2	14.1	15.5	499.5	659.6	1,158.4	3,193.2	605.0
Suburbs[1]	5,665.4	7.6	24.8	240.4	445.2	993.1	3,488.4	466.0
Metro[2]	5,746.5	8.7	23.2	284.2	481.4	1,021.0	3,438.5	489.4
U.S.	3,465.5	5.0	28.7	133.0	262.8	716.3	2,060.9	258.8

Note: Figures are crimes per 100,000 population; (1) All areas within the metro area that are located outside the city limits; (2) Metropolitan Division - see Appendix B for areas included
Source: FBI Uniform Crime Reports, 2009

Hate Crimes

Area	Number of Quarters Reported	Bias Motivation				
		Race	Religion	Sexual Orientation	Ethnicity	Disability
City	4	0	0	0	0	0

Source: Federal Bureau of Investigation, Hate Crime Statistics 2009

Identity Theft Consumer Complaints

Area	Complaints	Complaints per 100,000 Population	Rank[2]
MSA[1]	9,972	184.2	1
U.S.	250,854	81.3	-

Note: (1) Metropolitan Statistical Area - see Appendix B for areas included; (2) Rank ranges from 1 to 384 where 1 indicates greatest number of complaints per 100,000 population
Source: Federal Trade Commission, Consumer Sentinel Network Data Book for January - December 2010

RECREATION

Culture

Dance[1]	Theatre[1]	Instrumental Music[1]	Vocal Music[1]	Series/ Festivals	Museums	Zoos and Aquariums[2]
2	3	3	1	4	11	1

Note: (1) Number of professional perfoming groups; (2) AZA-accredited
Source: The Grey House Performing Arts Directory, 2011-2012; Official Museum Directory, 2010; American Association of Museums, AAM Member Museums, March 2011; Association of Zoos & Aquariums, AZA Member Zoos & Aquariums, May 2011

Professional Sports Teams

Team Name	League
Florida Marlins	Major League Baseball (MLB)
Florida Panthers	National Hockey League (NHL)
Miami Dolphins	National Football League (NFL)
Miami Heat	National Basketball Association (NBA)

Note: Includes teams located in the Miami-Fort Lauderdale metro area.
Source: Original research

CLIMATE

Average and Extreme Temperatures

Temperature	Jan	Feb	Mar	Apr	May	Jun	Jul	Aug	Sep	Oct	Nov	Dec	Yr.
Extreme High (°F)	88	89	92	96	95	98	98	98	97	95	89	87	98
Average High (°F)	75	77	79	82	85	88	89	90	88	85	80	77	83
Average Temp. (°F)	68	69	72	75	79	82	83	83	82	78	73	69	76
Average Low (°F)	59	60	64	68	72	75	76	76	76	72	66	61	69
Extreme Low (°F)	30	35	32	42	55	60	69	68	68	53	39	30	30

Note: Figures cover the years 1948-1990
Source: National Climatic Data Center, International Station Meteorological Climate Summary, 9/96

Average Precipitation/Snowfall/Humidity

Precip./Humidity	Jan	Feb	Mar	Apr	May	Jun	Jul	Aug	Sep	Oct	Nov	Dec	Yr.
Avg. Precip. (in.)	1.9	2.0	2.3	3.0	6.2	8.7	6.1	7.5	8.2	6.6	2.7	1.8	57.1
Avg. Snowfall (in.)	0	0	0	0	0	0	0	0	0	0	0	0	0
Avg. Rel. Hum. 7am (%)	84	84	82	80	81	84	84	86	88	87	85	84	84
Avg. Rel. Hum. 4pm (%)	59	57	57	57	62	68	66	67	69	65	63	60	63

Note: Figures cover the years 1948-1990; Tr = Trace amounts (<0.05 in. of rain; <0.5 in. of snow)
Source: National Climatic Data Center, International Station Meteorological Climate Summary, 9/96

Weather Conditions

Temperature			Daytime Sky			Precipitation		
32°F & below	45°F & below	90°F & above	Clear	Partly cloudy	Cloudy	0.01 inch or more precip.	0.1 inch or more snow/ice	Thunder-storms
< 1	7	55	48	263	54	128	0	74

Note: Figures are average number of days per year and cover the years 1948-1990
Source: National Climatic Data Center, International Station Meteorological Climate Summary, 9/96

HAZARDOUS WASTE

Superfund Sites

Miami has two hazardous waste sites on the EPA's Superfund Final National Priorities List: **Airco Plating Co.**; **Miami Drum Services**. *U.S. Environmental Protection Agency, Final National Priorities List, April 1, 2011*

**AIR & WATER
QUALITY**

Air Quality Index

Area	Percent of Days when Air Quality was...[2]				AQI Statistics	
	Good	Moderate	Unhealthy for Sensitive Groups	Unhealthy	Maximum	Median
Area[1]	90.5	8.0	1.5	0.0	139	33

*Note: The Air Quality Index (AQI) is an index for reporting daily air quality. EPA calculates the AQI for five major air pollutants regulated by the Clean Air Act: ground-level ozone, particle pollution (also known as particulate matter), carbon monoxide, sulfur dioxide, and nitrogen dioxide. The AQI runs from 0 to 500. The higher the AQI value, the greater the level of air pollution and the greater the health concern. There are six AQI categories: "Good" The AQI is between 0 and 50. Air quality is considered satisfactory; "Moderate" The AQI is between 51 and 100. Air quality is acceptable; "Unhealthy for Sensitive Groups" When AQI values are between 101 and 150, members of sensitive groups may experience health effects; "Unhealthy" When AQI values are between 151 and 200 everyone may begin to experience health effects; "Very Unhealthy" AQI values between 201 and 300 trigger a health alert; "Hazardous" AQI values over 300 trigger health warnings of emergency conditions; (1) Data covers Miami-Dade County; (2) Based on 275 days with AQI data in 2008; The EPA has suspended data updates while it assesses its data systems, including AirData reports and maps.
Source: U.S. Environmental Protection Agency, AirData Report, 2008*

Air Quality Index Pollutants

Area	Percent of Days when AQI Pollutant was...[2]					
	Carbon Monoxide	Nitrogen Dioxide	Ozone	Sulfur Dioxide	Particulate Matter 2.5	Particulate Matter 10
Area[1]	1.1	0.0	66.9	0.0	29.1	2.9

*Note: The Air Quality Index (AQI) is an index for reporting daily air quality. EPA calculates the AQI for five major air pollutants regulated by the Clean Air Act: ground-level ozone, particle pollution (also known as particulate matter), carbon monoxide, sulfur dioxide, and nitrogen dioxide. The AQI runs from 0 to 500. The higher the AQI value, the greater the level of air pollution and the greater the health concern; (1) Data covers Miami-Dade County; (2) Based on 275 days with AQI data in 2008; The EPA has suspended data updates while it assesses its data systems, including AirData reports and maps.
Source: U.S. Environmental Protection Agency, AirData Report, 2008*

Air Quality Index Trends

Area	Trend Sites (days)								All Sites (days)
	2002	2003	2004	2005	2006	2007	2008	2009	2009
MSA[1]	5	4	11	4	11	10	5	2	2

*Note: Figures are the number of days the AQI value exceeded 100 in a given year. An AQI value greater than 100 indicates that air quality would have been in the unhealthful range on that day. Data from exceptional events are included. These counts are presented in two ways. First, the counts are based on sites having an adequate record of monitoring data during the trend period (trend sites). These counts represent the relative change in the number of days with AQI values greater than 100. In the last column, the counts are based on all sites with data in the most recent year (because it is possible for a site to have data in the most recent year but not enough data to be a trend site); (1) Data covers the Miami-Fort Lauderdale-Miami Beach, FL Metropolitan Statistical Area - see Appendix B for areas included
Source: U.S. Environmental Protection Agency, Office of Air and Radiation, Air Quality Index Information, "Number of Days with Air Quality Index Values Greater than 100 and Trend Sites, 1990-2009, and at All Sites in 2009"*

Maximum Air Pollutant Concentrations

	Particulate Matter 10 (ug/m³)	Particulate Matter 2.5 (ug/m³)	Ozone (ppm)	Carbon Monoxide (ppm)	Sulfur Dioxide (ppm)	Nitrogen Dioxide (ppm)	Lead (ug/m³)
MSA[1] Level	65	16	0.064	2	0.014	0.009	n/a
NAAQS[2]	150	35	0.075	9	0.140	0.053	0.15
Met NAAQS[2]	Yes	Yes	Yes	Yes	Yes	Yes	n/a

*Note: Data from exceptional events are not included; (1) Data covers the Miami-Fort Lauderdale-Miami Beach, FL Metropolitan Statistical Area - see Appendix B for areas included; (2) National Ambient Air Quality Standards; n/a not available
Concentrations: Particulate Matter 10 (coarse particulate) - highest second maximum 24-hour concentration; Particulate Matter 2.5 (fine particulate) - highest 98th percentile 24-hour concentration; Ozone - highest fourth daily maximum 8-hour concentration; Carbon Monoxide - highest second maximum non-overlapping 8-hour concentration; Sulfur Dioxide - highest second maximum 24-hour concentration; Nitrogen Dioxide - highest arithmetic mean concentration; Lead - maximum running 3-month average
Units: ppm = parts per million; ug/m³ = micrograms per cubic meter
Source: U.S. Environmental Protection Agency, CBSA Factbook 2009, Air Quality Statistics by City, 2009*

Drinking Water

Water System Name	Pop. Served	Primary Water Source Type	Violations[1]	
			Health Based	Monitoring/ Reporting
MDWASA - Main System	2,100,000	Ground	0	0

Note: (1) Based on violation data from January 1, 2010 to December 31, 2010 (includes unresolved violations from earlier years)
Source: U.S. Environmental Protection Agency, Office of Ground Water and Drinking Water, Safe Drinking Water Information System (based on data extracted May 9, 2011)

Nashville, Tennessee

Background

Nashville, the capital of Tennessee, was founded on Christmas Day in 1779 by James Robertson and John Donelson, and sits in the minds of millions as the country music capital of the world. This is the place to record if you want to make it into the country music industry, and where the Grand Ole Opry—the longest-running radio show in the country—still captures the hearts of millions of devoted listeners. It is no wonder, given how profoundly this industry has touched people, names like Dolly, Chet, Loretta, Hank, and Johnny are more familiar than the city's true native sons: Andrew, James, and Sam. Jackson, Polk, and Houston, that is.

Nashville is home to Music Row, an area just to the southwest of downtown with hundreds of businesses related to the country music, gospel music, and contemporary Christian music industries. The USA Network's Nashville Star, a country music singing competition, is also held in the Acuff Theatre. The magnitude of Nashville's recording industry is impressive, but other industries are important to the city, such as health care management, automobile production, and printing and publishing.

Nashville is also a devoted patron of education. The Davidson Academy, forerunner of the George Peabody College for Teachers, was founded in Nashville, as were Vanderbilt and Fisk universities, the latter being the first private black university in the United States. Vanderbilt University and Medical Center is the region's largest non-governmental employer.

Nashville citizens take pride in their numerous museums, including the Adventure Science Center, with its new Sudekum Planetarium; the Aaron Douglas Gallery at Fisk University, which features a remarkable collection of African-American art; and the Carl Van Vechten Gallery, also at Fisk University, home to works by Alfred Stieglitz, Picasso, Cezanne, and Georgia O'Keefe. The Cheekwood Botanical Garden and Museum of Art includes 55 acres of gardens and contemporary art galleries.

Gracing the city are majestic mansions and plantations that testify to the mid nineteenth-century splendor for which the South came to be famous. Known as the "Queen of the Tennessee Plantations," the Belle Meade Plantation is an 1853 Greek Revival mansion crowning a 5,400-acre thoroughbred stud farm and nursery. The Belmont Mansion, built in 1850 by Adelicia Acklen, one of the wealthiest women in America, is constructed in the style of an Italian villa and was originally intended to be the summer home of the Acklens. Travelers' Rest Plantation served as a haven for weary travelers, past and present, and is Nashville's oldest plantation home open to the public. It features docents dressed in period costume who explain and demonstrate life in the plantations' heyday. Carnton Plantation was the site of the Civil War's Battle of Franklin, and The Hermitage was the home of Andrew Jackson, the seventh president of the United States. Tennessee's historic State Capitol Building, completed in 1859, has had much of its interior restored to its nineteenth-century appearance.

The Nashville area comprises many urban, suburban, rural, and historic districts, which can differ immensely from each other. Most of the best restaurants, clubs, and shops are on the west side of the Cumberland River, however, the east side encompasses fine neighborhoods, interesting homes, plenty of shopping, and good food, as well. Outdoor activities include camping, fishing, hiking, and biking at the many scenic and accessible lakes in the region.

Located on the Cumberland River in central Tennessee, Nashville's average relative humidity is moderate, as is its weather, with great temperature extremes a rarity. The city is not in the most common path of storms that cross the country, but is in a zone of moderate frequency for thunderstorms.

Rankings

General Rankings

- Nashville was ranked #281 out of 375 metro areas in *Cities Ranked & Rated*. Criteria: cost of living; climate; crime; transportation; economy and jobs; education; arts and culture; health and healthcare; leisure; quality of life. *Cities Ranked & Rated, 2nd Edition, 2007*

- Nashville was ranked #58 out of 379 metro areas in *Places Rated Almanac*. Criteria: health care; education; recreation; transportation; ambience; climate; crime; housing costs; jobs. *Places Rated Almanac, 7th Edition, 2007*

- *Men's Health Living* ranked 100 U.S. cities in terms of quality of life. Nashville was ranked #41 and received a grade of C. Criteria: number of fitness facilities; air quality; number of physicians; male/female ratio; education levels; household income; cost of living. *Men's Health Living, Spring 2008*

- Nashville was selected as one of "America's Top 100 Places to Live" by RelocateAmerica.com. Cities and towns nominated to be great places to live along with their key data regarding education, employment, economy, crime, parks, recreation and housing were reviewed, rated and judged by the Relocate-America.com editorial staff. *Relocate-America.com, "RelocateAmerica's Top 100 Places to Live in 2010"*

- Nashville was identified as one of the top places to live in the U.S. by Harris Interactive. The city ranked #7 out of 15. Criteria: 2,620 adults (age 18 and over) were polled and asked "if you could live in or near any city in the country except the one you live in or nearest to now, which city would you choose?" The poll was conducted online within the U.S. between September 14 and 20, 2010. *Harris Interactive, October 20, 2010*

- Nashville was selected as one of "America's Favorite Cities." The city ranked #10 in the "People" category. Respondents to an online survey were asked to rate 35 top urban destinations in the U.S. from a visitor's perspective. Criteria: attractive; friendly; stylish; intelligent; athletic/active; diverse. *Travelandleisure.com, "America's Favorite Cities 2010," November 2010*

- Nashville was selected as one of "America's Favorite Cities." The city ranked #5 in the "Nightlife" category. Respondents to an online survey were asked to rate 35 top urban destinations in the U.S. from a visitor's perspective. Criteria: cocktail hour; live music/concerts and bands; singles/bar scene. *Travelandleisure.com, "America's Favorite Cities 2010," November 2010*

Business/Finance Rankings

- A.G. Edwards ranked America's 500 top-performing communities based on their residents' personal savings and investing behavior. The Nashville metro area ranked #294 with an index score of 100.05 (national average = 100.00). A dozen statistical factors were measured including: participation in retirement savings plans; personal debt levels; and home ownership. *A.G. Edwards, "2007 Nest Egg Index," September 12, 2007*

- Nashville was selected as one of the "100 Best Places to Live and Launch" in the U.S. The city ranked #79. The editors at *Fortune Small Business* ranked 296 Census-designated metro areas by business friendliness (Launching Score, % New Businesses) and lifestyle offerings (Living Score). Then they picked the town within each of the top 100 metro areas that best blends business and pleasure. *Fortune Small Business, "100 Best Places to Live and Launch 2008," April 2008*

- *American City Business Journals* ranked America's 261 largest cities in terms of their resident's wealth. Nashville ranked #161. Criteria: per capita income; median household income; percentage of households with annual incomes of $200,000 or more; median home value. *American City Business Journals, www.bizjournals.com, "Where the Money Is: America's Wealth Centers," August 18, 2008*

- The Nashville metro area appeared on the Milken Institute "2010 Best Performing Metros" list. Rank: #84 out of 200 large metro areas. Criteria: job growth; wage and salary growth; high-tech output growth. *Milken Institute, "2010 Best Performing Metros"*

- The Nashville metro area was selected as one of the best cities for entrepreneurs in America by *Inc. Magazine*. Criteria: job-growth data for 335 metro areas was analyzed for: recent growth trend (the current and prior year's employment growth rates, with the current year emphasized); mid-term growth (the average annual 2002-2007 growth rate); long-term trend (the sum of the 2002-2007 and 1996-2001 employment growth rates multiplied by the ratio of the 1996-2001 growth rate over the 2002-2007 growth rate); current year growth. The Nashville metro area ranked #18 among large metro areas and #97 overall. *Inc. Magazine, "The Best Cities for Doing Business," July 2008*

- Nashville was ranked #92 out of 145 regions worldwide in terms of its "Knowledge Competitiveness Index." The index attempts to measure the knowledge-based development taking place throughout the world and is based on 19 measures of economic performance that indicate a region's ability to translate its knowledge capacity into economic value. *Centre for International Competitiveness, World Knowledge Competitiveness Index 2008*

- *Forbes* ranked the 200 most populous metro areas in the U.S. in terms of the "Best Places for Business and Careers." The Nashville metro area was ranked #31. Criteria: 12 metrics including costs (business and living), job growth (past and projected), income growth, educational attainment, projected economic growth, crime, cultural and recreational opportunities, net migration patterns, percentage of subprime mortgages handed out over a three-year period, and the number of highly ranked four-year colleges. *Forbes, "Best Places for Business and Careers," April 14, 2010*

Children/Family Rankings

- The Nashville metro area was selected as one of the "Best Cities for Relocating Families" by Worldwide ERC and Primacy Relocation. The 2008 study looked at nearly 50 factors important to relocating families including: recent job growth; nearby top-ranked colleges; in-state tuition for four-year public colleges; population growth since 2000; pediatricians per 100,000 population; and a Green Living index. *Worldwide ERC and Primacy Relocation, "2008 Best Cities for Relocating Families"*

- *Fit Pregnancy* magazine ranked the 50 best U.S. cities in which to have a baby. Nashville was ranked #33. Criteria: access to hospitals and doctors; affordability; birthing options; breastfeeding; child care; fertility laws/resources; maternal and infant health risk; parks/stroller friendliness; safety. *Fit Pregnancy, "The Best Cities in America to Have a Baby 2008"*

- Nashville was chosen as one of America's "100 Best Communities for Young People." The winners were selected based upon detailed information provided about each community's efforts to fulfill five essential promises critical to the well-being of young people: caring adults who are actively involved in their lives; safe places in which to learn and grow; a healthy start toward adulthood; an effective education that builds marketable skills; and opportunities to help others. *America's Promise Alliance, "100 Best Communities for Young People, 2010"*

Culture/Performing Arts Rankings

- The Nashville metro area was selected as one of the "Best Places for Artists in America" by *BusinessWeek.com*. Criteria: percentage of young people age 25 to 34; population diversity; concentration of museums, philharmonic orchestras, dance companies, theater troupes, library resources, and college arts programs. *BusinessWeek.com, "Best Places for Artists in America," February 26, 2007*

- Nashville was selected as one of "America's Top 25 Arts Destinations." The city ranked #18 in the big city (population 500,000 and over) category. Criteria: readers' top choices for arts travel destinations based on the richness and variety of visual arts sites, activities and events. *American Style, "America's Top 25 Arts Destinations," May 2010*

Dating/Romance Rankings

- Nashville appeared on *Men's Health's* list of the most sex-happy cities in America. The city ranked #18 of 100. Criteria: condom sales; birth rates; sex toy sales; rates of chlamydia, gonorrhea, and syphilis. *Men's Health, "America's Most Sex-Happy Cities," October 2010*

- *Men's Health* ranked 100 U.S. cities in terms of best (and worst) marriages. Nashville was ranked #43 (#1 = worst marriages). Criteria: rate of failed marriages; stringency of divorce laws; percentage of population who've split; number of licensed marriage and family therapists. *Men's Health, "Splitsville, USA," May 2010*

- Eli Lily and Company, in partnership with Sperling's BestPlaces, ranked the nation's 50 largest metro areas in terms of the "Most Romantic Cities for Baby Boomers." The Nashville metro area ranked #17. Criteria: marriage and divorce rates among "baby boomers" age 45 to 60; great restaurants; dance studios; chocolate, jewelry and flower sales. *Eli Lily and Company, "Most Romantic Cities for Baby Boomers," April 20, 2007*

- The Nashville metro area was selected as one of the "Best Cities for Relocating Singles" by Worldwide ERC and Primacy Relocation. The area ranked #41 out of the 100 largest metro areas in the U.S. Areas were selected based on the following criteria: recent job growth; recent singles population growth; overall population growth; affordable rental housing; cost-of-living index; expanded arts and recreation opportunities; ratio of single men and single women; affordability of quality higher education (including state residency requirements); diversity index; climate; population density. *Worldwide ERC and Primacy Relocation, "2008 Best Cities for Relocating Singles"*

Education Rankings

- Nashville was selected as one of "America's Most Literate Cities." The city ranked #22 out of the 75 largest U.S. cities. Criteria: number of booksellers; library resources; Internet resources; educational attainment; periodical publishing resources; newspaper circulation. *Central Connecticut State University, "America's Most Literate Cities 2010"*

- Nashville was identified as one of the 100 "smartest" metro areas in the U.S. The area ranked #59. Criteria: the editors rated the collective brainpower of the 100 largest metro area in the U.S based on their residents' educational attainment. *American City Business Journals, www.bizjournals.com, April 14, 2008*

- Nashville was identified as one of "America's Brainiest Bastions" by *Portfolio.com*. The metro area ranked #79 out of 200. Portfolio.com analyzed levels of educational attainment in the nation's 200 largest metropolitan areas. The editors established scores for five levels of educational attainment, based on relative earning power of adult workers age 25 or older. Scores were determined by comparing the median income for all workers with the median income for those workers at a specified educational level. *Portfolio.com, "America's Brainiest Bastions," December 1, 2010*

Environmental Rankings

- Nashville was selected as one of 22 "Smarter Cities" for energy by the Natural Resources Defense Council." Criteria: investment in green power; energy efficiency measures; conservation. *Natural Resources Defense Council, "2010 Smarter Cities," July 19, 2010*

- *American City Business Journal* ranked 43 metropolitan areas in terms of their "greenness." The Nashville metro area ranked #34. Criteria: Forty-one metros in which *ACBJ* has business weeklies, plus Indianapolis and Cleveland, were ranked based on 20 different indicators such as adoption of green technologies, utilization of environmentally sound practices, and air and water quality. *American City Business Journals, "Green City Index," March 11, 2010*

- 100 of the largest metro areas in the U.S. were analyzed in terms of their current drought severity. The Nashville metro area ranked #6 (#1 = driest). The rankings were based on statistics such as long-term precipitation trends and patterns and the Palmer drought indices. *Sperling's BestPlaces, www.BestPlaces.net, "America's Drought-Riskiest Cities," November 2007*

- The Nashville metro area appeared in *Country Home's* "Best Green Places" report. The area ranked #216 out of 379. Criteria: official energy policies; green power; green buildings; availability of fresh, locally grown food. *Country Home, "Best Green Places," 2008*

Health/Fitness Rankings

- Nashville was selected as one of the 25 fittest cities in America by *Men's Fitness Online*. It ranked #24 out of America's 50 largest cities. Criteria: fitness centers and sport stores; nutrition; sports participation; TV viewing; overweight/sedentary; junk food; air quality; geography; commute; parks and open space; city recreational facilities; access to healthcare; motivation; mayor and city initiatives; state obesity initiatives. *Men's Fitness Online, 2009 Fittest/Fattest Cities*

- Nashville was identified as a "2011 Asthma Capital." The area ranked #10 out of the nation's 100 largest metropolitan areas. Twelve factors were used to identify the most challenging places to live for people with asthma: estimated prevalence; self-reported prevalence; crude death rate for asthma; annual pollen score; annual air quality; public smoking laws; number of board-certified asthma specialists; school inhaler access laws; rescue medication use; controller medication use; uninsured rate; poverty rate. *Asthma and Allergy Foundation of America, "2011 Asthma Capitals"*

- Nashville was identified as a 2009 "Spring Allergy Capital." The area ranked #29 out of 100. Three groups of factors were used to identify the most severe cities for people with allergies during the spring season: annual pollen levels; medicine utilization; access to board-certified allergists. *Asthma and Allergy Foundation of America, "Spring Allergy Capitals 2009"*

- Nashville was identified as a 2010 "Fall Allergy Capital." The area ranked #49 out of 100. Three groups of factors were used to identify the most severe cities for people with allergies during the fall season: annual pollen levels; medicine utilization; access to board-certified allergists. *Asthma and Allergy Foundation of America, "Fall Allergy Capitals 2010"*

- *Men's Health* ranked 100 U.S. cities in terms of the quality of their tap water. Nashville was ranked #13 and received a grade of B. Criteria: levels of total coliform bacteria, arsenic, lead, total trihalomethanes (linked to cancer), and halo-acetic acids; number of EPA water-system violations from 1995 to 2005. *Men's Health, March 2007*

- Nashville was selected as one of the most accident-prone cities in America by *Men's Health*. The city ranked #4 of 10. Criteria: workplace accident rates; traffic fatalities; emergency room visits; accidental poisonings; incidents of drowning; fires; injury-producing falls. *Men's Health, "Ranking America's Cities: Accident City, USA," October 2009*

- Ortho-McNeil Neurologics, in partnership with Sperling's BestPlaces, analyzed 110 metro areas and identified those U.S. cities with the highest prevalence of factors that are most commonly associated with migraine headaches. The Nashville metro area ranked #6. Criteria: number of migraine-related drug prescriptions per capita; lifestyle factors that can contribute to migraines; environmental factors that can trigger migraines; and consumption of migraine-triggering foods. *Ortho-McNeil Neurologics, "America's Migraine Hot Spots," March 14, 2006*

- An analysis of the "Best & Worst Cities for Sleep" was conducted by Sperling's BestPlaces. The study ranked America's 50 most populated metro areas. The Nashville metro area ranked #49 (#1 = best city for sleep). Criteria: number of days residents didn't get enough rest or sleep during the past month; average length of daily commute; divorce rate; unemployment rate. *Sperling's BestPlaces, www.BestPlaces.net, "Best & Worst Cities for Sleep," 2006*

- *Men's Health* ranked 100 U.S. cities in terms of cities "Where the Food is Sickening." Nashville was ranked #57 and received a grade of C-. The magazine arrived at their ratings by looking at data compiled by the Community Health Status Indicator Project to determine outbreaks of E. coli, salmonella-, and shigella-related infections. They then checked the CDC's Wonder database to see how many people died from tainted food. Finally, the magazine found out which states have adopted the current version of the FDA's uniform Food Code, which contains the most up-to-date rules for keeping restaurant kitchens clean. *Men's Health, October 2005*

- *Men's Health* examined the nation's largest 100 cities and identified the cities with the best and worst teeth. Nashville was ranked among the ten best at #2. Criteria: annual dentist visits; canceled appointments; regular flossers; fluoride usage; dental extractions. *Men's Health, April 2008*

- The Nashville metro area was identified as one of "America's Most Obese Cities" by *Forbes*. The magazine analyzed BMI (body mass index) data from the CDC in the 50 most populated metro areas in the U.S. and ranked the top 20. The area ranked #7. *Forbes, "America's Most Obese Cities," November 26, 2007*

- The Nashville metro area appeared in the 2010 Gallup-Healthways Well-Being Index. The index, based on interviews with more than 353,000 Americans during 2009, asked individuals to assess their jobs, finances, physical health, emotional state of mind and communities. The metro area ranked #52 out of 162. Criteria: life evaluation; emotional health; work environment; physical health; healthy behaviors; basic access (basic needs optimal for a healthy life, such as access to food and medicine, having health insurance and feeling safe while walking at night). *Gallup-Healthways, "Well-Being Index 2010"*

- The Nashville metro area was identified as one of "America's Most Stressful Cities" by *Forbes*. The metro area ranked #38. Criteria: median home price drop; unemployment rates; cost of living; air quality; sunny days; population density. *Forbes.com, "America's Most Stressful Cities," August 20, 2009*

- The Nashville metro area was identified as one of "America's 20 Most Sedentary Cities" by *Forbes*. The metro area ranked #9. Criteria: percentage of overweight or obese people; percentage of people who had not engaged in any physical activity in the past 30 days; average number of hours of TV watched per week. *Forbes.com, "America's Most Sedentary Cities," October 29, 2007*

- 50 of the largest metro areas in the U.S. were analyzed in terms of their health and fitness by the American College of Sports Medicine in their "American Fitness Index." The Nashville metro area ranked #31 (#1 = healthiest). Criteria: preventative health behaviors; levels of chronic disease; health care access; community resources and policies that support physical activity. *American College of Sports Medicine, "Health and Community Fitness Status of the 50 Largest Metropolitan Areas," May 24, 2010*

- *The Daily Beast* identified the 30 U.S metro areas with the worst smoking habits. The Nashville metro area ranked #15. Sixty urban centers with populations of more than one million were ranked based on the following criteria: number of smokers; number of cigarettes smoked per day; fewest attempts to quit. *The Daily Beast, "30 Cities With Smoking Problems," January 3, 2011*

Pet Rankings

- Nashville was selected as one of the best places to live with pets by *Livability.com*. The city was ranked #9. Criteria: pet-friendly parks and trails; quality veterinary care; active animal welfare groups; abundance of pet boutiques and retail shops; excellent quality of life for pet owners. *Livability.com, "Top 10 Pet Friendly Cities," October 20, 2010*

- Nashville was identified as one of North America's most accommodating cities for travelers with pets. The city was ranked #9. Criteria: number of AAA Approved and Diamond rated pet-friendly hotels. *AAA, Traveling with your Pet: The AAA PetBook, 2006*

Real Estate Rankings

- *Fortune* ranked the 100 largest metro areas in the U.S. in terms of projected median home price change in 2010. The Nashville metro area ranked #48. *Fortune, "The 2010 Housing Outlook," December 9, 2009*

- Nashville appeared on ApartmentRatings.com "Top Cities for Renters" list in 2009." The area ranked #44. Overall satisfaction ratings were ranked using thousands of user submitted scores for hundreds of apartment complexes located in the 100 most populated U.S. municipalities. *ApartmentRatings.com, "2009 Renter Satisfaction Rankings"*

- The Nashville metro area was identified as one of the "Top 25 Real Estate Investment Markets" by *FinestExperts.com*. The metro area ranked #16. Over 10,000 real estate markets were analyzed to identify the most suitable places for real estate investors to seek stability and growth. Criteria: employment; rental markets; growth levels as offset by foreclosures. *FinestExperts.com, "Top 25 Real Estate Investment Markets," January 7, 2010*

- The nation's largest metro areas were analyzed in terms of the percentage of households entering some stage of foreclosure in 2010. The Nashville metro area ranked #107 out of 206 (#1 = highest foreclosure rate). *RealtyTrac, 2010 Year-End Metropolitan Foreclosure Market Report, January 27, 2011*

- The Nashville metro area was identified as one of the "Least Expensive U.S Cities for Renters" by *Forbes*. The metro area ranked #9. Criteria: renter-occupied units paying cash rent where gross rent is defined as contract rent plus utilities, if utilities were paid by the renter. *Forbes.com, "Most and Least Expensive U.S. Cities for Renters," September 23, 2008*

- The Nashville metro area appeared in a *Wall Street Journal* article ranking cities by "housing stress." The metro area was ranked #35 (#1 = most stress). Criteria: fraction of mortgage-holding homeowners with a monthly housing payment in excess of 30 percent of income; percentage of people without health insurance; unemployment rate. *The Wall Street Journal, "Which Cities Face Biggest Housing Risk," October 5, 2010*

- The Center for Housing Policy ranked 210 U.S metropolitan areas by the fair market rent for a two-bedroom unit. The Nashville metro area was ranked #112. (#1 = most expensive) with a rent of $807. Criteria: Fair Market Rent (FMR) in effect during the fourth quarter of 2009 based on HUD's fiscal year 2010 FMRs. *The Center for Housing Policy, "Paycheck to Paycheck: Most to Least Expensive Rental Markets in 2009"*

- The Nashville metro area was identified as one of the markets with the best expected performance in home prices over the next 12 months. *Local Market Monitor, "First Quarter Home Price Forecast for Largest US Markets," March 2, 2011*

Safety Rankings

- Symantec, the makers of Norton, in partnership with Sperling's BestPlaces, ranked the 50 largest cities in the U.S. in terms of their vulnerability to cybercrime. The city ranked #19. Criteria: number of cyberattacks and potential infections; level of Internet access; expenditures on computer hardware and software; wireless hotspots; broadband connectivity; Internet usage; online purchases. *Symantec, "10 Riskiest Cities for Cybercrime," March 22, 2010*

- Allstate ranked the 200 largest cities in America in terms of driver safety. Nashville ranked #21. In addition, drivers were 10.8% less likely to have had an accident compared to the national average. Allstate researchers analyzed internal property damage reported claims over a two-year period (from January 2007 to December 2008) to ensure the findings would not be affected by external influences such as weather or road construction. A weighted average of the two-year numbers determined the annual percentages. The report defines an auto crash as any collision resulting in a property damage claim. *Allstate, "The 2010 Allstate America's Best Drivers Report™"*

- The National Insurance Crime Bureau ranked 366 metro areas in the U.S. in terms of per capita rates of vehicle theft. The Nashville metro area ranked #156 (#1 = highest rate). Criteria: number of vehicle theft offenses per 100,000 inhabitants. *National Insurance Crime Bureau, "Hot Spots," May 17, 2010*

- The Nashville metro area was identified as one of the "The Most Dangerous Metro Areas for Pedestrians" by Transportation for America and the Surface Transportation Policy Partnership. The metro area ranked #28 out of 52 metro areas with over 1 million residents. Criteria: area's population divided by the number of pedestrian fatalities in that area. *Transportation for America and the Surface Transportation Policy Partnership, "Dangerous by Design: Solving the Epidemic of Preventable Pedestrian Deaths (and Making Great Neighborhoods)," November 11, 2009*

Seniors/Retirement Rankings

- The Nashville metro area was identified as one of "America's Most Affordable Places to Retire" by *Forbes*. The metro area ranked #10. Criteria: housing affordability; inflation; number of persons over 65 who are employed; net migration for persons over 65; percent of persons over 65 living below poverty level; doctors per capita; number of citizens tapping their Medicare benefits per thousand people. *Forbes.com, "America's Most Affordable Places to Retire," September 5, 2008*

- The Nashville metro area was selected as one of "America's Best Places to Grow Old" by *Forbes*. The area was ranked #10 out of 10. Criteria: housing affordability; inflationary pressures; number of persons over 65 who are currently employed; net migration for persons over 65; percent of seniors living below poverty level; doctors per capita; number of citizens tapping their Medicare benefits per 1,000 people. *Forbes, "America's Best Places to Grow Old," December 12, 2008*

Sports/Recreation Rankings

- Nashville was selected as one of "10 Great Golf Cities" by *Livability.com*. The city was ranked #5. Livability.com searched 200 of the most livable cities in America to find the top 10 best lesser-known cities for golfers. *Livability.com, "Golf's Best Kept Secrets: 10 Great Golf Cities," March 2, 2010*

- Nashville appeared on the *Sporting News* list of the "Best Sports Cities" for 2010. The area ranked #18 out of 402 cities in the U.S. *Sporting News* takes a 12-month snapshot, roughly October to October, of each city's sports, putting a heavy premium on regular-season won-lost records (from the most recently completed season). Other criteria include: playoff berths, bowl appearances and tournament bids; championships; applicable power ratings; quality of competition; overall fan fervor as measured in part by attendance as percentage of venue capacity; abundance of teams (rewarding quality over quantity); stadium and arena quality; ticket availability and prices; franchise ownership; and marquee appeal of athletes. *Sporting News, "Best Sports Cities 2010," October, 2010*

- *Golf Digest* ranked 330 metro areas in the U.S. in terms of golf. The Nashville metro area was ranked #188. Criteria: access to golf; weather; value of golf; and quality of golf. *Golf Digest, "Metro Golf Rankings," August 2005*

Transportation Rankings

- Nashville was identified as one of America's worst cities for speed traps by the National Motorists Association. One city from each state was selected based on data from the National Speed Trap Exchange. The NSTE collects driver reported speed trap locations. *National Motorists Association, "The Worst Speed Trap Cities in North America," September 2010*

- The Nashville metro area appeared on *Forbes* list of the best and worst cities for commuters. The metro area ranked #49 out of 60 (#1 is best). Criteria: travel time; road congestion; travel delays. *Forbes.com, "Best and Worst Cities for Commuters," February 16, 2010*

Women/Minorities Rankings

- Nashville was ranked #56 out of 100 metro areas in *SELF Magazine's* ranking of America's healthiest places for women." A panel of experts came up with more than 50 criteria including death and disease rates, environmental indicators, community resources, and lifestyle habits. *SELF Magazine, "Secrets of America's Healthiest Women," December 2008*

- Nashville appeared on *Black Enterprise's* list of the "Ten Best Cities for African Americans." The top picks were culled from more than 2,000 interactive surveys completed on www.blackenterprise.com and by editorial staff evaluation. The editors weighed the following criteria as it pertained to African Americans in each city: median household income; percentage of households earning more than $100,000; percentage of businesses owned; percentage of college graduates; unemployment rates; home loan rejections; and homeownership rates. *Black Enterprise, May 2007*

Miscellaneous Rankings

- Energizer Holdings, the makers of Edge® shave gel, in partnership with Sperling's BestPlaces, ranked 50 major metro areas in terms of everyday irritations. The Nashville metro area ranked #19. Criteria: humidity levels; weather conditions; incidence of traffic delays and congestion; average commute times; frequency of flight delays and cancellations; rates of sleeplessness; underemployment; pollens and allergens; pests; comedy clubs per capita. *Energizer Holdings, "Most Irritation Prone Cities," July 23, 2010*

- Mars Chocolate North America, the makers of COMBOS®, in partnership with Sperling's BestPlaces, ranked 50 major metro areas in terms of their "manliness." The Nashville metro area ranked #4. Criteria: number of home improvement stores, steak houses, pickup trucks, motorcycles, and manly occupations (fire fighters, police officers, construction workers, EMP personnel) per capita; salty snack sales; sports TV viewing habits. *Mars Chocolate North America, "America's Manliest Cities," June 22, 2010*

- The Nashville metro area appeared in AutoMD.com's ranking of the "Best and Worst Cities for Auto Repair." The metro area ranked #11 (#1 is best). The 50 most-populated metro areas in the U.S. were ranked on three critical factors: repair affordability; price disparity range; shop integrity factor. *AutoMD.com, "Advocacy for Repair Shop Fairness Report," February 24, 2010*

- Nashville was identified as one of "America's Vainest Cities" by Forbes.com. The city ranked #6. Criteria: highest number of cosmetic surgeons per 100,000 people in America's 50 largest cities. *Forbes.com, "America's Vainest Cities," November 29, 2007*

- The Nashville metro area appeared on *Forbes* list of "America's Drunkest Cities." The area ranked #35. Criteria: 35 of the largest continental U.S. metro areas were chosen based on availability of data and geographic diversity. Each metro was ranked in five areas: state laws; drinkers; heavy drinkers; binge drinkers; and alcoholism. *Forbes.com, "America's Drunkest Cities," August 22, 2006*

- Scarborough Research, a leading market research firm, identified the top local markets for frequent fast food restaurant patronage. The Nashville DMA (Designated Market Area) ranked in the top 10 with consumers reporting an average of 6.1 visits within the past 30 days. *Scarborough Research, May 31, 2006*

Business Environment

CITY FINANCES

City Government Finances

Component	2008 ($000)	2008 ($ per capita)
Total Revenues	3,226,731	5,462
Total Expenditures	3,538,813	5,990
Debt Outstanding	3,894,484	6,592
Cash and Securities[1]	4,281,873	7,247

Note: (1) Cash and security holdings of a government at the close of its fiscal year, including those of its dependent agencies, utilities, and liquor stores.
Source: U.S Census Bureau, State & Local Government Finances 2008

City Government Revenue by Source

Source	2008 ($000)	2008 ($ per capita)
General Revenue		
From Federal Government	10,553	18
From State Government	497,557	842
From Local Governments	0	0
Taxes		
Property	757,993	1,283
Sales and Gross Receipts	338,509	573
Personal Income	0	0
Corporate Income	0	0
Motor Vehicle License	12,654	21
Other Taxes	39,505	67
Current Charges	278,386	471
Liquor Store	0	0
Utility	1,145,576	1,939
Employee Retirement	-50,498	-85

Source: U.S Census Bureau, State & Local Government Finances 2008

City Government Expenditures by Function

Function	2008 ($000)	2008 ($ per capita)	2008 (%)
General Direct Expenditures			
Air Transportation	0	0	0.0
Corrections	60,039	102	1.7
Education	788,547	1,335	22.3
Employment Security Administration	0	0	0.0
Financial Administration	15,570	26	0.4
Fire Protection	119,649	203	3.4
General Public Buildings	0	0	0.0
Governmental Administration, Other	22,571	38	0.6
Health	54,706	93	1.5
Highways	60,587	103	1.7
Hospitals	146,027	247	4.1
Housing and Community Development	0	0	0.0
Interest on General Debt	161,483	273	4.6
Judicial and Legal	70,698	120	2.0
Libraries	22,684	38	0.6
Parking	0	0	0.0
Parks and Recreation	82,091	139	2.3
Police Protection	182,007	308	5.1
Public Welfare	29,629	50	0.8
Sewerage	81,933	139	2.3
Solid Waste Management	23,308	39	0.7
Veterans' Services	0	0	0.0
Liquor Store	0	0	0.0
Utility	1,168,385	1,978	33.0
Employee Retirement	155,968	264	4.4

Source: U.S Census Bureau, State & Local Government Finances 2008

Municipal Bond Ratings

Area	Moody's	S&P	Fitch
City	Aa2	AA	AA

Rating Systems (shown in declining order of credit quality): Moody's– Aaa, Aa, A, Baa, Ba, B, Caa, Ca, C (numerical modifiers 1, 2, and 3 are added to letter-rating); S&P– AAA, AA, A, BBB, BB, B, CCC, CC, C; Fitch– AAA, AA, A, BBB, BB, B, CCC, CC, C. Ratings may be modified by the addition of a plus or minus sign to show relative standing within the major rating categories.
Notes: n/a Not available; (1) Not reviewed; (2) Issuer Rating/No General Obligation; (3) Standard and Poor's Issue Credit Rating (ICR) is a current opinion of an obliger with respect to a specific financial obligation, a specific class of financial obligations, or a specific financial program.
Source: U.S. Census Bureau, 2011 Statistical Abstract, Bond Ratings for City Governments by Largest Cities: 2009

DEMOGRAPHICS

Population Growth

Area	1990 Census	2000 Census	2010 Estimate	2015 Projection	Population Growth (%) 2000-2010	2010-2015
City	488,364	545,524	605,658	631,132	11.0	4.2
MSA[1]	1,048,218	1,311,789	1,596,033	1,727,736	21.7	8.3
U.S.	248,709,873	281,421,906	309,038,974	321,675,005	9.8	4.1

Note: (1) Metropolitan Statistical Area - see Appendix B for areas included
Source: Claritas, Inc.

Number of Households and Average Household Size

Area	2010 Estimate	2010 Average Household Size
City	252,508	2.30
MSA[1]	624,143	2.49
U.S.	116,136,617	2.59

Note: (1) Metropolitan Statistical Area - see Appendix B for areas included
Source: Claritas, Inc.

Race and Ethnicity

Area	White Alone[2] (%)	Black Alone[2] (%)	Asian Alone[2] (%)	Other Race Alone[2] (%)	Hispanic[3] (%)
City	61.4	27.8	2.9	7.9	8.6
MSA[1]	77.6	15.3	2.0	5.1	5.8
U.S.	72.3	12.4	4.4	10.9	15.8

Note: Figures are 2010 estimates; (1) Metropolitan Statistical Area - see Appendix B for areas included (2) Alone is defined as not being in combination with one or more other races; (3) May be of any race.
Source: Claritas, Inc.

Segregation

Type	Segregation Indices[1] 1990	2000	2010	2010 Rank[2]	Percent Change 1990-2000	1990-2010	2000-2010
Black/White	60.7	58.1	56.2	49	-2.6	-4.4	-1.9
Asian/White	45.2	44.4	41.0	51	-0.8	-4.2	-3.4
Hispanic/White	24.3	46.0	47.9	34	21.6	23.5	1.9

Note: Figures are based on an analysis of 1990, 2000, and 2010 Census Decennial Census tract data by William H. Frey, Brookings Institution and the University of Michigan Social Science Data Analysis Network. In this analysis all racial groups (whites, blacks, and asians) are non-Hispanic members of those races. Hispanics are shown as a separate category; All figures cover the Metropolitan Statistical Area (see Appendix B for areas included); (1) Segregation Indices are Dissimilarity Indices that measure the degree to which the minority group is distributed differently than whites aross census tracts. They range from 0 (complete integration) to 100 (complete [segregation) where the value indicates the percentage of the minority group that needs to move to be distributed exactly like whites; (2) Ranges from 1 (most segregated) to 102 (least segregated); n/a not available.
Source: www.CensusScope.org

Ancestry

Area	German	Irish	English	American	Italian	Polish	French	Scottish
City	10.1	9.6	8.9	9.8	2.4	1.2	2.0	2.2
MSA[1]	11.8	12.1	11.7	13.4	2.6	1.3	2.3	2.6
U.S.	16.6	12.0	9.1	6.1	5.9	3.3	3.1	1.9

Note: The top eight ancestries in the U.S. are shown. Figures are percentages and include multiple ancestry (e.g. if a person reported being Irish and Italian, they were included in both columns); (1) Metropolitan Statistical Area - see Appendix B for areas included
Source: U.S. Census Bureau, 2007-2009 American Community Survey 3-Year Estimates

Foreign-Born Population

Area	Any Foreign Country	Mexico	Asia	Europe	Carribean	South America	Central America[2]	Africa	Canada
City	11.2	3.3	3.2	0.9	0.3	0.3	1.3	1.7	0.1
MSA[1]	7.0	2.1	2.0	0.7	0.2	0.2	0.8	0.8	0.2
U.S.	12.5	3.8	3.4	1.6	1.1	0.8	0.9	0.5	0.3

Note: (1) Metropolitan Statistical Area - see Appendix B for areas included; (2) Excludes Mexico.
Source: U.S. Census Bureau, 2007-2009 American Community Survey 3-Year Estimates

Marriage Status

Area	Never Married	Now Married[2]	Separated	Widowed	Divorced
City	38.1	40.2	2.5	5.8	13.3
MSA[1]	29.8	50.7	2.0	5.5	12.0
U.S.	31.4	49.7	2.2	6.2	10.6

Note: Figures are percentages and cover the population 15 years of age and older; (1) Metropolitan Statistical Area - see Appendix B for areas included; (2) Excludes separated
Source: U.S. Census Bureau, 2007-2009 American Community Survey 3-Year Estimates

Age Distribution and Median Age

Area	Under Age 5	Age 5 to 17	Age 18 to 34	Age 35 to 49	Age 50 to 64	Age 65 to 79	80 Years and Over	Median Age
City	7.5	14.7	29.5	21.2	16.6	7.3	3.2	33.9
MSA[1]	7.2	17.3	24.7	22.7	17.6	7.8	2.8	35.5
U.S.	6.9	17.5	23.3	21.4	18.1	9.1	3.7	36.7

Note: (1) Metropolitan Statistical Area - see Appendix B for areas included
Source: U.S. Census Bureau, 2007-2009 American Community Survey 3-Year Estimates

Male/Female Ratio

Area	Males	Females	Males per 100 Females
City	295,722	309,936	95.4
MSA[1]	785,255	810,778	96.9
U.S.	152,401,520	156,637,454	97.3

Note: Figures are 2010 estimates; (1) Metropolitan Statistical Area - see Appendix B for areas included
Source: Claritas, Inc.

Religion

Area	Catholic	Southern Baptist	United Methodist	ELCA[1]	LDS[2]	Presbyterian Church USA	Jewish Est.	Muslim Est.
County	4.9	17.0	5.7	0.4	0.3	1.9	1.1	1.6
U.S.	22.0	7.1	3.7	1.8	1.5	1.1	2.2	0.6

Note: Figures are the number of adherents as a percentage of the total population; Adherents are defined as all members, including full members, their children and the estimated number of other participants who are not considered members (e.g. the baptized, those not confirmed, those regularly attending services, etc.);
(1) Evangelical Lutheran Church in America; (2) The Church of Jesus Christ of Latter Day Saints
Source: Reprinted with permission from Religious Congregations and Membership in the United States 2000 (Nashville, Glenmary Research Center, 2002) Copyright Association of Statisticians of American Religious Bodies. All rights reserved.

ECONOMY

Gross Metropolitan Product

Area	2006	2007	2008	2009	2009 Rank[2]
MSA[1]	72.9	76.3	78.9	78.1	38

Note: Figures are in billions of dollars; (1) Nashville-Davidson—Murfreesboro, TN Metropolitan Statistical Area - see Appendix B for areas included; (2) Rank ranges from 1 to 363
Source: The U.S. Conference of Mayors, "Pace of Economic Recovery: GMP and Jobs," January 2010

Economic Growth

Area	2006-2008 (%)	2009 (%)	2010 (%)	Rank[2]
MSA[1]	1.9	-2.1	2.2	116
U.S.	1.3	-2.5	2.2	–

Note: Figures are real Gross Metropolitan Product growth rates and represent annual average percent change; (1) Nashville-Davidson—Murfreesboro, TN Metropolitan Statistical Area - see Appendix B for areas included; (2) Rank ranges from 1 to 363
Source: The U.S. Conference of Mayors, "Pace of Economic Recovery: GMP and Jobs," January 2010

Metropolitan Area Exports

Area	2005	2006	2007	2008	2009	2009 Rank[2]
MSA[1]	5,020.6	5,388.6	5,105.9	5,259.5	4,406.6	43

Note: Figures are in millions of dollars; (1) Nashville-Davidson—Murfreesboro, TN Metropolitan Statistical Area - see Appendix B for areas included; (2) Rank ranges from 1 to 374
Source: U.S. Department of Commerce, International Trade Administration, Office of Trade & Industry Information, Manufacturing & Services

INCOME

Per Capita/Median/Average Income

Area	Per Capita ($)	Median Household ($)	Average Household ($)
City	26,583	47,040	62,944
MSA[1]	27,418	52,798	69,518
U.S.	27,034	52,795	71,071

Note: Figures are 2010 estimates; (1) Metropolitan Statistical Area - see Appendix B for areas included
Source: Claritas, Inc.

Household Income Distribution

Area	Percent of Households Earning							
	Under $15,000	$15,000 -24,999	$25,000 -34,999	$35,000 -49,999	$50,000 -74,999	$75,000 -99,000	$100,000 -149,999	$150,000 and up
City	13.4	10.6	12.3	17.1	20.1	11.0	10.0	5.5
MSA[1]	11.4	9.5	10.8	15.9	21.1	12.6	11.7	6.9
U.S.	12.1	10.2	10.6	15.0	19.5	12.5	12.1	8.0

Note: Figures are 2010 estimates; (1) Metropolitan Statistical Area - see Appendix B for areas included
Source: Claritas, Inc.

Poverty Rates by Age

Area	All Ages	Under 18 Years Old	18 to 64 Years Old	65 Years and Over
City	16.7	6.1	9.5	1.1
MSA[1]	12.5	4.4	7.2	1.0
U.S.	13.6	4.7	7.7	1.2

Note: Figures are percent of population with income during the previous 12 months below poverty level and only include population for whom poverty status is determined; (1) Metropolitan Statistical Area - see Appendix B for areas included
Source: U.S. Census Bureau, 2007-2009 American Community Survey 3-Year Estimates

Personal Bankruptcy Filing Rate

Area	2006	2007	2008	2009	2010
Davidson County	4.54	5.35	6.45	7.13	6.69
U.S.	2.00	2.73	3.53	4.60	4.96

Note: Numbers are per 1,000 population and include Chapter 7 and Chapter 13 filings
Source: Federal Deposit Insurance Corporation, Regional Economic Conditions, March 17, 2011

EMPLOYMENT

Labor Force and Employment

Area	Civilian Labor Force			Workers Employed		
	Dec. 2009	Dec. 2010	% Chg.	Dec. 2009	Dec. 2010	% Chg.
City	323,840	332,223	2.6	294,817	305,276	3.5
MSA[1]	805,781	823,775	2.2	732,497	758,483	3.5
U.S.	152,693,000	153,156,000	0.3	137,953,000	139,159,000	0.9

Note: Data is not seasonally adjusted and covers workers 16 years of age and older;
(1) Metropolitan Statistical Area - see Appendix B for areas included
Source: Bureau of Labor Statistics, http://stats.bls.gov

Unemployment Rate

Area	2010											
	Jan.	Feb.	Mar.	Apr.	May	Jun.	Jul.	Aug.	Sep.	Oct.	Nov.	Dec.
City	9.3	9.0	8.9	8.5	8.4	8.7	9.1	9.4	8.9	8.5	8.4	8.1
MSA[1]	9.7	9.4	9.3	8.8	8.5	8.6	8.5	8.7	8.2	8.0	8.2	7.9
U.S.	10.6	10.4	10.2	9.5	9.3	9.6	9.7	9.5	9.2	9.0	9.3	9.1

Note: Data is not seasonally adjusted and covers workers 16 years of age and older; All figures are percentages; (1) Metropolitan Statistical Area - see Appendix B for areas included
Source: Bureau of Labor Statistics, http://stats.bls.gov

Projected Unemployment Rate

Area	2007 (%)	2009 (%)	2011 (%)	2013 (%)
MSA[1]	4.6	10.1	9.2	7.4

Note: (1) Metropolitan Statistical Area - see Appendix B for areas included
Source: The U.S. Conference of Mayors, "Pace of Economic Recovery: GMP and Jobs," January 2010

Employment by Occupation

Occupation Classification	City (%)	MSA[1] (%)	U.S. (%)
Sales and Office	27.7	27.3	25.4
Professional and Related	23.1	21.3	21.0
Service	16.9	15.2	17.2
Production, Transportation, and Material Moving	11.1	12.5	12.3
Management, Business, and Financial	13.8	14.6	14.1
Construction, Extraction, and Maintenance	7.3	8.9	9.2
Farming, Forestry, and Fishing	0.1	0.2	0.7

Note: Figures cover employed civilians 16 years of age and older;
(1) Metropolitan Statistical Area - see Appendix B for areas included
Source: U.S. Census Bureau, 2007-2009 American Community Survey 3-Year Estimates

Employment by Industry

| Sector | MSA[1] | | U.S. |
	Number of Employees	Percent of Total	Percent of Total
Government	110,100	14.7	17.2
Education and Health Services	120,500	16.1	15.2
Professional and Business Services	101,600	13.6	13.0
Retail Trade	86,600	11.6	11.4
Leisure and Hospitality	76,800	10.3	9.7
Manufacturing	60,100	8.0	8.8
Financial Activities	45,600	6.1	5.8
Wholesale Trade	35,800	4.8	4.2
Construction	n/a	n/a	4.1
Other Services	29,900	4.0	4.1
Transportation and Utilities	30,000	4.0	3.7
Information	19,600	2.6	2.1
Mining and Logging	n/a	n/a	0.6

Note: Figures cover non-farm employment as of December 2010 and are not seasonally adjusted;
(1) Metropolitan Statistical Area - see Appendix B for areas included; n/a not available
Source: Bureau of Labor Statistics, http://stats.bls.gov

Occupations with Greatest Projected Employment Growth: 2006 - 2016

Occupation[1]	2006 Employment	2016 Projected Employment	Numeric Employment Change	Percent Employment Change
Retail salespersons	85,980	104,710	18,730	21.8
Customer service representatives	48,360	62,400	14,040	29.0
Registered nurses	51,960	65,410	13,450	25.9
Combined food preparation and serving workers, including fast food	56,290	68,360	12,070	21.4
Truck drivers, heavy and tractor-trailer	73,170	83,140	9,970	13.6
Waiters and waitresses	49,750	58,960	9,210	18.5
Office clerks, general	56,220	64,620	8,400	14.9
Elementary school teachers, except special education	30,740	38,000	7,260	23.6
Nursing aides, orderlies, and attendants	31,850	38,580	6,730	21.1
Janitors and cleaners, except maids and housekeeping cleaners	42,750	48,660	5,910	13.8

Note: Projections cover Tennessee; (1) Sorted by numeric employment change
Source: www.projectionscentral.com, State Occupational Projections, 2006-2016 Long-Term Projections

Fastest Growing Occupations: 2006 - 2016

Occupation[1]	2006 Employment	2016 Projected Employment	Numeric Employment Change	Percent Employment Change
Pharmacy technicians	7,970	12,540	4,570	57.3
Environmental engineers	900	1,410	510	56.7
Network systems and data communications analysts	2,810	4,340	1,530	54.4
Home health aides	10,760	15,610	4,850	45.1
Animal trainers	730	1,040	310	42.5
Pharmacists	5,640	7,960	2,320	41.1
Computer software engineers, applications	3,310	4,630	1,320	39.9
Paralegals and legal assistants	3,730	5,180	1,450	38.9
Financial analysts	2,220	3,080	860	38.7
Personal financial advisors	1,440	1,980	540	37.5

Note: Projections cover Tennessee; (1) Sorted by percent employment change and excludes occupations with numeric employment change less than 300
Source: www.projectionscentral.com, State Occupational Projections, 2006-2016 Long-Term Projections

Average Wages

Occupation	$/Hr.	Occupation	$/Hr.
Accountants and Auditors	28.56	Maids and Housekeeping Cleaners	9.10
Automotive Mechanics	17.76	Maintenance and Repair Workers	17.15
Bookkeepers	16.21	Marketing Managers	42.83
Carpenters	17.31	Nuclear Medicine Technologists	29.40
Cashiers	8.74	Nurses, Licensed Practical	18.68
Clerks, General Office	13.65	Nurses, Registered	30.34
Clerks, Receptionists/Information	12.25	Nursing Aides/Orderlies/Attendants	11.59
Clerks, Shipping/Receiving	13.27	Packers and Packagers, Hand	9.81
Computer Programmers	29.44	Physical Therapists	35.63
Computer Support Specialists	21.31	Postal Service Mail Carriers	23.18
Computer Systems Analysts	32.86	Real Estate Brokers	27.91
Cooks, Restaurant	11.35	Retail Salespersons	10.99
Dentists	n/a	Sales Reps., Exc. Tech./Scientific	27.58
Electrical Engineers	39.02	Sales Reps., Tech./Scientific	28.32
Electricians	18.53	Secretaries, Exc. Legal/Med./Exec.	13.86
Financial Managers	41.41	Security Guards	11.57
First-Line Supervisors/Mgrs., Sales	19.25	Surgeons	n/a
Food Preparation Workers	9.66	Teacher Assistants	10.60
General and Operations Managers	48.03	Teachers, Elementary School	22.30
Hairdressers/Cosmetologists	14.54	Teachers, Secondary School	21.90
Internists	93.25	Telemarketers	13.86
Janitors and Cleaners	9.68	Truck Drivers, Heavy/Tractor-Trailer	18.38
Landscaping/Groundskeeping Workers	11.69	Truck Drivers, Light/Delivery Svcs.	16.28
Lawyers	54.02	Waiters and Waitresses	9.32

Note: Wage data covers the Nashville-Davidson—Murfreesboro—Franklin, TN - see Appendix B for areas included. Hourly wages for elementary/secondary school teachers and teacher assistants were calculated by the editors from annual wage data assuming a 40 hour work week; n/a not available.
Source: Bureau of Labor Statistics, Metro Area Occupational Employment and Wage Estimates, May 2009

RESIDENTIAL REAL ESTATE

Building Permits

Area	Single-Family			Multi-Family			Total		
	2009	2010	Pct. Chg.	2009	2010	Pct. Chg.	2009	2010	Pct. Chg.
City	1,068	1,001	-6.3	533	567	6.4	1,601	1,568	-2.1
MSA[1]	3,957	3,938	-0.5	976	1,154	18.2	4,933	5,092	3.2
U.S.	441,100	447,300	1.4	141,900	157,300	10.9	583,000	604,600	3.7

Note: (1) Metropolitan Statistical Area - see Appendix B for areas included; figures represent new, privately-owned housing units authorized (unadjusted data); All permit data are based on estimates with imputation.
Source: U.S. Census Bureau, Manufacturing, Mining, and Construction Statistics, Building Permits, 2009, 2010

Homeownership Rate

Area	2005 (%)	2006 (%)	2007 (%)	2008 (%)	2009 (%)	2010 (%)
MSA[1]	73.0	72.4	70.0	71.3	71.8	70.4
U.S.	68.9	68.8	68.1	67.8	67.4	66.9

Note: (1) Metropolitan Statistical Area - see Appendix B for areas included
Source: U.S. Census Bureau, Housing Vacancies and Homeownership Annual Statistics: 2010

Housing Vacancy Rates

Area	Gross Vacancy Rate[2] (%)			Year-Round Vacancy Rate[3] (%)			Rental Vacancy Rate[4] (%)			Homeowner Vacancy Rate[5] (%)		
	2008	2009	2010	2008	2009	2010	2008	2009	2010	2008	2009	2010
MSA[1]	9.9	8.7	10.9	9.3	8.1	10.5	10.6	8.3	8.2	2.2	1.9	2.4
U.S.	14.4	14.5	14.3	11.1	11.3	11.3	10.0	10.6	10.2	2.8	2.6	2.6

Note: (1) Metropolitan Statistical Area - see Appendix B for areas included; (2) The percentage of the total housing inventory that is vacant; (3) The percentage of the housing inventory (excluding seasonal units) that is year-round vacant; (4) The percentage of rental inventory that is vacant for rent; (5) The percentage of homeowner inventory that is vacant for sale; n/a not available
Source: U.S. Census Bureau, Housing Vacancies and Homeownership Annual Statistics: 2010

State Corporate Income Tax Rates

State	Tax Rate (%)	Income Brackets ($)	Num. of Brackets	Financial Institution Tax Rate (%)[a]	Federal Income Tax Ded.
Tennessee	6.5	Flat rate	1	6.5	No

Note: Tax rates as of January 1, 2011; (a) Rates listed are the tax rates applied to financial institutions or excise taxes based on income. Some states have other taxes based upon the value of deposits or shares.
Source: Federation of Tax Administrators, "State Corporate Income Tax Rates, 2011"

State Individual Income Tax Rates

State	Tax Rate (%)	Income Brackets ($)	Num. of Brackets	Personal Exempt. ($)[1] Single	Personal Exempt. ($)[1] Dependents	Fed. Inc. Tax Ded.

Tennessee – State Income Tax of 6% on Dividends and Interest Income Only

Note: Tax rates as of January 1, 2011; Local- and county-level taxes are not included; n/a not applicable;
(1) Married joint filers generally receive double the single exemption
Source: Federation of Tax Administrators, "State Individual Income Tax Rates, 2011"

Various State and Local Tax Rates

State	State and Local Sales and Use (%)	State Sales and Use (%)	Gasoline[1] (¢/gal.)	Cigarette[2] ($/pack)	Spirits[3] ($/gal.)	Wine[4] ($/gal.)	Beer[5] ($/gal.)
Tennessee	9.25	7.00	21.4	0.62	4.46	1.27	0.14

Note: All tax rates as of January 1, 2011 except Spirits (Sept. 1, 2010); (1) The American Petroleum Institute has developed a methodology for determining the average tax rate on a gallon of fuel. Rates may include any of the following: excise taxes, environmental fees, storage tank fees, other fees or taxes, general sales tax, and local taxes. In states where gasoline is subject to the general sales tax, or where the fuel tax is based on the average sale price, the average rate determined by API is sensitive to changes in the price of gasoline. States that fully or partially apply general sales taxes to gasoline: CA, CO, GA, IL, IN, MI, NY; (2) The federal excise tax of $1.0066 per pack and local taxes are not included; (3) Rates are those applicable to off-premise sales of 40% alcohol by volume (a.b.v.) distilled spirits in 750ml containers. Local excise taxes are excluded; (4) Rates are those applicable to off-premise sales of 11% a.b.v. non-carbonated wine in 750ml containers; (5) Rates are those applicable to off-premise sales of 4.7% a.b.v. beer in 12 ounce containers.
Source: Tax Foundation, 2011 Facts & Figures: How Does Your State Compare?

State-Local Tax Burdens

Area	Rate (%)	Rank[1]	Per Capita Taxes Paid to Home State ($)	Total State and Local Per Capita Taxes Paid ($)	Per Capita Income ($)
Tennessee	7.6	47	1,851	2,752	36,157
U.S. Average	9.8	-	3,057	4,160	42,539

Note: Figures cover 2009; (1) Rank ranges from 1 to 50 where 1 is highest tax burden
Source: Tax Foundation, State-Local Tax Burdens, All States, 2009

State Business Tax Climate Index Rankings

State	Overall Rank	Corporate Tax Index Rank	Individual Income Tax Index Rank	Sales Tax Index Rank	Unemployment Insurance Tax Index Rank	Property Tax Index Rank
Tennessee	27	11	8	47	35	50

Note: The index is a measure of how each state's tax laws affect economic performance. The lower the rank, the more favorable a state's tax system is for business. All ranks are for fiscal years. States without a given tax are given a ranking of 1.
Source: Tax Foundation, Tax Foundation Background Paper, No. 60, "2011 State Business Tax Climate Index"

COMMERCIAL UTILITIES

Typical Monthly Electric Bills

Area	Commercial Service ($/month)		Industrial Service ($/month)	
	40 kW demand 5,000 kWh	500 kW demand 100,000 kWh	5,000 kW demand 1,500,000 kWh	70,000 kW demand 50,000,000 kWh
City	437	10,807	116,945	2,160,900

Note: Based on rates in effect January 1, 2010
Source: Memphis Light, Gas and Water, 2010 Utility Bill Comparisons for Selected U.S. Cities

TRANSPORTATION

Means of Transportation to Work

Area	Car/Truck/Van		Public Transportation			Bicycle	Walked	Other Means	Worked at Home
	Drove Alone	Car-pooled	Bus	Subway	Railroad				
City	80.6	9.6	2.1	0.0	0.1	0.3	1.7	1.1	4.5
MSA[1]	81.3	10.6	1.0	0.0	0.1	0.2	1.2	1.1	4.5
U.S.	75.8	10.4	2.7	1.7	0.5	0.5	2.9	1.2	4.1

Note: Figures are percentages and cover workers 16 years of age and older;
(1) Metropolitan Statistical Area - see Appendix B for areas included
Source: U.S. Census Bureau, 2007-2009 American Community Survey 3-Year Estimates

Travel Time to Work

Area	Less Than 15 Minutes	15 to 29 Minutes	30 to 44 Minutes	45 to 59 Minutes	60 to 89 Minutes	90 Minutes or More
City	22.0	46.2	23.6	5.3	1.7	1.2
MSA[1]	22.9	37.8	23.9	9.4	4.3	1.7
U.S.	28.5	36.2	19.7	7.5	5.6	2.5

Note: Figures are percentages and include workers 16 years old and over;
(1) Metropolitan Statistical Area - see Appendix B for areas included
Source: U.S. Census Bureau, 2007-2009 American Community Survey 3-Year Estimates

Travel Time Index

Area	1982	1999	2008	2009
Urban Area[1]	1.11	1.17	1.14	1.15
Average[2]	1.08	1.20	1.20	1.20

Note: Travel Time Index—the ratio of travel time in the peak period to the travel time at
free-flow conditions. A value of 1.30 indicates a 20-minute free-flow trip takes 26 minutes
in the peak. Free-flow speeds (60 mph on freeways and 35 mph on principal arterials)
are used as the comparison threshold; (1) Covers the Nashville-Davidson—Murfreesboro urban area;
(2) average of 439 urban areas
Source: Texas Transportation Institute, Urban Mobility Report 2010, December 2010

Public Transportation

Agency Name / Mode of Transportation	Vehicles Operated in Maximum Service	Annual Unlinked Passenger Trips ('000)	Annual Passenger Miles ('000)
Metropolitan Transit Authority (MTA)			
Demand response	49	267.6	3,075.6
Demand response	83	68.6	829.1
Bus	108	10,236.5	50,227.4

Note: Figures include both directly operated and purchased transportation
Source: Federal Transit Administration, National Transit Database, 2009

Air Transportation

Airport Name and Code / Type of Service	Passenger Airlines[1]	Passenger Enplanements	Freight Carriers[2]	Freight (lbs.)
Nashville International (BNA)				
Domestic service (U.S. carriers - 2010)	37	4,409,267	19	50,939,053
International service (U.S. carriers - 2009)	12	3,644	1	3,408

Note: (1) Includes all U.S.-based major, minor and commuter airlines that carried at least one passenger during
the year; (2) Includes all U.S.-based airlines and freight carriers that transported at least one pound of freight
during the year
Source: Bureau of Transportation Statistics, The Intermodal Transportation Database, Air Carriers: T-100
Domestic Market (U.S. Carriers), 2010; Bureau of Transportation Statistics, The Intermodal Transportation
Database, Air Carriers: T-100 International Market (U.S. Carriers), 2009

Other Transportation Statistics

Interstate highways:	I-24; I-40; I-65
Amtrak service:	Bus connection
Major waterways/ports:	Cumberland River; Port of Nashville

Source: Amtrak.com; Google Maps

BUSINESSES

Major Business Headquarters

Company Name	Rankings	
	Fortune[1]	Forbes[2]
HCA	-	4
HCA Holdings	90	-
Vanguard Health Systems	-	109

*Note: (1) Fortune 500—companies that produce a 10-K are ranked 1 to 500
based on 2010 revenue; (2) all private companies with at least $2 billion in
annual revenue are ranked 1 to 223; companies listed are headquartered in
the city; dashes indicate no ranking
Source: Fortune, "Fortune 500," May 23, 2011; Forbes, "America's Largest
Private Companies," November 3, 2010*

Fast-Growing Businesses

According to *Inc.*, Nashville is home to one of America's 500 fastest-growing private
companies: **Randa Solutions**. Criteria: must be an independent, privately-held, for-profit,
U.S. corporation, proprietorship or partnership; revenues of at least $80,000 in 2006 and $2
million in 2009; four-year operating/sales history; holding companies, regulated banks, and
utilities were excluded. *Inc., "America's 500 Fastest-Growing Private Companies,"
September 2010*

According to *Fortune*, Nashville is home to one of America's 100 fastest-growing small
public companies: **HealthStream**. Companies were ranked by their three-year annualized
rates of revenue growth and total return to investors for the period ended December 31, 2008.
Criteria for inclusion: revenues of less than $200 million; stock price of at least $1. Banks,
real-estate firms and adult entertainment companies were excluded. Also excluded were
companies with losses in any of the four quarters ended on or before December 31, 2008.
*Fortune Small Business, "America's Fastest-Growing Small Public Companies," July/August
2009*

According to Deloitte, Nashville is home to one of North America's 500 fastest-growing
high-technology companies: **Cumberland Pharmaceuticals**. Companies are ranked by
percentage growth in revenue over a five-year period. Criteria for inclusion: company must be
headquartered within North America; company must own proprietary intellectual property or
proprietary technology that contributes to a significant portion of the company's operating
revenue or devotes a significant proportion of revenues to research and development of
technology; company must have been in business for a minumum of five years with 2005
operating revenues of at least $50,000 USD/CD and 2009 operating revenues of at least $5
million USD/CD. *Deloitte Touche Tohmatsu, 2010 Deloitte Technology Fast 500*[TM]

Minority Business Opportunity

Nashville is home to one company which is on the Black Enterprise Bank 25 list (25 largest
banks based on total assets, capital, deposits and loans, including mortgage-backed securities
for the calendar year): **Citizens Savings Bank & Trust Co.** Criteria: commercial banks or
savings and loans that are classified by the Federal Reserve as black institutions and have
been fully operational for the previous calendar year. *Black Enterprise, B.E. 100s, 2010*

Minority- and Women-Owned Businesses

Group	All Firms		Firms with Paid Employees			
	Firms	Sales ($000)	Firms	Sales ($000)	Employees	Payroll ($000)
Asian	2,148	613,454	604	535,979	3,943	95,979
Black	7,005	414,476	417	258,896	2,878	74,329
Hispanic	1,868	236,570	199	133,356	1,381	36,780
Women	16,502	5,695,700	1,745	5,205,388	16,751	538,220
All Firms	61,671	80,576,132	13,326	77,992,496	375,771	15,437,290

*Note: Figures cover firms located in the city; minority- and women-owned business are defined as firms in
which the corresponding group own 51% or more of the stock or equity of the company
Source: U.S. Census Bureau, 2007 Economic Census, Survey of Business Owners*

HOTELS

Hotels/Motels

Area	5 Star		4 Star		3 Star		2 Star		1 Star		Not Rated	
	Num.	Pct.3	Num.	Pct.3	Num.	Pct.3	Num.	Pct.3	Num.	Pct.3	Num.	Pct.3
City[1]	0	0.0	8	3.7	44	20.1	135	61.6	8	3.7	24	11.0
Total[2]	119	0.7	927	5.8	4,906	30.5	7,992	49.7	526	3.3	1,625	10.1

Note: (1) Figures cover Nashville and vicinity; (2) Figures cover all 100 cities in this book; (3) Percentage of hotels which are a given star rating; Star ratings are determined by expedia.com and offer an indication of the general quality of a particular hotel.
Source: expedia.com, May 5, 2011

The Nashville metro area is home to one of the top 218 hotels in the U.S. according to *Travel & Leisure*: **Hermitage Hotel** (#36). Criteria: service; location; rooms; food; and value.
Travel & Leisure, "T+L 500, The World's Best Hotels 2011"

EVENT SITES

Major Stadiums, Arenas, and Auditoriums

Name	Max. Capacity
Bridgestone Arena	20,000
Gentry Complex, Tennessee State University	10,500
Grand Ole Opry House	4,400
Herschel Greer Stadium	10,139
LP Field	68,798
Nashville Municipal Auditorium	9,654
Vanderbilt Stadium at Dudley Field	39,790

Source: Original research

Convention Centers

Name	Overall Space (sq. ft.)	Exhibit Space (sq. ft.)	Meeting Space (sq. ft.)	Meeting Rooms
Nashville Convention Center	n/a	n/a	118,675	25

Note: n/a not available
Source: Original research

Living Environment

COST OF LIVING

Cost of Living Index

Composite Index	Groceries	Housing	Utilities	Trans-portation	Health Care	Misc. Goods/ Services
88.9	91.7	71.3	82.6	92.5	87.3	104.5

Note: U.S. = 100; Figures cover Nashville-Franklin.
Source: The Council for Community and Economic Research, ACCRA Cost of Living Index, 2010

Grocery Prices

Area[1]	T-Bone Steak ($/pound)	Frying Chicken ($/pound)	Whole Milk ($/half gal.)	Eggs ($/dozen)	Orange Juice ($/64 oz.)	Coffee ($/11.5 oz.)
City[2]	8.77	1.12	1.99	1.24	2.78	3.22
Avg.	9.04	1.16	2.02	1.47	3.08	3.65
Min.	6.97	0.84	1.46	0.96	2.39	2.64
Max.	13.93	2.51	3.58	3.01	4.94	6.32

Note: (1) Values for the local area are compared with the average, minimum and maximum values for all 338 areas in the Cost of Living Index; (2) Figures cover Nashville-Franklin; **T-Bone Steak** (price per pound); **Frying Chicken** (price per pound, whole fryer); **Whole Milk** (half gallon carton); **Eggs** (price per dozen, Grade A, large); **Orange Juice** (64 oz. Tropicana or Florida Natural); **Coffee** (11.5 oz. can, vacuum-packed, Maxwell House, Hills Bros, or Folgers).
Source: The Council for Community and Economic Research, ACCRA Cost of Living Index, 2010

Housing and Utility Costs

Area[1]	New Home Price ($)	Apartment Rent ($/month)	All Electric ($/month)	Part Electric ($/month)	Other Energy ($/month)	Telephone ($/month)
City[2]	195,042	795	-	77.18	61.48	23.59
Avg.	293,442	810	166.39	91.93	83.82	26.93
Min.	182,545	453	119.21	44.47	36.85	17.98
Max.	1,123,114	2,776	307.53	218.20	313.90	39.15

Note: (1) Values for the local area are compared with the average, minimum and maximum values for all 338 areas in the Cost of Living Index; (2) Figures cover Nashville-Franklin; **New Home Price** (2,400 sf living area, 8,000 sf lot, in urban area with full utilities); **Apartment Rent** (950 sf 2 bedroom/1.5 or 2 bath, unfurnished, excluding all utilities except water); **All Electric** (average monthly cost for an all-electric home); **Part Electric** (average monthly cost for a part-electric home); **Other Energy** (average monthly cost for natural gas, fuel oil, coal, wood, and any other forms of energy except electricity); **Telephone** (price includes basic monthly rate for a private residential line plus additional local usage charges incurred by a family of four).
Source: The Council for Community and Economic Research, ACCRA Cost of Living Index, 2010

Health Care, Transportation, and Other Costs

Area[1]	Doctor ($/visit)	Dentist ($/visit)	Optometrist ($/visit)	Gasoline ($/gallon)	Beauty Salon ($/visit)	Men's Shirt ($)
City[2]	79.60	73.80	88.47	2.59	30.53	23.13
Avg.	89.44	78.95	87.40	2.73	31.92	24.83
Min.	57.00	54.25	48.32	2.44	19.17	13.67
Max.	149.90	136.73	174.22	3.75	62.81	47.89

Note: (1) Values for the local area are compared with the average, minimum and maximum values for all 338 areas in the Cost of Living Index; (2) Figures cover Nashville-Franklin; **Doctor** (general practitioners routine exam of an established patient); **Dentist** (adult teeth cleaning and periodic oral examination); **Optometrist** (full vision eye exam for established adult patient); **Gasoline** (one gallon regular unleaded, national brand, including all taxes, cash price at self-service pump if available); **Beauty Salon** (woman's shampoo, trim, and blow-dry); **Men's Shirt** (cotton/polyester dress shirt, pinpoint weave, long sleeves).
Source: The Council for Community and Economic Research, ACCRA Cost of Living Index, 2010

HOUSING

House Price Index (HPI)

Area	National Ranking[2]	Quarterly Change (%)	One-Year Change (%)	Five-Year Change (%)
MSA[1]	124	-0.62	-0.55	8.04
U.S.[3]	-	-0.84	-3.95	-11.45

Note: The HPI is a weighted repeat sales index. It measures average price changes in repeat sales or refinancings on the same properties. This information is obtained by reviewing repeat mortgage transactions on single-family properties whose mortgages have been purchased or securitized by Fannie Mae or Freddie Mac in January 1975; (1) Metropolitan/Micropolitan Statistical Area - see Appendix B for areas included; (2) Rankings are based on annual percentage change for all metro areas containing at least 15,000 transactions over the last 10 years and ranges from 1 to 309; (3) figures based on a weighted average of Census Division estimates; all figures are for the period ending December 31, 2010
Source: Federal Housing Finance Agency, House Price Index, February 24, 2011

House Price Valuations

Area	Q4 2005 Price ($000)	Q4 2005 Over-valuation	Q4 2006 Price ($000)	Q4 2006 Over-valuation	Q4 2007 Price ($000)	Q4 2007 Over-valuation	Q4 2008 Price ($000)	Q4 2008 Over-valuation	Q4 2009 Price ($000)	Q4 2009 Over-valuation
MSA[1]	155.2	-3.2	168.8	-1.1	173.3	-2.6	167.7	-4.7	164.6	-8.0

Note: Figures show the percentage of over- or under-valuation of single family homes relative to statistically normal house values (e.g. a value of 23.6 indicates that house values are 23.6% overvalued). Statistically normal house values are based on house prices, interest rates, household incomes, population densities, and any historical premiums or discounts metropolitan areas have exhibited over time; (1) Figures cover the Nashville-Davidson—Murfreesboro, TN Metropolitan Statistical Area - see Appendix B for areas included
Source: Global Insight/PNC Financial Services Group, House Prices in America: 4th Quarter 2009 Update

Median Single-Family Home Prices

Area	2008	2009	2010p	Percent Change 2009 to 2010
MSA[1]	n/a	n/a	n/a	n/a
U.S. Average	196.6	172.1	173.2	0.6

Note: Figures are median sales prices of existing single-family homes in thousands of dollars; (p) preliminary; n/a not available; (1) Metropolitan Statistical Area - see Appendix B for areas included
Source: National Association of Realtors, Median Sales Price of Existing Single-Family Homes for Metropolitan Areas, 4th Quarter 2010

Median Apartment Condo-Coop Home Prices

Area	2008	2009	2010p	Percent Change 2009 to 2010
MSA[1]	n/a	n/a	n/a	n/a
U.S. Average	209.8	175.6	171.7	-2.2

Note: Figures are median sales prices of existing apartment condo-coop homes in thousands of dollars; (p) preliminary; n/a not available; (1) Metropolitan Statistical Area - see Appendix B for areas included
Source: National Association of Realtors, Median Sales Price of Existing Apartment Condo-Coop Homes for Metropolitan Areas, 4th Quarter 2010

Year Housing Structure Built

Area	2000 or Later	1990 -1999	1980 -1989	1970 -1979	1960 -1969	1950 -1959	1940 -1949	Before 1940	Median Year
City	12.5	12.6	16.5	18.3	15.4	12.3	5.4	7.0	1975
MSA[1]	19.3	19.3	16.5	16.1	11.4	8.0	3.8	5.6	1983
U.S.	12.5	14.0	14.2	16.5	11.4	11.3	5.8	14.3	1974

Note: Figures are percentages except for Median Year; (1) Metropolitan Statistical Area - see Appendix B for areas included
Source: U.S. Census Bureau, 2007-2009 American Community Survey 3-Year Estimates

HEALTH

Health Risk Data

Category	MSA[1] (%)	U.S. (%)
Adults who have been told they have high blood pressure	26.3	28.7
Adults who have been told they have high blood cholesterol	28.2	37.5
Adults who have been told they have diabetes[3]	6.5	8.3
Adults who have been told they have arthritis	24.1	26.0
Adults who have been told they currently have asthma	6.5	8.8
Adults who are current smokers	21.8	17.9
Adults who are heavy drinkers[4]	2.4	5.1
Adults who are binge drinkers[5]	7.9	15.8
Adults who are overweight (BMI 25.0 - 29.9)	38.9	36.2
Adults who are obese (BMI 30.0 - 99.8)	27.1	26.9
Adults who participated in any physical activities in the past month	72.0	76.2
Adults 50+ who have ever had a sigmoidoscopy or colonoscopy[2]	59.7	62.2
Women 40+ who have had a mammogram within the past two years[2]	77.6	76.0
Adults age 18–64 who have any kind of health care coverage	82.4	83.1

Note: Data as of 2009 unless otherwise noted; (1) Figures cover the Nashville-Davidson—Murfreesboro, TN Metropolitan Statistical Area - see Appendix B for areas included; (2) Data as of 2008; (3) Figures do not include pregnancy-related, borderline, or pre-diabetes; (4) Heavy drinkers are classified as males having more than two drinks per day or females having more than one drink per day; (5) Binge drinkers are classified as males having five or more drinks on one occasion or females having four or more drinks on one occasion
Source: Centers for Disease Control and Prevention, Behaviorial Risk Factor Surveillance System, SMART: Selected Metropolitan/Micropolitan Area Risk Trends, 2008, 2009

Mortality Rates for the Top 10 Causes of Death in the U.S.

ICD-10[a] Sub-Chapter	ICD-10[a] Code	Age-Adjusted Mortality Rate[1] per 100,000 population	
		County[2]	U.S.
Malignant neoplasms	C00-C97	191.8	180.9
Ischaemic heart diseases	I20-I25	147.5	135.0
Other forms of heart disease	I30-I51	41.2	50.0
Cerebrovascular diseases	I60-I69	49.2	44.1
Chronic lower respiratory diseases	J40-J47	44.9	41.5
Other degenerative diseases of the nervous system	G30-G31	30.6	23.6
Diabetes mellitus	E10-E14	29.1	23.5
Other external causes of accidental injury	W00-X59	29.6	23.5
Organic, including symptomatic, mental disorders	F01-F09	27.7	22.2
Influenza and pneumonia	J09-J18	16.5	18.1

Note: (a) ICD-10 = International Classification of Diseases 10th Revision; (1) Mortality rates are a three year average covering 2005-2007; (2) Figures cover Davidson County
Source: Centers for Disease Control and Prevention, National Center for Health Statistics. Compressed Mortality File 1999-2007. CDC WONDER On-line Database, compiled from Compressed Mortality File 1999-2007 Series 20 No. 2M, 2010.

Mortality Rates for Selected Causes of Death

ICD-10[a] Sub-Chapter	ICD-10[a] Code	Age-Adjusted Mortality Rate[1] per 100,000 population	
		County[2]	U.S.
Assault	X85-Y09	13.3	6.0
Human immunodeficiency virus (HIV) disease	B20-B24	8.5	4.0
Hypertensive diseases	I10-I15	28.3	18.0
Intentional self-harm	X60-X84	11.3	11.0
Malnutrition	E40-E46	*1.0	0.8
Obesity and other hyperalimentation	E65-E68	2.9	1.5
Transport accidents	V01-V99	15.7	15.6
Viral hepatitis	B15-B19	2.9	2.1

Note: (a) ICD-10 = International Classification of Diseases 10th Revision; (1) Mortality rates are a three year average covering 2005-2007; (2) Figures cover Davidson County; (*) Unreliable data as per CDC
Source: Centers for Disease Control and Prevention, National Center for Health Statistics. Compressed Mortality File 1999-2007. CDC WONDER On-line Database, compiled from Compressed Mortality File 1999-2007 Series 20 No. 2M, 2010.

Distribution of Physicians and Dentists

Area[1]	Dentists[2]	D.O.[3]	M.D.[4]				
			Total	Family/ General Practice	Pediatrics	Medical Specialties	Surgical Specialties
Local (number)	355	45	2,062	106	148	811	563
Local (rate[5])	5.7	0.7	32.8	1.7	2.4	12.9	9.0
U.S. (rate[5])	4.5	1.9	18.3	2.5	1.4	6.8	4.1

Note: Data as of 2008 unless noted; (1) Local data covers Davidson County; (2) Data as of 2007; (3) Doctor of Osteopathic Medicine; (4) Includes active, non-federal, patient-care, office-based Doctors of Medicine; (5) rate per 10,000 population
Source: Area Resource File (ARF). 2009-2010 Release. U.S. Department of Health and Human Services, Health Resources and Services Administration, Bureau of Health Professions, Rockville, MD, August 2010

Hospitals

Nashville has the following hospitals: 9 general medical and surgical; 1 psychiatric; 1 rehabilitation; 2 long-term acute care.
AHA Guide to the Healthcare Field 2010

According to *U.S. News,* the Nashville-Davidson—Murfreesboro, TN Metropolitan Statistical Area is home to one of the best hospitals in the U.S.: **Vanderbilt University Medical Center**. The hospital listed was highly ranked in at least one adult specialty. *U.S. News Online, "America's Best Hospitals 2010-11"*

According to *U.S. News,* the Nashville-Davidson—Murfreesboro, TN Metropolitan Statistical Area is home to one of the best children's hospitals in the U.S.: **Monroe Carell Jr. Children's Hospital at Vanderbilt**. The hospital listed was highly ranked in at least one pediatric specialty. *U.S. News Online, "America's Best Children's Hospitals 2010-11"*

EDUCATION

Public School District Statistics

District Name	Schls	Pupils	Pupil/ Teacher Ratio	Minority Pupils[1] (%)	Free Lunch Eligible[2] (%)	IEP[3] (%)
Davidson County SD	139	74,312	14.0	66.8	57.6	11.1

Note: Table includes school districts with 2,000 or more students; (1) Percentage of students that are not non-Hispanic white; (2) Percentage of students that are eligible for the free lunch program; (3) Percentage of students that have an Individualized Education Program.
Source: U.S. Department of Education, National Center for Education Statistics, Common Core of Data, Local Education Agency (School District) Universe Survey: School Year 2008-2009; U.S. Department of Education, National Center for Education Statistics, Common Core of Data, Public Elementary/Secondary School Universe Survey: School Year 2008-2009

Top Public High Schools

High School Name	Index[1]	Rank[1]	Subsidized Lunch (%)[2]	E&E (%)[3]
Hillsboro[4]	1.783	871	45.0	15.8
Hume-Fogg Academic	5.735	32	18.0	90.2
Martin Luther King Academic Magnet	5.048	56	20.0	85.6

Note: (1) Public schools are ranked according to a ratio that is the number of Advanced Placement, International Baccalaureate, and/or Cambridge tests taken by all students at a school in 2009 divided by the number of graduating seniors. All of the schools on the list have an index of at least 1.000; they are in the top six percent of public schools measured this way. The rankings range from 1 to 1,734; (2) Percentage of students receiving federally subsidized meals; (3) E & E stands for equity and excellence percentage: the portion of all graduating seniors at a school that had at least one passing grade on one AP or IB test; (4) Schools that offer International Baccalaureate or Cambridge exams; (5) School is unranked, but has been identified by Newsweek as one of the nation's most elite public high schools.
Source: Newsweek Online, "Top High Schools 2010"

Highest Level of Education

Area	Less than H.S.	H.S. Diploma	Some College, No Deg.	Associate Degree	Bachelors Degree	Masters Degree	Profess. School Degree	Doctorate Degree
City	15.4	26.0	20.8	5.8	20.4	7.5	2.5	1.6
MSA[1]	14.5	29.4	21.1	6.0	19.4	6.4	2.0	1.2
U.S.	15.3	29.0	20.7	7.5	17.4	7.0	1.9	1.1

Note: Figures are 2010 estimated percentages and cover persons age 25 and over; (1) Metropolitan Statistical Area - see Appendix B for areas included
Source: Claritas, Inc.

Educational Attainment by Race

Area	High School Graduate (%)					Bachelor's Degree (%)				
	Total	White	Black	Asian	Hisp.[2]	Total	White	Black	Asian	Hisp.[2]
City	85.0	89.7	81.4	84.6	49.4	32.9	38.4	23.1	47.0	9.3
MSA[1]	85.9	88.2	81.8	87.0	54.6	29.8	31.6	22.8	46.4	11.3
U.S.	84.9	90.0	80.7	85.5	60.7	27.8	30.9	17.5	49.7	12.7

Note: Figures shown cover persons 25 years old and over; (1) Metropolitan Statistical Area - see Appendix B for areas included; (2) people of Hispanic origin can be of any race
Source: U.S. Census Bureau, 2007-2009 American Community Survey 3-Year Estimates

School Enrollment by Grade and Control

Area	Preschool (%)		Kindergarten (%)		Grades 1 - 4 (%)		Grades 5 - 8 (%)		Grades 9 - 12 (%)	
	Public	Private	Public	Private	Public	Private	Public	Private	Public	Private
City	46.5	53.5	75.6	24.4	84.2	15.8	77.8	22.2	81.9	18.1
MSA[1]	42.4	57.6	83.5	16.5	87.6	12.4	84.1	15.9	84.8	15.2
U.S.	54.3	45.7	86.4	13.6	88.9	11.1	89.1	10.9	90.2	9.8

Note: Figures shown cover persons 3 years old and over; (1) Metropolitan Statistical Area - see Appendix B for areas included
Source: U.S. Census Bureau, 2007-2009 American Community Survey 3-Year Estimates

Average Salaries of Public School Classroom Teachers

Area	2009-10		2010-11		Percent Change 2009-10 to 2010-11	Percent Change 2000-01 to 2010-11
	Dollars	Rank[1]	Dollars	Rank[1]		
Tennessee	46,290	40	47,043	43	1.63	25.7
U.S. Average	55,202	-	56,069	-	1.57	29.3

Note: (1) State rank ranges from 1 to 51 where 1 indicates highest salary.
Source: National Education Association, Rankings & Estimates: Rankings of the States 2010 and Estimates of School Statistics 2011, December 2010

Higher Education

Four-Year Colleges			Two-Year Colleges			Medical Schools[1]	Law Schools[2]	Voc/ Tech[3]
Public	Private Non-profit	Private For-profit	Public	Private Non-profit	Private For-profit			
1	9	6	2	1	6	2	1	3

Note: Figures cover institutions located within the city limits and include main campuses only; (1) includes schools accredited by the Liaison Committee on Medical Education and the American Osteopathic Association; (2) includes American Bar Association-accredited law schools; (3) includes all schools with programs that are less than 2 years.
Source: National Center for Education Statistics, Integrated Postsecondary Education System (IPEDS) Peer Analysis System, 2010-11; U.S. News & World Report, Medical School Directory, 2011; U.S. News & World Report, Law School Directory, 2011

According to *U.S. News & World Report,* the Nashville-Davidson—Murfreesboro, TN Metropolitan Statistical Area is home to one of the top 197 national universities in the U.S.: **Vanderbilt University** (#17). The rankings are based on quantitative measurements such as peer assessment, retention, faculty resources, student selectivity, financial resources, graduation rate, and alumni giving rate. *U.S. News & World Report, "America's Best Colleges 2011"*

According to *U.S. News & World Report,* the Nashville-Davidson—Murfreesboro, TN Metropolitan Statistical Area is home to one of the top 189 liberal arts colleges in the U.S.: **Fisk University** (#122). The rankings are based on quantitative measurements such as peer assessment, retention, faculty resources, student selectivity, financial resources, graduation rate, and alumni giving rate. *U.S. News & World Report, "America's Best Colleges 2011"*

According to *U.S. News & World Report,* the Nashville-Davidson—Murfreesboro, TN Metropolitan Statistical Area is home to one of the top 50 law schools in the U.S.: **Vanderbilt University** (#16). The rankings are based on a weighted average of 10 measures of quality: peer assessment score; assessment score by lawyers/judges; median LSAT scores; median undergrad GPA; acceptance rate; employment rates for graduates; bar passage rate; faculty resources; expenditures per student; student/faculty ratio; and library resources. *U.S. News & World Report, "America's Best Law Schools 2011"*

According to *Forbes,* the Nashville-Davidson—Murfreesboro, TN Metropolitan Statistical Area is home to one of the top 75 business schools in the U.S.: **Vanderbilt (Owen)** (#30). The rankings are based on the return on investment that graduates of the Class of 2004 received (median salary five years after graduation). *Forbes, "Best Business Schools," August 5, 2009*

PRESIDENTIAL ELECTION

2008 Presidential Election Results

Area	Obama	McCain	Nader	Other
Davidson County	59.9	38.9	0.4	0.8
U.S.	52.9	45.6	0.6	0.9

Note: Results are percentages and may not add to 100% due to rounding
Source: Dave Leip's Atlas of U.S. Presidential Elections, www.uselectionatlas.org

EMPLOYERS

Major Employers

Company Name	Industry	Type of Site
American Home Patients	Home health care services	Single
Asurion Corporation	Automotive services, nec	Headquarters
Baptist Hospital	General medical and surgical hospitals	Headquarters
Cloverleaf Partners	Home health care services	Single
Comdata Network	Data processing and preparation	Branch
County of Sumner	Executive offices	Headquarters
Gaylord Entertainment Company	Hotels and motels	Headquarters
Gaylord Opryland Usa	Hotels and motels	Headquarters
HCA Information Services	Data processing and preparation	Single
Hospital Administration	General medical and surgical hospitals	Single
Ingram Book Group	Books, periodicals, and newspapers	Headquarters
International Automotive	Automobile parking	Branch
Lifeway Christian Store	Book stores	Headquarters
Mazda America Credit	Personal credit institutions	Headquarters
Middle Tennessee State Univ	Colleges and universities	Headquarters
Nissan	Automobiles and other motor vehicles	Headquarters
Psychiatric Solutions	Offices and clinics of medical doctors	Headquarters
Rutherford Board of Education	Elementary and secondary schools	Branch
State Industries	Household appliances, nec	Headquarters
Tennessean The	Newspapers	Branch
Tennessee State University	Colleges and universities	Headquarters
Val Dor	Broadwoven fabric mills, wool	Single
Vanderbilt University Hospital	Colleges and universities	Headquarters

Note: Companies shown are located within the Nashville metropolitan area; nec = not elsewhere classified.
Source: www.zapdata.com, January 2011

Best Companies to Work For

HCA, headquartered in Nashville, is among the "100 Best Places to Work in IT." To qualify, companies, both public and private, had to have a minimum of 50 IT employees. Companies were selected based on average salary and bonus increases, the percentage of IT employees receiving promotions, IT staff turnover rates, training and development programs, and the percentage of women and minorities in IT staff and management positions. In addition, information was collected on how the organizations reward outstanding performance, how their retention programs are structured and what benefits they offer. *Computerworld, "100 Best Places to Work in IT 2010"*

PUBLIC SAFETY

Crime Rate

Area	All Crimes	Violent Crimes				Property Crimes		
		Murder	Forcible Rape	Robbery	Aggrav. Assault	Burglary	Larceny -Theft	Motor Vehicle Theft
City	5,918.8	12.6	42.9	323.0	761.9	1,035.4	3,460.1	282.7
Suburbs[1]	2,819.6	3.4	26.3	50.2	278.4	612.0	1,717.9	131.4
Metro[2]	4,012.9	6.9	32.7	155.2	464.6	775.0	2,388.8	189.7
U.S.	3,465.5	5.0	28.7	133.0	262.8	716.3	2,060.9	258.8

Note: Figures are crimes per 100,000 population; (1) All areas within the metro area that are located outside the city limits; (2) Metropolitan Statistical Area - see Appendix B for areas included
Source: FBI Uniform Crime Reports, 2009

Hate Crimes

Area	Number of Quarters Reported	Bias Motivation				
		Race	Religion	Sexual Orientation	Ethnicity	Disability
City	4	1	0	4	1	0

Source: Federal Bureau of Investigation, Hate Crime Statistics 2009

Identity Theft Consumer Complaints

Area	Complaints	Complaints per 100,000 Population	Rank[2]
MSA[1]	1,120	73.6	182
U.S.	250,854	81.3	-

Note: (1) Metropolitan Statistical Area - see Appendix B for areas included; (2) Rank ranges from 1 to 384 where 1 indicates greatest number of complaints per 100,000 population
Source: Federal Trade Commission, Consumer Sentinel Network Data Book for January - December 2010

RECREATION

Culture

Dance[1]	Theatre[1]	Instrumental Music[1]	Vocal Music[1]	Series/ Festivals	Museums	Zoos and Aquariums[2]
1	7	1	2	5	14	1

Note: (1) Number of professional perfoming groups; (2) AZA-accredited
Source: The Grey House Performing Arts Directory, 2011-2012; Official Museum Directory, 2010; American Association of Museums, AAM Member Museums, March 2011; Association of Zoos & Aquariums, AZA Member Zoos & Aquariums, May 2011

Professional Sports Teams

Team Name	League
Nashville Predators	National Hockey League (NHL)
Tennessee Titans	National Football League (NFL)

Note: Includes teams located in the Nashville metro area.
Source: Original research

CLIMATE

Average and Extreme Temperatures

Temperature	Jan	Feb	Mar	Apr	May	Jun	Jul	Aug	Sep	Oct	Nov	Dec	Yr.
Extreme High (°F)	78	84	86	91	95	106	107	104	105	94	84	79	107
Average High (°F)	47	51	60	71	79	87	90	89	83	72	60	50	70
Average Temp. (°F)	38	41	50	60	68	76	80	79	72	61	49	41	60
Average Low (°F)	28	31	39	48	57	65	69	68	61	48	39	31	49
Extreme Low (°F)	-17	-13	2	23	34	42	54	49	36	26	-1	-10	-17

Note: Figures cover the years 1948-1990
Source: National Climatic Data Center, International Station Meteorological Climate Summary, 9/96

Average Precipitation/Snowfall/Humidity

Precip./Humidity	Jan	Feb	Mar	Apr	May	Jun	Jul	Aug	Sep	Oct	Nov	Dec	Yr.
Avg. Precip. (in.)	4.4	4.2	5.0	4.1	4.6	3.7	3.8	3.3	3.2	2.6	3.9	4.6	47.4
Avg. Snowfall (in.)	4	3	1	Tr	0	0	0	0	0	Tr	1	1	11
Avg. Rel. Hum. 6am (%)	81	81	80	81	86	86	88	90	90	87	83	82	85
Avg. Rel. Hum. 3pm (%)	61	57	51	48	52	52	54	53	52	49	55	59	54

Note: Figures cover the years 1948-1990; Tr = Trace amounts (<0.05 in. of rain; <0.5 in. of snow)
Source: National Climatic Data Center, International Station Meteorological Climate Summary, 9/96

Weather Conditions

Temperature			Daytime Sky			Precipitation		
10°F & below	32°F & below	90°F & above	Clear	Partly cloudy	Cloudy	0.01 inch or more precip.	0.1 inch or more snow/ice	Thunder-storms
5	76	51	98	135	132	119	8	54

Note: Figures are average number of days per year and cover the years 1948-1990
Source: National Climatic Data Center, International Station Meteorological Climate Summary, 9/96

HAZARDOUS WASTE

Superfund Sites

Nashville has no sites on the EPA's Superfund Final National Priorities List.
U.S. Environmental Protection Agency, Final National Priorities List, April 1, 2011

AIR & WATER QUALITY

Air Quality Index

Area	Percent of Days when Air Quality was...[2]				AQI Statistics	
	Good	Moderate	Unhealthy for Sensitive Groups	Unhealthy	Maximum	Median
Area[1]	64.5	34.7	0.8	0.0	109	44

Note: The Air Quality Index (AQI) is an index for reporting daily air quality. EPA calculates the AQI for five major air pollutants regulated by the Clean Air Act: ground-level ozone, particle pollution (also known as particulate matter), carbon monoxide, sulfur dioxide, and nitrogen dioxide. The AQI runs from 0 to 500. The higher the AQI value, the greater the level of air pollution and the greater the health concern. There are six AQI categories: "Good" The AQI is between 0 and 50. Air quality is considered satisfactory; "Moderate" The AQI is between 51 and 100. Air quality is acceptable; "Unhealthy for Sensitive Groups" When AQI values are between 101 and 150, members of sensitive groups may experience health effects; "Unhealthy" When AQI values are between 151 and 200 everyone may begin to experience health effects; "Very Unhealthy" AQI values between 201 and 300 trigger a health alert; "Hazardous" AQI values over 300 trigger health warnings of emergency conditions; (1) Data covers Davidson County; (2) Based on 366 days with AQI data in 2008; The EPA has suspended data updates while it assesses its data systems, including AirData reports and maps.
Source: U.S. Environmental Protection Agency, AirData Report, 2008

Air Quality Index Pollutants

Area	Percent of Days when AQI Pollutant was...[2]					
	Carbon Monoxide	Nitrogen Dioxide	Ozone	Sulfur Dioxide	Particulate Matter 2.5	Particulate Matter 10
Area[1]	0.0	0.0	23.8	0.0	76.2	0.0

Note: The Air Quality Index (AQI) is an index for reporting daily air quality. EPA calculates the AQI for five major air pollutants regulated by the Clean Air Act: ground-level ozone, particle pollution (also known as particulate matter), carbon monoxide, sulfur dioxide, and nitrogen dioxide. The AQI runs from 0 to 500. The higher the AQI value, the greater the level of air pollution and the greater the health concern; (1) Data covers Davidson County; (2) Based on 366 days with AQI data in 2008; The EPA has suspended data updates while it assesses its data systems, including AirData reports and maps.
Source: U.S. Environmental Protection Agency, AirData Report, 2008

Air Quality Index Trends

| Area | Trend Sites (days) | | | | | | | | All Sites (days) |
	2002	2003	2004	2005	2006	2007	2008	2009	2009
MSA[1]	36	20	7	26	17	34	9	1	1

Note: Figures are the number of days the AQI value exceeded 100 in a given year. An AQI value greater than 100 indicates that air quality would have been in the unhealthful range on that day. Data from exceptional events are included. These counts are presented in two ways. First, the counts are based on sites having an adequate record of monitoring data during the trend period (trend sites). These counts represent the relative change in the number of days with AQI values greater than 100. In the last column, the counts are based on all sites with data in the most recent year (because it is possible for a site to have data in the most recent year but not enough data to be a trend site); (1) Data covers the Nashville-Davidson—Murfreesboro, TN Metropolitan Statistical Area - see Appendix B for areas included
Source: U.S. Environmental Protection Agency, Office of Air and Radiation, Air Quality Index Information, "Number of Days with Air Quality Index Values Greater than 100 and Trend Sites, 1990-2009, and at All Sites in 2009"

Maximum Air Pollutant Concentrations

	Particulate Matter 10 (ug/m^3)	Particulate Matter 2.5 (ug/m^3)	Ozone (ppm)	Carbon Monoxide (ppm)	Sulfur Dioxide (ppm)	Nitrogen Dioxide (ppm)	Lead (ug/m^3)
MSA[1] Level	34	21	0.07	2	0.007	0.012	n/a
NAAQS[2]	150	35	0.075	9	0.140	0.053	0.15
Met NAAQS[2]	Yes	Yes	Yes	Yes	Yes	Yes	n/a

Note: Data from exceptional events are not included; (1) Data covers the Nashville-Davidson—Murfreesboro, TN Metropolitan Statistical Area - see Appendix B for areas included; (2) National Ambient Air Quality Standards; n/a not available
Concentrations: Particulate Matter 10 (coarse particulate) - highest second maximum 24-hour concentration; Particulate Matter 2.5 (fine particulate) - highest 98th percentile 24-hour concentration; Ozone - highest fourth daily maximum 8-hour concentration; Carbon Monoxide - highest second maximum non-overlapping 8-hour concentration; Sulfur Dioxide - highest second maximum 24-hour concentration; Nitrogen Dioxide - highest arithmetic mean concentration; Lead - maximum running 3-month average
Units: ppm = parts per million; ug/m^3 = micrograms per cubic meter
Source: U.S. Environmental Protection Agency, CBSA Factbook 2009, Air Quality Statistics by City, 2009

Drinking Water

Water System Name	Pop. Served	Primary Water Source Type	Violations[1] Health Based	Monitoring/ Reporting
Nashville Water Dept. #1	582,341	Surface	0	0

Note: (1) Based on violation data from January 1, 2010 to December 31, 2010 (includes unresolved violations from earlier years)
Source: U.S. Environmental Protection Agency, Office of Ground Water and Drinking Water, Safe Drinking Water Information System (based on data extracted May 9, 2011)

New Orleans, Louisiana

Background

New Orleans, the old port city upriver from the mouth of the Mississippi River, is on a par with San Francisco and New York City as one of the United States' most interesting cities. The birthplace of jazz is rich in unique local history, distinctive neighborhoods, and an unmistakably individual character.

The failure of the federal levees following Hurricane Katrina in 2005 brought New Orleans to its knees and put 80 percent of the city under floodwaters for weeks. The Crescent City's revival since then is a testament to her unique spirit, an influx of federal dollars, and an outpouring from volunteers ranging from church groups to spring breakers who returned year after year to help rebuild.

New Orleans was founded on behalf of France by the brothers Le Moyne, Sieurs d'Iberville, and de Bienville, in 1718. Despite early travesties such as disease, starvation, and an unwilling working class, New Orleans nevertheless emerged as a genteel antebellum slave society, fashioning itself after the rigid social hierarchy of Versailles. Even after New Orleans was ceded to Spain after the French & Indian War, this unequal lifestyle, however gracious, persisted.

The port city briefly returned to French control, then became a crown jewel in the 1803 Louisiana Purchase to the U.S. The transfer of control changed New Orleans's Old World isolation. American settlers introduced aggressive business acumen to the area, as well as the idea of respect for the self-made man. As trade opened up with countries around the world, this made for a happy union. New Orleans became "Queen City of the South," growing prosperous from adventurous riverboat traders and speculators, as well as the cotton trade.

Today, much of the city's Old World charm remains, resulting from a polyglot of Southern, Creole, African-American, and European cultures. New Orleans' fine and native cuisine, indigenous music, unique festivals, and sultry, pleasing atmosphere, drew more than eight million visitors in 2010.

A major pillar of the city's economy is the enormous tourism trade that includes the Ernest N. Morial Convention Center's numerous convention goers who fill more than 35,000 rooms. A second economic pillar is the Port of New Orleans, one of the nation's leading general cargo ports. In recent years, it has seen $400 million invested in new facilities.

In addition, an influx of mostly young people who arrived after Katrina is giving rise to a new start-up spirit. Plus, state tax breaks have helped to turn New Orleans into "Hollywood South," where 35 films were in production in 2010.

New Orleans has given birth to a mother lode of cultural phenomena: Dixieland jazz, musicians Louis Armstrong, Mahalia Jackson, Dr. John, and chefs Emeril Lagasse and John Besh. The city is well aware of its "cultural economy," which employs 12.5 percent of the local workforce.

Popular tourist draws include the annual Mardi Gras celebration—which spans two long weekends leading up to Fat Tuesday—and the annual New Orleans Jazz & Heritage Festival. The Louisiana Superdome, home to the 2010 Super Bowl champion New Orleans Saints, also plays host to major events including the occasional Super Bowl. Tourists are likely to appreciate the nearly $75 million Consolidated Rental Car Facility project underway to expand rental capacity and bring scattered facilities under one roof at the Louis Armstrong New Orleans International Airport.

In addition, an effort to boost medical services—and a medical economy that suffered after the hurricane—is underway with a major new Louisiana State University teaching/Veterans Administration hospital for which ground was broken in spring 2011.

In his 2011 state of the city address, Mayor Mitch Landrieu said more than $13 billion in investments would unfold in coming years for bridge, airport, road and hospital repairs. School rebuilding was set for a $1.8 billion influx. Since Katrina, the majority of New Orleans public schools have become charter schools—a major experiment that is seeing some success. Higher education campuses include Tulane University (including a med school and law school), Loyola University, and the University of New Orleans. Louisiana State University has a medical school campus downtown.

Cultural amenities include the New Orleans Museum of Art located in the live-oak filled City Park, the Ogden Museum of Southern Art, and Audubon Park, designed by John Charles Olmsted (nephew and business partner of Frederick Law Olmsted) with its golf course and the Audubon Zoo.

The New Orleans metro area is virtually surrounded by water, which influences its climate. Between mid-June and September, temperatures are kept down by near-daily sporadic thunderstorms. Cold spells sometimes reach the area in winter but seldom last. Frequent and sometimes heavy rains are typical. Hurricane season officially runs from June 1 to November 30 but typically reaches its height in late summer.

Rankings

General Rankings

- New Orleans was ranked #39 out of 379 metro areas in *Places Rated Almanac*. Criteria: health care; education; recreation; transportation; ambience; climate; crime; housing costs; jobs. *Places Rated Almanac, 7th Edition, 2007*

- New Orleans was identified as one of seven American cities that have lost the most people in the past decade. The city ranked #1. Criteria: population change 2000-2009; percent population change 2000-2009; home vacancy rates. *24/7 Wall St., "American Cities that are Running Out of People," January 1, 2011*

- New Orleans was selected as one of "America's Favorite Cities." The city ranked #1 in the "Food/Dining" category. Respondents to an online survey were asked to rate 35 top urban destinations in the U.S. from a visitor's perspective. Criteria: big-name restaurants; ethnic food; farmers' markets; neighborhood joints and cafes. *Travelandleisure.com, "America's Favorite Cities 2010," November 2010*

- New Orleans was selected as one of "America's Favorite Cities." The city ranked #1 in the "Nightlife" category. Respondents to an online survey were asked to rate 35 top urban destinations in the U.S. from a visitor's perspective. Criteria: cocktail hour; live music/concerts and bands; singles/bar scene. *Travelandleisure.com, "America's Favorite Cities 2010," November 2010*

- New Orleans was selected as one of the "Best Places to Live" by *Men's Journal*. Criteria: "18 towns were selected that are perfecting the art of living well—places where conservation is more important than development, bike makers and breweries and farmers thrive, and Whole Foods is considered a big-box store." *Men's Journal, "Best Place to Live 2011: Think Small, Live Big," April 2011*

- New Orleans appeared on *Travel + Leisure's* list of the ten best cities in the continental U.S. and Canada. The city was ranked #7. Criteria: activities/attractions; culture/arts; restaurants/food; people; and value. *Travel + Leisure, "The World's Best Awards 2010"*

Business/Finance Rankings

- New Orleans was identified as one of the 20 weakest-performing metro areas during the recession and recovery from December 2007 through December 2010. Criteria: percent change in employment; percentage point change in unemployment rate; percent change in gross metropolitan product; percent change in House Price Index. *Brookings Institution, MetroMonitor: Tracking Economic Recession and Recovery in America's 100 Largest Metropolitan Areas, March 2011*

- New Orleans was selected as one of the best places to ride out a recession in the U.S. by *Business Week.* Twenty cities were identified as places where large portions of the population worked in anticyclical industries such as government, health care, education, agriculture, and legal services. *BusinessWeek, "Some Cities Will Be Safer in a Recession," October 14, 2008*

- New Orleans was cited as one of America's top metros for new and expanded facility projects in 2010. The area ranked #10 in the large metro area category (population over 1 million). *Site Selection, "2010 Top Metros," March 2011*

- *American City Business Journals* ranked America's 261 largest cities in terms of their resident's wealth. New Orleans ranked #98. Criteria: per capita income; median household income; percentage of households with annual incomes of $200,000 or more; median home value. *American City Business Journals, www.bizjournals.com, "Where the Money Is: America's Wealth Centers," August 18, 2008*

- The New Orleans metro area appeared on the Milken Institute "2010 Best Performing Metros" list. Rank: #123 out of 200 large metro areas. Criteria: job growth; wage and salary growth; high-tech output growth. *Milken Institute, "2010 Best Performing Metros"*

- The New Orleans metro area was selected as one of the best cities for entrepreneurs in America by *Inc. Magazine*. Criteria: job-growth data for 335 metro areas was analyzed for: recent growth trend (the current and prior year's employment growth rates, with the current year emphasized); mid-term growth (the average annual 2002-2007 growth rate); long-term trend (the sum of the 2002-2007 and 1996-2001 employment growth rates multiplied by the ratio of the 1996-2001 growth rate over the 2002-2007 growth rate); current year growth. The New Orleans metro area ranked #13 among large metro areas and #60 overall. *Inc. Magazine, "The Best Cities for Doing Business," July 2008*

- *Forbes* ranked the 200 most populous metro areas in the U.S. in terms of the "Best Places for Business and Careers." The New Orleans metro area was ranked #190. Criteria: 12 metrics including costs (business and living), job growth (past and projected), income growth, educational attainment, projected economic growth, crime, cultural and recreational opportunities, net migration patterns, percentage of subprime mortgages handed out over a three-year period, and the number of highly ranked four-year colleges. *Forbes, "Best Places for Business and Careers," April 14, 2010*

Children/Family Rankings

- New Orleans was selected as one of the least safe cities for children in America by *Men's Health*. The city ranked #2 of 10. Criteria: accidental death rates for kids ages 5 to 14; number of car seat inspection locations per child; sex offenders per capita; percentage of abused children protected from further abuse; strength of child-restraint and bike-helmet laws. *Men's Health, "The Safest (and Least Safe) Cities for Children," September 2010*

- New Orleans was selected as one of the 10 worst cities to raise children in the U.S. by *KidFriendlyCities.org*. Criteria: education; environment; health; employment; crime; diversity; cost of living. *KidFriendlyCities.org, "Top Rated Kid/Family Friendly Cities 2009"*

- The New Orleans metro area was selected as one of the "Best Cities for Relocating Families" by Worldwide ERC and Primacy Relocation. The 2008 study looked at nearly 50 factors important to relocating families including: recent job growth; nearby top-ranked colleges; in-state tuition for four-year public colleges; population growth since 2000; pediatricians per 100,000 population; and a Green Living index. *Worldwide ERC and Primacy Relocation, "2008 Best Cities for Relocating Families"*

Culture/Performing Arts Rankings

- New Orleans was selected as one of "America's Top 25 Arts Destinations." The city ranked #2 in the mid-sized city (population 100,000 to 499,999) category. Criteria: readers' top choices for arts travel destinations based on the richness and variety of visual arts sites, activities and events. *American Style, "America's Top 25 Arts Destinations," May 2010*

Dating/Romance Rankings

- New Orleans appeared on *Men's Health's* list of the most sex-happy cities in America. The city ranked #46 of 100. Criteria: condom sales; birth rates; sex toy sales; rates of chlamydia, gonorrhea, and syphilis. *Men's Health, "America's Most Sex-Happy Cities," October 2010*

- *Men's Health* ranked 100 U.S. cities in terms of best (and worst) marriages. New Orleans was ranked #88 (#1 = worst marriages). Criteria: rate of failed marriages; stringency of divorce laws; percentage of population who've split; number of licensed marriage and family therapists. *Men's Health, "Splitsville, USA," May 2010*

- The New Orleans metro area was selected as one of the "Best Cities for Relocating Singles" by Worldwide ERC and Primacy Relocation. The area ranked #19 out of the 100 largest metro areas in the U.S. Areas were selected based on the following criteria: recent job growth; recent singles population growth; overall population growth; affordable rental housing; cost-of-living index; expanded arts and recreation opportunities; ratio of single men and single women; affordability of quality higher education (including state residency requirements); diversity index; climate; population density. *Worldwide ERC and Primacy Relocation, "2008 Best Cities for Relocating Singles"*

Education Rankings

- New Orleans was selected as one of "America's Most Literate Cities." The city ranked #15 out of the 75 largest U.S. cities. Criteria: number of booksellers; library resources; Internet resources; educational attainment; periodical publishing resources; newspaper circulation. *Central Connecticut State University, "America's Most Literate Cities 2010"*

- New Orleans was identified as one of the 100 "smartest" metro areas in the U.S. The area ranked #78. Criteria: the editors rated the collective brainpower of the 100 largest metro area in the U.S based on their residents' educational attainment. *American City Business Journals, www.bizjournals.com, April 14, 2008*

- New Orleans was identified as one of "America's Brainiest Bastions" by *Portfolio.com*. The metro area ranked #123 out of 200. Portfolio.com analyzed levels of educational attainment in the nation's 200 largest metropolitan areas. The editors established scores for five levels of educational attainment, based on relative earning power of adult workers age 25 or older. Scores were determined by comparing the median income for all workers with the median income for those workers at a specified educational level. *Portfolio.com, "America's Brainiest Bastions," December 1, 2010*

Environmental Rankings

- Scarborough Research, a leading market research firm, identified the top local markets for green appliance households. The New Orleans DMA (Designated Market Area) ranked in the top 16 with 36% of consumers reporting that they own an energy-efficient appliance. *Scarborough Research, March 23, 2010*

- New Orleans was selected as one of 22 "Smarter Cities" for energy by the Natural Resources Defense Council." Criteria: investment in green power; energy efficiency measures; conservation. *Natural Resources Defense Council, "2010 Smarter Cities," July 19, 2010*

- New Orleans was selected as one of worst summer weather cities in the U.S. by the *Farmers' Almanac*. The city ranked #2 out of 5. Criteria: average summer and winter temperatures; humidity; precipitation; number of overcast days. The editors only considered cities with populations of 50,000 or more. *Farmers' Almanac, "America's Ten Worst Weather Cities," September 7, 2010*

- 100 of the largest metro areas in the U.S. were analyzed in terms of their current drought severity. The New Orleans metro area ranked #65 (#1 = driest). The rankings were based on statistics such as long-term precipitation trends and patterns and the Palmer drought indices. *Sperling's BestPlaces, www.BestPlaces.net, "America's Drought-Riskiest Cities," November 2007*

- The New Orleans metro area appeared in *Country Home's* "Best Green Places" report. The area ranked #304 out of 379. Criteria: official energy policies; green power; green buildings; availability of fresh, locally grown food. *Country Home, "Best Green Places," 2008*

Health/Fitness Rankings

- The American Podiatric Medical Association and *Prevention* magazine ranked 100 American cities based on walkability. Nineteen walking criteria were evaluated including the percentage of adults who walk to work, number of parks per square mile, number of trails for walking and hiking, air pollution, use of mass transit, crime rate, pedestrian fatalities, and percentage of adults who walk for fitness. New Orleans ranked #22. *Prevention, "The Best Walking Cities of 2009," May 2009; American Podiatric Medical Association, "2009 Best Fitness-Walking Cities," April 7, 2009*

- New Orleans was identified as a "2011 Asthma Capital." The area ranked #76 out of the nation's 100 largest metropolitan areas. Twelve factors were used to identify the most challenging places to live for people with asthma: estimated prevalence; self-reported prevalence; crude death rate for asthma; annual pollen score; annual air quality; public smoking laws; number of board-certified asthma specialists; school inhaler access laws; rescue medication use; controller medication use; uninsured rate; poverty rate. *Asthma and Allergy Foundation of America, "2011 Asthma Capitals"*

- New Orleans was identified as a 2009 "Spring Allergy Capital." The area ranked #23 out of 100. Three groups of factors were used to identify the most severe cities for people with allergies during the spring season: annual pollen levels; medicine utilization; access to board-certified allergists. *Asthma and Allergy Foundation of America, "Spring Allergy Capitals 2009"*

- New Orleans was identified as a 2010 "Fall Allergy Capital." The area ranked #21 out of 100. Three groups of factors were used to identify the most severe cities for people with allergies during the fall season: annual pollen levels; medicine utilization; access to board-certified allergists. *Asthma and Allergy Foundation of America, "Fall Allergy Capitals 2010"*

- *Men's Health* examined 100 U.S. cities and selected the best and worst cities for men. New Orleans was ranked among the ten worst at #9. Criteria: dozens of statistical parameters of long life in the categories of health, quality of life, and fitness. *Men's Health, "The 10 Best and Worst Cities for Men 2011," January/February 2011*

- Ortho-McNeil Neurologics, in partnership with Sperling's BestPlaces, analyzed 110 metro areas and identified those U.S. cities with the highest prevalence of factors that are most commonly associated with migraine headaches. The New Orleans metro area ranked #72. Criteria: number of migraine-related drug prescriptions per capita; lifestyle factors that can contribute to migraines; environmental factors that can trigger migraines; and consumption of migraine-triggering foods. *Ortho-McNeil Neurologics, "America's Migraine Hot Spots," March 14, 2006*

- An analysis of the "Best & Worst Cities for Sleep" was conducted by Sperling's BestPlaces. The study ranked America's 50 most populated metro areas. The New Orleans metro area ranked #17 (#1 = best city for sleep). Criteria: number of days residents didn't get enough rest or sleep during the past month; average length of daily commute; divorce rate; unemployment rate. *Sperling's BestPlaces, www.BestPlaces.net, "Best & Worst Cities for Sleep," 2006*

- The New Orleans metro area was identified as one of "America's Most Obese Cities" by *Forbes*. The magazine analyzed BMI (body mass index) data from the CDC in the 50 most populated metro areas in the U.S. and ranked the top 20. The area ranked #13. *Forbes, "America's Most Obese Cities," November 26, 2007*

- The New Orleans metro area appeared in the 2010 Gallup-Healthways Well-Being Index. The index, based on interviews with more than 353,000 Americans during 2009, asked individuals to assess their jobs, finances, physical health, emotional state of mind and communities. The metro area ranked #119 out of 162. Criteria: life evaluation; emotional health; work environment; physical health; healthy behaviors; basic access (basic needs optimal for a healthy life, such as access to food and medicine, having health insurance and feeling safe while walking at night). *Gallup-Healthways, "Well-Being Index 2010"*

- The New Orleans metro area was identified as one of "America's 20 Most Sedentary Cities" by *Forbes*. The metro area ranked #2. Criteria: percentage of overweight or obese people; percentage of people who had not engaged in any physical activity in the past 30 days; average number of hours of TV watched per week. *Forbes.com, "America's Most Sedentary Cities," October 29, 2007*

- 50 of the largest metro areas in the U.S. were analyzed in terms of their health and fitness by the American College of Sports Medicine in their "American Fitness Index." The New Orleans metro area ranked #41 (#1 = healthiest). Criteria: preventative health behaviors; levels of chronic disease; health care access; community resources and policies that support physical activity. *American College of Sports Medicine, "Health and Community Fitness Status of the 50 Largest Metropolitan Areas," May 24, 2010*

- New Orleans was selected as one of the "20 Most Livable U.S. Cities for Wheelchair Users" by the Christopher & Dana Reeve Foundation. The city ranked #18. Criteria: Medicaid eligibility and spending; access to physicians and rehabilitation facilities; access to fitness facilities and recreation; access to paratransit; percentage of people living with disabilities who are employed; clean air; climate. *Christopher & Dana Reeve Foundation, "20 Most Livable U.S. Cities for Wheelchair Users," July 26, 2010*

- *The Daily Beast* identified the 30 U.S metro areas with the worst smoking habits. The New Orleans metro area ranked #24. Sixty urban centers with populations of more than one million were ranked based on the following criteria: number of smokers; number of cigarettes smoked per day; fewest attempts to quit. *The Daily Beast, "30 Cities With Smoking Problems," January 3, 2011*

Real Estate Rankings

- *Fortune* ranked the 100 largest metro areas in the U.S. in terms of projected median home price change in 2010. The New Orleans metro area ranked #23. *Fortune, "The 2010 Housing Outlook," December 9, 2009*

- New Orleans was identified as one of the worst places for real estate investors by *Forbes.com*. Criteria: 700 real estate professional were asked to name the best (and worst) places to invest in commercial real estate in the coming year. *Forbes.com, "Real Estate Markets Most Likely to Rebound," October 29, 2008*

- New Orleans appeared on ApartmentRatings.com "Top Cities for Renters" list in 2009." The area ranked #72. Overall satisfaction ratings were ranked using thousands of user submitted scores for hundreds of apartment complexes located in the 100 most populated U.S. municipalities. *ApartmentRatings.com, "2009 Renter Satisfaction Rankings"*

- New Orleans appeared on CNNMoney.com's list of "Foreclosure Hotspots." The list includes the 10 cities with the fastest-growing foreclosure rates out of the 100 worst-hit places. *CNNMoney.com, "Foreclosure Hotspots," February 14, 2011*

- The New Orleans metro area was identified as one of the "Top 25 Real Estate Investment Markets" by *FinestExperts.com*. The metro area ranked #8. Over 10,000 real estate markets were analyzed to identify the most suitable places for real estate investors to seek stability and growth. Criteria: employment; rental markets; growth levels as offset by foreclosures. *FinestExperts.com, "Top 25 Real Estate Investment Markets," January 7, 2010*

- The nation's largest metro areas were analyzed in terms of the percentage of households entering some stage of foreclosure in 2010. The New Orleans metro area ranked #95 out of 206 (#1 = highest foreclosure rate). *RealtyTrac, 2010 Year-End Metropolitan Foreclosure Market Report, January 27, 2011*

- The New Orleans metro area appeared in a *Wall Street Journal* article ranking cities by "housing stress." The metro area was ranked #14 (#1 = most stress). Criteria: fraction of mortgage-holding homeowners with a monthly housing payment in excess of 30 percent of income; percentage of people without health insurance; unemployment rate. *The Wall Street Journal, "Which Cities Face Biggest Housing Risk," October 5, 2010*

- The Center for Housing Policy ranked 210 U.S metropolitan areas by the fair market rent for a two-bedroom unit. The New Orleans metro area was ranked #58. (#1 = most expensive) with a rent of $982. Criteria: Fair Market Rent (FMR) in effect during the fourth quarter of 2009 based on HUD's fiscal year 2010 FMRs. *The Center for Housing Policy, "Paycheck to Paycheck: Most to Least Expensive Rental Markets in 2009"*

Safety Rankings

- Allstate ranked the 200 largest cities in America in terms of driver safety. New Orleans ranked #148. In addition, drivers were 23.6% more likely to have had an accident compared to the national average. Allstate researchers analyzed internal property damage reported claims over a two-year period (from January 2007 to December 2008) to ensure the findings would not be affected by external influences such as weather or road construction. A weighted average of the two-year numbers determined the annual percentages. The report defines an auto crash as any collision resulting in a property damage claim. *Allstate, "The 2010 Allstate America's Best Drivers Report™"*

- New Orleans was identified as one of the most dangerous mid-size cities in America by CQ Press. All 234 cities with populations of 100,000 to 499,999 that reported crime rates in 2009 for murder, rape, robbery, aggravated assault, burglary, and motor vehicle thefts were ranked. The city ranked #7 out of the top 10. *CQ Press, City Crime Rankings 2010-2011*

- Sperling's BestPlaces analyzed the tracks of tropical storms for the past 100 years and ranked which areas are most likely to be hit by a major hurricane. The New Orleans metro area ranked #9 out of 10. *Sperling's BestPlaces, www.bestplaces.net, February 2, 2006*

- The National Insurance Crime Bureau ranked 366 metro areas in the U.S. in terms of per capita rates of vehicle theft. The New Orleans metro area ranked #38 (#1 = highest rate). Criteria: number of vehicle theft offenses per 100,000 inhabitants. *National Insurance Crime Bureau, "Hot Spots," May 17, 2010*

- The New Orleans metro area was identified as one of the "The Most Dangerous Metro Areas for Pedestrians" by Transportation for America and the Surface Transportation Policy Partnership. The metro area ranked #15 out of 52 metro areas with over 1 million residents. Criteria: area's population divided by the number of pedestrian fatalities in that area. *Transportation for America and the Surface Transportation Policy Partnership, "Dangerous by Design: Solving the Epidemic of Preventable Pedestrian Deaths (and Making Great Neighborhoods)," November 11, 2009*

Seniors/Retirement Rankings

- The New Orleans metro area was selected as one of the "10 Best Places for Single Seniors to Retire" by *U.S. News & World Report*. Criteria: metro areas with the most single seniors age 55 and over. *U.S. News & World Report, "10 Best Places for Single Seniors to Retire," November 1, 2010*

- New Orleans was selected as one of "10 Historic Places to Retire" by *U.S. News & World Report*. The editors looked for places filled with museums, libraries, and national historic monuments that also offer a good quality of life and plenty of amenities for seniors. *U.S. News & World Report, "10 Historic Places to Retire," September 6, 2010*

- The New Orleans metro area was selected as one of the "Best Places for Military Retirees" by *U.S. News*. The area was ranked #9 out of 10. Criteria: climate; health resources; health indicators; crime levels; local school performance; recreational resources; arts and culture; airport and mass transit resources; susceptibility to natural disasters; military facilities and base amenities; VA medical services; tax policies affecting military pensions, unemployment trends; higher education resources; overall affordability; housing costs; home price trends; economic stability. *U.S. News & Word Report, "Best Places for Military Retirees," December 8, 2010*

Sports/Recreation Rankings

- New Orleans appeared on the *Sporting News* list of the "Best Sports Cities" for 2010. The area ranked #22 out of 402 cities in the U.S. *Sporting News* takes a 12-month snapshot, roughly October to October, of each city's sports, putting a heavy premium on regular-season won-lost records (from the most recently completed season). Other criteria include: playoff berths, bowl appearances and tournament bids; championships; applicable power ratings; quality of competition; overall fan fervor as measured in part by attendance as percentage of venue capacity; abundance of teams (rewarding quality over quantity); stadium and arena quality; ticket availability and prices; franchise ownership; and marquee appeal of athletes. *Sporting News, "Best Sports Cities 2010," October, 2010*

- *Golf Digest* ranked 330 metro areas in the U.S. in terms of golf. The New Orleans metro area was ranked #275. Criteria: access to golf; weather; value of golf; and quality of golf. *Golf Digest, "Metro Golf Rankings," August 2005*

Technology Rankings

- The New Orleans metro area was selected as one of "America's Most Wired Cities" by *Forbes*. The metro area was ranked #13 out of 20. Criteria: percentage of Internet users with high-speed access; number of companies providing high-speed Internet; number of public wireless hot spots. *Forbes, "America's Most Wired Cities," March 2, 2010*

Transportation Rankings

- The New Orleans metro area appeared on *Forbes* list of the best and worst cities for commuters. The metro area ranked #32 out of 60 (#1 is best). Criteria: travel time; road congestion; travel delays. *Forbes.com, "Best and Worst Cities for Commuters," February 16, 2010*

Women/Minorities Rankings

- New Orleans was ranked #61 out of 100 metro areas in *SELF Magazine's* ranking of America's healthiest places for women." A panel of experts came up with more than 50 criteria including death and disease rates, environmental indicators, community resources, and lifestyle habits. *SELF Magazine, "Secrets of America's Healthiest Women," December 2008*

Miscellaneous Rankings

- Energizer Holdings, the makers of Edge® shave gel, in partnership with Sperling's BestPlaces, ranked 50 major metro areas in terms of everyday irritations. The New Orleans metro area ranked #31. Criteria: humidity levels; weather conditions; incidence of traffic delays and congestion; average commute times; frequency of flight delays and cancellations; rates of sleeplessness; underemployment; pollens and allergens; pests; comedy clubs per capita. *Energizer Holdings, "Most Irritation Prone Cities," July 23, 2010*

- Mars Chocolate North America, the makers of COMBOS®, in partnership with Sperling's BestPlaces, ranked 50 major metro areas in terms of their "manliness." The New Orleans metro area ranked #22. Criteria: number of home improvement stores, steak houses, pickup trucks, motorcycles, and manly occupations (fire fighters, police officers, construction workers, EMP personnel) per capita; salty snack sales; sports TV viewing habits. *Mars Chocolate North America, "America's Manliest Cities," June 22, 2010*

- New Orleans was selected as one of the "Worst Hair Cities" by naturallycurly.com. The city was ranked #10. Criteria: humidity levels; pollution; rainfall; average wind speeds; water hardness; beauty salons per capita. *naturallycurly.com, "Best/Worst Hair Cities," April 29, 2009*

- The New Orleans metro area appeared in AutoMD.com's ranking of the "Best and Worst Cities for Auto Repair." The metro area ranked #32 (#1 is best). The 50 most-populated metro areas in the U.S. were ranked on three critical factors: repair affordability; price disparity range; shop integrity factor. *AutoMD.com, "Advocacy for Repair Shop Fairness Report," February 24, 2010*

- New Orleans appeared on Procter & Gamble's list of the "Top-20 All-Time Sweatiest Cities." The city was ranked #6. The rankings are based on computer simulations of the amount of sweat a person of average height and weight would produce walking around for an hour in the average temperatures during the summer months, based on historical weather data during June, July and August from 2001-2008 for each city. *Procter & Gamble, Old Spice Press Release, "Top-20 All-Time Sweatiest Cities," July 1, 2009*

- The New Orleans metro area appeared on *Forbes* list of "America's Drunkest Cities." The area ranked #24. Criteria: 35 of the largest continental U.S. metro areas were chosen based on availability of data and geographic diversity. Each metro was ranked in five areas: state laws; drinkers; heavy drinkers; binge drinkers; and alcoholism. *Forbes.com, "America's Drunkest Cities," August 22, 2006*

Business Environment

CITY FINANCES

City Government Finances

Component	2008 ($000)	2008 ($ per capita)
Total Revenues	1,442,933	6,034
Total Expenditures	1,319,848	5,520
Debt Outstanding	2,140,302	8,951
Cash and Securities[1]	2,379,240	9,950

Note: (1) Cash and security holdings of a government at the close of its fiscal year, including those of its dependent agencies, utilities, and liquor stores.
Source: U.S Census Bureau, State & Local Government Finances 2008

City Government Revenue by Source

Source	2008 ($000)	2008 ($ per capita)
General Revenue		
From Federal Government	391,493	1,637
From State Government	106,046	443
From Local Governments	0	0
Taxes		
Property	203,539	851
Sales and Gross Receipts	190,602	797
Personal Income	0	0
Corporate Income	0	0
Motor Vehicle License	1,693	7
Other Taxes	27,799	116
Current Charges	254,422	1,064
Liquor Store	0	0
Utility	39,981	167
Employee Retirement	82,856	346

Source: U.S Census Bureau, State & Local Government Finances 2008

City Government Expenditures by Function

Function	2008 ($000)	2008 ($ per capita)	2008 (%)
General Direct Expenditures			
Air Transportation	53,520	224	4.1
Corrections	64,548	270	4.9
Education	0	0	0.0
Employment Security Administration	0	0	0.0
Financial Administration	50,532	211	3.8
Fire Protection	69,430	290	5.3
General Public Buildings	12,087	51	0.9
Governmental Administration, Other	82,286	344	6.2
Health	15,336	64	1.2
Highways	18,936	79	1.4
Hospitals	0	0	0.0
Housing and Community Development	157,821	660	12.0
Interest on General Debt	109,916	460	8.3
Judicial and Legal	41,887	175	3.2
Libraries	4,590	19	0.3
Parking	2,184	9	0.2
Parks and Recreation	58,158	243	4.4
Police Protection	132,645	555	10.1
Public Welfare	0	0	0.0
Sewerage	113,132	473	8.6
Solid Waste Management	33,129	139	2.5
Veterans' Services	0	0	0.0
Liquor Store	0	0	0.0
Utility	79,335	332	6.0
Employee Retirement	78,537	328	6.0

Source: U.S Census Bureau, State & Local Government Finances 2008

Municipal Bond Ratings

Area	Moody's	S&P	Fitch
City	Baa3	BBB	BBB

Rating Systems (shown in declining order of credit quality): Moody's– Aaa, Aa, A, Baa, Ba, B, Caa, Ca, C (numerical modifiers 1, 2, and 3 are added to letter-rating); S&P– AAA, AA, A, BBB, BB, B, CCC, CC, C; Fitch– AAA, AA, A, BBB, BB, B, CCC, CC, C. Ratings may be modified by the addition of a plus or minus sign to show relative standing within the major rating categories.
Notes: n/a Not available; (1) Not reviewed; (2) Issuer Rating/No General Obligation; (3) Standard and Poor's Issue Credit Rating (ICR) is a current opinion of an obliger with respect to a specific financial obligation, a specific class of financial obligations, or a specific financial program.
Source: U.S. Census Bureau, 2011 Statistical Abstract, Bond Ratings for City Governments by Largest Cities: 2009

DEMOGRAPHICS

Population Growth

Area	1990 Census	2000 Census	2010 Estimate	2015 Projection	Population Growth (%) 2000-2010	Population Growth (%) 2010-2015
City	496,938	484,674	357,104	390,479	-26.3	9.3
MSA[1]	1,264,391	1,316,510	1,194,196	1,264,365	-9.3	5.9
U.S.	248,709,873	281,421,906	309,038,974	321,675,005	9.8	4.1

Note: (1) Metropolitan Statistical Area - see Appendix B for areas included
Source: Claritas, Inc.

Number of Households and Average Household Size

Area	2010 Estimate	2010 Average Household Size
City	141,177	2.44
MSA[1]	457,187	2.57
U.S.	116,136,617	2.59

Note: (1) Metropolitan Statistical Area - see Appendix B for areas included
Source: Claritas, Inc.

Race and Ethnicity

Area	White Alone[2] (%)	Black Alone[2] (%)	Asian Alone[2] (%)	Other Race Alone[2] (%)	Hispanic[3] (%)
City	33.1	60.6	2.9	3.4	4.7
MSA[1]	58.5	34.7	2.6	4.2	6.4
U.S.	72.3	12.4	4.4	10.9	15.8

Note: Figures are 2010 estimates; (1) Metropolitan Statistical Area - see Appendix B for areas included (2) Alone is defined as not being in combination with one or more other races; (3) May be of any race.
Source: Claritas, Inc.

Segregation

Type	Segregation Indices[1] 1990	Segregation Indices[1] 2000	Segregation Indices[1] 2010	2010 Rank[2]	Percent Change 1990-2000	Percent Change 1990-2010	Percent Change 2000-2010
Black/White	68.3	69.2	63.9	28	0.9	-4.4	-5.3
Asian/White	49.6	50.4	48.6	9	0.8	-1.0	-1.8
Hispanic/White	31.1	35.6	38.3	74	4.5	7.2	2.7

Note: Figures are based on an analysis of 1990, 2000, and 2010 Census Decennial Census tract data by William H. Frey, Brookings Institution and the University of Michigan Social Science Data Analysis Network. In this analysis all racial groups (whites, blacks, and asians) are non-Hispanic members of those races. Hispanics are shown as a separate category; All figures cover the Metropolitan Statistical Area (see Appendix B for areas included); (1) Segregation Indices are Dissimilarity Indices that measure the degree to which the minority group is distributed differently than whites aross census tracts. They range from 0 (complete integration) to 100 (complete [segregation) where the value indicates the percentage of the minority group that needs to move to be distributed exactly like whites; (2) Ranges from 1 (most segregated) to 102 (least segregated); n/a not available.
Source: www.CensusScope.org

Ancestry

Area	German	Irish	English	American	Italian	Polish	French	Scottish
City	6.6	5.3	4.5	2.5	3.6	0.6	6.5	1.0
MSA[1]	12.6	8.5	5.5	4.3	9.5	0.7	16.3	1.0
U.S.	16.6	12.0	9.1	6.1	5.9	3.3	3.1	1.9

Note: The top eight ancestries in the U.S. are shown. Figures are percentages and include multiple ancestry (e.g. if a person reported being Irish and Italian, they were included in both columns); (1) Metropolitan Statistical Area - see Appendix B for areas included
Source: U.S. Census Bureau, 2007-2009 American Community Survey 3-Year Estimates

Foreign-Born Population

Area	Percent of Population Born in								
	Any Foreign Country	Mexico	Asia	Europe	Carribean	South America	Central America[2]	Africa	Canada
City	5.8	0.3	1.9	0.8	0.5	0.5	1.4	0.4	0.1
MSA[1]	6.6	0.5	2.0	0.6	0.6	0.5	2.1	0.2	0.1
U.S.	12.5	3.8	3.4	1.6	1.1	0.8	0.9	0.5	0.3

Note: (1) Metropolitan Statistical Area - see Appendix B for areas included; (2) Excludes Mexico.
Source: U.S. Census Bureau, 2007-2009 American Community Survey 3-Year Estimates

Marriage Status

Area	Never Married	Now Married[2]	Separated	Widowed	Divorced
City	46.4	30.8	3.3	7.0	12.5
MSA[1]	35.2	43.3	2.5	7.2	11.8
U.S.	31.4	49.7	2.2	6.2	10.6

Note: Figures are percentages and cover the population 15 years of age and older;
(1) Metropolitan Statistical Area - see Appendix B for areas included; (2) Excludes separated
Source: U.S. Census Bureau, 2007-2009 American Community Survey 3-Year Estimates

Age Distribution and Median Age

Area	Percent of Population							Median Age
	Under Age 5	Age 5 to 17	Age 18 to 34	Age 35 to 49	Age 50 to 64	Age 65 to 79	80 Years and Over	
City	7.1	13.9	26.1	20.9	20.2	8.1	3.7	37.2
MSA[1]	6.8	16.8	23.0	21.3	19.8	8.7	3.6	37.6
U.S.	6.9	17.5	23.3	21.4	18.1	9.1	3.7	36.7

Note: (1) Metropolitan Statistical Area - see Appendix B for areas included
Source: U.S. Census Bureau, 2007-2009 American Community Survey 3-Year Estimates

Male/Female Ratio

Area	Males	Females	Males per 100 Females
City	166,637	190,467	87.5
MSA[1]	571,739	622,457	91.9
U.S.	152,401,520	156,637,454	97.3

Note: Figures are 2010 estimates; (1) Metropolitan Statistical Area - see Appendix B for areas included
Source: Claritas, Inc.

Religion

Area	Catholic	Southern Baptist	United Methodist	ELCA[1]	LDS[2]	Presbyterian Church USA	Jewish Est.	Muslim Est.
County	28.1	5.7	2.3	0.2	0.1	0.7	1.8	0.8
U.S.	22.0	7.1	3.7	1.8	1.5	1.1	2.2	0.6

Note: Figures are the number of adherents as a percentage of the total population; Adherents are defined as all members, including full members, their children and the estimated number of other participants who are not considered members (e.g. the baptized, those not confirmed, those regularly attending services, etc.); (1) Evangelical Lutheran Church in America; (2) The Church of Jesus Christ of Latter Day Saints
Source: Reprinted with permission from Religious Congregations and Membership in the United States 2000 (Nashville, Glenmary Research Center, 2002) Copyright Association of Statisticians of American Religious Bodies. All rights reserved.

ECONOMY

Gross Metropolitan Product

Area	2006	2007	2008	2009	2009 Rank[2]
MSA[1]	64.3	67.5	72.4	73.3	40

Note: Figures are in billions of dollars; (1) New Orleans-Metairie-Kenner, LA Metropolitan Statistical Area - see Appendix B for areas included; (2) Rank ranges from 1 to 363
Source: The U.S. Conference of Mayors, "Pace of Economic Recovery: GMP and Jobs," January 2010

Economic Growth

Area	2006-2008 (%)	2009 (%)	2010 (%)	Rank[2]
MSA[1]	0.1	-0.5	2.5	260
U.S.	1.3	-2.5	2.2	–

Note: Figures are real Gross Metropolitan Product growth rates and represent annual average percent change; (1) New Orleans-Metairie-Kenner, LA Metropolitan Statistical Area - see Appendix B for areas included; (2) Rank ranges from 1 to 363
Source: The U.S. Conference of Mayors, "Pace of Economic Recovery: GMP and Jobs," January 2010

Metropolitan Area Exports

Area	2005	2006	2007	2008	2009	2009 Rank[2]
MSA[1]	4,857.8	6,717.2	8,449.1	12,664.5	10,145.1	19

Note: Figures are in millions of dollars; (1) New Orleans-Metairie-Kenner, LA Metropolitan Statistical Area - see Appendix B for areas included; (2) Rank ranges from 1 to 374
Source: U.S. Department of Commerce, International Trade Administration, Office of Trade & Industry Information, Manufacturing & Services

INCOME

Per Capita/Median/Average Income

Area	Per Capita ($)	Median Household ($)	Average Household ($)
City	24,535	39,530	60,945
MSA[1]	25,527	48,041	66,077
U.S.	27,034	52,795	71,071

Note: Figures are 2010 estimates; (1) Metropolitan Statistical Area - see Appendix B for areas included
Source: Claritas, Inc.

Household Income Distribution

Area	Under $15,000	$15,000 -24,999	$25,000 -34,999	$35,000 -49,999	$50,000 -74,999	$75,000 -99,000	$100,000 -149,999	$150,000 and up
City	22.0	12.8	10.9	14.3	15.5	8.9	8.4	7.2
MSA[1]	15.3	11.1	10.8	14.8	18.5	11.6	11.0	7.0
U.S.	12.1	10.2	10.6	15.0	19.5	12.5	12.1	8.0

Note: Figures are 2010 estimates; (1) Metropolitan Statistical Area - see Appendix B for areas included
Source: Claritas, Inc.

Poverty Rates by Age

Area	All Ages	Under 18 Years Old	18 to 64 Years Old	65 Years and Over
City	23.2	7.9	13.6	1.7
MSA[1]	15.6	5.5	8.7	1.3
U.S.	13.6	4.7	7.7	1.2

Note: Figures are percent of population with income during the previous 12 months below poverty level and only include population for whom poverty status is determined; (1) Metropolitan Statistical Area - see Appendix B for areas included
Source: U.S. Census Bureau, 2007-2009 American Community Survey 3-Year Estimates

Personal Bankruptcy Filing Rate

Area	2006	2007	2008	2009	2010
Orleans Parish	1.30	1.32	1.43	1.96	2.26
U.S.	2.00	2.73	3.53	4.60	4.96

Note: Numbers are per 1,000 population and include Chapter 7 and Chapter 13 filings
Source: Federal Deposit Insurance Corporation, Regional Economic Conditions, March 17, 2011

EMPLOYMENT

Labor Force and Employment

Area	Civilian Labor Force			Workers Employed		
	Dec. 2009	Dec. 2010	% Chg.	Dec. 2009	Dec. 2010	% Chg.
City	144,475	148,131	2.5	133,161	135,477	1.7
MSA[1]	530,817	541,914	2.1	495,173	503,787	1.7
U.S.	152,693,000	153,156,000	0.3	137,953,000	139,159,000	0.9

Note: Data is not seasonally adjusted and covers workers 16 years of age and older;
(1) Metropolitan Statistical Area - see Appendix B for areas included
Source: Bureau of Labor Statistics, http://stats.bls.gov

Unemployment Rate

Area	2010											
	Jan.	Feb.	Mar.	Apr.	May	Jun.	Jul.	Aug.	Sep.	Oct.	Nov.	Dec.
City	8.7	7.6	7.5	7.3	8.0	9.8	9.9	10.2	9.8	9.4	8.9	8.5
MSA[1]	7.6	6.6	6.6	6.5	7.1	8.2	7.9	8.2	7.7	7.6	7.3	7.0
U.S.	10.6	10.4	10.2	9.5	9.3	9.6	9.7	9.5	9.2	9.0	9.3	9.1

Note: Data is not seasonally adjusted and covers workers 16 years of age and older; All figures are percentages; (1) Metropolitan Statistical Area - see Appendix B for areas included
Source: Bureau of Labor Statistics, http://stats.bls.gov

Projected Unemployment Rate

Area	2007 (%)	2009 (%)	2011 (%)	2013 (%)
MSA[1]	3.2	7.3	6.9	6.0

Note: (1) Metropolitan Statistical Area - see Appendix B for areas included
Source: The U.S. Conference of Mayors, "Pace of Economic Recovery: GMP and Jobs," January 2010

Employment by Occupation

Occupation Classification	City (%)	MSA[1] (%)	U.S. (%)
Sales and Office	22.0	25.9	25.4
Professional and Related	25.0	20.9	21.0
Service	21.2	17.5	17.2
Production, Transportation, and Material Moving	10.0	10.6	12.3
Management, Business, and Financial	12.2	13.0	14.1
Construction, Extraction, and Maintenance	9.4	11.7	9.2
Farming, Forestry, and Fishing	0.2	0.4	0.7

Note: Figures cover employed civilians 16 years of age and older;
(1) Metropolitan Statistical Area - see Appendix B for areas included
Source: U.S. Census Bureau, 2007-2009 American Community Survey 3-Year Estimates

Employment by Industry

| Sector | MSA[1] | | U.S. |
	Number of Employees	Percent of Total	Percent of Total
Government	81,500	15.5	17.2
Education and Health Services	76,200	14.5	15.2
Professional and Business Services	67,600	12.9	13.0
Retail Trade	58,800	11.2	11.4
Leisure and Hospitality	71,300	13.6	9.7
Manufacturing	31,500	6.0	8.8
Financial Activities	25,900	4.9	5.8
Wholesale Trade	22,200	4.2	4.2
Construction	29,800	5.7	4.1
Other Services	18,900	3.6	4.1
Transportation and Utilities	24,800	4.7	3.7
Information	9,000	1.7	2.1
Mining and Logging	7,500	1.4	0.6

Note: Figures cover non-farm employment as of December 2010 and are not seasonally adjusted;
(1) Metropolitan Statistical Area - see Appendix B for areas included
Source: Bureau of Labor Statistics, http://stats.bls.gov

Occupations with Greatest Projected Employment Growth: 2006 - 2016

Occupation[1]	2006 Employment	2016 Projected Employment	Numeric Employment Change	Percent Employment Change
Registered nurses	39,510	52,060	12,550	31.8
Retail salespersons	60,330	70,020	9,690	16.1
Customer service representatives	25,430	33,810	8,380	33.0
Waiters and waitresses	30,870	38,870	8,000	25.9
Office clerks, general	37,680	45,030	7,350	19.5
Nursing aides, orderlies, and attendants	25,090	32,300	7,210	28.7
Food preparation workers	23,190	30,180	6,990	30.1
Personal and home care aides	11,120	17,680	6,560	59.0
Janitors and cleaners, except maids and housekeeping cleaners	29,740	35,930	6,190	20.8
Elementary school teachers, except special education	25,210	30,920	5,710	22.6

Note: Projections cover Louisiana; (1) Sorted by numeric employment change
Source: www.projectionscentral.com, State Occupational Projections, 2006-2016 Long-Term Projections

Fastest Growing Occupations: 2006 - 2016

Occupation[1]	2006 Employment	2016 Projected Employment	Numeric Employment Change	Percent Employment Change
Actors	1,270	2,450	1,180	92.9
Entertainers and performers, sports and related workers, all other	1,050	1,990	940	89.5
Ushers, lobby attendants, and ticket takers	920	1,590	670	72.8
Home health aides	8,210	13,900	5,690	69.3
Network systems and data communications analysts	2,150	3,430	1,280	59.5
Personal and home care aides	11,120	17,680	6,560	59.0
Athletes and sports competitors	690	1,090	400	58.0
Gaming surveillance officers and gaming investigators	560	850	290	51.8
Computer software engineers, applications	1,510	2,290	780	51.7
Gaming supervisors	1,860	2,720	860	46.2

Note: Projections cover Louisiana; (1) Sorted by percent employment change and excludes occupations with numeric employment change less than 250
Source: www.projectionscentral.com, State Occupational Projections, 2006-2016 Long-Term Projections

Average Wages

Occupation	$/Hr.	Occupation	$/Hr.
Accountants and Auditors	26.93	Maids and Housekeeping Cleaners	9.54
Automotive Mechanics	17.12	Maintenance and Repair Workers	16.79
Bookkeepers	16.60	Marketing Managers	37.12
Carpenters	19.28	Nuclear Medicine Technologists	30.99
Cashiers	8.39	Nurses, Licensed Practical	19.94
Clerks, General Office	11.55	Nurses, Registered	30.79
Clerks, Receptionists/Information	10.74	Nursing Aides/Orderlies/Attendants	10.96
Clerks, Shipping/Receiving	14.18	Packers and Packagers, Hand	10.21
Computer Programmers	24.32	Physical Therapists	35.72
Computer Support Specialists	21.36	Postal Service Mail Carriers	24.18
Computer Systems Analysts	26.70	Real Estate Brokers	n/a
Cooks, Restaurant	10.43	Retail Salespersons	11.16
Dentists	n/a	Sales Reps., Exc. Tech./Scientific	26.81
Electrical Engineers	42.26	Sales Reps., Tech./Scientific	30.32
Electricians	21.71	Secretaries, Exc. Legal/Med./Exec.	13.86
Financial Managers	38.16	Security Guards	12.11
First-Line Supervisors/Mgrs., Sales	16.97	Surgeons	n/a
Food Preparation Workers	8.46	Teacher Assistants	10.20
General and Operations Managers	49.78	Teachers, Elementary School	22.50
Hairdressers/Cosmetologists	16.41	Teachers, Secondary School	23.00
Internists	96.82	Telemarketers	11.63
Janitors and Cleaners	10.05	Truck Drivers, Heavy/Tractor-Trailer	17.24
Landscaping/Groundskeeping Workers	10.43	Truck Drivers, Light/Delivery Svcs.	15.09
Lawyers	51.40	Waiters and Waitresses	8.73

Note: Wage data covers the New Orleans-Metairie-Kenner, LA - see Appendix B for areas included. Hourly wages for elementary/secondary school teachers and teacher assistants were calculated by the editors from annual wage data assuming a 40 hour work week; n/a not available.
Source: Bureau of Labor Statistics, Metro Area Occupational Employment and Wage Estimates, May 2009

RESIDENTIAL REAL ESTATE

Building Permits

Area	Single-Family			Multi-Family			Total		
	2009	2010	Pct. Chg.	2009	2010	Pct. Chg.	2009	2010	Pct. Chg.
City	947	820	-13.4	614	260	-57.7	1,561	1,080	-30.8
MSA[1]	2,190	1,875	-14.4	642	296	-53.9	2,832	2,171	-23.3
U.S.	441,100	447,300	1.4	141,900	157,300	10.9	583,000	604,600	3.7

Note: (1) Metropolitan Statistical Area - see Appendix B for areas included; figures represent new, privately-owned housing units authorized (unadjusted data); All permit data are based on estimates with imputation.
Source: U.S. Census Bureau, Manufacturing, Mining, and Construction Statistics, Building Permits, 2009, 2010

Homeownership Rate

Area	2005 (%)	2006 (%)	2007 (%)	2008 (%)	2009 (%)	2010 (%)
MSA[1]	71.2	70.3	67.8	68.0	68.2	66.9
U.S.	68.9	68.8	68.1	67.8	67.4	66.9

Note: (1) Metropolitan Statistical Area - see Appendix B for areas included
Source: U.S. Census Bureau, Housing Vacancies and Homeownership Annual Statistics: 2010

Housing Vacancy Rates

Area	Gross Vacancy Rate[2] (%)			Year-Round Vacancy Rate[3] (%)			Rental Vacancy Rate[4] (%)			Homeowner Vacancy Rate[5] (%)		
	2008	2009	2010	2008	2009	2010	2008	2009	2010	2008	2009	2010
MSA[1]	16.5	16.1	14.6	16.3	15.9	14.4	12.3	18.0	15.2	3.7	2.5	2.6
U.S.	14.4	14.5	14.3	11.1	11.3	11.3	10.0	10.6	10.2	2.8	2.6	2.6

Note: (1) Metropolitan Statistical Area - see Appendix B for areas included; (2) The percentage of the total housing inventory that is vacant; (3) The percentage of the housing inventory (excluding seasonal units) that is year-round vacant; (4) The percentage of rental inventory that is vacant for rent; (5) The percentage of homeowner inventory that is vacant for sale; n/a not available
Source: U.S. Census Bureau, Housing Vacancies and Homeownership Annual Statistics: 2010

State Corporate Income Tax Rates

State	Tax Rate (%)	Income Brackets ($)	Num. of Brackets	Financial Institution Tax Rate (%)[a]	Federal Income Tax Ded.
Louisiana	4.0 - 8.0	25,000 - 200,001	5	4.0 - 8.0	Yes

Note: Tax rates as of January 1, 2011; (a) Rates listed are the tax rates applied to financial institutions or excise taxes based on income. Some states have other taxes based upon the value of deposits or shares.
Source: Federation of Tax Administrators, "State Corporate Income Tax Rates, 2011"

State Individual Income Tax Rates

State	Tax Rate (%)	Income Brackets ($)	Num. of Brackets	Personal Exempt. ($)[1] Single	Dependents	Fed. Inc. Tax Ded.
Louisiana	2.0 - 6.0	12,500 (b)-50,001 (b)	3	4,500 (l)	1,000	Yes

Note: Tax rates as of January 1, 2011; Local- and county-level taxes are not included; n/a not applicable; (1) Married joint filers generally receive double the single exemption; (b) For joint returns, taxes are twice the tax on half the couple's income; (l) The amounts reported for Louisiana are a combined personal exemption-standard deduction.
Source: Federation of Tax Administrators, "State Individual Income Tax Rates, 2011"

Various State and Local Tax Rates

State	State and Local Sales and Use (%)	State Sales and Use (%)	Gasoline[1] (¢/gal.)	Cigarette[2] ($/pack)	Spirits[3] ($/gal.)	Wine[4] ($/gal.)	Beer[5] ($/gal.)
Louisiana	8.75	4.00	20.0	0.36	2.50	0.11	0.32

Note: All tax rates as of January 1, 2011 except Spirits (Sept. 1, 2010); (1) The American Petroleum Institute has developed a methodology for determining the average tax rate on a gallon of fuel. Rates may include any of the following: excise taxes, environmental fees, storage tank fees, other fees or taxes, general sales tax, and local taxes. In states where gasoline is subject to the general sales tax, or where the fuel tax is based on the average sale price, the average rate determined by API is sensitive to changes in the price of gasoline. States that fully or partially apply general sales taxes to gasoline: CA, CO, GA, IL, IN, MI, NY; (2) The federal excise tax of $1.0066 per pack and local taxes are not included; (3) Rates are those applicable to off-premise sales of 40% alcohol by volume (a.b.v.) distilled spirits in 750ml containers. Local excise taxes are excluded; (4) Rates are those applicable to off-premise sales of 11% a.b.v. non-carbonated wine in 750ml containers; (5) Rates are those applicable to off-premise sales of 4.7% a.b.v. beer in 12 ounce containers.
Source: Tax Foundation, 2011 Facts & Figures: How Does Your State Compare?

State-Local Tax Burdens

Area	Rate (%)	Rank[1]	Per Capita Taxes Paid to Home State ($)	Total State and Local Per Capita Taxes Paid ($)	Per Capita Income ($)
Louisiana	8.2	42	2,034	3,037	37,109
U.S. Average	9.8	-	3,057	4,160	42,539

Note: Figures cover 2009; (1) Rank ranges from 1 to 50 where 1 is highest tax burden
Source: Tax Foundation, State-Local Tax Burdens, All States, 2009

State Business Tax Climate Index Rankings

State	Overall Rank	Corporate Tax Index Rank	Individual Income Tax Index Rank	Sales Tax Index Rank	Unemployment Insurance Tax Index Rank	Property Tax Index Rank
Louisiana	36	19	26	46	5	22

Note: The index is a measure of how each state's tax laws affect economic performance. The lower the rank, the more favorable a state's tax system is for business. All ranks are for fiscal years. States without a given tax are given a ranking of 1.
Source: Tax Foundation, Tax Foundation Background Paper, No. 60, "2011 State Business Tax Climate Index"

**COMMERCIAL
UTILITIES**

Typical Monthly Electric Bills

Area	Commercial Service ($/month)		Industrial Service ($/month)	
	3 kW demand 1,000 kWh	40 kW demand 14,000 kWh	1,000 kW demand 200,000 kWh	50,000 kW demand 15,000,000 kWh
City	128	1,510	23,724	1,545,216
Average[1]	135	1,576	23,741	1,402,202

Note: Based on total rates in effect July 1, 2010; (1) average based on 182 utilities surveyed
Source: Edison Electric Institute, Typical Bills and Average Rates Report, Summer 2010

TRANSPORTATION

Means of Transportation to Work

Area	Car/Truck/Van		Public Transportation			Bicycle	Walked	Other Means	Worked at Home
	Drove Alone	Car-pooled	Bus	Subway	Railroad				
City	66.3	13.2	6.2	0.1	0.0	1.7	5.8	2.2	3.6
MSA[1]	77.6	11.8	2.2	0.0	0.0	0.7	2.6	1.6	3.2
U.S.	75.8	10.4	2.7	1.7	0.5	0.5	2.9	1.2	4.1

Note: Figures are percentages and cover workers 16 years of age and older;
(1) Metropolitan Statistical Area - see Appendix B for areas included
Source: U.S. Census Bureau, 2007-2009 American Community Survey 3-Year Estimates

Travel Time to Work

Area	Less Than 15 Minutes	15 to 29 Minutes	30 to 44 Minutes	45 to 59 Minutes	60 to 89 Minutes	90 Minutes or More
City	25.9	44.2	20.2	4.7	3.1	1.9
MSA[1]	26.1	37.5	21.8	7.3	5.0	2.3
U.S.	28.5	36.2	19.7	7.5	5.6	2.5

Note: Figures are percentages and include workers 16 years old and over;
(1) Metropolitan Statistical Area - see Appendix B for areas included
Source: U.S. Census Bureau, 2007-2009 American Community Survey 3-Year Estimates

Travel Time Index

Area	1982	1999	2008	2009
Urban Area[1]	1.14	1.20	1.18	1.15
Average[2]	1.08	1.20	1.20	1.20

Note: Travel Time Index—the ratio of travel time in the peak period to the travel time at
free-flow conditions. A value of 1.30 indicates a 20-minute free-flow trip takes 26 minutes
in the peak. Free-flow speeds (60 mph on freeways and 35 mph on principal arterials)
are used as the comparison threshold; (1) Covers the New Orleans-Metairie-Kenner urban area;
(2) average of 439 urban areas
Source: Texas Transportation Institute, Urban Mobility Report 2010, December 2010

Public Transportation

Agency Name / Mode of Transportation	Vehicles Operated in Maximum Service	Annual Unlinked Passenger Trips ('000)	Annual Passenger Miles ('000)
New Orleans Regional Transit Authority (NORTA)			
Demand response	28	138.0	1,013.2
Light rail	23	5,342.1	12,303.6
Bus	62	9,988.5	28,422.9

Note: Figures include both directly operated and purchased transportation
Source: Federal Transit Administration, National Transit Database, 2009

Air Transportation

Airport Name and Code / Type of Service	Passenger Airlines[1]	Passenger Enplanements	Freight Carriers[2]	Freight (lbs.)
New Orleans International (MSY)				
Domestic service (U.S. carriers - 2010)	36	4,071,823	17	51,027,828
International service (U.S. carriers - 2009)	8	4,997	1	11,760

Note: (1) Includes all U.S.-based major, minor and commuter airlines that carried at least one passenger during the year; (2) Includes all U.S.-based airlines and freight carriers that transported at least one pound of freight during the year
Source: Bureau of Transportation Statistics, The Intermodal Transportation Database, Air Carriers: T-100 Domestic Market (U.S. Carriers), 2010; Bureau of Transportation Statistics, The Intermodal Transportation Database, Air Carriers: T-100 International Market (U.S. Carriers), 2009

Other Transportation Statistics

Interstate highways:	I-10; I-59
Amtrak service:	Yes
Major waterways/ports:	Port of New Orleans; Mississippi River

Source: Amtrak.com; Google Maps

BUSINESSES

Major Business Headquarters

Company Name	Rankings	
	Fortune[1]	Forbes[2]
Entergy	213	-

Note: (1) Fortune 500—companies that produce a 10-K are ranked 1 to 500 based on 2010 revenue; (2) all private companies with at least $2 billion in annual revenue are ranked 1 to 223; companies listed are headquartered in the city; dashes indicate no ranking
Source: Fortune, "Fortune 500," May 23, 2011; Forbes, "America's Largest Private Companies," November 3, 2010

Minority Business Opportunity

New Orleans is home to one company which is on the Black Enterprise Bank 25 list (25 largest banks based on total assets, capital, deposits and loans, including mortgage-backed securities for the calendar year): **Liberty Bank and Trust Co.** Criteria: commercial banks or savings and loans that are classified by the Federal Reserve as black institutions and have been fully operational for the previous calendar year. *Black Enterprise, B.E. 100s, 2010*

New Orleans is home to one company which is on the *Hispanic Business 500* list (500 largest U.S. Hispanic-owned companies based on 2009 revenue): **Pan-American Life Insurance Group**. Companies included must show at least 51 percent ownership by Hispanic U.S. citizens, and must maintain headquarters in one of the 50 states or Washington, D.C. *Hispanic Business, "Hispanic Business 500," June 2010*

Minority- and Women-Owned Businesses

Group	All Firms		Firms with Paid Employees			
	Firms	Sales ($000)	Firms	Sales ($000)	Employees	Payroll ($000)
Asian	1,403	310,414	388	268,702	1,755	39,419
Black	7,843	497,070	391	345,949	4,728	104,339
Hispanic	1,103	107,771	137	77,257	970	23,102
Women	8,245	1,418,443	1,048	1,236,470	9,907	300,668
All Firms	27,166	28,788,251	6,588	27,896,926	136,683	6,060,483

Note: Figures cover firms located in the city; minority- and women-owned business are defined as firms in which the corresponding group own 51% or more of the stock or equity of the company
Source: U.S. Census Bureau, 2007 Economic Census, Survey of Business Owners

HOTELS

Hotels/Motels

Area	5 Star		4 Star		3 Star		2 Star		1 Star		Not Rated	
	Num.	Pct.3	Num.	Pct.3	Num.	Pct.3	Num.	Pct.3	Num.	Pct.3	Num.	Pct.3
City[1]	0	0.0	21	10.7	82	41.8	69	35.2	7	3.6	17	8.7
Total[2]	119	0.7	927	5.8	4,906	30.5	7,992	49.7	526	3.3	1,625	10.1

Note: (1) Figures cover New Orleans and vicinity; (2) Figures cover all 100 cities in this book; (3) Percentage of hotels which are a given star rating; Star ratings are determined by expedia.com and offer an indication of the general quality of a particular hotel.
Source: expedia.com, May 5, 2011

The New Orleans metro area is home to two of the top 218 hotels in the U.S. according to *Travel & Leisure*: **Windsor Court Hotel** (#96); **Ritz-Carlton, New Orleans** (#179). Criteria: service; location; rooms; food; and value. *Travel & Leisure, "T+L 500, The World's Best Hotels 2011"*

The New Orleans metro area is home to two of the top 100 hotels in the U.S. according to *Condé Nast Traveler*: **Windsor Court Hotel** (#38); **Ritz-Carlton** (#99). The selections are based on over 25,000 responses to the magazine's annual Readers' Choice Survey. *Condé Nast Traveler, "2010 Readers' Choice Awards"*

EVENT SITES

Major Stadiums, Arenas, and Auditoriums

Name	Max. Capacity
Lakefront Arena	10,000
Louisiana Superdome	76,468
New Orleans Cultural Center	8,500
Tad Gormley Stadium/Alerion Field	26,500
The Conference Auditorium at the Morial Center	4,000

Source: Original research

Convention Centers

Name	Overall Space (sq. ft.)	Exhibit Space (sq. ft.)	Meeting Space (sq. ft.)	Meeting Rooms
Ernest N. Morial Convention Center	3,000,000	n/a	1,100,000	n/a

Note: n/a not available
Source: Original research

Living Environment

COST OF LIVING

Cost of Living Index

Composite Index	Groceries	Housing	Utilities	Trans- portation	Health Care	Misc. Goods/ Services
97.0	95.1	101.0	82.2	96.2	93.4	99.4

Note: U.S. = 100; Figures cover Slidell (data for New Orleans was not available).
Source: The Council for Community and Economic Research, ACCRA Cost of Living Index, 2010

Grocery Prices

Area[1]	T-Bone Steak ($/pound)	Frying Chicken ($/pound)	Whole Milk ($/half gal.)	Eggs ($/dozen)	Orange Juice ($/64 oz.)	Coffee ($/11.5 oz.)
City[2]	9.46	1.03	2.40	1.50	2.77	3.37
Avg.	9.04	1.16	2.02	1.47	3.08	3.65
Min.	6.97	0.84	1.46	0.96	2.39	2.64
Max.	13.93	2.51	3.58	3.01	4.94	6.32

Note: (1) Values for the local area are compared with the average, minimum and maximum values for all 338 areas in the Cost of Living Index; (2) Figures cover Slidell (data for New Orleans was not available); **T-Bone Steak** (price per pound); **Frying Chicken** (price per pound, whole fryer); **Whole Milk** (half gallon carton); **Eggs** (price per dozen, Grade A, large); **Orange Juice** (64 oz. Tropicana or Florida Natural); **Coffee** (11.5 oz. can, vacuum-packed, Maxwell House, Hills Bros, or Folgers).
Source: The Council for Community and Economic Research, ACCRA Cost of Living Index, 2010

Housing and Utility Costs

Area[1]	New Home Price ($)	Apartment Rent ($/month)	All Electric ($/month)	Part Electric ($/month)	Other Energy ($/month)	Telephone ($/month)
City[2]	272,114	1,019	137.12	-	-	23.70
Avg.	293,442	810	166.39	91.93	83.82	26.93
Min.	182,545	453	119.21	44.47	36.85	17.98
Max.	1,123,114	2,776	307.53	218.20	313.90	39.15

Note: (1) Values for the local area are compared with the average, minimum and maximum values for all 338 areas in the Cost of Living Index; (2) Figures cover Slidell (data for New Orleans was not available); **New Home Price** (2,400 sf living area, 8,000 sf lot, in urban area with full utilities); **Apartment Rent** (950 sf 2 bedroom/1.5 or 2 bath, unfurnished, excluding all utilities except water); **All Electric** (average monthly cost for an all-electric home); **Part Electric** (average monthly cost for a part-electric home); **Other Energy** (average monthly cost for natural gas, fuel oil, coal, wood, and any other forms of energy except electricity); **Telephone** (price includes basic monthly rate for a private residential line plus additional local usage charges incurred by a family of four).
Source: The Council for Community and Economic Research, ACCRA Cost of Living Index, 2010

Health Care, Transportation, and Other Costs

Area[1]	Doctor ($/visit)	Dentist ($/visit)	Optometrist ($/visit)	Gasoline ($/gallon)	Beauty Salon ($/visit)	Men's Shirt ($)
City[2]	83.99	67.07	75.35	2.62	37.04	28.38
Avg.	89.44	78.95	87.40	2.73	31.92	24.83
Min.	57.00	54.25	48.32	2.44	19.17	13.67
Max.	149.90	136.73	174.22	3.75	62.81	47.89

Note: (1) Values for the local area are compared with the average, minimum and maximum values for all 338 areas in the Cost of Living Index; (2) Figures cover Slidell (data for New Orleans was not available); **Doctor** (general practitioners routine exam of an established patient); **Dentist** (adult teeth cleaning and periodic oral examination); **Optometrist** (full vision eye exam for established adult patient); **Gasoline** (one gallon regular unleaded, national brand, including all taxes, cash price at self-service pump if available); **Beauty Salon** (woman's shampoo, trim, and blow-dry); **Men's Shirt** (cotton/polyester dress shirt, pinpoint weave, long sleeves).
Source: The Council for Community and Economic Research, ACCRA Cost of Living Index, 2010

HOUSING

House Price Index (HPI)

Area	National Ranking[2]	Quarterly Change (%)	One-Year Change (%)	Five-Year Change (%)
MSA[1]	173	-0.94	-1.54	3.40
U.S.[3]	-	-0.84	-3.95	-11.45

Note: The HPI is a weighted repeat sales index. It measures average price changes in repeat sales or refinancings on the same properties. This information is obtained by reviewing repeat mortgage transactions on single-family properties whose mortgages have been purchased or securitized by Fannie Mae or Freddie Mac in January 1975; (1) Metropolitan/Micropolitan Statistical Area - see Appendix B for areas included; (2) Rankings are based on annual percentage change for all metro areas containing at least 15,000 transactions over the last 10 years and ranges from 1 to 309; (3) figures based on a weighted average of Census Division estimates; all figures are for the period ending December 31, 2010
Source: Federal Housing Finance Agency, House Price Index, February 24, 2011

House Price Valuations

Area	Q4 2005 Price ($000)	Q4 2005 Over-valuation	Q4 2006 Price ($000)	Q4 2006 Over-valuation	Q4 2007 Price ($000)	Q4 2007 Over-valuation	Q4 2008 Price ($000)	Q4 2008 Over-valuation	Q4 2009 Price ($000)	Q4 2009 Over-valuation
MSA[1]	142.5	-30.2	156.1	-6.0	154.4	-9.8	149.0	-12.4	145.5	-12.5

Note: Figures show the percentage of over- or under-valuation of single family homes relative to statistically normal house values (e.g. a value of 23.6 indicates that house values are 23.6% overvalued). Statistically normal house values are based on house prices, interest rates, household incomes, population densities, and any historical premiums or discounts metropolitan areas have exhibited over time; (1) Figures cover the New Orleans-Metairie-Kenner, LA Metropolitan Statistical Area - see Appendix B for areas included
Source: Global Insight/PNC Financial Services Group, House Prices in America: 4th Quarter 2009 Update

Median Single-Family Home Prices

Area	2008	2009	2010[p]	Percent Change 2009 to 2010
MSA[1]	160.5	160.1	159.7	-0.2
U.S. Average	196.6	172.1	173.2	0.6

Note: Figures are median sales prices of existing single-family homes in thousands of dollars; (p) preliminary; n/a not available; (1) Metropolitan Statistical Area - see Appendix B for areas included
Source: National Association of Realtors, Median Sales Price of Existing Single-Family Homes for Metropolitan Areas, 4th Quarter 2010

Median Apartment Condo-Coop Home Prices

Area	2008	2009	2010[p]	Percent Change 2009 to 2010
MSA[1]	176.4	171.5	175.7	2.4
U.S. Average	209.8	175.6	171.7	-2.2

Note: Figures are median sales prices of existing apartment condo-coop homes in thousands of dollars; (p) preliminary; n/a not available; (1) Metropolitan Statistical Area - see Appendix B for areas included
Source: National Association of Realtors, Median Sales Price of Existing Apartment Condo-Coop Homes for Metropolitan Areas, 4th Quarter 2010

Year Housing Structure Built

Area	2000 or Later	1990 -1999	1980 -1989	1970 -1979	1960 -1969	1950 -1959	1940 -1949	Before 1940	Median Year
City	5.8	3.4	7.8	12.0	12.0	12.1	11.2	35.7	1953
MSA[1]	10.9	9.7	15.0	19.8	15.2	10.2	6.0	13.2	1973
U.S.	12.5	14.0	14.2	16.5	11.4	11.3	5.8	14.3	1974

Note: Figures are percentages except for Median Year; (1) Metropolitan Statistical Area - see Appendix B for areas included
Source: U.S. Census Bureau, 2007-2009 American Community Survey 3-Year Estimates

HEALTH

Health Risk Data

Category	MSA[1] (%)	U.S. (%)
Adults who have been told they have high blood pressure	36.1	28.7
Adults who have been told they have high blood cholesterol	35.0	37.5
Adults who have been told they have diabetes[3]	9.7	8.3
Adults who have been told they have arthritis	24.2	26.0
Adults who have been told they currently have asthma	4.7	8.8
Adults who are current smokers	20.6	17.9
Adults who are heavy drinkers[4]	6.2	5.1
Adults who are binge drinkers[5]	16.9	15.8
Adults who are overweight (BMI 25.0 - 29.9)	35.6	36.2
Adults who are obese (BMI 30.0 - 99.8)	28.8	26.9
Adults who participated in any physical activities in the past month	72.4	76.2
Adults 50+ who have ever had a sigmoidoscopy or colonoscopy[2]	56.4	62.2
Women 40+ who have had a mammogram within the past two years[2]	76.7	76.0
Adults age 18–64 who have any kind of health care coverage	80.8	83.1

Note: Data as of 2009 unless otherwise noted; (1) Figures cover the New Orleans-Metairie-Kenner, LA Metropolitan Statistical Area - see Appendix B for areas included; (2) Data as of 2008; (3) Figures do not include pregnancy-related, borderline, or pre-diabetes; (4) Heavy drinkers are classified as males having more than two drinks per day or females having more than one drink per day; (5) Binge drinkers are classified as males having five or more drinks on one occasion or females having four or more drinks on one occasion
Source: Centers for Disease Control and Prevention, Behaviorial Risk Factor Surveillance System, SMART: Selected Metropolitan/Micropolitan Area Risk Trends, 2008, 2009

Mortality Rates for the Top 10 Causes of Death in the U.S.

ICD-10[a] Sub-Chapter	ICD-10[a] Code	Age-Adjusted Mortality Rate[1] per 100,000 population	
		County[2]	U.S.
Malignant neoplasms	C00-C97	191.7	180.9
Ischaemic heart diseases	I20-I25	124.8	135.0
Other forms of heart disease	I30-I51	63.1	50.0
Cerebrovascular diseases	I60-I69	55.6	44.1
Chronic lower respiratory diseases	J40-J47	32.9	41.5
Other degenerative diseases of the nervous system	G30-G31	22.5	23.6
Diabetes mellitus	E10-E14	39.1	23.5
Other external causes of accidental injury	W00-X59	71.5	23.5
Organic, including symptomatic, mental disorders	F01-F09	25.2	22.2
Influenza and pneumonia	J09-J18	15.1	18.1

Note: (a) ICD-10 = International Classification of Diseases 10th Revision; (1) Mortality rates are a three year average covering 2005-2007; (2) Figures cover Orleans Parish
Source: Centers for Disease Control and Prevention, National Center for Health Statistics. Compressed Mortality File 1999-2007. CDC WONDER On-line Database, compiled from Compressed Mortality File 1999-2007 Series 20 No. 2M, 2010.

Mortality Rates for Selected Causes of Death

ICD-10[a] Sub-Chapter	ICD-10[a] Code	Age-Adjusted Mortality Rate[1] per 100,000 population	
		County[2]	U.S.
Assault	X85-Y09	56.6	6.0
Human immunodeficiency virus (HIV) disease	B20-B24	21.4	4.0
Hypertensive diseases	I10-I15	41.0	18.0
Intentional self-harm	X60-X84	9.2	11.0
Malnutrition	E40-E46	2.0	0.8
Obesity and other hyperalimentation	E65-E68	3.3	1.5
Transport accidents	V01-V99	15.7	15.6
Viral hepatitis	B15-B19	4.4	2.1

Note: (a) ICD-10 = International Classification of Diseases 10th Revision; (1) Mortality rates are a three year average covering 2005-2007; (2) Figures cover Orleans Parish
Source: Centers for Disease Control and Prevention, National Center for Health Statistics. Compressed Mortality File 1999-2007. CDC WONDER On-line Database, compiled from Compressed Mortality File 1999-2007 Series 20 No. 2M, 2010.

Distribution of Physicians and Dentists

Area[1]	Dentists[2]	D.O.[3]	M.D.[4]				
			Total	Family/ General Practice	Pediatrics	Medical Specialties	Surgical Specialties
Local (number)	99	26	1,082	62	77	399	269
Local (rate[5])	3.4	0.8	32.1	1.8	2.3	11.9	8.0
U.S. (rate[5])	4.5	1.9	18.3	2.5	1.4	6.8	4.1

Note: Data as of 2008 unless noted; (1) Local data covers Orleans Parish; (2) Data as of 2007; (3) Doctor of Osteopathic Medicine; (4) Includes active, non-federal, patient-care, office-based Doctors of Medicine; (5) rate per 10,000 population
Source: Area Resource File (ARF). 2009-2010 Release. U.S. Department of Health and Human Services, Health Resources and Services Administration, Bureau of Health Professions, Rockville, MD, August 2010

Hospitals

New Orleans has the following hospitals: 9 general medical and surgical; 1 psychiatric; 1 rehabilitation; 1 long-term acute care; 2 other specialty; 1 children's general; 1 children's psychiatric.
AHA Guide to the Healthcare Field 2010

According to *U.S. News,* the New Orleans-Metairie-Kenner, LA Metropolitan Statistical Area is home to two of the best hospitals in the U.S.: **Ochsner Medical Center**; **Tulane University Hospital and Clinic**. The hospitals listed were highly ranked in at least one adult specialty. *U.S. News Online, "America's Best Hospitals 2010-11"*

EDUCATION

Public School District Statistics

District Name	Schls	Pupils	Pupil/ Teacher Ratio	Minority Pupils[1] (%)	Free Lunch Eligible[2] (%)	IEP[3] (%)
Orleans Parish	21	10,109	13.8	84.9	62.0	7.4
RSD-Algiers Charter Schools	8	3,667	15.1	99.5	86.0	7.4
Recovery School District-LDE	35	12,675	15.3	99.4	85.1	11.9

Note: Table includes school districts with 2,000 or more students; (1) Percentage of students that are not non-Hispanic white; (2) Percentage of students that are eligible for the free lunch program; (3) Percentage of students that have an Individualized Education Program.
Source: U.S. Department of Education, National Center for Education Statistics, Common Core of Data, Local Education Agency (School District) Universe Survey: School Year 2008-2009; U.S. Department of Education, National Center for Education Statistics, Common Core of Data, Public Elementary/Secondary School Universe Survey: School Year 2008-2009

Top Public High Schools

High School Name	Index[1]	Rank[1]	Subsidized Lunch (%)[2]	E&E (%)[3]
Benjamin Franklin	3.472	163	29.0	95.0

Note: (1) Public schools are ranked according to a ratio that is the number of Advanced Placement, International Baccalaureate, and/or Cambridge tests taken by all students at a school in 2009 divided by the number of graduating seniors. All of the schools on the list have an index of at least 1.000; they are in the top six percent of public schools measured this way. The rankings range from 1 to 1,734; (2) Percentage of students receiving federally subsidized meals; (3) E & E stands for equity and excellence percentage: the portion of all graduating seniors at a school that had at least one passing grade on one AP or IB test; (4) Schools that offer International Baccalaureate or Cambridge exams; (5) School is unranked, but has been identified by Newsweek as one of the nation's most elite public high schools.
Source: Newsweek Online, "Top High Schools 2010"

Highest Level of Education

Area	Less than H.S.	H.S. Diploma	Some College, No Deg.	Associate Degree	Bachelors Degree	Masters Degree	Profess. School Degree	Doctorate Degree
City	17.8	30.0	20.6	3.8	16.2	6.5	3.3	1.8
MSA[1]	16.7	31.5	22.5	5.0	15.9	5.1	2.2	1.1
U.S.	15.3	29.0	20.7	7.5	17.4	7.0	1.9	1.1

Note: Figures are 2010 estimated percentages and cover persons age 25 and over; (1) Metropolitan Statistical Area - see Appendix B for areas included
Source: Claritas, Inc.

Educational Attainment by Race

Area	High School Graduate (%)					Bachelor's Degree (%)				
	Total	White	Black	Asian	Hisp.[2]	Total	White	Black	Asian	Hisp.[2]
City	82.9	93.4	78.3	54.3	71.9	29.2	52.6	14.1	29.6	30.8
MSA[1]	83.7	88.2	78.4	68.2	72.2	25.2	31.3	13.8	31.9	19.5
U.S.	84.9	90.0	80.7	85.5	60.7	27.8	30.9	17.5	49.7	12.7

Note: Figures shown cover persons 25 years old and over; (1) Metropolitan Statistical Area - see Appendix B for areas included; (2) people of Hispanic origin can be of any race
Source: U.S. Census Bureau, 2007-2009 American Community Survey 3-Year Estimates

School Enrollment by Grade and Control

Area	Preschool (%)		Kindergarten (%)		Grades 1 - 4 (%)		Grades 5 - 8 (%)		Grades 9 - 12 (%)	
	Public	Private	Public	Private	Public	Private	Public	Private	Public	Private
City	51.4	48.6	69.7	30.3	76.4	23.6	75.6	24.4	79.7	20.3
MSA[1]	50.5	49.5	70.3	29.7	75.5	24.5	72.7	27.3	74.7	25.3
U.S.	54.3	45.7	86.4	13.6	88.9	11.1	89.1	10.9	90.2	9.8

Note: Figures shown cover persons 3 years old and over; (1) Metropolitan Statistical Area - see Appendix B for areas included
Source: U.S. Census Bureau, 2007-2009 American Community Survey 3-Year Estimates

Average Salaries of Public School Classroom Teachers

Area	2009-10		2010-11		Percent Change 2009-10 to 2010-11	Percent Change 2000-01 to 2010-11
	Dollars	Rank[1]	Dollars	Rank[1]		
Louisiana	48,903	30	49,634	30	1.50	47.7
U.S. Average	55,202	-	56,069	-	1.57	29.3

Note: (1) State rank ranges from 1 to 51 where 1 indicates highest salary.
Source: National Education Association, Rankings & Estimates: Rankings of the States 2010 and Estimates of School Statistics 2011, December 2010

Higher Education

Four-Year Colleges			Two-Year Colleges			Medical Schools[1]	Law Schools[2]	Voc/ Tech[3]
Public	Private Non-profit	Private For-profit	Public	Private Non-profit	Private For-profit			
3	7	0	1	0	1	2	2	5

Note: Figures cover institutions located within the city limits and include main campuses only; (1) includes schools accredited by the Liaison Committee on Medical Education and the American Osteopathic Association; (2) includes American Bar Association-accredited law schools; (3) includes all schools with programs that are less than 2 years.
Source: National Center for Education Statistics, Integrated Postsecondary Education System (IPEDS) Peer Analysis System, 2010-11; U.S. News & World Report, Medical School Directory, 2011; U.S. News & World Report, Law School Directory, 2011

According to *U.S. News & World Report*, the New Orleans-Metairie-Kenner, LA Metropolitan Statistical Area is home to one of the top 197 national universities in the U.S.: **Tulane University** (#51). The rankings are based on quantitative measurements such as peer assessment, retention, faculty resources, student selectivity, financial resources, graduation rate, and alumni giving rate. *U.S. News & World Report, "America's Best Colleges 2011"*

According to *U.S. News & World Report*, the New Orleans-Metairie-Kenner, LA Metropolitan Statistical Area is home to one of the top 50 law schools in the U.S.: **Tulane University** (#47). The rankings are based on a weighted average of 10 measures of quality: peer assessment score; assessment score by lawyers/judges; median LSAT scores; median undergrad GPA; acceptance rate; employment rates for graduates; bar passage rate; faculty resources; expenditures per student; student/faculty ratio; and library resources. *U.S. News & World Report, "America's Best Law Schools 2011"*

According to *Forbes*, the New Orleans-Metairie-Kenner, LA Metropolitan Statistical Area is home to one of the top 75 business schools in the U.S.: **Tulane (Freeman)** (#52). The rankings are based on the return on investment that graduates of the Class of 2004 received (median salary five years after graduation). *Forbes, "Best Business Schools," August 5, 2009*

**PRESIDENTIAL
ELECTION**

2008 Presidential Election Results

Area	Obama	McCain	Nader	Other
Orleans Parish	79.4	19.1	0.3	1.2
U.S.	52.9	45.6	0.6	0.9

Note: Results are percentages and may not add to 100% due to rounding
Source: Dave Leip's Atlas of U.S. Presidential Elections, www.uselectionatlas.org

EMPLOYERS

Major Employers

Company Name	Industry	Type of Site
Acme Truck Line	Trucking, except local	Headquarters
Alton Ochsner Med Foundation	Home health care services	Single
Avondale Industries NY	Shipbuilding and repairing	Single
Charity Hospital	General medical and surgical hospitals	Headquarters
Chevron	Gasoline service stations	Branch
Commander Navl Rsrve Frce Cmnd	National security	Branch
East Jefferson Hospital	General medical and surgical hospitals	Headquarters
Elmwood Fitness Center	General medical and surgical hospitals	Headquarters
Harrahs Casino	Hotels and motels	Single
Lockheed Martin	Fabricated plate work (boiler shop)	Branch
Medi Lend Nursing Services	Employment agencies	Single
Ochsner Clinic Foundation	General medical and surgical hospitals	Single
St Tammany Parish Hospital	General medical and surgical hospitals	Headquarters
Tulane Univ Hosp & Clinic	General medical and surgical hospitals	Headquarters
Tulane University	Colleges and universities	Headquarters
University of New Orleans	Colleges and universities	Branch
US Post Office	U.S. postal service	Branch
USDA National Finance Center	Regulation of agricultural marketing	Branch
West Jefferson Medical Center	General medical and surgical hospitals	Headquarters

Note: Companies shown are located within the New Orleans metropolitan area; nec = not elsewhere classified.
Source: www.zapdata.com, January 2011

PUBLIC SAFETY

Crime Rate

Area	All Crimes	Violent Crimes				Property Crimes		
		Murder	Forcible Rape	Robbery	Aggrav. Assault	Burglary	Larceny -Theft	Motor Vehicle Theft
City	4,623.3	51.7	29.1	277.0	419.1	1,135.8	1,934.2	776.4
Suburbs[1]	n/a	9.3	21.8	103.9	321.1	n/a	2,356.7	n/a
Metro[2]	n/a	21.4	23.9	153.3	349.0	n/a	2,236.2	n/a
U.S.	3,465.5	5.0	28.7	133.0	262.8	716.3	2,060.9	258.8

Note: Figures are crimes per 100,000 population; (1) All areas within the metro area that are located outside the city limits; (2) Metropolitan Statistical Area - see Appendix B for areas included
Source: FBI Uniform Crime Reports, 2009

Hate Crimes

Area	Number of Quarters Reported	Bias Motivation				
		Race	Religion	Sexual Orientation	Ethnicity	Disability
City	4	0	0	0	0	0

Source: Federal Bureau of Investigation, Hate Crime Statistics 2009

Identity Theft Consumer Complaints

Area	Complaints	Complaints per 100,000 Population	Rank[2]
MSA[1]	986	95.7	76
U.S.	250,854	81.3	-

Note: (1) Metropolitan Statistical Area - see Appendix B for areas included; (2) Rank ranges from 1 to 384 where 1 indicates greatest number of complaints per 100,000 population
Source: Federal Trade Commission, Consumer Sentinel Network Data Book for January - December 2010

RECREATION

Culture

Dance[1]	Theatre[1]	Instrumental Music[1]	Vocal Music[1]	Series/ Festivals	Museums	Zoos and Aquariums[2]
2	5	3	2	5	16	2

Note: (1) Number of professional perfoming groups; (2) AZA-accredited
Source: The Grey House Performing Arts Directory, 2011-2012; Official Museum Directory, 2010; American Association of Museums, AAM Member Museums, March 2011; Association of Zoos & Aquariums, AZA Member Zoos & Aquariums, May 2011

Professional Sports Teams

Team Name	League
New Orleans Hornets	National Basketball Association (NBA)
New Orleans Saints	National Football League (NFL)

Note: Includes teams located in the New Orleans metro area.
Source: Original research

CLIMATE

Average and Extreme Temperatures

Temperature	Jan	Feb	Mar	Apr	May	Jun	Jul	Aug	Sep	Oct	Nov	Dec	Yr.
Extreme High (°F)	83	85	89	92	96	100	101	102	101	92	87	84	102
Average High (°F)	62	65	71	78	85	89	91	90	87	80	71	64	78
Average Temp. (°F)	53	56	62	69	75	81	82	82	79	70	61	55	69
Average Low (°F)	43	46	52	59	66	71	73	73	70	59	51	45	59
Extreme Low (°F)	14	19	25	32	41	50	60	60	42	35	24	11	11

Note: Figures cover the years 1948-1990
Source: National Climatic Data Center, International Station Meteorological Climate Summary, 9/96

Average Precipitation/Snowfall/Humidity

Precip./Humidity	Jan	Feb	Mar	Apr	May	Jun	Jul	Aug	Sep	Oct	Nov	Dec	Yr.
Avg. Precip. (in.)	4.7	5.6	5.2	4.7	4.4	5.4	6.4	5.9	5.5	2.8	4.4	5.5	60.6
Avg. Snowfall (in.)	Tr	Tr	Tr	0	0	0	0	0	0	0	0	Tr	Tr
Avg. Rel. Hum. 6am (%)	85	84	84	88	89	89	91	91	89	87	86	85	88
Avg. Rel. Hum. 3pm (%)	62	59	57	57	58	61	66	65	63	56	59	62	60

Note: Figures cover the years 1948-1990; Tr = Trace amounts (<0.05 in. of rain; <0.5 in. of snow)
Source: National Climatic Data Center, International Station Meteorological Climate Summary, 9/96

Weather Conditions

Temperature			Daytime Sky			Precipitation		
10°F & below	32°F & below	90°F & above	Clear	Partly cloudy	Cloudy	0.01 inch or more precip.	0.1 inch or more snow/ice	Thunder-storms
0	13	70	90	169	106	114	1	69

Note: Figures are average number of days per year and cover the years 1948-1990
Source: National Climatic Data Center, International Station Meteorological Climate Summary, 9/96

HAZARDOUS WASTE

Superfund Sites

New Orleans has one hazardous waste site on the EPA's Superfund Final National Priorities List: **Agriculture Street Landfill**. U.S. Environmental Protection Agency, Final National Priorities List, April 1, 2011

AIR & WATER QUALITY

Air Quality Index

Area	Percent of Days when Air Quality was...[2]				AQI Statistics	
	Good	Moderate	Unhealthy for Sensitive Groups	Unhealthy	Maximum	Median
Area[1]	85.8	13.9	0.3	0.0	114	36

Note: The Air Quality Index (AQI) is an index for reporting daily air quality. EPA calculates the AQI for five major air pollutants regulated by the Clean Air Act: ground-level ozone, particle pollution (also known as particulate matter), carbon monoxide, sulfur dioxide, and nitrogen dioxide. The AQI runs from 0 to 500. The higher the AQI value, the greater the level of air pollution and the greater the health concern. There are six AQI categories: "Good" The AQI is between 0 and 50. Air quality is considered satisfactory; "Moderate" The AQI is between 51 and 100. Air quality is acceptable; "Unhealthy for Sensitive Groups" When AQI values are between 101 and 150, members of sensitive groups may experience health effects; "Unhealthy" When AQI values are between 151 and 200 everyone may begin to experience health effects; "Very Unhealthy" AQI values between 201 and 300 trigger a health alert; "Hazardous" AQI values over 300 trigger health warnings of emergency conditions; (1) Data covers Orleans Parish; (2) Based on 346 days with AQI data in 2008; The EPA has suspended data updates while it assesses its data systems, including AirData reports and maps.
Source: U.S. Environmental Protection Agency, AirData Report, 2008

Air Quality Index Pollutants

Area	Percent of Days when AQI Pollutant was...[2]					
	Carbon Monoxide	Nitrogen Dioxide	Ozone	Sulfur Dioxide	Particulate Matter 2.5	Particulate Matter 10
Area[1]	0.0	0.0	69.7	0.0	30.3	0.0

Note: The Air Quality Index (AQI) is an index for reporting daily air quality. EPA calculates the AQI for five major air pollutants regulated by the Clean Air Act: ground-level ozone, particle pollution (also known as particulate matter), carbon monoxide, sulfur dioxide, and nitrogen dioxide. The AQI runs from 0 to 500. The higher the AQI value, the greater the level of air pollution and the greater the health concern; (1) Data covers Orleans Parish; (2) Based on 346 days with AQI data in 2008; The EPA has suspended data updates while it assesses its data systems, including AirData reports and maps.
Source: U.S. Environmental Protection Agency, AirData Report, 2008

Air Quality Index Trends

Area	Trend Sites (days)								All Sites (days)
	2002	2003	2004	2005	2006	2007	2008	2009	2009
MSA[1]	4	15	12	13	13	17	2	6	89

Note: Figures are the number of days the AQI value exceeded 100 in a given year. An AQI value greater than 100 indicates that air quality would have been in the unhealthful range on that day. Data from exceptional events are included. These counts are presented in two ways. First, the counts are based on sites having an adequate record of monitoring data during the trend period (trend sites). These counts represent the relative change in the number of days with AQI values greater than 100. In the last column, the counts are based on all sites with data in the most recent year (because it is possible for a site to have data in the most recent year but not enough data to be a trend site); (1) Data covers the New Orleans-Metairie-Kenner, LA Metropolitan Statistical Area - see Appendix B for areas included
Source: U.S. Environmental Protection Agency, Office of Air and Radiation, Air Quality Index Information, "Number of Days with Air Quality Index Values Greater than 100 and Trend Sites, 1990-2009, and at All Sites in 2009"

Maximum Air Pollutant Concentrations

	Particulate Matter 10 (ug/m^3)	Particulate Matter 2.5 (ug/m^3)	Ozone (ppm)	Carbon Monoxide (ppm)	Sulfur Dioxide (ppm)	Nitrogen Dioxide (ppm)	Lead (ug/m^3)
MSA[1] Level	40	22	0.077	n/a	0.108	0.008	n/a
NAAQS[2]	150	35	0.075	9	0.140	0.053	0.15
Met NAAQS[2]	Yes	Yes	No	n/a	Yes	Yes	n/a

Note: Data from exceptional events are not included; (1) Data covers the New Orleans-Metairie-Kenner, LA Metropolitan Statistical Area - see Appendix B for areas included; (2) National Ambient Air Quality Standards; n/a not available
Concentrations: Particulate Matter 10 (coarse particulate) - highest second maximum 24-hour concentration; Particulate Matter 2.5 (fine particulate) - highest 98th percentile 24-hour concentration; Ozone - highest fourth daily maximum 8-hour concentration; Carbon Monoxide - highest second maximum non-overlapping 8-hour concentration; Sulfur Dioxide - highest second maximum 24-hour concentration; Nitrogen Dioxide - highest arithmetic mean concentration; Lead - maximum running 3-month average
Units: ppm = parts per million; ug/m^3 = micrograms per cubic meter
Source: U.S. Environmental Protection Agency, CBSA Factbook 2009, Air Quality Statistics by City, 2009

Drinking Water

Water System Name	Pop. Served	Primary Water Source Type	Violations[1]	
			Health Based	Monitoring/ Reporting
New Orleans Carrollton WW	428,000	Surface	0	0

Note: (1) Based on violation data from January 1, 2010 to December 31, 2010 (includes unresolved violations from earlier years)
Source: U.S. Environmental Protection Agency, Office of Ground Water and Drinking Water, Safe Drinking Water Information System (based on data extracted May 9, 2011)

Orlando, Florida

Background

The city of Orlando can hold the viewer aghast with its rampant tourism. Not only is it home to the worldwide tourist attractions of Disney World, Epcot Center, and Sea World, but Orlando and its surrounding area also host such institutions as Medieval Times Dinner & Tournament, Wet-N-Wild, Ripley's Believe It or Not Museum, and Sleuths Mystery Dinner Shows, as well as thousands of T-shirt, citrus, and shell vendor shacks.

Orlando has its own high-tech corridor because of the University of Central Florida's College of Optics and Photonics. Manufacturing, government, business service, health care, high-tech research, and tourism supply significant numbers of jobs. Xenerga, a new biodiesel fuel manufacturer, built its flagship plant in Orlando with plans for dozens more sites across the United States.

Aside from the glitz that pumps most of the money into its economy, Orlando is also called "The City Beautiful." The warm climate and abundant rains produce a variety of lush flora and fauna, which provide an attractive setting for the many young people who settle in the area, spending their nights in the numerous jazz clubs, restaurants, and pubs along Orange Avenue and Church Street. Stereotypically the land of orange juice and sunshine, Orlando is becoming the city for young job seekers and professionals.

This genteel setting is a far cry from Orlando's rough-and-tumble origins. The city started out as a makeshift campsite in the middle of a cotton plantation. The Civil War and devastating rains brought an end to the cotton trade, and its settlers turned to raising livestock. The transition to a new livelihood did not insure any peace and serenity. Rustling, chaotic brawls, and senseless shootings were everyday occurrences. Martial law had to be imposed by a few large ranch families.

The greatest impetus toward modernity came from the installation of Cape Canaveral, 50 miles away, which brought missile assembly and electronic component production to the area, and Walt Disney World, created out of 27,000 acres of unexplored swampland, which set the tone for Orlando as a tourist-oriented economy.

Orlando is also a major film production site. Nickelodeon, the world's largest teleproduction studio dedicated to children's television programming, is based there, as are the Golf Channel, Sun Sports, House of Moves, and the America Channel. Disney's biggest theme-park competitor, Universal Studios, is also based in Orlando.

The city is also home to a variety of arts and entertainment facilities, including the Amway Arena, part of the Orlando Centroplex, home to the NBA's Orlando Magic and the Orlando Sharks of the Indoor Soccer League. The city vies with Chicago and Las Vegas for hosting the most convention attendees in the United States.

Orlando is surrounded by many lakes. Its relative humidity remains high year-round, though in winter the humidity may drop. June through September is the rainy season, during which time, scattered afternoon thunderstorms are an almost daily occurrence. During the winter months rainfall is light and the afternoons are most pleasant. Hurricanes are not usually considered a threat to the area.

Rankings

General Rankings

- Orlando was ranked #155 out of 375 metro areas in *Cities Ranked & Rated*. Criteria: cost of living; climate; crime; transportation; economy and jobs; education; arts and culture; health and healthcare; leisure; quality of life. *Cities Ranked & Rated, 2nd Edition, 2007*

- Orlando was ranked #49 out of 379 metro areas in *Places Rated Almanac*. Criteria: health care; education; recreation; transportation; ambience; climate; crime; housing costs; jobs. *Places Rated Almanac, 7th Edition, 2007*

- The Orlando metro area was identified as one of the 10 most popular big cities by Pew Research Center. The results are based on a telephone survey of 2,260 adults conducted during October 2008. The report explored a range of attitudes related to where Americans live, where they would like to live, and why. *Pew Research Center, "For Nearly Half of America, Grass is Greener Somewhere Else," January 29, 2009*

- *Men's Health Living* ranked 100 U.S. cities in terms of quality of life. Orlando was ranked #71 and received a grade of D+. Criteria: number of fitness facilities; air quality; number of physicians; male/female ratio; education levels; household income; cost of living. *Men's Health Living, Spring 2008*

- Orlando was identified as one of the top places to live in the U.S. by Harris Interactive. The city ranked #11 out of 15. Criteria: 2,620 adults (age 18 and over) were polled and asked "if you could live in or near any city in the country except the one you live in or nearest to now, which city would you choose?" The poll was conducted online within the U.S. between September 14 and 20, 2010. *Harris Interactive, October 20, 2010*

Business/Finance Rankings

- Experian ranked the top 20 major U.S metropolitan areas by average debt per consumer. The Orlando metro area was ranked #10. Criteria: average debt per consumer. Debt for this study includes credit cards, auto loans and personal loans. It does not include mortgages. *Experian, May 13, 2010*

- Orlando was identified as one of the top 25 U.S. cities with the most credit card debt by credit reporting bureau Experian. The city was ranked #25. *Experian, March 4, 2011*

- A.G. Edwards ranked America's 500 top-performing communities based on their residents' personal savings and investing behavior. The Orlando metro area ranked #368 with an index score of 97.88 (national average = 100.00). A dozen statistical factors were measured including: participation in retirement savings plans; personal debt levels; and home ownership. *A.G. Edwards, "2007 Nest Egg Index," September 12, 2007*

- Orlando was selected as one of the "100 Best Places to Live and Launch" in the U.S. The city ranked #73. The editors at *Fortune Small Business* ranked 296 Census-designated metro areas by business friendliness (Launching Score, % New Businesses) and lifestyle offerings (Living Score). Then they picked the town within each of the top 100 metro areas that best blends business and pleasure. *Fortune Small Business, "100 Best Places to Live and Launch 2008," April 2008*

- *American City Business Journals* ranked America's 261 largest cities in terms of their resident's wealth. Orlando ranked #124. Criteria: per capita income; median household income; percentage of households with annual incomes of $200,000 or more; median home value. *American City Business Journals, www.bizjournals.com, "Where the Money Is: America's Wealth Centers," August 18, 2008*

- The Orlando metro area appeared on the Milken Institute "2010 Best Performing Metros" list. Rank: #98 out of 200 large metro areas. Criteria: job growth; wage and salary growth; high-tech output growth. *Milken Institute, "2010 Best Performing Metros"*

- The Orlando metro area was selected as one of the best cities for entrepreneurs in America by *Inc. Magazine*. Criteria: job-growth data for 335 metro areas was analyzed for: recent growth trend (the current and prior year's employment growth rates, with the current year emphasized); mid-term growth (the average annual 2002-2007 growth rate); long-term trend (the sum of the 2002-2007 and 1996-2001 employment growth rates multiplied by the ratio of the 1996-2001 growth rate over the 2002-2007 growth rate); current year growth. The Orlando metro area ranked #6 among large metro areas and #45 overall. *Inc. Magazine, "The Best Cities for Doing Business," July 2008*

- Orlando was ranked #103 out of 145 regions worldwide in terms of its "Knowledge Competitiveness Index." The index attempts to measure the knowledge-based development taking place throughout the world and is based on 19 measures of economic performance that indicate a region's ability to translate its knowledge capacity into economic value. *Centre for International Competitiveness, World Knowledge Competitiveness Index 2008*

- *Forbes* ranked the 200 most populous metro areas in the U.S. in terms of the "Best Places for Business and Careers." The Orlando metro area was ranked #105. Criteria: 12 metrics including costs (business and living), job growth (past and projected), income growth, educational attainment, projected economic growth, crime, cultural and recreational opportunities, net migration patterns, percentage of subprime mortgages handed out over a three-year period, and the number of highly ranked four-year colleges. *Forbes, "Best Places for Business and Careers," April 14, 2010*

Children/Family Rankings

- Orlando was selected as one of the 10 worst cities to raise children in the U.S. by *KidFriendlyCities.org*. Criteria: education; environment; health; employment; crime; diversity; cost of living. *KidFriendlyCities.org, "Top Rated Kid/Family Friendly Cities 2009"*

- The Orlando metro area was selected as one of the "Best Cities for Relocating Families" by Worldwide ERC and Primacy Relocation. The 2008 study looked at nearly 50 factors important to relocating families including: recent job growth; nearby top-ranked colleges; in-state tuition for four-year public colleges; population growth since 2000; pediatricians per 100,000 population; and a Green Living index. *Worldwide ERC and Primacy Relocation, "2008 Best Cities for Relocating Families"*

Dating/Romance Rankings

- Orlando was selected as one of the most romantic cities in America by *Amazon.com*. The city ranked #3 of 20. Cities with populations greater than 100,000 were evaluated based on per capita sales of romance novels and relationship books, romantic comedy movies, Barry White albums, and sexual wellness products. *Amazon.com, "Top 20 Most Romantic Cities in America," February 8, 2011*

- Orlando appeared on *Men's Health's* list of the most sex-happy cities in America. The city ranked #71 of 100. Criteria: condom sales; birth rates; sex toy sales; rates of chlamydia, gonorrhea, and syphilis. *Men's Health, "America's Most Sex-Happy Cities," October 2010*

- *Men's Health* ranked 100 U.S. cities in terms of best (and worst) marriages. Orlando was ranked #18 (#1 = worst marriages). Criteria: rate of failed marriages; stringency of divorce laws; percentage of population who've split; number of licensed marriage and family therapists. *Men's Health, "Splitsville, USA," May 2010*

- Eli Lily and Company, in partnership with Sperling's BestPlaces, ranked the nation's 50 largest metro areas in terms of the "Most Romantic Cities for Baby Boomers." The Orlando metro area ranked #19. Criteria: marriage and divorce rates among "baby boomers" age 45 to 60; great restaurants; dance studios; chocolate, jewelry and flower sales. *Eli Lily and Company, "Most Romantic Cities for Baby Boomers," April 20, 2007*

- The Orlando metro area was selected as one of the "Best Cities for Relocating Singles" by Worldwide ERC and Primacy Relocation. The area ranked #13 out of the 100 largest metro areas in the U.S. Areas were selected based on the following criteria: recent job growth; recent singles population growth; overall population growth; affordable rental housing; cost-of-living index; expanded arts and recreation opportunities; ratio of single men and single women; affordability of quality higher education (including state residency requirements); diversity index; climate; population density. *Worldwide ERC and Primacy Relocation, "2008 Best Cities for Relocating Singles"*

- *Forbes* ranked the 40 most populous urbanized areas in the U.S. in terms of the "Best Cities for Singles." The Orlando metro area ranked #26. Criteria: number of singles; cost of living alone; nightlife; culture; job growth; coolness; and online dating participation. *Forbes.com, "Best Cities for Singles," July 27, 2009*

Education Rankings

- Orlando was identified as one of the 100 "smartest" metro areas in the U.S. The area ranked #47. Criteria: the editors rated the collective brainpower of the 100 largest metro area in the U.S based on their residents' educational attainment. *American City Business Journals, www.bizjournals.com, April 14, 2008*

- Orlando was identified as one of "America's Brainiest Bastions" by *Portfolio.com.* The metro area ranked #115 out of 200. Portfolio.com analyzed levels of educational attainment in the nation's 200 largest metropolitan areas. The editors established scores for five levels of educational attainment, based on relative earning power of adult workers age 25 or older. Scores were determined by comparing the median income for all workers with the median income for those workers at a specified educational level. *Portfolio.com, "America's Brainiest Bastions," December 1, 2010*

Environmental Rankings

- The Orlando metro area was identified as one of "The Ten Biggest American Cities that are Running Out of Water" by *24/7 Wall St.* The metro area ranked #10 out of 10. *24/7 Wall St.* did an analysis of the water supply and consumption in the 30 largest metropolitan areas in the U.S. Criteria include: projected water demand as a share of available precipitation; groundwater use as a share or projected available precipitation; susceptibility to drought; projected increase in freshwater withdrawls; projected increase in summer water deficit. The editors chose ten cities that are likely to face severe shortages in the relatively near-term future. *24/7 Wall St., "The Ten Biggest American Cities that are Running Out of Water," November 1, 2010*

- Scarborough Research, a leading market research firm, identified the top local markets for green appliance households. The Orlando DMA (Designated Market Area) ranked in the top 16 with 35% of consumers reporting that they own an energy-efficient appliance. *Scarborough Research, March 23, 2010*

- Orlando was selected as one of 22 "Smarter Cities" for energy by the Natural Resources Defense Council." Criteria: investment in green power; energy efficiency measures; conservation. *Natural Resources Defense Council, "2010 Smarter Cities," July 19, 2010*

- *American City Business Journal* ranked 43 metropolitan areas in terms of their "greenness." The Orlando metro area ranked #28. Criteria: Forty-one metros in which *ACBJ* has business weeklies, plus Indianapolis and Cleveland, were ranked based on 20 different indicators such as adoption of green technologies, utilization of environmentally sound practices, and air and water quality. *American City Business Journals, "Green City Index," March 11, 2010*

- The Orlando metro area was selected as one of "America's Cleanest Cities" by *Forbes.* The metro area ranked #4 out of 10. Criteria: air quality; water quality; per capita spending on Superfund site cleanup and solid-waste management. *Forbes.com, "America's Cleanest Cities," March 11, 2008*

- 100 of the largest metro areas in the U.S. were analyzed in terms of their current drought severity. The Orlando metro area ranked #15 (#1 = driest). The rankings were based on statistics such as long-term precipitation trends and patterns and the Palmer drought indices. *Sperling's BestPlaces, www.BestPlaces.net, "America's Drought-Riskiest Cities," November 2007*

- The Orlando metro area appeared in *Country Home's* "Best Green Places" report. The area ranked #236 out of 379. Criteria: official energy policies; green power; green buildings; availability of fresh, locally grown food. *Country Home, "Best Green Places," 2008*

- Orlando was highlighted as one of the top 25 cleanest metro areas for year-round particle pollution (Annual PM 2.5) in the U.S. The area ranked #24. *American Lung Association, State of the Air 2011*

Health/Fitness Rankings

- Orlando was identified as a "2011 Asthma Capital." The area ranked #26 out of the nation's 100 largest metropolitan areas. Twelve factors were used to identify the most challenging places to live for people with asthma: estimated prevalence; self-reported prevalence; crude death rate for asthma; annual pollen score; annual air quality; public smoking laws; number of board-certified asthma specialists; school inhaler access laws; rescue medication use; controller medication use; uninsured rate; poverty rate. *Asthma and Allergy Foundation of America, "2011 Asthma Capitals"*

- Orlando was identified as a 2009 "Spring Allergy Capital." The area ranked #83 out of 100. Three groups of factors were used to identify the most severe cities for people with allergies during the spring season: annual pollen levels; medicine utilization; access to board-certified allergists. *Asthma and Allergy Foundation of America, "Spring Allergy Capitals 2009"*

- Orlando was identified as a 2010 "Fall Allergy Capital." The area ranked #61 out of 100. Three groups of factors were used to identify the most severe cities for people with allergies during the fall season: annual pollen levels; medicine utilization; access to board-certified allergists. *Asthma and Allergy Foundation of America, "Fall Allergy Capitals 2010"*

- *Men's Health* ranked 100 U.S. cities in terms of the quality of their tap water. Orlando was ranked #80 and received a grade of C. Criteria: levels of total coliform bacteria, arsenic, lead, total trihalomethanes (linked to cancer), and halo-acetic acids; number of EPA water-system violations from 1995 to 2005. *Men's Health, March 2007*

- Ortho-McNeil Neurologics, in partnership with Sperling's BestPlaces, analyzed 110 metro areas and identified those U.S. cities with the highest prevalence of factors that are most commonly associated with migraine headaches. The Orlando metro area ranked #76. Criteria: number of migraine-related drug prescriptions per capita; lifestyle factors that can contribute to migraines; environmental factors that can trigger migraines; and consumption of migraine-triggering foods. *Ortho-McNeil Neurologics, "America's Migraine Hot Spots," March 14, 2006*

- An analysis of the "Best & Worst Cities for Sleep" was conducted by Sperling's BestPlaces. The study ranked America's 50 most populated metro areas. The Orlando metro area ranked #37 (#1 = best city for sleep). Criteria: number of days residents didn't get enough rest or sleep during the past month; average length of daily commute; divorce rate; unemployment rate. *Sperling's BestPlaces, www.BestPlaces.net, "Best & Worst Cities for Sleep," 2006*

- The Orlando metropolitan area was selected as one of the best metros for hospital care in America by HealthGrades. The rankings are based on a comprehensive study of patient death and complication rates in the nation's nearly 5,000 hospitals. Hospitals performing in the top 5% nationwide across 26 different medical procedures and diagnoses were identified. HealthGrades then ranked cities by the highest percentage of these Distinguished Hospitals for Clinical Excellence™. The Orlando metro area ranked #21. *HealthGrades.com, "America's Top 50 Cities for Hospital Care," January 26, 2011*

- *Men's Health* ranked 100 U.S. cities in terms of cities "Where the Food is Sickening." Orlando was ranked #66 and received a grade of C-. The magazine arrived at their ratings by looking at data compiled by the Community Health Status Indicator Project to determine outbreaks of E. coli, salmonella-, and shigella-related infections. They then checked the CDC's Wonder database to see how many people died from tainted food. Finally, the magazine found out which states have adopted the current version of the FDA's uniform Food Code, which contains the most up-to-date rules for keeping restaurant kitchens clean. *Men's Health, October 2005*

- Scarborough Research, a leading market research firm, identified the top local markets for diabetes medication purchasers. The Orlando DMA (Designated Market Area) ranked in the top 13 with 10% of consumers reporting that they purchased medication for diabetes within the past 12 months. *Scarborough Research, March 19, 2007*

- The Orlando metro area appeared in the 2010 Gallup-Healthways Well-Being Index. The index, based on interviews with more than 353,000 Americans during 2009, asked individuals to assess their jobs, finances, physical health, emotional state of mind and communities. The metro area ranked #66 out of 162. Criteria: life evaluation; emotional health; work environment; physical health; healthy behaviors; basic access (basic needs optimal for a healthy life, such as access to food and medicine, having health insurance and feeling safe while walking at night). *Gallup-Healthways, "Well-Being Index 2010"*

- The Orlando metro area was identified as one of "America's Most Stressful Cities" by *Forbes*. The metro area ranked #28. Criteria: median home price drop; unemployment rates; cost of living; air quality; sunny days; population density. *Forbes.com, "America's Most Stressful Cities," August 20, 2009*

- 50 of the largest metro areas in the U.S. were analyzed in terms of their health and fitness by the American College of Sports Medicine in their "American Fitness Index." The Orlando metro area ranked #19 (#1 = healthiest). Criteria: preventative health behaviors; levels of chronic disease; health care access; community resources and policies that support physical activity. *American College of Sports Medicine, "Health and Community Fitness Status of the 50 Largest Metropolitan Areas," May 24, 2010*

- Orlando was selected as one of the "20 Most Livable U.S. Cities for Wheelchair Users" by the Christopher & Dana Reeve Foundation. The city ranked #9. Criteria: Medicaid eligibility and spending; access to physicians and rehabilitation facilities; access to fitness facilities and recreation; access to paratransit; percentage of people living with disabilities who are employed; clean air; climate. *Christopher & Dana Reeve Foundation, "20 Most Livable U.S. Cities for Wheelchair Users," July 26, 2010*

Pet Rankings

- Orlando was identified as one of North America's most accommodating cities for travelers with pets. The city was ranked #8. Criteria: number of AAA Approved and Diamond rated pet-friendly hotels. *AAA, Traveling with your Pet: The AAA PetBook, 2006*

Real Estate Rankings

- *Fortune* ranked the 100 largest metro areas in the U.S. in terms of projected median home price change in 2010. The Orlando metro area ranked #99. *Fortune, "The 2010 Housing Outlook," December 9, 2009*

- Orlando was identified as one of the top 20 metro areas with the lowest rate of house price appreciation in 2010. The area ranked #295 with a one-year price appreciation of -8.0% through the 4th quarter 2010. *Federal Housing Finance Agency, House Price Index, 4th Quarter 2010*

- Orlando appeared on ApartmentRatings.com "Top College Towns & Cities" for renters list in 2010." The area ranked #61. Overall satisfaction ratings were ranked using thousands of user submitted scores for hundreds of apartment complexes located in cities and towns that are home to the 100 largest four-year institutions in the U.S. *ApartmentRatings.com, "2010 College Town Renter Satisfaction Rankings"*

- The Orlando metro area was identified as one of "America's 25 Weakest Housing Markets" by *Forbes*. The metro area ranked #9. Criteria: metro areas with populations over 500,000 were ranked based on projected home values through 2011. *Forbes.com, "America's 25 Weakest Housing Markets," January 7, 2009*

- The nation's largest metro areas were analyzed in terms of the percentage of households entering some stage of foreclosure in 2010. The Orlando metro area ranked #9 out of 206 (#1 = highest foreclosure rate). *RealtyTrac, 2010 Year-End Metropolitan Foreclosure Market Report, January 27, 2011*

- The Orlando metro area appeared in a *Wall Street Journal* article ranking cities by "housing stress." The metro area was ranked #6 (#1 = most stress). Criteria: fraction of mortgage-holding homeowners with a monthly housing payment in excess of 30 percent of income; percentage of people without health insurance; unemployment rate. *The Wall Street Journal, "Which Cities Face Biggest Housing Risk," October 5, 2010*

- The Center for Housing Policy ranked 210 U.S metropolitan areas by the fair market rent for a two-bedroom unit. The Orlando metro area was ranked #48. (#1 = most expensive) with a rent of $1,052. Criteria: Fair Market Rent (FMR) in effect during the fourth quarter of 2009 based on HUD's fiscal year 2010 FMRs. *The Center for Housing Policy, "Paycheck to Paycheck: Most to Least Expensive Rental Markets in 2009"*

- The Orlando metro area was identified as one of the top 20 cities in terms of decreasing home equity. The metro area was ranked #13. Criteria: percentage of home equity relative to the home's current value. *Forbes.com, "Where Americans are Losing Home Equity Most," May 1, 2010*

- The Orlando metro area was identified as one of the markets with the worst expected performance in home prices over the next 12 months. *Local Market Monitor, "First Quarter Home Price Forecast for Largest US Markets," March 2, 2011*

Safety Rankings

- Allstate ranked the 200 largest cities in America in terms of driver safety. Orlando ranked #145. In addition, drivers were 21.4% more likely to have had an accident compared to the national average. Allstate researchers analyzed internal property damage reported claims over a two-year period (from January 2007 to December 2008) to ensure the findings would not be affected by external influences such as weather or road construction. A weighted average of the two-year numbers determined the annual percentages. The report defines an auto crash as any collision resulting in a property damage claim. *Allstate, "The 2010 Allstate America's Best Drivers Report™"*

- Orlando was identified as one of America's "11 Most Dangerous Cities" by *U.S. News*. The city ranked #3. Criteria: crime risk was calculated using the most recent seven years (2003-2009) of FBI crime reporting data. The data includes both property crimes and violent crimes. *U.S. News & World Report, "The 11 Most Dangerous Cities," February 16, 2011*

- The National Insurance Crime Bureau ranked 366 metro areas in the U.S. in terms of per capita rates of vehicle theft. The Orlando metro area ranked #83 (#1 = highest rate). Criteria: number of vehicle theft offenses per 100,000 inhabitants. *National Insurance Crime Bureau, "Hot Spots," May 17, 2010*

- The Orlando metro area was identified as one of the "The Most Dangerous Metro Areas for Pedestrians" by Transportation for America and the Surface Transportation Policy Partnership. The metro area ranked #1 out of 52 metro areas with over 1 million residents. Criteria: area's population divided by the number of pedestrian fatalities in that area. *Transportation for America and the Surface Transportation Policy Partnership, "Dangerous by Design: Solving the Epidemic of Preventable Pedestrian Deaths (and Making Great Neighborhoods)," November 11, 2009*

Seniors/Retirement Rankings

- Orlando was identified as one of "The Top 100 Places to Retire" by *Topretirements.com* The list reflects the 100 cities (out of 625+ total cities reviewed) that visitors to the website are most interested in for retirement. *Topretirements.com, "2011 Best Places to Retire List: The Sunbelt Rules"*

- Orlando was selected as one of "Seven Places to Retire During an Economic Downturn." The city ranked #3. The editors at *Smart Money* selected seven recession-proof places soon-to-be retirees should consider. *SmartMoney.com, "Seven Places to Retire During an Economic Downturn," February 29, 2008*

Sports/Recreation Rankings

- Orlando appeared on the *Sporting News* list of the "Best Sports Cities" for 2010. The area ranked #24 out of 402 cities in the U.S. *Sporting News* takes a 12-month snapshot, roughly October to October, of each city's sports, putting a heavy premium on regular-season won-lost records (from the most recently completed season). Other criteria include: playoff berths, bowl appearances and tournament bids; championships; applicable power ratings; quality of competition; overall fan fervor as measured in part by attendance as percentage of venue capacity; abundance of teams (rewarding quality over quantity); stadium and arena quality; ticket availability and prices; franchise ownership; and marquee appeal of athletes. *Sporting News, "Best Sports Cities 2010," October, 2010*

- Orlando was chosen as a bicycle friendly community by the League of American Bicyclists. A Bicycle Friendly Community welcomes cyclists by providing safe accommodation for cycling and encouraging people to bike for transportation and recreation. There are four award levels: Platinum; Gold; Silver; and Bronze. The community achieved an award level of Bronze. *League of American Bicyclists, "Bicycle Friendly Community Master List," September 2010*

- Orlando was selected as one of the most playful cities in the U.S. by KaBOOM! The organization's Playful City USA initiative is a national recognition program that honors cities and towns across the nation for a vision, plan and commitment to creating an agenda for play. Cities were recognized based on a pledge to five specific commitments to play: creating a local play commission or task force; designing an annual action plan for play; conducting a play space audit; outlining a financial investment in play for the current fiscal year; and proclaiming and celebrating an annual "play day." *KaBOOM! National Campaign for Play, "2010 Playful City USA Communities"*

- *Golf Digest* ranked 330 metro areas in the U.S. in terms of golf. The Orlando metro area was ranked #73. Criteria: access to golf; weather; value of golf; and quality of golf. *Golf Digest, "Metro Golf Rankings," August 2005*

- *Golf.com* and the research arm of the National Golf Foundation analyzed the 50 largest metropolitan areas in the U.S. in terms of golf. The Orlando metro area ranked #5. Criteria: weather; affordability; quality of courses; accessibility; number of courses designed by esteemed architects; availability; crowdedness. *Golf.com, November 15, 2007*

Technology Rankings

- The Orlando metro area was selected as one of "America's Most Wired Cities" by *Forbes*. The metro area was ranked #9 out of 20. Criteria: percentage of Internet users with high-speed access; number of companies providing high-speed Internet; number of public wireless hot spots. *Forbes, "America's Most Wired Cities," March 2, 2010*

Transportation Rankings

- The Orlando metro area appeared on *Forbes* list of the best and worst cities for commuters. The metro area ranked #57 out of 60 (#1 is best). Criteria: travel time; road congestion; travel delays. *Forbes.com, "Best and Worst Cities for Commuters," February 16, 2010*

Women/Minorities Rankings

- Orlando was ranked #57 out of 100 metro areas in *SELF Magazine's* ranking of America's healthiest places for women." A panel of experts came up with more than 50 criteria including death and disease rates, environmental indicators, community resources, and lifestyle habits. *SELF Magazine, "Secrets of America's Healthiest Women," December 2008*

- Orlando was selected as one of the "Gayest Cities in America" by *The Advocate*. The city ranked #4 out of 15. Criteria: gay.com profiles; listed officiants for gay weddings within a 50 mile radius; elected openly gay officials; Tegan and Sara performances over the past five years; lesbian bars; gay and gay-friendly religious congregations; entries in YellowPages.com with "gay" in the business name or description. *The Advocate, "Gayest Cities in America," February 2011*

Miscellaneous Rankings

- Energizer Holdings, the makers of Edge® shave gel, in partnership with Sperling's BestPlaces, ranked 50 major metro areas in terms of everyday irritations. The Orlando metro area ranked #11. Criteria: humidity levels; weather conditions; incidence of traffic delays and congestion; average commute times; frequency of flight delays and cancellations; rates of sleeplessness; underemployment; pollens and allergens; pests; comedy clubs per capita. *Energizer Holdings, "Most Irritation Prone Cities," July 23, 2010*

- Mars Chocolate North America, the makers of COMBOS®, in partnership with Sperling's BestPlaces, ranked 50 major metro areas in terms of their "manliness." The Orlando metro area ranked #16. Criteria: number of home improvement stores, steak houses, pickup trucks, motorcycles, and manly occupations (fire fighters, police officers, construction workers, EMP personnel) per capita; salty snack sales; sports TV viewing habits. *Mars Chocolate North America, "America's Manliest Cities," June 22, 2010*

- Orlando appeared on Procter & Gamble's list of the "Top-20 All-Time Sweatiest Cities." The city was ranked #10. The rankings are based on computer simulations of the amount of sweat a person of average height and weight would produce walking around for an hour in the average temperatures during the summer months, based on historical weather data during June, July and August from 2001-2008 for each city. *Procter & Gamble, Old Spice Press Release, "Top-20 All-Time Sweatiest Cities," July 1, 2009*

- Orlando was selected as one of America's "10 Meanest Cities" by the National Coalition for the Homeless and The National Law Center on Homelessness & Poverty. The city was ranked #3. Criteria: the number of anti-homeless laws; the enforcement of those laws and severity of penalties; the general political climate towards homeless people; local advocate support for the meanest designation; the city's history of criminalization measures; and the existence of pending or recently enacted criminalization legislation in the city. *National Coalition for the Homeless and The National Law Center on Homelessness & Poverty, "Homes Not Handcuffs: The Criminalization of Homelessness in U.S. Cities," July 2009*

- The Orlando metro area appeared on *Forbes* list of "America's Drunkest Cities." The area ranked #31. Criteria: 35 of the largest continental U.S. metro areas were chosen based on availability of data and geographic diversity. Each metro was ranked in five areas: state laws; drinkers; heavy drinkers; binge drinkers; and alcoholism. *Forbes.com, "America's Drunkest Cities," August 22, 2006*

- Scarborough Research, a leading market research firm, identified the top local markets for frequent sit-down restaurant patronage. The Orlando DMA (Designated Market Area) ranked in the top 10 with consumers reporting an average of 4.5 visits within the past 30 days. *Scarborough Research, May 31, 2006*

Business Environment

CITY FINANCES

City Government Finances

Component	2008 ($000)	2008 ($ per capita)
Total Revenues	788,066	3,458
Total Expenditures	584,460	2,564
Debt Outstanding	507,706	2,228
Cash and Securities[1]	1,282,208	5,626

Note: (1) Cash and security holdings of a government at the close of its fiscal year, including those of its dependent agencies, utilities, and liquor stores.
Source: U.S Census Bureau, State & Local Government Finances 2008

City Government Revenue by Source

Source	2008 ($000)	2008 ($ per capita)
General Revenue		
From Federal Government	26,570	117
From State Government	49,674	218
From Local Governments	46,535	204
Taxes		
Property	117,844	517
Sales and Gross Receipts	54,217	238
Personal Income	0	0
Corporate Income	0	0
Motor Vehicle License	0	0
Other Taxes	71,322	313
Current Charges	146,106	641
Liquor Store	0	0
Utility	156	1
Employee Retirement	180,374	791

Source: U.S Census Bureau, State & Local Government Finances 2008

City Government Expenditures by Function

Function	2008 ($000)	2008 ($ per capita)	2008 (%)
General Direct Expenditures			
Air Transportation	0	0	0.0
Corrections	0	0	0.0
Education	0	0	0.0
Employment Security Administration	0	0	0.0
Financial Administration	48,036	211	8.2
Fire Protection	76,128	334	13.0
General Public Buildings	7,809	34	1.3
Governmental Administration, Other	14,754	65	2.5
Health	0	0	0.0
Highways	43,123	189	7.4
Hospitals	0	0	0.0
Housing and Community Development	14,746	65	2.5
Interest on General Debt	17,101	75	2.9
Judicial and Legal	3,497	15	0.6
Libraries	0	0	0.0
Parking	12,820	56	2.2
Parks and Recreation	58,865	258	10.1
Police Protection	112,989	496	19.3
Public Welfare	0	0	0.0
Sewerage	57,320	252	9.8
Solid Waste Management	22,243	98	3.8
Veterans' Services	0	0	0.0
Liquor Store	0	0	0.0
Utility	0	0	0.0
Employee Retirement	29,246	128	5.0

Source: U.S Census Bureau, State & Local Government Finances 2008

Municipal Bond Ratings

Area	Moody's	S&P	Fitch
City	Aa1	AA	AAA

Rating Systems (shown in declining order of credit quality): Moody's– Aaa, Aa, A, Baa, Ba, B, Caa, Ca, C (numerical modifiers 1, 2, and 3 are added to letter-rating); S&P– AAA, AA, A, BBB, BB, B, CCC, CC, C; Fitch– AAA, AA, A, BBB, BB, B, CCC, CC, C. Ratings may be modified by the addition of a plus or minus sign to show relative standing within the major rating categories.
Notes: n/a Not available; (1) Not reviewed; (2) Issuer Rating/No General Obligation; (3) Standard and Poor's Issue Credit Rating (ICR) is a current opinion of an obliger with respect to a specific financial obligation, a specific class of financial obligations, or a specific financial program.
Source: City of Orlando, Florida, Comprehensive Annual Financial Report, Fiscal Year Ended September 30, 2010

DEMOGRAPHICS

Population Growth

Area	1990 Census	2000 Census	2010 Estimate	2015 Projection	Population Growth (%) 2000-2010	2010-2015
City	161,172	185,951	229,589	251,720	23.5	9.6
MSA[1]	1,224,852	1,644,561	2,138,839	2,386,929	30.1	11.6
U.S.	248,709,873	281,421,906	309,038,974	321,675,005	9.8	4.1

Note: (1) Metropolitan Statistical Area - see Appendix B for areas included
Source: Claritas, Inc.

Number of Households and Average Household Size

Area	2010 Estimate	2010 Average Household Size
City	99,179	2.26
MSA[1]	805,054	2.61
U.S.	116,136,617	2.59

Note: (1) Metropolitan Statistical Area - see Appendix B for areas included
Source: Claritas, Inc.

Race and Ethnicity

Area	White Alone[2] (%)	Black Alone[2] (%)	Asian Alone[2] (%)	Other Race Alone[2] (%)	Hispanic[3] (%)
City	57.6	26.0	3.3	13.0	24.2
MSA[1]	69.9	15.0	3.6	11.6	23.8
U.S.	72.3	12.4	4.4	10.9	15.8

Note: Figures are 2010 estimates; (1) Metropolitan Statistical Area - see Appendix B for areas included (2) Alone is defined as not being in combination with one or more other races; (3) May be of any race.
Source: Claritas, Inc.

Segregation

Type	Segregation Indices[1] 1990	2000	2010	2010 Rank[2]	Percent Change 1990-2000	1990-2010	2000-2010
Black/White	59.1	55.9	50.7	69	-3.2	-8.4	-5.2
Asian/White	29.4	35.4	33.9	81	6.0	4.6	-1.4
Hispanic/White	29.2	38.7	40.2	64	9.5	11.0	1.5

Note: Figures are based on an analysis of 1990, 2000, and 2010 Census Decennial Census tract data by William H. Frey, Brookings Institution and the University of Michigan Social Science Data Analysis Network. In this analysis all racial groups (whites, blacks, and asians) are non-Hispanic members of those races. Hispanics are shown as a separate category; All figures cover the Metropolitan Statistical Area (see Appendix B for areas included); (1) Segregation Indices are Dissimilarity Indices that measure the degree to which the minority group is distributed differently than whites aross census tracts. They range from 0 (complete integration) to 100 (complete [segregation) where the value indicates the percentage of the minority group that needs to move to be distributed exactly like whites; (2) Ranges from 1 (most segregated) to 102 (least segregated); n/a not available.
Source: www.CensusScope.org

Ancestry

Area	German	Irish	English	American	Italian	Polish	French	Scottish
City	9.5	8.7	7.2	4.2	5.3	1.9	2.1	1.7
MSA[1]	11.9	10.0	8.5	7.3	5.9	2.4	2.5	1.7
U.S.	16.6	12.0	9.1	6.1	5.9	3.3	3.1	1.9

Note: The top eight ancestries in the U.S. are shown. Figures are percentages and include multiple ancestry (e.g. if a person reported being Irish and Italian, they were included in both columns); (1) Metropolitan Statistical Area - see Appendix B for areas included
Source: U.S. Census Bureau, 2007-2009 American Community Survey 3-Year Estimates

Foreign-Born Population

Area	Percent of Population Born in								
	Any Foreign Country	Mexico	Asia	Europe	Carribean	South America	Central America[2]	Africa	Canada
City	18.3	1.3	2.4	1.5	5.7	5.2	0.9	0.7	0.3
MSA[1]	15.8	1.7	2.6	1.7	4.3	3.6	0.9	0.5	0.5
U.S.	12.5	3.8	3.4	1.6	1.1	0.8	0.9	0.5	0.3

Note: (1) Metropolitan Statistical Area - see Appendix B for areas included; (2) Excludes Mexico.
Source: U.S. Census Bureau, 2007-2009 American Community Survey 3-Year Estimates

Marriage Status

Area	Never Married	Now Married[2]	Separated	Widowed	Divorced
City	41.3	36.8	3.8	4.8	13.3
MSA[1]	31.3	48.8	2.5	5.7	11.7
U.S.	31.4	49.7	2.2	6.2	10.6

Note: Figures are percentages and cover the population 15 years of age and older; (1) Metropolitan Statistical Area - see Appendix B for areas included; (2) Excludes separated
Source: U.S. Census Bureau, 2007-2009 American Community Survey 3-Year Estimates

Age Distribution and Median Age

Area	Percent of Population							Median Age
	Under Age 5	Age 5 to 17	Age 18 to 34	Age 35 to 49	Age 50 to 64	Age 65 to 79	80 Years and Over	
City	7.8	15.0	33.4	21.7	13.1	6.2	2.8	31.5
MSA[1]	6.9	17.2	24.5	21.8	16.6	9.4	3.6	36.0
U.S.	6.9	17.5	23.3	21.4	18.1	9.1	3.7	36.7

Note: (1) Metropolitan Statistical Area - see Appendix B for areas included
Source: U.S. Census Bureau, 2007-2009 American Community Survey 3-Year Estimates

Male/Female Ratio

Area	Males	Females	Males per 100 Females
City	113,184	116,405	97.2
MSA[1]	1,058,885	1,079,954	98.0
U.S.	152,401,520	156,637,454	97.3

Note: Figures are 2010 estimates; (1) Metropolitan Statistical Area - see Appendix B for areas included
Source: Claritas, Inc.

Religion

Area	Catholic	Southern Baptist	United Methodist	ELCA[1]	LDS[2]	Presbyterian Church USA	Jewish Est.	Muslim Est.
County	13.3	8.2	3.3	0.6	0.6	1.7	1.2	0.2
U.S.	22.0	7.1	3.7	1.8	1.5	1.1	2.2	0.6

Note: Figures are the number of adherents as a percentage of the total population; Adherents are defined as all members, including full members, their children and the estimated number of other participants who are not considered members (e.g. the baptized, those not confirmed, those regularly attending services, etc.);
(1) Evangelical Lutheran Church in America; (2) The Church of Jesus Christ of Latter Day Saints
Source: Reprinted with permission from Religious Congregations and Membership in the United States 2000 (Nashville, Glenmary Research Center, 2002) Copyright Association of Statisticians of American Religious Bodies. All rights reserved.

ECONOMY

Gross Metropolitan Product

Area	2006	2007	2008	2009	2009 Rank[2]
MSA[1]	97.8	102.1	104.0	101.6	26

Note: Figures are in billions of dollars; (1) Orlando-Kissimmee, FL Metropolitan Statistical Area - see Appendix B for areas included; (2) Rank ranges from 1 to 363
Source: The U.S. Conference of Mayors, "Pace of Economic Recovery: GMP and Jobs," January 2010

Economic Growth

Area	2006-2008 (%)	2009 (%)	2010 (%)	Rank[2]
MSA[1]	0.8	-3.2	2.4	212
U.S.	1.3	-2.5	2.2	–

Note: Figures are real Gross Metropolitan Product growth rates and represent annual average percent change; (1) Orlando-Kissimmee, FL Metropolitan Statistical Area - see Appendix B for areas included; (2) Rank ranges from 1 to 363
Source: The U.S. Conference of Mayors, "Pace of Economic Recovery: GMP and Jobs," January 2010

Metropolitan Area Exports

Area	2005	2006	2007	2008	2009	2009 Rank[2]
MSA[1]	2,183.2	2,474.3	3,045.1	3,388.0	2,947.1	59

Note: Figures are in millions of dollars; (1) Orlando-Kissimmee, FL Metropolitan Statistical Area - see Appendix B for areas included; (2) Rank ranges from 1 to 374
Source: U.S. Department of Commerce, International Trade Administration, Office of Trade & Industry Information, Manufacturing & Services

INCOME

Per Capita/Median/Average Income

Area	Per Capita ($)	Median Household ($)	Average Household ($)
City	25,195	43,787	57,689
MSA[1]	25,937	52,081	68,354
U.S.	27,034	52,795	71,071

Note: Figures are 2010 estimates; (1) Metropolitan Statistical Area - see Appendix B for areas included
Source: Claritas, Inc.

Household Income Distribution

Area	Percent of Households Earning							
	Under $15,000	$15,000 -24,999	$25,000 -34,999	$35,000 -49,999	$50,000 -74,999	$75,000 -99,000	$100,000 -149,999	$150,000 and up
City	13.2	12.3	13.5	18.7	20.2	9.8	7.9	4.4
MSA[1]	9.8	10.1	11.5	16.8	21.6	12.2	11.3	6.6
U.S.	12.1	10.2	10.6	15.0	19.5	12.5	12.1	8.0

Note: Figures are 2010 estimates; (1) Metropolitan Statistical Area - see Appendix B for areas included
Source: Claritas, Inc.

Poverty Rates by Age

Area	All Ages	Under 18 Years Old	18 to 64 Years Old	65 Years and Over
City	16.5	5.2	10.0	1.3
MSA[1]	12.0	3.9	7.0	1.1
U.S.	13.6	4.7	7.7	1.2

Note: Figures are percent of population with income during the previous 12 months below poverty level and only include population for whom poverty status is determined; (1) Metropolitan Statistical Area - see Appendix B for areas included
Source: U.S. Census Bureau, 2007-2009 American Community Survey 3-Year Estimates

Personal Bankruptcy Filing Rate

Area	2006	2007	2008	2009	2010
Orange County	1.21	2.21	3.97	6.78	7.98
U.S.	2.00	2.73	3.53	4.60	4.96

Note: Numbers are per 1,000 population and include Chapter 7 and Chapter 13 filings
Source: Federal Deposit Insurance Corporation, Regional Economic Conditions, March 17, 2011

EMPLOYMENT

Labor Force and Employment

Area	Civilian Labor Force			Workers Employed		
	Dec. 2009	Dec. 2010	% Chg.	Dec. 2009	Dec. 2010	% Chg.
City	133,121	136,757	2.7	118,865	121,383	2.1
MSA[1]	1,097,459	1,125,039	2.5	975,472	996,137	2.1
U.S.	152,693,000	153,156,000	0.3	137,953,000	139,159,000	0.9

Note: Data is not seasonally adjusted and covers workers 16 years of age and older;
(1) Metropolitan Statistical Area - see Appendix B for areas included
Source: Bureau of Labor Statistics, http://stats.bls.gov

Unemployment Rate

Area	2010											
	Jan.	Feb.	Mar.	Apr.	May	Jun.	Jul.	Aug.	Sep.	Oct.	Nov.	Dec.
City	11.1	10.9	10.8	10.6	10.5	11.0	11.4	11.6	11.4	11.4	11.8	11.2
MSA[1]	11.7	11.6	11.3	11.0	10.9	11.2	11.6	11.7	11.6	11.3	11.9	11.5
U.S.	10.6	10.4	10.2	9.5	9.3	9.6	9.7	9.5	9.2	9.0	9.3	9.1

Note: Data is not seasonally adjusted and covers workers 16 years of age and older; All figures are percentages; (1) Metropolitan Statistical Area - see Appendix B for areas included
Source: Bureau of Labor Statistics, http://stats.bls.gov

Projected Unemployment Rate

Area	2007 (%)	2009 (%)	2011 (%)	2013 (%)
MSA[1]	4.3	12.2	10.2	7.8

Note: (1) Metropolitan Statistical Area - see Appendix B for areas included
Source: The U.S. Conference of Mayors, "Pace of Economic Recovery: GMP and Jobs," January 2010

Employment by Occupation

Occupation Classification	City (%)	MSA[1] (%)	U.S. (%)
Sales and Office	28.2	28.7	25.4
Professional and Related	19.2	18.8	21.0
Service	21.7	19.0	17.2
Production, Transportation, and Material Moving	8.2	8.4	12.3
Management, Business, and Financial	13.6	15.1	14.1
Construction, Extraction, and Maintenance	8.8	9.8	9.2
Farming, Forestry, and Fishing	0.3	0.4	0.7

Note: Figures cover employed civilians 16 years of age and older;
(1) Metropolitan Statistical Area - see Appendix B for areas included
Source: U.S. Census Bureau, 2007-2009 American Community Survey 3-Year Estimates

Employment by Industry

| Sector | MSA[1] | | U.S. |
	Number of Employees	Percent of Total	Percent of Total
Government	117,000	11.5	17.2
Education and Health Services	122,300	12.0	15.2
Professional and Business Services	165,400	16.3	13.0
Retail Trade	120,400	11.9	11.4
Leisure and Hospitality	204,100	20.1	9.7
Manufacturing	37,300	3.7	8.8
Financial Activities	63,900	6.3	5.8
Wholesale Trade	37,900	3.7	4.2
Construction	45,100	4.4	4.1
Other Services	47,900	4.7	4.1
Transportation and Utilities	30,700	3.0	3.7
Information	23,600	2.3	2.1
Mining and Logging	200	<0.1	0.6

Note: Figures cover non-farm employment as of December 2010 and are not seasonally adjusted;
(1) Metropolitan Statistical Area - see Appendix B for areas included
Source: Bureau of Labor Statistics, http://stats.bls.gov

Occupations with Greatest Projected Employment Growth: 2006 - 2016

Occupation[1]	2006 Employment	2016 Projected Employment	Numeric Employment Change	Percent Employment Change
Retail salespersons	283,850	339,780	55,930	19.7
Customer service representatives	162,780	214,600	51,820	31.8
Registered nurses	148,390	190,020	41,630	28.1
Combined food preparation and serving workers, including fast food	163,780	202,670	38,890	23.7
Waiters and waitresses	197,920	232,430	34,510	17.4
Office clerks, general	188,190	221,750	33,560	17.8
Bookkeeping, accounting, and auditing clerks	128,340	153,830	25,490	19.9
Janitors and cleaners, except maids and housekeeping cleaners	124,030	147,970	23,940	19.3
Sales representatives, services, all other	73,650	97,390	23,740	32.2
Executive secretaries and administrative assistants	106,820	129,140	22,320	20.9

Note: Projections cover Florida; (1) Sorted by numeric employment change
Source: www.projectionscentral.com, State Occupational Projections, 2006-2016 Long-Term Projections

Fastest Growing Occupations: 2006 - 2016

Occupation[1]	2006 Employment	2016 Projected Employment	Numeric Employment Change	Percent Employment Change
Network systems and data communications analysts	20,830	33,090	12,260	58.9
Court reporters	2,170	3,430	1,260	58.1
Computer software engineers, applications	17,350	27,250	9,900	57.1
Veterinary technologists and technicians	5,720	8,880	3,160	55.2
Veterinarians	3,280	4,890	1,610	49.1
Home health aides	29,600	42,780	13,180	44.5
Personal and home care aides	10,640	15,220	4,580	43.0
Paralegals and legal assistants	19,240	27,360	8,120	42.2
Pharmacy technicians	21,110	29,950	8,840	41.9
Medical assistants	31,040	43,930	12,890	41.5

Note: Projections cover Florida; (1) Sorted by percent employment change and excludes occupations with numeric employment change less than 900
Source: www.projectionscentral.com, State Occupational Projections, 2006-2016 Long-Term Projections

Average Wages

Occupation	$/Hr.	Occupation	$/Hr.
Accountants and Auditors	29.32	Maids and Housekeeping Cleaners	9.35
Automotive Mechanics	17.79	Maintenance and Repair Workers	14.61
Bookkeepers	15.25	Marketing Managers	49.93
Carpenters	16.74	Nuclear Medicine Technologists	31.05
Cashiers	8.78	Nurses, Licensed Practical	18.64
Clerks, General Office	12.31	Nurses, Registered	27.87
Clerks, Receptionists/Information	11.78	Nursing Aides/Orderlies/Attendants	11.51
Clerks, Shipping/Receiving	12.28	Packers and Packagers, Hand	12.31
Computer Programmers	29.57	Physical Therapists	40.50
Computer Support Specialists	19.04	Postal Service Mail Carriers	23.62
Computer Systems Analysts	36.00	Real Estate Brokers	42.97
Cooks, Restaurant	11.86	Retail Salespersons	12.08
Dentists	n/a	Sales Reps., Exc. Tech./Scientific	26.07
Electrical Engineers	32.95	Sales Reps., Tech./Scientific	37.35
Electricians	17.99	Secretaries, Exc. Legal/Med./Exec.	13.79
Financial Managers	54.10	Security Guards	10.90
First-Line Supervisors/Mgrs., Sales	20.14	Surgeons	95.92
Food Preparation Workers	9.49	Teacher Assistants	11.10
General and Operations Managers	46.91	Teachers, Elementary School	24.80
Hairdressers/Cosmetologists	12.89	Teachers, Secondary School	25.90
Internists	85.24	Telemarketers	11.92
Janitors and Cleaners	10.14	Truck Drivers, Heavy/Tractor-Trailer	18.20
Landscaping/Groundskeeping Workers	11.38	Truck Drivers, Light/Delivery Svcs.	14.16
Lawyers	56.86	Waiters and Waitresses	9.93

Note: Wage data covers the Orlando-Kissimmee, FL - see Appendix B for areas included. Hourly wages for elementary/secondary school teachers and teacher assistants were calculated by the editors from annual wage data assuming a 40 hour work week; n/a not available.
Source: Bureau of Labor Statistics, Metro Area Occupational Employment and Wage Estimates, May 2009

RESIDENTIAL REAL ESTATE

Building Permits

Area	Single-Family			Multi-Family			Total		
	2009	2010	Pct. Chg.	2009	2010	Pct. Chg.	2009	2010	Pct. Chg.
City	235	224	-4.7	62	336	441.9	297	560	88.6
MSA[1]	3,707	4,221	13.9	780	1,033	32.4	4,487	5,254	17.1
U.S.	441,100	447,300	1.4	141,900	157,300	10.9	583,000	604,600	3.7

Note: (1) Metropolitan Statistical Area - see Appendix B for areas included; figures represent new, privately-owned housing units authorized (unadjusted data); All permit data are based on estimates with imputation.
Source: U.S. Census Bureau, Manufacturing, Mining, and Construction Statistics, Building Permits, 2009, 2010

Homeownership Rate

Area	2005 (%)	2006 (%)	2007 (%)	2008 (%)	2009 (%)	2010 (%)
MSA[1]	70.5	71.1	71.8	70.5	72.4	70.8
U.S.	68.9	68.8	68.1	67.8	67.4	66.9

Note: (1) Metropolitan Statistical Area - see Appendix B for areas included
Source: U.S. Census Bureau, Housing Vacancies and Homeownership Annual Statistics: 2010

Housing Vacancy Rates

Area	Gross Vacancy Rate[2] (%)			Year-Round Vacancy Rate[3] (%)			Rental Vacancy Rate[4] (%)			Homeowner Vacancy Rate[5] (%)		
	2008	2009	2010	2008	2009	2010	2008	2009	2010	2008	2009	2010
MSA[1]	21.4	21.2	19.9	17.8	17.5	16.6	21.9	22.8	19.0	6.8	5.8	5.9
U.S.	14.4	14.5	14.3	11.1	11.3	11.3	10.0	10.6	10.2	2.8	2.6	2.6

Note: (1) Metropolitan Statistical Area - see Appendix B for areas included; (2) The percentage of the total housing inventory that is vacant; (3) The percentage of the housing inventory (excluding seasonal units) that is year-round vacant; (4) The percentage of rental inventory that is vacant for rent; (5) The percentage of homeowner inventory that is vacant for sale; n/a not available
Source: U.S. Census Bureau, Housing Vacancies and Homeownership Annual Statistics: 2010

State Corporate Income Tax Rates

State	Tax Rate (%)	Income Brackets ($)	Num. of Brackets	Financial Institution Tax Rate (%)[a]	Federal Income Tax Ded.
Florida	5.5 (f)	Flat rate	1	5.5 (f)	No

Note: Tax rates as of January 1, 2011; (a) Rates listed are the tax rates applied to financial institutions or excise taxes based on income. Some states have other taxes based upon the value of deposits or shares; (f) An exemption of $5,000 is allowed. Florida's Alternative Minimum Tax rate is 3.3%.
Source: Federation of Tax Administrators, "State Corporate Income Tax Rates, 2011"

State Individual Income Tax Rates

State	Tax Rate (%)	Income Brackets ($)	Num. of Brackets	Personal Exempt. ($)[1] Single	Personal Exempt. ($)[1] Dependents	Fed. Inc. Tax Ded.
Florida – No State Income Tax						

Note: Tax rates as of January 1, 2011; Local- and county-level taxes are not included; n/a not applicable; (1) Married joint filers generally receive double the single exemption
Source: Federation of Tax Administrators, "State Individual Income Tax Rates, 2011"

Various State and Local Tax Rates

State	State and Local Sales and Use (%)	State Sales and Use (%)	Gasoline[1] (¢/gal.)	Cigarette[2] ($/pack)	Spirits[3] ($/gal.)	Wine[4] ($/gal.)	Beer[5] ($/gal.)
Florida	6.5	6.00	34.4	1.34	6.50	2.25	0.48

Note: All tax rates as of January 1, 2011 except Spirits (Sept. 1, 2010); (1) The American Petroleum Institute has developed a methodology for determining the average tax rate on a gallon of fuel. Rates may include any of the following: excise taxes, environmental fees, storage tank fees, other fees or taxes, general sales tax, and local taxes. In states where gasoline is subject to the general sales tax, or where the fuel tax is based on the average sale price, the average rate determined by API is sensitive to changes in the price of gasoline. States that fully or partially apply general sales taxes to gasoline: CA, CO, GA, IL, IN, MI, NY; (2) The federal excise tax of $1.0066 per pack and local taxes are not included; (3) Rates are those applicable to off-premise sales of 40% alcohol by volume (a.b.v.) distilled spirits in 750ml containers. Local excise taxes are excluded; (4) Rates are those applicable to off-premise sales of 11% a.b.v. non-carbonated wine in 750ml containers; (5) Rates are those applicable to off-premise sales of 4.7% a.b.v. beer in 12 ounce containers.
Source: Tax Foundation, 2011 Facts & Figures: How Does Your State Compare?

State-Local Tax Burdens

Area	Rate (%)	Rank[1]	Per Capita Taxes Paid to Home State ($)	Total State and Local Per Capita Taxes Paid ($)	Per Capita Income ($)
Florida	9.2	31	2,713	3,897	42,146
U.S. Average	9.8	-	3,057	4,160	42,539

Note: Figures cover 2009; (1) Rank ranges from 1 to 50 where 1 is highest tax burden
Source: Tax Foundation, State-Local Tax Burdens, All States, 2009

State Business Tax Climate Index Rankings

State	Overall Rank	Corporate Tax Index Rank	Individual Income Tax Index Rank	Sales Tax Index Rank	Unemployment Insurance Tax Index Rank	Property Tax Index Rank
Florida	5	15	1	30	3	28

Note: The index is a measure of how each state's tax laws affect economic performance. The lower the rank, the more favorable a state's tax system is for business. All ranks are for fiscal years. States without a given tax are given a ranking of 1.
Source: Tax Foundation, Tax Foundation Background Paper, No. 60, "2011 State Business Tax Climate Index"

COMMERCIAL REAL ESTATE

Office Market

Market Area	Inventory (sq. ft.)	Vacant (sq. ft.)	Vac. Rate (%)	Under Constr. (sq. ft.)	Asking Rent ($/sf/yr) Class A	Asking Rent ($/sf/yr) Class B
Orlando	54,140,414	10,159,725	18.8	353,356	22.73	18.63

Source: Grubb & Ellis, Office Markets Trends, 1st Quarter 2011

Industrial Market

Market Area	Inventory (sq. ft.)	Vacant (sq. ft.)	Vac. Rate (%)	Under Constr. (sq. ft.)	Asking Rent ($/sf/yr) WH/Dist	Asking Rent ($/sf/yr) R&D/Flex
Orlando	176,204,564	21,257,964	12.1	-	4.57	8.58

Source: Grubb & Ellis, Industrial Markets Trends, 4th Quarter 2010

COMMERCIAL UTILITIES

Typical Monthly Electric Bills

Area	Commercial Service ($/month) 3 kW demand 1,000 kWh	Commercial Service ($/month) 40 kW demand 14,000 kWh	Industrial Service ($/month) 1,000 kW demand 200,000 kWh	Industrial Service ($/month) 50,000 kW demand 15,000,000 kWh
City	106	1,214	21,777	945,149
Average[1]	135	1,576	23,741	1,402,202

Note: Based on total rates in effect July 1, 2010; (1) average based on 182 utilities surveyed
Source: Edison Electric Institute, Typical Bills and Average Rates Report, Summer 2010

TRANSPORTATION

Means of Transportation to Work

Area	Car/Truck/Van Drove Alone	Car/Truck/Van Car-pooled	Public Transportation Bus	Public Transportation Subway	Public Transportation Railroad	Bicycle	Walked	Other Means	Worked at Home
City	78.2	10.9	4.3	0.0	0.0	0.5	1.7	1.2	3.1
MSA[1]	80.7	9.7	1.7	0.0	0.0	0.4	1.1	1.7	4.7
U.S.	75.8	10.4	2.7	1.7	0.5	0.5	2.9	1.2	4.1

Note: Figures are percentages and cover workers 16 years of age and older;
(1) Metropolitan Statistical Area - see Appendix B for areas included
Source: U.S. Census Bureau, 2007-2009 American Community Survey 3-Year Estimates

Travel Time to Work

Area	Less Than 15 Minutes	15 to 29 Minutes	30 to 44 Minutes	45 to 59 Minutes	60 to 89 Minutes	90 Minutes or More
City	22.5	42.2	23.9	6.0	3.6	1.8
MSA[1]	20.3	37.9	26.1	9.1	4.7	1.9
U.S.	28.5	36.2	19.7	7.5	5.6	2.5

Note: Figures are percentages and include workers 16 years old and over;
(1) Metropolitan Statistical Area - see Appendix B for areas included
Source: U.S. Census Bureau, 2007-2009 American Community Survey 3-Year Estimates

Travel Time Index

Area	1982	1999	2008	2009
Urban Area[1]	1.07	1.23	1.19	1.20
Average[2]	1.08	1.20	1.20	1.20

Note: Travel Time Index—the ratio of travel time in the peak period to the travel time at free-flow conditions. A value of 1.30 indicates a 20-minute free-flow trip takes 26 minutes in the peak. Free-flow speeds (60 mph on freeways and 35 mph on principal arterials) are used as the comparison threshold; (1) Covers the Orlando-Kissimmee urban area; (2) average of 439 urban areas
Source: Texas Transportation Institute, Urban Mobility Report 2010, December 2010

Public Transportation

Agency Name / Mode of Transportation	Vehicles Operated in Maximum Service	Annual Unlinked Passenger Trips ('000)	Annual Passenger Miles ('000)
Central Florida Regional Transportation Authority (Lynx)			
Demand response	168	686.3	8,671.0
Bus	234	23,747.8	136,787.3
Vanpool	64	182.4	5,931.5

Note: Figures include both directly operated and purchased transportation
Source: Federal Transit Administration, National Transit Database, 2009

Air Transportation

Airport Name and Code / Type of Service	Passenger Airlines[1]	Passenger Enplanements	Freight Carriers[2]	Freight (lbs.)
Orlando International (MCO)				
Domestic service (U.S. carriers - 2010)	32	15,453,491	17	125,571,120
International service (U.S. carriers - 2009)	15	185,399	4	58,157

Note: (1) Includes all U.S.-based major, minor and commuter airlines that carried at least one passenger during the year; (2) Includes all U.S.-based airlines and freight carriers that transported at least one pound of freight during the year
Source: Bureau of Transportation Statistics, The Intermodal Transportation Database, Air Carriers: T-100 Domestic Market (U.S. Carriers), 2010; Bureau of Transportation Statistics, The Intermodal Transportation Database, Air Carriers: T-100 International Market (U.S. Carriers), 2009

Other Transportation Statistics

Interstate highways:	I-4
Amtrak service:	Yes
Major waterways/ports:	None

Source: Amtrak.com; Google Maps

BUSINESSES

Major Business Headquarters

Company Name	Rankings	
	Fortune[1]	Forbes[2]
Darden Restaurants	332	-

Note: (1) Fortune 500—companies that produce a 10-K are ranked 1 to 500 based on 2010 revenue; (2) all private companies with at least $2 billion in annual revenue are ranked 1 to 223; companies listed are headquartered in the city; dashes indicate no ranking
Source: Fortune, "Fortune 500," May 23, 2011; Forbes, "America's Largest Private Companies," November 3, 2010

Fast-Growing Businesses

According to *Inc.*, Orlando is home to two of America's 500 fastest-growing private companies: **LimitLess International; NPE**. Criteria: must be an independent, privately-held, for-profit, U.S. corporation, proprietorship or partnership; revenues of at least $80,000 in 2006 and $2 million in 2009; four-year operating/sales history; holding companies, regulated banks, and utilities were excluded. *Inc., "America's 500 Fastest-Growing Private Companies," September 2010*

According to Deloitte, Orlando is home to one of North America's 500 fastest-growing high-technology companies: **Engineering and Computer**. Companies are ranked by percentage growth in revenue over a five-year period. Criteria for inclusion: company must be headquartered within North America; company must own proprietary intellectual property or proprietary technology that contributes to a significant portion of the company's operating revenue or devotes a significant proportion of revenues to research and development of technology; company must have been in business for a minumum of five years with 2005 operating revenues of at least $50,000 USD/CD and 2009 operating revenues of at least $5 million USD/CD. *Deloitte Touche Tohmatsu, 2010 Deloitte Technology Fast 500*[TM]

Minority Business Opportunity

Orlando is home to one company which is on the Black Enterprise Industrial/Service 100 list (100 largest companies based on gross sales): **ZeroChaos**. Criteria: operational in previous calendar year; at least 51% black-owned and manufactures/owns the product it sells or provides industrial or consumer services. Brokerages, real estate firms and firms that provide professional services are not eligible. *Black Enterprise, B.E. 100s, 2010*

Orlando is home to two companies which are on the Black Enterprise Auto Dealer 60 list (60 largest dealers based on gross sales): **Boyland Auto Group**; **Massey Automotive Group**. Criteria: company must be operational in previous calendar year and at least 51% black-owned. *Black Enterprise, B.E. 100s, 2010*

Orlando is home to six companies which are on the *Hispanic Business 500* list (500 largest U.S. Hispanic-owned companies based on 2009 revenue): **Greenway Ford**; **Jardon & Howard Technologies**; **T&G Constructors**; **Advanced Xerographics Imaging Systems**; **Boat Tree**; **Exterior Walls**. Companies included must show at least 51 percent ownership by Hispanic U.S. citizens, and must maintain headquarters in one of the 50 states or Washington, D.C. *Hispanic Business, "Hispanic Business 500," June 2010*

Minority- and Women-Owned Businesses

Group	All Firms		Firms with Paid Employees			
	Firms	Sales ($000)	Firms	Sales ($000)	Employees	Payroll ($000)
Asian	1,522	774,833	467	715,806	2,957	77,699
Black	3,685	676,406	267	594,074	4,180	237,447
Hispanic	5,698	763,059	625	612,670	4,149	111,111
Women	8,731	1,491,871	1,376	1,231,467	9,795	283,759
All Firms	30,564	47,965,704	9,019	46,886,322	239,814	9,467,514

Note: Figures cover firms located in the city; minority- and women-owned business are defined as firms in which the corresponding group own 51% or more of the stock or equity of the company
Source: U.S. Census Bureau, 2007 Economic Census, Survey of Business Owners

HOTELS

Hotels/Motels

Area	5 Star		4 Star		3 Star		2 Star		1 Star		Not Rated	
	Num.	Pct.3	Num.	Pct.3	Num.	Pct.3	Num.	Pct.3	Num.	Pct.3	Num.	Pct.3
City[1]	3	0.7	35	7.6	183	39.7	181	39.3	8	1.7	51	11.1
Total[2]	119	0.7	927	5.8	4,906	30.5	7,992	49.7	526	3.3	1,625	10.1

Note: (1) Figures cover Orlando and vicinity; (2) Figures cover all 100 cities in this book; (3) Percentage of hotels which are a given star rating; Star ratings are determined by expedia.com and offer an indication of the general quality of a particular hotel.
Source: expedia.com, May 5, 2011

The Orlando metro area is home to six of the top 218 hotels in the U.S. according to *Travel & Leisure*: **Disney's Grand Floridian Resort & Spa** (#102); **Villas of Grand Cypress** (#131); **Disney's Boardwalk Inn and Villas** (#134); **Ritz-Carlton Orlando, Grande Lakes** (#136); **Disney's Animal Kingdom Lodge** (#161); **Disney's Wilderness Lodge** (#184). Criteria: service; location; rooms; food; and value. *Travel & Leisure, "T+L 500, The World's Best Hotels 2011"*

EVENT SITES

Major Stadiums, Arenas, and Auditoriums

Name	Max. Capacity
Amway Arena	17,282
Bob Carr Performing Arts Centre	2,518
Bright House Networks Stadium	45,301
The Florida Citrus Bowl	70,000
Tinker Field	5,000
U.C.F. Arena at Knights Plaza	10,000

Source: Original research

Convention Centers

Name	Overall Space (sq. ft.)	Exhibit Space (sq. ft.)	Meeting Space (sq. ft.)	Meeting Rooms
Orange County Convention Center	n/a	n/a	2,100,000	74

Note: n/a not available
Source: Original research

Living Environment

COST OF LIVING

Cost of Living Index

Composite Index	Groceries	Housing	Utilities	Trans-portation	Health Care	Misc. Goods/ Services
97.8	97.8	85.4	108.5	101.8	95.5	104.5

Note: U.S. = 100; Figures cover the Orlando FL urban area.
Source: The Council for Community and Economic Research, ACCRA Cost of Living Index, 2010

Grocery Prices

Area[1]	T-Bone Steak ($/pound)	Frying Chicken ($/pound)	Whole Milk ($/half gal.)	Eggs ($/dozen)	Orange Juice ($/64 oz.)	Coffee ($/11.5 oz.)
City[2]	9.32	1.20	2.63	1.49	2.93	3.28
Avg.	9.04	1.16	2.02	1.47	3.08	3.65
Min.	6.97	0.84	1.46	0.96	2.39	2.64
Max.	13.93	2.51	3.58	3.01	4.94	6.32

Note: (1) Values for the local area are compared with the average, minimum and maximum values for all 338 areas in the Cost of Living Index; (2) Figures cover the Orlando FL urban area; **T-Bone Steak** *(price per pound);* **Frying Chicken** *(price per pound, whole fryer);* **Whole Milk** *(half gallon carton);* **Eggs** *(price per dozen, Grade A, large);* **Orange Juice** *(64 oz. Tropicana or Florida Natural);* **Coffee** *(11.5 oz. can, vacuum-packed, Maxwell House, Hills Bros, or Folgers).*
Source: The Council for Community and Economic Research, ACCRA Cost of Living Index, 2010

Housing and Utility Costs

Area[1]	New Home Price ($)	Apartment Rent ($/month)	All Electric ($/month)	Part Electric ($/month)	Other Energy ($/month)	Telephone ($/month)
City[2]	238,078	803	190.04	-	-	28.95
Avg.	293,442	810	166.39	91.93	83.82	26.93
Min.	182,545	453	119.21	44.47	36.85	17.98
Max.	1,123,114	2,776	307.53	218.20	313.90	39.15

Note: (1) Values for the local area are compared with the average, minimum and maximum values for all 338 areas in the Cost of Living Index; (2) Figures cover the Orlando FL urban area; **New Home Price** *(2,400 sf living area, 8,000 sf lot, in urban area with full utilities);* **Apartment Rent** *(950 sf 2 bedroom/1.5 or 2 bath, unfurnished, excluding all utilities except water);* **All Electric** *(average monthly cost for an all-electric home);* **Part Electric** *(average monthly cost for a part-electric home);* **Other Energy** *(average monthly cost for natural gas, fuel oil, coal, wood, and any other forms of energy except electricity);* **Telephone** *(price includes basic monthly rate for a private residential line plus additional local usage charges incurred by a family of four).*
Source: The Council for Community and Economic Research, ACCRA Cost of Living Index, 2010

Health Care, Transportation, and Other Costs

Area[1]	Doctor ($/visit)	Dentist ($/visit)	Optometrist ($/visit)	Gasoline ($/gallon)	Beauty Salon ($/visit)	Men's Shirt ($)
City[2]	79.03	77.49	69.78	2.67	42.00	26.70
Avg.	89.44	78.95	87.40	2.73	31.92	24.83
Min.	57.00	54.25	48.32	2.44	19.17	13.67
Max.	149.90	136.73	174.22	3.75	62.81	47.89

Note: (1) Values for the local area are compared with the average, minimum and maximum values for all 338 areas in the Cost of Living Index; (2) Figures cover the Orlando FL urban area; **Doctor** *(general practitioners routine exam of an established patient);* **Dentist** *(adult teeth cleaning and periodic oral examination);* **Optometrist** *(full vision eye exam for established adult patient);* **Gasoline** *(one gallon regular unleaded, national brand, including all taxes, cash price at self-service pump if available);* **Beauty Salon** *(woman's shampoo, trim, and blow-dry);* **Men's Shirt** *(cotton/polyester dress shirt, pinpoint weave, long sleeves).*
Source: The Council for Community and Economic Research, ACCRA Cost of Living Index, 2010

HOUSING

House Price Index (HPI)

Area	National Ranking[2]	Quarterly Change (%)	One-Year Change (%)	Five-Year Change (%)
MSA[1]	295	-2.10	-8.05	-33.34
U.S.[3]	-	-0.84	-3.95	-11.45

Note: The HPI is a weighted repeat sales index. It measures average price changes in repeat sales or refinancings on the same properties. This information is obtained by reviewing repeat mortgage transactions on single-family properties whose mortgages have been purchased or securitized by Fannie Mae or Freddie Mac in January 1975; (1) Metropolitan/Micropolitan Statistical Area - see Appendix B for areas included; (2) Rankings are based on annual percentage change for all metro areas containing at least 15,000 transactions over the last 10 years and ranges from 1 to 309; (3) figures based on a weighted average of Census Division estimates; all figures are for the period ending December 31, 2010
Source: Federal Housing Finance Agency, House Price Index, February 24, 2011

House Price Valuations

Area	Q4 2005 Price ($000)	Q4 2005 Over-valuation	Q4 2006 Price ($000)	Q4 2006 Over-valuation	Q4 2007 Price ($000)	Q4 2007 Over-valuation	Q4 2008 Price ($000)	Q4 2008 Over-valuation	Q4 2009 Price ($000)	Q4 2009 Over-valuation
MSA[1]	205.6	28.6	220.5	29.0	203.9	17.6	156.0	-9.5	135.3	-20.4

Note: Figures show the percentage of over- or under-valuation of single family homes relative to statistically normal house values (e.g. a value of 23.6 indicates that house values are 23.6% overvalued). Statistically normal house values are based on house prices, interest rates, household incomes, population densities, and any historical premiums or discounts metropolitan areas have exhibited over time; (1) Figures cover the Orlando-Kissimmee, FL Metropolitan Statistical Area - see Appendix B for areas included
Source: Global Insight/PNC Financial Services Group, House Prices in America: 4th Quarter 2009 Update

Median Single-Family Home Prices

Area	2008	2009	2010[p]	Percent Change 2009 to 2010
MSA[1]	208.9	147.4	131.6	-10.7
U.S. Average	196.6	172.1	173.2	0.6

Note: Figures are median sales prices of existing single-family homes in thousands of dollars; (p) preliminary; n/a not available; (1) Metropolitan Statistical Area - see Appendix B for areas included
Source: National Association of Realtors, Median Sales Price of Existing Single-Family Homes for Metropolitan Areas, 4th Quarter 2010

Median Apartment Condo-Coop Home Prices

Area	2008	2009	2010[p]	Percent Change 2009 to 2010
MSA[1]	n/a	n/a	n/a	n/a
U.S. Average	209.8	175.6	171.7	-2.2

Note: Figures are median sales prices of existing apartment condo-coop homes in thousands of dollars; (p) preliminary; n/a not available; (1) Metropolitan Statistical Area - see Appendix B for areas included
Source: National Association of Realtors, Median Sales Price of Existing Apartment Condo-Coop Homes for Metropolitan Areas, 4th Quarter 2010

Year Housing Structure Built

Area	2000 or Later	1990 -1999	1980 -1989	1970 -1979	1960 -1969	1950 -1959	1940 -1949	Before 1940	Median Year
City	21.2	15.9	19.8	14.5	9.4	11.3	3.5	4.5	1983
MSA[1]	24.2	21.9	23.0	14.5	7.1	6.0	1.5	1.8	1988
U.S.	12.5	14.0	14.2	16.5	11.4	11.3	5.8	14.3	1974

Note: Figures are percentages except for Median Year; (1) Metropolitan Statistical Area - see Appendix B for areas included
Source: U.S. Census Bureau, 2007-2009 American Community Survey 3-Year Estimates

HEALTH

Health Risk Data

Category	MSA[1] (%)	U.S. (%)
Adults who have been told they have high blood pressure	27.3	28.7
Adults who have been told they have high blood cholesterol	35.3	37.5
Adults who have been told they have diabetes[3]	9.9	8.3
Adults who have been told they have arthritis	24.3	26.0
Adults who have been told they currently have asthma	6.0	8.8
Adults who are current smokers	14.3	17.9
Adults who are heavy drinkers[4]	4.7	5.1
Adults who are binge drinkers[5]	15.5	15.8
Adults who are overweight (BMI 25.0 - 29.9)	39.7	36.2
Adults who are obese (BMI 30.0 - 99.8)	24.7	26.9
Adults who participated in any physical activities in the past month	76.0	76.2
Adults 50+ who have ever had a sigmoidoscopy or colonoscopy[2]	64.7	62.2
Women 40+ who have had a mammogram within the past two years[2]	79.4	76.0
Adults age 18–64 who have any kind of health care coverage	75.0	83.1

Note: Data as of 2009 unless otherwise noted; (1) Figures cover the Orlando-Kissimmee, FL Metropolitan Statistical Area - see Appendix B for areas included; (2) Data as of 2008; (3) Figures do not include pregnancy-related, borderline, or pre-diabetes; (4) Heavy drinkers are classified as males having more than two drinks per day or females having more than one drink per day; (5) Binge drinkers are classified as males having five or more drinks on one occasion or females having four or more drinks on one occasion
Source: Centers for Disease Control and Prevention, Behaviorial Risk Factor Surveillance System, SMART: Selected Metropolitan/Micropolitan Area Risk Trends, 2008, 2009

Mortality Rates for the Top 10 Causes of Death in the U.S.

ICD-10[a] Sub-Chapter	ICD-10[a] Code	Age-Adjusted Mortality Rate[1] per 100,000 population	
		County[2]	U.S.
Malignant neoplasms	C00-C97	175.6	180.9
Ischaemic heart diseases	I20-I25	127.5	135.0
Other forms of heart disease	I30-I51	42.0	50.0
Cerebrovascular diseases	I60-I69	40.0	44.1
Chronic lower respiratory diseases	J40-J47	43.3	41.5
Other degenerative diseases of the nervous system	G30-G31	25.2	23.6
Diabetes mellitus	E10-E14	21.5	23.5
Other external causes of accidental injury	W00-X59	19.1	23.5
Organic, including symptomatic, mental disorders	F01-F09	26.0	22.2
Influenza and pneumonia	J09-J18	15.1	18.1

Note: (a) ICD-10 = International Classification of Diseases 10th Revision; (1) Mortality rates are a three year average covering 2005-2007; (2) Figures cover Orange County
Source: Centers for Disease Control and Prevention, National Center for Health Statistics. Compressed Mortality File 1999-2007. CDC WONDER On-line Database, compiled from Compressed Mortality File 1999-2007 Series 20 No. 2M, 2010.

Mortality Rates for Selected Causes of Death

ICD-10[a] Sub-Chapter	ICD-10[a] Code	Age-Adjusted Mortality Rate[1] per 100,000 population	
		County[2]	U.S.
Assault	X85-Y09	9.2	6.0
Human immunodeficiency virus (HIV) disease	B20-B24	9.1	4.0
Hypertensive diseases	I10-I15	19.7	18.0
Intentional self-harm	X60-X84	10.5	11.0
Malnutrition	E40-E46	*0.6	0.8
Obesity and other hyperalimentation	E65-E68	1.0	1.5
Transport accidents	V01-V99	17.3	15.6
Viral hepatitis	B15-B19	1.8	2.1

Note: (a) ICD-10 = International Classification of Diseases 10th Revision; (1) Mortality rates are a three year average covering 2005-2007; (2) Figures cover Orange County; (*) Unreliable data as per CDC
Source: Centers for Disease Control and Prevention, National Center for Health Statistics. Compressed Mortality File 1999-2007. CDC WONDER On-line Database, compiled from Compressed Mortality File 1999-2007 Series 20 No. 2M, 2010.

Distribution of Physicians and Dentists

Area[1]	Dentists[2]	D.O.[3]	M.D.[4]				
			Total	Family/ General Practice	Pediatrics	Medical Specialties	Surgical Specialties
Local (number)	427	206	2,124	264	192	820	462
Local (rate[5])	4.0	1.9	19.7	2.5	1.8	7.6	4.3
U.S. (rate[5])	4.5	1.9	18.3	2.5	1.4	6.8	4.1

Note: Data as of 2008 unless noted; (1) Local data covers Orange County; (2) Data as of 2007; (3) Doctor of Osteopathic Medicine; (4) Includes active, non-federal, patient-care, office-based Doctors of Medicine; (5) rate per 10,000 population
Source: Area Resource File (ARF). 2009-2010 Release. U.S. Department of Health and Human Services, Health Resources and Services Administration, Bureau of Health Professions, Rockville, MD, August 2010

Hospitals

Orlando has the following hospitals: 2 general medical and surgical; 1 long-term acute care. *AHA Guide to the Healthcare Field 2010*

According to *U.S. News,* the Orlando-Kissimmee, FL Metropolitan Statistical Area is home to one of the best children's hospitals in the U.S.: **Arnold Palmer Medical Center**. The hospital listed was highly ranked in at least one pediatric specialty. *U.S. News Online, "America's Best Children's Hospitals 2010-11"*

EDUCATION

Public School District Statistics

District Name	Schls	Pupils	Pupil/ Teacher Ratio	Minority Pupils[1] (%)	Free Lunch Eligible[2] (%)	IEP[3] (%)
Orange	236	172,257	15.7	66.4	38.7	14.2

Note: Table includes school districts with 2,000 or more students; (1) Percentage of students that are not non-Hispanic white; (2) Percentage of students that are eligible for the free lunch program; (3) Percentage of students that have an Individualized Education Program.
Source: U.S. Department of Education, National Center for Education Statistics, Common Core of Data, Local Education Agency (School District) Universe Survey: School Year 2008-2009; U.S. Department of Education, National Center for Education Statistics, Common Core of Data, Public Elementary/Secondary School Universe Survey: School Year 2008-2009

Top Public High Schools

High School Name	Index[1]	Rank[1]	Subsidized Lunch (%)[2]	E&E (%)[3]
Boone	1.584	1068	25.0	25.9
Cypress Creek[4]	3.109	228	60.0	24.0
Dr. Phillips	2.362	483	40.0	38.0
Edgewater	2.612	370	38.0	21.6
Freedom	1.445	1210	44.0	18.5
Olympia	3.163	215	33.0	42.3
Timber Creek	1.896	791	28.0	31.8
University[4]	3.034	246	37.0	25.2

Note: (1) Public schools are ranked according to a ratio that is the number of Advanced Placement, International Baccalaureate, and/or Cambridge tests taken by all students at a school in 2009 divided by the number of graduating seniors. All of the schools on the list have an index of at least 1.000; they are in the top six percent of public schools measured this way. The rankings range from 1 to 1,734; (2) Percentage of students receiving federally subsidized meals; (3) E & E stands for equity and excellence percentage: the portion of all graduating seniors at a school that had at least one passing grade on one AP or IB test; (4) Schools that offer International Baccalaureate or Cambridge exams; (5) School is unranked, but has been identified by Newsweek as one of the nation's most elite public high schools.
Source: Newsweek Online, "Top High Schools 2010"

Highest Level of Education

Area	Less than H.S.	H.S. Diploma	Some College, No Deg.	Associate Degree	Bachelors Degree	Masters Degree	Profess. School Degree	Doctorate Degree
City	13.7	27.0	18.9	10.1	20.7	6.9	2.0	0.6
MSA[1]	12.8	29.6	21.1	9.7	18.3	6.2	1.6	0.8
U.S.	15.3	29.0	20.7	7.5	17.4	7.0	1.9	1.1

Note: Figures are 2010 estimated percentages and cover persons age 25 and over; (1) Metropolitan Statistical Area - see Appendix B for areas included
Source: Claritas, Inc.

Educational Attainment by Race

Area	High School Graduate (%)					Bachelor's Degree (%)				
	Total	White	Black	Asian	Hisp.[2]	Total	White	Black	Asian	Hisp.[2]
City	86.5	95.0	77.8	88.0	76.8	31.7	44.0	14.1	44.4	20.8
MSA[1]	87.2	91.5	80.8	86.2	78.5	27.1	31.0	18.2	44.6	18.3
U.S.	84.9	90.0	80.7	85.5	60.7	27.8	30.9	17.5	49.7	12.7

Note: Figures shown cover persons 25 years old and over; (1) Metropolitan Statistical Area - see Appendix B for areas included; (2) people of Hispanic origin can be of any race
Source: U.S. Census Bureau, 2007-2009 American Community Survey 3-Year Estimates

School Enrollment by Grade and Control

Area	Preschool (%)		Kindergarten (%)		Grades 1 - 4 (%)		Grades 5 - 8 (%)		Grades 9 - 12 (%)	
	Public	Private	Public	Private	Public	Private	Public	Private	Public	Private
City	40.8	59.2	78.3	21.7	88.3	11.7	86.8	13.2	91.8	8.2
MSA[1]	43.4	56.6	80.3	19.7	86.2	13.8	88.0	12.0	91.0	9.0
U.S.	54.3	45.7	86.4	13.6	88.9	11.1	89.1	10.9	90.2	9.8

Note: Figures shown cover persons 3 years old and over; (1) Metropolitan Statistical Area - see Appendix B for areas included
Source: U.S. Census Bureau, 2007-2009 American Community Survey 3-Year Estimates

Average Salaries of Public School Classroom Teachers

Area	2009-10		2010-11		Percent Change 2009-10 to 2010-11	Percent Change 2000-01 to 2010-11
	Dollars	Rank[1]	Dollars	Rank[1]		
Florida	46,708	37	46,702	47	-0.01	22.2
U.S. Average	55,202	-	56,069	-	1.57	29.3

Note: (1) State rank ranges from 1 to 51 where 1 indicates highest salary.
Source: National Education Association, Rankings & Estimates: Rankings of the States 2010 and Estimates of School Statistics 2011, December 2010

Higher Education

Four-Year Colleges			Two-Year Colleges			Medical Schools[1]	Law Schools[2]	Voc/ Tech[3]
Public	Private Non-profit	Private For-profit	Public	Private Non-profit	Private For-profit			
1	1	4	3	0	10	0	2	0

Note: Figures cover institutions located within the city limits and include main campuses only; (1) includes schools accredited by the Liaison Committee on Medical Education and the American Osteopathic Association; (2) includes American Bar Association-accredited law schools; (3) includes all schools with programs that are less than 2 years.
Source: National Center for Education Statistics, Integrated Postsecondary Education System (IPEDS) Peer Analysis System, 2010-11; U.S. News & World Report, Medical School Directory, 2011; U.S. News & World Report, Law School Directory, 2011

According to *U.S. News & World Report,* the Orlando-Kissimmee, FL Metropolitan Statistical Area is home to one of the top 197 national universities in the U.S.: **University of Central Florida** (#179). The rankings are based on quantitative measurements such as peer assessment, retention, faculty resources, student selectivity, financial resources, graduation rate, and alumni giving rate. *U.S. News & World Report, "America's Best Colleges 2011"*

According to *Forbes,* the Orlando-Kissimmee, FL Metropolitan Statistical Area is home to one of the top 75 business schools in the U.S.: **Rollins (Crummer)** (#36). The rankings are based on the return on investment that graduates of the Class of 2004 received (median salary five years after graduation). *Forbes, "Best Business Schools," August 5, 2009*

PRESIDENTIAL ELECTION

2008 Presidential Election Results

Area	Obama	McCain	Nader	Other
Orange County	59.0	40.4	0.2	0.4
U.S.	52.9	45.6	0.6	0.9

Note: Results are percentages and may not add to 100% due to rounding
Source: Dave Leip's Atlas of U.S. Presidential Elections, www.uselectionatlas.org

EMPLOYERS

Major Employers

Company Name	Industry	Type of Site
Airtran Airways	Air transportation, scheduled	Headquarters
Central Florida Health Aliance	Management services	Headquarters
Connextions Health	Computer related services, nec	Headquarters
Discovery Cove	Amusement parks	Headquarters
FL Dept Children & Families	Individual and family services	Branch
Florida Hospital	General medical and surgical hospitals	Branch
Gaylord Palms Resort & Convent	Hotels and motels	Single
Health Cenral	General medical and surgical hospitals	Single
Houston Hotel	Management services	Single
Hughes Kitchen & Bath Collectn	Electrical apparatus and equipment	Single
Lockheed Martin Simulation	Guided missiles and space vehicles	Branch
New Life Publications	Religious organizations	Headquarters
Orlando Regional Medical Cente	General medical and surgical hospitals	Headquarters
Red Lobster	Eating places	Headquarters
Rosen Shingle Creek	Hotels and motels	Branch
Sears	Disinfecting and pest control services	Single
Seminole Community	Junior colleges	Headquarters
Sentinel Communications Co	Newspapers	Headquarters
Siemens Energy	Heavy construction, nec	Headquarters
Solid Resources	Management consulting services	Single
U C F	Colleges and universities	Headquarters
US Post Office	U.S. postal service	Branch
West Campus	Junior colleges	Headquarters
Winter Park Memorial Hospital	General medical and surgical hospitals	Headquarters

Note: Companies shown are located within the Orlando metropolitan area; nec = not elsewhere classified.
Source: www.zapdata.com, January 2011

Best Companies to Work For

Darden Restaurants, headquartered in Orlando, is among the "100 Best Companies to Work For." To pick the 100 Best Companies to Work For, *Fortune* partnered with the Great Place to Work Institute. Three hundred eleven companies participated in this year's survey. Most of a company's score (two-thirds) is based on the results of the Institute's Trust Index survey, which is sent to a random sample of employees from each company. The survey asks questions related to their attitudes about management's credibility, job satisfaction, and camaraderie. The other third of the scoring is based on the company's responses to the Institute's Culture Audit, which includes detailed questions about pay and benefit programs, and a series of open-ended questions about hiring practices, internal communication, training, recognition programs, and diversity efforts. Any company that is at least seven years old with more than 1,000 U.S. employees is eligible. *Fortune, "100 Best Companies to Work For," February 7, 2011*

PUBLIC SAFETY

Crime Rate

Area	All Crimes	Violent Crimes				Property Crimes		
		Murder	Forcible Rape	Robbery	Aggrav. Assault	Burglary	Larceny -Theft	Motor Vehicle Theft
City	8,579.4	11.9	49.8	326.2	809.0	1,603.5	5,245.2	533.8
Suburbs[1]	4,186.1	4.5	33.2	149.6	430.4	1,026.6	2,284.6	257.3
Metro[2]	4,680.9	5.3	35.0	169.5	473.0	1,091.6	2,618.1	288.5
U.S.	3,465.5	5.0	28.7	133.0	262.8	716.3	2,060.9	258.8

Note: Figures are crimes per 100,000 population; (1) All areas within the metro area that are located outside the city limits; (2) Metropolitan Statistical Area - see Appendix B for areas included
Source: FBI Uniform Crime Reports, 2009

Hate Crimes

Area	Number of Quarters Reported	Bias Motivation				
		Race	Religion	Sexual Orientation	Ethnicity	Disability
City	4	1	0	0	0	0

Source: Federal Bureau of Investigation, Hate Crime Statistics 2009

Identity Theft Consumer Complaints

Area	Complaints	Complaints per 100,000 Population	Rank[2]
MSA[1]	2,220	109.2	41
U.S.	250,854	81.3	-

Note: (1) Metropolitan Statistical Area - see Appendix B for areas included; (2) Rank ranges from 1 to 384 where 1 indicates greatest number of complaints per 100,000 population
Source: Federal Trade Commission, Consumer Sentinel Network Data Book for January - December 2010

RECREATION

Culture

Dance[1]	Theatre[1]	Instrumental Music[1]	Vocal Music[1]	Series/ Festivals	Museums	Zoos and Aquariums[2]
2	5	3	1	1	6	3

Note: (1) Number of professional performing groups; (2) AZA-accredited
Source: The Grey House Performing Arts Directory, 2011-2012; Official Museum Directory, 2010; American Association of Museums, AAM Member Museums, March 2011; Association of Zoos & Aquariums, AZA Member Zoos & Aquariums, May 2011

Professional Sports Teams

Team Name	League
Orlando Magic	National Basketball Association (NBA)

Note: Includes teams located in the Orlando metro area.
Source: Original research

CLIMATE

Average and Extreme Temperatures

Temperature	Jan	Feb	Mar	Apr	May	Jun	Jul	Aug	Sep	Oct	Nov	Dec	Yr.
Extreme High (°F)	86	89	90	95	100	100	99	100	98	95	89	90	100
Average High (°F)	70	72	77	82	87	90	91	91	89	83	78	72	82
Average Temp. (°F)	59	62	67	72	77	81	82	82	81	75	68	62	72
Average Low (°F)	48	51	56	60	66	71	73	74	72	66	58	51	62
Extreme Low (°F)	19	29	25	38	51	53	64	65	57	44	32	20	19

Note: Figures cover the years 1952-1990
Source: National Climatic Data Center, International Station Meteorological Climate Summary, 9/96

Average Precipitation/Snowfall/Humidity

Precip./Humidity	Jan	Feb	Mar	Apr	May	Jun	Jul	Aug	Sep	Oct	Nov	Dec	Yr.
Avg. Precip. (in.)	2.3	2.8	3.4	2.0	3.2	7.0	7.2	5.8	5.8	2.7	3.5	2.0	47.7
Avg. Snowfall (in.)	Tr	0	0	0	0	0	0	0	0	0	0	0	Tr
Avg. Rel. Hum. 7am (%)	87	87	88	87	88	89	90	92	92	89	89	87	89
Avg. Rel. Hum. 4pm (%)	53	51	49	47	51	61	65	66	66	59	56	55	57

Note: Figures cover the years 1952-1990; Tr = Trace amounts (<0.05 in. of rain; <0.5 in. of snow)
Source: National Climatic Data Center, International Station Meteorological Climate Summary, 9/96

Weather Conditions

Temperature			Daytime Sky			Precipitation		
32°F & below	45°F & below	90°F & above	Clear	Partly cloudy	Cloudy	0.01 inch or more precip.	0.1 inch or more snow/ice	Thunder-storms
3	35	90	76	208	81	115	0	80

Note: Figures are average number of days per year and cover the years 1952-1990
Source: National Climatic Data Center, International Station Meteorological Climate Summary, 9/96

HAZARDOUS WASTE

Superfund Sites

Orlando has two hazardous waste sites on the EPA's Superfund Final National Priorities List: **Chevron Chemical Co. (Ortho Division); City Industries, Inc.** *U.S. Environmental Protection Agency, Final National Priorities List, April 1, 2011*

AIR & WATER QUALITY

Air Quality Index

Area	Percent of Days when Air Quality was...[2]				AQI Statistics	
	Good	Moderate	Unhealthy for Sensitive Groups	Unhealthy	Maximum	Median
Area[1]	89.5	10.2	0.4	0.0	122	35

Note: The Air Quality Index (AQI) is an index for reporting daily air quality. EPA calculates the AQI for five major air pollutants regulated by the Clean Air Act: ground-level ozone, particle pollution (also known as particulate matter), carbon monoxide, sulfur dioxide, and nitrogen dioxide. The AQI runs from 0 to 500. The higher the AQI value, the greater the level of air pollution and the greater the health concern. There are six AQI categories: "Good" The AQI is between 0 and 50. Air quality is considered satisfactory; "Moderate" The AQI is between 51 and 100. Air quality is acceptable; "Unhealthy for Sensitive Groups" When AQI values are between 101 and 150, members of sensitive groups may experience health effects; "Unhealthy" When AQI values are between 151 and 200 everyone may begin to experience health effects; "Very Unhealthy" AQI values between 201 and 300 trigger a health alert; "Hazardous" AQI values over 300 trigger health warnings of emergency conditions; (1) Data covers Orange County; (2) Based on 275 days with AQI data in 2008; The EPA has suspended data updates while it assesses its data systems, including AirData reports and maps.
Source: U.S. Environmental Protection Agency, AirData Report, 2008

Air Quality Index Pollutants

Area	Percent of Days when AQI Pollutant was...[2]					
	Carbon Monoxide	Nitrogen Dioxide	Ozone	Sulfur Dioxide	Particulate Matter 2.5	Particulate Matter 10
Area[1]	0.4	0.0	78.5	0.0	20.4	0.7

Note: The Air Quality Index (AQI) is an index for reporting daily air quality. EPA calculates the AQI for five major air pollutants regulated by the Clean Air Act: ground-level ozone, particle pollution (also known as particulate matter), carbon monoxide, sulfur dioxide, and nitrogen dioxide. The AQI runs from 0 to 500. The higher the AQI value, the greater the level of air pollution and the greater the health concern; (1) Data covers Orange County; (2) Based on 275 days with AQI data in 2008; The EPA has suspended data updates while it assesses its data systems, including AirData reports and maps.
Source: U.S. Environmental Protection Agency, AirData Report, 2008

Air Quality Index Trends

Area	Trend Sites (days)								All Sites (days)
	2002	2003	2004	2005	2006	2007	2008	2009	2009
MSA[1]	5	4	5	8	8	8	1	0	1

Note: Figures are the number of days the AQI value exceeded 100 in a given year. An AQI value greater than 100 indicates that air quality would have been in the unhealthful range on that day. Data from exceptional events are included. These counts are presented in two ways. First, the counts are based on sites having an adequate record of monitoring data during the trend period (trend sites). These counts represent the relative change in the number of days with AQI values greater than 100. In the last column, the counts are based on all sites with data in the most recent year (because it is possible for a site to have data in the most recent year but not enough data to be a trend site); (1) Data covers the Orlando-Kissimmee, FL Metropolitan Statistical Area - see Appendix B for areas included
Source: U.S. Environmental Protection Agency, Office of Air and Radiation, Air Quality Index Information, "Number of Days with Air Quality Index Values Greater than 100 and Trend Sites, 1990-2009, and at All Sites in 2009"

Maximum Air Pollutant Concentrations

	Particulate Matter 10 (ug/m³)	Particulate Matter 2.5 (ug/m³)	Ozone (ppm)	Carbon Monoxide (ppm)	Sulfur Dioxide (ppm)	Nitrogen Dioxide (ppm)	Lead (ug/m³)
MSA[1] Level	34	17	0.066	1	0.002	0.006	n/a
NAAQS[2]	150	35	0.075	9	0.140	0.053	0.15
Met NAAQS[2]	Yes	Yes	Yes	Yes	Yes	Yes	n/a

Note: Data from exceptional events are not included; (1) Data covers the Orlando-Kissimmee, FL Metropolitan Statistical Area - see Appendix B for areas included; (2) National Ambient Air Quality Standards; n/a not available
Concentrations: Particulate Matter 10 (coarse particulate) - highest second maximum 24-hour concentration; Particulate Matter 2.5 (fine particulate) - highest 98th percentile 24-hour concentration; Ozone - highest fourth daily maximum 8-hour concentration; Carbon Monoxide - highest second maximum non-overlapping 8-hour concentration; Sulfur Dioxide - highest second maximum 24-hour concentration; Nitrogen Dioxide - highest arithmetic mean concentration; Lead - maximum running 3-month average
Units: ppm = parts per million; ug/m³ = micrograms per cubic meter
Source: U.S. Environmental Protection Agency, CBSA Factbook 2009, Air Quality Statistics by City, 2009

Drinking Water

Water System Name	Pop. Served	Primary Water Source Type	Violations[1]	
			Health Based	Monitoring/ Reporting
Orlando Utilities Commission	426,452	Ground	0	0

Note: (1) Based on violation data from January 1, 2010 to December 31, 2010 (includes unresolved violations from earlier years)
Source: U.S. Environmental Protection Agency, Office of Ground Water and Drinking Water, Safe Drinking Water Information System (based on data extracted May 9, 2011)

Plano, Texas

Background

Plano, just 20 miles north of downtown Dallas, is the largest city in Collin County. Its location, and the performance of its municipal government and local economy, help to explain why Plano proudly presents itself as a good choice for families and businesses of all types.

The city was first settled in the 1840s during the era of the Republic of Texas, mostly by migrants from Kentucky and Tennessee who were seeking new hunting and grazing areas. In 1846, William Foreman, an early entrepreneur, established a sawmill and gristmill at the site, and later a store and cotton gin. Such improvements began to attract new settlers and, by 1850, residents decided they needed an official post office. Their first application requesting the name Fillmore to the federal government, in honor of the president of the United States, was rejected, and in its place, Foreman's name was proposed. This alternative, however, was also rejected, and finally, the descriptive Plano (Spanish for plain) was suggested and adopted.

Cattle and other livestock were the mainstay of Plano's early economy, but gradually farmers began to exploit the rich, black soil of the area. Population and economic growth was slow and steady until the Civil War, but afterwards, with the growth of railroads and the adjacent towns, Plano began to assume its modern form. In 1872, with the completion of the Houston and Texas Railroad, Plano's economy took off, and the city was incorporated in 1873. Although for much its early life, Plano had been dependent on agriculture, all manner of building and business flourished toward the end of the nineteenth century. It was said locally that virtually anything could be bought, sold, or traded in the city. By the mid-twentieth century, Plano had almost completed its conversion from farming to trading, and by the 1960s, the expansion of Dallas had exerted a significant effect.

With the historic shift of manufacturing and labor from the North to the South, Plano achieved its economic maturity.

Today, Plano is headquarters of several large corporations, such as Pizza Hut, Frito Lay, J.C. Penney, Dr. Pepper Snapple Group, HP Enterprise Services (which includes the former EDS), and Ericsson.

The Plano Independent School District (PISD) serves the City of Plano, portions of Dallas and Richardson, the City of Parker, portions of Allen and Murphy, Carrollton, Garland, Lucas, and Wylie. The schools have consistently garnered awards, and the school district itself most recently garnered an "exemplary" rating from the Texas Education Agency in preliminary 2010 ratings.

In and around Plano are numerous institutions of higher learning, including Austin College, Collin College Spring Creek Campus and Courtyard Center, Dallas Baptist University-Frisco, Richland College, SMU-in-Plano, University of North Texas Irving, University of North Texas Denton, and the University of Texas Southwestern Medical School.

There are more than 65 parks and numerous acres of park land in the city. Also in Plano: Southfork Ranch, set of the iconic 1980s TV show "Dallas."

Plano can be hot in the summer. The good news, though, is that there is plenty of sunshine. Winters are generally mild, and cold snaps are infrequent and short-lived. Rainfall is relatively plentiful and usually falls more often at night than during daytime.

Rankings

General Rankings

- Dallas was ranked #132 out of 375 metro areas in *Cities Ranked & Rated*. Criteria: cost of living; climate; crime; transportation; economy and jobs; education; arts and culture; health and healthcare; leisure; quality of life. *Cities Ranked & Rated, 2nd Edition, 2007*

- Dallas was ranked #43 out of 379 metro areas in *Places Rated Almanac*. Criteria: health care; education; recreation; transportation; ambience; climate; crime; housing costs; jobs. *Places Rated Almanac, 7th Edition, 2007*

Business/Finance Rankings

- Dallas was identified as one of the 20 strongest-performing metro areas during the recession and recovery from December 2007 through December 2010. Criteria: percent change in employment; percentage point change in unemployment rate; percent change in gross metropolitan product; percent change in House Price Index. *Brookings Institution, MetroMonitor: Tracking Economic Recession and Recovery in America's 100 Largest Metropolitan Areas, March 2011*

- The Dallas metro area was identified as one of 10 "Cities Where the Recession is Easing." The metro area was ranked #3. Criteria: job growth; goods produced; home sale prices; unemployment rates. *Forbes.com, "Cities Where the Recession is Easing," March 3, 2010*

- The Dallas metro area was identified as one of the most affordable major metropolitan areas in America by *Forbes*. The metro area was ranked #14 out of 15. Criteria: median asking price of homes for sale; median salaries of workers with bachelor's degrees or higher compared to a cost-of-living index; unemployment rates. *Forbes.com, "The Most Affordable Cities in America," January 7, 2011*

- Experian ranked the top 20 major U.S metropolitan areas by average debt per consumer. The Dallas metro area was ranked #2. Criteria: average debt per consumer. Debt for this study includes credit cards, auto loans and personal loans. It does not include mortgages. *Experian, May 13, 2010*

- The Dallas metro area was identified as one of the "Best U.S. Cities for Earning a Living" by *Forbes*. The metro area ranked #8. Criteria: median income; cost of living; job growth; number of companies on *Forbes* 400 best big company and 200 best small company lists. *Forbes.com, "Best U.S. Cities for Earning a Living," August 21, 2008*

- A.G. Edwards ranked America's 500 top-performing communities based on their residents' personal savings and investing behavior. The Dallas metro area ranked #353 with an index score of 98.36 (national average = 100.00). A dozen statistical factors were measured including: participation in retirement savings plans; personal debt levels; and home ownership. *A.G. Edwards, "2007 Nest Egg Index," September 12, 2007*

- The Dallas metro area was identified as one of the 10 best cities to find a job in 2009 by *Forbes*. The metro area ranked #10. Criteria: city unemployment rate; number of new jobs created in the previous six months. *Forbes.com, "10 Cities for Job Growth in 2009," January 5, 2009*

- Dallas was cited as one of America's top metros for new and expanded facility projects in 2010. The area ranked #3 in the large metro area category (population over 1 million). *Site Selection, "2010 Top Metros," March 2011*

- *American City Business Journals* ranked America's 261 largest cities in terms of their resident's wealth. Plano ranked #22. Criteria: per capita income; median household income; percentage of households with annual incomes of $200,000 or more; median home value. *American City Business Journals, www.bizjournals.com, "Where the Money Is: America's Wealth Centers," August 18, 2008*

- The Dallas metro area appeared on the Milken Institute "2010 Best Performing Metros" list. Rank: #17 out of 200 large metro areas. Criteria: job growth; wage and salary growth; high-tech output growth. *Milken Institute, "2010 Best Performing Metros"*

- The Dallas metro area was selected as one of the best cities for entrepreneurs in America by *Inc. Magazine.* Criteria: job-growth data for 335 metro areas was analyzed for: recent growth trend (the current and prior year's employment growth rates, with the current year emphasized); mid-term growth (the average annual 2002-2007 growth rate); long-term trend (the sum of the 2002-2007 and 1996-2001 employment growth rates multiplied by the ratio of the 1996-2001 growth rate over the 2002-2007 growth rate); current year growth. The Dallas metro area ranked #12 among large metro areas and #57 overall. *Inc. Magazine, "The Best Cities for Doing Business," July 2008*

- Dallas was ranked #52 out of 145 regions worldwide in terms of its "Knowledge Competitiveness Index." The index attempts to measure the knowledge-based development taking place throughout the world and is based on 19 measures of economic performance that indicate a region's ability to translate its knowledge capacity into economic value. *Centre for International Competitiveness, World Knowledge Competitiveness Index 2008*

- *Forbes* ranked the 200 most populous metro areas in the U.S. in terms of the "Best Places for Business and Careers." The Dallas metro area was ranked #26. Criteria: 12 metrics including costs (business and living), job growth (past and projected), income growth, educational attainment, projected economic growth, crime, cultural and recreational opportunities, net migration patterns, percentage of subprime mortgages handed out over a three-year period, and the number of highly ranked four-year colleges. *Forbes, "Best Places for Business and Careers," April 14, 2010*

Children/Family Rankings

- The Dallas metro area was selected as one of the "Best Cities for Relocating Families" by Worldwide ERC and Primacy Relocation. The 2008 study looked at nearly 50 factors important to relocating families including: recent job growth; nearby top-ranked colleges; in-state tuition for four-year public colleges; population growth since 2000; pediatricians per 100,000 population; and a Green Living index. *Worldwide ERC and Primacy Relocation, "2008 Best Cities for Relocating Families"*

Dating/Romance Rankings

- Eli Lily and Company, in partnership with Sperling's BestPlaces, ranked the nation's 50 largest metro areas in terms of the "Most Romantic Cities for Baby Boomers." The Dallas metro area ranked #9. Criteria: marriage and divorce rates among "baby boomers" age 45 to 60; great restaurants; dance studios; chocolate, jewelry and flower sales. *Eli Lily and Company, "Most Romantic Cities for Baby Boomers," April 20, 2007*

- The Dallas metro area was selected as one of the "Best Cities for Relocating Singles" by Worldwide ERC and Primacy Relocation. The area ranked #37 out of the 100 largest metro areas in the U.S. Areas were selected based on the following criteria: recent job growth; recent singles population growth; overall population growth; affordable rental housing; cost-of-living index; expanded arts and recreation opportunities; ratio of single men and single women; affordability of quality higher education (including state residency requirements); diversity index; climate; population density. *Worldwide ERC and Primacy Relocation, "2008 Best Cities for Relocating Singles"*

- *Forbes* ranked the 40 most populous urbanized areas in the U.S. in terms of the "Best Cities for Singles." The Dallas metro area ranked #17. Criteria: number of singles; cost of living alone; nightlife; culture; job growth; coolness; and online dating participation. *Forbes.com, "Best Cities for Singles," July 27, 2009*

Education Rankings

- Plano was selected as one of "America's Most Literate Cities." The city ranked #54 out of the 75 largest U.S. cities. Criteria: number of booksellers; library resources; Internet resources; educational attainment; periodical publishing resources; newspaper circulation. *Central Connecticut State University, "America's Most Literate Cities 2010"*

- Dallas was identified as one of the 100 "smartest" metro areas in the U.S. The area ranked #72. Criteria: the editors rated the collective brainpower of the 100 largest metro area in the U.S based on their residents' educational attainment. *American City Business Journals, www.bizjournals.com, April 14, 2008*

- Dallas was identified as one of "America's Brainiest Bastions" by *Portfolio.com*. The metro area ranked #96 out of 200. Portfolio.com analyzed levels of educational attainment in the nation's 200 largest metropolitan areas. The editors established scores for five levels of educational attainment, based on relative earning power of adult workers age 25 or older. Scores were determined by comparing the median income for all workers with the median income for those workers at a specified educational level. *Portfolio.com, "America's Brainiest Bastions," December 1, 2010*

- *Forbes* ranked the largest metro areas in the U.S. in terms of the "Best Cities for Young Professionals." The Dallas metro area ranked #6out of 10. Graduates from six elite schools (Harvard, Stanford, Princeton, Rice, Northwestern and Duke) were tracked ten years after graduation to see where they settled down. Those rankings were combined with several other statistics: job growth; unemployment rate; average salary of college graduates; cost of living; number of large companies that are located in the city. *Forbes.com, "Best Cities for Young Professionals," June 17, 2010*

Environmental Rankings

- Plano was selected as one of 22 "Smarter Cities" for energy by the Natural Resources Defense Council." Criteria: investment in green power; energy efficiency measures; conservation. *Natural Resources Defense Council, "2010 Smarter Cities," July 19, 2010*

- *American City Business Journal* ranked 43 metropolitan areas in terms of their "greenness." The Dallas metro area ranked #37. Criteria: Forty-one metros in which *ACBJ* has business weeklies, plus Indianapolis and Cleveland, were ranked based on 20 different indicators such as adoption of green technologies, utilization of environmentally sound practices, and air and water quality. *American City Business Journals, "Green City Index," March 11, 2010*

- 100 of the largest metro areas in the U.S. were analyzed in terms of their current drought severity. The Dallas metro area ranked #97 (#1 = driest). The rankings were based on statistics such as long-term precipitation trends and patterns and the Palmer drought indices. *Sperling's BestPlaces, www.BestPlaces.net, "America's Drought-Riskiest Cities," November 2007*

- The Dallas metro area appeared in *Country Home's* "Best Green Places" report. The area ranked #94 out of 379. Criteria: official energy policies; green power; green buildings; availability of fresh, locally grown food. *Country Home, "Best Green Places," 2008*

- Dallas was highlighted as one of the 25 most ozone-polluted metro areas in the U.S. The area ranked #12. *American Lung Association, State of the Air 2011*

Health/Fitness Rankings

- Dallas was identified as a "2011 Asthma Capital." The area ranked #34 out of the nation's 100 largest metropolitan areas. Twelve factors were used to identify the most challenging places to live for people with asthma: estimated prevalence; self-reported prevalence; crude death rate for asthma; annual pollen score; annual air quality; public smoking laws; number of board-certified asthma specialists; school inhaler access laws; rescue medication use; controller medication use; uninsured rate; poverty rate. *Asthma and Allergy Foundation of America, "2011 Asthma Capitals"*

- Dallas was identified as a 2009 "Spring Allergy Capital." The area ranked #50 out of 100. Three groups of factors were used to identify the most severe cities for people with allergies during the spring season: annual pollen levels; medicine utilization; access to board-certified allergists. *Asthma and Allergy Foundation of America, "Spring Allergy Capitals 2009"*

- Dallas was identified as a 2010 "Fall Allergy Capital." The area ranked #33 out of 100. Three groups of factors were used to identify the most severe cities for people with allergies during the fall season: annual pollen levels; medicine utilization; access to board-certified allergists. *Asthma and Allergy Foundation of America, "Fall Allergy Capitals 2010"*

- *Men's Health* examined 100 U.S. cities and selected the best and worst cities for men. Plano was ranked among the ten best at #3. Criteria: dozens of statistical parameters of long life in the categories of health, quality of life, and fitness. *Men's Health, "The 10 Best and Worst Cities for Men 2011," January/February 2011*

- *Men's Health* examined 100 U.S. cities and selected the best and worst cities for women. Plano was ranked among the ten best at #1. Criteria: dozens of statistical parameters of long life in the categories of health, quality of life, and fitness. *Men's Health, "The 10 Best and Worst Cities for Women 2011," January/February 2011*

- Ortho-McNeil Neurologics, in partnership with Sperling's BestPlaces, analyzed 110 metro areas and identified those U.S. cities with the highest prevalence of factors that are most commonly associated with migraine headaches. The Dallas metro area ranked #82. Criteria: number of migraine-related drug prescriptions per capita; lifestyle factors that can contribute to migraines; environmental factors that can trigger migraines; and consumption of migraine-triggering foods. *Ortho-McNeil Neurologics, "America's Migraine Hot Spots," March 14, 2006*

- An analysis of the "Best & Worst Cities for Sleep" was conducted by Sperling's BestPlaces. The study ranked America's 50 most populated metro areas. The Dallas metro area ranked #21 (#1 = best city for sleep). Criteria: number of days residents didn't get enough rest or sleep during the past month; average length of daily commute; divorce rate; unemployment rate. *Sperling's BestPlaces, www.BestPlaces.net, "Best & Worst Cities for Sleep," 2006*

- The American Academy of Dermatology ranked 26 U.S. metropolitan regions in terms of their residents knowledge, attitude and behaviors towards tanning, sun protection and skin cancer detection. The Dallas metro area ranked #11. The results of the study are based on an online survey of over 7,000 adults nationwide. *American Academy of Dermatology, "Suntelligence: How Sun Smart is Your City," May 3, 2010*

- The Dallas metro area appeared in the 2010 Gallup-Healthways Well-Being Index. The index, based on interviews with more than 353,000 Americans during 2009, asked individuals to assess their jobs, finances, physical health, emotional state of mind and communities. The metro area ranked #41 out of 162. Criteria: life evaluation; emotional health; work environment; physical health; healthy behaviors; basic access (basic needs optimal for a healthy life, such as access to food and medicine, having health insurance and feeling safe while walking at night). *Gallup-Healthways, "Well-Being Index 2010"*

- The Dallas metro area was identified as one of "America's Most Stressful Cities" by *Forbes*. The metro area ranked #36. Criteria: median home price drop; unemployment rates; cost of living; air quality; sunny days; population density. *Forbes.com, "America's Most Stressful Cities," August 20, 2009*

- 50 of the largest metro areas in the U.S. were analyzed in terms of their health and fitness by the American College of Sports Medicine in their "American Fitness Index." The Dallas metro area ranked #40 (#1 = healthiest). Criteria: preventative health behaviors; levels of chronic disease; health care access; community resources and policies that support physical activity. *American College of Sports Medicine, "Health and Community Fitness Status of the 50 Largest Metropolitan Areas," May 24, 2010*

Real Estate Rankings

- *Fortune* ranked the 100 largest metro areas in the U.S. in terms of projected median home price change in 2010. The Dallas metro area ranked #13. *Fortune, "The 2010 Housing Outlook," December 9, 2009*

- Plano appeared on ApartmentRatings.com "Top Cities for Renters" list in 2009." The area ranked #14. Overall satisfaction ratings were ranked using thousands of user submitted scores for hundreds of apartment complexes located in the 100 most populated U.S. municipalities. *ApartmentRatings.com, "2009 Renter Satisfaction Rankings"*

- The Dallas metro area was identified as one of the "Top 25 Real Estate Investment Markets" by *FinestExperts.com*. The metro area ranked #1. Over 10,000 real estate markets were analyzed to identify the most suitable places for real estate investors to seek stability and growth. Criteria: employment; rental markets; growth levels as offset by foreclosures. *FinestExperts.com, "Top 25 Real Estate Investment Markets," January 7, 2010*

- The Dallas metro area was identified as one of "America's Best Housing Markets" by *Forbes*. The metro area ranked #9. Criteria: housing affordability; rising home prices; percentage of foreclosures. *Forbes.com, "America's Best Housing Markets," February 19, 2010*

- The nation's largest metro areas were analyzed in terms of the percentage of households entering some stage of foreclosure in 2010. The Dallas metro area ranked #98 out of 206 (#1 = highest foreclosure rate). *RealtyTrac, 2010 Year-End Metropolitan Foreclosure Market Report, January 27, 2011*

- The Dallas metro area was identified as one of the "Best Cities to Buy a Home" by *Forbes*. The metro area ranked #6. Criteria: 2-year home price appreciation; vacancy rates; spread between monthly rent and mortgage payment at the median level. *Forbes.com, "Best Cities to Buy a Home," July 22, 2008*

- The Dallas metro area appeared in a *Wall Street Journal* article ranking cities by "housing stress." The metro area was ranked #22 (#1 = most stress). Criteria: fraction of mortgage-holding homeowners with a monthly housing payment in excess of 30 percent of income; percentage of people without health insurance; unemployment rate. *The Wall Street Journal, "Which Cities Face Biggest Housing Risk," October 5, 2010*

- The Center for Housing Policy ranked 210 U.S metropolitan areas by the fair market rent for a two-bedroom unit. The Dallas metro area was ranked #82. (#1 = most expensive) with a rent of $894. Criteria: Fair Market Rent (FMR) in effect during the fourth quarter of 2009 based on HUD's fiscal year 2010 FMRs. *The Center for Housing Policy, "Paycheck to Paycheck: Most to Least Expensive Rental Markets in 2009"*

- The Dallas metro area was identified as one of the markets with the best expected performance in home prices over the next 12 months. *Local Market Monitor, "First Quarter Home Price Forecast for Largest US Markets," March 2, 2011*

Safety Rankings

- Allstate ranked the 200 largest cities in America in terms of driver safety. Plano ranked #155. In addition, drivers were 26.4% more likely to have had an accident compared to the national average. Allstate researchers analyzed internal property damage reported claims over a two-year period (from January 2007 to December 2008) to ensure the findings would not be affected by external influences such as weather or road construction. A weighted average of the two-year numbers determined the annual percentages. The report defines an auto crash as any collision resulting in a property damage claim. *Allstate, "The 2010 Allstate America's Best Drivers Report*™*"*

- Dallas was identified as one of the least safe places in the U.S. in terms of its vulnerability to natural disasters and weather extremes. The city ranked #2 out of 10. Sperling's BestPlaces analyzed data to show a metro areas' relative tendency to experience natural disasters (hail, tornadoes, high winds, hurricanes, earthquakes, and brush fires) or extreme weather (abundant rain or snowfall or days that are below freezing or above 90 degrees Fahrenheit). *Forbes, "Safest and Least Safe Places in the U.S.," August 30, 2005*

- Plano was selected as one of "America's Safest Cities" by *Forbes*. The city ranked #1 out of 10. Criteria: violent crime rates; traffic fatalities per 100,000 residents. The editors only considered cities with populations above 250,000. *Forbes, "America's Safest Cities," October 11, 2010*

- The National Insurance Crime Bureau ranked 366 metro areas in the U.S. in terms of per capita rates of vehicle theft. The Dallas metro area ranked #39 (#1 = highest rate). Criteria: number of vehicle theft offenses per 100,000 inhabitants. *National Insurance Crime Bureau, "Hot Spots," May 17, 2010*

- The Dallas metro area was identified as one of the "The Most Dangerous Metro Areas for Pedestrians" by Transportation for America and the Surface Transportation Policy Partnership. The metro area ranked #13 out of 52 metro areas with over 1 million residents. Criteria: area's population divided by the number of pedestrian fatalities in that area. *Transportation for America and the Surface Transportation Policy Partnership, "Dangerous by Design: Solving the Epidemic of Preventable Pedestrian Deaths (and Making Great Neighborhoods)," November 11, 2009*

Seniors/Retirement Rankings

- The Dallas metro area was identified as one of "America's Most Affordable Places to Retire" by *Forbes*. The metro area ranked #2. Criteria: housing affordability; inflation; number of persons over 65 who are employed; net migration for persons over 65; percent of persons over 65 living below poverty level; doctors per capita; number of citizens tapping their Medicare benefits per thousand people. *Forbes.com, "America's Most Affordable Places to Retire," September 5, 2008*

- The Dallas metro area was selected as one of "America's Best Places to Grow Old" by *Forbes*. The area was ranked #2 out of 10. Criteria: housing affordability; inflationary pressures; number of persons over 65 who are currently employed; net migration for persons over 65; percent of seniors living below poverty level; doctors per capita; number of citizens tapping their Medicare benefits per 1,000 people. *Forbes, "America's Best Places to Grow Old," December 12, 2008*

- The Dallas metro area was selected as one of "The 10 Most Affordable Cities for Long-Term Care" by *U.S. News & World Report*. Criteria: costs at nursing homes, assisted living facilities, and adult day health care facilities; cost for licensed home health aides. *U.S. News & Word Report, "The 10 Most Affordable Cities for Long-Term Care," May 17, 2010*

Sports/Recreation Rankings

- Scarborough Research, a leading market research firm, identified the top local markets for avid NBA fans. The Dallas DMA (Designated Market Area) ranked in the top 10 with 13% of consumers 18 years and over reporting that they are "very interested in the NBA." *Scarborough Research, April 24, 2006*

- *Golf Digest* ranked 330 metro areas in the U.S. in terms of golf. The Dallas metro area was ranked #256. Criteria: access to golf; weather; value of golf; and quality of golf. *Golf Digest, "Metro Golf Rankings," August 2005*

- *Golf.com* and the research arm of the National Golf Foundation analyzed the 50 largest metropolitan areas in the U.S. in terms of golf. The Dallas metro area ranked #4. Criteria: weather; affordability; quality of courses; accessibility; number of courses designed by esteemed architects; availability; crowdedness. *Golf.com, November 15, 2007*

Technology Rankings

- Plano was selected as a 2010 Digital Cities Survey winner. The city ranked #7 in the large city (250,000 or more population) category. The survey examined and assessed how city governments are utilizing information technology to operate and deliver quality service to their customers and citizens. Survey questions focused on implementation and adoption of online service delivery; planning and governance; and the infrastructure and architecture that make the transformation to digital government possible. *Center for Digital Government, "2010 Digital Cities Survey"*

- Scarborough Research, a leading market research firm, identified the Dallas DMA (Designated Market Area) as one of the top markets for text messaging with more than 50% of cell phone subscribers age 18+ utilizing the text messaging feature on their phone. *Scarborough Research, November 24, 2008*

Transportation Rankings

- The Dallas metro area appeared on *Forbes* list of the best and worst cities for commuters. The metro area ranked #56 out of 60 (#1 is best). Criteria: travel time; road congestion; travel delays. *Forbes.com, "Best and Worst Cities for Commuters," February 16, 2010*

Women/Minorities Rankings

- Dallas was ranked #68 out of 100 metro areas in *SELF Magazine's* ranking of America's healthiest places for women." A panel of experts came up with more than 50 criteria including death and disease rates, environmental indicators, community resources, and lifestyle habits. *SELF Magazine, "Secrets of America's Healthiest Women," December 2008*

- Dallas appeared on *Black Enterprise's* list of the "Ten Best Cities for African Americans." The top picks were culled from more than 2,000 interactive surveys completed on www.blackenterprise.com and by editorial staff evaluation. The editors weighed the following criteria as it pertained to African Americans in each city: median household income; percentage of households earning more than $100,000; percentage of businesses owned; percentage of college graduates; unemployment rates; home loan rejections; and homeownership rates. *Black Enterprise, May 2007*

Miscellaneous Rankings

- Energizer Holdings, the makers of Edge® shave gel, in partnership with Sperling's BestPlaces, ranked 50 major metro areas in terms of everyday irritations. The Dallas metro area ranked #13. Criteria: humidity levels; weather conditions; incidence of traffic delays and congestion; average commute times; frequency of flight delays and cancellations; rates of sleeplessness; underemployment; pollens and allergens; pests; comedy clubs per capita. *Energizer Holdings, "Most Irritation Prone Cities," July 23, 2010*

- Mars Chocolate North America, the makers of COMBOS®, in partnership with Sperling's BestPlaces, ranked 50 major metro areas in terms of their "manliness." The Dallas metro area ranked #39. Criteria: number of home improvement stores, steak houses, pickup trucks, motorcycles, and manly occupations (fire fighters, police officers, construction workers, EMP personnel) per capita; salty snack sales; sports TV viewing habits. *Mars Chocolate North America, "America's Manliest Cities," June 22, 2010*

- The Dallas metro area was selected as one of "America's Greediest Cities" by *Forbes*. The area was ranked #7 out of 10. Criteria: number of Forbes 400 (*Forbes* annual list of the richest Americans) members per capita. *Forbes, "America's Greediest Cities," December 7, 2007*

- The Dallas metro area appeared on *Forbes* list of "America's Drunkest Cities." The area ranked #27. Criteria: 35 of the largest continental U.S. metro areas were chosen based on availability of data and geographic diversity. Each metro was ranked in five areas: state laws; drinkers; heavy drinkers; binge drinkers; and alcoholism. *Forbes.com, "America's Drunkest Cities," August 22, 2006*

Business Environment

CITY FINANCES

City Government Finances

Component	2008 ($000)	2008 ($ per capita)
Total Revenues	374,983	1,438
Total Expenditures	386,538	1,482
Debt Outstanding	339,556	1,302
Cash and Securities[1]	209,555	804

Note: (1) Cash and security holdings of a government at the close of its fiscal year, including those of its dependent agencies, utilities, and liquor stores.
Source: U.S Census Bureau, State & Local Government Finances 2008

City Government Revenue by Source

Source	2008 ($000)	2008 ($ per capita)
General Revenue		
From Federal Government	0	0
From State Government	4,203	16
From Local Governments	697	3
Taxes		
Property	116,441	446
Sales and Gross Receipts	95,481	366
Personal Income	0	0
Corporate Income	0	0
Motor Vehicle License	0	0
Other Taxes	5,525	21
Current Charges	85,234	327
Liquor Store	0	0
Utility	40,669	156
Employee Retirement	0	0

Source: U.S Census Bureau, State & Local Government Finances 2008

City Government Expenditures by Function

Function	2008 ($000)	2008 ($ per capita)	2008 (%)
General Direct Expenditures			
Air Transportation	0	0	0.0
Corrections	0	0	0.0
Education	0	0	0.0
Employment Security Administration	0	0	0.0
Financial Administration	4,975	19	1.3
Fire Protection	39,097	150	10.1
General Public Buildings	13,195	51	3.4
Governmental Administration, Other	7,917	30	2.0
Health	3,161	12	0.8
Highways	22,921	88	5.9
Hospitals	0	0	0.0
Housing and Community Development	0	0	0.0
Interest on General Debt	14,221	55	3.7
Judicial and Legal	4,035	15	1.0
Libraries	10,251	39	2.7
Parking	0	0	0.0
Parks and Recreation	54,656	210	14.1
Police Protection	52,933	203	13.7
Public Welfare	0	0	0.0
Sewerage	11,298	43	2.9
Solid Waste Management	19,160	73	5.0
Veterans' Services	0	0	0.0
Liquor Store	0	0	0.0
Utility	24,515	94	6.3
Employee Retirement	0	0	0.0

Source: U.S Census Bureau, State & Local Government Finances 2008

Municipal Bond Ratings

Area	Moody's	S&P	Fitch
City	Aaa	AAA	AAA

Rating Systems (shown in declining order of credit quality): Moody's– Aaa, Aa, A, Baa, Ba, B, Caa, Ca, C (numerical modifiers 1, 2, and 3 are added to letter-rating); S&P– AAA, AA, A, BBB, BB, B, CCC, CC, C; Fitch– AAA, AA, A, BBB, BB, B, CCC, CC, C. Ratings may be modified by the addition of a plus or minus sign to show relative standing within the major rating categories.
Notes: n/a Not available; (1) Not reviewed; (2) Issuer Rating/No General Obligation; (3) Standard and Poor's Issue Credit Rating (ICR) is a current opinion of an obliger with respect to a specific financial obligation, a specific class of financial obligations, or a specific financial program.
Source: U.S. Census Bureau, 2011 Statistical Abstract, Bond Ratings for City Governments by Largest Cities: 2009

DEMOGRAPHICS

Population Growth

Area	1990 Census	2000 Census	2010 Estimate	2015 Projection	Population Growth (%) 2000-2010	Population Growth (%) 2010-2015
City	128,507	222,030	280,422	325,345	26.3	16.0
MSA[1]	3,989,294	5,161,544	6,493,230	7,129,430	25.8	9.8
U.S.	248,709,873	281,421,906	309,038,974	321,675,005	9.8	4.1

Note: (1) Metropolitan Statistical Area - see Appendix B for areas included
Source: Claritas, Inc.

Number of Households and Average Household Size

Area	2010 Estimate	2010 Average Household Size
City	105,438	2.65
MSA[1]	2,320,136	2.76
U.S.	116,136,617	2.59

Note: (1) Metropolitan Statistical Area - see Appendix B for areas included
Source: Claritas, Inc.

Race and Ethnicity

Area	White Alone[2] (%)	Black Alone[2] (%)	Asian Alone[2] (%)	Other Race Alone[2] (%)	Hispanic[3] (%)
City	64.0	8.7	17.4	9.9	14.9
MSA[1]	64.4	14.0	4.7	16.9	28.1
U.S.	72.3	12.4	4.4	10.9	15.8

Note: Figures are 2010 estimates; (1) Metropolitan Statistical Area - see Appendix B for areas included (2) Alone is defined as not being in combination with one or more other races; (3) May be of any race.
Source: Claritas, Inc.

Segregation

Type	Segregation Indices[1] 1990	2000	2010	2010 Rank[2]	Percent Change 1990-2000	1990-2010	2000-2010
Black/White	62.8	59.8	56.6	48	-3.1	-6.2	-3.2
Asian/White	41.8	45.6	46.6	19	3.8	4.8	1.0
Hispanic/White	48.8	52.3	50.3	24	3.5	1.5	-2.0

Note: Figures are based on an analysis of 1990, 2000, and 2010 Census Decennial Census tract data by William H. Frey, Brookings Institution and the University of Michigan Social Science Data Analysis Network. In this analysis all racial groups (whites, blacks, and asians) are non-Hispanic members of those races. Hispanics are shown as a separate category; All figures cover the Metropolitan Statistical Area (see Appendix B for areas included); (1) Segregation Indices are Dissimilarity Indices that measure the degree to which the minority group is distributed differently than whites aross census tracts. They range from 0 (complete integration) to 100 (complete [segregation) where the value indicates the percentage of the minority group that needs to move to be distributed exactly like whites; (2) Ranges from 1 (most segregated) to 102 (least segregated); n/a not available.
Source: www.CensusScope.org

Ancestry

Area	German	Irish	English	American	Italian	Polish	French	Scottish
City	14.3	11.0	9.6	7.1	3.7	1.7	3.0	2.4
MSA[1]	11.4	8.8	8.6	6.5	2.3	1.2	2.3	1.9
U.S.	16.6	12.0	9.1	6.1	5.9	3.3	3.1	1.9

*Note: The top eight ancestries in the U.S. are shown. Figures are percentages and include multiple ancestry
(e.g. if a person reported being Irish and Italian, they were included in both columns); (1) Metropolitan
Statistical Area - see Appendix B for areas included*
Source: U.S. Census Bureau, 2007-2009 American Community Survey 3-Year Estimates

Foreign-Born Population

Area	Percent of Population Born in								
	Any Foreign Country	Mexico	Asia	Europe	Carribean	South America	Central America[2]	Africa	Canada
City	22.7	5.3	12.3	1.4	0.1	0.7	1.1	1.0	0.5
MSA[1]	17.5	9.8	3.8	0.8	0.2	0.5	1.3	0.8	0.2
U.S.	12.5	3.8	3.4	1.6	1.1	0.8	0.9	0.5	0.3

Note: (1) Metropolitan Statistical Area - see Appendix B for areas included; (2) Excludes Mexico.
Source: U.S. Census Bureau, 2007-2009 American Community Survey 3-Year Estimates

Marriage Status

Area	Never Married	Now Married[2]	Separated	Widowed	Divorced
City	27.4	57.8	1.6	3.6	9.6
MSA[1]	30.9	50.7	2.6	4.7	11.1
U.S.	31.4	49.7	2.2	6.2	10.6

*Note: Figures are percentages and cover the population 15 years of age and older;
(1) Metropolitan Statistical Area - see Appendix B for areas included; (2) Excludes separated*
Source: U.S. Census Bureau, 2007-2009 American Community Survey 3-Year Estimates

Age Distribution and Median Age

Area	Percent of Population							Median Age
	Under Age 5	Age 5 to 17	Age 18 to 34	Age 35 to 49	Age 50 to 64	Age 65 to 79	80 Years and Over	
City	6.5	19.4	21.9	25.9	17.9	6.4	2.0	36.2
MSA[1]	8.4	19.6	25.3	22.8	15.4	6.2	2.2	32.9
U.S.	6.9	17.5	23.3	21.4	18.1	9.1	3.7	36.7

Note: (1) Metropolitan Statistical Area - see Appendix B for areas included
Source: U.S. Census Bureau, 2007-2009 American Community Survey 3-Year Estimates

Male/Female Ratio

Area	Males	Females	Males per 100 Females
City	140,508	139,914	100.4
MSA[1]	3,264,985	3,228,245	101.1
U.S.	152,401,520	156,637,454	97.3

*Note: Figures are 2010 estimates; (1) Metropolitan Statistical Area -
see Appendix B for areas included*
Source: Claritas, Inc.

Religion

Area	Catholic	Southern Baptist	United Methodist	ELCA[1]	LDS[2]	Presbyterian Church USA	Jewish Est.	Muslim Est.
County	18.3	16.0	6.1	0.6	1.3	0.7	1.4	1.2
U.S.	22.0	7.1	3.7	1.8	1.5	1.1	2.2	0.6

Note: Figures are the number of adherents as a percentage of the total population; Adherents are defined as all members, including full members, their children and the estimated number of other participants who are not considered members (e.g. the baptized, those not confirmed, those regularly attending services, etc.); (1) Evangelical Lutheran Church in America; (2) The Church of Jesus Christ of Latter Day Saints
Source: Reprinted with permission from Religious Congregations and Membership in the United States 2000 (Nashville, Glenmary Research Center, 2002) Copyright Association of Statisticians of American Religious Bodies. All rights reserved.

ECONOMY

Gross Metropolitan Product

Area	2006	2007	2008	2009	2009 Rank[2]
MSA[1]	340.6	362.1	379.9	384.8	6

Note: Figures are in billions of dollars; (1) Dallas-Fort Worth-Arlington, TX Metropolitan Statistical Area - see Appendix B for areas included; (2) Rank ranges from 1 to 363
Source: The U.S. Conference of Mayors, "Pace of Economic Recovery: GMP and Jobs," January 2010

Economic Growth

Area	2006-2008 (%)	2009 (%)	2010 (%)	Rank[2]
MSA[1]	2.7	-0.1	3.7	67
U.S.	1.3	-2.5	2.2	–

Note: Figures are real Gross Metropolitan Product growth rates and represent annual average percent change; (1) Dallas-Fort Worth-Arlington, TX Metropolitan Statistical Area - see Appendix B for areas included; (2) Rank ranges from 1 to 363
Source: The U.S. Conference of Mayors, "Pace of Economic Recovery: GMP and Jobs," January 2010

Metropolitan Area Exports

Area	2005	2006	2007	2008	2009	2009 Rank[2]
MSA[1]	20,541.2	22,461.6	22,079.1	22,503.7	19,881.8	10

Note: Figures are in millions of dollars; (1) Dallas-Fort Worth-Arlington, TX Metropolitan Statistical Area - see Appendix B for areas included; (2) Rank ranges from 1 to 374
Source: U.S. Department of Commerce, International Trade Administration, Office of Trade & Industry Information, Manufacturing & Services

INCOME

Per Capita/Median/Average Income

Area	Per Capita ($)	Median Household ($)	Average Household ($)
City	42,764	86,954	113,481
MSA[1]	27,980	58,202	77,740
U.S.	27,034	52,795	71,071

Note: Figures are 2010 estimates; (1) Metropolitan Statistical Area - see Appendix B for areas included
Source: Claritas, Inc.

Household Income Distribution

Area	Percent of Households Earning							
	Under $15,000	$15,000 -24,999	$25,000 -34,999	$35,000 -49,999	$50,000 -74,999	$75,000 -99,000	$100,000 -149,999	$150,000 and up
City	4.2	4.3	6.1	11.1	17.3	14.7	21.9	20.5
MSA[1]	9.4	8.6	10.2	15.3	19.6	13.3	14.1	9.4
U.S.	12.1	10.2	10.6	15.0	19.5	12.5	12.1	8.0

Note: Figures are 2010 estimates; (1) Metropolitan Statistical Area - see Appendix B for areas included
Source: Claritas, Inc.

Poverty Rates by Age

Area	All Ages	Under 18 Years Old	18 to 64 Years Old	65 Years and Over
City	6.9	2.5	3.9	0.6
MSA[1]	13.4	5.4	7.2	0.7
U.S.	13.6	4.7	7.7	1.2

Note: Figures are percent of population with income during the previous 12 months below poverty level and only include population for whom poverty status is determined; (1) Metropolitan Statistical Area - see Appendix B for areas included
Source: U.S. Census Bureau, 2007-2009 American Community Survey 3-Year Estimates

Personal Bankruptcy Filing Rate

Area	2006	2007	2008	2009	2010
Collin County	1.91	2.40	2.75	3.38	3.75
U.S.	2.00	2.73	3.53	4.60	4.96

Note: Numbers are per 1,000 population and include Chapter 7 and Chapter 13 filings
Source: Federal Deposit Insurance Corporation, Regional Economic Conditions, March 17, 2011

EMPLOYMENT

Labor Force and Employment

Area	Civilian Labor Force			Workers Employed		
	Dec. 2009	Dec. 2010	% Chg.	Dec. 2009	Dec. 2010	% Chg.
City	144,707	147,581	2.0	134,666	137,656	2.2
MD[1]	2,109,867	2,158,513	2.3	1,942,343	1,985,464	2.2
U.S.	152,693,000	153,156,000	0.3	137,953,000	139,159,000	0.9

Note: Data is not seasonally adjusted and covers workers 16 years of age and older;
(1) Metropolitan Division - see Appendix B for areas included
Source: Bureau of Labor Statistics, http://stats.bls.gov

Unemployment Rate

Area	2010											
	Jan.	Feb.	Mar.	Apr.	May	Jun.	Jul.	Aug.	Sep.	Oct.	Nov.	Dec.
City	7.5	7.4	7.4	7.1	7.2	7.5	7.4	7.3	7.1	7.0	7.0	6.7
MD[1]	8.7	8.5	8.4	8.1	8.0	8.5	8.5	8.4	8.1	8.0	8.3	8.0
U.S.	10.6	10.4	10.2	9.5	9.3	9.6	9.7	9.5	9.2	9.0	9.3	9.1

Note: Data is not seasonally adjusted and covers workers 16 years of age and older; All figures are percentages; (1) Metropolitan Division - see Appendix B for areas included
Source: Bureau of Labor Statistics, http://stats.bls.gov

Projected Unemployment Rate

Area	2007 (%)	2009 (%)	2011 (%)	2013 (%)
MSA[1]	4.4	8.9	8.3	7.0

Note: (1) Metropolitan Statistical Area - see Appendix B for areas included
Source: The U.S. Conference of Mayors, "Pace of Economic Recovery: GMP and Jobs," January 2010

Employment by Occupation

Occupation Classification	City (%)	MSA[1] (%)	U.S. (%)
Sales and Office	27.0	27.0	25.4
Professional and Related	27.6	19.5	21.0
Service	11.5	15.1	17.2
Production, Transportation, and Material Moving	5.2	11.8	12.3
Management, Business, and Financial	23.0	15.7	14.1
Construction, Extraction, and Maintenance	5.7	10.7	9.2
Farming, Forestry, and Fishing	0.0	0.2	0.7

Note: Figures cover employed civilians 16 years of age and older;
(1) Metropolitan Statistical Area - see Appendix B for areas included
Source: U.S. Census Bureau, 2007-2009 American Community Survey 3-Year Estimates

Employment by Industry

Sector	MSA[1]		U.S.
	Number of Employees	Percent of Total	Percent of Total
Government	276,100	13.4	17.2
Education and Health Services	255,300	12.4	15.2
Professional and Business Services	344,000	16.7	13.0
Retail Trade	210,300	10.2	11.4
Leisure and Hospitality	191,400	9.3	9.7
Manufacturing	162,400	7.9	8.8
Financial Activities	180,400	8.8	5.8
Wholesale Trade	119,900	5.8	4.2
Construction	n/a	n/a	4.1
Other Services	69,100	3.4	4.1
Transportation and Utilities	74,500	3.6	3.7
Information	64,200	3.1	2.1
Mining and Logging	n/a	n/a	0.6

Note: Figures cover non-farm employment as of December 2010 and are not seasonally adjusted;
(1) Metropolitan Statistical Area - see Appendix B for areas included; n/a not available
Source: Bureau of Labor Statistics, http://stats.bls.gov

Occupations with Greatest Projected Employment Growth: 2006 - 2016

Occupation[1]	2006 Employment	2016 Projected Employment	Numeric Employment Change	Percent Employment Change
Combined food preparation and serving workers, including fast food	270,530	359,050	88,520	32.7
Retail salespersons	332,750	411,350	78,600	23.6
Personal and home care aides	133,050	207,850	74,800	56.2
Customer service representatives	214,440	280,060	65,620	30.6
Elementary school teachers, except special education	145,430	207,710	62,280	42.8
Registered nurses	157,840	217,430	59,590	37.8
Waiters and waitresses	174,140	227,790	53,650	30.8
Child care workers	145,500	189,730	44,230	30.4
Office clerks, general	194,610	236,670	42,060	21.6
Postsecondary teachers	113,400	153,130	39,730	35.0

Note: Projections cover Texas; (1) Sorted by numeric employment change
Source: www.projectionscentral.com, State Occupational Projections, 2006-2016 Long-Term Projections

Fastest Growing Occupations: 2006 - 2016

Occupation[1]	2006 Employment	2016 Projected Employment	Numeric Employment Change	Percent Employment Change
Personal and home care aides	133,050	207,850	74,800	56.2
Network systems and data communications analysts	17,750	27,620	9,870	55.6
Medical assistants	34,790	53,500	18,710	53.8
Special education teachers, preschool, kindergarten, and elementary school	13,750	20,560	6,810	49.5
Physical therapist assistants	3,780	5,570	1,790	47.4
Special education teachers, middle school	6,270	9,170	2,900	46.3
Computer software engineers, applications	30,900	45,200	14,300	46.3
Physician assistants	3,810	5,540	1,730	45.4
Kindergarten teachers, except special education	12,850	18,690	5,840	45.4
Pharmacy technicians	24,420	35,050	10,630	43.5

Note: Projections cover Texas; (1) Sorted by percent employment change and excludes occupations with numeric employment change less than 1500
Source: www.projectionscentral.com, State Occupational Projections, 2006-2016 Long-Term Projections

Average Wages

Occupation	$/Hr.	Occupation	$/Hr.
Accountants and Auditors	32.90	Maids and Housekeeping Cleaners	8.89
Automotive Mechanics	18.35	Maintenance and Repair Workers	16.07
Bookkeepers	17.45	Marketing Managers	62.86
Carpenters	15.47	Nuclear Medicine Technologists	31.78
Cashiers	8.69	Nurses, Licensed Practical	22.59
Clerks, General Office	14.40	Nurses, Registered	32.47
Clerks, Receptionists/Information	12.90	Nursing Aides/Orderlies/Attendants	10.99
Clerks, Shipping/Receiving	13.87	Packers and Packagers, Hand	9.89
Computer Programmers	40.97	Physical Therapists	39.65
Computer Support Specialists	24.37	Postal Service Mail Carriers	23.77
Computer Systems Analysts	40.47	Real Estate Brokers	47.56
Cooks, Restaurant	9.77	Retail Salespersons	12.29
Dentists	n/a	Sales Reps., Exc. Tech./Scientific	29.08
Electrical Engineers	46.55	Sales Reps., Tech./Scientific	49.88
Electricians	20.47	Secretaries, Exc. Legal/Med./Exec.	14.58
Financial Managers	59.84	Security Guards	12.72
First-Line Supervisors/Mgrs., Sales	19.44	Surgeons	108.56
Food Preparation Workers	8.61	Teacher Assistants	11.00
General and Operations Managers	59.88	Teachers, Elementary School	25.80
Hairdressers/Cosmetologists	13.15	Teachers, Secondary School	27.00
Internists	100.60	Telemarketers	13.85
Janitors and Cleaners	9.85	Truck Drivers, Heavy/Tractor-Trailer	18.91
Landscaping/Groundskeeping Workers	11.05	Truck Drivers, Light/Delivery Svcs.	15.12
Lawyers	71.15	Waiters and Waitresses	8.67

Note: Wage data covers the Dallas-Plano-Irving, TX Metropolitan Division - see Appendix B for areas included. Hourly wages for elementary/secondary school teachers and teacher assistants were calculated by the editors from annual wage data assuming a 40 hour work week; n/a not available.
Source: Bureau of Labor Statistics, Metro Area Occupational Employment and Wage Estimates, May 2009

RESIDENTIAL REAL ESTATE

Building Permits

Area	Single-Family			Multi-Family			Total		
	2009	2010	Pct. Chg.	2009	2010	Pct. Chg.	2009	2010	Pct. Chg.
City	226	311	37.6	365	303	-17.0	591	614	3.9
MSA[1]	14,141	14,420	2.0	6,229	5,138	-17.5	20,370	19,558	-4.0
U.S.	441,100	447,300	1.4	141,900	157,300	10.9	583,000	604,600	3.7

Note: (1) Metropolitan Statistical Area - see Appendix B for areas included; figures represent new, privately-owned housing units authorized (unadjusted data); All permit data are based on estimates with imputation.
Source: U.S. Census Bureau, Manufacturing, Mining, and Construction Statistics, Building Permits, 2009, 2010

Homeownership Rate

Area	2005 (%)	2006 (%)	2007 (%)	2008 (%)	2009 (%)	2010 (%)
MSA[1]	62.3	60.7	60.9	60.9	61.6	63.8
U.S.	68.9	68.8	68.1	67.8	67.4	66.9

Note: (1) Metropolitan Statistical Area - see Appendix B for areas included
Source: U.S. Census Bureau, Housing Vacancies and Homeownership Annual Statistics: 2010

Housing Vacancy Rates

Area	Gross Vacancy Rate[2] (%)			Year-Round Vacancy Rate[3] (%)			Rental Vacancy Rate[4] (%)			Homeowner Vacancy Rate[5] (%)		
	2008	2009	2010	2008	2009	2010	2008	2009	2010	2008	2009	2010
MSA[1]	9.5	9.4	10.5	9.4	9.3	10.4	10.5	11.7	13.5	2.8	2.1	2.3
U.S.	14.4	14.5	14.3	11.1	11.3	11.3	10.0	10.6	10.2	2.8	2.6	2.6

Note: (1) Metropolitan Statistical Area - see Appendix B for areas included; (2) The percentage of the total housing inventory that is vacant; (3) The percentage of the housing inventory (excluding seasonal units) that is year-round vacant; (4) The percentage of rental inventory that is vacant for rent; (5) The percentage of homeowner inventory that is vacant for sale; n/a not available
Source: U.S. Census Bureau, Housing Vacancies and Homeownership Annual Statistics: 2010

State Corporate Income Tax Rates

State	Tax Rate (%)	Income Brackets ($)	Num. of Brackets	Financial Institution Tax Rate (%)[a]	Federal Income Tax Ded.
Texas	(y)	–	-	(y)	No

Note: Tax rates as of January 1, 2011; (a) Rates listed are the tax rates applied to financial institutions or excise taxes based on income. Some states have other taxes based upon the value of deposits or shares; (y) Texas imposes a Franchise Tax, otherwise known as margin tax, imposed on entities with more than $1,000,000 total revenues at rate of 1%, or 0.5% for entities primarily engaged in retail or wholesale trade, on lesser of 70% of total revenues or 100%of gross receipts after deductions for either compensation or cost of goods sold.
Source: Federation of Tax Administrators, "State Corporate Income Tax Rates, 2011"

State Individual Income Tax Rates

State	Tax Rate (%)	Income Brackets ($)	Num. of Brackets	Personal Exempt. ($)[1] Single	Personal Exempt. ($)[1] Dependents	Fed. Inc. Tax Ded.
Texas – No State Income Tax						

Note: Tax rates as of January 1, 2011; Local- and county-level taxes are not included; n/a not applicable;
(1) Married joint filers generally receive double the single exemption
Source: Federation of Tax Administrators, "State Individual Income Tax Rates, 2011"

Various State and Local Tax Rates

State	State and Local Sales and Use (%)	State Sales and Use (%)	Gasoline[1] (¢/gal.)	Cigarette[2] ($/pack)	Spirits[3] ($/gal.)	Wine[4] ($/gal.)	Beer[5] ($/gal.)
Texas	8.25	6.25	20.0	1.41	2.40	0.20	0.20

Note: All tax rates as of January 1, 2011 except Spirits (Sept. 1, 2010); (1) The American Petroleum Institute has developed a methodology for determining the average tax rate on a gallon of fuel. Rates may include any of the following: excise taxes, environmental fees, storage tank fees, other fees or taxes, general sales tax, and local taxes. In states where gasoline is subject to the general sales tax, or where the fuel tax is based on the average sale price, the average rate determined by API is sensitive to changes in the price of gasoline. States that fully or partially apply general sales taxes to gasoline: CA, CO, GA, IL, IN, MI, NY; (2) The federal excise tax of $1.0066 per pack and local taxes are not included; (3) Rates are those applicable to off-premise sales of 40% alcohol by volume (a.b.v.) distilled spirits in 750ml containers. Local excise taxes are excluded; (4) Rates are those applicable to off-premise sales of 11% a.b.v. non-carbonated wine in 750ml containers; (5) Rates are those applicable to off-premise sales of 4.7% a.b.v. beer in 12 ounce containers.
Source: Tax Foundation, 2011 Facts & Figures: How Does Your State Compare?

State-Local Tax Burdens

Area	Rate (%)	Rank[1]	Per Capita Taxes Paid to Home State ($)	Total State and Local Per Capita Taxes Paid ($)	Per Capita Income ($)
Texas	7.9	45	2,248	3,197	40,498
U.S. Average	9.8	-	3,057	4,160	42,539

Note: Figures cover 2009; (1) Rank ranges from 1 to 50 where 1 is highest tax burden
Source: Tax Foundation, State-Local Tax Burdens, All States, 2009

State Business Tax Climate Index Rankings

State	Overall Rank	Corporate Tax Index Rank	Individual Income Tax Index Rank	Sales Tax Index Rank	Unemployment Insurance Tax Index Rank	Property Tax Index Rank
Texas	13	46	7	37	15	29

Note: The index is a measure of how each state's tax laws affect economic performance. The lower the rank, the more favorable a state's tax system is for business. All ranks are for fiscal years. States without a given tax are given a ranking of 1.
Source: Tax Foundation, Tax Foundation Background Paper, No. 60, "2011 State Business Tax Climate Index"

COMMERCIAL REAL ESTATE

Office Market

Market Area	Inventory (sq. ft.)	Vacant (sq. ft.)	Vac. Rate (%)	Under Constr. (sq. ft.)	Asking Rent ($/sf/yr) Class A	Asking Rent ($/sf/yr) Class B
Dallas/Fort Worth	190,744,710	43,317,095	22.7	281,600	23.16	17.90

Source: Grubb & Ellis, Office Markets Trends, 1st Quarter 2011

Industrial Market

Market Area	Inventory (sq. ft.)	Vacant (sq. ft.)	Vac. Rate (%)	Under Constr. (sq. ft.)	Asking Rent ($/sf/yr) WH/Dist	R&D/Flex
Dallas/Fort Worth	662,799,900	76,917,306	11.6	1,403,552	3.53	6.46

Source: Grubb & Ellis, Industrial Markets Trends, 1st Quarter 2011

COMMERCIAL UTILITIES

Typical Monthly Electric Bills

Area	Commercial Service ($/month) 3 kW demand 1,000 kWh	40 kW demand 14,000 kWh	Industrial Service ($/month) 1,000 kW demand 200,000 kWh	50,000 kW demand 15,000,000 kWh
City	n/a	n/a	n/a	n/a
Average[1]	135	1,576	23,741	1,402,202

Note: Based on total rates in effect July 1, 2010; (1) average based on 182 utilities surveyed; n/a not available
Source: Edison Electric Institute, Typical Bills and Average Rates Report, Summer 2010

TRANSPORTATION

Means of Transportation to Work

Area	Car/Truck/Van Drove Alone	Car-pooled	Public Transportation Bus	Subway	Railroad	Bicycle	Walked	Other Means	Worked at Home
City	82.5	6.6	0.7	0.4	0.5	0.1	0.8	2.1	6.3
MSA[1]	80.4	11.0	1.2	0.2	0.2	0.2	1.3	1.4	4.1
U.S.	75.8	10.4	2.7	1.7	0.5	0.5	2.9	1.2	4.1

Note: Figures are percentages and cover workers 16 years of age and older;
(1) Metropolitan Statistical Area - see Appendix B for areas included
Source: U.S. Census Bureau, 2007-2009 American Community Survey 3-Year Estimates

Travel Time to Work

Area	Less Than 15 Minutes	15 to 29 Minutes	30 to 44 Minutes	45 to 59 Minutes	60 to 89 Minutes	90 Minutes or More
City	20.9	38.2	23.6	10.2	6.3	0.8
MSA[1]	22.5	36.3	24.0	9.6	5.9	1.7
U.S.	28.5	36.2	19.7	7.5	5.6	2.5

Note: Figures are percentages and include workers 16 years old and over;
(1) Metropolitan Statistical Area - see Appendix B for areas included
Source: U.S. Census Bureau, 2007-2009 American Community Survey 3-Year Estimates

Travel Time Index

Area	1982	1999	2008	2009
Urban Area[1]	1.05	1.19	1.23	1.22
Average[2]	1.08	1.20	1.20	1.20

Note: Travel Time Index—the ratio of travel time in the peak period to the travel time at free-flow conditions. A value of 1.30 indicates a 20-minute free-flow trip takes 26 minutes in the peak. Free-flow speeds (60 mph on freeways and 35 mph on principal arterials) are used as the comparison threshold; (1) Covers the Dallas-Fort Worth-Arlington urban area; (2) average of 439 urban areas
Source: Texas Transportation Institute, Urban Mobility Report 2010, December 2010

Public Transportation

Agency Name / Mode of Transportation	Vehicles Operated in Maximum Service	Annual Unlinked Passenger Trips ('000)	Annual Passenger Miles ('000)
Dallas Area Rapid Transit (DART)			
Commuter rail	21	1,607.2	18,965.4
Demand response	207	1,038.7	14,338.1
Light rail	85	18,965.2	133,364.3
Bus	564	42,517.3	173,242.2
Vanpool	162	880.7	35,337.8

Note: Figures include both directly operated and purchased transportation
Source: Federal Transit Administration, National Transit Database, 2009

Air Transportation

Airport Name and Code / Type of Service	Passenger Airlines[1]	Passenger Enplanements	Freight Carriers[2]	Freight (lbs.)
Dallas-Fort Worth International (DFW)				
Domestic service (U.S. carriers - 2010)	29	24,515,012	29	331,267,166
International service (U.S. carriers - 2009)	14	1,982,583	9	56,792,392
Dallas Love Field (DAL)				
Domestic service (U.S. carriers - 2010)	16	3,780,857	6	9,736,359
International service (U.S. carriers - 2009)	5	519	3	23,275

Note: (1) Includes all U.S.-based major, minor and commuter airlines that carried at least one passenger during the year; (2) Includes all U.S.-based airlines and freight carriers that transported at least one pound of freight during the year
Source: Bureau of Transportation Statistics, The Intermodal Transportation Database, Air Carriers: T-100 Domestic Market (U.S. Carriers), 2010; Bureau of Transportation Statistics, The Intermodal Transportation Database, Air Carriers: T-100 International Market (U.S. Carriers), 2009

Other Transportation Statistics

Interstate highways:	I-20; I-30; I-35E; I-45
Amtrak service:	No
Major waterways/ports:	None

Source: Amtrak.com; Google Maps

BUSINESSES

Major Business Headquarters

Company Name	Rankings	
	Fortune[1]	Forbes[2]
Dr Pepper Snapple Group	404	-
J.C. Penney	146	-

Note: (1) Fortune 500—companies that produce a 10-K are ranked 1 to 500 based on 2010 revenue; (2) all private companies with at least $2 billion in annual revenue are ranked 1 to 223; companies listed are headquartered in the city; dashes indicate no ranking
Source: Fortune, "Fortune 500," May 23, 2011; Forbes, "America's Largest Private Companies," November 3, 2010

Fast-Growing Businesses

According to *Inc.*, Plano is home to one of America's 500 fastest-growing private companies: **SoftLayer Technologies**. Criteria: must be an independent, privately-held, for-profit, U.S. corporation, proprietorship or partnership; revenues of at least $80,000 in 2006 and $2 million in 2009; four-year operating/sales history; holding companies, regulated banks, and utilities were excluded. *Inc., "America's 500 Fastest-Growing Private Companies," September 2010*

According to *Fortune*, Plano is home to one of America's 100 fastest-growing small public companies: **TGC Industries**. Companies were ranked by their three-year annualized rates of revenue growth and total return to investors for the period ended December 31, 2008. Criteria for inclusion: revenues of less than $200 million; stock price of at least $1. Banks, real-estate firms and adult entertainment companies were excluded. Also excluded were companies with losses in any of the four quarters ended on or before December 31, 2008. *Fortune Small Business, "America's Fastest-Growing Small Public Companies," July/August 2009*

According to Deloitte, Plano is home to one of North America's 500 fastest-growing high-technology companies: **GENBAND**. Companies are ranked by percentage growth in revenue over a five-year period. Criteria for inclusion: company must be headquartered within North America; company must own proprietary intellectual property or proprietary technology that contributes to a significant portion of the company's operating revenue or devotes a significant proportion of revenues to research and development of technology; company must have been in business for a minumum of five years with 2005 operating revenues of at least $50,000 USD/CD and 2009 operating revenues of at least $5 million USD/CD. *Deloitte Touche Tohmatsu, 2010 Deloitte Technology Fast 500*[TM]

Minority Business Opportunity

Plano is home to one company which is on the Black Enterprise Auto Dealer 60 list (60 largest dealers based on gross sales): **Stephens Automotive Group**. Criteria: company must be operational in previous calendar year and at least 51% black-owned. *Black Enterprise, B.E. 100s, 2010*

Plano is home to one company which is on the *Hispanic Business 500* list (500 largest U.S. Hispanic-owned companies based on 2009 revenue): **Goodman Networks**. Companies included must show at least 51 percent ownership by Hispanic U.S. citizens, and must maintain headquarters in one of the 50 states or Washington, D.C. *Hispanic Business, "Hispanic Business 500," June 2010*

Plano is home to one company which is on the *Hispanic Business* Fastest-Growing 100 list (greatest sales growth from 2005 to 2009): **Goodman Networks**. Companies included must show at least 51 percent ownership by Hispanic U.S. citizens, and must maintain headquarters in one of the 50 states or Washington, D.C. In addition, companies must have minimum revenues of $200,000 for calendar year 2005. *Hispanic Business, July/August 2010*

Minority- and Women-Owned Businesses

Group	All Firms		Firms with Paid Employees			
	Firms	Sales ($000)	Firms	Sales ($000)	Employees	Payroll ($000)
Asian	4,137	899,330	948	771,844	4,058	136,643
Black	1,322	143,194	107	110,598	391	20,675
Hispanic	1,786	339,648	165	228,866	1,756	65,304
Women	8,711	1,053,589	1,078	769,300	7,865	219,327
All Firms	31,253	57,697,657	6,292	56,193,861	143,711	8,321,423

Note: Figures cover firms located in the city; minority- and women-owned business are defined as firms in which the corresponding group own 51% or more of the stock or equity of the company
Source: U.S. Census Bureau, 2007 Economic Census, Survey of Business Owners

HOTELS

Hotels/Motels

Area	5 Star		4 Star		3 Star		2 Star		1 Star		Not Rated	
	Num.	Pct.3	Num.	Pct.3	Num.	Pct.3	Num.	Pct.3	Num.	Pct.3	Num.	Pct.3
City[1]	0	0.0	2	4.8	17	40.5	23	54.8	0	0.0	0	0.0
Total[2]	119	0.7	927	5.8	4,906	30.5	7,992	49.7	526	3.3	1,625	10.1

Note: (1) Figures cover Plano and vicinity; (2) Figures cover all 100 cities in this book; (3) Percentage of hotels which are a given star rating; Star ratings are determined by expedia.com and offer an indication of the general quality of a particular hotel.
Source: expedia.com, May 5, 2011

Living Environment

COST OF LIVING

Cost of Living Index

Composite Index	Groceries	Housing	Utilities	Trans-portation	Health Care	Misc. Goods/ Services
97.4	101.3	85.2	103.9	101.8	102.9	102.6

Note: U.S. = 100; Figures cover the Plano TX urban area.
Source: The Council for Community and Economic Research, ACCRA Cost of Living Index, 2010

Grocery Prices

Area[1]	T-Bone Steak ($/pound)	Frying Chicken ($/pound)	Whole Milk ($/half gal.)	Eggs ($/dozen)	Orange Juice ($/64 oz.)	Coffee ($/11.5 oz.)
City[2]	9.26	1.03	2.09	1.59	2.99	3.74
Avg.	9.04	1.16	2.02	1.47	3.08	3.65
Min.	6.97	0.84	1.46	0.96	2.39	2.64
Max.	13.93	2.51	3.58	3.01	4.94	6.32

Note: (1) Values for the local area are compared with the average, minimum and maximum values for all 338 areas in the Cost of Living Index; (2) Figures cover the Plano TX urban area; **T-Bone Steak** (price per pound); **Frying Chicken** (price per pound, whole fryer); **Whole Milk** (half gallon carton); **Eggs** (price per dozen, Grade A, large); **Orange Juice** (64 oz. Tropicana or Florida Natural); **Coffee** (11.5 oz. can, vacuum-packed, Maxwell House, Hills Bros, or Folgers).
Source: The Council for Community and Economic Research, ACCRA Cost of Living Index, 2010

Housing and Utility Costs

Area[1]	New Home Price ($)	Apartment Rent ($/month)	All Electric ($/month)	Part Electric ($/month)	Other Energy ($/month)	Telephone ($/month)
City[2]	228,377	940	-	139.88	48.73	26.01
Avg.	293,442	810	166.39	91.93	83.82	26.93
Min.	182,545	453	119.21	44.47	36.85	17.98
Max.	1,123,114	2,776	307.53	218.20	313.90	39.15

Note: (1) Values for the local area are compared with the average, minimum and maximum values for all 338 areas in the Cost of Living Index; (2) Figures cover the Plano TX urban area; **New Home Price** (2,400 sf living area, 8,000 sf lot, in urban area with full utilities); **Apartment Rent** (950 sf 2 bedroom/1.5 or 2 bath, unfurnished, excluding all utilities except water); **All Electric** (average monthly cost for an all-electric home); **Part Electric** (average monthly cost for a part-electric home); **Other Energy** (average monthly cost for natural gas, fuel oil, coal, wood, and any other forms of energy except electricity); **Telephone** (price includes basic monthly rate for a private residential line plus additional local usage charges incurred by a family of four).
Source: The Council for Community and Economic Research, ACCRA Cost of Living Index, 2010

Health Care, Transportation, and Other Costs

Area[1]	Doctor ($/visit)	Dentist ($/visit)	Optometrist ($/visit)	Gasoline ($/gallon)	Beauty Salon ($/visit)	Men's Shirt ($)
City[2]	93.54	85.49	79.53	2.52	30.92	22.21
Avg.	89.44	78.95	87.40	2.73	31.92	24.83
Min.	57.00	54.25	48.32	2.44	19.17	13.67
Max.	149.90	136.73	174.22	3.75	62.81	47.89

Note: (1) Values for the local area are compared with the average, minimum and maximum values for all 338 areas in the Cost of Living Index; (2) Figures cover the Plano TX urban area; **Doctor** (general practitioners routine exam of an established patient); **Dentist** (adult teeth cleaning and periodic oral examination); **Optometrist** (full vision eye exam for established adult patient); **Gasoline** (one gallon regular unleaded, national brand, including all taxes, cash price at self-service pump if available); **Beauty Salon** (woman's shampoo, trim, and blow-dry); **Men's Shirt** (cotton/polyester dress shirt, pinpoint weave, long sleeves).
Source: The Council for Community and Economic Research, ACCRA Cost of Living Index, 2010

HOUSING

House Price Index (HPI)

Area	National Ranking[2]	Quarterly Change (%)	One-Year Change (%)	Five-Year Change (%)
MD[1]	103	-0.43	-0.26	6.73
U.S.[3]	-	-0.84	-3.95	-11.45

Note: The HPI is a weighted repeat sales index. It measures average price changes in repeat sales or refinancings on the same properties. This information is obtained by reviewing repeat mortgage transactions on single-family properties whose mortgages have been purchased or securitized by Fannie Mae or Freddie Mac in January 1975; (1) Metropolitan Division - see Appendix B for areas included; (2) Rankings are based on annual percentage change for all metro areas containing at least 15,000 transactions over the last 10 years and ranges from 1 to 309; (3) figures based on a weighted average of Census Division estimates; all figures are for the period ending December 31, 2010
Source: Federal Housing Finance Agency, House Price Index, February 24, 2011

House Price Valuations

Area	Q4 2005 Price ($000)	Q4 2005 Over-valuation	Q4 2006 Price ($000)	Q4 2006 Over-valuation	Q4 2007 Price ($000)	Q4 2007 Over-valuation	Q4 2008 Price ($000)	Q4 2008 Over-valuation	Q4 2009 Price ($000)	Q4 2009 Over-valuation
MD[1]	127.1	-20.5	131.9	-22.2	134.1	-24.6	136.4	-24.0	137.1	-23.1

Note: Figures show the percentage of over- or under-valuation of single family homes relative to statistically normal house values (e.g. a value of 23.6 indicates that house values are 23.6% overvalued). Statistically normal house values are based on house prices, interest rates, household incomes, population densities, and any historical premiums or discounts metropolitan areas have exhibited over time; (1) Figures cover the Dallas-Plano-Irving, TX Metropolitan Division - see Appendix B for areas included
Source: Global Insight/PNC Financial Services Group, House Prices in America: 4th Quarter 2009 Update

Median Single-Family Home Prices

Area	2008	2009	2010[p]	Percent Change 2009 to 2010
MSA[1]	145.8	140.5	148.4	5.6
U.S. Average	196.6	172.1	173.2	0.6

Note: Figures are median sales prices of existing single-family homes in thousands of dollars; (p) preliminary; n/a not available; (1) Metropolitan Statistical Area - see Appendix B for areas included
Source: National Association of Realtors, Median Sales Price of Existing Single-Family Homes for Metropolitan Areas, 4th Quarter 2010

Median Apartment Condo-Coop Home Prices

Area	2008	2009	2010[p]	Percent Change 2009 to 2010
MSA[1]	137.4	130.5	132.6	1.6
U.S. Average	209.8	175.6	171.7	-2.2

Note: Figures are median sales prices of existing apartment condo-coop homes in thousands of dollars; (p) preliminary; n/a not available; (1) Metropolitan Statistical Area - see Appendix B for areas included
Source: National Association of Realtors, Median Sales Price of Existing Apartment Condo-Coop Homes for Metropolitan Areas, 4th Quarter 2010

Year Housing Structure Built

Area	2000 or Later	1990 -1999	1980 -1989	1970 -1979	1960 -1969	1950 -1959	1940 -1949	Before 1940	Median Year
City	14.0	37.0	27.5	16.3	3.5	1.0	0.4	0.4	1990
MSA[1]	20.5	17.0	20.3	16.1	10.4	8.8	3.3	3.5	1984
U.S.	12.5	14.0	14.2	16.5	11.4	11.3	5.8	14.3	1974

Note: Figures are percentages except for Median Year; (1) Metropolitan Statistical Area - see Appendix B for areas included
Source: U.S. Census Bureau, 2007-2009 American Community Survey 3-Year Estimates

HEALTH

Health Risk Data

Category	MSA[1] (%)	U.S. (%)
Adults who have been told they have high blood pressure	25.4	28.7
Adults who have been told they have high blood cholesterol	41.8	37.5
Adults who have been told they have diabetes[3]	8.3	8.3
Adults who have been told they have arthritis	18.5	26.0
Adults who have been told they currently have asthma	7.2	8.8
Adults who are current smokers	16.3	17.9
Adults who are heavy drinkers[4]	4.3	5.1
Adults who are binge drinkers[5]	7.9	15.8
Adults who are overweight (BMI 25.0 - 29.9)	37.0	36.2
Adults who are obese (BMI 30.0 - 99.8)	26.1	26.9
Adults who participated in any physical activities in the past month	77.4	76.2
Adults 50+ who have ever had a sigmoidoscopy or colonoscopy[2]	59.2	62.2
Women 40+ who have had a mammogram within the past two years[2]	76.5	76.0
Adults age 18–64 who have any kind of health care coverage	76.1	83.1

Note: Data as of 2009 unless otherwise noted; (1) Figures cover the Dallas-Plano-Irving, TX Metropolitan Division - see Appendix B for areas included; (2) Data as of 2008; (3) Figures do not include pregnancy-related, borderline, or pre-diabetes; (4) Heavy drinkers are classified as males having more than two drinks per day or females having more than one drink per day; (5) Binge drinkers are classified as males having five or more drinks on one occasion or females having four or more drinks on one occasion
Source: Centers for Disease Control and Prevention, Behaviorial Risk Factor Surveillance System, SMART: Selected Metropolitan/Micropolitan Area Risk Trends, 2008, 2009

Mortality Rates for the Top 10 Causes of Death in the U.S.

ICD-10[a] Sub-Chapter	ICD-10[a] Code	Age-Adjusted Mortality Rate[1] per 100,000 population	
		County[2]	U.S.
Malignant neoplasms	C00-C97	142.8	180.9
Ischaemic heart diseases	I20-I25	106.0	135.0
Other forms of heart disease	I30-I51	43.2	50.0
Cerebrovascular diseases	I60-I69	38.7	44.1
Chronic lower respiratory diseases	J40-J47	31.9	41.5
Other degenerative diseases of the nervous system	G30-G31	39.2	23.6
Diabetes mellitus	E10-E14	13.5	23.5
Other external causes of accidental injury	W00-X59	21.5	23.5
Organic, including symptomatic, mental disorders	F01-F09	38.0	22.2
Influenza and pneumonia	J09-J18	13.6	18.1

Note: (a) ICD-10 = International Classification of Diseases 10th Revision; (1) Mortality rates are a three year average covering 2005-2007; (2) Figures cover Collin County
Source: Centers for Disease Control and Prevention, National Center for Health Statistics. Compressed Mortality File 1999-2007. CDC WONDER On-line Database, compiled from Compressed Mortality File 1999-2007 Series 20 No. 2M, 2010.

Mortality Rates for Selected Causes of Death

ICD-10[a] Sub-Chapter	ICD-10[a] Code	Age-Adjusted Mortality Rate[1] per 100,000 population	
		County[2]	U.S.
Assault	X85-Y09	1.7	6.0
Human immunodeficiency virus (HIV) disease	B20-B24	1.0	4.0
Hypertensive diseases	I10-I15	10.4	18.0
Intentional self-harm	X60-X84	8.3	11.0
Malnutrition	E40-E46	*1.3	0.8
Obesity and other hyperalimentation	E65-E68	*1.1	1.5
Transport accidents	V01-V99	7.7	15.6
Viral hepatitis	B15-B19	*0.8	2.1

Note: (a) ICD-10 = International Classification of Diseases 10th Revision; (1) Mortality rates are a three year average covering 2005-2007; (2) Figures cover Collin County; (*) Unreliable data as per CDC
Source: Centers for Disease Control and Prevention, National Center for Health Statistics. Compressed Mortality File 1999-2007. CDC WONDER On-line Database, compiled from Compressed Mortality File 1999-2007 Series 20 No. 2M, 2010.

Distribution of Physicians and Dentists

Area[1]	Dentists[2]	D.O.[3]	M.D.[4]				
			Total	Family/ General Practice	Pediatrics	Medical Specialties	Surgical Specialties
Local (number)	415	109	1,427	176	135	562	305
Local (rate[5])	5.7	1.4	18.7	2.3	1.8	7.4	4.0
U.S. (rate[5])	4.5	1.9	18.3	2.5	1.4	6.8	4.1

Note: Data as of 2008 unless noted; (1) Local data covers Collin County; (2) Data as of 2007; (3) Doctor of Osteopathic Medicine; (4) Includes active, non-federal, patient-care, office-based Doctors of Medicine; (5) rate per 10,000 population
Source: Area Resource File (ARF). 2009-2010 Release. U.S. Department of Health and Human Services, Health Resources and Services Administration, Bureau of Health Professions, Rockville, MD, August 2010

Hospitals

Plano has the following hospitals: 2 general medical and surgical; 1 rehabilitation; 2 long-term acute care.
AHA Guide to the Healthcare Field 2010

According to *U.S. News,* the Dallas-Plano-Irving, TX Metropolitan Division is home to four of the best hospitals in the U.S.: **Baylor Institute for Rehabilitation**; **Baylor University Medical Center**; **Parkland Memorial Hospital**; **University of Texas Southwestern Medical Center**. The hospitals listed were highly ranked in at least one adult specialty. *U.S. News Online, "America's Best Hospitals 2010-11"*

According to *U.S. News,* the Dallas-Plano-Irving, TX Metropolitan Division is home to two of the best children's hospitals in the U.S.: **Children's Medical Center Dallas**; **Children's Medical Center-Texas Scottish Rite Hospital for Children**. The hospitals listed were highly ranked in at least one pediatric specialty. *U.S. News Online, "America's Best Children's Hospitals 2010-11"*

EDUCATION

Public School District Statistics

District Name	Schls	Pupils	Pupil/ Teacher Ratio	Minority Pupils[1] (%)	Free Lunch Eligible[2] (%)	IEP[3] (%)
Plano ISD	75	54,203	13.3	49.2	16.2	11.2

Note: Table includes school districts with 2,000 or more students; (1) Percentage of students that are not non-Hispanic white; (2) Percentage of students that are eligible for the free lunch program; (3) Percentage of students that have an Individualized Education Program.
Source: U.S. Department of Education, National Center for Education Statistics, Common Core of Data, Local Education Agency (School District) Universe Survey: School Year 2008-2009; U.S. Department of Education, National Center for Education Statistics, Common Core of Data, Public Elementary/Secondary School Universe Survey: School Year 2008-2009

Top Public High Schools

High School Name	Index[1]	Rank[1]	Subsidized Lunch (%)[2]	E&E (%)[3]
Plano	2.150	614	10.0	45.6
Plano East[4]	1.747	909	26.0	29.1
Plano West	2.640	363	9.0	50.2

Note: (1) Public schools are ranked according to a ratio that is the number of Advanced Placement, International Baccalaureate, and/or Cambridge tests taken by all students at a school in 2009 divided by the number of graduating seniors. All of the schools on the list have an index of at least 1.000; they are in the top six percent of public schools measured this way. The rankings range from 1 to 1,734; (2) Percentage of students receiving federally subsidized meals; (3) E & E stands for equity and excellence percentage: the portion of all graduating seniors at a school that had at least one passing grade on one AP or IB test; (4) Schools that offer International Baccalaureate or Cambridge exams; (5) School is unranked, but has been identified by Newsweek as one of the nation's most elite public high schools.
Source: Newsweek Online, "Top High Schools 2010"

Highest Level of Education

Area	Less than H.S.	H.S. Diploma	Some College, No Deg.	Associate Degree	Bachelors Degree	Masters Degree	Profess. School Degree	Doctorate Degree
City	5.8	12.6	20.5	6.9	35.3	14.6	2.3	1.9
MSA[1]	18.5	23.3	22.2	6.3	20.3	7.0	1.5	0.9
U.S.	15.3	29.0	20.7	7.5	17.4	7.0	1.9	1.1

Note: Figures are 2010 estimated percentages and cover persons age 25 and over; (1) Metropolitan Statistical Area - see Appendix B for areas included
Source: Claritas, Inc.

Educational Attainment by Race

Area	High School Graduate (%)					Bachelor's Degree (%)				
	Total	White	Black	Asian	Hisp.[2]	Total	White	Black	Asian	Hisp.[2]
City	92.3	97.6	98.2	94.9	60.5	52.6	54.9	45.7	76.4	18.6
MSA[1]	81.9	92.7	86.3	88.2	49.9	30.2	38.0	21.2	56.4	9.9
U.S.	84.9	90.0	80.7	85.5	60.7	27.8	30.9	17.5	49.7	12.7

Note: Figures shown cover persons 25 years old and over; (1) Metropolitan Statistical Area - see Appendix B for areas included; (2) people of Hispanic origin can be of any race
Source: U.S. Census Bureau, 2007-2009 American Community Survey 3-Year Estimates

School Enrollment by Grade and Control

Area	Preschool (%)		Kindergarten (%)		Grades 1 - 4 (%)		Grades 5 - 8 (%)		Grades 9 - 12 (%)	
	Public	Private	Public	Private	Public	Private	Public	Private	Public	Private
City	38.5	61.5	88.1	11.9	87.5	12.5	90.2	9.8	91.7	8.3
MSA[1]	50.2	49.8	88.8	11.2	91.4	8.6	92.1	7.9	92.4	7.6
U.S.	54.3	45.7	86.4	13.6	88.9	11.1	89.1	10.9	90.2	9.8

Note: Figures shown cover persons 3 years old and over; (1) Metropolitan Statistical Area - see Appendix B for areas included
Source: U.S. Census Bureau, 2007-2009 American Community Survey 3-Year Estimates

Average Salaries of Public School Classroom Teachers

Area	2009-10		2010-11		Percent Change 2009-10 to 2010-11	Percent Change 2000-01 to 2010-11
	Dollars	Rank[1]	Dollars	Rank[1]		
Texas	48,261	31	48,261	34	0.00	25.8
U.S. Average	55,202	-	56,069	-	1.57	29.3

Note: (1) State rank ranges from 1 to 51 where 1 indicates highest salary.
Source: National Education Association, Rankings & Estimates: Rankings of the States 2010 and Estimates of School Statistics 2011, December 2010

Higher Education

Four-Year Colleges			Two-Year Colleges			Medical Schools[1]	Law Schools[2]	Voc/ Tech[3]
Public	Private Non-profit	Private For-profit	Public	Private Non-profit	Private For-profit			
0	0	0	0	0	0	0	0	0

Note: Figures cover institutions located within the city limits and include main campuses only; (1) includes schools accredited by the Liaison Committee on Medical Education and the American Osteopathic Association; (2) includes American Bar Association-accredited law schools; (3) includes all schools with programs that are less than 2 years.
Source: National Center for Education Statistics, Integrated Postsecondary Education System (IPEDS) Peer Analysis System, 2010-11; U.S. News & World Report, Medical School Directory, 2011; U.S. News & World Report, Law School Directory, 2011

According to *U.S. News & World Report,* the Dallas-Plano-Irving, TX Metropolitan Division is home to two of the top 197 national universities in the U.S.: **Southern Methodist University** (#56); **University of Texas—Dallas** (#143). The rankings are based on quantitative measurements such as peer assessment, retention, faculty resources, student selectivity, financial resources, graduation rate, and alumni giving rate. *U.S. News & World Report, "America's Best Colleges 2011"*

According to *U.S. News & World Report,* the Dallas-Plano-Irving, TX Metropolitan Division is home to one of the top 50 law schools in the U.S.: **Southern Methodist University (Dedman)** (#50). The rankings are based on a weighted average of 10 measures of quality: peer assessment score; assessment score by lawyers/judges; median LSAT scores; median undergrad GPA; acceptance rate; employment rates for graduates; bar passage rate; faculty resources; expenditures per student; student/faculty ratio; and library resources. *U.S. News & World Report, "America's Best Law Schools 2011"*

According to *Forbes,* the Dallas-Plano-Irving, TX Metropolitan Division is home to one of the top 75 business schools in the U.S.: **SMU (Cox)** (#33). The rankings are based on the return on investment that graduates of the Class of 2004 received (median salary five years after graduation). *Forbes, "Best Business Schools," August 5, 2009*

PRESIDENTIAL ELECTION

2008 Presidential Election Results

Area	Obama	McCain	Nader	Other
Collin County	36.7	62.2	0.1	1.1
U.S.	52.9	45.6	0.6	0.9

Note: Results are percentages and may not add to 100% due to rounding
Source: Dave Leip's Atlas of U.S. Presidential Elections, www.uselectionatlas.org

EMPLOYERS

Major Employers

Company Name	Industry	Type of Site
Associates Corp North America	Personal credit institutions	Headquarters
Associates First Capital Corp	Mortgage bankers and correspondents	Headquarters
Baylor University Medical Ctr	General medical and surgical hospitals	Headquarters
Dallas Cnty Commissioners Crt	Executive offices	Branch
Dallas County Sheriffs Dept	Police protection	Branch
Emergency Department	General medical and surgical hospitals	Branch
HP Enterprise Services	Data processing and preparation	Headquarters
JC Penney	Department stores	Headquarters
Lockheed Martin Missiles	Aircraft	Branch
North Texas Hcs	Administration of veterans' affairs	Branch
Odyssey Healthcare	Skilled nursing care facilities	Headquarters
Palm Harbor Homes I	Prefabricated wood buildings	Single
Parkland Health & Hospital Sys	General medical and surgical hospitals	Headquarters
Presbyterian Hospital Dallas	General medical and surgical hospitals	Branch
Romanos Macaroni Grill	Eating places	Single
SFG Management Ltd Lblty Co	Fluid milk	Single
South Central Region	Detective and armored car services	Branch
Southwest Airlines	Air transportation, scheduled	Headquarters
Teaching Assistance Office	Colleges and universities	Branch
Texas Instruments	Semiconductors and related devices	Headquarters
The University of Texas At El	Accident and health insurance	Headquarters
Verizon	Telephone communication, except radio	Branch
Verizon	Business consulting, nec	Branch
Verizon Business	Telephone communication, except radio	Branch

Note: Companies shown are located within the Dallas metropolitan area; nec = not elsewhere classified.
Source: www.zapdata.com, January 2011

PUBLIC SAFETY

Crime Rate

Area	All Crimes	Violent Crimes				Property Crimes		
		Murder	Forcible Rape	Robbery	Aggrav. Assault	Burglary	Larceny -Theft	Motor Vehicle Theft
City	3,100.7	1.5	16.5	52.4	99.7	541.5	2,217.1	172.0
Suburbs[1]	4,295.3	5.7	27.9	186.9	195.8	994.0	2,450.8	434.3
Metro[2]	4,220.1	5.4	27.2	178.4	189.7	965.5	2,436.0	417.8
U.S.	3,465.5	5.0	28.7	133.0	262.8	716.3	2,060.9	258.8

Note: Figures are crimes per 100,000 population; (1) All areas within the metro area that are located outside the city limits; (2) Metropolitan Division - see Appendix B for areas included
Source: FBI Uniform Crime Reports, 2009

Hate Crimes

Area	Number of Quarters Reported	Bias Motivation				
		Race	Religion	Sexual Orientation	Ethnicity	Disability
City	4	2	1	0	0	0

Source: Federal Bureau of Investigation, Hate Crime Statistics 2009

Identity Theft Consumer Complaints

Area	Complaints	Complaints per 100,000 Population	Rank[2]
MSA[1]	6,920	112.6	36
U.S.	250,854	81.3	-

Note: (1) Metropolitan Statistical Area - see Appendix B for areas included; (2) Rank ranges from 1 to 384 where 1 indicates greatest number of complaints per 100,000 population
Source: Federal Trade Commission, Consumer Sentinel Network Data Book for January - December 2010

RECREATION

Culture

Dance[1]	Theatre[1]	Instrumental Music[1]	Vocal Music[1]	Series/ Festivals	Museums	Zoos and Aquariums[2]
0	1	0	0	0	2	0

Note: (1) Number of professional perfoming groups; (2) AZA-accredited
Source: The Grey House Performing Arts Directory, 2011-2012; Official Museum Directory, 2010; American Association of Museums, AAM Member Museums, March 2011; Association of Zoos & Aquariums, AZA Member Zoos & Aquariums, May 2011

Professional Sports Teams

Team Name	League
Dallas Cowboys	National Football League (NFL)
Dallas Mavericks	National Basketball Association (NBA)
Dallas Stars	National Hockey League (NHL)
FC Dallas	Major League Soccer (MLS)
Texas Rangers	Major League Baseball (MLB)

Note: Includes teams located in the Dallas-Fort Worth metro area.
Source: Original research

CLIMATE

Average and Extreme Temperatures

Temperature	Jan	Feb	Mar	Apr	May	Jun	Jul	Aug	Sep	Oct	Nov	Dec	Yr.
Extreme High (°F)	85	90	100	100	101	112	111	109	107	101	91	87	112
Average High (°F)	55	60	68	76	84	92	96	96	89	79	67	58	77
Average Temp. (°F)	45	50	57	66	74	82	86	86	79	68	56	48	67
Average Low (°F)	35	39	47	56	64	72	76	75	68	57	46	38	56
Extreme Low (°F)	-2	9	12	30	39	53	58	58	42	24	16	0	-2

Note: Figures cover the years 1945-1993
Source: National Climatic Data Center, International Station Meteorological Climate Summary, 9/96

Average Precipitation/Snowfall/Humidity

Precip./Humidity	Jan	Feb	Mar	Apr	May	Jun	Jul	Aug	Sep	Oct	Nov	Dec	Yr.
Avg. Precip. (in.)	1.9	2.3	2.6	3.8	4.9	3.4	2.1	2.3	2.9	3.3	2.3	2.1	33.9
Avg. Snowfall (in.)	1	1	Tr	Tr	0	0	0	0	0	Tr	Tr	Tr	3
Avg. Rel. Hum. 6am (%)	78	77	75	77	82	81	77	76	80	79	78	77	78
Avg. Rel. Hum. 3pm (%)	53	51	47	49	51	48	43	41	46	46	48	51	48

Note: Figures cover the years 1945-1993; Tr = Trace amounts (<0.05 in. of rain; <0.5 in. of snow)
Source: National Climatic Data Center, International Station Meteorological Climate Summary, 9/96

Weather Conditions

Temperature			Daytime Sky			Precipitation		
10°F & below	32°F & below	90°F & above	Clear	Partly cloudy	Cloudy	0.01 inch or more precip.	0.1 inch or more snow/ice	Thunder-storms
1	34	102	108	160	97	78	2	49

Note: Figures are average number of days per year and cover the years 1945-1993
Source: National Climatic Data Center, International Station Meteorological Climate Summary, 9/96

HAZARDOUS WASTE

Superfund Sites

Plano has no sites on the EPA's Superfund Final National Priorities List.
U.S. Environmental Protection Agency, Final National Priorities List, April 1, 2011

AIR & WATER QUALITY

Air Quality Index

Area	Percent of Days when Air Quality was...[2]				AQI Statistics	
	Good	Moderate	Unhealthy for Sensitive Groups	Unhealthy	Maximum	Median
Area[1]	80.7	17.7	1.6	0.0	145	40

Note: The Air Quality Index (AQI) is an index for reporting daily air quality. EPA calculates the AQI for five major air pollutants regulated by the Clean Air Act: ground-level ozone, particle pollution (also known as particulate matter), carbon monoxide, sulfur dioxide, and nitrogen dioxide. The AQI runs from 0 to 500. The higher the AQI value, the greater the level of air pollution and the greater the health concern. There are six AQI categories: "Good" The AQI is between 0 and 50. Air quality is considered satisfactory; "Moderate" The AQI is between 51 and 100. Air quality is acceptable; "Unhealthy for Sensitive Groups" When AQI values are between 101 and 150, members of sensitive groups may experience health effects; "Unhealthy" When AQI values are between 151 and 200 everyone may begin to experience health effects; "Very Unhealthy" AQI values between 201 and 300 trigger a health alert; "Hazardous" AQI values over 300 trigger health warnings of emergency conditions; (1) Data covers Collin County; (2) Based on 305 days with AQI data in 2008; The EPA has suspended data updates while it assesses its data systems, including AirData reports and maps.
Source: U.S. Environmental Protection Agency, AirData Report, 2008

Air Quality Index Pollutants

Area	Percent of Days when AQI Pollutant was...[2]					
	Carbon Monoxide	Nitrogen Dioxide	Ozone	Sulfur Dioxide	Particulate Matter 2.5	Particulate Matter 10
Area[1]	0.0	0.0	100.0	0.0	0.0	0.0

Note: The Air Quality Index (AQI) is an index for reporting daily air quality. EPA calculates the AQI for five major air pollutants regulated by the Clean Air Act: ground-level ozone, particle pollution (also known as particulate matter), carbon monoxide, sulfur dioxide, and nitrogen dioxide. The AQI runs from 0 to 500. The higher the AQI value, the greater the level of air pollution and the greater the health concern; (1) Data covers Collin County; (2) Based on 305 days with AQI data in 2008; The EPA has suspended data updates while it assesses its data systems, including AirData reports and maps.
Source: U.S. Environmental Protection Agency, AirData Report, 2008

Air Quality Index Trends

Area	Trend Sites (days)								All Sites (days)
	2002	2003	2004	2005	2006	2007	2008	2009	2009
MSA[1]	40	40	32	56	39	16	20	19	33

Note: Figures are the number of days the AQI value exceeded 100 in a given year. An AQI value greater than 100 indicates that air quality would have been in the unhealthful range on that day. Data from exceptional events are included. These counts are presented in two ways. First, the counts are based on sites having an adequate record of monitoring data during the trend period (trend sites). These counts represent the relative change in the number of days with AQI values greater than 100. In the last column, the counts are based on all sites with data in the most recent year (because it is possible for a site to have data in the most recent year but not enough data to be a trend site); (1) Data covers the Dallas-Fort Worth-Arlington, TX Metropolitan Statistical Area - see Appendix B for areas included
Source: U.S. Environmental Protection Agency, Office of Air and Radiation, Air Quality Index Information, "Number of Days with Air Quality Index Values Greater than 100 and Trend Sites, 1990-2009, and at All Sites in 2009"

Maximum Air Pollutant Concentrations

	Particulate Matter 10 (ug/m^3)	Particulate Matter 2.5 (ug/m^3)	Ozone (ppm)	Carbon Monoxide (ppm)	Sulfur Dioxide (ppm)	Nitrogen Dioxide (ppm)	Lead (ug/m^3)
MSA[1] Level	43	38	0.091	2	0.004	0.012	0.65
NAAQS[2]	150	35	0.075	9	0.140	0.053	0.15
Met NAAQS[2]	Yes	No	No	Yes	Yes	Yes	No

Note: Data from exceptional events are not included; (1) Data covers the Dallas-Fort Worth-Arlington, TX Metropolitan Statistical Area - see Appendix B for areas included; (2) National Ambient Air Quality Standards; n/a not available; (a) Localized impact from an industrial source in Dallas. Concentration from highest nonpoint source site is 0.14 ug/m^3 in Collin County
Concentrations: Particulate Matter 10 (coarse particulate) - highest second maximum 24-hour concentration; Particulate Matter 2.5 (fine particulate) - highest 98th percentile 24-hour concentration; Ozone - highest fourth daily maximum 8-hour concentration; Carbon Monoxide - highest second maximum non-overlapping 8-hour concentration; Sulfur Dioxide - highest second maximum 24-hour concentration; Nitrogen Dioxide - highest arithmetic mean concentration; Lead - maximum running 3-month average
Units: ppm = parts per million; ug/m^3 = micrograms per cubic meter
Source: U.S. Environmental Protection Agency, CBSA Factbook 2009, Air Quality Statistics by City, 2009

Drinking Water

Water System Name	Pop. Served	Primary Water Source Type	Violations[1] Health Based	Violations[1] Monitoring/ Reporting
City of Plano	260,000	Purchased Surface	1	1

Note: (1) Based on violation data from January 1, 2010 to December 31, 2010 (includes unresolved violations from earlier years)
Source: U.S. Environmental Protection Agency, Office of Ground Water and Drinking Water, Safe Drinking Water Information System (based on data extracted May 9, 2011)

Saint Petersburg, Florida

Background

St. Petersburg, located in Pinellas County in western Florida, is the state's fourth-largest city, offering Gulf beaches, a vibrant economy, major league baseball, and a host of year-round recreational resources.

The city is also a regional economic power with a thriving business environment built on retailing, high-tech manufacturing, finance, and insurance. Major employers in the area include the Pinellas County School District and Pinellas County Government, the City of St. Petersburg, the Home Shopping Network, and the Sony Ericsson WTA Tour, previously known as the Women's Tennis Association, world headquarters is consolidated in the city.

During the age of exploration in the sixteenth-century, St. Petersburg was visited by a distinguished group of Spanish adventurers and colonialists, including Juan Ponce de Leon in 1521, who thought the mythical Fountain of Youth might be nearby.

Actual European settlements, however, were not established until much later. In 1843, Antonio Maximo set up a fishing village at what is now called Maximo Point. Rancher James Hay built the first house within what in not the city limits in 1856. Settlement accelerated rapidly after this time, and even more so after 1881, when Hamilton Disston sparked St. Pete's first real-estate explosion by purchasing four million acres of land from the state of Florida. Disston built the first hotel and went to great lengths to popularize the town up and down the eastern seaboard. The railroad magnate Peter Demens, born Piotr Alexeitch Dementieff in St. Petersburg, Russia, who gave the city its present name, did the same.

Tourist excursions began in 1890, when the Orange Belt Railroad opened a link to St. Petersburg, carrying great stores of mackerel and snapper to eastern cities. By the end of the century, millions of pounds of fish were being shipped annually. Since 1914, when the city was chosen by the St. Louis Browns as a spring training site, St. Petersburg strengthened its position as a major U.S. sports capital. It is home to the Tampa Bay Devil Rays baseball team, the Tampa Bay Buccaneers, the Tampa Bay Lightning, and the Tampa Bay Storm.

Tropicana Field initially opened in 1990 as Florida Suncoast Dome, becoming the ThunderDome in 1993, and Tropicana Field in 1996, when it was extensively renovated. The home of the Tampa Bay Devil Rays, it recalls several aspects of Brooklyn's 1913 Ebbets Field, including Ebbet's asymmetrical outfield dimensions, and a rotunda entrance built directly from Ebbets Field blueprints. The park is distinctive in other ways as well, being the first Major League Baseball stadium to install the synthetic grass FieldTurf, and the first and only to host a Cuesta-Rey Cigar Bar.

The city has also hosted the X-Games, and is the site of the annual St. Anthony's Triathlon, attended by athletes from all over the world.

Other sporting opportunities are available at 40 local golf courses, at marinas where deep-sea fishing trips originate daily, and at horse and greyhound tracks. The city parks are spread over 2,400 acres, including the seven-mile preserved downtown waterfront, and St. Petersburg boasts the longest urban hiking/biking trail in the Eastern U.S., at 47 miles.

Cultural life is vibrant in the area, with the Florida International Museum a premier venue for world-class exhibitions, and the Salvador Dali Museum featuring the world's largest collection of the artist's works. The Museum of Fine Arts offers many works by Cezanne, Monet, Gauguin, Renoir, Rodin, George Wesley Bellows, and Georgia O'Keeffe.

Great Explorations, which has been called by the *Miami Herald* the most "user-friendly museum of its kind in the country," offers ever-changing arts and science exhibits for children. The museum is located next to Sunken Gardens, home to some of the oldest tropical plants in the region, and a stretch of fine dining on newly developed 4th Street, which includes many nationally recognized restaurants as well as numerous local specialties. At the St. Petersburg Museum of History, one can see a splendid exhibit that explains the beginnings of commercial aviation, which began in this city in 1914. Finally, the Florida Holocaust Museum presents important exhibits from around the world.

The weather is subtropical, with only four days a year on average without sunshine. Daytime temperatures are quite pleasant and mild.

Rankings

General Rankings

- Tampa was ranked #220 out of 375 metro areas in *Cities Ranked & Rated*. Criteria: cost of living; climate; crime; transportation; economy and jobs; education; arts and culture; health and healthcare; leisure; quality of life. *Cities Ranked & Rated, 2nd Edition, 2007*

- Tampa was ranked #68 out of 379 metro areas in *Places Rated Almanac*. Criteria: health care; education; recreation; transportation; ambience; climate; crime; housing costs; jobs. *Places Rated Almanac, 7th Edition, 2007*

- The Tampa metro area was identified as one of the 10 most popular big cities by Pew Research Center. The results are based on a telephone survey of 2,260 adults conducted during October 2008. The report explored a range of attitudes related to where Americans live, where they would like to live, and why. *Pew Research Center, "For Nearly Half of America, Grass is Greener Somewhere Else," January 29, 2009*

- *Men's Health Living* ranked 100 U.S. cities in terms of quality of life. Saint Petersburg was ranked #66 and received a grade of C-. Criteria: number of fitness facilities; air quality; number of physicians; male/female ratio; education levels; household income; cost of living. *Men's Health Living, Spring 2008*

Business/Finance Rankings

- Tampa was identified as one of the 20 weakest-performing metro areas during the recession and recovery from December 2007 through December 2010. Criteria: percent change in employment; percentage point change in unemployment rate; percent change in gross metropolitan product; percent change in House Price Index. *Brookings Institution, MetroMonitor: Tracking Economic Recession and Recovery in America's 100 Largest Metropolitan Areas, March 2011*

- Experian ranked the top 20 major U.S metropolitan areas by average debt per consumer. The Tampa metro area was ranked #8. Criteria: average debt per consumer. Debt for this study includes credit cards, auto loans and personal loans. It does not include mortgages. *Experian, May 13, 2010*

- A.G. Edwards ranked America's 500 top-performing communities based on their residents' personal savings and investing behavior. The Tampa metro area ranked #383 with an index score of 97.38 (national average = 100.00). A dozen statistical factors were measured including: participation in retirement savings plans; personal debt levels; and home ownership. *A.G. Edwards, "2007 Nest Egg Index," September 12, 2007*

- *American City Business Journals* ranked America's 261 largest cities in terms of their resident's wealth. Saint Petersburg ranked #150. Criteria: per capita income; median household income; percentage of households with annual incomes of $200,000 or more; median home value. *American City Business Journals, www.bizjournals.com, "Where the Money Is: America's Wealth Centers," August 18, 2008*

- The Tampa metro area appeared on the Milken Institute "2010 Best Performing Metros" list. Rank: #155 out of 200 large metro areas. Criteria: job growth; wage and salary growth; high-tech output growth. *Milken Institute, "2010 Best Performing Metros"*

- Tampa was ranked #98 out of 145 regions worldwide in terms of its "Knowledge Competitiveness Index." The index attempts to measure the knowledge-based development taking place throughout the world and is based on 19 measures of economic performance that indicate a region's ability to translate its knowledge capacity into economic value. *Centre for International Competitiveness, World Knowledge Competitiveness Index 2008*

- *Forbes* ranked the 200 most populous metro areas in the U.S. in terms of the "Best Places for Business and Careers." The Tampa metro area was ranked #104. Criteria: 12 metrics including costs (business and living), job growth (past and projected), income growth, educational attainment, projected economic growth, crime, cultural and recreational opportunities, net migration patterns, percentage of subprime mortgages handed out over a three-year period, and the number of highly ranked four-year colleges. *Forbes, "Best Places for Business and Careers," April 14, 2010*

Children/Family Rankings

- The Tampa metro area was selected as one of the "Best Cities for Relocating Families" by Worldwide ERC and Primacy Relocation. The 2008 study looked at nearly 50 factors important to relocating families including: recent job growth; nearby top-ranked colleges; in-state tuition for four-year public colleges; population growth since 2000; pediatricians per 100,000 population; and a Green Living index. *Worldwide ERC and Primacy Relocation, "2008 Best Cities for Relocating Families"*

- Saint Petersburg was chosen as one of America's "100 Best Communities for Young People." The winners were selected based upon detailed information provided about each community's efforts to fulfill five essential promises critical to the well-being of young people: caring adults who are actively involved in their lives; safe places in which to learn and grow; a healthy start toward adulthood; an effective education that builds marketable skills; and opportunities to help others. *America's Promise Alliance, "100 Best Communities for Young People, 2010"*

Culture/Performing Arts Rankings

- Saint Petersburg was selected as one of "America's Top 25 Arts Destinations." The city ranked #1 in the mid-sized city (population 100,000 to 499,999) category. Criteria: readers' top choices for arts travel destinations based on the richness and variety of visual arts sites, activities and events. *American Style, "America's Top 25 Arts Destinations," May 2010*

Dating/Romance Rankings

- Saint Petersburg appeared on *Men's Health's* list of the most sex-happy cities in America. The city ranked #95 of 100. Criteria: condom sales; birth rates; sex toy sales; rates of chlamydia, gonorrhea, and syphilis. *Men's Health, "America's Most Sex-Happy Cities," October 2010*

- *Men's Health* ranked 100 U.S. cities in terms of best (and worst) marriages. Saint Petersburg was ranked #33 (#1 = worst marriages). Criteria: rate of failed marriages; stringency of divorce laws; percentage of population who've split; number of licensed marriage and family therapists. *Men's Health, "Splitsville, USA," May 2010*

- Eli Lily and Company, in partnership with Sperling's BestPlaces, ranked the nation's 50 largest metro areas in terms of the "Most Romantic Cities for Baby Boomers." The Tampa metro area ranked #44. Criteria: marriage and divorce rates among "baby boomers" age 45 to 60; great restaurants; dance studios; chocolate, jewelry and flower sales. *Eli Lily and Company, "Most Romantic Cities for Baby Boomers," April 20, 2007*

- The Tampa metro area was selected as one of the "Best Cities for Relocating Singles" by Worldwide ERC and Primacy Relocation. The area ranked #11 out of the 100 largest metro areas in the U.S. Areas were selected based on the following criteria: recent job growth; recent singles population growth; overall population growth; affordable rental housing; cost-of-living index; expanded arts and recreation opportunities; ratio of single men and single women; affordability of quality higher education (including state residency requirements); diversity index; climate; population density. *Worldwide ERC and Primacy Relocation, "2008 Best Cities for Relocating Singles"*

- *Forbes* ranked the 40 most populous urbanized areas in the U.S. in terms of the "Best Cities for Singles." The Tampa metro area ranked #33. Criteria: number of singles; cost of living alone; nightlife; culture; job growth; coolness; and online dating participation. *Forbes.com, "Best Cities for Singles," July 27, 2009*

Education Rankings

- Tampa was identified as one of the 100 "smartest" metro areas in the U.S. The area ranked #64. Criteria: the editors rated the collective brainpower of the 100 largest metro area in the U.S based on their residents' educational attainment. *American City Business Journals, www.bizjournals.com, April 14, 2008*

- Tampa was identified as one of "America's Brainiest Bastions" by *Portfolio.com*. The metro area ranked #134 out of 200. Portfolio.com analyzed levels of educational attainment in the nation's 200 largest metropolitan areas. The editors established scores for five levels of educational attainment, based on relative earning power of adult workers age 25 or older. Scores were determined by comparing the median income for all workers with the median income for those workers at a specified educational level. *Portfolio.com, "America's Brainiest Bastions," December 1, 2010*

Environmental Rankings

- Saint Petersburg was selected as one of 22 "Smarter Cities" for energy by the Natural Resources Defense Council." Criteria: investment in green power; energy efficiency measures; conservation. *Natural Resources Defense Council, "2010 Smarter Cities," July 19, 2010*

- *American City Business Journal* ranked 43 metropolitan areas in terms of their "greenness." The Tampa metro area ranked #41. Criteria: Forty-one metros in which *ACBJ* has business weeklies, plus Indianapolis and Cleveland, were ranked based on 20 different indicators such as adoption of green technologies, utilization of environmentally sound practices, and air and water quality. *American City Business Journals, "Green City Index," March 11, 2010*

- The Tampa metro area was selected as one of "America's Cleanest Cities" by *Forbes*. The metro area ranked #8 out of 10. Criteria: air quality; water quality; per capita spending on Superfund site cleanup and solid-waste management. *Forbes.com, "America's Cleanest Cities," March 11, 2008*

- 100 of the largest metro areas in the U.S. were analyzed in terms of their current drought severity. The Tampa metro area ranked #16 (#1 = driest). The rankings were based on statistics such as long-term precipitation trends and patterns and the Palmer drought indices. *Sperling's BestPlaces, www.BestPlaces.net, "America's Drought-Riskiest Cities," November 2007*

- The Tampa metro area appeared in *Country Home's* "Best Green Places" report. The area ranked #176 out of 379. Criteria: official energy policies; green power; green buildings; availability of fresh, locally grown food. *Country Home, "Best Green Places," 2008*

Health/Fitness Rankings

- Tampa was identified as a "2011 Asthma Capital." The area ranked #86 out of the nation's 100 largest metropolitan areas. Twelve factors were used to identify the most challenging places to live for people with asthma: estimated prevalence; self-reported prevalence; crude death rate for asthma; annual pollen score; annual air quality; public smoking laws; number of board-certified asthma specialists; school inhaler access laws; rescue medication use; controller medication use; uninsured rate; poverty rate. *Asthma and Allergy Foundation of America, "2011 Asthma Capitals"*

- Tampa was identified as a 2009 "Spring Allergy Capital." The area ranked #66 out of 100. Three groups of factors were used to identify the most severe cities for people with allergies during the spring season: annual pollen levels; medicine utilization; access to board-certified allergists. *Asthma and Allergy Foundation of America, "Spring Allergy Capitals 2009"*

- Tampa was identified as a 2010 "Fall Allergy Capital." The area ranked #73 out of 100. Three groups of factors were used to identify the most severe cities for people with allergies during the fall season: annual pollen levels; medicine utilization; access to board-certified allergists. *Asthma and Allergy Foundation of America, "Fall Allergy Capitals 2010"*

- *Men's Health* examined 100 U.S. cities and selected the best and worst cities for men. Saint Petersburg was ranked among the ten worst at #6. Criteria: dozens of statistical parameters of long life in the categories of health, quality of life, and fitness. *Men's Health, "The 10 Best and Worst Cities for Men 2011," January/February 2011*

- *Men's Health* examined 100 U.S. cities and selected the best and worst cities for women. Saint Petersburg was ranked among the ten worst at #8. Criteria: dozens of statistical parameters of long life in the categories of health, quality of life, and fitness. *Men's Health, "The 10 Best and Worst Cities for Women 2011," January/February 2011*

- *Men's Health* ranked 100 U.S. cities in terms of the quality of their tap water. Saint Petersburg was ranked #8 and received a grade of A. Criteria: levels of total coliform bacteria, arsenic, lead, total trihalomethanes (linked to cancer), and halo-acetic acids; number of EPA water-system violations from 1995 to 2005. *Men's Health, March 2007*

- Saint Petersburg was selected as one of the most accident-prone cities in America by *Men's Health*. The city ranked #6 of 10. Criteria: workplace accident rates; traffic fatalities; emergency room visits; accidental poisonings; incidents of drowning; fires; injury-producing falls. *Men's Health, "Ranking America's Cities: Accident City, USA," October 2009*

- Ortho-McNeil Neurologics, in partnership with Sperling's BestPlaces, analyzed 110 metro areas and identified those U.S. cities with the highest prevalence of factors that are most commonly associated with migraine headaches. The Tampa metro area ranked #52. Criteria: number of migraine-related drug prescriptions per capita; lifestyle factors that can contribute to migraines; environmental factors that can trigger migraines; and consumption of migraine-triggering foods. *Ortho-McNeil Neurologics, "America's Migraine Hot Spots," March 14, 2006*

- An analysis of the "Best & Worst Cities for Sleep" was conducted by Sperling's BestPlaces. The study ranked America's 50 most populated metro areas. The Tampa metro area ranked #30 (#1 = best city for sleep). Criteria: number of days residents didn't get enough rest or sleep during the past month; average length of daily commute; divorce rate; unemployment rate. *Sperling's BestPlaces, www.BestPlaces.net, "Best & Worst Cities for Sleep," 2006*

- *Men's Health* ranked 100 U.S. cities in terms of cities "Where the Food is Sickening." Saint Petersburg was ranked #11 and received a grade of B+. The magazine arrived at their ratings by looking at data compiled by the Community Health Status Indicator Project to determine outbreaks of E. coli, salmonella-, and shigella-related infections. They then checked the CDC's Wonder database to see how many people died from tainted food. Finally, the magazine found out which states have adopted the current version of the FDA's uniform Food Code, which contains the most up-to-date rules for keeping restaurant kitchens clean. *Men's Health, October 2005*

- The American Academy of Dermatology ranked 26 U.S. metropolitan regions in terms of their residents knowledge, attitude and behaviors towards tanning, sun protection and skin cancer detection. The Tampa metro area ranked #4. The results of the study are based on an online survey of over 7,000 adults nationwide. *American Academy of Dermatology, "Suntelligence: How Sun Smart is Your City," May 3, 2010*

- Scarborough Research, a leading market research firm, identified the top local markets for diabetes medication purchasers. The Tampa DMA (Designated Market Area) ranked in the top 13 with 10% of consumers reporting that they purchased medication for diabetes within the past 12 months. *Scarborough Research, March 19, 2007*

- The Tampa metro area appeared in the 2010 Gallup-Healthways Well-Being Index. The index, based on interviews with more than 353,000 Americans during 2009, asked individuals to assess their jobs, finances, physical health, emotional state of mind and communities. The metro area ranked #132 out of 162. Criteria: life evaluation; emotional health; work environment; physical health; healthy behaviors; basic access (basic needs optimal for a healthy life, such as access to food and medicine, having health insurance and feeling safe while walking at night). *Gallup-Healthways, "Well-Being Index 2010"*

- The Tampa metro area was identified as one of "America's Most Stressful Cities" by *Forbes*. The metro area ranked #17. Criteria: median home price drop; unemployment rates; cost of living; air quality; sunny days; population density. *Forbes.com, "America's Most Stressful Cities," August 20, 2009*

- The Tampa metro area was identified as one of "America's 20 Most Sedentary Cities" by *Forbes*. The metro area ranked #12. Criteria: percentage of overweight or obese people; percentage of people who had not engaged in any physical activity in the past 30 days; average number of hours of TV watched per week. *Forbes.com, "America's Most Sedentary Cities," October 29, 2007*

- 50 of the largest metro areas in the U.S. were analyzed in terms of their health and fitness by the American College of Sports Medicine in their "American Fitness Index." The Tampa metro area ranked #30 (#1 = healthiest). Criteria: preventative health behaviors; levels of chronic disease; health care access; community resources and policies that support physical activity. *American College of Sports Medicine, "Health and Community Fitness Status of the 50 Largest Metropolitan Areas," May 24, 2010*

- *The Daily Beast* identified the 30 U.S metro areas with the worst smoking habits. The Tampa metro area ranked #19. Sixty urban centers with populations of more than one million were ranked based on the following criteria: number of smokers; number of cigarettes smoked per day; fewest attempts to quit. *The Daily Beast, "30 Cities With Smoking Problems," January 3, 2011*

Real Estate Rankings

- *Fortune* ranked the 100 largest metro areas in the U.S. in terms of projected median home price change in 2010. The Tampa metro area ranked #94. *Fortune, "The 2010 Housing Outlook," December 9, 2009*

- Saint Petersburg appeared on ApartmentRatings.com "Top Cities for Renters" list in 2009." The area ranked #69. Overall satisfaction ratings were ranked using thousands of user submitted scores for hundreds of apartment complexes located in the 100 most populated U.S. municipalities. *ApartmentRatings.com, "2009 Renter Satisfaction Rankings"*

- The Tampa metro area was identified as one of "America's 25 Weakest Housing Markets" by *Forbes*. The metro area ranked #14. Criteria: metro areas with populations over 500,000 were ranked based on projected home values through 2011. *Forbes.com, "America's 25 Weakest Housing Markets," January 7, 2009*

- The nation's largest metro areas were analyzed in terms of the percentage of households entering some stage of foreclosure in 2010. The Tampa metro area ranked #17 out of 206 (#1 = highest foreclosure rate). *RealtyTrac, 2010 Year-End Metropolitan Foreclosure Market Report, January 27, 2011*

- The Tampa metro area appeared in a *Wall Street Journal* article ranking cities by "housing stress." The metro area was ranked #7 (#1 = most stress). Criteria: fraction of mortgage-holding homeowners with a monthly housing payment in excess of 30 percent of income; percentage of people without health insurance; unemployment rate. *The Wall Street Journal, "Which Cities Face Biggest Housing Risk," October 5, 2010*

- The Center for Housing Policy ranked 210 U.S metropolitan areas by the fair market rent for a two-bedroom unit. The Tampa metro area was ranked #63. (#1 = most expensive) with a rent of $959. Criteria: Fair Market Rent (FMR) in effect during the fourth quarter of 2009 based on HUD's fiscal year 2010 FMRs. *The Center for Housing Policy, "Paycheck to Paycheck: Most to Least Expensive Rental Markets in 2009"*

- The Tampa metro area was identified as one of the markets with the worst expected performance in home prices over the next 12 months. *Local Market Monitor, "First Quarter Home Price Forecast for Largest US Markets," March 2, 2011*

Safety Rankings

- Allstate ranked the 200 largest cities in America in terms of driver safety. Saint Petersburg ranked #80. In addition, drivers were 2.6% more likely to have had an accident compared to the national average. Allstate researchers analyzed internal property damage reported claims over a two-year period (from January 2007 to December 2008) to ensure the findings would not be affected by external influences such as weather or road construction. A weighted average of the two-year numbers determined the annual percentages. The report defines an auto crash as any collision resulting in a property damage claim. *Allstate, "The 2010 Allstate America's Best Drivers Report™"*

- Sperling's BestPlaces analyzed the tracks of tropical storms for the past 100 years and ranked which areas are most likely to be hit by a major hurricane. The Tampa metro area ranked #4 out of 10. *Sperling's BestPlaces, www.bestplaces.net, February 2, 2006*

- The National Insurance Crime Bureau ranked 366 metro areas in the U.S. in terms of per capita rates of vehicle theft. The Tampa metro area ranked #87 (#1 = highest rate). Criteria: number of vehicle theft offenses per 100,000 inhabitants. *National Insurance Crime Bureau, "Hot Spots," May 17, 2010*

- The Tampa metro area was identified as one of the "The Most Dangerous Metro Areas for Pedestrians" by Transportation for America and the Surface Transportation Policy Partnership. The metro area ranked #2 out of 52 metro areas with over 1 million residents. Criteria: area's population divided by the number of pedestrian fatalities in that area. *Transportation for America and the Surface Transportation Policy Partnership, "Dangerous by Design: Solving the Epidemic of Preventable Pedestrian Deaths (and Making Great Neighborhoods)," November 11, 2009*

Seniors/Retirement Rankings

- Saint Petersburg was identified as one of "The Top 100 Places to Retire" by *Topretirements.com* The list reflects the 100 cities (out of 625+ total cities reviewed) that visitors to the website are most interested in for retirement. *Topretirements.com, "2011 Best Places to Retire List: The Sunbelt Rules"*

- Saint Petersburg was selected as one of the best places to retire by *Money*. The city was ranked #7 out of 25. Criteria: notable lifelong-learning programs; low taxes; affordable housing; high-quality health care; rich intellectual environment. *CNNMoney, "Best Places to Retire 2010"*

Sports/Recreation Rankings

- Saint Petersburg appeared on the *Sporting News* list of the "Best Sports Cities" for 2010. The area ranked #27 out of 402 cities in the U.S. *Sporting News* takes a 12-month snapshot, roughly October to October, of each city's sports, putting a heavy premium on regular-season won-lost records (from the most recently completed season). Other criteria include: playoff berths, bowl appearances and tournament bids; championships; applicable power ratings; quality of competition; overall fan fervor as measured in part by attendance as percentage of venue capacity; abundance of teams (rewarding quality over quantity); stadium and arena quality; ticket availability and prices; franchise ownership; and marquee appeal of athletes. *Sporting News, "Best Sports Cities 2010," October, 2010*

- Saint Petersburg was selected as one of the five best boat cities to live in (in the U.S.). The city ranked #4. Criteria: climate; scenery; fishing; boat communities with water access. *Best Boat Ne.ws, "The 5 Best Boat Cities to Live In (in the U.S.)," April 16, 2010*

- Saint Petersburg was chosen as a bicycle friendly community by the League of American Bicyclists. A Bicycle Friendly Community welcomes cyclists by providing safe accommodation for cycling and encouraging people to bike for transportation and recreation. There are four award levels: Platinum; Gold; Silver; and Bronze. The community achieved an award level of Bronze. *League of American Bicyclists, "Bicycle Friendly Community Master List," September 2010*

- Saint Petersburg was chosen as one of America's 10 best places to live and boat. Criteria: boating opportunities; boat-friendly regulations; water access; availability of waterfront homes; health of the local economy; and overall lifestyle for boaters. *Boating Magazine, "10 Best Places to Live and Boat," June 2010*

- Saint Petersburg was selected as one of the most playful cities in the U.S. by KaBOOM! The organization's Playful City USA initiative is a national recognition program that honors cities and towns across the nation for a vision, plan and commitment to creating an agenda for play. Cities were recognized based on a pledge to five specific commitments to play: creating a local play commission or task force; designing an annual action plan for play; conducting a play space audit; outlining a financial investment in play for the current fiscal year; and proclaiming and celebrating an annual "play day." *KaBOOM! National Campaign for Play, "2010 Playful City USA Communities"*

- *Golf Digest* ranked 330 metro areas in the U.S. in terms of golf. The Tampa metro area was ranked #148. Criteria: access to golf; weather; value of golf; and quality of golf. *Golf Digest, "Metro Golf Rankings," August 2005*

Transportation Rankings

- The Tampa metro area appeared on *Forbes* list of the best and worst cities for commuters. The metro area ranked #60 out of 60 (#1 is best). Criteria: travel time; road congestion; travel delays. *Forbes.com, "Best and Worst Cities for Commuters," February 16, 2010*

Women/Minorities Rankings

- Tampa was ranked #71 out of 100 metro areas in *SELF Magazine's* ranking of America's healthiest places for women." A panel of experts came up with more than 50 criteria including death and disease rates, environmental indicators, community resources, and lifestyle habits. *SELF Magazine, "Secrets of America's Healthiest Women," December 2008*

Miscellaneous Rankings

- Energizer Holdings, the makers of Edge® shave gel, in partnership with Sperling's BestPlaces, ranked 50 major metro areas in terms of everyday irritations. The Tampa metro area ranked #7. Criteria: humidity levels; weather conditions; incidence of traffic delays and congestion; average commute times; frequency of flight delays and cancellations; rates of sleeplessness; underemployment; pollens and allergens; pests; comedy clubs per capita. *Energizer Holdings, "Most Irritation Prone Cities," July 23, 2010*

- Mars Chocolate North America, the makers of COMBOS®, in partnership with Sperling's BestPlaces, ranked 50 major metro areas in terms of their "manliness." The Tampa metro area ranked #44. Criteria: number of home improvement stores, steak houses, pickup trucks, motorcycles, and manly occupations (fire fighters, police officers, construction workers, EMP personnel) per capita; salty snack sales; sports TV viewing habits. *Mars Chocolate North America, "America's Manliest Cities," June 22, 2010*

- Saint Petersburg was selected as one of America's "10 Meanest Cities" by the National Coalition for the Homeless and The National Law Center on Homelessness & Poverty. The city was ranked #2. Criteria: the number of anti-homeless laws; the enforcement of those laws and severity of penalties; the general political climate towards homeless people; local advocate support for the meanest designation; the city's history of criminalization measures; and the existence of pending or recently enacted criminalization legislation in the city. *National Coalition for the Homeless and The National Law Center on Homelessness & Poverty, "Homes Not Handcuffs: The Criminalization of Homelessness in U.S. Cities," July 2009*

- The Tampa metro area appeared on *Forbes* list of "America's Drunkest Cities." The area ranked #24. Criteria: 35 of the largest continental U.S. metro areas were chosen based on availability of data and geographic diversity. Each metro was ranked in five areas: state laws; drinkers; heavy drinkers; binge drinkers; and alcoholism. *Forbes.com, "America's Drunkest Cities," August 22, 2006*

- Scarborough Research, a leading market research firm, identified the top local markets for frequent sit-down restaurant patronage. The Tampa DMA (Designated Market Area) ranked in the top 10 with consumers reporting an average of 4.1 visits within the past 30 days. *Scarborough Research, May 31, 2006*

Business Environment

CITY FINANCES

City Government Finances

Component	2008 ($000)	2008 ($ per capita)
Total Revenues	578,278	2,347
Total Expenditures	488,067	1,981
Debt Outstanding	555,113	2,253
Cash and Securities[1]	1,337,231	5,427

Note: (1) Cash and security holdings of a government at the close of its fiscal year, including those of its dependent agencies, utilities, and liquor stores.
Source: U.S Census Bureau, State & Local Government Finances 2008

City Government Revenue by Source

Source	2008 ($000)	2008 ($ per capita)
General Revenue		
From Federal Government	13,548	55
From State Government	33,183	135
From Local Governments	45,673	185
Taxes		
Property	104,355	424
Sales and Gross Receipts	55,883	227
Personal Income	0	0
Corporate Income	0	0
Motor Vehicle License	0	0
Other Taxes	9,727	39
Current Charges	117,181	476
Liquor Store	0	0
Utility	41,822	170
Employee Retirement	101,395	411

Source: U.S Census Bureau, State & Local Government Finances 2008

City Government Expenditures by Function

Function	2008 ($000)	2008 ($ per capita)	2008 (%)
General Direct Expenditures			
Air Transportation	1,215	5	0.2
Corrections	0	0	0.0
Education	0	0	0.0
Employment Security Administration	0	0	0.0
Financial Administration	15,217	62	3.1
Fire Protection	33,723	137	6.9
General Public Buildings	2,015	8	0.4
Governmental Administration, Other	1,566	6	0.3
Health	10,714	43	2.2
Highways	27,386	111	5.6
Hospitals	0	0	0.0
Housing and Community Development	7,092	29	1.5
Interest on General Debt	3,994	16	0.8
Judicial and Legal	2,999	12	0.6
Libraries	6,649	27	1.4
Parking	4,185	17	0.9
Parks and Recreation	66,192	269	13.6
Police Protection	84,552	343	17.3
Public Welfare	0	0	0.0
Sewerage	51,190	208	10.5
Solid Waste Management	36,543	148	7.5
Veterans' Services	0	0	0.0
Liquor Store	0	0	0.0
Utility	51,871	211	10.6
Employee Retirement	39,313	160	8.1

Source: U.S Census Bureau, State & Local Government Finances 2008

Municipal Bond Ratings

Area	Moody's	S&P	Fitch
City	A1	(1)	n/a

Rating Systems (shown in declining order of credit quality): Moody's– Aaa, Aa, A, Baa, Ba, B, Caa, Ca, C (numerical modifiers 1, 2, and 3 are added to letter-rating); S&P– AAA, AA, A, BBB, BB, B, CCC, CC, C; Fitch– AAA, AA, A, BBB, BB, B, CCC, CC, C. Ratings may be modified by the addition of a plus or minus sign to show relative standing within the major rating categories.
Notes: n/a Not available; (1) Not reviewed; (2) Issuer Rating/No General Obligation; (3) Standard and Poor's Issue Credit Rating (ICR) is a current opinion of an obliger with respect to a specific financial obligation, a specific class of financial obligations, or a specific financial program.
Source: U.S. Census Bureau, 2011 Statistical Abstract, Bond Ratings for City Governments by Largest Cities: 2009

DEMOGRAPHICS

Population Growth

Area	1990 Census	2000 Census	2010 Estimate	2015 Projection	Population Growth (%) 2000-2010	Population Growth (%) 2010-2015
City	238,846	248,232	249,120	250,370	0.4	0.5
MSA[1]	2,067,959	2,395,997	2,782,113	2,979,241	16.1	7.1
U.S.	248,709,873	281,421,906	309,038,974	321,675,005	9.8	4.1

Note: (1) Metropolitan Statistical Area - see Appendix B for areas included
Source: Claritas, Inc.

Number of Households and Average Household Size

Area	2010 Estimate	2010 Average Household Size
City	108,643	2.23
MSA[1]	1,156,562	2.36
U.S.	116,136,617	2.59

Note: (1) Metropolitan Statistical Area - see Appendix B for areas included
Source: Claritas, Inc.

Race and Ethnicity

Area	White Alone[2] (%)	Black Alone[2] (%)	Asian Alone[2] (%)	Other Race Alone[2] (%)	Hispanic[3] (%)
City	66.8	24.6	3.5	5.1	6.3
MSA[1]	78.9	11.5	2.6	7.0	15.2
U.S.	72.3	12.4	4.4	10.9	15.8

Note: Figures are 2010 estimates; (1) Metropolitan Statistical Area - see Appendix B for areas included (2) Alone is defined as not being in combination with one or more other races; (3) May be of any race.
Source: Claritas, Inc.

Segregation

Type	Segregation Indices[1] 1990	2000	2010	2010 Rank[2]	Percent Change 1990-2000	1990-2010	2000-2010
Black/White	69.7	64.6	56.2	50	-5.1	-13.5	-8.3
Asian/White	33.8	35.4	35.3	78	1.6	1.5	-0.1
Hispanic/White	45.3	44.4	40.7	62	-0.9	-4.6	-3.7

Note: Figures are based on an analysis of 1990, 2000, and 2010 Census Decennial Census tract data by William H. Frey, Brookings Institution and the University of Michigan Social Science Data Analysis Network. In this analysis all racial groups (whites, blacks, and asians) are non-Hispanic members of those races. Hispanics are shown as a separate category; All figures cover the Metropolitan Statistical Area (see Appendix B for areas included); (1) Segregation Indices are Dissimilarity Indices that measure the degree to which the minority group is distributed differently than whites aross census tracts. They range from 0 (complete integration) to 100 (complete [segregation) where the value indicates the percentage of the minority group that needs to move to be distributed exactly like whites; (2) Ranges from 1 (most segregated) to 102 (least segregated); n/a not available.
Source: www.CensusScope.org

Ancestry

Area	German	Irish	English	American	Italian	Polish	French	Scottish
City	14.5	14.1	10.8	3.2	6.9	3.3	3.4	2.4
MSA[1]	16.2	14.2	10.9	5.9	9.0	3.5	3.5	2.3
U.S.	16.6	12.0	9.1	6.1	5.9	3.3	3.1	1.9

Note: The top eight ancestries in the U.S. are shown. Figures are percentages and include multiple ancestry (e.g. if a person reported being Irish and Italian, they were included in both columns); (1) Metropolitan Statistical Area - see Appendix B for areas included
Source: U.S. Census Bureau, 2007-2009 American Community Survey 3-Year Estimates

Foreign-Born Population

Area	Percent of Population Born in								
	Any Foreign Country	Mexico	Asia	Europe	Carribean	South America	Central America[2]	Africa	Canada
City	10.0	0.5	2.5	3.4	1.5	0.7	0.3	0.5	0.6
MSA[1]	11.9	1.5	2.2	2.4	2.6	1.4	0.6	0.4	0.8
U.S.	12.5	3.8	3.4	1.6	1.1	0.8	0.9	0.5	0.3

Note: (1) Metropolitan Statistical Area - see Appendix B for areas included; (2) Excludes Mexico.
Source: U.S. Census Bureau, 2007-2009 American Community Survey 3-Year Estimates

Marriage Status

Area	Never Married	Now Married[2]	Separated	Widowed	Divorced
City	33.3	40.6	2.5	8.3	15.3
MSA[1]	28.4	48.1	2.2	7.9	13.4
U.S.	31.4	49.7	2.2	6.2	10.6

Note: Figures are percentages and cover the population 15 years of age and older;
(1) Metropolitan Statistical Area - see Appendix B for areas included; (2) Excludes separated
Source: U.S. Census Bureau, 2007-2009 American Community Survey 3-Year Estimates

Age Distribution and Median Age

Area	Percent of Population							Median Age
	Under Age 5	Age 5 to 17	Age 18 to 34	Age 35 to 49	Age 50 to 64	Age 65 to 79	80 Years and Over	
City	5.9	15.0	21.6	22.1	20.0	10.1	5.2	40.6
MSA[1]	6.1	15.7	21.1	21.2	18.8	11.6	5.5	40.5
U.S.	6.9	17.5	23.3	21.4	18.1	9.1	3.7	36.7

Note: (1) Metropolitan Statistical Area - see Appendix B for areas included
Source: U.S. Census Bureau, 2007-2009 American Community Survey 3-Year Estimates

Male/Female Ratio

Area	Males	Females	Males per 100 Females
City	120,043	129,077	93.0
MSA[1]	1,354,345	1,427,768	94.9
U.S.	152,401,520	156,637,454	97.3

Note: Figures are 2010 estimates; (1) Metropolitan Statistical Area - see Appendix B for areas included
Source: Claritas, Inc.

Religion

Area	Catholic	Southern Baptist	United Methodist	ELCA[1]	LDS[2]	Presbyterian Church USA	Jewish Est.	Muslim Est.
County	12.2	3.9	4.4	0.9	0.2	1.3	2.6	0.5
U.S.	22.0	7.1	3.7	1.8	1.5	1.1	2.2	0.6

Note: Figures are the number of adherents as a percentage of the total population; Adherents are defined as all members, including full members, their children and the estimated number of other participants who are not considered members (e.g. the baptized, those not confirmed, those regularly attending services, etc.);
(1) Evangelical Lutheran Church in America; (2) The Church of Jesus Christ of Latter Day Saints
Source: Reprinted with permission from Religious Congregations and Membership in the United States 2000 (Nashville, Glenmary Research Center, 2002) Copyright Association of Statisticians of American Religious Bodies. All rights reserved.

ECONOMY

Gross Metropolitan Product

Area	2006	2007	2008	2009	2009 Rank[2]
MSA[1]	108.2	110.7	110.5	107.4	25

Note: Figures are in billions of dollars; (1) Tampa-St. Petersburg-Clearwater, FL Metropolitan Statistical Area - see Appendix B for areas included; (2) Rank ranges from 1 to 363
Source: The U.S. Conference of Mayors, "Pace of Economic Recovery: GMP and Jobs," January 2010

Economic Growth

Area	2006-2008 (%)	2009 (%)	2010 (%)	Rank[2]
MSA[1]	-1.2	-3.7	1.8	320
U.S.	1.3	-2.5	2.2	–

Note: Figures are real Gross Metropolitan Product growth rates and represent annual average percent change; (1) Tampa-St. Petersburg-Clearwater, FL Metropolitan Statistical Area - see Appendix B for areas included; (2) Rank ranges from 1 to 363
Source: The U.S. Conference of Mayors, "Pace of Economic Recovery: GMP and Jobs," January 2010

Metropolitan Area Exports

Area	2005	2006	2007	2008	2009	2009 Rank[2]
MSA[1]	4,423.8	4,738.5	5,711.2	7,153.5	6,463.6	34

Note: Figures are in millions of dollars; (1) Tampa-St. Petersburg-Clearwater, FL Metropolitan Statistical Area - see Appendix B for areas included; (2) Rank ranges from 1 to 374
Source: U.S. Department of Commerce, International Trade Administration, Office of Trade & Industry Information, Manufacturing & Services

INCOME

Per Capita/Median/Average Income

Area	Per Capita ($)	Median Household ($)	Average Household ($)
City	26,167	43,640	59,099
MSA[1]	27,068	47,630	64,446
U.S.	27,034	52,795	71,071

Note: Figures are 2010 estimates; (1) Metropolitan Statistical Area - see Appendix B for areas included
Source: Claritas, Inc.

Household Income Distribution

Area	Percent of Households Earning							
	Under $15,000	$15,000 -24,999	$25,000 -34,999	$35,000 -49,999	$50,000 -74,999	$75,000 -99,000	$100,000 -149,999	$150,000 and up
City	14.2	12.5	13.5	17.1	18.9	10.1	8.7	5.0
MSA[1]	11.7	11.6	12.5	16.9	20.0	11.3	9.8	6.2
U.S.	12.1	10.2	10.6	15.0	19.5	12.5	12.1	8.0

Note: Figures are 2010 estimates; (1) Metropolitan Statistical Area - see Appendix B for areas included
Source: Claritas, Inc.

Poverty Rates by Age

Area	All Ages	Under 18 Years Old	18 to 64 Years Old	65 Years and Over
City	13.3	4.0	7.5	1.7
MSA[1]	12.7	4.0	7.2	1.5
U.S.	13.6	4.7	7.7	1.2

Note: Figures are percent of population with income during the previous 12 months below poverty level and only include population for whom poverty status is determined; (1) Metropolitan Statistical Area - see Appendix B for areas included
Source: U.S. Census Bureau, 2007-2009 American Community Survey 3-Year Estimates

Personal Bankruptcy Filing Rate

Area	2006	2007	2008	2009	2010
Pinellas County	1.96	3.00	4.25	5.76	5.89
U.S.	2.00	2.73	3.53	4.60	4.96

Note: Numbers are per 1,000 population and include Chapter 7 and Chapter 13 filings
Source: Federal Deposit Insurance Corporation, Regional Economic Conditions, March 17, 2011

EMPLOYMENT

Labor Force and Employment

Area	Civilian Labor Force			Workers Employed		
	Dec. 2009	Dec. 2010	% Chg.	Dec. 2009	Dec. 2010	% Chg.
City	120,698	122,039	1.1	106,990	107,572	0.5
MSA[1]	1,284,093	1,298,265	1.1	1,134,329	1,140,498	0.5
U.S.	152,693,000	153,156,000	0.3	137,953,000	139,159,000	0.9

Note: Data is not seasonally adjusted and covers workers 16 years of age and older;
(1) Metropolitan Statistical Area - see Appendix B for areas included
Source: Bureau of Labor Statistics, http://stats.bls.gov

Unemployment Rate

Area	2010											
	Jan.	Feb.	Mar.	Apr.	May	Jun.	Jul.	Aug.	Sep.	Oct.	Nov.	Dec.
City	12.1	11.8	11.6	11.2	11.0	11.5	11.9	11.9	11.7	11.5	12.4	11.9
MSA[1]	12.4	12.1	11.9	11.6	11.5	11.9	12.3	12.4	12.2	12.0	12.6	12.2
U.S.	10.6	10.4	10.2	9.5	9.3	9.6	9.7	9.5	9.2	9.0	9.3	9.1

Note: Data is not seasonally adjusted and covers workers 16 years of age and older; All figures are percentages; (1) Metropolitan Statistical Area - see Appendix B for areas included
Source: Bureau of Labor Statistics, http://stats.bls.gov

Projected Unemployment Rate

Area	2007 (%)	2009 (%)	2011 (%)	2013 (%)
MSA[1]	4.8	12.5	10.3	7.8

Note: (1) Metropolitan Statistical Area - see Appendix B for areas included
Source: The U.S. Conference of Mayors, "Pace of Economic Recovery: GMP and Jobs," January 2010

Employment by Occupation

Occupation Classification	City (%)	MSA[1] (%)	U.S. (%)
Sales and Office	28.0	29.5	25.4
Professional and Related	22.5	20.4	21.0
Service	18.7	17.0	17.2
Production, Transportation, and Material Moving	10.3	8.8	12.3
Management, Business, and Financial	13.5	14.9	14.1
Construction, Extraction, and Maintenance	6.9	8.9	9.2
Farming, Forestry, and Fishing	0.1	0.5	0.7

Note: Figures cover employed civilians 16 years of age and older;
(1) Metropolitan Statistical Area - see Appendix B for areas included
Source: U.S. Census Bureau, 2007-2009 American Community Survey 3-Year Estimates

Employment by Industry

Sector	MSA[1] Number of Employees	MSA[1] Percent of Total	U.S. Percent of Total
Government	155,600	13.9	17.2
Education and Health Services	181,500	16.2	15.2
Professional and Business Services	191,900	17.1	13.0
Retail Trade	141,200	12.6	11.4
Leisure and Hospitality	117,800	10.5	9.7
Manufacturing	57,200	5.1	8.8
Financial Activities	86,400	7.7	5.8
Wholesale Trade	45,400	4.0	4.2
Construction	51,100	4.6	4.1
Other Services	42,900	3.8	4.1
Transportation and Utilities	25,600	2.3	3.7
Information	25,300	2.3	2.1
Mining and Logging	400	<0.1	0.6

Note: Figures cover non-farm employment as of December 2010 and are not seasonally adjusted;
(1) Metropolitan Statistical Area - see Appendix B for areas included
Source: Bureau of Labor Statistics, http://stats.bls.gov

Occupations with Greatest Projected Employment Growth: 2006 - 2016

Occupation[1]	2006 Employment	2016 Projected Employment	Numeric Employment Change	Percent Employment Change
Retail salespersons	283,850	339,780	55,930	19.7
Customer service representatives	162,780	214,600	51,820	31.8
Registered nurses	148,390	190,020	41,630	28.1
Combined food preparation and serving workers, including fast food	163,780	202,670	38,890	23.7
Waiters and waitresses	197,920	232,430	34,510	17.4
Office clerks, general	188,190	221,750	33,560	17.8
Bookkeeping, accounting, and auditing clerks	128,340	153,830	25,490	19.9
Janitors and cleaners, except maids and housekeeping cleaners	124,030	147,970	23,940	19.3
Sales representatives, services, all other	73,650	97,390	23,740	32.2
Executive secretaries and administrative assistants	106,820	129,140	22,320	20.9

Note: Projections cover Florida; (1) Sorted by numeric employment change
Source: www.projectionscentral.com, State Occupational Projections, 2006-2016 Long-Term Projections

Fastest Growing Occupations: 2006 - 2016

Occupation[1]	2006 Employment	2016 Projected Employment	Numeric Employment Change	Percent Employment Change
Network systems and data communications analysts	20,830	33,090	12,260	58.9
Court reporters	2,170	3,430	1,260	58.1
Computer software engineers, applications	17,350	27,250	9,900	57.1
Veterinary technologists and technicians	5,720	8,880	3,160	55.2
Veterinarians	3,280	4,890	1,610	49.1
Home health aides	29,600	42,780	13,180	44.5
Personal and home care aides	10,640	15,220	4,580	43.0
Paralegals and legal assistants	19,240	27,360	8,120	42.2
Pharmacy technicians	21,110	29,950	8,840	41.9
Medical assistants	31,040	43,930	12,890	41.5

Note: Projections cover Florida; (1) Sorted by percent employment change and excludes occupations with numeric employment change less than 900
Source: www.projectionscentral.com, State Occupational Projections, 2006-2016 Long-Term Projections

Average Wages

Occupation	$/Hr.	Occupation	$/Hr.
Accountants and Auditors	28.37	Maids and Housekeeping Cleaners	9.12
Automotive Mechanics	17.69	Maintenance and Repair Workers	14.94
Bookkeepers	15.60	Marketing Managers	54.78
Carpenters	16.76	Nuclear Medicine Technologists	31.56
Cashiers	8.60	Nurses, Licensed Practical	20.05
Clerks, General Office	12.11	Nurses, Registered	30.78
Clerks, Receptionists/Information	12.21	Nursing Aides/Orderlies/Attendants	11.45
Clerks, Shipping/Receiving	12.63	Packers and Packagers, Hand	9.80
Computer Programmers	32.73	Physical Therapists	38.46
Computer Support Specialists	21.17	Postal Service Mail Carriers	23.34
Computer Systems Analysts	35.41	Real Estate Brokers	26.08
Cooks, Restaurant	11.18	Retail Salespersons	12.63
Dentists	n/a	Sales Reps., Exc. Tech./Scientific	28.60
Electrical Engineers	35.99	Sales Reps., Tech./Scientific	35.33
Electricians	18.45	Secretaries, Exc. Legal/Med./Exec.	13.70
Financial Managers	53.06	Security Guards	10.29
First-Line Supervisors/Mgrs., Sales	21.52	Surgeons	n/a
Food Preparation Workers	9.64	Teacher Assistants	10.10
General and Operations Managers	49.91	Teachers, Elementary School	24.50
Hairdressers/Cosmetologists	11.46	Teachers, Secondary School	26.30
Internists	90.16	Telemarketers	11.52
Janitors and Cleaners	10.15	Truck Drivers, Heavy/Tractor-Trailer	16.69
Landscaping/Groundskeeping Workers	11.15	Truck Drivers, Light/Delivery Svcs.	13.98
Lawyers	53.98	Waiters and Waitresses	9.86

Note: Wage data covers the Tampa-St. Petersburg-Clearwater, FL - see Appendix B for areas included. Hourly wages for elementary/secondary school teachers and teacher assistants were calculated by the editors from annual wage data assuming a 40 hour work week; n/a not available.
Source: Bureau of Labor Statistics, Metro Area Occupational Employment and Wage Estimates, May 2009

RESIDENTIAL REAL ESTATE

Building Permits

Area	Single-Family			Multi-Family			Total		
	2009	2010	Pct. Chg.	2009	2010	Pct. Chg.	2009	2010	Pct. Chg.
City	47	70	48.9	716	268	-62.6	763	338	-55.7
MSA[1]	3,923	4,396	12.1	3,039	2,105	-30.7	6,962	6,501	-6.6
U.S.	441,100	447,300	1.4	141,900	157,300	10.9	583,000	604,600	3.7

Note: (1) Metropolitan Statistical Area - see Appendix B for areas included; figures represent new, privately-owned housing units authorized (unadjusted data); All permit data are based on estimates with imputation.
Source: U.S. Census Bureau, Manufacturing, Mining, and Construction Statistics, Building Permits, 2009, 2010

Homeownership Rate

Area	2005 (%)	2006 (%)	2007 (%)	2008 (%)	2009 (%)	2010 (%)
MSA[1]	71.7	71.6	72.9	70.5	68.3	68.3
U.S.	68.9	68.8	68.1	67.8	67.4	66.9

Note: (1) Metropolitan Statistical Area - see Appendix B for areas included
Source: U.S. Census Bureau, Housing Vacancies and Homeownership Annual Statistics: 2010

Housing Vacancy Rates

Area	Gross Vacancy Rate[2] (%)			Year-Round Vacancy Rate[3] (%)			Rental Vacancy Rate[4] (%)			Homeowner Vacancy Rate[5] (%)		
	2008	2009	2010	2008	2009	2010	2008	2009	2010	2008	2009	2010
MSA[1]	18.7	20.5	20.2	13.3	14.7	14.2	15.4	12.4	12.6	3.0	4.1	4.0
U.S.	14.4	14.5	14.3	11.1	11.3	11.3	10.0	10.6	10.2	2.8	2.6	2.6

Note: (1) Metropolitan Statistical Area - see Appendix B for areas included; (2) The percentage of the total housing inventory that is vacant; (3) The percentage of the housing inventory (excluding seasonal units) that is year-round vacant; (4) The percentage of rental inventory that is vacant for rent; (5) The percentage of homeowner inventory that is vacant for sale; n/a not available
Source: U.S. Census Bureau, Housing Vacancies and Homeownership Annual Statistics: 2010

State Corporate Income Tax Rates

State	Tax Rate (%)	Income Brackets ($)	Num. of Brackets	Financial Institution Tax Rate (%)[a]	Federal Income Tax Ded.
Florida	5.5 (f)	Flat rate	1	5.5 (f)	No

Note: Tax rates as of January 1, 2011; (a) Rates listed are the tax rates applied to financial institutions or excise taxes based on income. Some states have other taxes based upon the value of deposits or shares; (f) An exemption of $5,000 is allowed. Florida's Alternative Minimum Tax rate is 3.3%.
Source: Federation of Tax Administrators, "State Corporate Income Tax Rates, 2011"

State Individual Income Tax Rates

State	Tax Rate (%)	Income Brackets ($)	Num. of Brackets	Personal Exempt. ($)[1] Single	Personal Exempt. ($)[1] Dependents	Fed. Inc. Tax Ded.
Florida – No State Income Tax						

Note: Tax rates as of January 1, 2011; Local- and county-level taxes are not included; n/a not applicable; (1) Married joint filers generally receive double the single exemption
Source: Federation of Tax Administrators, "State Individual Income Tax Rates, 2011"

Various State and Local Tax Rates

State	State and Local Sales and Use (%)	State Sales and Use (%)	Gasoline[1] (¢/gal.)	Cigarette[2] ($/pack)	Spirits[3] ($/gal.)	Wine[4] ($/gal.)	Beer[5] ($/gal.)
Florida	7.0	6.00	34.4	1.34	6.50	2.25	0.48

Note: All tax rates as of January 1, 2011 except Spirits (Sept. 1, 2010); (1) The American Petroleum Institute has developed a methodology for determining the average tax rate on a gallon of fuel. Rates may include any of the following: excise taxes, environmental fees, storage tank fees, other fees or taxes, general sales tax, and local taxes. In states where gasoline is subject to the general sales tax, or where the fuel tax is based on the average sale price, the average rate determined by API is sensitive to changes in the price of gasoline. States that fully or partially apply general sales taxes to gasoline: CA, CO, GA, IL, IN, MI, NY; (2) The federal excise tax of $1.0066 per pack and local taxes are not included; (3) Rates are those applicable to off-premise sales of 40% alcohol by volume (a.b.v.) distilled spirits in 750ml containers. Local excise taxes are excluded; (4) Rates are those applicable to off-premise sales of 11% a.b.v. non-carbonated wine in 750ml containers; (5) Rates are those applicable to off-premise sales of 4.7% a.b.v. beer in 12 ounce containers.
Source: Tax Foundation, 2011 Facts & Figures: How Does Your State Compare?

State-Local Tax Burdens

Area	Rate (%)	Rank[1]	Per Capita Taxes Paid to Home State ($)	Total State and Local Per Capita Taxes Paid ($)	Per Capita Income ($)
Florida	9.2	31	2,713	3,897	42,146
U.S. Average	9.8	-	3,057	4,160	42,539

Note: Figures cover 2009; (1) Rank ranges from 1 to 50 where 1 is highest tax burden
Source: Tax Foundation, State-Local Tax Burdens, All States, 2009

State Business Tax Climate Index Rankings

State	Overall Rank	Corporate Tax Index Rank	Individual Income Tax Index Rank	Sales Tax Index Rank	Unemployment Insurance Tax Index Rank	Property Tax Index Rank
Florida	5	15	1	30	3	28

Note: The index is a measure of how each state's tax laws affect economic performance. The lower the rank, the more favorable a state's tax system is for business. All ranks are for fiscal years. States without a given tax are given a ranking of 1.
Source: Tax Foundation, Tax Foundation Background Paper, No. 60, "2011 State Business Tax Climate Index"

COMMERCIAL REAL ESTATE

Office Market

Market Area	Inventory (sq. ft.)	Vacant (sq. ft.)	Vac. Rate (%)	Under Constr. (sq. ft.)	Asking Rent ($/sf/yr) Class A	Asking Rent ($/sf/yr) Class B
Tampa/Saint Petersburg	63,407,168	12,447,184	19.6	88,000	21.86	17.47

Source: Grubb & Ellis, Office Markets Trends, 1st Quarter 2011

Industrial Market

Market Area	Inventory (sq. ft.)	Vacant (sq. ft.)	Vac. Rate (%)	Under Constr. (sq. ft.)	Asking Rent ($/sf/yr) WH/Dist	R&D/Flex
Tampa/Saint Petersburg	268,177,434	28,669,471	10.7	-	4.91	7.96

Source: Grubb & Ellis, Industrial Markets Trends, 1st Quarter 2011

COMMERCIAL UTILITIES

Typical Monthly Electric Bills

Area	Commercial Service ($/month)		Industrial Service ($/month)	
	3 kW demand 1,000 kWh	40 kW demand 14,000 kWh	1,000 kW demand 200,000 kWh	50,000 kW demand 15,000,000 kWh
City	130	1,757	18,650	1,271,366
Average[1]	135	1,576	23,741	1,402,202

Note: Based on total rates in effect July 1, 2010; (1) average based on 182 utilities surveyed
Source: Edison Electric Institute, Typical Bills and Average Rates Report, Summer 2010

TRANSPORTATION

Means of Transportation to Work

Area	Car/Truck/Van Drove Alone	Car-pooled	Public Transportation Bus	Subway	Railroad	Bicycle	Walked	Other Means	Worked at Home
City	80.6	8.5	1.9	0.0	0.0	0.9	2.5	1.4	4.1
MSA[1]	80.5	9.4	1.4	0.0	0.0	0.6	1.6	1.5	5.0
U.S.	75.8	10.4	2.7	1.7	0.5	0.5	2.9	1.2	4.1

Note: Figures are percentages and cover workers 16 years of age and older;
(1) Metropolitan Statistical Area - see Appendix B for areas included
Source: U.S. Census Bureau, 2007-2009 American Community Survey 3-Year Estimates

Travel Time to Work

Area	Less Than 15 Minutes	15 to 29 Minutes	30 to 44 Minutes	45 to 59 Minutes	60 to 89 Minutes	90 Minutes or More
City	27.3	44.0	19.7	5.6	2.1	1.3
MSA[1]	24.6	38.0	22.1	8.5	5.1	1.7
U.S.	28.5	36.2	19.7	7.5	5.6	2.5

Note: Figures are percentages and include workers 16 years old and over;
(1) Metropolitan Statistical Area - see Appendix B for areas included
Source: U.S. Census Bureau, 2007-2009 American Community Survey 3-Year Estimates

Travel Time Index

Area	1982	1999	2008	2009
Urban Area[1]	1.13	1.16	1.16	1.16
Average[2]	1.08	1.20	1.20	1.20

Note: Travel Time Index—the ratio of travel time in the peak period to the travel time at
free-flow conditions. A value of 1.30 indicates a 20-minute free-flow trip takes 26 minutes
in the peak. Free-flow speeds (60 mph on freeways and 35 mph on principal arterials)
are used as the comparison threshold; (1) Covers the Tampa-St. Petersburg-Clearwater urban area;
(2) average of 439 urban areas
Source: Texas Transportation Institute, Urban Mobility Report 2010, December 2010

Public Transportation

Agency Name / Mode of Transportation	Vehicles Operated in Maximum Service	Annual Unlinked Passenger Trips ('000)	Annual Passenger Miles ('000)
Pinellas Suncoast Transit Authority (PSTA)			
Demand response	117	228.5	1,746.2
Bus	170	11,865.5	61,548.6
Bus	2	87.6	177.0

Note: Figures include both directly operated and purchased transportation
Source: Federal Transit Administration, National Transit Database, 2009

Air Transportation

Airport Name and Code / Type of Service	Passenger Airlines[1]	Passenger Enplanements	Freight Carriers[2]	Freight (lbs.)
Tampa International (TPA)				
Domestic service (U.S. carriers - 2010)	25	7,940,755	11	75,535,446
International service (U.S. carriers - 2009)	8	22,304	1	491
St. Petersburg-Clearwater International (PIE)				
Domestic service (U.S. carriers - 2010)	13	381,601	5	16,882,111
International service (U.S. carriers - 2009)	4	370	2	63,744

Note: (1) Includes all U.S.-based major, minor and commuter airlines that carried at least one passenger during the year; (2) Includes all U.S.-based airlines and freight carriers that transported at least one pound of freight during the year
Source: Bureau of Transportation Statistics, The Intermodal Transportation Database, Air Carriers: T-100 Domestic Market (U.S. Carriers), 2010; Bureau of Transportation Statistics, The Intermodal Transportation Database, Air Carriers: T-100 International Market (U.S. Carriers), 2009

Other Transportation Statistics

Interstate highways:	I-275 connecting to I-75 and I-4
Amtrak service:	Bus connection
Major waterways/ports:	Gulf of Mexico; Tampa Bay

Source: Amtrak.com; Google Maps

BUSINESSES

Major Business Headquarters

Company Name	Rankings	
	Fortune[1]	Forbes[2]
Jabil Circuit	182	-

Note: (1) Fortune 500—companies that produce a 10-K are ranked 1 to 500 based on 2010 revenue; (2) all private companies with at least $2 billion in annual revenue are ranked 1 to 223; companies listed are headquartered in the city; dashes indicate no ranking
Source: Fortune, "Fortune 500," May 23, 2011; Forbes, "America's Largest Private Companies," November 3, 2010

Minority Business Opportunity

Saint Petersburg is home to one company which is on the *Hispanic Business 500* list (500 largest U.S. Hispanic-owned companies based on 2009 revenue): **Gemini Power Systems**. Companies included must show at least 51 percent ownership by Hispanic U.S. citizens, and must maintain headquarters in one of the 50 states or Washington, D.C. *Hispanic Business, "Hispanic Business 500," June 2010*

Minority- and Women-Owned Businesses

Group	All Firms		Firms with Paid Employees			
	Firms	Sales ($000)	Firms	Sales ($000)	Employees	Payroll ($000)
Asian	965	198,751	197	181,183	1,336	35,674
Black	2,558	97,708	170	51,110	696	12,696
Hispanic	1,363	194,206	242	154,370	1,318	44,230
Women	7,812	1,125,963	878	923,987	22,823	479,523
All Firms	25,606	28,929,780	5,957	27,973,666	207,540	7,468,928

Note: Figures cover firms located in the city; minority- and women-owned business are defined as firms in which the corresponding group own 51% or more of the stock or equity of the company
Source: U.S. Census Bureau, 2007 Economic Census, Survey of Business Owners

HOTELS

Hotels/Motels

Area	5 Star		4 Star		3 Star		2 Star		1 Star		Not Rated	
	Num.	Pct.3	Num.	Pct.3	Num.	Pct.3	Num.	Pct.3	Num.	Pct.3	Num.	Pct.3
City[1]	0	0.0	6	3.7	51	31.3	73	44.8	9	5.5	24	14.7
Total[2]	119	0.7	927	5.8	4,906	30.5	7,992	49.7	526	3.3	1,625	10.1

Note: (1) Figures cover Saint Petersburg and vicinity; (2) Figures cover all 100 cities in this book; (3) Percentage of hotels which are a given star rating; Star ratings are determined by expedia.com and offer an indication of the general quality of a particular hotel.
Source: expedia.com, May 5, 2011

EVENT SITES

Major Stadiums, Arenas, and Auditoriums

Name	Max. Capacity
Progress Energy Center for the Arts-Mahaffey Theater	2,030
Progress Energy Park/Al Lang Field	6,439
The Coliseum	2,000
Tropicana Field	45,000

Source: Original research

Convention Centers

Name	Overall Space (sq. ft.)	Exhibit Space (sq. ft.)	Meeting Space (sq. ft.)	Meeting Rooms

There are no major convention centers.

Source: Original research

Living Environment

COST OF LIVING

Cost of Living Index

Composite Index	Groceries	Housing	Utilities	Trans-portation	Health Care	Misc. Goods/ Services
92.4	96.3	84.7	93.8	103.3	98.4	93.4

Note: U.S. = 100; Figures cover the Tampa urban area.
Source: The Council for Community and Economic Research, ACCRA Cost of Living Index, 2010

Grocery Prices

Area[1]	T-Bone Steak ($/pound)	Frying Chicken ($/pound)	Whole Milk ($/half gal.)	Eggs ($/dozen)	Orange Juice ($/64 oz.)	Coffee ($/11.5 oz.)
City[2]	8.57	1.06	2.36	1.45	2.77	3.26
Avg.	9.04	1.16	2.02	1.47	3.08	3.65
Min.	6.97	0.84	1.46	0.96	2.39	2.64
Max.	13.93	2.51	3.58	3.01	4.94	6.32

Note: (1) Values for the local area are compared with the average, minimum and maximum values for all 338 areas in the Cost of Living Index; (2) Figures cover the Tampa urban area; **T-Bone Steak** *(price per pound);* **Frying Chicken** *(price per pound, whole fryer);* **Whole Milk** *(half gallon carton);* **Eggs** *(price per dozen, Grade A, large);* **Orange Juice** *(64 oz. Tropicana or Florida Natural);* **Coffee** *(11.5 oz. can, vacuum-packed, Maxwell House, Hills Bros, or Folgers).*
Source: The Council for Community and Economic Research, ACCRA Cost of Living Index, 2010

Housing and Utility Costs

Area[1]	New Home Price ($)	Apartment Rent ($/month)	All Electric ($/month)	Part Electric ($/month)	Other Energy ($/month)	Telephone ($/month)
City[2]	233,346	838	173.22	-	-	22.72
Avg.	293,442	810	166.39	91.93	83.82	26.93
Min.	182,545	453	119.21	44.47	36.85	17.98
Max.	1,123,114	2,776	307.53	218.20	313.90	39.15

Note: (1) Values for the local area are compared with the average, minimum and maximum values for all 338 areas in the Cost of Living Index; (2) Figures cover the Tampa urban area; **New Home Price** *(2,400 sf living area, 8,000 sf lot, in urban area with full utilities);* **Apartment Rent** *(950 sf 2 bedroom/1.5 or 2 bath, unfurnished, excluding all utilities except water);* **All Electric** *(average monthly cost for an all-electric home);* **Part Electric** *(average monthly cost for a part-electric home);* **Other Energy** *(average monthly cost for natural gas, fuel oil, coal, wood, and any other forms of energy except electricity);* **Telephone** *(price includes basic monthly rate for a private residential line plus additional local usage charges incurred by a family of four).*
Source: The Council for Community and Economic Research, ACCRA Cost of Living Index, 2010

Health Care, Transportation, and Other Costs

Area[1]	Doctor ($/visit)	Dentist ($/visit)	Optometrist ($/visit)	Gasoline ($/gallon)	Beauty Salon ($/visit)	Men's Shirt ($)
City[2]	84.14	81.87	68.10	2.68	33.62	19.85
Avg.	89.44	78.95	87.40	2.73	31.92	24.83
Min.	57.00	54.25	48.32	2.44	19.17	13.67
Max.	149.90	136.73	174.22	3.75	62.81	47.89

Note: (1) Values for the local area are compared with the average, minimum and maximum values for all 338 areas in the Cost of Living Index; (2) Figures cover the Tampa urban area; **Doctor** *(general practitioners routine exam of an established patient);* **Dentist** *(adult teeth cleaning and periodic oral examination);* **Optometrist** *(full vision eye exam for established adult patient);* **Gasoline** *(one gallon regular unleaded, national brand, including all taxes, cash price at self-service pump if available);* **Beauty Salon** *(woman's shampoo, trim, and blow-dry);* **Men's Shirt** *(cotton/polyester dress shirt, pinpoint weave, long sleeves).*
Source: The Council for Community and Economic Research, ACCRA Cost of Living Index, 2010

HOUSING

House Price Index (HPI)

Area	National Ranking[2]	Quarterly Change (%)	One-Year Change (%)	Five-Year Change (%)
MSA[1]	286	-3.29	-6.53	-30.69
U.S.[3]	-	-0.84	-3.95	-11.45

Note: The HPI is a weighted repeat sales index. It measures average price changes in repeat sales or refinancings on the same properties. This information is obtained by reviewing repeat mortgage transactions on single-family properties whose mortgages have been purchased or securitized by Fannie Mae or Freddie Mac in January 1975; (1) Metropolitan/Micropolitan Statistical Area - see Appendix B for areas included; (2) Rankings are based on annual percentage change for all metro areas containing at least 15,000 transactions over the last 10 years and ranges from 1 to 309; (3) figures based on a weighted average of Census Division estimates; all figures are for the period ending December 31, 2010
Source: Federal Housing Finance Agency, House Price Index, February 24, 2011

House Price Valuations

Area	Q4 2005		Q4 2006		Q4 2007		Q4 2008		Q4 2009	
	Price ($000)	Over-valuation	Price ($000)	Over-valuation	Price ($000)	Over-valuation	Price ($000)	Over-valuation	Price ($000)	Over-valuation
MSA[1]	181.8	30.2	188.8	26.4	169.9	11.8	130.8	-13.6	120.4	-19.9

Note: Figures show the percentage of over- or under-valuation of single family homes relative to statistically normal house values (e.g. a value of 23.6 indicates that house values are 23.6% overvalued). Statistically normal house values are based on house prices, interest rates, household incomes, population densities, and any historical premiums or discounts metropolitan areas have exhibited over time; (1) Figures cover the Tampa-St. Petersburg-Clearwater, FL Metropolitan Statistical Area - see Appendix B for areas included
Source: Global Insight/PNC Financial Services Group, House Prices in America: 4th Quarter 2009 Update

Median Single-Family Home Prices

Area	2008	2009	2010p	Percent Change 2009 to 2010
MSA[1]	173.0	140.7	134.2	-4.6
U.S. Average	196.6	172.1	173.2	0.6

Note: Figures are median sales prices of existing single-family homes in thousands of dollars; (p) preliminary; n/a not available; (1) Metropolitan Statistical Area - see Appendix B for areas included
Source: National Association of Realtors, Median Sales Price of Existing Single-Family Homes for Metropolitan Areas, 4th Quarter 2010

Median Apartment Condo-Coop Home Prices

Area	2008	2009	2010p	Percent Change 2009 to 2010
MSA[1]	141.3	107.1	93.2	-13.0
U.S. Average	209.8	175.6	171.7	-2.2

Note: Figures are median sales prices of existing apartment condo-coop homes in thousands of dollars; (p) preliminary; n/a not available; (1) Metropolitan Statistical Area - see Appendix B for areas included
Source: National Association of Realtors, Median Sales Price of Existing Apartment Condo-Coop Homes for Metropolitan Areas, 4th Quarter 2010

Year Housing Structure Built

Area	2000 or Later	1990 -1999	1980 -1989	1970 -1979	1960 -1969	1950 -1959	1940 -1949	Before 1940	Median Year
City	4.8	4.3	9.8	20.3	20.0	26.3	6.4	8.2	1965
MSA[1]	15.3	14.2	22.8	21.5	11.6	9.4	2.4	2.7	1981
U.S.	12.5	14.0	14.2	16.5	11.4	11.3	5.8	14.3	1974

Note: Figures are percentages except for Median Year; (1) Metropolitan Statistical Area - see Appendix B for areas included
Source: U.S. Census Bureau, 2007-2009 American Community Survey 3-Year Estimates

HEALTH

Health Risk Data

Category	MSA[1] (%)	U.S. (%)
Adults who have been told they have high blood pressure	30.7	28.7
Adults who have been told they have high blood cholesterol	39.9	37.5
Adults who have been told they have diabetes[3]	10.9	8.3
Adults who have been told they have arthritis	29.7	26.0
Adults who have been told they currently have asthma	6.9	8.8
Adults who are current smokers	21.3	17.9
Adults who are heavy drinkers[4]	7.3	5.1
Adults who are binge drinkers[5]	17.2	15.8
Adults who are overweight (BMI 25.0 - 29.9)	35.5	36.2
Adults who are obese (BMI 30.0 - 99.8)	29.2	26.9
Adults who participated in any physical activities in the past month	74.7	76.2
Adults 50+ who have ever had a sigmoidoscopy or colonoscopy[2]	61.6	62.2
Women 40+ who have had a mammogram within the past two years[2]	75.9	76.0
Adults age 18–64 who have any kind of health care coverage	78.1	83.1

Note: Data as of 2009 unless otherwise noted; (1) Figures cover the Tampa-St. Petersburg-Clearwater, FL Metropolitan Statistical Area - see Appendix B for areas included; (2) Data as of 2008; (3) Figures do not include pregnancy-related, borderline, or pre-diabetes; (4) Heavy drinkers are classified as males having more than two drinks per day or females having more than one drink per day; (5) Binge drinkers are classified as males having five or more drinks on one occasion or females having four or more drinks on one occasion
Source: Centers for Disease Control and Prevention, Behaviorial Risk Factor Surveillance System, SMART: Selected Metropolitan/Micropolitan Area Risk Trends, 2008, 2009

Mortality Rates for the Top 10 Causes of Death in the U.S.

ICD-10[a] Sub-Chapter	ICD-10[a] Code	Age-Adjusted Mortality Rate[1] per 100,000 population	
		County[2]	U.S.
Malignant neoplasms	C00-C97	175.6	180.9
Ischaemic heart diseases	I20-I25	123.3	135.0
Other forms of heart disease	I30-I51	25.7	50.0
Cerebrovascular diseases	I60-I69	33.7	44.1
Chronic lower respiratory diseases	J40-J47	40.2	41.5
Other degenerative diseases of the nervous system	G30-G31	14.2	23.6
Diabetes mellitus	E10-E14	22.4	23.5
Other external causes of accidental injury	W00-X59	36.6	23.5
Organic, including symptomatic, mental disorders	F01-F09	14.5	22.2
Influenza and pneumonia	J09-J18	8.9	18.1

Note: (a) ICD-10 = International Classification of Diseases 10th Revision; (1) Mortality rates are a three year average covering 2005-2007; (2) Figures cover Pinellas County
Source: Centers for Disease Control and Prevention, National Center for Health Statistics. Compressed Mortality File 1999-2007. CDC WONDER On-line Database, compiled from Compressed Mortality File 1999-2007 Series 20 No. 2M, 2010.

Mortality Rates for Selected Causes of Death

ICD-10[a] Sub-Chapter	ICD-10[a] Code	Age-Adjusted Mortality Rate[1] per 100,000 population	
		County[2]	U.S.
Assault	X85-Y09	6.8	6.0
Human immunodeficiency virus (HIV) disease	B20-B24	6.4	4.0
Hypertensive diseases	I10-I15	18.3	18.0
Intentional self-harm	X60-X84	15.8	11.0
Malnutrition	E40-E46	*0.3	0.8
Obesity and other hyperalimentation	E65-E68	2.3	1.5
Transport accidents	V01-V99	15.4	15.6
Viral hepatitis	B15-B19	3.9	2.1

Note: (a) ICD-10 = International Classification of Diseases 10th Revision; (1) Mortality rates are a three year average covering 2005-2007; (2) Figures cover Pinellas County; (*) Unreliable data as per CDC
Source: Centers for Disease Control and Prevention, National Center for Health Statistics. Compressed Mortality File 1999-2007. CDC WONDER On-line Database, compiled from Compressed Mortality File 1999-2007 Series 20 No. 2M, 2010.

Distribution of Physicians and Dentists

Area[1]	Dentists[2]	D.O.[3]	M.D.[4]				
			Total	Family/ General Practice	Pediatrics	Medical Specialties	Surgical Specialties
Local (number)	425	413	2,039	235	136	810	456
Local (rate[5])	4.7	4.5	22.4	2.6	1.5	8.9	5.0
U.S. (rate[5])	4.5	1.9	18.3	2.5	1.4	6.8	4.1

Note: Data as of 2008 unless noted; (1) Local data covers Pinellas County; (2) Data as of 2007; (3) Doctor of Osteopathic Medicine; (4) Includes active, non-federal, patient-care, office-based Doctors of Medicine; (5) rate per 10,000 population
Source: Area Resource File (ARF). 2009-2010 Release. U.S. Department of Health and Human Services, Health Resources and Services Administration, Bureau of Health Professions, Rockville, MD, August 2010

Hospitals

Saint Petersburg has the following hospitals: 6 general medical and surgical; 1 children's general.
AHA Guide to the Healthcare Field 2010

According to *U.S. News,* the Tampa-St. Petersburg-Clearwater, FL Metropolitan Statistical Area is home to two of the best hospitals in the U.S.: **Moffitt Cancer Center; Tampa General Hospital**. The hospitals listed were highly ranked in at least one adult specialty. *U.S. News Online, "America's Best Hospitals 2010-11"*

According to *U.S. News,* the Tampa-St. Petersburg-Clearwater, FL Metropolitan Statistical Area is home to one of the best children's hospitals in the U.S.: **All Children's Hospital**. The hospital listed was highly ranked in at least one pediatric specialty. *U.S. News Online, "America's Best Children's Hospitals 2010-11"*

EDUCATION

Public School District Statistics

District Name	Schls	Pupils	Pupil/ Teacher Ratio	Minority Pupils[1] (%)	Free Lunch Eligible[2] (%)	IEP[3] (%)
Pinellas	173	106,061	13.5	38.1	35.0	14.9

Note: Table includes school districts with 2,000 or more students; (1) Percentage of students that are not non-Hispanic white; (2) Percentage of students that are eligible for the free lunch program; (3) Percentage of students that have an Individualized Education Program.
Source: U.S. Department of Education, National Center for Education Statistics, Common Core of Data, Local Education Agency (School District) Universe Survey: School Year 2008-2009; U.S. Department of Education, National Center for Education Statistics, Common Core of Data, Public Elementary/Secondary School Universe Survey: School Year 2008-2009

Top Public High Schools

High School Name	Index[1]	Rank[1]	Subsidized Lunch (%)[2]	E&E (%)[3]
Center for Advanced Technologies	7.575	16	20.0	100.0

Note: (1) Public schools are ranked according to a ratio that is the number of Advanced Placement, International Baccalaureate, and/or Cambridge tests taken by all students at a school in 2009 divided by the number of graduating seniors. All of the schools on the list have an index of at least 1.000; they are in the top six percent of public schools measured this way. The rankings range from 1 to 1,734; (2) Percentage of students receiving federally subsidized meals; (3) E & E stands for equity and excellence percentage: the portion of all graduating seniors at a school that had at least one passing grade on one AP or IB test; (4) Schools that offer International Baccalaureate or Cambridge exams; (5) School is unranked, but has been identified by Newsweek as one of the nation's most elite public high schools.
Source: Newsweek Online, "Top High Schools 2010"

Highest Level of Education

Area	Less than H.S.	H.S. Diploma	Some College, No Deg.	Associate Degree	Bachelors Degree	Masters Degree	Profess. School Degree	Doctorate Degree
City	13.8	29.0	21.7	9.0	17.6	6.2	1.8	0.9
MSA[1]	13.6	30.9	21.1	8.8	17.1	5.9	1.7	0.9
U.S.	15.3	29.0	20.7	7.5	17.4	7.0	1.9	1.1

Note: Figures are 2010 estimated percentages and cover persons age 25 and over; (1) Metropolitan Statistical Area - see Appendix B for areas included
Source: Claritas, Inc.

Educational Attainment by Race

Area	High School Graduate (%)					Bachelor's Degree (%)				
	Total	White	Black	Asian	Hisp.[2]	Total	White	Black	Asian	Hisp.[2]
City	87.3	91.7	76.7	68.4	77.1	27.1	31.5	12.7	27.2	22.8
MSA[1]	86.6	89.5	80.2	83.3	73.9	25.5	27.1	17.2	47.6	17.3
U.S.	84.9	90.0	80.7	85.5	60.7	27.8	30.9	17.5	49.7	12.7

Note: Figures shown cover persons 25 years old and over; (1) Metropolitan Statistical Area - see Appendix B for areas included; (2) people of Hispanic origin can be of any race
Source: U.S. Census Bureau, 2007-2009 American Community Survey 3-Year Estimates

School Enrollment by Grade and Control

Area	Preschool (%)		Kindergarten (%)		Grades 1 - 4 (%)		Grades 5 - 8 (%)		Grades 9 - 12 (%)	
	Public	Private	Public	Private	Public	Private	Public	Private	Public	Private
City	58.1	41.9	80.5	19.5	82.6	17.4	84.3	15.7	92.2	7.8
MSA[1]	49.5	50.5	84.6	15.4	88.5	11.5	88.2	11.8	91.0	9.0
U.S.	54.3	45.7	86.4	13.6	88.9	11.1	89.1	10.9	90.2	9.8

Note: Figures shown cover persons 3 years old and over; (1) Metropolitan Statistical Area - see Appendix B for areas included
Source: U.S. Census Bureau, 2007-2009 American Community Survey 3-Year Estimates

Average Salaries of Public School Classroom Teachers

Area	2009-10		2010-11		Percent Change 2009-10 to 2010-11	Percent Change 2000-01 to 2010-11
	Dollars	Rank[1]	Dollars	Rank[1]		
Florida	46,708	37	46,702	47	-0.01	22.2
U.S. Average	55,202	-	56,069	-	1.57	29.3

Note: (1) State rank ranges from 1 to 51 where 1 indicates highest salary.
Source: National Education Association, Rankings & Estimates: Rankings of the States 2010 and Estimates of School Statistics 2011, December 2010

Higher Education

Four-Year Colleges			Two-Year Colleges			Medical Schools[1]	Law Schools[2]	Voc/ Tech[3]
Public	Private Non-profit	Private For-profit	Public	Private Non-profit	Private For-profit			
1	2	1	1	0	1	0	0	2

Note: Figures cover institutions located within the city limits and include main campuses only; (1) includes schools accredited by the Liaison Committee on Medical Education and the American Osteopathic Association; (2) includes American Bar Association-accredited law schools; (3) includes all schools with programs that are less than 2 years.
Source: National Center for Education Statistics, Integrated Postsecondary Education System (IPEDS) Peer Analysis System, 2010-11; U.S. News & World Report, Medical School Directory, 2011; U.S. News & World Report, Law School Directory, 2011

According to *U.S. News & World Report,* the Tampa-St. Petersburg-Clearwater, FL Metropolitan Statistical Area is home to one of the top 197 national universities in the U.S.: **University of South Florida** (#183). The rankings are based on quantitative measurements such as peer assessment, retention, faculty resources, student selectivity, financial resources, graduation rate, and alumni giving rate. *U.S. News & World Report, "America's Best Colleges 2011"*

According to *U.S. News & World Report,* the Tampa-St. Petersburg-Clearwater, FL Metropolitan Statistical Area is home to one of the top 189 liberal arts colleges in the U.S.: **Eckerd College** (#137). The rankings are based on quantitative measurements such as peer assessment, retention, faculty resources, student selectivity, financial resources, graduation rate, and alumni giving rate. *U.S. News & World Report, "America's Best Colleges 2011"*

PRESIDENTIAL ELECTION

2008 Presidential Election Results

Area	Obama	McCain	Nader	Other
Pinellas County	53.4	45.2	0.5	0.9
U.S.	52.9	45.6	0.6	0.9

Note: Results are percentages and may not add to 100% due to rounding
Source: Dave Leip's Atlas of U.S. Presidential Elections, www.uselectionatlas.org

EMPLOYERS

Major Employers

Company Name	Industry	Type of Site
All Childrens Hospital	Specialty hospitals, except psychiatric	Branch
American Staff Management	Help supply services	Single
Bayfront Cancer Center	General medical and surgical hospitals	Headquarters
Bayfront Medical Center	General medical and surgical hospitals	Branch
Chase Manhattan	National commercial banks	Branch
Diversified Maint Systems	Building maintenance services, nec	Single
Employee Benefit & Risk Mgt	Administration of educational programs	Branch
Honeywell	Aircraft engines and engine parts	Branch
HSN	Television broadcasting stations	Headquarters
IF Music	Miscellaneous publishing	Single
James Haley Vamc	Administration of veterans' affairs	Branch
Moffitt Cancer Center	Offices and clinics of medical doctors	Single
Morton Plant Hospital	General medical and surgical hospitals	Headquarters
Pen Power	Engineering services	Branch
St Petersburg Times	Newspapers	Branch
Sykes Enterprises Incorporated	Computer related services, nec	Headquarters
Tech Data Corporation	Computers, peripherals, and software	Headquarters
University Community Health	General medical and surgical hospitals	Headquarters
University of South Florida	Colleges and universities	Headquarters
US Post Office	U.S. postal service	Branch
USANI Sub	Television broadcasting stations	Single
VA Bay Pines Healthcare System	General medical and surgical hospitals	Branch
Verizon	Business services, nec	Branch
Verizon	Data processing and preparation	Headquarters
Veterans Health Administration	Administration of public health programs	Branch

Note: Companies shown are located within the Tampa metropolitan area; nec = not elsewhere classified.
Source: www.zapdata.com, January 2011

Best Companies to Work For

Raymond James Financial, headquartered in Saint Petersburg, is among the "100 Best Places to Work in IT." To qualify, companies, both public and private, had to have a minimum of 50 IT employees. Companies were selected based on average salary and bonus increases, the percentage of IT employees receiving promotions, IT staff turnover rates, training and development programs, and the percentage of women and minorities in IT staff and management positions. In addition, information was collected on how the organizations reward outstanding performance, how their retention programs are structured and what benefits they offer. *Computerworld, "100 Best Places to Work in IT 2010"*

PUBLIC SAFETY

Crime Rate

Area	All Crimes	Violent Crimes				Property Crimes		
		Murder	Forcible Rape	Robbery	Aggrav. Assault	Burglary	Larceny -Theft	Motor Vehicle Theft
City	8,382.7	4.5	45.7	370.3	940.7	1,782.5	4,317.5	921.5
Suburbs[1]	4,069.8	3.5	27.7	135.0	347.2	906.7	2,403.2	246.5
Metro[2]	4,453.8	3.6	29.3	155.9	400.0	984.7	2,573.6	306.6
U.S.	3,465.5	5.0	28.7	133.0	262.8	716.3	2,060.9	258.8

Note: Figures are crimes per 100,000 population; (1) All areas within the metro area that are located outside the city limits; (2) Metropolitan Statistical Area - see Appendix B for areas included
Source: FBI Uniform Crime Reports, 2009

Hate Crimes

Area	Number of Quarters Reported	Bias Motivation				
		Race	Religion	Sexual Orientation	Ethnicity	Disability
City	4	1	0	0	0	0

Source: Federal Bureau of Investigation, Hate Crime Statistics 2009

Identity Theft Consumer Complaints

Area	Complaints	Complaints per 100,000 Population	Rank[2]
MSA[1]	2,710	99.5	61
U.S.	250,854	81.3	-

Note: (1) Metropolitan Statistical Area - see Appendix B for areas included; (2) Rank ranges from 1 to 384 where 1 indicates greatest number of complaints per 100,000 population
Source: Federal Trade Commission, Consumer Sentinel Network Data Book for January - December 2010

RECREATION

Culture

Dance[1]	Theatre[1]	Instrumental Music[1]	Vocal Music[1]	Series/ Festivals	Museums	Zoos and Aquariums[2]
1	2	1	0	3	8	0

Note: (1) Number of professional perfoming groups; (2) AZA-accredited
Source: The Grey House Performing Arts Directory, 2011-2012; Official Museum Directory, 2010; American Association of Museums, AAM Member Museums, March 2011; Association of Zoos & Aquariums, AZA Member Zoos & Aquariums, May 2011

Professional Sports Teams

Team Name	League
Tampa Bay Buccaneers	National Football League (NFL)
Tampa Bay Lightning	National Hockey League (NHL)
Tampa Bay Rays	Major League Baseball (MLB)

Note: Includes teams located in the Tampa-Saint Petersburg metro area.
Source: Original research

CLIMATE

Average and Extreme Temperatures

Temperature	Jan	Feb	Mar	Apr	May	Jun	Jul	Aug	Sep	Oct	Nov	Dec	Yr.
Extreme High (°F)	85	88	91	93	98	99	97	98	96	94	90	86	99
Average High (°F)	70	72	76	82	87	90	90	90	89	84	77	72	82
Average Temp. (°F)	60	62	67	72	78	81	82	83	81	75	68	62	73
Average Low (°F)	50	52	56	61	67	73	74	74	73	66	57	52	63
Extreme Low (°F)	21	24	29	40	49	53	63	67	57	40	23	18	18

Note: Figures cover the years 1948-1990
Source: National Climatic Data Center, International Station Meteorological Climate Summary, 9/96

Average Precipitation/Snowfall/Humidity

Precip./Humidity	Jan	Feb	Mar	Apr	May	Jun	Jul	Aug	Sep	Oct	Nov	Dec	Yr.
Avg. Precip. (in.)	2.1	2.8	3.5	1.8	3.0	5.6	7.3	7.9	6.5	2.3	1.8	2.1	46.7
Avg. Snowfall (in.)	Tr	Tr	Tr	0	0	0	0	0	0	0	0	Tr	Tr
Avg. Rel. Hum. 7am (%)	87	87	86	86	85	86	88	90	91	89	88	87	88
Avg. Rel. Hum. 4pm (%)	56	55	54	51	52	60	65	66	64	57	56	57	58

Note: Figures cover the years 1948-1990; Tr = Trace amounts (<0.05 in. of rain; <0.5 in. of snow)
Source: National Climatic Data Center, International Station Meteorological Climate Summary, 9/96

Weather Conditions

Temperature			Daytime Sky			Precipitation		
32°F & below	45°F & below	90°F & above	Clear	Partly cloudy	Cloudy	0.01 inch or more precip.	0.1 inch or more snow/ice	Thunder-storms
3	35	85	81	204	80	107	< 1	87

Note: Figures are average number of days per year and cover the years 1948-1990
Source: National Climatic Data Center, International Station Meteorological Climate Summary, 9/96

HAZARDOUS WASTE

Superfund Sites

Saint Petersburg has no sites on the EPA's Superfund Final National Priorities List.
U.S. Environmental Protection Agency, Final National Priorities List, April 1, 2011

**AIR & WATER
QUALITY**

Air Quality Index

Area	Percent of Days when Air Quality was...[2]				AQI Statistics	
	Good	Moderate	Unhealthy for Sensitive Groups	Unhealthy	Maximum	Median
Area[1]	91.6	7.6	0.7	0.0	116	36

*Note: The Air Quality Index (AQI) is an index for reporting daily air quality. EPA calculates the AQI for five major air pollutants regulated by the Clean Air Act: ground-level ozone, particle pollution (also known as particulate matter), carbon monoxide, sulfur dioxide, and nitrogen dioxide. The AQI runs from 0 to 500. The higher the AQI value, the greater the level of air pollution and the greater the health concern. There are six AQI categories: "Good" The AQI is between 0 and 50. Air quality is considered satisfactory; "Moderate" The AQI is between 51 and 100. Air quality is acceptable; "Unhealthy for Sensitive Groups" When AQI values are between 101 and 150, members of sensitive groups may experience health effects; "Unhealthy" When AQI values are between 151 and 200 everyone may begin to experience health effects; "Very Unhealthy" AQI values between 201 and 300 trigger a health alert; "Hazardous" AQI values over 300 trigger health warnings of emergency conditions; (1) Data covers Pinellas County; (2) Based on 275 days with AQI data in 2008; The EPA has suspended data updates while it assesses its data systems, including AirData reports and maps.
Source: U.S. Environmental Protection Agency, AirData Report, 2008*

Air Quality Index Pollutants

Area	Percent of Days when AQI Pollutant was...[2]					
	Carbon Monoxide	Nitrogen Dioxide	Ozone	Sulfur Dioxide	Particulate Matter 2.5	Particulate Matter 10
Area[1]	0.4	0.0	74.2	0.0	24.4	1.1

*Note: The Air Quality Index (AQI) is an index for reporting daily air quality. EPA calculates the AQI for five major air pollutants regulated by the Clean Air Act: ground-level ozone, particle pollution (also known as particulate matter), carbon monoxide, sulfur dioxide, and nitrogen dioxide. The AQI runs from 0 to 500. The higher the AQI value, the greater the level of air pollution and the greater the health concern; (1) Data covers Pinellas County; (2) Based on 275 days with AQI data in 2008; The EPA has suspended data updates while it assesses its data systems, including AirData reports and maps.
Source: U.S. Environmental Protection Agency, AirData Report, 2008*

Air Quality Index Trends

Area	Trend Sites (days)								All Sites (days)
	2002	2003	2004	2005	2006	2007	2008	2009	2009
MSA[1]	81	69	38	30	21	31	10	6	18

*Note: Figures are the number of days the AQI value exceeded 100 in a given year. An AQI value greater than 100 indicates that air quality would have been in the unhealthful range on that day. Data from exceptional events are included. These counts are presented in two ways. First, the counts are based on sites having an adequate record of monitoring data during the trend period (trend sites). These counts represent the relative change in the number of days with AQI values greater than 100. In the last column, the counts are based on all sites with data in the most recent year (because it is possible for a site to have data in the most recent year but not enough data to be a trend site); (1) Data covers the Tampa-St. Petersburg-Clearwater, FL Metropolitan Statistical Area - see Appendix B for areas included
Source: U.S. Environmental Protection Agency, Office of Air and Radiation, Air Quality Index Information, "Number of Days with Air Quality Index Values Greater than 100 and Trend Sites, 1990-2009, and at All Sites in 2009"*

Maximum Air Pollutant Concentrations

	Particulate Matter 10 (ug/m³)	Particulate Matter 2.5 (ug/m³)	Ozone (ppm)	Carbon Monoxide (ppm)	Sulfur Dioxide (ppm)	Nitrogen Dioxide (ppm)	Lead (ug/m³)
MSA[1] Level	42	17	0.073	1	0.028	0.007	0.25
NAAQS[2]	150	35	0.075	9	0.140	0.053	0.15
Met NAAQS[2]	Yes	Yes	Yes	Yes	Yes	Yes	No

*Note: Data from exceptional events are not included; (1) Data covers the Tampa-St. Petersburg-Clearwater, FL Metropolitan Statistical Area - see Appendix B for areas included; (2) National Ambient Air Quality Standards; n/a not available; (a) Localized impact from an industrial source in Tampa. Concentration from highest nonpoint source site is 0.01 ug/m³ in Pinellas County
Concentrations: Particulate Matter 10 (coarse particulate) - highest second maximum 24-hour concentration; Particulate Matter 2.5 (fine particulate) - highest 98th percentile 24-hour concentration; Ozone - highest fourth daily maximum 8-hour concentration; Carbon Monoxide - highest second maximum non-overlapping 8-hour concentration; Sulfur Dioxide - highest second maximum 24-hour concentration; Nitrogen Dioxide - highest arithmetic mean concentration; Lead - maximum running 3-month average
Units: ppm = parts per million; ug/m³ = micrograms per cubic meter
Source: U.S. Environmental Protection Agency, CBSA Factbook 2009, Air Quality Statistics by City, 2009*

Drinking Water

Water System Name	Pop. Served	Primary Water Source Type	Violations[1]	
			Health Based	Monitoring/ Reporting
City of St. Petersburg	300,075	Purchased Surface	0	0

Note: (1) Based on violation data from January 1, 2010 to December 31, 2010 (includes unresolved violations from earlier years)
Source: U.S. Environmental Protection Agency, Office of Ground Water and Drinking Water, Safe Drinking Water Information System (based on data extracted May 9, 2011)

San Antonio, Texas

Background

San Antonio is a charming preservation of its Mexican-Spanish heritage. Walking along its famous Paseo Del Rio at night, with cream-colored stucco structures, sea shell ornamented facades, and gently illuminating tiny lights is very romantic.

Emotional intensity is nothing new to San Antonio. The city began in the early eighteenth century as a cohesion of different Spanish missions, whose zealous aim was to convert the Coahuiltecan natives to Christianity, and to European ways of farming. A debilitating epidemic, however, killed most of the natives, as well as the missions' goal, causing the city to be abandoned.

In 1836, San Antonio became the site of interest again, when a small band of American soldiers were unable to successfully defend themselves against an army of 4,000 Mexican soldiers, led by General Antonio de Lopez Santa Anna. Fighting desperately from within the walls of the Mission San Antonio de Valero, or The Alamo, all 183 men were killed. This inspired the cry "Remember the Alamo" from the throats of every American soldier led by General Sam Houston, who was determined to wrest Texas territory and independence from Mexico.

Despite the Anglo victory over the Mexicans more than 150 years ago, the Mexican culture and its influence remain strong. We see evidence of this in the architecture, the Franciscan educational system, the variety of Spanish-language media, and the racial composition of the population, in which over half the city's residents are Latino.

This picturesque and practical blend of old and new makes San Antonio unique among American cities.

The city continues to draw tourists who come to visit not just the Alamo, but the nearby theme parks like Six Flags Fiesta Texas and SeaWorld, or to take in the famed River Walk, the charming promenade of shops, restaurants, and pubs. In addition, the city has used ingenuity to diversify its traditional economy. For instance, Kelly Air Force Base, which was decommissioned in 2001, was developed into a successful, nearly 5,000-acre business park, called Kelly USA. The name has since changed to Port San Antonio and a warehouse on the site was used to house refugees from Hurricane Katrina. Businesses at the port receive favorable property tax and pay no state, city or corporate income taxes.

Toyota is a major employer in the city. Since 2003, Toyota's San Antonio plant has produced Tundra trucks and other Toyota products. Other employers include Clear Channel Communication, Southwest Research Institute, and Zachry Construction.

San Antonio's location on the edge of the Gulf Coastal Plains exposes it to a modified subtropical climate. Summers are hot, although extremely high temperatures are rare. Winters are mild. Since the city is only 140 miles from the Gulf of Mexico, tropical storms occasionally occur, bringing strong winds and heavy rains. Relative humidity is high in the morning, but tends to drop by late afternoon.

Rankings

General Rankings

- San Antonio was ranked #51 out of 375 metro areas in *Cities Ranked & Rated*. Criteria: cost of living; climate; crime; transportation; economy and jobs; education; arts and culture; health and healthcare; leisure; quality of life. *Cities Ranked & Rated, 2nd Edition, 2007*

- San Antonio was ranked #24 out of 379 metro areas in *Places Rated Almanac*. Criteria: health care; education; recreation; transportation; ambience; climate; crime; housing costs; jobs. *Places Rated Almanac, 7th Edition, 2007*

- The San Antonio metro area was identified as one of the 10 most popular big cities by Pew Research Center. The results are based on a telephone survey of 2,260 adults conducted during October 2008. The report explored a range of attitudes related to where Americans live, where they would like to live, and why. *Pew Research Center, "For Nearly Half of America, Grass is Greener Somewhere Else," January 29, 2009*

- *Men's Health Living* ranked 100 U.S. cities in terms of quality of life. San Antonio was ranked #43 and received a grade of C. Criteria: number of fitness facilities; air quality; number of physicians; male/female ratio; education levels; household income; cost of living. *Men's Health Living, Spring 2008*

- San Antonio was selected as one of "America's Top 100 Places to Live" by RelocateAmerica.com. Cities and towns nominated to be great places to live along with their key data regarding education, employment, economy, crime, parks, recreation and housing were reviewed, rated and judged by the Relocate-America.com editorial staff. *Relocate-America.com, "RelocateAmerica's Top 100 Places to Live in 2010"*

- San Antonio was selected as one of "America's Favorite Cities." The city ranked #10 in the "Food/Dining" category. Respondents to an online survey were asked to rate 35 top urban destinations in the U.S. from a visitor's perspective. Criteria: big-name restaurants; ethnic food; farmers' markets; neighborhood joints and cafes. *Travelandleisure.com, "America's Favorite Cities 2010," November 2010*

- San Antonio appeared on *National Geographic Adventure's* list of the "50 Best Places to Live + Play." *National Geographic Adventure, September 2008*

Business/Finance Rankings

- San Antonio was identified as one of the 20 strongest-performing metro areas during the recession and recovery from December 2007 through December 2010. Criteria: percent change in employment; percentage point change in unemployment rate; percent change in gross metropolitan product; percent change in House Price Index. *Brookings Institution, MetroMonitor: Tracking Economic Recession and Recovery in America's 100 Largest Metropolitan Areas, March 2011*

- The San Antonio metro area was identified as one of 10 "Cities Where the Recession is Easing." The metro area was ranked #7. Criteria: job growth; goods produced; home sale prices; unemployment rates. *Forbes.com, "Cities Where the Recession is Easing," March 3, 2010*

- San Antonio was identified as one of the top 25 U.S. cities with the most credit card debt by credit reporting bureau Experian. The city was ranked #1. *Experian, March 4, 2011*

- San Antonio was selected as one of the "100 Best Places to Live and Launch" in the U.S. The city ranked #34. The editors at *Fortune Small Business* ranked 296 Census-designated metro areas by business friendliness (Launching Score, % New Businesses) and lifestyle offerings (Living Score). Then they picked the town within each of the top 100 metro areas that best blends business and pleasure. *Fortune Small Business, "100 Best Places to Live and Launch 2008," April 2008*

- *American City Business Journals* ranked America's 261 largest cities in terms of their resident's wealth. San Antonio ranked #215. Criteria: per capita income; median household income; percentage of households with annual incomes of $200,000 or more; median home value. *American City Business Journals, www.bizjournals.com, "Where the Money Is: America's Wealth Centers," August 18, 2008*

- The San Antonio metro area appeared on the Milken Institute "2010 Best Performing Metros" list. Rank: #14 out of 200 large metro areas. Criteria: job growth; wage and salary growth; high-tech output growth. *Milken Institute, "2010 Best Performing Metros"*

- The San Antonio metro area was selected as one of the best cities for entrepreneurs in America by *Inc. Magazine.* Criteria: job-growth data for 335 metro areas was analyzed for: recent growth trend (the current and prior year's employment growth rates, with the current year emphasized); mid-term growth (the average annual 2002-2007 growth rate); long-term trend (the sum of the 2002-2007 and 1996-2001 employment growth rates multiplied by the ratio of the 1996-2001 growth rate over the 2002-2007 growth rate); current year growth. The San Antonio metro area ranked #7 among large metro areas and #48 overall. *Inc. Magazine, "The Best Cities for Doing Business," July 2008*

- San Antonio was ranked #88 out of 145 regions worldwide in terms of its "Knowledge Competitiveness Index." The index attempts to measure the knowledge-based development taking place throughout the world and is based on 19 measures of economic performance that indicate a region's ability to translate its knowledge capacity into economic value. *Centre for International Competitiveness, World Knowledge Competitiveness Index 2008*

- *Forbes* ranked the 200 most populous metro areas in the U.S. in terms of the "Best Places for Business and Careers." The San Antonio metro area was ranked #16. Criteria: 12 metrics including costs (business and living), job growth (past and projected), income growth, educational attainment, projected economic growth, crime, cultural and recreational opportunities, net migration patterns, percentage of subprime mortgages handed out over a three-year period, and the number of highly ranked four-year colleges. *Forbes, "Best Places for Business and Careers," April 14, 2010*

Children/Family Rankings

- San Antonio was selected as one of the 10 worst cities to raise children in the U.S. by *KidFriendlyCities.org.* Criteria: education; environment; health; employment; crime; diversity; cost of living. *KidFriendlyCities.org, "Top Rated Kid/Family Friendly Cities 2009"*

- The San Antonio metro area was selected as one of the "Best Cities for Relocating Families" by Worldwide ERC and Primacy Relocation. The 2008 study looked at nearly 50 factors important to relocating families including: recent job growth; nearby top-ranked colleges; in-state tuition for four-year public colleges; population growth since 2000; pediatricians per 100,000 population; and a Green Living index. *Worldwide ERC and Primacy Relocation, "2008 Best Cities for Relocating Families"*

- *Fit Pregnancy* magazine ranked the 50 best U.S. cities in which to have a baby. San Antonio was ranked #38. Criteria: access to hospitals and doctors; affordability; birthing options; breastfeeding; child care; fertility laws/resources; maternal and infant health risk; parks/stroller friendliness; safety. *Fit Pregnancy, "The Best Cities in America to Have a Baby 2008"*

Culture/Performing Arts Rankings

- San Antonio was selected as one of "America's Top 25 Arts Destinations." The city ranked #21 in the big city (population 500,000 and over) category. Criteria: readers' top choices for arts travel destinations based on the richness and variety of visual arts sites, activities and events. *American Style, "America's Top 25 Arts Destinations," May 2010*

Dating/Romance Rankings

- San Antonio appeared on *Men's Health's* list of the most sex-happy cities in America. The city ranked #15 of 100. Criteria: condom sales; birth rates; sex toy sales; rates of chlamydia, gonorrhea, and syphilis. *Men's Health, "America's Most Sex-Happy Cities," October 2010*

- *Men's Health* ranked 100 U.S. cities in terms of best (and worst) marriages. San Antonio was ranked #91 (#1 = worst marriages). Criteria: rate of failed marriages; stringency of divorce laws; percentage of population who've split; number of licensed marriage and family therapists. *Men's Health, "Splitsville, USA," May 2010*

- Eli Lily and Company, in partnership with Sperling's BestPlaces, ranked the nation's 50 largest metro areas in terms of the "Most Romantic Cities for Baby Boomers." The San Antonio metro area ranked #31. Criteria: marriage and divorce rates among "baby boomers" age 45 to 60; great restaurants; dance studios; chocolate, jewelry and flower sales. *Eli Lily and Company, "Most Romantic Cities for Baby Boomers," April 20, 2007*

- The San Antonio metro area was selected as one of the "Best Cities for Relocating Singles" by Worldwide ERC and Primacy Relocation. The area ranked #61 out of the 100 largest metro areas in the U.S. Areas were selected based on the following criteria: recent job growth; recent singles population growth; overall population growth; affordable rental housing; cost-of-living index; expanded arts and recreation opportunities; ratio of single men and single women; affordability of quality higher education (including state residency requirements); diversity index; climate; population density. *Worldwide ERC and Primacy Relocation, "2008 Best Cities for Relocating Singles"*

- *Forbes* ranked the 40 most populous urbanized areas in the U.S. in terms of the "Best Cities for Singles." The San Antonio metro area ranked #27. Criteria: number of singles; cost of living alone; nightlife; culture; job growth; coolness; and online dating participation. *Forbes.com, "Best Cities for Singles," July 27, 2009*

- San Antonio was identified as one of "America's Most Lustful Cities" by Forbes.com. The city ranked #2. Criteria: highest per capita over-the-counter contraceptive purchases in America's 50 largest cities. *Forbes.com, "America's Most Lustful Cities," December 17, 2007*

Education Rankings

- San Antonio was selected as one of "America's Most Literate Cities." The city ranked #62 out of the 75 largest U.S. cities. Criteria: number of booksellers; library resources; Internet resources; educational attainment; periodical publishing resources; newspaper circulation. *Central Connecticut State University, "America's Most Literate Cities 2010"*

- San Antonio was identified as one of the 100 "smartest" metro areas in the U.S. The area ranked #86. Criteria: the editors rated the collective brainpower of the 100 largest metro area in the U.S based on their residents' educational attainment. *American City Business Journals, www.bizjournals.com, April 14, 2008*

- San Antonio was identified as one of "America's Brainiest Bastions" by *Portfolio.com*. The metro area ranked #140 out of 200. Portfolio.com analyzed levels of educational attainment in the nation's 200 largest metropolitan areas. The editors established scores for five levels of educational attainment, based on relative earning power of adult workers age 25 or older. Scores were determined by comparing the median income for all workers with the median income for those workers at a specified educational level. *Portfolio.com, "America's Brainiest Bastions," December 1, 2010*

Environmental Rankings

- The San Antonio metro area was identified as one of "The Ten Biggest American Cities that are Running Out of Water" by *24/7 Wall St.* The metro area ranked #4 out of 10. *24/7 Wall St.* did an analysis of the water supply and consumption in the 30 largest metropolitan areas in the U.S. Criteria include: projected water demand as a share of available precipitation; groundwater use as a share or projected available precipitation; susceptibility to drought; projected increase in freshwater withdrawls; projected increase in summer water deficit. The editors chose ten cities that are likely to face severe shortages in the relatively near-term future. *24/7 Wall St., "The Ten Biggest American Cities that are Running Out of Water," November 1, 2010*

- San Antonio was selected as one of 22 "Smarter Cities" for energy by the Natural Resources Defense Council." Criteria: investment in green power; energy efficiency measures; conservation. *Natural Resources Defense Council, "2010 Smarter Cities," July 19, 2010*

- *American City Business Journal* ranked 43 metropolitan areas in terms of their "greenness." The San Antonio metro area ranked #19. Criteria: Forty-one metros in which *ACBJ* has business weeklies, plus Indianapolis and Cleveland, were ranked based on 20 different indicators such as adoption of green technologies, utilization of environmentally sound practices, and air and water quality. *American City Business Journals, "Green City Index," March 11, 2010*

- 100 of the largest metro areas in the U.S. were analyzed in terms of their current drought severity. The San Antonio metro area ranked #99 (#1 = driest). The rankings were based on statistics such as long-term precipitation trends and patterns and the Palmer drought indices. *Sperling's BestPlaces, www.BestPlaces.net, "America's Drought-Riskiest Cities," November 2007*

- The San Antonio metro area appeared in *Country Home's* "Best Green Places" report. The area ranked #114 out of 379. Criteria: official energy policies; green power; green buildings; availability of fresh, locally grown food. *Country Home, "Best Green Places," 2008*

Health/Fitness Rankings

- San Antonio was selected as one of the 25 fattest cities in America by *Men's Fitness Online*. It ranked #3 out of America's 50 largest cities. Criteria: fitness centers and sport stores; nutrition; sports participation; TV viewing; overweight/sedentary; junk food; air quality; geography; commute; parks and open space; city recreational facilities; access to healthcare; motivation; mayor and city initiatives; state obesity initiatives. *Men's Fitness Online, 2009 Fittest/Fattest Cities*

- San Antonio was identified as a "2011 Asthma Capital." The area ranked #22 out of the nation's 100 largest metropolitan areas. Twelve factors were used to identify the most challenging places to live for people with asthma: estimated prevalence; self-reported prevalence; crude death rate for asthma; annual pollen score; annual air quality; public smoking laws; number of board-certified asthma specialists; school inhaler access laws; rescue medication use; controller medication use; uninsured rate; poverty rate. *Asthma and Allergy Foundation of America, "2011 Asthma Capitals"*

- San Antonio was identified as a 2009 "Spring Allergy Capital." The area ranked #40 out of 100. Three groups of factors were used to identify the most severe cities for people with allergies during the spring season: annual pollen levels; medicine utilization; access to board-certified allergists. *Asthma and Allergy Foundation of America, "Spring Allergy Capitals 2009"*

- San Antonio was identified as a 2010 "Fall Allergy Capital." The area ranked #30 out of 100. Three groups of factors were used to identify the most severe cities for people with allergies during the fall season: annual pollen levels; medicine utilization; access to board-certified allergists. *Asthma and Allergy Foundation of America, "Fall Allergy Capitals 2010"*

- *Men's Health* ranked 100 U.S. cities in terms of the quality of their tap water. San Antonio was ranked #39 and received a grade of B. Criteria: levels of total coliform bacteria, arsenic, lead, total trihalomethanes (linked to cancer), and halo-acetic acids; number of EPA water-system violations from 1995 to 2005. *Men's Health, March 2007*

- Ortho-McNeil Neurologics, in partnership with Sperling's BestPlaces, analyzed 110 metro areas and identified those U.S. cities with the highest prevalence of factors that are most commonly associated with migraine headaches. The San Antonio metro area ranked #100. Criteria: number of migraine-related drug prescriptions per capita; lifestyle factors that can contribute to migraines; environmental factors that can trigger migraines; and consumption of migraine-triggering foods. *Ortho-McNeil Neurologics, "America's Migraine Hot Spots," March 14, 2006*

- An analysis of the "Best & Worst Cities for Sleep" was conducted by Sperling's BestPlaces. The study ranked America's 50 most populated metro areas. The San Antonio metro area ranked #35 (#1 = best city for sleep). Criteria: number of days residents didn't get enough rest or sleep during the past month; average length of daily commute; divorce rate; unemployment rate. *Sperling's BestPlaces, www.BestPlaces.net, "Best & Worst Cities for Sleep," 2006*

- *Men's Health* ranked 100 U.S. cities in terms of cities "Where the Food is Sickening." San Antonio was ranked #60 and received a grade of C-. The magazine arrived at their ratings by looking at data compiled by the Community Health Status Indicator Project to determine outbreaks of E. coli, salmonella-, and shigella-related infections. They then checked the CDC's Wonder database to see how many people died from tainted food. Finally, the magazine found out which states have adopted the current version of the FDA's uniform Food Code, which contains the most up-to-date rules for keeping restaurant kitchens clean. *Men's Health, October 2005*

- The San Antonio metro area was identified as one of "America's Most Obese Cities" by *Forbes*. The magazine analyzed BMI (body mass index) data from the CDC in the 50 most populated metro areas in the U.S. and ranked the top 20. The area ranked #3. *Forbes, "America's Most Obese Cities," November 26, 2007*

- The San Antonio metro area appeared in the 2010 Gallup-Healthways Well-Being Index. The index, based on interviews with more than 353,000 Americans during 2009, asked individuals to assess their jobs, finances, physical health, emotional state of mind and communities. The metro area ranked #36 out of 162. Criteria: life evaluation; emotional health; work environment; physical health; healthy behaviors; basic access (basic needs optimal for a healthy life, such as access to food and medicine, having health insurance and feeling safe while walking at night). *Gallup-Healthways, "Well-Being Index 2010"*

- The San Antonio metro area was identified as one of "America's Most Stressful Cities" by *Forbes*. The metro area ranked #39. Criteria: median home price drop; unemployment rates; cost of living; air quality; sunny days; population density. *Forbes.com, "America's Most Stressful Cities," August 20, 2009*

- The San Antonio metro area was identified as one of "America's 20 Most Sedentary Cities" by *Forbes*. The metro area ranked #7. Criteria: percentage of overweight or obese people; percentage of people who had not engaged in any physical activity in the past 30 days; average number of hours of TV watched per week. *Forbes.com, "America's Most Sedentary Cities," October 29, 2007*

- 50 of the largest metro areas in the U.S. were analyzed in terms of their health and fitness by the American College of Sports Medicine in their "American Fitness Index." The San Antonio metro area ranked #43 (#1 = healthiest). Criteria: preventative health behaviors; levels of chronic disease; health care access; community resources and policies that support physical activity. *American College of Sports Medicine, "Health and Community Fitness Status of the 50 Largest Metropolitan Areas," May 24, 2010*

- *The Daily Beast* identified the 30 U.S metro areas with the worst smoking habits. The San Antonio metro area ranked #17. Sixty urban centers with populations of more than one million were ranked based on the following criteria: number of smokers; number of cigarettes smoked per day; fewest attempts to quit. *The Daily Beast, "30 Cities With Smoking Problems," January 3, 2011*

Pet Rankings

- San Antonio was identified as one of North America's most accommodating cities for travelers with pets. The city was ranked #2. Criteria: number of AAA Approved and Diamond rated pet-friendly hotels. *AAA, Traveling with your Pet: The AAA PetBook, 2006*

Real Estate Rankings

- *Fortune* ranked the 100 largest metro areas in the U.S. in terms of projected median home price change in 2010. The San Antonio metro area ranked #28. *Fortune, "The 2010 Housing Outlook," December 9, 2009*

- The San Antonio metro area was identified as one of the "25 Hottest Housing Markets" in the U.S. The area ranked #19 out of 160 markets with a home price appreciation rate of 7.0%. Criteria: year-over-year change of median sales price of existing single-family homes between the 4th quarter of 2009 and the 4th quarter of 2010. *National Association of Realtors, Median Sales Price of Existing Single-Family Homes for Metropolitan Areas, 4th Quarter 2010*

- San Antonio appeared on ApartmentRatings.com "Top Cities for Renters" list in 2009." The area ranked #82. Overall satisfaction ratings were ranked using thousands of user submitted scores for hundreds of apartment complexes located in the 100 most populated U.S. municipalities. *ApartmentRatings.com, "2009 Renter Satisfaction Rankings"*

- San Antonio appeared on ApartmentRatings.com "Top College Towns & Cities" for renters list in 2010." The area ranked #80. Overall satisfaction ratings were ranked using thousands of user submitted scores for hundreds of apartment complexes located in cities and towns that are home to the 100 largest four-year institutions in the U.S. *ApartmentRatings.com, "2010 College Town Renter Satisfaction Rankings"*

- The San Antonio metro area was identified as one of the "Top 25 Real Estate Investment Markets" by *FinestExperts.com*. The metro area ranked #10. Over 10,000 real estate markets were analyzed to identify the most suitable places for real estate investors to seek stability and growth. Criteria: employment; rental markets; growth levels as offset by foreclosures. *FinestExperts.com, "Top 25 Real Estate Investment Markets," January 7, 2010*

- The nation's largest metro areas were analyzed in terms of the percentage of households entering some stage of foreclosure in 2010. The San Antonio metro area ranked #115 out of 206 (#1 = highest foreclosure rate). *RealtyTrac, 2010 Year-End Metropolitan Foreclosure Market Report, January 27, 2011*

- The San Antonio metro area was identified as one of the "Best Cities to Buy a Home" by *Forbes*. The metro area ranked #5. Criteria: 2-year home price appreciation; vacancy rates; spread between monthly rent and mortgage payment at the median level. *Forbes.com, "Best Cities to Buy a Home," July 22, 2008*

- The San Antonio metro area was identified as one of the "Least Expensive U.S Cities for Renters" by *Forbes*. The metro area ranked #6. Criteria: renter-occupied units paying cash rent where gross rent is defined as contract rent plus utilities, if utilities were paid by the renter. *Forbes.com, "Most and Least Expensive U.S. Cities for Renters," September 23, 2008*

- The San Antonio metro area appeared in a *Wall Street Journal* article ranking cities by "housing stress." The metro area was ranked #24 (#1 = most stress). Criteria: fraction of mortgage-holding homeowners with a monthly housing payment in excess of 30 percent of income; percentage of people without health insurance; unemployment rate. *The Wall Street Journal, "Which Cities Face Biggest Housing Risk," October 5, 2010*

- The Center for Housing Policy ranked 210 U.S metropolitan areas by the fair market rent for a two-bedroom unit. The San Antonio metro area was ranked #118. (#1 = most expensive) with a rent of $796. Criteria: Fair Market Rent (FMR) in effect during the fourth quarter of 2009 based on HUD's fiscal year 2010 FMRs. *The Center for Housing Policy, "Paycheck to Paycheck: Most to Least Expensive Rental Markets in 2009"*

- The San Antonio metro area was identified as one of the markets with the best expected performance in home prices over the next 12 months. *Local Market Monitor, "First Quarter Home Price Forecast for Largest US Markets," March 2, 2011*

Safety Rankings

- Symantec, the makers of Norton, in partnership with Sperling's BestPlaces, ranked the 50 largest cities in the U.S. in terms of their vulnerability to cybercrime. The city ranked #41. Criteria: number of cyberattacks and potential infections; level of Internet access; expenditures on computer hardware and software; wireless hotspots; broadband connectivity; Internet usage; online purchases. *Symantec, "10 Riskiest Cities for Cybercrime," March 22, 2010*

- Allstate ranked the 200 largest cities in America in terms of driver safety. San Antonio ranked #163. In addition, drivers were 30.2% more likely to have had an accident compared to the national average. Allstate researchers analyzed internal property damage reported claims over a two-year period (from January 2007 to December 2008) to ensure the findings would not be affected by external influences such as weather or road construction. A weighted average of the two-year numbers determined the annual percentages. The report defines an auto crash as any collision resulting in a property damage claim. *Allstate, "The 2010 Allstate America's Best Drivers Report™"*

- The National Insurance Crime Bureau ranked 366 metro areas in the U.S. in terms of per capita rates of vehicle theft. The San Antonio metro area ranked #54 (#1 = highest rate). Criteria: number of vehicle theft offenses per 100,000 inhabitants. *National Insurance Crime Bureau, "Hot Spots," May 17, 2010*

- The San Antonio metro area was identified as one of the "The Most Dangerous Metro Areas for Pedestrians" by Transportation for America and the Surface Transportation Policy Partnership. The metro area ranked #30 out of 52 metro areas with over 1 million residents. Criteria: area's population divided by the number of pedestrian fatalities in that area. *Transportation for America and the Surface Transportation Policy Partnership, "Dangerous by Design: Solving the Epidemic of Preventable Pedestrian Deaths (and Making Great Neighborhoods)," November 11, 2009*

Seniors/Retirement Rankings

- San Antonio was selected as one of "5 Great Places to Retire" by *Fortune*. The city ranked #3. Criteria: cost of living; culture; tax rates; health care; attractive real estate markets that have come down significantly in price. *Fortune, "5 Great Places to Retire," June 14, 2010*

- San Antonio was identified as one of "The Top 100 Places to Retire" by *Topretirements.com* The list reflects the 100 cities (out of 625+ total cities reviewed) that visitors to the website are most interested in for retirement. *Topretirements.com, "2011 Best Places to Retire List: The Sunbelt Rules"*

- San Antonio was selected as one of "Seven Places to Retire During an Economic Downturn." The city ranked #6. The editors at *Smart Money* selected seven recession-proof places soon-to-be retirees should consider. *SmartMoney.com, "Seven Places to Retire During an Economic Downturn," February 29, 2008*

- The San Antonio metro area was selected as one of "The 10 Most Affordable Cities for Long-Term Care" by *U.S. News & World Report*. Criteria: costs at nursing homes, assisted living facilities, and adult day health care facilities; cost for licensed home health aides. *U.S. News & Word Report, "The 10 Most Affordable Cities for Long-Term Care," May 17, 2010*

Sports/Recreation Rankings

- San Antonio appeared on the *Sporting News* list of the "Best Sports Cities" for 2010. The area ranked #36 out of 402 cities in the U.S. *Sporting News* takes a 12-month snapshot, roughly October to October, of each city's sports, putting a heavy premium on regular-season won-lost records (from the most recently completed season). Other criteria include: playoff berths, bowl appearances and tournament bids; championships; applicable power ratings; quality of competition; overall fan fervor as measured in part by attendance as percentage of venue capacity; abundance of teams (rewarding quality over quantity); stadium and arena quality; ticket availability and prices; franchise ownership; and marquee appeal of athletes. *Sporting News, "Best Sports Cities 2010," October, 2010*

- Scarborough Sports Marketing, a leading market research firm, identified the San Antonio DMA (Designated Market Area) as one of the top markets for sports with more than 60% of adults reporting that they are "very" interested in any of the sports measured by Scarborough. *Scarborough Sports Marketing, October 1, 2008*

- San Antonio was chosen as a bicycle friendly community by the League of American Bicyclists. A Bicycle Friendly Community welcomes cyclists by providing safe accommodation for cycling and encouraging people to bike for transportation and recreation. There are four award levels: Platinum; Gold; Silver; and Bronze. The community achieved an award level of Bronze. *League of American Bicyclists, "Bicycle Friendly Community Master List," September 2010*

- San Antonio was selected as one of the most playful cities in the U.S. by KaBOOM! The organization's Playful City USA initiative is a national recognition program that honors cities and towns across the nation for a vision, plan and commitment to creating an agenda for play. Cities were recognized based on a pledge to five specific commitments to play: creating a local play commission or task force; designing an annual action plan for play; conducting a play space audit; outlining a financial investment in play for the current fiscal year; and proclaiming and celebrating an annual "play day." *KaBOOM! National Campaign for Play, "2010 Playful City USA Communities"*

- Scarborough Research, a leading market research firm, identified the top local markets for avid NBA fans. The San Antonio DMA (Designated Market Area) ranked in the top 10 with 33% of consumers 18 years and over reporting that they are "very interested in the NBA." *Scarborough Research, April 24, 2006*

- *Golf Digest* ranked 330 metro areas in the U.S. in terms of golf. The San Antonio metro area was ranked #250. Criteria: access to golf; weather; value of golf; and quality of golf. *Golf Digest, "Metro Golf Rankings," August 2005*

Technology Rankings

- San Antonio was selected as a 2010 Digital Cities Survey winner. The city ranked #8 in the large city (250,000 or more population) category. The survey examined and assessed how city governments are utilizing information technology to operate and deliver quality service to their customers and citizens. Survey questions focused on implementation and adoption of online service delivery; planning and governance; and the infrastructure and architecture that make the transformation to digital government possible. *Center for Digital Government, "2010 Digital Cities Survey"*

Transportation Rankings

- The San Antonio metro area appeared on *Forbes* list of the best and worst cities for commuters. The metro area ranked #23 out of 60 (#1 is best). Criteria: travel time; road congestion; travel delays. *Forbes.com, "Best and Worst Cities for Commuters," February 16, 2010*

Women/Minorities Rankings

- San Antonio was ranked #76 out of 100 metro areas in *SELF Magazine's* ranking of America's healthiest places for women." A panel of experts came up with more than 50 criteria including death and disease rates, environmental indicators, community resources, and lifestyle habits. *SELF Magazine, "Secrets of America's Healthiest Women," December 2008*

- San Antonio was selected as one of the 25 healthiest cities for Latinas by *Latina Magazine*. The city ranked #6. Criteria: access to health care; community risk; family and home statistics; air quality; number of parks. *Latina Magazine, May 2007*

- San Antonio was selected as one of the "Top 10 Cities for Hispanics." Criteria: the prospect of a good job; a safe place to raise a family; a manageable cost of living; the ability to buy and keep a home; a culture of inclusion where Hispanics are highly represented; resources to help start a business; the presence of Hispanic or Spanish-language media; representation of Hispanic needs on local government; a thriving arts and culture community; air quality; energy costs; city's state of health and rates of obesity. *Hispanic Magazine, August 2008*

Miscellaneous Rankings

- Energizer Holdings, the makers of Edge® shave gel, in partnership with Sperling's BestPlaces, ranked 50 major metro areas in terms of everyday irritations. The San Antonio metro area ranked #29. Criteria: humidity levels; weather conditions; incidence of traffic delays and congestion; average commute times; frequency of flight delays and cancellations; rates of sleeplessness; underemployment; pollens and allergens; pests; comedy clubs per capita. *Energizer Holdings, "Most Irritation Prone Cities," July 23, 2010*

- San Antonio was selected as one of the best cities for shopping in the U.S. by *Forbes*. The city was ranked #8. Criteria: number of major shopping centers; retail locations; Consumer Price Index (CPI); combined state and local sales tax. *Forbes, "America's 25 Best Cities for Shopping," December 13, 2010*

- The San Antonio metro area appeared in AutoMD.com's ranking of the "Best and Worst Cities for Auto Repair." The metro area ranked #4 (#1 is best). The 50 most-populated metro areas in the U.S. were ranked on three critical factors: repair affordability; price disparity range; shop integrity factor. *AutoMD.com, "Advocacy for Repair Shop Fairness Report," February 24, 2010*

- *Men's Health* examined the nation's largest 100 cities and identified "America's Most Political Cities." San Antonio was ranked among the ten least political at #8. Criteria: percentage of active registered voters; percentage of ballots counted of active registration; percentage of income donated to 2008 presidential election; campaign spending; percentage of registrants who voted in the 2008 primaries; percentage of voters in the 2004/2006 Senate election; percentage of voters in the 2004-2007 gubernatorial election. *Men's Health, "Ranking America's Cities: America's Most Political Cities," October 2008*

- San Antonio was identified as one of "America's Most Jealous Cities" by Forbes.com. The city ranked #3. Criteria: highest per capita incidences of property crimes in America's 50 largest cities. *Forbes.com, "America's Most Jealous Cities," December 10, 2007*

- San Antonio was selected as one of the "Top 10 Places to Eat Classic American Chow." *USA Weekend, "Summer Travel Report," May 18-20, 2007*

- San Antonio appeared on Procter & Gamble's list of the "Top-20 All-Time Sweatiest Cities." The city was ranked #2. The rankings are based on computer simulations of the amount of sweat a person of average height and weight would produce walking around for an hour in the average temperatures during the summer months, based on historical weather data during June, July and August from 2001-2008 for each city. *Procter & Gamble, Old Spice Press Release, "Top-20 All-Time Sweatiest Cities," July 1, 2009*

- The San Antonio metro area appeared on *Forbes* list of "America's Drunkest Cities." The area ranked #12. Criteria: 35 of the largest continental U.S. metro areas were chosen based on availability of data and geographic diversity. Each metro was ranked in five areas: state laws; drinkers; heavy drinkers; binge drinkers; and alcoholism. *Forbes.com, "America's Drunkest Cities," August 22, 2006*

- Scarborough Research, a leading market research firm, identified the top local markets for frequent fast food restaurant patronage. The San Antonio DMA (Designated Market Area) ranked in the top 10 with consumers reporting an average of 6.2 visits within the past 30 days. *Scarborough Research, May 31, 2006*

- Scarborough Research, a leading market research firm, identified the top local markets for frequent sit-down restaurant patronage. The San Antonio DMA (Designated Market Area) ranked in the top 10 with consumers reporting an average of 4.0 visits within the past 30 days. *Scarborough Research, May 31, 2006*

Business Environment

CITY FINANCES

City Government Finances

Component	2008 ($000)	2008 ($ per capita)
Total Revenues	3,931,355	2,958
Total Expenditures	4,243,509	3,193
Debt Outstanding	6,874,000	5,172
Cash and Securities[1]	4,718,556	3,550

Note: (1) Cash and security holdings of a government at the close of its fiscal year, including those of its dependent agencies, utilities, and liquor stores.
Source: U.S Census Bureau, State & Local Government Finances 2008

City Government Revenue by Source

Source	2008 ($000)	2008 ($ per capita)
General Revenue		
From Federal Government	78,287	59
From State Government	98,666	74
From Local Governments	27,447	21
Taxes		
Property	326,390	246
Sales and Gross Receipts	304,859	229
Personal Income	0	0
Corporate Income	0	0
Motor Vehicle License	0	0
Other Taxes	33,887	25
Current Charges	454,869	342
Liquor Store	0	0
Utility	1,964,489	1,478
Employee Retirement	350,139	263

Source: U.S Census Bureau, State & Local Government Finances 2008

City Government Expenditures by Function

Function	2008 ($000)	2008 ($ per capita)	2008 (%)
General Direct Expenditures			
Air Transportation	96,749	73	2.3
Corrections	0	0	0.0
Education	46,922	35	1.1
Employment Security Administration	0	0	0.0
Financial Administration	31,897	24	0.8
Fire Protection	176,681	133	4.2
General Public Buildings	9,874	7	0.2
Governmental Administration, Other	11,305	9	0.3
Health	50,673	38	1.2
Highways	134,075	101	3.2
Hospitals	0	0	0.0
Housing and Community Development	47,600	36	1.1
Interest on General Debt	78,730	59	1.9
Judicial and Legal	19,417	15	0.5
Libraries	32,595	25	0.8
Parking	6,363	5	0.1
Parks and Recreation	183,236	138	4.3
Police Protection	256,025	193	6.0
Public Welfare	43,025	32	1.0
Sewerage	200,832	151	4.7
Solid Waste Management	66,522	50	1.6
Veterans' Services	0	0	0.0
Liquor Store	0	0	0.0
Utility	2,528,091	1,902	59.6
Employee Retirement	79,130	60	1.9

Source: U.S Census Bureau, State & Local Government Finances 2008

Municipal Bond Ratings

Area	Moody's	S&P	Fitch
City	Aa1	AAA	AA+

Rating Systems (shown in declining order of credit quality): Moody's– Aaa, Aa, A, Baa, Ba, B, Caa, Ca, C (numerical modifiers 1, 2, and 3 are added to letter-rating); S&P– AAA, AA, A, BBB, BB, B, CCC, CC, C; Fitch– AAA, AA, A, BBB, BB, B, CCC, CC, C. Ratings may be modified by the addition of a plus or minus sign to show relative standing within the major rating categories.

Notes: n/a Not available; (1) Not reviewed; (2) Issuer Rating/No General Obligation; (3) Standard and Poor's Issue Credit Rating (ICR) is a current opinion of an obliger with respect to a specific financial obligation, a specific class of financial obligations, or a specific financial program.

Source: U.S. Census Bureau, 2011 Statistical Abstract, Bond Ratings for City Governments by Largest Cities: 2009

DEMOGRAPHICS

Population Growth

Area	1990 Census	2000 Census	2010 Estimate	2015 Projection	Population Growth (%) 2000-2010	Population Growth (%) 2010-2015
City	997,258	1,144,646	1,323,124	1,420,762	15.6	7.4
MSA[1]	1,407,745	1,711,703	2,090,028	2,270,338	22.1	8.6
U.S.	248,709,873	281,421,906	309,038,974	321,675,005	9.8	4.1

Note: (1) Metropolitan Statistical Area - see Appendix B for areas included
Source: Claritas, Inc.

Number of Households and Average Household Size

Area	2010 Estimate	2010 Average Household Size
City	467,597	2.77
MSA[1]	733,645	2.79
U.S.	116,136,617	2.59

Note: (1) Metropolitan Statistical Area - see Appendix B for areas included
Source: Claritas, Inc.

Race and Ethnicity

Area	White Alone[2] (%)	Black Alone[2] (%)	Asian Alone[2] (%)	Other Race Alone[2] (%)	Hispanic[3] (%)
City	65.5	6.5	1.9	26.1	62.8
MSA[1]	69.4	6.2	1.8	22.6	53.4
U.S.	72.3	12.4	4.4	10.9	15.8

Note: Figures are 2010 estimates; (1) Metropolitan Statistical Area - see Appendix B for areas included (2) Alone is defined as not being in combination with one or more other races; (3) May be of any race.
Source: Claritas, Inc.

Segregation

Type	Segregation Indices[1] 1990	2000	2010	2010 Rank[2]	Percent Change 1990-2000	1990-2010	2000-2010
Black/White	56.1	52.8	49.0	73	-3.3	-7.1	-3.8
Asian/White	33.8	35.4	38.3	66	1.6	4.5	2.9
Hispanic/White	52.1	49.7	46.1	43	-2.4	-6.0	-3.6

Note: Figures are based on an analysis of 1990, 2000, and 2010 Census Decennial Census tract data by William H. Frey, Brookings Institution and the University of Michigan Social Science Data Analysis Network. In this analysis all racial groups (whites, blacks, and asians) are non-Hispanic members of those races. Hispanics are shown as a separate category; All figures cover the Metropolitan Statistical Area (see Appendix B for areas included); (1) Segregation Indices are Dissimilarity Indices that measure the degree to which the minority group is distributed differently than whites aross census tracts. They range from 0 (complete integration) to 100 (complete [segregation) where the value indicates the percentage of the minority group that needs to move to be distributed exactly like whites; (2) Ranges from 1 (most segregated) to 102 (least segregated); n/a not available.
Source: www.CensusScope.org

Ancestry

Area	German	Irish	English	American	Italian	Polish	French	Scottish
City	9.2	5.4	5.0	3.9	1.9	1.2	1.9	1.2
MSA[1]	12.7	7.0	6.3	4.1	2.1	1.7	2.2	1.5
U.S.	16.6	12.0	9.1	6.1	5.9	3.3	3.1	1.9

Note: The top eight ancestries in the U.S. are shown. Figures are percentages and include multiple ancestry (e.g. if a person reported being Irish and Italian, they were included in both columns); (1) Metropolitan Statistical Area - see Appendix B for areas included
Source: U.S. Census Bureau, 2007-2009 American Community Survey 3-Year Estimates

Foreign-Born Population

Area	Percent of Population Born in								
	Any Foreign Country	Mexico	Asia	Europe	Carribean	South America	Central America[2]	Africa	Canada
City	13.3	9.4	1.6	0.7	0.2	0.3	0.7	0.3	0.1
MSA[1]	11.2	7.6	1.4	0.7	0.2	0.3	0.6	0.3	0.1
U.S.	12.5	3.8	3.4	1.6	1.1	0.8	0.9	0.5	0.3

Note: (1) Metropolitan Statistical Area - see Appendix B for areas included; (2) Excludes Mexico.
Source: U.S. Census Bureau, 2007-2009 American Community Survey 3-Year Estimates

Marriage Status

Area	Never Married	Now Married[2]	Separated	Widowed	Divorced
City	34.5	44.3	3.1	5.6	12.5
MSA[1]	31.6	48.2	2.9	5.7	11.7
U.S.	31.4	49.7	2.2	6.2	10.6

Note: Figures are percentages and cover the population 15 years of age and older;
(1) Metropolitan Statistical Area - see Appendix B for areas included; (2) Excludes separated
Source: U.S. Census Bureau, 2007-2009 American Community Survey 3-Year Estimates

Age Distribution and Median Age

Area	Percent of Population							Median Age
	Under Age 5	Age 5 to 17	Age 18 to 34	Age 35 to 49	Age 50 to 64	Age 65 to 79	80 Years and Over	
City	8.2	19.5	25.9	20.3	15.6	7.4	3.0	32.3
MSA[1]	8.0	19.5	24.3	20.8	16.4	7.9	3.0	33.6
U.S.	6.9	17.5	23.3	21.4	18.1	9.1	3.7	36.7

Note: (1) Metropolitan Statistical Area - see Appendix B for areas included
Source: U.S. Census Bureau, 2007-2009 American Community Survey 3-Year Estimates

Male/Female Ratio

Area	Males	Females	Males per 100 Females
City	643,568	679,556	94.7
MSA[1]	1,024,476	1,065,552	96.1
U.S.	152,401,520	156,637,454	97.3

Note: Figures are 2010 estimates; (1) Metropolitan Statistical Area -
see Appendix B for areas included
Source: Claritas, Inc.

Religion

Area	Catholic	Southern Baptist	United Meth-odist	ELCA[1]	LDS[2]	Presby-terian Church USA	Jewish Est.	Muslim Est.
County	41.2	8.6	3.0	1.0	0.7	0.8	0.8	0.2
U.S.	22.0	7.1	3.7	1.8	1.5	1.1	2.2	0.6

Note: Figures are the number of adherents as a percentage of the total population; Adherents are defined as all members, including full members, their children and the estimated number of other participants who are not considered members (e.g. the baptized, those not confirmed, those regularly attending services, etc.);
(1) Evangelical Lutheran Church in America; (2) The Church of Jesus Christ of Latter Day Saints
Source: Reprinted with permission from Religious Congregations and Membership in the United States 2000 (Nashville, Glenmary Research Center, 2002) Copyright Association of Statisticians of American Religious Bodies. All rights reserved.

ECONOMY

Gross Metropolitan Product

Area	2006	2007	2008	2009	2009 Rank[2]
MSA[1]	72.1	76.8	80.9	82.3	34

Note: Figures are in billions of dollars; (1) San Antonio, TX Metropolitan Statistical Area - see Appendix B for areas included; (2) Rank ranges from 1 to 363
Source: The U.S. Conference of Mayors, "Pace of Economic Recovery: GMP and Jobs," January 2010

Economic Growth

Area	2006-2008 (%)	2009 (%)	2010 (%)	Rank[2]
MSA[1]	2.8	0.3	3.7	59
U.S.	1.3	-2.5	2.2	–

Note: Figures are real Gross Metropolitan Product growth rates and represent annual average percent change; (1) San Antonio, TX Metropolitan Statistical Area - see Appendix B for areas included; (2) Rank ranges from 1 to 363
Source: The U.S. Conference of Mayors, "Pace of Economic Recovery: GMP and Jobs," January 2010

Metropolitan Area Exports

Area	2005	2006	2007	2008	2009	2009 Rank[2]
MSA[1]	2,347.0	3,093.7	3,567.8	5,049.5	4,390.0	44

Note: Figures are in millions of dollars; (1) San Antonio, TX Metropolitan Statistical Area - see Appendix B for areas included; (2) Rank ranges from 1 to 374
Source: U.S. Department of Commerce, International Trade Administration, Office of Trade & Industry Information, Manufacturing & Services

INCOME

Per Capita/Median/Average Income

Area	Per Capita ($)	Median Household ($)	Average Household ($)
City	20,873	43,723	58,165
MSA[1]	22,895	48,395	64,361
U.S.	27,034	52,795	71,071

Note: Figures are 2010 estimates; (1) Metropolitan Statistical Area - see Appendix B for areas included
Source: Claritas, Inc.

Household Income Distribution

Area	Percent of Households Earning							
	Under $15,000	$15,000 -24,999	$25,000 -34,999	$35,000 -49,999	$50,000 -74,999	$75,000 -99,000	$100,000 -149,999	$150,000 and up
City	15.1	12.4	12.7	16.8	19.1	10.1	9.2	4.6
MSA[1]	12.8	11.1	11.6	16.3	20.0	11.7	10.7	5.9
U.S.	12.1	10.2	10.6	15.0	19.5	12.5	12.1	8.0

Note: Figures are 2010 estimates; (1) Metropolitan Statistical Area - see Appendix B for areas included
Source: Claritas, Inc.

Poverty Rates by Age

Area	All Ages	Under 18 Years Old	18 to 64 Years Old	65 Years and Over
City	19.2	7.7	10.1	1.4
MSA[1]	16.3	6.4	8.6	1.3
U.S.	13.6	4.7	7.7	1.2

Note: Figures are percent of population with income during the previous 12 months below poverty level and only include population for whom poverty status is determined; (1) Metropolitan Statistical Area - see Appendix B for areas included
Source: U.S. Census Bureau, 2007-2009 American Community Survey 3-Year Estimates

Personal Bankruptcy Filing Rate

Area	2006	2007	2008	2009	2010
Bexar County	1.48	1.76	1.96	2.44	2.38
U.S.	2.00	2.73	3.53	4.60	4.96

Note: Numbers are per 1,000 population and include Chapter 7 and Chapter 13 filings
Source: Federal Deposit Insurance Corporation, Regional Economic Conditions, March 17, 2011

EMPLOYMENT

Labor Force and Employment

Area	Civilian Labor Force			Workers Employed		
	Dec. 2009	Dec. 2010	% Chg.	Dec. 2009	Dec. 2010	% Chg.
City	635,724	646,232	1.7	594,647	602,179	1.3
MSA[1]	972,595	989,732	1.8	906,553	918,035	1.3
U.S.	152,693,000	153,156,000	0.3	137,953,000	139,159,000	0.9

Note: Data is not seasonally adjusted and covers workers 16 years of age and older;
(1) Metropolitan Statistical Area - see Appendix B for areas included
Source: Bureau of Labor Statistics, http://stats.bls.gov

Unemployment Rate

Area	2010											
	Jan.	Feb.	Mar.	Apr.	May	Jun.	Jul.	Aug.	Sep.	Oct.	Nov.	Dec.
City	7.2	7.0	6.8	6.7	6.6	7.2	7.3	7.2	7.0	6.9	7.1	6.8
MSA[1]	7.6	7.3	7.2	7.0	6.9	7.5	7.6	7.5	7.3	7.3	7.5	7.2
U.S.	10.6	10.4	10.2	9.5	9.3	9.6	9.7	9.5	9.2	9.0	9.3	9.1

Note: Data is not seasonally adjusted and covers workers 16 years of age and older; All figures are percentages; (1) Metropolitan Statistical Area - see Appendix B for areas included
Source: Bureau of Labor Statistics, http://stats.bls.gov

Projected Unemployment Rate

Area	2007 (%)	2009 (%)	2011 (%)	2013 (%)
MSA[1]	4.1	7.5	7.1	6.2

Note: (1) Metropolitan Statistical Area - see Appendix B for areas included
Source: The U.S. Conference of Mayors, "Pace of Economic Recovery: GMP and Jobs," January 2010

Employment by Occupation

Occupation Classification	City (%)	MSA[1] (%)	U.S. (%)
Sales and Office	28.3	27.5	25.4
Professional and Related	18.8	19.4	21.0
Service	19.5	18.1	17.2
Production, Transportation, and Material Moving	10.0	10.2	12.3
Management, Business, and Financial	12.6	13.6	14.1
Construction, Extraction, and Maintenance	10.6	10.8	9.2
Farming, Forestry, and Fishing	0.3	0.3	0.7

Note: Figures cover employed civilians 16 years of age and older;
(1) Metropolitan Statistical Area - see Appendix B for areas included
Source: U.S. Census Bureau, 2007-2009 American Community Survey 3-Year Estimates

Employment by Industry

| Sector | MSA[1] | | U.S. |
	Number of Employees	Percent of Total	Percent of Total
Government	164,100	19.4	17.2
Education and Health Services	131,200	15.5	15.2
Professional and Business Services	101,900	12.0	13.0
Retail Trade	96,500	11.4	11.4
Leisure and Hospitality	100,400	11.8	9.7
Manufacturing	44,800	5.3	8.8
Financial Activities	65,600	7.7	5.8
Wholesale Trade	28,300	3.3	4.2
Construction	41,500	4.9	4.1
Other Services	31,500	3.7	4.1
Transportation and Utilities	20,200	2.4	3.7
Information	17,900	2.1	2.1
Mining and Logging	3,500	0.4	0.6

Note: Figures cover non-farm employment as of December 2010 and are not seasonally adjusted;
(1) Metropolitan Statistical Area - see Appendix B for areas included
Source: Bureau of Labor Statistics, http://stats.bls.gov

Occupations with Greatest Projected Employment Growth: 2006 - 2016

Occupation[1]	2006 Employment	2016 Projected Employment	Numeric Employment Change	Percent Employment Change
Combined food preparation and serving workers, including fast food	270,530	359,050	88,520	32.7
Retail salespersons	332,750	411,350	78,600	23.6
Personal and home care aides	133,050	207,850	74,800	56.2
Customer service representatives	214,440	280,060	65,620	30.6
Elementary school teachers, except special education	145,430	207,710	62,280	42.8
Registered nurses	157,840	217,430	59,590	37.8
Waiters and waitresses	174,140	227,790	53,650	30.8
Child care workers	145,500	189,730	44,230	30.4
Office clerks, general	194,610	236,670	42,060	21.6
Postsecondary teachers	113,400	153,130	39,730	35.0

Note: Projections cover Texas; (1) Sorted by numeric employment change
Source: www.projectionscentral.com, State Occupational Projections, 2006-2016 Long-Term Projections

Fastest Growing Occupations: 2006 - 2016

Occupation[1]	2006 Employment	2016 Projected Employment	Numeric Employment Change	Percent Employment Change
Personal and home care aides	133,050	207,850	74,800	56.2
Network systems and data communications analysts	17,750	27,620	9,870	55.6
Medical assistants	34,790	53,500	18,710	53.8
Special education teachers, preschool, kindergarten, and elementary school	13,750	20,560	6,810	49.5
Physical therapist assistants	3,780	5,570	1,790	47.4
Special education teachers, middle school	6,270	9,170	2,900	46.3
Computer software engineers, applications	30,900	45,200	14,300	46.3
Physician assistants	3,810	5,540	1,730	45.4
Kindergarten teachers, except special education	12,850	18,690	5,840	45.4
Pharmacy technicians	24,420	35,050	10,630	43.5

Note: Projections cover Texas; (1) Sorted by percent employment change and excludes occupations with numeric employment change less than 1500
Source: www.projectionscentral.com, State Occupational Projections, 2006-2016 Long-Term Projections

Average Wages

Occupation	$/Hr.	Occupation	$/Hr.
Accountants and Auditors	28.58	Maids and Housekeeping Cleaners	8.87
Automotive Mechanics	17.75	Maintenance and Repair Workers	13.86
Bookkeepers	15.91	Marketing Managers	57.91
Carpenters	15.70	Nuclear Medicine Technologists	29.23
Cashiers	8.45	Nurses, Licensed Practical	19.18
Clerks, General Office	12.18	Nurses, Registered	31.32
Clerks, Receptionists/Information	11.43	Nursing Aides/Orderlies/Attendants	11.00
Clerks, Shipping/Receiving	13.32	Packers and Packagers, Hand	9.71
Computer Programmers	34.97	Physical Therapists	45.28
Computer Support Specialists	20.56	Postal Service Mail Carriers	23.83
Computer Systems Analysts	n/a	Real Estate Brokers	27.88
Cooks, Restaurant	10.72	Retail Salespersons	10.70
Dentists	n/a	Sales Reps., Exc. Tech./Scientific	26.41
Electrical Engineers	43.32	Sales Reps., Tech./Scientific	38.00
Electricians	18.17	Secretaries, Exc. Legal/Med./Exec.	13.73
Financial Managers	52.88	Security Guards	11.64
First-Line Supervisors/Mgrs., Sales	18.60	Surgeons	n/a
Food Preparation Workers	8.22	Teacher Assistants	10.10
General and Operations Managers	48.19	Teachers, Elementary School	25.90
Hairdressers/Cosmetologists	11.41	Teachers, Secondary School	26.70
Internists	n/a	Telemarketers	9.75
Janitors and Cleaners	10.17	Truck Drivers, Heavy/Tractor-Trailer	16.33
Landscaping/Groundskeeping Workers	10.74	Truck Drivers, Light/Delivery Svcs.	12.69
Lawyers	51.75	Waiters and Waitresses	8.70

Note: Wage data covers the San Antonio, TX - see Appendix B for areas included. Hourly wages for elementary/secondary school teachers and teacher assistants were calculated by the editors from annual wage data assuming a 40 hour work week; n/a not available.
Source: Bureau of Labor Statistics, Metro Area Occupational Employment and Wage Estimates, May 2009

RESIDENTIAL REAL ESTATE

Building Permits

Area	Single-Family 2009	2010	Pct. Chg.	Multi-Family 2009	2010	Pct. Chg.	Total 2009	2010	Pct. Chg.
City	2,836	2,337	-17.6	330	1,237	274.8	3,166	3,574	12.9
MSA[1]	5,486	5,144	-6.2	438	1,721	292.9	5,924	6,865	15.9
U.S.	441,100	447,300	1.4	141,900	157,300	10.9	583,000	604,600	3.7

Note: (1) Metropolitan Statistical Area - see Appendix B for areas included; figures represent new, privately-owned housing units authorized (unadjusted data); All permit data are based on estimates with imputation.
Source: U.S. Census Bureau, Manufacturing, Mining, and Construction Statistics, Building Permits, 2009, 2010

Homeownership Rate

Area	2005 (%)	2006 (%)	2007 (%)	2008 (%)	2009 (%)	2010 (%)
MSA[1]	66.0	62.6	62.4	66.1	69.8	70.1
U.S.	68.9	68.8	68.1	67.8	67.4	66.9

Note: (1) Metropolitan Statistical Area - see Appendix B for areas included
Source: U.S. Census Bureau, Housing Vacancies and Homeownership Annual Statistics: 2010

Housing Vacancy Rates

Area	Gross Vacancy Rate[2] (%) 2008	2009	2010	Year-Round Vacancy Rate[3] (%) 2008	2009	2010	Rental Vacancy Rate[4] (%) 2008	2009	2010	Homeowner Vacancy Rate[5] (%) 2008	2009	2010
MSA[1]	11.1	10.6	11.1	10.7	10.3	10.6	11.5	12.1	14.0	1.5	1.2	1.6
U.S.	14.4	14.5	14.3	11.1	11.3	11.3	10.0	10.6	10.2	2.8	2.6	2.6

Note: (1) Metropolitan Statistical Area - see Appendix B for areas included; (2) The percentage of the total housing inventory that is vacant; (3) The percentage of the housing inventory (excluding seasonal units) that is year-round vacant; (4) The percentage of rental inventory that is vacant for rent; (5) The percentage of homeowner inventory that is vacant for sale; n/a not available
Source: U.S. Census Bureau, Housing Vacancies and Homeownership Annual Statistics: 2010

State Corporate Income Tax Rates

State	Tax Rate (%)	Income Brackets ($)	Num. of Brackets	Financial Institution Tax Rate (%)[a]	Federal Income Tax Ded.
Texas	(y)	–	–	(y)	No

Note: Tax rates as of January 1, 2011; (a) Rates listed are the tax rates applied to financial institutions or excise taxes based on income. Some states have other taxes based upon the value of deposits or shares; (y) Texas imposes a Franchise Tax, otherwise known as margin tax, imposed on entities with more than $1,000,000 total revenues at rate of 1%, or 0.5% for entities primarily engaged in retail or wholesale trade, on lesser of 70% of total revenues or 100%of gross receipts after deductions for either compensation or cost of goods sold.
Source: Federation of Tax Administrators, "State Corporate Income Tax Rates, 2011"

State Individual Income Tax Rates

State	Tax Rate (%)	Income Brackets ($)	Num. of Brackets	Personal Exempt. ($)[1] Single	Personal Exempt. ($)[1] Dependents	Fed. Inc. Tax Ded.
Texas – No State Income Tax						

Note: Tax rates as of January 1, 2011; Local- and county-level taxes are not included; n/a not applicable;
(1) Married joint filers generally receive double the single exemption
Source: Federation of Tax Administrators, "State Individual Income Tax Rates, 2011"

Various State and Local Tax Rates

State	State and Local Sales and Use (%)	State Sales and Use (%)	Gasoline[1] (¢/gal.)	Cigarette[2] ($/pack)	Spirits[3] ($/gal.)	Wine[4] ($/gal.)	Beer[5] ($/gal.)
Texas	8.125	6.25	20.0	1.41	2.40	0.20	0.20

Note: All tax rates as of January 1, 2011 except Spirits (Sept. 1, 2010); (1) The American Petroleum Institute has developed a methodology for determining the average tax rate on a gallon of fuel. Rates may include any of the following: excise taxes, environmental fees, storage tank fees, other fees or taxes, general sales tax, and local taxes. In states where gasoline is subject to the general sales tax, or where the fuel tax is based on the average sale price, the average rate determined by API is sensitive to changes in the price of gasoline. States that fully or partially apply general sales taxes to gasoline: CA, CO, GA, IL, IN, MI, NY; (2) The federal excise tax of $1.0066 per pack and local taxes are not included; (3) Rates are those applicable to off-premise sales of 40% alcohol by volume (a.b.v.) distilled spirits in 750ml containers. Local excise taxes are excluded; (4) Rates are those applicable to off-premise sales of 11% a.b.v. non-carbonated wine in 750ml containers; (5) Rates are those applicable to off-premise sales of 4.7% a.b.v. beer in 12 ounce containers.
Source: Tax Foundation, 2011 Facts & Figures: How Does Your State Compare?

State-Local Tax Burdens

Area	Rate (%)	Rank[1]	Per Capita Taxes Paid to Home State ($)	Total State and Local Per Capita Taxes Paid ($)	Per Capita Income ($)
Texas	7.9	45	2,248	3,197	40,498
U.S. Average	9.8	-	3,057	4,160	42,539

Note: Figures cover 2009; (1) Rank ranges from 1 to 50 where 1 is highest tax burden
Source: Tax Foundation, State-Local Tax Burdens, All States, 2009

State Business Tax Climate Index Rankings

State	Overall Rank	Corporate Tax Index Rank	Individual Income Tax Index Rank	Sales Tax Index Rank	Unemployment Insurance Tax Index Rank	Property Tax Index Rank
Texas	13	46	7	37	15	29

Note: The index is a measure of how each state's tax laws affect economic performance. The lower the rank, the more favorable a state's tax system is for business. All ranks are for fiscal years. States without a given tax are given a ranking of 1.
Source: Tax Foundation, Tax Foundation Background Paper, No. 60, "2011 State Business Tax Climate Index"

COMMERCIAL REAL ESTATE

Office Market

Market Area	Inventory (sq. ft.)	Vacant (sq. ft.)	Vac. Rate (%)	Under Constr. (sq. ft.)	Asking Rent ($/sf/yr) Class A	Asking Rent ($/sf/yr) Class B
San Antonio	25,860,617	4,612,573	17.8	175,110	26.28	18.52

Source: Grubb & Ellis, Office Markets Trends, 1st Quarter 2011

Industrial Market

Market Area	Inventory (sq. ft.)	Vacant (sq. ft.)	Vac. Rate (%)	Under Constr. (sq. ft.)	Asking Rent ($/sf/yr)	
					WH/Dist	R&D/Flex
San Antonio	67,770,869	6,679,807	9.9	584,400	4.26	8.45

Source: Grubb & Ellis, Industrial Markets Trends, 1st Quarter 2011

COMMERCIAL UTILITIES

Typical Monthly Electric Bills

Area	Commercial Service ($/month)		Industrial Service ($/month)	
	3 kW demand 1,000 kWh	40 kW demand 14,000 kWh	1,000 kW demand 200,000 kWh	50,000 kW demand 15,000,000 kWh
City	n/a	n/a	n/a	n/a
Average[1]	135	1,576	23,741	1,402,202

Note: Based on total rates in effect July 1, 2010; (1) average based on 182 utilities surveyed; n/a not available
Source: Edison Electric Institute, Typical Bills and Average Rates Report, Summer 2010

TRANSPORTATION

Means of Transportation to Work

Area	Car/Truck/Van		Public Transportation			Bicycle	Walked	Other Means	Worked at Home
	Drove Alone	Car-pooled	Bus	Subway	Railroad				
City	78.8	11.6	3.4	0.0	0.0	0.1	2.0	1.7	2.4
MSA[1]	79.0	11.7	2.4	0.0	0.0	0.2	2.1	1.5	3.2
U.S.	75.8	10.4	2.7	1.7	0.5	0.5	2.9	1.2	4.1

Note: Figures are percentages and cover workers 16 years of age and older;
(1) Metropolitan Statistical Area - see Appendix B for areas included
Source: U.S. Census Bureau, 2007-2009 American Community Survey 3-Year Estimates

Travel Time to Work

Area	Less Than 15 Minutes	15 to 29 Minutes	30 to 44 Minutes	45 to 59 Minutes	60 to 89 Minutes	90 Minutes or More
City	23.2	44.0	23.1	5.2	2.9	1.6
MSA[1]	23.8	40.1	23.2	7.2	3.9	1.8
U.S.	28.5	36.2	19.7	7.5	5.6	2.5

Note: Figures are percentages and include workers 16 years old and over;
(1) Metropolitan Statistical Area - see Appendix B for areas included
Source: U.S. Census Bureau, 2007-2009 American Community Survey 3-Year Estimates

Travel Time Index

Area	1982	1999	2008	2009
Urban Area[1]	1.03	1.16	1.16	1.16
Average[2]	1.08	1.20	1.20	1.20

Note: Travel Time Index—the ratio of travel time in the peak period to the travel time at
free-flow conditions. A value of 1.30 indicates a 20-minute free-flow trip takes 26 minutes
in the peak. Free-flow speeds (60 mph on freeways and 35 mph on principal arterials)
are used as the comparison threshold; (1) Covers the San Antonio urban area;
(2) average of 439 urban areas
Source: Texas Transportation Institute, Urban Mobility Report 2010, December 2010

Public Transportation

Agency Name / Mode of Transportation	Vehicles Operated in Maximum Service	Annual Unlinked Passenger Trips ('000)	Annual Passenger Miles ('000)
VIA Metropolitan Transit (VIA)			
Demand response	91	533.3	5,987.9
Demand response	110	545.3	6,691.6
Bus	346	43,296.3	171,668.7
Vanpool	36	125.3	8,425.5

Note: Figures include both directly operated and purchased transportation
Source: Federal Transit Administration, National Transit Database, 2009

Air Transportation

Airport Name and Code / Type of Service	Passenger Airlines[1]	Passenger Enplanements	Freight Carriers[2]	Freight (lbs.)
San Antonio International (SAT)				
Domestic service (U.S. carriers - 2010)	33	3,851,576	23	111,513,092
International service (U.S. carriers - 2009)	10	3,538	6	7,900,578

Note: (1) Includes all U.S.-based major, minor and commuter airlines that carried at least one passenger during the year; (2) Includes all U.S.-based airlines and freight carriers that transported at least one pound of freight during the year
Source: Bureau of Transportation Statistics, The Intermodal Transportation Database, Air Carriers: T-100 Domestic Market (U.S. Carriers), 2010; Bureau of Transportation Statistics, The Intermodal Transportation Database, Air Carriers: T-100 International Market (U.S. Carriers), 2009

Other Transportation Statistics

Interstate highways:	I-10; I-35; I-37
Amtrak service:	Yes
Major waterways/ports:	None

Source: Amtrak.com; Google Maps

BUSINESSES

Major Business Headquarters

Company Name	Rankings	
	Fortune[1]	Forbes[2]
CC Media Holdings	391	-
HE Butt Grocery	-	13
NuStar Energy	497	-
Tesoro	128	-
United Services Automobile Assn.	145	-
Valero Energy	24	-

Note: (1) Fortune 500—companies that produce a 10-K are ranked 1 to 500 based on 2010 revenue; (2) all private companies with at least $2 billion in annual revenue are ranked 1 to 223; companies listed are headquartered in the city; dashes indicate no ranking
Source: Fortune, "Fortune 500," May 23, 2011; Forbes, "America's Largest Private Companies," November 3, 2010

Fast-Growing Businesses

According to *Inc.*, San Antonio is home to five of America's 500 fastest-growing private companies: **Abacus Solutions Group; CareNet; Interlex Communications; P3S; Pyramed Health Services**. Criteria: must be an independent, privately-held, for-profit, U.S. corporation, proprietorship or partnership; revenues of at least $80,000 in 2006 and $2 million in 2009; four-year operating/sales history; holding companies, regulated banks, and utilities were excluded. *Inc., "America's 500 Fastest-Growing Private Companies," September 2010*

According to Deloitte, San Antonio is home to one of North America's 500 fastest-growing high-technology companies: **GlobalSCAPE**. Companies are ranked by percentage growth in revenue over a five-year period. Criteria for inclusion: company must be headquartered within North America; company must own proprietary intellectual property or proprietary technology that contributes to a significant portion of the company's operating revenue or devotes a significant proportion of revenues to research and development of technology; company must have been in business for a minumum of five years with 2005 operating revenues of at least $50,000 USD/CD and 2009 operating revenues of at least $5 million USD/CD. *Deloitte Touche Tohmatsu, 2010 Deloitte Technology Fast 500*[TM]

Minority Business Opportunity

San Antonio is home to two companies which are on the Black Enterprise Industrial/Service 100 list (100 largest companies based on gross sales): **Millennium Steel Service**; **Millennium Steel of Texas**. Criteria: operational in previous calendar year; at least 51% black-owned and manufactures/owns the product it sells or provides industrial or consumer services. Brokerages, real estate firms and firms that provide professional services are not eligible. *Black Enterprise, B.E. 100s, 2010*

San Antonio is home to 10 companies which are on the *Hispanic Business 500* list (500 largest U.S. Hispanic-owned companies based on 2009 revenue): **Ancira Enterprises**; **The Alamo Travel Group**; **Maldonado Nursery & Landscaping**; **Genesis Networks Enterprises**; **Davila Pharmacy**; **P3S Corporation**; **Garcia Foods**; **Kell Muñoz Architects**; **Cacheaux, Cavazos & Newton**; **J.R. Ramon & Sons**. Companies included must show at least 51 percent ownership by Hispanic U.S. citizens, and must maintain headquarters in one of the 50 states or Washington, D.C. *Hispanic Business, "Hispanic Business 500," June 2010*

San Antonio is home to one company which is on the *Hispanic Business* Fastest-Growing 100 list (greatest sales growth from 2005 to 2009): **The Alamo Travel Group**. Companies included must show at least 51 percent ownership by Hispanic U.S. citizens, and must maintain headquarters in one of the 50 states or Washington, D.C. In addition, companies must have minimum revenues of $200,000 for calendar year 2005. *Hispanic Business, July/August 2010*

Minority- and Women-Owned Businesses

Group	All Firms		Firms with Paid Employees			
	Firms	Sales ($000)	Firms	Sales ($000)	Employees	Payroll ($000)
Asian	3,893	1,370,455	1,258	1,273,871	7,827	226,171
Black	3,870	247,723	405	185,861	3,241	73,771
Hispanic	43,099	5,679,041	4,527	4,390,071	49,857	1,143,331
Women	30,582	5,470,505	3,715	4,752,339	40,608	944,891
All Firms	109,196	116,494,521	20,853	112,708,777	560,807	21,252,253

Note: Figures cover firms located in the city; minority- and women-owned business are defined as firms in which the corresponding group own 51% or more of the stock or equity of the company
Source: U.S. Census Bureau, 2007 Economic Census, Survey of Business Owners

HOTELS

Hotels/Motels

Area	5 Star		4 Star		3 Star		2 Star		1 Star		Not Rated	
	Num.	Pct.3	Num.	Pct.3	Num.	Pct.3	Num.	Pct.3	Num.	Pct.3	Num.	Pct.3
City[1]	0	0.0	19	6.3	84	27.9	164	54.5	10	3.3	24	8.0
Total[2]	119	0.7	927	5.8	4,906	30.5	7,992	49.7	526	3.3	1,625	10.1

Note: (1) Figures cover San Antonio and vicinity; (2) Figures cover all 100 cities in this book; (3) Percentage of hotels which are a given star rating; Star ratings are determined by expedia.com and offer an indication of the general quality of a particular hotel.
Source: expedia.com, May 5, 2011

The San Antonio metro area is home to four of the top 218 hotels in the U.S. according to *Travel & Leisure*: **JW Marriott San Antonio Hill Country Resort & Spa** (#165); **Westin La Cantera Resort** (#180); **Omni La Mansion del Rio** (#198); **Hotel Valencia Riverwalk** (#208). Criteria: service; location; rooms; food; and value. *Travel & Leisure, "T+L 500, The World's Best Hotels 2011"*

The San Antonio metro area is home to three of the top 100 hotels in the U.S. according to *Condé Nast Traveler*: **Watermark Hotel & Spa** (#21); **Omni La Mansion del Rio** (#60); **Hotel Valencia Riverwalk** (#63). The selections are based on over 25,000 responses to the magazine's annual Readers' Choice Survey. *Condé Nast Traveler, "2010 Readers' Choice Awards"*

EVENT SITES

Major Stadiums, Arenas, and Auditoriums

Name	Max. Capacity
AT&T Center	18,797
Alamodome	65,000
Freeman Coliseum	12,000
Municipal Auditorium/San Antonio Convention Facilities	4,884
Nelson W. Wolff Municipal Stadium	9,200
Verizon Wireless Amphitheatre	n/a

Note: n/a not available
Source: Original research

Convention Centers

Name	Overall Space (sq. ft.)	Exhibit Space (sq. ft.)	Meeting Space (sq. ft.)	Meeting Rooms
Henry B. Gonzalez Convention Center	1,300,000	n/a	440,000	59

Note: n/a not available
Source: Original research

Living Environment

COST OF LIVING

Cost of Living Index

Composite Index	Groceries	Housing	Utilities	Trans-portation	Health Care	Misc. Goods/Services
95.7	84.9	95.3	82.8	100.7	99.9	102.2

Note: U.S. = 100; Figures cover the San Antonio TX urban area.
Source: The Council for Community and Economic Research, ACCRA Cost of Living Index, 2010

Grocery Prices

Area[1]	T-Bone Steak ($/pound)	Frying Chicken ($/pound)	Whole Milk ($/half gal.)	Eggs ($/dozen)	Orange Juice ($/64 oz.)	Coffee ($/11.5 oz.)
City[2]	7.73	1.03	2.04	1.22	2.92	3.02
Avg.	9.04	1.16	2.02	1.47	3.08	3.65
Min.	6.97	0.84	1.46	0.96	2.39	2.64
Max.	13.93	2.51	3.58	3.01	4.94	6.32

Note: (1) Values for the local area are compared with the average, minimum and maximum values for all 338 areas in the Cost of Living Index; (2) Figures cover the San Antonio TX urban area; **T-Bone Steak** *(price per pound);* **Frying Chicken** *(price per pound, whole fryer);* **Whole Milk** *(half gallon carton);* **Eggs** *(price per dozen, Grade A, large);* **Orange Juice** *(64 oz. Tropicana or Florida Natural);* **Coffee** *(11.5 oz. can, vacuum-packed, Maxwell House, Hills Bros, or Folgers).*
Source: The Council for Community and Economic Research, ACCRA Cost of Living Index, 2010

Housing and Utility Costs

Area[1]	New Home Price ($)	Apartment Rent ($/month)	All Electric ($/month)	Part Electric ($/month)	Other Energy ($/month)	Telephone ($/month)
City[2]	254,957	1,018	-	89.68	40.06	26.01
Avg.	293,442	810	166.39	91.93	83.82	26.93
Min.	182,545	453	119.21	44.47	36.85	17.98
Max.	1,123,114	2,776	307.53	218.20	313.90	39.15

Note: (1) Values for the local area are compared with the average, minimum and maximum values for all 338 areas in the Cost of Living Index; (2) Figures cover the San Antonio TX urban area; **New Home Price** *(2,400 sf living area, 8,000 sf lot, in urban area with full utilities);* **Apartment Rent** *(950 sf 2 bedroom/1.5 or 2 bath, unfurnished, excluding all utilities except water);* **All Electric** *(average monthly cost for an all-electric home);* **Part Electric** *(average monthly cost for a part-electric home);* **Other Energy** *(average monthly cost for natural gas, fuel oil, coal, wood, and any other forms of energy except electricity);* **Telephone** *(price includes basic monthly rate for a private residential line plus additional local usage charges incurred by a family of four).*
Source: The Council for Community and Economic Research, ACCRA Cost of Living Index, 2010

Health Care, Transportation, and Other Costs

Area[1]	Doctor ($/visit)	Dentist ($/visit)	Optometrist ($/visit)	Gasoline ($/gallon)	Beauty Salon ($/visit)	Men's Shirt ($)
City[2]	85.61	83.00	84.75	2.57	50.58	38.59
Avg.	89.44	78.95	87.40	2.73	31.92	24.83
Min.	57.00	54.25	48.32	2.44	19.17	13.67
Max.	149.90	136.73	174.22	3.75	62.81	47.89

Note: (1) Values for the local area are compared with the average, minimum and maximum values for all 338 areas in the Cost of Living Index; (2) Figures cover the San Antonio TX urban area; **Doctor** *(general practitioners routine exam of an established patient);* **Dentist** *(adult teeth cleaning and periodic oral examination);* **Optometrist** *(full vision eye exam for established adult patient);* **Gasoline** *(one gallon regular unleaded, national brand, including all taxes, cash price at self-service pump if available);* **Beauty Salon** *(woman's shampoo, trim, and blow-dry);* **Men's Shirt** *(cotton/polyester dress shirt, pinpoint weave, long sleeves).*
Source: The Council for Community and Economic Research, ACCRA Cost of Living Index, 2010

HOUSING

House Price Index (HPI)

Area	National Ranking[2]	Quarterly Change (%)	One-Year Change (%)	Five-Year Change (%)
MSA[1]	49	0.37	0.67	14.37
U.S.[3]	-	-0.84	-3.95	-11.45

Note: The HPI is a weighted repeat sales index. It measures average price changes in repeat sales or refinancings on the same properties. This information is obtained by reviewing repeat mortgage transactions on single-family properties whose mortgages have been purchased or securitized by Fannie Mae or Freddie Mac in January 1975; (1) Metropolitan/Micropolitan Statistical Area - see Appendix B for areas included; (2) Rankings are based on annual percentage change for all metro areas containing at least 15,000 transactions over the last 10 years and ranges from 1 to 309; (3) figures based on a weighted average of Census Division estimates; all figures are for the period ending December 31, 2010
Source: Federal Housing Finance Agency, House Price Index, February 24, 2011

House Price Valuations

Area	Q4 2005 Price ($000)	Over-valuation	Q4 2006 Price ($000)	Over-valuation	Q4 2007 Price ($000)	Over-valuation	Q4 2008 Price ($000)	Over-valuation	Q4 2009 Price ($000)	Over-valuation
MSA[1]	99.0	-12.2	106.4	-10.1	113.5	-7.8	110.7	-11.1	111.6	-10.9

Note: Figures show the percentage of over- or under-valuation of single family homes relative to statistically normal house values (e.g. a value of 23.6 indicates that house values are 23.6% overvalued). Statistically normal house values are based on house prices, interest rates, household incomes, population densities, and any historical premiums or discounts metropolitan areas have exhibited over time; (1) Figures cover the San Antonio, TX Metropolitan Statistical Area - see Appendix B for areas included
Source: Global Insight/PNC Financial Services Group, House Prices in America: 4th Quarter 2009 Update

Median Single-Family Home Prices

Area	2008	2009	2010p	Percent Change 2009 to 2010
MSA[1]	152.8	149.3	151.0	1.1
U.S. Average	196.6	172.1	173.2	0.6

Note: Figures are median sales prices of existing single-family homes in thousands of dollars; (p) preliminary; n/a not available; (1) Metropolitan Statistical Area - see Appendix B for areas included
Source: National Association of Realtors, Median Sales Price of Existing Single-Family Homes for Metropolitan Areas, 4th Quarter 2010

Median Apartment Condo-Coop Home Prices

Area	2008	2009	2010p	Percent Change 2009 to 2010
MSA[1]	n/a	n/a	n/a	n/a
U.S. Average	209.8	175.6	171.7	-2.2

Note: Figures are median sales prices of existing apartment condo-coop homes in thousands of dollars; (p) preliminary; n/a not available; (1) Metropolitan Statistical Area - see Appendix B for areas included
Source: National Association of Realtors, Median Sales Price of Existing Apartment Condo-Coop Homes for Metropolitan Areas, 4th Quarter 2010

Year Housing Structure Built

Area	2000 or Later	1990 -1999	1980 -1989	1970 -1979	1960 -1969	1950 -1959	1940 -1949	Before 1940	Median Year
City	16.6	13.4	17.6	18.5	11.1	11.0	5.5	6.3	1979
MSA[1]	20.3	15.4	17.5	17.5	10.0	9.1	4.7	5.7	1982
U.S.	12.5	14.0	14.2	16.5	11.4	11.3	5.8	14.3	1974

Note: Figures are percentages except for Median Year; (1) Metropolitan Statistical Area - see Appendix B for areas included
Source: U.S. Census Bureau, 2007-2009 American Community Survey 3-Year Estimates

HEALTH

Health Risk Data

Category	MSA[1] (%)	U.S. (%)
Adults who have been told they have high blood pressure	27.7	28.7
Adults who have been told they have high blood cholesterol	34.7	37.5
Adults who have been told they have diabetes[3]	7.5	8.3
Adults who have been told they have arthritis	24.9	26.0
Adults who have been told they currently have asthma	8.3	8.8
Adults who are current smokers	14.0	17.9
Adults who are heavy drinkers[4]	5.8	5.1
Adults who are binge drinkers[5]	21.0	15.8
Adults who are overweight (BMI 25.0 - 29.9)	38.5	36.2
Adults who are obese (BMI 30.0 - 99.8)	25.2	26.9
Adults who participated in any physical activities in the past month	75.0	76.2
Adults 50+ who have ever had a sigmoidoscopy or colonoscopy[2]	62.1	62.2
Women 40+ who have had a mammogram within the past two years[2]	75.9	76.0
Adults age 18–64 who have any kind of health care coverage	78.1	83.1

Note: Data as of 2009 unless otherwise noted; (1) Figures cover the San Antonio, TX Metropolitan Statistical Area - see Appendix B for areas included; (2) Data as of 2008; (3) Figures do not include pregnancy-related, borderline, or pre-diabetes; (4) Heavy drinkers are classified as males having more than two drinks per day or females having more than one drink per day; (5) Binge drinkers are classified as males having five or more drinks on one occasion or females having four or more drinks on one occasion
Source: Centers for Disease Control and Prevention, Behaviorial Risk Factor Surveillance System, SMART: Selected Metropolitan/Micropolitan Area Risk Trends, 2008, 2009

Mortality Rates for the Top 10 Causes of Death in the U.S.

ICD-10[a] Sub-Chapter	ICD-10[a] Code	Age-Adjusted Mortality Rate[1] per 100,000 population	
		County[2]	U.S.
Malignant neoplasms	C00-C97	167.1	180.9
Ischaemic heart diseases	I20-I25	137.5	135.0
Other forms of heart disease	I30-I51	43.6	50.0
Cerebrovascular diseases	I60-I69	47.0	44.1
Chronic lower respiratory diseases	J40-J47	35.0	41.5
Other degenerative diseases of the nervous system	G30-G31	22.7	23.6
Diabetes mellitus	E10-E14	34.4	23.5
Other external causes of accidental injury	W00-X59	27.4	23.5
Organic, including symptomatic, mental disorders	F01-F09	26.9	22.2
Influenza and pneumonia	J09-J18	13.0	18.1

Note: (a) ICD-10 = International Classification of Diseases 10th Revision; (1) Mortality rates are a three year average covering 2005-2007; (2) Figures cover Bexar County
Source: Centers for Disease Control and Prevention, National Center for Health Statistics. Compressed Mortality File 1999-2007. CDC WONDER On-line Database, compiled from Compressed Mortality File 1999-2007 Series 20 No. 2M, 2010.

Mortality Rates for Selected Causes of Death

ICD-10[a] Sub-Chapter	ICD-10[a] Code	Age-Adjusted Mortality Rate[1] per 100,000 population	
		County[2]	U.S.
Assault	X85-Y09	7.7	6.0
Human immunodeficiency virus (HIV) disease	B20-B24	4.8	4.0
Hypertensive diseases	I10-I15	15.9	18.0
Intentional self-harm	X60-X84	10.2	11.0
Malnutrition	E40-E46	0.9	0.8
Obesity and other hyperalimentation	E65-E68	1.3	1.5
Transport accidents	V01-V99	13.3	15.6
Viral hepatitis	B15-B19	3.0	2.1

Note: (a) ICD-10 = International Classification of Diseases 10th Revision; (1) Mortality rates are a three year average covering 2005-2007; (2) Figures cover Bexar County
Source: Centers for Disease Control and Prevention, National Center for Health Statistics. Compressed Mortality File 1999-2007. CDC WONDER On-line Database, compiled from Compressed Mortality File 1999-2007 Series 20 No. 2M, 2010.

Distribution of Physicians and Dentists

Area[1]	Dentists[2]	D.O.[3]	M.D.[4] Total	Family/ General Practice	Pediatrics	Medical Specialties	Surgical Specialties
Local (number)	737	278	3,354	437	245	1,177	770
Local (rate[5])	4.6	1.7	20.7	2.7	1.5	7.3	4.7
U.S. (rate[5])	4.5	1.9	18.3	2.5	1.4	6.8	4.1

Note: Data as of 2008 unless noted; (1) Local data covers Bexar County; (2) Data as of 2007; (3) Doctor of Osteopathic Medicine; (4) Includes active, non-federal, patient-care, office-based Doctors of Medicine; (5) rate per 10,000 population
Source: Area Resource File (ARF). 2009-2010 Release. U.S. Department of Health and Human Services, Health Resources and Services Administration, Bureau of Health Professions, Rockville, MD, August 2010

Hospitals

San Antonio has the following hospitals: 12 general medical and surgical; 3 psychiatric; 1 tuberculosis and other respiratory disease; 2 rehabilitation; 1 heart; 1 surgical; 4 long-term acute care; 1 other specialty; 1 children's general; 1 children's psychiatric.
AHA Guide to the Healthcare Field 2010

According to *U.S. News,* the San Antonio, TX Metropolitan Statistical Area is home to one of the best hospitals in the U.S.: **University Hospital**. The hospital listed was highly ranked in at least one adult specialty. *U.S. News Online, "America's Best Hospitals 2010-11"*

EDUCATION

Public School District Statistics

District Name	Schls	Pupils	Pupil/ Teacher Ratio	Minority Pupils[1] (%)	Free Lunch Eligible[2] (%)	IEP[3] (%)
Alamo Heights ISD	6	4,660	14.5	38.0	13.3	6.0
East Central ISD	13	9,112	15.9	72.2	46.6	10.9
Edgewood ISD	20	11,644	14.5	99.2	9.6	11.3
Harlandale ISD	30	14,399	15.1	96.9	4.7	10.3
North East ISD	73	63,452	14.7	62.1	31.1	10.5
Northside ISD	101	89,000	15.4	75.4	36.3	12.4
San Antonio ISD	100	54,696	16.5	97.2	42.2	11.7
School Of Excellence In Education	8	2,287	13.3	93.4	71.8	9.6
South San Antonio ISD	18	9,976	14.7	97.6	15.6	9.0
Southside ISD	10	5,107	14.2	88.1	80.2	10.0
Southwest ISD	15	11,393	16.4	93.1	68.7	11.1

Note: Table includes school districts with 2,000 or more students; (1) Percentage of students that are not non-Hispanic white; (2) Percentage of students that are eligible for the free lunch program; (3) Percentage of students that have an Individualized Education Program.
Source: U.S. Department of Education, National Center for Education Statistics, Common Core of Data, Local Education Agency (School District) Universe Survey: School Year 2008-2009; U.S. Department of Education, National Center for Education Statistics, Common Core of Data, Public Elementary/Secondary School Universe Survey: School Year 2008-2009

Top Public High Schools

High School Name	Index[1]	Rank[1]	Subsidized Lunch (%)[2]	E&E (%)[3]
Alamo Heights	2.701	335	15.0	45.5
Burbank[4]	2.150	612	82.0	19.5
Clark	1.981	734	27.0	33.7
Communication Arts	7.198	19	16.0	74.0
Douglas Macarthur	1.480	1176	26.0	21.9
Earl Warren	1.262	1412	38.0	18.5
Health Careers	3.298	197	22.0	59.1
International School of the Americas	4.357	82	20.0	33.0
James Madison	1.289	1386	38.0	16.7
John Jay	2.951	262	64.0	21.0
John Marshall	1.074	1636	34.0	16.2
Johnson	3.315	192	10.0	15.8
Reagan	2.533	393	1.0	73.4
Sandra Day O'Connor	1.206	1485	19.0	26.9
Theodore Roosevelt	1.770	888	61.5	12.2
Winston Churchill	2.677	346	24.0	37.6

Note: (1) Public schools are ranked according to a ratio that is the number of Advanced Placement, International Baccalaureate, and/or Cambridge tests taken by all students at a school in 2009 divided by the number of graduating seniors. All of the schools on the list have an index of at least 1.000; they are in the top six percent of public schools measured this way. The rankings range from 1 to 1,734; (2) Percentage of students receiving federally subsidized meals; (3) E & E stands for equity and excellence percentage: the portion of all graduating seniors at a school that had at least one passing grade on one AP or IB test; (4) Schools that offer International Baccalaureate or Cambridge exams; (5) School is unranked, but has been identified by Newsweek as one of the nation's most elite public high schools.
Source: Newsweek Online, "Top High Schools 2010"

Highest Level of Education

Area	Less than H.S.	H.S. Diploma	Some College, No Deg.	Associate Degree	Bachelors Degree	Masters Degree	Profess. School Degree	Doctorate Degree
City	21.4	26.4	22.6	6.5	15.0	5.6	1.6	0.8
MSA[1]	18.6	27.2	23.2	6.8	15.8	6.0	1.7	0.8
U.S.	15.3	29.0	20.7	7.5	17.4	7.0	1.9	1.1

Note: Figures are 2010 estimated percentages and cover persons age 25 and over; (1) Metropolitan Statistical Area - see Appendix B for areas included
Source: Claritas, Inc.

Educational Attainment by Race

Area	High School Graduate (%)					Bachelor's Degree (%)				
	Total	White	Black	Asian	Hisp.[2]	Total	White	Black	Asian	Hisp.[2]
City	79.2	94.0	85.0	86.0	69.3	23.2	39.8	20.3	50.1	12.7
MSA[1]	81.5	93.6	86.5	84.8	69.8	24.4	37.1	21.9	46.9	12.7
U.S.	84.9	90.0	80.7	85.5	60.7	27.8	30.9	17.5	49.7	12.7

Note: Figures shown cover persons 25 years old and over; (1) Metropolitan Statistical Area - see Appendix B for areas included; (2) people of Hispanic origin can be of any race
Source: U.S. Census Bureau, 2007-2009 American Community Survey 3-Year Estimates

School Enrollment by Grade and Control

Area	Preschool (%)		Kindergarten (%)		Grades 1 - 4 (%)		Grades 5 - 8 (%)		Grades 9 - 12 (%)	
	Public	Private	Public	Private	Public	Private	Public	Private	Public	Private
City	66.8	33.2	90.0	10.0	91.7	8.3	92.0	8.0	92.9	7.1
MSA[1]	62.7	37.3	89.4	10.6	91.5	8.5	91.8	8.2	93.0	7.0
U.S.	54.3	45.7	86.4	13.6	88.9	11.1	89.1	10.9	90.2	9.8

Note: Figures shown cover persons 3 years old and over; (1) Metropolitan Statistical Area - see Appendix B for areas included
Source: U.S. Census Bureau, 2007-2009 American Community Survey 3-Year Estimates

Average Salaries of Public School Classroom Teachers

Area	2009-10		2010-11		Percent Change 2009-10 to 2010-11	Percent Change 2000-01 to 2010-11
	Dollars	Rank[1]	Dollars	Rank[1]		
Texas	48,261	31	48,261	34	0.00	25.8
U.S. Average	55,202	-	56,069	-	1.57	29.3

Note: (1) State rank ranges from 1 to 51 where 1 indicates highest salary.
Source: National Education Association, Rankings & Estimates: Rankings of the States 2010
and Estimates of School Statistics 2011, December 2010

Higher Education

Four-Year Colleges			Two-Year Colleges			Medical Schools[1]	Law Schools[2]	Voc/ Tech[3]
Public	Private Non-profit	Private For-profit	Public	Private Non-profit	Private For-profit			
2	6	5	4	0	9	1	1	15

Note: Figures cover institutions located within the city limits and include main campuses only; (1) includes schools accredited by the Liaison Committee on Medical Education and the American Osteopathic Association; (2) includes American Bar Association-accredited law schools; (3) includes all schools with programs that are less than 2 years.
Source: National Center for Education Statistics, Integrated Postsecondary Education System (IPEDS) Peer Analysis System, 2010-11; U.S. News & World Report, Medical School Directory, 2011; U.S. News & World Report, Law School Directory, 2011

PRESIDENTIAL ELECTION

2008 Presidential Election Results

Area	Obama	McCain	Nader	Other
Bexar County	52.2	46.7	0.0	1.0
U.S.	52.9	45.6	0.6	0.9

Note: Results are percentages and may not add to 100% due to rounding
Source: Dave Leip's Atlas of U.S. Presidential Elections, www.uselectionatlas.org

EMPLOYERS

Major Employers

Company Name	Industry	Type of Site
Air Education Training Command	National security	Branch
Air Force Services Agency	National security	Branch
AT&T	Telephone communication, except radio	Branch
Boeing	Vocational schools, nec	Branch
Boeing	Repair services, nec	Branch
Cardell Cabinetry	Wood kitchen cabinets	Headquarters
Diamond Shamrock	Gasoline service stations	Headquarters
Frost Capital Group The	National commercial banks	Headquarters
Jay Science Academy	Business services, nec	Branch
Northeast Baptist Hospital	General medical and surgical hospitals	Headquarters
P B X	General medical and surgical hospitals	Branch
Santa Rosa Childrens Hospital	Offices and clinics of medical doctors	Branch
Security Forces 37	National security	Branch
Six Flags Festa Texas Theme Pk	Amusement parks	Single
South Texas Veterans Hcs	Administration of veterans' affairs	Branch
Southwest Research Institute	Commercial physical research	Headquarters
Temic Automotive of North Amer	Semiconductors and related devices	Branch
The University of Texas	Colleges and universities	Headquarters
Toyota Motor Mfg Texas	Motor vehicles and car bodies	Single
University Hospital	General medical and surgical hospitals	Headquarters
University of Texas Health Sci	Colleges and universities	Headquarters

Note: Companies shown are located within the San Antonio metropolitan area; nec = not elsewhere classified.
Source: www.zapdata.com, January 2011

Best Companies to Work For

NuStar Energy; Rackspace Hosting; USAA, headquartered in San Antonio, are among the "100 Best Companies to Work For." To pick the 100 Best Companies to Work For, *Fortune* partnered with the Great Place to Work Institute. Three hundred eleven companies participated in this year's survey. Most of a company's score (two-thirds) is based on the results of the Institute's Trust Index survey, which is sent to a random sample of employees from each company. The survey asks questions related to their attitudes about management's credibility, job satisfaction, and camaraderie. The other third of the scoring is based on the company's responses to the Institute's Culture Audit, which includes detailed questions about pay and benefit programs, and a series of open-ended questions about hiring practices, internal communication, training, recognition programs, and diversity efforts. Any company that is at least seven years old with more than 1,000 U.S. employees is eligible. *Fortune, "100 Best Companies to Work For," February 7, 2011*

San Antonio Lighthouse for the Blind, headquartered in San Antonio, is among the "50 Best Employers for Workers Over 50." Criteria: recruiting practices; opportunities for training, education, and career development; workplace accommodations; alternative work options, such as flexible scheduling, job sharing, and phased retirement; employee health and pension benefits; and retiree benefits. Any employer with at least 50 employees based in the U.S. is eligible. This includes for-profit companies, not-for-profit organizations, and government employers. *AARP, "2009 AARP Best Employers for Workers Over 50"*

GlobalScape; Rackspace US; USAA, headquartered in San Antonio, are among the "100 Best Places to Work in IT." To qualify, companies, both public and private, had to have a minimum of 50 IT employees. Companies were selected based on average salary and bonus increases, the percentage of IT employees receiving promotions, IT staff turnover rates, training and development programs, and the percentage of women and minorities in IT staff and management positions. In addition, information was collected on how the organizations reward outstanding performance, how their retention programs are structured and what benefits they offer. *Computerworld, "100 Best Places to Work in IT 2010"*

PUBLIC SAFETY

Crime Rate

Area	All Crimes	Violent Crimes				Property Crimes		
		Murder	Forcible Rape	Robbery	Aggrav. Assault	Burglary	Larceny -Theft	Motor Vehicle Theft
City	7,241.6	7.2	45.7	195.3	322.7	1,322.0	4,926.3	422.4
Suburbs[1]	3,418.5	4.4	34.5	50.0	181.4	779.1	2,213.8	155.3
Metro[2]	5,953.6	6.3	41.9	146.3	275.1	1,139.1	4,012.4	332.4
U.S.	3,465.5	5.0	28.7	133.0	262.8	716.3	2,060.9	258.8

Note: Figures are crimes per 100,000 population; (1) All areas within the metro area that are located outside the city limits; (2) Metropolitan Statistical Area - see Appendix B for areas included
Source: FBI Uniform Crime Reports, 2009

Hate Crimes

Area	Number of Quarters Reported	Bias Motivation				
		Race	Religion	Sexual Orientation	Ethnicity	Disability
City	4	3	1	3	2	0

Source: Federal Bureau of Investigation, Hate Crime Statistics 2009

Identity Theft Consumer Complaints

Area	Complaints	Complaints per 100,000 Population	Rank[2]
MSA[1]	2,068	103.9	53
U.S.	250,854	81.3	-

Note: (1) Metropolitan Statistical Area - see Appendix B for areas included; (2) Rank ranges from 1 to 384 where 1 indicates greatest number of complaints per 100,000 population
Source: Federal Trade Commission, Consumer Sentinel Network Data Book for January - December 2010

RECREATION

Culture

Dance[1]	Theatre[1]	Instrumental Music[1]	Vocal Music[1]	Series/ Festivals	Museums	Zoos and Aquariums[2]
1	4	3	1	5	15	2

Note: (1) Number of professional perfoming groups; (2) AZA-accredited
Source: The Grey House Performing Arts Directory, 2011-2012; Official Museum Directory, 2010; American Association of Museums, AAM Member Museums, March 2011; Association of Zoos & Aquariums, AZA Member Zoos & Aquariums, May 2011

Professional Sports Teams

Team Name	League
San Antonio Spurs	National Basketball Association (NBA)

Note: Includes teams located in the San Antonio metro area.
Source: Original research

CLIMATE

Average and Extreme Temperatures

Temperature	Jan	Feb	Mar	Apr	May	Jun	Jul	Aug	Sep	Oct	Nov	Dec	Yr.
Extreme High (°F)	89	97	100	100	103	105	106	108	103	98	94	90	108
Average High (°F)	62	66	74	80	86	92	95	95	90	82	71	64	80
Average Temp. (°F)	51	55	62	70	76	82	85	85	80	71	60	53	69
Average Low (°F)	39	43	50	58	66	72	74	74	69	59	49	41	58
Extreme Low (°F)	0	6	19	31	43	53	62	61	46	33	21	6	0

Note: Figures cover the years 1948-1990
Source: National Climatic Data Center, International Station Meteorological Climate Summary, 9/96

Average Precipitation/Snowfall/Humidity

Precip./Humidity	Jan	Feb	Mar	Apr	May	Jun	Jul	Aug	Sep	Oct	Nov	Dec	Yr.
Avg. Precip. (in.)	1.5	1.8	1.5	2.6	3.8	3.6	2.0	2.5	3.3	3.2	2.3	1.4	29.6
Avg. Snowfall (in.)	1	Tr	Tr	0	0	0	0	0	0	0	Tr	Tr	1
Avg. Rel. Hum. 6am (%)	79	80	79	82	87	87	87	86	85	83	81	79	83
Avg. Rel. Hum. 3pm (%)	51	48	45	48	51	48	43	42	47	46	48	49	47

Note: Figures cover the years 1948-1990; Tr = Trace amounts (<0.05 in. of rain; <0.5 in. of snow)
Source: National Climatic Data Center, International Station Meteorological Climate Summary, 9/96

Weather Conditions

Temperature			Daytime Sky			Precipitation		
32°F & below	45°F & below	90°F & above	Clear	Partly cloudy	Cloudy	0.01 inch or more precip.	0.1 inch or more snow/ice	Thunder-storms
23	91	112	97	153	115	81	1	36

Note: Figures are average number of days per year and cover the years 1948-1990
Source: National Climatic Data Center, International Station Meteorological Climate Summary, 9/96

HAZARDOUS WASTE

Superfund Sites

San Antonio has no sites on the EPA's Superfund Final National Priorities List.
U.S. Environmental Protection Agency, Final National Priorities List, April 1, 2011

AIR & WATER QUALITY

Air Quality Index

Area	Percent of Days when Air Quality was...[2]				AQI Statistics	
	Good	Moderate	Unhealthy for Sensitive Groups	Unhealthy	Maximum	Median
Area[1]	71.2	25.5	3.3	0.0	116	42

Note: The Air Quality Index (AQI) is an index for reporting daily air quality. EPA calculates the AQI for five major air pollutants regulated by the Clean Air Act: ground-level ozone, particle pollution (also known as particulate matter), carbon monoxide, sulfur dioxide, and nitrogen dioxide. The AQI runs from 0 to 500. The higher the AQI value, the greater the level of air pollution and the greater the health concern. There are six AQI categories: "Good" The AQI is between 0 and 50. Air quality is considered satisfactory; "Moderate" The AQI is between 51 and 100. Air quality is acceptable; "Unhealthy for Sensitive Groups" When AQI values are between 101 and 150, members of sensitive groups may experience health effects; "Unhealthy" When AQI values are between 151 and 200 everyone may begin to experience health effects; "Very Unhealthy" AQI values between 201 and 300 trigger a health alert; "Hazardous" AQI values over 300 trigger health warnings of emergency conditions; (1) Data covers Bexar County; (2) Based on 306 days with AQI data in 2008; The EPA has suspended data updates while it assesses its data systems, including AirData reports and maps.
Source: U.S. Environmental Protection Agency, AirData Report, 2008

Air Quality Index Pollutants

Area	Percent of Days when AQI Pollutant was...[2]					
	Carbon Monoxide	Nitrogen Dioxide	Ozone	Sulfur Dioxide	Particulate Matter 2.5	Particulate Matter 10
Area[1]	0.3	0.0	61.4	0.0	37.9	0.3

Note: The Air Quality Index (AQI) is an index for reporting daily air quality. EPA calculates the AQI for five major air pollutants regulated by the Clean Air Act: ground-level ozone, particle pollution (also known as particulate matter), carbon monoxide, sulfur dioxide, and nitrogen dioxide. The AQI runs from 0 to 500. The higher the AQI value, the greater the level of air pollution and the greater the health concern; (1) Data covers Bexar County; (2) Based on 306 days with AQI data in 2008; The EPA has suspended data updates while it assesses its data systems, including AirData reports and maps.
Source: U.S. Environmental Protection Agency, AirData Report, 2008

Air Quality Index Trends

Area	Trend Sites (days)								All Sites (days)
	2002	2003	2004	2005	2006	2007	2008	2009	2009
MSA[1]	26	18	6	10	8	3	7	3	3

Note: Figures are the number of days the AQI value exceeded 100 in a given year. An AQI value greater than 100 indicates that air quality would have been in the unhealthful range on that day. Data from exceptional events are included. These counts are presented in two ways. First, the counts are based on sites having an adequate record of monitoring data during the trend period (trend sites). These counts represent the relative change in the number of days with AQI values greater than 100. In the last column, the counts are based on all sites with data in the most recent year (because it is possible for a site to have data in the most recent year but not enough data to be a trend site); (1) Data covers the San Antonio, TX Metropolitan Statistical Area - see Appendix B for areas included
Source: U.S. Environmental Protection Agency, Office of Air and Radiation, Air Quality Index Information, "Number of Days with Air Quality Index Values Greater than 100 and Trend Sites, 1990-2009, and at All Sites in 2009"

Maximum Air Pollutant Concentrations

	Particulate Matter 10 (ug/m^3)	Particulate Matter 2.5 (ug/m^3)	Ozone (ppm)	Carbon Monoxide (ppm)	Sulfur Dioxide (ppm)	Nitrogen Dioxide (ppm)	Lead (ug/m^3)
MSA[1] Level	n/a	n/a	n/a	n/a	n/a	n/a	n/a
NAAQS[2]	150	35	0.075	9	0.140	0.053	0.15
Met NAAQS[2]	Yes	Yes	Yes	Yes	Yes	Yes	Yes

Note: Data from exceptional events are not included; (1) Data covers the San Antonio, TX Metropolitan Statistical Area - see Appendix B for areas included; (2) National Ambient Air Quality Standards; n/a not available
Concentrations: Particulate Matter 10 (coarse particulate) - highest second maximum 24-hour concentration; Particulate Matter 2.5 (fine particulate) - highest 98th percentile 24-hour concentration; Ozone - highest fourth daily maximum 8-hour concentration; Carbon Monoxide - highest second maximum non-overlapping 8-hour concentration; Sulfur Dioxide - highest second maximum 24-hour concentration; Nitrogen Dioxide - highest arithmetic mean concentration; Lead - maximum running 3-month average
Units: ppm = parts per million; ug/m^3 = micrograms per cubic meter
Source: U.S. Environmental Protection Agency, CBSA Factbook 2009, Air Quality Statistics by City, 2009

Drinking Water

Water System Name	Pop. Served	Primary Water Source Type	Violations[1]	
			Health Based	Monitoring/ Reporting
San Antonio Water System	1,342,747	Purchased Surface	0	0

Note: (1) Based on violation data from January 1, 2010 to December 31, 2010 (includes unresolved violations from earlier years)
Source: U.S. Environmental Protection Agency, Office of Ground Water and Drinking Water, Safe Drinking Water Information System (based on data extracted May 9, 2011)

Savannah, Georgia

Background

Savannah, at the mouth of the Savannah River on the border between Georgia and South Carolina, is Georgia's second fastest-growing city. It was established in 1733 when General James Oglethorpe landed with a group of settlers in the sailing vessel Anne, after a voyage of more than three months. City Hall now stands at the spot where Oglethorpe and his followers first camped on a small bluff overlooking the river.

Savannah is unique among American cities in that it was extensively planned while Oglethorpe was still in England. Each new settler was given a package of property, including a town lot, a garden space, and an outlying farm area. The town was planned in quadrants, the north and south for residences, and the east and west for public buildings.

The quadrant design was inspired in part by considerations of public defense, given the unsettled character of relations with Native Americans, but in fact an early treaty between the settlers and the Creek Indian Chief Tomochichi allowed Savannah to develop quite peacefully, with little of the hostility between Europeans and Indians that marred much of the development elsewhere in the colonies.

Savannah was taken by the British during the American Revolution, and in the patriotic siege that followed, many lives were lost. Count Pulaski, among other Revolutionary heroes, lost his life during the battle, but Savannah was eventually retaken in 1782 by the American Generals Nathaniel Greene and Anthony Wayne.

In the post-Revolutionary period, Savannah grew dramatically, its economic strength being driven in large part by Eli Whitney's cotton gin. As the world's leader in the cotton trade, Savannah also hosted a great development in export activity, and the first American steamboat built in the United States to cross the Atlantic was launched in its busy port.

Savannah's physical structure had been saved from the worst ravages of war, but the destruction of the area's infrastructure slowed its further development for an extended period, and "sleepy" became a common adjective applied to the once-vibrant economic center. In the long period of slow recovery that followed, one of the great Savannah success stories was the establishment of the Girl Scouts in 1912 by Juliette Gordon Low.

In 1954, an extensive fire destroyed a large portion of the historic City Market, and the area was bulldozed to make room for a parking garage. The Historic Savannah Foundation has worked unceasingly since then to maintain and improve Savannah's considerable architectural charms.

As a result, Savannah's Historic District was designated a Registered National Historic Landmark. Savannah has also been one of the favored sites for movie makers for decades. More than forty major movies have been filmed in Savannah including *Roots* (1976), *East of Eden* (1980), *Forrest Gump* (1994), *Midnight in the Garden of Good and Evil* (1997) and *The Legend of Bagger Vance* (2000), and a segment of the Colbert Report (2005).

Tourism, military services, port operations, and arts & culture industries are major employers in the city. Savannah's port facilities, operated by the Georgia Ports Authority, have seen notable growth in container tonnage in recent years. Garden City Terminal is the fourth largest container port in the United States, and the largest single-terminal operation in North America. Military installations in the area include Hunter Army Airfield and Fort Stewart military bases, employing a combined 42,000 people. Museums include Juliette Gordon Low Museum, Telfair Museum of Art and the Mighty 8th Air Forth Museum.

In addition, the city's beauty draws not just tourists, but conventioneers. The Savannah International Trade & Convention Center is a state-of-the-art facility with more than 100,000 square feet of exhibition space, accommodating nearly 10,000 people.

Colleges and universities in the city include the Savannah College of Art and Design, Savannah State University, and South University.

Savannah's climate is subtropical, with hot summers and mild winters, making the city an ideal locale for all-year outside activities.

Rankings

General Rankings

- Savannah was ranked #91 out of 375 metro areas in *Cities Ranked & Rated*. Criteria: cost of living; climate; crime; transportation; economy and jobs; education; arts and culture; health and healthcare; leisure; quality of life. *Cities Ranked & Rated, 2nd Edition, 2007*

- Savannah was ranked #115 out of 379 metro areas in *Places Rated Almanac*. Criteria: health care; education; recreation; transportation; ambience; climate; crime; housing costs; jobs. *Places Rated Almanac, 7th Edition, 2007*

- Savannah was selected as one of "America's Favorite Cities." The city ranked #1 in the "Quality of Life and Visitor Experience" category. Respondents to an online survey were asked to rate 35 top urban destinations in the U.S from a visitor's perspective. Criteria: noteworthy neighborhoods; skyline/views; public parks and outdoor access; cleanliness; public transportation and pedestrian friendliness; safety; weather; peace and quiet; people-watching; environmental friendliness. *Travelandleisure.com, "America's Favorite Cities 2010," November 2010*

- Savannah was selected as one of "America's Favorite Cities." The city ranked #1 in the "People" category. Respondents to an online survey were asked to rate 35 top urban destinations in the U.S. from a visitor's perspective. Criteria: attractive; friendly; stylish; intelligent; athletic/active; diverse. *Travelandleisure.com, "America's Favorite Cities 2010," November 2010*

- Savannah was selected as one of "America's Favorite Cities." The city ranked #8 in the "Food/Dining" category. Respondents to an online survey were asked to rate 35 top urban destinations in the U.S. from a visitor's perspective. Criteria: big-name restaurants; ethnic food; farmers' markets; neighborhood joints and cafes. *Travelandleisure.com, "America's Favorite Cities 2010," November 2010*

- Savannah was selected as one of "America's Favorite Cities." The city ranked #9 in the "Nightlife" category. Respondents to an online survey were asked to rate 35 top urban destinations in the U.S. from a visitor's perspective. Criteria: cocktail hour; live music/concerts and bands; singles/bar scene. *Travelandleisure.com, "America's Favorite Cities 2010," November 2010*

- *Condé Nast Traveler* polled thousands of readers for travel satisfaction. American cities were ranked based on the following criteria: friendliness; atmosphere/ambiance; culture/sites; restaurants; lodging; and shopping. Savannah appeared in the top 10, ranking #7. *Condé Nast Traveler, 2010 Readers' Choice Awards*

Business/Finance Rankings

- Savannah was identified as one of the top 25 U.S. cities with the most credit card debt by credit reporting bureau Experian. The city was ranked #21. *Experian, March 4, 2011*

- Savannah was selected as one of the "100 Best Places to Live and Launch" in the U.S. The city ranked #99. The editors at *Fortune Small Business* ranked 296 Census-designated metro areas by business friendliness (Launching Score, % New Businesses) and lifestyle offerings (Living Score). Then they picked the town within each of the top 100 metro areas that best blends business and pleasure. *Fortune Small Business, "100 Best Places to Live and Launch 2008," April 2008*

- *American City Business Journals* ranked America's 261 largest cities in terms of their resident's wealth. Savannah ranked #229. Criteria: per capita income; median household income; percentage of households with annual incomes of $200,000 or more; median home value. *American City Business Journals, www.bizjournals.com, "Where the Money Is: America's Wealth Centers," August 18, 2008*

- The Savannah metro area appeared on the Milken Institute "2010 Best Performing Metros" list. Rank: #40 out of 200 large metro areas. Criteria: job growth; wage and salary growth; high-tech output growth. *Milken Institute, "2010 Best Performing Metros"*

- The Savannah metro area was selected as one of the best cities for entrepreneurs in America by *Inc. Magazine*. Criteria: job-growth data for 335 metro areas was analyzed for: recent growth trend (the current and prior year's employment growth rates, with the current year emphasized); mid-term growth (the average annual 2002-2007 growth rate); long-term trend (the sum of the 2002-2007 and 1996-2001 employment growth rates multiplied by the ratio of the 1996-2001 growth rate over the 2002-2007 growth rate); current year growth. The Savannah metro area ranked #3 among mid-sized metro areas and #15 overall. *Inc. Magazine, "The Best Cities for Doing Business," July 2008*

- *Forbes* ranked the 200 most populous metro areas in the U.S. in terms of the "Best Places for Business and Careers." The Savannah metro area was ranked #61. Criteria: 12 metrics including costs (business and living), job growth (past and projected), income growth, educational attainment, projected economic growth, crime, cultural and recreational opportunities, net migration patterns, percentage of subprime mortgages handed out over a three-year period, and the number of highly ranked four-year colleges. *Forbes, "Best Places for Business and Careers," April 14, 2010*

Culture/Performing Arts Rankings

- Savannah was selected as one of "America's Favorite Cities." The city ranked #6 in the "Culture" category. Respondents to an online survey were asked to rate 35 top urban destinations in the U.S. from a visitor's perspective. Criteria: classical music; live music/bands; theater; museums/galleries; historical sites/monuments. *Travelandleisure.com, "America's Favorite Cities 2010," November 2010*

- Savannah was selected as one of "America's Top 25 Arts Destinations." The city ranked #6 in the mid-sized city (population 100,000 to 499,999) category. Criteria: readers' top choices for arts travel destinations based on the richness and variety of visual arts sites, activities and events. *American Style, "America's Top 25 Arts Destinations," May 2010*

Education Rankings

- Savannah was identified as one of "America's Brainiest Bastions" by *Portfolio.com*. The metro area ranked #107 out of 200. Portfolio.com analyzed levels of educational attainment in the nation's 200 largest metropolitan areas. The editors established scores for five levels of educational attainment, based on relative earning power of adult workers age 25 or older. Scores were determined by comparing the median income for all workers with the median income for those workers at a specified educational level. *Portfolio.com, "America's Brainiest Bastions," December 1, 2010*

Environmental Rankings

- Savannah was selected as one of 22 "Smarter Cities" for energy by the Natural Resources Defense Council." Criteria: investment in green power; energy efficiency measures; conservation. *Natural Resources Defense Council, "2010 Smarter Cities," July 19, 2010*

- The Savannah metro area appeared in *Country Home's* "Best Green Places" report. The area ranked #277 out of 379. Criteria: official energy policies; green power; green buildings; availability of fresh, locally grown food. *Country Home, "Best Green Places," 2008*

- Savannah was highlighted as one of the cleanest metro areas for ozone air pollution in the U.S. The list represents cities with no monitored ozone air pollution in unhealthful ranges. *American Lung Association, State of the Air 2011*

Health/Fitness Rankings

- The Savannah metropolitan area was selected as one of the best metros for hospital care in America by HealthGrades. The rankings are based on a comprehensive study of patient death and complication rates in the nation's nearly 5,000 hospitals. Hospitals performing in the top 5% nationwide across 26 different medical procedures and diagnoses were identified. HealthGrades then ranked cities by the highest percentage of these Distinguished Hospitals for Clinical Excellence™. The Savannah metro area ranked #33. *HealthGrades.com, "America's Top 50 Cities for Hospital Care," January 26, 2011*

- The Savannah metro area appeared in the 2010 Gallup-Healthways Well-Being Index. The index, based on interviews with more than 353,000 Americans during 2009, asked individuals to assess their jobs, finances, physical health, emotional state of mind and communities. The metro area ranked #144 out of 162. Criteria: life evaluation; emotional health; work environment; physical health; healthy behaviors; basic access (basic needs optimal for a healthy life, such as access to food and medicine, having health insurance and feeling safe while walking at night). *Gallup-Healthways, "Well-Being Index 2010"*

Real Estate Rankings

- Savannah was identified as one of the top 20 metro areas with the lowest rate of house price appreciation in 2010. The area ranked #296 with a one-year price appreciation of -8.1% through the 4th quarter 2010. *Federal Housing Finance Agency, House Price Index, 4th Quarter 2010*

- Savannah appeared on CNNMoney.com's list of "Foreclosure Hotspots." The list includes the 10 cities with the fastest-growing foreclosure rates out of the 100 worst-hit places. *CNNMoney.com, "Foreclosure Hotspots," February 14, 2011*

- The nation's largest metro areas were analyzed in terms of the percentage of households entering some stage of foreclosure in 2010. The Savannah metro area ranked #59 out of 206 (#1 = highest foreclosure rate). *RealtyTrac, 2010 Year-End Metropolitan Foreclosure Market Report, January 27, 2011*

- The Savannah metro area was identified as one of the markets with the worst expected performance in home prices over the next 12 months. *Local Market Monitor, "First Quarter Home Price Forecast for Smallest US Markets," March 2, 2011*

Safety Rankings

- Allstate ranked the 200 largest cities in America in terms of driver safety. Savannah ranked #94. In addition, drivers were 4.9% more likely to have had an accident compared to the national average. Allstate researchers analyzed internal property damage reported claims over a two-year period (from January 2007 to December 2008) to ensure the findings would not be affected by external influences such as weather or road construction. A weighted average of the two-year numbers determined the annual percentages. The report defines an auto crash as any collision resulting in a property damage claim. *Allstate, "The 2010 Allstate America's Best Drivers Report™"*

- The National Insurance Crime Bureau ranked 366 metro areas in the U.S. in terms of per capita rates of vehicle theft. The Savannah metro area ranked #28 (#1 = highest rate). Criteria: number of vehicle theft offenses per 100,000 inhabitants. *National Insurance Crime Bureau, "Hot Spots," May 17, 2010*

Seniors/Retirement Rankings

- Savannah was selected as one of "10 Historic Places to Retire" by *U.S. News & World Report.* The editors looked for places filled with museums, libraries, and national historic monuments that also offer a good quality of life and plenty of amenities for seniors. *U.S. News & World Report, "10 Historic Places to Retire," September 6, 2010*

- Savannah was identified as one of the best places to retire in *Retirement Places Rated.* Criteria: population above 10,000; attractiveness to older adults; affordability; climate and natural endowments; personal safety. The city was ranked #17 out of 200. *Retirement Places Rated, 7th Edition, 2007*

Sports/Recreation Rankings

- Savannah appeared on the *Sporting News* list of the "Best Sports Cities" for 2010. The area ranked #244 out of 402 cities in the U.S. *Sporting News* takes a 12-month snapshot, roughly October to October, of each city's sports, putting a heavy premium on regular-season won-lost records (from the most recently completed season). Other criteria include: playoff berths, bowl appearances and tournament bids; championships; applicable power ratings; quality of competition; overall fan fervor as measured in part by attendance as percentage of venue capacity; abundance of teams (rewarding quality over quantity); stadium and arena quality; ticket availability and prices; franchise ownership; and marquee appeal of athletes. *Sporting News, "Best Sports Cities 2010," October, 2010*

- Savannah was selected as one of the most playful cities in the U.S. by KaBOOM! The organization's Playful City USA initiative is a national recognition program that honors cities and towns across the nation for a vision, plan and commitment to creating an agenda for play. Cities were recognized based on a pledge to five specific commitments to play: creating a local play commission or task force; designing an annual action plan for play; conducting a play space audit; outlining a financial investment in play for the current fiscal year; and proclaiming and celebrating an annual "play day." *KaBOOM! National Campaign for Play, "2010 Playful City USA Communities"*

- *Golf Digest* ranked 330 metro areas in the U.S. in terms of golf. The Savannah metro area was ranked #37. Criteria: access to golf; weather; value of golf; and quality of golf. *Golf Digest, "Metro Golf Rankings," August 2005*

Miscellaneous Rankings

- Savannah was selected as one of the "Top 10 Cities to Defy Death" by Livability.com. The city was ranked #9. Livability.com scoured the U.S. for the best adventure cities. Criteria includes: extreme sports; surfing; rock-climbing; haunted cities. *Livability.com, "Top 10 Cities to Defy Death," February 22, 2011*

- Savannah was selected as one of America's best-mannered cities. The area ranked #2. The general public determined the winners by casting votes online and by mail. *The Charleston School of Protocol and Etiquette, "2010 Most Mannerly City in America Contest," February 7, 2011*

Business Environment

CITY FINANCES

City Government Finances

Component	2008 ($000)	2008 ($ per capita)
Total Revenues	407,159	3,124
Total Expenditures	424,810	3,259
Debt Outstanding	207,755	1,594
Cash and Securities[1]	580,666	4,455

Note: (1) Cash and security holdings of a government at the close of its fiscal year, including those of its dependent agencies, utilities, and liquor stores.
Source: U.S Census Bureau, State & Local Government Finances 2008

City Government Revenue by Source

Source	2008 ($000)	2008 ($ per capita)
General Revenue		
From Federal Government	11,298	87
From State Government	8,035	62
From Local Governments	84,743	650
Taxes		
Property	56,225	431
Sales and Gross Receipts	33,443	257
Personal Income	0	0
Corporate Income	0	0
Motor Vehicle License	0	0
Other Taxes	11,374	87
Current Charges	100,693	773
Liquor Store	0	0
Utility	35,604	273
Employee Retirement	23,077	177

Source: U.S Census Bureau, State & Local Government Finances 2008

City Government Expenditures by Function

Function	2008 ($000)	2008 ($ per capita)	2008 (%)
General Direct Expenditures			
Air Transportation	53,694	412	12.6
Corrections	0	0	0.0
Education	0	0	0.0
Employment Security Administration	0	0	0.0
Financial Administration	5,023	39	1.2
Fire Protection	23,290	179	5.5
General Public Buildings	13,759	106	3.2
Governmental Administration, Other	5,524	42	1.3
Health	0	0	0.0
Highways	15,055	116	3.5
Hospitals	0	0	0.0
Housing and Community Development	28,861	221	6.8
Interest on General Debt	5,354	41	1.3
Judicial and Legal	2,031	16	0.5
Libraries	0	0	0.0
Parking	5,058	39	1.2
Parks and Recreation	22,920	176	5.4
Police Protection	53,365	409	12.6
Public Welfare	1,053	8	0.2
Sewerage	44,347	340	10.4
Solid Waste Management	40,423	310	9.5
Veterans' Services	0	0	0.0
Liquor Store	0	0	0.0
Utility	40,816	313	9.6
Employee Retirement	13,892	107	3.3

Source: U.S Census Bureau, State & Local Government Finances 2008

Municipal Bond Ratings

Area	Moody's	S&P	Fitch
City	Aa3	AA	n/a

Rating Systems (shown in declining order of credit quality): Moody's– Aaa, Aa, A, Baa, Ba, B, Caa, Ca, C (numerical modifiers 1, 2, and 3 are added to letter-rating); S&P– AAA, AA, A, BBB, BB, B, CCC, CC, C; Fitch– AAA, AA, A, BBB, BB, B, CCC, CC, C. Ratings may be modified by the addition of a plus or minus sign to show relative standing within the major rating categories.

Notes: n/a Not available; (1) Not reviewed; (2) Issuer Rating/No General Obligation; (3) Standard and Poor's Issue Credit Rating (ICR) is a current opinion of an obliger with respect to a specific financial obligation, a specific class of financial obligations, or a specific financial program.

Source: City of Savannah, Georgia, Comprehensive Annual Financial Report, Fiscal Year Ended December 31, 2009

DEMOGRAPHICS

Population Growth

Area	1990 Census	2000 Census	2010 Estimate	2015 Projection	Population Growth (%)	
					2000-2010	2010-2015
City	138,038	131,510	131,346	134,046	-0.1	2.1
MSA[1]	258,060	293,000	342,793	366,584	17.0	6.9
U.S.	248,709,873	281,421,906	309,038,974	321,675,005	9.8	4.1

Note: (1) Metropolitan Statistical Area - see Appendix B for areas included
Source: Claritas, Inc.

Number of Households and Average Household Size

Area	2010 Estimate	2010 Average Household Size
City	51,619	2.40
MSA[1]	130,387	2.53
U.S.	116,136,617	2.59

Note: (1) Metropolitan Statistical Area - see Appendix B for areas included
Source: Claritas, Inc.

Race and Ethnicity

Area	White Alone[2] (%)	Black Alone[2] (%)	Asian Alone[2] (%)	Other Race Alone[2] (%)	Hispanic[3] (%)
City	36.8	57.9	1.8	3.5	3.0
MSA[1]	61.1	33.7	1.9	3.3	3.1
U.S.	72.3	12.4	4.4	10.9	15.8

Note: Figures are 2010 estimates; (1) Metropolitan Statistical Area - see Appendix B for areas included (2) Alone is defined as not being in combination with one or more other races; (3) May be of any race.
Source: Claritas, Inc.

Segregation

Type	Segregation Indices[1]				Percent Change		
	1990	2000	2010	2010 Rank[2]	1990-2000	1990-2010	2000-2010
Black/White	n/a	n/a	n/a	n/a	n/a	n/a	n/a
Asian/White	n/a	n/a	n/a	n/a	n/a	n/a	n/a
Hispanic/White	n/a	n/a	n/a	n/a	n/a	n/a	n/a

Note: Figures are based on an analysis of 1990, 2000, and 2010 Census Decennial Census tract data by William H. Frey, Brookings Institution and the University of Michigan Social Science Data Analysis Network. In this analysis all racial groups (whites, blacks, and asians) are non-Hispanic members of those races. Hispanics are shown as a separate category; All figures cover the Metropolitan Statistical Area (see Appendix B for areas included); (1) Segregation Indices are Dissimilarity Indices that measure the degree to which the minority group is distributed differently than whites aross census tracts. They range from 0 (complete integration) to 100 (complete [segregation) where the value indicates the percentage of the minority group that needs to move to be distributed exactly like whites; (2) Ranges from 1 (most segregated) to 102 (least segregated); n/a not available.
Source: www.CensusScope.org

Ancestry

Area	German	Irish	English	American	Italian	Polish	French	Scottish
City	6.0	8.0	7.4	3.3	1.8	0.5	1.3	1.3
MSA[1]	10.4	12.1	10.3	5.9	2.4	1.1	2.0	2.4
U.S.	16.6	12.0	9.1	6.1	5.9	3.3	3.1	1.9

Note: The top eight ancestries in the U.S. are shown. Figures are percentages and include multiple ancestry (e.g. if a person reported being Irish and Italian, they were included in both columns); (1) Metropolitan Statistical Area - see Appendix B for areas included
Source: U.S. Census Bureau, 2007-2009 American Community Survey 3-Year Estimates

Foreign-Born Population

Area	Percent of Population Born in								
	Any Foreign Country	Mexico	Asia	Europe	Carribean	South America	Central America[2]	Africa	Canada
City	n/a	n/a	n/a	n/a	n/a	n/a	n/a	n/a	n/a
MSA[1]	4.1	0.6	1.5	0.7	0.3	0.3	0.2	0.2	0.2
U.S.	12.5	3.8	3.4	1.6	1.1	0.8	0.9	0.5	0.3

Note: (1) Metropolitan Statistical Area - see Appendix B for areas included; (2) Excludes Mexico.
Source: U.S. Census Bureau, 2007-2009 American Community Survey 3-Year Estimates

Marriage Status

Area	Never Married	Now Married[2]	Separated	Widowed	Divorced
City	41.7	35.6	2.5	8.6	11.7
MSA[1]	32.4	48.0	2.2	6.3	11.1
U.S.	31.4	49.7	2.2	6.2	10.6

Note: Figures are percentages and cover the population 15 years of age and older;
(1) Metropolitan Statistical Area - see Appendix B for areas included; (2) Excludes separated
Source: U.S. Census Bureau, 2007-2009 American Community Survey 3-Year Estimates

Age Distribution and Median Age

Area	Percent of Population							Median Age
	Under Age 5	Age 5 to 17	Age 18 to 34	Age 35 to 49	Age 50 to 64	Age 65 to 79	80 Years and Over	
City	7.9	15.5	30.0	17.8	16.1	8.3	4.4	32.0
MSA[1]	7.5	17.4	26.0	20.2	17.3	8.3	3.2	34.2
U.S.	6.9	17.5	23.3	21.4	18.1	9.1	3.7	36.7

Note: (1) Metropolitan Statistical Area - see Appendix B for areas included
Source: U.S. Census Bureau, 2007-2009 American Community Survey 3-Year Estimates

Male/Female Ratio

Area	Males	Females	Males per 100 Females
City	62,207	69,139	90.0
MSA[1]	166,169	176,624	94.1
U.S.	152,401,520	156,637,454	97.3

Note: Figures are 2010 estimates; (1) Metropolitan Statistical Area - see Appendix B for areas included
Source: Claritas, Inc.

Religion

Area	Catholic	Southern Baptist	United Meth-odist	ELCA[1]	LDS[2]	Presby-terian Church USA	Jewish Est.	Muslim Est.
County	9.0	14.9	6.7	1.5	0.3	1.4	1.3	0.3
U.S.	22.0	7.1	3.7	1.8	1.5	1.1	2.2	0.6

Note: Figures are the number of adherents as a percentage of the total population; Adherents are defined as all members, including full members, their children and the estimated number of other participants who are not considered members (e.g. the baptized, those not confirmed, those regularly attending services, etc.); (1) Evangelical Lutheran Church in America; (2) The Church of Jesus Christ of Latter Day Saints
Source: Reprinted with permission from Religious Congregations and Membership in the United States 2000 (Nashville, Glenmary Research Center, 2002) Copyright Association of Statisticians of American Religious Bodies. All rights reserved.

ECONOMY

Gross Metropolitan Product

Area	2006	2007	2008	2009	2009 Rank[2]
MSA[1]	12.2	12.8	13.2	13.2	143

Note: Figures are in billions of dollars; (1) Savannah, GA Metropolitan Statistical Area - see Appendix B for areas included; (2) Rank ranges from 1 to 363
Source: The U.S. Conference of Mayors, "Pace of Economic Recovery: GMP and Jobs," January 2010

Economic Growth

Area	2006-2008 (%)	2009 (%)	2010 (%)	Rank[2]
MSA[1]	1.2	-0.6	2.3	172
U.S.	1.3	-2.5	2.2	–

Note: Figures are real Gross Metropolitan Product growth rates and represent annual average percent change; (1) Savannah, GA Metropolitan Statistical Area - see Appendix B for areas included; (2) Rank ranges from 1 to 363
Source: The U.S. Conference of Mayors, "Pace of Economic Recovery: GMP and Jobs," January 2010

Metropolitan Area Exports

Area	2005	2006	2007	2008	2009	2009 Rank[2]
MSA[1]	1,647.9	1,951.1	2,520.2	3,598.5	2,724.7	62

Note: Figures are in millions of dollars; (1) Savannah, GA Metropolitan Statistical Area - see Appendix B for areas included; (2) Rank ranges from 1 to 374
Source: U.S. Department of Commerce, International Trade Administration, Office of Trade & Industry Information, Manufacturing & Services

INCOME

Per Capita/Median/Average Income

Area	Per Capita ($)	Median Household ($)	Average Household ($)
City	20,189	34,366	49,899
MSA[1]	25,795	49,308	66,807
U.S.	27,034	52,795	71,071

Note: Figures are 2010 estimates; (1) Metropolitan Statistical Area - see Appendix B for areas included
Source: Claritas, Inc.

Household Income Distribution

Area	Under $15,000	$15,000 -24,999	$25,000 -34,999	$35,000 -49,999	$50,000 -74,999	$75,000 -99,000	$100,000 -149,999	$150,000 and up
City	22.4	14.8	13.7	14.9	16.3	8.0	6.4	3.5
MSA[1]	14.3	10.7	11.4	14.1	19.1	12.2	11.3	6.7
U.S.	12.1	10.2	10.6	15.0	19.5	12.5	12.1	8.0

Note: Figures are 2010 estimates; (1) Metropolitan Statistical Area - see Appendix B for areas included
Source: Claritas, Inc.

Poverty Rates by Age

Area	All Ages	Under 18 Years Old	18 to 64 Years Old	65 Years and Over
City	22.8	7.7	12.8	2.4
MSA[1]	14.4	4.8	8.2	1.4
U.S.	13.6	4.7	7.7	1.2

Note: Figures are percent of population with income during the previous 12 months below poverty level and only include population for whom poverty status is determined; (1) Metropolitan Statistical Area - see Appendix B for areas included
Source: U.S. Census Bureau, 2007-2009 American Community Survey 3-Year Estimates

Personal Bankruptcy Filing Rate

Area	2006	2007	2008	2009	2010
Chatham County	4.91	5.33	6.43	7.12	6.67
U.S.	2.00	2.73	3.53	4.60	4.96

Note: Numbers are per 1,000 population and include Chapter 7 and Chapter 13 filings
Source: Federal Deposit Insurance Corporation, Regional Economic Conditions, March 17, 2011

EMPLOYMENT

Labor Force and Employment

Area	Civilian Labor Force			Workers Employed		
	Dec. 2009	Dec. 2010	% Chg.	Dec. 2009	Dec. 2010	% Chg.
City	63,160	63,625	0.7	56,660	56,977	0.6
MSA[1]	174,003	175,491	0.9	158,829	159,717	0.6
U.S.	152,693,000	153,156,000	0.3	137,953,000	139,159,000	0.9

Note: Data is not seasonally adjusted and covers workers 16 years of age and older;
(1) Metropolitan Statistical Area - see Appendix B for areas included
Source: Bureau of Labor Statistics, http://stats.bls.gov

Unemployment Rate

Area	2010											
	Jan.	Feb.	Mar.	Apr.	May	Jun.	Jul.	Aug.	Sep.	Oct.	Nov.	Dec.
City	10.7	10.2	9.6	9.4	9.6	10.3	10.9	11.0	10.4	10.2	10.4	10.4
MSA[1]	9.3	9.0	8.6	8.3	8.3	8.8	10.1	9.3	9.0	8.9	9.0	9.0
U.S.	10.6	10.4	10.2	9.5	9.3	9.6	9.7	9.5	9.2	9.0	9.3	9.1

Note: Data is not seasonally adjusted and covers workers 16 years of age and older; All figures are percentages; (1) Metropolitan Statistical Area - see Appendix B for areas included
Source: Bureau of Labor Statistics, http://stats.bls.gov

Projected Unemployment Rate

Area	2007 (%)	2009 (%)	2011 (%)	2013 (%)
MSA[1]	4.2	8.4	8.5	7.0

Note: (1) Metropolitan Statistical Area - see Appendix B for areas included
Source: The U.S. Conference of Mayors, "Pace of Economic Recovery: GMP and Jobs," January 2010

Employment by Occupation

Occupation Classification	City (%)	MSA[1] (%)	U.S. (%)
Sales and Office	23.4	25.4	25.4
Professional and Related	19.3	20.0	21.0
Service	24.3	18.1	17.2
Production, Transportation, and Material Moving	12.4	13.0	12.3
Management, Business, and Financial	11.1	13.4	14.1
Construction, Extraction, and Maintenance	9.3	10.0	9.2
Farming, Forestry, and Fishing	0.3	0.2	0.7

Note: Figures cover employed civilians 16 years of age and older;
(1) Metropolitan Statistical Area - see Appendix B for areas included
Source: U.S. Census Bureau, 2007-2009 American Community Survey 3-Year Estimates

Employment by Industry

Sector	MSA[1]		U.S.
	Number of Employees	Percent of Total	Percent of Total
Government	23,100	15.4	17.2
Education and Health Services	23,200	15.4	15.2
Professional and Business Services	17,600	11.7	13.0
Retail Trade	18,000	12.0	11.4
Leisure and Hospitality	19,400	12.9	9.7
Manufacturing	13,700	9.1	8.8
Financial Activities	5,400	3.6	5.8
Wholesale Trade	5,900	3.9	4.2
Construction	n/a	n/a	4.1
Other Services	6,800	4.5	4.1
Transportation and Utilities	9,900	6.6	3.7
Information	1,500	1.0	2.1
Mining and Logging	n/a	n/a	0.6

Note: Figures cover non-farm employment as of December 2010 and are not seasonally adjusted;
(1) Metropolitan Statistical Area - see Appendix B for areas included; n/a not available
Source: Bureau of Labor Statistics, http://stats.bls.gov

Occupations with Greatest Projected Employment Growth: 2006 - 2016

Occupation[1]	2006 Employment	2016 Projected Employment	Numeric Employment Change	Percent Employment Change
Combined food preparation and serving workers, including fast food	95,500	124,650	29,150	30.5
Retail salespersons	127,750	153,800	26,050	20.4
Customer service representatives	83,640	105,060	21,420	25.6
Registered nurses	61,770	81,670	19,900	32.2
Waiters and waitresses	67,030	85,420	18,390	27.4
Elementary school teachers, except special education	54,220	70,440	16,220	29.9
Office clerks, general	88,680	102,290	13,610	15.3
Janitors and cleaners, except maids and housekeeping cleaners	60,840	73,160	12,320	20.2
Nursing aides, orderlies, and attendants	38,510	48,910	10,400	27.0
Child care workers	35,890	45,770	9,880	27.5

Note: Projections cover Georgia; (1) Sorted by numeric employment change
Source: www.projectionscentral.com, State Occupational Projections, 2006-2016 Long-Term Projections

Fastest Growing Occupations: 2006 - 2016

Occupation[1]	2006 Employment	2016 Projected Employment	Numeric Employment Change	Percent Employment Change
Skin care specialists	1,570	2,560	990	63.1
Network systems and data communications analysts	8,570	13,260	4,690	54.7
Home health aides	7,720	11,780	4,060	52.6
Medical assistants	11,990	17,450	5,460	45.5
Veterinary technologists and technicians	2,160	3,140	980	45.4
Mental health and substance abuse social workers	1,260	1,780	520	41.3
Computer software engineers, applications	11,160	15,730	4,570	40.9
Physician assistants	2,160	3,020	860	39.8
Veterinarians	1,820	2,530	710	39.0
Physical therapist assistants	1,350	1,870	520	38.5

Note: Projections cover Georgia; (1) Sorted by percent employment change and excludes occupations with numeric employment change less than 400
Source: www.projectionscentral.com, State Occupational Projections, 2006-2016 Long-Term Projections

Average Wages

Occupation	$/Hr.	Occupation	$/Hr.
Accountants and Auditors	30.29	Maids and Housekeeping Cleaners	8.35
Automotive Mechanics	17.82	Maintenance and Repair Workers	16.10
Bookkeepers	15.36	Marketing Managers	45.32
Carpenters	17.12	Nuclear Medicine Technologists	n/a
Cashiers	8.37	Nurses, Licensed Practical	18.32
Clerks, General Office	11.33	Nurses, Registered	31.28
Clerks, Receptionists/Information	10.78	Nursing Aides/Orderlies/Attendants	10.32
Clerks, Shipping/Receiving	15.99	Packers and Packagers, Hand	7.94
Computer Programmers	31.28	Physical Therapists	34.65
Computer Support Specialists	19.44	Postal Service Mail Carriers	22.86
Computer Systems Analysts	28.39	Real Estate Brokers	n/a
Cooks, Restaurant	10.48	Retail Salespersons	10.21
Dentists	n/a	Sales Reps., Exc. Tech./Scientific	36.37
Electrical Engineers	43.30	Sales Reps., Tech./Scientific	36.95
Electricians	21.26	Secretaries, Exc. Legal/Med./Exec.	12.97
Financial Managers	45.61	Security Guards	10.44
First-Line Supervisors/Mgrs., Sales	17.21	Surgeons	n/a
Food Preparation Workers	10.50	Teacher Assistants	11.30
General and Operations Managers	44.28	Teachers, Elementary School	23.60
Hairdressers/Cosmetologists	16.71	Teachers, Secondary School	23.20
Internists	105.17	Telemarketers	n/a
Janitors and Cleaners	10.02	Truck Drivers, Heavy/Tractor-Trailer	18.68
Landscaping/Groundskeeping Workers	12.51	Truck Drivers, Light/Delivery Svcs.	16.22
Lawyers	52.35	Waiters and Waitresses	9.76

Note: Wage data covers the Savannah, GA - see Appendix B for areas included. Hourly wages for elementary/secondary school teachers and teacher assistants were calculated by the editors from annual wage data assuming a 40 hour work week; n/a not available.
Source: Bureau of Labor Statistics, Metro Area Occupational Employment and Wage Estimates, May 2009

RESIDENTIAL REAL ESTATE

Building Permits

Area	Single-Family			Multi-Family			Total		
	2009	2010	Pct. Chg.	2009	2010	Pct. Chg.	2009	2010	Pct. Chg.
City	330	241	-27.0	326	279	-14.4	656	520	-20.7
MSA[1]	1,241	1,020	-17.8	364	281	-22.8	1,605	1,301	-18.9
U.S.	441,100	447,300	1.4	141,900	157,300	10.9	583,000	604,600	3.7

Note: (1) Metropolitan Statistical Area - see Appendix B for areas included; figures represent new, privately-owned housing units authorized (unadjusted data); All permit data are based on estimates with imputation.
Source: U.S. Census Bureau, Manufacturing, Mining, and Construction Statistics, Building Permits, 2009, 2010

Homeownership Rate

Area	2005 (%)	2006 (%)	2007 (%)	2008 (%)	2009 (%)	2010 (%)
MSA[1]	n/a	n/a	n/a	n/a	n/a	n/a
U.S.	68.9	68.8	68.1	67.8	67.4	66.9

Note: (1) Metropolitan Statistical Area - see Appendix B for areas included
Source: U.S. Census Bureau, Housing Vacancies and Homeownership Annual Statistics: 2010

Housing Vacancy Rates

Area	Gross Vacancy Rate[2] (%)			Year-Round Vacancy Rate[3] (%)			Rental Vacancy Rate[4] (%)			Homeowner Vacancy Rate[5] (%)		
	2008	2009	2010	2008	2009	2010	2008	2009	2010	2008	2009	2010
MSA[1]	n/a	n/a	n/a	n/a	n/a	n/a	n/a	n/a	n/a	n/a	n/a	n/a
U.S.	14.4	14.5	14.3	11.1	11.3	11.3	10.0	10.6	10.2	2.8	2.6	2.6

Note: (1) Metropolitan Statistical Area - see Appendix B for areas included; (2) The percentage of the total housing inventory that is vacant; (3) The percentage of the housing inventory (excluding seasonal units) that is year-round vacant; (4) The percentage of rental inventory that is vacant for rent; (5) The percentage of homeowner inventory that is vacant for sale; n/a not available
Source: U.S. Census Bureau, Housing Vacancies and Homeownership Annual Statistics: 2010

State Corporate Income Tax Rates

State	Tax Rate (%)	Income Brackets ($)	Num. of Brackets	Financial Institution Tax Rate (%)[a]	Federal Income Tax Ded.
Georgia	6.0	Flat rate	1	6.0	No

Note: Tax rates as of January 1, 2011; (a) Rates listed are the tax rates applied to financial institutions or excise taxes based on income. Some states have other taxes based upon the value of deposits or shares.
Source: Federation of Tax Administrators, "State Corporate Income Tax Rates, 2011"

State Individual Income Tax Rates

State	Tax Rate (%)	Income Brackets ($)	Num. of Brackets	Personal Exempt. ($)[1] Single	Personal Exempt. ($)[1] Dependents	Fed. Inc. Tax Ded.
Georgia	1.0 - 6.0	750 (h) - 7,001 (h)	6	2,700	3,000	No

Note: Tax rates as of January 1, 2011; Local- and county-level taxes are not included; n/a not applicable; (1) Married joint filers generally receive double the single exemption; (h) The Georgia income brackets reported are for single individuals. For married couples filing jointly, the same tax rates apply to income brackets ranging from $1,000, to $10,000.
Source: Federation of Tax Administrators, "State Individual Income Tax Rates, 2011"

Various State and Local Tax Rates

State	State and Local Sales and Use (%)	State Sales and Use (%)	Gasoline[1] (¢/gal.)	Cigarette[2] ($/pack)	Spirits[3] ($/gal.)	Wine[4] ($/gal.)	Beer[5] ($/gal.)
Georgia	7.0	4.00	20.8	0.37	3.79	1.51	1.01 (l)

Note: All tax rates as of January 1, 2011 except Spirits (Sept. 1, 2010); (1) The American Petroleum Institute has developed a methodology for determining the average tax rate on a gallon of fuel. Rates may include any of the following: excise taxes, environmental fees, storage tank fees, other fees or taxes, general sales tax, and local taxes. In states where gasoline is subject to the general sales tax, or where the fuel tax is based on the average sale price, the average rate determined by API is sensitive to changes in the price of gasoline. States that fully or partially apply general sales taxes to gasoline: CA, CO, GA, IL, IN, MI, NY; (2) The federal excise tax of $1.0066 per pack and local taxes are not included; (3) Rates are those applicable to off-premise sales of 40% alcohol by volume (a.b.v.) distilled spirits in 750ml containers. Local excise taxes are excluded; (4) Rates are those applicable to off-premise sales of 11% a.b.v. non-carbonated wine in 750ml containers; (5) Rates are those applicable to off-premise sales of 4.7% a.b.v. beer in 12 ounce containers; (l) Includes statewide local rates in Alabama ($0.52) and Georgia ($0.53).
Source: Tax Foundation, 2011 Facts & Figures: How Does Your State Compare?

State-Local Tax Burdens

Area	Rate (%)	Rank[1]	Per Capita Taxes Paid to Home State ($)	Total State and Local Per Capita Taxes Paid ($)	Per Capita Income ($)
Georgia	9.1	32	2,411	3,350	36,738
U.S. Average	9.8	-	3,057	4,160	42,539

Note: Figures cover 2009; (1) Rank ranges from 1 to 50 where 1 is highest tax burden
Source: Tax Foundation, State-Local Tax Burdens, All States, 2009

State Business Tax Climate Index Rankings

State	Overall Rank	Corporate Tax Index Rank	Individual Income Tax Index Rank	Sales Tax Index Rank	Unemployment Insurance Tax Index Rank	Property Tax Index Rank
Georgia	25	8	30	23	22	38

Note: The index is a measure of how each state's tax laws affect economic performance. The lower the rank, the more favorable a state's tax system is for business. All ranks are for fiscal years. States without a given tax are given a ranking of 1.
Source: Tax Foundation, Tax Foundation Background Paper, No. 60, "2011 State Business Tax Climate Index"

COMMERCIAL UTILITIES

Typical Monthly Electric Bills

Area	Commercial Service ($/month)		Industrial Service ($/month)	
	3 kW demand 1,000 kWh	40 kW demand 14,000 kWh	1,000 kW demand 200,000 kWh	50,000 kW demand 15,000,000 kWh
City	153	1,980	25,423	1,372,795
Average[1]	135	1,576	23,741	1,402,202

Note: Based on total rates in effect July 1, 2010; (1) average based on 182 utilities surveyed
Source: Edison Electric Institute, Typical Bills and Average Rates Report, Summer 2010

TRANSPORTATION

Means of Transportation to Work

Area	Car/Truck/Van		Public Transportation			Bicycle	Walked	Other Means	Worked at Home
	Drove Alone	Car-pooled	Bus	Subway	Railroad				
City	77.6	9.7	4.2	0.0	0.0	1.0	3.3	1.4	2.8
MSA[1]	81.1	10.5	1.9	0.0	0.0	0.4	1.8	1.2	3.1
U.S.	75.8	10.4	2.7	1.7	0.5	0.5	2.9	1.2	4.1

Note: Figures are percentages and cover workers 16 years of age and older;
(1) Metropolitan Statistical Area - see Appendix B for areas included
Source: U.S. Census Bureau, 2007-2009 American Community Survey 3-Year Estimates

Travel Time to Work

Area	Less Than 15 Minutes	15 to 29 Minutes	30 to 44 Minutes	45 to 59 Minutes	60 to 89 Minutes	90 Minutes or More
City	30.7	52.7	12.8	1.5	1.6	0.7
MSA[1]	24.3	47.1	19.9	5.5	2.1	1.1
U.S.	28.5	36.2	19.7	7.5	5.6	2.5

Note: Figures are percentages and include workers 16 years old and over;
(1) Metropolitan Statistical Area - see Appendix B for areas included
Source: U.S. Census Bureau, 2007-2009 American Community Survey 3-Year Estimates

Travel Time Index

Area	1982	1999	2008	2009
Urban Area[1]	n/a	n/a	n/a	n/a
Average[2]	1.08	1.20	1.20	1.20

Note: Travel Time Index—the ratio of travel time in the peak period to the travel time at free-flow conditions. A value of 1.30 indicates a 20-minute free-flow trip takes 26 minutes in the peak. Free-flow speeds (60 mph on freeways and 35 mph on principal arterials) are used as the comparison threshold; (1) Covers the Savannah urban area; (2) average of 439 urban areas
Source: Texas Transportation Institute, Urban Mobility Report 2010, December 2010

Public Transportation

Agency Name / Mode of Transportation	Vehicles Operated in Maximum Service	Annual Unlinked Passenger Trips ('000)	Annual Passenger Miles ('000)
Chatham Area Transit Authority (CAT)			
Demand response	19	63.0	585.4
Ferryboat	2	452.2	171.8
Bus	47	3,277.5	12,049.9

Note: Figures include both directly operated and purchased transportation
Source: Federal Transit Administration, National Transit Database, 2009

Air Transportation

Airport Name and Code / Type of Service	Passenger Airlines[1]	Passenger Enplanements	Freight Carriers[2]	Freight (lbs.)
Savannah International (SAV)				
Domestic service (U.S. carriers - 2010)	28	797,563	13	4,794,172
International service (U.S. carriers - 2009)	4	160	0	0

Note: (1) Includes all U.S.-based major, minor and commuter airlines that carried at least one passenger during the year; (2) Includes all U.S.-based airlines and freight carriers that transported at least one pound of freight during the year
Source: Bureau of Transportation Statistics, The Intermodal Transportation Database, Air Carriers: T-100 Domestic Market (U.S. Carriers), 2010; Bureau of Transportation Statistics, The Intermodal Transportation Database, Air Carriers: T-100 International Market (U.S. Carriers), 2009

Other Transportation Statistics

Interstate highways:	I-16; I-95
Amtrak service:	Yes
Major waterways/ports:	Savannah River (Atlantic Ocean)

Source: Amtrak.com; Google Maps

BUSINESSES

Major Business Headquarters

Company Name	Rankings	
	Fortune[1]	Forbes[2]
Colonial Group	-	87

Note: (1) Fortune 500—companies that produce a 10-K are ranked 1 to 500 based on 2010 revenue; (2) all private companies with at least $2 billion in annual revenue are ranked 1 to 223; companies listed are headquartered in the city; dashes indicate no ranking
Source: Fortune, "Fortune 500," May 23, 2011; Forbes, "America's Largest Private Companies," November 3, 2010

Minority- and Women-Owned Businesses

Group	All Firms		Firms with Paid Employees			
	Firms	Sales ($000)	Firms	Sales ($000)	Employees	Payroll ($000)
Asian	639	240,363	290	222,341	3,076	38,001
Black	4,185	316,962	211	193,454	839	21,492
Hispanic	139	47,330	39	39,932	727	6,988
Women	4,332	717,594	628	633,948	7,500	147,281
All Firms	13,722	14,667,749	3,980	14,215,679	89,874	2,946,574

Note: Figures cover firms located in the city; minority- and women-owned business are defined as firms in which the corresponding group own 51% or more of the stock or equity of the company
Source: U.S. Census Bureau, 2007 Economic Census, Survey of Business Owners

HOTELS

Hotels/Motels

Area	5 Star		4 Star		3 Star		2 Star		1 Star		Not Rated	
	Num.	Pct.3	Num.	Pct.3	Num.	Pct.3	Num.	Pct.3	Num.	Pct.3	Num.	Pct.3
City[1]	0	0.0	7	4.6	40	26.3	88	57.9	4	2.6	13	8.6
Total[2]	119	0.7	927	5.8	4,906	30.5	7,992	49.7	526	3.3	1,625	10.1

Note: (1) Figures cover Savannah and vicinity; (2) Figures cover all 100 cities in this book; (3) Percentage of hotels which are a given star rating; Star ratings are determined by expedia.com and offer an indication of the general quality of a particular hotel.
Source: expedia.com, May 5, 2011

The Savannah metro area is home to one of the top 218 hotels in the U.S. according to *Travel & Leisure*: **Mansion on Forsyth Park** (#127). Criteria: service; location; rooms; food; and value. *Travel & Leisure, "T+L 500, The World's Best Hotels 2011"*

The Savannah metro area is home to one of the top 100 hotels in the U.S. according to *Condé Nast Traveler*: **Mansion on Forsyth Park** (#78). The selections are based on over 25,000 responses to the magazine's annual Readers' Choice Survey. *Condé Nast Traveler, "2010 Readers' Choice Awards"*

EVENT SITES

Major Stadiums, Arenas, and Auditoriums

Name	Max. Capacity
Grayson Stadium	8,000
Johnny Mercer Theatre, Savannah Civic Center	2,506
MLK Jr. Arena, Savannah Civic Center	9,600

Source: Original research

Convention Centers

Name	Overall Space (sq. ft.)	Exhibit Space (sq. ft.)	Meeting Space (sq. ft.)	Meeting Rooms
Savannah Intl Trade & Convention Center	330,000	50,000	100,000	13

Source: Original research

Living Environment

COST OF LIVING

Cost of Living Index

Composite Index	Groceries	Housing	Utilities	Trans- portation	Health Care	Misc. Goods/ Services
93.5	94.7	84.0	94.0	98.4	99.0	99.1

Note: U.S. = 100; Figures cover the Savannah GA urban area.
Source: The Council for Community and Economic Research, ACCRA Cost of Living Index, 2010

Grocery Prices

Area[1]	T-Bone Steak ($/pound)	Frying Chicken ($/pound)	Whole Milk ($/half gal.)	Eggs ($/dozen)	Orange Juice ($/64 oz.)	Coffee ($/11.5 oz.)
City[2]	8.21	1.08	2.02	1.32	2.68	3.28
Avg.	9.04	1.16	2.02	1.47	3.08	3.65
Min.	6.97	0.84	1.46	0.96	2.39	2.64
Max.	13.93	2.51	3.58	3.01	4.94	6.32

*Note: (1) Values for the local area are compared with the average, minimum and maximum values for all 338 areas in the Cost of Living Index; (2) Figures cover the Savannah GA urban area; **T-Bone Steak** (price per pound); **Frying Chicken** (price per pound, whole fryer); **Whole Milk** (half gallon carton); **Eggs** (price per dozen, Grade A, large); **Orange Juice** (64 oz. Tropicana or Florida Natural); **Coffee** (11.5 oz. can, vacuum-packed, Maxwell House, Hills Bros, or Folgers).*
Source: The Council for Community and Economic Research, ACCRA Cost of Living Index, 2010

Housing and Utility Costs

Area[1]	New Home Price ($)	Apartment Rent ($/month)	All Electric ($/month)	Part Electric ($/month)	Other Energy ($/month)	Telephone ($/month)
City[2]	248,019	694	155.51	-	-	27.42
Avg.	293,442	810	166.39	91.93	83.82	26.93
Min.	182,545	453	119.21	44.47	36.85	17.98
Max.	1,123,114	2,776	307.53	218.20	313.90	39.15

*Note: (1) Values for the local area are compared with the average, minimum and maximum values for all 338 areas in the Cost of Living Index; (2) Figures cover the Savannah GA urban area; **New Home Price** (2,400 sf living area, 8,000 sf lot, in urban area with full utilities); **Apartment Rent** (950 sf 2 bedroom/1.5 or 2 bath, unfurnished, excluding all utilities except water); **All Electric** (average monthly cost for an all-electric home); **Part Electric** (average monthly cost for a part-electric home); **Other Energy** (average monthly cost for natural gas, fuel oil, coal, wood, and any other forms of energy except electricity); **Telephone** (price includes basic monthly rate for a private residential line plus additional local usage charges incurred by a family of four).*
Source: The Council for Community and Economic Research, ACCRA Cost of Living Index, 2010

Health Care, Transportation, and Other Costs

Area[1]	Doctor ($/visit)	Dentist ($/visit)	Optometrist ($/visit)	Gasoline ($/gallon)	Beauty Salon ($/visit)	Men's Shirt ($)
City[2]	88.60	71.20	71.51	2.66	38.38	21.59
Avg.	89.44	78.95	87.40	2.73	31.92	24.83
Min.	57.00	54.25	48.32	2.44	19.17	13.67
Max.	149.90	136.73	174.22	3.75	62.81	47.89

*Note: (1) Values for the local area are compared with the average, minimum and maximum values for all 338 areas in the Cost of Living Index; (2) Figures cover the Savannah GA urban area; **Doctor** (general practitioners routine exam of an established patient); **Dentist** (adult teeth cleaning and periodic oral examination); **Optometrist** (full vision eye exam for established adult patient); **Gasoline** (one gallon regular unleaded, national brand, including all taxes, cash price at self-service pump if available); **Beauty Salon** (woman's shampoo, trim, and blow-dry); **Men's Shirt** (cotton/polyester dress shirt, pinpoint weave, long sleeves).*
Source: The Council for Community and Economic Research, ACCRA Cost of Living Index, 2010

HOUSING

House Price Index (HPI)

Area	National Ranking[2]	Quarterly Change (%)	One-Year Change (%)	Five-Year Change (%)
MSA[1]	296	-3.52	-8.13	-2.24
U.S.[3]	-	-0.84	-3.95	-11.45

Note: The HPI is a weighted repeat sales index. It measures average price changes in repeat sales or refinancings on the same properties. This information is obtained by reviewing repeat mortgage transactions on single-family properties whose mortgages have been purchased or securitized by Fannie Mae or Freddie Mac in January 1975; (1) Metropolitan/Micropolitan Statistical Area - see Appendix B for areas included; (2) Rankings are based on annual percentage change for all metro areas containing at least 15,000 transactions over the last 10 years and ranges from 1 to 309; (3) figures based on a weighted average of Census Division estimates; all figures are for the period ending December 31, 2010
Source: Federal Housing Finance Agency, House Price Index, February 24, 2011

House Price Valuations

Area	Q4 2005 Price ($000)	Q4 2005 Over-valuation	Q4 2006 Price ($000)	Q4 2006 Over-valuation	Q4 2007 Price ($000)	Q4 2007 Over-valuation	Q4 2008 Price ($000)	Q4 2008 Over-valuation	Q4 2009 Price ($000)	Q4 2009 Over-valuation
MSA[1]	137.6	11.8	150.0	13.8	148.7	7.2	135.5	-2.4	135.3	-3.0

Note: Figures show the percentage of over- or under-valuation of single family homes relative to statistically normal house values (e.g. a value of 23.6 indicates that house values are 23.6% overvalued). Statistically normal house values are based on house prices, interest rates, household incomes, population densities, and any historical premiums or discounts metropolitan areas have exhibited over time; (1) Figures cover the Savannah, GA Metropolitan Statistical Area - see Appendix B for areas included
Source: Global Insight/PNC Financial Services Group, House Prices in America: 4th Quarter 2009 Update

Median Single-Family Home Prices

Area	2008	2009	2010[p]	Percent Change 2009 to 2010
MSA[1]	n/a	n/a	n/a	n/a
U.S. Average	196.6	172.1	173.2	0.6

Note: Figures are median sales prices of existing single-family homes in thousands of dollars; (p) preliminary; n/a not available; (1) Metropolitan Statistical Area - see Appendix B for areas included
Source: National Association of Realtors, Median Sales Price of Existing Single-Family Homes for Metropolitan Areas, 4th Quarter 2010

Median Apartment Condo-Coop Home Prices

Area	2008	2009	2010[p]	Percent Change 2009 to 2010
MSA[1]	n/a	n/a	n/a	n/a
U.S. Average	209.8	175.6	171.7	-2.2

Note: Figures are median sales prices of existing apartment condo-coop homes in thousands of dollars; (p) preliminary; n/a not available; (1) Metropolitan Statistical Area - see Appendix B for areas included
Source: National Association of Realtors, Median Sales Price of Existing Apartment Condo-Coop Homes for Metropolitan Areas, 4th Quarter 2010

Year Housing Structure Built

Area	2000 or Later	1990 -1999	1980 -1989	1970 -1979	1960 -1969	1950 -1959	1940 -1949	Before 1940	Median Year
City	9.3	6.8	10.6	16.0	15.2	17.0	7.7	17.3	1965
MSA[1]	20.5	17.8	14.5	12.9	10.3	9.9	4.6	9.5	1982
U.S.	12.5	14.0	14.2	16.5	11.4	11.3	5.8	14.3	1974

Note: Figures are percentages except for Median Year; (1) Metropolitan Statistical Area - see Appendix B for areas included
Source: U.S. Census Bureau, 2007-2009 American Community Survey 3-Year Estimates

HEALTH

Health Risk Data

Category	MSA[1] (%)	U.S. (%)
Adults who have been told they have high blood pressure	n/a	28.7
Adults who have been told they have high blood cholesterol	n/a	37.5
Adults who have been told they have diabetes[3]	n/a	8.3
Adults who have been told they have arthritis	n/a	26.0
Adults who have been told they currently have asthma	n/a	8.8
Adults who are current smokers	n/a	17.9
Adults who are heavy drinkers[4]	n/a	5.1
Adults who are binge drinkers[5]	n/a	15.8
Adults who are overweight (BMI 25.0 - 29.9)	n/a	36.2
Adults who are obese (BMI 30.0 - 99.8)	n/a	26.9
Adults who participated in any physical activities in the past month	n/a	76.2
Adults 50+ who have ever had a sigmoidoscopy or colonoscopy[2]	n/a	62.2
Women 40+ who have had a mammogram within the past two years[2]	n/a	76.0
Adults age 18–64 who have any kind of health care coverage	n/a	83.1

Note: Data as of 2009 unless otherwise noted; n/a not available; (1) Figures cover the Savannah, GA Metropolitan Statistical Area - see Appendix B for areas included; (2) Data as of 2008; (3) Figures do not include pregnancy-related, borderline, or pre-diabetes; (4) Heavy drinkers are classified as males having more than two drinks per day or females having more than one drink per day; (5) Binge drinkers are classified as males having five or more drinks on one occasion or females having four or more drinks on one occasion
Source: Centers for Disease Control and Prevention, Behaviorial Risk Factor Surveillance System, SMART: Selected Metropolitan/Micropolitan Area Risk Trends, 2008, 2009

Mortality Rates for the Top 10 Causes of Death in the U.S.

ICD-10[a] Sub-Chapter	ICD-10[a] Code	Age-Adjusted Mortality Rate[1] per 100,000 population	
		County[2]	U.S.
Malignant neoplasms	C00-C97	193.7	180.9
Ischaemic heart diseases	I20-I25	120.2	135.0
Other forms of heart disease	I30-I51	98.2	50.0
Cerebrovascular diseases	I60-I69	46.4	44.1
Chronic lower respiratory diseases	J40-J47	38.2	41.5
Other degenerative diseases of the nervous system	G30-G31	20.7	23.6
Diabetes mellitus	E10-E14	13.9	23.5
Other external causes of accidental injury	W00-X59	22.8	23.5
Organic, including symptomatic, mental disorders	F01-F09	21.4	22.2
Influenza and pneumonia	J09-J18	17.1	18.1

Note: (a) ICD-10 = International Classification of Diseases 10th Revision; (1) Mortality rates are a three year average covering 2005-2007; (2) Figures cover Chatham County
Source: Centers for Disease Control and Prevention, National Center for Health Statistics. Compressed Mortality File 1999-2007. CDC WONDER On-line Database, compiled from Compressed Mortality File 1999-2007 Series 20 No. 2M, 2010.

Mortality Rates for Selected Causes of Death

ICD-10[a] Sub-Chapter	ICD-10[a] Code	Age-Adjusted Mortality Rate[1] per 100,000 population	
		County[2]	U.S.
Assault	X85-Y09	13.7	6.0
Human immunodeficiency virus (HIV) disease	B20-B24	15.3	4.0
Hypertensive diseases	I10-I15	19.6	18.0
Intentional self-harm	X60-X84	10.3	11.0
Malnutrition	E40-E46	*0.6	0.8
Obesity and other hyperalimentation	E65-E68	*1.9	1.5
Transport accidents	V01-V99	18.8	15.6
Viral hepatitis	B15-B19	*1.5	2.1

Note: (a) ICD-10 = International Classification of Diseases 10th Revision; (1) Mortality rates are a three year average covering 2005-2007; (2) Figures cover Chatham County; (*) Unreliable data as per CDC
Source: Centers for Disease Control and Prevention, National Center for Health Statistics. Compressed Mortality File 1999-2007. CDC WONDER On-line Database, compiled from Compressed Mortality File 1999-2007 Series 20 No. 2M, 2010.

Distribution of Physicians and Dentists

Area[1]	Dentists[2]	D.O.[3]	M.D.[4]				
			Total	Family/ General Practice	Pediatrics	Medical Specialties	Surgical Specialties
Local (number)	114	33	671	67	48	238	185
Local (rate[5])	4.6	1.3	26.7	2.7	1.9	9.5	7.4
U.S. (rate[5])	4.5	1.9	18.3	2.5	1.4	6.8	4.1

Note: Data as of 2008 unless noted; (1) Local data covers Chatham County; (2) Data as of 2007; (3) Doctor of Osteopathic Medicine; (4) Includes active, non-federal, patient-care, office-based Doctors of Medicine; (5) rate per 10,000 population
Source: Area Resource File (ARF). 2009-2010 Release. U.S. Department of Health and Human Services, Health Resources and Services Administration, Bureau of Health Professions, Rockville, MD, August 2010

Hospitals

Savannah has the following hospitals: 3 general medical and surgical; 1 psychiatric; 1 long-term acute care; 1 children's psychiatric.
AHA Guide to the Healthcare Field 2010

EDUCATION

Public School District Statistics

District Name	Schls	Pupils	Pupil/ Teacher Ratio	Minority Pupils[1] (%)	Free Lunch Eligible[2] (%)	IEP[3] (%)
Chatham County	58	33,994	12.5	74.7	52.7	11.0

Note: Table includes school districts with 2,000 or more students; (1) Percentage of students that are not non-Hispanic white; (2) Percentage of students that are eligible for the free lunch program; (3) Percentage of students that have an Individualized Education Program.
Source: U.S. Department of Education, National Center for Education Statistics, Common Core of Data, Local Education Agency (School District) Universe Survey: School Year 2008-2009; U.S. Department of Education, National Center for Education Statistics, Common Core of Data, Public Elementary/Secondary School Universe Survey: School Year 2008-2009

Top Public High Schools

High School Name	Index[1]	Rank[1]	Subsidized Lunch (%)[2]	E&E (%)[3]
Johnson[4]	1.454	1201	54.0	15.1

Note: (1) Public schools are ranked according to a ratio that is the number of Advanced Placement, International Baccalaureate, and/or Cambridge tests taken by all students at a school in 2009 divided by the number of graduating seniors. All of the schools on the list have an index of at least 1.000; they are in the top six percent of public schools measured this way. The rankings range from 1 to 1,734; (2) Percentage of students receiving federally subsidized meals; (3) E & E stands for equity and excellence percentage: the portion of all graduating seniors at a school that had at least one passing grade on one AP or IB test; (4) Schools that offer International Baccalaureate or Cambridge exams; (5) School is unranked, but has been identified by Newsweek as one of the nation's most elite public high schools.
Source: Newsweek Online, "Top High Schools 2010"

Highest Level of Education

Area	Less than H.S.	H.S. Diploma	Some College, No Deg.	Associate Degree	Bachelors Degree	Masters Degree	Profess. School Degree	Doctorate Degree
City	15.2	30.9	20.8	7.7	16.5	6.2	2.0	0.9
MSA[1]	13.3	32.0	20.7	7.5	17.6	6.1	2.1	1.0
U.S.	15.3	29.0	20.7	7.5	17.4	7.0	1.9	1.1

Note: Figures are 2010 estimated percentages and cover persons age 25 and over; (1) Metropolitan Statistical Area - see Appendix B for areas included
Source: Claritas, Inc.

Educational Attainment by Race

Area	High School Graduate (%)					Bachelor's Degree (%)				
	Total	White	Black	Asian	Hisp.[2]	Total	White	Black	Asian	Hisp.[2]
City	84.5	92.7	78.8	85.2	65.1	23.7	38.1	11.7	46.6	16.7
MSA[1]	87.7	91.3	81.5	87.4	76.2	26.7	32.9	13.6	37.0	19.1
U.S.	84.9	90.0	80.7	85.5	60.7	27.8	30.9	17.5	49.7	12.7

Note: Figures shown cover persons 25 years old and over; (1) Metropolitan Statistical Area - see Appendix B for areas included; (2) people of Hispanic origin can be of any race
Source: U.S. Census Bureau, 2007-2009 American Community Survey 3-Year Estimates

School Enrollment by Grade and Control

Area	Preschool (%)		Kindergarten (%)		Grades 1 - 4 (%)		Grades 5 - 8 (%)		Grades 9 - 12 (%)	
	Public	Private	Public	Private	Public	Private	Public	Private	Public	Private
City	69.5	30.5	84.3	15.7	87.8	12.2	85.0	15.0	88.1	11.9
MSA[1]	59.1	40.9	80.2	19.8	82.6	17.4	83.9	16.1	84.1	15.9
U.S.	54.3	45.7	86.4	13.6	88.9	11.1	89.1	10.9	90.2	9.8

Note: Figures shown cover persons 3 years old and over; (1) Metropolitan Statistical Area - see Appendix B for areas included
Source: U.S. Census Bureau, 2007-2009 American Community Survey 3-Year Estimates

Average Salaries of Public School Classroom Teachers

Area	2009-10		2010-11		Percent Change 2009-10 to 2010-11	Percent Change 2000-01 to 2010-11
	Dollars	Rank[1]	Dollars	Rank[1]		
Georgia	53,112	18	53,906	18	1.50	27.7
U.S. Average	55,202	-	56,069	-	1.57	29.3

Note: (1) State rank ranges from 1 to 51 where 1 indicates highest salary.
Source: National Education Association, Rankings & Estimates: Rankings of the States 2010 and Estimates of School Statistics 2011, December 2010

Higher Education

Four-Year Colleges			Two-Year Colleges			Medical Schools[1]	Law Schools[2]	Voc/ Tech[3]
Public	Private Non-profit	Private For-profit	Public	Private Non-profit	Private For-profit			
2	1	2	1	0	0	0	0	1

Note: Figures cover institutions located within the city limits and include main campuses only; (1) includes schools accredited by the Liaison Committee on Medical Education and the American Osteopathic Association; (2) includes American Bar Association-accredited law schools; (3) includes all schools with programs that are less than 2 years.
Source: National Center for Education Statistics, Integrated Postsecondary Education System (IPEDS) Peer Analysis System, 2010-11; U.S. News & World Report, Medical School Directory, 2011; U.S. News & World Report, Law School Directory, 2011

PRESIDENTIAL ELECTION

2008 Presidential Election Results

Area	Obama	McCain	Nader	Other
Chatham County	56.8	42.4	0.0	0.7
U.S.	52.9	45.6	0.6	0.9

Note: Results are percentages and may not add to 100% due to rounding
Source: Dave Leip's Atlas of U.S. Presidential Elections, www.uselectionatlas.org

EMPLOYERS

Major Employers

Company Name	Industry	Type of Site
Armstrong Atlantic State Univ	Colleges and universities	Headquarters
Bain Medical Supply Group	Shoe stores	Single
Candler Hospital	General medical and surgical hospitals	Headquarters
Care One Home Health	General medical and surgical hospitals	Headquarters
Chatham County Sherriffs Off	Police protection	Branch
City of Savannah	Executive offices	Headquarters
Fort McIlster State Hstoric Pk	Land, mineral, and wildlife conservation	Branch
Garden City Terminal	Regulation, administration of transportation	Headquarters
Great Dane Trailers	Truck trailers	Branch
Great Dane Trailers	Truck trailers	Headquarters
Gulfstream Aerospace Corp	Aircraft	Headquarters
NE Trade Del Authority	Railroads, line-haul operating	Branch
Saint Josephs Hospital	General medical and surgical hospitals	Headquarters
Savannah Chatham Metro Police	Police protection	Branch
Savannah Morning News	Books, periodicals, and newspapers	Branch
Savannah State University	Colleges and universities	Headquarters
Savannah State University	Elementary and secondary schools	Branch
Smurfit-Stone Cont Entps	Paperboard mills	Branch
Sullivan Group	Employment agencies	Single
Tidelnds Cmnty Mental Hlth Ctr	Administration of public health programs	Branch
Tronox Oklahoma	Inorganic pigments	Single
Wal-Mart	Department stores	Branch

Note: Companies shown are located within the Savannah metropolitan area; nec = not elsewhere classified.
Source: www.zapdata.com, January 2011

PUBLIC SAFETY

Crime Rate

Area	All Crimes	Violent Crimes				Property Crimes		
		Murder	Forcible Rape	Robbery	Aggrav. Assault	Burglary	Larceny -Theft	Motor Vehicle Theft
City	5,539.0	14.1	21.6	301.8	192.7	1,246.8	3,228.3	533.6
Suburbs[1]	3,095.9	0.8	24.0	55.1	175.7	749.2	1,881.0	210.1
Metro[2]	4,633.8	9.2	22.5	210.4	186.4	1,062.4	2,729.1	413.7
U.S.	3,465.5	5.0	28.7	133.0	262.8	716.3	2,060.9	258.8

Note: Figures are crimes per 100,000 population; (1) All areas within the metro area that are located outside the city limits; (2) Metropolitan Statistical Area - see Appendix B for areas included
Source: FBI Uniform Crime Reports, 2009

Hate Crimes

Area	Number of Quarters Reported	Bias Motivation				
		Race	Religion	Sexual Orientation	Ethnicity	Disability
Area[2]	4	0	0	0	0	0

Note: (2) Figures cover Savannah-Chatham Metropolitan.
Source: Federal Bureau of Investigation, Hate Crime Statistics 2009

Identity Theft Consumer Complaints

Area	Complaints	Complaints per 100,000 Population	Rank[2]
MSA[1]	326	99.0	62
U.S.	250,854	81.3	-

Note: (1) Metropolitan Statistical Area - see Appendix B for areas included; (2) Rank ranges from 1 to 384 where 1 indicates greatest number of complaints per 100,000 population
Source: Federal Trade Commission, Consumer Sentinel Network Data Book for January - December 2010

RECREATION

Culture

Dance[1]	Theatre[1]	Instrumental Music[1]	Vocal Music[1]	Series/ Festivals	Museums	Zoos and Aquariums[2]
0	0	0	0	3	12	0

Note: (1) Number of professional perfoming groups; (2) AZA-accredited
Source: The Grey House Performing Arts Directory, 2011-2012; Official Museum Directory, 2010; American Association of Museums, AAM Member Museums, March 2011; Association of Zoos & Aquariums, AZA Member Zoos & Aquariums, May 2011

Professional Sports Teams

Team Name	League

No teams are located in the metro area
Source: Original research

CLIMATE

Average and Extreme Temperatures

Temperature	Jan	Feb	Mar	Apr	May	Jun	Jul	Aug	Sep	Oct	Nov	Dec	Yr.
Extreme High (°F)	84	86	91	95	100	104	105	104	98	97	89	83	105
Average High (°F)	60	64	70	78	84	89	92	90	86	78	70	62	77
Average Temp. (°F)	49	53	59	66	74	79	82	81	77	68	59	52	67
Average Low (°F)	38	41	48	54	62	69	72	72	68	57	47	40	56
Extreme Low (°F)	3	14	20	32	39	51	61	57	43	28	15	9	3

Note: Figures cover the years 1950-1995
Source: National Climatic Data Center, International Station Meteorological Climate Summary, 9/96

Average Precipitation/Snowfall/Humidity

Precip./Humidity	Jan	Feb	Mar	Apr	May	Jun	Jul	Aug	Sep	Oct	Nov	Dec	Yr.
Avg. Precip. (in.)	3.5	3.1	3.9	3.2	4.2	5.6	6.8	7.2	5.0	2.9	2.2	2.7	50.3
Avg. Snowfall (in.)	Tr	Tr	Tr	0	0	0	0	0	0	0	Tr	Tr	Tr
Avg. Rel. Hum. 7am (%)	83	82	83	84	85	87	88	91	91	88	86	83	86
Avg. Rel. Hum. 4pm (%)	53	50	49	48	52	58	61	63	62	55	53	54	55

Note: Figures cover the years 1950-1995; Tr = Trace amounts (<0.05 in. of rain; <0.5 in. of snow)
Source: National Climatic Data Center, International Station Meteorological Climate Summary, 9/96

Weather Conditions

Temperature			Daytime Sky			Precipitation		
10°F & below	32°F & below	90°F & above	Clear	Partly cloudy	Cloudy	0.01 inch or more precip.	0.1 inch or more snow/ice	Thunder-storms
< 1	29	70	97	155	113	111	< 1	63

Note: Figures are average number of days per year and cover the years 1950-1995
Source: National Climatic Data Center, International Station Meteorological Climate Summary, 9/96

HAZARDOUS WASTE

Superfund Sites

Savannah has no sites on the EPA's Superfund Final National Priorities List.
U.S. Environmental Protection Agency, Final National Priorities List, April 1, 2011

**AIR & WATER
QUALITY**

Air Quality Index

Area	Percent of Days when Air Quality was...[2]				AQI Statistics	
	Good	Moderate	Unhealthy for Sensitive Groups	Unhealthy	Maximum	Median
Area[1]	75.1	24.6	0.3	0.0	119	39

*Note: The Air Quality Index (AQI) is an index for reporting daily air quality. EPA calculates the AQI for five major air pollutants regulated by the Clean Air Act: ground-level ozone, particle pollution (also known as particulate matter), carbon monoxide, sulfur dioxide, and nitrogen dioxide. The AQI runs from 0 to 500. The higher the AQI value, the greater the level of air pollution and the greater the health concern. There are six AQI categories: "Good" The AQI is between 0 and 50. Air quality is considered satisfactory; "Moderate" The AQI is between 51 and 100. Air quality is acceptable; "Unhealthy for Sensitive Groups" When AQI values are between 101 and 150, members of sensitive groups may experience health effects; "Unhealthy" When AQI values are between 151 and 200 everyone may begin to experience health effects; "Very Unhealthy" AQI values between 201 and 300 trigger a health alert; "Hazardous" AQI values over 300 trigger health warnings of emergency conditions; (1) Data covers Chatham County; (2) Based on 305 days with AQI data in 2008; The EPA has suspended data updates while it assesses its data systems, including AirData reports and maps.
Source: U.S. Environmental Protection Agency, AirData Report, 2008*

Air Quality Index Pollutants

Area	Percent of Days when AQI Pollutant was...[2]					
	Carbon Monoxide	Nitrogen Dioxide	Ozone	Sulfur Dioxide	Particulate Matter 2.5	Particulate Matter 10
Area[1]	0.0	0.0	39.7	2.3	56.1	2.0

*Note: The Air Quality Index (AQI) is an index for reporting daily air quality. EPA calculates the AQI for five major air pollutants regulated by the Clean Air Act: ground-level ozone, particle pollution (also known as particulate matter), carbon monoxide, sulfur dioxide, and nitrogen dioxide. The AQI runs from 0 to 500. The higher the AQI value, the greater the level of air pollution and the greater the health concern; (1) Data covers Chatham County; (2) Based on 305 days with AQI data in 2008; The EPA has suspended data updates while it assesses its data systems, including AirData reports and maps.
Source: U.S. Environmental Protection Agency, AirData Report, 2008*

Air Quality Index Trends

Area	Trend Sites (days)								All Sites (days)
	2002	2003	2004	2005	2006	2007	2008	2009	2009
MSA[1]	n/a	n/a	n/a	n/a	n/a	n/a	n/a	n/a	n/a

*Note: Figures are the number of days the AQI value exceeded 100 in a given year. An AQI value greater than 100 indicates that air quality would have been in the unhealthful range on that day. Data from exceptional events are included. These counts are presented in two ways. First, the counts are based on sites having an adequate record of monitoring data during the trend period (trend sites). These counts represent the relative change in the number of days with AQI values greater than 100. In the last column, the counts are based on all sites with data in the most recent year (because it is possible for a site to have data in the most recent year but not enough data to be a trend site); (1) Data covers the Savannah, GA Metropolitan Statistical Area - see Appendix B for areas included; n/a not available.
Source: U.S. Environmental Protection Agency, Office of Air and Radiation, Air Quality Index Information, "Number of Days with Air Quality Index Values Greater than 100 and Trend Sites, 1990-2009, and at All Sites in 2009"*

Maximum Air Pollutant Concentrations

	Particulate Matter 10 (ug/m³)	Particulate Matter 2.5 (ug/m³)	Ozone (ppm)	Carbon Monoxide (ppm)	Sulfur Dioxide (ppm)	Nitrogen Dioxide (ppm)	Lead (ug/m³)
MSA[1] Level	32	25	0.062	n/a	0.022	n/a	n/a
NAAQS[2]	150	35	0.075	9	0.140	0.053	0.15
Met NAAQS[2]	Yes	Yes	Yes	n/a	Yes	n/a	n/a

*Note: Data from exceptional events are not included; (1) Data covers the Savannah, GA Metropolitan Statistical Area - see Appendix B for areas included; (2) National Ambient Air Quality Standards; n/a not available
Concentrations: Particulate Matter 10 (coarse particulate) - highest second maximum 24-hour concentration; Particulate Matter 2.5 (fine particulate) - highest 98th percentile 24-hour concentration; Ozone - highest fourth daily maximum 8-hour concentration; Carbon Monoxide - highest second maximum non-overlapping 8-hour concentration; Sulfur Dioxide - highest second maximum 24-hour concentration; Nitrogen Dioxide - highest arithmetic mean concentration; Lead - maximum running 3-month average
Units: ppm = parts per million; ug/m³ = micrograms per cubic meter
Source: U.S. Environmental Protection Agency, CBSA Factbook 2009, Air Quality Statistics by City, 2009*

Drinking Water

Water System Name	Pop. Served	Primary Water Source Type	Violations[1]	
			Health Based	Monitoring/ Reporting
Savannah-Main	163,688	Ground	1	0

Note: (1) Based on violation data from January 1, 2010 to December 31, 2010 (includes unresolved violations from earlier years)
Source: U.S. Environmental Protection Agency, Office of Ground Water and Drinking Water, Safe Drinking Water Information System (based on data extracted May 9, 2011)

Tampa, Florida

Background

Although Tampa was visited by Spanish explorers, such as Ponce de Leon and Hernando de Soto as early as 1521, this city, located on the mouth of the Hillsborough River on Tampa Bay, did not see significant growth until the mid-nineteenth century.

Like many cities in northern Florida such as Jacksonville, Tampa was a fort during the Seminole War, and during the Civil War it was captured by the Union Army. Later, Tampa enjoyed prosperity and development when the railroad transported tourists from up north to enjoy the warmth and sunshine of Florida.

Two historical events in the late nineteenth century set Tampa apart from other Florida cities. First, Tampa played a significant role during the Spanish-American War in 1898 as a chief port of embarkation for American troops to Cuba. During that time, Colonel Theodore Roosevelt occupied a Tampa hotel as his military headquarters. Second, a cigar factory in nearby Ybor City, named after owner Vicente Martinez Ybor, was the site where Jose Marti (the George Washington of Cuba) exhorted workers to take up arms against the tyranny of Spanish rule in the late 1800s.

Today, Tampa enjoys its role as a U.S. port and is host to many cruise ships. Major industries in and around Tampa include services, retail trade, government and finance, insurance and real estate. Like most of Florida, its economy is also heavily based on tourism. Significant employers include the Hillsborough County School District, Verizon Communications, the University of South Florida, Hillsborough County Government, Publix (in nearby Lakeland) and MacDill Air Force Base. It is also home to servers at Wikipedia, the online encyclopedia.

The city boasts NFL's Tampa Bay Buccaneers, the Devil Rays baseball team, and the NHL's Lightning. Other attractions include Florida's Latin Quarter known as Ybor City (a National Historic Landmark District), Busch Gardens, and a Museum of Science and Industry. MacDill Air Force Base also hosts a popular air show every year.

Tampa has received high marks in various surveys throughout the years, including being top cleanest and outdoor cities, as well as the best place for 20-somethings.

Winters are mild, while summers are long, warm, and humid. Freezing temperatures occur on one or two mornings per year during November through March. A dramatic feature of the Tampa climate is the summer thunderstorm season. Most occur during the late afternoon, sometimes causing temperatures to drop dramatically. The area is vulnerable to tidal surges, as the land has an elevation of less than 15 feet above sea level. The city has not experienced a direct hit from a hurricane since the 1930s.

Rankings

General Rankings

- Tampa was ranked #220 out of 375 metro areas in *Cities Ranked & Rated*. Criteria: cost of living; climate; crime; transportation; economy and jobs; education; arts and culture; health and healthcare; leisure; quality of life. *Cities Ranked & Rated, 2nd Edition, 2007*

- Tampa was ranked #68 out of 379 metro areas in *Places Rated Almanac*. Criteria: health care; education; recreation; transportation; ambience; climate; crime; housing costs; jobs. *Places Rated Almanac, 7th Edition, 2007*

- The Tampa metro area was identified as one of the 10 most popular big cities by Pew Research Center. The results are based on a telephone survey of 2,260 adults conducted during October 2008. The report explored a range of attitudes related to where Americans live, where they would like to live, and why. *Pew Research Center, "For Nearly Half of America, Grass is Greener Somewhere Else," January 29, 2009*

- *Men's Health Living* ranked 100 U.S. cities in terms of quality of life. Tampa was ranked #72 and received a grade of D+. Criteria: number of fitness facilities; air quality; number of physicians; male/female ratio; education levels; household income; cost of living. *Men's Health Living, Spring 2008*

- Tampa was selected as one of "America's Top 100 Places to Live" by RelocateAmerica.com. Cities and towns nominated to be great places to live along with their key data regarding education, employment, economy, crime, parks, recreation and housing were reviewed, rated and judged by the Relocate-America.com editorial staff. *Relocate-America.com, "RelocateAmerica's Top 100 Places to Live in 2010"*

Business/Finance Rankings

- Tampa was identified as one of the 20 weakest-performing metro areas during the recession and recovery from December 2007 through December 2010. Criteria: percent change in employment; percentage point change in unemployment rate; percent change in gross metropolitan product; percent change in House Price Index. *Brookings Institution, MetroMonitor: Tracking Economic Recession and Recovery in America's 100 Largest Metropolitan Areas, March 2011*

- Experian ranked the top 20 major U.S metropolitan areas by average debt per consumer. The Tampa metro area was ranked #8. Criteria: average debt per consumer. Debt for this study includes credit cards, auto loans and personal loans. It does not include mortgages. *Experian, May 13, 2010*

- A.G. Edwards ranked America's 500 top-performing communities based on their residents' personal savings and investing behavior. The Tampa metro area ranked #383 with an index score of 97.38 (national average = 100.00). A dozen statistical factors were measured including: participation in retirement savings plans; personal debt levels; and home ownership. *A.G. Edwards, "2007 Nest Egg Index," September 12, 2007*

- Tampa was identified as one of the "Unhappiest Cities to Work" by CareerBliss.com, an online community for career advancement. The city ranked #10 out of 10. CareerBliss.com conducted independent company reviews from employees all over the country to collect data on eight specific factors of workplace happiness: growth opportunities, compensation, benefits, work-life balance, career advancement, senior management, job security, and whether the employee would recommend the company to others. The numbers were combined to find an average rating of overall workplace happiness for each city. *CareerBliss.com, "Happiest and Unhappiest Cities to Work," February 1, 2011*

- *American City Business Journals* ranked America's 261 largest cities in terms of their resident's wealth. Tampa ranked #81. Criteria: per capita income; median household income; percentage of households with annual incomes of $200,000 or more; median home value. *American City Business Journals, www.bizjournals.com, "Where the Money Is: America's Wealth Centers," August 18, 2008*

- The Tampa metro area appeared on the Milken Institute "2010 Best Performing Metros" list. Rank: #155 out of 200 large metro areas. Criteria: job growth; wage and salary growth; high-tech output growth. *Milken Institute, "2010 Best Performing Metros"*

- Tampa was ranked #98 out of 145 regions worldwide in terms of its "Knowledge Competitiveness Index." The index attempts to measure the knowledge-based development taking place throughout the world and is based on 19 measures of economic performance that indicate a region's ability to translate its knowledge capacity into economic value. *Centre for International Competitiveness, World Knowledge Competitiveness Index 2008*

- *Forbes* ranked the 200 most populous metro areas in the U.S. in terms of the "Best Places for Business and Careers." The Tampa metro area was ranked #104. Criteria: 12 metrics including costs (business and living), job growth (past and projected), income growth, educational attainment, projected economic growth, crime, cultural and recreational opportunities, net migration patterns, percentage of subprime mortgages handed out over a three-year period, and the number of highly ranked four-year colleges. *Forbes, "Best Places for Business and Careers," April 14, 2010*

Children/Family Rankings

- The Tampa metro area was selected as one of the "Best Cities for Relocating Families" by Worldwide ERC and Primacy Relocation. The 2008 study looked at nearly 50 factors important to relocating families including: recent job growth; nearby top-ranked colleges; in-state tuition for four-year public colleges; population growth since 2000; pediatricians per 100,000 population; and a Green Living index. *Worldwide ERC and Primacy Relocation, "2008 Best Cities for Relocating Families"*

- Tampa was chosen as one of America's "100 Best Communities for Young People." The winners were selected based upon detailed information provided about each community's efforts to fulfill five essential promises critical to the well-being of young people: caring adults who are actively involved in their lives; safe places in which to learn and grow; a healthy start toward adulthood; an effective education that builds marketable skills; and opportunities to help others. *America's Promise Alliance, "100 Best Communities for Young People, 2010"*

Culture/Performing Arts Rankings

- Tampa was selected as one of "America's Top 25 Arts Destinations." The city ranked #11 in the mid-sized city (population 100,000 to 499,999) category. Criteria: readers' top choices for arts travel destinations based on the richness and variety of visual arts sites, activities and events. *American Style, "America's Top 25 Arts Destinations," May 2010*

Dating/Romance Rankings

- Tampa appeared on *Men's Health's* list of the most sex-happy cities in America. The city ranked #83 of 100. Criteria: condom sales; birth rates; sex toy sales; rates of chlamydia, gonorrhea, and syphilis. *Men's Health, "America's Most Sex-Happy Cities," October 2010*

- *Men's Health* ranked 100 U.S. cities in terms of best (and worst) marriages. Tampa was ranked #12 (#1 = worst marriages). Criteria: rate of failed marriages; stringency of divorce laws; percentage of population who've split; number of licensed marriage and family therapists. *Men's Health, "Splitsville, USA," May 2010*

- Eli Lily and Company, in partnership with Sperling's BestPlaces, ranked the nation's 50 largest metro areas in terms of the "Most Romantic Cities for Baby Boomers." The Tampa metro area ranked #44. Criteria: marriage and divorce rates among "baby boomers" age 45 to 60; great restaurants; dance studios; chocolate, jewelry and flower sales. *Eli Lily and Company, "Most Romantic Cities for Baby Boomers," April 20, 2007*

- The Tampa metro area was selected as one of the "Best Cities for Relocating Singles" by Worldwide ERC and Primacy Relocation. The area ranked #11 out of the 100 largest metro areas in the U.S. Areas were selected based on the following criteria: recent job growth; recent singles population growth; overall population growth; affordable rental housing; cost-of-living index; expanded arts and recreation opportunities; ratio of single men and single women; affordability of quality higher education (including state residency requirements); diversity index; climate; population density. *Worldwide ERC and Primacy Relocation, "2008 Best Cities for Relocating Singles"*

- *Forbes* ranked the 40 most populous urbanized areas in the U.S. in terms of the "Best Cities for Singles." The Tampa metro area ranked #33. Criteria: number of singles; cost of living alone; nightlife; culture; job growth; coolness; and online dating participation. *Forbes.com, "Best Cities for Singles," July 27, 2009*

Education Rankings

- Tampa was selected as one of "America's Most Literate Cities." The city ranked #19 out of the 75 largest U.S. cities. Criteria: number of booksellers; library resources; Internet resources; educational attainment; periodical publishing resources; newspaper circulation. *Central Connecticut State University, "America's Most Literate Cities 2010"*

- Tampa was identified as one of the 100 "smartest" metro areas in the U.S. The area ranked #64. Criteria: the editors rated the collective brainpower of the 100 largest metro area in the U.S based on their residents' educational attainment. *American City Business Journals, www.bizjournals.com, April 14, 2008*

- Tampa was identified as one of "America's Brainiest Bastions" by *Portfolio.com*. The metro area ranked #134 out of 200. Portfolio.com analyzed levels of educational attainment in the nation's 200 largest metropolitan areas. The editors established scores for five levels of educational attainment, based on relative earning power of adult workers age 25 or older. Scores were determined by comparing the median income for all workers with the median income for those workers at a specified educational level. *Portfolio.com, "America's Brainiest Bastions," December 1, 2010*

Environmental Rankings

- Tampa was selected as one of 22 "Smarter Cities" for energy by the Natural Resources Defense Council." Criteria: investment in green power; energy efficiency measures; conservation. *Natural Resources Defense Council, "2010 Smarter Cities," July 19, 2010*

- *American City Business Journal* ranked 43 metropolitan areas in terms of their "greenness." The Tampa metro area ranked #41. Criteria: Forty-one metros in which *ACBJ* has business weeklies, plus Indianapolis and Cleveland, were ranked based on 20 different indicators such as adoption of green technologies, utilization of environmentally sound practices, and air and water quality. *American City Business Journals, "Green City Index," March 11, 2010*

- The Tampa metro area was selected as one of "America's Cleanest Cities" by *Forbes*. The metro area ranked #8 out of 10. Criteria: air quality; water quality; per capita spending on Superfund site cleanup and solid-waste management. *Forbes.com, "America's Cleanest Cities," March 11, 2008*

- 100 of the largest metro areas in the U.S. were analyzed in terms of their current drought severity. The Tampa metro area ranked #16 (#1 = driest). The rankings were based on statistics such as long-term precipitation trends and patterns and the Palmer drought indices. *Sperling's BestPlaces, www.BestPlaces.net, "America's Drought-Riskiest Cities," November 2007*

- The Tampa metro area appeared in *Country Home's* "Best Green Places" report. The area ranked #176 out of 379. Criteria: official energy policies; green power; green buildings; availability of fresh, locally grown food. *Country Home, "Best Green Places," 2008*

Health/Fitness Rankings

- Tampa was selected as one of the 25 fittest cities in America by *Men's Fitness Online*. It ranked #23 out of America's 50 largest cities. Criteria: fitness centers and sport stores; nutrition; sports participation; TV viewing; overweight/sedentary; junk food; air quality; geography; commute; parks and open space; city recreational facilities; access to healthcare; motivation; mayor and city initiatives; state obesity initiatives. *Men's Fitness Online, 2009 Fittest/Fattest Cities*

- Tampa was identified as a "2011 Asthma Capital." The area ranked #86 out of the nation's 100 largest metropolitan areas. Twelve factors were used to identify the most challenging places to live for people with asthma: estimated prevalence; self-reported prevalence; crude death rate for asthma; annual pollen score; annual air quality; public smoking laws; number of board-certified asthma specialists; school inhaler access laws; rescue medication use; controller medication use; uninsured rate; poverty rate. *Asthma and Allergy Foundation of America, "2011 Asthma Capitals"*

- Tampa was identified as a 2009 "Spring Allergy Capital." The area ranked #66 out of 100. Three groups of factors were used to identify the most severe cities for people with allergies during the spring season: annual pollen levels; medicine utilization; access to board-certified allergists. *Asthma and Allergy Foundation of America, "Spring Allergy Capitals 2009"*

- Tampa was identified as a 2010 "Fall Allergy Capital." The area ranked #73 out of 100. Three groups of factors were used to identify the most severe cities for people with allergies during the fall season: annual pollen levels; medicine utilization; access to board-certified allergists. *Asthma and Allergy Foundation of America, "Fall Allergy Capitals 2010"*

- *Men's Health* ranked 100 U.S. cities in terms of the quality of their tap water. Tampa was ranked #66 and received a grade of C. Criteria: levels of total coliform bacteria, arsenic, lead, total trihalomethanes (linked to cancer), and halo-acetic acids; number of EPA water-system violations from 1995 to 2005. *Men's Health, March 2007*

- Ortho-McNeil Neurologics, in partnership with Sperling's BestPlaces, analyzed 110 metro areas and identified those U.S. cities with the highest prevalence of factors that are most commonly associated with migraine headaches. The Tampa metro area ranked #52. Criteria: number of migraine-related drug prescriptions per capita; lifestyle factors that can contribute to migraines; environmental factors that can trigger migraines; and consumption of migraine-triggering foods. *Ortho-McNeil Neurologics, "America's Migraine Hot Spots," March 14, 2006*

- An analysis of the "Best & Worst Cities for Sleep" was conducted by Sperling's BestPlaces. The study ranked America's 50 most populated metro areas. The Tampa metro area ranked #30 (#1 = best city for sleep). Criteria: number of days residents didn't get enough rest or sleep during the past month; average length of daily commute; divorce rate; unemployment rate. *Sperling's BestPlaces, www.BestPlaces.net, "Best & Worst Cities for Sleep," 2006*

- *Men's Health* ranked 100 U.S. cities in terms of cities "Where the Food is Sickening." Tampa was ranked #74 and received a grade of D+. The magazine arrived at their ratings by looking at data compiled by the Community Health Status Indicator Project to determine outbreaks of E. coli, salmonella-, and shigella-related infections. They then checked the CDC's Wonder database to see how many people died from tainted food. Finally, the magazine found out which states have adopted the current version of the FDA's uniform Food Code, which contains the most up-to-date rules for keeping restaurant kitchens clean. *Men's Health, October 2005*

- The American Academy of Dermatology ranked 26 U.S. metropolitan regions in terms of their residents knowledge, attitude and behaviors towards tanning, sun protection and skin cancer detection. The Tampa metro area ranked #4. The results of the study are based on an online survey of over 7,000 adults nationwide. *American Academy of Dermatology, "Suntelligence: How Sun Smart is Your City," May 3, 2010*

- Scarborough Research, a leading market research firm, identified the top local markets for diabetes medication purchasers. The Tampa DMA (Designated Market Area) ranked in the top 13 with 10% of consumers reporting that they purchased medication for diabetes within the past 12 months. *Scarborough Research, March 19, 2007*

- The Tampa metro area appeared in the 2010 Gallup-Healthways Well-Being Index. The index, based on interviews with more than 353,000 Americans during 2009, asked individuals to assess their jobs, finances, physical health, emotional state of mind and communities. The metro area ranked #132 out of 162. Criteria: life evaluation; emotional health; work environment; physical health; healthy behaviors; basic access (basic needs optimal for a healthy life, such as access to food and medicine, having health insurance and feeling safe while walking at night). *Gallup-Healthways, "Well-Being Index 2010"*

- The Tampa metro area was identified as one of "America's Most Stressful Cities" by *Forbes*. The metro area ranked #17. Criteria: median home price drop; unemployment rates; cost of living; air quality; sunny days; population density. *Forbes.com, "America's Most Stressful Cities," August 20, 2009*

- The Tampa metro area was identified as one of "America's 20 Most Sedentary Cities" by *Forbes*. The metro area ranked #12. Criteria: percentage of overweight or obese people; percentage of people who had not engaged in any physical activity in the past 30 days; average number of hours of TV watched per week. *Forbes.com, "America's Most Sedentary Cities," October 29, 2007*

- 50 of the largest metro areas in the U.S. were analyzed in terms of their health and fitness by the American College of Sports Medicine in their "American Fitness Index." The Tampa metro area ranked #30 (#1 = healthiest). Criteria: preventative health behaviors; levels of chronic disease; health care access; community resources and policies that support physical activity. *American College of Sports Medicine, "Health and Community Fitness Status of the 50 Largest Metropolitan Areas," May 24, 2010*

- Tampa was selected as one of the "20 Most Livable U.S. Cities for Wheelchair Users" by the Christopher & Dana Reeve Foundation. The city ranked #12. Criteria: Medicaid eligibility and spending; access to physicians and rehabilitation facilities; access to fitness facilities and recreation; access to paratransit; percentage of people living with disabilities who are employed; clean air; climate. *Christopher & Dana Reeve Foundation, "20 Most Livable U.S. Cities for Wheelchair Users," July 26, 2010*

- *The Daily Beast* identified the 30 U.S metro areas with the worst smoking habits. The Tampa metro area ranked #19. Sixty urban centers with populations of more than one million were ranked based on the following criteria: number of smokers; number of cigarettes smoked per day; fewest attempts to quit. *The Daily Beast, "30 Cities With Smoking Problems," January 3, 2011*

Pet Rankings

- Tampa was selected as one of "The Best Cities for Dogs." The city was ranked #9. Criteria: number of dogs, dog parks, pet (and pet supply) stores, animal shelters, boarding and daycare facilities, and veterinarians; incidence of heartworm. *Men's Health, "The Best Cities for Dogs," June 2007*

Real Estate Rankings

- *Fortune* ranked the 100 largest metro areas in the U.S. in terms of projected median home price change in 2010. The Tampa metro area ranked #94. *Fortune, "The 2010 Housing Outlook," December 9, 2009*

- Tampa appeared on ApartmentRatings.com "Top Cities for Renters" list in 2009." The area ranked #79. Overall satisfaction ratings were ranked using thousands of user submitted scores for hundreds of apartment complexes located in the 100 most populated U.S. municipalities. *ApartmentRatings.com, "2009 Renter Satisfaction Rankings"*

- Tampa appeared on ApartmentRatings.com "Top College Towns & Cities" for renters list in 2010." The area ranked #67. Overall satisfaction ratings were ranked using thousands of user submitted scores for hundreds of apartment complexes located in cities and towns that are home to the 100 largest four-year institutions in the U.S. *ApartmentRatings.com, "2010 College Town Renter Satisfaction Rankings"*

- The Tampa metro area was identified as one of "America's 25 Weakest Housing Markets" by *Forbes*. The metro area ranked #14. Criteria: metro areas with populations over 500,000 were ranked based on projected home values through 2011. *Forbes.com, "America's 25 Weakest Housing Markets," January 7, 2009*

- The nation's largest metro areas were analyzed in terms of the percentage of households entering some stage of foreclosure in 2010. The Tampa metro area ranked #17 out of 206 (#1 = highest foreclosure rate). *RealtyTrac, 2010 Year-End Metropolitan Foreclosure Market Report, January 27, 2011*

- The Tampa metro area appeared in a *Wall Street Journal* article ranking cities by "housing stress." The metro area was ranked #7 (#1 = most stress). Criteria: fraction of mortgage-holding homeowners with a monthly housing payment in excess of 30 percent of income; percentage of people without health insurance; unemployment rate. *The Wall Street Journal, "Which Cities Face Biggest Housing Risk," October 5, 2010*

- The Center for Housing Policy ranked 210 U.S metropolitan areas by the fair market rent for a two-bedroom unit. The Tampa metro area was ranked #63. (#1 = most expensive) with a rent of $959. Criteria: Fair Market Rent (FMR) in effect during the fourth quarter of 2009 based on HUD's fiscal year 2010 FMRs. *The Center for Housing Policy, "Paycheck to Paycheck: Most to Least Expensive Rental Markets in 2009"*

- The Tampa metro area was identified as one of the markets with the worst expected performance in home prices over the next 12 months. *Local Market Monitor, "First Quarter Home Price Forecast for Largest US Markets," March 2, 2011*

Safety Rankings

- Allstate ranked the 200 largest cities in America in terms of driver safety. Tampa ranked #154. In addition, drivers were 26.0% more likely to have had an accident compared to the national average. Allstate researchers analyzed internal property damage reported claims over a two-year period (from January 2007 to December 2008) to ensure the findings would not be affected by external influences such as weather or road construction. A weighted average of the two-year numbers determined the annual percentages. The report defines an auto crash as any collision resulting in a property damage claim. *Allstate, "The 2010 Allstate America's Best Drivers Report™"*

- Sperling's BestPlaces analyzed the tracks of tropical storms for the past 100 years and ranked which areas are most likely to be hit by a major hurricane. The Tampa metro area ranked #4 out of 10. *Sperling's BestPlaces, www.bestplaces.net, February 2, 2006*

- The National Insurance Crime Bureau ranked 366 metro areas in the U.S. in terms of per capita rates of vehicle theft. The Tampa metro area ranked #87 (#1 = highest rate). Criteria: number of vehicle theft offenses per 100,000 inhabitants. *National Insurance Crime Bureau, "Hot Spots," May 17, 2010*

- The Tampa metro area was identified as one of the "The Most Dangerous Metro Areas for Pedestrians" by Transportation for America and the Surface Transportation Policy Partnership. The metro area ranked #2 out of 52 metro areas with over 1 million residents. Criteria: area's population divided by the number of pedestrian fatalities in that area. *Transportation for America and the Surface Transportation Policy Partnership, "Dangerous by Design: Solving the Epidemic of Preventable Pedestrian Deaths (and Making Great Neighborhoods)," November 11, 2009*

Seniors/Retirement Rankings

- Tampa was identified as one of "The Top 100 Places to Retire" by *Topretirements.com* The list reflects the 100 cities (out of 625+ total cities reviewed) that visitors to the website are most interested in for retirement. *Topretirements.com, "2011 Best Places to Retire List: The Sunbelt Rules"*

Sports/Recreation Rankings

- Tampa appeared on the *Sporting News* list of the "Best Sports Cities" for 2010. The area ranked #27 out of 402 cities in the U.S. *Sporting News* takes a 12-month snapshot, roughly October to October, of each city's sports, putting a heavy premium on regular-season won-lost records (from the most recently completed season). Other criteria include: playoff berths, bowl appearances and tournament bids; championships; applicable power ratings; quality of competition; overall fan fervor as measured in part by attendance as percentage of venue capacity; abundance of teams (rewarding quality over quantity); stadium and arena quality; ticket availability and prices; franchise ownership; and marquee appeal of athletes. *Sporting News, "Best Sports Cities 2010," October, 2010*

- Tampa was selected as one of the five best boat cities to live in (in the U.S.). The city ranked #4. Criteria: climate; scenery; fishing; boat communities with water access. *Best Boat Ne.ws, "The 5 Best Boat Cities to Live In (in the U.S.)," April 16, 2010*

- Tampa was chosen as one of America's 10 best places to live and boat. Criteria: boating opportunities; boat-friendly regulations; water access; availability of waterfront homes; health of the local economy; and overall lifestyle for boaters. *Boating Magazine, "10 Best Places to Live and Boat," June 2010*

- *Golf Digest* ranked 330 metro areas in the U.S. in terms of golf. The Tampa metro area was ranked #148. Criteria: access to golf; weather; value of golf; and quality of golf. *Golf Digest, "Metro Golf Rankings," August 2005*

Technology Rankings

- Tampa was selected as one of the best cities for broadband by Ookla, the company behind the broadband speed testing site Speedtest.net. The city ranked #6 out of 10. Criteria: U.S. cities were ranked based on their 30-day average speeds. Only cities with more than 75,000 people connecting for more than three months were measured. *Ookla, "The Top 10 Cities With the Best Broadband," May 25, 2010*

Transportation Rankings

- The Tampa metro area appeared on *Forbes* list of the best and worst cities for commuters. The metro area ranked #60 out of 60 (#1 is best). Criteria: travel time; road congestion; travel delays. *Forbes.com, "Best and Worst Cities for Commuters," February 16, 2010*

Women/Minorities Rankings

- Tampa was ranked #71 out of 100 metro areas in *SELF Magazine's* ranking of America's healthiest places for women." A panel of experts came up with more than 50 criteria including death and disease rates, environmental indicators, community resources, and lifestyle habits. *SELF Magazine, "Secrets of America's Healthiest Women," December 2008*

Miscellaneous Rankings

- Energizer Holdings, the makers of Edge® shave gel, in partnership with Sperling's BestPlaces, ranked 50 major metro areas in terms of everyday irritations. The Tampa metro area ranked #7. Criteria: humidity levels; weather conditions; incidence of traffic delays and congestion; average commute times; frequency of flight delays and cancellations; rates of sleeplessness; underemployment; pollens and allergens; pests; comedy clubs per capita. *Energizer Holdings, "Most Irritation Prone Cities," July 23, 2010*

- Mars Chocolate North America, the makers of COMBOS®, in partnership with Sperling's BestPlaces, ranked 50 major metro areas in terms of their "manliness." The Tampa metro area ranked #44. Criteria: number of home improvement stores, steak houses, pickup trucks, motorcycles, and manly occupations (fire fighters, police officers, construction workers, EMP personnel) per capita; salty snack sales; sports TV viewing habits. *Mars Chocolate North America, "America's Manliest Cities," June 22, 2010*

- Tampa appeared on Procter & Gamble's list of the "Top-20 All-Time Sweatiest Cities." The city was ranked #9. The rankings are based on computer simulations of the amount of sweat a person of average height and weight would produce walking around for an hour in the average temperatures during the summer months, based on historical weather data during June, July and August from 2001-2008 for each city. *Procter & Gamble, Old Spice Press Release, "Top-20 All-Time Sweatiest Cities," July 1, 2009*

- The Tampa metro area appeared on *Forbes* list of "America's Drunkest Cities." The area ranked #24. Criteria: 35 of the largest continental U.S. metro areas were chosen based on availability of data and geographic diversity. Each metro was ranked in five areas: state laws; drinkers; heavy drinkers; binge drinkers; and alcoholism. *Forbes.com, "America's Drunkest Cities," August 22, 2006*

- Scarborough Research, a leading market research firm, identified the top local markets for frequent sit-down restaurant patronage. The Tampa DMA (Designated Market Area) ranked in the top 10 with consumers reporting an average of 4.1 visits within the past 30 days. *Scarborough Research, May 31, 2006*

Business Environment

CITY FINANCES

City Government Finances

Component	2008 ($000)	2008 ($ per capita)
Total Revenues	1,143,513	3,395
Total Expenditures	734,255	2,180
Debt Outstanding	1,500,248	4,454
Cash and Securities[1]	2,947,128	8,750

Note: (1) Cash and security holdings of a government at the close of its fiscal year, including those of its dependent agencies, utilities, and liquor stores.
Source: U.S Census Bureau, State & Local Government Finances 2008

City Government Revenue by Source

Source	2008 ($000)	2008 ($ per capita)
General Revenue		
From Federal Government	7,101	21
From State Government	78,696	234
From Local Governments	37,696	112
Taxes		
Property	166,238	494
Sales and Gross Receipts	122,657	364
Personal Income	0	0
Corporate Income	0	0
Motor Vehicle License	0	0
Other Taxes	43,366	129
Current Charges	206,402	613
Liquor Store	0	0
Utility	69,336	206
Employee Retirement	340,702	1,012

Source: U.S Census Bureau, State & Local Government Finances 2008

City Government Expenditures by Function

Function	2008 ($000)	2008 ($ per capita)	2008 (%)
General Direct Expenditures			
Air Transportation	0	0	0.0
Corrections	0	0	0.0
Education	0	0	0.0
Employment Security Administration	0	0	0.0
Financial Administration	12,114	36	1.6
Fire Protection	57,192	170	7.8
General Public Buildings	10,830	32	1.5
Governmental Administration, Other	4,502	13	0.6
Health	0	0	0.0
Highways	94,410	280	12.9
Hospitals	0	0	0.0
Housing and Community Development	26,422	78	3.6
Interest on General Debt	31,002	92	4.2
Judicial and Legal	3,345	10	0.5
Libraries	0	0	0.0
Parking	16,965	50	2.3
Parks and Recreation	50,060	149	6.8
Police Protection	142,115	422	19.4
Public Welfare	0	0	0.0
Sewerage	86,391	256	11.8
Solid Waste Management	58,877	175	8.0
Veterans' Services	0	0	0.0
Liquor Store	0	0	0.0
Utility	80,593	239	11.0
Employee Retirement	38,683	115	5.3

Source: U.S Census Bureau, State & Local Government Finances 2008

Municipal Bond Ratings

Area	Moody's	S&P	Fitch
City	Aa2	(1)	n/a

Rating Systems (shown in declining order of credit quality): Moody's– Aaa, Aa, A, Baa, Ba, B, Caa, Ca, C (numerical modifiers 1, 2, and 3 are added to letter-rating); S&P– AAA, AA, A, BBB, BB, B, CCC, CC, C; Fitch– AAA, AA, A, BBB, BB, B, CCC, CC, C. Ratings may be modified by the addition of a plus or minus sign to show relative standing within the major rating categories.
Notes: n/a Not available; (1) Not reviewed; (2) Issuer Rating/No General Obligation; (3) Standard and Poor's Issue Credit Rating (ICR) is a current opinion of an obliger with respect to a specific financial obligation, a specific class of financial obligations, or a specific financial program.
Source: U.S. Census Bureau, 2011 Statistical Abstract, Bond Ratings for City Governments by Largest Cities: 2009

DEMOGRAPHICS

Population Growth

Area	1990 Census	2000 Census	2010 Estimate	2015 Projection	Population Growth (%)	
					2000-2010	2010-2015
City	279,960	303,447	350,061	377,104	15.4	7.7
MSA[1]	2,067,959	2,395,997	2,782,113	2,979,241	16.1	7.1
U.S.	248,709,873	281,421,906	309,038,974	321,675,005	9.8	4.1

Note: (1) Metropolitan Statistical Area - see Appendix B for areas included
Source: Claritas, Inc.

Number of Households and Average Household Size

Area	2010 Estimate	2010 Average Household Size
City	144,002	2.36
MSA[1]	1,156,562	2.36
U.S.	116,136,617	2.59

Note: (1) Metropolitan Statistical Area - see Appendix B for areas included
Source: Claritas, Inc.

Race and Ethnicity

Area	White Alone[2] (%)	Black Alone[2] (%)	Asian Alone[2] (%)	Other Race Alone[2] (%)	Hispanic[3] (%)
City	60.9	26.6	3.1	9.4	23.7
MSA[1]	78.9	11.5	2.6	7.0	15.2
U.S.	72.3	12.4	4.4	10.9	15.8

Note: Figures are 2010 estimates; (1) Metropolitan Statistical Area - see Appendix B for areas included (2) Alone is defined as not being in combination with one or more other races; (3) May be of any race.
Source: Claritas, Inc.

Segregation

Type	Segregation Indices[1]				Percent Change		
	1990	2000	2010	2010 Rank[2]	1990-2000	1990-2010	2000-2010
Black/White	69.7	64.6	56.2	50	-5.1	-13.5	-8.3
Asian/White	33.8	35.4	35.3	78	1.6	1.5	-0.1
Hispanic/White	45.3	44.4	40.7	62	-0.9	-4.6	-3.7

Note: Figures are based on an analysis of 1990, 2000, and 2010 Census Decennial Census tract data by William H. Frey, Brookings Institution and the University of Michigan Social Science Data Analysis Network. In this analysis all racial groups (whites, blacks, and asians) are non-Hispanic members of those races. Hispanics are shown as a separate category; All figures cover the Metropolitan Statistical Area (see Appendix B for areas included); (1) Segregation Indices are Dissimilarity Indices that measure the degree to which the minority group is distributed differently than whites aross census tracts. They range from 0 (complete integration) to 100 (complete [segregation) where the value indicates the percentage of the minority group that needs to move to be distributed exactly like whites; (2) Ranges from 1 (most segregated) to 102 (least segregated); n/a not available.
Source: www.CensusScope.org

Ancestry

Area	German	Irish	English	American	Italian	Polish	French	Scottish
City	11.2	9.0	7.1	3.8	6.7	2.1	2.3	1.8
MSA[1]	16.2	14.2	10.9	5.9	9.0	3.5	3.5	2.3
U.S.	16.6	12.0	9.1	6.1	5.9	3.3	3.1	1.9

Note: The top eight ancestries in the U.S. are shown. Figures are percentages and include multiple ancestry (e.g. if a person reported being Irish and Italian, they were included in both columns); (1) Metropolitan Statistical Area - see Appendix B for areas included
Source: U.S. Census Bureau, 2007-2009 American Community Survey 3-Year Estimates

Foreign-Born Population

Area	Percent of Population Born in								
	Any Foreign Country	Mexico	Asia	Europe	Carribean	South America	Central America[2]	Africa	Canada
City	14.4	1.7	2.5	1.4	5.2	1.5	1.1	0.5	0.4
MSA[1]	11.9	1.5	2.2	2.4	2.6	1.4	0.6	0.4	0.8
U.S.	12.5	3.8	3.4	1.6	1.1	0.8	0.9	0.5	0.3

Note: (1) Metropolitan Statistical Area - see Appendix B for areas included; (2) Excludes Mexico.
Source: U.S. Census Bureau, 2007-2009 American Community Survey 3-Year Estimates

Marriage Status

Area	Never Married	Now Married[2]	Separated	Widowed	Divorced
City	39.0	38.6	3.2	5.3	13.9
MSA[1]	28.4	48.1	2.2	7.9	13.4
U.S.	31.4	49.7	2.2	6.2	10.6

Note: Figures are percentages and cover the population 15 years of age and older;
(1) Metropolitan Statistical Area - see Appendix B for areas included; (2) Excludes separated
Source: U.S. Census Bureau, 2007-2009 American Community Survey 3-Year Estimates

Age Distribution and Median Age

Area	Percent of Population							Median Age
	Under Age 5	Age 5 to 17	Age 18 to 34	Age 35 to 49	Age 50 to 64	Age 65 to 79	80 Years and Over	
City	7.3	16.6	26.9	22.9	15.7	7.4	3.2	34.5
MSA[1]	6.1	15.7	21.1	21.2	18.8	11.6	5.5	40.5
U.S.	6.9	17.5	23.3	21.4	18.1	9.1	3.7	36.7

Note: (1) Metropolitan Statistical Area - see Appendix B for areas included
Source: U.S. Census Bureau, 2007-2009 American Community Survey 3-Year Estimates

Male/Female Ratio

Area	Males	Females	Males per 100 Females
City	172,976	177,085	97.7
MSA[1]	1,354,345	1,427,768	94.9
U.S.	152,401,520	156,637,454	97.3

Note: Figures are 2010 estimates; (1) Metropolitan Statistical Area -
see Appendix B for areas included
Source: Claritas, Inc.

Religion

Area	Catholic	Southern Baptist	United Meth-odist	ELCA[1]	LDS[2]	Presby-terian Church USA	Jewish Est.	Muslim Est.
County	16.6	10.3	3.3	0.7	0.4	1.0	2.0	0.5
U.S.	22.0	7.1	3.7	1.8	1.5	1.1	2.2	0.6

Note: Figures are the number of adherents as a percentage of the total population; Adherents are defined as all members, including full members, their children and the estimated number of other participants who are not considered members (e.g. the baptized, those not confirmed, those regularly attending services, etc.);
(1) Evangelical Lutheran Church in America; (2) The Church of Jesus Christ of Latter Day Saints
Source: Reprinted with permission from Religious Congregations and Membership in the United States 2000 (Nashville, Glenmary Research Center, 2002) Copyright Association of Statisticians of American Religious Bodies. All rights reserved.

ECONOMY

Gross Metropolitan Product

Area	2006	2007	2008	2009	2009 Rank[2]
MSA[1]	108.2	110.7	110.5	107.4	25

Note: Figures are in billions of dollars; (1) Tampa-St. Petersburg-Clearwater, FL Metropolitan Statistical Area - see Appendix B for areas included; (2) Rank ranges from 1 to 363
Source: The U.S. Conference of Mayors, "Pace of Economic Recovery: GMP and Jobs," January 2010

Economic Growth

Area	2006-2008 (%)	2009 (%)	2010 (%)	Rank[2]
MSA[1]	-1.2	-3.7	1.8	320
U.S.	1.3	-2.5	2.2	–

Note: Figures are real Gross Metropolitan Product growth rates and represent annual average percent change; (1) Tampa-St. Petersburg-Clearwater, FL Metropolitan Statistical Area - see Appendix B for areas included; (2) Rank ranges from 1 to 363
Source: The U.S. Conference of Mayors, "Pace of Economic Recovery: GMP and Jobs," January 2010

Metropolitan Area Exports

Area	2005	2006	2007	2008	2009	2009 Rank[2]
MSA[1]	4,423.8	4,738.5	5,711.2	7,153.5	6,463.6	34

Note: Figures are in millions of dollars; (1) Tampa-St. Petersburg-Clearwater, FL Metropolitan Statistical Area - see Appendix B for areas included; (2) Rank ranges from 1 to 374
Source: U.S. Department of Commerce, International Trade Administration, Office of Trade & Industry Information, Manufacturing & Services

INCOME

Per Capita/Median/Average Income

Area	Per Capita ($)	Median Household ($)	Average Household ($)
City	26,855	43,677	64,337
MSA[1]	27,068	47,630	64,446
U.S.	27,034	52,795	71,071

Note: Figures are 2010 estimates; (1) Metropolitan Statistical Area - see Appendix B for areas included
Source: Claritas, Inc.

Household Income Distribution

Area	Percent of Households Earning							
	Under $15,000	$15,000 -24,999	$25,000 -34,999	$35,000 -49,999	$50,000 -74,999	$75,000 -99,000	$100,000 -149,999	$150,000 and up
City	16.6	11.9	12.3	16.0	17.8	9.5	8.5	7.4
MSA[1]	11.7	11.6	12.5	16.9	20.0	11.3	9.8	6.2
U.S.	12.1	10.2	10.6	15.0	19.5	12.5	12.1	8.0

Note: Figures are 2010 estimates; (1) Metropolitan Statistical Area - see Appendix B for areas included
Source: Claritas, Inc.

Poverty Rates by Age

Area	All Ages	Under 18 Years Old	18 to 64 Years Old	65 Years and Over
City	18.3	6.6	10.2	1.5
MSA[1]	12.7	4.0	7.2	1.5
U.S.	13.6	4.7	7.7	1.2

Note: Figures are percent of population with income during the previous 12 months below poverty level and only include population for whom poverty status is determined; (1) Metropolitan Statistical Area - see Appendix B for areas included
Source: U.S. Census Bureau, 2007-2009 American Community Survey 3-Year Estimates

Personal Bankruptcy Filing Rate

Area	2006	2007	2008	2009	2010
Hillsborough County	1.82	2.79	4.15	5.63	6.33
U.S.	2.00	2.73	3.53	4.60	4.96

Note: Numbers are per 1,000 population and include Chapter 7 and Chapter 13 filings
Source: Federal Deposit Insurance Corporation, Regional Economic Conditions, March 17, 2011

EMPLOYMENT

Labor Force and Employment

Area	Civilian Labor Force			Workers Employed		
	Dec. 2009	Dec. 2010	% Chg.	Dec. 2009	Dec. 2010	% Chg.
City	161,072	162,264	0.7	142,359	143,133	0.5
MSA[1]	1,284,093	1,298,265	1.1	1,134,329	1,140,498	0.5
U.S.	152,693,000	153,156,000	0.3	137,953,000	139,159,000	0.9

Note: Data is not seasonally adjusted and covers workers 16 years of age and older;
(1) Metropolitan Statistical Area - see Appendix B for areas included
Source: Bureau of Labor Statistics, http://stats.bls.gov

Unemployment Rate

Area	2010											
	Jan.	Feb.	Mar.	Apr.	May	Jun.	Jul.	Aug.	Sep.	Oct.	Nov.	Dec.
City	12.2	11.9	11.7	11.6	11.7	12.1	12.5	12.5	12.2	11.8	12.6	11.8
MSA[1]	12.4	12.1	11.9	11.6	11.5	11.9	12.3	12.4	12.2	12.0	12.6	12.2
U.S.	10.6	10.4	10.2	9.5	9.3	9.6	9.7	9.5	9.2	9.0	9.3	9.1

Note: Data is not seasonally adjusted and covers workers 16 years of age and older; All figures are percentages; (1) Metropolitan Statistical Area - see Appendix B for areas included
Source: Bureau of Labor Statistics, http://stats.bls.gov

Projected Unemployment Rate

Area	2007 (%)	2009 (%)	2011 (%)	2013 (%)
MSA[1]	4.8	12.5	10.3	7.8

Note: (1) Metropolitan Statistical Area - see Appendix B for areas included
Source: The U.S. Conference of Mayors, "Pace of Economic Recovery: GMP and Jobs," January 2010

Employment by Occupation

Occupation Classification	City (%)	MSA[1] (%)	U.S. (%)
Sales and Office	28.1	29.5	25.4
Professional and Related	22.0	20.4	21.0
Service	17.8	17.0	17.2
Production, Transportation, and Material Moving	8.7	8.8	12.3
Management, Business, and Financial	15.2	14.9	14.1
Construction, Extraction, and Maintenance	8.0	8.9	9.2
Farming, Forestry, and Fishing	0.2	0.5	0.7

Note: Figures cover employed civilians 16 years of age and older;
(1) Metropolitan Statistical Area - see Appendix B for areas included
Source: U.S. Census Bureau, 2007-2009 American Community Survey 3-Year Estimates

Employment by Industry

Sector	MSA[1]		U.S.
	Number of Employees	Percent of Total	Percent of Total
Government	155,600	13.9	17.2
Education and Health Services	181,500	16.2	15.2
Professional and Business Services	191,900	17.1	13.0
Retail Trade	141,200	12.6	11.4
Leisure and Hospitality	117,800	10.5	9.7
Manufacturing	57,200	5.1	8.8
Financial Activities	86,400	7.7	5.8
Wholesale Trade	45,400	4.0	4.2
Construction	51,100	4.6	4.1
Other Services	42,900	3.8	4.1
Transportation and Utilities	25,600	2.3	3.7
Information	25,300	2.3	2.1
Mining and Logging	400	<0.1	0.6

Note: Figures cover non-farm employment as of December 2010 and are not seasonally adjusted;
(1) Metropolitan Statistical Area - see Appendix B for areas included
Source: Bureau of Labor Statistics, http://stats.bls.gov

Occupations with Greatest Projected Employment Growth: 2006 - 2016

Occupation[1]	2006 Employment	2016 Projected Employment	Numeric Employment Change	Percent Employment Change
Retail salespersons	283,850	339,780	55,930	19.7
Customer service representatives	162,780	214,600	51,820	31.8
Registered nurses	148,390	190,020	41,630	28.1
Combined food preparation and serving workers, including fast food	163,780	202,670	38,890	23.7
Waiters and waitresses	197,920	232,430	34,510	17.4
Office clerks, general	188,190	221,750	33,560	17.8
Bookkeeping, accounting, and auditing clerks	128,340	153,830	25,490	19.9
Janitors and cleaners, except maids and housekeeping cleaners	124,030	147,970	23,940	19.3
Sales representatives, services, all other	73,650	97,390	23,740	32.2
Executive secretaries and administrative assistants	106,820	129,140	22,320	20.9

Note: Projections cover Florida; (1) Sorted by numeric employment change
Source: www.projectionscentral.com, State Occupational Projections, 2006-2016 Long-Term Projections

Fastest Growing Occupations: 2006 - 2016

Occupation[1]	2006 Employment	2016 Projected Employment	Numeric Employment Change	Percent Employment Change
Network systems and data communications analysts	20,830	33,090	12,260	58.9
Court reporters	2,170	3,430	1,260	58.1
Computer software engineers, applications	17,350	27,250	9,900	57.1
Veterinary technologists and technicians	5,720	8,880	3,160	55.2
Veterinarians	3,280	4,890	1,610	49.1
Home health aides	29,600	42,780	13,180	44.5
Personal and home care aides	10,640	15,220	4,580	43.0
Paralegals and legal assistants	19,240	27,360	8,120	42.2
Pharmacy technicians	21,110	29,950	8,840	41.9
Medical assistants	31,040	43,930	12,890	41.5

Note: Projections cover Florida; (1) Sorted by percent employment change and excludes occupations with numeric employment change less than 900
Source: www.projectionscentral.com, State Occupational Projections, 2006-2016 Long-Term Projections

Average Wages

Occupation	$/Hr.	Occupation	$/Hr.
Accountants and Auditors	28.37	Maids and Housekeeping Cleaners	9.12
Automotive Mechanics	17.69	Maintenance and Repair Workers	14.94
Bookkeepers	15.60	Marketing Managers	54.78
Carpenters	16.76	Nuclear Medicine Technologists	31.56
Cashiers	8.60	Nurses, Licensed Practical	20.05
Clerks, General Office	12.11	Nurses, Registered	30.78
Clerks, Receptionists/Information	12.21	Nursing Aides/Orderlies/Attendants	11.45
Clerks, Shipping/Receiving	12.63	Packers and Packagers, Hand	9.80
Computer Programmers	32.73	Physical Therapists	38.46
Computer Support Specialists	21.17	Postal Service Mail Carriers	23.34
Computer Systems Analysts	35.41	Real Estate Brokers	26.08
Cooks, Restaurant	11.18	Retail Salespersons	12.63
Dentists	n/a	Sales Reps., Exc. Tech./Scientific	28.60
Electrical Engineers	35.99	Sales Reps., Tech./Scientific	35.33
Electricians	18.45	Secretaries, Exc. Legal/Med./Exec.	13.70
Financial Managers	53.06	Security Guards	10.29
First-Line Supervisors/Mgrs., Sales	21.52	Surgeons	n/a
Food Preparation Workers	9.64	Teacher Assistants	10.10
General and Operations Managers	49.91	Teachers, Elementary School	24.50
Hairdressers/Cosmetologists	11.46	Teachers, Secondary School	26.30
Internists	90.16	Telemarketers	11.52
Janitors and Cleaners	10.15	Truck Drivers, Heavy/Tractor-Trailer	16.69
Landscaping/Groundskeeping Workers	11.15	Truck Drivers, Light/Delivery Svcs.	13.98
Lawyers	53.98	Waiters and Waitresses	9.86

Note: Wage data covers the Tampa-St. Petersburg-Clearwater, FL - see Appendix B for areas included. Hourly wages for elementary/secondary school teachers and teacher assistants were calculated by the editors from annual wage data assuming a 40 hour work week; n/a not available.
Source: Bureau of Labor Statistics, Metro Area Occupational Employment and Wage Estimates, May 2009

RESIDENTIAL REAL ESTATE

Building Permits

Area	Single-Family			Multi-Family			Total		
	2009	2010	Pct. Chg.	2009	2010	Pct. Chg.	2009	2010	Pct. Chg.
City	445	455	2.2	349	643	84.2	794	1,098	38.3
MSA[1]	3,923	4,396	12.1	3,039	2,105	-30.7	6,962	6,501	-6.6
U.S.	441,100	447,300	1.4	141,900	157,300	10.9	583,000	604,600	3.7

Note: (1) Metropolitan Statistical Area - see Appendix B for areas included; figures represent new, privately-owned housing units authorized (unadjusted data); All permit data are based on estimates with imputation.
Source: U.S. Census Bureau, Manufacturing, Mining, and Construction Statistics, Building Permits, 2009, 2010

Homeownership Rate

Area	2005 (%)	2006 (%)	2007 (%)	2008 (%)	2009 (%)	2010 (%)
MSA[1]	71.7	71.6	72.9	70.5	68.3	68.3
U.S.	68.9	68.8	68.1	67.8	67.4	66.9

Note: (1) Metropolitan Statistical Area - see Appendix B for areas included
Source: U.S. Census Bureau, Housing Vacancies and Homeownership Annual Statistics: 2010

Housing Vacancy Rates

Area	Gross Vacancy Rate[2] (%)			Year-Round Vacancy Rate[3] (%)			Rental Vacancy Rate[4] (%)			Homeowner Vacancy Rate[5] (%)		
	2008	2009	2010	2008	2009	2010	2008	2009	2010	2008	2009	2010
MSA[1]	18.7	20.5	20.2	13.3	14.7	14.2	15.4	12.4	12.6	3.0	4.1	4.0
U.S.	14.4	14.5	14.3	11.1	11.3	11.3	10.0	10.6	10.2	2.8	2.6	2.6

Note: (1) Metropolitan Statistical Area - see Appendix B for areas included; (2) The percentage of the total housing inventory that is vacant; (3) The percentage of the housing inventory (excluding seasonal units) that is year-round vacant; (4) The percentage of rental inventory that is vacant for rent; (5) The percentage of homeowner inventory that is vacant for sale; n/a not available
Source: U.S. Census Bureau, Housing Vacancies and Homeownership Annual Statistics: 2010

State Corporate Income Tax Rates

State	Tax Rate (%)	Income Brackets ($)	Num. of Brackets	Financial Institution Tax Rate (%)[a]	Federal Income Tax Ded.
Florida	5.5 (f)	Flat rate	1	5.5 (f)	No

Note: Tax rates as of January 1, 2011; (a) Rates listed are the tax rates applied to financial institutions or excise taxes based on income. Some states have other taxes based upon the value of deposits or shares; (f) An exemption of $5,000 is allowed. Florida's Alternative Minimum Tax rate is 3.3%.
Source: Federation of Tax Administrators, "State Corporate Income Tax Rates, 2011"

State Individual Income Tax Rates

State	Tax Rate (%)	Income Brackets ($)	Num. of Brackets	Personal Exempt. ($)[1] Single	Personal Exempt. ($)[1] Dependents	Fed. Inc. Tax Ded.
Florida – No State Income Tax						

Note: Tax rates as of January 1, 2011; Local- and county-level taxes are not included; n/a not applicable;
(1) Married joint filers generally receive double the single exemption
Source: Federation of Tax Administrators, "State Individual Income Tax Rates, 2011"

Various State and Local Tax Rates

State	State and Local Sales and Use (%)	State Sales and Use (%)	Gasoline[1] (¢/gal.)	Cigarette[2] ($/pack)	Spirits[3] ($/gal.)	Wine[4] ($/gal.)	Beer[5] ($/gal.)
Florida	7.0	6.00	34.4	1.34	6.50	2.25	0.48

Note: All tax rates as of January 1, 2011 except Spirits (Sept. 1, 2010); (1) The American Petroleum Institute has developed a methodology for determining the average tax rate on a gallon of fuel. Rates may include any of the following: excise taxes, environmental fees, storage tank fees, other fees or taxes, general sales tax, and local taxes. In states where gasoline is subject to the general sales tax, or where the fuel tax is based on the average sale price, the average rate determined by API is sensitive to changes in the price of gasoline. States that fully or partially apply general sales taxes to gasoline: CA, CO, GA, IL, IN, MI, NY; (2) The federal excise tax of $1.0066 per pack and local taxes are not included; (3) Rates are those applicable to off-premise sales of 40% alcohol by volume (a.b.v.) distilled spirits in 750ml containers. Local excise taxes are excluded; (4) Rates are those applicable to off-premise sales of 11% a.b.v. non-carbonated wine in 750ml containers; (5) Rates are those applicable to off-premise sales of 4.7% a.b.v. beer in 12 ounce containers.
Source: Tax Foundation, 2011 Facts & Figures: How Does Your State Compare?

State-Local Tax Burdens

Area	Rate (%)	Rank[1]	Per Capita Taxes Paid to Home State ($)	Total State and Local Per Capita Taxes Paid ($)	Per Capita Income ($)
Florida	9.2	31	2,713	3,897	42,146
U.S. Average	9.8	-	3,057	4,160	42,539

Note: Figures cover 2009; (1) Rank ranges from 1 to 50 where 1 is highest tax burden
Source: Tax Foundation, State-Local Tax Burdens, All States, 2009

State Business Tax Climate Index Rankings

State	Overall Rank	Corporate Tax Index Rank	Individual Income Tax Index Rank	Sales Tax Index Rank	Unemployment Insurance Tax Index Rank	Property Tax Index Rank
Florida	5	15	1	30	3	28

Note: The index is a measure of how each state's tax laws affect economic performance. The lower the rank, the more favorable a state's tax system is for business. All ranks are for fiscal years. States without a given tax are given a ranking of 1.
Source: Tax Foundation, Tax Foundation Background Paper, No. 60, "2011 State Business Tax Climate Index"

COMMERCIAL REAL ESTATE

Office Market

Market Area	Inventory (sq. ft.)	Vacant (sq. ft.)	Vac. Rate (%)	Under Constr. (sq. ft.)	Asking Rent ($/sf/yr) Class A	Asking Rent ($/sf/yr) Class B
Tampa/Saint Petersburg	63,407,168	12,447,184	19.6	88,000	21.86	17.47

Source: Grubb & Ellis, Office Markets Trends, 1st Quarter 2011

Industrial Market

Market Area	Inventory (sq. ft.)	Vacant (sq. ft.)	Vac. Rate (%)	Under Constr. (sq. ft.)	Asking Rent ($/sf/yr) WH/Dist	Asking Rent ($/sf/yr) R&D/Flex
Tampa/Saint Petersburg	268,177,434	28,669,471	10.7	-	4.91	7.96

Source: Grubb & Ellis, Industrial Markets Trends, 1st Quarter 2011

COMMERCIAL UTILITIES

Typical Monthly Electric Bills

Area	Commercial Service ($/month) 3 kW demand 1,000 kWh	Commercial Service ($/month) 40 kW demand 14,000 kWh	Industrial Service ($/month) 1,000 kW demand 200,000 kWh	Industrial Service ($/month) 50,000 kW demand 15,000,000 kWh
City	120	1,536	24,879	1,578,776
Average[1]	135	1,576	23,741	1,402,202

Note: Based on total rates in effect July 1, 2010; (1) average based on 182 utilities surveyed
Source: Edison Electric Institute, Typical Bills and Average Rates Report, Summer 2010

TRANSPORTATION

Means of Transportation to Work

Area	Car/Truck/Van Drove Alone	Car/Truck/Van Car-pooled	Public Transportation Bus	Public Transportation Subway	Public Transportation Railroad	Bicycle	Walked	Other Means	Worked at Home
City	77.3	9.8	2.7	0.0	0.0	1.0	2.8	1.3	5.2
MSA[1]	80.5	9.4	1.4	0.0	0.0	0.6	1.6	1.5	5.0
U.S.	75.8	10.4	2.7	1.7	0.5	0.5	2.9	1.2	4.1

Note: Figures are percentages and cover workers 16 years of age and older;
(1) Metropolitan Statistical Area - see Appendix B for areas included
Source: U.S. Census Bureau, 2007-2009 American Community Survey 3-Year Estimates

Travel Time to Work

Area	Less Than 15 Minutes	15 to 29 Minutes	30 to 44 Minutes	45 to 59 Minutes	60 to 89 Minutes	90 Minutes or More
City	28.1	42.5	19.9	5.0	3.0	1.5
MSA[1]	24.6	38.0	22.1	8.5	5.1	1.7
U.S.	28.5	36.2	19.7	7.5	5.6	2.5

Note: Figures are percentages and include workers 16 years old and over;
(1) Metropolitan Statistical Area - see Appendix B for areas included
Source: U.S. Census Bureau, 2007-2009 American Community Survey 3-Year Estimates

Travel Time Index

Area	1982	1999	2008	2009
Urban Area[1]	1.13	1.16	1.16	1.16
Average[2]	1.08	1.20	1.20	1.20

Note: Travel Time Index—the ratio of travel time in the peak period to the travel time at
free-flow conditions. A value of 1.30 indicates a 20-minute free-flow trip takes 26 minutes
in the peak. Free-flow speeds (60 mph on freeways and 35 mph on principal arterials)
are used as the comparison threshold; (1) Covers the Tampa-St. Petersburg-Clearwater urban area;
(2) average of 439 urban areas
Source: Texas Transportation Institute, Urban Mobility Report 2010, December 2010

Public Transportation

Agency Name / Mode of Transportation	Vehicles Operated in Maximum Service	Annual Unlinked Passenger Trips ('000)	Annual Passenger Miles ('000)
Hillsborough Area Regional Transit Authority (HART)			
Demand response	30	97.0	856.1
Light rail	8	505.7	776.7
Bus	159	13,125.5	63,652.0
Vanpool	30	83.1	3,258.6

Note: Figures include both directly operated and purchased transportation
Source: Federal Transit Administration, National Transit Database, 2009

Air Transportation

Airport Name and Code / Type of Service	Passenger Airlines[1]	Passenger Enplanements	Freight Carriers[2]	Freight (lbs.)
Tampa International (TPA)				
Domestic service (U.S. carriers - 2010)	25	7,940,755	11	75,535,446
International service (U.S. carriers - 2009)	8	22,304	1	491

Note: (1) Includes all U.S.-based major, minor and commuter airlines that carried at least one passenger during the year; (2) Includes all U.S.-based airlines and freight carriers that transported at least one pound of freight during the year
Source: Bureau of Transportation Statistics, The Intermodal Transportation Database, Air Carriers: T-100 Domestic Market (U.S. Carriers), 2010; Bureau of Transportation Statistics, The Intermodal Transportation Database, Air Carriers: T-100 International Market (U.S. Carriers), 2009

Other Transportation Statistics

Interstate highways:	I-4; I-75
Amtrak service:	Yes
Major waterways/ports:	Port of Tampa

Source: Amtrak.com; Google Maps

BUSINESSES

Major Business Headquarters

Company Name	Rankings	
	Fortune[1]	Forbes[2]
OSI Restaurant Partners	-	98
WellCare Health Plans	420	-

Note: (1) Fortune 500—companies that produce a 10-K are ranked 1 to 500 based on 2010 revenue; (2) all private companies with at least $2 billion in annual revenue are ranked 1 to 223; companies listed are headquartered in the city; dashes indicate no ranking
Source: Fortune, "Fortune 500," May 23, 2011; Forbes, "America's Largest Private Companies," November 3, 2010

Fast-Growing Businesses

According to *Inc.*, Tampa is home to three of America's 500 fastest-growing private companies: **Archimedes Global; Freedom Health; Telovations**. Criteria: must be an independent, privately-held, for-profit, U.S. corporation, proprietorship or partnership; revenues of at least $80,000 in 2006 and $2 million in 2009; four-year operating/sales history; holding companies, regulated banks, and utilities were excluded. *Inc., "America's 500 Fastest-Growing Private Companies," September 2010*

According to Deloitte, Tampa is home to one of North America's 500 fastest-growing high-technology companies: **Acclaris**. Companies are ranked by percentage growth in revenue over a five-year period. Criteria for inclusion: company must be headquartered within North America; company must own proprietary intellectual property or proprietary technology that contributes to a significant portion of the company's operating revenue or devotes a significant proportion of revenues to research and development of technology; company must have been in business for a minumum of five years with 2005 operating revenues of at least $50,000 USD/CD and 2009 operating revenues of at least $5 million USD/CD. *Deloitte Touche Tohmatsu, 2010 Deloitte Technology Fast 500*[TM]

Minority Business Opportunity

Tampa is home to one company which is on the Black Enterprise Industrial/Service 100 list (100 largest companies based on gross sales): **Sun State International Trucks**. Criteria: operational in previous calendar year; at least 51% black-owned and manufactures/owns the product it sells or provides industrial or consumer services. Brokerages, real estate firms and firms that provide professional services are not eligible. *Black Enterprise, B.E. 100s, 2010*

Tampa is home to four companies which are on the *Hispanic Business 500* list (500 largest U.S. Hispanic-owned companies based on 2009 revenue): **J2 Engineering**; **Paul J. Sierra Construction**; **MarkMaster**; **Apex Office Products**. Companies included must show at least 51 percent ownership by Hispanic U.S. citizens, and must maintain headquarters in one of the 50 states or Washington, D.C. *Hispanic Business, "Hispanic Business 500," June 2010*

Minority- and Women-Owned Businesses

Group	All Firms		Firms with Paid Employees			
	Firms	Sales ($000)	Firms	Sales ($000)	Employees	Payroll ($000)
Asian	1,552	605,434	521	483,557	3,663	95,944
Black	4,378	455,594	338	351,483	2,814	63,365
Hispanic	7,947	1,642,003	1,395	1,338,467	7,318	288,902
Women	10,798	3,708,549	1,626	3,373,231	13,263	369,989
All Firms	38,665	67,668,675	11,088	66,207,395	301,506	13,047,915

Note: Figures cover firms located in the city; minority- and women-owned business are defined as firms in which the corresponding group own 51% or more of the stock or equity of the company
Source: U.S. Census Bureau, 2007 Economic Census, Survey of Business Owners

HOTELS

Hotels/Motels

Area	5 Star		4 Star		3 Star		2 Star		1 Star		Not Rated	
	Num.	Pct.3	Num.	Pct.3	Num.	Pct.3	Num.	Pct.3	Num.	Pct.3	Num.	Pct.3
City[1]	0	0.0	7	4.6	51	33.3	85	55.6	2	1.3	8	5.2
Total[2]	119	0.7	927	5.8	4,906	30.5	7,992	49.7	526	3.3	1,625	10.1

Note: (1) Figures cover Tampa and vicinity; (2) Figures cover all 100 cities in this book; (3) Percentage of hotels which are a given star rating; Star ratings are determined by expedia.com and offer an indication of the general quality of a particular hotel.
Source: expedia.com, May 5, 2011

The Tampa metro area is home to one of the top 218 hotels in the U.S. according to *Travel & Leisure*: **Sandpearl Resort** (#79). Criteria: service; location; rooms; food; and value. *Travel & Leisure, "T+L 500, The World's Best Hotels 2011"*

EVENT SITES

Major Stadiums, Arenas, and Auditoriums

Name	Max. Capacity
George M Steinbrenner Field	11,000
Plant City Stadium	6,700
Raymond James Stadium	65,000
St. Pete Times Forum	21,500
USF Sun Dome	10,411

Source: Original research

Convention Centers

Name	Overall Space (sq. ft.)	Exhibit Space (sq. ft.)	Meeting Space (sq. ft.)	Meeting Rooms
Tampa Convention Center	600,000	42,000	200,000	36

Source: Original research

Living Environment

COST OF LIVING

Cost of Living Index

Composite Index	Groceries	Housing	Utilities	Trans-portation	Health Care	Misc. Goods/ Services
92.4	96.3	84.7	93.8	103.3	98.4	93.4

Note: U.S. = 100; Figures cover the Tampa FL urban area.
Source: The Council for Community and Economic Research, ACCRA Cost of Living Index, 2010

Grocery Prices

Area[1]	T-Bone Steak ($/pound)	Frying Chicken ($/pound)	Whole Milk ($/half gal.)	Eggs ($/dozen)	Orange Juice ($/64 oz.)	Coffee ($/11.5 oz.)
City[2]	8.57	1.06	2.36	1.45	2.77	3.26
Avg.	9.04	1.16	2.02	1.47	3.08	3.65
Min.	6.97	0.84	1.46	0.96	2.39	2.64
Max.	13.93	2.51	3.58	3.01	4.94	6.32

Note: (1) Values for the local area are compared with the average, minimum and maximum values for all 338 areas in the Cost of Living Index; (2) Figures cover the Tampa FL urban area; **T-Bone Steak** *(price per pound);* **Frying Chicken** *(price per pound, whole fryer);* **Whole Milk** *(half gallon carton);* **Eggs** *(price per dozen, Grade A, large);* **Orange Juice** *(64 oz. Tropicana or Florida Natural);* **Coffee** *(11.5 oz. can, vacuum-packed, Maxwell House, Hills Bros, or Folgers).*
Source: The Council for Community and Economic Research, ACCRA Cost of Living Index, 2010

Housing and Utility Costs

Area[1]	New Home Price ($)	Apartment Rent ($/month)	All Electric ($/month)	Part Electric ($/month)	Other Energy ($/month)	Telephone ($/month)
City[2]	233,346	838	173.22	-	-	22.72
Avg.	293,442	810	166.39	91.93	83.82	26.93
Min.	182,545	453	119.21	44.47	36.85	17.98
Max.	1,123,114	2,776	307.53	218.20	313.90	39.15

Note: (1) Values for the local area are compared with the average, minimum and maximum values for all 338 areas in the Cost of Living Index; (2) Figures cover the Tampa FL urban area; **New Home Price** *(2,400 sf living area, 8,000 sf lot, in urban area with full utilities);* **Apartment Rent** *(950 sf 2 bedroom/1.5 or 2 bath, unfurnished, excluding all utilities except water);* **All Electric** *(average monthly cost for an all-electric home);* **Part Electric** *(average monthly cost for a part-electric home);* **Other Energy** *(average monthly cost for natural gas, fuel oil, coal, wood, and any other forms of energy except electricity);* **Telephone** *(price includes basic monthly rate for a private residential line plus additional local usage charges incurred by a family of four).*
Source: The Council for Community and Economic Research, ACCRA Cost of Living Index, 2010

Health Care, Transportation, and Other Costs

Area[1]	Doctor ($/visit)	Dentist ($/visit)	Optometrist ($/visit)	Gasoline ($/gallon)	Beauty Salon ($/visit)	Men's Shirt ($)
City[2]	84.14	81.87	68.10	2.68	33.62	19.85
Avg.	89.44	78.95	87.40	2.73	31.92	24.83
Min.	57.00	54.25	48.32	2.44	19.17	13.67
Max.	149.90	136.73	174.22	3.75	62.81	47.89

Note: (1) Values for the local area are compared with the average, minimum and maximum values for all 338 areas in the Cost of Living Index; (2) Figures cover the Tampa FL urban area; **Doctor** *(general practitioners routine exam of an established patient);* **Dentist** *(adult teeth cleaning and periodic oral examination);* **Optometrist** *(full vision eye exam for established adult patient);* **Gasoline** *(one gallon regular unleaded, national brand, including all taxes, cash price at self-service pump if available);* **Beauty Salon** *(woman's shampoo, trim, and blow-dry);* **Men's Shirt** *(cotton/polyester dress shirt, pinpoint weave, long sleeves).*
Source: The Council for Community and Economic Research, ACCRA Cost of Living Index, 2010

HOUSING

House Price Index (HPI)

Area	National Ranking[2]	Quarterly Change (%)	One-Year Change (%)	Five-Year Change (%)
MSA[1]	286	-3.29	-6.53	-30.69
U.S.[3]	-	-0.84	-3.95	-11.45

Note: The HPI is a weighted repeat sales index. It measures average price changes in repeat sales or refinancings on the same properties. This information is obtained by reviewing repeat mortgage transactions on single-family properties whose mortgages have been purchased or securitized by Fannie Mae or Freddie Mac in January 1975; (1) Metropolitan/Micropolitan Statistical Area - see Appendix B for areas included; (2) Rankings are based on annual percentage change for all metro areas containing at least 15,000 transactions over the last 10 years and ranges from 1 to 309; (3) figures based on a weighted average of Census Division estimates; all figures are for the period ending December 31, 2010
Source: Federal Housing Finance Agency, House Price Index, February 24, 2011

House Price Valuations

Area	Q4 2005 Price ($000)	Q4 2005 Over-valuation	Q4 2006 Price ($000)	Q4 2006 Over-valuation	Q4 2007 Price ($000)	Q4 2007 Over-valuation	Q4 2008 Price ($000)	Q4 2008 Over-valuation	Q4 2009 Price ($000)	Q4 2009 Over-valuation
MSA[1]	181.8	30.2	188.8	26.4	169.9	11.8	130.8	-13.6	120.4	-19.9

Note: Figures show the percentage of over- or under-valuation of single family homes relative to statistically normal house values (e.g. a value of 23.6 indicates that house values are 23.6% overvalued). Statistically normal house values are based on house prices, interest rates, household incomes, population densities, and any historical premiums or discounts metropolitan areas have exhibited over time; (1) Figures cover the Tampa-St. Petersburg-Clearwater, FL Metropolitan Statistical Area - see Appendix B for areas included
Source: Global Insight/PNC Financial Services Group, House Prices in America: 4th Quarter 2009 Update

Median Single-Family Home Prices

Area	2008	2009	2010p	Percent Change 2009 to 2010
MSA[1]	173.0	140.7	134.2	-4.6
U.S. Average	196.6	172.1	173.2	0.6

Note: Figures are median sales prices of existing single-family homes in thousands of dollars; (p) preliminary; n/a not available; (1) Metropolitan Statistical Area - see Appendix B for areas included
Source: National Association of Realtors, Median Sales Price of Existing Single-Family Homes for Metropolitan Areas, 4th Quarter 2010

Median Apartment Condo-Coop Home Prices

Area	2008	2009	2010p	Percent Change 2009 to 2010
MSA[1]	141.3	107.1	93.2	-13.0
U.S. Average	209.8	175.6	171.7	-2.2

Note: Figures are median sales prices of existing apartment condo-coop homes in thousands of dollars; (p) preliminary; n/a not available; (1) Metropolitan Statistical Area - see Appendix B for areas included
Source: National Association of Realtors, Median Sales Price of Existing Apartment Condo-Coop Homes for Metropolitan Areas, 4th Quarter 2010

Year Housing Structure Built

Area	2000 or Later	1990 -1999	1980 -1989	1970 -1979	1960 -1969	1950 -1959	1940 -1949	Before 1940	Median Year
City	16.4	10.3	13.0	13.6	13.4	17.4	7.2	8.7	1972
MSA[1]	15.3	14.2	22.8	21.5	11.6	9.4	2.4	2.7	1981
U.S.	12.5	14.0	14.2	16.5	11.4	11.3	5.8	14.3	1974

Note: Figures are percentages except for Median Year; (1) Metropolitan Statistical Area - see Appendix B for areas included
Source: U.S. Census Bureau, 2007-2009 American Community Survey 3-Year Estimates

HEALTH

Health Risk Data

Category	MSA[1] (%)	U.S. (%)
Adults who have been told they have high blood pressure	30.7	28.7
Adults who have been told they have high blood cholesterol	39.9	37.5
Adults who have been told they have diabetes[3]	10.9	8.3
Adults who have been told they have arthritis	29.7	26.0
Adults who have been told they currently have asthma	6.9	8.8
Adults who are current smokers	21.3	17.9
Adults who are heavy drinkers[4]	7.3	5.1
Adults who are binge drinkers[5]	17.2	15.8
Adults who are overweight (BMI 25.0 - 29.9)	35.5	36.2
Adults who are obese (BMI 30.0 - 99.8)	29.2	26.9
Adults who participated in any physical activities in the past month	74.7	76.2
Adults 50+ who have ever had a sigmoidoscopy or colonoscopy[2]	61.6	62.2
Women 40+ who have had a mammogram within the past two years[2]	75.9	76.0
Adults age 18–64 who have any kind of health care coverage	78.1	83.1

Note: Data as of 2009 unless otherwise noted; (1) Figures cover the Tampa-St. Petersburg-Clearwater, FL Metropolitan Statistical Area - see Appendix B for areas included; (2) Data as of 2008; (3) Figures do not include pregnancy-related, borderline, or pre-diabetes; (4) Heavy drinkers are classified as males having more than two drinks per day or females having more than one drink per day; (5) Binge drinkers are classified as males having five or more drinks on one occasion or females having four or more drinks on one occasion
Source: Centers for Disease Control and Prevention, Behaviorial Risk Factor Surveillance System, SMART: Selected Metropolitan/Micropolitan Area Risk Trends, 2008, 2009

Mortality Rates for the Top 10 Causes of Death in the U.S.

ICD-10[a] Sub-Chapter	ICD-10[a] Code	Age-Adjusted Mortality Rate[1] per 100,000 population	
		County[2]	U.S.
Malignant neoplasms	C00-C97	186.2	180.9
Ischaemic heart diseases	I20-I25	147.9	135.0
Other forms of heart disease	I30-I51	31.2	50.0
Cerebrovascular diseases	I60-I69	41.6	44.1
Chronic lower respiratory diseases	J40-J47	48.5	41.5
Other degenerative diseases of the nervous system	G30-G31	24.2	23.6
Diabetes mellitus	E10-E14	29.9	23.5
Other external causes of accidental injury	W00-X59	31.0	23.5
Organic, including symptomatic, mental disorders	F01-F09	33.7	22.2
Influenza and pneumonia	J09-J18	7.8	18.1

Note: (a) ICD-10 = International Classification of Diseases 10th Revision; (1) Mortality rates are a three year average covering 2005-2007; (2) Figures cover Hillsborough County
Source: Centers for Disease Control and Prevention, National Center for Health Statistics. Compressed Mortality File 1999-2007. CDC WONDER On-line Database, compiled from Compressed Mortality File 1999-2007 Series 20 No. 2M, 2010.

Mortality Rates for Selected Causes of Death

ICD-10[a] Sub-Chapter	ICD-10[a] Code	Age-Adjusted Mortality Rate[1] per 100,000 population	
		County[2]	U.S.
Assault	X85-Y09	5.4	6.0
Human immunodeficiency virus (HIV) disease	B20-B24	8.4	4.0
Hypertensive diseases	I10-I15	31.8	18.0
Intentional self-harm	X60-X84	13.3	11.0
Malnutrition	E40-E46	0.7	0.8
Obesity and other hyperalimentation	E65-E68	1.6	1.5
Transport accidents	V01-V99	18.2	15.6
Viral hepatitis	B15-B19	3.0	2.1

Note: (a) ICD-10 = International Classification of Diseases 10th Revision; (1) Mortality rates are a three year average covering 2005-2007; (2) Figures cover Hillsborough County
Source: Centers for Disease Control and Prevention, National Center for Health Statistics. Compressed Mortality File 1999-2007. CDC WONDER On-line Database, compiled from Compressed Mortality File 1999-2007 Series 20 No. 2M, 2010.

Distribution of Physicians and Dentists

Area[1]	Dentists[2]	D.O.[3]	M.D.[4]				
			Total	Family/ General Practice	Pediatrics	Medical Specialties	Surgical Specialties
Local (number)	487	271	2,617	209	225	1,043	601
Local (rate[5])	4.2	2.3	22.2	1.8	1.9	8.8	5.1
U.S. (rate[5])	4.5	1.9	18.3	2.5	1.4	6.8	4.1

Note: Data as of 2008 unless noted; (1) Local data covers Hillsborough County; (2) Data as of 2007; (3) Doctor of Osteopathic Medicine; (4) Includes active, non-federal, patient-care, office-based Doctors of Medicine; (5) rate per 10,000 population
Source: Area Resource File (ARF). 2009-2010 Release. U.S. Department of Health and Human Services, Health Resources and Services Administration, Bureau of Health Professions, Rockville, MD, August 2010

Hospitals

Tampa has the following hospitals: 7 general medical and surgical; 1 cancer; 2 long-term acute care; 1 children's orthopedic.
AHA Guide to the Healthcare Field 2010

According to *U.S. News,* the Tampa-St. Petersburg-Clearwater, FL Metropolitan Statistical Area is home to two of the best hospitals in the U.S.: **Moffitt Cancer Center**; **Tampa General Hospital**. The hospitals listed were highly ranked in at least one adult specialty. *U.S. News Online, "America's Best Hospitals 2010-11"*

According to *U.S. News,* the Tampa-St. Petersburg-Clearwater, FL Metropolitan Statistical Area is home to one of the best children's hospitals in the U.S.: **All Children's Hospital**. The hospital listed was highly ranked in at least one pediatric specialty. *U.S. News Online, "America's Best Children's Hospitals 2010-11"*

EDUCATION

Public School District Statistics

District Name	Schls	Pupils	Pupil/ Teacher Ratio	Minority Pupils[1] (%)	Free Lunch Eligible[2] (%)	IEP[3] (%)
Hillsborough	285	192,007	13.7	58.8	41.2	15.0

Note: Table includes school districts with 2,000 or more students; (1) Percentage of students that are not non-Hispanic white; (2) Percentage of students that are eligible for the free lunch program; (3) Percentage of students that have an Individualized Education Program.
Source: U.S. Department of Education, National Center for Education Statistics, Common Core of Data, Local Education Agency (School District) Universe Survey: School Year 2008-2009; U.S. Department of Education, National Center for Education Statistics, Common Core of Data, Public Elementary/Secondary School Universe Survey: School Year 2008-2009

Top Public High Schools

High School Name	Index[1]	Rank[1]	Subsidized Lunch (%)[2]	E&E (%)[3]
Braulio Alonso	1.991	723	44.4	25.3
C. Leon King Magnet[4]	4.620	68	49.0	70.0
Chamberlain	2.175	598	61.0	18.3
Freedom	2.223	563	45.0	35.8
Gaither	2.781	306	31.0	28.0
Hillsborough[4]	5.407	44	61.0	45.1
Plant	5.292	48	13.0	35.3
T. R. Robinson	3.790	113	44.0	19.8
Tampa Bay Tech	1.864	808	51.0	20.5
Walter Sickles	2.163	607	28.0	37.9
Wharton	3.544	148	38.0	23.3

Note: (1) Public schools are ranked according to a ratio that is the number of Advanced Placement, International Baccalaureate, and/or Cambridge tests taken by all students at a school in 2009 divided by the number of graduating seniors. All of the schools on the list have an index of at least 1.000; they are in the top six percent of public schools measured this way. The rankings range from 1 to 1,734; (2) Percentage of students receiving federally subsidized meals; (3) E & E stands for equity and excellence percentage: the portion of all graduating seniors at a school that had at least one passing grade on one AP or IB test; (4) Schools that offer International Baccalaureate or Cambridge exams; (5) School is unranked, but has been identified by Newsweek as one of the nation's most elite public high schools.
Source: Newsweek Online, "Top High Schools 2010"

Highest Level of Education

Area	Less than H.S.	H.S. Diploma	Some College, No Deg.	Associate Degree	Bachelors Degree	Masters Degree	Profess. School Degree	Doctorate Degree
City	17.4	26.7	17.3	8.7	19.2	6.8	2.9	1.1
MSA[1]	13.6	30.9	21.1	8.8	17.1	5.9	1.7	0.9
U.S.	15.3	29.0	20.7	7.5	17.4	7.0	1.9	1.1

Note: Figures are 2010 estimated percentages and cover persons age 25 and over; (1) Metropolitan Statistical Area - see Appendix B for areas included
Source: Claritas, Inc.

Educational Attainment by Race

Area	High School Graduate (%)					Bachelor's Degree (%)				
	Total	White	Black	Asian	Hisp.[2]	Total	White	Black	Asian	Hisp.[2]
City	83.8	91.4	77.4	86.1	70.3	31.9	43.6	13.1	62.3	17.4
MSA[1]	86.6	89.5	80.2	83.3	73.9	25.5	27.1	17.2	47.6	17.3
U.S.	84.9	90.0	80.7	85.5	60.7	27.8	30.9	17.5	49.7	12.7

Note: Figures shown cover persons 25 years old and over; (1) Metropolitan Statistical Area - see Appendix B for areas included; (2) people of Hispanic origin can be of any race
Source: U.S. Census Bureau, 2007-2009 American Community Survey 3-Year Estimates

School Enrollment by Grade and Control

Area	Preschool (%)		Kindergarten (%)		Grades 1 - 4 (%)		Grades 5 - 8 (%)		Grades 9 - 12 (%)	
	Public	Private	Public	Private	Public	Private	Public	Private	Public	Private
City	50.4	49.6	80.6	19.4	90.0	10.0	89.5	10.5	91.7	8.3
MSA[1]	49.5	50.5	84.6	15.4	88.5	11.5	88.2	11.8	91.0	9.0
U.S.	54.3	45.7	86.4	13.6	88.9	11.1	89.1	10.9	90.2	9.8

Note: Figures shown cover persons 3 years old and over; (1) Metropolitan Statistical Area - see Appendix B for areas included
Source: U.S. Census Bureau, 2007-2009 American Community Survey 3-Year Estimates

Average Salaries of Public School Classroom Teachers

Area	2009-10		2010-11		Percent Change 2009-10 to 2010-11	Percent Change 2000-01 to 2010-11
	Dollars	Rank[1]	Dollars	Rank[1]		
Florida	46,708	37	46,702	47	-0.01	22.2
U.S. Average	55,202	-	56,069	-	1.57	29.3

Note: (1) State rank ranges from 1 to 51 where 1 indicates highest salary.
Source: National Education Association, Rankings & Estimates: Rankings of the States 2010 and Estimates of School Statistics 2011, December 2010

Higher Education

Four-Year Colleges			Two-Year Colleges			Medical Schools[1]	Law Schools[2]	Voc/ Tech[3]
Public	Private Non-profit	Private For-profit	Public	Private Non-profit	Private For-profit			
1	1	9	3	0	4	1	0	6

Note: Figures cover institutions located within the city limits and include main campuses only; (1) includes schools accredited by the Liaison Committee on Medical Education and the American Osteopathic Association; (2) includes American Bar Association-accredited law schools; (3) includes all schools with programs that are less than 2 years.
Source: National Center for Education Statistics, Integrated Postsecondary Education System (IPEDS) Peer Analysis System, 2010-11; U.S. News & World Report, Medical School Directory, 2011; U.S. News & World Report, Law School Directory, 2011

According to *U.S. News & World Report,* the Tampa-St. Petersburg-Clearwater, FL Metropolitan Statistical Area is home to one of the top 197 national universities in the U.S.: **University of South Florida** (#183). The rankings are based on quantitative measurements such as peer assessment, retention, faculty resources, student selectivity, financial resources, graduation rate, and alumni giving rate. *U.S. News & World Report, "America's Best Colleges 2011"*

According to *U.S. News & World Report,* the Tampa-St. Petersburg-Clearwater, FL Metropolitan Statistical Area is home to one of the top 189 liberal arts colleges in the U.S.: **Eckerd College** (#137). The rankings are based on quantitative measurements such as peer assessment, retention, faculty resources, student selectivity, financial resources, graduation rate, and alumni giving rate. *U.S. News & World Report, "America's Best Colleges 2011"*

PRESIDENTIAL ELECTION

2008 Presidential Election Results

Area	Obama	McCain	Nader	Other
Hillsborough County	53.1	45.9	0.4	0.7
U.S.	52.9	45.6	0.6	0.9

Note: Results are percentages and may not add to 100% due to rounding
Source: Dave Leip's Atlas of U.S. Presidential Elections, www.uselectionatlas.org

EMPLOYERS

Major Employers

Company Name	Industry	Type of Site
All Childrens Hospital	Specialty hospitals, except psychiatric	Branch
American Staff Management	Help supply services	Single
Bayfront Cancer Center	General medical and surgical hospitals	Headquarters
Bayfront Medical Center	General medical and surgical hospitals	Branch
Chase Manhattan	National commercial banks	Branch
Diversified Maint Systems	Building maintenance services, nec	Single
Employee Benefit & Risk Mgt	Administration of educational programs	Branch
Honeywell	Aircraft engines and engine parts	Branch
HSN	Television broadcasting stations	Headquarters
IF Music	Miscellaneous publishing	Single
James Haley Vamc	Administration of veterans' affairs	Branch
Moffitt Cancer Center	Offices and clinics of medical doctors	Single
Morton Plant Hospital	General medical and surgical hospitals	Headquarters
Pen Power	Engineering services	Branch
St Petersburg Times	Newspapers	Branch
Sykes Enterprises Incorporated	Computer related services, nec	Headquarters
Tech Data Corporation	Computers, peripherals, and software	Headquarters
University Community Health	General medical and surgical hospitals	Headquarters
University of South Florida	Colleges and universities	Headquarters
US Post Office	U.S. postal service	Branch
USANI Sub	Television broadcasting stations	Single
VA Bay Pines Healthcare System	General medical and surgical hospitals	Branch
Verizon	Business services, nec	Branch
Verizon	Data processing and preparation	Headquarters
Veterans Health Administration	Administration of public health programs	Branch

Note: Companies shown are located within the Tampa metropolitan area; nec = not elsewhere classified.
Source: www.zapdata.com, January 2011

Best Companies to Work For

Moffitt Cancer Center, headquartered in Tampa, is among the "100 Best Companies for Working Mothers." Criteria: workforce profile; benefits; child care; women's issues and advancement; flexible work; paid time off and leaves; company culture; and work-life programs. This year *Working Mother* gave particular weight to child care, flexibility, and paid time off and leaves. *Working Mother, "100 Best Companies 2010"*

H. Lee Moffitt Cancer Center & Research Institute, headquartered in Tampa, is among the "100 Best Places to Work in IT." To qualify, companies, both public and private, had to have a minimum of 50 IT employees. Companies were selected based on average salary and bonus increases, the percentage of IT employees receiving promotions, IT staff turnover rates, training and development programs, and the percentage of women and minorities in IT staff and management positions. In addition, information was collected on how the organizations reward outstanding performance, how their retention programs are structured and what benefits they offer. *Computerworld, "100 Best Places to Work in IT 2010"*

Moffit Cancer Center, located in Tampa, is among the "Top Companies for Executive Women." To be named to the list, companies with a minimum of two women on the board complete a comprehensive application that focuses on the number of women in senior ranks (compared to men and to the company population). In addition to assessing corporate programs and policies dedicated to advancing women, NAFE measured results, examining the number of women in each company overall, in senior management, and on its board of directors. They drew particular attention to the number of women with profit-and-loss responsibility. *National Association for Female Executives, "2011 NAFE Top Companies for Executive Women"*

PUBLIC SAFETY

Crime Rate

Area	All Crimes	Violent Crimes				Property Crimes		
		Murder	Forcible Rape	Robbery	Aggrav. Assault	Burglary	Larceny -Theft	Motor Vehicle Theft
City	4,506.2	5.8	23.2	263.3	460.0	1,014.1	2,345.7	394.2
Suburbs[1]	4,446.3	3.3	30.2	140.5	391.4	980.5	2,606.3	294.0
Metro[2]	4,453.8	3.6	29.3	155.9	400.0	984.7	2,573.6	306.6
U.S.	3,465.5	5.0	28.7	133.0	262.8	716.3	2,060.9	258.8

Note: Figures are crimes per 100,000 population; (1) All areas within the metro area that are located outside the city limits; (2) Metropolitan Statistical Area - see Appendix B for areas included
Source: FBI Uniform Crime Reports, 2009

Hate Crimes

Area	Number of Quarters Reported	Bias Motivation				
		Race	Religion	Sexual Orientation	Ethnicity	Disability
City	4	3	0	2	0	0

Source: Federal Bureau of Investigation, Hate Crime Statistics 2009

Identity Theft Consumer Complaints

Area	Complaints	Complaints per 100,000 Population	Rank[2]
MSA[1]	2,710	99.5	61
U.S.	250,854	81.3	-

Note: (1) Metropolitan Statistical Area - see Appendix B for areas included; (2) Rank ranges from 1 to 384 where 1 indicates greatest number of complaints per 100,000 population
Source: Federal Trade Commission, Consumer Sentinel Network Data Book for January - December 2010

RECREATION

Culture

Dance[1]	Theatre[1]	Instrumental Music[1]	Vocal Music[1]	Series/ Festivals	Museums	Zoos and Aquariums[2]
0	5	0	2	0	8	3

Note: (1) Number of professional perfoming groups; (2) AZA-accredited
Source: The Grey House Performing Arts Directory, 2011-2012; Official Museum Directory, 2010; American Association of Museums, AAM Member Museums, March 2011; Association of Zoos & Aquariums, AZA Member Zoos & Aquariums, May 2011

Professional Sports Teams

Team Name	League
Tampa Bay Buccaneers	National Football League (NFL)
Tampa Bay Lightning	National Hockey League (NHL)
Tampa Bay Rays	Major League Baseball (MLB)

Note: Includes teams located in the Tampa-Saint Petersburg metro area.
Source: Original research

CLIMATE

Average and Extreme Temperatures

Temperature	Jan	Feb	Mar	Apr	May	Jun	Jul	Aug	Sep	Oct	Nov	Dec	Yr.
Extreme High (°F)	85	88	91	93	98	99	97	98	96	94	90	86	99
Average High (°F)	70	72	76	82	87	90	90	90	89	84	77	72	82
Average Temp. (°F)	60	62	67	72	78	81	82	83	81	75	68	62	73
Average Low (°F)	50	52	56	61	67	73	74	74	73	66	57	52	63
Extreme Low (°F)	21	24	29	40	49	53	63	67	57	40	23	18	18

Note: Figures cover the years 1948-1990
Source: National Climatic Data Center, International Station Meteorological Climate Summary, 9/96

Average Precipitation/Snowfall/Humidity

Precip./Humidity	Jan	Feb	Mar	Apr	May	Jun	Jul	Aug	Sep	Oct	Nov	Dec	Yr.
Avg. Precip. (in.)	2.1	2.8	3.5	1.8	3.0	5.6	7.3	7.9	6.5	2.3	1.8	2.1	46.7
Avg. Snowfall (in.)	Tr	Tr	Tr	0	0	0	0	0	0	0	0	Tr	Tr
Avg. Rel. Hum. 7am (%)	87	87	86	86	85	86	88	90	91	89	88	87	88
Avg. Rel. Hum. 4pm (%)	56	55	54	51	52	60	65	66	64	57	56	57	58

Note: Figures cover the years 1948-1990; Tr = Trace amounts (<0.05 in. of rain; <0.5 in. of snow)
Source: National Climatic Data Center, International Station Meteorological Climate Summary, 9/96

Weather Conditions

Temperature			Daytime Sky			Precipitation		
32°F & below	45°F & below	90°F & above	Clear	Partly cloudy	Cloudy	0.01 inch or more precip.	0.1 inch or more snow/ice	Thunder-storms
3	35	85	81	204	80	107	< 1	87

Note: Figures are average number of days per year and cover the years 1948-1990
Source: National Climatic Data Center, International Station Meteorological Climate Summary, 9/96

HAZARDOUS WASTE

Superfund Sites

Tampa has eight hazardous waste sites on the EPA's Superfund Final National Priorities List: **Alaric Area Ground Water Plume; Helena Chemical Co. (Tampa Plant); MRI Corp (Tampa); Peak Oil Co./Bay Drum Co.; Raleigh Street Dump; Reeves Southeastern Galvanizing Corp.; Southern Solvents, Inc.; Stauffer Chemical Co (Tampa).** *U.S. Environmental Protection Agency, Final National Priorities List, April 1, 2011*

AIR & WATER QUALITY

Air Quality Index

Area	Percent of Days when Air Quality was...[2]				AQI Statistics	
	Good	Moderate	Unhealthy for Sensitive Groups	Unhealthy	Maximum	Median
Area[1]	81.8	16.0	1.8	0.4	161	40

Note: The Air Quality Index (AQI) is an index for reporting daily air quality. EPA calculates the AQI for five major air pollutants regulated by the Clean Air Act: ground-level ozone, particle pollution (also known as particulate matter), carbon monoxide, sulfur dioxide, and nitrogen dioxide. The AQI runs from 0 to 500. The higher the AQI value, the greater the level of air pollution and the greater the health concern. There are six AQI categories: "Good" The AQI is between 0 and 50. Air quality is considered satisfactory; "Moderate" The AQI is between 51 and 100. Air quality is acceptable; "Unhealthy for Sensitive Groups" When AQI values are between 101 and 150, members of sensitive groups may experience health effects; "Unhealthy" When AQI values are between 151 and 200 everyone may begin to experience health effects; "Very Unhealthy" AQI values between 201 and 300 trigger a health alert; "Hazardous" AQI values over 300 trigger health warnings of emergency conditions; (1) Data covers Hillsborough County; (2) Based on 275 days with AQI data in 2008; The EPA has suspended data updates while it assesses its data systems, including AirData reports and maps.
Source: U.S. Environmental Protection Agency, AirData Report, 2008

Air Quality Index Pollutants

Area	Percent of Days when AQI Pollutant was...[2]					
	Carbon Monoxide	Nitrogen Dioxide	Ozone	Sulfur Dioxide	Particulate Matter 2.5	Particulate Matter 10
Area[1]	0.4	0.0	66.9	0.4	15.6	16.7

Note: The Air Quality Index (AQI) is an index for reporting daily air quality. EPA calculates the AQI for five major air pollutants regulated by the Clean Air Act: ground-level ozone, particle pollution (also known as particulate matter), carbon monoxide, sulfur dioxide, and nitrogen dioxide. The AQI runs from 0 to 500. The higher the AQI value, the greater the level of air pollution and the greater the health concern; (1) Data covers Hillsborough County; (2) Based on 275 days with AQI data in 2008; The EPA has suspended data updates while it assesses its data systems, including AirData reports and maps.
Source: U.S. Environmental Protection Agency, AirData Report, 2008

Air Quality Index Trends

Area	Trend Sites (days)								All Sites (days)
	2002	2003	2004	2005	2006	2007	2008	2009	2009
MSA[1]	81	69	38	30	21	31	10	6	18

Note: Figures are the number of days the AQI value exceeded 100 in a given year. An AQI value greater than 100 indicates that air quality would have been in the unhealthful range on that day. Data from exceptional events are included. These counts are presented in two ways. First, the counts are based on sites having an adequate record of monitoring data during the trend period (trend sites). These counts represent the relative change in the number of days with AQI values greater than 100. In the last column, the counts are based on all sites with data in the most recent year (because it is possible for a site to have data in the most recent year but not enough data to be a trend site); (1) Data covers the Tampa-St. Petersburg-Clearwater, FL Metropolitan Statistical Area - see Appendix B for areas included
Source: U.S. Environmental Protection Agency, Office of Air and Radiation, Air Quality Index Information, "Number of Days with Air Quality Index Values Greater than 100 and Trend Sites, 1990-2009, and at All Sites in 2009"

Maximum Air Pollutant Concentrations

	Particulate Matter 10 (ug/m^3)	Particulate Matter 2.5 (ug/m^3)	Ozone (ppm)	Carbon Monoxide (ppm)	Sulfur Dioxide (ppm)	Nitrogen Dioxide (ppm)	Lead (ug/m^3)
MSA[1] Level	42	17	0.073	1	0.028	0.007	0.25
NAAQS[2]	150	35	0.075	9	0.140	0.053	0.15
Met NAAQS[2]	Yes	Yes	Yes	Yes	Yes	Yes	No

Note: Data from exceptional events are not included; (1) Data covers the Tampa-St. Petersburg-Clearwater, FL Metropolitan Statistical Area - see Appendix B for areas included; (2) National Ambient Air Quality Standards; n/a not available; (a) Localized impact from an industrial source in Tampa. Concentration from highest nonpoint source site is 0.01 ug/m³ in Pinellas County
Concentrations: Particulate Matter 10 (coarse particulate) - highest second maximum 24-hour concentration; Particulate Matter 2.5 (fine particulate) - highest 98th percentile 24-hour concentration; Ozone - highest fourth daily maximum 8-hour concentration; Carbon Monoxide - highest second maximum non-overlapping 8-hour concentration; Sulfur Dioxide - highest second maximum 24-hour concentration; Nitrogen Dioxide - highest arithmetic mean concentration; Lead - maximum running 3-month average
Units: ppm = parts per million; ug/m³ = micrograms per cubic meter
Source: U.S. Environmental Protection Agency, CBSA Factbook 2009, Air Quality Statistics by City, 2009

Drinking Water

Water System Name	Pop. Served	Primary Water Source Type	Violations[1]	
			Health Based	Monitoring/ Reporting
City of Tampa-Water Dept.	550,000	Surface	0	0

Note: (1) Based on violation data from January 1, 2010 to December 31, 2010 (includes unresolved violations from earlier years)
Source: U.S. Environmental Protection Agency, Office of Ground Water and Drinking Water, Safe Drinking Water Information System (based on data extracted May 9, 2011)

Appendix A: Counties

Albuquerque, NM
Bernalillo County

Anchorage, AK
Anchorage County

Ann Arbor, MI
Washtenaw County

Athens, GA
Clarke County

Atlanta, GA
Fulton County

Austin, TX
Travis County

Baltimore, MD
Baltimore City

Bellevue, WA
King County

Birmingham, AL
Jefferson County

Boise City, ID
Ada County

Boston, MA
Suffolk County

Boulder, CO
Boulder County

Cambridge, MA
Middlesex County

Cary, NC
Wake County

Charleston, SC
Charleston County

Charlotte, NC
Mecklenburg County

Chattanooga, TN
Hamilton County

Chicago, IL
Cook County

Cincinnati, OH
Hamilton County

Cleveland, OH
Cuyahoga County

Colorado Springs, CO
El Paso County

Columbia, SC
Richland County

Columbus, OH
Franklin County

Dallas, TX
Dallas County

Denver, CO
Denver County

Des Moines, IA
Polk County

Durham, NC
Durham County

Edison, NJ
Middlesex County

El Paso, TX
El Paso County

Eugene, OR
Lane County

Evansville, IN
Vanderburgh County

Fargo, ND
Cass County

Fort Collins, CO
Larimer County

Fort Lauderdale, FL
Broward County

Fort Wayne, IN
Allen County

Fort Worth, TX
Tarrant County

Gainesville, FL
Alachua County

Greensboro, NC
Guilford County

Honolulu, HI
Honolulu County

Houston, TX
Harris County

Huntsville, AL
Madison County

Indianapolis, IN
Marion County

Irvine, CA
Orange County

Jackson, MS
Hinds County

Jacksonville, FL
Duval County

Kansas City, MO
Jackson County

Knoxville, TN
Knox County

Las Vegas, NV
Clark County

Lexington, KY
Fayette County

Lincoln, NE
Lancaster County

Little Rock, AR
Pulaski County

Los Angeles, CA
Los Angeles County

Louisville, KY
Jefferson County

Madison, WI
Dane County

Manchester, NH
Hillsborough County

Miami, FL
Dade County

Milwaukee, WI
Milwaukee County

Minneapolis, MN
Hennepin County

Naperville, IL
DuPage County

Nashville, TN
Davidson County

New Orleans, LA
Orleans Parish

New York, NY
Bronx, Kings, New York, Queens, and
Richmond Counties

Oakland, CA
Alameda County

Oklahoma City, OK
Oklahoma County

Omaha, NE
Douglas County

Orlando, FL
Orange County

Overland Park, KS
Johnson County

Oxnard, CA
Ventura County

Philadelphia, PA
Philadelphia County

Phoenix, AZ
Maricopa County

Pittsburgh, PA
Allegheny County

Plano, TX
Collin County

Portland, OR
Multnomah County

Providence, RI
Providence County

Provo, UT
Utah County

Raleigh, NC
Wake County

Reno, NV
Washoe County

Richmond, VA
Richmond City

Riverside, CA
Riverside County

Rochester, NY
Monroe County

Sacramento, CA
Sacramento County

Saint Louis, MO
Saint Louis City

Saint Paul, MN
Ramsey County

Saint Petersburg, FL
Pinellas County

Salt Lake City, UT
Salt Lake County

San Antonio, TX
Bexar County

San Diego, CA
San Diego County

San Francisco, CA
San Francisco County

San Jose, CA
Santa Clara County

Santa Ana, CA
Orange County

Savannah, GA
Chatham County

Seattle, WA
King County

Spokane, WA
Spokane County

Springfield, MO
Greene County

Tampa, FL
Hillsborough County

Tulsa, OK
Tulsa County

Virginia Beach, VA
Virginia Beach City

Warren, MI
Macomb County

Washington, DC
District of Columbia

Wichita, KS
Sedgwick County

*Note: In cases where a city's population is
split over multiple counties (except New York),
data in this book reflects the county where the
majority of the population resides.*

Appendix B: Metropolitan Area Definitions

Metropolitan Statistical Areas (MSA), Metropolitan Divisions (MD), New England City and Town Areas (NECTA), and New England City and Town Area Divisions (NECTA Division)

These metropolitan area definitions went into effect June 6, 2003 and are current as of December 2009.

Albuquerque, NM MSA
Bernalillo, Sandoval, Torrance, and Valencia Counties

Anchorage, AK MSA
Anchorage Municipality and Matanuska-Susitna Borough

Ann Arbor, MI MSA
Washtenaw County

Athens, GA MSA
Clarke, Madison, Oconee, and Oglethorpe Counties

Atlanta-Sandy Springs-Marietta, GA MSA
Barrow, Bartow, Butts, Carroll, Cherokee, Clayton, Cobb, Coweta, Dawson, DeKalb, Douglas, Fayette, Forsyth, Fulton, Gwinnett, Haralson, Heard, Henry, Jasper, Lamar, Meriwether, Newton, Paulding, Pickens, Pike, Rockdale, Spalding, and Walton Counties

Austin-Round Rock, TX MSA
Bastrop, Caldwell, Hays, Travis, and Williamson Counties

Baltimore-Towson, MD MSA
Baltimore city; Anne Arundel, Baltimore, Carroll, Harford, Howard, and Queen Anne's Counties

Bellevue, WA
See Seattle, WA

Birmingham-Hoover, AL MSA
Bibb, Blount, Chilton, Jefferson, Shelby, St. Clair, and Walker Counties

Boise City-Nampa, ID MSA
Ada, Boise, Canyon, Gem, and Owyhee Counties

Boston, MA
Boston-Cambridge-Quincy, MA-NH MSA
Essex, Middlesex, Norfolk, Plymouth, and Suffolk Counties, MA; Rockingham and Strafford Counties, NH
Boston-Quincy, MA MD
Norfolk, Plymouth, and Suffolk Counties
Boston-Cambridge-Quincy, MA-NH NECTA
Includes 155 cities and towns in Massachusetts and 38 cities and towns in New Hampshire
Boston-Cambridge-Quincy, MA NECTA Division
Includes 97 cities and towns in Massachusetts

Boulder, CO MSA
Boulder County

Charleston-North Charleston, SC MSA
Berkeley, Charleston, and Dorchester Counties

Cambridge, MA
See Boston, MA

Cary, NC
See Raleigh-Cary, NC MSA

Charlotte-Gastonia-Concord, NC-SC MSA
Anson, Cabarrus, Gaston, Mecklenburg, Union, and York Counties

Chattanooga, TN-GA MSA
Catoosa, Dade, and Walker Counties, GA; Hamilton, Marion, and Sequatchie Counties, TN

Chicago, IL
Chicago-Naperville-Joliet, IL-IN-WI MSA
Cook, DeKalb, DuPage, Grundy, Kane, Kendall, Lake, McHenry, and Will Counties, IL; Jasper, Lake, Newton, and Porter Counties, IN; Kenosha County, WI
Chicago-Naperville-Joliet, IL MD
Cook, DeKalb, DuPage, Grundy, Kane, Kendall, McHenry, and Will Counties

Cincinnati-Middletown, OH-KY-IN MSA
Dearborn, Franklin, and Ohio Counties, IN; Boone, Bracken, Campbell, Gallatin, Grant, Kenton, and Pendleton Counties, KY; Brown, Butler, Clermont, Hamilton, and Warren Counties, OH

Cleveland-Elyria-Mentor, OH MSA
Cuyahoga, Geauga, Lake, Lorain, and Medina Counties

Colorado Springs, CO MSA
El Paso and Teller Counties

Columbia, SC MSA
Calhoun, Fairfield, Kershaw, Lexington, Richland, and Saluda Counties

Columbus, OH MSA
Delaware, Fairfield, Franklin, Licking, Madison, Morrow, Pickaway, and Union Counties

Dallas, TX
Dallas-Fort Worth-Arlington, TX MSA
Collin, Dallas, Delta, Denton, Ellis, Hunt, Johnson, Kaufman, Parker, Rockwall, Tarrant, and Wise Counties
Dallas-Plano-Irving, TX MD
Collin, Dallas, Delta, Denton, Ellis, Hunt, Kaufman, and Rockwall Counties

Denver-Aurora, CO MSA
Adams, Arapahoe, Broomfield, Clear Creek, Denver, Douglas, Elbert, Gilpin, Jefferson, and Park Counties

Des Moines, IA MSA
Dallas, Guthrie, Madison, Polk, and Warren Counties

Detroit, MI
Detroit-Warren-Livonia, MI MSA
Lapeer, Livingston, Macomb, Oakland, and St. Clair, and Wayne Counties
Warren-Troy-Farmington Hills, MI MD
Lapeer, Livingston, Macomb, Oakland, and St. Clair Counties

Durham, NC MSA
Chatham, Durham, Orange, and and Person Counties

Edison, NJ
Edison, NJ MD
Hunterdon, Middlesex and Somerset Counties
See also New York-Northern New Jersey-Long Island, NY-NJ-PA MSA

El Paso, TX MSA
El Paso County

Eugene-Springfield, OR MSA
Lane County

Evansville, IN-KY MSA
Gibson, Posey, Vanderburgh and Warrick Counties, IN; Henderson and Webster Counties, KY

Fargo-Moorhead, ND-MN MSA
Cass County, ND; Clay County, MN

Fort Collins-Loveland, CO MSA
Larimer County

Fort Lauderdale, FL
Fort Lauderdale-Pompano Beach-Deerfield Beach, FL MD
Broward County
See also Miami-Fort Lauderdale-Miami Beach, FL MSA

Fort Wayne, IN MSA
Allen, Wells, and Whitley Counties

Fort Worth, TX
Fort Worth-Arlington, TX MD
Johnson, Parker, Tarrant, and Wise Counties
See also Dallas-Fort Worth-Arlington, TX MSA

Gainesville, FL
Alachua and Gilchrist Counties

Greensboro-High Point, NC MSA
Guilford, Randolph, and Rockingham Counties

Honolulu, HI MSA
Honolulu County

Houston-Baytown-Sugar Land, TX MSA
Austin, Brazoria, Chambers, Fort Bend, Galveston, Harris, Liberty, Montgomery, San Jacinto, and Waller Counties

Huntsville, AL MSA
Limestone and Madison Counties

Indianapolis, IN MSA
Boone, Brown, Hamilton, Hancock, Hendricks, Johnson, Marion, Morgan, Putnam, and Shelby Counties

Irvine, CA
See Los Angeles, CA

Jackson, MS MSA
Copiah, Hinds, Madison, Rankin and Simpson Counties, MS

Jacksonville, FL MSA
Baker, Clay, Duval, Nassau, and St. Johns Counties

Kansas City, MO-KS MSA
Franklin, Johnson, Leavenworth, Linn, Miami, and Wyandotte Counties, KS; Bates, Caldwell, Cass, Clay, Clinton, Jackson, Lafayette, Platte, and Ray Counties, MO

Knoxville, TN MSA
Anderson, Blount, Knox, Loudon, and Union Counties

Las Vegas-Paradise, NV MSA
Clark County

Lexington-Fayette, KY MSA
Bourbon, Clark, Fayette, Jessamine, Scott, and Woodford Counties

Lincoln, NE MSA
Lancaster and Seward Counties

Little Rock-North Little Rock-Conway, AR MSA
Faulkner, Grant, Lonoke, Perry, Pulaski and Saline Counties, AR

Los Angeles, CA
Los Angeles-Long Beach-Santa Ana, CA MSA
Los Angeles and Orange Counties
Los Angeles-Long Beach-Glendale, CA MD
Los Angeles County
Santa Ana-Anaheim-Irvine, CA MD
Orange County

Louisville, KY-IN MSA
Clark, Floyd, Harrison, and Washington Counties, IN; Bullitt, Henry, Jefferson, Meade, Nelson, Oldham, Shelby, Spencer, and Trimble Counties, KY

Madison, WI MSA
Columbia, Dane, and Iowa Counties

Manchester-Nashua, NH MSA
Hillsborough County
Manchester, NH NECTA
Includes 9 cities and towns in New Hampshire

Miami, FL
Miami-Fort Lauderdale-Miami Beach, FL MSA
Broward, Miami-Dade, and Palm Beach Counties
Miami-Miami Beach-Kendall, FL MD
Miami-Dade County

Milwaukee-Waukesha-West Allis, WI MSA
Milwaukee, Ozaukee, Washington, and Waukesha Counties

Minneapolis-St. Paul-Bloomington, MN-WI MSA
Anoka, Carver, Chisago, Dakota, Hennepin, Isanti, Ramsey, Scott, Sherburne, Washington, and Wright Counties, MN; Pierce and St. Croix Counties, WI

Naperville, IL
See Chicago, IL

Nashville-Davidson— Murfreesboro, TN MSA
Cannon, Cheatham, Davidson, Dickson, Hickman, Macon, Robertson, Rutherford, Smith, Sumner, Trousdale, Williamson, and Wilson Counties

New Orleans, LA
Jefferson, Orleans, Plaquemines, St. Bernard, St. Charles, St. John the Baptist, and St. Tammany Parish

New York, NY
New York-Northern New Jersey-Long Island, NY-NJ-PA MSA
Bergen, Essex, Hudson, Hunterdon, Middlesex, Monmouth, Morris, Ocean, Passaic, Somerset, Sussex, and Union Counties, NJ; Bronx, Kings, Nassau, New York, Putnam, Queens, Richmond, Rockland, Suffolk, and Westchester Counties, NY; Pike County, PA
New York-Wayne-White Plains, NY-NJ MD
Bergen, Hudson, and Passaic Counties, NJ; Bronx, Kings, New York, Putnam, Queens, Richmond, Rockland, and Westchester Counties, NY

Oakland, CA
Oakland-Fremont-Hayward, CA MD
Alameda and Contra Costa Counties
See also San Francisco-Oakland-Fremont, CA MSA

Oklahoma City, OK MSA
Canadian, Cleveland, Grady, Lincoln, Logan, McClain, and Oklahoma Counties

Omaha-Council Bluffs, NE-IA MSA
Harrison, Mills, and Pottawattamie Counties, IA; Cass, Douglas, Sarpy, Saunders, and Washington Counties, NE

Orlando, FL MSA
Lake, Orange, Osceola, and Seminole Counties

Overland Park, KS
See Kansas City, MO-KS MSA

Oxnard-Thousand Oaks-Ventura, CA MSA
Ventura County

Philadelphia, PA
Philadelphia-Camden-Wilmington, PA-NJ-DE-MD MSA
New Castle County, DE; Cecil County, MD; Burlington, Camden, Gloucester, and Salem Counties, NJ; Bucks, Chester, Delaware, Montgomery, and Philadelphia Counties, PA
Philadelphia, PA MD
Bucks, Chester, Delaware, Montgomery, and Philadelphia Counties

Phoenix-Mesa-Scottsdale, AZ MSA
Maricopa and Pinal Counties

Pittsburgh, PA MSA
Allegheny, Armstrong, Beaver, Butler, Fayette, Washington, and Westmoreland Counties

Plano, TX
See Dallas, TX

Portland-Vancouver-Beaverton, OR-WA MSA

Clackamas, Columbia, Multnomah, Washington, and Yamhill Counties, OR; Clark and Skamania Counties, WA

Providence-New Bedford-Fall River, RI-MA MSA

Bristol County, MA; Bristol, Kent, Newport, Providence, and Washington Counties, RI

Providence-Fall River-Warwick, RI-MA NECTA

Includes 12 cities and towns in Massachusetts and 37 cities and towns in Rhode Island

Provo-Orem, UT MSA

Juab and Utah Counties

Raleigh-Cary, NC MSA

Franklin, Johnston, and Wake Counties

Reno-Sparks, NV MSA

Storey and Washoe Counties

Richmond, VA MSA

Petersburg, Colonial Heights, Hopewell, and Richmond cities; Amelia, Caroline, Charles City, Chesterfield, Cumberland, Dinwiddie, Goochland, Hanover, Henrico, King William, King and Queen, Louisa, New Kent, Powhatan, Prince George, and Sussex Counties

Riverside-San Bernardino-Ontario, CA MSA

Riverside and San Bernardino Counties

Rochester, NY MSA

Livingston, Monroe, Ontario, Orleans, and Wayne Counties

Sacramento—Arden-Arcade—Roseville, CA MSA

El Dorado, Placer, Sacramento, and Yolo Counties

Saint Louis, MO-IL MSA

Bond, Calhoun, Clinton, Jersey, Macoupin, Madison, Monroe, and St. Clair Counties, IL; St. Louis city; Crawford (part), Franklin, Jefferson, Lincoln, St. Charles, St. Louis, Warren, and Washington Counties, MO

Saint Paul, MN

See Minneapolis-St. Paul-Bloomington, MN-WI MSA

Saint Petersburg, FL

See Tampa-St. Petersburg-Clearwater, FL MSA

Salt Lake City, UT MSA

Salt Lake, Summit, and Tooele Counties

San Antonio, TX MSA

Atascosa, Bandera, Bexar, Comal, Guadalupe, Kendall, Medina, and Wilson Counties

San Diego-Carlsbad-San Marcos, CA MSA

San Diego County

San Francisco, CA

San Francisco-Oakland-Fremont, CA MSA

Alameda, Contra Costa, Marin, San Francisco, and San Mateo Counties

San Francisco-San Mateo-Redwood City, CA MD

Marin, San Francisco, and San Mateo Counties

San Jose-Sunnyvale-Santa Clara, CA MSA

San Benito and Santa Clara Counties

Santa Ana, CA

Santa Ana-Anaheim-Irvine, CA MD

Orange County

See also Los Angeles-Long Beach-Santa Ana, CA MSA

Savannah, GA MSA

Bryan, Chatham, and Effingham Counties

Seattle, WA

Seattle-Tacoma-Bellevue, WA MSA

King, Pierce, and Snohomish Counties

Seattle-Bellevue-Everett, WA MD

King and Snohomish Counties

Spokane, WA MSA

Spokane County

Springfield, MO MSA

Christian, Dallas, Greene, Polk, and Webster Counties

Tampa-St. Petersburg-Clearwater, FL MSA

Hernando, Hillsborough, Pasco, and Pinellas Counties

Tulsa, OK MSA

Creek, Okmulgee, Osage, Pawnee, Rogers, Tulsa, and Wagoner Counties

Virginia Beach-Norfolk-Newport News, VA-NC MSA

Currituck County, NC; Chesapeake, Hampton, Newport News, Norfolk, Poquoson, Portsmouth, Suffolk, Virginia Beach and Williamsburg cities, VA; Gloucester, Isle of Wight, James City, Mathews, Surry, and York Counties, VA

Warren, MI

See Detroit, MI

Washington, DC

Washington-Arlington-Alexandria, DC-VA-MD-WV MSA

District of Columbia; Calvert, Charles, Frederick, Montgomery, and Prince George's Counties, MD; Alexandria, Fairfax, Falls Church, Fredericksburg, Manassas Park, and Manassas cities, VA; Arlington, Clarke, Fairfax, Fauquier, Loudoun, Prince William, Spotsylvania, Stafford, and Warren Counties, VA; Jefferson County, WV

Washington-Arlington-Alexandria, DC-VA-MD-WV MD

District of Columbia; Calvert, Charles, and Prince George's Counties, MD; Alexandria, Fairfax, Falls Church, Fredericksburg, Manassas Park, and Manassas cities, VA; Arlington, Clarke, Fairfax, Fauquier, Loudoun, Prince William, Spotsylvania, Stafford, and Warren Counties, VA; Jefferson County, WV

Wichita, KS MSA

Butler, Harvey, Sedgwick, and Sumner Counties

Appendix C: Chambers of Commerce & Economic Development Departments

Albuquerque, NM

Albuquerque Chamber of Commerce
P.O. Box 25100
Albuquerque, NM 87125
Phone: (505) 764-3700
Fax: (505) 764-3714
www.abqchamber.com

Albuquerque Economic Development Dept
851 University Blvd SE
Suite 203
Albuquerque, NM 87106
Phone: (505) 246-6200
Fax: (505) 246-6219
www.cabq.gov/econdev

Anchorage, AK

Anchorage Chamber of Commerce
1016 W Sixth Avenue
Suite 303
Anchorage, AK 99501
Phone: (907) 272-2401
Fax: (907) 272-4117
www.anchoragechamber.org

Anchorage Economic Development Dept
900 W 5th Avenue
Suite 300
Anchorage, AK 99501
Phone: (907) 258-3700
Fax: (907) 258-6646
www.aedcweb.com/aedcdig

Ann Arbor, MI

Ann Arbor Area Chamber of Commerce
115 West Huron
3rd Floor
Ann Arbor, MI 48104
Phone: (734) 665-4433
Fax: (734) 665-4191
www.annarborchamber.org

Ann Arbor Economic Development
201 S Division
Suite 430
Ann Arbor, MI 48104
Phone: (734) 761-9317
www.annarborspark.org

Athens, GA

Athens Area Chamber of Commerce
246 W Hancock Avenue
Athens, GA 30601
Phone: (706) 549-6800
Fax: (706) 549-5636
www.aacoc.org

Athens-Clarke Economic Development
150 E. Hancock Avenue
P.O. Box 1692
Athens, GA 30603
Phone: (706) 613-3810
Fax: (706) 613-3812
www.athensbusiness.org/contact.aspx

Atlanta, GA

Metro Atlanta Chamber of Commerce
235 Andrew Young International Blvd NW
Atlanta, GA 30303
Phone: (404) 880-9000
Fax: (404) 586-8464
www.metroatlantachamber.com/contact_us.html

Austin, TX

Greater Austin Chamber of Commerce
210 Barton Springs Road
Suite 400
Austin, TX 78704
Phone: (512) 478-9383
Fax: (512) 478-6389
www.austin-chamber.org

Baltimore, MD

Baltimore City Chamber of Commerce
312 Martin Luther King Jr Blvd
Baltimore, MD 21201
Phone: (410) 837-7101
Fax: (410) 837-7104
www.baltimorecitychamber.com

City of Baltimore Development Corporation
36 South Charles Street
Suite 1600
Baltimore, MD 21201
Phone: (410) 837-9305
Fax: (410) 837-6363
www.baltimoredevelopment.com

Bellevue, WA

Bellevue Chamber of Commerce
302 Bellevue Square
Bellevue, WA 98004
Phone: (425) 454-2464
www.bellevuechamber.org

Birmingham, AL

Birmingham Area Chamber of Commerce
505 North 20th Street
Suite 200
Birmingham, AL 35203
Phone: (205) 324-2100
Fax: (205) 324-2314
www.birminghamchamber.com

Birmingham Office of Economic Development
710 North 20th Street
Birmingham, AL 35203
Phone: (205) 254-2799
Fax: (205) 254-7741
www.informationbirmingham.com

Boise City, ID

Boise Metro Chamber of Commerce
250 S 5th Street
Suite 800
Boise City, ID 83701
Phone: (208) 472-5200
Fax: (208) 472-5201
www.bisechamber.org

Boise Metro Office of Economic Development
150 N Capitol Blvd.
Boise, ID 83702
Phone: (208) 384-3843
Fax: (208) 384-3753
www.cityofboise.org

Boston, MA

Greater Boston Chamber of Commerce
265 Franklin Street
12th Floor
Boston, MA 02110
Phone: (617) 227-4500
Fax: (617) 227-7505
www.bostonchamber.com

Boulder, CO

Boulder Chamber of Commerce
2440 Pearl Street
Boulder, CO 80302
Phone: (303) 442-1044
Fax: (303) 938-8837
www.boulderchamber.com

City of Boulder Economic Vitality Program
P.O. Box 791
Boulder, CO 80306
Phone: (303) 441-3090
www.bouldercolorado.gov

Cary, NC

Cary Chamber of Commerce
307 North Academy Street
Cary, NC 27513-4539
Tol-Free: (800) 919-CARY
Phone: (919) 467-1016
Fax: (919) 469-2375
www.carychamber.com

Cambridge, MA

Cambridge Chamber of Commerce
859 Massachusetts Avenue
Cambridge, MA 02139
Phone: (617) 876-4100
Fax: (617) 354-9874
www.cambridgechamber.org

Charleston, SC

Central Midlands Council of Government
Research Data Center
236 Stoneridge Drive
Columbia, SC 29210
Phone: (803) 376-5390
Fax: (803) 376-5394
www.centralmidlands.org

Charlotte, NC

Charlotte Chamber of Commerce
330 S Tryon Street
P.O. Box 32785
Charlotte, NC 28232
Phone: (704) 378-1300
Fax: (704) 374-1903
www.charlottechamber.com

Charlotte Regional Partnership
1001 Morehead Square Drive
Suite 200
Charlotte, NC 28203
Phone: (704) 347-8942
Fax: (704) 347-8981
www.charlotteusa.com

Chattanooga, TN

Chattanooga Chamber of Commerce
811 Broad Street #100
Chattanooga, TN 37402
Phone: (423) 756-2121
Fax: (423) 267-7242
www.chattanooga-chamber.com

Chicago, IL

Chicagoland Chamber of Commerce
200 E Randolph Street
Suite 2200
Chicago, IL 60601-6436
Phone: (312) 494-6700
Fax: (312) 861-0660
www.chicagolandchamber.org

City of Chicago Department of Planning and
Development
City Hall, Room 1000
121 North La Salle Street
Chicago, IL 60602
Phone: (312) 744-4190
Fax: (312) 744-2271
egov.cityofchicago.org

Cincinnati, OH

Greater Cincinnati Chamber of Commerce
441 Vine Street
Suite 300
Cincinnati, OH 45202
Phone: (513) 579-3100
Fax: (513) 579-3101
www.cincinnatichamber.com

Cleveland, OH

Cleveland Department of Economic
Development
601 Lakeside Avenue
Room 210
Cleveland, OH 44114
Phone: (216) 664-2406
Fax: (216) 664-3681
www.city.cleveland.oh.us

Greater Cleveland Growth Association
50 Public Square
Suite 200
Cleveland, OH 44113
Phone: (216) 621-3300
Fax: (216) 621-6013
www.gcpartnership.com

Colorado Springs, CO

Greater Colorado Springs Chamber of
Commerce
6 S. Tejon Street
Suite 700
Colorado Springs, CO 80903
Phone: (719) 635-1551
Fax: (719) 635-1571
gcsco.wliinc3.com

Greater Colorado Springs Economic
Development Corp
90 South Cascade Avenue
Suite 1050
Colorado Springs, CO 80903
Phone: (719) 471-8183
Fax: (719) 471-9733
www.coloradosprings.org

Columbia, SC

Columbia Office of Economic Development
1201 Main Street
Suite 250
Columbia, SC 29201
Phone: (803) 734-2700
Fax: (803) 734-2702
www.columbiascdevelopment.com

Columbia Chamber of Commerce
930 Richmond Street
Columbia, SC 20201
Phone: (803) 733-1110
Fax: (803) 733-1149
www.columbiachamber.com

Columbus, OH

Greater Columbus Chamber
37 North High Street
Columbus, OH 43215
Phone: (614) 221-1321
Fax: (614) 221-1408
www.columbus.org

Dallas, TX

City of Dallas Economic Development
Department
1500 Marilla Street
5C South
Dallas, TX 75201
Phone: (214) 670-1685
Fax: (214) 670-0158
www.dallas-edd.org

City of Kyle Economic Development Dept
100 N Front Street
P.O. Box 900
Kyle, TX 78640
Phone: (512) 268-4220
Fax: (800) 903-1564
www.kylechamber.org

Greater Dallas Chamber of Commerce
700 North Pearl Street
Suite1200
Dallas, TX 75201
Phone: (214) 746-6600
Fax: (214) 746-6799
www.dallaschamber.org

Denver, CO

Denver Metro Chamber of Commerce
1445 Market Street
Denver, CO 80202
Phone: (303) 534-8500
Fax: (303) 534-3200
www.denverchamber.org

Downtown Denver Partnership
511 16th Street
Suite 200
Denver, CO 80202
Phone: (303) 534-6161
Fax: (303) 534-2803
www.downtowndenver.com

Des Moines, IA

Greater Des Moines Partnership
700 Locust Street
Suite 100
Des Moines, IA 50309
Phone: (515) 286-4950
Fax: (515) 286-4974
www.desmoinesmetro.com

Durham, NC

Durham Chamber of Commerce
PO Box 3829
Durham, NC 27702
Phone: (919) 682-2133
Fax: (919) 688-8351
www.durhamchamber.org

North Carolina Institute of Minority Economic
Development
114 W Parish Street
Durham, NC 27701
Phone: (919) 956-8889
Fax: (919) 688-7668
www.ncimed.com

Edison, NJ

Edison Chamber of Commerce
336 Raritan Center Parkway
Campus Plaza 6
Edison, NJ 08837
Phone: (732) 738-9482
Fax: (732) 738-9485
www.edisonchamber.com

New Jersey Economic Development Authority
36 West State Street
Trenton, NJ 08625
Phone: (609) 292-1800
www.njeda.com

El Paso, TX

City of El Paso Department of Economic
Development
2 Civic Center Plaza
El Paso, TX 79901
Phone: (915) 541-4000
Fax: (915) 541-1316
www.elpasotexas.gov

Greater El Paso Chamber of Commerce
10 Civic Center Plaza
El Paso, TX 79901
Phone: (915) 534-0500
Fax: (915) 534-0510
www.elpaso.org

Eugene, OR

Eugene Area Chamber of Commerce
1401 Williamette Street
Eugene, OR 97401
Phone: (541) 484-1314
Fax: (541) 484-4942
www.eugenechamber.com

Evansville, IN

Metropolitan Development
Civic Center Complex
Room 306
Evansvile, IN 47706
Phone: (812) 436-7823
Fax: (812) 436-7809
www.evansvillegov.org

Metropolitan Evansville Chamber of
Commerce
100 NW 2nd Street
Suite 100
Evansville, IN 47706-2101
Phone: (812) 425-8147
Fax: (812) 421-5883
evansvillechamber.com

Fargo, ND

Chamber of Commerce of Fargo Moorhead
202 First Avenue North
Fargo, ND 56560
Phone: (218) 233-1100
Fax: (218) 233-1200
www.fmchamber.com

Greater Fargo-Moorhead Economic
Development Corporation
51 Broadway, Suite 500
Fargo, ND 58102
Phone: (701) 364-1900
Fax: (701) 293-7819
www.gfmedc.com

Fort Collins, CO

Fort Collins Chamber of Commerce
225 South Meldrum
Fort Collins, CO 80521
Phone: (970) 482-3746
Fax: (970) 482-3774
www.fcchamber.org

Fort Lauderdale, FL

Fort Lauderdale Chamber of Commerce
512 NE 3rd Avenue
Fort Lauderdale, FL 33301
Phone: (954) 462-6000
Fax: (954) 527-8766
ftlchamber.com

Fort Wayne, IN

City of Fort Wayne Economic Development
1 Main St
1 Main Street
Fort Wayne, IN 46802
Phone: (260) 427-1111
Fax: (260) 427-1375
www.cityoffortwayne.org

Greater Fort Wayne Chamber of Commerce
826 Ewing Street
Fort Wayne, IN 46802
Phone: (260) 424-1435
Fax: (260) 426-7232
www.fwchamber.org

Fort Worth, TX

City of Fort Worth Economic Development
City Hall
900 Monroe Street, Suite 301
Fort Worth, TX 76102
Phone: (817) 392-6103
Fax: (817) 392-2431
www.fortworthgov.org

Fort Worth Chamber of Commerce
777 Taylor Street
Suite 900
Fort Worth, TX 76102-4997
Phone: (817) 336-2491
Fax: (817) 877-4034
www.fortworthchamber.com

Gainesville, FL

Gainesville Area Chamber of Commerce
300 East University Avenue, Suite 100
Gainesville, FL 32601
Phone: (352) 334-7100
Fax: (352) 334-7141
www.gainesvillechamber.com

Greensboro, NC

Greensboro Area Chamber of Commerce
342 N Elm St.
Greensboro, NC 27401
Phone: (336) 387-8301
Fax: (336) 275-9299
www.greensboro.org

Honolulu, HI

The Chamber of Commerce of Hawaii
1132 Bishop Street
Suite 402
Honolulu, HI 96813
Phone: (808) 545-4300
Fax: (808) 545-4369
www.cochawaii.com

Houston, TX

Greater Houston Partnership
1200 Smith Street
Suite 700
Houston, TX 77002-4400
Phone: (713) 844-3600
Fax: (713) 844-0200
www.houston.org

Huntsville, AL

Chamber of Commerce of Huntsville/Madison
County
225 Church Street
Huntsville, AL 35801
Phone: (256) 535-2000
Fax: (256) 535-2015
www.huntsvillealabamausa.com

Indianapolis, IN

Greater Indianapolis Chamber of Commerce
111 Monument Circle
Suite 1950
Indianapolis, IN 46204
Phone: (317) 464-2222
Fax: (317) 464-2217
www.indychamber.com

The Indy Partnership
111 Monument Circle
Suite 1800
Indianapolis, IN 46204
Phone: (317) 236-6262
Fax: (317) 236-6275
www.indypartnership.com

Irvine, CA

Irvine Chamber
2485 McCabe Way, Suite 150
Irvine, CA 92614
Phone: (949) 660-9112
Fax: (949) 660-0829
www.irvinechamber.com

Jackson, MS

MetroJackson Chamber of Commerce
PO Box 22548
Jackson, MS 39225
Phone: (601) 948-7575
Fax: (601) 352-5539
www.metrochamber.com

Jacksonville, FL

Jacksonville Chamber of Commerce
3 Independent Drive
Jacksonville, FL 32202
Phone: (904) 366-6600
Fax: (904) 632-0617
www.myjaxchamber.com

Kansas City, MO

Greater Kansas City Chamber of Commerce
2600 Commerce Tower
911 Main Street
Kansas City, MO 64105
Phone: (816) 221-2424
Fax: (816) 221-7440
www.kcchamber.com

Kansas City Area Development Council
2600 Commerce Tower
911 Main Street
Kansas City, MO 64105
Phone: (816) 221-2121
Fax: (816) 842-2865
www.thinkkc.com

Knoxville, TN

Knoxville Area Chamber Partnership
17 Market Square
Suite 201
Knoxville, TN 37902-2021
Phone: (865) 637-4550
Fax: (865) 523-2071
www.knoxvillechamber.com

Las Vegas, NV

Las Vegas Chamber of Commerce
6671 Las Vegas Blvd South
Suite 300
Las Vegas, NV 89119
Phone: (702) 735-1616
Fax: (702) 735-0406
www.lvchamber.org

Las Vegas Office of Business Development
400 Stewart Avenue
City Hall
Las Vegas, NV 89101
Phone: (702) 229-6011
Fax: (702) 385-3128
www.lasvegasnevada.gov

Lexington, KY

Greater Lexington Chamber of Commerce
330 East Main Street
Suite 100
Lexington, KY 40507
Phone: (859) 254-4447
Fax: (859) 233-3304
www.commercelexington.com

Lexington Downtown Development Authority
101 East Vine Street
Suite 500
Lexington, KY 40507
Phone: (859) 425-2296
Fax: (859) 425-2292
www.lexingtondda.com

Lincoln, NE

Lincoln Chamber of Commerce
1135 M Street
Suite 200
Lincoln, NE 68508
Phone: (402) 436-2350
Fax: (402) 436-2360
www.lcoc.com

Little Rock, AR

Little Rock Regional Chamber of Commerce
One Chamber Plaza
Little Rock, AR 72201-1618
Phone: (501) 374-2001
www.littlerockchamber.com

Los Angeles, CA

Los Angeles Area Chamber of Commerce
350 South Bixel Street
Los Angeles, CA 90017
Phone: (213) 580-7500
Fax: (213) 580-7511
www.lachamber.org

Los Angeles County Economic Development
Corporation
444 South Flower Street
34th Floor
Los Angeles, CA 90071
Phone: (213) 622-4300
Fax: (213) 622-7100
www.laedc.org

Louisville, KY

The Greater Louisville Chamber of Commerce
614 West Main Street
Suite 6000
Louisville, KY 40202
Phone: (502) 625-0000
Fax: (502) 625-0010
www.greaterlouisville.com

Madison, WI

Greater Madison Chamber of Commerce
615 East Washington Avenue
P.O. Box 71
Madison, WI 53701-0071
Phone: (608) 256-8348
Fax: (608) 256-0333
www.greatermadisonchamber.com

Manchester, NH

Greater Manchester Chamber of Commerce
889 Elm Street
Manchester, NH 03101
Phone: (603) 666-6600
Fax: (603) 626-0910
www.manchester-chamber.org

Manchester Economic Development Office
One City Hall Plaza
Manchester, NH 03101
Phone: (603) 624-6505
Fax: (603) 624-6308
www.yourmanchesternh.com

Miami, FL

Greater Miami Chamber of Commerce
1601 Biscayne Boulevard
Ballroom Level
Miami, FL 33132-1260
Phone: (305) 350-7700
Fax: (305) 374-6902
www.greatermiami.com

The Beacon Council
80 Southwest 8th Street
Suite 2400
Miami, FL 33130
Phone: (305) 579-1300
Fax: (305) 375-0271
www.beaconcouncil.com

Milwaukee, WI

City of Milwaukee Economic Development
Department
809 North Broadway
2nd Floor
Milwaukee, WI 53202
Phone: (414) 286-5840
Fax: (414) 286-5778
www.medconline.com

Metropolitan Milwaukee Association of
Commerce
756 North Milwaukee Street
Suite 400
Milwaukee, WI 53202
Phone: (414) 287-4100
Fax: (414) 271-7753
www.mmac.org

Minneapolis, MN

Bloomington Chamber of Commerce
9633 Lyndale Avenue
Suite 200
Bloomington, MN 55420
Phone: (952) 888-8818
Fax: (952) 888-0508
www.minneapolischamber.org

Minneapolis Community Development
Agency
Crown Roller Mill
105 5th Avenue South, Suite 200
Minneapolis, MN 55401
Phone: (612) 673-5095
Fax: (612) 673-5100
www.ci.minneapolis.mn.us

Naperville, IL

Naperville Area Chamber of Commerce
Main Street Promenade
55 S. Main St., Suite 351
Naperville, IL, 60540
Phone: (630) 355-4141
www.naperville.net

Nashville, TN

Community Development Department
312 Eighth Avenue North
Eleventh Floor
Nashville, TN 37243
Phone: (615) 741-2626
Fax: (615) 532-8715
www.state.tn.us

Nashville Area Chamber of Commerce
211 Commerce Street
Suite 100
Nashville, TN 37201
Phone: (615) 743-3000
Fax: (615) 256-3074
www.nashvillechamber.cm

Tennessee Valley Authority Economic
Development Corp.
P.O. Box 292409
Nashville, TN 37229-2409
Phone: (615) 232-6225
www.tvaed.com

New Orleans, LA

New Orleans Chamber of Commerce
1515 Poydras St., Suite 1010
New Orleans, LA 70112
Phone: (504) 799-4260
Fax: (504) 799-4259
www.neworleanschamber.org

New York, NY

New York City Economic Development
Corporation
110 William Street
New York, NY 10038
Phone: (212) 619-5000
www.nycedc.com

The Partnership for New York City
One Battery Park Plaza
5th Floor
New York, NY 10004
Phone: (212) 493-7400
Fax: (212) 344-3344
www.pfnyc.org

Oakland, CA

Oakland Metropolitan Chamber of Commerce
475 14th Street
Oakland, CA 94612
Phone: (510) 874-4800
Fax: (510) 839-8817
www.oaklandchamber.com

Oklahoma City, OK

Greater Oklahoma City Chamber of
Commerce
123 Park Avenue
Oklahoma City, OK 73102
Phone: (405) 297-8900
Fax: (405) 297-8916
www.okcchamber.com

Omaha, NE

Omaha Chamber of Commerce
1301 Harney Street
Omaha, NE 68102
Phone: (402) 346-5000
Fax: (402) 346-7050
www.omahachamber.org

Orlando, FL

Metro Orlando Economic Development
Commission of Mid-Florida
301 East Pine Street
Suite 900
Orlando, FL 32801
Phone: (407) 422-7159
Fax: (407) 425.6428
www.orlandoedc.com

Orlando Regional Chamber of Commerce
75 South Ivanhoe Boulevard
PO Box 1234
Orlando, FL 32802
Phone: (407) 425-1234
Fax: (407) 839-5020
www.orlando.org

Overland Park, KS

Overland Park Chamber of Commerce
9001 W. 110th Street, Suite 150
Overland Park, KS 66210
Phone: (913) 491-3600
www.opks.org

Oxnard, CA

Oxnard Chamber of Commerce
400 E Esplanade Drive
Suite 302
Oxnard, CA 93036
Phone: (805) 983-6118
Fax: (805) 604-7331
www.oxnardchamber.org

Philadelphia, PA

Greater Philadelphia Chamber of Commerce
200 South Broad Street
Suite 700
Philadelphia, PA 19102
Phone: (215) 545-1234
Fax: (215) 790-3600
www.greaterphilachamber.com

Phoenix, AZ

Greater Phoenix Chamber of Commerce
201 North Central Avenue
27th Floor
Phoenix, AZ 85073
Phone: (602) 495-2195
Fax: (602) 495-8913
www.phoenixchamber.com

Greater Phoenix Economic Council
2 North Central Avenue
Suite 2500
Phoenix, AZ 85004
Phone: (602) 256-7700
Fax: (602) 256-7744
www.gpec.org

Pittsburgh, PA

Allegheny County Industrial Development
Authority
425 6th Avenue
Suite 800
Pittsburgh, PA 15219
Phone: (412) 350-1067
Fax: (412) 642-2217
www.alleghenycounty.us

Greater Pittsburgh Chamber of Commerce
425 6th Avenue, 12th Floor
Pittsburgh, PA 15219
Phone: (412) 392-4500
Fax: (412) 392-4520
www.alleghenyconference.org

Plano, TX

Plano Chamber of Commerce
1200 E 15th St
Plano, TX 75074
Phone: (972) 424-7547
Fax: (972) 422-5182
www.planochamber.org

Portland, OR

Portland Business Alliance
200 SW Market Street
Suite 1770
Portland, OR 97201
Phone: (503) 224-8684
Fax: (503) 323-9186
www.portlandalliance.com

Providence, RI

Greater Providence Chamber of Commerce
30 Exchange Terrace
Fourth Floor
Providence, RI 02903
Phone: (401) 521-5000
Fax: (401) 351-2090
www.provchamber.com

Rhode Island Economic Development
Corporation
Providence City Hall
25 Dorrance Street
Providence, RI 02903
Phone: (401) 421-7740
Fax: (401) 751-0203
www.providenceri.com

Provo, UT

Provo-Orem Chamber of Commerce
51 South University Avenue
Suite 215
Provo, UT 84601
Phone: (801) 851-2555
Fax: (801) 851-2557
www.thechamber.org/

Raleigh, NC

Greater Raleigh Chamber of Commerce
800 South Salisbury Street
Raleigh, NC 27601-2978
Phone: (919) 664-7000
Fax: (919) 664-7099
www.raleighchamber.org

Reno, NV

Greater Reno-Sparks Chamber of Commerce
1 East First Street
16th Floor
Reno, NV 89505
Phone: (775) 337-3030
Fax: (775) 337-3038
www.reno-sparkschamber.org

Richmond, VA

Greater Richmond Chamber of Commerce
P.O. Box 12280
Richmond, VA 23241-2280
Phone: (804) 648-1234
Fax: (804) 783-9366
www.grcc.com/

Greater Richmond Partnership
901 East Byrd Street
Suite 801
Richmond, VA 23219-4070
Phone: (804) 643-3227
Fax: (804) 343-7167
www.grpva.com/New_pages/home_ted.shtm

Riverside, CA

Greater Riveside Chamber of Commerce
3985 University Ave.
Riverside, CA 92501
Phone: (951) 683-7100
Fax: (951) 683-2670
www.riverside-chamber.com

Rochester, NY

Rochester Business Alliance
150 State Street
Rochester, NY 14614
Phone: (585) 244.1800
Fax: (585) 263-3679
www.rochesterbusinessalliance.com

Rochester Economic Development Department
30 Church Street
Room 005A
Rochester, NY 14614
Phone: (585) 428-6808
Fax: (585) 428-6042
www.cityofrochester.gov

Sacramento, CA

Sacramento Chamber of Commerce
917 7th Street
Sacramento, CA 95814
Phone: (916) 552-6808
Fax: (916) 443-2672
www.metrochamber.org/CWT/Index.aspx

Saint Louis, MO

St. Louis Regional Chamber & Growth Assn
One Metropolitan Square
Suite 1300
Saint Louis, MO 63102
Phone: (314) 231-5555
Fax: (314) 206-3222
www.gotostlouis.org

Saint Paul, MN

Department of Trade and Economic
Development
500 Metro Square
121 7th Place East
Saint Paul, MN 55101
Phone: (651) 297-1291
Fax: (651) 284-0088
www.deed.state.mn.us

Saint Paul Area Chamber of Commerce
401 North Robert Street
Suite 150
Saint Paul, MN 55101
Phone: (651) 223-5000
Fax: (651) 223-5119
www.saintpaulchamber.com

Saint Petersburg, FL

Saint Petersburg Area Chamber of Commerce
100 2nd Avenue North
Suite 150
Saint Petersburg, FL 33701
Phone: (727) 821-4069
Fax: (727) 895-6326
www.pleasure.stpete.com

Salt Lake City, UT

Department of Economic Development
451 South State Street
Room 345
Salt Lake City, UT 84111
Phone: (801) 535-6306
Fax: (801) 535-6331
www.slcgov.com/mayor/ED

Salt Lake Area Chamber of Commerce
175 East 400 South
Suite 600
Salt Lake City, UT 84111
Phone: (801) 364-3631
Fax: (801) 328-5098
www.saltlakechamber.org

San Antonio, TX

San Antonio Economic Development
Department
P.O. Box 839966
San Antonio, TX 78283-3966
Phone: (210) 207-8080
Fax: (210) 207-8151
www.sanantonio.gov/edd

The Greater San Antonio Chamber of
Commerce
602 E. Commerce Street
San Antonio, TX 78205
Phone: (210) 229-2100
Fax: (210) 229-1600
www.sachamber.org

San Diego, CA

San Diego Economic Development
Corporation
401 B Street
Suite 1100
San Diego, CA 92101
Phone: (619) 234-8484
Fax: (619) 234-1935
www.sandiegobusiness.org

San Diego Regional Chamber of Commerce
402 West Broadway
Suite 1000
San Diego, CA 92101-3585
Phone: (619) 544-1300
Fax: (619) 744-7481
www.sdchamber.org

San Francisco, CA

San Francisco Chamber of Commerce
235 Montgomery Street
12th Floor
San Francisco, CA 94104
Phone: (415) 392-4520
Fax: (415) 392-0485
www.sfchamber.com

San Jose, CA

Office of Economic Development
60 South Market Street
Suite 470
San Jose, CA 95113
Phone: (408) 277-5880
Fax: (408) 277-3615
www.sba.gov

San Jose-Silicone Valley Chamber of
Commerce
310 South First Street
San Jose, CA 95113
Phone: (408) 291-5250
Fax: (408) 286-5019
www.sjchamber.com

Santa Ana, CA

Santa Ana Chamber of Commerce
2020 N Broadway
2nd Floor
Santa Ana, CA 92706
Phone: (714) 541-5353
Fax: (714) 541-2238
www.santaanachamber.com

Savannah, GA

Economic Development Authority
131 Hutchinson Island Road
4th Floor
Savannah, GA 31421
Phone: (912) 447-8450
Fax: (912) 447-8455
www.Seda.org

Savannah Chamber of Commerce
101 E. Bay Street
Savannah, GA 31402
Phone: (912) 644-6400
Fax: (912) 644-6499
www.savannahchamber.com

Seattle, WA

Greater Seattle Chamber of Commerce
1301 Fifth Avenue
Suite 2500
Seattle, WA 98101
Phone: (206) 389-7200
Fax: (206) 389-7288
www.seattlechamber.com

Spokane, WA

Greater Spokane
801 W Riverside
Suite 100
Spokane, WA 99201
Phone: (509) 624-1393
Fax: (509) 747-0077
www.spokanechamber.org

Springfield, MO

City of Springfield
Department of Planning & Development
840 Booneville
Springfield, MO 65802
Phone: (417) 864-1000
Fax: (417) 864-1882
www.springfieldmo.gov/home

Springfield Area Chamber of Commerce
P.O. Box 1687
Springfield, MO 65801-1687
Phone: (417) 862-5567
Fax: (417) 862-1611
www.springfield-chamber.org

Tampa, FL

Greater Tampa Chamber of Commerce
P.O. Box 420
Tampa, FL 33601-0420
Phone: (813) 276-9401
Fax: (813) 229-7855
www.tampachamber.com

Tulsa, OK

Tulsa Metro Chamber
2 West 2nd Street
Williams Tower 2, Suite 150
Tulsa, OK 74103
Phone: (918) 585-1201
Fax: (918) 585-8016
ww3.tulsachamber.com

Virginia Beach, VA

Hampton Roads Chamber of Commerce
420 Bank Street
Norfolk, VA 23510
Phone: (757) 622-2312
Fax: (757) 622-5563
www.hamptonroadschamber.com

Warren, MI

Macomb County Chamber
28 First Street
Suite B
Mount Clemens, MI 48043
Phone: (586) 493-7600
www.macombcountychamber.com

Washington, DC

District of Columbia Chamber of Commerce
1213 K Street NW
Washington, DC 20005
Phone: (202) 347-7201
Fax: (202) 638-6762
www.dcchamber.org

District of Columbia Office of Planning and
Economic Development
J.A. Wilson Building
1350 Pennsylvania Ave NW, Suite 317
Washington, DC 20004
Phone: (202) 727-6365
Fax: (202) 727-6703
dcbiz.dc.gov/dmped/site/default.asp

Wichita, KS

City of Wichita Economic Development
Department
City Hall, 12th Floor
455 North Main Street
Wichita, KS 67202
Phone: (316) 268-4524
Fax: (316) 268-4656
www.wichitagov.org

Wichita Chamber of Commerce
350 West Douglas
Wichita, KS 67202
Phone: (316) 265-7771
Fax: (316) 265-7502
www.wichitakansas.org

Appendix D: State Departments of Labor

Alabama

Jim Bennett, Commissioner
Alabama Department of Labor
P.O. Box 303500
Montgomery, AL 36130-3500
Phone: (334) 242-3072
www.Alalabor.state.al.us

Alaska

Clark Bishop, Commissioner
Dept of Labor and Workforce Devel.
P.O. Box 11149
Juneau, AK 99822-2249
Phone: (907) 465-2700
www.labor.state.AK.us

Arizona

Brian C. Delfs, Director
Arizona Industrial Commission
800 West Washington Street
Phoenix, AZ 85007
Phone: (602) 542-4515
www.ica.state.AZ.us

Arkansas

James Salkeld, Director
Department of Labor
10421 West Markham
Little Rock, AR 72205
Phone: (501) 682-4500
www.Arkansas.gov/labor

California

Victoria Bradshaw, Director
Labor and Workforce Development
445 Golden Gate Ave., 10th Floor
San Francisco, CA 94102
Phone: (916) 263-1811
www.labor.CA.gov

Colorado

Donald J. Mares, Executive Director
Dept of Labor and Employment
633 17th St., 2nd Floor
Denver, CO 80202-3660
Phone: (888) 390-7936
www.COworkforce.com

Connecticut

Patricia H. Mayfield, Commissioner
Department of Labor
200 Folly Brook Blvd.
Wethersfield, CT 06109-1114
Phone: (860) 263-6000
www.CT.gov/dol

Delaware

Thomas B. Sharp, Secretary of Labor
Department of Labor
4425 N. Market St., 4th Floor
Wilmington, DE 19802
Phone: (302) 451-3423
www.Delawareworks.com

District of Columbia

Ms. Summer Spencer, Director
Employment Services Department
614 New York Ave., NE, Suite 300
Washington, DC 20002
Phone: (202) 671-1900
www.DOES.DC.gov

Florida

Monesia T. Brown, Director
Agency for Workforce Innovation
The Caldwell Building
107 East Madison St. Suite 100
Tallahassee, FL 32399-4120
Phone: (800) 342-3450
www.Floridajobs.org

Georgia

Michael Thurmond, Commissioner
Department of Labor
Sussex Place, Room 600
148 Andrew Young Intl Blvd., NE
Atlanta, GA 30303
Phone: (404) 656-3011
www.dol.state.GA.us

Hawaii

Director
Dept of Labor & Industrial Relations
830 Punchbowl Street
Honolulu, HI 96813
Phone: (808) 586-8842
wwwHawaii.gov/labor

Idaho

Robert B. Madsen, Director
Department of Labor
317 W. Main St.
Boise, ID 83735-0001
Phone: (208) 332-3579
www.labor.Idaho.gov

Illinois

Catherine M. Shannon, Director
Department of Labor
160 N. LaSalle Street, 13th Floor
Suite C-1300
Chicago, IL 60601
Phone: (312) 793-2800
www.state.IL.us/agency/idol

Indiana

Lori Torres, Dept of Labor
Indiana Government Center South
402 W. Washington Street
Room W195
Indianapolis, IN 46204
Phone: (317) 232-2655
www.IN.gov/labor

Iowa

David Neil, Labor Commissioner
Iowa Workforce Development
1000 East Grand Avenue
Des Moines, IA 50319-0209
Phone: (515) 242-5870
www.Iowaworkforce.org/labor

Kansas

Jim Garner, Secretary
Department of Labor
401 S.W. Topeka Blvd.
Topeka, KS 66603-3182
Phone: (785) 296-5000
www.dol.KS.gov

Kentucky

Philip Anderson, Commissioner
Department of Labor
1047 U.S. Hwy 127 South, Suite 4
Frankfort, KY 40601-4381
Phone: (502) 564-3070
www.labor.KY.gov

Louisiana

John Warner Smith, Secretary
Department of Labor
P.O. Box 94094
Baton Rouge, LA 70804-9094
Phone: (225) 342-3111
www.LAworks.net

Maine

Laura Fortman, Commissioner
Department of Labor
45 Commerce Street
Augusta, ME 04330
Phone: (207) 623-7900
www.state.ME.us/labor

Maryland

Tom Perez, Secretary
Department of Labor and Industry
500 N. Calvert Street
Suite 401
Baltimore, MD 21202
Phone: (410) 767-2357
www.dllr.state.MD.us

Massachusetts

Greg Noel, Secretary
Dept of Labor & Work Force Devel.
One Ashburton Place
Room 2112
Boston, MA 02108
Phone: (617) 626-7100
www.Mass.gov/eolwd

Michigan

Keith Cooley, Director
Dept of Labor & Economic Growth
P.O. Box 30004
Lansing, MI 48909
Phone: (517) 335-0400
www.Michigan.gov/cis

Minnesota

Steven A. Sviggum, Commissioner
Dept of Labor and Industry
443 Lafayette Road North
Saint Paul, MN 55155
Phone: (651) 284-5070
www.doli.state.MN.us

Mississippi

Tommye Dale Favre, Executive Director
Dept of Employment Security
P.O. Box 1699
Jackson, MS 39215-1699
Phone: (601) 321-6000
www.mdes.MS.gov

Missouri

Todd Smith, Director
Labor and Industrial Relations
P.O. Box 599
3315 W. Truman Boulevard
Jefferson City, MO 65102-0599
Phone: (573) 751-7500
www.dolir.MO.gov/lirc

Montana

Keith Kelly, Commissioner
Dept of Labor and Industry
P.O. Box 1728
Helena, MT 59624-1728
Phone: (406) 444-9091
www.dli.MT.gov

Nebraska

Fernando Lecuona, Commissioner
Department of Labor
550 South 16th Street
Box 94600
Lincoln, NE 68509-4600
Phone: (402) 471-9000
www.Nebraskaworkforce.com

Nevada

Michael Tanchek, Commissioner
Dept of Business and Industry
555 E. Washington Ave.
Suite 4100
Las Vegas, NV 89101-1050
Phone: (702) 486-2650
www.laborcommissioner.com

New Hampshire

George N. Copadis, Commissioner
Department of Labor
State Office Park South
95 Pleasant Street
Concord, NH 03301
Phone: (603) 271-3176
www.labor.state.NH.us

New Jersey

David Socolow, Commissioner
Department of Labor
John Fitch Plaza, 13th Floor
Suite D
Trenton, NJ 08625-0110
Phone: (609) 777-3200
lwd.dol.state.nj.us/labor

New Mexico

Betty D. Sparrow, Secretary
Department of Labor
401 Broadway, NE
Albuquerque, NM 87103-1928
Phone: (505) 841-8450
www.dol.state.NM.us

New York

M. Patricia Smith, Commissioner
Department of Labor
State Office Bldg. # 12
W.A. Harriman Campus
Albany, NY 12240
Phone: (518) 457-5519
www.labor.state.NY.us

North Carolina

Cherie K. Berry, Commissioner
Department of Labor
4 West Edenton Street
Raleigh, NC 27601-1092
Phone: (919) 733-7166
www.nclabor.com

North Dakota

Lisa Fair McEvers, Commissioner
Department of Labor
State Capitol Building
600 East Boulevard, Dept 406
Bismark, ND 58505-0340
Phone: (701) 328-2660
www.nd.gov/labor

Ohio

Kimberly A. Zurz, Director
Department of Commerce
77 South High Street, 22nd Floor
Columbus, OH 43215
Phone: (614) 644-2239
www.com.state.OH.us

Oklahoma

Lloyd Fields, Commissioner
Department of Labor
4001 N. Lincoln Blvd.
Oklahoma City, OK 73105-5212
Phone: (405) 528-1500
www.state.OK.us/~okdol

Oregon

Dan Gardner, Commissioner
Bureau of Labor and Industries
800 NE Oregon St., #32
Portland, OR 97232
Phone: (971) 673-0761
www.Oregon.gov/boli

Pennsylvania

Stephen M. Schmerin, Secretary
Dept of Labor and Industry
1700 Labor and Industry Bldg
7th and Forster Streets
Harrisburg, PA 17120
Phone: (717) 787-5279
www.dli.state.PA.us

Rhode Island

Adelita S. Orefice, Director
Department of Labor and Training
1511 Pontiac Avenue
Cranston, RI 02920
Phone: (401) 462-8000
www.dlt.state.RI.us

South Carolina

Adrienne R. Youmans, Director
Dept of Labor, Licensing & Regulations
P.O. Box 11329
Columbia, SC 29211-1329
Phone: (803) 896-4300
www.llr.state.SC.us

South Dakota

Pamela S. Roberts, Secretary
Department of Labor
700 Governors Drive
Pierre, SD 57501-2291
Phone: (605) 773-3682
www.state.SD.us

Tennessee

James G. Neeley, Commissioner
Dept of Labor & Workforce Development
Andrew Johnson Tower
710 James Robertson Pkwy
Nashville, TN 37243-0655
Phone: (615) 741-6642
www.state.TN.us/labor-wfd

Texas

Ronald Congleton, Labor Commissioner
Texas Workforce Commission
101 East 15th St.
Austin, TX 78778
Phone: (512) 475-2670
www.twc.state.TX.us

Utah

Sherrie Hayashi, Commissioner
Utah Labor Commission
P.O. Box 146610
Salt Lake City, UT 84114-6610
Phone: (801) 530-6800
Laborcommission.Utah.gov

Vermont

Patricia Moulton Pow, Commissioner
Department of Labor
5 Green Mountain Drive
P.O. Box 488
Montpelier, VT 05601-0488
Phone: (802) 828-4000
www.labor.verMont.gov

Virginia

C. Ray Davenport, Commissioner
Dept of Labor and Industry
Powers-Taylor Building
13 S. 13th Street
Richmond, VA 23219
Phone: (804) 371-2327
www.doli.Virginia.gov

Washington

Judy Schurke, Acting Director
Dept of Labor and Industries
P.O. Box 44001
Olympia, WA 98504-4001
Phone: (360) 902-4200
www.lni.WA.gov

West Virginia

David Mullens, Commissioner
Division of Labor
State Capitol Complex, Building #6
1900 Kanawha Blvd.
Charleston, WV 25305
Phone: (304) 558-7890
www.labor.state.WV.us

Wisconsin

Roberta Gassman, Secretary
Dept of Workforce Development
201 E. Washington Ave., #A400
P.O. Box 7946
Madison, WI 53707-7946
Phone: (608) 266-6861
www.dwd.state.WI.us

Wyoming

Cynthia Pomeroy, Director
Department of Employment
1510 East Pershing Blvd.
Cheyenne, WY 82002
Phone: (307) 777-7261
www.doe.state.WY.us

Source: U.S. Department of Labor
http://www.dol.gov/esa/contacts/state_of.htm

Appendix E: Comparative Statistics

Population Growth: City

City	1990 Census	2000 Census	2010 Estimate	2015 Projection	Population Growth (%) 1990-2000	Population Growth (%) 2000-2015
Albuquerque	388,375	448,607	528,683	563,552	15.5	25.6
Anchorage	226,338	260,283	286,430	296,930	15.0	14.1
Ann Arbor	111,018	114,024	112,805	111,634	2.7	-2.1
Athens	86,561	100,266	115,741	122,911	15.8	22.6
Atlanta	394,092	416,474	541,696	602,248	5.7	44.6
Austin	499,053	656,562	764,479	824,376	31.6	25.6
Baltimore	736,014	651,154	634,206	622,117	-11.5	-4.5
Bellevue	99,057	109,569	119,279	123,441	10.6	12.7
Birmingham	266,532	242,820	227,529	220,329	-8.9	-9.3
Boise City	144,317	185,787	198,213	212,040	28.7	14.1
Boston	574,283	589,141	633,224	645,191	2.6	9.5
Boulder	87,737	94,673	95,588	97,139	7.9	2.6
Cambridge	95,959	101,355	106,501	108,435	5.6	7.0
Cary	49,835	94,536	132,674	151,479	89.7	60.2
Charleston	96,102	96,650	111,528	116,709	0.6	20.8
Charlotte	428,283	540,828	660,839	735,940	26.3	36.1
Chattanooga	152,695	155,554	172,489	179,545	1.9	15.4
Chicago	2,783,726	2,896,016	2,848,389	2,814,480	4.0	-2.8
Cincinnati	363,974	331,285	327,360	323,484	-9.0	-2.4
Cleveland	505,333	478,403	428,633	402,724	-5.3	-15.8
Colorado Spgs.	283,798	360,890	393,737	412,792	27.2	14.4
Columbia	115,475	116,278	124,815	130,760	0.7	12.5
Columbus	648,656	711,470	752,929	769,467	9.7	8.2
Dallas	1,006,971	1,188,580	1,297,289	1,357,127	18.0	14.2
Denver	467,153	554,636	612,145	639,277	18.7	15.3
Des Moines	193,569	198,682	197,155	199,968	2.6	0.6
Durham	151,737	187,035	226,017	246,070	23.3	31.6
Edison	88,680	97,687	99,491	100,108	10.2	2.5
El Paso	515,541	563,662	614,938	640,686	9.3	13.7
Eugene	118,073	137,893	151,153	156,944	16.8	13.8
Evansville	126,272	121,582	114,593	111,463	-3.7	-8.3
Fargo	74,372	90,599	95,943	100,007	21.8	10.4
Ft. Collins	89,555	118,652	136,749	145,570	32.5	22.7
Ft. Lauderdale	149,908	152,397	158,684	161,790	1.7	6.2
Ft. Wayne	205,671	205,727	200,606	199,029	0.0	-3.3
Ft. Worth	448,311	534,694	696,039	764,598	19.3	43.0
Gainesville	90,519	95,447	100,710	104,346	5.4	9.3
Greensboro	193,389	223,891	250,874	265,204	15.8	18.5
Honolulu	376,465	371,657	373,040	373,866	-1.3	0.6
Houston	1,697,610	1,953,631	2,269,768	2,451,441	15.1	25.5
Huntsville	161,842	158,216	176,195	185,173	-2.2	17.0
Indianapolis	730,993	781,870	802,032	807,668	7.0	3.3
Irvine	111,754	143,072	215,191	239,991	28.0	67.7
Jackson	196,469	184,256	172,029	164,415	-6.2	-10.8
Jacksonville	635,221	735,617	846,695	902,808	15.8	22.7
Kansas City	434,967	441,545	455,672	460,074	1.5	4.2
Knoxville	173,288	173,890	185,041	190,587	0.3	9.6
Las Vegas	261,374	478,434	564,650	617,115	83.0	29.0
Lexington	225,366	260,512	286,728	298,393	15.6	14.5
Lincoln	193,629	225,581	245,653	256,067	16.5	13.5
Little Rock	177,519	183,133	191,692	195,512	3.2	6.8
Los Angeles	3,487,671	3,694,820	3,947,805	4,107,461	5.9	11.2
Louisville	269,160	256,231	238,504	231,755	-4.8	-9.6
Madison	193,451	208,054	225,284	232,525	7.5	11.8
Manchester	99,567	107,006	108,958	109,014	7.5	1.9

Table continued on next page.

City	1990 Census	2000 Census	2010 Estimate	2015 Projection	Population Growth (%) 1990-2000	2000-2015
Miami	358,843	362,470	411,168	434,131	1.0	19.8
Milwaukee	628,095	596,974	598,356	595,169	-5.0	-0.3
Minneapolis	368,383	382,618	384,997	385,578	3.9	0.8
Naperville	90,506	128,358	147,227	155,212	41.8	20.9
Nashville	488,364	545,524	605,658	631,132	11.7	15.7
New Orleans	496,938	484,674	357,104	390,479	-2.5	-19.4
New York	7,322,552	8,008,278	8,430,691	8,581,158	9.4	7.2
Oakland	372,199	399,484	414,678	426,722	7.3	6.8
Oklahoma City	445,065	506,132	563,693	588,317	13.7	16.2
Omaha	371,972	390,007	383,452	388,670	4.8	-0.3
Orlando	161,172	185,951	229,589	251,720	15.4	35.4
Overland Park	111,803	149,080	177,149	189,684	33.3	27.2
Oxnard	143,271	170,358	192,924	204,351	18.9	20.0
Philadelphia	1,585,577	1,517,550	1,493,866	1,486,767	-4.3	-2.0
Phoenix	989,873	1,321,045	1,567,579	1,734,388	33.5	31.3
Pittsburgh	369,785	334,563	306,679	292,852	-9.5	-12.5
Plano	128,507	222,030	280,422	325,345	72.8	46.5
Portland	485,833	529,121	571,902	591,797	8.9	11.8
Providence	160,734	173,618	172,270	170,412	8.0	-1.8
Provo	87,148	105,166	123,547	139,344	20.7	32.5
Raleigh	226,841	276,093	380,890	440,315	21.7	59.5
Reno	139,950	180,480	215,785	233,934	29.0	29.6
Richmond	202,783	197,790	199,893	199,490	-2.5	0.9
Riverside	226,232	255,166	299,335	335,140	12.8	31.3
Rochester	231,642	219,773	206,897	200,044	-5.1	-9.0
Sacramento	368,923	407,018	477,071	512,550	10.3	25.9
St. Louis	396,685	348,189	354,685	355,030	-12.2	2.0
St. Paul	272,235	287,151	283,979	280,754	5.5	-2.2
St. Petersburg	238,846	248,232	249,120	250,370	3.9	0.9
Salt Lake City	159,796	181,743	183,609	189,468	13.7	4.3
San Antonio	997,258	1,144,646	1,323,124	1,420,762	14.8	24.1
San Diego	1,111,048	1,223,400	1,321,313	1,384,863	10.1	13.2
San Francisco	723,959	776,733	823,166	853,083	7.3	9.8
San Jose	784,324	894,943	977,014	1,025,560	14.1	14.6
Santa Ana	293,667	337,977	344,451	353,677	15.1	4.6
Savannah	138,038	131,510	131,346	134,046	-4.7	1.9
Seattle	516,262	563,374	604,715	626,520	9.1	11.2
Spokane	178,202	195,629	202,260	206,249	9.8	5.4
Springfield	142,557	151,580	157,166	160,512	6.3	5.9
Tampa	279,960	303,447	350,061	377,104	8.4	24.3
Tulsa	367,241	393,049	389,179	390,784	7.0	-0.6
Virginia Beach	393,069	425,257	433,144	434,048	8.2	2.1
Warren	144,864	138,247	132,292	129,759	-4.6	-6.1
Washington	606,900	572,059	595,933	604,219	-5.7	5.6
Wichita	313,693	344,284	361,238	369,794	9.8	7.4
U.S.	248,709,873	281,421,906	309,038,974	321,675,005	13.2	14.3

Source: Claritas, Inc.

Population Growth: Metro Area

Metro Area	1990 Census	2000 Census	2010 Estimate	2015 Projection	Population Growth (%)	
					1990-2000	2000-2015
Albuquerque	599,416	729,649	867,318	930,048	21.7	27.5
Anchorage	266,021	319,605	374,724	398,570	20.1	24.7
Ann Arbor	282,937	322,895	348,885	356,825	14.1	10.5
Athens	136,025	166,079	193,746	206,795	22.1	24.5
Atlanta	3,069,411	4,247,981	5,569,195	6,182,135	38.4	45.5
Austin	846,217	1,249,763	1,703,994	1,921,939	47.7	53.8
Baltimore	2,382,172	2,552,994	2,677,198	2,711,907	7.2	6.2
Bellevue	2,559,164	3,043,878	3,419,662	3,592,543	18.9	18.0
Birmingham	956,894	1,052,238	1,130,075	1,161,967	10.0	10.4
Boise City	319,596	464,840	623,694	698,345	45.4	50.2
Boston	4,133,895	4,391,344	4,562,075	4,611,141	6.2	5.0
Boulder	208,898	269,758	299,149	311,973	29.1	15.6
Cambridge	4,133,895	4,391,344	4,562,075	4,611,141	6.2	5.0
Cary	541,081	797,071	1,149,177	1,322,544	47.3	65.9
Charleston	506,875	549,033	663,996	718,900	8.3	30.9
Charlotte	1,024,331	1,330,448	1,780,697	2,002,801	29.9	50.5
Chattanooga	433,166	476,531	525,589	546,663	10.0	14.7
Chicago	8,182,076	9,098,316	9,651,162	9,856,994	11.2	8.3
Cincinnati	1,844,917	2,009,632	2,177,460	2,240,244	8.9	11.5
Cleveland	2,102,219	2,148,143	2,075,531	2,024,031	2.2	-5.8
Colorado Spgs.	409,482	537,484	632,543	677,441	31.3	26.0
Columbia	548,325	647,158	744,816	790,857	18.0	22.2
Columbus	1,405,176	1,612,694	1,800,112	1,876,062	14.8	16.3
Dallas	3,989,294	5,161,544	6,493,230	7,129,430	29.4	38.1
Denver	1,666,935	2,179,296	2,582,000	2,768,229	30.7	27.0
Des Moines	416,346	481,394	570,780	611,223	15.6	27.0
Durham	344,646	426,493	504,182	543,569	23.7	27.5
Edison	16,845,992	18,323,002	19,104,202	19,331,734	8.8	5.5
El Paso	591,610	679,622	764,048	803,756	14.9	18.3
Eugene	282,912	322,959	351,400	364,154	14.2	12.8
Evansville	324,858	342,815	351,391	353,275	5.5	3.1
Fargo	153,296	174,367	199,797	210,986	13.7	21.0
Ft. Collins	186,136	251,494	300,353	323,474	35.1	28.6
Ft. Lauderdale	4,056,100	5,007,564	5,519,882	5,786,816	23.5	15.6
Ft. Wayne	354,435	390,156	414,696	423,864	10.1	8.6
Ft. Worth	3,989,294	5,161,544	6,493,230	7,129,430	29.4	38.1
Gainesville	191,263	232,392	268,606	287,115	21.5	23.5
Greensboro	540,257	643,430	719,617	756,342	19.1	17.5
Honolulu	836,231	876,156	909,071	918,745	4.8	4.9
Houston	3,767,335	4,715,407	5,909,705	6,480,092	25.2	37.4
Huntsville	293,047	342,376	407,220	437,840	16.8	27.9
Indianapolis	1,294,217	1,525,104	1,748,230	1,844,166	17.8	20.9
Irvine	11,273,720	12,365,627	13,255,498	13,807,018	9.7	11.7
Jackson	446,941	497,197	542,333	555,584	11.2	11.7
Jacksonville	925,213	1,122,750	1,372,183	1,498,271	21.4	33.4
Kansas City	1,636,528	1,836,038	2,031,038	2,112,261	12.2	15.0
Knoxville	534,919	616,079	705,932	747,061	15.2	21.3
Las Vegas	741,459	1,375,765	1,904,738	2,112,594	85.5	53.6
Lexington	348,428	408,326	462,703	487,357	17.2	19.4
Lincoln	229,091	266,787	300,735	315,371	16.5	18.2
Little Rock	535,034	610,518	687,976	722,825	14.1	18.4
Los Angeles	11,273,720	12,365,627	13,255,498	13,807,018	9.7	11.7
Louisville	1,055,973	1,161,975	1,261,213	1,303,139	10.0	12.1
Madison	432,323	501,774	563,337	589,153	16.1	17.4
Manchester	336,073	380,841	404,052	411,262	13.3	8.0

Table continued on next page.

Metro Area	1990 Census	2000 Census	2010 Estimate	2015 Projection	Population Growth (%) 1990-2000	2000-2015
Miami	4,056,100	5,007,564	5,519,882	5,786,816	23.5	15.6
Milwaukee	1,432,149	1,500,741	1,542,181	1,551,343	4.8	3.4
Minneapolis	2,538,834	2,968,806	3,279,181	3,408,830	16.9	14.8
Naperville	8,182,076	9,098,316	9,651,162	9,856,994	11.2	8.3
Nashville	1,048,218	1,311,789	1,596,033	1,727,736	25.1	31.7
New Orleans	1,264,391	1,316,510	1,194,196	1,264,365	4.1	-4.0
New York	16,845,992	18,323,002	19,104,202	19,331,734	8.8	5.5
Oakland	3,686,592	4,123,740	4,377,542	4,539,970	11.9	10.1
Oklahoma City	971,042	1,095,421	1,228,544	1,288,100	12.8	17.6
Omaha	685,797	767,041	851,194	887,017	11.8	15.6
Orlando	1,224,852	1,644,561	2,138,839	2,386,929	34.3	45.1
Overland Park	1,636,528	1,836,038	2,031,038	2,112,261	12.2	15.0
Oxnard	669,016	753,197	820,970	861,351	12.6	14.4
Philadelphia	5,435,470	5,687,147	5,913,308	5,987,829	4.6	5.3
Phoenix	2,238,480	3,251,876	4,448,760	5,021,248	45.3	54.4
Pittsburgh	2,468,289	2,431,087	2,339,954	2,282,539	-1.5	-6.1
Plano	3,989,294	5,161,544	6,493,230	7,129,430	29.4	38.1
Portland	1,523,741	1,927,881	2,250,194	2,400,163	26.5	24.5
Providence	1,509,789	1,582,997	1,591,898	1,580,421	4.8	-0.2
Provo	269,407	376,774	561,831	652,719	39.9	73.2
Raleigh	541,081	797,071	1,149,177	1,322,544	47.3	65.9
Reno	257,193	342,885	425,316	462,058	33.3	34.8
Richmond	949,244	1,096,957	1,241,094	1,302,514	15.6	18.7
Riverside	2,588,793	3,254,821	4,253,554	4,781,112	25.7	46.9
Rochester	1,002,410	1,037,831	1,033,458	1,024,577	3.5	-1.3
Sacramento	1,481,126	1,796,857	2,166,538	2,366,916	21.3	31.7
St. Louis	2,580,897	2,698,687	2,835,186	2,881,864	4.6	6.8
St. Paul	2,538,834	2,968,806	3,279,181	3,408,830	16.9	14.8
St. Petersburg	2,067,959	2,395,997	2,782,113	2,979,241	15.9	24.3
Salt Lake City	768,075	968,858	1,150,758	1,240,742	26.1	28.1
San Antonio	1,407,745	1,711,703	2,090,028	2,270,338	21.6	32.6
San Diego	2,498,016	2,813,833	3,109,270	3,281,275	12.6	16.6
San Francisco	3,686,592	4,123,740	4,377,542	4,539,970	11.9	10.1
San Jose	1,534,280	1,735,819	1,879,279	1,965,999	13.1	13.3
Santa Ana	11,273,720	12,365,627	13,255,498	13,807,018	9.7	11.7
Savannah	258,060	293,000	342,793	366,584	13.5	25.1
Seattle	2,559,164	3,043,878	3,419,662	3,592,543	18.9	18.0
Spokane	361,364	417,939	468,349	491,518	15.7	17.6
Springfield	298,818	368,374	436,923	467,824	23.3	27.0
Tampa	2,067,959	2,395,997	2,782,113	2,979,241	15.9	24.3
Tulsa	761,019	859,532	930,074	962,351	12.9	12.0
Virginia Beach	1,449,389	1,576,370	1,670,719	1,704,900	8.8	8.2
Warren	4,248,699	4,452,557	4,392,431	4,312,504	4.8	-3.1
Washington	4,122,914	4,796,183	5,438,913	5,701,636	16.3	18.9
Wichita	511,111	571,166	612,430	631,209	11.7	10.5
U.S.	248,709,873	281,421,906	309,038,974	321,675,005	13.2	14.3

Note: Figures cover the Metropolitan Statistical Area (MSA) - see Appendix B for areas included
Source: Claritas, Inc.

Number of Households and Average Household Size: City

City	2010 Estimate	2010 Average Household Size
Albuquerque	218,918	2.37
Anchorage	104,174	2.67
Ann Arbor	45,853	2.19
Athens	45,380	2.35
Atlanta	217,657	2.34
Austin	308,268	2.41
Baltimore	248,610	2.44
Bellevue	51,124	2.32
Birmingham	94,113	2.32
Boise City	81,897	2.35
Boston	252,289	2.34
Boulder	40,523	2.18
Cambridge	44,844	2.03
Cary	48,855	2.71
Charleston	47,704	2.21
Charlotte	268,531	2.41
Chattanooga	73,828	2.26
Chicago	1,045,666	2.66
Cincinnati	145,600	2.14
Cleveland	172,252	2.40
Colorado Spgs.	154,941	2.50
Columbia	46,278	2.12
Columbus	321,436	2.29
Dallas	482,467	2.64
Denver	257,531	2.32
Des Moines	80,832	2.35
Durham	90,792	2.38
Edison	35,636	2.73
El Paso	202,980	3.00
Eugene	64,514	2.25
Evansville	50,063	2.19
Fargo	43,236	2.11
Ft. Collins	53,651	2.44
Ft. Lauderdale	70,385	2.18
Ft. Wayne	82,367	2.37
Ft. Worth	248,820	2.73
Gainesville	39,809	2.23
Greensboro	104,525	2.28
Honolulu	144,869	2.50
Houston	818,151	2.73
Huntsville	76,367	2.23
Indianapolis	329,676	2.37
Irvine	76,389	2.71
Jackson	63,694	2.59
Jacksonville	333,499	2.50
Kansas City	191,536	2.33
Knoxville	83,624	2.09
Las Vegas	204,035	2.72
Lexington	121,915	2.25
Lincoln	99,004	2.35
Little Rock	81,739	2.28
Los Angeles	1,346,368	2.87
Louisville	105,291	2.18
Madison	97,178	2.18
Manchester	45,455	2.33

Table continued on next page.

City	2010 Estimate	2010 Average Household Size
Miami	155,735	2.55
Milwaukee	233,182	2.50
Minneapolis	164,318	2.23
Naperville	49,838	2.91
Nashville	252,508	2.30
New Orleans	141,177	2.44
New York	3,131,885	2.63
Oakland	154,128	2.64
Oklahoma City	227,427	2.42
Omaha	154,996	2.40
Orlando	99,179	2.26
Overland Park	69,974	2.51
Oxnard	48,420	3.94
Philadelphia	586,527	2.44
Phoenix	537,929	2.87
Pittsburgh	134,086	2.11
Plano	105,438	2.65
Portland	244,163	2.28
Providence	60,961	2.61
Provo	34,984	3.26
Raleigh	154,898	2.34
Reno	87,831	2.41
Richmond	83,482	2.24
Riverside	94,062	3.10
Rochester	83,585	2.34
Sacramento	179,047	2.61
St. Louis	148,897	2.31
St. Paul	110,839	2.45
St. Petersburg	108,643	2.23
Salt Lake City	72,979	2.45
San Antonio	467,597	2.77
San Diego	486,433	2.61
San Francisco	347,648	2.31
San Jose	299,575	3.22
Santa Ana	73,159	4.62
Savannah	51,619	2.40
Seattle	279,248	2.07
Spokane	84,424	2.32
Springfield	69,681	2.11
Tampa	144,002	2.36
Tulsa	165,249	2.29
Virginia Beach	161,614	2.63
Warren	55,345	2.37
Washington	262,976	2.13
Wichita	146,410	2.43
U.S.	116,136,617	2.59

Source: Claritas, Inc.

Number of Households and Average Household Size: Metro Area

Metro Area	2010 Estimate	2010 Average Household Size
Albuquerque	340,379	2.50
Anchorage	135,413	2.70
Ann Arbor	136,353	2.40
Athens	74,219	2.48
Atlanta	2,005,649	2.73
Austin	629,606	2.64
Baltimore	1,026,868	2.54
Bellevue	1,347,944	2.48
Birmingham	449,542	2.46
Boise City	228,835	2.67
Boston	1,746,622	2.52
Boulder	117,845	2.47
Cambridge	1,746,622	2.52
Cary	438,411	2.57
Charleston	258,984	2.48
Charlotte	687,844	2.54
Chattanooga	212,905	2.41
Chicago	3,467,425	2.73
Cincinnati	848,820	2.51
Cleveland	833,947	2.43
Colorado Spgs.	235,767	2.61
Columbia	290,699	2.44
Columbus	715,478	2.45
Dallas	2,320,136	2.76
Denver	996,177	2.56
Des Moines	226,213	2.47
Durham	200,343	2.40
Edison	6,904,091	2.71
El Paso	240,413	3.12
Eugene	143,731	2.39
Evansville	142,729	2.39
Fargo	83,226	2.29
Ft. Collins	117,729	2.49
Ft. Lauderdale	2,058,462	2.64
Ft. Wayne	162,213	2.52
Ft. Worth	2,320,136	2.76
Gainesville	107,906	2.35
Greensboro	289,364	2.42
Honolulu	303,401	2.90
Houston	2,041,580	2.85
Huntsville	162,099	2.45
Indianapolis	682,376	2.51
Irvine	4,297,861	3.03
Jackson	200,786	2.60
Jacksonville	536,105	2.52
Kansas City	796,129	2.51
Knoxville	295,527	2.33
Las Vegas	702,509	2.68
Lexington	189,839	2.35
Lincoln	118,969	2.40
Little Rock	274,189	2.45
Los Angeles	4,297,861	3.03
Louisville	510,456	2.43
Madison	228,224	2.39
Manchester	154,538	2.56

Table continued on next page.

Metro Area	2010 Estimate	2010 Average Household Size
Miami	2,058,462	2.64
Milwaukee	614,655	2.46
Minneapolis	1,265,079	2.54
Naperville	3,467,425	2.73
Nashville	624,143	2.49
New Orleans	457,187	2.57
New York	6,904,091	2.71
Oakland	1,623,622	2.65
Oklahoma City	485,038	2.47
Omaha	329,423	2.53
Orlando	805,054	2.61
Overland Park	796,129	2.51
Oxnard	262,938	3.07
Philadelphia	2,242,863	2.55
Phoenix	1,586,897	2.76
Pittsburgh	973,462	2.32
Plano	2,320,136	2.76
Portland	867,887	2.55
Providence	621,836	2.47
Provo	152,991	3.59
Raleigh	438,411	2.57
Reno	163,984	2.56
Richmond	484,006	2.48
Riverside	1,310,346	3.18
Rochester	399,870	2.46
Sacramento	797,203	2.67
St. Louis	1,117,149	2.49
St. Paul	1,265,079	2.54
St. Petersburg	1,156,562	2.36
Salt Lake City	376,585	3.01
San Antonio	733,645	2.79
San Diego	1,091,399	2.75
San Francisco	1,623,622	2.65
San Jose	622,000	2.97
Santa Ana	4,297,861	3.03
Savannah	130,387	2.53
Seattle	1,347,944	2.48
Spokane	184,166	2.46
Springfield	176,309	2.39
Tampa	1,156,562	2.36
Tulsa	364,818	2.50
Virginia Beach	626,274	2.55
Warren	1,686,703	2.57
Washington	2,044,883	2.61
Wichita	237,110	2.54
U.S.	116,136,617	2.59

Note: Figures cover the Metropolitan Statistical Area (MSA) - see Appendix B for areas included
Source: Claritas, Inc.

Race and Ethnicity: City

City	White alone[2] (%)	Black alone[2] (%)	Asian alone[2] (%)	Other Race alone[2] (%)	Hispanic[3] (%)
Albuquerque	67.3	3.5	2.3	26.8	45.0
Anchorage	68.0	6.9	6.5	18.5	8.4
Ann Arbor	71.8	7.5	15.6	5.1	4.1
Athens	65.0	24.9	3.4	6.7	9.5
Atlanta	37.0	54.6	2.8	5.6	7.2
Austin	62.0	8.0	5.9	24.1	36.2
Baltimore	31.6	63.2	2.0	3.3	2.8
Bellevue	66.8	1.9	23.2	8.1	8.0
Birmingham	21.2	75.0	1.0	2.8	3.3
Boise City	88.7	1.5	2.5	7.3	7.4
Boston	55.1	22.5	7.9	14.5	17.0
Boulder	86.3	1.4	4.2	8.1	10.9
Cambridge	63.5	11.4	15.3	9.8	8.4
Cary	77.3	6.5	10.8	5.4	6.6
Charleston	66.4	29.8	1.3	2.4	2.5
Charlotte	51.7	34.7	4.1	9.6	13.2
Chattanooga	59.4	34.6	1.8	4.1	4.0
Chicago	41.4	34.6	4.9	19.0	29.5
Cincinnati	50.0	44.9	1.8	3.3	2.2
Cleveland	37.5	52.9	1.8	7.8	9.7
Colorado Spgs.	78.1	6.5	3.4	12.0	15.1
Columbia	48.1	45.3	2.3	4.4	4.3
Columbus	63.8	26.2	4.4	5.6	4.7
Dallas	48.1	23.0	3.0	25.9	45.8
Denver	64.9	9.2	3.3	22.6	34.5
Des Moines	76.4	9.3	4.1	10.1	11.7
Durham	45.8	38.6	4.8	10.8	14.4
Edison	47.5	7.8	38.9	5.8	9.0
El Paso	72.2	2.8	1.2	23.7	80.4
Eugene	84.8	1.6	5.2	8.4	6.8
Evansville	84.3	11.8	0.9	2.9	1.6
Fargo	90.8	2.5	2.0	4.7	2.4
Ft. Collins	87.3	1.7	2.8	8.3	10.6
Ft. Lauderdale	60.5	30.6	1.2	7.7	12.4
Ft. Wayne	71.4	18.5	2.0	8.1	9.2
Ft. Worth	57.8	18.5	3.2	20.5	35.9
Gainesville	65.6	23.9	5.4	5.1	8.3
Greensboro	50.7	39.3	3.4	6.6	7.5
Honolulu	20.9	2.7	54.0	22.4	5.3
Houston	47.2	23.6	5.4	23.7	44.6
Huntsville	61.5	32.3	2.5	3.7	3.3
Indianapolis	65.3	26.6	1.6	6.6	7.9
Irvine	51.3	1.3	36.8	10.6	7.9
Jackson	19.9	77.7	0.7	1.7	1.4
Jacksonville	60.4	30.8	3.5	5.3	6.6
Kansas City	59.6	29.8	2.2	8.4	10.2
Knoxville	76.6	17.2	1.9	4.2	3.3
Las Vegas	62.6	11.2	6.2	19.9	32.9
Lexington	78.6	13.6	3.1	4.7	6.1
Lincoln	86.7	3.6	3.4	6.2	5.5
Little Rock	49.8	42.9	2.5	4.8	5.1
Los Angeles	45.7	9.5	10.5	34.4	50.7
Louisville	58.3	36.1	1.9	3.7	3.5
Madison	80.4	6.1	7.5	6.0	6.5
Manchester	86.4	3.7	4.0	5.9	8.1

Table continued on next page.

City	White alone[2] (%)	Black alone[2] (%)	Asian alone[2] (%)	Other Race alone[2] (%)	Hispanic[3] (%)
Miami	70.0	18.2	0.7	11.1	68.9
Milwaukee	45.8	38.0	3.4	12.8	16.5
Minneapolis	60.3	19.0	6.5	14.2	12.7
Naperville	77.1	5.1	14.0	3.7	6.0
Nashville	61.4	27.8	2.9	7.9	8.6
New Orleans	33.1	60.6	2.9	3.4	4.7
New York	44.2	24.6	11.5	19.7	27.7
Oakland	33.1	28.8	16.9	21.2	28.0
Oklahoma City	65.5	15.2	4.2	15.1	15.1
Omaha	73.1	14.2	2.6	10.1	12.4
Orlando	57.6	26.0	3.3	13.0	24.2
Overland Park	86.2	4.2	5.3	4.3	5.9
Oxnard	37.3	3.1	7.7	51.9	71.2
Philadelphia	41.6	43.2	5.6	9.6	11.6
Phoenix	63.7	5.6	2.5	28.1	44.2
Pittsburgh	64.4	27.8	4.1	3.7	2.4
Plano	64.0	8.7	17.4	9.9	14.9
Portland	75.6	6.5	6.5	11.4	10.1
Providence	47.5	15.1	5.8	31.6	39.8
Provo	83.4	0.8	2.5	13.4	17.0
Raleigh	59.1	28.2	3.9	8.9	12.0
Reno	73.2	2.7	5.8	18.3	25.1
Richmond	41.8	51.1	1.6	5.5	5.1
Riverside	52.0	6.7	8.2	33.2	47.9
Rochester	43.6	41.0	2.5	12.9	14.7
Sacramento	45.7	13.9	17.7	22.8	26.4
St. Louis	46.0	48.4	2.0	3.5	3.0
St. Paul	62.6	14.4	12.4	10.6	10.1
St. Petersburg	66.8	24.6	3.5	5.1	6.3
Salt Lake City	74.7	2.4	3.8	19.1	26.5
San Antonio	65.5	6.5	1.9	26.1	62.8
San Diego	58.6	6.3	14.8	20.4	29.2
San Francisco	51.0	6.2	30.8	12.0	14.1
San Jose	41.7	3.2	31.5	23.7	32.4
Santa Ana	37.1	1.5	8.6	52.8	80.0
Savannah	36.8	57.9	1.8	3.5	3.0
Seattle	67.8	7.7	14.8	9.7	7.3
Spokane	87.5	2.3	2.6	7.6	4.5
Springfield	89.6	4.1	1.6	4.7	3.6
Tampa	60.9	26.6	3.1	9.4	23.7
Tulsa	65.7	16.9	2.2	15.2	13.0
Virginia Beach	68.5	19.8	5.4	6.3	6.1
Warren	81.7	9.7	4.7	3.8	1.6
Washington	36.5	52.5	3.3	7.6	8.7
Wichita	71.4	11.9	4.5	12.2	13.8
U.S.	72.3	12.4	4.4	10.9	15.8

Note: Figures are 2010 estimates; (2) Alone is defined as not being in combination with one or more other races;
(3) May be of any race
Source: Claritas, Inc.

Race and Ethnicity: Metro Area

Metro Area	White alone[2] (%)	Black alone[2] (%)	Asian alone[2] (%)	Other Race alone[2] (%)	Hispanic[3] (%)
Albuquerque	66.8	3.0	1.8	28.5	44.9
Anchorage	72.0	5.6	5.3	17.1	7.3
Ann Arbor	75.0	12.1	8.3	4.6	3.4
Athens	73.3	18.9	2.5	5.2	7.1
Atlanta	57.9	31.0	4.1	7.0	9.9
Austin	69.5	7.3	4.5	18.7	30.5
Baltimore	63.7	28.8	3.9	3.6	3.5
Bellevue	74.1	5.4	10.5	10.0	7.9
Birmingham	68.0	28.1	1.1	2.8	3.4
Boise City	86.6	1.1	1.6	10.7	12.0
Boston	79.9	6.5	6.0	7.6	8.3
Boulder	85.5	1.1	3.8	9.7	13.7
Cambridge	79.9	6.5	6.0	7.6	8.3
Cary	69.1	19.8	3.8	7.3	9.5
Charleston	66.3	28.2	1.6	3.9	3.9
Charlotte	67.4	23.3	2.6	6.7	9.3
Chattanooga	82.0	14.0	1.2	2.8	2.6
Chicago	64.8	17.5	5.3	12.5	20.3
Cincinnati	83.7	12.1	1.7	2.4	2.0
Cleveland	74.8	19.5	1.8	4.0	4.4
Colorado Spgs.	79.6	6.2	2.8	11.4	13.6
Columbia	61.1	33.5	1.6	3.8	4.1
Columbus	79.0	14.0	3.2	3.8	3.2
Dallas	64.4	14.0	4.7	16.9	28.1
Denver	77.0	5.3	3.4	14.3	22.8
Des Moines	87.8	4.1	2.5	5.5	6.2
Durham	60.9	26.8	4.2	8.1	10.4
Edison	59.2	17.3	9.2	14.3	21.8
El Paso	72.9	2.7	1.1	23.3	82.2
Eugene	88.0	1.0	2.9	8.0	6.6
Evansville	91.2	5.9	0.9	2.0	1.4
Fargo	92.7	1.6	1.3	4.3	2.6
Ft. Collins	89.4	1.1	1.8	7.7	10.2
Ft. Lauderdale	69.7	19.4	2.1	8.9	40.3
Ft. Wayne	83.3	9.9	1.7	5.1	5.6
Ft. Worth	64.4	14.0	4.7	16.9	28.1
Gainesville	72.5	18.5	4.3	4.7	7.3
Greensboro	67.0	24.8	2.3	6.0	7.4
Honolulu	22.1	3.8	44.3	29.8	8.0
Houston	59.0	16.6	5.6	18.8	34.5
Huntsville	72.2	22.1	1.9	3.8	3.3
Indianapolis	79.2	14.6	1.9	4.4	5.1
Irvine	49.8	7.1	13.6	29.5	44.7
Jackson	50.5	46.9	0.9	1.7	1.7
Jacksonville	70.1	22.2	2.9	4.7	6.2
Kansas City	79.9	11.9	2.0	6.2	7.5
Knoxville	89.1	6.6	1.4	2.9	2.5
Las Vegas	65.0	9.7	7.2	18.1	29.2
Lexington	83.6	10.3	2.2	3.9	4.9
Lincoln	88.5	3.1	3.0	5.5	4.8
Little Rock	72.3	22.3	1.3	4.0	3.8
Los Angeles	49.8	7.1	13.6	29.5	44.7
Louisville	82.1	13.4	1.3	3.1	3.0
Madison	87.6	3.9	4.1	4.5	4.7
Manchester	90.7	2.0	3.1	4.2	5.2

Table continued on next page.

Metro Area	White alone[2] (%)	Black alone[2] (%)	Asian alone[2] (%)	Other Race alone[2] (%)	Hispanic[3] (%)
Miami	69.7	19.4	2.1	8.9	40.3
Milwaukee	74.5	16.0	2.6	6.9	8.7
Minneapolis	83.0	6.4	4.9	5.6	4.9
Naperville	64.8	17.5	5.3	12.5	20.3
Nashville	77.6	15.3	2.0	5.1	5.8
New Orleans	58.5	34.7	2.6	4.2	6.4
New York	59.2	17.3	9.2	14.3	21.8
Oakland	53.0	8.5	22.0	16.6	20.7
Oklahoma City	73.9	10.7	3.0	12.5	10.0
Omaha	83.8	7.6	2.0	6.6	7.9
Orlando	69.9	15.0	3.6	11.6	23.8
Overland Park	79.9	11.9	2.0	6.2	7.5
Oxnard	65.7	1.8	6.5	26.0	38.5
Philadelphia	69.3	20.6	4.4	5.7	7.0
Phoenix	71.5	4.4	2.8	21.3	31.5
Pittsburgh	88.3	8.3	1.6	1.8	1.2
Plano	64.4	14.0	4.7	16.9	28.1
Portland	81.2	2.9	5.4	10.5	10.8
Providence	83.8	4.4	2.3	9.5	9.7
Provo	89.7	0.6	1.4	8.3	9.8
Raleigh	69.1	19.8	3.8	7.3	9.5
Reno	76.6	2.3	4.8	16.3	21.6
Richmond	63.4	29.7	2.6	4.3	4.2
Riverside	55.7	7.4	5.5	31.4	46.6
Rochester	81.9	11.1	2.2	4.9	5.3
Sacramento	65.1	7.3	10.9	16.8	19.3
St. Louis	77.3	18.1	1.9	2.7	2.3
St. Paul	83.0	6.4	4.9	5.6	4.9
St. Petersburg	78.9	11.5	2.6	7.0	15.2
Salt Lake City	82.6	1.5	2.8	13.2	16.3
San Antonio	69.4	6.2	1.8	22.6	53.4
San Diego	63.2	4.9	10.1	21.8	31.3
San Francisco	53.0	8.5	22.0	16.6	20.7
San Jose	47.4	2.5	30.4	19.7	27.0
Santa Ana	49.8	7.1	13.6	29.5	44.7
Savannah	61.1	33.7	1.9	3.3	3.1
Seattle	74.1	5.4	10.5	10.0	7.9
Spokane	89.7	1.8	2.1	6.4	4.2
Springfield	93.5	2.1	1.0	3.4	2.5
Tampa	78.9	11.5	2.6	7.0	15.2
Tulsa	73.8	9.0	1.5	15.7	7.8
Virginia Beach	60.4	31.6	3.0	4.9	4.4
Warren	69.8	22.8	3.2	4.2	3.8
Washington	56.4	25.4	8.6	9.6	12.7
Wichita	79.8	7.8	3.1	9.3	10.0
U.S.	72.3	12.4	4.4	10.9	15.8

Note: Figures are 2010 estimates and cover the Metropolitan Statistical Area (MSA) - see Appendix B for areas included
(2) Alone is defined as not being in combination with one or more other races; (3) May be of any race
Source: Claritas, Inc.

Age Distribution: City

City	Percent of Population							Median Age
	Under Age 5	Age 5 to 17	Age 18 to 34	Age 35 to 49	Age 50 to 64	Age 65 to 79	80 Years and Over	
Albuquerque	7.7	16.3	27.2	19.9	17.1	8.1	3.6	34.1
Anchorage	7.7	18.2	28.0	21.6	17.5	5.6	1.4	32.2
Ann Arbor	4.0	10.1	49.7	14.8	13.4	5.6	2.4	24.7
Athens	6.7	11.7	47.2	14.1	11.8	6.0	2.5	24.5
Atlanta	6.6	13.5	31.9	23.9	15.9	5.9	2.3	33.9
Austin	7.7	14.2	36.5	21.4	13.5	4.6	2.0	30.9
Baltimore	7.0	15.7	28.3	20.1	17.1	8.4	3.4	34.1
Bellevue	5.3	15.4	24.3	22.9	18.2	9.7	4.2	38.5
Birmingham	6.6	15.3	27.2	19.3	18.7	8.7	4.2	35.7
Boise City	6.8	16.1	28.6	20.5	17.6	7.1	3.4	33.9
Boston	5.7	12.0	38.5	19.5	14.2	7.0	3.1	31.9
Boulder	4.1	9.3	46.2	17.8	14.7	5.4	2.6	27.0
Cambridge	4.7	9.3	42.5	18.5	15.1	6.9	3.0	31.5
Cary	7.6	21.1	19.7	26.2	17.1	6.3	1.9	36.0
Charleston	6.5	13.2	34.4	17.2	16.5	8.5	3.6	32.3
Charlotte	8.3	17.3	27.6	23.1	15.3	6.1	2.3	33.2
Chattanooga	6.7	14.7	25.4	19.3	18.9	10.6	4.3	37.9
Chicago	7.5	16.4	29.6	20.9	15.4	7.5	2.8	32.9
Cincinnati	7.2	14.6	30.2	19.5	16.9	7.5	4.1	33.4
Cleveland	6.8	17.9	23.6	21.2	18.0	8.8	3.8	36.3
Colorado Spgs.	7.1	18.2	24.3	22.1	18.0	7.2	3.0	35.3
Columbia	5.5	12.7	41.4	17.1	13.8	6.6	2.9	29.0
Columbus	7.9	15.2	33.6	19.9	14.7	6.1	2.5	31.4
Dallas	9.5	17.4	29.7	21.0	13.8	5.9	2.7	31.0
Denver	8.4	14.4	30.4	21.1	15.4	6.8	3.5	33.2
Des Moines	8.2	16.4	26.7	20.0	16.9	8.0	3.8	34.0
Durham	8.2	15.5	31.6	21.4	14.6	5.8	2.8	32.1
Edison	7.6	16.6	23.3	21.7	17.7	8.4	4.6	36.6
El Paso	9.6	21.1	23.3	19.6	15.0	8.3	3.1	31.8
Eugene	5.3	13.0	32.6	18.2	18.3	7.9	4.6	34.1
Evansville	7.2	15.0	27.1	18.7	17.7	9.6	4.7	35.6
Fargo	6.2	12.9	40.8	16.2	13.9	6.4	3.6	28.7
Ft. Collins	5.2	14.4	39.2	18.9	14.2	5.4	2.6	28.0
Ft. Lauderdale	6.3	13.9	21.6	24.0	20.4	9.4	4.5	40.7
Ft. Wayne	7.9	18.2	24.3	19.8	17.8	7.8	4.1	34.7
Ft. Worth	9.8	19.8	27.0	21.3	13.9	5.9	2.3	31.0
Gainesville	4.7	9.4	55.1	12.5	10.9	4.6	2.7	23.1
Greensboro	6.8	16.0	29.2	19.8	16.3	8.4	3.5	33.5
Honolulu	5.0	12.4	23.2	20.4	19.8	12.2	6.9	42.1
Houston	8.8	18.0	27.9	21.2	15.2	6.5	2.4	32.0
Huntsville	6.1	16.0	25.3	20.1	17.8	11.0	3.6	37.0
Indianapolis	8.2	17.2	26.7	20.7	16.5	7.6	3.2	33.7
Irvine	6.0	15.1	31.6	23.4	16.0	5.7	2.3	33.2
Jackson	8.4	20.0	27.1	18.8	15.7	6.8	3.2	30.9
Jacksonville	7.7	17.3	25.6	21.6	17.2	7.6	2.9	34.5
Kansas City	7.6	16.1	26.3	21.1	17.4	7.9	3.5	35.0
Knoxville	6.4	12.8	32.8	18.9	15.5	9.2	4.3	32.8
Las Vegas	8.2	19.1	23.2	21.9	16.3	8.6	2.7	34.6
Lexington	6.8	14.5	30.6	20.9	16.6	7.6	3.0	33.4
Lincoln	7.5	15.1	32.9	18.6	15.6	7.0	3.4	30.3
Little Rock	7.3	17.3	25.5	20.2	17.7	7.9	4.1	34.9
Los Angeles	7.5	16.9	28.0	22.3	15.2	7.0	3.1	33.5
Louisville	7.1	16.9	23.3	21.4	18.5	8.9	4.0	37.1
Madison	5.8	10.8	40.9	18.5	15.0	6.1	2.9	29.6

Table continued on next page.

City	Percent of Population							Median Age
	Under Age 5	Age 5 to 17	Age 18 to 34	Age 35 to 49	Age 50 to 64	Age 65 to 79	80 Years and Over	
Manchester	7.1	15.4	27.0	21.8	16.9	7.4	4.5	35.4
Miami	6.9	13.2	24.7	21.5	17.1	11.2	5.4	38.7
Milwaukee	8.2	18.5	29.5	19.4	15.0	6.5	3.0	31.0
Minneapolis	7.1	12.4	35.1	21.2	15.8	5.6	2.8	32.4
Naperville	6.8	22.9	19.0	24.9	18.3	5.9	2.2	35.9
Nashville	7.5	14.7	29.5	21.2	16.6	7.3	3.2	33.9
New Orleans	7.1	13.9	26.1	20.9	20.2	8.1	3.7	37.2
New York	6.9	15.8	26.1	22.0	17.1	8.6	3.5	35.7
Oakland	7.6	14.7	26.3	23.5	17.2	7.3	3.3	35.8
Oklahoma City	8.4	17.1	25.7	20.2	16.9	8.5	3.2	34.1
Omaha	8.1	17.6	26.5	19.9	16.7	7.7	3.5	33.4
Orlando	7.8	15.0	33.4	21.7	13.1	6.2	2.8	31.5
Overland Park	6.1	17.6	23.4	22.8	18.1	7.7	4.3	37.2
Oxnard	9.6	20.1	25.9	20.2	14.7	7.0	2.6	30.8
Philadelphia	7.1	16.6	27.4	20.0	16.4	8.5	4.0	34.1
Phoenix	9.3	19.8	26.9	21.9	14.4	5.6	2.1	31.2
Pittsburgh	5.0	12.2	33.2	17.7	17.3	9.1	5.4	34.6
Plano	6.5	19.4	21.9	25.9	17.9	6.4	2.0	36.2
Portland	6.6	13.1	29.3	22.6	18.1	6.6	3.6	35.6
Providence	7.1	17.5	35.5	18.3	13.2	5.8	2.6	29.1
Provo	8.2	12.2	58.6	8.7	7.1	3.8	1.5	22.7
Raleigh	7.7	15.6	32.1	22.3	14.1	5.9	2.2	32.0
Reno	7.7	16.4	27.2	20.7	16.7	8.1	3.2	33.7
Richmond	7.2	13.2	31.6	18.3	15.3	9.5	5.0	33.6
Riverside	8.1	20.3	28.1	21.5	13.7	6.1	2.1	30.3
Rochester	6.9	17.8	29.3	20.2	16.3	6.5	3.1	31.9
Sacramento	8.0	16.7	27.7	20.4	16.5	7.3	3.4	33.4
St. Louis	7.1	15.5	28.0	20.8	17.2	7.5	3.9	34.6
St. Paul	8.2	16.4	29.7	19.8	15.7	6.6	3.6	32.0
St. Petersburg	5.9	15.0	21.6	22.1	20.0	10.1	5.2	40.6
Salt Lake City	8.5	13.8	34.3	19.5	13.8	6.6	3.4	31.3
San Antonio	8.2	19.5	25.9	20.3	15.6	7.4	3.0	32.3
San Diego	6.8	15.3	29.7	21.6	15.9	7.5	3.2	33.8
San Francisco	5.1	9.3	29.2	24.4	18.0	9.5	4.5	38.3
San Jose	7.9	17.3	25.5	23.7	15.9	7.1	2.6	34.6
Santa Ana	10.1	21.5	29.4	21.9	10.9	4.6	1.6	28.4
Savannah	7.9	15.5	30.0	17.8	16.1	8.3	4.4	32.0
Seattle	5.2	9.9	32.3	23.4	18.3	7.0	4.0	36.4
Spokane	6.8	15.9	27.8	19.0	17.8	8.6	4.1	34.7
Springfield	5.8	12.6	34.6	16.6	15.7	9.6	5.2	31.8
Tampa	7.3	16.6	26.9	22.9	15.7	7.4	3.2	34.5
Tulsa	8.0	16.5	25.9	19.0	17.5	8.8	4.2	34.6
Virginia Beach	7.0	17.9	26.0	21.9	16.8	7.8	2.5	34.3
Warren	5.6	17.0	21.6	22.7	17.2	11.0	4.9	39.5
Washington	6.2	13.0	30.2	21.4	17.5	8.3	3.4	35.4
Wichita	8.1	18.1	25.1	19.4	17.5	8.1	3.6	34.0
U.S.	6.9	17.5	23.3	21.4	18.1	9.1	3.7	36.7

Source: U.S. Census Bureau, 2007-2009 American Community Survey 3-Year Estimates

Age Distribution: Metro Area

Metro Area	Percent of Population							Median Age
	Under Age 5	Age 5 to 17	Age 18 to 34	Age 35 to 49	Age 50 to 64	Age 65 to 79	80 Years and Over	
Albuquerque	7.3	17.5	24.6	20.6	18.1	8.6	3.3	35.4
Anchorage	7.7	18.7	27.3	21.4	17.8	5.7	1.4	32.3
Ann Arbor	5.8	15.1	31.4	21.0	17.3	6.7	2.7	32.7
Athens	6.6	14.9	36.3	17.5	15.0	7.3	2.4	28.5
Atlanta	7.9	19.3	24.0	24.1	16.4	6.3	2.1	34.2
Austin	7.9	17.3	29.7	22.5	14.9	5.7	2.1	32.2
Baltimore	6.5	17.0	23.3	22.2	18.8	8.8	3.5	37.5
Bellevue	6.7	16.3	24.8	23.3	18.5	7.4	3.1	36.5
Birmingham	6.9	17.3	23.0	21.3	18.6	9.2	3.6	37.1
Boise City	8.2	19.5	24.6	20.9	16.5	7.3	3.0	33.4
Boston	6.0	16.0	23.7	23.0	18.7	8.8	4.0	38.2
Boulder	6.0	15.4	28.1	22.6	19.0	6.5	2.4	35.3
Cambridge	6.0	16.0	23.7	23.0	18.7	8.8	4.0	38.2
Cary	7.9	18.7	24.5	24.4	16.1	6.4	2.0	34.4
Charleston	7.1	16.5	26.6	20.8	17.8	8.4	2.9	34.9
Charlotte	7.8	18.6	23.6	23.7	16.5	7.3	2.5	35.0
Chattanooga	6.3	16.6	22.0	20.9	19.9	10.7	3.7	38.9
Chicago	7.2	18.4	23.9	22.1	17.3	7.9	3.2	35.3
Cincinnati	6.9	17.9	22.9	22.0	18.2	8.6	3.4	36.7
Cleveland	6.1	17.5	20.0	21.8	19.9	10.1	4.7	39.9
Colorado Spgs.	7.3	18.7	23.8	22.3	18.2	7.2	2.5	35.1
Columbia	6.9	17.6	24.9	21.2	18.1	8.3	3.0	35.5
Columbus	7.3	17.4	25.8	22.2	16.9	7.6	2.8	34.7
Dallas	8.4	19.6	25.3	22.8	15.4	6.2	2.2	32.9
Denver	7.7	17.6	24.3	23.0	17.7	7.1	2.7	35.3
Des Moines	7.8	17.8	24.2	21.8	17.2	7.9	3.3	35.2
Durham	7.1	15.5	28.2	21.3	17.3	7.6	3.0	34.4
Edison	6.6	16.8	22.9	22.6	18.2	9.1	3.8	37.6
El Paso	9.9	21.6	23.8	19.5	14.6	7.7	2.9	30.8
Eugene	5.4	14.8	25.8	19.0	20.8	9.8	4.4	38.3
Evansville	6.6	16.6	22.4	20.6	19.6	9.9	4.3	38.6
Fargo	6.8	15.2	33.5	18.5	15.6	7.1	3.4	30.8
Ft. Collins	6.1	15.4	28.5	20.1	18.9	8.0	3.0	35.0
Ft. Lauderdale	6.6	16.2	21.6	22.2	17.6	10.4	5.4	39.0
Ft. Wayne	7.5	19.0	22.4	20.9	18.2	8.2	3.8	35.8
Ft. Worth	8.4	19.6	25.3	22.8	15.4	6.2	2.2	32.9
Gainesville	5.6	13.1	38.0	16.7	15.8	7.5	3.3	28.1
Greensboro	6.6	17.3	22.8	21.8	18.5	9.3	3.6	37.3
Honolulu	6.9	15.4	25.1	20.3	17.5	10.0	4.8	37.0
Houston	8.5	20.1	24.6	22.1	16.4	6.3	2.0	32.8
Huntsville	6.4	17.7	22.8	22.8	18.0	9.5	2.8	37.3
Indianapolis	7.6	18.6	23.4	22.5	17.2	7.8	3.0	35.3
Irvine	7.4	18.2	25.3	22.3	16.1	7.5	3.1	34.4
Jackson	7.5	19.1	24.8	20.4	17.1	8.0	3.1	33.9
Jacksonville	7.0	17.5	23.3	22.1	18.4	8.4	3.2	36.5
Kansas City	7.3	18.1	22.9	22.0	18.1	8.1	3.5	36.2
Knoxville	6.1	15.9	23.0	21.3	19.5	10.5	3.7	38.7
Las Vegas	8.0	18.4	24.5	21.9	16.7	8.2	2.3	34.4
Lexington	6.8	15.8	27.7	21.4	17.3	7.9	3.0	34.7
Lincoln	7.2	15.7	30.9	18.9	16.6	7.4	3.3	31.5
Little Rock	7.2	17.7	24.4	20.9	17.8	8.7	3.3	35.5
Los Angeles	7.4	18.2	25.3	22.3	16.1	7.5	3.1	34.4
Louisville	6.7	17.4	22.2	22.0	19.1	9.0	3.6	37.6
Madison	6.3	15.0	29.0	21.6	17.8	7.2	3.2	34.8

Table continued on next page.

Metro Area	Percent of Population							Median Age
	Under Age 5	Age 5 to 17	Age 18 to 34	Age 35 to 49	Age 50 to 64	Age 65 to 79	80 Years and Over	
Manchester	6.4	17.5	21.5	24.1	18.8	8.0	3.5	38.2
Miami	6.6	16.2	21.6	22.2	17.6	10.4	5.4	39.0
Milwaukee	7.0	17.8	23.0	21.5	18.4	8.4	4.0	36.8
Minneapolis	7.2	17.7	24.1	23.0	17.8	7.2	3.0	35.8
Naperville	7.2	18.4	23.9	22.1	17.3	7.9	3.2	35.3
Nashville	7.2	17.3	24.7	22.7	17.6	7.8	2.8	35.5
New Orleans	6.8	16.8	23.0	21.3	19.8	8.7	3.6	37.6
New York	6.6	16.8	22.9	22.6	18.2	9.1	3.8	37.6
Oakland	6.5	15.2	23.5	23.6	18.8	8.6	3.8	38.0
Oklahoma City	7.6	17.3	26.0	20.0	17.3	8.6	3.2	34.3
Omaha	7.9	18.3	24.6	21.0	17.2	7.8	3.2	34.4
Orlando	6.9	17.2	24.5	21.8	16.6	9.4	3.6	36.0
Overland Park	7.3	18.1	22.9	22.0	18.1	8.1	3.5	36.2
Oxnard	7.5	18.9	21.9	22.0	18.1	8.1	3.4	36.3
Philadelphia	6.5	17.3	22.7	22.0	18.5	9.0	4.1	37.7
Phoenix	8.3	19.0	24.9	21.0	15.5	8.1	3.1	33.5
Pittsburgh	5.2	15.2	20.6	21.0	20.7	11.5	5.7	42.1
Plano	8.4	19.6	25.3	22.8	15.4	6.2	2.2	32.9
Portland	6.8	17.2	24.2	22.3	18.8	7.5	3.2	36.2
Providence	5.8	16.3	22.4	22.4	19.1	9.4	4.6	39.0
Provo	11.3	23.4	33.2	15.4	10.3	4.9	1.5	23.4
Raleigh	7.9	18.7	24.5	24.4	16.1	6.4	2.0	34.4
Reno	7.4	17.2	23.9	20.8	18.9	8.9	3.0	36.2
Richmond	6.6	17.3	23.0	22.4	18.8	8.5	3.3	37.2
Riverside	8.1	21.7	24.1	21.1	15.1	7.3	2.6	31.9
Rochester	5.7	17.1	22.0	21.7	19.8	9.4	4.3	39.3
Sacramento	7.1	18.2	23.8	21.4	17.7	8.4	3.3	35.6
St. Louis	6.6	17.6	22.3	21.7	18.8	9.1	3.9	37.7
St. Paul	7.2	17.7	24.1	23.0	17.8	7.2	3.0	35.8
St. Petersburg	6.1	15.7	21.1	21.2	18.8	11.6	5.5	40.5
Salt Lake City	9.3	20.1	27.9	19.6	14.7	6.1	2.3	30.7
San Antonio	8.0	19.5	24.3	20.8	16.4	7.9	3.0	33.6
San Diego	7.5	16.9	26.2	21.3	16.8	7.8	3.4	34.6
San Francisco	6.5	15.2	23.5	23.6	18.8	8.6	3.8	38.0
San Jose	7.6	17.0	24.4	23.9	16.4	7.7	3.1	35.6
Santa Ana	7.4	18.2	25.3	22.3	16.1	7.5	3.1	34.4
Savannah	7.5	17.4	26.0	20.2	17.3	8.3	3.2	34.2
Seattle	6.7	16.3	24.8	23.3	18.5	7.4	3.1	36.5
Spokane	6.5	17.0	24.7	20.1	18.9	9.1	3.7	36.5
Springfield	6.8	16.5	26.1	19.7	17.4	9.7	3.9	35.5
Tampa	6.1	15.7	21.1	21.2	18.8	11.6	5.5	40.5
Tulsa	7.4	18.3	23.0	20.5	18.3	9.1	3.4	36.0
Virginia Beach	7.0	17.6	25.9	21.3	17.1	8.4	2.8	34.7
Warren	6.3	18.4	20.8	22.7	19.3	8.7	3.8	38.2
Washington	7.3	17.3	23.8	23.7	18.0	7.3	2.6	36.0
Wichita	7.8	19.1	23.1	20.2	17.7	8.4	3.7	35.0
U.S.	6.9	17.5	23.3	21.4	18.1	9.1	3.7	36.7

Note: Figures cover the Metropolitan Statistical Area (MSA) - see Appendix B for areas included
Source: U.S. Census Bureau, 2007-2009 American Community Survey 3-Year Estimates

Segregation

Area	Black/White		Asian/White		Hispanic/White	
	Index[1]	Rank[2]	Index[1]	Rank[2]	Index[1]	Rank[2]
Albuquerque	30.9	99	28.5	93	36.4	79
Anchorage	n/a	n/a	n/a	n/a	n/a	n/a
Ann Arbor	n/a	n/a	n/a	n/a	n/a	n/a
Athens	n/a	n/a	n/a	n/a	n/a	n/a
Atlanta	59.0	41	48.5	10	49.5	27
Austin	50.1	70	41.2	49	43.2	51
Baltimore	65.4	19	43.6	33	39.8	67
Bellevue	49.1	72	37.6	69	32.8	87
Birmingham	65.8	16	47.1	15	44.5	47
Boise City	30.2	101	27.6	95	36.2	80
Boston	64.0	27	45.4	23	59.6	5
Boulder	n/a	n/a	n/a	n/a	n/a	n/a
Cambridge	64.0	27	45.4	23	59.6	5
Cary	42.1	87	46.7	16	37.1	76
Charleston	41.5	88	33.4	84	39.8	66
Charlotte	53.8	56	43.6	34	47.6	35
Chattanooga	64.6	25	37.7	68	38.8	72
Chicago	76.4	3	44.9	26	56.3	10
Cincinnati	69.4	8	46.0	21	36.9	77
Cleveland	74.1	5	41.3	48	52.3	20
Colorado Spgs.	39.3	92	24.1	98	30.3	95
Columbia	48.8	74	41.9	46	34.9	82
Columbus	62.2	33	43.3	35	41.5	59
Dallas	56.6	48	46.6	19	50.3	24
Denver	62.6	31	33.4	83	48.8	31
Des Moines	51.6	66	35.5	76	46.7	40
Durham	48.1	75	44.0	30	48.0	33
Edison	78.0	2	51.9	3	62.0	3
El Paso	30.7	100	22.2	100	43.3	50
Eugene	n/a	n/a	n/a	n/a	n/a	n/a
Evansville	n/a	n/a	n/a	n/a	n/a	n/a
Fargo	n/a	n/a	n/a	n/a	n/a	n/a
Ft. Collins	n/a	n/a	n/a	n/a	n/a	n/a
Ft. Lauderdale	64.8	23	34.2	80	57.4	8
Ft. Wayne	n/a	n/a	n/a	n/a	n/a	n/a
Ft. Worth	56.6	48	46.6	19	50.3	24
Gainesville	n/a	n/a	n/a	n/a	n/a	n/a
Greensboro	54.7	53	47.7	14	41.1	61
Honolulu	36.9	95	42.1	44	31.9	91
Houston	61.4	36	50.4	7	52.5	18
Huntsville	n/a	n/a	n/a	n/a	n/a	n/a
Indianapolis	66.4	15	41.6	47	47.3	37
Irvine	67.8	10	48.4	12	62.2	2
Jackson	56.0	51	38.9	63	42.9	52
Jacksonville	53.1	59	37.5	71	27.6	98
Kansas City	61.2	39	38.4	65	44.4	48
Knoxville	54.1	54	43.3	36	33.6	86
Las Vegas	37.6	94	28.8	92	42.0	58
Lexington	n/a	n/a	n/a	n/a	n/a	n/a
Lincoln	n/a	n/a	n/a	n/a	n/a	n/a
Little Rock	58.8	42	39.7	59	39.7	68
Los Angeles	67.8	10	48.4	12	62.2	2
Louisville	58.1	43	42.2	43	38.7	73
Madison	49.6	71	44.2	29	40.1	65
Manchester	n/a	n/a	n/a	n/a	n/a	n/a

Table continued on next page.

Area	Black/White		Asian/White		Hispanic/White	
	Index[1]	Rank[2]	Index[1]	Rank[2]	Index[1]	Rank[2]
Miami	64.8	23	34.2	80	57.4	8
Milwaukee	81.5	1	40.7	52	57.0	9
Minneapolis	52.9	60	42.8	39	42.5	54
Naperville	76.4	3	44.9	26	56.3	10
Nashville	56.2	49	41.0	51	47.9	34
New Orleans	63.9	28	48.6	9	38.3	74
New York	78.0	2	51.9	3	62.0	3
Oakland	62.0	34	46.6	18	49.6	26
Oklahoma City	51.4	67	39.2	60	47.0	38
Omaha	61.3	38	36.3	74	48.8	30
Orlando	50.7	69	33.9	81	40.2	64
Overland Park	61.2	39	38.4	65	44.4	48
Oxnard	39.9	91	31.2	87	54.6	13
Philadelphia	68.4	9	42.3	42	55.1	12
Phoenix	43.6	86	32.7	85	49.3	28
Pittsburgh	65.8	17	52.4	2	28.6	97
Plano	56.6	48	46.6	19	50.3	24
Portland	46.0	81	35.8	75	34.3	83
Providence	53.5	57	40.1	55	60.1	4
Provo	21.9	102	28.2	94	30.9	93
Raleigh	42.1	87	46.7	16	37.1	76
Reno	n/a	n/a	n/a	n/a	n/a	n/a
Richmond	52.4	63	43.9	32	44.9	46
Riverside	45.7	82	40.7	53	42.4	55
Rochester	65.3	21	45.1	24	48.9	29
Sacramento	56.9	46	49.9	8	38.9	71
St. Louis	72.3	7	44.3	28	30.7	94
St. Paul	52.9	60	42.8	39	42.5	54
St. Petersburg	56.2	50	35.3	78	40.7	62
Salt Lake City	39.3	93	31.0	88	42.9	53
San Antonio	49.0	73	38.3	66	46.1	43
San Diego	51.2	68	48.2	13	49.6	25
San Francisco	62.0	34	46.6	18	49.6	26
San Jose	40.9	89	45.0	25	47.6	36
Santa Ana	67.8	10	48.4	12	62.2	2
Savannah	n/a	n/a	n/a	n/a	n/a	n/a
Seattle	49.1	72	37.6	69	32.8	87
Spokane	n/a	n/a	n/a	n/a	n/a	n/a
Springfield	n/a	n/a	n/a	n/a	n/a	n/a
Tampa	56.2	50	35.3	78	40.7	62
Tulsa	56.6	47	42.6	40	45.3	45
Virginia Beach	47.8	76	34.3	79	32.2	90
Warren	75.3	4	50.6	6	43.3	49
Washington	62.3	32	38.9	64	48.3	32
Wichita	58.0	44	46.5	20	42.3	56

Note: Figures are based on an analysis of 1990, 2000, and 2010 Census Decennial Census tract data by William H. Frey, Brookings Institution and the University of Michigan Social Science Data Analysis Network. In this analysis all racial groups (whites, blacks, and asians) are non-Hispanic members of those races. Hispanics are shown as a separate category; All figures cover the Metropolitan Statistical Area (see Appendix B for areas included); (1) Segregation Indices are Dissimilarity Indices that measure the degree to which the minority group is distributed differently than whites aross census tracts. They range from 0 (complete integration) to 100 (complete [segregation) where the value indicates the percentage of the minority group that needs to move to be distributed exactly like whites; (2) Ranges from 1 (most segregated) to 102 (least segregated); n/a not available.
Source: www.CensusScope.org

Religion

City	County/Parish	Catholic	Southern Baptist	United Methodist	ELCA[1]	LDS[2]	Presbyterian Church	Jewish Est.	Muslim Est.
Albuquerque	Bernalillo	34.4	4.0	2.0	1.4	1.5	0.9	1.4	0.3
Anchorage	Anchorage	8.8	4.6	0.9	1.8	3.2	0.8	0.9	0.5
Ann Arbor	Washtenaw	12.9	0.7	2.2	1.7	0.5	1.4	2.2	1.5
Athens	Clarke	4.9	12.8	7.0	0.4	0.5	2.5	0.4	0.3
Atlanta	Fulton	8.8	10.0	9.2	0.8	0.3	3.7	8.1	2.7
Austin	Travis	20.4	9.5	2.7	1.5	0.6	1.3	1.7	0.4
Baltimore	Baltimore City	12.5	0.8	2.7	1.8	0.1	1.5	8.7	1.6
Bellevue	King	16.2	0.7	1.1	2.0	2.3	1.6	1.9	0.5
Birmingham	Jefferson	6.7	29.7	8.0	0.2	0.3	1.5	0.8	0.3
Boise City	Ada	12.3	1.0	2.0	1.0	15.2	0.7	0.3	0.1
Boston	Suffolk	45.0	0.6	0.2	0.1	0.1	0.1	3.6	2.0
Boulder	Boulder	20.2	1.0	1.8	3.0	1.6	1.8	4.5	1.4
Cambridge	Middlesex	54.2	0.2	1.2	0.4	0.4	0.1	7.8	0.9
Cary	Wake	9.5	12.6	7.4	0.9	0.6	2.7	1.0	0.5
Charleston	Charleston	7.7	11.6	5.7	1.9	0.5	3.9	1.6	0.7
Charlotte	Mecklenburg	8.5	10.8	6.7	1.2	0.5	6.0	1.2	1.1
Chattanooga	Hamilton	3.2	21.6	8.0	0.3	0.2	1.3	0.5	0.7
Chicago	Cook	39.9	1.2	0.8	1.2	0.2	0.7	4.4	1.8
Cincinnati	Hamilton	26.8	1.8	3.6	0.7	0.4	2.3	2.7	0.1
Cleveland	Cuyahoga	34.9	0.3	2.2	1.4	0.2	1.1	5.7	1.5
Colorado Spgs.	El Paso	11.3	4.0	2.0	1.6	2.2	1.7	0.3	0.1
Columbia	Richland	4.0	13.5	7.0	2.7	0.3	3.1	0.9	0.4
Columbus	Franklin	13.7	2.1	4.1	2.8	0.4	1.5	1.5	0.6
Dallas	Dallas	21.7	12.7	4.8	0.5	0.5	1.3	1.7	1.0
Denver	Denver	28.7	1.3	1.6	0.9	0.6	1.1	6.9	1.1
Des Moines	Polk	15.5	0.2	5.3	6.3	0.5	1.9	0.6	0.3
Durham	Durham	4.4	12.8	5.6	0.5	0.8	2.0	1.8	0.9
Edison	Middlesex	45.7	0.1	0.8	0.6	0.2	1.0	6.0	0.9
El Paso	El Paso	51.5	3.6	1.3	0.2	0.8	0.4	0.7	0.1
Eugene	Lane	4.8	1.3	1.0	1.3	2.6	0.5	1.0	0.2
Evansville	Vanderburgh	18.3	11.2	4.2	0.7	0.6	0.9	0.2	0.5
Fargo	Cass	14.5	0.2	2.4	27.6	0.3	2.0	0.5	0.5
Ft. Collins	Larimer	12.8	0.9	2.1	2.1	2.5	1.8	0.4	0.5
Ft. Lauderdale	Broward	21.1	3.6	1.2	0.3	0.3	0.4	13.1	0.4
Ft. Wayne	Allen	17.4	1.1	4.5	3.8	0.3	1.0	0.3	0.2
Ft. Worth	Tarrant	11.5	18.7	6.8	0.6	0.8	0.8	0.4	1.0
Gainesville	Alachua	7.3	11.2	5.4	0.4	0.7	1.1	1.0	0.2
Greensboro	Guilford	5.1	12.8	10.5	1.1	0.4	3.9	0.6	0.9
Honolulu	Honolulu	17.6	1.9	0.8	0.3	3.3	0.0	0.7	0.1
Houston	Harris	18.2	14.3	5.0	0.5	0.7	1.1	1.1	1.4
Huntsville	Madison	5.8	22.4	7.7	0.7	0.8	1.6	0.3	0.4
Indianapolis	Marion	12.7	1.7	3.7	0.7	0.3	1.8	1.2	0.3
Irvine	Orange	27.4	1.2	0.6	0.8	1.7	0.9	2.1	1.4
Jackson	Hinds	3.0	30.1	10.6	0.2	0.3	0.8	0.2	0.5
Jacksonville	Duval	8.3	18.4	3.7	0.5	0.7	1.7	0.8	0.3
Kansas City	Jackson	15.5	11.5	4.2	0.4	0.9	1.8	1.1	1.0
Knoxville	Knox	4.0	31.5	8.4	0.7	0.4	2.6	0.5	0.9
Las Vegas	Clark	17.2	1.9	0.4	0.6	6.0	0.3	5.5	0.1
Lexington	Fayette	10.0	14.1	6.1	0.5	0.7	1.8	0.8	0.4
Lincoln	Lancaster	10.5	0.9	6.3	5.1	0.9	2.3	0.3	0.5
Little Rock	Pulaski	8.2	22.2	9.1	0.1	0.6	1.2	0.3	0.3
Los Angeles	Los Angeles	40.0	1.2	0.6	0.3	1.0	0.6	5.9	1.0
Louisville	Jefferson	22.6	15.6	2.9	0.5	0.4	1.5	1.3	0.3
Madison	Dane	28.0	0.1	2.0	11.6	0.3	1.0	1.1	0.3
Manchester	Hillsborough	45.5	0.2	1.0	0.4	0.5	0.4	1.6	n/a

Table continued on next page.

City	County/Parish	Catholic	Southern Baptist	United Meth- odist	ELCA[1]	LDS[2]	Presby- terian Church	Jewish Est.	Muslim Est.
Miami	Miami-Dade	24.1	3.6	0.8	0.3	0.3	0.2	5.5	0.3
Milwaukee	Milwaukee	27.8	1.0	1.0	3.0	0.2	0.5	1.8	0.3
Minneapolis	Hennepin	23.4	0.2	2.1	13.7	0.4	1.6	2.8	0.7
Naperville	DuPage	38.7	0.2	2.2	3.0	0.3	1.1	0.2	1.7
Nashville	Davidson	4.9	17.0	5.7	0.4	0.3	1.9	1.1	1.6
New Orleans	Orleans	28.1	5.7	2.3	0.2	0.1	0.7	1.8	0.8
New York	Bronx	43.7	0.2	0.5	0.2	0.2	0.2	6.3	0.9
New York	Kings	37.0	0.1	0.5	0.3	0.1	0.1	15.4	2.3
New York	New York	36.7	0.1	0.8	0.3	0.3	0.7	20.5	2.4
New York	Queens	28.9	0.1	0.5	0.4	0.3	0.3	10.7	2.3
New York	Richmond	59.7	0.0	0.7	0.9	0.2	0.2	7.6	1.8
Oakland	Alameda	21.2	1.6	0.7	0.5	1.2	0.7	2.3	1.6
Oklahoma City	Oklahoma	6.5	26.4	9.4	0.6	0.7	1.3	0.4	0.4
Omaha	Douglas	27.7	1.7	2.8	5.4	1.0	2.3	1.4	0.4
Orlando	Orange	13.3	8.2	3.3	0.6	0.6	1.7	1.2	0.2
Overland Park	Johnson	21.3	3.1	4.5	1.8	0.8	3.5	2.7	n/a
Oxnard	Ventura	29.3	0.8	0.9	1.1	2.1	0.9	2.0	0.3
Philadelphia	Philadelphia	32.4	1.2	1.3	1.0	0.1	0.7	5.7	2.8
Phoenix	Maricopa	17.3	2.5	1.1	1.7	5.0	0.6	2.0	0.3
Pittsburgh	Allegheny	49.4	0.2	3.7	2.5	0.2	4.7	2.7	0.6
Plano	Collin	18.3	16.0	6.1	0.6	1.3	0.7	1.4	1.2
Portland	Multnomah	22.7	0.7	0.9	1.2	1.6	1.6	2.9	0.6
Providence	Providence	52.1	0.0	0.6	0.3	0.2	0.1	1.7	0.3
Provo	Utah	1.0	0.1	n/a	0.0	88.1	0.1	n/a	n/a
Raleigh	Wake	9.5	12.6	7.4	0.9	0.6	2.7	1.0	0.5
Reno	Washoe	16.2	1.1	0.8	0.6	3.5	0.5	0.6	0.2
Richmond	Richmond City	5.1	12.5	5.8	0.3	n/a	0.4	7.6	0.4
Riverside	Riverside	28.2	1.4	0.5	0.5	2.2	0.3	1.3	0.5
Rochester	Monroe	35.7	0.1	2.0	1.4	0.4	1.9	3.1	0.6
Sacramento	Sacramento	18.3	1.7	0.6	0.7	2.5	0.9	1.4	0.5
St. Louis	Saint Louis City	20.3	4.4	1.4	1.4	0.1	0.8	1.3	1.2
St. Paul	Ramsey	31.2	0.1	1.6	12.2	0.4	1.2	1.6	0.5
St. Petersburg	Pinellas	12.2	3.9	4.4	0.9	0.2	1.3	2.6	0.5
Salt Lake City	Salt Lake	6.0	0.6	0.5	0.4	56.0	0.4	0.5	0.4
San Antonio	Bexar	41.2	8.6	3.0	1.0	0.7	0.8	0.8	0.2
San Diego	San Diego	29.5	1.0	0.7	0.6	1.6	0.9	2.5	0.3
San Francisco	San Francisco	23.3	0.4	1.7	0.2	0.2	0.5	6.4	2.9
San Jose	Santa Clara	28.7	1.0	0.9	0.6	1.2	0.6	3.2	1.1
Santa Ana	Orange	27.4	1.2	0.6	0.8	1.7	0.9	2.1	1.4
Savannah	Chatham	9.0	14.9	6.7	1.5	0.3	1.4	1.3	0.3
Seattle	King	16.2	0.7	1.1	2.0	2.3	1.6	1.9	0.5
Spokane	Spokane	13.7	2.1	1.4	2.6	3.4	1.9	0.4	0.2
Springfield	Greene	6.0	21.7	5.4	0.5	0.9	1.9	0.1	0.3
Tampa	Hillsborough	16.6	10.3	3.3	0.7	0.4	1.0	2.0	0.5
Tulsa	Tulsa	7.3	19.5	11.7	0.6	0.8	1.8	0.5	0.4
Virginia Beach	Virginia Beach City	9.6	4.7	4.6	0.5	0.5	1.4	1.8	n/a
Warren	Macomb	30.9	0.7	0.7	1.8	0.1	0.5	0.5	n/a
Washington	District of Columbia	28.0	6.8	2.7	0.7	0.1	1.5	4.5	10.6
Wichita	Sedgwick	13.8	7.0	6.0	0.7	0.8	1.6	0.3	0.4
U.S.		22.0	7.1	3.7	1.8	1.5	1.1	2.2	0.6

Note: Figures shown are the number of adherents as a percentage of the total population; Adherents are defined as all members, including full members, their children and the estimated number of other participants who are not considered members (e.g. the baptized, those not confirmed, those not eligible for communion, those regularly attending services, etc.); (1) Evangelical Lutheran Church in America; (2) The Church of Jesus Christ of Latter Day Saints
Source: Reprinted with permission from Religious Congregations and Membership in the United States 2000 (Nashville, Glenmary Research Center, 2002) Copyright Association of Statisticians of American Religious Bodies. All rights reserved.

Ancestry: City

City	German	Irish	English	American	Italian	Polish	French	Scottish
Albuquerque	12.1	8.9	7.6	2.5	3.2	1.8	2.1	1.9
Anchorage	20.7	13.7	9.6	3.5	3.9	2.9	3.6	3.3
Ann Arbor	19.2	11.2	12.1	2.8	4.2	6.8	3.4	3.0
Athens	9.8	9.3	11.3	6.2	2.4	1.4	1.8	3.4
Atlanta	7.5	6.2	8.4	6.5	2.4	1.3	2.1	2.1
Austin	13.1	8.6	9.2	3.1	2.8	1.7	2.9	2.5
Baltimore	8.1	6.9	3.9	3.9	3.1	2.7	1.0	0.8
Bellevue	13.1	8.5	11.6	2.8	3.5	2.5	3.3	2.8
Birmingham	3.2	4.5	4.5	3.5	1.0	0.5	1.0	1.5
Boise City	19.4	13.3	15.5	9.4	3.6	1.7	3.2	3.5
Boston	4.7	17.5	5.6	1.8	8.8	2.6	2.4	1.5
Boulder	24.8	14.8	16.5	2.3	6.3	4.9	3.7	4.3
Cambridge	9.8	14.7	10.6	1.8	8.5	4.2	3.8	3.0
Cary	16.0	13.4	15.2	7.3	7.4	3.4	2.5	3.0
Charleston	12.7	11.6	12.7	10.9	3.9	1.8	2.6	3.7
Charlotte	10.9	8.3	8.7	4.4	4.3	1.8	1.9	2.6
Chattanooga	8.5	8.2	8.2	11.7	1.7	0.9	1.8	2.1
Chicago	7.9	7.9	2.4	1.2	3.8	6.6	1.0	0.6
Cincinnati	20.5	11.5	5.6	6.7	3.2	1.3	1.9	1.4
Cleveland	11.3	10.5	3.9	2.0	5.0	4.7	1.2	0.9
Colorado Spgs.	22.9	13.9	12.8	4.2	5.3	2.4	3.8	3.0
Columbia	9.8	8.1	9.6	6.3	2.0	1.5	1.8	2.8
Columbus	22.1	13.3	7.8	4.0	5.0	2.5	2.2	1.8
Dallas	6.3	4.9	5.4	2.8	1.5	0.9	1.5	1.2
Denver	14.7	10.0	8.3	3.4	4.2	2.1	2.7	2.0
Des Moines	24.5	15.4	9.1	4.1	4.5	1.0	2.1	1.8
Durham	9.2	7.2	8.6	4.1	3.1	1.9	1.6	2.6
Edison	6.7	7.7	2.4	3.7	9.9	5.7	1.1	0.6
El Paso	4.1	2.8	2.4	3.4	1.0	0.5	0.7	0.5
Eugene	21.9	13.9	14.7	3.9	4.1	2.4	3.5	3.8
Evansville	29.3	12.2	8.4	20.4	2.2	1.4	2.6	1.5
Fargo	43.4	9.4	4.1	1.6	1.4	2.7	4.6	1.3
Ft. Collins	31.4	15.4	13.0	3.7	6.0	2.6	3.1	3.4
Ft. Lauderdale	9.4	10.4	7.5	7.8	7.8	2.8	2.0	1.8
Ft. Wayne	31.1	11.5	7.7	9.1	3.0	2.5	3.9	1.9
Ft. Worth	9.3	7.2	7.1	7.1	1.9	0.9	1.8	1.8
Gainesville	14.0	11.6	10.8	1.7	5.8	3.6	2.5	2.3
Greensboro	8.9	7.1	8.6	4.7	2.4	1.4	1.8	2.3
Honolulu	4.9	4.0	3.8	0.6	1.6	1.0	1.2	1.0
Houston	6.2	4.4	4.8	2.6	1.6	0.9	1.8	1.1
Huntsville	9.7	10.6	11.5	10.5	2.3	1.0	2.1	2.4
Indianapolis	19.2	12.1	8.6	6.3	2.6	1.7	2.0	1.8
Irvine	9.2	6.7	6.4	3.3	3.8	1.9	1.9	1.4
Jackson	2.3	3.3	3.6	2.4	0.6	0.2	0.9	0.7
Jacksonville	10.4	10.6	8.6	6.6	3.7	1.9	2.4	2.1
Kansas City	18.9	12.5	8.3	11.5	4.0	1.3	2.2	1.8
Knoxville	16.4	12.4	16.2	9.7	2.1	1.4	2.1	2.5
Las Vegas	11.9	8.7	7.3	2.5	6.7	2.7	2.2	1.7
Lexington	15.4	13.7	13.4	12.1	3.0	1.4	2.4	3.0
Lincoln	44.6	14.8	10.7	3.2	1.9	3.0	2.7	2.1
Little Rock	9.1	7.9	10.4	4.9	1.4	0.8	2.5	1.8
Los Angeles	4.8	4.0	3.5	1.7	2.7	1.6	1.3	0.8
Louisville	18.8	13.9	9.4	10.8	2.8	1.2	2.1	1.6
Madison	35.9	14.2	8.8	2.1	4.1	5.5	3.1	2.1
Manchester	5.7	21.4	10.0	2.8	9.4	5.7	22.8	2.9
Miami	1.9	1.7	1.1	2.0	1.8	0.6	1.0	0.3

Table continued on next page.

City	German	Irish	English	American	Italian	Polish	French	Scottish
Milwaukee	20.9	6.9	2.8	0.9	2.9	8.4	1.8	0.6
Minneapolis	24.1	11.6	6.6	1.4	2.4	4.0	3.2	1.5
Naperville	23.1	18.6	8.3	2.1	10.8	11.7	2.0	1.8
Nashville	10.1	9.6	8.9	9.8	2.4	1.2	2.0	2.2
New Orleans	6.6	5.3	4.5	2.5	3.6	0.6	6.5	1.0
New York	3.6	5.3	1.9	2.6	8.2	2.8	0.9	0.5
Oakland	5.8	5.1	4.4	1.0	2.9	1.3	1.5	1.2
Oklahoma City	15.0	11.7	8.6	6.2	2.0	0.8	2.3	1.8
Omaha	31.5	17.7	8.8	2.7	5.1	4.5	2.9	1.5
Orlando	9.5	8.7	7.2	4.2	5.3	1.9	2.1	1.7
Overland Park	31.0	18.1	14.1	4.7	4.1	2.3	3.8	3.0
Oxnard	4.5	4.2	2.9	1.2	1.4	0.9	1.2	0.7
Philadelphia	8.6	13.8	3.2	1.4	8.8	4.1	0.9	0.6
Phoenix	12.4	8.9	7.0	3.4	4.0	2.3	2.3	1.5
Pittsburgh	21.8	17.1	5.8	2.3	13.6	7.9	1.3	1.7
Plano	14.3	11.0	9.6	7.1	3.7	1.7	3.0	2.4
Portland	19.3	12.8	11.7	4.5	4.3	2.3	4.0	3.5
Providence	4.1	9.7	5.3	0.9	10.8	2.6	3.6	1.1
Provo	11.4	5.3	29.1	2.5	3.2	0.9	2.3	6.1
Raleigh	10.3	8.6	10.7	10.1	3.9	2.0	1.7	2.9
Reno	16.0	12.2	10.3	4.3	7.1	1.7	3.2	2.5
Richmond	8.0	6.8	9.0	4.4	2.9	1.6	1.7	2.6
Riverside	10.1	6.9	6.8	2.2	4.2	1.2	2.3	1.2
Rochester	11.8	9.8	7.3	1.9	10.1	3.0	2.2	1.6
Sacramento	9.4	7.8	6.1	1.6	4.1	1.2	2.1	1.9
St. Louis	17.5	10.5	4.9	3.7	3.9	2.2	3.1	1.0
St. Paul	25.4	12.9	5.8	1.7	3.3	3.8	3.7	1.5
St. Petersburg	14.5	14.1	10.8	3.2	6.9	3.3	3.4	2.4
Salt Lake City	11.9	7.0	20.9	2.6	2.9	1.6	2.3	3.9
San Antonio	9.2	5.4	5.0	3.9	1.9	1.2	1.9	1.2
San Diego	11.6	8.8	7.4	2.4	4.9	2.1	2.6	2.0
San Francisco	8.6	8.7	6.1	1.0	5.0	2.2	2.3	1.7
San Jose	6.9	5.2	4.7	1.2	4.5	1.0	1.5	1.0
Santa Ana	2.1	1.5	1.7	1.3	0.8	0.4	0.6	0.4
Savannah	6.0	8.0	7.4	3.3	1.8	0.5	1.3	1.3
Seattle	16.9	12.4	11.8	2.7	4.3	2.3	3.4	3.9
Spokane	25.7	16.7	12.6	4.1	5.1	2.0	4.6	3.7
Springfield	22.8	15.0	11.6	14.4	2.7	1.8	3.4	3.0
Tampa	11.2	9.0	7.1	3.8	6.7	2.1	2.3	1.8
Tulsa	14.9	11.7	10.3	7.0	2.1	1.1	2.6	2.4
Virginia Beach	14.3	13.1	11.4	10.2	7.2	2.8	2.7	3.1
Warren	21.0	12.3	6.9	3.2	9.9	19.6	5.5	2.0
Washington	6.6	6.7	5.1	1.6	3.1	2.0	1.5	1.3
Wichita	25.6	12.9	10.6	4.8	2.2	1.1	3.1	1.9
U.S.	16.6	12.0	9.1	6.1	5.9	3.3	3.1	1.9

Note: The top eight ancestries in the U.S. are shown; Figures are percentages and include multiple ancestry (e.g. if a person reported being Irish and Italian, they were included in both columns);
Source: U.S. Census Bureau, 2007-2009 American Community Survey 3-Year Estimates

Ancestry: Metro Area

Metro Area	German	Irish	English	American	Italian	Polish	French	Scottish
Albuquerque	12.1	8.7	7.7	2.7	3.2	1.7	2.3	2.0
Anchorage	22.0	14.0	11.0	3.7	4.1	2.9	4.1	3.3
Ann Arbor	22.0	11.9	12.7	4.6	4.2	7.2	3.7	3.2
Athens	9.6	10.2	11.8	10.3	2.1	1.3	1.6	3.2
Atlanta	8.6	8.8	8.6	9.3	2.9	1.4	1.8	2.0
Austin	16.1	9.8	9.9	4.1	2.8	1.7	3.0	2.7
Baltimore	19.8	14.6	9.4	4.7	6.7	4.8	2.0	1.9
Bellevue	19.0	12.3	11.8	3.2	3.9	2.1	3.7	3.3
Birmingham	8.0	10.3	10.3	11.5	2.5	0.8	1.8	2.5
Boise City	19.1	11.3	15.2	12.7	3.1	1.5	2.8	3.4
Boston	6.8	25.3	11.9	3.0	15.3	3.9	6.6	2.9
Boulder	24.6	14.1	15.0	2.8	6.0	4.0	4.0	4.2
Cambridge	6.8	25.3	11.9	3.0	15.3	3.9	6.6	2.9
Cary	12.0	10.7	12.1	11.0	5.0	2.3	2.1	2.9
Charleston	11.8	10.3	10.3	11.4	3.5	1.6	2.7	2.8
Charlotte	13.4	10.0	9.5	8.1	4.2	1.9	2.0	2.6
Chattanooga	10.7	13.2	11.1	17.3	1.6	0.9	2.1	2.5
Chicago	17.1	12.8	4.9	2.2	7.3	10.2	1.7	1.1
Cincinnati	31.9	16.2	9.6	9.4	4.5	1.6	2.5	2.0
Cleveland	21.7	15.1	8.3	3.5	10.3	8.7	1.9	1.8
Colorado Spgs.	23.0	13.9	12.5	4.6	5.3	2.6	3.7	2.9
Columbia	12.2	9.1	9.7	11.6	2.3	1.2	2.0	2.1
Columbus	27.8	15.1	10.6	6.6	5.5	2.5	2.3	2.3
Dallas	11.4	8.8	8.6	6.5	2.3	1.2	2.3	1.9
Denver	21.7	12.5	11.2	4.5	5.2	2.7	3.3	2.7
Des Moines	32.8	16.2	11.1	4.7	4.2	1.3	2.5	1.8
Durham	11.5	9.2	12.1	6.1	3.3	2.3	2.1	3.1
Edison	8.0	11.5	3.5	2.9	15.0	4.7	1.2	0.8
El Paso	3.8	2.6	2.2	3.3	0.9	0.5	0.7	0.5
Eugene	22.4	13.9	14.8	5.1	3.9	2.0	3.8	3.4
Evansville	31.0	12.9	10.8	17.1	2.0	1.5	2.8	2.0
Fargo	43.7	8.6	4.6	1.7	1.2	3.1	4.3	1.4
Ft. Collins	31.9	15.2	13.8	4.2	5.2	2.8	3.5	3.5
Ft. Lauderdale	6.2	6.0	4.2	4.2	5.9	2.5	1.7	0.9
Ft. Wayne	35.1	11.8	8.4	10.1	3.0	2.4	4.2	1.9
Ft. Worth	11.4	8.8	8.6	6.5	2.3	1.2	2.3	1.9
Gainesville	13.8	12.2	11.0	5.0	5.4	2.7	2.7	2.5
Greensboro	9.9	8.3	10.1	9.0	2.4	1.1	1.5	2.2
Honolulu	6.4	4.8	4.1	0.8	1.9	0.9	1.5	1.0
Houston	10.0	6.9	6.6	4.5	2.3	1.3	2.8	1.4
Huntsville	10.6	11.9	11.1	13.0	2.4	1.2	2.1	2.4
Indianapolis	24.0	13.6	11.1	7.8	2.9	2.0	2.3	2.3
Irvine	6.9	5.4	4.9	2.2	3.3	1.4	1.6	1.1
Jackson	5.8	8.7	7.5	7.5	1.4	0.4	2.0	1.8
Jacksonville	12.1	12.4	10.3	8.6	4.6	2.2	2.7	2.4
Kansas City	25.7	15.5	11.3	8.1	3.7	1.8	2.9	2.3
Knoxville	16.1	13.4	14.8	14.9	2.4	1.5	2.1	2.9
Las Vegas	11.8	9.1	7.7	2.8	6.4	2.6	2.2	1.6
Lexington	15.2	14.2	13.5	15.4	2.7	1.4	2.2	2.8
Lincoln	45.9	14.4	10.9	3.3	1.8	2.8	2.6	2.0
Little Rock	12.2	11.8	10.1	9.7	1.9	1.0	2.6	2.0
Los Angeles	6.9	5.4	4.9	2.2	3.3	1.4	1.6	1.1
Louisville	21.0	14.6	10.7	14.1	2.7	1.2	2.4	2.0
Madison	42.6	15.2	9.4	2.8	3.6	5.2	3.1	1.9
Manchester	8.6	23.4	15.0	3.4	10.2	4.9	17.7	3.9
Miami	6.2	6.0	4.2	4.2	5.9	2.5	1.7	0.9

Table continued on next page.

Metro Area	German	Irish	English	American	Italian	Polish	French	Scottish
Milwaukee	38.9	11.2	5.1	1.9	4.8	12.5	3.1	1.1
Minneapolis	35.2	12.9	6.8	2.4	2.9	5.1	4.4	1.5
Naperville	17.1	12.8	4.9	2.2	7.3	10.2	1.7	1.1
Nashville	11.8	12.1	11.7	13.4	2.6	1.3	2.3	2.6
New Orleans	12.6	8.5	5.5	4.3	9.5	0.7	16.3	1.0
New York	8.0	11.5	3.5	2.9	15.0	4.7	1.2	0.8
Oakland	9.7	8.8	7.2	1.6	5.5	1.7	2.4	1.8
Oklahoma City	16.9	13.3	9.4	7.4	1.9	1.0	2.4	2.0
Omaha	35.9	18.1	9.5	3.2	4.6	4.3	3.1	1.7
Orlando	11.9	10.0	8.5	7.3	5.9	2.4	2.5	1.7
Overland Park	25.7	15.5	11.3	8.1	3.7	1.8	2.9	2.3
Oxnard	12.6	9.8	9.1	4.5	5.1	2.5	2.7	2.0
Philadelphia	17.9	21.5	8.7	2.8	14.6	5.9	1.7	1.5
Phoenix	15.9	10.6	9.6	4.5	4.9	2.8	2.7	1.9
Pittsburgh	31.0	19.9	9.4	3.3	17.1	9.4	2.0	2.2
Plano	11.4	8.8	8.6	6.5	2.3	1.2	2.3	1.9
Portland	22.4	12.9	13.1	4.1	3.9	2.0	3.9	3.5
Providence	5.8	19.8	12.7	2.2	16.0	4.4	12.8	2.1
Provo	11.4	4.8	31.1	4.7	2.4	0.6	2.0	6.0
Raleigh	12.0	10.7	12.1	11.0	5.0	2.3	2.1	2.9
Reno	17.1	13.0	11.9	4.6	7.0	1.8	3.3	2.8
Richmond	11.2	10.1	14.0	9.5	3.6	1.8	2.1	2.5
Riverside	10.1	7.6	6.8	2.6	3.9	1.3	2.2	1.3
Rochester	23.6	17.5	14.9	3.2	17.7	5.5	3.7	2.3
Sacramento	15.0	11.7	10.6	2.6	5.8	1.6	3.0	2.4
St. Louis	32.3	15.5	9.1	5.7	5.2	2.8	4.7	1.6
St. Paul	35.2	12.9	6.8	2.4	2.9	5.1	4.4	1.5
St. Petersburg	16.2	14.2	10.9	5.9	9.0	3.5	3.5	2.3
Salt Lake City	12.1	6.6	24.0	5.4	3.3	1.0	2.2	3.9
San Antonio	12.7	7.0	6.3	4.1	2.1	1.7	2.2	1.5
San Diego	13.0	9.8	8.8	2.4	4.9	2.1	2.8	2.1
San Francisco	9.7	8.8	7.2	1.6	5.5	1.7	2.4	1.8
San Jose	8.2	6.3	6.1	1.3	4.8	1.3	1.9	1.4
Santa Ana	6.9	5.4	4.9	2.2	3.3	1.4	1.6	1.1
Savannah	10.4	12.1	10.3	5.9	2.4	1.1	2.0	2.4
Seattle	19.0	12.3	11.8	3.2	3.9	2.1	3.7	3.3
Spokane	27.1	15.7	13.5	4.1	4.9	1.9	4.4	3.4
Springfield	22.4	13.8	12.2	15.8	2.5	1.5	3.3	2.5
Tampa	16.2	14.2	10.9	5.9	9.0	3.5	3.5	2.3
Tulsa	16.1	13.3	9.8	8.3	1.9	1.0	2.7	2.2
Virginia Beach	11.7	10.6	11.2	10.4	4.7	2.1	2.3	2.5
Warren	18.0	11.2	8.2	3.4	6.6	11.2	4.4	2.4
Washington	11.9	10.4	8.8	4.1	4.7	2.6	2.1	2.0
Wichita	28.9	13.7	11.4	5.9	2.0	1.1	3.2	2.1
U.S.	16.6	12.0	9.1	6.1	5.9	3.3	3.1	1.9

Note: The top eight ancestries in the U.S. are shown; Figures are percentages and cover the Metropolitan Statistical Area (MSA) - see Appendix B for areas included; Figures include multiple ancestry (e.g. if a person reported being Irish and Italian, they were included in both columns)
Source: U.S. Census Bureau, 2007-2009 American Community Survey 3-Year Estimates

Foreign-Born Population: City

City	Any Foreign Country	Mexico	Asia	Europe	Carribean	South America	Central America[1]	Africa	Canada
Albuquerque	10.7	6.6	1.9	0.8	0.3	0.3	0.3	0.2	0.2
Anchorage	9.0	0.6	4.6	1.3	0.5	0.6	0.3	0.2	0.6
Ann Arbor	16.3	0.3	10.6	3.2	0.1	0.4	0.0	1.0	0.6
Athens	10.2	3.3	2.5	1.4	0.4	1.1	0.7	0.5	0.3
Atlanta	7.4	1.8	2.1	1.3	0.5	0.5	0.4	0.6	0.2
Austin	19.8	10.9	4.4	1.1	0.3	0.5	1.7	0.6	0.3
Baltimore	6.2	0.6	1.5	1.1	1.1	0.3	0.5	1.1	0.1
Bellevue	31.4	2.4	19.9	5.2	0.1	0.7	0.5	0.9	1.5
Birmingham	n/a	n/a	n/a	n/a	n/a	n/a	n/a	n/a	n/a
Boise City	n/a	n/a	n/a	n/a	n/a	n/a	n/a	n/a	n/a
Boston	26.8	0.4	6.4	4.4	6.9	2.9	2.5	2.8	0.4
Boulder	n/a	n/a	n/a	n/a	n/a	n/a	n/a	n/a	n/a
Cambridge	25.7	0.7	8.9	6.7	2.8	1.6	0.8	3.1	0.9
Cary	17.3	2.7	8.8	2.4	0.3	0.8	0.9	0.9	0.5
Charleston	n/a	n/a	n/a	n/a	n/a	n/a	n/a	n/a	n/a
Charlotte	13.8	3.2	3.5	1.4	0.6	1.2	2.3	1.3	0.3
Chattanooga	n/a	n/a	n/a	n/a	n/a	n/a	n/a	n/a	n/a
Chicago	21.0	9.6	4.0	4.0	0.4	1.0	0.8	0.9	0.2
Cincinnati	3.9	0.4	1.0	0.8	0.2	0.1	0.3	0.9	0.2
Cleveland	4.5	0.1	1.5	1.5	0.3	0.3	0.2	0.4	0.1
Colorado Spgs.	7.9	2.3	2.4	1.8	0.2	0.3	0.3	0.3	0.4
Columbia	n/a	n/a	n/a	n/a	n/a	n/a	n/a	n/a	n/a
Columbus	9.9	1.8	3.4	1.0	0.3	0.3	0.4	2.5	0.1
Dallas	25.2	18.2	2.3	0.7	0.2	0.4	2.3	1.0	0.1
Denver	17.4	10.4	2.8	1.6	0.1	0.4	0.7	0.9	0.2
Des Moines	n/a	n/a	n/a	n/a	n/a	n/a	n/a	n/a	n/a
Durham	13.8	4.0	3.5	1.4	0.5	0.7	2.4	0.9	0.5
Edison	37.5	0.7	29.1	3.4	1.7	1.5	0.2	0.7	0.2
El Paso	25.4	22.7	1.1	0.7	0.2	0.2	0.3	0.1	0.0
Eugene	7.8	1.5	3.8	1.1	0.0	0.2	0.2	0.2	0.6
Evansville	n/a	n/a	n/a	n/a	n/a	n/a	n/a	n/a	n/a
Fargo	n/a	n/a	n/a	n/a	n/a	n/a	n/a	n/a	n/a
Ft. Collins	n/a	n/a	n/a	n/a	n/a	n/a	n/a	n/a	n/a
Ft. Lauderdale	21.5	0.9	1.7	3.4	8.5	3.2	2.4	0.5	0.9
Ft. Wayne	6.4	2.2	1.7	1.3	0.2	0.1	0.3	0.3	0.2
Ft. Worth	18.3	12.6	2.6	0.8	0.2	0.4	0.9	0.6	0.1
Gainesville	10.5	0.3	3.6	1.8	1.4	1.7	0.6	0.4	0.5
Greensboro	9.4	2.6	2.8	0.8	0.4	0.5	0.5	1.6	0.2
Honolulu	25.7	0.3	21.0	1.4	0.1	0.3	0.1	0.1	0.5
Houston	28.1	13.9	4.9	1.2	0.5	1.0	5.2	1.1	0.2
Huntsville	n/a	n/a	n/a	n/a	n/a	n/a	n/a	n/a	n/a
Indianapolis	7.1	3.3	1.5	0.6	0.2	0.2	0.6	0.7	0.1
Irvine	34.1	1.3	26.6	2.9	0.1	1.0	0.5	0.7	0.7
Jackson	n/a	n/a	n/a	n/a	n/a	n/a	n/a	n/a	n/a
Jacksonville	8.8	0.7	2.9	1.8	1.4	0.8	0.4	0.5	0.1
Kansas City	7.4	2.9	1.8	0.8	0.3	0.2	0.5	0.8	0.1
Knoxville	n/a	n/a	n/a	n/a	n/a	n/a	n/a	n/a	n/a
Las Vegas	21.7	11.5	4.4	1.8	0.7	0.6	1.9	0.3	0.4
Lexington	8.0	3.1	2.6	1.1	0.1	0.3	0.2	0.4	0.2
Lincoln	6.6	1.2	3.1	0.7	0.2	0.2	0.4	0.7	0.1
Little Rock	n/a	n/a	n/a	n/a	n/a	n/a	n/a	n/a	n/a
Los Angeles	39.6	15.2	10.7	2.5	0.3	1.2	8.6	0.6	0.4
Louisville	5.5	0.8	1.7	1.0	0.9	0.1	0.2	0.6	0.1
Madison	9.5	1.7	5.0	1.3	0.1	0.5	0.2	0.4	0.2

Table continued on next page.

City	Percent of Population Born in								
	Any Foreign Country	Mexico	Asia	Europe	Carribean	South America	Central America[1]	Africa	Canada
Manchester	10.9	0.8	2.4	2.6	0.6	1.0	0.7	1.6	1.1
Miami	56.7	1.0	0.9	1.6	31.8	7.0	13.9	0.4	0.2
Milwaukee	9.8	5.3	2.1	1.1	0.2	0.2	0.2	0.5	0.1
Minneapolis	14.6	3.7	3.6	1.1	0.2	1.5	0.4	3.9	0.3
Naperville	15.8	1.7	9.4	2.8	0.1	0.3	0.1	0.7	0.6
Nashville	11.2	3.3	3.2	0.9	0.3	0.3	1.3	1.7	0.1
New Orleans	5.8	0.3	1.9	0.8	0.5	0.5	1.4	0.4	0.1
New York	36.0	2.1	9.3	6.2	9.9	5.2	1.4	1.5	0.3
Oakland	28.2	10.4	11.3	1.5	0.3	0.6	2.6	1.1	0.2
Oklahoma City	11.3	6.0	3.2	0.5	0.0	0.3	0.8	0.4	0.1
Omaha	8.4	3.8	2.0	0.7	0.1	0.1	0.8	0.7	0.1
Orlando	18.3	1.3	2.4	1.5	5.7	5.2	0.9	0.7	0.3
Overland Park	8.9	1.0	5.1	1.5	0.0	0.3	0.3	0.4	0.2
Oxnard	n/a	n/a	n/a	n/a	n/a	n/a	n/a	n/a	n/a
Philadelphia	11.0	0.4	4.0	2.4	1.8	0.7	0.3	1.1	0.1
Phoenix	23.3	17.1	2.3	1.5	0.2	0.3	0.8	0.7	0.3
Pittsburgh	7.1	0.1	3.3	2.0	0.5	0.3	0.1	0.6	0.2
Plano	22.7	5.3	12.3	1.4	0.1	0.7	1.1	1.0	0.5
Portland	12.9	2.8	4.7	3.0	0.2	0.2	0.6	0.6	0.5
Providence	28.9	0.9	3.7	2.0	9.9	1.7	7.0	3.5	0.3
Provo	n/a	n/a	n/a	n/a	n/a	n/a	n/a	n/a	n/a
Raleigh	13.1	3.8	3.6	1.2	0.6	0.7	1.2	1.8	0.3
Reno	18.2	8.1	5.2	1.6	0.1	0.4	1.7	0.3	0.5
Richmond	6.2	0.7	1.3	0.9	0.4	0.4	1.6	0.8	0.2
Riverside	23.9	15.4	4.0	0.8	0.3	0.8	1.7	0.5	0.2
Rochester	7.0	0.2	2.2	1.5	1.6	0.3	0.3	0.7	0.2
Sacramento	22.3	7.0	10.2	1.9	0.1	0.2	0.8	0.6	0.2
St. Louis	6.3	0.9	2.4	1.6	0.3	0.1	0.1	0.8	0.1
St. Paul	15.4	2.6	7.4	1.0	0.1	0.3	0.7	2.8	0.2
St. Petersburg	10.0	0.5	2.5	3.4	1.5	0.7	0.3	0.5	0.6
Salt Lake City	18.4	8.4	3.8	2.1	0.1	1.1	0.9	1.0	0.3
San Antonio	13.3	9.4	1.6	0.7	0.2	0.3	0.7	0.3	0.1
San Diego	25.2	9.7	10.6	2.3	0.2	0.6	0.5	0.7	0.5
San Francisco	34.4	2.9	21.4	4.9	0.1	0.8	3.0	0.4	0.5
San Jose	38.5	11.1	22.4	2.3	0.1	0.5	1.1	0.5	0.4
Santa Ana	49.6	38.6	6.7	0.3	0.1	0.5	3.1	0.1	0.0
Savannah	n/a	n/a	n/a	n/a	n/a	n/a	n/a	n/a	n/a
Seattle	16.6	1.6	8.7	2.4	0.1	0.4	0.3	1.8	1.0
Spokane	5.5	0.5	1.8	1.8	0.3	0.2	0.0	0.2	0.3
Springfield	n/a	n/a	n/a	n/a	n/a	n/a	n/a	n/a	n/a
Tampa	14.4	1.7	2.5	1.4	5.2	1.5	1.1	0.5	0.4
Tulsa	9.4	5.1	1.8	0.7	0.1	0.2	0.6	0.5	0.2
Virginia Beach	8.6	0.3	4.4	1.6	0.7	0.5	0.5	0.4	0.3
Warren	n/a	n/a	n/a	n/a	n/a	n/a	n/a	n/a	n/a
Washington	12.5	0.5	2.3	2.2	1.4	1.0	3.0	1.7	0.3
Wichita	8.5	3.4	3.2	0.5	0.1	0.2	0.3	0.5	0.2
U.S.	12.5	3.8	3.4	1.6	1.1	0.8	0.9	0.5	0.3

Note: (1) Excludes Mexico.
Source: U.S. Census Bureau, 2007-2009 American Community Survey 3-Year Estimates

Foreign-Born Population: Metro Area

Metro Area	Any Foreign Country	Mexico	Asia	Europe	Carribean	South America	Central America[2]	Africa	Canada
Albuquerque	9.6	6.3	1.4	0.7	0.2	0.3	0.2	0.1	0.2
Anchorage	7.5	0.5	3.8	1.3	0.4	0.5	0.2	0.2	0.5
Ann Arbor	10.9	0.5	6.3	2.2	0.1	0.3	0.3	0.8	0.5
Athens	7.4	2.5	1.8	1.0	0.3	0.8	0.4	0.3	0.2
Atlanta	12.8	3.4	3.4	1.3	1.2	1.0	1.1	1.2	0.2
Austin	14.5	7.7	3.3	1.1	0.2	0.4	1.0	0.5	0.2
Baltimore	8.1	0.5	3.1	1.4	0.7	0.4	0.6	1.0	0.1
Bellevue	15.6	2.4	7.5	2.7	0.1	0.3	0.3	1.0	0.8
Birmingham	3.7	1.6	1.0	0.4	0.1	0.2	0.2	0.2	0.1
Boise City	7.4	3.4	1.5	1.3	0.1	0.1	0.2	0.3	0.3
Boston	15.9	0.2	4.7	3.5	2.5	1.9	1.2	1.3	0.5
Boulder	11.1	4.2	2.7	2.5	0.1	0.4	0.5	0.1	0.5
Cambridge	15.9	0.2	4.7	3.5	2.5	1.9	1.2	1.3	0.5
Cary	10.9	3.4	3.2	1.2	0.4	0.5	0.9	0.9	0.4
Charleston	4.8	1.2	1.2	1.1	0.2	0.4	0.3	0.1	0.2
Charlotte	9.4	2.6	2.2	1.1	0.4	0.9	1.2	0.7	0.3
Chattanooga	3.3	0.6	1.0	0.7	0.1	0.2	0.3	0.2	0.1
Chicago	17.3	7.0	4.2	4.1	0.3	0.6	0.5	0.5	0.2
Cincinnati	3.7	0.4	1.4	0.8	0.1	0.1	0.2	0.4	0.2
Cleveland	5.5	0.3	1.7	2.6	0.2	0.2	0.1	0.2	0.2
Colorado Spgs.	7.0	1.9	2.1	1.8	0.2	0.2	0.3	0.2	0.3
Columbia	4.7	1.3	1.4	0.8	0.2	0.2	0.4	0.2	0.1
Columbus	6.6	0.9	2.4	1.0	0.2	0.2	0.2	1.3	0.2
Dallas	17.5	9.8	3.8	0.8	0.2	0.5	1.3	0.8	0.2
Denver	12.2	6.0	2.7	1.5	0.1	0.3	0.5	0.6	0.3
Des Moines	6.3	1.8	1.9	1.3	0.1	0.2	0.5	0.5	0.1
Durham	11.6	3.7	3.2	1.5	0.4	0.5	1.4	0.6	0.4
Edison	27.7	1.6	7.4	5.1	6.3	4.3	1.7	1.1	0.2
El Paso	26.3	24.0	1.0	0.6	0.2	0.2	0.3	0.1	0.0
Eugene	5.6	1.7	2.0	0.9	0.0	0.2	0.2	0.1	0.4
Evansville	n/a	n/a	n/a	n/a	n/a	n/a	n/a	n/a	n/a
Fargo	n/a	n/a	n/a	n/a	n/a	n/a	n/a	n/a	n/a
Ft. Collins	5.1	1.8	1.3	1.2	0.1	0.2	0.1	0.1	0.2
Ft. Lauderdale	36.7	1.2	1.9	2.3	18.6	7.3	4.4	0.4	0.6
Ft. Wayne	4.7	1.5	1.4	1.0	0.2	0.1	0.2	0.2	0.2
Ft. Worth	17.5	9.8	3.8	0.8	0.2	0.5	1.3	0.8	0.2
Gainesville	9.2	0.3	3.2	1.7	1.6	1.1	0.5	0.5	0.5
Greensboro	7.6	3.0	2.0	0.7	0.3	0.4	0.4	0.8	0.1
Honolulu	19.2	0.2	15.3	0.9	0.2	0.3	0.1	0.1	0.3
Houston	21.5	10.2	4.6	1.0	0.5	1.0	3.1	0.8	0.2
Huntsville	4.4	1.1	1.6	0.8	0.3	0.1	0.1	0.3	0.2
Indianapolis	5.4	1.9	1.6	0.6	0.1	0.2	0.3	0.4	0.1
Irvine	34.4	14.3	11.7	1.8	0.3	1.0	4.3	0.5	0.3
Jackson	n/a	n/a	n/a	n/a	n/a	n/a	n/a	n/a	n/a
Jacksonville	7.5	0.6	2.4	1.7	1.1	0.7	0.4	0.3	0.2
Kansas City	5.9	2.2	1.7	0.7	0.1	0.2	0.4	0.4	0.1
Knoxville	3.2	0.6	1.2	0.6	0.0	0.1	0.2	0.2	0.2
Las Vegas	21.9	9.9	5.8	1.9	0.8	0.6	1.8	0.6	0.4
Lexington	6.2	2.4	1.9	0.9	0.1	0.2	0.3	0.3	0.2
Lincoln	5.9	1.0	2.8	0.7	0.1	0.2	0.3	0.6	0.1
Little Rock	3.7	1.3	1.2	0.5	0.0	0.1	0.2	0.2	0.1
Los Angeles	34.4	14.3	11.7	1.8	0.3	1.0	4.3	0.5	0.3
Louisville	4.0	0.9	1.2	0.7	0.5	0.1	0.2	0.3	0.1
Madison	6.2	1.3	2.8	1.0	0.1	0.4	0.2	0.2	0.2

Table continued on next page.

Metro Area	Percent of Population Born in								
	Any Foreign Country	Mexico	Asia	Europe	Carribean	South America	Central America[2]	Africa	Canada
Manchester	8.0	0.5	2.3	1.8	0.6	1.1	0.3	0.8	0.8
Miami	36.7	1.2	1.9	2.3	18.6	7.3	4.4	0.4	0.6
Milwaukee	6.8	2.4	1.9	1.6	0.1	0.2	0.1	0.3	0.1
Minneapolis	9.0	1.5	3.4	1.2	0.1	0.5	0.3	1.8	0.3
Naperville	17.3	7.0	4.2	4.1	0.3	0.6	0.5	0.5	0.2
Nashville	7.0	2.1	2.0	0.7	0.2	0.2	0.8	0.8	0.2
New Orleans	6.6	0.5	2.0	0.6	0.6	0.5	2.1	0.2	0.1
New York	27.7	1.6	7.4	5.1	6.3	4.3	1.7	1.1	0.2
Oakland	29.3	6.1	15.4	2.9	0.2	0.8	2.4	0.6	0.5
Oklahoma City	7.2	3.4	2.1	0.5	0.1	0.2	0.5	0.3	0.1
Omaha	6.1	2.5	1.6	0.6	0.1	0.1	0.5	0.5	0.1
Orlando	15.8	1.7	2.6	1.7	4.3	3.6	0.9	0.5	0.5
Overland Park	5.9	2.2	1.7	0.7	0.1	0.2	0.4	0.4	0.1
Oxnard	22.8	13.4	5.0	2.0	0.1	0.6	1.0	0.2	0.4
Philadelphia	9.0	0.8	3.4	2.1	1.0	0.5	0.3	0.8	0.2
Phoenix	16.4	10.4	2.4	1.5	0.2	0.3	0.5	0.4	0.6
Pittsburgh	3.1	0.1	1.3	1.1	0.1	0.1	0.0	0.2	0.1
Plano	17.5	9.8	3.8	0.8	0.2	0.5	1.3	0.8	0.2
Portland	12.2	3.6	4.0	2.6	0.1	0.2	0.5	0.3	0.5
Providence	12.6	0.3	1.8	4.7	1.7	1.0	1.3	1.4	0.4
Provo	6.6	2.4	1.0	0.6	0.0	1.3	0.4	0.1	0.5
Raleigh	10.9	3.4	3.2	1.2	0.4	0.5	0.9	0.9	0.4
Reno	15.3	7.3	3.9	1.4	0.1	0.3	1.3	0.2	0.4
Richmond	6.1	0.6	2.1	1.0	0.3	0.4	0.9	0.5	0.2
Riverside	21.7	13.6	4.0	1.0	0.2	0.5	1.6	0.3	0.4
Rochester	6.4	0.2	2.1	2.3	0.7	0.3	0.1	0.3	0.4
Sacramento	17.0	5.0	7.0	2.6	0.1	0.2	0.7	0.4	0.3
St. Louis	4.0	0.5	1.6	1.2	0.1	0.1	0.1	0.3	0.1
St. Paul	9.0	1.5	3.4	1.2	0.1	0.5	0.3	1.8	0.3
St. Petersburg	11.9	1.5	2.2	2.4	2.6	1.4	0.6	0.4	0.8
Salt Lake City	11.5	5.0	2.3	1.3	0.1	1.0	0.6	0.4	0.3
San Antonio	11.2	7.6	1.4	0.7	0.2	0.3	0.6	0.3	0.1
San Diego	22.6	10.8	7.7	1.9	0.2	0.5	0.5	0.4	0.5
San Francisco	29.3	6.1	15.4	2.9	0.2	0.8	2.4	0.6	0.5
San Jose	36.1	9.0	21.4	3.0	0.1	0.6	0.9	0.5	0.5
Santa Ana	34.4	14.3	11.7	1.8	0.3	1.0	4.3	0.5	0.3
Savannah	4.1	0.6	1.5	0.7	0.3	0.3	0.2	0.2	0.2
Seattle	15.6	2.4	7.5	2.7	0.1	0.3	0.3	1.0	0.8
Spokane	4.9	0.5	1.7	1.5	0.1	0.1	0.1	0.2	0.5
Springfield	2.1	0.5	0.7	0.5	0.1	0.1	0.1	0.1	0.1
Tampa	11.9	1.5	2.2	2.4	2.6	1.4	0.6	0.4	0.8
Tulsa	5.3	2.7	1.2	0.5	0.1	0.1	0.3	0.3	0.1
Virginia Beach	5.9	0.4	2.6	1.1	0.5	0.3	0.5	0.3	0.2
Warren	8.7	0.9	4.2	2.4	0.1	0.2	0.1	0.3	0.6
Washington	20.2	0.8	7.1	2.0	1.0	2.1	4.1	2.8	0.2
Wichita	6.0	2.4	2.2	0.4	0.1	0.2	0.2	0.3	0.2
U.S.	12.5	3.8	3.4	1.6	1.1	0.8	0.9	0.5	0.3

Note: Figures cover the Metropolitan Statistical Area - see Appendix B for areas included; (2) Excludes Mexico.
Source: U.S. Census Bureau, 2007-2009 American Community Survey 3-Year Estimates

Marriage Status: City

City	Never Married	Now Married[1]	Separated	Widowed	Divorced
Albuquerque	34.6	44.9	1.8	5.4	13.4
Anchorage	32.8	50.3	2.2	3.0	11.7
Ann Arbor	56.8	33.3	0.5	2.6	6.7
Athens	56.3	30.0	1.7	3.8	8.2
Atlanta	53.7	27.4	2.4	5.1	11.4
Austin	42.5	41.8	2.0	3.4	10.3
Baltimore	50.8	26.5	4.4	7.5	10.9
Bellevue	27.7	55.9	1.6	4.8	9.9
Birmingham	42.7	31.4	3.9	8.3	13.7
Boise City	31.7	49.5	1.5	4.4	12.9
Boston	56.6	28.1	3.0	4.7	7.5
Boulder	56.0	32.2	0.7	2.5	8.6
Cambridge	52.0	35.4	1.8	3.3	7.4
Cary	25.9	61.1	1.7	3.0	8.3
Charleston	42.4	39.2	3.2	5.8	9.4
Charlotte	36.1	46.7	3.0	4.6	9.6
Chattanooga	34.4	40.8	3.1	8.0	13.7
Chicago	46.8	35.7	2.8	5.7	9.0
Cincinnati	48.6	29.0	3.5	7.0	11.9
Cleveland	46.0	28.2	3.3	7.8	14.8
Colorado Spgs.	29.1	50.6	2.3	4.9	13.2
Columbia	53.6	29.6	2.9	5.2	8.6
Columbus	41.7	37.9	2.5	4.9	13.0
Dallas	39.1	40.9	3.6	5.2	11.2
Denver	40.2	39.6	2.5	5.2	12.6
Des Moines	33.6	45.3	2.5	6.0	12.6
Durham	41.3	40.3	2.9	5.2	10.3
Edison	28.8	56.7	1.3	6.1	7.1
El Paso	30.9	49.1	3.5	6.0	10.5
Eugene	40.3	40.0	1.3	5.6	12.8
Evansville	32.0	42.2	1.3	7.2	17.3
Fargo	43.2	42.9	0.9	4.9	8.1
Ft. Collins	44.3	42.0	1.2	3.5	9.0
Ft. Lauderdale	39.0	36.6	2.9	6.2	15.3
Ft. Wayne	32.0	46.1	1.9	6.3	13.7
Ft. Worth	31.6	48.4	3.0	5.0	12.0
Gainesville	65.1	22.3	1.3	3.9	7.4
Greensboro	40.2	38.9	3.1	6.5	11.3
Honolulu	32.8	48.3	1.3	7.7	9.8
Houston	36.9	44.5	3.5	5.0	10.0
Huntsville	32.1	44.5	3.3	6.7	13.4
Indianapolis	37.4	40.7	2.4	6.3	13.3
Irvine	37.8	49.5	1.3	3.6	7.8
Jackson	46.5	31.1	4.1	6.4	12.0
Jacksonville	32.2	46.2	2.6	6.0	13.0
Kansas City	37.4	40.4	2.9	6.0	13.3
Knoxville	40.9	36.7	1.8	7.3	13.3
Las Vegas	30.4	48.0	2.6	5.1	13.9
Lexington	37.1	44.6	1.7	5.0	11.6
Lincoln	36.7	47.3	1.1	4.6	10.3
Little Rock	35.6	43.3	2.4	6.1	12.6
Los Angeles	43.2	40.2	3.0	5.1	8.5
Louisville	32.5	45.0	2.3	7.3	12.8
Madison	49.5	37.6	1.2	3.6	8.1
Manchester	37.1	41.1	1.6	5.8	14.5

Table continued on next page.

City	Never Married	Now Married[1]	Separated	Widowed	Divorced
Miami	37.4	37.6	4.3	7.6	13.0
Milwaukee	49.9	31.3	2.4	5.5	10.9
Minneapolis	50.5	33.2	1.9	4.1	10.2
Naperville	26.0	63.0	0.7	4.0	6.2
Nashville	38.1	40.2	2.5	5.8	13.3
New Orleans	46.4	30.8	3.3	7.0	12.5
New York	42.2	39.9	3.7	6.2	8.0
Oakland	43.7	37.2	2.9	5.6	10.8
Oklahoma City	29.4	48.6	2.5	6.4	13.1
Omaha	37.0	44.2	1.8	5.6	11.5
Orlando	41.3	36.8	3.8	4.8	13.3
Overland Park	27.6	55.2	1.1	5.4	10.8
Oxnard	34.7	49.1	2.5	4.9	8.7
Philadelphia	48.7	30.4	3.8	8.0	9.0
Phoenix	37.4	43.4	2.2	4.4	12.7
Pittsburgh	48.3	32.0	2.3	7.9	9.5
Plano	27.4	57.8	1.6	3.6	9.6
Portland	39.4	41.1	2.0	4.9	12.7
Providence	51.5	30.8	4.0	5.1	8.7
Provo	57.6	35.0	0.7	2.3	4.4
Raleigh	41.3	41.8	3.2	3.9	9.8
Reno	33.9	43.3	2.5	5.7	14.6
Richmond	48.4	27.0	3.8	8.3	12.5
Riverside	37.1	45.9	2.4	4.6	9.9
Rochester	51.5	26.2	4.4	6.0	11.9
Sacramento	38.4	40.4	2.8	6.3	12.0
St. Louis	48.2	27.5	4.2	7.3	12.8
St. Paul	43.3	38.4	1.8	5.2	11.2
St. Petersburg	33.3	40.6	2.5	8.3	15.3
Salt Lake City	37.7	43.3	2.1	4.5	12.3
San Antonio	34.5	44.3	3.1	5.6	12.5
San Diego	39.4	43.4	2.2	4.7	10.2
San Francisco	47.5	36.7	1.6	5.8	8.4
San Jose	34.1	50.9	1.7	4.8	8.5
Santa Ana	41.8	45.4	3.1	3.7	6.0
Savannah	41.7	35.6	2.5	8.6	11.7
Seattle	43.6	39.2	1.3	4.5	11.4
Spokane	33.0	44.0	1.6	6.0	15.5
Springfield	38.2	39.4	1.8	6.9	13.7
Tampa	39.0	38.6	3.2	5.3	13.9
Tulsa	31.8	44.3	2.6	6.8	14.6
Virginia Beach	30.2	51.1	2.7	5.0	11.1
Warren	33.2	45.8	0.9	8.6	11.6
Washington	54.9	26.2	3.2	5.8	9.9
Wichita	30.2	48.0	1.8	5.9	14.1
U.S.	31.4	49.7	2.2	6.2	10.6

Note: Figures are percentages and cover the population 15 years of age and older; (1) Excludes separated
Source: U.S. Census Bureau, 2007-2009 American Community Survey 3-Year Estimates

Marriage Status: Metro Area

Metro Area	Never Married	Now Married[1]	Separated	Widowed	Divorced
Albuquerque	32.4	47.6	1.6	5.5	12.9
Anchorage	33.3	49.0	2.1	3.3	12.3
Ann Arbor	41.1	45.5	0.9	3.9	8.7
Athens	45.1	40.2	1.8	4.2	8.7
Atlanta	33.5	48.4	2.2	4.7	11.1
Austin	35.3	48.3	1.9	3.8	10.7
Baltimore	34.8	46.3	2.8	6.4	9.7
Bellevue	31.3	50.5	1.7	4.6	11.9
Birmingham	28.0	50.3	2.4	7.3	12.0
Boise City	25.7	56.2	1.7	4.4	12.1
Boston	36.1	47.6	1.7	5.8	8.8
Boulder	37.2	47.9	1.1	3.2	10.5
Cambridge	36.1	47.6	1.7	5.8	8.8
Cary	30.9	53.0	2.6	4.4	9.1
Charleston	34.2	46.5	3.1	5.8	10.4
Charlotte	30.0	52.2	2.9	5.3	9.7
Chattanooga	26.1	52.0	2.1	7.3	12.4
Chicago	35.3	48.1	1.8	5.8	9.0
Cincinnati	31.0	49.5	2.1	6.1	11.3
Cleveland	32.5	46.6	1.8	7.3	11.7
Colorado Spgs.	27.4	54.1	1.9	4.4	12.2
Columbia	33.9	47.3	3.1	6.2	9.5
Columbus	32.3	48.9	2.1	5.1	11.7
Dallas	30.9	50.7	2.6	4.7	11.1
Denver	30.8	51.0	1.8	4.6	11.8
Des Moines	27.2	55.1	1.7	5.2	10.8
Durham	36.5	46.6	2.5	5.0	9.4
Edison	36.5	46.5	2.7	6.5	7.8
El Paso	30.9	49.8	3.6	5.8	9.9
Eugene	32.6	46.8	1.5	5.8	13.3
Evansville	24.9	54.6	0.9	6.5	13.1
Fargo	36.9	49.5	0.6	4.9	8.0
Ft. Collins	32.7	52.0	1.0	4.1	10.2
Ft. Lauderdale	31.9	45.5	2.9	7.5	12.3
Ft. Wayne	28.4	52.2	1.6	5.9	11.9
Ft. Worth	30.9	50.7	2.6	4.7	11.1
Gainesville	47.3	37.5	1.3	4.9	9.0
Greensboro	29.9	48.8	3.2	6.9	11.1
Honolulu	31.9	52.0	1.4	6.2	8.5
Houston	31.1	51.3	2.8	4.7	10.0
Huntsville	27.4	52.0	2.7	5.7	12.2
Indianapolis	30.3	50.3	1.8	5.7	11.9
Irvine	37.8	45.8	2.6	5.2	8.6
Jackson	34.7	44.4	2.9	6.6	11.4
Jacksonville	29.3	49.8	2.4	5.9	12.6
Kansas City	28.7	51.6	1.9	5.7	12.1
Knoxville	27.3	52.4	1.6	6.7	12.0
Las Vegas	31.0	48.6	2.3	4.8	13.4
Lexington	32.2	49.1	1.9	5.4	11.4
Lincoln	34.7	50.1	1.0	4.5	9.7
Little Rock	28.5	50.7	2.3	6.1	12.4
Los Angeles	37.8	45.8	2.6	5.2	8.6
Louisville	28.4	50.3	2.0	6.5	12.8
Madison	36.6	48.9	1.0	4.3	9.2
Manchester	29.3	52.0	1.6	5.3	11.9

Table continued on next page.

Metro Area	Never Married	Now Married[1]	Separated	Widowed	Divorced
Miami	31.9	45.5	2.9	7.5	12.3
Milwaukee	35.6	47.1	1.4	6.1	9.9
Minneapolis	32.5	52.1	1.2	4.5	9.7
Naperville	35.3	48.1	1.8	5.8	9.0
Nashville	29.8	50.7	2.0	5.5	12.0
New Orleans	35.2	43.3	2.5	7.2	11.8
New York	36.5	46.5	2.7	6.5	7.8
Oakland	35.9	47.2	1.9	5.5	9.5
Oklahoma City	28.7	50.3	2.1	6.2	12.6
Omaha	31.7	51.0	1.5	5.3	10.5
Orlando	31.3	48.8	2.5	5.7	11.7
Overland Park	28.7	51.6	1.9	5.7	12.1
Oxnard	30.3	52.8	1.7	5.1	10.2
Philadelphia	35.6	46.3	2.3	7.0	8.7
Phoenix	32.2	48.8	1.7	5.2	12.1
Pittsburgh	30.3	50.1	2.0	8.4	9.2
Plano	30.9	50.7	2.6	4.7	11.1
Portland	30.6	50.5	1.8	4.9	12.2
Providence	33.2	47.1	2.1	7.1	10.5
Provo	35.9	54.4	1.1	2.9	5.7
Raleigh	30.9	53.0	2.6	4.4	9.1
Reno	29.4	49.1	2.2	5.4	13.7
Richmond	32.8	48.1	2.8	6.1	10.2
Riverside	33.0	49.5	2.6	5.0	10.0
Rochester	34.0	47.6	2.3	6.3	9.8
Sacramento	32.3	48.8	2.3	5.4	11.3
St. Louis	31.1	49.4	2.0	6.5	10.9
St. Paul	32.5	52.1	1.2	4.5	9.7
St. Petersburg	28.4	48.1	2.2	7.9	13.4
Salt Lake City	29.7	54.1	1.5	3.8	10.9
San Antonio	31.6	48.2	2.9	5.7	11.7
San Diego	34.4	47.9	2.1	5.2	10.5
San Francisco	35.9	47.2	1.9	5.5	9.5
San Jose	32.5	52.8	1.6	4.9	8.2
Santa Ana	37.8	45.8	2.6	5.2	8.6
Savannah	32.4	48.0	2.2	6.3	11.1
Seattle	31.3	50.5	1.7	4.6	11.9
Spokane	29.1	50.5	1.4	5.5	13.5
Springfield	27.7	53.0	1.5	5.9	11.9
Tampa	28.4	48.1	2.2	7.9	13.4
Tulsa	25.6	53.5	2.0	6.2	12.7
Virginia Beach	32.0	48.9	3.1	5.7	10.3
Warren	33.5	47.1	1.7	6.6	11.1
Washington	35.2	49.0	2.3	4.7	8.8
Wichita	26.8	53.1	1.5	6.0	12.7
U.S.	31.4	49.7	2.2	6.2	10.6

Note: Figures are percentages and cover the population 15 years of age and older in the Metropolitan Statistical Area - see Appendix B for areas included; (1) Excludes separated
Source: U.S. Census Bureau, 2007-2009 American Community Survey 3-Year Estimates

Male/Female Ratio: City

City	Males	Females	Males per 100 Females
Albuquerque	258,252	270,431	95.5
Anchorage	146,060	140,370	104.1
Ann Arbor	56,263	56,542	99.5
Athens	56,697	59,044	96.0
Atlanta	271,536	270,160	100.5
Austin	392,918	371,561	105.7
Baltimore	297,145	337,061	88.2
Bellevue	59,343	59,936	99.0
Birmingham	106,257	121,272	87.6
Boise City	99,349	98,864	100.5
Boston	307,497	325,727	94.4
Boulder	49,637	45,951	108.0
Cambridge	52,645	53,856	97.8
Cary	66,051	66,623	99.1
Charleston	53,386	58,142	91.8
Charlotte	324,342	336,497	96.4
Chattanooga	82,066	90,423	90.8
Chicago	1,397,882	1,450,507	96.4
Cincinnati	156,507	170,853	91.6
Cleveland	204,570	224,063	91.3
Colorado Spgs.	193,126	200,611	96.3
Columbia	61,996	62,819	98.7
Columbus	370,652	382,277	97.0
Dallas	664,980	632,309	105.2
Denver	310,008	302,137	102.6
Des Moines	96,284	100,871	95.5
Durham	110,468	115,549	95.6
Edison	49,205	50,286	97.9
El Paso	291,638	323,300	90.2
Eugene	74,271	76,882	96.6
Evansville	54,306	60,287	90.1
Fargo	48,573	47,370	102.5
Ft. Collins	69,085	67,664	102.1
Ft. Lauderdale	83,393	75,291	110.8
Ft. Wayne	97,910	102,696	95.3
Ft. Worth	347,246	348,793	99.6
Gainesville	49,965	50,745	98.5
Greensboro	119,393	131,481	90.8
Honolulu	182,796	190,244	96.1
Houston	1,143,799	1,125,969	101.6
Huntsville	85,298	90,897	93.8
Indianapolis	390,849	411,183	95.1
Irvine	106,205	108,986	97.4
Jackson	80,500	91,529	88.0
Jacksonville	410,299	436,396	94.0
Kansas City	221,997	233,675	95.0
Knoxville	88,777	96,264	92.2
Las Vegas	287,367	277,283	103.6
Lexington	141,767	144,961	97.8
Lincoln	123,247	122,406	100.7
Little Rock	90,751	100,941	89.9
Los Angeles	1,974,547	1,973,258	100.1
Louisville	113,734	124,770	91.2
Madison	112,268	113,016	99.3
Manchester	53,861	55,097	97.8

Table continued on next page.

City	Males	Females	Males per 100 Females
Miami	205,016	206,152	99.4
Milwaukee	289,501	308,855	93.7
Minneapolis	195,983	189,014	103.7
Naperville	72,556	74,671	97.2
Nashville	295,722	309,936	95.4
New Orleans	166,637	190,467	87.5
New York	4,031,533	4,399,158	91.6
Oakland	201,968	212,710	94.9
Oklahoma City	276,754	286,939	96.5
Omaha	188,934	194,518	97.1
Orlando	113,184	116,405	97.2
Overland Park	86,941	90,208	96.4
Oxnard	98,698	94,226	104.7
Philadelphia	700,838	793,028	88.4
Phoenix	800,729	766,850	104.4
Pittsburgh	147,958	158,721	93.2
Plano	140,508	139,914	100.4
Portland	283,750	288,152	98.5
Providence	83,257	89,013	93.5
Provo	59,811	63,736	93.8
Raleigh	189,411	191,479	98.9
Reno	110,661	105,124	105.3
Richmond	93,518	106,375	87.9
Riverside	148,496	150,839	98.4
Rochester	99,917	106,980	93.4
Sacramento	232,966	244,105	95.4
St. Louis	169,400	185,285	91.4
St. Paul	138,439	145,540	95.1
St. Petersburg	120,043	129,077	93.0
Salt Lake City	94,205	89,404	105.4
San Antonio	643,568	679,556	94.7
San Diego	669,070	652,243	102.6
San Francisco	418,965	404,201	103.7
San Jose	500,821	476,193	105.2
Santa Ana	179,027	165,424	108.2
Savannah	62,207	69,139	90.0
Seattle	305,052	299,663	101.8
Spokane	98,184	104,076	94.3
Springfield	76,277	80,889	94.3
Tampa	172,976	177,085	97.7
Tulsa	190,201	198,978	95.6
Virginia Beach	212,159	220,985	96.0
Warren	64,808	67,484	96.0
Washington	282,102	313,831	89.9
Wichita	178,918	182,320	98.1
U.S.	152,401,520	156,637,454	97.3

Note: Figures are 2010 estimates
Source: Claritas, Inc.

Male/Female Ratio: Metro Area

Metro Area	Males	Females	Males per 100 Females
Albuquerque	426,991	440,327	97.0
Anchorage	192,045	182,679	105.1
Ann Arbor	174,439	174,446	100.0
Athens	95,037	98,709	96.3
Atlanta	2,751,690	2,817,505	97.7
Austin	863,629	840,365	102.8
Baltimore	1,291,108	1,386,090	93.1
Bellevue	1,709,734	1,709,928	100.0
Birmingham	545,521	584,554	93.3
Boise City	314,202	309,492	101.5
Boston	2,220,915	2,341,160	94.9
Boulder	151,891	147,258	103.1
Cambridge	2,220,915	2,341,160	94.9
Cary	571,092	578,085	98.8
Charleston	324,572	339,424	95.6
Charlotte	875,282	905,415	96.7
Chattanooga	253,697	271,892	93.3
Chicago	4,755,984	4,895,178	97.2
Cincinnati	1,063,504	1,113,956	95.5
Cleveland	999,055	1,076,476	92.8
Colorado Spgs.	314,683	317,860	99.0
Columbia	360,873	383,943	94.0
Columbus	888,387	911,725	97.4
Dallas	3,264,985	3,228,245	101.1
Denver	1,295,073	1,286,927	100.6
Des Moines	279,635	291,145	96.0
Durham	244,886	259,296	94.4
Edison	9,254,996	9,849,206	94.0
El Paso	367,257	396,791	92.6
Eugene	172,989	178,411	97.0
Evansville	170,091	181,300	93.8
Fargo	99,963	99,834	100.1
Ft. Collins	150,487	149,866	100.4
Ft. Lauderdale	2,682,549	2,837,333	94.5
Ft. Wayne	204,203	210,493	97.0
Ft. Worth	3,264,985	3,228,245	101.1
Gainesville	132,771	135,835	97.7
Greensboro	348,452	371,165	93.9
Honolulu	456,016	453,055	100.7
Houston	2,958,164	2,951,541	100.2
Huntsville	200,275	206,945	96.8
Indianapolis	859,213	889,017	96.6
Irvine	6,582,650	6,672,848	98.6
Jackson	259,905	282,428	92.0
Jacksonville	670,200	701,983	95.5
Kansas City	997,831	1,033,207	96.6
Knoxville	342,840	363,092	94.4
Las Vegas	967,057	937,681	103.1
Lexington	227,700	235,003	96.9
Lincoln	151,244	149,491	101.2
Little Rock	333,990	353,986	94.4
Los Angeles	6,582,650	6,672,848	98.6
Louisville	613,873	647,340	94.8
Madison	281,446	281,891	99.8
Manchester	200,270	203,782	98.3

Table continued on next page.

Metro Area	Males	Females	Males per 100 Females
Miami	2,682,549	2,837,333	94.5
Milwaukee	754,471	787,710	95.8
Minneapolis	1,631,474	1,647,707	99.0
Naperville	4,755,984	4,895,178	97.2
Nashville	785,255	810,778	96.9
New Orleans	571,739	622,457	91.9
New York	9,254,996	9,849,206	94.0
Oakland	2,177,120	2,200,422	98.9
Oklahoma City	605,156	623,388	97.1
Omaha	421,184	430,010	97.9
Orlando	1,058,885	1,079,954	98.0
Overland Park	997,831	1,033,207	96.6
Oxnard	410,933	410,037	100.2
Philadelphia	2,860,817	3,052,491	93.7
Phoenix	2,240,796	2,207,964	101.5
Pittsburgh	1,126,830	1,213,124	92.9
Plano	3,264,985	3,228,245	101.1
Portland	1,121,416	1,128,778	99.3
Providence	770,346	821,552	93.8
Provo	278,906	282,925	98.6
Raleigh	571,092	578,085	98.8
Reno	215,680	209,636	102.9
Richmond	603,694	637,400	94.7
Riverside	2,124,677	2,128,877	99.8
Rochester	504,586	528,872	95.4
Sacramento	1,065,453	1,101,085	96.8
St. Louis	1,373,208	1,461,978	93.9
St. Paul	1,631,474	1,647,707	99.0
St. Petersburg	1,354,345	1,427,768	94.9
Salt Lake City	584,720	566,038	103.3
San Antonio	1,024,476	1,065,552	96.1
San Diego	1,563,763	1,545,507	101.2
San Francisco	2,177,120	2,200,422	98.9
San Jose	961,760	917,519	104.8
Santa Ana	6,582,650	6,672,848	98.6
Savannah	166,169	176,624	94.1
Seattle	1,709,734	1,709,928	100.0
Spokane	230,670	237,679	97.1
Springfield	213,422	223,501	95.5
Tampa	1,354,345	1,427,768	94.9
Tulsa	456,789	473,285	96.5
Virginia Beach	822,778	847,941	97.0
Warren	2,146,881	2,245,550	95.6
Washington	2,655,817	2,783,096	95.4
Wichita	304,055	308,375	98.6
U.S.	152,401,520	156,637,454	97.3

Note: Figures are 2010 estimates and cover the Metropolitan Statistical Area (MSA) - see Appendix B for areas included
Source: Claritas, Inc.

Gross Metropolitan Product

MSA[1]	2006	2007	2008	2009	2009 Rank[2]
Albuquerque	32.8	33.8	34.9	34.5	59
Anchorage	23.9	24.8	26.3	26.4	80
Ann Arbor	17.6	18.2	17.9	17.5	112
Athens	5.7	5.9	6.3	6.3	227
Atlanta	255.4	267.3	269.8	262.7	10
Austin	71.3	75.8	80.1	81.6	35
Baltimore	123.5	128.8	133.0	132.0	19
Bellevue	195.2	210.4	218.8	217.5	12
Birmingham	51.2	53.1	54.3	54.2	49
Boise City	23.2	24.3	24.0	22.9	88
Boston	274.0	289.4	299.6	297.0	9
Boulder	16.0	17.1	17.8	17.5	111
Cambridge	274.0	289.4	299.6	297.0	9
Cary	48.0	51.3	53.5	53.8	50
Charleston	23.9	25.4	26.3	26.3	81
Charlotte	113.5	116.5	118.4	115.0	21
Chattanooga	19.6	20.4	20.8	20.7	96
Chicago	488.3	510.7	520.7	514.1	3
Cincinnati	92.7	96.1	98.8	97.1	29
Cleveland	100.1	103.0	104.4	101.0	27
Colorado Spgs.	22.1	22.9	24.1	24.3	86
Columbia	28.1	29.0	30.1	30.4	69
Columbus	84.5	87.8	89.8	90.0	33
Dallas	340.6	362.1	379.9	384.8	6
Denver	138.4	143.9	150.8	149.7	17
Des Moines	31.5	33.3	34.3	34.2	60
Durham	28.8	31.6	32.3	32.1	66
Edison	1,134.2	1,210.1	1,264.9	1,259.7	1
El Paso	23.2	24.6	26.4	26.9	79
Eugene	10.7	11.2	11.4	11.0	161
Evansville	15.2	15.3	15.7	15.7	122
Fargo	8.7	9.3	10.1	10.5	164
Ft. Collins	10.0	10.5	11.0	11.1	159
Ft. Lauderdale	251.5	260.0	261.3	257.2	11
Ft. Wayne	16.1	16.8	16.8	16.5	116
Ft. Worth	340.6	362.1	379.9	384.8	6
Gainesville	8.9	9.4	9.6	9.5	177
Greensboro	31.7	32.4	33.2	32.5	64
Honolulu	44.3	46.4	48.1	48.0	51
Houston	346.3	375.5	403.2	407.8	4
Huntsville	17.2	18.1	19.3	19.6	99
Indianapolis	90.0	93.1	96.4	95.8	30
Irvine	677.9	699.8	717.9	708.9	2
Jackson	21.4	22.3	23.1	23.4	87
Jacksonville	58.2	59.6	59.7	58.6	46
Kansas City	93.3	97.5	101.0	101.0	28
Knoxville	27.4	28.4	29.6	29.5	70
Las Vegas	89.9	95.7	97.1	94.5	31
Lexington	21.1	22.2	22.7	22.7	89
Lincoln	12.6	13.0	13.6	13.6	136
Little Rock	28.4	30.2	31.0	31.0	68
Los Angeles	677.9	699.8	717.9	708.9	2
Louisville	53.1	55.5	56.3	55.9	48
Madison	30.4	31.9	33.0	33.3	62
Manchester	19.0	19.7	20.8	20.9	95
Miami	251.5	260.0	261.3	257.2	11

Table continued on next page.

MSA[1]	2006	2007	2008	2009	2009 Rank[2]
Milwaukee	78.0	80.1	82.7	81.1	36
Minneapolis	178.5	186.7	193.9	192.4	13
Naperville	488.3	510.7	520.7	514.1	3
Nashville	72.9	76.3	78.9	78.1	38
New Orleans	64.3	67.5	72.4	73.3	40
New York	1,134.2	1,210.1	1,264.9	1,259.7	1
Oakland	287.5	302.8	310.8	306.1	8
Oklahoma City	50.6	52.8	57.1	58.3	47
Omaha	41.5	43.2	44.9	45.1	54
Orlando	97.8	102.1	104.0	101.6	26
Overland Park	93.3	97.5	101.0	101.0	28
Oxnard	34.2	35.9	35.1	34.0	61
Philadelphia	310.0	322.3	331.9	329.5	7
Phoenix	179.8	186.6	187.4	180.9	15
Pittsburgh	105.5	110.5	114.7	114.6	22
Plano	340.6	362.1	379.9	384.8	6
Portland	104.4	109.6	112.4	109.6	24
Providence	62.3	63.9	65.2	64.2	42
Provo	12.2	13.2	13.7	13.5	137
Raleigh	48.0	51.3	53.5	53.8	50
Reno	19.7	20.7	20.6	19.6	98
Richmond	57.3	59.9	61.4	59.8	45
Riverside	109.6	111.9	113.1	110.4	23
Rochester	43.4	43.8	45.4	45.7	53
Sacramento	90.1	92.3	93.7	91.5	32
St. Louis	117.8	122.1	128.5	127.8	20
St. Paul	178.5	186.7	193.9	192.4	13
St. Petersburg	108.2	110.7	110.5	107.4	25
Salt Lake City	56.3	60.6	62.5	61.6	44
San Antonio	72.1	76.8	80.9	82.3	34
San Diego	155.5	162.1	169.3	168.7	16
San Francisco	287.5	302.8	310.8	306.1	8
San Jose	135.3	145.3	146.7	142.6	18
Santa Ana	677.9	699.8	717.9	708.9	2
Savannah	12.2	12.8	13.2	13.2	143
Seattle	195.2	210.4	218.8	217.5	12
Spokane	16.2	17.0	17.6	17.5	110
Springfield	13.3	13.9	14.3	14.3	132
Tampa	108.2	110.7	110.5	107.4	25
Tulsa	40.8	42.6	45.2	45.7	52
Virginia Beach	71.3	74.8	77.1	76.5	39
Warren	198.5	200.7	200.9	190.8	14
Washington	363.2	379.6	395.7	396.2	5
Wichita	25.7	26.9	28.5	28.6	73

Note: Figures are in billions of dollars; (1) Metropolitan Statistical Area - see Appendix B for areas included; (2) Rank ranges from 1 to 363.
Source: The U.S. Conference of Mayors, "Pace of Economic Recovery: GMP and Jobs," January 2010

Per Capita/Median/Average Income: City

City	Per Capita ($)	Median Household ($)	Average Household ($)
Albuquerque	25,759	46,458	61,558
Anchorage	33,421	72,242	90,461
Ann Arbor	29,961	50,830	72,228
Athens	20,572	34,179	51,390
Atlanta	32,441	46,961	79,465
Austin	28,216	49,571	69,121
Baltimore	21,745	39,366	54,660
Bellevue	44,419	76,389	103,201
Birmingham	19,179	32,829	44,974
Boise City	28,170	50,512	67,237
Boston	30,100	52,716	73,867
Boulder	31,613	51,142	73,224
Cambridge	39,971	63,866	91,558
Cary	39,621	86,940	107,345
Charleston	28,499	46,576	65,745
Charlotte	30,502	52,359	74,382
Chattanooga	23,775	39,230	54,822
Chicago	24,664	47,233	66,345
Cincinnati	24,039	35,453	52,876
Cleveland	16,549	30,182	40,363
Colorado Spgs.	27,199	54,404	68,505
Columbia	23,506	38,709	58,989
Columbus	24,466	44,970	56,809
Dallas	24,273	43,066	64,560
Denver	28,035	47,220	65,965
Des Moines	23,087	44,976	55,348
Durham	25,599	47,281	62,841
Edison	39,394	88,169	109,036
El Paso	17,492	38,566	52,557
Eugene	24,839	41,916	57,372
Evansville	20,779	35,984	46,457
Fargo	25,861	41,935	56,389
Ft. Collins	26,503	51,012	66,625
Ft. Lauderdale	33,686	49,118	74,854
Ft. Wayne	20,360	39,804	48,890
Ft. Worth	22,786	46,649	62,573
Gainesville	21,283	35,378	52,342
Greensboro	25,640	43,686	60,669
Honolulu	32,017	58,382	81,208
Houston	23,910	44,923	65,640
Huntsville	29,064	47,856	66,403
Indianapolis	24,937	45,657	59,953
Irvine	44,826	96,755	125,463
Jackson	18,952	33,672	50,312
Jacksonville	25,890	50,252	65,168
Kansas City	24,755	44,795	58,345
Knoxville	21,750	32,768	47,008
Las Vegas	26,669	55,805	72,843
Lexington	29,043	48,581	67,306
Lincoln	25,615	48,901	62,351
Little Rock	28,251	44,904	65,591
Los Angeles	25,164	47,353	72,785
Louisville	21,076	32,991	46,799
Madison	29,164	51,489	66,354
Manchester	26,744	50,725	63,086

Table continued on next page.

City	Per Capita ($)	Median Household ($)	Average Household ($)
Miami	19,806	30,447	50,898
Milwaukee	19,164	38,330	48,470
Minneapolis	28,129	46,947	64,650
Naperville	42,321	101,695	124,373
Nashville	26,583	47,040	62,944
New Orleans	24,535	39,530	60,945
New York	28,215	50,063	75,198
Oakland	27,737	50,706	73,662
Oklahoma City	24,282	44,822	59,607
Omaha	24,605	46,178	60,146
Orlando	25,195	43,787	57,689
Overland Park	39,698	74,850	99,870
Oxnard	19,590	62,854	76,896
Philadelphia	20,364	37,509	50,815
Phoenix	23,458	48,918	67,641
Pittsburgh	23,841	35,984	52,797
Plano	42,764	86,954	113,481
Portland	28,542	49,504	66,048
Providence	19,016	33,982	52,262
Provo	15,946	40,431	54,707
Raleigh	28,647	52,938	69,515
Reno	26,889	49,210	65,293
Richmond	24,823	39,684	57,783
Riverside	22,875	55,228	71,700
Rochester	16,996	29,977	40,972
Sacramento	24,947	49,568	65,720
St. Louis	19,816	33,960	46,550
St. Paul	24,623	46,716	61,600
St. Petersburg	26,167	43,640	59,099
Salt Lake City	25,035	44,298	62,279
San Antonio	20,873	43,723	58,165
San Diego	31,777	62,518	84,761
San Francisco	44,419	73,509	103,945
San Jose	33,321	85,445	107,928
Santa Ana	15,236	55,962	68,958
Savannah	20,189	34,366	49,899
Seattle	37,949	59,136	80,798
Spokane	23,049	41,279	54,529
Springfield	22,292	35,651	49,100
Tampa	26,855	43,677	64,337
Tulsa	25,920	42,289	60,451
Virginia Beach	30,664	65,633	81,264
Warren	22,490	45,196	53,419
Washington	39,871	58,137	88,708
Wichita	23,796	45,723	58,163
U.S.	27,034	52,795	71,071

Note: Figures are 2010 estimates
Source: Claritas, Inc.

Per Capita/Median/Average Income: Metro Area

Metro Area	Per Capita ($)	Median Household ($)	Average Household ($)
Albuquerque	25,042	47,775	63,213
Anchorage	32,355	71,204	88,329
Ann Arbor	31,684	60,447	79,742
Athens	22,696	41,542	58,456
Atlanta	28,777	60,647	79,200
Austin	28,552	58,887	76,594
Baltimore	33,212	66,711	85,691
Bellevue	33,400	65,890	83,856
Birmingham	26,848	48,852	66,891
Boise City	24,823	52,454	66,834
Boston	36,214	70,675	93,513
Boulder	35,293	67,160	88,829
Cambridge	36,214	70,675	93,513
Cary	29,874	61,130	77,784
Charleston	26,406	51,277	66,897
Charlotte	28,418	55,666	73,049
Chattanooga	24,326	45,291	59,503
Chicago	29,402	62,177	81,110
Cincinnati	28,009	54,949	71,270
Cleveland	26,838	49,991	66,111
Colorado Spgs.	27,473	58,287	72,764
Columbia	25,589	49,462	64,489
Columbus	28,200	54,577	70,392
Dallas	27,980	58,202	77,740
Denver	31,029	61,853	79,855
Des Moines	29,320	58,404	73,250
Durham	27,967	50,771	69,548
Edison	33,113	64,976	90,841
El Paso	16,178	36,981	50,645
Eugene	24,095	44,793	58,311
Evansville	24,612	46,765	59,796
Fargo	25,577	46,998	60,552
Ft. Collins	28,416	57,110	71,849
Ft. Lauderdale	27,136	50,324	72,073
Ft. Wayne	24,378	48,809	61,814
Ft. Worth	27,980	58,202	77,740
Gainesville	23,875	40,780	58,453
Greensboro	24,365	45,121	59,990
Honolulu	30,049	69,293	88,300
Houston	26,961	57,150	77,540
Huntsville	27,794	53,544	69,313
Indianapolis	28,179	55,163	71,449
Irvine	27,686	60,649	84,480
Jackson	23,298	45,912	62,215
Jacksonville	27,961	54,624	71,023
Kansas City	28,534	56,699	72,163
Knoxville	26,117	45,934	61,768
Las Vegas	27,642	58,452	74,371
Lexington	27,685	49,516	66,577
Lincoln	26,249	51,743	65,244
Little Rock	24,611	46,936	61,187
Los Angeles	27,686	60,649	84,480
Louisville	26,110	48,731	63,946
Madison	31,027	61,262	75,730
Manchester	33,314	69,228	86,318

Table continued on next page.

Metro Area	Per Capita ($)	Median Household ($)	Average Household ($)
Miami	27,136	50,324	72,073
Milwaukee	28,341	55,101	70,443
Minneapolis	32,425	66,604	83,246
Naperville	29,402	62,177	81,110
Nashville	27,418	52,798	69,518
New Orleans	25,527	48,041	66,077
New York	33,113	64,976	90,841
Oakland	39,503	77,877	105,503
Oklahoma City	24,794	47,307	62,119
Omaha	27,467	56,143	70,415
Orlando	25,937	52,081	68,354
Overland Park	28,534	56,699	72,163
Oxnard	32,220	77,539	99,659
Philadelphia	31,172	61,681	81,112
Phoenix	26,798	56,890	74,534
Pittsburgh	26,915	47,453	63,762
Plano	27,980	58,202	77,740
Portland	28,885	58,575	74,210
Providence	28,434	56,206	71,897
Provo	19,883	58,454	72,462
Raleigh	29,874	61,130	77,784
Reno	29,247	57,989	75,180
Richmond	30,253	60,072	76,491
Riverside	22,956	57,457	73,444
Rochester	26,405	52,765	67,128
Sacramento	29,656	62,145	79,816
St. Louis	27,646	54,139	69,453
St. Paul	32,425	66,604	83,246
St. Petersburg	27,068	47,630	64,446
Salt Lake City	25,247	60,773	76,523
San Antonio	22,895	48,395	64,361
San Diego	30,858	64,890	86,332
San Francisco	39,503	77,877	105,503
San Jose	39,147	90,089	117,279
Santa Ana	27,686	60,649	84,480
Savannah	25,795	49,308	66,807
Seattle	33,400	65,890	83,856
Spokane	24,700	47,892	61,900
Springfield	23,247	43,329	56,804
Tampa	27,068	47,630	64,446
Tulsa	24,679	47,225	62,418
Virginia Beach	27,779	57,979	72,274
Warren	27,280	54,474	70,468
Washington	41,699	85,983	110,131
Wichita	24,404	49,995	62,423
U.S.	27,034	52,795	71,071

Note: Figures are 2010 estimates and cover the Metropolitan Statistical Area (MSA) - see Appendix B for areas included
Source: Claritas, Inc.

Household Income Distribution: City

City	Percent of Households Earning							
	Under $15,000	$15,000 -24,999	$25,000 -34,999	$35,000 -49,999	$50,000 -74,999	$75,000 -99,000	$100,000 -149,999	$150,000 and up
Albuquerque	13.4	11.8	12.1	16.7	19.3	11.0	10.6	5.2
Anchorage	5.4	6.4	8.0	12.4	19.9	16.1	18.3	13.3
Ann Arbor	14.7	10.2	9.6	15.0	17.0	11.6	12.9	9.0
Athens	25.5	13.7	11.7	14.0	15.6	7.4	7.3	4.7
Atlanta	19.0	10.9	9.9	12.8	14.4	9.7	10.4	12.8
Austin	12.9	10.1	11.5	15.9	19.1	11.5	11.3	7.7
Baltimore	21.3	12.6	11.7	15.3	16.9	9.8	7.7	4.7
Bellevue	6.1	5.1	7.0	11.6	19.4	14.6	18.9	17.3
Birmingham	24.8	14.8	13.2	16.6	15.6	7.1	5.2	2.7
Boise City	9.7	11.1	11.9	16.9	20.6	12.3	11.1	6.5
Boston	17.4	9.2	8.8	12.7	17.2	12.2	12.5	10.0
Boulder	14.3	10.3	10.3	14.3	17.1	11.1	13.1	9.4
Cambridge	13.0	7.9	7.9	11.9	16.6	12.1	15.1	15.4
Cary	3.4	4.5	5.7	10.8	17.8	16.5	22.9	18.5
Charleston	17.6	10.5	10.6	14.6	17.9	10.9	10.3	7.6
Charlotte	10.3	9.4	11.8	16.6	20.0	11.9	11.2	8.8
Chattanooga	18.9	13.6	13.0	16.1	17.4	9.2	7.1	4.7
Chicago	17.0	10.5	10.3	14.9	18.3	10.9	10.9	7.3
Cincinnati	22.4	13.9	13.3	15.4	15.2	8.1	7.1	4.7
Cleveland	26.9	15.8	14.1	15.7	15.1	6.5	4.4	1.6
Colorado Spgs.	9.2	9.4	11.5	16.0	22.1	13.3	12.3	6.2
Columbia	20.4	13.6	12.1	15.8	16.2	8.1	7.1	6.7
Columbus	14.4	11.4	12.6	17.4	20.5	11.2	8.8	3.6
Dallas	14.6	12.4	13.5	17.5	16.9	9.1	8.6	7.4
Denver	13.5	10.7	12.1	16.8	18.9	10.8	10.5	6.8
Des Moines	13.0	11.7	13.5	17.8	22.3	10.9	8.0	2.8
Durham	14.8	10.7	11.6	15.8	19.2	11.6	10.7	5.7
Edison	5.2	4.9	5.2	9.2	17.0	16.4	22.7	19.6
El Paso	18.7	14.1	13.3	16.2	17.7	8.9	7.5	3.6
Eugene	17.8	12.5	12.1	16.4	18.3	9.4	8.6	4.9
Evansville	17.8	16.1	15.0	18.3	18.6	7.5	4.6	2.2
Fargo	14.2	14.0	13.5	17.9	18.8	9.4	8.0	4.2
Ft. Collins	12.1	11.1	10.5	15.5	19.6	12.8	12.2	6.1
Ft. Lauderdale	14.1	11.2	11.2	14.4	18.4	10.7	9.6	10.4
Ft. Wayne	14.9	14.4	14.5	19.5	20.0	8.9	5.7	2.1
Ft. Worth	13.4	11.3	12.1	17.0	19.0	11.2	10.5	5.6
Gainesville	23.8	13.7	12.2	14.1	15.4	8.2	7.8	4.8
Greensboro	13.6	12.5	13.7	17.5	19.0	9.6	8.3	5.7
Honolulu	11.7	8.3	9.6	14.2	18.5	12.1	13.6	12.0
Houston	15.0	11.7	12.5	16.3	17.6	9.7	9.7	7.5
Huntsville	14.5	11.6	11.5	14.6	18.3	11.1	11.5	7.1
Indianapolis	12.9	12.0	12.7	17.5	19.9	11.1	9.3	4.7
Irvine	6.6	4.2	4.4	7.7	15.3	13.4	21.1	27.2
Jackson	23.2	15.0	13.6	16.1	15.3	7.1	5.4	4.3
Jacksonville	12.0	9.9	11.5	16.5	21.3	12.4	10.7	5.7
Kansas City	15.0	11.4	12.7	16.7	19.7	10.8	9.5	4.2
Knoxville	23.9	15.5	13.6	15.6	15.1	7.3	5.7	3.4
Las Vegas	9.8	9.2	10.7	15.5	20.7	13.3	12.9	7.8
Lexington	13.5	11.4	11.7	14.9	18.7	11.6	11.3	6.9
Lincoln	10.8	11.0	12.4	17.1	21.2	12.7	10.2	4.7
Little Rock	14.7	12.4	12.2	16.1	17.6	9.9	9.7	7.3
Los Angeles	15.9	11.5	10.9	14.2	16.5	10.4	10.5	10.1
Louisville	23.7	15.1	14.0	16.1	15.3	6.9	5.8	3.1
Madison	12.4	9.4	10.4	16.5	20.5	13.0	11.6	6.2

Table continued on next page.

City	Percent of Households Earning							
	Under $15,000	$15,000 -24,999	$25,000 -34,999	$35,000 -49,999	$50,000 -74,999	$75,000 -99,000	$100,000 -149,999	$150,000 and up
Manchester	11.5	10.0	11.3	16.6	21.6	14.0	10.5	4.5
Miami	28.3	15.1	12.1	13.4	13.0	6.5	6.2	5.4
Milwaukee	18.6	13.9	13.6	17.6	18.4	9.2	6.5	2.2
Minneapolis	14.0	11.1	11.9	16.3	18.7	11.0	10.6	6.3
Naperville	2.9	3.3	4.3	7.4	15.1	16.1	26.8	24.2
Nashville	13.4	10.6	12.3	17.1	20.1	11.0	10.0	5.5
New Orleans	22.0	12.8	10.9	14.3	15.5	8.9	8.4	7.2
New York	18.3	9.9	9.0	12.8	16.5	11.2	11.6	10.8
Oakland	15.8	9.8	9.9	14.1	17.1	11.3	11.8	10.2
Oklahoma City	14.4	12.3	12.5	16.5	19.2	10.8	9.3	5.0
Omaha	12.5	11.7	12.7	17.6	20.0	11.4	9.6	4.5
Orlando	13.2	12.3	13.5	18.7	20.2	9.8	7.9	4.4
Overland Park	4.4	5.4	7.3	13.2	19.8	15.0	19.2	15.7
Oxnard	8.0	7.7	8.6	14.6	21.7	15.4	16.0	8.1
Philadelphia	22.5	13.0	11.9	15.3	16.9	9.2	7.8	3.4
Phoenix	11.3	10.9	12.1	16.9	19.8	11.1	10.6	7.2
Pittsburgh	21.9	14.5	12.6	14.7	16.1	8.6	6.9	4.7
Plano	4.2	4.3	6.1	11.1	17.3	14.7	21.9	20.5
Portland	12.7	10.3	11.2	16.3	20.2	12.1	10.8	6.4
Providence	25.5	14.3	11.4	13.9	15.2	8.1	6.8	4.8
Provo	13.0	14.9	15.1	19.3	17.3	8.5	7.9	4.0
Raleigh	10.3	9.5	11.4	16.5	20.2	12.4	12.8	6.9
Reno	11.4	10.7	12.2	16.5	21.1	11.8	10.4	5.9
Richmond	19.2	13.0	12.8	15.9	17.0	8.6	7.6	5.8
Riverside	12.2	9.3	9.8	14.8	18.7	13.9	13.2	8.1
Rochester	26.6	16.7	13.5	15.6	14.5	6.7	4.4	2.0
Sacramento	13.6	10.8	10.2	15.9	19.3	12.6	10.6	7.0
St. Louis	23.2	14.9	13.3	15.7	16.4	7.6	6.0	2.9
St. Paul	13.7	11.3	12.2	16.5	19.8	11.3	10.1	5.2
St. Petersburg	14.2	12.5	13.5	17.1	18.9	10.1	8.7	5.0
Salt Lake City	15.0	12.5	12.7	15.9	18.5	10.2	9.1	6.2
San Antonio	15.1	12.4	12.7	16.8	19.1	10.1	9.2	4.6
San Diego	9.8	8.7	9.2	13.3	18.1	13.6	14.6	12.8
San Francisco	11.2	7.0	6.6	10.3	15.9	12.8	16.3	19.9
San Jose	6.3	5.2	5.7	9.8	16.7	15.0	21.7	19.6
Santa Ana	8.2	9.1	10.9	16.6	21.8	14.3	13.0	6.1
Savannah	22.4	14.8	13.7	14.9	16.3	8.0	6.4	3.5
Seattle	11.1	8.4	9.4	14.2	18.8	12.8	14.1	11.1
Spokane	16.2	13.5	12.9	17.7	18.5	9.7	7.5	4.1
Springfield	17.3	16.7	15.2	18.7	16.2	6.9	5.5	3.4
Tampa	16.6	11.9	12.3	16.0	17.8	9.5	8.5	7.4
Tulsa	14.8	13.6	13.4	16.9	17.8	9.3	8.4	5.9
Virginia Beach	5.2	5.9	8.5	15.7	23.5	17.4	14.6	9.2
Warren	11.0	13.0	13.8	18.0	22.7	11.8	7.9	1.9
Washington	15.5	8.0	8.2	13.0	16.1	11.2	12.8	15.1
Wichita	12.9	12.1	12.7	17.2	20.9	11.4	9.0	3.8
U.S.	12.1	10.2	10.6	15.0	19.5	12.5	12.1	8.0

Note: Figures are 2010 estimates
Source: Claritas, Inc.

Household Income Distribution: Metro Area

Metro Area	Percent of Households Earning							
	Under $15,000	$15,000 -24,999	$25,000 -34,999	$35,000 -49,999	$50,000 -74,999	$75,000 -99,000	$100,000 -149,999	$150,000 and up
Albuquerque	12.7	11.5	11.8	16.4	19.8	11.4	10.8	5.5
Anchorage	6.1	6.8	8.0	12.4	19.7	16.3	18.1	12.6
Ann Arbor	10.9	8.5	9.2	13.8	18.2	13.4	15.8	10.2
Athens	19.8	12.3	11.4	14.7	17.4	9.5	9.1	5.7
Atlanta	9.0	7.8	9.3	14.9	21.1	14.1	14.2	9.6
Austin	10.0	8.3	9.7	14.9	20.2	13.9	14.2	8.9
Baltimore	9.4	7.3	8.2	12.6	18.7	14.9	16.5	12.3
Bellevue	7.9	7.1	8.5	13.6	20.3	15.4	16.5	10.7
Birmingham	14.5	10.5	10.9	15.3	18.9	11.8	11.0	7.1
Boise City	9.3	10.2	11.8	16.6	21.8	13.1	11.5	5.8
Boston	9.7	7.2	7.2	11.2	17.6	14.4	17.5	15.1
Boulder	8.9	7.3	8.2	13.0	18.4	13.9	17.4	12.9
Cambridge	9.7	7.2	7.2	11.2	17.6	14.4	17.5	15.1
Cary	9.0	7.9	9.4	14.6	20.4	14.3	15.5	9.0
Charleston	12.9	9.9	10.7	15.5	20.2	13.0	11.2	6.6
Charlotte	10.0	8.8	10.6	15.8	21.1	13.3	12.6	7.7
Chattanooga	14.6	11.8	12.4	16.4	20.4	10.7	8.9	4.8
Chicago	10.0	8.0	8.7	13.7	19.8	14.3	15.6	10.0
Cincinnati	11.0	9.5	10.3	15.1	20.5	13.4	13.0	7.2
Cleveland	12.7	10.6	11.1	15.6	20.0	12.5	11.5	6.0
Colorado Spgs.	7.9	8.3	10.7	15.5	22.7	13.9	13.8	7.1
Columbia	12.6	10.5	11.2	16.3	20.5	12.4	11.0	5.5
Columbus	10.6	9.3	10.7	15.7	20.6	13.4	13.0	6.8
Dallas	9.4	8.6	10.2	15.3	19.6	13.3	14.1	9.4
Denver	8.0	7.5	9.5	15.1	20.8	14.5	15.3	9.3
Des Moines	8.4	8.5	10.4	15.3	21.9	14.9	13.5	7.1
Durham	13.6	9.9	10.9	15.0	19.4	11.9	11.4	7.9
Edison	12.6	8.1	7.8	11.6	16.6	12.8	15.5	15.1
El Paso	18.8	15.2	13.9	16.4	17.1	8.4	6.9	3.3
Eugene	14.7	12.2	12.0	17.1	20.2	10.7	8.8	4.3
Evansville	13.1	12.3	11.9	16.2	20.5	12.2	9.6	4.2
Fargo	12.3	12.0	12.2	16.8	20.9	11.9	9.4	4.5
Ft. Collins	9.4	9.4	10.0	15.1	21.5	13.9	13.9	6.8
Ft. Lauderdale	13.4	10.7	10.9	14.8	18.6	11.4	11.4	8.8
Ft. Wayne	10.6	11.2	12.1	17.5	21.7	12.6	10.1	4.2
Ft. Worth	9.4	8.6	10.2	15.3	19.6	13.3	14.1	9.4
Gainesville	20.4	12.2	11.9	14.1	16.8	9.7	8.9	5.9
Greensboro	13.5	11.9	12.8	17.6	20.1	10.4	8.7	5.0
Honolulu	8.5	6.6	8.0	12.6	18.5	14.9	17.4	13.5
Houston	11.0	9.1	10.1	14.5	18.6	12.6	14.0	10.0
Huntsville	12.0	10.2	10.5	14.6	19.1	13.0	13.5	7.1
Indianapolis	9.8	9.8	10.6	15.6	20.5	13.5	13.1	7.1
Irvine	11.1	9.0	9.2	13.2	17.7	12.8	14.2	12.8
Jackson	15.9	11.3	11.4	15.8	18.7	11.4	9.8	5.8
Jacksonville	10.4	9.3	10.7	15.7	21.3	13.2	12.1	7.3
Kansas City	9.6	8.8	10.4	15.5	21.2	14.0	13.5	7.0
Knoxville	14.9	11.6	12.0	15.7	19.2	11.0	9.9	5.6
Las Vegas	8.8	8.4	10.2	15.3	21.6	14.4	13.4	8.0
Lexington	13.1	11.0	11.3	15.1	19.2	12.3	11.6	6.3
Lincoln	10.1	10.3	11.6	16.4	21.6	13.5	11.1	5.3
Little Rock	13.2	11.4	11.9	16.9	20.7	11.3	9.7	4.8
Los Angeles	11.1	9.0	9.2	13.2	17.7	12.8	14.2	12.8
Louisville	13.0	10.9	11.6	15.9	20.5	11.8	10.8	5.6
Madison	8.5	7.7	9.3	14.8	21.6	15.7	14.6	7.8

Table continued on next page.

Metro Area	Percent of Households Earning							
	Under $15,000	$15,000 -24,999	$25,000 -34,999	$35,000 -49,999	$50,000 -74,999	$75,000 -99,000	$100,000 -149,999	$150,000 and up
Manchester	7.1	6.9	8.0	12.5	20.2	16.6	17.3	11.5
Miami	13.4	10.7	10.9	14.8	18.6	11.4	11.4	8.8
Milwaukee	10.7	9.7	10.2	15.2	20.5	13.8	13.3	6.6
Minneapolis	7.0	7.0	8.4	13.6	21.1	16.1	17.3	9.6
Naperville	10.0	8.0	8.7	13.7	19.8	14.3	15.6	10.0
Nashville	11.4	9.5	10.8	15.9	21.1	12.6	11.7	6.9
New Orleans	15.3	11.1	10.8	14.8	18.5	11.6	11.0	7.0
New York	12.6	8.1	7.8	11.6	16.6	12.8	15.5	15.1
Oakland	8.3	6.2	6.5	10.6	16.7	14.0	18.3	19.3
Oklahoma City	13.0	11.5	12.0	16.5	20.1	11.7	10.0	5.3
Omaha	9.0	9.2	10.8	15.7	21.7	14.2	13.1	6.3
Orlando	9.8	10.1	11.5	16.8	21.6	12.2	11.3	6.6
Overland Park	9.6	8.8	10.4	15.5	21.2	14.0	13.5	7.0
Oxnard	6.1	6.1	6.8	11.3	18.1	15.2	19.6	16.7
Philadelphia	11.1	8.4	8.8	13.1	18.5	13.8	15.4	10.9
Phoenix	9.1	9.1	10.4	15.6	20.9	13.3	13.2	8.4
Pittsburgh	13.4	12.1	11.8	15.3	19.2	11.9	10.3	6.0
Plano	9.4	8.6	10.2	15.3	19.6	13.3	14.1	9.4
Portland	8.9	8.5	9.8	15.3	21.6	14.2	14.0	7.7
Providence	12.8	10.2	9.2	13.1	18.8	14.2	13.5	8.1
Provo	7.0	8.6	10.3	16.2	23.3	14.3	13.4	6.9
Raleigh	9.0	7.9	9.4	14.6	20.4	14.3	15.5	9.0
Reno	9.0	8.6	10.7	14.9	21.4	13.9	13.4	8.2
Richmond	9.2	8.1	9.6	14.8	20.5	14.6	14.5	8.6
Riverside	10.5	9.8	10.0	14.0	19.3	14.2	13.6	8.6
Rochester	11.7	10.5	10.5	15.2	20.3	13.2	12.8	5.9
Sacramento	9.3	8.4	8.9	13.9	19.6	14.5	15.0	10.4
St. Louis	10.9	9.7	10.5	15.4	20.7	13.5	12.6	6.7
St. Paul	7.0	7.0	8.4	13.6	21.1	16.1	17.3	9.6
St. Petersburg	11.7	11.6	12.5	16.9	20.0	11.3	9.8	6.2
Salt Lake City	7.4	7.8	9.5	15.4	22.8	14.7	14.4	7.9
San Antonio	12.8	11.1	11.6	16.3	20.0	11.7	10.7	5.9
San Diego	8.3	8.1	8.9	13.5	18.7	14.4	15.2	12.9
San Francisco	8.3	6.2	6.5	10.6	16.7	14.0	18.3	19.3
San Jose	5.9	4.9	5.4	9.2	15.9	14.4	21.4	22.9
Santa Ana	11.1	9.0	9.2	13.2	17.7	12.8	14.2	12.8
Savannah	14.3	10.7	11.4	14.1	19.1	12.2	11.3	6.7
Seattle	7.9	7.1	8.5	13.6	20.3	15.4	16.5	10.7
Spokane	12.6	11.5	11.9	16.4	20.4	12.1	10.0	5.2
Springfield	13.3	13.2	13.5	18.0	20.0	10.1	7.7	4.2
Tampa	11.7	11.6	12.5	16.9	20.0	11.3	9.8	6.2
Tulsa	12.8	11.9	11.9	16.5	19.8	11.7	10.1	5.3
Virginia Beach	9.4	8.6	9.8	15.3	21.5	15.0	13.0	7.4
Warren	11.9	9.8	10.3	14.5	19.7	13.4	13.2	7.2
Washington	5.8	4.4	5.5	10.2	17.2	15.6	20.6	20.7
Wichita	11.0	10.6	11.7	16.7	21.8	13.1	10.8	4.3
U.S.	12.1	10.2	10.6	15.0	19.5	12.5	12.1	8.0

Note: Figures are 2010 estimates and cover the Metropolitan Statistical Area (MSA) - see Appendix B for areas included
Source: Claritas, Inc.

Poverty Rates by Age: City

City	All Ages	Under 18 Years Old	18 to 64 Years Old	65 Years and Over
Albuquerque	15.9	5.4	9.3	1.2
Anchorage	7.0	2.5	4.3	0.2
Ann Arbor	23.3	1.9	20.9	0.6
Athens	34.7	6.5	27.2	1.1
Atlanta	20.8	6.2	13.1	1.5
Austin	17.4	5.5	11.3	0.6
Baltimore	20.1	6.5	11.5	2.1
Bellevue	5.7	1.1	3.6	1.0
Birmingham	24.7	8.2	14.2	2.3
Boise City	11.7	3.2	7.9	0.6
Boston	18.3	4.9	11.4	2.0
Boulder	22.5	1.6	20.5	0.4
Cambridge	15.4	2.6	11.6	1.1
Cary	3.8	1.1	2.3	0.4
Charleston	17.1	5.1	10.6	1.4
Charlotte	13.3	4.6	8.0	0.7
Chattanooga	22.1	7.4	12.5	2.2
Chicago	20.7	7.4	11.6	1.8
Cincinnati	24.6	8.5	14.2	1.8
Cleveland	31.4	11.2	17.5	2.7
Colorado Spgs.	12.0	4.1	7.1	0.7
Columbia	21.3	5.5	14.3	1.6
Columbus	20.8	6.8	12.8	1.2
Dallas	22.2	9.2	11.9	1.1
Denver	18.1	6.2	10.5	1.4
Des Moines	15.9	5.9	9.2	0.9
Durham	16.9	5.3	10.6	1.0
Edison	8.8	2.9	5.2	0.8
El Paso	24.8	10.8	11.6	2.4
Eugene	20.7	3.0	16.6	1.1
Evansville	19.1	6.4	11.5	1.3
Fargo	16.7	3.0	12.8	0.9
Ft. Collins	19.3	2.2	16.5	0.6
Ft. Lauderdale	18.2	6.1	10.4	1.7
Ft. Wayne	15.4	5.7	9.0	0.8
Ft. Worth	17.3	7.5	8.9	0.9
Gainesville	36.8	3.9	32.1	0.8
Greensboro	18.1	5.7	11.2	1.2
Honolulu	10.0	1.8	6.7	1.5
Houston	20.2	8.3	10.6	1.2
Huntsville	15.2	5.1	9.3	0.9
Indianapolis	17.8	6.6	10.2	1.0
Irvine	9.1	1.4	7.1	0.6
Jackson	27.2	11.4	14.2	1.5
Jacksonville	13.8	5.0	7.8	1.1
Kansas City	17.0	6.1	9.7	1.2
Knoxville	24.9	6.7	16.8	1.4
Las Vegas	13.2	5.0	7.2	1.0
Lexington	17.0	4.4	11.7	0.9
Lincoln	14.4	3.6	10.2	0.6
Little Rock	18.0	6.6	9.9	1.5
Los Angeles	19.2	6.9	10.9	1.3
Louisville	16.9	6.2	9.5	1.2
Madison	20.1	2.8	16.9	0.5
Manchester	15.1	5.8	8.3	1.0

Table continued on next page.

City	All Ages	Under 18 Years Old	18 to 64 Years Old	65 Years and Over
Miami	25.8	6.9	13.7	5.1
Milwaukee	24.8	9.6	13.9	1.2
Minneapolis	21.3	6.1	14.0	1.1
Naperville	3.5	1.3	2.0	0.3
Nashville	16.7	6.1	9.5	1.1
New Orleans	23.2	7.9	13.6	1.7
New York	18.5	6.2	10.1	2.2
Oakland	17.3	5.6	10.3	1.3
Oklahoma City	17.0	6.6	9.5	0.9
Omaha	13.9	4.9	8.0	1.0
Orlando	16.5	5.2	10.0	1.3
Overland Park	4.8	1.5	2.7	0.5
Oxnard	14.9	6.5	7.7	0.7
Philadelphia	24.0	8.1	13.6	2.3
Phoenix	19.4	8.2	10.4	0.8
Pittsburgh	21.5	5.4	14.0	2.0
Plano	6.9	2.5	3.9	0.6
Portland	15.5	3.9	10.3	1.3
Providence	25.9	9.1	14.8	1.9
Provo	33.6	3.7	29.5	0.5
Raleigh	13.7	4.5	8.5	0.7
Reno	15.4	5.1	9.4	0.8
Richmond	24.7	8.3	14.0	2.3
Riverside	13.4	5.1	7.7	0.6
Rochester	29.4	10.9	16.8	1.6
Sacramento	16.3	5.5	9.8	0.9
St. Louis	23.7	8.3	13.6	1.7
St. Paul	19.8	7.7	10.8	1.3
St. Petersburg	13.3	4.0	7.5	1.7
Salt Lake City	15.6	3.8	10.1	1.7
San Antonio	19.2	7.7	10.1	1.4
San Diego	13.3	3.9	8.6	0.9
San Francisco	11.1	1.7	7.8	1.6
San Jose	10.4	3.5	6.1	0.8
Santa Ana	18.4	7.9	9.7	0.8
Savannah	22.8	7.7	12.8	2.4
Seattle	11.8	1.6	8.9	1.3
Spokane	19.0	5.6	12.0	1.3
Springfield	22.0	5.5	15.2	1.3
Tampa	18.3	6.6	10.2	1.5
Tulsa	19.2	7.6	10.3	1.2
Virginia Beach	6.4	2.5	3.5	0.5
Warren	13.0	4.4	7.4	1.2
Washington	17.4	5.3	10.4	1.7
Wichita	14.9	5.4	8.4	1.1
U.S.	13.6	4.7	7.7	1.2

Note: Figures are percent of population with income during the previous 12 months below poverty level and only include population for whom poverty status is determined
Source: U.S. Census Bureau, 2007-2009 American Community Survey 3-Year Estimates

Poverty Rates by Age: Metro Area

Metro Area	All Ages	Under 18 Years Old	18 to 64 Years Old	65 Years and Over
Albuquerque	15.2	5.4	8.6	1.3
Anchorage	7.5	2.7	4.5	0.2
Ann Arbor	14.4	2.7	11.0	0.6
Athens	25.5	5.3	18.8	1.4
Atlanta	12.2	4.6	6.8	0.8
Austin	13.2	4.3	8.3	0.5
Baltimore	9.6	3.0	5.5	1.1
Bellevue	9.8	2.8	6.1	0.9
Birmingham	13.3	4.5	7.5	1.3
Boise City	12.4	4.5	7.1	0.8
Boston	9.2	2.4	5.6	1.2
Boulder	12.9	2.6	9.9	0.5
Cambridge	9.2	2.4	5.6	1.2
Cary	10.3	3.6	6.0	0.7
Charleston	14.1	5.1	7.8	1.2
Charlotte	12.1	4.4	6.8	0.9
Chattanooga	14.9	5.0	8.4	1.5
Chicago	12.0	4.4	6.6	1.0
Cincinnati	11.9	4.1	6.8	0.9
Cleveland	14.0	4.9	7.7	1.4
Colorado Spgs.	10.8	3.9	6.2	0.6
Columbia	13.0	4.1	7.7	1.2
Columbus	13.8	4.7	8.3	0.9
Dallas	13.4	5.4	7.2	0.7
Denver	11.6	4.2	6.6	0.9
Des Moines	9.3	3.3	5.4	0.7
Durham	15.0	4.2	9.8	0.9
Edison	12.5	4.1	6.8	1.5
El Paso	25.9	11.4	12.2	2.3
Eugene	16.3	3.1	11.9	1.3
Evansville	13.3	4.4	7.7	1.2
Fargo	13.0	2.8	9.3	0.9
Ft. Collins	14.3	2.8	10.8	0.7
Ft. Lauderdale	14.2	4.4	7.5	2.3
Ft. Wayne	11.8	4.4	6.8	0.7
Ft. Worth	13.4	5.4	7.2	0.7
Gainesville	23.7	3.6	19.1	1.0
Greensboro	16.0	5.5	9.3	1.2
Honolulu	8.8	2.5	5.3	1.0
Houston	14.7	6.1	7.7	0.9
Huntsville	11.8	4.1	6.9	0.9
Indianapolis	12.1	4.5	6.9	0.8
Irvine	14.1	5.2	7.9	1.0
Jackson	17.8	6.8	9.6	1.4
Jacksonville	12.0	4.2	6.8	1.0
Kansas City	10.7	3.9	6.0	0.8
Knoxville	14.4	4.2	9.0	1.1
Las Vegas	11.2	4.2	6.2	0.8
Lexington	15.9	4.6	10.4	0.9
Lincoln	13.0	3.2	9.2	0.6
Little Rock	15.0	5.4	8.4	1.2
Los Angeles	14.1	5.2	7.9	1.0
Louisville	13.4	4.6	7.7	1.1
Madison	11.9	2.3	9.0	0.6
Manchester	7.8	2.6	4.5	0.7

Table continued on next page.

Metro Area	All Ages	Under 18 Years Old	18 to 64 Years Old	65 Years and Over
Miami	14.2	4.4	7.5	2.3
Milwaukee	13.0	4.7	7.3	1.0
Minneapolis	9.0	2.9	5.4	0.7
Naperville	12.0	4.4	6.6	1.0
Nashville	12.5	4.4	7.2	1.0
New Orleans	15.6	5.5	8.7	1.3
New York	12.5	4.1	6.8	1.5
Oakland	9.6	2.6	6.0	1.0
Oklahoma City	14.6	5.1	8.6	0.9
Omaha	11.0	3.9	6.2	0.9
Orlando	12.0	3.9	7.0	1.1
Overland Park	10.7	3.9	6.0	0.8
Oxnard	9.2	3.4	5.0	0.8
Philadelphia	11.7	3.8	6.7	1.2
Phoenix	14.0	5.5	7.7	0.8
Pittsburgh	11.9	3.4	7.0	1.5
Plano	13.4	5.4	7.2	0.7
Portland	11.6	3.7	7.0	0.9
Providence	11.6	3.7	6.5	1.3
Provo	12.7	3.2	9.2	0.3
Raleigh	10.3	3.6	6.0	0.7
Reno	12.4	4.2	7.4	0.8
Richmond	10.9	3.7	6.1	1.1
Riverside	13.6	5.6	7.1	0.8
Rochester	12.5	4.1	7.4	1.0
Sacramento	12.3	4.1	7.3	0.8
St. Louis	11.6	4.1	6.6	0.9
St. Paul	9.0	2.9	5.4	0.7
St. Petersburg	12.7	4.0	7.2	1.5
Salt Lake City	8.9	3.2	5.0	0.7
San Antonio	16.3	6.4	8.6	1.3
San Diego	11.9	3.9	7.1	0.9
San Francisco	9.6	2.6	6.0	1.0
San Jose	8.6	2.6	5.3	0.7
Santa Ana	14.1	5.2	7.9	1.0
Savannah	14.4	4.8	8.2	1.4
Seattle	9.8	2.8	6.1	0.9
Spokane	14.0	3.9	8.9	1.1
Springfield	15.7	5.0	9.6	1.2
Tampa	12.7	4.0	7.2	1.5
Tulsa	13.7	5.3	7.3	1.0
Virginia Beach	10.3	3.9	5.6	0.9
Warren	15.1	5.4	8.6	1.1
Washington	7.1	2.2	4.3	0.7
Wichita	12.2	4.5	6.8	0.9
U.S.	13.6	4.7	7.7	1.2

Note: Figures are percent of population with income during the previous 12 months below poverty level and only include population for whom poverty status is determined; Figures cover the Metropolitan Statistical Area - see Appendix B for areas included
Source: U.S. Census Bureau, 2007-2009 American Community Survey 3-Year Estimates

Personal Bankruptcy Filing Rate

City	Area Covered	2006	2007	2008	2009	2010
Albuquerque	Bernalillo County	1.37	1.98	2.71	3.51	3.74
Anchorage	Anchorage Borough	1.13	1.24	1.69	1.80	1.95
Ann Arbor	Washtenaw County	2.07	3.04	3.94	4.76	4.90
Athens	Clarke County	2.19	2.67	2.91	3.47	3.50
Atlanta	Fulton County	3.32	4.29	4.99	6.53	7.25
Austin	Travis County	1.25	1.31	1.33	1.78	1.83
Baltimore	Baltimore City County	2.17	2.75	3.42	5.09	5.61
Bellevue	King County	1.44	1.78	2.41	3.75	4.31
Birmingham	Jefferson County	6.78	7.50	7.93	8.87	8.75
Boise City	Ada County	2.48	3.00	4.30	6.23	6.13
Boston	Suffolk County	1.11	1.77	1.84	2.21	2.59
Boulder	Boulder County	1.37	2.17	2.88	3.79	4.17
Cambridge	Middlesex County	0.09	1.50	1.78	2.28	2.57
Cary	Wake County	1.84	2.32	2.63	3.40	3.06
Charleston	Charleston County	0.89	1.22	1.42	1.67	1.84
Charlotte	Mecklenburg County	1.65	1.88	1.97	2.49	2.66
Chattanooga	Hamilton County	5.63	6.80	8.05	9.25	8.60
Chicago	Cook County	2.39	3.28	4.63	6.28	7.30
Cincinnati	Hamilton County	3.08	4.01	4.38	5.15	5.41
Cleveland	Cuyahoga County	3.66	5.76	5.83	6.76	6.92
Colorado Spgs.	El Paso County	1.94	3.27	4.58	5.56	6.21
Columbia	Richland County	2.11	2.24	2.46	2.42	2.32
Columbus	Franklin County	3.60	4.60	5.44	6.23	6.29
Dallas	Dallas County	2.13	2.30	2.29	2.77	2.73
Denver	Denver County	2.18	3.15	4.23	5.32	6.17
Des Moines	Polk County	2.41	3.33	3.89	4.54	4.81
Durham	Durham County	2.16	2.16	2.32	2.75	2.91
Edison	Middlesex County	1.06	1.65	2.34	3.33	3.93
El Paso	El Paso County	2.11	2.28	3.00	3.89	3.59
Eugene	Lane County	1.82	2.45	3.25	4.30	4.87
Evansville	Vanderburgh County	3.36	4.55	5.44	6.38	6.43
Fargo	Cass County	1.32	2.57	2.90	3.52	3.43
Ft. Collins	Larimer County	2.36	3.47	4.26	5.34	6.21
Ft. Lauderdale	Broward County	1.32	2.21	3.69	5.37	6.71
Ft. Wayne	Allen County	3.76	5.52	6.64	8.22	7.67
Ft. Worth	Tarrant County	2.44	2.91	3.01	3.73	3.75
Gainesville	Alachua County	0.85	1.07	1.48	1.93	1.98
Greensboro	Guilford County	1.79	2.02	2.30	2.70	2.56
Honolulu	Honolulu County	0.85	1.11	1.49	2.06	2.52
Houston	Harris County	1.48	1.72	1.50	1.76	2.07
Huntsville	Madison County	3.21	3.67	4.49	4.99	5.22
Indianapolis	Marion County	4.67	6.73	8.59	9.06	9.85
Irvine	Orange County	0.87	1.02	2.26	3.13	4.57
Jackson	Hinds County	5.24	6.88	5.82	6.49	6.37
Jacksonville	Duval County	2.39	3.47	4.45	5.82	5.91
Kansas City	Jackson County	3.86	4.54	4.94	5.60	6.12
Knoxville	Knox County	2.86	3.97	5.23	5.83	5.42
Las Vegas	Clark County	2.47	4.88	8.40	12.93	12.51
Lexington	Fayette County	2.17	2.84	3.53	4.52	4.54
Lincoln	Lancaster County	2.60	3.23	4.04	4.40	4.48
Little Rock	Pulaski County	4.75	5.50	6.07	6.78	7.12
Los Angeles	Los Angeles County	1.01	1.82	3.41	5.53	7.25
Louisville	Jefferson County	3.91	4.78	5.53	6.18	6.35
Madison	Dane County	1.56	2.13	2.63	3.33	3.66
Manchester	Hillsborough County	1.51	2.24	3.27	3.93	4.51
Miami	Miami-Dade County	n/a	n/a	n/a	n/a	n/a

Table continued on next page.

City	Area Covered	2006	2007	2008	2009	2010
Milwaukee	Milwaukee County	3.51	4.75	6.27	7.66	9.06
Minneapolis	Hennepin County	1.47	2.13	2.94	3.85	4.16
Naperville	DuPage County	1.36	2.06	3.24	4.77	5.69
Nashville	Davidson County	4.54	5.35	6.45	7.13	6.69
New Orleans	Orleans Parish	1.30	1.32	1.43	1.96	2.26
New York	Bronx County	1.17	1.62	1.97	2.33	2.32
New York	Kings County	0.99	1.20	1.44	1.76	1.80
New York	New York County	0.92	1.13	1.38	2.09	1.90
New York	Queens County	1.02	1.52	1.91	2.46	2.65
New York	Richmond County	0.93	1.34	1.83	2.70	2.88
Oakland	Alameda County	1.06	1.66	2.66	4.20	5.24
Oklahoma City	Oklahoma County	2.60	3.08	3.74	4.51	4.67
Omaha	Douglas County	3.00	3.58	4.40	4.45	4.70
Orlando	Orange County	1.21	2.21	3.97	6.78	7.98
Overland Park	Johnson County	1.97	2.59	3.10	4.10	4.09
Oxnard	Ventura County	0.78	1.70	3.22	5.11	6.46
Philadelphia	Philadelphia County	2.06	2.14	1.97	1.84	2.29
Phoenix	Maricopa County	1.35	1.79	3.31	5.88	7.23
Pittsburgh	Allegheny County	2.97	3.58	3.55	3.85	3.70
Plano	Collin County	1.91	2.40	2.75	3.38	3.75
Portland	Multnomah County	2.18	2.63	3.18	4.30	4.84
Providence	Providence County	1.65	2.86	4.49	5.22	5.56
Provo	Utah County	1.48	1.60	2.43	4.25	5.58
Raleigh	Wake County	1.84	2.32	2.63	3.40	3.06
Reno	Washoe County	1.55	2.78	4.30	7.94	8.30
Richmond	Richmond City	3.96	3.60	4.28	4.35	7.95
Riverside	Riverside County	1.21	2.53	5.38	8.73	11.10
Rochester	Monroe County	2.20	2.66	2.72	2.85	2.55
Sacramento	Sacramento County	1.76	3.72	5.80	8.14	9.06
St. Louis	Saint Louis City County	3.10	3.67	4.19	4.94	5.35
St. Paul	Ramsey County	1.67	2.16	2.94	3.95	4.09
St. Petersburg	Pinellas County	1.96	3.00	4.25	5.76	5.89
Salt Lake City	Salt Lake County	2.61	2.90	4.02	6.11	7.33
San Antonio	Bexar County	1.48	1.76	1.96	2.44	2.38
San Diego	San Diego County	1.40	2.55	4.47	6.52	7.25
San Francisco	San Francisco County	0.88	1.16	1.49	2.25	2.69
San Jose	Santa Clara County	0.96	1.36	2.34	3.94	4.87
Santa Ana	Orange County	0.87	1.02	2.26	3.13	4.57
Savannah	Chatham County	4.91	5.33	6.43	7.12	6.67
Seattle	King County	1.44	1.78	2.41	3.75	4.31
Spokane	Spokane County	2.46	3.14	4.18	5.42	5.49
Springfield	Greene County	2.45	3.42	4.07	4.78	5.16
Tampa	Hillsborough County	1.82	2.79	4.15	5.63	6.33
Tulsa	Tulsa County	2.37	2.88	3.27	4.20	4.51
Virginia Beach	Virginia Beach City	1.72	2.64	4.07	5.01	5.46
Warren	Macomb County	3.88	5.97	7.59	9.79	9.72
Washington	District of Columbia	n/a	n/a	n/a	n/a	n/a
Wichita	Sedgwick County	2.87	3.41	3.66	4.45	4.61
U.S.	U.S.	2.00	2.73	3.53	4.60	4.96

Note: Numbers are per 1,000 population and include Chapter 7 and Chapter 13 filings; n/a not available
Source: Federal Deposit Insurance Corporation (FDIC),
Regional Economic Conditions (RECON), March 17, 2011

Building Permits: City

City	Single-Family			Multi-Family			Total		
	2009	2010	Pct. Chg.	2009	2010	Pct. Chg.	2009	2010	Pct. Chg.
Albuquerque	784	814	3.8	159	202	27.0	943	1,016	7.7
Anchorage	241	381	58.1	250	99	-60.4	491	480	-2.2
Ann Arbor	65	96	47.7	35	45	28.6	100	141	41.0
Athens	90	94	4.4	18	0	-100.0	108	94	-13.0
Atlanta	169	83	-50.9	750	196	-73.9	919	279	-69.6
Austin	1,951	1,664	-14.7	1,588	1,110	-30.1	3,539	2,774	-21.6
Baltimore	137	118	-13.9	204	251	23.0	341	369	8.2
Bellevue	63	75	19.0	159	129	-18.9	222	204	-8.1
Birmingham	75	110	46.7	62	347	459.7	137	457	233.6
Boise City	177	352	98.9	106	0	-100.0	283	352	24.4
Boston	38	23	-39.5	294	328	11.6	332	351	5.7
Boulder	43	115	167.4	76	338	344.7	119	453	280.7
Cambridge	11	8	-27.3	0	30	-	11	38	245.5
Cary	1,176	1,083	-7.9	0	276	-	1,176	1,359	15.6
Charleston	399	400	0.3	162	164	1.2	561	564	0.5
Charlotte	n/a	n/a	n/a	n/a	n/a	n/a	n/a	n/a	n/a
Chattanooga	207	206	-0.5	62	67	8.1	269	273	1.5
Chicago	129	164	27.1	1,128	1,713	51.9	1,257	1,877	49.3
Cincinnati	39	82	110.3	6	99	1,550.0	45	181	302.2
Cleveland	87	91	4.6	36	36	0.0	123	127	3.3
Colorado Spgs.	n/a	n/a	n/a	n/a	n/a	n/a	n/a	n/a	n/a
Columbia	265	203	-23.4	38	96	152.6	303	299	-1.3
Columbus	852	716	-16.0	1,354	1,391	2.7	2,206	2,107	-4.5
Dallas	734	865	17.8	1,037	1,744	68.2	1,771	2,609	47.3
Denver	485	632	30.3	403	600	48.9	888	1,232	38.7
Des Moines	134	143	6.7	108	261	141.7	242	404	66.9
Durham	739	891	20.6	824	296	-64.1	1,563	1,187	-24.1
Edison	27	28	3.7	0	n/a	-	27	22	-18.5
El Paso	2,330	2,478	6.4	551	1,584	187.5	2,881	4,062	41.0
Eugene	114	168	47.4	186	70	-62.4	300	238	-20.7
Evansville	37	39	5.4	35	39	11.4	72	78	8.3
Fargo	353	334	-5.4	731	497	-32.0	1,084	831	-23.3
Ft. Collins	154	180	16.9	79	66	-16.5	233	246	5.6
Ft. Lauderdale	38	42	10.5	0	0	-	38	42	10.5
Ft. Wayne	86	8	-90.7	20	0	-100.0	106	8	-92.5
Ft. Worth	3,070	2,759	-10.1	973	818	-15.9	4,043	3,577	-11.5
Gainesville	45	45	0.0	145	123	-15.2	190	168	-11.6
Greensboro	470	430	-8.5	528	511	-3.2	998	941	-5.7
Honolulu	n/a	n/a	n/a	n/a	n/a	n/a	n/a	n/a	n/a
Houston	2,579	2,452	-4.9	1,710	2,139	25.1	4,289	4,591	7.0
Huntsville	1,096	1,073	-2.1	324	0	-100.0	1,420	1,073	-24.4
Indianapolis	587	619	5.5	454	723	59.3	1,041	1,342	28.9
Irvine	188	641	241.0	168	1,113	562.5	356	1,754	392.7
Jackson	45	42	-6.7	4	88	2,100.0	49	130	165.3
Jacksonville	1,467	1,397	-4.8	1,171	68	-94.2	2,638	1,465	-44.5
Kansas City	48	68	41.7	529	212	-59.9	577	280	-51.5
Knoxville	194	192	-1.0	214	650	203.7	408	842	106.4
Las Vegas	744	926	24.5	381	362	-5.0	1,125	1,288	14.5
Lexington	770	628	-18.4	332	194	-41.6	1,102	822	-25.4
Lincoln	558	501	-10.2	46	332	621.7	604	833	37.9
Little Rock	329	344	4.6	328	84	-74.4	657	428	-34.9
Los Angeles	518	636	22.8	2,089	3,473	66.3	2,607	4,109	57.6
Louisville	759	633	-16.6	89	342	284.3	848	975	15.0
Madison	191	186	-2.6	516	340	-34.1	707	526	-25.6

Table continued on next page.

City	Single-Family			Multi-Family			Total		
	2009	2010	Pct. Chg.	2009	2010	Pct. Chg.	2009	2010	Pct. Chg.
Manchester	34	45	32.4	64	155	142.2	98	200	104.1
Miami	28	27	-3.6	280	685	144.6	308	712	131.2
Milwaukee	78	83	6.4	389	610	56.8	467	693	48.4
Minneapolis	28	41	46.4	370	837	126.2	398	878	120.6
Naperville	86	94	9.3	0	0	-	86	94	9.3
Nashville	1,068	1,001	-6.3	533	567	6.4	1,601	1,568	-2.1
New Orleans	947	820	-13.4	614	260	-57.7	1,561	1,080	-30.8
New York	316	325	2.8	5,741	6,402	11.5	6,057	6,727	11.1
Oakland	105	144	37.1	176	380	115.9	281	524	86.5
Oklahoma City	1,371	1,312	-4.3	94	96	2.1	1,465	1,408	-3.9
Omaha	1,542	1,191	-22.8	326	388	19.0	1,868	1,579	-15.5
Orlando	235	224	-4.7	62	336	441.9	297	560	88.6
Overland Park	127	211	66.1	815	11	-98.7	942	222	-76.4
Oxnard	59	61	3.4	98	119	21.4	157	180	14.6
Philadelphia	291	447	53.6	656	537	-18.1	947	984	3.9
Phoenix	1,336	1,111	-16.8	370	584	57.8	1,706	1,695	-0.6
Pittsburgh	118	147	24.6	0	0	-	118	147	24.6
Plano	226	311	37.6	365	303	-17.0	591	614	3.9
Portland	427	435	1.9	366	665	81.7	793	1,100	38.7
Providence	4	8	100.0	69	13	-81.2	73	21	-71.2
Provo	64	76	18.8	0	238	-	64	314	390.6
Raleigh	1,032	1,024	-0.8	421	226	-46.3	1,453	1,250	-14.0
Reno	301	351	16.6	234	134	-42.7	535	485	-9.3
Richmond	139	126	-9.4	222	481	116.7	361	607	68.1
Riverside	56	107	91.1	23	266	1,056.5	79	373	372.2
Rochester	33	33	0.0	146	0	-100.0	179	33	-81.6
Sacramento	199	95	-52.3	54	96	77.8	253	191	-24.5
St. Louis	91	102	12.1	163	157	-3.7	254	259	2.0
St. Paul	21	18	-14.3	171	4	-97.7	192	22	-88.5
St. Petersburg	47	70	48.9	716	268	-62.6	763	338	-55.7
Salt Lake City	27	30	11.1	115	150	30.4	142	180	26.8
San Antonio	2,836	2,337	-17.6	330	1,237	274.8	3,166	3,574	12.9
San Diego	374	557	48.9	761	519	-31.8	1,135	1,076	-5.2
San Francisco	17	22	29.4	283	757	167.5	300	779	159.7
San Jose	31	74	138.7	238	2,348	886.6	269	2,422	800.4
Santa Ana	7	8	14.3	0	0	-	7	8	14.3
Savannah	330	241	-27.0	326	279	-14.4	656	520	-20.7
Seattle	216	241	11.6	562	2,456	337.0	778	2,697	246.7
Spokane	175	195	11.4	87	20	-77.0	262	215	-17.9
Springfield	103	105	1.9	400	376	-6.0	503	481	-4.4
Tampa	445	455	2.2	349	643	84.2	794	1,098	38.3
Tulsa	372	335	-9.9	350	111	-68.3	722	446	-38.2
Virginia Beach	503	529	5.2	726	100	-86.2	1,229	629	-48.8
Warren	7	20	185.7	0	0	-	7	20	185.7
Washington	151	177	17.2	975	562	-42.4	1,126	739	-34.4
Wichita	709	531	-25.1	132	146	10.6	841	677	-19.5
U.S.	441,100	447,300	1.4	141,900	157,300	10.9	583,000	604,600	3.7

Note: Figures represent new, privately-owned housing units authorized (unadjusted data); All permit data are based on estimates with imputation
Source: U.S. Census Bureau, Manufacturing, Mining, and Construction Statistics, Building Permits, 2009, 2010

Building Permits: Metro Area

Metro Area	Single-Family			Multi-Family			Total		
	2009	2010	Pct. Chg.	2009	2010	Pct. Chg.	2009	2010	Pct. Chg.
Albuquerque	1,519	1,553	2.2	173	211	22.0	1,692	1,764	4.3
Anchorage	297	424	42.8	254	109	-57.1	551	533	-3.3
Ann Arbor	210	317	51.0	43	51	18.6	253	368	45.5
Athens	277	226	-18.4	20	0	-100.0	297	226	-23.9
Atlanta	5,421	6,384	17.8	1,112	1,191	7.1	6,533	7,575	15.9
Austin	6,678	6,200	-7.2	2,080	2,586	24.3	8,758	8,786	0.3
Baltimore	3,099	3,554	14.7	2,016	2,040	1.2	5,115	5,594	9.4
Bellevue	5,036	6,139	21.9	2,383	3,901	63.7	7,419	10,040	35.3
Birmingham	1,683	1,563	-7.1	124	361	191.1	1,807	1,924	6.5
Boise City	1,769	1,630	-7.9	135	63	-53.3	1,904	1,693	-11.1
Boston	3,073	3,748	22.0	2,403	2,924	21.7	5,476	6,672	21.8
Boulder	136	276	102.9	209	381	82.3	345	657	90.4
Cambridge	3,073	3,748	22.0	2,403	2,924	21.7	5,476	6,672	21.8
Cary	4,377	4,653	6.3	517	560	8.3	4,894	5,213	6.5
Charleston	2,732	2,787	2.0	217	273	25.8	2,949	3,060	3.8
Charlotte	4,426	4,338	-2.0	2,665	950	-64.4	7,091	5,288	-25.4
Chattanooga	994	955	-3.9	132	131	-0.8	1,126	1,086	-3.6
Chicago	4,383	4,244	-3.2	1,714	3,023	76.4	6,097	7,267	19.2
Cincinnati	3,109	2,824	-9.2	406	382	-5.9	3,515	3,206	-8.8
Cleveland	1,809	1,853	2.4	260	88	-66.2	2,069	1,941	-6.2
Colorado Spgs.	1,353	1,676	23.9	16	84	425.0	1,369	1,760	28.6
Columbia	2,583	2,527	-2.2	915	415	-54.6	3,498	2,942	-15.9
Columbus	2,574	2,887	12.2	1,485	1,557	4.8	4,059	4,444	9.5
Dallas	14,141	14,420	2.0	6,229	5,138	-17.5	20,370	19,558	-4.0
Denver	2,723	3,660	34.4	1,389	1,382	-0.5	4,112	5,042	22.6
Des Moines	1,799	2,206	22.6	679	609	-10.3	2,478	2,815	13.6
Durham	1,324	1,530	15.6	1,333	383	-71.3	2,657	1,913	-28.0
Edison	6,496	7,010	7.9	10,211	11,658	14.2	16,707	18,668	11.7
El Paso	2,640	2,961	12.2	551	1,588	188.2	3,191	4,549	42.6
Eugene	428	464	8.4	188	86	-54.3	616	550	-10.7
Evansville	530	547	3.2	188	97	-48.4	718	644	-10.3
Fargo	803	760	-5.4	875	558	-36.2	1,678	1,318	-21.5
Ft. Collins	361	477	32.1	90	676	651.1	451	1,153	155.7
Ft. Lauderdale	2,289	3,171	38.5	1,586	2,706	70.6	3,875	5,877	51.7
Ft. Wayne	764	809	5.9	120	76	-36.7	884	885	0.1
Ft. Worth	14,141	14,420	2.0	6,229	5,138	-17.5	20,370	19,558	-4.0
Gainesville	384	367	-4.4	145	123	-15.2	529	490	-7.4
Greensboro	1,363	1,234	-9.5	712	669	-6.0	2,075	1,903	-8.3
Honolulu	862	879	2.0	174	1,012	481.6	1,036	1,891	82.5
Houston	22,369	22,330	-0.2	4,957	5,122	3.3	27,326	27,452	0.5
Huntsville	2,293	2,275	-0.8	695	0	-100.0	2,988	2,275	-23.9
Indianapolis	3,601	3,793	5.3	1,999	2,128	6.5	5,600	5,921	5.7
Irvine	3,609	4,008	11.1	3,672	6,386	73.9	7,281	10,394	42.8
Jackson	1,182	1,303	10.2	6	88	1,366.7	1,188	1,391	17.1
Jacksonville	3,323	3,387	1.9	1,343	219	-83.7	4,666	3,606	-22.7
Kansas City	1,858	2,155	16.0	1,548	559	-63.9	3,406	2,714	-20.3
Knoxville	1,367	1,452	6.2	560	821	46.6	1,927	2,273	18.0
Las Vegas	3,777	4,623	22.4	1,911	851	-55.5	5,688	5,474	-3.8
Lexington	1,279	1,155	-9.7	354	206	-41.8	1,633	1,361	-16.7
Lincoln	682	648	-5.0	46	384	734.8	728	1,032	41.8
Little Rock	1,781	1,896	6.5	1,268	1,663	31.2	3,049	3,559	16.7
Los Angeles	3,609	4,008	11.1	3,672	6,386	73.9	7,281	10,394	42.8
Louisville	2,154	2,009	-6.7	256	516	101.6	2,410	2,525	4.8
Madison	779	794	1.9	624	404	-35.3	1,403	1,198	-14.6

Table continued on next page.

Metro Area	Single-Family			Multi-Family			Total		
	2009	2010	Pct. Chg.	2009	2010	Pct. Chg.	2009	2010	Pct. Chg.
Manchester	321	367	14.3	192	315	64.1	513	682	32.9
Miami	2,289	3,171	38.5	1,586	2,706	70.6	3,875	5,877	51.7
Milwaukee	875	955	9.1	552	974	76.4	1,427	1,929	35.2
Minneapolis	3,629	3,805	4.8	1,041	1,921	84.5	4,670	5,726	22.6
Naperville	4,383	4,244	-3.2	1,714	3,023	76.4	6,097	7,267	19.2
Nashville	3,957	3,938	-0.5	976	1,154	18.2	4,933	5,092	3.2
New Orleans	2,190	1,875	-14.4	642	296	-53.9	2,832	2,171	-23.3
New York	6,496	7,010	7.9	10,211	11,658	14.2	16,707	18,668	11.7
Oakland	2,271	2,118	-6.7	1,279	2,503	95.7	3,550	4,621	30.2
Oklahoma City	3,119	3,032	-2.8	333	603	81.1	3,452	3,635	5.3
Omaha	3,081	2,305	-25.2	383	918	139.7	3,464	3,223	-7.0
Orlando	3,707	4,221	13.9	780	1,033	32.4	4,487	5,254	17.1
Overland Park	1,858	2,155	16.0	1,548	559	-63.9	3,406	2,714	-20.3
Oxnard	204	209	2.5	148	381	157.4	352	590	67.6
Philadelphia	4,963	5,186	4.5	2,130	1,867	-12.3	7,093	7,053	-0.6
Phoenix	8,598	7,212	-16.1	674	1,088	61.4	9,272	8,300	-10.5
Pittsburgh	2,681	3,398	26.7	352	217	-38.4	3,033	3,615	19.2
Plano	14,141	14,420	2.0	6,229	5,138	-17.5	20,370	19,558	-4.0
Portland	3,011	3,359	11.6	1,009	1,117	10.7	4,020	4,476	11.3
Providence	1,158	1,205	4.1	279	234	-16.1	1,437	1,439	0.1
Provo	1,260	1,553	23.3	264	432	63.6	1,524	1,985	30.2
Raleigh	4,377	4,653	6.3	517	560	8.3	4,894	5,213	6.5
Reno	497	472	-5.0	276	134	-51.4	773	606	-21.6
Richmond	2,682	2,472	-7.8	614	984	60.3	3,296	3,456	4.9
Riverside	4,887	5,287	8.2	1,448	1,049	-27.6	6,335	6,336	0.0
Rochester	1,157	1,129	-2.4	468	320	-31.6	1,625	1,449	-10.8
Sacramento	2,415	2,166	-10.3	295	536	81.7	2,710	2,702	-0.3
St. Louis	4,050	4,253	5.0	1,112	1,407	26.5	5,162	5,660	9.6
St. Paul	3,629	3,805	4.8	1,041	1,921	84.5	4,670	5,726	22.6
St. Petersburg	3,923	4,396	12.1	3,039	2,105	-30.7	6,962	6,501	-6.6
Salt Lake City	1,627	1,882	15.7	3,065	1,107	-63.9	4,692	2,989	-36.3
San Antonio	5,486	5,144	-6.2	438	1,721	292.9	5,924	6,865	15.9
San Diego	1,778	2,270	27.7	1,168	1,224	4.8	2,946	3,494	18.6
San Francisco	2,271	2,118	-6.7	1,279	2,503	95.7	3,550	4,621	30.2
San Jose	642	861	34.1	452	3,318	634.1	1,094	4,179	282.0
Santa Ana	3,609	4,008	11.1	3,672	6,386	73.9	7,281	10,394	42.8
Savannah	1,241	1,020	-17.8	364	281	-22.8	1,605	1,301	-18.9
Seattle	5,036	6,139	21.9	2,383	3,901	63.7	7,419	10,040	35.3
Spokane	809	939	16.1	977	670	-31.4	1,786	1,609	-9.9
Springfield	693	904	30.4	503	434	-13.7	1,196	1,338	11.9
Tampa	3,923	4,396	12.1	3,039	2,105	-30.7	6,962	6,501	-6.6
Tulsa	2,680	2,269	-15.3	660	347	-47.4	3,340	2,616	-21.7
Virginia Beach	2,999	3,149	5.0	2,303	817	-64.5	5,302	3,966	-25.2
Warren	1,261	2,430	92.7	72	780	983.3	1,333	3,210	140.8
Washington	8,954	9,488	6.0	3,375	3,577	6.0	12,329	13,065	6.0
Wichita	1,372	1,046	-23.8	504	213	-57.7	1,876	1,259	-32.9
U.S.	441,100	447,300	1.4	141,900	157,300	10.9	583,000	604,600	3.7

Note: Figures cover the Metropolitan Statistical Area - see Appendix B for areas included; Figures represent new, privately-owned housing units authorized (unadjusted data); All permit data are based on estimates with imputation
Source: U.S. Census Bureau, Manufacturing, Mining, and Construction Statistics, Building Permits, 2009, 2010

Homeownership Rate

Metro Area	2005	2006	2007	2008	2009	2010
Albuquerque	69.2	70.0	70.5	68.2	65.7	65.5
Anchorage	n/a	n/a	n/a	n/a	n/a	n/a
Ann Arbor	n/a	n/a	n/a	n/a	n/a	n/a
Athens	n/a	n/a	n/a	n/a	n/a	n/a
Atlanta	66.4	67.9	66.4	67.5	67.7	67.2
Austin	63.9	66.7	66.4	65.5	64.0	65.8
Baltimore	70.6	72.9	71.2	69.3	67.7	65.7
Bellevue	64.5	63.7	62.8	61.3	61.2	60.9
Birmingham	75.1	76.1	75.0	73.3	75.1	76.2
Boise City	n/a	n/a	n/a	n/a	n/a	n/a
Boston	63.0	64.7	64.8	66.2	65.5	66.0
Boulder	n/a	n/a	n/a	n/a	n/a	n/a
Cambridge	63.0	64.7	64.8	66.2	65.5	66.0
Cary	71.4	71.1	72.8	70.7	65.7	65.9
Charleston	n/a	n/a	n/a	n/a	n/a	n/a
Charlotte	65.8	66.1	66.5	65.4	66.1	66.1
Chattanooga	n/a	n/a	n/a	n/a	n/a	n/a
Chicago	70.0	69.6	69.0	68.4	69.2	68.2
Cincinnati	68.4	65.5	67.6	64.7	62.4	62.8
Cleveland	74.4	76.9	74.3	73.1	70.9	70.7
Colorado Spgs.	n/a	n/a	n/a	n/a	n/a	n/a
Columbia	76.3	72.2	71.1	71.4	71.5	74.1
Columbus	68.9	65.8	66.1	61.2	61.5	62.2
Dallas	62.3	60.7	60.9	60.9	61.6	63.8
Denver	70.7	70.0	69.5	66.9	65.3	65.7
Des Moines	n/a	n/a	n/a	n/a	n/a	n/a
Durham	n/a	n/a	n/a	n/a	n/a	n/a
Edison	54.6	53.6	53.8	52.6	51.7	51.6
El Paso	72.6	65.0	68.2	64.8	63.8	70.1
Eugene	n/a	n/a	n/a	n/a	n/a	n/a
Evansville	n/a	n/a	n/a	n/a	n/a	n/a
Fargo	n/a	n/a	n/a	n/a	n/a	n/a
Ft. Collins	n/a	n/a	n/a	n/a	n/a	n/a
Ft. Lauderdale	69.2	67.4	66.6	66.0	67.1	63.8
Ft. Wayne	n/a	n/a	n/a	n/a	n/a	n/a
Ft. Worth	62.3	60.7	60.9	60.9	61.6	63.8
Gainesville	n/a	n/a	n/a	n/a	n/a	n/a
Greensboro	66.3	62.2	62.1	68.0	70.7	68.8
Honolulu	58.0	58.4	58.8	57.2	57.6	54.9
Houston	61.7	63.5	64.5	64.8	63.6	61.4
Huntsville	n/a	n/a	n/a	n/a	n/a	n/a
Indianapolis	77.1	79.0	75.9	75.0	71.0	68.8
Irvine	54.6	54.4	52.3	52.1	50.4	49.7
Jackson	n/a	n/a	n/a	n/a	n/a	n/a
Jacksonville	67.9	70.0	70.9	72.1	72.6	70.0
Kansas City	71.3	69.5	71.3	70.2	69.5	68.8
Knoxville	n/a	n/a	n/a	n/a	n/a	n/a
Las Vegas	61.4	63.3	60.5	60.3	59.0	55.7
Lexington	n/a	n/a	n/a	n/a	n/a	n/a
Lincoln	n/a	n/a	n/a	n/a	n/a	n/a
Little Rock	n/a	n/a	n/a	n/a	n/a	n/a
Los Angeles	54.6	54.4	52.3	52.1	50.4	49.7
Louisville	62.9	66.4	67.2	67.9	67.7	63.4
Madison	n/a	n/a	n/a	n/a	n/a	n/a
Manchester	n/a	n/a	n/a	n/a	n/a	n/a
Miami	69.2	67.4	66.6	66.0	67.1	63.8

Table continued on next page.

Metro Area	2005	2006	2007	2008	2009	2010
Milwaukee	65.7	65.2	64.8	60.9	61.6	62.4
Minneapolis	74.9	73.4	70.7	69.9	70.9	71.2
Naperville	70.0	69.6	69.0	68.4	69.2	68.2
Nashville	73.0	72.4	70.0	71.3	71.8	70.4
New Orleans	71.2	70.3	67.8	68.0	68.2	66.9
New York	54.6	53.6	53.8	52.6	51.7	51.6
Oakland	57.8	59.4	58.0	56.4	57.3	58.0
Oklahoma City	72.9	71.8	68.2	69.5	69.0	70.0
Omaha	69.7	68.1	67.9	72.5	73.1	73.2
Orlando	70.5	71.1	71.8	70.5	72.4	70.8
Overland Park	71.3	69.5	71.3	70.2	69.5	68.8
Oxnard	73.4	69.8	71.4	71.7	73.1	67.1
Philadelphia	73.5	73.1	73.1	71.8	69.7	70.7
Phoenix	71.2	72.5	70.8	70.2	69.8	66.5
Pittsburgh	73.1	72.2	73.6	73.2	71.7	70.4
Plano	62.3	60.7	60.9	60.9	61.6	63.8
Portland	68.3	66.0	61.2	62.6	64.0	63.7
Providence	63.1	65.5	64.1	63.9	61.7	61.0
Provo	n/a	n/a	n/a	n/a	n/a	n/a
Raleigh	71.4	71.1	72.8	70.7	65.7	65.9
Reno	n/a	n/a	n/a	n/a	n/a	n/a
Richmond	69.7	68.9	72.7	72.4	72.2	68.1
Riverside	68.5	68.3	66.6	65.8	65.9	63.9
Rochester	74.9	73.4	74.4	75.0	74.7	71.4
Sacramento	64.1	64.2	60.8	61.1	64.3	61.1
St. Louis	74.4	72.8	72.1	72.2	72.5	72.2
St. Paul	74.9	73.4	70.7	69.9	70.9	71.2
St. Petersburg	71.7	71.6	72.9	70.5	68.3	68.3
Salt Lake City	68.8	69.6	71.8	72.0	68.8	65.5
San Antonio	66.0	62.6	62.4	66.1	69.8	70.1
San Diego	60.5	61.2	59.6	57.1	56.4	54.4
San Francisco	57.8	59.4	58.0	56.4	57.3	58.0
San Jose	59.2	59.4	57.6	54.6	57.2	58.9
Santa Ana	54.6	54.4	52.3	52.1	50.4	49.7
Savannah	n/a	n/a	n/a	n/a	n/a	n/a
Seattle	64.5	63.7	62.8	61.3	61.2	60.9
Spokane	n/a	n/a	n/a	n/a	n/a	n/a
Springfield	n/a	n/a	n/a	n/a	n/a	n/a
Tampa	71.7	71.6	72.9	70.5	68.3	68.3
Tulsa	71.7	67.9	66.7	66.8	67.8	64.2
Virginia Beach	68.0	68.3	66.0	63.9	63.5	61.4
Warren	75.1	75.8	76.1	75.5	73.9	73.6
Washington	68.4	68.9	69.2	68.1	67.2	67.3
Wichita	n/a	n/a	n/a	n/a	n/a	n/a
U.S.	68.9	68.8	68.1	67.8	67.4	66.9

Note: Figures are percentages and cover the Metropolitan Statistical Area - see Appendix B for areas included
Source: U.S. Census Bureau, Housing Vacancies and Homeownership Annual Statistics: 2010

Housing Vacancy Rates

Area	Gross Vacancy Rate[2] (%)			Year-Round Vacancy Rate[3] (%)			Rental Vacancy Rate[4] (%)			Homeowner Vacancy Rate[5] (%)		
	2008	2009	2010	2008	2009	2010	2008	2009	2010	2008	2009	2010
Albuquerque	8.5	8.5	7.4	7.6	7.8	6.6	8.1	8.0	5.0	1.9	1.9	1.7
Anchorage	n/a	n/a	n/a	n/a	n/a	n/a	n/a	n/a	n/a	n/a	n/a	n/a
Ann Arbor	n/a	n/a	n/a	n/a	n/a	n/a	n/a	n/a	n/a	n/a	n/a	n/a
Athens	n/a	n/a	n/a	n/a	n/a	n/a	n/a	n/a	n/a	n/a	n/a	n/a
Atlanta	12.6	13.0	11.7	12.4	12.8	11.4	16.1	16.6	13.8	4.8	4.1	3.0
Austin	11.4	12.8	15.8	11.0	12.7	15.7	11.8	12.2	11.8	2.3	1.6	1.9
Baltimore	11.9	12.3	11.0	11.8	12.1	10.9	12.4	13.4	11.8	2.3	1.9	2.2
Bellevue	6.6	9.0	8.8	6.6	8.8	8.6	4.5	8.0	7.4	1.9	2.8	3.2
Birmingham	14.3	12.9	14.8	13.2	11.4	13.5	10.6	13.1	8.8	3.3	2.2	2.3
Boise City	n/a	n/a	n/a	n/a	n/a	n/a	n/a	n/a	n/a	n/a	n/a	n/a
Boston	8.4	8.2	8.5	7.1	6.8	7.0	5.9	6.0	6.2	1.5	1.5	1.2
Boulder	n/a	n/a	n/a	n/a	n/a	n/a	n/a	n/a	n/a	n/a	n/a	n/a
Cambridge	8.4	8.2	8.5	7.1	6.8	7.0	5.9	6.0	6.2	1.5	1.5	1.2
Cary	10.6	10.5	11.0	10.6	10.5	11.0	9.9	10.3	11.4	3.2	2.8	5.0
Charleston	n/a	n/a	n/a	n/a	n/a	n/a	n/a	n/a	n/a	n/a	n/a	n/a
Charlotte	11.6	12.9	11.7	11.2	12.7	11.5	12.1	12.1	11.2	4.0	5.1	3.1
Chattanooga	n/a	n/a	n/a	n/a	n/a	n/a	n/a	n/a	n/a	n/a	n/a	n/a
Chicago	10.7	11.4	11.9	10.5	11.2	11.6	9.9	12.0	12.1	3.1	2.9	3.4
Cincinnati	12.8	12.9	13.2	11.7	11.7	12.1	8.5	11.3	12.0	4.4	4.0	4.0
Cleveland	12.8	13.9	11.4	12.8	13.9	11.3	13.4	12.5	11.3	2.7	3.0	3.1
Colorado Spgs.	n/a	n/a	n/a	n/a	n/a	n/a	n/a	n/a	n/a	n/a	n/a	n/a
Columbia	13.2	13.3	11.1	12.6	13.0	10.9	6.8	8.4	9.4	3.2	3.1	2.5
Columbus	11.6	10.8	11.7	11.4	10.2	11.7	9.2	7.6	8.0	3.2	2.0	4.2
Dallas	9.5	9.4	10.5	9.4	9.3	10.4	10.5	11.7	13.5	2.8	2.1	2.3
Denver	8.5	9.2	7.2	7.5	8.7	6.8	7.1	10.2	8.2	3.1	2.7	1.7
Des Moines	n/a	n/a	n/a	n/a	n/a	n/a	n/a	n/a	n/a	n/a	n/a	n/a
Durham	n/a	n/a	n/a	n/a	n/a	n/a	n/a	n/a	n/a	n/a	n/a	n/a
Edison	9.0	9.4	9.6	7.7	8.1	8.3	5.2	5.9	6.6	1.9	2.8	2.1
El Paso	9.0	8.6	7.0	9.0	8.4	6.9	9.5	9.6	5.8	3.0	2.5	1.4
Eugene	n/a	n/a	n/a	n/a	n/a	n/a	n/a	n/a	n/a	n/a	n/a	n/a
Evansville	n/a	n/a	n/a	n/a	n/a	n/a	n/a	n/a	n/a	n/a	n/a	n/a
Fargo	n/a	n/a	n/a	n/a	n/a	n/a	n/a	n/a	n/a	n/a	n/a	n/a
Ft. Collins	n/a	n/a	n/a	n/a	n/a	n/a	n/a	n/a	n/a	n/a	n/a	n/a
Ft. Lauderdale	22.1	23.1	21.8	13.1	13.7	13.0	12.1	13.2	10.1	3.8	3.2	3.5
Ft. Wayne	n/a	n/a	n/a	n/a	n/a	n/a	n/a	n/a	n/a	n/a	n/a	n/a
Ft. Worth	9.5	9.4	10.5	9.4	9.3	10.4	10.5	11.7	13.5	2.8	2.1	2.3
Gainesville	n/a	n/a	n/a	n/a	n/a	n/a	n/a	n/a	n/a	n/a	n/a	n/a
Greensboro	14.7	13.8	12.8	14.7	13.8	12.6	17.6	15.2	12.8	5.6	6.3	4.1
Honolulu	9.9	10.9	11.5	8.6	9.4	10.0	5.1	6.9	7.2	1.0	0.8	1.0
Houston	12.7	12.5	12.2	12.5	12.3	11.9	15.6	15.6	16.2	2.7	1.9	2.8
Huntsville	n/a	n/a	n/a	n/a	n/a	n/a	n/a	n/a	n/a	n/a	n/a	n/a
Indianapolis	12.6	10.0	12.1	12.6	9.7	11.8	19.3	12.6	14.1	4.2	2.6	3.0
Irvine	5.8	6.6	7.2	5.7	6.3	6.9	5.3	6.4	6.7	1.5	1.3	1.8
Jackson	n/a	n/a	n/a	n/a	n/a	n/a	n/a	n/a	n/a	n/a	n/a	n/a
Jacksonville	14.7	14.3	14.9	14.1	13.6	14.6	15.3	15.9	13.9	5.4	3.7	4.6
Kansas City	10.9	11.0	10.7	10.3	10.7	10.5	14.1	14.4	14.0	3.4	3.4	2.7
Knoxville	n/a	n/a	n/a	n/a	n/a	n/a	n/a	n/a	n/a	n/a	n/a	n/a
Las Vegas	16.7	16.7	17.2	16.2	16.5	16.8	14.9	14.3	13.8	6.1	5.0	5.1
Lexington	n/a	n/a	n/a	n/a	n/a	n/a	n/a	n/a	n/a	n/a	n/a	n/a
Lincoln	n/a	n/a	n/a	n/a	n/a	n/a	n/a	n/a	n/a	n/a	n/a	n/a
Little Rock	n/a	n/a	n/a	n/a	n/a	n/a	n/a	n/a	n/a	n/a	n/a	n/a
Los Angeles	5.8	6.6	7.2	5.7	6.3	6.9	5.3	6.4	6.7	1.5	1.3	1.8
Louisville	9.6	10.0	9.7	9.5	9.9	9.7	10.2	12.1	9.6	2.5	2.4	1.9
Madison	n/a	n/a	n/a	n/a	n/a	n/a	n/a	n/a	n/a	n/a	n/a	n/a

Table continued on next page.

Area	Gross Vacancy Rate[2] (%)			Year-Round Vacancy Rate[3] (%)			Rental Vacancy Rate[4] (%)			Homeowner Vacancy Rate[5] (%)		
	2008	2009	2010	2008	2009	2010	2008	2009	2010	2008	2009	2010
Manchester	n/a	n/a	n/a	n/a	n/a	n/a	n/a	n/a	n/a	n/a	n/a	n/a
Miami	22.1	23.1	21.8	13.1	13.7	13.0	12.1	13.2	10.1	3.8	3.2	3.5
Milwaukee	9.2	9.8	7.8	7.8	8.6	7.1	7.8	8.7	7.6	1.1	1.4	1.2
Minneapolis	7.6	7.6	6.8	7.2	7.1	6.3	7.2	8.5	7.4	2.8	2.2	1.4
Naperville	10.7	11.4	11.9	10.5	11.2	11.6	9.9	12.0	12.1	3.1	2.9	3.4
Nashville	9.9	8.7	10.9	9.3	8.1	10.5	10.6	8.3	8.2	2.2	1.9	2.4
New Orleans	16.5	16.1	14.6	16.3	15.9	14.4	12.3	18.0	15.2	3.7	2.5	2.6
New York	9.0	9.4	9.6	7.7	8.1	8.3	5.2	5.9	6.6	1.9	2.8	2.1
Oakland	8.9	10.3	9.1	8.8	10.1	9.0	5.4	6.7	6.0	2.1	1.8	1.8
Oklahoma City	13.9	12.6	13.3	13.8	12.2	13.2	9.9	8.3	9.6	3.5	2.8	2.7
Omaha	8.7	8.3	9.6	8.7	8.2	9.1	12.6	11.7	10.1	3.2	2.0	3.3
Orlando	21.4	21.2	19.9	17.8	17.5	16.6	21.9	22.8	19.0	6.8	5.8	5.9
Overland Park	10.9	11.0	10.7	10.3	10.7	10.5	14.1	14.4	14.0	3.4	3.4	2.7
Oxnard	4.9	5.9	7.3	4.9	5.5	6.6	4.2	5.0	6.4	2.0	1.5	1.1
Philadelphia	9.0	8.9	9.9	8.9	8.7	9.6	11.8	11.4	11.6	2.5	1.6	1.5
Phoenix	17.6	18.6	18.4	10.9	13.2	12.9	15.0	18.3	16.3	3.7	3.1	2.9
Pittsburgh	12.6	13.2	12.7	11.7	12.1	11.7	7.8	9.7	7.8	2.6	1.6	2.7
Plano	9.5	9.4	10.5	9.4	9.3	10.4	10.5	11.7	13.5	2.8	2.1	2.3
Portland	7.1	8.2	7.2	6.2	7.9	7.0	5.5	4.3	4.2	1.9	4.8	3.2
Providence	13.2	12.8	12.7	10.1	9.2	9.4	9.6	8.5	7.5	1.9	1.7	1.3
Provo	n/a	n/a	n/a	n/a	n/a	n/a	n/a	n/a	n/a	n/a	n/a	n/a
Raleigh	10.6	10.5	11.0	10.6	10.5	11.0	9.9	10.3	11.4	3.2	2.8	5.0
Reno	n/a	n/a	n/a	n/a	n/a	n/a	n/a	n/a	n/a	n/a	n/a	n/a
Richmond	12.8	12.7	11.7	12.3	12.0	11.2	20.8	18.5	13.5	2.0	2.2	3.1
Riverside	18.1	18.7	19.9	10.8	12.2	13.9	9.4	12.3	12.3	5.2	4.0	4.7
Rochester	13.1	13.1	12.0	8.9	8.7	7.2	7.0	8.0	6.3	1.7	1.3	1.1
Sacramento	16.9	15.2	14.0	15.2	12.7	11.3	10.4	10.6	8.4	4.8	4.0	2.9
St. Louis	11.1	9.4	11.3	11.0	9.1	11.2	10.7	11.2	11.2	3.1	1.8	2.1
St. Paul	7.6	7.6	6.8	7.2	7.1	6.3	7.2	8.5	7.4	2.8	2.2	1.4
St. Petersburg	18.7	20.5	20.2	13.3	14.7	14.2	15.4	12.4	12.6	3.0	4.1	4.0
Salt Lake City	7.4	8.7	6.4	6.1	7.8	6.0	9.2	10.2	6.0	1.8	2.3	2.2
San Antonio	11.1	10.6	11.1	10.7	10.3	10.6	11.5	12.1	14.0	1.5	1.2	1.6
San Diego	10.8	10.4	10.5	9.8	9.8	10.0	7.2	8.8	7.8	2.7	2.1	2.9
San Francisco	8.9	10.3	9.1	8.8	10.1	9.0	5.4	6.7	6.0	2.1	1.8	1.8
San Jose	5.8	6.3	6.4	5.8	6.3	6.4	5.6	7.7	8.2	2.0	1.4	0.9
Santa Ana	5.8	6.6	7.2	5.7	6.3	6.9	5.3	6.4	6.7	1.5	1.3	1.8
Savannah	n/a	n/a	n/a	n/a	n/a	n/a	n/a	n/a	n/a	n/a	n/a	n/a
Seattle	6.6	9.0	8.8	6.6	8.8	8.6	4.5	8.0	7.4	1.9	2.8	3.2
Spokane	n/a	n/a	n/a	n/a	n/a	n/a	n/a	n/a	n/a	n/a	n/a	n/a
Springfield	n/a	n/a	n/a	n/a	n/a	n/a	n/a	n/a	n/a	n/a	n/a	n/a
Tampa	18.7	20.5	20.2	13.3	14.7	14.2	15.4	12.4	12.6	3.0	4.1	4.0
Tulsa	11.6	12.7	13.3	10.4	11.8	12.7	9.8	15.1	15.9	3.0	2.4	1.4
Virginia Beach	10.9	10.4	11.1	10.8	9.9	10.4	6.7	6.2	8.8	3.2	2.3	2.8
Warren	12.9	12.1	12.7	12.7	12.0	12.6	18.3	15.8	16.4	4.6	3.3	2.6
Washington	11.0	10.3	10.2	10.7	10.0	10.0	10.0	10.0	8.8	2.7	2.3	2.1
Wichita	n/a	n/a	n/a	n/a	n/a	n/a	n/a	n/a	n/a	n/a	n/a	n/a
U.S.	14.4	14.5	14.3	11.1	11.3	11.3	10.0	10.6	10.2	2.8	2.6	2.6

Note: (1) Metropolitan Statistical Area - see Appendix B for areas included; (2) The percentage of the total housing inventory that is vacant; (3) The percentage of the housing inventory (excluding seasonal units) that is year-round vacant; (4) The percentage of rental inventory that is vacant for rent; (5) The percentage of homeowner inventory that is vacant for sale; n/a not available
Source: U.S. Census Bureau, Housing Vacancies and Homeownership Annual Statistics: 2010

Employment by Industry

Metro Area[1]	(A)	(B)	(C)	(D)	(E)	(F)	(G)	(H)	(I)	(J)	(K)	(L)	(M)
Albuquerque	22.7	14.7	15.0	11.4	4.6	10.1	4.7	n/a	3.3	3.1	2.6	2.2	n/a
Anchorage	21.2	15.0	11.5	12.1	1.2	10.7	5.6	5.2	2.6	3.7	7.0	2.7	1.6
Ann Arbor	38.5	12.4	12.9	8.6	6.5	6.5	3.1	n/a	2.7	3.6	1.7	2.0	n/a
Athens	30.0	n/a	8.4	11.6	n/a	9.5	n/a	n/a	n/a	n/a	n/a	n/a	n/a
Atlanta	14.2	12.3	16.8	11.2	6.4	9.6	6.1	3.8	6.4	4.1	5.6	3.5	0.1
Austin	22.2	11.6	14.1	10.9	6.2	10.7	5.5	n/a	5.2	4.4	1.7	2.5	n/a
Baltimore	18.2	18.8	14.7	10.8	4.8	8.5	5.6	n/a	4.1	4.3	3.5	1.7	n/a
Bellevue[2]	14.7	12.1	14.5	10.4	11.0	9.2	5.6	4.5	4.8	3.6	3.4	6.2	0.1
Birmingham	17.1	13.5	12.0	12.2	7.0	8.6	7.5	4.9	5.8	4.8	4.2	1.9	0.6
Boise City	17.3	15.4	14.6	12.0	9.0	8.6	5.3	n/a	4.3	3.6	3.3	1.7	n/a
Boston[4]	12.1	22.9	17.4	8.8	5.5	9.0	8.5	2.9	3.4	3.7	2.4	3.4	<0.1
Boulder	20.5	12.3	17.4	9.7	9.4	10.4	4.5	n/a	3.1	3.3	1.1	5.5	n/a
Cambridge[4]	12.1	22.9	17.4	8.8	5.5	9.0	8.5	2.9	3.4	3.7	2.4	3.4	<0.1
Cary	18.0	12.3	17.4	11.6	5.4	10.4	5.4	n/a	4.0	4.7	2.2	3.3	n/a
Charleston	20.6	11.6	14.7	12.5	7.4	11.8	4.3	n/a	2.8	3.7	4.0	1.8	n/a
Charlotte	14.5	10.0	16.6	11.4	8.1	10.2	8.7	n/a	5.5	3.8	4.1	2.7	n/a
Chattanooga	15.6	13.6	9.5	10.6	12.1	9.9	7.5	n/a	3.6	4.7	7.5	1.6	n/a
Chicago[2]	13.0	15.1	16.8	10.2	8.7	8.9	7.1	3.2	5.4	4.6	4.8	2.0	<0.1
Cincinnati	13.3	15.1	15.5	10.5	10.5	10.0	6.3	n/a	5.6	4.1	4.0	1.4	n/a
Cleveland	14.1	19.2	13.2	10.4	11.7	8.7	6.2	n/a	5.1	4.2	3.0	1.5	n/a
Colorado Spgs.	19.7	12.0	15.9	11.7	5.1	11.9	6.2	n/a	2.0	5.9	1.9	2.9	n/a
Columbia	22.8	12.5	11.6	11.4	7.8	9.0	7.9	n/a	4.0	4.0	3.1	1.6	n/a
Columbus	17.5	13.8	16.4	11.0	6.9	9.3	7.4	n/a	4.1	3.9	4.9	1.8	n/a
Dallas[2]	13.4	12.4	16.7	10.2	7.9	9.3	8.8	n/a	5.8	3.4	3.6	3.1	n/a
Denver	14.9	12.1	17.1	10.5	5.1	10.5	7.5	n/a	5.2	4.0	4.0	3.6	n/a
Des Moines	13.9	13.5	11.9	11.7	5.7	8.0	16.4	n/a	5.5	4.0	3.2	2.5	n/a
Durham	18.0	12.3	17.4	11.6	5.4	10.4	5.4	n/a	4.0	4.7	2.2	3.3	n/a
Edison[2]	15.1	15.4	16.4	12.7	6.3	8.1	5.8	n/a	5.7	4.3	4.1	2.6	n/a
El Paso	25.5	12.8	11.1	12.5	5.9	9.8	4.1	n/a	3.5	3.3	4.4	1.8	n/a
Eugene	22.2	15.4	10.1	13.1	8.5	9.7	5.2	3.7	3.8	3.5	2.0	2.3	0.5
Evansville	10.8	17.1	11.4	11.0	15.8	9.4	3.3	n/a	4.0	4.1	4.9	1.4	n/a
Fargo	15.1	15.2	10.6	12.8	7.2	10.4	7.1	n/a	6.2	4.1	3.6	2.8	n/a
Ft. Collins	22.5	13.3	12.9	12.3	7.9	11.7	4.2	n/a	2.2	3.6	1.9	1.9	n/a
Ft. Lauderdale[2]	14.3	13.5	16.7	13.7	3.3	10.9	7.5	4.3	6.1	4.3	3.2	2.3	n/a
Ft. Wayne	10.9	17.8	10.3	10.8	16.0	8.9	5.6	n/a	5.4	3.6	4.6	1.5	n/a
Ft. Worth[2]	14.8	12.7	10.7	11.9	10.0	10.5	6.0	n/a	4.5	3.7	7.4	1.6	n/a
Gainesville	33.3	17.6	8.3	10.6	3.5	10.4	4.8	n/a	1.9	3.5	1.8	1.2	n/a
Greensboro	13.3	13.7	13.5	10.4	15.2	8.5	6.1	n/a	5.4	4.1	4.5	1.6	n/a
Honolulu	22.7	13.7	13.3	10.3	2.3	13.8	4.7	n/a	3.2	4.7	4.4	2.1	n/a
Houston	15.0	12.2	14.3	10.6	8.5	9.1	5.3	6.8	5.2	3.6	5.0	1.2	3.3
Huntsville	23.7	8.2	22.9	10.9	11.0	8.3	2.9	n/a	2.5	3.5	1.2	1.2	n/a
Indianapolis	14.0	14.9	14.1	10.6	9.3	9.8	6.6	4.1	5.0	3.8	5.9	1.7	0.1
Irvine[2]	11.2	11.6	17.9	10.6	11.0	12.5	7.7	4.8	5.7	3.1	2.0	1.8	<0.1
Jackson	22.7	15.6	10.9	11.4	6.3	8.4	6.0	4.4	4.3	3.7	4.1	1.8	0.4
Jacksonville	13.2	14.8	14.9	12.1	4.6	11.0	9.5	4.6	4.3	4.0	5.2	1.7	0.1
Kansas City	16.0	13.6	14.3	11.1	7.6	9.2	7.4	n/a	4.9	4.2	4.6	3.3	n/a
Knoxville	15.7	13.9	13.8	12.7	9.0	10.5	5.1	n/a	4.8	4.3	3.5	1.7	n/a
Las Vegas	12.0	8.9	12.6	11.8	2.3	31.6	4.9	5.2	2.5	2.9	4.2	1.1	<0.1
Lexington	20.8	12.3	12.5	11.3	11.7	10.6	4.0	n/a	3.6	3.9	3.4	2.2	n/a
Lincoln	22.6	14.7	10.4	10.7	7.4	9.2	7.6	n/a	2.3	4.0	6.0	1.3	n/a
Little Rock	21.0	15.2	13.0	10.7	5.8	8.8	5.5	n/a	4.9	4.3	3.6	2.3	n/a
Los Angeles[2]	15.0	14.0	14.0	10.5	9.8	10.2	5.5	2.6	5.4	3.6	4.0	5.4	0.1
Louisville	13.9	14.1	12.5	10.6	10.9	9.6	6.7	n/a	4.7	4.2	7.1	1.6	n/a
Madison	24.7	12.4	10.4	11.2	8.0	8.3	7.5	n/a	3.4	5.5	2.3	3.1	n/a
Manchester[3]	12.7	19.3	13.4	12.3	8.0	8.4	7.4	n/a	4.3	4.0	n/a	3.3	n/a
Miami[2]	15.2	16.2	13.2	12.8	3.5	10.9	6.4	3.1	6.9	4.0	6.0	1.8	<0.1

Table continued on next page.

Metro Area[1]	(A)	(B)	(C)	(D)	(E)	(F)	(G)	(H)	(I)	(J)	(K)	(L)	(M)
Milwaukee	11.4	18.3	12.9	9.6	14.2	8.7	6.7	2.8	4.5	5.6	3.4	1.9	<0.1
Minneapolis	14.2	15.9	15.1	10.2	10.1	8.7	7.8	n/a	4.7	4.4	3.7	2.3	n/a
Naperville[2]	13.0	15.1	16.8	10.2	8.7	8.9	7.1	3.2	5.4	4.6	4.8	2.0	<0.1
Nashville	14.7	16.1	13.6	11.6	8.0	10.3	6.1	n/a	4.8	4.0	4.0	2.6	n/a
New Orleans	15.5	14.5	12.9	11.2	6.0	13.6	4.9	5.7	4.2	3.6	4.7	1.7	1.4
New York[2]	14.7	20.0	15.2	9.3	3.1	8.4	10.3	n/a	4.3	4.2	3.5	3.8	n/a
Oakland[2]	17.5	14.8	15.8	10.8	8.1	9.0	5.1	4.9	4.4	3.6	3.4	2.5	0.1
Oklahoma City	21.6	13.5	12.7	11.0	5.6	10.2	5.8	4.4	3.9	4.0	2.7	1.8	2.7
Omaha	14.2	15.3	14.0	11.6	6.8	9.1	8.7	n/a	3.7	3.9	6.1	2.4	n/a
Orlando	11.5	12.0	16.3	11.9	3.7	20.1	6.3	4.4	3.7	4.7	3.0	2.3	<0.1
Overland Park	16.0	13.6	14.3	11.1	7.6	9.2	7.4	n/a	4.9	4.2	4.6	3.3	n/a
Oxnard	15.6	12.2	13.0	13.3	11.5	11.1	7.4	3.9	4.3	3.2	2.0	1.9	0.5
Philadelphia[2]	11.7	22.9	15.3	10.4	7.0	8.1	7.0	n/a	4.3	4.4	3.3	2.0	n/a
Phoenix	13.9	14.4	16.1	12.4	6.5	10.2	8.0	4.6	4.8	3.6	3.8	1.6	0.2
Pittsburgh	11.4	21.1	13.9	11.6	7.8	9.3	6.1	4.1	4.2	4.5	3.9	1.6	0.7
Plano[2]	13.4	12.4	16.7	10.2	7.9	9.3	8.8	n/a	5.8	3.4	3.6	3.1	n/a
Portland	15.2	14.7	13.1	10.8	11.0	9.5	6.3	4.5	5.3	3.6	3.5	2.3	0.1
Providence[3]	13.1	21.9	10.7	12.1	9.3	10.5	5.9	3.5	3.7	4.6	2.4	2.2	<0.1
Provo	15.3	23.6	12.1	12.9	9.0	7.6	3.4	n/a	2.7	2.3	1.4	4.4	n/a
Raleigh	18.0	12.3	17.4	11.6	5.4	10.4	5.4	n/a	4.0	4.7	2.2	3.3	n/a
Reno	15.1	11.6	13.5	11.4	5.6	17.9	4.5	4.7	4.6	3.6	6.1	1.2	0.2
Richmond	18.7	14.2	15.6	10.9	5.5	8.1	6.7	n/a	4.4	5.3	3.3	1.6	n/a
Riverside	19.8	12.2	11.1	14.4	7.5	11.0	3.7	5.0	4.4	3.3	6.1	1.4	0.1
Rochester	16.4	22.8	12.0	11.1	11.6	7.8	3.9	3.2	3.4	3.8	2.0	1.8	0.1
Sacramento	28.2	12.4	12.6	11.2	4.1	9.9	5.8	4.5	2.8	3.5	2.9	2.1	<0.1
Salt Lake City	15.6	11.1	15.8	11.5	8.5	9.2	7.8	n/a	4.7	3.0	4.6	2.7	n/a
San Antonio	19.4	15.5	12.0	11.4	5.3	11.8	7.7	4.9	3.3	3.7	2.4	2.1	0.4
San Diego	18.5	12.2	17.3	10.9	7.4	12.5	5.4	4.4	3.2	3.9	2.3	2.0	<0.1
San Francisco[2]	14.3	11.7	21.4	9.6	4.0	13.0	8.1	3.3	2.6	4.0	3.9	4.1	<0.1
San Jose	10.8	13.2	19.2	9.4	17.8	8.6	3.6	3.7	4.1	3.0	1.4	5.3	<0.1
Santa Ana[2]	11.2	11.6	17.9	10.6	11.0	12.5	7.7	4.8	5.7	3.1	2.0	1.8	<0.1
Savannah	15.4	15.4	11.7	12.0	9.1	12.9	3.6	n/a	3.9	4.5	6.6	1.0	n/a
Seattle[2]	14.7	12.1	14.5	10.4	11.0	9.2	5.6	4.5	4.8	3.6	3.4	6.2	0.1
Spokane	17.6	19.7	10.3	12.5	6.9	9.3	5.8	n/a	4.6	4.3	2.9	1.4	n/a
Springfield	15.0	19.5	10.4	13.1	6.5	9.1	5.9	n/a	5.1	4.4	5.4	2.0	n/a
St. Louis	13.4	17.4	14.0	11.0	8.2	10.4	6.1	n/a	4.6	4.2	3.7	2.3	n/a
St. Paul	14.2	15.9	15.1	10.2	10.1	8.7	7.8	n/a	4.7	4.4	3.7	2.3	n/a
St. Petersburg	13.9	16.2	17.1	12.6	5.1	10.5	7.7	4.6	4.0	3.8	2.3	2.3	<0.1
Tampa	13.9	16.2	17.1	12.6	5.1	10.5	7.7	4.6	4.0	3.8	2.3	2.3	<0.1
Tulsa	13.7	14.7	13.5	11.4	10.9	8.9	5.6	4.9	3.7	4.0	5.0	2.0	1.7
Virginia Beach	21.7	12.9	13.4	11.7	7.1	10.7	4.9	n/a	2.8	4.7	3.4	1.7	n/a
Warren[2]	9.9	15.3	19.1	12.3	11.9	8.9	6.2	n/a	4.7	4.6	1.9	1.9	n/a
Washington[2]	24.5	11.7	23.2	8.7	1.4	8.7	4.3	n/a	2.1	6.1	2.3	2.6	n/a
Wichita	14.9	15.2	10.4	10.9	18.2	9.3	3.8	n/a	3.8	3.8	3.0	1.7	n/a
U.S.	17.2	15.2	13.0	11.4	9.7	8.8	5.8	4.2	4.1	4.1	3.7	2.1	0.6

Note: All figures are percentages covering non-farm employment as of December 2010 and are not seasonally adjusted;
(1) Figures cover the Metropolitan Statistical Area (MSA) except where noted. See Appendix B for areas included; (2) Metropolitan Division; (3) New England City and Town Area; (4) New England City and Town Area Division; (A) Government; (B) Education and Health Services; (C) Professional and Business Services; (D) Retail Trade; (E) Leisure and Hospitality; (F) Manufacturing; (G) Finance Activities; (H) Wholesale Trade; (I) Construction; (J) Other Services; (K) Transportation and Utilities; (L) Information; (M) Natural Resources and Mining; n/a not available
Source: Bureau of Labor Statistics, http://stats.bls.gov

Labor Force, Employment and Job Growth: City

City	Civilian Labor Force			Workers Employed		
	Dec. 2009	Dec. 2010	% Chg.	Dec. 2009	Dec. 2010	% Chg.
Albuquerque	259,975	263,601	1.4	241,791	242,952	0.5
Anchorage	156,114	158,312	1.4	145,869	148,244	1.6
Ann Arbor	62,912	63,099	0.3	57,279	58,664	2.4
Athens	64,003	64,416	0.6	59,181	59,484	0.5
Atlanta	233,074	232,329	-0.3	207,104	206,028	-0.5
Austin	423,893	429,920	1.4	397,108	402,844	1.4
Baltimore	274,569	274,017	-0.2	245,561	245,658	0.0
Bellevue	70,372	70,387	0.0	65,299	65,672	0.6
Birmingham	96,666	95,172	-1.5	85,595	85,368	-0.3
Boise City	107,242	106,962	-0.3	98,173	97,521	-0.7
Boston	323,425	327,437	1.2	298,493	303,503	1.7
Boulder	62,302	61,762	-0.9	57,301	56,942	-0.6
Cambridge	60,777	61,690	1.5	57,550	58,516	1.7
Cary	67,059	67,380	0.5	62,753	63,838	1.7
Charleston	57,124	58,080	1.7	52,237	53,354	2.1
Charlotte	345,524	344,387	-0.3	310,918	315,035	1.3
Chattanooga	78,201	79,478	1.6	70,720	72,941	3.1
Chicago	1,301,920	1,314,404	1.0	1,151,757	1,189,884	3.3
Cincinnati	159,600	158,829	-0.5	143,926	144,495	0.4
Cleveland	176,528	179,338	1.6	157,523	160,679	2.0
Colorado Spgs.	212,879	209,764	-1.5	193,477	190,593	-1.5
Columbia	54,943	54,922	0.0	49,716	49,714	0.0
Columbus	419,446	424,902	1.3	383,267	392,390	2.4
Dallas	588,889	602,997	2.4	539,610	551,590	2.2
Denver	321,157	319,329	-0.6	289,777	288,061	-0.6
Des Moines	106,468	106,442	0.0	98,765	98,400	-0.4
Durham	117,331	116,938	-0.3	108,543	109,337	0.7
Edison	54,494	53,777	-1.3	50,667	50,546	-0.2
El Paso	265,934	274,211	3.1	244,163	249,990	2.4
Eugene	81,211	82,033	1.0	73,441	74,723	1.7
Evansville	57,085	58,045	1.7	51,852	52,967	2.2
Fargo	58,521	57,385	-1.9	56,114	55,304	-1.4
Ft. Collins	83,246	82,975	-0.3	76,194	76,097	-0.1
Ft. Lauderdale	102,833	103,747	0.9	93,969	94,060	0.1
Ft. Wayne	122,982	123,247	0.2	108,828	111,032	2.0
Ft. Worth	332,708	338,904	1.9	306,145	311,270	1.7
Gainesville	59,685	60,405	1.2	55,174	55,274	0.2
Greensboro	128,094	127,009	-0.8	114,547	115,000	0.4
Honolulu	435,945	441,056	1.2	412,338	419,892	1.8
Houston	1,054,206	1,080,233	2.5	972,933	994,389	2.2
Huntsville	91,279	90,774	-0.6	84,445	84,297	-0.2
Indianapolis	402,964	403,445	0.1	363,686	366,365	0.7
Irvine	81,683	81,631	-0.1	75,964	76,110	0.2
Jackson	79,941	82,262	2.9	71,929	74,537	3.6
Jacksonville	411,812	417,935	1.5	366,869	371,136	1.2
Kansas City	229,342	227,884	-0.6	206,699	204,805	-0.9
Knoxville	92,633	94,018	1.5	84,013	86,557	3.0
Las Vegas	282,156	277,063	-1.8	239,347	233,762	-2.3
Lexington	153,043	157,131	2.7	141,425	145,319	2.8
Lincoln	141,922	142,326	0.3	136,084	137,422	1.0
Little Rock	96,128	98,119	2.1	89,447	91,248	2.0
Los Angeles	1,899,435	1,920,895	1.1	1,652,029	1,653,729	0.1
Louisville	361,836	363,899	0.6	322,927	327,627	1.5
Madison	145,007	144,027	-0.7	136,949	137,726	0.6
Manchester	61,672	61,974	0.5	57,151	58,202	1.8

Table continued on next page.

City	Civilian Labor Force			Workers Employed		
	Dec. 2009	Dec. 2010	% Chg.	Dec. 2009	Dec. 2010	% Chg.
Miami	189,231	200,338	5.9	166,259	172,181	3.6
Milwaukee	273,819	272,145	-0.6	242,330	245,679	1.4
Minneapolis	212,921	213,279	0.2	198,090	200,008	1.0
Naperville	74,968	75,809	1.1	69,170	71,459	3.3
Nashville	323,840	332,223	2.6	294,817	305,276	3.5
New Orleans	144,475	148,131	2.5	133,161	135,477	1.7
New York	3,991,922	3,963,982	-0.7	3,597,655	3,624,399	0.7
Oakland	202,240	200,841	-0.7	169,772	168,386	-0.8
Oklahoma City	253,543	255,315	0.7	237,129	239,645	1.1
Omaha	235,610	236,084	0.2	224,048	225,948	0.8
Orlando	133,121	136,757	2.7	118,865	121,383	2.1
Overland Park	96,122	95,913	-0.2	89,652	90,071	0.5
Oxnard	90,045	90,068	0.0	77,080	77,114	0.0
Philadelphia	644,489	646,182	0.3	578,843	578,561	0.0
Phoenix	794,711	800,878	0.8	707,851	722,214	2.0
Pittsburgh	151,348	152,110	0.5	140,292	140,667	0.3
Plano	144,707	147,581	2.0	134,666	137,656	2.2
Portland	306,837	310,800	1.3	275,851	282,198	2.3
Providence	79,135	80,643	1.9	68,801	70,192	2.0
Provo	69,255	68,637	-0.9	63,690	63,343	-0.5
Raleigh	205,212	206,489	0.6	189,532	192,821	1.7
Reno	115,607	114,717	-0.8	99,832	98,519	-1.3
Richmond	101,258	101,190	-0.1	91,047	91,741	0.8
Riverside	160,624	159,900	-0.5	137,874	136,997	-0.6
Rochester	93,390	93,371	0.0	83,475	84,025	0.7
Sacramento	214,799	211,580	-1.5	184,586	180,227	-2.4
Salt Lake City	115,637	114,289	-1.2	105,975	105,060	-0.9
San Antonio	635,724	646,232	1.7	594,647	602,179	1.3
San Diego	692,134	694,225	0.3	622,204	623,902	0.3
San Francisco	455,380	455,883	0.1	413,757	414,567	0.2
San Jose	456,952	457,821	0.2	401,128	405,177	1.0
Santa Ana	159,766	159,222	-0.3	136,466	136,730	0.2
Savannah	63,160	63,625	0.7	56,660	56,977	0.6
Seattle	377,351	375,788	-0.4	346,328	348,306	0.6
Spokane	104,138	103,841	-0.3	93,533	94,682	1.2
Springfield	79,314	79,385	0.1	72,582	72,756	0.2
St. Louis	155,436	156,863	0.9	137,215	138,490	0.9
St. Paul	142,246	142,440	0.1	131,375	132,648	1.0
St. Petersburg	120,698	122,039	1.1	106,990	107,572	0.5
Tampa	161,072	162,264	0.7	142,359	143,133	0.5
Tulsa	185,541	184,938	-0.3	172,084	172,059	0.0
Virginia Beach	219,544	219,880	0.2	205,444	206,492	0.5
Warren	68,420	66,720	-2.5	56,798	58,111	2.3
Washington	331,016	327,457	-1.1	296,376	297,348	0.3
Wichita	191,932	191,031	-0.5	174,110	174,811	0.4
U.S.	152,693,000	153,156,000	0.3	137,953,000	139,159,000	0.9

Note: Data is not seasonally adjusted and covers workers 16 years of age and older
Source: Bureau of Labor Statistics, http://stats.bls.gov

Labor Force, Employment and Job Growth: Metro Area

Metro Area[1]	Civilian Labor Force			Workers Employed		
	Dec. 2009	Dec. 2010	% Chg.	Dec. 2009	Dec. 2010	% Chg.
Albuquerque	404,059	409,834	1.4	373,136	374,929	0.5
Anchorage	199,483	202,320	1.4	185,139	188,153	1.6
Ann Arbor	182,281	183,061	0.4	166,958	170,996	2.4
Athens	106,230	106,744	0.5	98,149	98,651	0.5
Atlanta	2,678,487	2,661,869	-0.6	2,404,347	2,391,846	-0.5
Austin	890,415	902,646	1.4	828,542	840,510	1.4
Baltimore	1,385,890	1,383,128	-0.2	1,279,771	1,280,277	0.0
Bellevue[2]	1,490,064	1,486,730	-0.2	1,349,455	1,357,162	0.6
Birmingham	522,117	514,559	-1.4	473,277	472,020	-0.3
Boise City	292,460	292,392	0.0	265,415	263,652	-0.7
Boston[4]	1,526,126	1,542,443	1.1	1,413,994	1,437,727	1.7
Boulder	173,339	171,897	-0.8	161,375	160,365	-0.6
Cambridge[4]	1,526,126	1,542,443	1.1	1,413,994	1,437,727	1.7
Cary	555,352	557,030	0.3	505,357	514,126	1.7
Charleston	315,516	319,849	1.4	284,914	291,009	2.1
Charlotte	854,740	851,629	-0.4	751,369	760,716	1.2
Chattanooga	256,306	260,152	1.5	232,609	238,684	2.6
Chicago[2]	4,039,187	4,078,556	1.0	3,608,123	3,727,566	3.3
Cincinnati	1,114,485	1,112,850	-0.1	1,005,548	1,011,903	0.6
Cleveland	1,052,384	1,068,328	1.5	958,645	977,848	2.0
Colorado Spgs.	308,491	304,273	-1.4	279,705	275,536	-1.5
Columbia	368,248	366,913	-0.4	333,617	333,605	0.0
Columbus	959,341	970,812	1.2	875,086	895,916	2.4
Dallas[2]	2,109,867	2,158,513	2.3	1,942,343	1,985,464	2.2
Denver	1,374,790	1,366,243	-0.6	1,252,743	1,245,326	-0.6
Des Moines	312,714	312,317	-0.1	294,135	293,050	-0.4
Durham	555,352	557,030	0.3	505,357	514,126	1.7
Edison[2]	1,195,546	1,183,238	-1.0	1,091,087	1,088,479	-0.2
El Paso	312,104	322,362	3.3	284,426	291,214	2.4
Eugene	182,564	183,649	0.6	161,732	164,556	1.7
Evansville	177,495	180,360	1.6	162,344	166,152	2.3
Fargo	118,995	118,139	-0.7	113,935	113,300	-0.6
Ft. Collins	173,723	173,200	-0.3	160,865	160,659	-0.1
Ft. Lauderdale[2]	976,384	985,607	0.9	884,149	885,009	0.1
Ft. Wayne	203,564	203,560	0.0	181,040	184,705	2.0
Ft. Worth[2]	1,054,949	1,072,202	1.6	971,158	987,399	1.7
Gainesville	137,500	138,752	0.9	126,680	126,908	0.2
Greensboro	360,353	355,892	-1.2	318,630	319,890	0.4
Honolulu	435,945	441,056	1.2	412,338	419,892	1.8
Houston	2,849,041	2,917,366	2.4	2,618,530	2,676,277	2.2
Huntsville	208,152	206,531	-0.8	192,028	191,689	-0.2
Indianapolis	876,469	876,004	-0.1	796,707	802,574	0.7
Irvine[2]	1,575,303	1,572,994	-0.1	1,429,072	1,431,831	0.2
Jackson	262,148	269,419	2.8	239,852	248,550	3.6
Jacksonville	676,626	688,236	1.7	604,876	611,911	1.2
Kansas City	1,029,858	1,021,911	-0.8	937,608	934,486	-0.3
Knoxville	360,112	366,095	1.7	329,208	339,180	3.0
Las Vegas	969,256	952,734	-1.7	827,843	808,526	-2.3
Lexington	238,595	244,730	2.6	218,934	224,961	2.8
Lincoln	165,716	166,153	0.3	158,657	160,218	1.0
Little Rock	336,174	343,271	2.1	313,775	320,094	2.0
Los Angeles[2]	4,845,237	4,895,337	1.0	4,273,027	4,277,424	0.1
Louisville	630,159	633,093	0.5	564,414	571,338	1.2
Madison	344,054	341,563	-0.7	322,877	324,709	0.6
Manchester[3]	107,165	107,716	0.5	100,187	102,028	1.8

Table continued on next page.

Metro Area[1]	Civilian Labor Force			Workers Employed		
	Dec. 2009	Dec. 2010	% Chg.	Dec. 2009	Dec. 2010	% Chg.
Miami[2]	1,236,009	1,303,792	5.5	1,093,648	1,132,600	3.6
Milwaukee	792,615	788,717	-0.5	721,253	731,223	1.4
Minneapolis	1,826,567	1,824,877	-0.1	1,689,297	1,705,057	0.9
Naperville[2]	4,039,187	4,078,556	1.0	3,608,123	3,727,566	3.3
Nashville	805,781	823,775	2.2	732,497	758,483	3.5
New Orleans	530,817	541,914	2.1	495,173	503,787	1.7
New York[2]	5,695,569	5,658,379	-0.7	5,155,095	5,184,743	0.6
Oakland[2]	1,277,504	1,267,842	-0.8	1,140,269	1,130,954	-0.8
Oklahoma City	564,046	567,828	0.7	527,482	533,083	1.1
Omaha	442,984	444,254	0.3	419,931	423,346	0.8
Orlando	1,097,459	1,125,039	2.5	975,472	996,137	2.1
Overland Park	1,029,858	1,021,911	-0.8	937,608	934,486	-0.3
Oxnard	427,244	427,369	0.0	381,652	381,818	0.0
Philadelphia[2]	1,940,059	1,940,214	0.0	1,783,186	1,782,318	0.0
Phoenix	2,106,077	2,125,593	0.9	1,905,524	1,944,188	2.0
Pittsburgh	1,205,885	1,208,450	0.2	1,114,450	1,117,431	0.3
Plano[2]	2,109,867	2,158,513	2.3	1,942,343	1,985,464	2.2
Portland	1,179,509	1,193,027	1.1	1,052,674	1,076,210	2.2
Providence[3]	705,449	713,425	1.1	624,187	636,018	1.9
Provo	227,656	225,671	-0.9	210,986	209,836	-0.5
Raleigh	555,352	557,030	0.3	505,357	514,126	1.7
Reno	224,167	220,569	-1.6	192,609	190,077	-1.3
Richmond	648,023	647,263	-0.1	596,058	600,602	0.8
Riverside	1,769,228	1,760,229	-0.5	1,523,712	1,514,019	-0.6
Rochester	523,208	523,609	0.1	479,656	482,815	0.7
Sacramento	1,043,551	1,026,223	-1.7	918,616	896,923	-2.4
Salt Lake City	609,680	602,516	-1.2	565,872	560,990	-0.9
San Antonio	972,595	989,732	1.8	906,553	918,035	1.3
San Diego	1,550,490	1,555,176	0.3	1,393,771	1,397,575	0.3
San Francisco[2]	956,966	956,168	-0.1	872,887	874,596	0.2
San Jose	894,203	897,165	0.3	793,947	801,961	1.0
Santa Ana[2]	1,575,303	1,572,994	-0.1	1,429,072	1,431,831	0.2
Savannah	174,003	175,491	0.9	158,829	159,717	0.6
Seattle[2]	1,490,064	1,486,730	-0.2	1,349,455	1,357,162	0.6
Spokane	240,698	241,174	0.2	216,589	219,251	1.2
Springfield	215,900	216,099	0.1	197,202	197,675	0.2
St. Louis	1,415,340	1,430,943	1.1	1,272,738	1,297,099	1.9
St. Paul	1,826,567	1,824,877	-0.1	1,689,297	1,705,057	0.9
St. Petersburg	1,284,093	1,298,265	1.1	1,134,329	1,140,498	0.5
Tampa	1,284,093	1,298,265	1.1	1,134,329	1,140,498	0.5
Tulsa	436,208	434,239	-0.5	402,311	402,253	0.0
Virginia Beach	814,981	816,488	0.2	755,224	759,028	0.5
Warren[2]	1,216,521	1,195,732	-1.7	1,047,233	1,071,444	2.3
Washington[2]	2,400,196	2,417,159	0.7	2,247,378	2,277,413	1.3
Wichita	313,119	311,314	-0.6	286,115	287,267	0.4
U.S.	152,693,000	153,156,000	0.3	137,953,000	139,159,000	0.9

Note: Data is not seasonally adjusted and covers workers 16 years of age and older; (1) Figures cover the Metropolitan Statistical Area (MSA) except where noted. See Appendix B for areas included; (2) Metropolitan Division; (3) New England City and Town Area; (4) New England City and Town Area Division
Source: Bureau of Labor Statistics, http://stats.bls.gov

Unemployment Rate: City

City	2010											
	Jan.	Feb.	Mar.	Apr.	May	Jun.	Jul.	Aug.	Sep.	Oct.	Nov.	Dec.
Albuquerque	7.7	7.8	7.8	7.6	7.9	8.4	8.6	8.4	8.1	8.1	8.1	7.8
Anchorage	7.4	7.7	7.6	7.1	6.8	7.0	6.5	6.6	6.7	6.3	6.4	6.4
Ann Arbor	9.2	9.0	9.5	8.6	9.0	9.6	10.0	8.7	8.2	7.6	7.3	7.0
Athens	8.3	8.3	7.9	7.5	7.7	8.4	8.3	8.0	7.6	7.6	7.6	7.7
Atlanta	11.8	11.3	10.8	10.4	10.8	11.5	11.6	11.7	11.3	11.2	11.4	11.3
Austin	6.9	6.7	6.5	6.3	6.3	6.8	6.8	6.7	6.5	6.4	6.6	6.3
Baltimore	11.5	11.4	10.6	10.0	10.3	10.9	11.5	11.5	10.8	10.6	10.9	10.3
Bellevue	7.3	7.5	7.2	6.4	6.7	7.1	6.8	6.8	7.2	7.1	7.2	6.7
Birmingham	12.1	11.6	11.4	10.9	10.9	11.5	11.6	11.7	11.2	10.9	10.8	10.3
Boise City	9.2	9.1	9.0	8.7	8.3	8.7	9.0	9.0	8.7	9.0	9.3	8.8
Boston	8.4	7.9	7.7	7.6	7.7	8.4	8.5	8.1	8.1	7.6	7.7	7.3
Boulder	9.0	8.8	8.7	8.0	7.8	8.4	8.3	8.2	7.7	7.8	8.3	7.8
Cambridge	5.7	5.2	5.1	5.3	5.5	6.3	6.2	5.6	5.8	5.4	5.5	5.1
Cary	7.1	7.1	6.8	6.6	6.6	6.5	6.2	6.0	5.7	5.4	5.7	5.3
Charleston	9.1	9.1	8.4	7.6	8.2	8.6	8.7	9.0	8.1	8.3	8.3	8.1
Charlotte	10.6	10.6	10.2	9.7	9.8	9.9	10.0	9.5	8.6	8.8	8.9	8.5
Chattanooga	10.4	10.1	10.1	9.4	9.0	9.7	9.1	9.5	8.4	8.5	8.7	8.2
Chicago	12.4	11.9	11.6	11.4	11.3	11.3	11.3	10.8	10.6	10.1	10.1	9.5
Cincinnati	10.7	10.4	10.1	9.9	9.6	10.2	10.4	10.3	9.7	9.6	9.6	9.0
Cleveland	11.7	11.9	11.3	10.8	11.4	11.9	11.7	12.0	11.4	10.7	11.1	10.4
Colorado Spgs.	10.0	9.9	10.0	9.2	9.1	9.5	9.4	9.3	8.9	9.0	9.3	9.1
Columbia	9.6	9.8	9.8	8.9	10.1	10.9	10.8	11.3	9.7	9.9	9.7	9.5
Columbus	9.3	9.2	9.1	9.0	8.4	8.9	8.7	8.3	8.3	8.2	8.0	7.7
Dallas	9.2	9.0	8.9	8.6	8.6	9.0	9.0	8.8	8.6	8.5	8.8	8.5
Denver	10.4	10.3	10.6	9.5	9.4	9.6	9.5	9.4	9.3	9.3	9.8	9.8
Des Moines	8.1	7.7	7.5	7.2	6.6	6.8	6.8	7.2	7.1	7.0	7.3	7.6
Durham	8.1	8.1	7.8	7.4	7.5	7.6	7.5	7.2	6.7	6.7	6.9	6.5
Edison	7.4	7.5	7.4	7.3	7.2	7.6	8.2	7.6	7.2	6.9	6.8	6.0
El Paso	8.8	8.6	8.5	8.2	8.1	8.8	9.0	8.9	8.7	8.7	9.0	8.8
Eugene	10.4	10.4	10.8	10.0	9.2	9.3	10.0	9.8	9.1	9.1	9.3	8.9
Evansville	10.2	10.3	10.0	9.6	9.5	9.3	9.7	9.8	8.9	8.9	9.0	8.7
Fargo	4.6	4.4	4.8	4.0	3.6	4.2	3.8	3.9	3.4	3.2	3.5	3.6
Ft. Collins	9.7	9.4	9.4	8.4	8.0	8.4	8.3	8.1	7.7	7.8	8.4	8.3
Ft. Lauderdale	9.2	8.9	8.8	8.6	8.5	8.8	9.4	9.5	9.4	9.4	9.9	9.3
Ft. Wayne	12.2	12.5	12.3	11.4	11.0	11.0	10.9	10.9	10.1	10.0	10.7	9.9
Ft. Worth	8.7	8.5	8.4	8.3	8.2	8.7	8.9	8.7	8.3	8.2	8.4	8.2
Gainesville	8.1	8.3	7.7	7.0	7.3	8.6	9.5	8.7	8.1	7.7	8.9	8.5
Greensboro	10.9	10.9	10.6	10.3	10.5	10.8	10.8	10.3	9.4	9.3	9.8	9.5
Honolulu	6.0	5.7	5.6	5.4	5.3	6.1	5.9	5.7	5.6	5.5	5.5	4.8
Houston	8.4	8.2	8.2	7.9	7.9	8.4	8.5	8.3	8.1	8.0	8.2	7.9
Huntsville	8.2	7.9	7.7	7.0	7.0	7.7	7.6	7.5	7.3	7.1	7.1	7.1
Indianapolis	10.6	10.6	10.7	10.2	10.0	10.1	10.0	10.1	9.5	9.5	9.6	9.2
Irvine	7.5	7.4	7.5	7.1	7.0	7.2	7.5	7.4	7.2	7.0	7.1	6.8
Jackson	11.3	10.6	10.2	9.6	10.2	10.6	10.9	9.3	9.9	9.8	9.6	9.4
Jacksonville	11.7	11.5	11.5	11.1	11.0	11.4	12.2	12.2	11.5	11.2	11.6	11.2
Kansas City	10.5	10.5	10.4	10.2	10.1	10.3	10.9	11.1	10.7	10.6	11.4	10.1
Knoxville	9.8	9.6	9.6	9.2	8.7	9.0	8.7	8.9	8.2	8.0	8.2	7.9
Las Vegas	15.9	15.8	15.6	15.6	15.2	15.7	16.2	16.0	16.2	15.3	15.3	15.6
Lexington	8.7	8.8	8.5	7.9	8.0	8.1	8.2	8.4	7.8	7.4	7.8	7.5
Lincoln	5.0	4.8	4.8	4.2	4.0	4.5	4.0	3.7	3.8	3.6	3.4	3.4
Little Rock	7.9	7.9	7.4	6.9	7.0	7.3	7.7	7.5	7.0	6.6	6.8	7.0
Los Angeles	14.1	13.7	13.7	13.3	13.4	13.7	14.8	14.6	14.0	14.0	14.2	13.9
Louisville	11.7	12.3	11.2	10.5	10.6	10.5	10.2	10.4	10.1	9.9	10.2	10.0
Madison	6.1	6.0	6.2	5.5	5.5	6.0	5.7	5.5	5.1	5.0	4.8	4.4
Manchester	8.3	8.4	7.9	7.2	6.9	6.9	6.7	6.7	6.4	6.2	6.1	6.1

Table continued on next page.

City	2010											
	Jan.	Feb.	Mar.	Apr.	May	Jun.	Jul.	Aug.	Sep.	Oct.	Nov.	Dec.
Miami	11.7	11.8	12.4	12.3	12.7	13.3	13.7	14.5	13.5	14.1	13.6	14.1
Milwaukee	12.6	12.8	12.8	11.8	11.4	11.8	12.0	11.7	10.7	10.2	10.5	9.7
Minneapolis	7.4	7.1	7.2	6.7	6.6	7.2	7.3	7.3	7.0	6.7	6.6	6.2
Naperville	8.3	8.1	7.9	8.0	7.9	8.3	8.2	7.5	7.0	6.7	6.4	5.7
Nashville	9.3	9.0	8.9	8.5	8.4	8.7	9.1	9.4	8.9	8.5	8.4	8.1
New Orleans	8.7	7.6	7.5	7.3	8.0	9.8	9.9	10.2	9.8	9.4	8.9	8.5
New York	10.4	10.2	10.0	9.5	9.3	9.4	9.7	9.4	9.1	9.0	8.9	8.6
Oakland	17.3	17.0	17.2	16.9	16.6	17.0	17.4	17.4	16.9	16.6	16.8	16.2
Oklahoma City	7.2	7.3	6.7	6.3	6.6	6.7	6.5	6.3	6.1	6.2	6.3	6.1
Omaha	5.7	5.6	5.5	5.0	4.7	5.2	5.1	4.6	4.5	4.3	4.2	4.3
Orlando	11.1	10.9	10.8	10.6	10.5	11.0	11.4	11.6	11.4	11.4	11.8	11.2
Overland Park	7.3	7.0	7.4	6.4	6.2	6.5	6.8	6.5	6.7	6.4	6.4	6.1
Oxnard	15.2	14.8	14.7	13.9	13.7	14.3	15.2	15.2	14.7	14.3	14.7	14.4
Philadelphia	11.1	11.1	11.0	10.5	10.8	10.9	11.1	11.0	10.7	10.9	10.9	10.5
Phoenix	11.5	11.2	10.9	10.4	10.3	10.7	10.9	10.7	10.4	10.2	10.2	9.8
Pittsburgh	8.6	8.8	8.6	8.1	8.4	8.5	8.5	8.4	7.9	8.0	7.9	7.5
Plano	7.5	7.4	7.4	7.1	7.2	7.5	7.4	7.3	7.1	7.0	7.0	6.7
Portland	11.0	11.0	10.9	10.0	10.0	10.1	10.0	10.0	9.6	9.5	9.7	9.2
Providence	14.3	13.9	13.7	13.3	13.8	13.9	14.4	14.3	13.2	13.5	13.3	13.0
Provo	9.0	9.4	9.1	8.4	8.5	8.9	8.7	9.1	8.0	8.1	7.9	7.7
Raleigh	8.3	8.3	8.0	7.7	7.8	8.0	7.8	7.6	6.9	6.7	7.0	6.6
Reno	14.7	14.1	14.3	14.3	14.1	14.4	14.4	14.0	14.1	13.6	13.9	14.1
Richmond	10.7	10.5	10.4	9.6	9.7	10.2	10.5	10.7	10.0	9.7	9.8	9.3
Riverside	15.0	14.9	14.8	14.1	14.1	14.6	15.5	15.5	15.1	15.0	14.9	14.3
Rochester	11.4	11.2	10.8	10.5	10.5	10.6	11.0	10.5	10.5	10.0	10.2	10.0
Sacramento	15.2	15.1	15.0	14.5	14.3	14.8	15.4	15.2	14.9	14.8	15.1	14.8
Salt Lake City	9.2	9.3	9.1	8.6	8.4	8.7	8.7	8.9	8.2	8.3	8.3	8.1
San Antonio	7.2	7.0	6.8	6.7	6.6	7.2	7.3	7.2	7.0	6.9	7.1	6.8
San Diego	10.9	10.6	10.8	10.3	10.1	10.5	10.9	10.7	10.5	10.4	10.6	10.1
San Francisco	10.1	9.8	10.0	9.3	9.1	9.5	9.5	9.6	9.3	9.3	9.6	9.1
San Jose	13.1	12.9	12.9	12.4	12.1	12.4	12.6	12.5	12.1	11.9	12.1	11.5
Santa Ana	15.6	15.3	15.5	14.8	14.5	15.0	15.5	15.3	14.9	14.6	14.8	14.1
Savannah	10.7	10.2	9.6	9.4	9.6	10.3	10.9	11.0	10.4	10.2	10.4	10.4
Seattle	8.4	8.3	8.0	7.3	7.5	7.9	7.6	7.6	7.9	7.8	7.9	7.3
Spokane	11.1	11.3	10.8	9.4	9.1	8.8	9.0	9.1	8.3	7.9	8.5	8.8
Springfield	9.0	8.9	9.4	8.0	8.1	8.7	8.8	9.0	8.6	8.4	8.6	8.4
St. Louis	12.0	12.2	12.3	11.7	11.5	12.6	13.3	13.2	12.4	12.2	12.1	11.7
St. Paul	8.3	8.1	8.2	7.5	7.3	7.9	7.9	8.1	7.7	7.2	7.1	6.9
St. Petersburg	12.1	11.8	11.6	11.2	11.0	11.5	11.9	11.9	11.7	11.5	12.4	11.9
Tampa	12.2	11.9	11.7	11.6	11.7	12.1	12.5	12.5	12.2	11.8	12.6	11.8
Tulsa	8.2	8.2	7.7	7.2	7.6	7.7	7.4	7.4	7.2	7.2	7.1	7.0
Virginia Beach	7.0	6.9	6.7	6.1	6.2	6.4	6.3	6.3	6.1	6.1	6.2	6.1
Warren	18.4	17.8	17.8	16.5	15.5	16.1	16.7	15.3	14.6	14.3	13.8	12.9
Washington	10.7	10.6	10.1	9.3	9.4	10.2	10.2	9.8	9.5	9.5	10.0	9.2
Wichita	10.1	9.7	9.7	9.2	9.3	9.4	9.8	9.5	9.2	8.9	9.2	8.5
U.S.	10.6	10.4	10.2	9.5	9.3	9.6	9.7	9.5	9.2	9.0	9.3	9.1

Note: Data is not seasonally adjusted and covers workers 16 years of age and older; All figures are percentages
Source: Bureau of Labor Statistics, http://stats.bls.gov

Unemployment Rate: Metro Area

Metro Area[1]	2010											
	Jan.	Feb.	Mar.	Apr.	May	Jun.	Jul.	Aug.	Sep.	Oct.	Nov.	Dec.
Albuquerque	8.3	8.6	8.6	8.3	8.5	9.2	9.4	9.2	8.8	8.8	8.8	8.5
Anchorage	8.2	8.5	8.4	7.6	7.1	7.4	6.8	6.9	6.9	6.6	6.9	7.0
Ann Arbor	8.6	8.5	8.9	8.1	8.5	9.0	9.4	8.2	7.7	7.1	6.9	6.6
Athens	8.3	8.3	7.8	7.4	7.5	8.0	8.0	7.9	7.5	7.6	7.6	7.6
Atlanta	10.7	10.5	10.1	9.7	9.8	10.3	10.4	10.4	10.3	10.2	10.3	10.1
Austin	7.6	7.3	7.2	6.9	6.9	7.3	7.3	7.2	7.0	6.9	7.1	6.9
Baltimore	8.6	8.6	8.0	7.4	7.5	7.8	8.2	8.0	7.6	7.6	7.8	7.4
Bellevue[2]	9.7	9.7	9.4	8.7	8.9	9.3	8.9	8.8	9.1	9.2	9.3	8.7
Birmingham	10.1	9.8	9.5	8.7	8.6	9.3	8.9	9.0	8.7	8.5	8.5	8.3
Boise City	10.2	10.0	9.8	9.5	9.0	9.3	9.6	9.7	9.4	9.5	9.9	9.8
Boston[4]	8.1	7.8	7.6	7.3	7.3	7.6	7.7	7.2	7.4	6.9	7.0	6.8
Boulder	7.8	7.5	7.5	6.8	6.7	7.3	7.2	7.0	6.7	6.7	7.1	6.7
Cambridge[4]	8.1	7.8	7.6	7.3	7.3	7.6	7.7	7.2	7.4	6.9	7.0	6.8
Cary	9.8	9.8	9.4	8.9	8.9	8.9	8.6	8.4	7.9	7.7	8.1	7.7
Charleston	10.2	10.1	9.4	8.7	8.9	9.4	9.4	9.8	9.1	9.1	9.3	9.0
Charlotte	12.8	12.9	12.4	11.8	11.7	11.8	11.7	11.4	10.7	10.5	11.0	10.7
Chattanooga	9.7	9.5	9.2	8.7	8.4	8.7	8.5	8.8	8.2	8.2	8.4	8.3
Chicago[2]	11.6	11.2	11.1	10.7	10.4	10.6	10.5	9.7	9.3	8.8	8.9	8.6
Cincinnati	10.8	10.7	10.4	9.9	9.4	9.8	9.8	9.4	9.2	9.2	9.2	9.1
Cleveland	9.9	10.2	9.5	8.8	9.1	9.5	9.2	9.4	9.1	8.3	8.6	8.5
Colorado Spgs.	10.2	10.1	10.3	9.5	9.3	9.7	9.7	9.5	9.2	9.2	9.6	9.4
Columbia	9.8	9.7	9.3	8.5	8.9	9.4	9.5	9.8	9.1	9.1	9.3	9.1
Columbus	9.6	9.5	9.3	9.0	8.4	8.8	8.7	8.3	8.1	8.1	8.0	7.7
Dallas[2]	8.7	8.5	8.4	8.1	8.0	8.5	8.5	8.4	8.1	8.0	8.3	8.0
Denver	9.5	9.5	9.7	8.8	8.7	8.9	8.9	8.8	8.6	8.6	9.0	8.9
Des Moines	6.6	6.4	6.4	6.1	5.6	5.9	5.8	6.0	5.9	5.8	6.0	6.2
Durham	9.8	9.8	9.4	8.9	8.9	8.9	8.6	8.4	7.9	7.7	8.1	7.7
Edison[2]	9.6	9.7	9.5	8.7	8.6	8.6	9.2	8.5	8.3	8.1	8.2	8.0
El Paso	9.6	9.4	9.3	8.9	9.0	9.6	9.9	9.8	9.6	9.5	9.9	9.7
Eugene	12.2	12.2	12.4	11.4	10.6	10.9	11.1	11.0	10.4	10.4	10.7	10.4
Evansville	9.7	9.6	9.2	8.5	8.5	8.7	8.6	8.7	8.1	7.9	8.1	7.9
Fargo	5.0	4.8	5.1	4.2	3.8	4.4	3.9	3.9	3.5	3.3	3.6	4.1
Ft. Collins	8.5	8.2	8.3	7.3	7.0	7.3	7.3	7.1	6.7	6.8	7.3	7.2
Ft. Lauderdale[2]	10.1	9.9	9.8	9.5	9.5	9.9	10.4	10.5	10.3	10.1	10.7	10.2
Ft. Wayne	11.8	11.9	11.9	10.8	10.3	10.2	10.2	10.1	9.4	9.3	10.2	9.3
Ft. Worth[2]	8.6	8.5	8.4	8.0	8.0	8.5	8.5	8.3	8.1	8.0	8.2	7.9
Gainesville	8.4	8.3	8.0	7.3	7.5	8.4	9.1	8.8	8.3	8.0	8.8	8.5
Greensboro	12.5	12.6	12.0	11.4	11.4	11.3	11.1	10.7	10.0	9.9	10.4	10.1
Honolulu	6.0	5.7	5.6	5.4	5.3	6.1	5.9	5.7	5.6	5.5	5.5	4.8
Houston	8.8	8.6	8.6	8.2	8.2	8.7	8.7	8.6	8.3	8.2	8.5	8.3
Huntsville	8.5	8.3	7.9	7.2	7.1	7.5	7.5	7.4	7.3	7.1	7.2	7.2
Indianapolis	10.0	10.1	10.1	9.3	9.1	9.2	9.1	9.0	8.6	8.4	8.6	8.4
Irvine[2]	10.0	9.7	9.9	9.4	9.2	9.6	9.9	9.8	9.5	9.3	9.5	9.0
Jackson	9.7	9.0	8.6	8.0	8.5	8.8	9.0	7.6	8.1	8.1	7.9	7.7
Jacksonville	11.4	11.3	11.2	10.7	10.6	11.0	11.6	11.7	11.2	11.0	11.5	11.1
Kansas City	9.8	9.7	9.7	8.7	8.7	8.9	9.2	9.1	8.9	8.7	9.1	8.6
Knoxville	9.1	8.9	8.8	8.2	7.7	7.9	7.7	7.8	7.3	7.2	7.4	7.4
Las Vegas	15.4	15.2	15.1	15.1	14.9	15.3	15.7	15.5	15.6	14.8	14.9	15.1
Lexington	9.4	9.4	9.1	8.4	8.4	8.6	8.8	8.7	8.2	7.9	8.3	8.1
Lincoln	5.2	5.0	4.9	4.3	4.0	4.6	4.2	3.9	3.9	3.6	3.6	3.6
Little Rock	7.7	7.8	7.3	6.7	6.8	7.1	7.4	7.1	6.7	6.4	6.5	6.8
Los Angeles[2]	12.8	12.4	12.4	12.1	12.2	12.4	13.4	13.2	12.7	12.7	12.9	12.6
Louisville	11.5	12.4	11.0	10.1	10.0	10.0	9.9	10.1	9.8	9.6	9.8	9.8
Madison	7.1	7.1	7.2	6.0	5.9	6.1	5.8	5.7	5.3	5.1	5.0	4.9
Manchester[3]	7.3	7.4	7.1	6.4	6.0	6.1	6.1	6.1	5.6	5.4	5.5	5.3

Table continued on next page.

Metro Area[1]	2010											
	Jan.	Feb.	Mar.	Apr.	May	Jun.	Jul.	Aug.	Sep.	Oct.	Nov.	Dec.
Miami[2]	11.1	11.2	11.9	11.8	12.1	12.7	12.9	13.6	12.6	13.1	12.6	13.1
Milwaukee	10.0	10.2	10.2	9.1	8.8	9.0	8.8	8.5	7.8	7.5	7.6	7.3
Minneapolis	8.3	8.1	8.2	7.2	6.9	7.2	7.1	7.1	6.9	6.5	6.6	6.6
Naperville[2]	11.6	11.2	11.1	10.7	10.4	10.6	10.5	9.7	9.3	8.8	8.9	8.6
Nashville	9.7	9.4	9.3	8.8	8.5	8.6	8.5	8.7	8.2	8.0	8.2	7.9
New Orleans	7.6	6.6	6.6	6.5	7.1	8.2	7.9	8.2	7.7	7.6	7.3	7.0
New York[2]	10.1	9.9	9.7	9.2	9.1	9.1	9.5	9.2	8.9	8.7	8.7	8.4
Oakland[2]	11.7	11.5	11.5	11.2	11.0	11.3	11.6	11.5	11.2	11.0	11.2	10.8
Oklahoma City	7.3	7.4	6.8	6.3	6.7	6.9	6.6	6.4	6.1	6.3	6.3	6.1
Omaha	6.2	5.9	5.8	5.2	4.9	5.3	5.2	4.8	4.8	4.6	4.6	4.7
Orlando	11.7	11.6	11.3	11.0	10.9	11.2	11.6	11.7	11.6	11.3	11.9	11.5
Overland Park	9.8	9.7	9.7	8.7	8.7	8.9	9.2	9.1	8.9	8.7	9.1	8.6
Oxnard	11.3	11.0	10.9	10.3	10.1	10.6	11.3	11.3	10.9	10.6	10.9	10.7
Philadelphia[2]	9.1	9.2	9.1	8.6	8.8	8.8	8.9	8.8	8.3	8.4	8.5	8.1
Phoenix	10.0	9.7	9.5	9.0	8.9	9.3	9.6	9.4	9.1	8.9	8.8	8.5
Pittsburgh	8.9	9.4	8.9	7.9	8.0	8.0	8.0	7.8	7.2	7.3	7.5	7.5
Plano[2]	8.7	8.5	8.4	8.1	8.0	8.5	8.5	8.4	8.1	8.0	8.3	8.0
Portland	11.7	11.6	11.7	10.8	10.4	10.5	10.5	10.5	9.9	9.8	10.1	9.8
Providence[3]	13.0	12.9	12.8	11.8	11.6	11.3	11.7	11.6	10.9	11.0	11.0	10.9
Provo	8.2	8.6	8.3	7.6	7.7	8.0	7.9	8.2	7.3	7.3	7.2	7.0
Raleigh	9.8	9.8	9.4	8.9	8.9	8.9	8.6	8.4	7.9	7.7	8.1	7.7
Reno	15.1	14.8	14.5	14.4	14.1	14.1	14.2	13.9	13.9	13.3	13.6	13.8
Richmond	8.6	8.5	8.1	7.4	7.5	7.7	7.7	7.8	7.5	7.3	7.5	7.2
Riverside	14.7	14.6	14.6	14.0	13.9	14.4	15.1	14.9	14.6	14.4	14.5	14.0
Rochester	9.2	9.1	8.7	8.0	7.8	7.9	8.1	7.7	7.7	7.4	7.7	7.8
Sacramento	13.0	12.9	12.9	12.3	12.1	12.4	12.8	12.6	12.3	12.2	12.8	12.6
Salt Lake City	7.9	8.0	7.9	7.5	7.3	7.5	7.5	7.6	7.0	7.1	7.2	6.9
San Antonio	7.6	7.3	7.2	7.0	6.9	7.5	7.6	7.5	7.3	7.3	7.5	7.2
San Diego	10.9	10.6	10.8	10.3	10.1	10.5	10.9	10.7	10.5	10.4	10.6	10.1
San Francisco[2]	9.6	9.4	9.6	9.0	8.8	9.1	9.2	9.2	8.9	8.8	9.0	8.5
San Jose	12.1	11.9	11.9	11.4	11.1	11.3	11.5	11.3	11.0	10.8	11.0	10.6
Santa Ana[2]	10.0	9.7	9.9	9.4	9.2	9.6	9.9	9.8	9.5	9.3	9.5	9.0
Savannah	9.3	9.0	8.6	8.3	8.3	8.8	10.1	9.3	9.0	8.9	9.0	9.0
Seattle[2]	9.7	9.7	9.4	8.7	8.9	9.3	8.9	8.8	9.1	9.2	9.3	8.7
Spokane	11.5	11.7	11.0	9.7	9.4	9.1	9.1	9.2	8.5	8.1	8.8	9.1
Springfield	9.4	9.5	9.5	8.1	8.1	8.7	8.9	8.9	8.5	8.3	8.5	8.5
St. Louis	10.9	11.1	10.8	9.6	9.4	10.1	10.3	10.1	9.6	9.4	9.5	9.4
St. Paul	8.3	8.1	8.2	7.2	6.9	7.2	7.1	7.1	6.9	6.5	6.6	6.6
St. Petersburg	12.4	12.1	11.9	11.6	11.5	11.9	12.3	12.4	12.2	12.0	12.6	12.2
Tampa	12.4	12.1	11.9	11.6	11.5	11.9	12.3	12.4	12.2	12.0	12.6	12.2
Tulsa	8.9	8.9	8.3	7.6	7.9	8.0	7.7	7.7	7.5	7.5	7.5	7.4
Virginia Beach	8.1	8.0	7.7	7.1	7.2	7.5	7.4	7.4	7.1	7.0	7.2	7.0
Warren[2]	15.0	14.6	14.5	13.3	12.7	13.1	13.4	12.5	11.8	11.5	10.9	10.4
Washington[2]	7.0	7.0	6.7	6.1	6.2	6.4	6.4	6.3	6.0	6.0	6.1	5.8
Wichita	9.5	8.9	8.9	8.5	8.5	8.6	9.0	8.7	8.4	8.1	8.4	7.7
U.S.	10.6	10.4	10.2	9.5	9.3	9.6	9.7	9.5	9.2	9.0	9.3	9.1

Note: Data is not seasonally adjusted and covers workers 16 years of age and older; All figures are percentages; (1) Figures cover the Metropolitan Statistical Area (MSA) except where noted. See Appendix B for areas included; (2) Metropolitan Division; (3) New England City and Town Area; (4) New England City and Town Area Division
Source: Bureau of Labor Statistics, http://stats.bls.gov

Average Hourly Wages: Occupations A - C

Metro Area	Accountants/ Auditors	Automotive Mechanics	Book- keepers	Carpenters	Cashiers	Clerks, Gen. Office	Clerks, Recep./Info.
Albuquerque	29.38	16.86	15.08	18.80	9.65	12.09	11.39
Anchorage	34.12	24.58	19.24	28.36	10.66	16.13	13.98
Ann Arbor	29.45	25.65	17.49	26.54	9.81	13.63	12.81
Athens	23.32	19.39	14.66	18.82	8.48	11.71	11.38
Atlanta	34.69	18.42	17.23	18.27	8.78	12.46	12.89
Austin	33.18	19.83	17.32	15.33	9.03	14.90	13.37
Baltimore	35.84	20.23	18.40	20.12	9.58	14.25	13.51
Bellevue	32.48	19.91	18.90	24.97	11.75	15.22	13.97
Birmingham	29.30	17.60	16.00	16.90	8.45	10.70	11.94
Boise City	25.90	15.88	15.40	18.13	8.80	12.94	11.94
Boston	36.54	22.20	19.67	26.92	9.97	16.30	14.23
Boulder	35.18	18.62	17.46	20.04	10.43	14.17	13.38
Cambridge	36.54	22.20	19.67	26.92	9.97	16.30	14.23
Cary	30.60	20.59	17.23	16.11	8.60	12.86	12.61
Charleston	27.47	17.68	15.90	17.07	8.31	12.24	11.86
Charlotte	32.26	22.06	16.14	16.42	8.76	12.98	12.44
Chattanooga	26.11	15.57	14.79	15.63	7.98	12.50	11.47
Chicago	34.80	20.48	17.92	29.66	9.37	14.11	13.50
Cincinnati	30.74	18.51	16.70	18.98	9.00	13.46	11.45
Cleveland	31.42	18.17	16.08	20.89	8.80	13.40	12.37
Colorado Spgs.	31.85	21.77	15.83	23.91	9.52	12.59	12.51
Columbia	28.07	16.60	15.90	16.01	8.08	12.81	12.46
Columbus	29.72	17.68	16.71	19.90	9.20	13.98	11.94
Dallas	32.90	18.35	17.45	15.47	8.69	14.40	12.90
Denver	33.69	19.01	17.76	19.69	10.14	13.92	13.28
Des Moines	30.13	19.99	16.53	19.10	8.99	14.37	12.33
Durham	33.02	18.10	17.22	16.07	9.28	14.04	12.17
Edison	39.97	19.47	18.33	25.14	9.48	14.25	12.90
El Paso	26.06	14.53	13.72	12.34	8.01	11.05	9.73
Eugene	27.28	17.14	15.89	22.51	10.42	13.74	12.05
Evansville	27.27	18.68	15.24	18.21	8.07	11.63	11.13
Fargo	25.01	16.75	15.45	16.20	8.38	12.47	11.52
Ft. Collins	32.49	17.92	16.40	18.83	9.46	12.07	12.32
Ft. Lauderdale	30.97	17.83	17.04	17.86	9.13	12.33	13.15
Ft. Wayne	29.19	18.12	14.88	19.13	8.65	12.35	12.10
Ft. Worth	33.24	17.40	16.37	15.32	8.82	12.69	12.20
Gainesville	26.67	18.76	15.14	16.34	8.81	11.88	12.07
Greensboro	29.67	17.77	15.84	15.71	8.24	12.63	11.56
Honolulu	27.62	20.43	16.74	31.61	10.00	13.72	14.12
Houston	33.75	19.89	17.13	16.57	8.56	13.55	12.55
Huntsville	31.87	17.06	14.25	14.36	8.14	10.79	10.99
Indianapolis	32.49	19.68	17.01	20.48	8.68	12.72	12.35
Irvine	33.07	20.39	18.92	25.18	10.37	14.52	13.87
Jackson	25.46	15.01	16.67	14.00	8.39	11.34	10.84
Jacksonville	28.12	17.86	15.57	17.53	8.65	12.07	12.16
Kansas City	27.88	18.55	16.30	22.96	8.96	14.31	12.50
Knoxville	27.11	14.50	14.79	16.24	8.43	13.38	11.81
Las Vegas	28.20	19.58	16.94	26.57	10.14	14.51	12.69
Lexington	26.36	15.53	15.01	17.98	8.65	13.31	11.44
Lincoln	26.95	16.06	14.48	16.47	8.30	10.11	11.43
Little Rock	26.09	16.91	14.79	16.34	8.39	10.94	11.08
Los Angeles	34.32	18.46	18.27	24.03	10.54	14.11	13.43
Louisville	28.31	16.11	15.57	17.82	8.51	12.92	11.56
Madison	29.06	20.17	16.85	20.86	9.27	14.50	13.34
Manchester	29.62	20.04	17.79	21.94	9.10	15.44	13.23

Table continued on next page.

Metro Area	Accountants/ Auditors	Automotive Mechanics	Book-keepers	Carpenters	Cashiers	Clerks, Gen. Office	Clerks, Recep./Info.
Miami	33.45	18.46	16.08	16.30	8.88	12.03	11.45
Milwaukee	31.41	19.92	16.50	23.30	8.48	14.00	13.14
Minneapolis	30.16	20.16	18.07	23.92	9.24	14.42	13.82
Naperville	34.80	20.48	17.92	29.66	9.37	14.11	13.50
Nashville	28.56	17.76	16.21	17.31	8.74	13.65	12.25
New Orleans	26.93	17.12	16.60	19.28	8.39	11.55	10.74
New York	42.28	18.80	19.81	27.87	10.05	13.95	14.04
Oakland	37.05	24.13	20.42	28.96	11.63	17.23	15.34
Oklahoma City	26.89	15.53	14.68	15.32	8.38	11.27	10.83
Omaha	30.20	18.05	15.57	16.59	8.63	12.37	12.27
Orlando	29.32	17.79	15.25	16.74	8.78	12.31	11.78
Overland Park	27.88	18.55	16.30	22.96	8.96	14.31	12.50
Oxnard	32.42	20.45	18.96	23.31	10.81	14.65	13.05
Philadelphia	36.75	19.32	18.56	25.16	9.26	15.03	13.16
Phoenix	27.90	17.98	17.53	18.51	10.31	14.18	13.19
Pittsburgh	31.15	16.54	15.78	20.19	8.66	12.77	11.51
Plano	32.90	18.35	17.45	15.47	8.69	14.40	12.90
Portland	30.38	19.28	17.66	22.06	10.92	14.52	12.95
Providence	31.38	18.58	17.52	20.89	9.39	13.93	12.94
Provo	26.37	18.60	13.89	18.49	8.68	11.38	10.84
Raleigh	30.60	20.59	17.23	16.11	8.60	12.86	12.61
Reno	29.21	22.36	18.50	23.60	10.06	15.18	13.02
Richmond	31.07	20.84	17.57	18.79	8.74	14.18	12.21
Riverside	30.45	19.23	17.55	24.27	10.42	13.77	12.94
Rochester	34.50	16.41	16.21	18.26	8.63	12.20	12.16
Sacramento	31.73	21.06	18.91	25.75	11.09	15.48	13.59
Salt Lake City	29.93	19.05	15.27	18.14	8.99	12.44	11.02
San Antonio	28.58	17.75	15.91	15.70	8.45	12.18	11.43
San Diego	33.73	20.41	18.19	23.35	10.28	14.48	13.55
San Francisco	39.25	22.86	22.08	31.30	12.40	16.47	16.65
San Jose	41.18	24.31	21.44	27.75	11.74	16.32	15.65
Santa Ana	33.07	20.39	18.92	25.18	10.37	14.52	13.87
Savannah	30.29	17.82	15.36	17.12	8.37	11.33	10.78
Seattle	32.48	19.91	18.90	24.97	11.75	15.22	13.97
Spokane	29.34	18.38	16.30	21.99	10.88	13.40	12.48
Springfield	25.19	16.15	13.69	15.55	8.65	12.10	10.19
St. Louis	30.81	17.97	16.70	25.54	9.14	14.59	12.17
St. Paul	30.16	20.16	18.07	23.92	9.24	14.42	13.82
St. Petersburg	28.37	17.69	15.60	16.76	8.60	12.11	12.21
Tampa	28.37	17.69	15.60	16.76	8.60	12.11	12.21
Tulsa	26.10	16.31	14.60	14.74	8.23	11.45	11.42
Virginia Beach	28.73	18.55	16.21	18.23	8.24	12.67	11.67
Warren	30.67	20.10	17.58	23.01	9.38	13.41	12.87
Washington	37.91	22.44	20.51	21.30	10.13	15.77	14.69
Wichita	28.03	18.17	15.03	16.85	8.28	12.60	11.27

Notes: Wage data is for May 2010 and covers the Metropolitan Statistical Area - see Appendix B for areas included; n/a not available
Source: Bureau of Labor Statistics, May 2010 Metro Area Occupational Employment and Wage Estimates

Average Hourly Wages: Occupations C - E

Metro Area	Clerks, Ship./Rec.	Computer Programmers	Computer Support Specialists	Computer Systems Analysts	Cooks, Restaurant	Dentists	Electrical Engineers
Albuquerque	13.42	43.65	22.06	35.27	10.22	n/a	43.36
Anchorage	18.49	34.92	22.65	36.36	12.93	n/a	43.62
Ann Arbor	16.42	33.69	19.90	36.09	11.82	n/a	37.90
Athens	14.02	22.69	19.12	30.78	10.10	n/a	36.85
Atlanta	14.20	36.34	23.74	40.47	10.59	n/a	41.82
Austin	13.36	40.31	23.20	38.45	9.84	n/a	48.73
Baltimore	15.53	37.15	24.87	40.85	12.13	n/a	41.97
Bellevue	18.30	45.25	25.18	41.63	12.78	n/a	42.14
Birmingham	13.64	34.26	22.28	33.65	9.60	n/a	39.66
Boise City	13.24	28.11	19.37	32.53	11.72	n/a	40.95
Boston	16.61	44.57	29.98	43.47	12.80	n/a	49.35
Boulder	14.64	44.96	24.86	44.54	11.98	n/a	41.96
Cambridge	16.61	44.57	29.98	43.47	12.80	n/a	49.35
Cary	14.05	36.12	23.70	36.16	10.12	n/a	41.10
Charleston	14.27	30.73	20.22	30.71	11.14	n/a	37.24
Charlotte	14.26	37.00	22.32	41.54	11.49	n/a	37.19
Chattanooga	13.00	27.35	19.96	28.82	10.03	n/a	37.88
Chicago	14.75	36.93	25.66	37.75	10.90	n/a	42.58
Cincinnati	14.42	33.10	21.53	37.43	10.75	n/a	35.93
Cleveland	14.74	30.97	21.56	34.85	11.16	n/a	38.31
Colorado Spgs.	14.00	40.34	24.46	37.73	11.00	n/a	38.05
Columbia	13.48	30.60	20.06	29.00	9.61	n/a	42.11
Columbus	14.83	37.36	19.07	40.49	10.30	n/a	35.40
Dallas	13.87	40.97	24.37	40.47	9.77	n/a	46.55
Denver	15.85	39.92	25.61	39.57	10.48	n/a	40.42
Des Moines	16.24	34.12	19.96	35.10	9.98	n/a	31.46
Durham	13.31	41.99	24.32	40.65	11.54	n/a	40.51
Edison	15.32	39.35	24.68	43.05	11.33	n/a	40.96
El Paso	10.33	26.78	18.53	28.71	9.13	n/a	37.87
Eugene	13.88	25.14	21.82	31.25	11.47	n/a	39.94
Evansville	14.33	32.91	17.29	42.35	9.28	n/a	36.08
Fargo	14.08	24.88	16.73	30.66	9.85	n/a	34.41
Ft. Collins	13.65	31.11	23.88	38.19	11.14	n/a	38.56
Ft. Lauderdale	13.09	30.17	17.34	33.24	12.19	n/a	34.90
Ft. Wayne	13.81	30.11	21.42	29.48	9.80	n/a	38.61
Ft. Worth	14.52	36.58	21.45	39.28	9.57	n/a	33.73
Gainesville	11.66	25.72	17.01	28.91	10.54	n/a	38.34
Greensboro	14.43	34.44	22.19	36.34	10.08	n/a	37.23
Honolulu	15.21	31.55	23.24	32.06	13.92	n/a	40.47
Houston	13.76	34.99	23.98	39.00	8.85	n/a	43.50
Huntsville	13.25	35.81	20.78	36.17	10.63	n/a	42.30
Indianapolis	14.10	34.57	20.52	34.35	10.80	n/a	35.41
Irvine	14.59	37.54	25.16	37.93	12.30	n/a	43.13
Jackson	15.92	23.99	19.99	28.09	9.27	n/a	36.37
Jacksonville	14.16	36.10	19.86	32.67	10.88	n/a	35.97
Kansas City	14.92	35.46	21.47	35.09	10.41	n/a	37.41
Knoxville	12.68	30.19	19.46	33.40	10.39	n/a	43.28
Las Vegas	14.63	32.57	22.82	35.82	14.55	n/a	38.49
Lexington	16.06	33.65	19.20	34.73	9.90	n/a	52.54
Lincoln	14.45	28.27	19.41	28.15	9.65	n/a	38.23
Little Rock	13.47	31.87	18.75	30.48	10.74	n/a	37.07
Los Angeles	13.76	39.12	23.31	39.21	11.75	n/a	43.07
Louisville	15.18	33.82	20.67	36.04	10.11	n/a	35.45
Madison	14.49	35.02	22.39	31.14	10.92	n/a	38.11
Manchester	14.55	36.75	23.89	45.01	11.99	n/a	37.85

Table continued on next page.

Metro Area	Clerks, Ship./Rec.	Computer Programmers	Computer Support Specialists	Computer Systems Analysts	Cooks, Restaurant	Dentists	Electrical Engineers
Miami	12.85	34.09	20.14	33.73	11.96	n/a	40.21
Milwaukee	15.02	31.64	21.94	35.77	11.07	n/a	35.31
Minneapolis	16.04	32.41	23.72	36.67	11.69	n/a	41.47
Naperville	14.75	36.93	25.66	37.75	10.90	n/a	42.58
Nashville	13.27	29.44	21.31	32.86	11.35	n/a	39.02
New Orleans	14.18	24.32	21.36	26.70	10.43	n/a	42.26
New York	15.48	38.65	27.49	42.83	14.36	n/a	44.69
Oakland	15.72	36.49	27.85	42.55	12.01	n/a	47.11
Oklahoma City	13.76	26.94	18.29	31.51	9.62	n/a	36.84
Omaha	14.85	33.55	19.81	34.50	10.54	n/a	36.75
Orlando	12.28	29.57	19.04	36.00	11.86	n/a	32.95
Overland Park	14.92	35.46	21.47	35.09	10.41	n/a	37.41
Oxnard	15.09	33.58	23.40	43.08	12.11	n/a	40.46
Philadelphia	16.58	43.27	22.74	42.58	15.35	n/a	42.88
Phoenix	12.26	35.37	23.35	41.39	10.82	n/a	42.19
Pittsburgh	14.49	32.35	19.56	35.60	12.22	n/a	39.96
Plano	13.87	40.97	24.37	40.47	9.77	n/a	46.55
Portland	15.37	34.28	21.76	38.37	11.44	n/a	43.12
Providence	14.65	33.47	21.26	42.78	12.22	n/a	41.90
Provo	13.04	29.09	17.38	32.40	10.96	n/a	38.94
Raleigh	14.05	36.12	23.70	36.16	10.12	n/a	41.10
Reno	14.28	34.67	20.56	33.15	12.84	n/a	44.37
Richmond	15.29	37.23	22.33	37.39	10.11	n/a	37.90
Riverside	14.61	31.62	22.03	35.01	11.43	n/a	39.15
Rochester	13.50	31.64	22.21	34.50	12.10	n/a	34.34
Sacramento	15.44	33.92	25.89	37.83	11.60	n/a	53.94
Salt Lake City	13.78	42.74	21.91	33.49	10.82	n/a	38.32
San Antonio	13.32	34.97	20.56	n/a	10.72	n/a	43.32
San Diego	14.09	38.45	23.39	38.82	12.24	n/a	46.00
San Francisco	16.18	45.21	29.79	45.43	13.65	n/a	48.11
San Jose	16.92	52.49	32.67	44.63	11.43	n/a	51.11
Santa Ana	14.59	37.54	25.16	37.93	12.30	n/a	43.13
Savannah	15.99	31.28	19.44	28.39	10.48	n/a	43.30
Seattle	18.30	45.25	25.18	41.63	12.78	n/a	42.14
Spokane	13.91	28.08	21.20	32.22	10.90	n/a	37.08
Springfield	12.43	22.22	16.83	28.03	9.08	n/a	39.02
St. Louis	14.86	34.02	21.83	35.75	10.41	n/a	38.00
St. Paul	16.04	32.41	23.72	36.67	11.69	n/a	41.47
St. Petersburg	12.63	32.73	21.17	35.41	11.18	n/a	35.99
Tampa	12.63	32.73	21.17	35.41	11.18	n/a	35.99
Tulsa	13.65	29.09	18.78	34.90	9.93	n/a	33.68
Virginia Beach	14.24	31.04	21.21	34.87	10.75	n/a	36.34
Warren	15.17	36.16	21.71	39.31	10.91	n/a	41.44
Washington	15.54	39.43	25.65	46.42	12.18	n/a	47.99
Wichita	13.71	28.76	19.25	37.90	10.11	n/a	35.03

Notes: Wage data is for May 2010 and covers the Metropolitan Statistical Area - see Appendix B for areas included; n/a not available
Source: Bureau of Labor Statistics, May 2010 Metro Area Occupational Employment and Wage Estimates

Average Hourly Wages: Occupations E - I

Metro Area	Electricians	Financial Managers	First-Line Supervisors/ Mgrs., Sales	Food Preparation Workers	General/ Operations Managers	Hairdressers/ Cosmetolo- gists	Internists
Albuquerque	21.67	43.83	17.43	9.91	44.63	13.51	101.16
Anchorage	33.18	42.97	19.19	13.09	39.59	9.84	n/a
Ann Arbor	33.71	50.12	20.13	10.40	54.98	15.54	n/a
Athens	19.37	46.62	16.47	9.64	41.13	13.85	66.22
Atlanta	20.97	54.94	18.05	9.90	50.36	13.28	88.19
Austin	19.58	56.64	19.14	8.94	57.02	13.80	78.95
Baltimore	23.30	48.72	19.54	10.11	54.89	13.97	101.94
Bellevue	32.30	57.35	20.95	11.41	68.72	16.70	84.41
Birmingham	20.08	52.31	17.64	8.66	50.35	16.66	102.88
Boise City	21.72	38.48	15.36	9.10	37.66	14.27	n/a
Boston	28.81	63.88	20.80	11.14	60.29	14.67	97.53
Boulder	22.62	60.23	20.97	10.59	55.57	15.68	n/a
Cambridge	28.81	63.88	20.80	11.14	60.29	14.67	97.53
Cary	18.31	50.42	17.38	8.76	59.01	13.65	81.99
Charleston	19.36	45.45	19.16	8.76	46.29	17.92	101.56
Charlotte	19.22	60.26	17.68	8.77	62.02	11.92	95.20
Chattanooga	21.53	36.52	16.54	8.41	44.57	11.59	93.68
Chicago	34.28	59.25	19.77	10.25	59.68	13.31	93.61
Cincinnati	22.15	52.52	18.20	10.21	53.77	12.10	71.07
Cleveland	26.01	55.91	19.08	9.73	57.94	13.14	48.34
Colorado Spgs.	21.82	53.56	20.06	10.01	46.64	11.74	70.03
Columbia	18.41	45.80	18.68	8.08	49.81	14.80	106.84
Columbus	21.13	57.05	18.72	10.18	57.79	11.23	76.93
Dallas	20.47	59.84	19.44	8.61	59.88	13.15	100.60
Denver	22.11	57.63	20.34	10.03	56.68	13.73	82.22
Des Moines	22.74	50.58	18.70	9.73	53.38	13.67	n/a
Durham	18.95	52.26	17.57	9.17	61.99	19.18	77.59
Edison	29.51	61.87	21.47	10.31	73.86	14.82	98.44
El Paso	18.30	38.11	18.31	7.68	41.98	9.77	105.34
Eugene	27.85	46.23	19.24	10.05	44.29	11.33	n/a
Evansville	23.86	47.10	17.03	8.28	48.93	12.05	82.48
Fargo	21.20	42.20	16.45	9.11	51.62	11.19	n/a
Ft. Collins	20.98	53.77	18.09	9.47	43.88	11.79	n/a
Ft. Lauderdale	19.36	55.87	21.57	9.86	50.46	13.85	93.92
Ft. Wayne	25.52	49.54	18.43	9.15	50.90	10.88	105.33
Ft. Worth	20.06	53.16	19.55	8.61	51.90	12.95	74.08
Gainesville	19.55	51.42	19.79	9.09	39.63	11.02	n/a
Greensboro	17.63	48.95	17.48	8.43	55.68	10.03	100.66
Honolulu	32.86	42.92	19.40	9.81	49.36	19.61	73.47
Houston	21.13	58.21	20.21	9.51	57.93	12.57	88.74
Huntsville	18.36	53.12	17.80	8.24	50.47	11.90	n/a
Indianapolis	25.27	52.29	18.88	9.97	55.10	13.36	86.75
Irvine	24.89	62.10	20.26	10.46	63.71	10.83	88.06
Jackson	21.46	39.13	16.82	8.02	44.32	12.60	n/a
Jacksonville	20.88	52.14	20.05	9.09	45.64	14.87	n/a
Kansas City	27.52	48.42	18.59	10.00	46.49	12.72	98.38
Knoxville	18.98	40.21	17.81	9.97	42.56	15.07	92.73
Las Vegas	30.01	47.04	18.84	12.79	51.33	12.17	83.06
Lexington	18.62	40.76	19.05	10.36	42.32	11.69	105.65
Lincoln	18.57	45.07	18.11	9.18	45.33	10.04	115.84
Little Rock	19.27	40.73	16.39	8.78	48.01	14.44	n/a
Los Angeles	25.64	62.68	20.12	9.83	60.91	12.07	84.53
Louisville	19.46	44.00	17.50	9.61	45.49	11.05	91.24
Madison	24.11	50.70	19.13	9.90	49.53	11.94	102.05
Manchester	23.57	47.70	19.29	9.80	53.28	11.36	n/a

Table continued on next page.

Metro Area	Electricians	Financial Managers	First-Line Supervisors/ Mgrs., Sales	Food Preparation Workers	General/ Operations Managers	Hairdressers/ Cosmetologists	Internists
Miami	20.52	59.51	20.44	9.71	50.23	12.86	97.31
Milwaukee	27.24	53.05	18.83	9.79	57.89	13.23	101.84
Minneapolis	29.44	58.69	17.56	10.59	58.38	13.26	96.35
Naperville	34.28	59.25	19.77	10.25	59.68	13.31	93.61
Nashville	18.53	41.41	19.25	9.66	48.03	14.54	93.25
New Orleans	21.71	38.16	16.97	8.46	49.78	16.41	96.82
New York	35.57	77.25	22.87	11.34	74.85	16.12	70.21
Oakland	35.46	62.70	20.29	10.35	62.01	12.94	100.01
Oklahoma City	17.29	40.79	16.61	8.20	41.44	9.76	101.07
Omaha	23.59	57.53	20.62	10.14	51.21	12.76	92.35
Orlando	17.99	54.10	20.14	9.49	46.91	12.89	85.24
Overland Park	27.52	48.42	18.59	10.00	46.49	12.72	98.38
Oxnard	23.63	58.38	19.53	10.23	60.57	13.33	n/a
Philadelphia	34.26	57.78	22.53	10.68	58.38	13.97	54.93
Phoenix	22.03	46.60	20.11	10.80	52.21	13.92	84.14
Pittsburgh	25.35	47.80	20.53	10.09	48.70	10.80	106.90
Plano	20.47	59.84	19.44	8.61	59.88	13.15	100.60
Portland	30.57	52.68	19.30	10.88	53.91	13.96	82.93
Providence	25.98	53.40	20.84	10.45	54.84	13.60	83.98
Provo	22.06	43.12	15.28	8.22	38.66	14.41	n/a
Raleigh	18.31	50.42	17.38	8.76	59.01	13.65	81.99
Reno	25.21	44.93	17.88	9.77	48.71	8.96	89.57
Richmond	21.73	53.67	20.11	9.86	53.27	14.79	n/a
Riverside	24.63	51.12	19.40	10.30	51.83	10.45	98.08
Rochester	23.55	51.18	19.48	9.47	53.22	12.04	63.31
Sacramento	22.99	52.18	18.75	10.49	55.22	13.17	101.97
Salt Lake City	20.42	48.54	17.77	9.18	42.23	12.02	114.11
San Antonio	18.17	52.88	18.60	8.22	48.19	11.41	n/a
San Diego	24.22	59.92	19.42	10.24	59.36	11.93	83.12
San Francisco	38.48	70.98	22.34	11.34	68.17	18.05	85.01
San Jose	33.82	71.99	20.19	9.89	69.86	10.72	n/a
Santa Ana	24.89	62.10	20.26	10.46	63.71	10.83	88.06
Savannah	21.26	45.61	17.21	10.50	44.28	16.71	105.17
Seattle	32.30	57.35	20.95	11.41	68.72	16.70	84.41
Spokane	23.11	45.11	21.26	11.01	55.32	16.45	88.44
Springfield	17.65	45.37	18.35	8.81	41.10	10.35	n/a
St. Louis	30.55	54.28	18.91	9.32	52.40	12.13	98.34
St. Paul	29.44	58.69	17.56	10.59	58.38	13.26	96.35
St. Petersburg	18.45	53.06	21.52	9.64	49.91	11.46	90.16
Tampa	18.45	53.06	21.52	9.64	49.91	11.46	90.16
Tulsa	19.92	43.28	16.41	8.35	43.60	10.61	98.93
Virginia Beach	20.98	46.89	17.93	9.69	51.19	14.08	85.24
Warren	27.41	52.58	21.01	10.38	54.02	13.08	67.21
Washington	26.15	59.63	21.56	10.35	61.68	15.90	78.16
Wichita	22.35	41.97	16.00	8.50	41.11	10.87	115.49

Notes: Wage data is for May 2010 and covers the Metropolitan Statistical Area - see Appendix B for areas included; n/a not available
Source: Bureau of Labor Statistics, May 2010 Metro Area Occupational Employment and Wage Estimates

Average Hourly Wages: Occupations J - N

Metro Area	Janitors/ Cleaners	Landscapers	Lawyers	Maids/ House- keepers	Main- tenance Repairers	Marketing Managers	Nuclear Medicine Technologists
Albuquerque	10.12	10.53	45.13	8.97	15.77	38.29	17.82
Anchorage	14.61	13.82	49.68	11.85	21.67	38.90	n/a
Ann Arbor	13.89	12.26	53.41	11.35	18.72	50.19	32.14
Athens	10.92	11.32	n/a	9.06	16.00	42.63	n/a
Atlanta	10.44	11.55	70.58	8.86	18.06	54.65	32.23
Austin	10.32	11.31	57.65	8.55	15.69	68.24	35.72
Baltimore	11.58	12.90	63.70	10.37	18.69	51.36	38.02
Bellevue	13.83	14.93	59.70	11.85	20.24	61.19	39.33
Birmingham	9.71	11.06	63.17	8.68	16.68	47.83	28.93
Boise City	11.56	11.54	43.98	9.56	14.83	47.40	n/a
Boston	14.78	15.62	63.14	12.87	21.23	64.07	34.37
Boulder	13.87	12.90	53.77	9.70	18.95	49.36	n/a
Cambridge	14.78	15.62	63.14	12.87	21.23	64.07	34.37
Cary	10.31	10.60	60.01	8.97	18.06	56.27	29.53
Charleston	9.51	10.91	56.44	9.29	16.27	51.12	30.41
Charlotte	9.96	11.09	62.75	9.00	17.56	55.86	30.96
Chattanooga	11.83	10.16	71.32	8.56	15.99	35.49	30.29
Chicago	12.62	12.87	68.97	10.73	21.05	58.32	34.43
Cincinnati	11.60	11.62	55.12	10.01	18.63	53.56	30.57
Cleveland	11.95	11.59	52.19	10.06	17.65	55.23	30.66
Colorado Spgs.	11.47	12.41	45.07	9.35	17.13	54.55	32.27
Columbia	9.75	10.92	57.22	8.89	17.32	41.13	29.62
Columbus	11.74	11.04	48.10	9.51	17.24	56.17	30.98
Dallas	9.85	11.05	71.15	8.89	16.07	62.86	31.78
Denver	10.62	12.61	62.47	9.65	17.99	57.87	39.10
Des Moines	10.93	12.63	60.68	9.54	16.66	49.55	n/a
Durham	10.42	10.86	55.04	9.30	18.06	62.67	31.17
Edison	12.81	12.47	60.07	10.16	19.00	71.25	40.48
El Paso	9.45	9.68	63.58	7.90	12.63	46.65	28.66
Eugene	11.58	13.18	46.52	10.00	16.84	35.42	n/a
Evansville	11.09	10.90	42.96	9.04	19.32	48.04	29.62
Fargo	11.07	12.02	59.42	8.92	17.56	41.82	n/a
Ft. Collins	11.39	11.98	58.91	9.80	17.18	59.73	n/a
Ft. Lauderdale	10.26	11.52	57.21	9.54	16.13	56.51	37.48
Ft. Wayne	11.61	10.78	43.13	9.24	17.07	49.60	31.76
Ft. Worth	10.79	10.84	55.25	8.58	15.89	51.80	32.89
Gainesville	10.03	10.82	35.20	9.57	14.94	51.96	30.56
Greensboro	9.80	11.12	65.42	8.55	18.40	59.74	30.88
Honolulu	12.00	13.77	46.33	13.87	19.20	37.73	36.10
Houston	9.60	10.28	68.96	8.51	15.70	62.51	31.14
Huntsville	9.95	11.54	60.29	9.09	16.86	50.18	29.80
Indianapolis	10.78	11.55	50.96	9.07	17.48	52.98	32.65
Irvine	12.16	12.08	75.94	10.28	18.90	61.94	44.48
Jackson	9.99	10.08	51.56	7.89	14.51	39.66	29.01
Jacksonville	10.93	11.31	46.55	9.21	16.29	57.19	31.80
Kansas City	11.68	11.94	57.22	9.43	17.65	53.54	32.12
Knoxville	10.11	12.39	55.71	8.69	15.66	38.33	28.59
Las Vegas	12.83	12.55	58.91	12.89	20.68	51.28	38.52
Lexington	10.40	11.10	49.41	9.26	15.46	46.90	29.34
Lincoln	11.02	11.31	47.35	8.56	16.62	45.98	29.71
Little Rock	9.48	11.00	53.47	8.43	15.38	44.75	31.93
Los Angeles	12.23	13.82	74.58	10.97	19.71	66.25	39.59
Louisville	10.57	11.25	49.60	9.04	16.19	47.80	27.96
Madison	11.50	13.66	50.79	10.01	18.08	46.74	33.65
Manchester	12.20	15.62	52.16	9.63	17.64	45.05	n/a

Table continued on next page.

Metro Area	Janitors/ Cleaners	Landscapers	Lawyers	Maids/ House- keepers	Main- tenance Repairers	Marketing Managers	Nuclear Medicine Technologists
Miami	9.84	10.50	59.91	9.44	15.30	54.19	30.26
Milwaukee	11.99	13.61	55.29	9.75	18.90	55.60	34.52
Minneapolis	12.44	13.85	65.09	10.89	20.04	59.36	34.17
Naperville	12.62	12.87	68.97	10.73	21.05	58.32	34.43
Nashville	9.68	11.69	54.02	9.10	17.15	42.83	29.40
New Orleans	10.05	10.43	51.40	9.54	16.79	37.12	30.99
New York	14.12	15.22	79.87	15.48	19.51	74.12	36.04
Oakland	14.16	15.55	70.01	11.59	21.37	64.47	45.30
Oklahoma City	9.43	10.82	42.76	8.42	15.37	36.71	34.29
Omaha	10.48	11.58	49.22	9.30	16.66	56.97	30.39
Orlando	10.14	11.38	56.86	9.35	14.61	49.93	31.05
Overland Park	11.68	11.94	57.22	9.43	17.65	53.54	32.12
Oxnard	13.07	12.46	72.52	10.36	19.82	60.87	n/a
Philadelphia	13.03	13.88	69.79	11.10	18.66	62.81	33.91
Phoenix	10.59	11.13	57.07	9.83	17.70	42.93	34.63
Pittsburgh	11.29	11.92	61.23	9.76	16.81	56.22	24.79
Plano	9.85	11.05	71.15	8.89	16.07	62.86	31.78
Portland	12.19	13.14	49.47	10.49	18.37	53.57	37.16
Providence	12.86	13.48	57.18	11.63	18.36	46.45	36.74
Provo	10.16	11.86	52.18	9.34	16.25	44.09	n/a
Raleigh	10.31	10.60	60.01	8.97	18.06	56.27	29.53
Reno	10.66	12.60	65.83	9.75	17.11	48.96	n/a
Richmond	10.77	11.48	62.66	8.74	18.14	63.14	31.01
Riverside	13.21	12.20	60.04	10.00	18.72	50.21	38.85
Rochester	11.64	12.89	45.39	10.07	17.72	57.88	30.29
Sacramento	13.04	12.56	55.87	10.99	19.72	48.59	44.69
Salt Lake City	10.43	11.97	60.10	9.04	17.01	46.44	31.29
San Antonio	10.17	10.74	51.75	8.87	13.86	57.91	29.23
San Diego	12.22	12.90	68.89	10.06	17.84	58.64	39.92
San Francisco	13.47	15.96	80.35	13.66	22.50	75.60	44.89
San Jose	12.78	15.18	92.32	11.57	22.62	72.91	45.59
Santa Ana	12.16	12.08	75.94	10.28	18.90	61.94	44.48
Savannah	10.02	12.51	52.35	8.35	16.10	45.32	n/a
Seattle	13.83	14.93	59.70	11.85	20.24	61.19	39.33
Spokane	12.91	13.76	45.28	10.15	18.41	53.96	n/a
Springfield	10.93	10.98	42.63	9.21	14.54	38.42	31.04
St. Louis	11.10	13.15	54.99	10.11	18.51	53.08	31.36
St. Paul	12.44	13.85	65.09	10.89	20.04	59.36	34.17
St. Petersburg	10.15	11.15	53.98	9.12	14.94	54.78	31.56
Tampa	10.15	11.15	53.98	9.12	14.94	54.78	31.56
Tulsa	9.56	10.21	52.22	8.59	16.91	44.31	31.96
Virginia Beach	9.76	11.29	58.88	9.19	16.59	45.18	28.79
Warren	13.20	12.37	60.79	10.46	17.62	50.74	32.33
Washington	11.84	12.48	73.19	11.56	22.04	63.43	36.38
Wichita	10.80	10.75	49.12	8.84	17.48	44.79	26.05

Notes: Wage data is for May 2010 and covers the Metropolitan Statistical Area - see Appendix B for areas included; n/a not available
Source: Bureau of Labor Statistics, May 2010 Metro Area Occupational Employment and Wage Estimates

Average Hourly Wages: Occupations N - R

Metro Area	Nurses, Licensed Practical	Nurses, Registered	Nursing Aides/ Orderlies/ Attendants	Packers/ Packagers	Physical Therapists	Postal Mail Carriers	R.E. Brokers
Albuquerque	26.96	31.93	12.01	9.16	30.73	23.70	31.24
Anchorage	22.14	36.78	15.24	11.92	43.98	24.96	n/a
Ann Arbor	21.53	32.00	13.99	10.25	31.74	23.35	n/a
Athens	18.29	27.10	9.71	10.11	30.60	22.52	13.14
Atlanta	18.51	30.40	11.04	10.62	36.36	23.04	45.55
Austin	20.21	30.08	10.97	9.92	31.37	23.42	n/a
Baltimore	24.27	38.05	13.87	12.86	41.66	23.68	28.49
Bellevue	22.43	36.66	14.16	12.05	36.95	24.35	49.72
Birmingham	17.28	29.32	10.69	9.24	35.41	22.96	27.08
Boise City	19.93	31.37	11.40	10.68	33.46	22.87	21.10
Boston	23.87	42.66	14.54	11.91	34.90	24.62	41.49
Boulder	21.42	33.36	14.31	11.44	30.84	23.93	n/a
Cambridge	23.87	42.66	14.54	11.91	34.90	24.62	41.49
Cary	18.72	29.34	11.90	10.12	32.93	22.94	27.29
Charleston	18.77	31.18	11.15	9.63	32.54	22.71	26.40
Charlotte	19.81	28.17	11.14	9.92	35.72	22.82	26.96
Chattanooga	17.14	27.68	10.68	10.52	38.23	23.58	n/a
Chicago	21.60	33.35	12.16	10.41	39.34	24.41	29.45
Cincinnati	20.31	29.69	12.02	10.39	34.77	23.73	50.08
Cleveland	20.77	30.01	11.62	11.31	36.98	24.58	24.78
Colorado Spgs.	19.04	30.18	12.62	9.77	35.19	23.80	20.68
Columbia	19.07	28.76	9.96	10.00	37.11	22.76	21.11
Columbus	20.17	29.76	12.00	10.36	34.49	23.27	42.07
Dallas	22.59	32.47	10.99	9.89	39.65	23.77	47.56
Denver	22.06	33.54	13.95	10.29	34.84	24.38	26.22
Des Moines	18.36	26.87	12.12	11.03	32.02	23.91	37.92
Durham	20.30	29.88	12.58	9.48	34.84	23.35	30.03
Edison	24.54	35.37	13.26	10.32	40.13	24.26	n/a
El Paso	20.24	29.25	9.42	7.99	45.85	24.22	n/a
Eugene	20.70	35.17	12.42	9.78	37.90	23.88	n/a
Evansville	17.65	25.18	11.63	12.66	30.22	23.15	15.97
Fargo	16.30	29.67	11.75	9.74	32.59	23.51	n/a
Ft. Collins	16.90	31.07	11.54	10.85	30.48	23.68	n/a
Ft. Lauderdale	19.56	31.98	11.18	9.73	39.43	24.64	31.35
Ft. Wayne	17.61	24.73	11.25	10.12	33.87	23.79	42.40
Ft. Worth	20.16	30.48	11.06	10.47	39.23	23.73	21.41
Gainesville	19.17	29.95	11.06	10.50	37.58	22.54	n/a
Greensboro	19.45	28.40	11.30	10.00	37.87	22.89	29.09
Honolulu	22.03	39.49	14.32	10.70	26.16	25.08	n/a
Houston	20.81	33.26	10.86	9.54	38.52	23.98	41.68
Huntsville	16.58	28.25	9.69	10.43	40.91	23.46	26.82
Indianapolis	19.42	30.16	12.31	11.16	32.55	23.58	25.11
Irvine	24.41	36.73	12.86	10.77	41.67	24.81	43.66
Jackson	17.20	28.54	9.62	9.05	35.77	23.03	n/a
Jacksonville	19.30	29.53	11.71	10.60	39.56	23.53	42.61
Kansas City	18.04	29.27	11.76	9.71	33.06	23.72	24.57
Knoxville	15.98	27.15	10.70	8.88	33.76	22.90	24.66
Las Vegas	23.30	35.07	15.68	11.11	41.37	24.13	n/a
Lexington	18.40	30.48	11.84	9.10	35.81	24.12	n/a
Lincoln	17.78	n/a	11.87	9.16	33.30	23.70	27.66
Little Rock	18.19	30.37	10.54	8.74	36.04	23.26	34.24
Los Angeles	23.11	38.99	12.10	9.77	39.19	24.92	35.45
Louisville	18.10	28.27	11.55	9.81	35.34	23.35	n/a
Madison	20.02	33.79	13.38	14.49	36.32	23.07	n/a
Manchester	20.55	31.49	13.55	9.93	34.08	24.38	n/a

Table continued on next page.

Metro Area	Nurses, Licensed Practical	Nurses, Registered	Nursing Aides/ Orderlies/ Attendants	Packers/ Packagers	Physical Therapists	Postal Mail Carriers	R.E. Brokers
Miami	19.83	32.90	10.74	9.47	35.87	24.70	36.01
Milwaukee	21.97	30.16	12.45	11.53	33.96	24.23	39.62
Minneapolis	20.20	36.07	13.87	11.52	32.68	23.72	47.83
Naperville	21.60	33.35	12.16	10.41	39.34	24.41	29.45
Nashville	18.68	30.34	11.59	9.81	35.63	23.18	27.91
New Orleans	19.94	30.79	10.96	10.21	35.72	24.18	n/a
New York	23.52	39.11	15.71	10.29	39.24	24.54	72.78
Oakland	27.47	46.77	15.84	10.58	42.14	24.74	64.07
Oklahoma City	16.10	26.53	10.07	8.72	34.36	23.28	21.34
Omaha	18.59	27.76	12.19	10.12	31.39	23.63	37.75
Orlando	18.64	27.87	11.51	12.31	40.50	23.62	42.97
Overland Park	18.04	29.27	11.76	9.71	33.06	23.72	24.57
Oxnard	25.64	37.05	13.60	10.04	45.48	24.17	26.70
Philadelphia	22.86	34.34	13.06	10.58	35.57	24.40	69.53
Phoenix	22.29	32.79	12.29	10.25	33.30	23.61	25.70
Pittsburgh	19.04	29.18	12.56	11.04	36.04	23.83	57.83
Plano	22.59	32.47	10.99	9.89	39.65	23.77	47.56
Portland	22.56	36.54	13.45	10.81	34.51	23.95	31.19
Providence	24.02	33.03	13.73	10.42	37.74	24.18	n/a
Provo	17.66	28.48	10.41	9.27	32.50	23.33	n/a
Raleigh	18.72	29.34	11.90	10.12	32.93	22.94	27.29
Reno	22.23	34.90	13.39	11.46	40.38	23.86	n/a
Richmond	19.36	30.39	11.66	8.83	33.31	22.86	n/a
Riverside	21.31	36.45	11.95	11.18	39.58	23.96	27.59
Rochester	18.16	28.84	12.16	10.43	31.69	23.52	40.61
Sacramento	25.83	43.16	14.02	11.33	40.23	23.50	35.05
Salt Lake City	20.37	29.29	11.22	10.46	30.11	24.09	43.20
San Antonio	19.18	31.32	11.00	9.71	45.28	23.83	27.88
San Diego	22.80	39.12	11.96	9.83	38.90	24.47	30.85
San Francisco	27.37	47.55	17.74	10.77	45.92	25.06	63.55
San Jose	27.48	52.92	15.38	10.08	40.15	24.77	51.50
Santa Ana	24.41	36.73	12.86	10.77	41.67	24.81	43.66
Savannah	18.32	31.28	10.32	7.94	34.65	22.86	n/a
Seattle	22.43	36.66	14.16	12.05	36.95	24.35	49.72
Spokane	22.04	32.61	12.10	11.40	32.21	23.45	41.82
Springfield	15.54	25.45	10.02	9.98	35.14	22.51	25.75
St. Louis	18.59	28.37	11.14	10.76	30.50	23.60	26.20
St. Paul	20.20	36.07	13.87	11.52	32.68	23.72	47.83
St. Petersburg	20.05	30.78	11.45	9.80	38.46	23.34	26.08
Tampa	20.05	30.78	11.45	9.80	38.46	23.34	26.08
Tulsa	15.81	24.39	10.17	9.44	29.81	23.57	27.20
Virginia Beach	17.26	29.04	10.66	9.67	36.39	24.09	50.44
Warren	23.29	32.69	13.07	10.61	36.46	24.04	28.74
Washington	21.69	35.21	13.03	10.57	39.18	23.86	39.93
Wichita	17.97	25.52	10.74	9.44	36.36	23.72	n/a

Notes: Wage data is for May 2010 and covers the Metropolitan Statistical Area - see Appendix B for areas included; n/a not available
Source: Bureau of Labor Statistics, May 2010 Metro Area Occupational Employment and Wage Estimates

Average Hourly Wages: Occupations R - T

Metro Area	Retail Salespersons	Sales Reps., Except Tech./Scien.	Sales Reps., Tech./Scien.	Secretaries, Exc. Leg./Med./Exec.	Security Guards	Surgeons	Teacher Assistants
Albuquerque	11.43	25.95	36.09	13.87	12.37	104.03	8.70
Anchorage	12.31	25.96	39.05	18.83	15.73	n/a	n/a
Ann Arbor	11.88	30.90	37.89	16.82	12.59	n/a	11.90
Athens	10.66	25.81	26.79	12.80	13.07	105.18	9.30
Atlanta	11.77	30.49	40.13	14.10	11.16	104.46	9.80
Austin	11.55	32.49	31.01	14.13	12.84	102.13	11.70
Baltimore	11.98	31.68	38.41	17.48	14.44	n/a	12.30
Bellevue	13.03	31.34	40.22	18.11	18.76	104.97	15.00
Birmingham	11.51	26.29	33.34	14.90	10.29	105.78	9.40
Boise City	11.36	21.59	38.65	15.08	12.79	102.68	10.00
Boston	12.11	34.31	45.61	19.89	13.89	108.11	13.90
Boulder	12.36	28.56	46.28	16.26	12.01	100.84	n/a
Cambridge	12.11	34.31	45.61	19.89	13.89	108.11	13.90
Cary	11.07	27.19	32.38	15.66	11.39	96.71	10.00
Charleston	12.13	25.55	31.99	15.19	12.21	n/a	10.00
Charlotte	11.51	27.58	37.14	15.05	11.70	n/a	10.30
Chattanooga	11.62	26.59	33.14	13.72	12.40	112.14	8.20
Chicago	11.97	32.79	33.40	16.43	12.25	102.05	11.50
Cincinnati	11.87	32.28	41.10	15.23	12.75	n/a	11.90
Cleveland	11.67	30.17	32.94	15.39	12.02	104.15	13.40
Colorado Spgs.	12.18	28.22	31.70	14.88	13.26	n/a	11.40
Columbia	11.04	29.91	33.69	13.98	12.42	110.88	9.20
Columbus	11.30	27.73	40.41	15.64	13.90	108.56	13.60
Dallas	12.29	29.08	49.88	14.58	12.72	108.56	11.00
Denver	13.09	31.80	38.66	16.58	14.35	108.62	13.40
Des Moines	13.10	28.54	48.01	15.10	11.37	n/a	10.40
Durham	10.98	26.67	38.73	15.72	15.09	114.96	10.80
Edison	12.80	34.34	48.23	16.73	13.39	n/a	12.10
El Paso	10.16	20.50	32.72	11.84	11.74	105.11	11.60
Eugene	12.51	28.34	33.45	15.04	11.70	113.21	12.90
Evansville	10.73	26.15	36.63	13.74	15.28	n/a	9.80
Fargo	12.14	22.68	41.83	15.22	10.71	99.50	12.00
Ft. Collins	11.10	35.08	40.20	14.96	10.76	n/a	11.90
Ft. Lauderdale	13.64	26.45	34.49	14.38	10.71	115.99	9.60
Ft. Wayne	11.26	25.77	37.23	14.44	11.57	111.02	11.20
Ft. Worth	11.12	29.06	42.57	14.55	14.11	89.78	9.10
Gainesville	12.63	27.69	35.00	13.52	12.80	n/a	10.30
Greensboro	11.72	25.59	28.93	14.40	10.11	n/a	9.80
Honolulu	12.06	22.35	26.32	17.53	12.31	92.67	n/a
Houston	11.22	31.19	41.06	14.22	11.25	54.05	9.80
Huntsville	10.66	22.84	36.31	15.05	12.85	n/a	8.80
Indianapolis	10.69	29.16	38.50	15.14	12.58	107.59	11.10
Irvine	12.66	33.96	40.99	18.04	12.65	104.21	15.90
Jackson	11.59	24.78	35.52	13.05	9.37	n/a	8.40
Jacksonville	12.14	26.71	41.13	13.97	10.42	n/a	11.10
Kansas City	11.70	29.72	36.46	14.27	14.43	109.69	10.50
Knoxville	11.56	27.78	32.41	13.28	10.39	n/a	8.40
Las Vegas	11.95	28.54	37.09	16.90	12.90	104.43	13.70
Lexington	11.27	27.66	42.63	13.47	10.28	115.38	12.20
Lincoln	10.32	24.84	32.85	13.82	10.89	n/a	10.90
Little Rock	10.91	28.44	34.56	13.12	11.90	109.16	9.40
Los Angeles	12.19	29.52	38.30	16.87	12.37	101.05	14.90
Louisville	10.93	27.26	38.78	13.31	12.74	101.93	13.30
Madison	11.53	29.68	34.19	16.17	12.00	n/a	12.30
Manchester	12.33	28.62	40.09	15.14	11.97	111.01	12.20

Table continued on next page.

Metro Area	Retail Salespersons	Sales Reps., Except Tech./Scien.	Sales Reps., Tech./Scien.	Secretaries, Exc. Leg./ Med./Exec.	Security Guards	Surgeons	Teacher Assistants
Miami	13.23	27.65	31.24	14.59	11.08	97.02	10.70
Milwaukee	11.70	31.96	44.02	15.56	12.46	112.19	12.10
Minneapolis	11.24	36.71	45.18	18.33	13.96	n/a	13.30
Naperville	11.97	32.79	33.40	16.43	12.25	102.05	11.50
Nashville	10.99	27.58	28.32	13.86	11.57	n/a	10.60
New Orleans	11.16	26.81	30.32	13.86	12.11	n/a	10.20
New York	12.96	36.78	47.52	17.27	13.34	92.05	13.10
Oakland	13.23	33.40	42.44	19.56	13.00	114.81	15.20
Oklahoma City	11.13	21.69	28.84	12.83	12.48	110.76	9.80
Omaha	11.74	28.30	36.53	13.70	12.96	111.93	9.90
Orlando	12.08	26.07	37.35	13.79	10.90	95.92	11.10
Overland Park	11.70	29.72	36.46	14.27	14.43	109.69	10.50
Oxnard	11.49	34.90	38.18	17.58	12.99	n/a	14.40
Philadelphia	12.94	32.88	40.53	15.73	14.28	78.25	11.90
Phoenix	12.43	28.24	34.88	15.19	11.81	91.50	11.50
Pittsburgh	11.67	30.30	37.31	14.01	11.81	83.21	10.30
Plano	12.29	29.08	49.88	14.58	12.72	108.56	11.00
Portland	12.68	32.03	48.49	16.41	12.78	110.66	13.70
Providence	12.12	31.49	37.28	16.67	12.16	112.53	13.60
Provo	10.77	25.67	38.77	13.10	13.00	n/a	11.00
Raleigh	11.07	27.19	32.38	15.66	11.39	96.71	10.00
Reno	13.14	29.62	40.82	17.23	13.19	n/a	12.80
Richmond	12.23	31.88	42.06	16.27	13.00	101.19	10.30
Riverside	12.15	29.87	34.89	16.06	11.45	104.62	13.10
Rochester	11.46	29.92	43.96	14.59	12.34	103.06	10.70
Sacramento	11.61	30.80	53.83	17.19	11.89	103.89	13.40
Salt Lake City	12.09	27.55	39.79	13.80	12.66	105.51	10.30
San Antonio	10.70	26.41	38.00	13.73	11.64	n/a	10.10
San Diego	12.37	30.95	37.55	16.85	13.01	112.22	13.70
San Francisco	14.39	30.54	44.49	19.24	14.83	n/a	16.20
San Jose	12.16	38.98	48.29	19.05	14.11	116.52	15.70
Santa Ana	12.66	33.96	40.99	18.04	12.65	104.21	15.90
Savannah	10.21	36.37	36.95	12.97	10.44	n/a	11.30
Seattle	13.03	31.34	40.22	18.11	18.76	104.97	15.00
Spokane	12.47	27.16	30.31	16.06	13.03	n/a	12.90
Springfield	11.70	25.29	33.60	12.17	10.91	n/a	9.80
St. Louis	12.48	31.64	35.22	14.80	12.63	104.91	11.50
St. Paul	11.24	36.71	45.18	18.33	13.96	n/a	13.30
St. Petersburg	12.63	28.60	35.33	13.70	10.29	n/a	10.10
Tampa	12.63	28.60	35.33	13.70	10.29	n/a	10.10
Tulsa	11.72	25.41	32.51	12.64	11.53	89.37	10.30
Virginia Beach	10.82	26.66	37.70	15.45	12.25	97.54	10.00
Warren	12.27	32.16	45.11	16.30	11.74	n/a	12.60
Washington	12.53	34.48	46.47	20.73	17.11	107.54	13.70
Wichita	11.86	25.74	34.69	12.96	13.23	n/a	11.70

Notes: Wage data is for May 2010 and covers the Metropolitan Statistical Area - see Appendix B for areas included; hourly wages for teacher assistants were calculated by the editors from annual wage data assuming a 40 hour work week; n/a not available
Source: Bureau of Labor Statistics, May 2010 Metro Area Occupational Employment and Wage Estimates

Average Hourly Wages: Occupations T - Z

Metro Area	Teachers, Elementary School	Teachers, Secondary School	Tele-marketers	Truck Driv., Heavy/ Trac. Trail.	Truck Drivers, Light	Waiters/ Waitresses
Albuquerque	23.20	28.30	11.04	19.10	13.73	8.20
Anchorage	n/a	n/a	n/a	23.30	17.93	10.02
Ann Arbor	27.00	27.60	10.13	17.36	17.76	9.40
Athens	26.20	27.20	9.19	18.59	15.23	7.84
Atlanta	25.70	26.40	15.43	20.50	15.18	9.44
Austin	23.40	24.40	14.04	16.91	14.15	8.51
Baltimore	27.40	29.40	12.64	19.02	17.22	9.22
Bellevue	27.40	28.60	12.73	21.43	16.16	13.96
Birmingham	23.50	23.90	11.42	19.17	13.84	7.88
Boise City	26.00	25.60	10.11	15.02	13.21	8.28
Boston	31.00	30.90	17.45	20.69	16.80	14.14
Boulder	24.50	n/a	n/a	20.00	15.82	11.36
Cambridge	31.00	30.90	17.45	20.69	16.80	14.14
Cary	20.50	22.30	14.79	18.58	14.61	9.18
Charleston	20.70	23.30	10.94	17.24	12.76	9.48
Charlotte	21.00	21.80	12.75	19.86	15.21	9.07
Chattanooga	23.00	23.00	11.30	18.21	15.64	8.35
Chicago	30.70	35.80	13.73	20.83	16.88	10.22
Cincinnati	24.60	26.30	12.65	18.98	15.37	9.39
Cleveland	26.90	29.60	10.25	19.42	13.85	8.77
Colorado Spgs.	21.30	22.10	10.64	16.35	14.56	9.76
Columbia	22.50	24.30	11.99	18.31	13.78	7.67
Columbus	26.90	27.30	10.77	19.49	15.39	9.05
Dallas	25.80	27.00	13.85	18.91	15.12	8.67
Denver	24.60	25.20	12.83	20.09	16.13	10.77
Des Moines	22.60	23.20	12.03	19.91	15.29	9.21
Durham	21.70	23.60	10.33	18.13	15.54	10.07
Edison	28.90	30.50	12.92	20.12	16.76	11.04
El Paso	24.80	25.40	9.30	18.92	11.49	7.85
Eugene	25.40	24.60	14.61	16.63	14.48	13.17
Evansville	23.10	23.10	11.76	17.56	13.33	8.63
Fargo	22.70	22.60	8.65	18.81	13.07	8.12
Ft. Collins	22.70	n/a	15.06	17.10	14.32	11.68
Ft. Lauderdale	n/a	n/a	10.83	18.32	14.33	10.07
Ft. Wayne	23.10	23.60	15.01	19.77	13.73	8.71
Ft. Worth	24.30	25.30	10.19	19.53	14.57	9.89
Gainesville	n/a	n/a	8.53	14.54	13.62	9.63
Greensboro	20.90	21.80	11.11	18.73	14.56	8.50
Honolulu	23.10	23.00	11.46	19.55	14.30	12.03
Houston	24.70	26.30	14.46	17.68	15.59	8.80
Huntsville	24.10	21.10	10.72	16.10	13.91	8.97
Indianapolis	23.50	22.10	15.22	18.21	14.78	9.02
Irvine	31.80	35.50	13.59	20.14	16.06	10.54
Jackson	20.30	20.40	12.22	20.01	13.87	7.70
Jacksonville	22.00	22.70	11.12	17.97	13.80	9.71
Kansas City	21.90	21.40	13.31	19.16	14.75	9.85
Knoxville	21.70	22.70	10.10	18.33	14.28	7.98
Las Vegas	23.30	n/a	12.90	22.45	16.18	10.62
Lexington	22.50	23.70	14.52	18.78	14.68	9.22
Lincoln	22.80	22.60	8.66	n/a	12.86	8.64
Little Rock	21.80	23.40	10.40	17.45	13.36	8.10
Los Angeles	28.50	30.50	13.46	19.93	15.58	9.99
Louisville	24.00	24.50	11.27	17.63	14.93	8.16
Madison	22.90	24.40	13.35	19.04	16.34	9.79
Manchester	24.20	24.60	13.03	18.64	13.12	10.23

Table continued on next page.

Metro Area	Teachers, Elementary School	Teachers, Secondary School	Tele- marketers	Truck Driv., Heavy/ Trac. Trail.	Truck Drivers, Light	Waiters/ Waitresses
Miami	n/a	n/a	12.55	18.01	13.06	9.77
Milwaukee	27.10	26.30	12.60	19.95	14.59	8.85
Minneapolis	25.60	24.50	13.64	20.48	16.77	11.66
Naperville	30.70	35.80	13.73	20.83	16.88	10.22
Nashville	22.30	21.90	13.86	18.38	16.28	9.32
New Orleans	22.50	23.00	11.63	17.24	15.09	8.73
New York	31.80	34.20	13.85	22.47	17.64	13.54
Oakland	30.10	31.10	15.05	20.72	16.23	9.69
Oklahoma City	21.30	21.30	9.32	19.70	12.92	8.48
Omaha	20.40	20.80	12.36	21.77	14.42	8.32
Orlando	24.80	25.90	11.92	18.20	14.16	9.93
Overland Park	21.90	21.40	13.31	19.16	14.75	9.85
Oxnard	29.80	28.10	18.22	21.33	16.24	10.29
Philadelphia	25.90	28.00	13.89	20.83	16.16	9.62
Phoenix	20.90	21.40	12.44	19.67	15.70	10.98
Pittsburgh	24.60	26.40	10.45	19.53	14.77	9.46
Plano	25.80	27.00	13.85	18.91	15.12	8.67
Portland	24.90	25.30	11.78	19.61	16.14	11.63
Providence	32.00	30.90	15.31	19.58	15.26	10.19
Provo	21.40	22.50	11.15	19.24	11.68	9.21
Raleigh	20.50	22.30	14.79	18.58	14.61	9.18
Reno	n/a	n/a	13.64	21.22	15.55	8.58
Richmond	25.60	26.10	14.08	19.29	14.58	9.71
Riverside	30.20	30.00	13.40	20.98	16.24	9.79
Rochester	25.70	26.40	11.56	17.75	14.32	10.19
Sacramento	27.10	28.40	13.98	19.71	15.31	10.25
Salt Lake City	22.60	20.30	11.41	19.41	12.97	10.31
San Antonio	25.90	26.70	9.75	16.33	12.69	8.70
San Diego	33.20	32.10	12.38	20.27	15.85	10.07
San Francisco	29.60	30.80	16.47	23.49	19.97	11.39
San Jose	29.10	33.80	16.25	19.58	17.36	10.56
Santa Ana	31.80	35.50	13.59	20.14	16.06	10.54
Savannah	23.60	23.20	n/a	18.68	16.22	9.76
Seattle	27.40	28.60	12.73	21.43	16.16	13.96
Spokane	26.90	27.40	11.25	19.85	14.05	13.35
Springfield	19.10	20.20	9.19	16.14	13.26	9.22
St. Louis	23.90	24.20	13.13	20.14	15.10	9.11
St. Paul	25.60	24.50	13.64	20.48	16.77	11.66
St. Petersburg	24.50	26.30	11.52	16.69	13.98	9.86
Tampa	24.50	26.30	11.52	16.69	13.98	9.86
Tulsa	20.80	21.30	10.07	19.11	13.29	8.54
Virginia Beach	26.10	26.60	9.80	16.59	13.25	9.39
Warren	28.60	28.30	11.19	18.86	15.65	9.40
Washington	32.30	32.90	12.08	19.63	16.94	11.37
Wichita	22.20	22.90	10.49	18.41	13.28	8.26

Notes: Wage data is for May 2010 and covers the Metropolitan Statistical Area - see Appendix B for areas included; hourly wages for elementary and secondary school teachers were calculated by the editors from annual wage data assuming a 40 hour work week; n/a not available
Source: Bureau of Labor Statistics, May 2010 Metro Area Occupational Employment and Wage Estimates

Means of Transportation to Work: City

City	Car/Truck/Van		Public Transportation			Bicycle	Walked	Other Means	Worked at Home
	Drove Alone	Car-pooled	Bus	Subway	Railroad				
Albuquerque	77.7	11.4	2.0	0.0	0.1	1.3	2.1	1.4	4.1
Anchorage	76.4	12.8	1.5	0.0	0.0	1.0	2.9	2.0	3.5
Ann Arbor	56.7	7.4	9.4	0.1	0.0	3.2	16.4	0.9	5.9
Athens	72.7	11.6	4.2	0.0	0.0	1.4	5.6	1.1	3.3
Atlanta	67.2	7.6	9.2	2.5	0.3	0.8	4.2	1.5	6.4
Austin	71.2	12.0	5.1	0.0	0.0	1.2	2.0	3.1	5.4
Baltimore	59.1	10.8	15.5	1.4	1.5	0.7	6.7	1.1	2.9
Bellevue	68.7	8.6	10.5	0.0	0.0	0.5	5.2	0.9	5.6
Birmingham	79.2	14.4	2.4	0.0	0.0	0.1	2.2	0.4	1.3
Boise City	78.1	8.3	0.8	0.1	0.1	4.2	2.6	1.6	4.2
Boston	39.8	7.2	12.7	17.4	1.3	1.5	13.9	1.2	3.2
Boulder	52.7	5.7	10.4	0.0	0.0	10.8	9.4	1.5	9.4
Cambridge	31.4	5.0	6.8	19.2	0.7	6.9	22.4	1.0	6.2
Cary	80.5	7.6	0.7	0.0	0.0	0.4	1.5	1.5	7.8
Charleston	78.7	7.8	2.8	0.0	0.0	1.3	4.5	1.4	3.4
Charlotte	76.4	11.8	3.3	0.3	0.1	0.2	2.0	0.9	5.0
Chattanooga	80.9	10.9	2.0	0.0	0.0	0.4	2.5	1.1	2.1
Chicago	50.5	10.1	15.1	9.8	1.9	1.1	5.8	1.5	4.0
Cincinnati	70.4	9.9	9.8	0.0	0.0	0.4	4.8	0.7	4.0
Cleveland	70.1	9.5	11.1	0.7	0.2	0.5	4.4	0.6	2.8
Colorado Spgs.	78.9	10.4	1.8	0.0	0.0	0.5	2.5	1.2	4.7
Columbia	65.5	8.8	2.2	0.2	0.0	0.5	4.1	1.7	16.9
Columbus	81.3	8.2	2.9	0.0	0.0	0.8	2.6	0.8	3.3
Dallas	76.4	12.7	3.6	0.3	0.4	0.1	1.8	1.2	3.6
Denver	69.0	10.4	7.2	0.7	0.2	1.8	4.1	1.3	5.2
Des Moines	76.3	13.2	3.3	0.0	0.0	0.3	3.1	0.8	2.9
Durham	72.8	15.0	3.7	0.0	0.0	0.5	3.0	0.8	4.1
Edison	69.5	8.9	0.6	1.2	13.0	0.0	2.3	0.6	3.9
El Paso	80.0	10.4	2.2	0.0	0.0	0.2	2.2	2.5	2.5
Eugene	65.4	8.0	5.8	0.0	0.0	8.7	7.0	0.7	4.2
Evansville	81.8	10.7	1.9	0.0	0.0	0.4	2.5	0.7	1.8
Fargo	81.6	7.8	1.0	0.0	0.0	1.3	4.6	0.8	2.9
Ft. Collins	71.3	8.8	1.2	0.0	0.0	7.9	3.6	1.3	5.9
Ft. Lauderdale	74.0	9.8	4.2	0.0	0.2	1.7	2.4	2.2	5.4
Ft. Wayne	84.9	9.1	0.8	0.0	0.0	0.3	1.2	0.7	2.9
Ft. Worth	80.4	12.1	1.0	0.0	0.2	0.2	1.2	1.9	3.1
Gainesville	69.8	9.2	5.3	0.0	0.0	5.7	5.5	1.6	2.7
Greensboro	81.8	9.0	2.0	0.0	0.0	0.3	2.0	1.4	3.5
Honolulu	59.6	13.9	10.7	0.0	0.0	1.7	8.0	2.5	3.6
Houston	74.6	13.5	4.3	0.1	0.1	0.4	2.2	1.6	3.2
Huntsville	84.4	9.7	0.6	0.0	0.0	0.1	1.1	1.2	3.0
Indianapolis	82.0	10.1	1.9	0.0	0.0	0.3	2.1	0.7	2.8
Irvine	76.1	7.6	0.9	0.1	0.4	1.7	5.2	1.3	6.7
Jackson	81.9	11.4	0.8	0.0	0.0	0.2	1.5	1.3	2.9
Jacksonville	81.1	11.1	1.6	0.0	0.0	0.4	1.5	1.2	3.0
Kansas City	80.1	9.3	3.8	0.0	0.0	0.3	2.1	1.2	3.0
Knoxville	83.1	8.5	1.3	0.0	0.0	0.7	2.6	1.0	2.8
Las Vegas	77.6	11.4	4.3	0.0	0.0	0.4	2.0	1.5	2.8
Lexington	79.8	10.5	1.5	0.0	0.0	0.8	3.8	0.5	3.0
Lincoln	81.4	9.0	1.4	0.0	0.0	1.5	3.6	0.5	2.5
Little Rock	81.5	11.0	1.2	0.0	0.0	0.0	1.5	1.2	3.5
Los Angeles	67.2	10.7	10.6	0.5	0.1	0.9	3.5	1.4	5.1
Louisville	80.1	9.9	4.1	0.0	0.0	0.4	2.3	0.9	2.4
Madison	63.3	9.6	8.2	0.0	0.0	4.5	10.6	0.8	2.9

Table continued on next page.

City	Car/Truck/Van		Public Transportation			Bicycle	Walked	Other Means	Worked at Home
	Drove Alone	Car-pooled	Bus	Subway	Railroad				
Manchester	83.3	9.4	0.5	0.0	0.0	0.7	2.6	0.9	2.5
Miami	68.9	10.1	10.7	0.5	0.4	0.4	3.8	1.6	3.5
Milwaukee	71.6	11.7	8.2	0.0	0.1	0.8	4.6	0.7	2.3
Minneapolis	61.6	8.7	12.6	0.6	0.5	4.1	6.4	0.8	4.7
Naperville	75.6	5.9	0.5	0.5	8.3	0.2	1.8	1.0	6.3
Nashville	80.6	9.6	2.1	0.0	0.1	0.3	1.7	1.1	4.5
New Orleans	66.3	13.2	6.2	0.1	0.0	1.7	5.8	2.2	3.6
New York	23.3	5.4	12.3	40.2	1.8	0.7	10.3	1.8	3.8
Oakland	57.5	10.0	7.9	8.2	0.4	2.1	4.4	2.6	6.5
Oklahoma City	82.1	11.9	0.7	0.0	0.0	0.1	1.4	0.9	3.0
Omaha	80.0	11.3	1.3	0.0	0.0	0.2	2.7	0.9	3.6
Orlando	78.2	10.9	4.3	0.0	0.0	0.5	1.7	1.2	3.1
Overland Park	85.8	5.7	0.4	0.0	0.0	0.3	1.0	0.9	5.9
Oxnard	72.4	19.2	1.4	0.0	0.0	0.7	1.6	1.2	3.5
Philadelphia	51.3	9.1	18.1	4.5	2.7	1.6	8.4	1.0	2.8
Phoenix	73.3	14.3	3.7	0.0	0.0	0.7	1.8	1.7	4.5
Pittsburgh	54.6	9.8	18.4	0.3	0.0	1.1	11.8	0.7	3.0
Plano	82.5	6.6	0.7	0.4	0.5	0.1	0.8	2.1	6.3
Portland	61.5	8.9	10.2	0.5	0.3	5.5	5.2	0.9	6.1
Providence	62.7	12.4	6.9	0.2	1.0	1.0	9.8	0.9	5.2
Provo	59.3	11.9	4.1	0.0	0.0	3.0	16.8	0.6	4.3
Raleigh	77.3	11.0	2.1	0.0	0.0	0.5	2.6	1.0	5.4
Reno	75.3	10.6	4.3	0.0	0.1	0.7	4.0	2.2	2.7
Richmond	69.5	12.0	8.0	0.0	0.0	1.5	3.9	1.1	4.0
Riverside	75.6	13.4	1.8	0.0	0.5	0.8	2.5	1.1	4.1
Rochester	70.1	11.0	8.1	0.1	0.0	1.3	5.8	0.8	2.8
Sacramento	72.5	14.1	2.7	0.3	0.2	2.2	3.3	1.1	3.3
St. Louis	69.8	12.0	9.5	0.7	0.1	0.6	3.5	1.1	2.7
St. Paul	69.1	11.2	9.1	0.1	0.1	1.3	4.4	0.8	4.0
St. Petersburg	80.6	8.5	1.9	0.0	0.0	0.9	2.5	1.4	4.1
Salt Lake City	69.8	11.7	4.7	0.1	0.1	2.2	5.1	1.6	4.3
San Antonio	78.8	11.6	3.4	0.0	0.0	0.1	2.0	1.7	2.4
San Diego	75.8	9.3	3.6	0.1	0.1	0.9	2.9	1.1	6.1
San Francisco	38.3	7.5	22.5	6.6	1.1	2.8	10.0	1.9	6.8
San Jose	77.5	10.6	2.6	0.2	0.6	0.9	1.9	1.9	3.6
Santa Ana	66.7	20.4	7.7	0.0	0.0	1.0	1.8	0.6	1.7
Savannah	77.6	9.7	4.2	0.0	0.0	1.0	3.3	1.4	2.8
Seattle	52.9	9.9	18.7	0.1	0.0	2.9	8.6	1.3	5.5
Spokane	74.5	11.3	4.3	0.0	0.0	1.2	3.2	1.1	4.3
Springfield	79.1	10.0	1.0	0.0	0.0	0.9	4.4	0.9	3.7
Tampa	77.3	9.8	2.7	0.0	0.0	1.0	2.8	1.3	5.2
Tulsa	79.7	12.1	1.0	0.0	0.0	0.4	2.2	1.0	3.5
Virginia Beach	81.9	9.3	0.8	0.1	0.0	0.5	2.1	1.0	4.2
Warren	84.0	10.1	1.5	0.0	0.0	0.1	1.3	0.6	2.5
Washington	37.5	6.8	15.5	19.9	0.5	2.0	11.4	1.2	4.9
Wichita	84.9	9.4	0.7	0.0	0.0	0.3	1.3	0.7	2.7
U.S.	75.8	10.4	2.7	1.7	0.5	0.5	2.9	1.2	4.1

Note: Figures shown are percentages and cover workers 16 years of age and older
Source: U.S. Census Bureau, 2007-2009 American Community Survey 3-Year Estimates

Means of Transportation to Work: Metro Area

MSA[1]	Car/Truck/Van		Public Transportation			Bicycle	Walked	Other Means	Worked at Home
	Drove Alone	Car-pooled	Bus	Subway	Railroad				
Albuquerque	77.7	11.9	1.5	0.0	0.2	0.9	1.8	1.5	4.4
Anchorage	75.0	13.4	1.3	0.0	0.0	0.8	2.9	2.5	4.1
Ann Arbor	74.0	8.2	3.9	0.0	0.0	1.2	6.7	0.8	5.2
Athens	75.6	12.1	2.6	0.0	0.0	0.9	3.7	0.9	4.1
Atlanta	77.1	10.8	2.7	0.7	0.1	0.2	1.4	1.6	5.3
Austin	74.5	12.4	2.9	0.0	0.0	0.7	1.6	2.2	5.7
Baltimore	76.3	9.7	4.5	0.9	0.9	0.3	2.9	0.9	3.6
Bellevue	69.4	11.6	7.9	0.0	0.3	0.9	3.7	1.1	5.0
Birmingham	83.3	11.5	0.7	0.0	0.0	0.1	1.1	0.6	2.7
Boise City	78.2	10.2	0.5	0.1	0.0	1.8	2.1	2.3	4.9
Boston	68.9	8.1	3.8	5.8	2.0	0.8	5.1	0.8	4.2
Boulder	65.6	8.4	5.6	0.0	0.0	4.4	4.5	1.4	10.1
Cambridge	68.9	8.1	3.8	5.8	2.0	0.8	5.1	0.8	4.2
Cary	79.6	10.6	0.9	0.0	0.0	0.3	1.6	1.2	5.7
Charleston	81.2	9.6	1.3	0.0	0.0	0.5	2.4	1.2	3.7
Charlotte	79.6	11.1	1.8	0.1	0.0	0.1	1.4	0.9	4.8
Chattanooga	82.9	10.7	0.8	0.0	0.0	0.2	1.7	0.8	2.9
Chicago	70.6	9.0	5.1	3.4	3.1	0.6	3.1	1.1	4.0
Cincinnati	81.6	9.1	2.6	0.0	0.0	0.1	2.2	0.7	3.7
Cleveland	81.7	7.9	3.6	0.3	0.1	0.3	2.1	0.7	3.3
Colorado Spgs.	77.1	9.9	1.3	0.0	0.0	0.4	4.1	1.2	5.9
Columbia	79.5	9.9	0.8	0.1	0.0	0.2	1.6	2.1	5.8
Columbus	82.5	8.2	1.6	0.0	0.0	0.5	2.1	0.8	4.3
Dallas	80.4	11.0	1.2	0.2	0.2	0.2	1.3	1.4	4.1
Denver	75.2	9.9	4.0	0.4	0.2	0.8	2.2	1.2	6.0
Des Moines	80.8	10.8	1.6	0.0	0.0	0.2	2.0	0.7	3.9
Durham	73.6	13.2	3.6	0.0	0.0	0.7	3.4	0.8	4.7
Edison	50.2	7.2	8.4	18.0	3.7	0.4	6.2	1.6	3.7
El Paso	79.5	10.8	1.9	0.0	0.0	0.2	2.1	2.7	2.8
Eugene	71.1	9.6	3.9	0.0	0.0	4.6	4.5	0.7	5.6
Evansville	84.9	9.3	0.7	0.0	0.0	0.2	1.7	0.8	2.4
Fargo	81.4	8.3	0.7	0.0	0.0	0.8	4.1	0.9	3.7
Ft. Collins	74.4	9.4	0.9	0.0	0.0	4.3	2.7	1.4	6.9
Ft. Lauderdale	78.1	10.1	3.3	0.2	0.2	0.5	1.8	1.5	4.3
Ft. Wayne	84.8	8.7	0.5	0.0	0.0	0.3	1.3	1.0	3.3
Ft. Worth	80.4	11.0	1.2	0.2	0.2	0.2	1.3	1.4	4.1
Gainesville	75.4	11.3	2.8	0.0	0.0	2.9	2.8	1.3	3.4
Greensboro	82.6	10.1	1.2	0.0	0.0	0.2	1.5	1.0	3.4
Honolulu	65.2	15.2	7.5	0.0	0.0	1.1	5.5	2.2	3.2
Houston	78.3	12.3	2.5	0.0	0.0	0.3	1.5	1.6	3.4
Huntsville	85.5	9.7	0.3	0.0	0.0	0.1	1.1	1.0	2.2
Indianapolis	83.5	9.2	1.0	0.0	0.0	0.2	1.7	0.8	3.5
Irvine	73.5	11.0	5.6	0.3	0.2	0.8	2.6	1.3	4.6
Jackson	84.1	9.9	0.5	0.0	0.0	0.1	1.1	1.1	3.1
Jacksonville	81.1	10.5	1.1	0.0	0.0	0.6	1.5	1.5	3.7
Kansas City	82.6	9.2	1.4	0.0	0.0	0.2	1.4	1.2	3.9
Knoxville	84.7	8.9	0.4	0.0	0.0	0.2	1.4	1.1	3.2
Las Vegas	78.5	11.3	3.5	0.0	0.0	0.4	1.9	1.5	2.9
Lexington	80.2	10.9	1.0	0.0	0.0	0.5	3.3	0.6	3.4
Lincoln	81.2	9.0	1.3	0.0	0.0	1.4	3.4	0.5	3.3
Little Rock	81.9	11.7	0.8	0.0	0.0	0.1	1.4	0.9	3.2
Los Angeles	73.5	11.0	5.6	0.3	0.2	0.8	2.6	1.3	4.6
Louisville	82.3	9.9	2.3	0.0	0.0	0.2	1.8	0.8	2.7
Madison	73.5	10.0	4.0	0.0	0.0	2.2	5.5	0.8	3.9

Table continued on next page.

MSA[1]	Car/Truck/Van		Public Transportation			Bicycle	Walked	Other Means	Worked at Home
	Drove Alone	Car-pooled	Bus	Subway	Railroad				
Manchester	82.9	8.4	0.7	0.0	0.1	0.3	2.1	0.8	4.8
Miami	78.1	10.1	3.3	0.2	0.2	0.5	1.8	1.5	4.3
Milwaukee	80.2	9.0	3.6	0.0	0.0	0.5	2.7	0.8	3.1
Minneapolis	78.1	8.8	4.4	0.1	0.1	0.9	2.3	0.8	4.6
Naperville	70.6	9.0	5.1	3.4	3.1	0.6	3.1	1.1	4.0
Nashville	81.3	10.6	1.0	0.0	0.1	0.2	1.2	1.1	4.5
New Orleans	77.6	11.8	2.2	0.0	0.0	0.7	2.6	1.6	3.2
New York	50.2	7.2	8.4	18.0	3.7	0.4	6.2	1.6	3.7
Oakland	62.0	10.1	7.8	5.2	1.0	1.5	4.4	1.6	5.7
Oklahoma City	82.7	10.7	0.5	0.0	0.0	0.3	1.6	1.0	3.2
Omaha	81.8	10.2	0.8	0.0	0.0	0.2	2.3	0.8	3.9
Orlando	80.7	9.7	1.7	0.0	0.0	0.4	1.1	1.7	4.7
Overland Park	82.6	9.2	1.4	0.0	0.0	0.2	1.4	1.2	3.9
Oxnard	78.4	11.8	0.8	0.0	0.2	0.6	1.9	1.2	5.0
Philadelphia	73.2	8.7	5.5	1.5	2.1	0.6	3.8	0.8	3.6
Phoenix	75.3	13.0	2.4	0.0	0.0	0.8	1.7	1.7	5.0
Pittsburgh	77.0	9.4	5.3	0.2	0.0	0.2	3.8	0.7	3.1
Plano	80.4	11.0	1.2	0.2	0.2	0.2	1.3	1.4	4.1
Portland	71.7	10.3	4.9	0.3	0.3	2.0	3.2	0.9	5.8
Providence	80.9	9.0	1.7	0.1	0.9	0.3	2.8	1.0	3.3
Provo	71.8	12.8	2.3	0.0	0.0	0.9	5.3	1.1	5.7
Raleigh	79.6	10.6	0.9	0.0	0.0	0.3	1.6	1.2	5.7
Reno	77.6	10.4	3.0	0.0	0.0	0.6	2.9	1.8	3.7
Richmond	81.2	9.8	1.8	0.0	0.0	0.4	1.5	0.9	4.4
Riverside	75.8	14.6	1.1	0.1	0.4	0.3	1.9	1.1	4.6
Rochester	81.1	9.0	2.0	0.1	0.0	0.5	3.3	0.7	3.3
Sacramento	75.3	12.0	2.0	0.2	0.2	1.6	2.1	1.2	5.1
St. Louis	81.9	9.1	2.1	0.4	0.1	0.2	1.6	0.9	3.6
St. Paul	78.1	8.8	4.4	0.1	0.1	0.9	2.3	0.8	4.6
St. Petersburg	80.5	9.4	1.4	0.0	0.0	0.6	1.6	1.5	5.0
Salt Lake City	75.8	12.2	2.5	0.2	0.2	0.8	2.2	1.1	4.9
San Antonio	79.0	11.7	2.4	0.0	0.0	0.2	2.1	1.5	3.2
San Diego	75.2	10.6	2.8	0.0	0.3	0.6	2.9	1.2	6.1
San Francisco	62.0	10.1	7.8	5.2	1.0	1.5	4.4	1.6	5.7
San Jose	76.6	10.2	2.4	0.2	0.7	1.4	2.3	1.8	4.3
Santa Ana	73.5	11.0	5.6	0.3	0.2	0.8	2.6	1.3	4.6
Savannah	81.1	10.5	1.9	0.0	0.0	0.4	1.8	1.2	3.1
Seattle	69.4	11.6	7.9	0.0	0.3	0.9	3.7	1.1	5.0
Spokane	76.9	10.3	3.0	0.0	0.0	0.8	2.6	1.1	5.2
Springfield	81.7	10.2	0.5	0.0	0.0	0.4	2.4	1.0	3.9
Tampa	80.5	9.4	1.4	0.0	0.0	0.6	1.6	1.5	5.0
Tulsa	81.6	11.4	0.5	0.0	0.0	0.2	1.6	1.3	3.4
Virginia Beach	80.4	9.4	1.6	0.0	0.0	0.4	2.8	1.1	4.4
Warren	84.1	8.6	1.7	0.0	0.0	0.3	1.6	0.8	3.0
Washington	66.5	10.8	5.3	7.7	0.7	0.5	3.1	0.9	4.5
Wichita	84.6	9.1	0.5	0.0	0.0	0.4	1.4	0.8	3.2
U.S.	75.8	10.4	2.7	1.7	0.5	0.5	2.9	1.2	4.1

Note: Figures shown are percentages and cover workers 16 years of age and older; (1) Metropolitan Statistical Area - see Appendix B for areas included
Source: U.S. Census Bureau, 2007-2009 American Community Survey 3-Year Estimates

Travel Time to Work: City

City	Less Than 15 Minutes	15 to 29 Minutes	30 to 44 Minutes	45 to 59 Minutes	60 to 89 Minutes	90 Minutes or More
Albuquerque	27.9	48.6	16.3	3.3	2.4	1.6
Anchorage	38.7	45.1	11.2	2.4	1.3	1.3
Ann Arbor	40.6	39.6	12.0	4.0	3.1	0.7
Athens	47.9	35.4	9.5	2.1	2.5	2.7
Atlanta	23.9	42.4	20.5	6.1	4.3	2.9
Austin	26.4	44.6	19.7	4.7	2.9	1.7
Baltimore	18.4	38.5	24.2	7.3	7.5	4.2
Bellevue	28.8	42.4	21.1	4.3	2.8	0.7
Birmingham	25.0	49.2	19.1	3.5	2.1	1.2
Boise City	39.0	48.5	9.0	1.7	1.1	0.7
Boston	17.0	33.8	30.2	10.3	6.7	1.9
Boulder	45.9	35.5	10.5	4.4	2.7	1.0
Cambridge	24.4	37.4	25.9	8.3	3.3	0.7
Cary	25.7	48.2	19.1	3.9	1.8	1.2
Charleston	31.0	46.9	15.6	3.8	1.4	1.3
Charlotte	24.1	43.1	22.7	5.5	2.9	1.7
Chattanooga	36.2	47.6	12.0	2.1	1.0	1.0
Chicago	13.3	27.3	29.6	14.3	11.7	3.9
Cincinnati	28.6	45.5	18.1	3.5	2.6	1.7
Cleveland	24.0	45.2	19.5	4.9	4.1	2.3
Colorado Spgs.	30.7	47.8	14.1	3.1	2.8	1.5
Columbia	41.2	42.9	10.2	2.9	1.4	1.4
Columbus	26.8	50.9	16.8	2.7	1.6	1.3
Dallas	22.2	40.5	23.7	7.0	4.9	1.8
Denver	22.0	42.6	21.8	8.0	3.6	2.0
Des Moines	37.0	47.2	10.7	2.3	1.6	1.2
Durham	30.9	45.6	15.2	3.6	2.8	1.8
Edison	20.5	28.1	18.7	9.5	13.7	9.5
El Paso	24.9	47.0	21.3	3.7	1.9	1.2
Eugene	44.3	44.5	6.7	1.5	1.8	1.2
Evansville	42.1	43.7	9.2	2.4	1.8	0.9
Fargo	54.1	39.8	3.4	1.1	0.9	0.8
Ft. Collins	43.8	38.9	8.6	3.8	3.3	1.6
Ft. Lauderdale	27.7	39.8	20.3	4.9	5.4	1.9
Ft. Wayne	29.5	54.4	10.5	2.9	1.4	1.4
Ft. Worth	23.3	40.2	21.7	7.7	5.2	1.8
Gainesville	45.4	41.7	8.9	1.8	1.5	0.7
Greensboro	35.9	46.6	11.7	2.7	1.4	1.7
Honolulu	23.4	39.1	27.6	6.4	3.0	0.6
Houston	20.9	39.4	24.9	7.6	5.1	2.0
Huntsville	37.2	47.6	11.4	1.3	1.2	1.3
Indianapolis	25.0	47.2	20.1	4.0	2.4	1.3
Irvine	27.6	45.9	16.0	4.1	4.8	1.7
Jackson	24.6	53.1	17.8	2.3	1.2	1.0
Jacksonville	21.4	45.8	23.2	5.5	2.8	1.3
Kansas City	27.0	46.7	20.1	3.9	1.6	0.9
Knoxville	33.7	49.3	13.0	1.8	1.5	0.7
Las Vegas	18.3	45.6	25.6	5.6	3.3	1.6
Lexington	32.5	48.2	13.2	2.8	2.0	1.4
Lincoln	40.8	47.2	7.4	2.2	1.7	0.7
Little Rock	37.5	48.0	10.2	1.8	1.4	1.1
Los Angeles	18.4	33.9	27.4	9.1	8.2	3.1
Louisville	24.9	51.2	17.6	3.4	1.6	1.4
Madison	37.0	46.3	11.6	2.5	1.7	0.9
Manchester	34.2	40.4	14.6	5.5	3.6	1.7

Table continued on next page.

City	Less Than 15 Minutes	15 to 29 Minutes	30 to 44 Minutes	45 to 59 Minutes	60 to 89 Minutes	90 Minutes or More
Miami	19.2	39.9	24.8	8.4	5.9	1.9
Milwaukee	26.8	46.0	19.1	4.2	2.6	1.3
Minneapolis	23.9	50.1	18.5	4.0	2.5	1.1
Naperville	21.8	29.9	19.1	9.5	14.4	5.3
Nashville	22.0	46.2	23.6	5.3	1.7	1.2
New Orleans	25.9	44.2	20.2	4.7	3.1	1.9
New York	11.1	22.2	26.5	15.0	18.5	6.8
Oakland	18.9	38.1	23.4	9.5	7.6	2.5
Oklahoma City	30.2	50.1	15.0	2.1	1.3	1.4
Omaha	37.2	48.8	10.7	1.6	1.1	0.7
Orlando	22.5	42.2	23.9	6.0	3.6	1.8
Overland Park	34.7	46.4	14.1	2.7	0.9	1.2
Oxnard	26.3	41.6	19.5	5.9	4.0	2.8
Philadelphia	16.6	32.5	27.4	11.5	8.2	3.8
Phoenix	22.2	39.5	25.8	6.9	4.2	1.5
Pittsburgh	27.2	44.1	18.1	5.7	3.2	1.7
Plano	20.9	38.2	23.6	10.2	6.3	0.8
Portland	23.0	45.6	20.6	5.3	3.6	1.8
Providence	33.3	40.8	13.5	5.7	4.7	2.0
Provo	52.6	33.4	8.1	2.8	2.1	1.0
Raleigh	27.7	47.5	17.7	3.6	1.9	1.5
Reno	39.4	43.3	10.1	3.3	2.4	1.5
Richmond	30.1	48.5	13.7	2.4	3.0	2.2
Riverside	24.3	35.6	20.3	7.3	8.7	3.8
Rochester	37.7	45.6	10.5	2.9	2.4	1.0
Sacramento	26.5	44.6	18.4	5.0	3.1	2.4
St. Louis	24.0	42.8	21.8	5.6	3.9	2.0
St. Paul	28.4	46.6	16.9	4.3	2.4	1.4
St. Petersburg	27.3	44.0	19.7	5.6	2.1	1.3
Salt Lake City	33.8	47.1	13.4	2.8	1.5	1.3
San Antonio	23.2	44.0	23.1	5.2	2.9	1.6
San Diego	25.3	47.3	19.3	3.8	2.6	1.6
San Francisco	15.4	35.5	28.5	10.9	8.0	1.8
San Jose	19.4	43.4	24.3	6.6	4.6	1.7
Santa Ana	20.5	43.3	23.3	4.8	6.1	2.0
Savannah	30.7	52.7	12.8	1.5	1.6	0.7
Seattle	21.4	42.3	24.5	6.5	4.1	1.2
Spokane	34.6	45.1	13.2	3.3	2.3	1.4
Springfield	41.1	46.6	7.8	1.6	1.5	1.5
Tampa	28.1	42.5	19.9	5.0	3.0	1.5
Tulsa	36.7	50.3	8.7	1.9	1.2	1.1
Virginia Beach	24.5	45.2	22.2	4.8	1.9	1.4
Warren	23.2	42.8	23.7	6.6	2.9	0.9
Washington	14.8	36.3	28.5	10.5	7.6	2.3
Wichita	38.1	49.4	9.5	1.1	0.8	1.0
U.S.	28.5	36.2	19.7	7.5	5.6	2.5

Note: Figures are percentages and include workers 16 years old and over
Source: U.S. Census Bureau, 2007-2009 American Community Survey 3-Year Estimates

Travel Time to Work: Metro Area

MSA[1]	Less Than 15 Minutes	15 to 29 Minutes	30 to 44 Minutes	45 to 59 Minutes	60 to 89 Minutes	90 Minutes or More
Albuquerque	25.8	42.7	20.2	6.1	3.5	1.8
Anchorage	37.1	41.5	10.9	4.2	4.3	2.0
Ann Arbor	29.4	41.4	17.8	6.1	4.0	1.2
Athens	40.3	38.2	12.6	3.4	3.0	2.5
Atlanta	19.2	33.0	24.3	11.3	8.8	3.4
Austin	24.7	39.0	22.3	7.6	4.5	1.8
Baltimore	19.9	35.2	24.0	9.9	7.7	3.4
Bellevue	21.5	36.2	23.9	9.2	6.9	2.4
Birmingham	21.7	39.7	23.2	8.8	4.5	2.0
Boise City	31.8	42.7	17.1	4.7	2.5	1.1
Boston	22.7	31.7	24.3	10.6	8.3	2.4
Boulder	35.7	37.7	15.3	6.4	3.5	1.3
Cambridge	22.7	31.7	24.3	10.6	8.3	2.4
Cary	23.3	42.3	22.3	7.0	3.4	1.6
Charleston	25.0	39.5	22.6	7.8	3.5	1.6
Charlotte	23.6	40.4	23.2	7.6	3.6	1.7
Chattanooga	27.0	43.9	20.2	5.4	2.3	1.4
Chicago	20.3	29.6	24.6	11.7	10.3	3.5
Cincinnati	26.1	40.6	22.2	6.5	3.0	1.5
Cleveland	25.8	40.5	22.3	6.9	3.1	1.4
Colorado Spgs.	29.5	44.2	16.9	4.6	3.1	1.6
Columbia	25.9	42.0	21.1	6.5	2.9	1.6
Columbus	26.4	44.5	19.9	5.5	2.3	1.5
Dallas	22.5	36.3	24.0	9.6	5.9	1.7
Denver	21.0	38.5	24.3	9.8	4.5	1.9
Des Moines	34.1	45.9	13.9	3.4	1.6	1.0
Durham	28.5	41.9	18.7	5.9	3.3	1.7
Edison	18.1	27.1	23.1	11.7	13.9	6.0
El Paso	24.3	45.5	22.6	4.4	2.2	1.2
Eugene	37.5	43.7	11.8	3.0	2.4	1.7
Evansville	34.7	42.0	15.7	4.1	2.3	1.2
Fargo	47.5	41.1	7.3	2.0	1.0	1.1
Ft. Collins	36.1	39.3	13.2	5.1	4.4	1.9
Ft. Lauderdale	19.9	36.0	27.0	8.9	6.3	2.0
Ft. Wayne	28.3	50.1	14.8	3.6	1.6	1.5
Ft. Worth	22.5	36.3	24.0	9.6	5.9	1.7
Gainesville	32.0	43.4	17.0	3.7	2.7	1.2
Greensboro	30.9	43.7	16.8	5.0	2.0	1.7
Honolulu	21.6	33.8	26.7	9.7	6.5	1.8
Houston	20.6	34.7	24.9	10.1	7.4	2.3
Huntsville	28.5	44.3	19.2	5.1	1.6	1.2
Indianapolis	25.3	40.7	22.7	6.8	3.1	1.4
Irvine	20.9	34.9	24.6	8.8	7.9	2.9
Jackson	23.6	45.5	22.0	4.8	2.6	1.5
Jacksonville	22.1	40.0	23.9	8.4	4.0	1.6
Kansas City	27.8	41.7	20.9	6.1	2.4	1.2
Knoxville	27.6	45.6	19.3	4.5	2.0	1.1
Las Vegas	20.4	45.7	24.3	5.1	3.1	1.4
Lexington	32.4	43.5	16.7	3.9	2.2	1.3
Lincoln	39.2	46.5	9.5	2.4	1.6	0.8
Little Rock	30.9	39.5	19.6	6.0	2.9	1.1
Los Angeles	20.9	34.9	24.6	8.8	7.9	2.9
Louisville	25.1	45.0	20.3	5.7	2.5	1.4
Madison	32.9	42.8	16.3	4.4	2.1	1.4
Manchester	28.7	34.8	19.3	8.1	6.5	2.6

Table continued on next page.

MSA[1]	Less Than 15 Minutes	15 to 29 Minutes	30 to 44 Minutes	45 to 59 Minutes	60 to 89 Minutes	90 Minutes or More
Miami	19.9	36.0	27.0	8.9	6.3	2.0
Milwaukee	28.3	42.7	20.4	5.1	2.2	1.2
Minneapolis	25.2	40.7	21.7	7.6	3.7	1.3
Naperville	20.3	29.6	24.6	11.7	10.3	3.5
Nashville	22.9	37.8	23.9	9.4	4.3	1.7
New Orleans	26.1	37.5	21.8	7.3	5.0	2.3
New York	18.1	27.1	23.1	11.7	13.9	6.0
Oakland	21.1	33.4	23.6	10.8	8.7	2.4
Oklahoma City	31.2	43.1	17.7	4.5	2.0	1.4
Omaha	34.4	46.1	14.1	3.1	1.4	0.9
Orlando	20.3	37.9	26.1	9.1	4.7	1.9
Overland Park	27.8	41.7	20.9	6.1	2.4	1.2
Oxnard	29.7	34.7	18.8	7.5	6.1	3.2
Philadelphia	23.4	33.9	22.8	10.0	7.1	2.8
Phoenix	22.8	36.3	25.3	8.8	5.2	1.6
Pittsburgh	27.5	36.0	21.0	8.6	5.2	1.9
Plano	22.5	36.3	24.0	9.6	5.9	1.7
Portland	25.7	39.0	21.7	7.4	4.4	1.8
Providence	30.2	38.1	17.4	7.2	4.9	2.2
Provo	41.0	34.1	14.7	5.3	3.4	1.5
Raleigh	23.3	42.3	22.3	7.0	3.4	1.6
Reno	32.2	45.3	14.5	4.1	2.4	1.6
Richmond	23.7	43.2	21.8	6.0	3.1	2.2
Riverside	25.4	32.4	18.6	8.2	9.8	5.6
Rochester	33.2	43.7	16.0	3.9	2.1	1.0
Sacramento	26.1	38.0	21.5	7.1	4.3	3.0
St. Louis	24.8	38.6	23.0	8.1	3.9	1.5
St. Paul	25.2	40.7	21.7	7.6	3.7	1.3
St. Petersburg	24.6	38.0	22.1	8.5	5.1	1.7
Salt Lake City	26.7	45.0	19.8	4.6	2.5	1.3
San Antonio	23.8	40.1	23.2	7.2	3.9	1.8
San Diego	24.7	41.8	21.0	6.2	4.2	2.1
San Francisco	21.1	33.4	23.6	10.8	8.7	2.4
San Jose	22.9	43.3	21.6	6.2	4.4	1.7
Santa Ana	20.9	34.9	24.6	8.8	7.9	2.9
Savannah	24.3	47.1	19.9	5.5	2.1	1.1
Seattle	21.5	36.2	23.9	9.2	6.9	2.4
Spokane	30.1	45.2	17.1	4.4	1.9	1.3
Springfield	30.8	43.6	17.3	4.5	2.3	1.6
Tampa	24.6	38.0	22.1	8.5	5.1	1.7
Tulsa	31.3	44.5	16.3	4.5	2.1	1.3
Virginia Beach	26.5	42.0	20.5	6.4	3.3	1.4
Warren	23.1	37.7	23.6	8.9	4.9	1.8
Washington	15.8	29.7	25.3	13.4	12.0	3.8
Wichita	36.0	45.9	13.7	2.4	1.0	1.0
U.S.	28.5	36.2	19.7	7.5	5.6	2.5

Note: Figures are percentages and include workers 16 years old and over; (1) Metropolitan Statistical Area - see Appendix B for areas included
Source: U.S. Census Bureau, 2007-2009 American Community Survey 3-Year Estimates

2008 Presidential Election Results

City	Area Covered	Obama	McCain	Nader	Other
Albuquerque	Bernalillo County	60.0	38.7	0.6	0.7
Anchorage	Districts 18 - 32	43.0	55.9	1.0	0.0
Ann Arbor	Washtenaw County	69.6	28.8	0.5	1.1
Athens	Clarke County	64.8	33.6	0.1	1.5
Atlanta	Fulton County	67.1	32.1	0.0	0.8
Austin	Travis County	63.5	34.3	0.2	2.0
Baltimore	Baltimore Independent City	87.2	11.7	0.4	0.8
Bellevue	King County	70.0	28.0	0.8	1.2
Birmingham	Jefferson County	52.2	47.1	0.2	0.6
Boise City	Ada County	45.5	51.6	1.1	1.8
Boston	Suffolk County	77.5	21.1	0.7	0.7
Boulder	Boulder County	72.3	26.1	0.5	1.1
Cambridge	Middlesex County	64.0	34.3	0.8	0.9
Cary	Wake County	56.7	42.3	0.0	0.9
Charleston	Charleston County	53.5	45.2	0.3	1.0
Charlotte	Mecklenburg County	61.8	37.4	0.0	0.7
Chattanooga	Hamilton County	43.6	55.4	0.3	0.7
Chicago	Cook County	76.2	22.8	0.4	0.6
Cincinnati	Hamilton County	53.0	46.0	0.4	0.6
Cleveland	Cuyahoga County	68.7	30.0	0.5	0.8
Colorado Spgs.	El Paso County	39.9	58.7	0.4	1.0
Columbia	Richland County	64.0	35.1	0.2	0.7
Columbus	Franklin County	59.6	38.9	0.5	1.0
Dallas	Dallas County	57.2	41.9	0.1	0.9
Denver	Denver County	75.5	23.0	0.6	0.9
Des Moines	Polk County	56.4	41.8	0.4	1.3
Durham	Durham County	75.6	23.6	0.1	0.7
Edison	Middlesex County	60.2	38.4	0.6	0.7
El Paso	El Paso County	65.7	33.3	0.1	0.9
Eugene	Lane County	62.3	34.9	1.0	1.8
Evansville	Vanderburgh County	50.8	48.3	0.0	0.9
Fargo	Cass County	52.4	45.3	1.1	1.2
Ft. Collins	Larimer County	54.0	44.3	0.5	1.2
Ft. Lauderdale	Broward County	67.0	32.3	0.2	0.4
Ft. Wayne	Allen County	47.4	51.8	0.1	0.8
Ft. Worth	Tarrant County	43.7	55.4	0.1	0.8
Gainesville	Alachua County	60.0	38.5	0.5	1.0
Greensboro	Guilford County	58.8	40.4	0.0	0.8
Honolulu	Honolulu County	69.8	28.7	0.8	0.6
Houston	Harris County	50.4	48.8	0.1	0.7
Huntsville	Madison County	41.9	56.9	0.3	0.9
Indianapolis	Marion County	63.7	35.3	0.0	1.0
Irvine	Orange County	47.6	50.2	0.7	1.5
Jackson	Hinds County	69.2	30.3	0.1	0.4
Jacksonville	Duval County	48.6	50.5	0.2	0.6
Kansas City	Jackson County	62.1	36.8	0.5	0.6
Knoxville	Knox County	37.7	60.7	0.5	1.0
Las Vegas	Clark County	58.5	39.5	0.6	1.4
Lexington	Fayette County	51.7	46.9	0.6	0.7
Lincoln	Lancaster County	51.6	46.6	0.7	1.2
Little Rock	Pulaski County	55.1	43.5	0.6	0.8
Los Angeles	Los Angeles County	69.2	28.8	0.8	1.2
Louisville	Jefferson County	55.3	43.4	0.6	0.7
Madison	Dane County	72.8	25.8	0.5	0.8
Manchester	Hillsborough County	51.2	47.5	0.5	0.9
Miami	Miami-Dade County	57.8	41.7	0.2	0.3

Table continued on next page.

City	Area Covered	Obama	McCain	Nader	Other
Milwaukee	Milwaukee County	67.3	31.4	0.5	0.8
Minneapolis	Hennepin County	63.4	34.8	0.8	1.0
Naperville	Du Page County	54.7	43.9	0.5	0.8
Nashville	Davidson County	59.9	38.9	0.4	0.8
New Orleans	Orleans Parish	79.4	19.1	0.3	1.2
New York	Bronx County	88.7	10.9	0.1	0.2
New York	Kings County	79.4	20.0	0.2	0.4
New York	New York County	85.7	13.5	0.3	0.5
New York	Queens County	74.9	24.4	0.3	0.4
New York	Richmond County	47.6	51.7	0.4	0.4
Oakland	Alameda County	78.5	19.2	0.9	1.4
Oklahoma City	Oklahoma County	41.6	58.4	0.0	0.0
Omaha	Douglas County	51.5	46.9	0.6	1.0
Orlando	Orange County	59.0	40.4	0.2	0.4
Overland Park	Johnson County	44.7	53.7	0.5	1.1
Oxnard	Ventura County	55.0	42.8	0.7	1.6
Philadelphia	Philadelphia County	83.0	16.3	0.4	0.2
Phoenix	Maricopa County	43.9	54.4	0.4	1.2
Pittsburgh	Allegheny County	57.1	41.6	0.6	0.7
Plano	Collin County	36.7	62.2	0.1	1.1
Portland	Multnomah County	76.7	20.6	1.1	1.6
Providence	Providence County	66.3	32.1	1.0	0.6
Provo	Utah County	18.8	77.7	0.7	2.8
Raleigh	Wake County	56.7	42.3	0.0	0.9
Reno	Washoe County	55.2	42.6	0.6	1.5
Richmond	Richmond Independent City	79.1	20.0	0.2	0.6
Riverside	Riverside County	50.2	47.9	0.7	1.1
Rochester	Monroe County	58.2	40.5	0.6	0.8
Sacramento	Sacramento County	58.3	39.3	0.9	1.5
St. Louis	Saint Louis city	83.5	15.5	0.4	0.6
St. Paul	Ramsey County	66.0	32.1	0.9	1.1
St. Petersburg	Pinellas County	53.4	45.2	0.5	0.9
Salt Lake City	Salt Lake County	48.2	48.1	1.0	2.7
San Antonio	Bexar County	52.2	46.7	0.0	1.0
San Diego	San Diego County	54.1	43.9	0.7	1.2
San Francisco	San Francisco County	84.2	13.7	1.0	1.2
San Jose	Santa Clara County	69.4	28.6	0.7	1.3
Santa Ana	Orange County	47.6	50.2	0.7	1.5
Savannah	Chatham County	56.8	42.4	0.0	0.7
Seattle	King County	70.0	28.0	0.8	1.2
Spokane	Spokane County	48.2	49.3	1.2	1.3
Springfield	Greene County	41.3	57.1	0.6	1.1
Tampa	Hillsborough County	53.1	45.9	0.4	0.7
Tulsa	Tulsa County	37.8	62.2	0.0	0.0
Virginia Beach	Virginia Beach Independent City	49.1	49.8	0.3	0.7
Warren	Macomb County	53.4	44.8	0.8	1.0
Washington	District of Columbia	92.5	6.5	0.4	0.6
Wichita	Sedgwick County	42.5	55.2	0.8	1.5
U.S.	U.S.	52.9	45.6	0.6	0.9

Note: Results are percentages and may not add to 100% due to rounding
Source: Dave Leip's Atlas of U.S. Presidential Elections, www.uselectionatlas.org

House Price Index (HPI)

Metro Area[1]	National Ranking[3]	Quarterly Change (%)	One-Year Change (%)	Five-Year Change (%)
Albuquerque	213	-1.04	-2.49	5.20
Anchorage	59	0.42	0.46	8.17
Ann Arbor	85	0.24	0.08	-21.01
Athens	209	-0.77	-2.38	-0.02
Atlanta	257	-1.69	-4.34	-9.92
Austin	139	-1.05	-0.74	18.78
Baltimore	190	-1.34	-1.95	-8.70
Bellevue[2]	252	-1.90	-4.14	-3.74
Birmingham	220	-0.48	-2.71	2.11
Boise City	306	-2.39	-9.81	-15.96
Boston[2]	44	0.03	0.78	-12.71
Boulder	87	-0.03	0.06	4.77
Cambridge[2]	42	0.18	0.88	-9.41
Cary	174	-0.58	-1.55	8.94
Charleston	228	-1.13	-2.96	-3.61
Charlotte	223	-1.29	-2.81	5.49
Chattanooga	65	-0.75	0.37	5.48
Chicago[2]	230	-0.77	-3.02	-13.19
Cincinnati	83	-0.13	0.09	-2.33
Cleveland	166	-0.58	-1.37	-10.45
Colorado Spgs.	169	-1.01	-1.44	-2.69
Columbia	199	-0.75	-2.09	6.07
Columbus	110	-0.33	-0.34	-3.24
Dallas[2]	103	-0.43	-0.26	6.73
Denver	80	-0.14	0.12	-2.67
Des Moines	107	-0.56	-0.28	-0.16
Durham	217	-1.91	-2.67	7.57
Edison[2]	104	-0.03	-0.27	-11.38
El Paso	99	0.47	-0.21	17.20
Eugene	255	-2.66	-4.22	-3.31
Evansville	39	-0.79	1.01	2.64
Fargo	10	1.23	2.07	8.88
Ft. Collins	153	-1.42	-1.12	-1.82
Ft. Lauderdale[2]	142	-1.77	-0.80	-37.99
Ft. Wayne	37	0.15	1.07	-1.48
Ft. Worth[2]	151	-1.07	-1.04	6.70
Gainesville	247	1.36	-4.00	-9.19
Greensboro	115	-0.99	-0.48	2.25
Honolulu	11	0.10	1.98	0.61
Houston	122	-0.02	-0.53	14.40
Huntsville	131	-0.42	-0.65	15.55
Indianapolis	98	0.26	-0.20	-0.76
Irvine[2]	75	-0.51	0.18	-24.69
Jackson	123	-1.05	-0.53	6.25
Jacksonville	292	-2.38	-7.28	-19.37
Kansas City	134	-0.79	-0.69	-3.09
Knoxville	130	-0.19	-0.65	8.81
Las Vegas	282	-2.55	-5.93	-51.18
Lexington	109	0.39	-0.34	4.92
Lincoln	31	-0.90	1.20	0.26
Little Rock	149	-0.88	-1.01	6.53
Los Angeles[2]	90	-0.68	-0.04	-23.44
Louisville	93	-0.76	-0.11	3.60
Madison	136	-0.30	-0.71	-0.20
Manchester	158	-0.68	-1.24	-14.77

Table continued on next page.

Metro Area[1]	National Ranking[3]	Quarterly Change (%)	One-Year Change (%)	Five-Year Change (%)
Miami[2]	249	-1.52	-4.05	-30.80
Milwaukee	178	-0.89	-1.66	-4.85
Minneapolis	195	-2.03	-1.99	-17.00
Naperville[2]	230	-0.77	-3.02	-13.19
Nashville	124	-0.62	-0.55	8.04
New Orleans	173	-0.94	-1.54	3.40
New York[2]	147	-0.17	-0.97	-8.27
Oakland[2]	60	-1.00	0.46	-30.44
Oklahoma City	43	-0.43	0.81	9.53
Omaha	86	-0.72	0.06	0.37
Orlando	295	-2.10	-8.05	-33.34
Overland Park	134	-0.79	-0.69	-3.09
Oxnard	137	-0.70	-0.72	-29.96
Philadelphia[2]	114	-0.51	-0.47	-0.59
Phoenix	301	-3.60	-8.92	-38.59
Pittsburgh	17	-0.21	1.63	9.03
Plano[2]	103	-0.43	-0.26	6.73
Portland	254	-1.66	-4.21	-4.50
Providence	148	-0.12	-1.00	-17.55
Provo	211	-0.30	-2.43	4.99
Raleigh	174	-0.58	-1.55	8.94
Reno	309	-2.87	-10.28	-45.36
Richmond	235	-0.48	-3.24	-0.55
Riverside	106	-0.70	-0.28	-40.70
Rochester	53	-0.09	0.61	5.45
Sacramento	258	-1.75	-4.35	-40.91
St. Louis	113	-0.62	-0.43	-1.83
St. Paul	195	-2.03	-1.99	-17.00
St. Petersburg	286	-3.29	-6.53	-30.69
Salt Lake City	196	-0.48	-2.01	8.86
San Antonio	49	0.37	0.67	14.37
San Diego	82	-0.54	0.11	-29.09
San Francisco[2]	127	-0.75	-0.59	-16.39
San Jose	8	-0.66	2.18	-18.69
Santa Ana[2]	75	-0.51	0.18	-24.69
Savannah	296	-3.52	-8.13	-2.24
Seattle[2]	252	-1.90	-4.14	-3.74
Spokane	237	-1.31	-3.58	6.60
Springfield	163	-0.89	-1.32	1.52
Tampa	286	-3.29	-6.53	-30.69
Tulsa	81	0.00	0.12	10.88
Virginia Beach	219	-1.44	-2.70	-1.31
Warren[2]	214	0.05	-2.56	-31.92
Washington[2]	88	-0.51	0.02	-16.96
Wichita	72	-0.60	0.26	9.10
U.S.[4]	-	-0.84	-3.95	-11.45

Note: The HPI is a weighted repeat sales index. It measures average price changes in repeat sales or refinancings on the same properties. This information is obtained by reviewing repeat mortgage transactions on single-family properties whose mortgages have been purchased or securitized by Fannie Mae or Freddie Mac in January 1975; (1) figures cover the Metropolitan Statistical Area (MSA) unless noted otherwise - see Appendix B for areas included; (2) Metropolitan Division - see Appendix B for areas included; (3) Rankings are based on annual percentage change, for all MSAs containing at least 15,000 transactions over the last 10 years and ranges from 1 to 309; (4) figures based on a weighted division average; all figures are for the period ended December 31, 2010; n/a not available; n/r not ranked
Source: Federal Housing Finance Agency, House Price Index, February 24, 2011

Year Housing Structure Built: City

City	2000 or Later	1990 -2000	1980 -1989	1970 -1979	1960 -1969	1950 -1959	1940 -1949	Before 1940	Median Year
Albuquerque	16.5	15.0	15.4	21.4	10.8	13.4	4.5	3.0	1979
Anchorage	12.2	11.0	27.4	28.7	11.4	7.2	1.7	0.3	1980
Ann Arbor	5.7	10.4	11.1	18.8	20.5	12.9	6.1	14.5	1968
Athens	20.4	18.7	15.3	17.1	11.8	7.2	3.1	6.5	1983
Atlanta	18.7	9.4	8.6	10.5	15.4	14.4	7.2	15.8	1968
Austin	17.8	15.7	22.3	21.7	9.5	6.4	3.4	3.3	1983
Baltimore	3.5	3.1	4.2	6.1	9.0	17.7	15.0	41.4	1946
Bellevue	8.9	15.7	19.6	22.8	18.9	12.2	1.3	0.6	1977
Birmingham	4.6	5.5	10.7	16.0	16.0	19.6	10.2	17.5	1962
Boise City	13.2	21.0	15.1	21.8	7.9	8.1	4.6	8.3	1980
Boston	5.4	3.5	4.9	7.2	7.8	6.9	6.1	58.3	1939
Boulder	5.2	11.2	16.6	24.8	20.9	9.9	1.6	9.8	1973
Cambridge	6.4	4.8	7.0	9.1	6.0	4.1	4.6	58.1	1939
Cary	25.9	35.9	21.2	11.4	3.2	1.4	0.5	0.5	1993
Charleston	22.6	13.3	13.4	11.9	9.2	8.3	5.0	16.4	1979
Charlotte	22.3	21.3	16.7	13.9	10.6	8.4	3.3	3.5	1986
Chattanooga	9.4	9.0	11.4	15.9	15.7	14.6	8.1	16.0	1967
Chicago	6.7	4.0	3.9	7.0	10.0	12.9	10.4	45.1	1945
Cincinnati	3.7	2.7	4.0	8.9	12.8	13.0	9.5	45.5	1945
Cleveland	3.1	2.1	1.9	4.9	7.1	12.6	12.2	56.1	1939
Colorado Spgs.	17.4	15.0	19.2	20.8	11.0	8.2	1.9	6.5	1981
Columbia	12.3	9.2	12.0	11.8	15.0	18.9	9.9	11.0	1967
Columbus	11.9	14.8	12.3	13.6	13.0	14.1	6.2	14.0	1972
Dallas	10.7	9.3	18.0	19.0	15.6	15.3	6.1	5.9	1974
Denver	11.2	6.4	8.0	15.1	12.4	16.7	7.8	22.4	1963
Des Moines	6.7	6.3	6.6	13.1	11.1	16.8	9.6	29.7	1956
Durham	23.1	18.9	16.8	12.5	10.5	6.8	4.1	7.3	1985
Edison	5.7	8.6	25.6	14.3	16.3	18.7	4.9	5.8	1973
El Paso	13.7	13.4	15.5	20.5	13.3	13.2	4.2	6.1	1976
Eugene	11.5	17.8	8.4	23.4	14.1	10.8	6.2	7.8	1975
Evansville	3.6	4.9	8.2	11.6	11.8	16.8	13.3	29.7	1954
Fargo	15.0	22.0	14.4	17.3	7.1	9.7	3.2	11.3	1981
Ft. Collins	18.5	21.8	17.3	22.3	8.0	4.1	1.7	6.2	1984
Ft. Lauderdale	11.1	4.9	6.7	22.2	26.2	23.3	4.1	1.5	1968
Ft. Wayne	6.1	12.2	11.1	13.6	17.0	13.1	6.8	20.0	1966
Ft. Worth	25.3	10.7	14.9	11.1	9.7	12.8	6.9	8.7	1981
Gainesville	12.2	15.6	19.2	23.0	14.2	10.3	3.0	2.4	1979
Greensboro	13.4	18.2	17.8	16.3	13.6	11.1	5.0	4.7	1980
Honolulu	5.7	7.7	9.7	28.9	21.7	13.9	6.5	5.9	1971
Houston	13.5	9.0	14.4	26.8	15.2	11.8	4.9	4.5	1975
Huntsville	11.8	11.3	15.8	18.1	24.7	11.6	3.3	3.3	1974
Indianapolis	8.9	11.5	11.1	14.0	14.4	13.6	7.4	19.0	1967
Irvine	29.3	16.9	21.2	26.5	4.7	0.7	0.2	0.5	1988
Jackson	5.0	7.7	13.8	25.9	21.6	16.3	6.1	3.7	1971
Jacksonville	19.0	15.6	17.9	13.4	11.4	11.7	5.8	5.3	1981
Kansas City	8.9	8.8	9.4	12.3	12.7	14.5	8.1	25.4	1962
Knoxville	10.3	11.6	14.0	20.1	14.2	14.0	7.1	8.7	1973
Las Vegas	20.9	34.6	17.9	11.5	8.7	4.8	1.4	0.2	1992
Lexington	14.8	16.6	16.3	16.3	13.8	10.5	3.9	7.8	1979
Lincoln	14.5	16.3	11.2	17.5	10.2	12.5	3.6	14.3	1975
Little Rock	9.6	10.4	16.0	22.5	14.8	12.2	5.5	9.0	1974
Los Angeles	4.5	5.5	10.3	14.4	14.5	18.4	11.4	21.0	1960
Louisville	11.9	10.7	6.5	13.9	14.4	15.9	8.3	18.5	1965
Madison	14.6	12.2	10.1	16.9	14.0	11.4	4.9	15.9	1972
Manchester	6.9	6.2	12.9	11.6	8.9	9.6	7.3	36.4	1956

Table continued on next page.

City	2000 or Later	1990 -2000	1980 -1989	1970 -1979	1960 -1969	1950 -1959	1940 -1949	Before 1940	Median Year
Miami	13.3	6.7	7.9	15.3	11.6	17.5	17.6	10.2	1964
Milwaukee	2.8	2.5	3.4	8.1	11.0	20.1	10.4	41.8	1948
Minneapolis	6.6	2.6	6.4	9.5	7.8	10.4	7.8	48.9	1941
Naperville	12.8	27.7	27.9	17.9	7.0	2.8	1.1	3.0	1987
Nashville	12.5	12.6	16.5	18.3	15.4	12.3	5.4	7.0	1975
New Orleans	5.8	3.4	7.8	12.0	12.0	12.1	11.2	35.7	1953
New York	4.2	3.5	4.6	7.1	12.1	14.4	11.5	42.7	1946
Oakland	4.5	4.4	4.4	7.6	11.2	12.9	15.5	39.5	1947
Oklahoma City	12.2	10.0	16.4	18.6	14.3	11.8	6.9	9.8	1974
Omaha	6.0	9.3	9.5	17.5	16.3	13.0	5.7	22.6	1965
Orlando	21.2	15.9	19.8	14.5	9.4	11.3	3.5	4.5	1983
Overland Park	14.7	23.8	20.0	14.0	14.4	9.1	2.3	1.8	1984
Oxnard	12.1	8.1	12.0	21.1	24.0	15.0	5.0	2.6	1972
Philadelphia	2.9	2.3	3.7	6.7	10.6	17.8	16.3	39.7	1946
Phoenix	16.2	15.7	18.9	22.0	10.7	11.4	3.3	1.8	1980
Pittsburgh	2.8	2.6	4.5	6.7	7.2	14.1	10.4	51.7	1939
Plano	14.0	37.0	27.5	16.3	3.5	1.0	0.4	0.4	1990
Portland	9.7	8.2	5.6	11.3	9.8	12.9	9.2	33.1	1956
Providence	4.0	3.3	5.5	7.0	4.6	7.1	7.3	61.2	1939
Provo	13.0	17.2	11.4	24.5	10.6	8.6	6.6	8.0	1977
Raleigh	25.6	19.5	20.5	13.0	9.2	6.2	2.3	3.6	1988
Reno	21.0	19.6	15.1	17.4	11.4	8.1	3.6	3.8	1984
Richmond	5.9	3.0	7.2	12.6	12.4	15.0	11.2	32.8	1954
Riverside	13.6	10.0	15.0	20.6	11.6	18.4	4.0	6.7	1974
Rochester	1.6	1.9	2.5	7.2	6.6	9.9	7.5	62.8	1939
Sacramento	15.4	6.6	15.1	15.4	12.3	14.0	8.9	12.3	1972
St. Louis	3.5	2.4	3.6	4.5	6.2	10.5	10.2	59.2	1939
St. Paul	4.8	2.8	6.1	9.4	9.4	13.7	8.6	45.1	1946
St. Petersburg	4.8	4.3	9.8	20.3	20.0	26.3	6.4	8.2	1965
Salt Lake City	5.5	5.3	6.1	15.3	9.8	14.8	10.6	32.6	1955
San Antonio	16.6	13.4	17.6	18.5	11.1	11.0	5.5	6.3	1979
San Diego	9.6	10.5	18.0	23.5	13.1	13.3	5.0	7.0	1975
San Francisco	5.0	4.1	5.4	7.3	7.8	9.2	10.1	51.1	1939
San Jose	9.5	10.3	13.8	25.3	19.6	12.1	3.8	5.7	1973
Santa Ana	2.5	4.1	10.6	25.9	21.2	20.5	8.1	7.2	1967
Savannah	9.3	6.8	10.6	16.0	15.2	17.0	7.7	17.3	1965
Seattle	10.7	8.4	8.6	9.5	9.6	12.6	10.5	30.1	1957
Spokane	7.2	9.2	7.4	14.5	7.7	15.6	11.2	27.2	1957
Springfield	9.9	12.4	12.7	19.3	12.7	11.8	6.6	14.7	1972
Tampa	16.4	10.3	13.0	13.6	13.4	17.4	7.2	8.7	1972
Tulsa	5.3	8.2	14.9	22.9	15.2	17.5	7.7	8.2	1971
Virginia Beach	10.1	12.4	28.4	25.9	13.8	6.8	1.5	1.1	1980
Warren	3.6	3.6	5.2	14.2	36.7	25.5	8.0	3.3	1964
Washington	6.1	2.4	4.0	7.8	13.3	15.8	15.7	34.9	1950
Wichita	8.9	12.9	13.3	12.7	8.7	22.9	8.8	11.9	1967
U.S.	8.9	12.9	13.3	12.7	8.7	22.9	8.8	11.9	1967

Note: Figures are percentages except for Median Year
Source: U.S. Census Bureau, 2007-2009 American Community Survey 3-Year Estimates

Year Housing Structure Built: Metro Area

MSA[1]	2000 or Later	1990 -2000	1980 -1989	1970 -1979	1960 -1969	1950 -1959	1940 -1949	Before 1940	Median Year
Albuquerque	17.6	18.2	16.8	20.0	9.6	10.5	3.9	3.3	1982
Anchorage	13.8	12.5	28.3	26.6	10.4	6.4	1.5	0.4	1982
Ann Arbor	12.7	16.5	11.3	17.4	14.1	10.8	4.9	12.2	1975
Athens	17.1	22.0	18.4	17.1	10.1	5.5	2.7	7.2	1984
Atlanta	23.7	21.8	19.2	13.8	9.2	6.0	2.4	3.9	1988
Austin	26.6	20.7	20.1	16.3	6.4	4.6	2.4	2.9	1989
Baltimore	9.5	13.5	14.2	13.8	10.7	14.2	7.8	16.3	1971
Bellevue	13.9	16.6	15.9	16.1	12.0	8.7	5.3	11.5	1978
Birmingham	13.0	17.1	14.2	18.0	12.4	11.4	5.6	8.1	1977
Boise City	26.6	22.6	10.3	19.3	5.8	5.6	3.7	6.0	1989
Boston	6.7	7.0	10.6	11.3	10.6	11.0	5.9	37.0	1956
Boulder	11.8	20.3	16.5	22.8	13.6	6.2	1.4	7.4	1979
Cambridge	6.7	7.0	10.6	11.3	10.6	11.0	5.9	37.0	1956
Cary	27.4	25.8	18.4	11.2	7.2	4.8	2.0	3.3	1991
Charleston	21.1	17.3	20.0	15.8	9.9	6.8	3.7	5.4	1984
Charlotte	24.5	21.7	15.9	12.9	9.3	7.6	3.6	4.4	1988
Chattanooga	13.0	15.5	14.4	17.6	12.9	11.4	6.5	8.8	1976
Chicago	10.5	10.4	8.9	14.1	12.3	13.8	7.0	23.0	1965
Cincinnati	11.2	14.3	10.6	13.5	11.3	12.9	6.0	20.3	1970
Cleveland	6.5	8.1	6.3	12.2	13.1	18.7	8.7	26.4	1958
Colorado Spgs.	19.6	16.9	18.7	19.8	10.2	7.3	1.6	5.9	1983
Columbia	17.7	19.1	16.0	18.4	11.3	8.9	4.0	4.6	1982
Columbus	14.5	16.2	11.4	14.2	12.3	12.7	5.2	13.6	1974
Dallas	20.5	17.0	20.3	16.1	10.4	8.8	3.3	3.5	1984
Denver	16.3	15.6	14.9	20.7	11.0	10.6	3.3	7.7	1978
Des Moines	17.1	14.3	9.1	15.6	9.9	10.5	5.3	18.1	1974
Durham	20.1	19.6	17.6	15.3	10.4	6.6	3.8	6.4	1984
Edison	5.6	5.7	7.6	9.8	13.8	17.2	10.4	29.9	1956
El Paso	15.5	14.7	16.4	19.7	12.3	11.8	4.1	5.5	1978
Eugene	11.3	15.9	8.9	25.2	14.2	10.0	6.8	7.8	1974
Evansville	10.4	11.6	12.0	15.4	10.2	12.9	8.2	19.3	1969
Fargo	18.0	17.0	12.3	19.4	8.5	9.6	3.7	11.6	1979
Ft. Collins	20.0	20.9	14.8	22.8	8.2	4.6	1.9	6.8	1984
Ft. Lauderdale	12.4	14.6	19.7	23.5	13.0	10.9	3.6	2.2	1979
Ft. Wayne	9.7	13.6	10.6	13.7	14.5	11.7	6.4	19.8	1968
Ft. Worth	20.5	17.0	20.3	16.1	10.4	8.8	3.3	3.5	1984
Gainesville	18.8	19.8	21.8	19.4	9.1	6.4	2.1	2.5	1985
Greensboro	15.1	19.9	15.6	16.0	11.8	10.3	5.0	6.2	1980
Honolulu	8.8	11.8	12.2	27.1	19.3	11.9	4.8	4.1	1974
Houston	21.0	14.5	17.5	22.3	10.4	7.9	3.3	3.0	1982
Huntsville	18.7	18.8	17.7	14.8	16.0	7.9	2.7	3.5	1983
Indianapolis	15.2	17.3	11.1	13.8	11.8	11.0	5.3	14.5	1975
Irvine	5.5	7.2	12.7	17.1	16.5	19.2	9.4	12.4	1965
Jackson	15.7	19.1	16.2	20.5	12.9	8.8	3.6	3.3	1981
Jacksonville	21.9	18.1	19.2	14.1	9.3	9.0	4.3	4.2	1985
Kansas City	13.6	14.4	12.6	15.9	12.1	12.4	5.2	13.8	1974
Knoxville	14.5	19.7	15.7	17.5	11.2	9.3	6.1	6.0	1980
Las Vegas	32.1	29.7	15.9	12.8	6.0	2.5	0.8	0.2	1994
Lexington	16.8	17.7	15.2	16.0	12.6	9.0	3.9	8.8	1980
Lincoln	14.3	16.4	10.9	18.2	10.2	11.4	3.5	15.0	1975
Little Rock	16.9	17.1	16.3	20.5	12.1	8.6	4.0	4.6	1980
Los Angeles	5.5	7.2	12.7	17.1	16.5	19.2	9.4	12.4	1965
Louisville	13.3	15.0	9.6	16.1	13.0	13.1	6.5	13.6	1972
Madison	16.5	15.7	11.1	17.0	11.4	8.4	4.1	15.7	1976
Manchester	9.0	10.3	19.9	16.8	9.9	7.3	4.5	22.3	1974

Table continued on next page.

MSA[1]	2000 or Later	1990 -2000	1980 -1989	1970 -1979	1960 -1969	1950 -1959	1940 -1949	Before 1940	Median Year
Miami	12.4	14.6	19.7	23.5	13.0	10.9	3.6	2.2	1979
Milwaukee	7.3	10.7	7.7	13.6	11.6	16.6	7.4	25.2	1961
Minneapolis	14.3	14.7	14.7	15.7	10.3	10.5	4.3	15.7	1976
Naperville	10.5	10.4	8.9	14.1	12.3	13.8	7.0	23.0	1965
Nashville	19.3	19.3	16.5	16.1	11.4	8.0	3.8	5.6	1983
New Orleans	10.9	9.7	15.0	19.8	15.2	10.2	6.0	13.2	1973
New York	5.6	5.7	7.6	9.8	13.8	17.2	10.4	29.9	1956
Oakland	6.7	7.7	10.9	15.0	14.0	15.1	9.4	21.3	1963
Oklahoma City	13.5	11.8	16.4	19.5	14.1	11.2	5.9	7.8	1976
Omaha	11.8	12.2	9.9	17.2	13.7	10.5	4.5	20.3	1971
Orlando	24.2	21.9	23.0	14.5	7.1	6.0	1.5	1.8	1988
Overland Park	13.6	14.4	12.6	15.9	12.1	12.4	5.2	13.8	1974
Oxnard	10.2	10.6	16.6	23.6	21.9	10.1	3.2	3.6	1975
Philadelphia	7.2	9.2	10.3	12.7	12.4	16.6	9.4	22.2	1961
Phoenix	24.5	21.5	19.6	18.2	7.6	6.1	1.7	1.0	1988
Pittsburgh	5.6	7.2	7.4	12.0	11.0	17.0	10.1	29.8	1956
Plano	20.5	17.0	20.3	16.1	10.4	8.8	3.3	3.5	1984
Portland	14.8	19.5	11.5	18.3	9.4	7.7	5.2	13.7	1978
Providence	5.5	7.5	11.5	12.1	10.6	11.0	7.0	34.8	1957
Provo	25.4	23.6	10.6	18.4	6.1	5.6	4.4	5.8	1989
Raleigh	27.4	25.8	18.4	11.2	7.2	4.8	2.0	3.3	1991
Reno	22.4	20.6	16.7	19.2	9.5	6.4	2.6	2.7	1986
Richmond	14.1	15.8	16.8	16.9	11.1	10.2	4.8	10.3	1978
Riverside	20.3	14.8	23.6	16.9	9.5	9.1	2.8	3.0	1984
Rochester	6.2	9.0	10.2	13.3	13.0	11.7	5.5	31.2	1961
Sacramento	17.1	13.8	17.0	19.7	11.8	11.5	4.2	4.9	1979
St. Louis	10.7	12.1	11.5	14.2	12.7	13.8	6.8	18.2	1969
St. Paul	14.3	14.7	14.7	15.7	10.3	10.5	4.3	15.7	1976
St. Petersburg	15.3	14.2	22.8	21.5	11.6	9.4	2.4	2.7	1981
Salt Lake City	14.6	17.6	14.8	21.3	8.9	9.7	3.8	9.1	1979
San Antonio	20.3	15.4	17.5	17.5	10.0	9.1	4.7	5.7	1982
San Diego	11.1	11.5	19.3	25.0	12.8	11.8	4.1	4.4	1977
San Francisco	6.7	7.7	10.9	15.0	14.0	15.1	9.4	21.3	1963
San Jose	9.0	10.4	13.1	23.0	18.9	15.7	4.4	5.6	1972
Santa Ana	5.5	7.2	12.7	17.1	16.5	19.2	9.4	12.4	1965
Savannah	20.5	17.8	14.5	12.9	10.3	9.9	4.6	9.5	1982
Seattle	13.9	16.6	15.9	16.1	12.0	8.7	5.3	11.5	1978
Spokane	11.9	15.5	9.6	19.4	7.9	11.6	7.8	16.4	1973
Springfield	19.3	19.8	13.9	17.4	8.4	6.9	3.8	10.3	1982
Tampa	15.3	14.2	22.8	21.5	11.6	9.4	2.4	2.7	1981
Tulsa	12.6	12.8	15.8	21.9	11.9	12.0	5.7	7.3	1976
Virginia Beach	11.4	14.5	19.5	18.0	13.5	11.4	5.6	6.1	1977
Warren	8.1	10.7	8.9	14.1	12.2	19.7	11.7	14.8	1963
Washington	13.8	14.5	16.6	15.8	13.5	10.8	6.2	8.8	1977
Wichita	10.6	14.0	13.3	13.3	8.3	19.7	7.3	13.4	1971
U.S.	12.5	14.0	14.2	16.5	11.4	11.3	5.8	14.3	1974

Note: Figures are percentages; (1) Metropolitan Statistical Area - see Appendix B for areas included
Source: U.S. Census Bureau, 2007-2009 American Community Survey 3-Year Estimates

Highest Level of Education: City

City	Less than H.S.	H.S. Diploma	Some College, No Deg.	Associate Degree	Bachelors Degree	Masters Degree	Profess. School Degree	Doctorate Degree
Albuquerque	12.9	23.7	24.0	7.2	17.7	10.1	2.4	2.0
Anchorage	7.3	22.9	28.4	8.6	21.2	7.6	2.6	1.5
Ann Arbor	3.2	7.9	12.1	4.0	29.7	24.8	6.9	11.4
Athens	15.5	22.0	16.4	4.9	22.4	10.5	3.4	5.1
Atlanta	16.7	24.1	14.7	3.9	24.5	10.6	3.7	1.9
Austin	15.9	16.8	18.9	5.6	26.1	11.1	3.0	2.5
Baltimore	23.1	30.0	18.4	4.1	12.5	7.5	2.6	1.8
Bellevue	4.6	11.3	18.1	7.3	35.4	16.2	4.3	2.8
Birmingham	17.0	29.2	24.6	7.1	13.8	5.4	1.9	1.1
Boise City	7.1	20.6	27.2	8.0	24.6	8.5	2.6	1.5
Boston	17.1	23.7	13.7	4.2	22.1	12.7	4.0	2.4
Boulder	5.2	7.8	13.4	4.0	36.5	22.0	3.7	7.3
Cambridge	7.7	11.7	7.5	3.2	26.9	25.5	6.1	11.3
Cary	4.2	11.7	14.8	7.1	37.6	17.9	3.0	3.6
Charleston	11.6	22.5	18.7	7.2	24.1	9.5	4.1	2.4
Charlotte	12.5	20.6	20.7	7.3	26.4	9.0	2.5	1.0
Chattanooga	15.5	28.6	24.1	6.0	16.9	5.7	2.0	1.2
Chicago	22.3	24.2	17.9	5.6	17.9	8.2	2.7	1.2
Cincinnati	18.4	27.1	18.2	6.8	17.7	7.9	2.2	1.7
Cleveland	24.4	34.7	21.4	5.7	8.9	3.4	1.0	0.5
Colorado Spgs.	8.3	22.0	24.2	8.9	22.7	10.9	1.9	1.1
Columbia	13.6	21.0	19.9	6.6	22.0	10.8	3.7	2.4
Columbus	12.7	26.7	21.3	6.3	21.6	7.7	2.2	1.5
Dallas	30.6	20.8	17.3	4.5	17.2	6.3	2.3	0.9
Denver	17.4	21.6	17.9	4.9	22.7	10.0	3.8	1.6
Des Moines	14.4	32.3	21.9	8.0	16.8	4.2	1.7	0.6
Durham	14.4	19.0	16.3	6.7	23.4	11.9	3.7	4.7
Edison	8.9	22.7	14.2	6.3	28.0	14.9	2.8	2.3
El Paso	25.8	23.8	22.2	6.6	14.2	5.4	1.4	0.6
Eugene	7.0	19.4	26.3	8.3	22.4	11.0	2.8	2.8
Evansville	16.2	36.0	22.4	7.6	12.0	4.3	0.9	0.7
Fargo	6.0	20.9	23.0	11.3	28.6	6.6	2.3	1.5
Ft. Collins	6.0	16.4	20.7	7.2	29.2	14.0	2.8	3.7
Ft. Lauderdale	17.0	25.9	18.8	6.9	19.9	7.2	3.2	1.0
Ft. Wayne	14.4	32.0	22.7	8.6	15.2	5.3	1.1	0.7
Ft. Worth	24.7	25.2	21.1	5.5	15.7	5.6	1.4	0.8
Gainesville	10.7	17.2	14.7	9.8	23.0	14.7	4.1	6.0
Greensboro	12.2	23.9	22.0	6.5	23.6	8.4	1.8	1.6
Honolulu	11.0	26.4	19.7	8.3	21.8	7.8	3.4	1.7
Houston	27.2	22.6	18.3	4.6	17.3	6.4	2.2	1.4
Huntsville	12.0	21.8	21.5	6.3	25.0	9.8	2.1	1.6
Indianapolis	15.8	29.9	20.1	6.5	17.9	6.7	2.3	0.9
Irvine	3.8	10.2	15.4	7.8	36.6	17.2	4.6	4.5
Jackson	17.4	23.8	23.8	7.1	17.6	6.6	2.6	1.2
Jacksonville	13.2	31.3	23.8	8.4	15.5	5.3	1.6	0.9
Kansas City	13.7	27.3	23.2	6.9	18.4	7.7	1.9	1.0
Knoxville	14.8	28.3	20.3	6.5	18.8	7.4	2.2	1.8
Las Vegas	18.8	29.0	24.0	6.6	14.3	4.8	1.8	0.6
Lexington	10.8	21.1	22.1	7.1	22.6	9.7	3.9	2.7
Lincoln	7.4	22.3	24.6	9.6	24.4	7.3	2.3	2.1
Little Rock	9.7	23.7	23.0	5.6	22.8	9.3	4.1	2.0
Los Angeles	27.9	20.0	17.4	5.9	18.8	6.2	2.6	1.2
Louisville	17.8	30.9	21.8	5.6	13.6	6.8	2.4	1.1
Madison	5.5	17.1	18.3	7.8	27.8	14.4	4.0	5.0
Manchester	15.2	31.7	18.4	8.2	18.0	6.5	1.5	0.4

Table continued on next page.

City	Less than H.S.	H.S. Diploma	Some College, No Deg.	Associate Degree	Bachelors Degree	Masters Degree	Profess. School Degree	Doctorate Degree
Miami	36.3	25.0	11.2	5.6	13.1	4.7	2.8	1.3
Milwaukee	19.9	30.9	21.3	6.0	14.2	5.5	1.3	1.0
Minneapolis	12.9	20.0	19.4	6.2	25.7	10.1	3.3	2.2
Naperville	2.8	11.1	16.9	6.6	36.7	20.0	3.0	2.8
Nashville	15.4	26.0	20.8	5.8	20.4	7.5	2.5	1.6
New Orleans	17.8	30.0	20.6	3.8	16.2	6.5	3.3	1.8
New York	21.5	25.8	14.1	6.0	19.2	9.1	3.0	1.3
Oakland	22.4	19.9	17.8	5.7	19.5	9.8	2.8	2.1
Oklahoma City	15.2	25.7	26.5	6.1	17.6	6.0	1.9	0.8
Omaha	11.6	25.9	23.7	6.8	21.0	7.0	2.8	1.2
Orlando	13.7	27.0	18.9	10.1	20.7	6.9	2.0	0.6
Overland Park	3.2	13.1	20.1	6.3	37.5	14.4	3.6	1.9
Oxnard	37.6	20.4	19.5	6.5	10.7	3.6	1.2	0.5
Philadelphia	21.4	35.7	16.3	5.5	12.1	5.7	1.9	1.3
Phoenix	22.8	24.3	22.2	7.1	15.3	5.7	1.9	0.7
Pittsburgh	11.5	31.6	16.6	7.8	16.6	9.7	3.2	3.0
Plano	5.8	12.6	20.5	6.9	35.3	14.6	2.3	1.9
Portland	10.9	20.2	23.1	6.3	24.1	10.2	3.3	1.8
Providence	28.1	24.9	14.3	5.1	15.2	7.9	2.2	2.4
Provo	8.4	13.5	28.7	10.8	27.6	6.9	1.4	2.7
Raleigh	9.3	16.9	19.5	7.0	30.9	11.5	2.8	2.0
Reno	16.6	22.7	25.8	7.2	18.0	6.3	1.9	1.4
Richmond	20.0	24.6	18.7	4.5	19.0	8.2	3.3	1.8
Riverside	21.7	24.7	22.9	7.7	14.0	6.0	1.6	1.5
Rochester	21.7	29.2	16.7	8.7	13.7	7.2	1.7	1.1
Sacramento	20.4	21.9	23.4	8.3	16.9	5.6	2.4	1.1
St. Louis	20.3	26.6	22.3	5.3	15.1	7.0	2.1	1.2
St. Paul	13.2	24.4	19.6	6.6	21.7	9.0	3.5	2.1
St. Petersburg	13.8	29.0	21.7	9.0	17.6	6.2	1.8	0.9
Salt Lake City	16.4	19.8	19.8	6.7	21.1	9.8	3.6	2.8
San Antonio	21.4	26.4	22.6	6.5	15.0	5.6	1.6	0.8
San Diego	14.8	16.9	21.0	7.9	24.0	9.3	3.4	2.8
San Francisco	15.6	14.3	13.8	5.4	30.7	12.6	4.9	2.6
San Jose	18.7	19.5	18.7	7.8	22.0	9.7	1.8	1.7
Santa Ana	53.4	18.2	13.1	4.4	7.5	2.1	1.0	0.2
Savannah	15.2	30.9	20.8	7.7	16.5	6.2	2.0	0.9
Seattle	9.2	14.1	18.4	6.9	30.8	13.3	4.5	2.9
Spokane	9.0	25.1	27.3	11.5	17.3	6.6	2.3	0.9
Springfield	13.3	29.4	25.2	5.6	17.1	6.6	1.7	1.1
Tampa	17.4	26.7	17.3	8.7	19.2	6.8	2.9	1.1
Tulsa	13.1	26.4	23.6	7.1	19.9	5.8	2.8	1.3
Virginia Beach	7.6	25.0	26.6	9.7	20.4	7.9	2.0	0.7
Warren	18.0	35.9	22.5	7.4	11.2	3.9	0.7	0.3
Washington	14.5	20.3	14.4	3.2	21.4	15.2	7.2	4.0
Wichita	12.9	27.3	25.7	6.5	18.4	6.7	1.7	0.8
U.S.	15.3	29.0	20.7	7.5	17.4	7.0	1.9	1.1

Figures are 2010 estimates and cover persons age 25 and over; (1) Metropolitan Statistical Area - see Appendix B for areas included
Source: Claritas, Inc.

Highest Level of Education: Metro Area

Metro Area	Less than H.S.	H.S. Diploma	Some College, No Deg.	Associate Degree	Bachelors Degree	Masters Degree	Profess. School Degree	Doctorate Degree
Albuquerque	13.8	25.4	24.5	7.3	16.1	8.9	2.1	1.9
Anchorage	7.9	24.9	28.7	8.7	19.2	7.1	2.1	1.3
Ann Arbor	6.4	16.4	19.6	6.5	24.9	16.3	4.2	5.8
Athens	17.1	26.7	16.6	4.7	18.8	9.1	2.8	4.1
Atlanta	13.0	26.1	20.1	6.6	22.5	8.4	2.1	1.1
Austin	13.7	20.2	21.3	6.6	24.7	9.4	2.3	1.8
Baltimore	12.8	27.1	20.0	6.2	19.4	10.1	2.8	1.7
Bellevue	8.7	22.0	24.0	9.0	23.6	8.9	2.4	1.4
Birmingham	15.1	29.6	22.5	6.8	16.8	6.2	2.2	0.9
Boise City	11.4	26.1	26.9	7.6	19.4	6.0	1.7	1.0
Boston	10.3	25.4	15.6	7.1	23.4	12.6	3.2	2.5
Boulder	7.1	13.4	17.1	6.1	32.3	16.7	2.9	4.5
Cambridge	10.3	25.4	15.6	7.1	23.4	12.6	3.2	2.5
Cary	10.8	20.9	19.3	8.0	27.2	10.1	2.0	1.7
Charleston	12.5	29.3	20.8	8.7	18.1	7.1	2.2	1.3
Charlotte	13.8	24.7	21.7	8.0	22.0	7.3	1.7	0.8
Chattanooga	17.0	30.5	23.6	6.7	14.8	5.1	1.6	0.8
Chicago	14.7	25.7	20.3	6.7	20.3	8.9	2.3	1.1
Cincinnati	12.8	32.4	19.4	7.6	17.7	7.3	1.7	1.1
Cleveland	12.2	31.7	22.0	7.3	16.7	7.0	2.2	0.9
Colorado Spgs.	7.8	23.0	25.3	9.2	21.3	10.5	1.7	1.1
Columbia	12.8	27.6	21.1	8.7	18.6	8.0	1.9	1.3
Columbus	10.7	29.8	20.4	6.6	21.2	7.8	2.2	1.3
Dallas	18.5	23.3	22.2	6.3	20.3	7.0	1.5	0.9
Denver	11.6	22.5	21.8	7.1	24.1	9.3	2.4	1.2
Des Moines	8.6	28.3	21.8	9.6	23.0	5.8	2.1	0.8
Durham	13.8	21.4	16.1	6.6	22.5	11.5	3.5	4.5
Edison	16.2	27.1	15.3	6.3	20.7	10.0	3.0	1.3
El Paso	29.0	24.2	21.2	6.3	12.7	4.8	1.2	0.5
Eugene	10.2	26.0	27.7	8.5	16.5	7.6	1.9	1.6
Evansville	13.3	36.9	21.2	9.0	12.6	5.3	1.2	0.6
Fargo	6.4	23.9	23.1	11.6	26.1	5.8	1.7	1.3
Ft. Collins	7.1	20.5	22.3	8.1	25.5	11.7	2.3	2.6
Ft. Lauderdale	17.5	27.6	17.7	8.1	18.7	6.5	2.8	1.1
Ft. Wayne	11.7	32.5	22.2	9.2	16.6	5.8	1.4	0.5
Ft. Worth	18.5	23.3	22.2	6.3	20.3	7.0	1.5	0.9
Gainesville	10.9	21.6	16.2	9.9	21.4	11.7	3.7	4.6
Greensboro	17.4	29.4	21.3	6.8	17.6	5.5	1.2	0.9
Honolulu	9.9	28.1	21.5	9.6	20.2	6.9	2.7	1.1
Houston	20.2	24.6	21.3	6.0	18.7	6.3	1.8	1.2
Huntsville	13.6	24.8	21.2	6.5	22.5	8.8	1.4	1.2
Indianapolis	11.7	29.6	20.4	7.2	20.5	7.4	2.1	1.1
Irvine	23.1	20.7	19.3	7.1	19.5	6.8	2.4	1.2
Jackson	14.9	24.9	22.7	8.4	19.4	6.3	2.3	1.2
Jacksonville	12.3	30.6	23.7	8.5	16.5	5.8	1.7	0.9
Kansas City	9.9	28.2	23.1	7.1	20.6	8.3	1.9	0.9
Knoxville	13.5	30.4	20.6	6.9	18.4	6.9	1.8	1.5
Las Vegas	17.0	29.5	25.0	6.9	14.6	4.8	1.5	0.6
Lexington	12.6	25.7	21.3	7.1	19.7	8.5	2.9	2.2
Lincoln	7.1	23.5	24.3	10.2	23.5	7.1	2.3	2.0
Little Rock	12.2	31.8	23.8	6.1	16.9	6.1	2.1	1.1
Los Angeles	23.1	20.7	19.3	7.1	19.5	6.8	2.4	1.2
Louisville	13.8	33.5	22.1	7.1	14.3	6.5	2.0	0.7
Madison	6.2	23.9	20.2	9.4	24.3	10.2	3.0	3.1
Manchester	9.8	27.9	18.5	9.0	22.9	9.5	1.5	0.9

Table continued on next page.

Metro Area	Less than H.S.	H.S. Diploma	Some College, No Deg.	Associate Degree	Bachelors Degree	Masters Degree	Profess. School Degree	Doctorate Degree
Miami	17.5	27.6	17.7	8.1	18.7	6.5	2.8	1.1
Milwaukee	11.4	29.0	21.7	7.3	20.2	7.5	2.0	1.0
Minneapolis	7.3	24.3	22.3	8.9	25.2	8.1	2.5	1.3
Naperville	14.7	25.7	20.3	6.7	20.3	8.9	2.3	1.1
Nashville	14.5	29.4	21.1	6.0	19.4	6.4	2.0	1.2
New Orleans	16.7	31.5	22.5	5.0	15.9	5.1	2.2	1.1
New York	16.2	27.1	15.3	6.3	20.7	10.0	3.0	1.3
Oakland	13.1	18.1	18.7	7.0	26.2	11.0	3.5	2.5
Oklahoma City	13.0	27.9	26.2	6.3	17.6	6.3	1.8	0.9
Omaha	9.1	27.2	24.4	7.9	21.2	7.0	2.2	1.0
Orlando	12.8	29.6	21.1	9.7	18.3	6.2	1.6	0.8
Overland Park	9.9	28.2	23.1	7.1	20.6	8.3	1.9	0.9
Oxnard	18.0	19.9	23.8	8.2	19.5	7.2	2.2	1.3
Philadelphia	12.7	31.5	17.5	6.5	19.3	8.5	2.5	1.6
Phoenix	16.2	24.7	24.6	7.8	17.3	6.7	1.7	0.9
Pittsburgh	9.5	36.9	16.3	9.0	17.7	7.4	2.0	1.2
Plano	18.5	23.3	22.2	6.3	20.3	7.0	1.5	0.9
Portland	10.3	22.7	26.1	8.0	21.2	8.0	2.3	1.3
Providence	17.9	29.0	17.4	7.8	17.8	7.3	1.8	1.0
Provo	6.9	18.3	29.0	11.6	24.1	7.2	1.4	1.6
Raleigh	10.8	20.9	19.3	8.0	27.2	10.1	2.0	1.7
Reno	14.6	24.1	27.0	7.7	17.5	6.1	1.8	1.2
Richmond	14.9	27.4	21.2	6.1	19.6	7.6	1.9	1.2
Riverside	22.0	26.9	24.4	7.8	12.7	4.4	1.3	0.6
Rochester	11.7	28.1	17.8	11.0	18.2	10.1	2.0	1.1
Sacramento	12.9	22.3	25.6	9.3	20.1	6.3	2.1	1.3
St. Louis	12.1	28.4	23.2	7.7	18.0	7.7	1.9	1.1
St. Paul	7.3	24.3	22.3	8.9	25.2	8.1	2.5	1.3
St. Petersburg	13.6	30.9	21.1	8.8	17.1	5.9	1.7	0.9
Salt Lake City	11.1	25.0	25.3	8.6	19.6	7.1	2.1	1.3
San Antonio	18.6	27.2	23.2	6.8	15.8	6.0	1.7	0.8
San Diego	14.9	19.7	23.3	8.1	21.2	8.0	2.8	2.0
San Francisco	13.1	18.1	18.7	7.0	26.2	11.0	3.5	2.5
San Jose	14.6	16.9	17.5	7.4	24.4	13.6	2.4	3.1
Santa Ana	23.1	20.7	19.3	7.1	19.5	6.8	2.4	1.2
Savannah	13.3	32.0	20.7	7.5	17.6	6.1	2.1	1.0
Seattle	8.7	22.0	24.0	9.0	23.6	8.9	2.4	1.4
Spokane	8.0	25.2	27.7	11.9	17.9	6.5	2.0	0.8
Springfield	12.5	32.1	24.5	5.8	16.6	6.1	1.6	0.9
Tampa	13.6	30.9	21.1	8.8	17.1	5.9	1.7	0.9
Tulsa	12.6	30.6	23.8	8.3	17.0	5.0	1.8	0.8
Virginia Beach	11.5	27.6	25.3	8.5	17.0	7.7	1.6	0.9
Warren	12.9	29.5	23.6	7.6	16.1	7.6	1.9	0.8
Washington	10.6	19.6	17.5	5.7	24.9	14.7	4.2	2.9
Wichita	11.2	28.5	26.2	7.2	18.2	6.5	1.5	0.7
U.S.	15.3	29.0	20.7	7.5	17.4	7.0	1.9	1.1

Note: Figures cover persons age 25 and over; Figures are 2010 estimates and cover the Metropolitan Statistical Area (MSA) - see Appendix B for areas included
Source: Claritas, Inc.

School Enrollment by Grade and Control: City

City	Preschool (%)		Kindergarten (%)		Grades 1 - 4 (%)		Grades 5 - 8 (%)		Grades 9 - 12 (%)	
	Public	Private	Public	Private	Public	Private	Public	Private	Public	Private
Albuquerque	56.0	44.0	85.1	14.9	88.3	11.7	86.0	14.0	89.5	10.5
Anchorage	43.7	56.3	91.1	8.9	93.0	7.0	91.9	8.1	95.0	5.0
Ann Arbor	33.1	66.9	84.0	16.0	88.2	11.8	85.3	14.7	93.0	7.0
Athens	62.3	37.7	79.3	20.7	89.8	10.2	87.4	12.6	91.3	8.7
Atlanta	44.5	55.5	74.8	25.2	83.2	16.8	81.1	18.9	78.8	21.2
Austin	56.9	43.1	91.7	8.3	91.9	8.1	92.1	7.9	93.2	6.8
Baltimore	63.9	36.1	83.9	16.1	84.4	15.6	81.8	18.2	85.0	15.0
Bellevue	33.9	66.1	86.2	13.8	81.0	19.0	84.6	15.4	89.0	11.0
Birmingham	53.1	46.9	82.1	17.9	89.9	10.1	84.8	15.2	89.4	10.6
Boise City	50.5	49.5	79.7	20.3	88.7	11.3	89.8	10.2	92.1	7.9
Boston	56.2	43.8	80.8	19.2	81.0	19.0	77.1	22.9	85.6	14.4
Boulder	38.9	61.1	81.1	18.9	91.1	8.9	93.1	6.9	88.4	11.6
Cambridge	28.8	71.2	83.4	16.6	76.5	23.5	78.4	21.6	84.4	15.6
Cary	27.6	72.4	86.1	13.9	87.5	12.5	84.5	15.5	86.3	13.7
Charleston	44.8	55.2	65.2	34.8	82.6	17.4	83.8	16.2	78.3	21.7
Charlotte	41.5	58.5	83.5	16.5	86.8	13.2	85.5	14.5	85.2	14.8
Chattanooga	67.9	32.1	93.1	6.9	87.2	12.8	82.5	17.5	76.6	23.4
Chicago	63.6	36.4	81.1	18.9	84.4	15.6	86.2	13.8	85.0	15.0
Cincinnati	72.8	27.2	89.4	10.6	78.4	21.6	81.4	18.6	80.3	19.7
Cleveland	63.0	37.0	79.1	20.9	74.9	25.1	76.7	23.3	80.9	19.1
Colorado Spgs.	55.4	44.6	88.1	11.9	93.4	6.6	90.8	9.2	93.2	6.8
Columbia	47.1	52.9	78.5	21.5	79.6	20.4	82.6	17.4	93.1	6.9
Columbus	52.3	47.7	87.6	12.4	90.0	10.0	90.0	10.0	89.8	10.2
Dallas	63.8	36.2	88.5	11.5	89.4	10.6	89.9	10.1	89.8	10.2
Denver	54.4	45.6	88.7	11.3	88.3	11.7	87.1	12.9	89.1	10.9
Des Moines	55.1	44.9	94.4	5.6	90.8	9.2	91.0	9.0	93.1	6.9
Durham	38.1	61.9	83.8	16.2	87.2	12.8	86.6	13.4	90.3	9.7
Edison	20.4	79.6	80.4	19.6	90.8	9.2	87.9	12.1	93.0	7.0
El Paso	81.1	18.9	91.2	8.8	95.6	4.4	94.5	5.5	96.0	4.0
Eugene	41.5	58.5	93.2	6.8	91.0	9.0	91.9	8.1	91.5	8.5
Evansville	59.9	40.1	88.9	11.1	86.1	13.9	85.6	14.4	84.6	15.4
Fargo	54.0	46.0	85.5	14.5	85.6	14.4	88.1	11.9	91.7	8.3
Ft. Collins	29.9	70.1	97.7	2.3	92.5	7.5	90.7	9.3	95.7	4.3
Ft. Lauderdale	46.8	53.2	81.2	18.8	84.4	15.6	81.4	18.6	79.6	20.4
Ft. Wayne	50.6	49.4	80.5	19.5	81.7	18.3	84.3	15.7	85.5	14.5
Ft. Worth	58.1	41.9	90.1	9.9	91.5	8.5	92.2	7.8	90.3	9.7
Gainesville	42.4	57.6	85.3	14.7	86.4	13.6	93.1	6.9	93.6	6.4
Greensboro	58.5	41.5	89.3	10.7	91.7	8.3	88.7	11.3	92.6	7.4
Honolulu	34.9	65.1	67.0	33.0	74.7	25.3	73.6	26.4	73.8	26.2
Houston	68.3	31.7	91.9	8.1	92.6	7.4	92.6	7.4	92.6	7.4
Huntsville	44.2	55.8	85.0	15.0	88.9	11.1	84.3	15.7	91.7	8.3
Indianapolis	44.1	55.9	78.6	21.4	84.1	15.9	85.0	15.0	86.8	13.2
Irvine	23.3	76.7	90.7	9.3	90.4	9.6	93.1	6.9	93.4	6.6
Jackson	76.1	23.9	82.2	17.8	88.7	11.3	83.5	16.5	86.0	14.0
Jacksonville	50.0	50.0	80.4	19.6	84.5	15.5	80.7	19.3	82.6	17.4
Kansas City	60.5	39.5	89.5	10.5	84.7	15.3	84.2	15.8	83.9	16.1
Knoxville	45.3	54.7	83.3	16.7	83.8	16.2	86.1	13.9	87.9	12.1
Las Vegas	55.2	44.8	90.6	9.4	93.7	6.3	94.6	5.4	95.8	4.2
Lexington	42.4	57.6	80.1	19.9	85.1	14.9	83.6	16.4	88.6	11.4
Lincoln	35.0	65.0	83.0	17.0	84.0	16.0	82.1	17.9	87.2	12.8
Little Rock	46.1	53.9	77.2	22.8	78.1	21.9	76.0	24.0	76.9	23.1
Los Angeles	61.0	39.0	86.7	13.3	88.4	11.6	88.6	11.4	89.5	10.5
Louisville	55.0	45.0	85.4	14.6	81.2	18.8	80.4	19.6	81.7	18.3
Madison	30.1	69.9	92.3	7.7	89.8	10.2	89.2	10.8	89.8	10.2
Manchester	43.6	56.4	73.0	27.0	86.2	13.8	89.6	10.4	94.7	5.3

Table continued on next page.

City	Preschool (%)		Kindergarten (%)		Grades 1 - 4 (%)		Grades 5 - 8 (%)		Grades 9 - 12 (%)	
	Public	Private	Public	Private	Public	Private	Public	Private	Public	Private
Miami	61.4	38.6	86.0	14.0	89.2	10.8	91.2	8.8	89.7	10.3
Milwaukee	75.4	24.6	83.0	17.0	82.8	17.2	78.2	21.8	83.3	16.7
Minneapolis	52.3	47.7	81.4	18.6	87.4	12.6	85.8	14.2	89.9	10.1
Naperville	40.2	59.8	84.1	15.9	93.1	6.9	92.7	7.3	92.1	7.9
Nashville	46.5	53.5	75.6	24.4	84.2	15.8	77.8	22.2	81.9	18.1
New Orleans	51.4	48.6	69.7	30.3	76.4	23.6	75.6	24.4	79.7	20.3
New York	53.1	46.9	75.8	24.2	78.9	21.1	79.4	20.6	81.5	18.5
Oakland	50.1	49.9	89.5	10.5	88.4	11.6	87.2	12.8	84.9	15.1
Oklahoma City	67.6	32.4	87.7	12.3	90.1	9.9	90.1	9.9	91.3	8.7
Omaha	52.7	47.3	80.6	19.4	82.5	17.5	81.8	18.2	87.0	13.0
Orlando	40.8	59.2	78.3	21.7	88.3	11.7	86.8	13.2	91.8	8.2
Overland Park	28.7	71.3	78.8	21.2	80.4	19.6	82.4	17.6	85.0	15.0
Oxnard	73.7	26.3	92.8	7.2	96.6	3.4	94.5	5.5	94.5	5.5
Philadelphia	56.3	43.7	72.0	28.0	78.2	21.8	76.2	23.8	80.3	19.7
Phoenix	62.1	37.9	92.6	7.4	93.6	6.4	93.0	7.0	93.5	6.5
Pittsburgh	52.3	47.7	74.4	25.6	75.2	24.8	80.1	19.9	80.6	19.4
Plano	38.5	61.5	88.1	11.9	87.5	12.5	90.2	9.8	91.7	8.3
Portland	40.8	59.2	82.3	17.7	85.5	14.5	86.3	13.7	87.3	12.7
Providence	52.7	47.3	81.4	18.6	83.0	17.0	88.1	11.9	89.1	10.9
Provo	40.9	59.1	92.8	7.2	96.9	3.1	95.8	4.2	94.4	5.6
Raleigh	32.1	67.9	82.5	17.5	86.8	13.2	91.3	8.7	89.2	10.8
Reno	49.3	50.7	82.8	17.2	95.3	4.7	94.1	5.9	91.1	8.9
Richmond	55.1	44.9	77.0	23.0	86.6	13.4	82.1	17.9	88.6	11.4
Riverside	68.2	31.8	89.4	10.6	94.5	5.5	94.7	5.3	94.2	5.8
Rochester	74.3	25.7	87.5	12.5	92.9	7.1	90.1	9.9	89.7	10.3
Sacramento	59.5	40.5	87.5	12.5	92.0	8.0	92.9	7.1	90.6	9.4
St. Louis	63.6	36.4	69.6	30.4	77.6	22.4	76.8	23.2	78.7	21.3
St. Paul	50.0	50.0	87.5	12.5	85.5	14.5	84.4	15.6	88.2	11.8
St. Petersburg	58.1	41.9	80.5	19.5	82.6	17.4	84.3	15.7	92.2	7.8
Salt Lake City	58.1	41.9	79.6	20.4	90.9	9.1	89.9	10.1	89.6	10.4
San Antonio	66.8	33.2	90.0	10.0	91.7	8.3	92.0	8.0	92.9	7.1
San Diego	54.8	45.2	91.1	8.9	91.6	8.4	91.1	8.9	93.1	6.9
San Francisco	31.2	68.8	74.9	25.1	72.8	27.2	75.4	24.6	79.1	20.9
San Jose	43.5	56.5	85.5	14.5	86.8	13.2	87.7	12.3	90.1	9.9
Santa Ana	83.4	16.6	98.5	1.5	96.3	3.7	97.2	2.8	97.0	3.0
Savannah	69.5	30.5	84.3	15.7	87.8	12.2	85.0	15.0	88.1	11.9
Seattle	30.7	69.3	74.5	25.5	78.9	21.1	72.0	28.0	78.8	21.2
Spokane	43.6	56.4	85.5	14.5	89.1	10.9	88.6	11.4	91.9	8.1
Springfield	47.3	52.7	81.4	18.6	91.9	8.1	92.4	7.6	91.3	8.7
Tampa	50.4	49.6	80.6	19.4	90.0	10.0	89.5	10.5	91.7	8.3
Tulsa	67.3	32.7	88.5	11.5	87.5	12.5	85.8	14.2	84.3	15.7
Virginia Beach	26.1	73.9	82.4	17.6	89.8	10.2	90.3	9.7	92.0	8.0
Warren	64.7	35.3	92.5	7.5	93.1	6.9	92.7	7.3	93.3	6.7
Washington	59.3	40.7	76.8	23.2	79.7	20.3	79.8	20.2	81.9	18.1
Wichita	47.9	52.1	81.9	18.1	85.1	14.9	86.5	13.5	87.1	12.9
U.S.	54.3	45.7	86.4	13.6	88.9	11.1	89.1	10.9	90.2	9.8

Note: Figures shown cover persons 3 years old and over
Source: U.S. Census Bureau, 2007-2009 American Community Survey 3-Year Estimates

School Enrollment by Grade and Control: Metro Area

MSA[1]	Preschool (%)		Kindergarten (%)		Grades 1 - 4 (%)		Grades 5 - 8 (%)		Grades 9 - 12 (%)	
	Public	Private	Public	Private	Public	Private	Public	Private	Public	Private
Albuquerque	57.5	42.5	87.0	13.0	88.7	11.3	87.0	13.0	89.5	10.5
Anchorage	46.6	53.4	89.6	10.4	91.8	8.2	90.5	9.5	92.5	7.5
Ann Arbor	44.0	56.0	82.0	18.0	86.5	13.5	88.4	11.6	91.6	8.4
Athens	52.9	47.1	82.5	17.5	89.2	10.8	89.6	10.4	91.1	8.9
Atlanta	46.2	53.8	84.7	15.3	89.0	11.0	88.6	11.4	89.4	10.6
Austin	49.9	50.1	90.8	9.2	92.2	7.8	91.9	8.1	93.4	6.6
Baltimore	44.3	55.7	81.7	18.3	82.5	17.5	82.6	17.4	84.4	15.6
Bellevue	38.5	61.5	84.0	16.0	88.8	11.2	88.0	12.0	89.8	10.2
Birmingham	41.8	58.2	84.2	15.8	90.1	9.9	89.0	11.0	87.6	12.4
Boise City	43.3	56.7	89.0	11.0	91.4	8.6	91.4	8.6	91.5	8.5
Boston	38.5	61.5	82.7	17.3	88.3	11.7	87.3	12.7	85.3	14.7
Boulder	37.0	63.0	87.1	12.9	90.8	9.2	91.8	8.2	91.1	8.9
Cambridge	38.5	61.5	82.7	17.3	88.3	11.7	87.3	12.7	85.3	14.7
Cary	33.5	66.5	85.3	14.7	88.8	11.2	89.0	11.0	90.0	10.0
Charleston	46.9	53.1	80.8	19.2	85.5	14.5	85.7	14.3	86.8	13.2
Charlotte	43.1	56.9	86.4	13.6	88.3	11.7	87.8	12.2	88.3	11.7
Chattanooga	59.7	40.3	89.7	10.3	88.1	11.9	82.9	17.1	78.6	21.4
Chicago	55.9	44.1	83.0	17.0	87.2	12.8	88.2	11.8	89.3	10.7
Cincinnati	49.9	50.1	81.7	18.3	83.1	16.9	83.1	16.9	83.5	16.5
Cleveland	48.3	51.7	79.9	20.1	80.5	19.5	81.6	18.4	84.7	15.3
Colorado Spgs.	62.1	37.9	86.4	13.6	92.2	7.8	91.1	8.9	93.0	7.0
Columbia	55.3	44.7	84.2	15.8	90.3	9.7	91.5	8.5	91.8	8.2
Columbus	47.0	53.0	85.5	14.5	87.4	12.6	89.1	10.9	90.3	9.7
Dallas	50.2	49.8	88.8	11.2	91.4	8.6	92.1	7.9	92.4	7.6
Denver	51.8	48.2	87.9	12.1	91.5	8.5	91.6	8.4	91.7	8.3
Des Moines	55.3	44.7	92.9	7.1	90.8	9.2	90.7	9.3	92.0	8.0
Durham	37.0	63.0	82.8	17.2	86.3	13.7	87.1	12.9	91.9	8.1
Edison	46.4	53.6	80.0	20.0	84.2	15.8	84.4	15.6	84.7	15.3
El Paso	83.8	16.2	92.5	7.5	96.1	3.9	95.2	4.8	96.4	3.6
Eugene	43.0	57.0	91.4	8.6	90.5	9.5	90.0	10.0	92.5	7.5
Evansville	46.3	53.7	85.1	14.9	84.0	16.0	87.7	12.3	88.8	11.2
Fargo	56.4	43.6	88.1	11.9	88.5	11.5	90.5	9.5	92.6	7.4
Ft. Collins	32.3	67.7	89.7	10.3	91.6	8.4	91.5	8.5	94.2	5.8
Ft. Lauderdale	43.2	56.8	82.2	17.8	86.8	13.2	86.1	13.9	87.1	12.9
Ft. Wayne	50.6	49.4	82.0	18.0	78.6	21.4	82.8	17.2	85.6	14.4
Ft. Worth	50.2	49.8	88.8	11.2	91.4	8.6	92.1	7.9	92.4	7.6
Gainesville	45.1	54.9	88.9	11.1	85.6	14.4	85.8	14.2	88.4	11.6
Greensboro	56.5	43.5	88.4	11.6	92.4	7.6	90.3	9.7	92.3	7.7
Honolulu	34.9	65.1	79.3	20.7	82.6	17.4	77.6	22.4	77.6	22.4
Houston	56.6	43.4	90.0	10.0	92.9	7.1	93.0	7.0	93.4	6.6
Huntsville	41.4	58.6	87.4	12.6	89.7	10.3	83.9	16.1	90.0	10.0
Indianapolis	40.8	59.2	80.3	19.7	86.8	13.2	87.1	12.9	89.1	10.9
Irvine	56.7	43.3	86.4	13.6	89.5	10.5	90.3	9.7	91.3	8.7
Jackson	56.0	44.0	79.4	20.6	86.4	13.6	83.5	16.5	86.6	13.4
Jacksonville	47.0	53.0	83.8	16.2	86.4	13.6	83.9	16.1	86.4	13.6
Kansas City	51.1	48.9	86.5	13.5	87.6	12.4	88.4	11.6	88.8	11.2
Knoxville	44.6	55.4	83.3	16.7	88.0	12.0	86.5	13.5	88.3	11.7
Las Vegas	55.0	45.0	92.5	7.5	93.9	6.1	95.8	4.2	95.4	4.6
Lexington	45.3	54.7	82.7	17.3	86.9	13.1	86.0	14.0	89.7	10.3
Lincoln	34.7	65.3	83.6	16.4	83.1	16.9	81.9	18.1	87.5	12.5
Little Rock	53.1	46.9	81.6	18.4	86.5	13.5	86.2	13.8	85.4	14.6
Los Angeles	56.7	43.3	86.4	13.6	89.5	10.5	90.3	9.7	91.3	8.7
Louisville	52.3	47.7	84.9	15.1	82.8	17.2	82.6	17.4	84.2	15.8
Madison	45.7	54.3	89.1	10.9	89.0	11.0	92.0	8.0	93.9	6.1
Manchester	30.9	69.1	66.7	33.3	89.7	10.3	89.5	10.5	90.0	10.0

Table continued on next page.

MSA[1]	Preschool (%)		Kindergarten (%)		Grades 1 - 4 (%)		Grades 5 - 8 (%)		Grades 9 - 12 (%)	
	Public	Private	Public	Private	Public	Private	Public	Private	Public	Private
Miami	43.2	56.8	82.2	17.8	86.8	13.2	86.1	13.9	87.1	12.9
Milwaukee	49.9	50.1	80.0	20.0	81.2	18.8	79.7	20.3	85.1	14.9
Minneapolis	53.3	46.7	85.0	15.0	86.0	14.0	87.5	12.5	91.0	9.0
Naperville	55.9	44.1	83.0	17.0	87.2	12.8	88.2	11.8	89.3	10.7
Nashville	42.4	57.6	83.5	16.5	87.6	12.4	84.1	15.9	84.8	15.2
New Orleans	50.5	49.5	70.3	29.7	75.5	24.5	72.7	27.3	74.7	25.3
New York	46.4	53.6	80.0	20.0	84.2	15.8	84.4	15.6	84.7	15.3
Oakland	40.3	59.7	84.4	15.6	84.7	15.3	85.2	14.8	86.3	13.7
Oklahoma City	68.6	31.4	87.2	12.8	90.4	9.6	91.5	8.5	92.2	7.8
Omaha	53.1	46.9	83.7	16.3	84.2	15.8	84.3	15.7	88.0	12.0
Orlando	43.4	56.6	80.3	19.7	86.2	13.8	88.0	12.0	91.0	9.0
Overland Park	51.1	48.9	86.5	13.5	87.6	12.4	88.4	11.6	88.8	11.2
Oxnard	46.9	53.1	88.2	11.8	90.6	9.4	90.0	10.0	91.5	8.5
Philadelphia	41.5	58.5	76.0	24.0	81.9	18.1	81.3	18.7	82.9	17.1
Phoenix	54.6	45.4	90.9	9.1	93.0	7.0	93.3	6.7	94.0	6.0
Pittsburgh	45.7	54.3	84.8	15.2	86.2	13.8	88.1	11.9	90.5	9.5
Plano	50.2	49.8	88.8	11.2	91.4	8.6	92.1	7.9	92.4	7.6
Portland	38.4	61.6	83.5	16.5	88.5	11.5	89.9	10.1	91.6	8.4
Providence	47.8	52.2	84.6	15.4	89.3	10.7	89.2	10.8	87.7	12.3
Provo	40.3	59.7	93.2	6.8	95.3	4.7	95.4	4.6	96.7	3.3
Raleigh	33.5	66.5	85.3	14.7	88.8	11.2	89.0	11.0	90.0	10.0
Reno	55.1	44.9	86.9	13.1	94.5	5.5	93.4	6.6	92.0	8.0
Richmond	38.1	61.9	88.6	11.4	91.0	9.0	89.9	10.1	91.8	8.2
Riverside	60.4	39.6	91.4	8.6	93.7	6.3	93.5	6.5	93.8	6.2
Rochester	54.9	45.1	87.1	12.9	90.6	9.4	91.9	8.1	92.3	7.7
Sacramento	53.1	46.9	87.3	12.7	90.5	9.5	91.7	8.3	91.6	8.4
St. Louis	53.7	46.3	77.0	23.0	81.2	18.8	81.4	18.6	84.8	15.2
St. Paul	53.3	46.7	85.0	15.0	86.0	14.0	87.5	12.5	91.0	9.0
St. Petersburg	49.5	50.5	84.6	15.4	88.5	11.5	88.2	11.8	91.0	9.0
Salt Lake City	45.3	54.7	88.9	11.1	92.2	7.8	93.8	6.2	94.1	5.9
San Antonio	62.7	37.3	89.4	10.6	91.5	8.5	91.8	8.2	93.0	7.0
San Diego	53.7	46.3	90.2	9.8	91.6	8.4	91.2	8.8	93.1	6.9
San Francisco	40.3	59.7	84.4	15.6	84.7	15.3	85.2	14.8	86.3	13.7
San Jose	36.6	63.4	83.3	16.7	85.5	14.5	86.7	13.3	89.3	10.7
Santa Ana	56.7	43.3	86.4	13.6	89.5	10.5	90.3	9.7	91.3	8.7
Savannah	59.1	40.9	80.2	19.8	82.6	17.4	83.9	16.1	84.1	15.9
Seattle	38.5	61.5	84.0	16.0	88.8	11.2	88.0	12.0	89.8	10.2
Spokane	45.1	54.9	86.1	13.9	90.3	9.7	89.3	10.7	90.3	9.7
Springfield	51.9	48.1	85.9	14.1	91.7	8.3	90.9	9.1	92.7	7.3
Tampa	49.5	50.5	84.6	15.4	88.5	11.5	88.2	11.8	91.0	9.0
Tulsa	68.9	31.1	87.8	12.2	88.7	11.3	89.2	10.8	88.1	11.9
Virginia Beach	45.2	54.8	86.2	13.8	89.1	10.9	88.9	11.1	91.8	8.2
Warren	64.6	35.4	86.4	13.6	88.4	11.6	89.6	10.4	91.2	8.8
Washington	35.5	64.5	80.8	19.2	85.5	14.5	85.9	14.1	88.2	11.8
Wichita	51.5	48.5	83.2	16.8	85.4	14.6	88.6	11.4	90.0	10.0
U.S.	54.3	45.7	86.4	13.6	88.9	11.1	89.1	10.9	90.2	9.8

Note: Figures shown cover persons 3 years old and over; (1) Metropolitan Statistical Area - see Appendix B for areas included
Source: U.S. Census Bureau, 2007-2009 American Community Survey 3-Year Estimates

Educational Attainment by Race: City

City	High School Graduate (%)					Bachelor's Degree (%)				
	Total	White	Black	Asian	Hisp.[1]	Total	White	Black	Asian	Hisp.[1]
Albuquerque	87.0	95.5	92.7	85.5	75.7	31.8	44.5	28.7	44.3	16.4
Anchorage	92.3	95.7	93.4	81.8	78.8	32.2	37.5	20.7	24.6	18.2
Ann Arbor	97.1	97.9	91.4	96.8	97.8	70.8	73.0	34.5	85.3	60.6
Athens	84.7	93.3	74.5	96.7	51.8	40.9	55.6	12.3	81.7	18.2
Atlanta	86.9	97.7	78.4	88.9	62.7	47.1	76.2	18.9	70.9	27.8
Austin	84.0	96.2	83.1	92.5	59.3	43.3	57.6	20.7	71.1	16.9
Baltimore	78.3	84.6	74.9	92.3	62.5	25.8	45.9	13.3	70.8	21.4
Bellevue	95.8	97.8	97.7	95.3	72.6	60.5	60.0	31.8	71.8	30.3
Birmingham	82.9	88.8	81.0	n/a	57.8	21.7	38.9	13.6	n/a	18.4
Boise City	92.9	94.5	79.8	85.8	74.3	36.1	37.2	20.2	49.9	20.2
Boston	84.1	93.6	78.2	74.2	61.4	43.7	59.6	18.0	45.7	15.6
Boulder	95.5	98.5	n/a	94.8	60.1	69.5	72.9	n/a	80.3	30.7
Cambridge	95.0	97.1	85.3	96.7	84.3	72.4	78.0	35.9	81.4	53.8
Cary	94.6	97.6	94.0	93.6	63.8	62.8	65.3	50.6	80.1	20.2
Charleston	91.2	96.2	76.1	95.5	80.6	46.7	56.5	18.6	57.1	18.7
Charlotte	88.3	95.5	85.1	84.3	58.7	40.1	53.0	23.7	51.1	15.6
Chattanooga	82.7	87.1	76.7	88.7	45.4	26.2	33.3	11.9	54.4	7.2
Chicago	79.6	92.3	79.8	85.5	56.2	32.3	53.9	17.1	53.2	11.5
Cincinnati	83.0	88.7	75.1	89.7	63.3	31.1	43.0	12.7	67.8	21.9
Cleveland	75.7	79.1	74.2	78.9	63.0	13.8	19.9	7.8	45.8	6.6
Colorado Spgs.	91.9	95.4	89.6	84.0	72.7	35.8	40.6	20.4	35.6	13.8
Columbia	86.1	94.6	75.3	n/a	80.8	40.1	59.4	15.5	n/a	16.5
Columbus	87.2	89.6	83.5	89.7	63.9	33.0	38.0	16.9	61.7	15.5
Dallas	71.8	94.4	80.2	87.4	41.0	28.1	53.7	13.5	60.9	7.4
Denver	83.8	95.6	85.1	83.8	56.3	39.7	55.0	22.3	54.4	10.1
Des Moines	86.0	90.5	80.7	74.1	47.8	23.9	26.3	14.3	28.8	6.3
Durham	85.6	94.9	82.8	93.7	48.4	46.1	62.6	30.6	78.1	14.7
Edison	92.1	92.7	85.9	93.2	88.3	48.0	32.7	31.8	75.5	23.0
El Paso	74.0	94.3	93.4	84.4	68.2	21.8	38.3	26.0	50.6	17.2
Eugene	93.2	94.6	96.7	94.1	69.1	39.8	39.7	61.1	64.7	25.1
Evansville	83.7	84.7	77.9	n/a	50.8	18.7	19.5	10.2	n/a	12.7
Fargo	93.5	94.5	62.2	90.4	84.8	38.1	39.0	9.7	52.0	20.7
Ft. Collins	94.3	96.2	n/a	97.7	76.1	49.3	52.2	n/a	73.1	20.3
Ft. Lauderdale	84.7	94.3	65.8	90.1	73.4	31.2	41.6	8.3	51.2	21.2
Ft. Wayne	87.6	91.4	80.5	77.9	55.4	25.0	28.1	11.7	43.9	9.4
Ft. Worth	77.4	91.9	82.4	83.8	47.4	25.0	37.2	15.5	38.7	7.6
Gainesville	87.5	91.6	77.1	90.3	83.0	42.7	52.2	13.5	65.1	43.0
Greensboro	87.3	93.0	84.9	72.5	52.7	34.1	45.9	20.4	31.5	9.8
Honolulu	89.4	96.6	98.0	86.3	89.0	35.1	51.3	23.1	33.2	28.0
Houston	74.2	94.8	81.7	84.3	47.9	28.6	52.0	16.9	53.2	9.2
Huntsville	87.6	92.4	78.4	92.2	57.5	38.2	45.3	20.9	64.6	17.8
Indianapolis	83.8	87.7	81.2	83.7	48.1	28.3	34.0	15.0	52.9	9.0
Irvine	96.3	97.5	92.5	95.9	89.2	64.4	62.0	35.4	76.3	40.5
Jackson	82.1	93.1	78.8	n/a	49.0	27.3	51.8	18.9	n/a	15.1
Jacksonville	86.9	90.1	81.9	85.3	78.1	24.1	26.9	15.2	44.9	21.1
Kansas City	86.1	91.7	80.7	81.7	57.4	30.0	38.9	12.6	45.1	11.1
Knoxville	85.4	87.2	79.4	86.4	59.0	29.0	32.1	11.5	63.1	14.7
Las Vegas	81.1	91.4	83.7	90.6	52.8	21.2	26.3	13.8	40.9	7.3
Lexington	88.0	90.9	79.6	95.5	59.2	38.8	42.6	16.2	77.1	13.4
Lincoln	92.6	94.8	84.0	75.0	66.4	35.7	37.0	19.3	47.9	16.1
Little Rock	88.1	94.1	83.9	96.2	46.6	37.6	51.2	18.5	74.7	12.5
Los Angeles	73.4	93.6	84.8	88.4	48.8	29.9	49.4	21.5	50.9	9.1
Louisville	85.9	87.5	82.6	85.0	69.2	25.0	28.1	12.4	51.9	16.5
Madison	93.7	96.5	72.6	88.6	74.5	50.3	53.3	16.7	66.2	21.8
Manchester	85.8	87.1	83.2	81.3	71.1	25.0	25.3	15.9	48.6	15.2

Table continued on next page.

City	High School Graduate (%)					Bachelor's Degree (%)				
	Total	White	Black	Asian	Hisp.[1]	Total	White	Black	Asian	Hisp.[1]
Miami	67.9	93.7	62.6	87.1	63.9	23.3	58.9	9.8	62.6	19.3
Milwaukee	80.7	90.6	77.4	73.8	51.9	21.6	31.9	10.9	31.1	7.1
Minneapolis	87.6	95.8	71.8	74.3	49.6	43.6	53.1	13.4	42.7	14.9
Naperville	96.2	97.5	95.3	94.7	78.9	63.8	63.3	48.3	81.2	29.7
Nashville	85.0	89.7	81.4	84.6	49.4	32.9	38.4	23.1	47.0	9.3
New Orleans	82.9	93.4	78.3	54.3	71.9	29.2	52.6	14.1	29.6	30.8
New York	79.0	90.6	79.4	74.0	61.7	33.6	50.6	20.6	40.0	14.6
Oakland	78.6	95.8	84.1	68.6	51.0	36.6	67.9	19.7	32.4	13.7
Oklahoma City	84.6	90.5	86.4	82.1	47.8	27.1	32.1	16.2	39.2	7.6
Omaha	88.6	93.5	85.2	90.3	45.6	32.4	36.8	12.9	58.9	7.9
Orlando	86.5	95.0	77.8	88.0	76.8	31.7	44.0	14.1	44.4	20.8
Overland Park	96.0	97.0	91.7	93.1	77.7	55.0	55.6	39.5	68.7	35.9
Oxnard	62.4	93.7	87.3	83.8	44.9	15.4	31.5	17.2	39.5	5.5
Philadelphia	79.8	85.6	78.5	69.2	61.0	22.4	32.2	12.2	33.7	10.2
Phoenix	77.8	91.9	86.0	85.9	52.5	23.7	33.1	20.4	52.0	7.1
Pittsburgh	88.6	90.0	83.2	95.9	89.0	34.3	38.1	14.9	80.2	45.2
Plano	92.3	97.6	98.2	94.9	60.5	52.6	54.9	45.7	76.4	18.6
Portland	89.9	93.9	84.7	76.9	60.6	41.1	45.5	19.6	35.2	19.0
Providence	74.2	88.1	76.8	70.3	55.3	29.6	48.5	20.6	36.7	9.0
Provo	92.6	96.7	n/a	100.0	67.8	40.3	44.1	n/a	51.5	19.6
Raleigh	90.7	97.0	87.7	86.8	54.6	47.5	59.4	26.9	62.2	16.4
Reno	84.6	92.6	86.1	92.0	48.7	28.1	31.1	28.8	45.1	10.1
Richmond	79.6	92.2	71.3	72.2	38.2	32.1	55.8	11.7	47.8	9.6
Riverside	77.3	91.7	92.1	86.2	57.9	21.6	29.0	24.0	48.0	9.3
Rochester	78.4	87.8	70.4	65.1	58.9	24.5	37.2	9.0	29.8	9.5
Sacramento	81.4	92.1	87.7	74.9	60.7	29.3	39.7	17.7	31.8	13.9
St. Louis	81.0	87.4	74.6	74.5	63.0	26.4	38.3	11.8	45.6	17.9
St. Paul	87.5	95.2	80.2	58.4	56.2	38.3	46.8	14.9	20.1	13.9
St. Petersburg	87.3	91.7	76.7	68.4	77.1	27.1	31.5	12.7	27.2	22.8
Salt Lake City	85.3	92.9	71.5	91.6	52.1	38.2	44.9	14.5	64.6	8.9
San Antonio	79.2	94.0	85.0	86.0	69.3	23.2	39.8	20.3	50.1	12.7
San Diego	86.2	95.9	88.4	86.5	61.8	40.8	51.6	22.8	47.9	15.8
San Francisco	85.4	96.9	84.1	72.9	70.5	51.5	70.0	25.1	37.6	25.0
San Jose	81.6	93.3	90.0	85.0	60.6	35.6	44.0	27.6	47.7	11.2
Santa Ana	50.5	90.4	92.9	73.3	38.3	11.6	32.8	25.2	26.6	5.0
Savannah	84.5	92.7	78.8	85.2	65.1	23.7	38.1	11.7	46.6	16.7
Seattle	92.5	96.5	80.5	82.6	72.6	55.0	61.7	21.8	48.8	30.5
Spokane	91.3	92.4	85.7	85.5	79.7	27.8	27.8	21.4	53.4	22.9
Springfield	86.7	87.6	74.0	71.0	74.9	24.9	25.5	6.7	43.2	18.0
Tampa	83.8	91.4	77.4	86.1	70.3	31.9	43.6	13.1	62.3	17.4
Tulsa	85.9	91.0	84.9	82.0	50.4	29.3	35.2	14.8	44.0	8.9
Virginia Beach	92.4	94.0	89.2	89.4	84.8	31.5	34.7	19.1	38.9	18.3
Warren	84.4	84.0	92.8	79.2	78.5	15.3	14.4	13.6	38.3	14.8
Washington	86.4	98.7	81.5	92.9	58.1	48.3	86.9	21.8	75.9	33.7
Wichita	87.1	91.4	85.7	74.2	59.4	27.8	31.7	13.5	34.1	11.7
U.S.	87.1	91.4	85.7	74.2	59.4	27.8	31.7	13.5	34.1	11.7

Note: Figures shown cover persons 25 years old and over; (1) people of Hispanic origin can be of any race
Source: U.S. Census Bureau, 2007-2009 American Community Survey 3-Year Estimates

Educational Attainment by Race: Metro Area

MSA[1]	High School Graduate (%)					Bachelor's Degree (%)				
	Total	White	Black	Asian	Hisp.[2]	Total	White	Black	Asian	Hisp.[2]
Albuquerque	86.1	95.0	92.0	86.1	74.7	28.9	41.1	26.9	43.4	14.5
Anchorage	92.0	94.8	93.6	81.3	78.6	29.4	33.3	19.8	24.5	17.2
Ann Arbor	93.6	94.7	88.4	95.1	81.8	50.2	51.2	27.1	82.0	40.6
Athens	82.8	87.6	72.0	97.2	50.0	34.1	40.4	11.5	77.8	16.6
Atlanta	86.8	90.6	87.2	86.5	56.8	34.2	39.9	25.5	51.9	15.6
Austin	86.3	95.6	85.5	91.4	63.0	38.4	47.7	21.3	66.9	15.7
Baltimore	87.4	90.5	81.4	89.4	71.2	34.3	38.9	19.9	61.0	28.0
Bellevue	91.3	94.3	86.6	85.9	67.5	36.9	38.5	20.1	47.4	17.4
Birmingham	84.8	86.5	82.4	94.2	58.3	26.3	29.7	16.7	67.2	16.2
Boise City	89.1	92.4	87.7	83.6	58.0	27.8	29.6	23.0	44.4	9.6
Boston	90.1	93.3	81.4	83.2	64.8	42.2	44.7	23.0	56.4	17.5
Boulder	93.3	97.4	99.1	94.2	59.7	56.9	61.0	47.8	72.4	19.5
Cambridge	90.1	93.3	81.4	83.2	64.8	42.2	44.7	23.0	56.4	17.5
Cary	89.3	93.9	85.4	90.8	53.2	41.9	47.5	25.2	68.8	15.2
Charleston	87.5	91.9	78.9	83.0	66.1	29.7	36.2	13.7	40.9	15.5
Charlotte	86.3	90.1	83.2	84.9	58.0	32.5	36.7	21.7	51.4	16.0
Chattanooga	82.7	84.1	77.8	87.7	53.5	22.6	23.8	13.7	54.5	12.4
Chicago	85.7	92.9	82.8	90.5	59.0	33.3	40.2	19.1	61.4	11.4
Cincinnati	87.0	88.3	79.2	88.6	67.3	28.3	29.3	15.5	61.9	25.5
Cleveland	87.4	90.1	79.3	86.9	69.2	26.7	29.8	12.7	60.1	12.5
Colorado Spgs.	92.6	95.4	91.1	82.6	75.7	34.9	38.6	22.4	34.4	15.8
Columbia	87.4	90.9	82.4	86.4	63.6	30.3	34.9	20.6	59.3	16.3
Columbus	89.4	90.8	84.3	91.3	67.3	32.9	34.4	18.8	64.3	18.7
Dallas	81.9	92.7	86.3	88.2	49.9	30.2	38.0	21.2	56.4	9.9
Denver	88.7	95.3	87.3	84.7	62.9	37.4	44.1	23.0	48.1	12.5
Des Moines	91.6	94.0	81.6	82.2	57.2	33.2	34.6	17.1	48.1	11.5
Durham	86.6	93.0	82.1	90.0	48.0	43.1	51.9	26.9	71.9	14.5
Edison	84.1	91.8	81.1	82.1	65.2	35.5	43.7	21.4	51.8	15.5
El Paso	71.3	94.0	92.6	83.6	65.4	19.7	37.1	25.6	49.0	15.3
Eugene	90.1	91.4	96.1	92.4	64.6	27.6	27.5	53.4	59.7	17.2
Evansville	86.9	87.5	81.5	94.3	63.8	19.9	20.2	13.5	55.3	13.0
Fargo	93.6	94.4	65.1	89.6	78.1	34.4	35.2	9.6	53.1	14.5
Ft. Collins	93.3	95.7	88.3	97.4	66.5	41.2	43.3	19.3	70.7	14.3
Ft. Lauderdale	82.5	92.2	75.7	87.1	74.5	28.6	36.9	17.2	48.0	23.6
Ft. Wayne	88.2	90.5	81.5	77.7	58.4	23.5	24.9	12.4	44.6	10.8
Ft. Worth	81.9	92.7	86.3	88.2	49.9	30.2	38.0	21.2	56.4	9.9
Gainesville	88.7	91.3	77.6	94.9	83.3	38.5	42.8	14.6	70.4	37.4
Greensboro	83.0	85.9	82.2	77.7	51.6	25.8	28.8	19.7	34.7	10.6
Honolulu	90.4	96.7	98.8	87.3	90.6	30.9	46.0	26.4	30.7	21.1
Houston	79.9	92.8	85.1	86.2	53.8	28.3	38.5	20.6	52.4	10.2
Huntsville	86.8	88.9	80.7	92.6	63.2	34.0	36.3	25.4	54.0	19.4
Indianapolis	87.8	90.2	82.4	90.1	54.1	30.9	33.4	16.8	59.4	13.0
Irvine	77.4	93.9	87.5	86.6	54.5	30.3	44.1	23.0	48.9	10.0
Jackson	84.5	90.4	77.9	84.8	47.6	29.0	36.8	18.4	63.7	11.5
Jacksonville	87.9	90.3	82.0	86.6	78.9	25.9	28.3	15.2	45.3	21.6
Kansas City	89.9	92.7	84.2	86.4	62.8	32.0	35.2	15.8	51.5	12.6
Knoxville	86.5	87.1	84.5	89.1	64.8	28.2	28.5	18.6	65.4	20.8
Las Vegas	83.0	91.8	85.9	89.1	57.0	21.7	25.7	15.9	37.4	8.2
Lexington	86.9	88.9	79.6	94.8	59.0	33.5	35.4	17.2	71.8	12.0
Lincoln	93.1	95.1	84.4	75.2	67.1	35.3	36.3	19.7	47.6	17.2
Little Rock	87.6	89.8	82.8	93.6	60.8	26.5	29.1	16.6	55.8	15.0
Los Angeles	77.4	93.9	87.5	86.6	54.5	30.3	44.1	23.0	48.9	10.0
Louisville	86.4	87.4	83.2	89.0	64.6	24.3	25.6	14.1	54.3	15.1
Madison	93.6	95.2	75.6	90.8	74.5	40.3	41.3	16.6	63.8	20.2
Manchester	90.2	91.2	82.7	89.2	71.4	33.9	33.5	21.2	69.9	21.5

Table continued on next page.

MSA[1]	High School Graduate (%)					Bachelor's Degree (%)				
	Total	White	Black	Asian	Hisp.[2]	Total	White	Black	Asian	Hisp.[2]
Miami	82.5	92.2	75.7	87.1	74.5	28.6	36.9	17.2	48.0	23.6
Milwaukee	88.8	93.3	78.0	84.5	58.9	30.9	35.1	12.5	52.3	11.3
Minneapolis	92.6	95.4	80.2	79.9	60.8	37.5	39.3	20.1	42.4	17.3
Naperville	85.7	92.9	82.8	90.5	59.0	33.3	40.2	19.1	61.4	11.4
Nashville	85.9	88.2	81.8	87.0	54.6	29.8	31.6	22.8	46.4	11.3
New Orleans	83.7	88.2	78.4	68.2	72.2	25.2	31.3	13.8	31.9	19.5
New York	84.1	91.8	81.1	82.1	65.2	35.5	43.7	21.4	51.8	15.5
Oakland	87.0	95.6	86.7	84.0	65.2	43.3	53.8	22.9	49.0	16.0
Oklahoma City	87.1	90.3	86.9	84.3	55.3	27.0	29.4	18.4	44.1	9.7
Omaha	90.5	93.5	86.0	88.9	52.9	31.0	33.1	15.0	54.9	10.4
Orlando	87.2	91.5	80.8	86.2	78.5	27.1	31.0	18.2	44.6	18.3
Overland Park	89.9	92.7	84.2	86.4	62.8	32.0	35.2	15.8	51.5	12.6
Oxnard	82.3	95.3	91.1	91.3	55.7	30.8	39.6	26.4	53.4	10.0
Philadelphia	87.5	91.2	81.8	82.3	62.6	32.0	36.2	16.5	52.0	14.2
Phoenix	84.1	93.3	88.2	88.6	58.2	27.1	33.1	23.6	54.4	9.6
Pittsburgh	90.6	91.0	85.8	91.3	85.5	28.2	28.5	15.4	73.1	33.4
Plano	81.9	92.7	86.3	88.2	49.9	30.2	38.0	21.2	56.4	9.9
Portland	89.9	93.3	86.8	86.1	57.4	33.5	35.1	21.0	46.4	13.3
Providence	82.5	84.6	75.5	79.8	60.9	28.0	29.5	20.2	45.7	11.8
Provo	93.2	95.5	89.0	93.1	70.6	34.3	35.6	23.7	49.3	19.2
Raleigh	89.3	93.9	85.4	90.8	53.2	41.9	47.5	25.2	68.8	15.2
Reno	86.1	93.0	87.3	89.2	52.4	26.5	29.1	24.0	44.1	9.4
Richmond	85.3	90.2	77.5	83.8	57.5	30.7	37.1	16.3	51.4	16.3
Riverside	78.4	91.1	88.3	89.4	59.1	19.4	25.1	20.3	45.3	8.1
Rochester	88.4	91.4	72.9	80.8	64.5	31.4	33.8	12.6	49.3	15.1
Sacramento	86.9	93.4	87.5	81.7	63.5	29.7	33.5	18.8	38.8	13.5
St. Louis	88.1	89.9	80.2	86.3	75.4	28.9	30.9	15.9	61.7	24.3
St. Paul	92.6	95.4	80.2	79.9	60.8	37.5	39.3	20.1	42.4	17.3
St. Petersburg	86.6	89.5	80.2	83.3	73.9	25.5	27.1	17.2	47.6	17.3
Salt Lake City	89.0	93.6	81.9	84.2	62.0	29.7	32.9	21.1	41.4	9.8
San Antonio	81.5	93.6	86.5	84.8	69.8	24.4	37.1	21.9	46.9	12.7
San Diego	85.3	94.7	88.9	87.2	61.8	34.1	41.9	22.1	45.2	14.2
San Francisco	87.0	95.6	86.7	84.0	65.2	43.3	53.8	22.9	49.0	16.0
San Jose	85.3	94.9	91.6	88.9	61.0	43.3	50.1	27.9	57.9	12.4
Santa Ana	77.4	93.9	87.5	86.6	54.5	30.3	44.1	23.0	48.9	10.0
Savannah	87.7	91.3	81.5	87.4	76.2	26.7	32.9	13.6	37.0	19.1
Seattle	91.3	94.3	86.6	85.9	67.5	36.9	38.5	20.1	47.4	17.4
Spokane	92.1	93.0	89.7	84.7	79.8	27.4	27.5	19.8	49.2	19.4
Springfield	87.5	88.2	77.0	81.3	73.1	24.5	24.9	10.2	43.2	16.1
Tampa	86.6	89.5	80.2	83.3	73.9	25.5	27.1	17.2	47.6	17.3
Tulsa	87.4	90.2	84.5	81.4	56.2	25.1	27.6	15.8	39.6	11.3
Virginia Beach	88.8	91.9	82.7	87.9	83.7	27.1	31.7	16.5	39.1	19.8
Warren	86.7	89.3	81.2	87.6	62.4	26.2	28.6	14.4	63.0	14.5
Washington	89.6	95.4	88.3	89.4	63.0	47.0	57.9	28.9	60.5	23.3
Wichita	89.1	92.1	86.3	74.8	62.6	26.9	29.1	15.7	32.5	11.8
U.S.	89.1	92.1	86.3	74.8	62.6	26.9	29.1	15.7	32.5	11.8

Note: Figures shown cover persons 25 years old and over; (1) Metropolitan Statistical Area - see Appendix B for areas included; (2) people of Hispanic origin can be of any race
Source: U.S. Census Bureau, 2007-2009 American Community Survey 3-Year Estimates

Cost of Living Index

Area	Composite	Groceries	Housing	Utilities	Transp.	Health	Misc.
Albuquerque[2]	95.1	92.0	90.5	88.6	94.7	100.2	101.8
Anchorage	128.4	134.5	142.9	94.1	122.0	135.7	124.8
Ann Arbor	n/a	n/a	n/a	n/a	n/a	n/a	n/a
Athens	n/a	n/a	n/a	n/a	n/a	n/a	n/a
Atlanta	95.6	96.2	90.7	86.3	99.3	103.3	100.3
Austin	95.5	89.3	85.1	110.7	100.2	100.3	100.4
Baltimore	119.4	110.8	155.4	112.5	105.3	97.9	100.0
Bellevue[3]	121.4	115.1	140.3	85.7	118.8	119.9	119.1
Birmingham	90.8	93.5	73.2	105.7	93.5	87.9	100.3
Boise City	97.2	98.5	84.0	99.6	108.0	106.6	103.3
Boston	132.5	116.7	152.7	138.6	104.5	123.5	128.6
Boulder	n/a	n/a	n/a	n/a	n/a	n/a	n/a
Cambridge[4]	132.5	116.7	152.7	138.6	104.5	123.5	128.6
Cary[5]	98.2	104.2	88.8	105.6	96.7	101.0	101.9
Charleston[6]	98.3	105.7	92.6	96.6	93.9	104.4	101.5
Charlotte	93.2	97.1	79.5	91.2	95.7	110.3	101.4
Chattanooga	91.1	97.4	84.0	82.5	96.4	93.3	95.7
Chicago	116.9	111.2	134.8	117.3	116.5	108.5	104.4
Cincinnati	93.8	96.4	81.9	103.8	98.0	95.8	98.7
Cleveland	101.0	108.1	93.3	109.0	101.4	104.3	102.1
Colorado Springs	92.8	95.4	92.0	86.8	96.2	102.3	92.1
Columbia	100.4	105.2	82.3	109.0	102.0	106.2	110.6
Columbus	92.0	91.6	86.2	100.2	99.1	107.7	90.6
Dallas	91.9	96.2	70.7	105.5	100.9	103.8	100.4
Denver	103.2	101.0	107.5	101.9	95.4	105.9	102.7
Des Moines	90.9	90.9	89.6	90.2	95.9	90.8	90.9
Durham	96.6	97.9	86.8	96.3	105.5	108.5	100.6
Edison[7]	124.8	108.9	154.1	128.6	103.9	108.9	112.2
El Paso	90.4	99.9	86.0	88.1	97.0	95.4	88.5
Eugene	109.8	93.8	132.3	85.3	110.0	118.2	102.9
Evansville	96.2	97.9	86.3	120.0	97.1	97.4	96.4
Fargo[8]	92.7	99.8	87.4	78.7	95.8	102.4	96.6
Fort Collins[9]	91.0	102.7	79.3	89.6	91.4	100.3	95.7
Fort Lauderdale	115.7	112.5	144.0	92.5	106.3	102.4	103.7
Fort Wayne[10]	94.4	93.3	89.3	87.3	106.9	93.4	98.0
Fort Worth	91.1	89.8	78.0	106.2	97.6	93.8	96.1
Gainesville	99.8	106.3	101.8	99.2	103.3	92.7	95.5
Greensboro[11]	92.4	98.5	82.9	88.5	83.3	99.3	101.5
Honolulu	165.7	160.1	249.0	146.6	126.2	120.0	117.9
Houston	92.2	85.1	82.0	97.7	99.2	94.6	99.9
Huntsville	91.2	94.9	78.7	86.1	99.7	92.0	99.8
Indianapolis	87.2	91.4	73.4	86.7	100.5	93.6	93.1
Irvine[12]	146.4	104.5	242.8	103.2	114.6	111.6	105.2
Jackson	96.9	93.0	94.0	118.1	92.0	95.7	96.1
Jacksonville	92.9	102.8	80.0	91.9	103.6	94.5	97.3
Kansas City[13]	97.8	94.8	89.2	99.8	100.8	97.2	105.1
Knoxville	89.4	91.4	82.0	95.1	84.2	88.4	95.1
Las Vegas	101.9	106.8	94.1	97.7	104.9	109.0	106.2
Lexington	92.8	86.9	88.7	93.9	97.6	93.7	97.1
Lincoln	91.7	94.4	81.7	98.4	106.3	96.9	92.5
Little Rock[14]	96.5	92.9	92.2	104.1	94.0	93.5	100.4
Los Angeles[15]	136.4	106.0	207.1	101.7	113.6	109.1	107.0
Louisville	87.7	81.6	78.7	99.1	96.9	87.2	91.9
Madison	109.8	104.8	118.0	95.0	109.5	115.2	108.6
Manchester	116.8	102.3	117.0	124.5	100.1	116.1	125.0
Miami	106.0	110.9	107.7	91.9	108.8	105.7	106.2

Table continued on next page.

Area	Composite	Groceries	Housing	Utilities	Transp.	Health	Misc.
Milwaukee[16]	101.9	98.1	112.7	98.6	99.2	108.1	94.8
Minneapolis	111.0	111.6	116.8	104.7	103.7	105.4	110.4
Naperville[17]	102.2	100.9	102.3	116.1	111.3	106.5	95.2
Nashville[18]	88.9	91.7	71.3	82.6	92.5	87.3	104.5
New Orleans[19]	97.0	95.1	101.0	82.2	96.2	93.4	99.4
New York[20]	216.7	154.3	386.7	169.6	120.3	130.2	145.7
Oakland	139.1	116.8	198.8	94.7	113.6	119.9	119.0
Oklahoma City	91.7	92.9	86.0	88.1	92.6	99.4	96.2
Omaha	88.3	92.0	79.3	89.9	100.0	96.8	89.7
Orlando	97.8	97.8	85.4	108.5	101.8	95.5	104.5
Overland Park[21]	97.8	94.8	89.2	99.8	100.8	97.2	105.1
Oxnard	n/a	n/a	n/a	n/a	n/a	n/a	n/a
Philadelphia	126.5	124.9	141.3	135.9	105.8	108.2	119.6
Phoenix	100.7	108.1	90.4	96.6	108.9	108.8	104.6
Pittsburgh	91.5	104.1	74.4	97.0	105.9	90.1	95.8
Plano	97.4	101.3	85.2	103.9	101.8	102.9	102.6
Portland	111.3	105.8	130.8	87.1	105.8	113.6	105.1
Providence	123.3	113.4	129.0	129.0	102.5	113.2	128.1
Provo	n/a	n/a	n/a	n/a	n/a	n/a	n/a
Raleigh	98.2	104.2	88.8	105.6	96.7	101.0	101.9
Reno[22]	101.1	105.4	101.5	91.2	107.3	101.8	100.0
Richmond	104.5	103.6	103.2	113.9	100.8	112.6	103.2
Riverside	112.5	104.9	136.3	99.9	113.4	104.4	99.1
Rochester	100.0	94.6	94.2	114.4	108.7	99.7	100.2
Sacramento	116.2	114.7	135.7	109.6	114.4	110.8	102.8
Saint Louis[23]	90.4	98.4	74.6	92.9	99.0	100.8	96.5
Saint Paul	110.0	107.0	112.9	106.8	103.4	106.7	112.2
Saint Petersburg[24]	92.4	96.3	84.7	93.8	103.3	98.4	93.4
Salt Lake City	100.6	100.1	108.0	72.5	102.1	98.8	102.9
San Antonio	95.7	84.9	95.3	82.8	100.7	99.9	102.2
San Diego	132.3	105.5	194.4	101.9	113.1	111.5	105.8
San Francisco	164.0	111.9	281.0	94.5	113.0	117.0	124.3
San Jose	156.1	115.3	260.3	137.2	114.0	119.0	103.6
Santa Ana[25]	146.4	104.5	242.8	103.2	114.6	111.6	105.2
Savannah	93.5	94.7	84.0	94.0	98.4	99.0	99.1
Seattle	121.4	115.1	140.3	85.7	118.8	119.9	119.1
Spokane	93.9	92.4	85.7	89.5	109.1	110.0	96.5
Springfield	88.0	93.2	76.8	83.2	96.8	95.3	93.8
Tampa	92.4	96.3	84.7	93.8	103.3	98.4	93.4
Tulsa	88.4	91.9	66.5	95.2	99.1	94.6	100.5
Virginia Beach[26]	111.7	106.6	121.9	108.4	104.1	109.6	108.4
Warren[27]	99.4	92.7	95.2	129.5	101.3	94.2	96.6
Washington[28]	140.1	107.9	226.4	97.3	109.3	103.4	103.7
Wichita	91.8	90.5	83.6	89.7	100.6	96.7	97.1
U.S.	100.0	100.0	100.0	100.0	100.0	100.0	100.0

Note: In cases where data is not available for the city, data for the metro area or for a neighboring city has been provided and noted below; (2) Rio Rancho (data for Albuquerque was not available); (3) Seattle urban area; (4) Boston urban area; (5) Raleigh urban area; (6) Charleston-North Charleston metro area; (7) Middlesex-Monmouth NJ metro area; (8) Fargo-Moorhead ND-MN metro area; (9) Loveland (data for Fort Collins was not available); (10) Fort Wayne-Allen County; (11) Winston-Salem (data for Greensboro was not available); (12) Orange County; (13) Kansas City MO-KS metro area; (14) Little Rock-North Little Rock metro area; (15) Los Angeles-Long Beach metro area; (16) Milwaukee-Waukesha metro area; (17) Joliet (data for Naperville was not available); (18) Nashville-Franklin; (19) Slidell (data for New Orleans was not available); (20) Manhattan; (21) Kansas City MO-KS metro area; (22) Reno-Sparks NV metro area; (23) St. Louis MO-IL metro area; (24) Tampa urban area; (25) Orange County; (26) Hampton Roads/SE Virginia area; (27) Detroit (data for Warren was not available); (28) Washington-Arlington-Alexandria DC-VA metro area
Source: The Council for Community and Economic Research (formerly ACCRA), Cost of Living Index, 2010

Grocery Prices

Area	T-Bone Steak ($/pound)	Frying Chicken ($/pound)	Whole Milk ($/half gal.)	Eggs ($/dozen)	Orange Juice ($/64 oz.)	Coffee ($/11.5 oz.)
Albuquerque[2]	7.81	0.94	1.95	1.33	2.75	4.06
Anchorage	10.18	1.39	2.43	2.31	4.48	4.53
Ann Arbor	n/a	n/a	n/a	n/a	n/a	n/a
Athens	n/a	n/a	n/a	n/a	n/a	n/a
Atlanta	9.76	1.17	1.75	1.16	3.18	3.49
Austin	8.82	1.13	2.29	1.32	2.72	3.08
Baltimore	10.01	1.43	2.22	2.13	3.18	3.71
Bellevue[3]	9.35	1.20	2.03	1.75	3.72	4.59
Birmingham	8.04	1.10	2.14	1.50	2.82	3.29
Boise City	8.72	1.13	1.76	1.57	3.08	3.76
Boston	11.01	1.43	2.23	2.00	3.43	3.71
Boulder	n/a	n/a	n/a	n/a	n/a	n/a
Cambridge[4]	11.01	1.43	2.23	2.00	3.43	3.71
Cary[5]	9.52	1.21	2.14	1.62	3.02	3.51
Charleston[6]	8.36	1.27	2.28	1.51	3.11	3.42
Charlotte	9.26	1.19	2.19	1.51	2.96	3.41
Chattanooga	9.11	1.12	2.29	1.34	2.96	3.45
Chicago	8.69	1.16	2.25	1.35	3.13	4.81
Cincinnati	9.66	1.13	1.68	1.18	2.91	3.57
Cleveland	10.26	1.40	1.96	1.51	3.43	3.91
Colorado Springs	8.98	0.99	1.81	1.26	2.78	3.91
Columbia	9.62	1.28	2.21	1.32	3.22	3.47
Columbus	10.68	1.02	1.64	1.02	2.89	3.43
Dallas	8.66	0.98	2.03	1.40	2.89	3.81
Denver	9.79	1.08	1.74	1.25	2.85	4.94
Des Moines	7.44	1.12	1.83	1.34	2.99	3.55
Durham	8.39	1.04	2.24	1.42	3.00	3.25
Edison[7]	8.64	1.27	2.04	2.20	3.11	3.76
El Paso	8.78	0.90	1.88	1.59	2.88	3.91
Eugene	8.45	1.05	1.71	1.49	2.91	4.09
Evansville	8.84	1.07	2.09	1.32	3.00	3.72
Fargo[8]	8.49	1.32	2.56	1.14	3.17	3.90
Fort Collins[9]	10.18	1.00	1.66	1.22	2.76	4.84
Fort Lauderdale	10.42	1.43	2.50	1.67	3.13	3.28
Fort Wayne[10]	9.67	0.92	1.71	1.21	3.03	3.72
Fort Worth	8.27	1.03	1.88	1.33	2.83	3.24
Gainesville	9.99	1.24	2.43	1.41	3.06	3.57
Greensboro[11]	8.93	1.18	2.21	1.45	2.87	3.21
Honolulu	9.49	1.64	3.58	2.75	4.50	6.32
Houston	6.97	0.94	1.98	1.31	2.64	2.93
Huntsville	9.05	1.12	2.03	1.41	2.66	3.14
Indianapolis	8.18	1.01	1.75	1.34	2.86	3.34
Irvine[12]	9.60	0.89	2.02	1.88	3.23	4.81
Jackson	9.13	1.01	2.09	1.33	2.85	3.02
Jacksonville	9.38	1.27	2.39	1.47	3.03	3.46
Kansas City[13]	9.22	1.26	1.99	1.37	3.06	3.50
Knoxville	8.86	0.99	2.08	1.25	2.76	3.00
Las Vegas	9.42	1.19	2.11	1.71	3.20	4.42
Lexington	8.62	0.97	1.60	1.08	2.59	3.30
Lincoln	8.71	1.33	1.81	1.27	3.10	3.40
Little Rock[14]	9.69	1.01	1.82	1.25	2.88	3.39
Los Angeles[15]	10.36	1.17	2.01	1.97	3.16	4.84
Louisville	8.01	0.96	1.57	1.19	2.60	3.48
Madison	8.60	1.60	1.85	1.16	3.47	3.80
Manchester	9.90	1.17	1.98	1.49	2.91	3.63

Table continued on next page.

Area	T-Bone Steak ($/pound)	Frying Chicken ($/pound)	Whole Milk ($/half gal.)	Eggs ($/dozen)	Orange Juice ($/64 oz.)	Coffee ($/11.5 oz.)
Miami	9.76	1.26	2.44	1.63	3.15	3.44
Milwaukee[16]	9.01	1.36	1.83	1.07	3.21	3.60
Minneapolis	13.82	2.51	2.63	1.96	3.14	3.89
Naperville[17]	9.12	1.13	2.22	1.29	2.90	4.28
Nashville[18]	8.77	1.12	1.99	1.24	2.78	3.22
New Orleans[19]	9.46	1.03	2.40	1.50	2.77	3.37
New York[20]	13.93	1.77	2.47	2.67	4.94	5.82
Oakland	10.55	1.43	1.98	2.30	3.28	5.39
Oklahoma City	8.81	0.99	1.87	1.21	2.66	3.42
Omaha	8.11	1.22	1.71	1.25	2.92	3.26
Orlando	9.32	1.20	2.63	1.49	2.93	3.28
Overland Park[21]	9.22	1.26	1.99	1.37	3.06	3.50
Oxnard	n/a	n/a	n/a	n/a	n/a	n/a
Philadelphia	10.01	1.58	1.92	1.97	4.04	3.87
Phoenix	9.05	1.32	2.05	1.59	3.17	4.76
Pittsburgh	8.50	1.47	1.83	1.69	3.23	4.02
Plano	9.26	1.03	2.09	1.59	2.99	3.74
Portland	9.52	1.25	1.68	1.57	3.17	4.44
Providence	10.07	1.09	2.16	1.92	3.06	3.56
Provo	n/a	n/a	n/a	n/a	n/a	n/a
Raleigh	9.52	1.21	2.14	1.62	3.02	3.51
Reno[22]	9.27	1.16	2.08	1.58	3.41	4.63
Richmond	9.64	1.02	2.08	1.47	2.90	3.58
Riverside	8.79	1.04	2.03	1.92	3.34	4.52
Rochester	10.40	1.08	1.69	1.38	2.92	2.74
Sacramento	9.49	1.31	1.98	1.95	3.30	4.92
Saint Louis[23]	8.54	1.31	2.23	1.54	3.00	3.81
Saint Paul	11.91	2.13	2.43	1.84	3.04	3.77
Saint Petersburg[24]	8.57	1.06	2.36	1.45	2.77	3.26
Salt Lake City	7.91	1.37	1.68	1.30	2.95	3.82
San Antonio	7.73	1.03	2.04	1.22	2.92	3.02
San Diego	10.29	0.91	2.03	2.00	3.10	4.85
San Francisco	10.54	1.23	1.78	2.08	3.44	5.36
San Jose	9.62	1.27	1.52	1.95	2.78	5.33
Santa Ana[25]	9.60	0.89	2.02	1.88	3.23	4.81
Savannah	8.21	1.08	2.02	1.32	2.68	3.28
Seattle	9.35	1.20	2.03	1.75	3.72	4.59
Spokane	7.67	1.00	1.84	1.50	3.08	3.63
Springfield	9.65	1.06	1.92	1.19	3.05	3.35
Tampa	8.57	1.06	2.36	1.45	2.77	3.26
Tulsa	7.86	0.95	1.97	1.34	3.43	3.35
Virginia Beach[26]	9.46	1.23	2.10	1.81	3.18	4.04
Warren[27]	9.36	0.93	1.70	1.23	2.87	3.29
Washington[28]	9.74	1.52	2.16	1.87	3.06	3.79
Wichita	8.49	1.04	1.93	1.28	3.00	3.26
Average[99]	9.04	1.16	2.02	1.47	3.08	3.65
Minimum[99]	6.97	0.84	1.46	0.96	2.39	2.64
Maximum[99]	13.93	2.51	3.58	3.01	4.94	6.32

Note: **T-Bone Steak** (price per pound); **Frying Chicken** (price per pound, whole fryer); **Whole Milk** (half gallon carton); **Eggs** (price per dozen, Grade A, large); **Orange Juice** (64 oz. Tropicana or Florida Natural); **Coffee** (11.5 oz. can, vacuum-packed, Maxwell House, Hills Bros, or Folgers); (99) Values for the local area are compared with the average, minimum, and maximum values for all 331 areas in the Cost of Living Index report; n/a not available; In cases where data is not available for the city, data for the metro area or for a neighboring city has been provided and noted below; (2) Rio Rancho (data for Albuquerque was not available); (3) Seattle urban area; (4) Boston urban area; (5) Raleigh urban area; (6) Charleston-North Charleston metro area; (7) Middlesex-Monmouth NJ metro area; (8) Fargo-Moorhead ND-MN metro area; (9) Loveland (data for Fort Collins was not available); (10) Fort Wayne-Allen County; (11) Winston-Salem (data for Greensboro was not available); (12) Orange County; (13) Kansas City MO-KS metro area; (14) Little Rock-North Little Rock metro area; (15) Los Angeles-Long Beach metro area; (16) Milwaukee-Waukesha metro area; (17) Joliet (data for Naperville was not available); (18) Nashville-Franklin; (19) Slidell (data for New Orleans was not available); (20) Manhattan; (21) Kansas City MO-KS metro area; (22) Reno-Sparks NV metro area; (23) St. Louis MO-IL metro area; (24) Tampa urban area; (25) Orange County; (26) Hampton Roads/SE Virginia area; (27) Detroit (data for Warren was not available); (28) Washington-Arlington-Alexandria DC-VA metro area
Source: The Council for Community and Economic Research (formerly ACCRA), Cost of Living Index, 2010

Housing and Utility Costs

Area	New Home Price ($)	Apartment Rent ($/month)	All Electric ($/month)	Part Electric ($/month)	Other Energy ($/month)	Telephone ($/month)
Albuquerque[2]	269,216	700	-	90.02	70.99	22.15
Anchorage	423,830	1,106	-	68.50	106.56	22.41
Ann Arbor	n/a	n/a	n/a	n/a	n/a	n/a
Athens	n/a	n/a	n/a	n/a	n/a	n/a
Atlanta	261,224	790	-	88.54	54.81	25.06
Austin	231,855	925	-	97.77	116.32	24.18
Baltimore	440,849	1,415	-	109.71	93.93	28.32
Bellevue[3]	383,117	1,365	141.71	-	-	24.99
Birmingham	205,371	694	-	114.09	85.95	24.33
Boise City	254,424	718	-	87.40	74.57	30.00
Boston	418,700	1,492	-	104.91	132.52	38.32
Boulder	n/a	n/a	n/a	n/a	n/a	n/a
Cambridge[4]	418,700	1,492	-	104.91	132.52	38.32
Cary[5]	263,999	676	-	98.33	70.48	32.33
Charleston[6]	264,161	899	176.55	-	-	23.82
Charlotte	238,497	636	145.02	-	-	28.13
Chattanooga	242,572	716	-	63.46	80.12	22.23
Chicago	360,966	1,455	-	109.50	104.03	29.15
Cincinnati	233,664	762	-	124.09	66.86	25.32
Cleveland	254,654	986	-	101.95	112.98	22.87
Colorado Springs	261,466	783	-	58.35	66.68	30.15
Columbia	235,945	752	-	92.81	105.96	27.00
Columbus	247,893	731	-	98.41	72.17	27.99
Dallas	197,358	702	-	139.74	44.85	28.15
Denver	328,601	783	-	80.90	98.81	26.81
Des Moines	277,033	586	-	64.80	80.37	27.37
Durham	253,572	733	144.51	-	-	31.90
Edison[7]	446,782	1,309	-	136.02	106.80	29.75
El Paso	235,174	825	-	102.64	38.19	26.95
Eugene	420,648	820	-	60.11	81.66	24.71
Evansville	255,106	688	-	103.19	130.13	26.01
Fargo[8]	259,446	704	-	57.46	64.79	25.01
Fort Collins[9]	215,820	818	-	45.62	68.15	34.95
Fort Lauderdale	396,553	1,299	170.81	-	-	22.37
Fort Wayne[10]	270,867	650	-	61.06	72.83	28.16
Fort Worth	203,993	902	-	133.63	45.92	29.95
Gainesville	282,583	883	-	133.02	50.67	24.00
Greensboro[11]	247,228	616	145.37	-	-	26.07
Honolulu	695,539	2,480	307.53	-	-	25.95
Houston	224,048	858	-	107.28	49.34	29.82
Huntsville	226,779	736	127.90	-	-	28.90
Indianapolis	199,433	789	-	73.06	84.58	22.01
Irvine[12]	732,021	1,673	-	129.61	55.54	26.35
Jackson	273,992	730	-	94.24	118.02	30.00
Jacksonville	205,252	933	163.38	-	-	23.88
Kansas City[13]	261,976	751	-	83.68	79.26	29.67
Knoxville	243,677	640	-	69.25	94.34	26.11
Las Vegas	272,475	801	-	126.18	69.95	19.55
Lexington	258,943	774	-	74.75	76.65	28.40
Lincoln	229,311	728	-	64.44	86.68	31.74
Little Rock[14]	261,610	746	-	84.88	77.51	32.90
Los Angeles[15]	585,580	1,841	-	122.63	58.45	26.35
Louisville	220,296	770	-	66.42	98.63	28.66
Madison	360,679	818	-	93.91	74.82	25.01
Manchester	335,686	1,052	-	102.93	103.33	36.25

Table continued on next page.

Area	New Home Price ($)	Apartment Rent ($/month)	All Electric ($/month)	Part Electric ($/month)	Other Energy ($/month)	Telephone ($/month)
Miami	266,107	1,433	169.06	-	-	22.44
Milwaukee[16]	341,177	804	-	101.00	73.89	25.88
Minneapolis	332,330	1,059	-	79.76	114.98	24.99
Naperville[17]	278,110	998	-	108.43	103.92	28.62
Nashville[18]	195,042	795	-	77.18	61.48	23.59
New Orleans[19]	272,114	1,019	137.12	-	-	23.70
New York[20]	1,123,114	2,776	-	193.01	163.08	29.95
Oakland	604,992	1,516	-	113.71	61.24	22.91
Oklahoma City	250,492	693	-	70.76	70.02	27.01
Omaha	231,995	661	-	86.59	67.95	24.71
Orlando	238,078	803	190.04	-	-	28.95
Overland Park[21]	261,976	751	-	83.68	79.26	29.67
Oxnard	n/a	n/a	n/a	n/a	n/a	n/a
Philadelphia	392,622	1,314	-	147.68	88.26	36.75
Phoenix	265,399	795	182.92	-	-	22.17
Pittsburgh	204,467	790	-	91.42	89.92	22.90
Plano	228,377	940	-	139.88	48.73	26.01
Portland	391,472	1,015	-	64.22	81.66	24.95
Providence	358,133	1,246	-	99.56	119.39	36.19
Provo	n/a	n/a	n/a	n/a	n/a	n/a
Raleigh	263,999	676	-	98.33	70.48	32.33
Reno[22]	286,757	883	-	80.91	97.72	19.43
Richmond	297,373	958	-	95.90	81.91	35.95
Riverside	399,770	1,078	-	115.27	65.09	25.23
Rochester	268,508	824	-	108.24	94.10	29.99
Sacramento	399,608	1,074	-	157.89	45.30	26.35
Saint Louis[23]	206,539	743	-	70.75	73.84	29.43
Saint Paul	321,547	1,022	-	79.55	121.00	24.99
Saint Petersburg[24]	233,346	838	173.22	-	-	22.72
Salt Lake City	318,482	821	-	59.46	61.12	21.01
San Antonio	254,957	1,018	-	89.68	40.06	26.01
San Diego	562,945	1,655	-	81.47	100.17	26.35
San Francisco	813,300	2,264	-	112.84	61.02	23.07
San Jose	781,361	1,537	-	218.20	60.80	26.36
Santa Ana[25]	732,021	1,673	-	129.61	55.54	26.35
Savannah	248,019	694	155.51	-	-	27.42
Seattle	383,117	1,365	141.71	-	-	24.99
Spokane	248,473	730	-	48.02	109.24	23.73
Springfield	226,377	619	-	53.95	67.76	28.37
Tampa	233,346	838	173.22	-	-	22.72
Tulsa	191,384	590	-	72.87	72.19	30.97
Virginia Beach[26]	352,318	969	-	98.38	73.83	33.45
Warren[27]	276,971	757	-	95.04	153.48	28.95
Washington[28]	668,633	1,783	-	87.02	98.13	22.14
Wichita	246,259	671	-	74.71	65.17	28.56
Average[99]	293,442	810	166.39	91.93	83.82	26.93
Minimum[99]	182,545	453	119.21	44.47	36.85	17.98
Maximum[99]	1,123,114	2,776	307.53	218.20	313.90	39.15

Note: *New Home Price* (2,400 sf living area, 8,000 sf lot, in urban area with full utilities); *Apartment Rent* (950 sf 2 bedroom/1.5 or 2 bath, unfurnished, excluding all utilities except water); *All Electric* (average monthly cost for an all-electric home); *Part Electric* (average monthly cost for a part-electric home); *Other Energy* (average monthly cost for natural gas, fuel oil, coal, wood, and any other forms of energy except electricity); *Telephone* (price includes basic monthly rate for a private residential line plus additional local usage charges incurred by a family of four); (99) Values for the local area are compared with the average, minimum, and maximum values for all 331 areas in the Cost of Living Index report; n/a not available; In cases where data is not available for the city, data for the metro area or for a neighboring city has been provided and noted below; (2) Rio Rancho (data for Albuquerque was not available); (3) Seattle urban area; (4) Boston urban area; (5) Raleigh urban area; (6) Charleston-North Charleston metro area; (7) Middlesex-Monmouth NJ metro area; (8) Fargo-Moorhead ND-MN metro area; (9) Loveland (data for Fort Collins was not available); (10) Fort Wayne-Allen County; (11) Winston-Salem (data for Greensboro was not available); (12) Orange County; (13) Kansas City MO-KS metro area; (14) Little Rock-North Little Rock metro area; (15) Los Angeles-Long Beach metro area; (16) Milwaukee-Waukesha metro area; (17) Joliet (data for Naperville was not available); (18) Nashville-Franklin; (19) Slidell (data for New Orleans was not available); (20) Manhattan; (21) Kansas City MO-KS metro area; (22) Reno-Sparks NV metro area; (23) St. Louis MO-IL metro area; (24) Tampa urban area; (25) Orange County; (26) Hampton Roads/SE Virginia area; (27) Detroit (data for Warren was not available); (28) Washington-Arlington-Alexandria DC-VA metro area
Source: The Council for Community and Economic Research (formerly ACCRA), Cost of Living Index, 2010

Health Care, Transportation, and Other Costs

Area	Doctor ($/visit)	Dentist ($/visit)	Optometrist ($/visit)	Gasoline ($/gallon)	Beauty Salon ($/visit)	Men's Shirt ($)
Albuquerque[2]	87.47	86.26	90.61	2.67	32.72	25.09
Anchorage	133.17	120.42	170.17	3.31	43.27	25.15
Ann Arbor	n/a	n/a	n/a	n/a	n/a	n/a
Athens	n/a	n/a	n/a	n/a	n/a	n/a
Atlanta	87.08	88.73	70.82	2.63	42.99	22.31
Austin	84.28	82.40	94.34	2.61	46.72	21.07
Baltimore	78.83	78.41	68.89	2.74	43.70	25.55
Bellevue[3]	113.67	104.49	110.96	3.13	40.57	34.64
Birmingham	75.67	64.72	91.35	2.63	31.44	30.25
Boise City	99.86	91.28	89.28	2.88	25.25	27.32
Boston	149.00	103.02	91.45	2.78	44.00	37.99
Boulder	n/a	n/a	n/a	n/a	n/a	n/a
Cambridge[4]	149.00	103.02	91.45	2.78	44.00	37.99
Cary[5]	100.28	83.96	83.76	2.61	31.23	21.24
Charleston[6]	92.61	83.33	91.20	2.57	44.42	25.75
Charlotte	94.78	99.67	97.44	2.72	35.00	22.07
Chattanooga	96.93	60.00	89.47	2.55	38.33	25.56
Chicago	86.66	98.99	97.82	3.13	36.73	27.60
Cincinnati	84.39	71.22	81.89	2.80	32.30	18.66
Cleveland	93.00	82.33	85.40	2.79	30.33	25.59
Colorado Springs	95.20	81.80	86.83	2.48	30.40	25.11
Columbia	91.89	86.67	94.83	2.57	30.67	28.29
Columbus	106.85	88.45	107.02	2.76	36.00	24.74
Dallas	92.71	84.90	90.40	2.58	29.10	24.60
Denver	106.13	84.83	96.72	2.53	35.30	20.38
Des Moines	83.51	65.12	74.94	2.58	26.33	17.43
Durham	106.11	84.05	91.67	2.70	33.33	20.31
Edison[7]	73.55	108.25	89.10	2.72	32.67	37.62
El Paso	85.28	74.89	74.25	2.69	31.89	23.91
Eugene	138.40	87.60	103.89	2.86	31.27	26.52
Evansville	88.42	68.67	79.13	2.71	29.33	28.49
Fargo[8]	108.17	77.33	73.70	2.65	25.60	31.50
Fort Collins[9]	88.00	83.75	91.59	2.44	29.73	19.67
Fort Lauderdale	81.32	86.62	98.08	2.80	40.80	18.84
Fort Wayne[10]	81.67	67.44	88.11	2.79	32.00	36.22
Fort Worth	84.00	76.34	55.72	2.57	34.89	26.37
Gainesville	71.87	75.15	77.39	2.78	37.86	17.76
Greensboro[11]	86.67	77.18	83.00	2.63	34.60	24.45
Honolulu	131.02	84.96	117.83	3.38	46.03	41.08
Houston	76.66	78.10	86.17	2.57	40.20	22.48
Huntsville	61.56	73.56	94.33	2.73	33.61	20.24
Indianapolis	79.31	71.39	93.43	2.89	32.69	15.96
Irvine[12]	93.67	96.07	100.94	3.12	56.87	24.86
Jackson	84.10	76.53	79.21	2.51	31.89	24.62
Jacksonville	71.32	82.84	54.53	2.67	41.87	21.38
Kansas City[13]	84.50	73.23	76.55	2.66	23.80	38.45
Knoxville	77.17	66.13	80.80	2.55	33.60	21.38
Las Vegas	100.78	89.80	109.17	2.85	39.43	27.90
Lexington	82.49	71.84	66.34	2.64	31.87	19.49
Lincoln	107.00	60.33	104.50	2.80	23.50	27.50
Little Rock[14]	91.44	67.44	80.83	2.53	39.17	23.68
Los Angeles[15]	86.67	92.60	110.07	3.13	56.67	23.31
Louisville	71.63	71.63	73.37	2.68	26.80	22.73
Madison	147.72	85.74	49.36	2.76	34.93	23.10
Manchester	149.00	87.00	90.60	2.74	38.67	36.80

Table continued on next page.

Area	Doctor ($/visit)	Dentist ($/visit)	Optometrist ($/visit)	Gasoline ($/gallon)	Beauty Salon ($/visit)	Men's Shirt ($)
Miami	90.57	89.88	79.93	2.80	45.87	24.40
Milwaukee[16]	128.58	77.47	48.32	2.75	30.35	19.23
Minneapolis	108.67	81.50	80.79	2.70	39.42	23.20
Naperville[17]	100.87	83.37	106.05	2.86	30.48	17.20
Nashville[18]	79.60	73.80	88.47	2.59	30.53	23.13
New Orleans[19]	83.99	67.07	75.35	2.62	37.04	28.38
New York[20]	120.23	119.19	150.67	3.01	47.40	43.58
Oakland	119.87	103.75	119.49	3.06	46.66	44.56
Oklahoma City	85.33	85.04	89.69	2.47	33.95	20.57
Omaha	99.37	65.83	87.53	2.74	27.25	19.16
Orlando	79.03	77.49	69.78	2.67	42.00	26.70
Overland Park[21]	84.50	73.23	76.55	2.66	23.80	38.45
Oxnard	n/a	n/a	n/a	n/a	n/a	n/a
Philadelphia	114.01	89.01	100.28	2.74	57.52	38.19
Phoenix	86.05	96.56	95.97	2.79	44.11	27.09
Pittsburgh	67.07	70.67	72.40	2.76	34.33	22.32
Plano	93.54	85.49	79.53	2.52	30.92	22.21
Portland	113.58	94.28	105.22	2.79	29.63	25.33
Providence	149.00	77.60	98.26	2.81	43.00	36.87
Provo	n/a	n/a	n/a	n/a	n/a	n/a
Raleigh	100.28	83.96	83.76	2.61	31.23	21.24
Reno[22]	80.33	92.00	102.00	3.03	29.17	20.86
Richmond	94.33	98.00	99.97	2.61	37.42	21.11
Riverside	82.75	86.67	88.28	3.16	35.99	26.26
Rochester	93.53	83.22	88.43	2.90	28.59	28.13
Sacramento	96.93	92.13	107.93	3.07	48.03	26.34
Saint Louis[23]	80.86	89.08	72.96	2.69	29.19	16.90
Saint Paul	109.90	82.31	83.33	2.68	40.87	26.94
Saint Petersburg[24]	84.14	81.87	68.10	2.68	33.62	19.85
Salt Lake City	87.45	79.67	83.11	2.80	33.89	29.22
San Antonio	85.61	83.00	84.75	2.57	50.58	38.59
San Diego	92.76	96.90	96.38	3.11	45.63	25.11
San Francisco	120.47	96.31	109.71	3.06	62.81	43.81
San Jose	107.99	100.70	129.27	3.08	52.55	22.25
Santa Ana[25]	93.67	96.07	100.94	3.12	56.87	24.86
Savannah	88.60	71.20	71.51	2.66	38.38	21.59
Seattle	113.67	104.49	110.96	3.13	40.57	34.64
Spokane	94.56	90.57	97.24	2.97	31.33	17.02
Springfield	81.87	73.47	82.44	2.55	24.97	18.92
Tampa	84.14	81.87	68.10	2.68	33.62	19.85
Tulsa	84.50	71.00	84.22	2.52	30.83	26.64
Virginia Beach[26]	99.05	96.33	103.60	2.62	28.84	28.24
Warren[27]	75.09	78.93	72.23	2.79	39.50	21.07
Washington[28]	89.27	86.73	75.52	2.89	48.80	26.46
Wichita	85.10	71.35	103.54	2.62	35.81	30.78
Average[99]	89.44	78.95	87.40	2.73	31.92	24.83
Minimum[99]	57.00	54.25	48.32	2.44	19.17	13.67
Maximum[99]	149.90	136.73	174.22	3.75	62.81	47.89

*Note: **Doctor** (general practitioners routine exam of an established patient); **Dentist** (adult teeth cleaning and periodic oral examination); **Optometrist** (full vision eye exam for established adult patient); **Gasoline** (one gallon regular unleaded, national brand, including all taxes, cash price at self-service pump if available); **Beauty Salon** (woman's shampoo, trim, and blow-dry); **Men's Shirt** (cotton/polyester dress shirt, pinpoint weave, long sleeves); (99) Values for the local area are compared with the average, minimum, and maximum values for all 331 areas in the Cost of Living Index report; n/a not available; In cases where data is not available for the city, data for the metro area or for a neighboring city has been provided and noted below; (2) Rio Rancho (data for Albuquerque was not available); (3) Seattle urban area; (4) Boston urban area; (5) Raleigh urban area; (6) Charleston-North Charleston metro area; (7) Middlesex-Monmouth NJ metro area; (8) Fargo-Moorhead ND-MN metro area; (9) Loveland (data for Fort Collins was not available); (10) Fort Wayne-Allen County; (11) Winston-Salem (data for Greensboro was not available); (12) Orange County; (13) Kansas City MO-KS metro area; (14) Little Rock-North Little Rock metro area; (15) Los Angeles-Long Beach metro area; (16) Milwaukee-Waukesha metro area; (17) Joliet (data for Naperville was not available); (18) Nashville-Franklin; (19) Slidell (data for New Orleans was not available); (20) Manhattan; (21) Kansas City MO-KS metro area; (22) Reno-Sparks NV metro area; (23) St. Louis MO-IL metro area; (24) Tampa urban area; (25) Orange County; (26) Hampton Roads/SE Virginia area; (27) Detroit (data for Warren was not available); (28) Washington-Arlington-Alexandria DC-VA metro area*
Source: The Council for Community and Economic Research (formerly ACCRA), Cost of Living Index, 2010

Distribution of Physicians and Dentists

City	Area Covered	Dentists[1]	D.O.[2]	M.D.[3]				
				Total	Family/General Practice	Pediatrics	Medical Specialties	Surgical Specialties
Albuquerque	Bernalillo County	4.2	1.5	25.2	3.3	1.9	9.0	5.1
Anchorage	Anchorage Borough	5.8	2.2	23.9	4.4	1.8	6.5	6.2
Ann Arbor	Washtenaw County	9.0	3.0	47.5	2.9	3.5	19.1	9.0
Athens	Clarke County	4.8	1.0	23.3	1.9	1.0	7.6	7.4
Atlanta	Fulton County	5.7	0.8	31.2	1.8	2.2	11.5	8.5
Austin	Travis County	4.5	1.2	22.6	2.9	1.7	7.7	5.2
Baltimore	Baltimore City	3.2	1.6	29.3	1.3	1.8	12.5	6.2
Bellevue	King County	7.6	1.1	29.4	4.6	1.9	10.2	5.7
Birmingham	Jefferson County	5.7	1.0	31.7	2.1	2.4	12.6	8.5
Boise City	Ada County	6.5	1.6	22.5	3.6	1.0	6.4	6.5
Boston	Suffolk County	7.8	1.1	44.4	1.1	3.0	20.4	8.2
Boulder	Boulder County	6.1	2.0	28.4	5.4	2.1	8.3	6.4
Cambridge	Middlesex County	7.4	0.6	32.2	1.5	2.9	14.4	5.7
Cary	Wake County	5.4	0.6	20.4	2.4	2.2	8.0	4.7
Charleston	Charleston County	7.1	2.1	40.7	3.3	2.7	13.6	10.1
Charlotte	Mecklenburg County	5.4	0.7	23.2	2.4	2.0	9.1	5.6
Chattanooga	Hamilton County	4.8	1.9	27.2	2.7	2.1	10.4	7.0
Chicago	Cook County	5.5	2.3	21.5	2.2	1.6	9.1	4.4
Cincinnati	Hamilton County	4.7	1.5	28.6	2.5	2.3	10.9	6.9
Cleveland	Cuyahoga County	5.8	4.1	29.9	1.9	2.0	12.6	6.7
Colorado Spgs.	El Paso County	5.6	2.6	16.0	2.0	1.1	4.9	4.0
Columbia	Richland County	4.9	0.6	26.1	2.9	2.0	9.9	6.3
Columbus	Franklin County	5.6	5.8	22.2	2.9	1.6	8.2	5.1
Dallas	Dallas County	4.5	1.8	18.7	1.5	1.2	6.8	4.6
Denver	Denver County	5.4	2.6	35.3	2.9	2.3	13.2	7.7
Des Moines	Polk County	4.9	10.6	16.9	2.0	1.3	6.1	4.6
Durham	Durham County	5.4	0.9	42.5	2.8	3.3	16.9	9.3
Edison	Middlesex County	6.6	1.8	22.2	1.3	2.5	11.2	4.5
El Paso	El Paso County	1.7	1.3	11.5	1.3	1.1	4.4	3.1
Eugene	Lane County	3.6	0.8	22.2	4.2	1.6	6.9	4.7
Evansville	Vanderburgh County	4.1	1.5	24.5	5.5	1.0	6.5	6.1
Fargo	Cass County	5.2	0.9	29.4	4.7	1.9	10.8	6.3
Ft. Collins	Larimer County	5.1	2.1	19.1	4.6	1.1	5.1	4.3
Ft. Lauderdale	Broward County	5.0	3.4	19.5	1.6	1.6	8.3	4.5
Ft. Wayne	Allen County	3.9	1.5	21.4	3.0	0.8	6.5	5.2
Ft. Worth	Tarrant County	3.7	3.6	13.7	1.7	0.9	4.7	3.6
Gainesville	Alachua County	8.3	2.3	39.7	4.6	3.0	14.7	7.6
Greensboro	Guilford County	4.2	0.5	21.5	2.7	1.5	8.2	5.5
Honolulu	Honolulu County	6.3	1.5	24.1	2.2	2.1	9.6	5.3
Houston	Harris County	4.1	0.8	18.2	1.9	1.4	6.8	4.3
Huntsville	Madison County	4.4	0.9	20.9	3.7	1.4	6.9	5.0
Indianapolis	Marion County	4.5	1.4	24.5	2.9	1.7	9.0	5.5
Irvine	Orange County	8.2	1.5	23.3	3.2	1.9	8.6	5.2
Jackson	Hinds County	4.9	0.7	27.6	2.5	1.8	10.1	7.4
Jacksonville	Duval County	3.7	2.0	22.1	3.2	1.5	8.0	5.0
Kansas City	Jackson County	4.6	4.3	14.9	1.7	1.4	6.1	3.2
Knoxville	Knox County	4.3	1.7	32.8	3.9	2.0	12.7	7.8
Las Vegas	Clark County	4.0	2.1	14.2	1.6	0.9	5.6	3.0
Lexington	Fayette County	8.1	2.6	39.4	3.7	2.2	14.0	9.8
Lincoln	Lancaster County	5.5	0.9	19.9	3.9	1.3	6.5	4.4
Little Rock	Pulaski County	5.1	1.3	37.9	4.3	2.2	12.6	8.8
Los Angeles	Los Angeles County	6.1	1.0	19.7	2.2	1.5	7.7	4.3
Louisville	Jefferson County	6.3	0.7	31.0	2.7	2.3	11.7	7.5
Madison	Dane County	5.1	1.6	29.9	4.7	1.8	10.3	5.8

Table continued on next page.

City	Area Covered	Dentists[1]	D.O.[2]	M.D.[3]				
				Total	Family/ General Practice	Pediatrics	Medical Specialties	Surgical Specialties
Manchester	Hillsborough County	5.3	1.5	18.3	2.5	1.6	7.0	4.3
Miami	Miami-Dade County	4.4	1.4	22.0	2.7	1.9	9.0	4.7
Milwaukee	Milwaukee County	4.5	1.5	21.1	2.5	1.4	7.7	5.0
Minneapolis	Hennepin County	5.9	1.1	31.0	4.5	2.2	10.8	6.7
Naperville	DuPage County	7.4	3.0	32.9	3.6	2.5	13.0	6.8
Nashville	Davidson County	5.7	0.7	32.8	1.7	2.4	12.9	9.0
New Orleans	Orleans Parish	3.4	0.8	32.1	1.8	2.3	11.9	8.0
New York	Kings County	3.8	1.1	12.4	0.8	1.4	6.5	2.3
Oakland	Alameda County	6.5	0.8	22.2	2.2	2.5	9.8	4.4
Oklahoma City	Oklahoma County	6.1	3.5	25.1	3.2	1.2	8.2	6.2
Omaha	Douglas County	5.9	2.0	29.6	3.8	2.1	10.2	7.6
Orlando	Orange County	4.0	1.9	19.7	2.5	1.8	7.6	4.3
Overland Park	Johnson County	7.1	3.6	30.4	3.6	1.9	10.4	7.0
Oxnard	Ventura County	5.5	0.8	17.8	3.4	1.2	6.2	4.0
Philadelphia	Philadelphia County	4.2	5.3	17.8	1.0	1.3	7.4	3.9
Phoenix	Maricopa County	4.5	3.1	16.3	1.8	1.1	6.1	3.6
Pittsburgh	Allegheny County	6.5	3.3	31.6	2.8	2.0	12.7	6.9
Plano	Collin County	5.7	1.4	18.7	2.3	1.8	7.4	4.0
Portland	Multnomah County	5.5	2.4	33.3	3.1	2.0	12.6	7.2
Providence	Providence County	3.7	1.5	22.4	1.4	1.8	10.5	5.2
Provo	Utah County	5.0	1.1	9.4	2.0	0.9	2.6	2.4
Raleigh	Wake County	5.4	0.6	20.4	2.4	2.2	8.0	4.7
Reno	Washoe County	4.8	1.7	21.7	2.8	1.0	6.6	5.3
Richmond	Richmond City	6.1	2.0	33.0	2.9	2.4	12.1	8.7
Riverside	Riverside County	3.1	0.9	9.8	1.7	0.7	3.3	2.3
Rochester	Monroe County	5.0	1.3	25.2	1.9	2.4	11.4	5.5
Sacramento	Sacramento County	5.5	0.9	19.6	2.5	1.5	7.3	4.3
St. Louis	St. Louis City	2.4	1.9	24.1	1.2	1.9	9.3	5.6
St. Paul	Ramsey County	5.4	0.6	25.8	4.7	1.6	9.5	4.5
St. Petersburg	Pinellas County	4.7	4.5	22.4	2.6	1.5	8.9	5.0
Salt Lake City	Salt Lake County	5.3	0.9	21.1	2.4	1.9	7.2	5.0
San Antonio	Bexar County	4.6	1.7	20.7	2.7	1.5	7.3	4.7
San Diego	San Diego County	6.0	1.3	21.0	2.7	1.6	7.5	4.5
San Francisco	San Francisco County	10.2	0.8	42.4	2.8	2.9	17.2	8.4
San Jose	Santa Clara County	8.7	0.6	25.1	2.1	2.6	10.9	5.4
Santa Ana	Orange County	8.2	1.5	23.3	3.2	1.9	8.6	5.2
Savannah	Chatham County	4.6	1.3	26.7	2.7	1.9	9.5	7.4
Seattle	King County	7.6	1.1	29.4	4.6	1.9	10.2	5.7
Spokane	Spokane County	5.3	1.7	21.6	3.7	1.0	6.4	4.9
Springfield	Greene County	5.1	3.6	24.2	2.8	1.2	7.9	6.6
Tampa	Hillsborough County	4.2	2.3	22.2	1.8	1.9	8.8	5.1
Tulsa	Tulsa County	5.1	11.2	20.4	2.4	1.3	7.6	4.9
Virginia Beach	Virginia Beach City	5.7	0.8	19.5	3.3	1.6	6.2	4.4
Warren	Macomb County	5.1	5.9	9.5	1.6	0.8	4.1	2.3
Washington	The District County	7.4	1.7	36.1	2.1	2.9	15.4	7.7
Wichita	Sedgwick County	3.8	3.1	18.5	3.7	1.0	5.7	4.2
U.S.	U.S.	4.5	1.9	18.3	2.5	1.4	6.8	4.1

Note: All figures are rates per 100,000 population; Data as of 2008 unless noted; (1) Data as of 2007; (2) Doctor of Osteopathic Medicine; (3) Includes active, non-federal, patient-care, office-based Doctors of Medicine
Source: Area Resource File (ARF). 2009-2010 Release. U.S. Department of Health and Human Services, Health Resources and Services Administration, Bureau of Health Professions, Rockville, MD, August 2010

Crime Rate: City

City	All Crimes	Violent Crimes				Property Crimes		
		Murder	Forcible Rape	Robbery	Aggrav. Assault	Burglary	Larceny -Theft	Motor Vehicle Theft
Albuquerque	6,260.8	10.6	61.4	207.9	489.4	1,201.6	3,649.4	640.6
Anchorage	4,519.6	4.9	99.5	188.5	585.2	569.4	2,765.6	306.4
Ann Arbor	2,815.5	0.9	25.4	55.1	154.8	532.5	1,937.6	109.3
Athens	5,339.6	8.7	36.7	135.3	231.4	1,673.7	3,014.7	239.2
Atlanta	7,362.6	14.5	24.4	492.9	618.4	1,648.0	3,528.8	1,035.6
Austin	6,768.8	2.9	34.5	184.0	302.0	1,138.3	4,818.7	288.6
Baltimore	6,078.5	37.3	24.7	580.3	870.6	1,220.8	2,620.9	723.9
Bellevue	3,288.2	1.6	20.0	48.8	59.2	496.6	2,518.9	143.1
Birmingham	9,223.2	28.6	87.1	505.8	615.3	2,207.4	5,078.0	701.1
Boise City	3,049.4	3.4	33.9	30.0	193.3	506.7	2,197.8	84.3
Boston	4,315.9	8.0	43.1	364.8	576.1	473.4	2,484.2	366.4
Boulder	3,019.9	5.0	32.0	51.0	156.9	563.8	2,092.3	119.0
Cambridge	3,544.4	1.9	20.4	174.0	286.8	421.9	2,453.7	185.7
Cary	1,597.7	0.0	9.0	35.9	53.8	350.6	1,087.0	61.3
Charleston	4,034.1	7.9	27.3	191.8	296.4	497.9	2,772.7	240.1
Charlotte	5,678.0	7.5	39.0	301.7	375.2	1,262.3	3,263.3	429.1
Chattanooga	8,485.8	9.9	30.7	310.1	688.0	1,731.2	5,186.7	529.2
Chicago	n/a	16.1	n/a	557.4	552.1	930.1	2,753.9	543.1
Cincinnati	7,294.8	16.5	70.5	681.1	423.9	1,884.8	3,751.3	466.8
Cleveland	7,016.6	20.0	86.9	828.2	460.4	2,149.4	2,532.6	939.1
Colorado Springs	4,155.9	3.7	85.7	130.7	269.9	822.9	2,578.8	264.2
Columbia	7,058.7	10.2	53.2	296.4	686.6	1,312.1	4,160.8	539.6
Columbus	7,131.1	10.9	75.6	447.1	169.6	1,920.4	3,956.3	551.2
Dallas	6,323.1	12.9	37.6	426.3	315.4	1,505.7	3,214.9	810.3
Denver	4,030.6	6.4	56.7	156.4	358.0	787.7	2,088.4	576.8
Des Moines	4,957.0	3.0	77.7	124.0	337.4	929.9	3,123.1	361.8
Durham	5,870.1	9.2	27.7	312.1	350.3	1,601.4	3,237.9	331.4
Edison	2,471.9	1.0	4.0	97.6	163.1	425.7	1,595.3	185.2
El Paso	3,451.5	1.9	29.4	73.0	352.9	321.7	2,367.0	305.4
Eugene	6,009.3	0.7	48.2	132.8	128.8	1,234.0	3,878.2	586.6
Evansville	5,016.8	2.6	51.8	117.5	201.3	958.8	3,488.0	196.9
Fargo	3,719.5	2.1	57.6	36.2	227.0	681.0	2,453.4	262.2
Fort Collins	3,697.8	1.4	62.8	49.1	272.9	543.0	2,602.4	166.1
Fort Lauderdale	6,480.2	7.1	30.6	374.4	397.4	1,589.0	3,706.1	375.5
Fort Wayne	4,076.2	7.2	29.8	192.8	118.4	901.9	2,656.4	169.7
Fort Worth	5,545.1	6.1	51.1	200.3	327.5	1,408.2	3,257.1	294.7
Gainesville	6,541.4	2.6	82.4	207.3	710.5	1,290.1	3,866.7	381.7
Greensboro	6,810.3	9.5	30.0	358.6	368.1	1,891.5	3,818.5	334.1
Honolulu	n/a	n/a	n/a	n/a	n/a	n/a	n/a	n/a
Houston	6,444.2	12.6	36.2	499.9	576.8	1,287.7	3,389.0	641.9
Huntsville	6,133.2	7.3	49.8	242.4	352.2	1,411.0	3,569.4	501.1
Indianapolis	7,029.0	12.3	56.5	483.0	648.0	1,870.6	3,407.3	551.3
Irvine	1,460.1	1.4	13.0	25.5	31.1	223.0	1,096.6	69.5
Jackson	8,505.3	21.4	71.8	554.4	229.2	2,644.1	4,047.5	936.9
Jacksonville	5,993.7	12.2	26.9	291.2	505.6	1,395.7	3,426.1	335.9
Kansas City	6,808.1	20.6	56.9	406.5	816.4	1,491.9	3,288.1	727.7
Knoxville	7,418.3	11.8	79.1	355.1	611.8	1,393.1	4,602.1	365.3
Las Vegas	4,407.7	8.1	50.7	326.4	561.6	981.1	1,831.8	648.2
Lexington	4,009.4	4.4	36.1	195.0	358.3	818.8	2,413.6	183.2
Lincoln	4,390.9	1.6	49.5	77.4	329.4	635.9	3,181.5	115.5
Little Rock	9,791.0	16.8	89.9	420.1	942.7	2,319.6	5,390.5	611.4
Los Angeles	3,074.0	8.1	23.5	317.4	276.4	479.0	1,491.7	477.8
Louisville	4,859.5	9.8	36.4	248.7	302.1	1,122.4	2,866.3	273.7
Madison	3,726.4	1.7	11.9	155.2	194.9	649.6	2,565.5	147.6

Table continued on next page.

City	All Crimes	Violent Crimes				Property Crimes		
		Murder	Forcible Rape	Robbery	Aggrav. Assault	Burglary	Larceny -Theft	Motor Vehicle Theft
Manchester	3,911.8	1.8	65.3	157.4	269.6	699.4	2,568.3	150.0
Miami	6,145.2	14.1	15.5	499.5	659.6	1,158.4	3,193.2	605.0
Milwaukee	6,842.5	11.9	33.7	516.3	526.9	1,080.6	3,869.4	803.7
Minneapolis	5,776.3	4.7	107.9	434.6	561.4	1,239.1	2,958.6	469.9
Naperville	n/a	0.0	n/a	15.2	53.9	204.5	1,414.3	42.1
Nashville	5,918.8	12.6	42.9	323.0	761.9	1,035.4	3,460.1	282.7
New Orleans	4,623.3	51.7	29.1	277.0	419.1	1,135.8	1,934.2	776.4
New York	2,242.1	5.6	9.9	221.4	314.9	223.5	1,339.5	127.3
Oakland	6,665.6	25.7	80.6	716.3	856.5	1,186.0	2,183.4	1,617.1
Oklahoma City	7,028.6	11.7	52.8	224.3	641.5	1,902.2	3,509.2	687.0
Omaha	4,661.9	6.8	43.3	201.3	281.9	728.6	2,920.3	479.6
Orlando	8,579.4	11.9	49.8	326.2	809.0	1,603.5	5,245.2	533.8
Overland Park	2,772.2	1.7	16.1	29.4	130.1	307.4	2,088.8	198.6
Oxnard	2,592.9	6.9	12.8	205.0	186.8	375.8	1,563.3	242.3
Philadelphia	4,849.5	19.5	57.9	583.9	576.9	708.8	2,451.6	450.9
Phoenix	4,654.3	7.6	32.7	235.2	271.0	1,019.2	2,481.7	606.8
Pittsburgh	4,759.9	12.5	37.2	437.8	501.2	900.3	2,605.1	265.8
Plano	3,100.7	1.5	16.5	52.4	99.7	541.5	2,217.1	172.0
Portland	5,277.2	3.4	44.9	184.9	320.4	658.9	3,498.6	566.0
Providence	5,343.0	13.4	29.1	230.1	415.9	1,063.1	2,963.9	627.4
Provo	2,583.0	0.8	29.3	26.8	82.9	340.7	1,981.2	121.4
Raleigh	3,896.0	3.4	24.4	204.9	260.1	785.0	2,422.1	196.1
Reno	4,652.7	4.1	38.0	185.1	439.3	836.2	2,809.4	340.7
Richmond	4,910.6	18.2	17.2	418.2	348.9	765.1	2,864.7	478.3
Riverside	3,709.9	5.0	32.7	222.4	251.8	673.6	2,080.6	443.9
Rochester	6,341.0	13.6	47.2	411.6	521.1	1,410.5	3,469.0	468.0
Sacramento	5,351.0	6.4	38.1	341.5	499.7	1,091.8	2,492.0	881.5
Saint Louis	10,401.8	40.3	70.4	766.0	1,193.4	1,923.9	5,010.9	1,396.9
Saint Paul	4,842.4	4.6	58.9	247.7	451.5	1,045.3	2,395.8	638.5
Saint Petersburg	8,382.7	4.5	45.7	370.3	940.7	1,782.5	4,317.5	921.5
Salt Lake City	8,731.0	1.7	55.3	227.4	421.6	1,202.4	6,024.7	797.9
San Antonio	7,241.6	7.2	45.7	195.3	322.7	1,322.0	4,926.3	422.4
San Diego	2,903.7	3.1	24.2	144.9	278.9	509.1	1,373.4	570.1
San Francisco	4,997.3	5.6	22.1	422.7	285.3	641.8	3,013.1	606.7
San Jose	2,745.7	2.9	27.0	107.4	223.1	392.1	1,429.2	563.8
Santa Ana	2,513.0	7.4	22.7	256.2	222.6	342.0	1,227.9	434.3
Savannah	5,539.0	14.1	21.6	301.8	192.7	1,246.8	3,228.3	533.6
Seattle	6,464.6	3.7	16.9	297.4	322.8	1,113.5	4,164.9	545.4
Spokane	7,113.7	3.4	37.0	218.3	367.1	1,264.0	4,368.0	856.0
Springfield	9,708.3	3.8	71.5	190.9	497.9	1,477.1	6,931.6	535.6
Tampa	4,506.2	5.8	23.2	263.3	460.0	1,014.1	2,345.7	394.2
Tulsa	7,149.5	17.7	66.0	290.2	742.1	1,721.7	3,773.1	538.7
Virginia Beach	3,271.4	4.1	16.0	103.6	84.8	468.4	2,464.8	129.5
Warren	3,418.4	3.0	50.2	156.6	373.1	664.5	1,421.1	749.9
Washington	5,768.8	23.8	25.0	666.7	549.5	616.4	3,003.7	883.7
Wichita	6,213.2	6.8	69.1	143.3	663.4	1,100.3	3,777.1	453.2
U.S.	3,465.5	5.0	28.7	133.0	262.8	716.3	2,060.9	258.8

Note: Figures are crimes per 100,000 population in 2009 except where noted; n/a not available
Source: FBI Uniform Crime Reports, 2009

Crime Rate: Suburbs

Suburbs[1]	All Crimes	Violent Crimes				Property Crimes		
		Murder	Forcible Rape	Robbery	Aggrav. Assault	Burglary	Larceny -Theft	Motor Vehicle Theft
Albuquerque	2,947.0	3.6	28.7	49.5	383.6	869.8	1,328.0	283.8
Anchorage	4,603.3	0.0	31.8	40.9	464.0	504.9	3,343.3	218.3
Ann Arbor	3,095.1	2.1	55.1	68.3	238.2	764.6	1,786.2	180.6
Athens	2,987.4	1.3	15.7	24.8	297.8	590.4	1,929.3	128.0
Atlanta	3,601.8	5.0	20.9	140.7	193.6	912.2	1,998.9	330.4
Austin	2,420.3	2.0	20.3	27.2	169.3	496.5	1,617.1	87.9
Baltimore	3,377.9	2.9	19.2	135.6	319.0	505.9	2,181.4	213.9
Bellevue	4,458.1	2.7	32.5	146.7	212.1	856.9	2,781.5	425.8
Birmingham	4,024.9	4.4	26.0	114.7	212.8	988.3	2,464.0	214.8
Boise City	1,804.0	0.7	35.6	15.9	169.0	392.3	1,111.7	78.8
Boston	2,342.9	1.9	20.9	97.4	258.3	429.1	1,395.9	139.3
Boulder	2,463.8	1.0	17.8	33.7	189.2	409.4	1,710.2	102.5
Cambridge	2,061.5	1.1	14.8	54.7	195.1	390.2	1,277.8	127.7
Cary	3,090.2	2.6	18.2	108.5	173.0	740.0	1,877.1	170.7
Charleston	n/a	4.9	34.2	153.8	442.7	n/a	2,555.0	328.7
Charlotte	3,434.7	4.1	20.0	78.9	269.5	778.1	2,090.4	193.6
Chattanooga	3,117.7	2.0	21.9	28.5	317.2	674.4	1,897.5	176.2
Chicago	n/a	n/a	n/a	n/a	n/a	n/a	n/a	n/a
Cincinnati	2,987.5	1.8	26.3	70.9	89.0	585.6	2,102.9	111.1
Cleveland	2,299.5	2.2	20.9	74.3	82.0	505.8	1,503.4	111.1
Colorado Springs	1,746.5	2.6	34.0	15.9	331.2	361.7	880.1	121.0
Columbia	4,273.3	5.5	35.8	108.0	552.0	886.5	2,374.8	310.6
Columbus	2,854.4	1.9	24.9	54.4	45.8	610.9	2,025.6	90.9
Dallas	3,327.4	2.3	22.8	73.2	136.4	736.1	2,105.4	251.2
Denver	2,869.0	3.1	45.3	63.0	163.7	456.2	1,873.2	264.4
Des Moines	2,010.5	0.3	22.6	13.6	96.0	341.1	1,463.7	73.2
Durham	3,266.8	3.0	21.1	60.9	142.2	949.8	1,968.4	121.5
Edison	1,998.2	1.3	9.0	58.1	90.8	353.7	1,408.6	76.7
El Paso	2,938.7	3.1	37.4	45.0	275.3	611.5	1,776.6	189.9
Eugene	3,143.9	1.5	20.8	35.5	239.9	681.2	1,878.3	286.6
Evansville	1,960.5	1.7	17.8	25.0	122.9	310.3	1,410.3	72.5
Fargo	n/a	0.0	n/a	10.4	73.9	353.5	1,383.7	86.2
Fort Collins	2,475.9	2.5	35.1	24.4	108.4	378.4	1,822.5	104.6
Fort Lauderdale	4,294.5	4.0	24.4	171.7	315.7	832.7	2,662.4	283.6
Fort Wayne	1,440.7	2.5	14.1	16.6	55.4	289.1	987.9	75.0
Fort Worth	4,011.3	2.2	28.4	84.9	236.1	837.7	2,584.0	238.1
Gainesville	3,901.3	2.8	37.5	95.8	486.2	1,036.3	2,054.5	188.2
Greensboro	3,686.8	2.4	16.3	101.8	201.0	1,011.1	2,197.3	156.9
Honolulu	n/a	n/a	n/a	n/a	n/a	n/a	n/a	n/a
Houston	3,802.3	4.9	24.9	134.2	277.1	876.1	2,197.5	287.6
Huntsville	2,334.9	3.6	17.3	52.4	136.9	587.0	1,405.0	132.9
Indianapolis	2,200.1	1.2	11.8	25.2	88.6	331.8	1,638.9	102.6
Irvine	2,318.7	2.4	15.3	102.5	139.5	373.2	1,468.3	217.5
Jackson	2,287.9	1.9	25.4	36.3	100.1	594.1	1,397.4	132.6
Jacksonville	3,447.3	4.1	21.9	71.9	377.1	668.3	2,162.5	141.6
Kansas City	n/a	4.0	26.9	65.6	204.3	n/a	2,079.7	253.8
Knoxville	2,802.7	1.7	17.6	52.1	220.1	801.1	1,563.4	146.7
Las Vegas	3,086.9	4.2	21.3	171.7	258.6	693.2	1,583.8	354.1
Lexington	3,531.4	0.6	20.1	45.9	112.9	697.1	2,538.5	116.4
Lincoln	1,494.8	0.0	24.4	4.4	48.9	268.8	1,108.3	40.0
Little Rock	4,639.3	3.8	39.2	89.1	396.0	1,206.0	2,657.6	247.6
Los Angeles	2,965.9	6.4	20.1	204.7	278.8	534.0	1,449.3	472.5
Louisville	2,524.0	1.1	21.0	49.4	69.9	583.7	1,658.6	140.3
Madison	2,237.1	2.1	17.4	31.5	81.8	308.8	1,728.9	66.6

Table continued on next page.

Suburbs[1]	All Crimes	Violent Crimes				Property Crimes		
		Murder	Forcible Rape	Robbery	Aggrav. Assault	Burglary	Larceny -Theft	Motor Vehicle Theft
Manchester	1,977.1	1.4	16.9	22.3	80.8	297.7	1,485.6	72.4
Miami	5,665.4	7.6	24.8	240.4	445.2	993.1	3,488.4	466.0
Milwaukee	2,389.6	0.9	10.3	36.7	67.4	301.0	1,892.6	80.6
Minneapolis	n/a	1.3	n/a	55.0	104.1	450.1	2,141.5	167.8
Naperville	n/a	n/a	n/a	n/a	n/a	n/a	n/a	n/a
Nashville	2,819.6	3.4	26.3	50.2	278.4	612.0	1,717.9	131.4
New Orleans	n/a	9.3	21.8	103.9	321.1	n/a	2,356.7	n/a
New York	2,004.4	2.4	7.9	119.7	149.5	303.4	1,285.3	136.4
Oakland	3,609.8	5.9	20.3	192.6	192.8	667.9	1,925.5	604.9
Oklahoma City	n/a	2.7	30.9	41.7	n/a	799.8	2,110.2	189.0
Omaha	2,768.6	0.7	34.6	35.3	170.5	495.4	1,812.3	219.7
Orlando	4,186.1	4.5	33.2	149.6	430.4	1,026.6	2,284.6	257.3
Overland Park	n/a	8.5	35.6	156.5	368.4	n/a	2,389.3	380.6
Oxnard	2,040.0	2.6	15.0	60.9	125.6	367.4	1,354.2	114.3
Philadelphia	2,195.0	2.0	25.5	76.6	151.2	298.7	1,547.0	94.1
Phoenix	3,615.8	3.9	21.3	84.2	196.0	720.0	2,281.9	308.5
Pittsburgh	2,022.4	3.5	15.5	58.9	165.9	376.0	1,316.0	86.6
Plano	4,295.3	5.7	27.9	186.9	195.8	994.0	2,450.8	434.3
Portland	2,502.4	1.7	33.9	51.1	86.5	358.3	1,749.4	221.5
Providence	2,642.7	1.7	27.8	83.0	224.5	533.8	1,608.7	163.2
Provo	2,184.5	0.7	16.8	12.0	29.5	311.3	1,721.4	92.7
Raleigh	2,360.5	1.7	13.0	40.9	102.0	642.6	1,424.2	136.2
Reno	2,760.1	4.6	22.3	63.9	260.6	690.0	1,525.6	193.2
Richmond	2,642.2	3.4	15.9	75.7	98.9	506.9	1,787.7	153.6
Riverside	3,211.1	5.1	21.2	128.1	251.9	788.7	1,575.9	440.1
Rochester	2,247.6	1.1	17.3	28.6	71.4	338.9	1,727.1	63.2
Sacramento	3,239.6	3.4	26.8	124.3	247.8	676.1	1,806.1	355.0
Saint Louis	n/a	2.7	n/a	59.0	168.6	432.7	1,836.6	157.9
Saint Paul	n/a	1.4	n/a	85.6	130.1	495.3	2,222.3	162.3
Saint Petersburg	4,069.8	3.5	27.7	135.0	347.2	906.7	2,403.2	246.5
Salt Lake City	4,394.5	1.9	40.3	58.9	178.3	700.4	3,026.4	388.4
San Antonio	3,418.5	4.4	34.5	50.0	181.4	779.1	2,213.8	155.3
San Diego	2,614.1	2.0	25.2	125.5	250.8	461.6	1,369.1	379.8
San Francisco	2,581.0	2.1	17.3	97.4	161.6	453.7	1,576.4	272.5
San Jose	2,641.6	2.1	15.9	60.8	130.9	437.6	1,751.6	242.6
Santa Ana	2,224.9	1.6	14.1	76.9	120.2	365.0	1,468.9	178.1
Savannah	3,095.9	0.8	24.0	55.1	175.7	749.2	1,881.0	210.1
Seattle	3,611.9	1.9	32.1	91.9	123.2	703.1	2,310.3	349.4
Spokane	2,768.3	1.1	15.3	35.5	136.8	562.7	1,821.5	195.4
Springfield	2,054.7	0.7	15.2	14.5	199.7	500.3	1,235.7	88.6
Tampa	4,446.3	3.3	30.2	140.5	391.4	980.5	2,606.3	294.0
Tulsa	2,321.3	2.2	29.8	24.1	215.0	552.8	1,345.0	152.4
Virginia Beach	n/a	n/a	n/a	n/a	n/a	n/a	n/a	n/a
Warren	2,321.8	1.9	28.6	55.6	176.6	429.3	1,453.0	176.8
Washington	2,867.4	4.4	16.3	139.2	151.8	382.4	1,878.5	294.9
Wichita	2,542.2	0.4	26.6	21.2	226.3	584.5	1,558.4	124.8
U.S.	3,465.5	5.0	28.7	133.0	262.8	716.3	2,060.9	258.8

Note: Figures are crimes per 100,000 population in 2009 except where noted; n/a not available; (1) All areas within the metro area that are located outside the city limits
Source: FBI Uniform Crime Reports, 2009

Crime Rate: Metro Area

Metro Area[1]	All Crimes	Violent Crimes				Property Crimes		
		Murder	Forcible Rape	Robbery	Aggrav. Assault	Burglary	Larceny -Theft	Motor Vehicle Theft
Albuquerque	4,986.5	7.9	48.8	147.0	448.7	1,074.0	2,756.7	503.4
Anchorage	4,525.6	4.6	94.7	177.9	576.5	564.7	2,807.2	300.0
Ann Arbor	3,003.4	1.7	45.3	64.0	210.8	688.5	1,835.9	157.2
Athens	4,397.3	5.8	28.3	91.1	258.0	1,239.7	2,579.9	194.7
Atlanta	3,980.2	5.9	21.3	176.1	236.4	986.3	2,152.8	401.4
Austin	4,380.9	2.4	26.7	97.9	229.1	785.9	3,060.6	178.4
Baltimore	4,018.4	11.1	20.5	241.1	449.8	675.5	2,285.7	334.9
Bellevue	4,415.1	2.6	32.1	143.1	206.5	843.6	2,771.8	415.4
Birmingham	5,070.2	9.3	38.3	193.3	293.7	1,233.4	2,989.6	312.5
Boise City	2,222.7	1.6	35.0	20.7	177.2	430.8	1,476.8	80.6
Boston[2]	2,986.9	3.9	28.1	184.7	362.0	443.5	1,751.2	213.4
Boulder	2,651.7	2.4	22.6	39.5	178.3	461.6	1,839.3	108.1
Cambridge[2]	2,162.9	1.2	15.2	62.8	201.4	392.4	1,358.2	131.7
Cary	2,913.2	2.3	17.1	99.9	158.9	693.9	1,783.4	157.7
Charleston	n/a	5.5	33.0	160.4	417.5	n/a	2,592.5	313.5
Charlotte	4,430.4	5.6	28.4	177.8	316.4	993.0	2,611.0	298.1
Chattanooga	4,886.0	4.6	24.8	121.2	439.3	1,022.6	2,981.0	292.5
Chicago	n/a	n/a	n/a	n/a	n/a	n/a	n/a	n/a
Cincinnati	3,647.1	4.1	33.1	164.4	140.3	784.5	2,355.3	165.6
Cleveland	3,266.8	5.8	34.4	228.9	159.6	842.8	1,714.4	280.9
Colorado Springs	3,287.2	3.3	67.0	89.3	292.0	656.6	1,966.3	212.6
Columbia	4,753.6	6.3	38.8	140.5	575.2	959.9	2,682.8	350.0
Columbus	4,661.2	5.7	46.3	220.3	98.1	1,164.1	2,841.3	285.4
Dallas[2]	4,220.1	5.4	27.2	178.4	189.7	965.5	2,436.0	417.8
Denver	3,144.4	3.9	48.0	85.2	209.7	534.8	1,924.2	338.5
Des Moines	3,037.8	1.2	41.8	52.1	180.2	546.4	2,042.3	173.8
Durham	4,455.4	5.8	24.1	175.6	237.2	1,247.3	2,548.0	217.4
Edison[2]	2,018.3	1.3	8.8	59.8	93.9	356.8	1,416.5	81.3
El Paso	3,361.8	2.1	30.8	68.1	339.4	372.4	2,263.7	285.2
Eugene	4,388.5	1.1	32.7	77.8	191.7	921.3	2,747.0	416.9
Evansville	2,966.6	2.0	29.0	55.4	148.7	523.8	2,094.2	113.5
Fargo	n/a	1.0	n/a	22.6	146.0	507.7	1,887.2	169.1
Fort Collins	3,043.5	2.0	48.0	35.9	184.8	454.9	2,184.8	133.2
Fort Lauderdale[2]	4,523.1	4.3	25.1	192.9	324.3	911.8	2,771.5	293.2
Fort Wayne	3,041.7	5.3	23.7	123.6	93.7	661.4	2,001.5	132.6
Fort Worth[2]	4,534.7	3.5	36.1	124.3	267.3	1,032.4	2,813.7	257.4
Gainesville	5,075.2	2.7	57.5	145.4	585.9	1,149.1	2,860.3	274.3
Greensboro	4,794.6	4.9	21.2	192.9	260.3	1,323.3	2,772.3	219.8
Honolulu	3,958.9	1.5	26.8	95.8	155.5	661.3	2,606.8	411.1
Houston	4,827.6	7.9	29.3	276.2	393.4	1,035.8	2,659.9	425.1
Huntsville	4,015.5	5.2	31.7	136.5	232.1	951.5	2,362.6	295.8
Indianapolis	4,455.0	6.4	32.7	239.0	349.8	1,050.3	2,464.6	312.2
Irvine[2]	2,257.3	2.3	15.1	97.0	131.7	362.4	1,441.8	206.9
Jackson	4,269.2	8.1	40.2	201.4	141.3	1,247.4	2,241.9	388.9
Jacksonville	5,004.1	9.1	25.0	206.0	455.7	1,113.0	2,935.1	260.4
Kansas City	n/a	7.9	34.0	145.8	348.3	n/a	2,363.9	365.3
Knoxville	4,024.6	4.4	33.9	132.3	323.8	957.8	2,367.8	204.5
Las Vegas	4,042.4	7.0	42.5	283.6	477.8	901.4	1,763.2	566.8
Lexington	3,832.3	3.0	30.2	139.7	267.4	773.7	2,459.8	158.4
Lincoln	3,955.4	1.3	45.7	66.5	287.2	580.7	2,869.8	104.2
Little Rock	6,069.0	7.4	53.3	180.9	547.7	1,515.1	3,416.0	348.6
Los Angeles[2]	3,008.0	7.1	21.4	248.7	277.8	512.6	1,465.9	474.6
Louisville	3,697.6	5.5	28.7	149.6	186.6	854.4	2,265.5	207.4
Madison	2,851.8	1.9	15.1	82.6	128.5	449.5	2,074.2	100.0

Table continued on next page.

Metro Area[1]	All Crimes	Violent Crimes				Property Crimes		
		Murder	Forcible Rape	Robbery	Aggrav. Assault	Burglary	Larceny -Theft	Motor Vehicle Theft
Manchester	2,497.1	1.5	29.9	58.6	131.6	405.6	1,776.6	93.2
Miami[2]	5,746.5	8.7	23.2	284.2	481.4	1,021.0	3,438.5	489.4
Milwaukee	4,122.4	5.2	19.4	223.3	246.2	604.4	2,661.9	362.0
Minneapolis	n/a	1.7	n/a	99.5	157.6	542.5	2,237.2	203.2
Naperville	n/a	n/a	n/a	n/a	n/a	n/a	n/a	n/a
Nashville	4,012.9	6.9	32.7	155.2	464.6	775.0	2,388.8	189.7
New Orleans	n/a	21.4	23.9	153.3	349.0	n/a	2,236.2	n/a
New York[2]	2,174.6	4.7	9.3	192.5	267.9	246.2	1,324.0	129.9
Oakland[2]	4,103.0	9.1	30.0	277.1	299.9	751.5	1,967.1	768.3
Oklahoma City	n/a	6.8	40.9	124.6	n/a	1,300.4	2,745.5	415.1
Omaha	3,758.1	3.9	39.2	122.1	228.7	617.3	2,391.3	355.5
Orlando	4,680.9	5.3	35.0	169.5	473.0	1,091.6	2,618.1	288.5
Overland Park	n/a	7.9	34.0	145.8	348.3	n/a	2,363.9	365.3
Oxnard	2,169.6	3.6	14.5	94.7	139.9	369.4	1,403.2	144.3
Philadelphia[2]	3,219.2	8.8	38.0	272.3	315.4	456.9	1,896.0	231.7
Phoenix	3,996.0	5.3	25.4	139.5	223.4	829.6	2,355.1	417.7
Pittsburgh	2,386.3	4.7	18.4	109.3	210.4	445.7	1,487.4	110.4
Plano[2]	4,220.1	5.4	27.2	178.4	189.7	965.5	2,436.0	417.8
Portland	3,197.5	2.1	36.7	84.6	145.0	433.6	2,187.6	307.8
Providence	2,931.2	2.9	27.9	98.8	245.0	590.3	1,753.4	212.8
Provo	2,269.6	0.7	19.5	15.2	40.9	317.6	1,776.9	98.8
Raleigh	2,913.2	2.3	17.1	99.9	158.9	693.9	1,783.4	157.7
Reno	3,760.2	4.3	30.6	127.9	355.1	767.3	2,204.0	271.1
Richmond	3,012.4	5.8	16.1	131.6	139.7	549.1	1,963.5	206.6
Riverside	3,246.6	5.1	22.1	134.9	251.9	780.5	1,611.8	440.4
Rochester	3,062.1	3.6	23.2	104.8	160.9	552.1	2,073.7	143.8
Sacramento	3,703.7	4.0	29.3	172.0	303.2	767.5	1,956.9	470.8
Saint Louis	n/a	7.4	n/a	147.8	297.2	619.9	2,235.0	313.5
Saint Paul	n/a	1.7	n/a	99.5	157.6	542.5	2,237.2	203.2
Saint Petersburg	4,453.8	3.6	29.3	155.9	400.0	984.7	2,573.6	306.6
Salt Lake City	5,089.9	1.9	42.7	85.9	217.3	780.9	3,507.2	454.1
San Antonio	5,953.6	6.3	41.9	146.3	275.1	1,139.1	4,012.4	332.4
San Diego	2,740.5	2.5	24.8	134.0	263.1	482.3	1,371.0	462.9
San Francisco[2]	3,687.4	3.7	19.5	246.4	218.2	539.8	2,234.2	425.6
San Jose	2,696.1	2.5	21.7	85.2	179.1	413.8	1,582.8	410.8
Santa Ana[2]	2,257.3	2.3	15.1	97.0	131.7	362.4	1,441.8	206.9
Savannah	4,633.8	9.2	22.5	210.4	186.4	1,062.4	2,729.1	413.7
Seattle[2]	4,273.2	2.3	28.6	139.5	169.5	798.3	2,740.3	394.9
Spokane	4,642.2	2.1	24.7	114.3	236.1	865.1	2,919.7	480.3
Springfield	4,823.1	1.8	35.6	78.3	307.6	853.6	3,296.0	250.3
Tampa	4,453.8	3.6	29.3	155.9	400.0	984.7	2,573.6	306.6
Tulsa	4,323.4	8.6	44.8	134.5	433.6	1,037.5	2,351.9	312.6
Virginia Beach	n/a	n/a	n/a	n/a	n/a	n/a	n/a	n/a
Warren[2]	2,381.0	2.0	29.7	61.1	187.2	442.0	1,451.3	207.8
Washington[2]	3,276.1	7.1	17.5	213.5	207.8	415.3	2,037.0	377.8
Wichita	4,761.9	4.3	52.3	95.1	490.6	896.4	2,899.9	323.3
U.S.	3,465.5	5.0	28.7	133.0	262.8	716.3	2,060.9	258.8

Note: Figures are crimes per 100,000 population in 2009 except where noted; n/a not available; (1) Figures cover the Metropolitan Statistical Area except where noted; (2) Metropolitan Division (MD); See Appendix B for counties included in MSAs and MDs
Source: FBI Uniform Crime Reports, 2009

Temperature & Precipitation: Yearly Averages and Extremes

City	Extreme Low (°F)	Average Low (°F)	Average Temp. (°F)	Average High (°F)	Extreme High (°F)	Average Precip. (in.)	Average Snow (in.)
Albuquerque	-17	43	57	70	105	8.5	11
Anchorage	-34	29	36	43	85	15.7	71
Ann Arbor	-21	39	49	58	104	32.4	41
Athens[1]	-8	52	62	72	105	49.8	2
Atlanta	-8	52	62	72	105	49.8	2
Austin	-2	58	69	79	109	31.1	1
Baltimore	-7	45	56	65	105	41.2	21
Bellevue	0	44	52	59	99	38.4	13
Birmingham	-6	51	63	74	106	53.5	2
Boise City	-25	39	51	63	111	11.8	22
Boston	-12	44	52	59	102	42.9	41
Boulder	-25	37	51	64	103	15.5	63
Cambridge	-12	44	52	59	102	42.9	41
Cary	-9	48	60	71	105	42.0	8
Charleston	6	55	66	76	104	52.1	1
Charlotte	-5	50	61	71	104	42.8	6
Chattanooga	-10	49	60	71	106	53.3	4
Chicago	-27	40	49	59	104	35.4	39
Cincinnati	-25	44	54	64	103	40.9	23
Cleveland	-19	41	50	59	104	37.1	55
Colorado Springs	-24	36	49	62	99	17.0	48
Columbia	-1	51	64	75	107	48.3	2
Columbus	-19	42	52	62	104	37.9	28
Dallas	-2	56	67	77	112	33.9	3
Denver	-25	37	51	64	103	15.5	63
Des Moines	-24	40	50	60	108	31.8	33
Durham	-9	48	60	71	105	42.0	8
Edison	-2	47	55	62	104	47.0	23
El Paso	-8	50	64	78	114	8.6	6
Eugene	-12	42	53	63	108	47.3	7
Evansville	-23	42	53	62	104	40.2	25
Fargo	-36	31	41	52	106	19.6	40
Fort Collins[2]	-25	37	51	64	103	15.5	63
Fort Lauderdale[3]	30	69	76	83	98	57.1	0
Fort Wayne	-22	40	50	60	106	35.9	33
Fort Worth	-1	55	66	76	113	32.3	3
Gainesville	10	58	69	79	102	50.9	Trace
Greensboro	-8	47	58	69	103	42.5	10
Honolulu	52	70	77	84	94	22.4	0
Houston	7	58	69	79	107	46.9	Trace
Huntsville	-11	50	61	71	104	56.8	4
Indianapolis	-23	42	53	62	104	40.2	25
Irvine	25	53	64	75	112	11.9	Trace
Jackson	2	53	65	76	106	55.4	1
Jacksonville	7	58	69	79	103	52.0	0
Kansas City	-23	44	54	64	109	38.1	21
Knoxville	-24	48	59	69	103	46.7	13
Las Vegas	8	53	67	80	116	4.0	1
Lexington	-21	45	55	65	103	45.1	17
Lincoln	-33	39	51	62	108	29.1	27
Little Rock	-5	51	62	73	112	50.7	5
Los Angeles	27	55	63	70	110	11.3	Trace
Louisville	-20	46	57	67	105	43.9	17
Madison	-37	35	46	57	104	31.1	42
Manchester	-33	34	46	57	102	36.9	63

Table continued on next page.